UNIVERSITY TREATISE SERIES

Fundamentals of Legal Research

TENTH EDITION

by

STEVEN M. BARKAN
Voss Bascom Professor of Law
Director of the Law Library
University of Wisconsin Law School

BARBARA A. BINTLIFF
Joseph C. Hutcheson Professor in Law
Director, Tarlton Law Library and Jamail Center for Legal Research
The University of Texas at Austin School of Law

MARY WHISNER
Reference Librarian
University of Washington School of Law

Mat #41181444

© 1977, 1981, 1985, 1987, 1990, 1994, 1998, 2002 FOUNDATION PRESS
© 2009 THOMSON REUTERS/FOUNDATION PRESS
© 2015 LEG, Inc. d/b/a West Academic
    444 Cedar Street, Suite 700
    St. Paul, MN 55101
    1-877-888-1330

West, West Academic Publishing, and West Academic are trademarks of West Publishing Corporation, used under license.

Printed in the United States of America

ISBN: 978-1-60930-056-2

This book is dedicated

To my parents Ruth and Irving Barkan and to my children Daniel and Davida Fernandez-Barkan

S.M.B

To the men in my life—John, Brad, and Bruce—who can always be counted on.

B.B.

To my colleagues and to my spouse, who is a colleague as well as so much more.

M.W.

Research is formalized curiosity. It is poking and prying with a purpose.

Zora Neale Hurston

Preface

Fundamentals of Legal Research has a distinguished history[1] as both a teaching tool and a guide to legal research. Those two uses serve readers' different needs, at different stages of their development. Beginning legal researchers can read the chapters and look at the illustrations of sources to pick up the basics, such as how federal statutes are published. Later, they can use the book as a reference, looking up detailed answers to specific questions. Curious students and expert researchers can mine the footnotes for sources to take them deeper into the field of legal research—for example, examining the policy issues related to state publication of statues online, the history of law review publishing, or the effects of statutory codification.

As in the past, the chapters in *Fundamentals of Legal Research* have been ordered to reflect a "jurisprudential" approach to teaching legal research—that is, with primary law first. Since most law students begin the study of law by reading and analyzing judicial opinions, the book begins with a discussion of the process of publishing court reports and the methods for locating them. Next follow chapters on other primary sources of law, then secondary sources. *Fundamentals of Legal Research* can also be used effectively to support a "process" approach to teaching legal research in which resources are presented in the order in lawyers tend to conduct research—that is, secondary authority before primary authority. Instructors who prefer that order can begin with introductory chapters 1–3, and then cover secondary sources in chapters 16–19 before covering primary sources.[2]

Several chapters address research areas that most law students do not reach in their first year but may find very important to them in their second and third years and in practice. These include public international law and human rights law, the law of the United Kingdom, and federal tax research. For the first time, this volume includes a chapter on Native American tribal law research, an area that is becoming more important as tribes exercise their sovereign authority in various ways. Many law schools have added to or expanded their curricular offerings to support more in-depth study of Native American law, and *Fundamentals of Legal Research* now supports that study

Assignments to Accompany Fundamentals of Legal Research, 10th and *Legal Research Illustrated, 10th* is available as a separate pamphlet. These assignments, produced by Professor Susan T. Phillips of the Texas A&M University School of Law, are designed to help students understand the resources described in this book.

---

[1] The history began with ERVIN POLLACK, FUNDAMENTALS OF LEGAL RESEARCH (1956). Although labeled the tenth edition, the present volume could be considered the fourteenth. The numbering of editions was reinitiated in 1977 with a change in authorship. For a history of this and other legal research textbooks, see Steven M. Barkan, *On Describing Legal Research*, 80 MICH. L. REV. 925 (1982) (reviewing J. MYRON JACOBSTEIN & ROY M. MERSKY, FUNDAMENTALS OF LEGAL RESEARCH (2d ed. 1981)).

[2] For a dialogue on the two approaches, see Donald J. Dunn, *Why We Should Teach Primary Sources First*, 8 PERSP.: TEACHING LEGAL RES. & WRITING 10 (1999); Penny A. Hazelton, *Why Don't We Teach Secondary Sources First?*, 8 PERSP.: TEACHING LEGAL RES. & WRITING 8 (1999).

Legal research changes, as landforms do, by different processes and at different rates. Some changes are fairly minor, as when the wind creates shifting patterns on the surface of the sand—for instance, when the U.S. Government Printing Office began releasing the 2012 edition of the *United States Code*, there was little that someone familiar with the 2006 edition needed to learn in order to use it effectively. Other changes require some addition to our knowledge, as when a familiar source becomes available on an online platform; think of a river that carves a new channel while the original channel remains. But when familiar sources cease to exist or totally new platforms are introduced, it sometimes feels as though the legal research landscape has been affected by an earthquake that shifts the ground we stand on or a volcano that creates totally new features. We don't want to carry this metaphor too far—we believe that many of the changes we see in legal research are salutary, not cataclysmic—but the field is dynamic and the resources used to teach it must also change.

The changes in the legal research landscape have been and will continue to be dramatic. Here are a few changes since the prior edition of *Fundamentals*. Industry giants *Westlaw* and *LexisNexis* restructured their search interfaces, creating *WestlawNext* and *Lexis Advance*.[3] *Bloomberg Law* made a strong entrance into the law school market. The Government Printing Office revamped and expanded its website, introducing *FDsys*. After twenty years of developing the very useful *THOMAS*, the Library of Congress replaced it with *Congress.gov*. And, although many researchers won't be as astonished as we were, the IRS stopped compiling the *Cumulative Bulletin*. Oh, and Scotland nearly left the United Kingdom, a move that would have changed the research in the law of those nations in multiple ways.

This book is the work of many hands, including the authors and contributors from all the past editions. In 2011, more than 18 contributors reviewed all the chapters of the ninth edition. (See the Acknowledgements for a list.) Many of them had been involved with one or more earlier editions. Beginning in 2013, we went over every chapter, reviewing and revising the content and style of each. Information in this volume is generally current as of late 2013 or early 2014.

Our goal was to make the content useful to contemporary readers who are familiar with online tools (and indeed prefer them) while also covering print resources sufficiently to ground students in the structure of legal authority and provide a useful reference for those needing information about print legal materials. Some of our changes were minor, likely to be noticed only by someone who carefully compares this edition with the last. Others are greater. Although we pondered whether it was necessary to have a separate chapter on electronic legal research when electronic sources are discussed throughout the book, we decided instead to revise it substantially. The chapter now has few specifics about *LexisNexis* and *Westlaw* and offers analysis and commentary to help even digital natives be more thoughtful about online research. The citators chapter now only briefly mentions *Shepard's Citations* in print, and focuses on online citators. In recognition that what we have long called "looseleaf services" are no longer printed on single sheets of paper (i.e., loose leaves) and are widely available, often only available, electronically, we

---

[3] Between the time we sent the manuscript to the publisher and the first page proofs, the *Lexis Advance* interface was reshaped. What we say about the system—its content, the general method of searching—is still valid, even though the look of screens has changed. For the details of how to navigate any given system, we invite readers to use help screens and attend training. This book is offering a broader view.

have used the term "topical services" to describe this resource. This edition of *Fundamentals*, like a new map, reflects changes in the landscape.

A note about our citations: In general we follow *The Bluebook: A Uniform System of Citation* (19th ed. 2010), with three chief exceptions. First, we often provide publishers' names when we are listing works in the text. Second, we do not provide the dates we visited the many websites we cite. Most were visited during the process of editing and revision during the fall of 2013 and early 2014. Finally, we cite the *Bluebook* itself so often that we shorten its citation. A full citation to the *Bluebook* in a footnote would be:

> THE BLUEBOOK: A UNIFORM SYSTEM OF CITATION R. 1.4(e), at 50 (Columbia Law Review Ass'n et al. eds., 19th ed. 2010).[4]

This is cumbersome for a book that so often cites the *Bluebook*. We usually shorten *Bluebook* references to:

> BLUEBOOK R. 1.4(e), at 50.

STEVEN M. BARKAN
Madison, Wisconsin

BARBARA A. BINTLIFF
Austin, Texas

MARY WHISNER
Seattle, Washington

October 2014

---

[4] THE BLUEBOOK: A UNIFORM SYSTEM OF CITATION R. 15.8(c)(v), at 145 (Columbia Law Review Ass'n et al. eds., 19th ed. 2010).

Acknowledgments

For over 50 years, *Fundamentals of Legal Research* has been a work-in-progress. This edition builds on the work of Professors Ervin H. Pollack, J. Myron Jacobstein, Roy M. Mersky, Donald J. Dunn, and numerous contributing authors. Along with the primary and contributing authors, the law library staffs at Ohio State, Stanford, Texas, Western New England, Washington, and Wisconsin have supported the research and development of this book.

The following people were primarily responsible for preparing specific chapters or sections of this edition. We are grateful for their contributions and for their commitment to this project.

Melissa Bernstein, Library Director & Professor of Law, S.J. Quinney Law Library, University of Utah (Chapters 16, 17, 19).

Nancy Carol Carter, Professor of Law (Retired), University of San Diego (Chapter 25).

Casey Duncan, Assistant Director for Technical Services, Tarlton Law Library, Jamail Center for Legal Research, University of Texas School of Law (Illustrations).

Mary A. Hotchkiss, Associate Dean for Students, University of Washington School of Law (Chapter 3).

Susan Nevelow Mart, Associate Professor and Director of the Law Library, University of Colorado Law School (Chapter 2).

Daniel W. Martin, Professor of Law and Director, Raines Law Library, Loyola Law School, Los Angeles (Appendix A).

David McClure, Head of Research and Curriculum Services and Assistant Professor, Wiener-Rogers Law Library, William S. Boyd School of Law, University of Nevada, Las Vegas (Glossary).

Pat Newcombe, Associate Dean for Library and Information Resources, Western New England University School of Law (Chapter 24).

Jane O'Connell, Deputy Director, Tarlton Law Library, Jamail Center for Legal Research, University of Texas School of Law (Chapter 20 and Illustrations).

George H. Pike, Director, Pritzker Legal Research Center and Senior Lecturer, Northwestern University School of Law (Chapter 23).

Jonathan Pratter, Foreign and International Law Librarian, Tarlton Law Library, Jamail Center for Legal Research, University of Texas School of Law (Chapter 21, Appendix C).

Jeanne F. Price, Associate Professor of Law and Director of the Law Library, William S. Boyd School of Law, University of Nevada, Las Vegas (Chapter 15).

Gail Levin Richmond, Professor of Law, Nova Southeastern University Law Center (Chapter 26). In addition, Gail, proofreader *par excellence*, meticulously proofread the entire book.

Bonnie Shucha, Assistant Director for Public Services, University of Wisconsin Law Library (Chapters 11, 18, Appendix B).

Matthew Steinke, Assistant Director for Public Services, Tarlton Law Library, Jamail Center for Legal Research, University of Texas School of Law (Illustrations).

Keith Ann Stiverson, Director of the Law Library, IIT Chicago–Kent College of Law (Chapter 13).

Jane Thompson, Associate Director of Faculty Services and Research, William A. Wise Law Library, University of Colorado Law School (Chapters 9, 10).

Stephen Young, Senior Reference Librarian, Judge Kathryn J. DuFour Law Library, Catholic University of America, Columbus School of Law (Chapter 22).

We also express our appreciation to the staff of West Academic, especially Tessa Boury, Christina Eschbach, and Greg Olson, for their patience and support in moving this project forward and to the publishers' representatives who provided information about their products and services. We would like to acknowledge those publishers who permitted us to reprint copyrighted material in this book, notably Thomson Reuters and LexisNexis.

Fundamentals of Legal Research is a book for students learning to do legal research. Therefore, we thank and acknowledge law librarians and all teachers of legal research, both in and out of the classroom. Their efforts to teach law students and lawyers how to find the information upon which legal decisions are made contribute to the betterment of our legal system. Their suggestions and feedback for improving this book will always be appreciated.

Finally, we thank all of the law students who read and use the book and who continue to sustain our intellectual interests and curiosity. We are gratified when lawyers indicate that the book they used in their first-year legal research class or in an advanced course in legal research is still in their personal library, and that they continue referring to it. Ultimately, we are grateful for having the opportunity to make our contributions to the body of legal literature.

Summary of Contents

Table of Contents

———————

Glossary of Terms Used in Legal Research*

This glossary is limited in scope, and the definitions of words are restricted in meaning, to a legal or legal research context. Words such as "index," whose meanings conform to general usage and are obvious, are omitted.

ACQUITTAL—

the verdict in a criminal trial in which the defendant is found not guilty.

ACT—

an alternative name for statutory law. When introduced in a legislature, a piece of proposed legislation is typically described as a "bill." After a bill is enacted, the terms "law" and "act" may be used interchangeably to describe it. An act has the same legislative force as a joint resolution but is technically distinguishable, being of a different form and introduced with the words "Be it enacted" instead of "Be it resolved."

ACTION—

the formal legal demand of one's rights from another person brought in court.

ADJUDICATION—

the formal pronouncing or recording of a judgment or decree by a court.

ADMINISTRATIVE AGENCY—

a governmental authority, other than a legislature or court, which issues rules and regulations or adjudicates disputes arising under designated statutes and regulations. Administrative agencies usually act under authority delegated by the legislature.

ADMINISTRATIVE LAW—

law that governs, or is promulgated by, governmental administrative agencies other than courts or legislative bodies. These administrative agencies derive their power from legislative enactments and are subject to judicial review.

ADVANCE SHEETS—

current pamphlets containing the most recently reported opinions of a court or the courts of several jurisdictions. The volume and page numbers usually are the same as in the subsequently bound volumes of the series, which cover several of the previously issued advance sheets.

ADVISORY OPINION—

an opinion rendered by a court at the request of the government or an interested party that indicates how the court would likely rule on a matter should adversary litigation develop. An advisory opinion is thus an interpretation of the law without binding effect.

---

* This glossary was revised by David McClure, Head of Research and Curriculum Services, Wiener-Rogers Law Library, William S. Boyd School of Law, University of Nevada, Las Vegas.

The International Court of Justice and some state courts will render advisory opinions; the Supreme Court of the United States and other federal courts will not.

AFFIDAVIT—

a written statement or declaration of facts sworn to by the maker, taken before a person officially permitted by law to administer oaths.

ALTERNATIVE DISPUTE RESOLUTION—

the process of resolving disputes through such means as mediation or arbitration rather than through litigation.

AMICUS CURIAE—

literally, "friend of the court." A person or entity with strong interest in or views on the subject matter of a dispute involving other parties that petitions the court for permission to file a brief in the case, ostensibly on behalf of one of the parties, but actually to suggest a rationale consistent with its own views.

ANNOTATIONS—

(1) brief summaries of the law and facts of cases interpreting statutes passed by Congress or state legislatures that are compiled in codes (i.e., in annotated codes); or (2) expository essays of varying length on significant legal topics chosen from selected cases or statutes, chiefly in the series of *American Law Reports*.

ANSWER—

the pleading filed by the defendant in response to the plaintiff's complaint.

APPEAL PAPERS—

the record of lower court proceedings and briefs filed by attorneys with courts for the purpose of appealing a lower court's actions in a litigated matter.

APPELLANT—

the party who requests that a higher court review the actions of a lower court. Compare with APPELLEE.

APPELLATE COURT—

a court that has legal authority to review the actions and decisions of a lower court or an administrative agency on appeal.

APPELLEE—

the party against whom an appeal is taken (usually, but not always, the winner in the lower court). It should be noted that a party's status as appellant or appellee bears no relation to his, her or its status as plaintiff or defendant in the lower court. Sometimes termed "respondent."

ARBITRATION—

the hearing and settlement of a dispute between opposing parties by one or more neutral and non-judicial third parties. The third party's decision is often binding by prior agreement of the opposing parties. Arbitration is an alternative to litigation as a means of resolving disputes.

ATTORNEY GENERAL OPINION—

an opinion issued by the chief counsel of the federal or state government at the request of the president, governor, or other governmental official on behalf of an agency, interpreting the law for the requesting official or agency in the same manner as a private attorney would for his or her client. The opinion is not binding on a court but is usually accorded some degree of persuasive authority.

AUTHORITY—

that which can bind or influence a court. Case law, legislation, constitutions, administrative regulations, and writings about the law are all legal authority. See PRIMARY AUTHORITY; MANDATORY AUTHORITY; PERSUASIVE AUTHORITY.

BILL—

a legislative proposal introduced in a legislature. The term distinguishes unfinished legislation from enacted law.

BLACK LETTER LAW—

an informal term indicating the basic principles of law generally accepted by the courts and/or embodied in the statutes of a particular jurisdiction.

BOOLEAN LOGIC—

a form of search strategy used in many databases, such as *Westlaw* and *LexisNexis*. In a Boolean search, connectors such as AND, OR, and NOT are used to construct a complex search command. The search "fungible and gasoline" for example, retrieves documents in which the term "fungible" and the term "gasoline" both appear. Compare with NATURAL LANGUAGE.

BRIEF—

(1) in American law practice, a written statement prepared by the counsel arguing a case in court. It contains a summary of the facts of the case, the pertinent laws, and an argument of how the law applies to the facts supporting counsel's position; (2) a summary of a published legal opinion prepared for the purpose of studying the opinion in law school.

BRIEFS AND RECORDS—

See APPEAL PAPERS.

CALENDAR—

a list or schedule that states the order in which cases are to be heard during a term of court.

CALR—

an acronym for Computer-Assisted Legal Research. *Bloomberg Law, Fastcase, Casemaker, LexisNexis, Loislaw, Westlaw, and VersusLaw* are examples of CALR services.

CAPTION—

See STYLE OF A CASE.

xxxvi   GLOSSARY OF TERMS USED IN LEGAL RESEARCH

CASE IN POINT—

a judicial opinion which deals with a fact situation similar to the one being researched and substantiates a point of law to be asserted. It is also referred to as "case on all fours."

CASE LAW—

the law of reported judicial opinions as distinguished from statutes or administrative law.

CASEBOOK—

a textbook used to instruct law students in a particular area of law. The text consists of a collection of judicial opinions, usually from appellate courts, and notes by the author(s).

CAUSE OF ACTION—

a claim in law and in fact sufficient to bring a case to court; the grounds of an action. (Example: breach of contract.)

CERTIORARI—

a writ issued by a higher court to a lower court requiring the latter to produce the records of a particular case tried therein. It is most commonly used to refer to the Supreme Court of the United States, which uses the writ of certiorari as a discretionary device to choose the cases it wishes to hear. The term's origin is Latin, meaning "to be informed of."

CHARTER—

a document issued by a governmental entity that gives a corporation legal existence. A corporation's charter may be referred to as the "articles of incorporation" or the "certificate of incorporation," depending on the terminology used in the state where the corporation was incorporated.

CITATION—

a reference to an authority. Citations to authority and supporting references are both important and extensive in any form of legal writing. Citation form—as prescribed by a manual such as the *Bluebook* or the *ALWD Citation Manual*—is also given emphasis in legal writing.

CITATORS—

books or online services that provide the subsequent judicial history and interpretation of reported cases or lists of cases and legislative enactments construing, applying, or affecting statutes. Citators indicate where a specific source (cited source) is cited by another source (citing source). In the United States, the most widely used citators are *Shepard's* and *KeyCite*.

CITED CASE—

a case that is referred to by other cases.

CITING CASE—

the case that refers to the cited case.

CIVIL LAW—

(1) Roman law embodied in the Code of Justinian, which is the basis of law in most Latin American countries and most countries of Western Europe other than Great Britain and is the foundation of the law of Louisiana and Quebec; (2) the law concerning noncriminal matters in both common law and civil law jurisdictions, such as those described in (1).

CLAIM—

(1) the assertion of a right, as to money or property; (2) the accumulation of facts that give rise to a right enforceable in court.

CLASS ACTION—

a lawsuit brought by a representative party on behalf of a group, all of whose members have the same or a similar grievance against the defendant.

CODE—

a compilation of statutory laws or regulations. In a code, the current laws are rewritten and arranged in classified order by subject. Repealed and temporary acts are eliminated and the revision is reenacted. See also COMPILED STATUTES; CONSOLIDATED STATUTES; REVISED STATUTES.

CODIFICATION—

the process of collecting and arranging systematically, usually by subject, the laws of a state or country.

COMMON LAW—

the basis of the Anglo-American legal systems. In theory, the common law courts did not create law but rather discovered it in the customs and habits of the English people. English common law was largely customary, unwritten law until discovered, applied, and reported by the courts of law. The strength of the English judicial system in pre-parliamentary days is one reason for the continued emphasis in common law systems on case law. In a narrow sense, common law is the phrase sometimes used to distinguish case law from statutory law.

COMPILED STATUTES—

in popular usage, a code. Technically, it is a compilation of acts printed verbatim as originally enacted but in a new classified order. The text is not modified; however, repealed and temporary acts are omitted. See also CODE; CONSOLIDATED STATUTES; REVISED STATUTES.

COMPLAINT—

the plaintiff's initial pleading. In general, a complaint need only contain a short and plain statement of the claim upon which relief is sought, an indication of the type of relief requested, and an indication that the court has jurisdiction to hear the case.

CONNECTOR—

See BOOLEAN LOGIC.

CONSOLIDATED STATUTES—

a compilation of statutes arranged in classified order by subject and subdivided as necessary into parts, articles, chapters, and sections for clarity and consistency of style. In the process of preparing consolidated statutes, all temporary and repealed statutes are deleted. A collection of statutes is sometimes referred to in popular usage as "consolidated laws," "compiled statutes," "revised statutes," or a "code." See also CODE; COMPILED STATUTES; REVISED STATUTES.

CONSOLIDATING STATUTE—

a law that gathers various statutes on a certain topic and organizes them into a single statutory act, making minor textual revisions and eliminating repealed and temporary acts in the process.

CONSTITUTION—

the system of fundamental principles by which a political body or organization governs itself. Most national constitutions are written; the constitutions of Israel, the United Kingdom, and New Zealand are unwritten.

COUNT—

a separate and independent claim. A civil complaint or a criminal indictment may contain several counts.

COUNTERCLAIM—

a claim made by a defendant against a plaintiff in a civil lawsuit; it constitutes a separate cause of action.

COURT DECISION—

the disposition of a case by a court. See OPINION.

COURT RULES—

rules of procedure promulgated to govern civil, criminal, and appellate practice before the courts.

DAMAGES—

monetary compensation awarded by a court for an injury caused by the act of another. Damages may be actual or compensatory (equal to the amount of loss shown), exemplary or punitive (in excess of the actual loss given to punish the person for the malicious conduct that caused the injury), or nominal (a trivial amount given because the injury is slight or because the exact amount of injury has not been determined satisfactorily).

DATABASE—

a collection of information organized for retrieval by computer. In legal research, it usually refers to a commercial service that may be searched online. A full-text database provides the complete text of documents such as judicial opinions or newspaper articles. *Westlaw* and *LexisNexis* are full-text databases for cases, statutes, and many other resources. A bibliographic database provides citations or abstracts of articles, books, reports, or patents.

DECISION—

See COURT DECISION.

DECREE—

a determination by a court of the rights and duties of the parties before it. Formerly, decrees were issued by courts of equity and distinguished from judgments, which were issued by courts of law. See EQUITY.

DEFENDANT—

the person against whom a civil or criminal action is brought.

DEMURRER—

a means of objecting to the sufficiency in law of a pleading by admitting the actual allegations made, but disputing that they frame an adequate legal claim. A demurrer is more commonly referred to in most jurisdictions today as a "motion to dismiss for failure to state a claim."

DICTUM, DICTA—

See OBITER DICTUM.

DIGEST—

an index to reported cases, providing brief, unconnected statements of court holdings on points of law, which are arranged by subject and subdivided by jurisdiction and courts.

DOCKET NUMBER—

an identifying number, sequentially assigned by the court clerk at the outset of a lawsuit submitted to the court for adjudication.

EN BANC—

a session in which the entire bench of the court participates in the decision rather than the regular quorum In the United States, each federal circuit court of appeals usually sits in groups of three judges but for important cases may expand the bench to include all circuit judges in regular active service for that circuit, which can range from six to twenty-nine judges. In such instances, the court is said to be "sitting en banc."

ENCYCLOPEDIA—

a work containing expository statements on principles of law, topically arranged, with supporting footnote references to cases and statutes on point.

EQUITY—

justice administered according to fairness as contrasted with strict adherence to the common law or statutes. Equity is based on a system of rules and principles that originated in England as an alternative to the harsh rules of common law and that were based on what was fair in a particular situation. One sought relief under this system in courts of equity rather than in courts of law.

EXECUTIVE AGREEMENT—

an international agreement, not a treaty, concluded by the president on the president's authority as commander-in-chief and director of foreign relations. An executive agreement is not submitted to the Senate for its advice and consent. The distinction between treaty and executive agreement is complicated and believed by some to be of questionable constitutionality, but the import of such agreements as that of Yalta, Potsdam, the Algiers Accords, the North American Free Trade Agreement (NAFTA), and the General Agreement on Tariffs and Trade (GATT), among many others, is unquestionably great.

EXECUTIVE ORDER—

an order issued by the president under specific authority granted by Congress. There is no precise distinction between a presidential proclamation and an executive order; however, a proclamation generally cover matters of widespread interest, and an executive order often relates to the conduct of government business or to organization of the executive branch of government. Every act of the president authorizing or directing the performance of an act, in its general context, is an executive order. Governors also issue executive orders. See PRESIDENTIAL PROCLAMATION.

FICHE—

See MICROFICHE.

FORM BOOKS—

books containing sample documents to aid drafting.

FORMS OF ACTION—

conventions that governed English common law pleadings that included the only theories of liability on which a plaintiff's claims could be based. The common law forms of action were usually considered to be eleven in number: trespass, trespass on the case, trover, ejectment, detinue, replevin, debt, covenant, account, special assumpsit, and general assumpsit. Many of these terms are still used today.

GRAND JURY—

a jury of five to twenty-three persons that sits for a specified period of time and hears criminal accusations and evidence, and then determines whether indictments should be made. Compare with PETIT JURY.

HEADNOTES—

brief summaries of the points of law in a case that precede the printed opinion in reports. Headnotes are often numbered and usually do not exceed one or two sentences in length. They may be prepared by an official reporter, the judges of the court, or by commercial publishers of court reports. More than one topic or key number may be assigned to a single headnote. Headnotes typically do not constitute part of the court's opinion and may not be relied upon as legal authority. See KEY NUMBER.

HEARINGS—

proceedings extensively employed by both legislative and administrative agencies to elicit facts or to make authorized determinations. Adjudicative hearings of administrative agencies can be appealed in a court of law. Investigative hearings are often held by congressional committees prior to enactment of legislation, and are important sources of legislative history.

HOLDING—

the declaration of the conclusion of law reached by the court as to the legal effect of the facts of the case.

HOLOGRAPH (OR OLOGRAPH)—

a will, deed, or other legal document that is entirely in the handwriting of the signer.

HORNBOOK—

a basic or rudimentary treatise that reviews a certain field of law in summary, textual form, as opposed to a casebook that is designed as a teaching tool and typically includes many reprints of judicial opinions. The trademarked "Hornbook Series" is published by West Academic.

INDICTMENT—

a formal accusation of a crime made by a grand jury at the request of a prosecuting attorney.

INFORMATION—

an accusation based not on the action of a grand jury but rather on the affirmation of a public official.

INJUNCTION—

a judge's order that a person do or, more commonly, refrain from doing, a certain act. An injunction may be preliminary or temporary, pending trial of the issue presented, or it may be final if the issue has already been decided in court.

JUDGMENT—

See COURT DECISION.

JURISDICTION—

(1) the power given to a court by a constitution or a legislative body to make legally binding decisions over certain persons, property, or subject matter, or (2) the geographical area in which a court's decisions or legislative enactments are binding.

JURISPRUDENCE—

(1) the science or philosophy of law; (2) a collective term for case law as opposed to legislation.

KEYCITE—

Westlaw's electronic citator. See CITATORS.

KEY NUMBER—

a category of the major indexing system devised for American case law, developed by West Publishing Company (now Thomson Reuters). The key number is a permanent number given to a specific point of law.

LAW REVIEW/LAW JOURNAL—

a legal periodical. The term "law review" usually describes a scholarly periodical edited by students at a law school.

LEGISLATIVE HISTORY—

information embodied in legislative documents and other materials that provides background information and insight into the purpose and intent of statutes.

LIABILITY—

responsibility either for damages resulting from an injury or for discharging an obligation or debt.

LIBEL—

(1) written or visual defamation of a person's character; (2) in an admiralty court, the plaintiff's statement of the cause of action and the relief sought.

LITIGATE—

to bring a civil action in court.

LOOSELEAF SERVICES AND REPORTERS—

publications that contain specialized materials focusing on an area of law, which may include federal or state regulations, statutes, decisions, and analysis of legal topics. They traditionally consist of separate pages or pamphlet-sized inserts in special binders, designed for frequent insertion or substitution of new material. Many looseleaf services and reporters are available online. Looseleaf services or reporters are typically referred to as services or topical services.

MANDATORY AUTHORITY—

authority that a given court is bound to follow. Mandatory authority is found in constitutional provisions, legislation, and judicial opinions. Compare with PERSUASIVE AUTHORITY.

MEMORANDUM—

(1) an informal record; (2) a written document that may be used to prove that a contract exists; (3) an exposition of all the points of law pertaining to a particular case (referred to as a "memorandum of law"); or (4) an informal written discussion of the merits of a matter pending in a lawyer's office, usually written by a law clerk or junior associate for a senior associate or partner (referred to as an "office memorandum").

MICROFICHE—

a sheet of film, usually 4 x 6 inches or 3 x 5 inches in size, containing miniaturized photographic images of printed text. The term "fiche" is synonymous with microfiche. "Ultrafiche" is a type of microfiche containing images that are reduced by a factor of 90 or more.

MICROFILM—

a film containing miniaturized photographic images of printed text. This is usually in a reel, but may also be in a cartridge or cassette form.

MICROFORM—

a general term describing miniaturized reproduction of printed text on film or paper. Microfilm and microfiche are specific types of microform.

MODEL CODES—

codes formulated by various groups or institutions to serve as guidelines or models for legislative drafting on a particular topic. Model codes are intended to improve existing laws or unify diverse state legislation.

MOOT POINT—

a point that is not a subject of contention and that is raised only for the purpose of discussion or hypothesis. Many law schools conduct moot courts where students gain practice by arguing hypothetical or moot cases.

MOTION—

a formal request made to a court during the course of a lawsuit for a decision or an action.

NATIONAL REPORTER SYSTEM—

the collection of reporters published by Thomson Reuters (formerly West Publishing) which attempts to publish and digest all cases of precedential value from all U.S. state and federal courts.

NATURAL LANGUAGE—

an online search strategy using English-language sentences or phrases instead of Boolean commands. Compare BOOLEAN LOGIC.

NISI PRIUS—

generally, a court where a case is first tried, as distinguished from an appellate court.

NOTER UP—

the term used in the British Commonwealth countries for a citator.

OBITER DICTUM—

an incidental comment, not necessary to the formulation of the decision, made by the judge in his or her opinion. Such comments are not binding as precedent.

OFFICIAL REPORTS—

court reports mandated by statute or court rule. Compare with UNOFFICIAL REPORTS.

OPINION—

(1) an expression of the reasons why a certain decision (the judgment) was reached in a case. A *majority opinion* is usually written by one judge and represents the principles of law that a majority of his or her colleagues on the court deem operative in a given decision; it has more precedential value than any of the following types of opinions. A *separate opinion* may be written by one or more judges in which he, she, or they concur in or dissent from the majority opinion. A *concurring opinion* agrees with the result reached by the majority, but disagrees with the precise reasoning leading to that result. A *dissenting opinion* disagrees with the result reached by the majority and thus disagrees with the reasoning and/or the principles of law used by the majority in deciding the case. A *plurality opinion* (called a "judgment" by the Supreme Court) is agreed to by less than a majority as to the reasoning of the decision, but is agreed to by a majority as to the result. A *per curiam opinion* is an opinion by the court that expresses its decision

in the case but whose author is not identified. A *memorandum opinion* is a holding of the whole court in which the opinion is very concise. (2) a lawyer's analysis of a legal situation, often communicated to the client in an opinion letter.

ORAL ARGUMENT—

a spoken presentation of reasons for a desired decision directed to an appellate court by attorneys for the parties.

ORDINANCE—

a law passed by a city or county council.

PAMPHLET SUPPLEMENT—

a paperbound supplement to a larger bound volume or a set, usually intended to be discarded when superseded by the next supplement or new bound volume.

PARALLEL CITATION—

a citation reference to the same case printed in two or more different reports.

PER CURIAM—

literally, "by the court." Usually a short opinion written on behalf of the majority of the court but whose author is not identified. It may be accompanied by concurring or dissenting opinions.

PERIODICAL—

a publication appearing at regular intervals. Legal periodicals include law reviews, law school alumni magazines, bar association journals, commercially published journals, and legal newspapers.

PERSUASIVE AUTHORITY—

a law or reasoning which a given court may, but is not bound to, follow. For example, decisions from one jurisdiction may be persuasive authority in the courts of another jurisdiction. Compare with MANDATORY AUTHORITY.

PETIT JURY—

a group of six to twelve persons that decides questions of fact in civil and criminal trials. Compare with GRAND JURY.

PETITION—

a formal, written application to a court requesting judicial action on a certain matter.

PETITIONER—

the person presenting a petition to a court, officer, or legislative body; the one who starts an equity proceeding or the one who takes an appeal from a judgment.

PLAINTIFF—

the person who brings a lawsuit against another.

PLEA BARGAINING—

the process whereby the accused and the prosecutor in a criminal case work out a mutually satisfactory disposition of the case. It usually involves the defendant's pleading guilty to a lesser offense or to only one or some of the counts of a multi-count indictment in return for a lighter sentence than that possible for the graver charge.

PLEADINGS—

the technical documents by which parties to a dispute frame the issue for the court. The plaintiff's complaint or declaration is followed by the defendant's answer; subsequent papers may be filed as needed.

POCKET PART/ POCKET SUPPLEMENT—

a paperbound supplement to a book, inserted in the book through a slit in its back cover. Depending on the type of publication, it may have textual, case, or statutory references keyed to the original publication.

POPULAR NAME TABLE—

a table listing names by which certain cases or statutes have become known, and identifying for each popular name the citation of the case or statute.

POWER OF ATTORNEY—

a document authorizing one person to act as another's agent.

PRECEDENT—

See STARE DECISIS.

PRELIMINARY PRINTS—

the name given to the advance sheets of the official *United States Reports*.

PRESENTMENT—

in criminal law, a written accusation made by the grand jury without the consent or participation of a prosecutor.

PRESIDENTIAL PROCLAMATION—

a declaration issued under specific authority granted to the president by Congress. Generally, it relates to matters of widespread interest. Some proclamations have no legal effect but merely are appeals to the public, e.g., the observance of American Education Week. See EXECUTIVE ORDER.

PRESIDENTIAL SIGNING STATEMENT—

a written statement issued by the president upon signing a bill into law. In the modern era, presidents have often contested the constitutionality of certain provisions and expressed their intention to reconstrue or disregard the provisions under the executive branch's constitutional authority. Legal scholars and others have debated the significance and constitutionality of such statements.

PRIMARY AUTHORITY—

the law itself: constitutions, statutes, case law, ordinances, and administrative regulations issued pursuant to enabling legislation. Primary authority may be either mandatory or persuasive. All other legal writings are secondary authority and are never binding on courts. See AUTHORITY; MANDATORY AUTHORITY; PERSUASIVE AUTHORITY.

PRIVATE LAW—

(1) an act that relates to a specific person, or (2) that body of law that concerns relations between private parties rather than governmental powers and functions. Compare PUBLIC LAW.

PROCEDURAL LAW—

the law which governs the operation of the legal system, including court rules and rules of procedure, as distinguished from substantive law.

PUBLIC LAW—

(1) an act that affects the public as a whole. It may be: (a) general (applicable to each person in the jurisdiction); (b) local (applicable to a specific geographic area); or (c) special (concerning an entity charged with a public interest), or (2) that body of law that concerns governmental powers and functions rather than relations between private parties.

RATIO DECIDENDI—

the point in a case that determines the result—the basis of the decision.

RECORD—

the documentation, prepared for an appeal, of the trial court proceedings (pleadings, motions, transcript of examination of witnesses, objections to evidence, rulings, jury instructions, opinion, etc.).

RECORDS AND BRIEFS—

See APPEAL PAPERS.

REGIONAL REPORTER—

a unit of the *National Reporter System* that reports state court cases from a defined geographical area.

REGULATIONS—

rules or orders issued by various governmental departments to carry out the provisions of statutory law. Agencies issue regulations to guide the activity of their employees and to ensure uniform application of the law.

RELIEF—

the remedy or redress sought by a complainant from a court.

REMAND—

the act of sending back for further proceedings, as when a higher court sends a case or claim back to a lower court.

REPORTS—

(1) court reports—published judicial decisions organized on the basis of jurisdiction, court, period of time, subject matter, case significance, or some other grouping; and (2) administrative reports or decisions—published decisions of an administrative agency.

RESOLUTION—

a formal expression of the opinion or policy of a rule-making body. For example, the United States Senate uses "simple resolutions" to express nonbinding opinions or to deal with internal Senate business.

RESPONDENT—

the party who makes an answer to a bill in an equity proceeding or who contends against an appeal.

RESTATEMENTS OF THE LAW—

systematic restatements of the existing common law in certain areas, published by the American Law Institute since 1923. The restatements are valuable secondary research sources, but are not binding as law.

REVISED STATUTES—

in some jurisdictions, the name for a statutory code. See also CODE; COMPILED STATUTES; CONSOLIDATED STATUTES.

RULES OF COURT—

the rules regulating practice and procedure before a court. Rules may be issued by an individual court, by the highest court in the jurisdiction, or by the legislature.

SANCTION—

(1) to assent to another's actions; (2) a penalty for violating a law.

SCOPE NOTE—

a notation appearing below a topic heading in a publication that identifies the content of the topic.

SECONDARY AUTHORITY—

See PRIMARY AUTHORITY.

SECTION LINE—

the subject of a key number in West's key number digests, printed after the key number.

SESSION LAWS—

laws enacted by a legislature, typically published in order of passage in bound or pamphlet volumes after the adjournment of each regular or special session.

SHEPARDIZING—

the act of using *Shepard's Citations* to update or verify the status of an authority. The term is a trademark of Reed Elsevier Properties Inc. and describes the general use of its *Shepard's* publications and citator services. In common usage, the term refers to the use of any citator. See CITATORS.

SLIP LAW—

a single legislative enactment published in a pamphlet or on a single page immediately after its passage.

SLIP OPINION—

an individual judicial opinion published separately soon after it is decided.

SQUIB—

a very brief summary of a case or a single point of law from a case. Compare with HEADNOTES and SYLLABUS.

STAR PAGINATION—

a system used in many unofficial editions of court reports to show where the pages of the text of the official edition begin and end.

STARE DECISIS—

the common law doctrine that, when a court has formulated a principle of law as applicable to a given set of facts, it will follow that principle and apply it in future cases where the facts are substantially the same. It grounds the decision of present cases on the basis of past precedent.

STATUTE—

enacted legislation. Depending upon its context in usage, statute may mean a single act of a legislature or a body of acts that are collected and arranged according to a defined system or for a session of a legislature or parliament.

STATUTES AT LARGE—

the official compilation of acts passed by the U.S. Congress. The Statutes at Large from an individual Congressional session are published in chronological order of passage at the end of each session.

STATUTES OF LIMITATIONS—

laws setting time limits after which a dispute cannot be taken to court or a crime prosecuted.

STATUTORY INSTRUMENTS—

administrative rules and regulations from England, Canada, and several other common law nations. The term applies especially to *Statutory Instruments,* the annual publication of England's administrative rules and regulations.

STYLE OF A CASE—

the names of the parties to a lawsuit as they are written in the heading at the beginning of a written court document. It is also referred to as the "caption" of a case.

SUBPOENA—

a court order compelling a witness to appear and testify in a certain proceeding. A *subpoena duces tecum* compels production of documents or other tangible items.

SUBSTANTIVE LAW—

the law which establishes rights and obligations, as distinguished from procedural law.

SUMMONS—

a notice delivered by a sheriff or other authorized individual informing a person that he or she is the defendant in a civil action, and specifying a time and place to appear in court to answer to the plaintiff.

SUPERSEDE—

to displace or to supplant a publication or one of its segments with another.

SUPREME COURT—

(1) the court of last resort in the federal judicial system; (2) in state judicial systems, except New York and Massachusetts, the highest appellate court or court of last resort.

SYLLABUS—

a brief summary of the significant facts, procedural history, and holding in a case that precedes the printed opinion in reports, often in paragraph form. The syllabus typically does not constitute part of the court's opinion and may not be relied upon as legal authority; however, certain courts, such as the Ohio Supreme Court, have adopted rules that make the syllabus the authoritative statement of the binding legal principles of the case.

TABLE OF CASES—

a list of cases, arranged alphabetically by name, with citations and references to where the cases are published or discussed in a publication.

TABLE OF STATUTES—

a list of statutes, arranged alphabetically, with references to where the statutes are published or discussed in a publication.

TEMPORARY LAW—

an act in force for a limited period of time.

TERM OF COURT—

the period of time prescribed by law during which a court holds session. For example, the October Term of the Supreme Court of the United States, the only term during which the Court currently sits, begins in October and continues to June or July.

TRANSCRIPT OF RECORD—

the official printed record compiled in each case of the proceedings and pleadings, necessary for the appellate court to review the history of the case.

TREATISE—

a book on a legal subject which may be critical, evaluative, or interpretative.

TREATY—

an agreement between two or more sovereign nations.

ULTRAFICHE—

See MICROFICHE.

UNIFORM LAWS—

proposed statutes drafted with the intention of presenting them for adoption by the several states in the interest of uniformity. A considerable number of uniform laws on various subjects have been approved by the Uniform Law Commission (ULC, also referred to as the National Conference of Commissioners on Uniform State Laws, or NCCUSL), and have been adopted by jurisdictions in the United States and its possessions. An example of a uniform law is the Uniform Commercial Code, which has been adopted, in whole or in part, by every state.

UNIFORM SYSTEM OF CITATION—

See BLUEBOOK.

UNOFFICIAL REPORTS—

court reports published without statutory direction. Unofficial reports typically reproduce the complete text of the court decisions and include additional features (headnotes, finding aids, indexes, etc.) not provided by the official reports.

VENUE—

the particular geographical area where a court with jurisdiction may hear a case.

VERDICT—

the finding or decision of a jury in a civil or criminal case on the questions of fact submitted to them.

WESTLAW—

the CALR service produced by Thomson Reuters (previously produced by West Publishing). *Westlaw* provides the full text of court decisions, statutes, administrative materials, *ALR* annotations, law review articles, Supreme Court briefs, and many other items, arranged in databases and searched by words, with Boolean operators, or via natural language searches. *WestlawNext* is a version of *Westlaw* that searches across multiple databases, primarily with word or natural language searches.

WESTLAWNEXT—

See WESTLAW.

WRIT—

a written court order, of which there are many types, directed to an official or party, requiring the performance of an act or giving the authority to perform an act.

Fundamentals of Legal Research

TENTH EDITION

Chapter 1

AN INTRODUCTION TO LEGAL RESEARCH

Legal research is the process of identifying and retrieving the law-related information necessary to support legal decision-making. In its broadest sense, legal research includes each step of a course of action that begins with an analysis of the facts of a problem and concludes with the application and communication of the results of the investigation.

Many types of information are needed to support legal decision-making. Although this book focuses on information sources that are concerned explicitly with law, legal decisions cannot be made out of their economic, social, historical, and political contexts. Today, legal decisions often involve business, scientific, medical, psychological, and technological information. Consequently, the process of legal research often involves investigation into other relevant disciplines.

This chapter, an introduction to legal research, explains why researchers seek certain types of information. This chapter explains the basic jurisprudential model upon which legal resources are designed, created, and collected, and introduces materials that are covered more comprehensively in subsequent chapters.

A. SOURCES OF LAW

American law, like the law of other countries, comes from a variety of sources. In the context of legal research, the term "sources of law" can refer to three different concepts. In one sense, the term sources of law refers to the origins of legal concepts and ideas. Custom, tradition, principles of morality, and economic, political, philosophical, and religious thought may manifest themselves in law. Legal research frequently must extend to these areas, especially when historical or policy issues are involved.

The term sources of law can also refer to the governmental institutions that formulate legal rules. The United States incorporates one national (federal) government, fifty autonomous state governments, and the local government of the District of Columbia. Also within the United States are more than 560 federally recognized Indian tribes.[1] Although there are some variations in their structures, each of these governments has legislative, executive, and judicial components that interact with one another. Because all three branches of government "make law" and create legal information that is the subject of legal research, researchers must understand the types of information created by each branch and the processes through which that information is created.

---

[1] http://bia.gov/WhoWeAre/BIA/OIS/TribalGovernmentServices/TribalDirectory/.

Finally, sources of law can refer to the published manifestations of the law. The books, electronic databases, microforms, CD-ROMs, DVDs, and other media that contain legal information are all sources of law.

1.   The Nature of Legal Authority

Legal authority is any published source of law setting forth legal rules, legal doctrine, or legal reasoning that can be used as a basis for legal decisions.[2] In discussions about legal research, the term *authority* is used to refer both to the types of legal information and to the degree of persuasiveness of legal information.

When the term is used to describe types of information, legal authority can be categorized as *primary* or *secondary*.[3] Primary authorities are authorized statements of the law formulated by governmental institutions. Such authorities include the written opinions of courts (case law), constitutions, legislation, rules of court, and the rules, regulations, and opinions of administrative agencies. Secondary authorities are statements about the law and are used to explain, interpret, develop, locate, or update primary authorities. Treatises, articles in law reviews and other scholarly journals, *American Law Reports (A.L.R.)* annotations, restatements of the law, and looseleaf services are examples of secondary authorities.[4]

When the term is used to describe the degree of persuasiveness of legal information, authority is an estimation of the power of information to influence a legal decision. In this sense, authority can be termed *binding* (also called *mandatory*), meaning that a court or other decision-maker believes the authority applies to the case before it and must be followed; or authority can be considered *persuasive*, meaning that a decision-maker can, if so persuaded, follow it.

Only primary authority can be binding; but some primary authority will be merely persuasive, depending on the source of the authority and its content. Secondary authority can never be binding, but it can be persuasive. The application of legal authority to individual problems is a complex and often controversial process. Variations in the facts of individual cases enable judges, influenced by their own philosophies and perspectives, to exercise wide discretion in interpreting and applying legal authority.[5]

2.   The Common Law Tradition

The American legal system, like those of most English-speaking countries, is part of the *common law* tradition. The common law is the body of law that originated and developed in England and spread to those countries that England settled or controlled. Historically, the common law was considered to be the "unwritten law" and was distinguished from the "written," or statutory, law. The common law was an oral tradition derived from general customs, principles, and rules handed down from generation to generation and was eventually reflected in the reports of the decisions of

---

[2] THOMAS B. MARVELL, APPELLATE COURTS AND LAWYERS 129 (1978).

[3] When used in this sense, the terms *authority* and *source* are interchangeable.

[4] Other types of relevant information, such as historical, economic, and social science information, are also sometimes referred to as secondary authorities. Such materials are often used in legal argument.

[5] For a classic explanation of why courts cite authority and a discussion of the authority of various legal sources, see John Henry Merryman, *The Authority of Authority,* 6 STAN. L. REV. 613 (1954). For an examination of how one noted jurist used authority, see William H. Manz, *Cardozo's Use of Authority: An Empirical Study,* 32 CAL. W. L. REV. 31 (1995).

courts. The English common law arrived in America with the colonists, who used it as a basis for developing their own law and legal institutions.[6] English common law is still cited as authority in American courts.[7]

The common law tradition should be contrasted with the *civil law* tradition, which is based on Roman law and predominates in continental Europe and Latin America. Common and civil law systems differ in their theories about the sources of law, the relative persuasiveness of the sources, and the ways in which the sources are used in legal reasoning. For example, in legal systems that are part of the civil law tradition, the legislature creates a comprehensive code of legal principles that represents the highest form of law, and there is a presumption that code provisions apply to every legal problem.[8] In common law systems, there is no presumption that statutes or codes cover all legal problems; many legal principles are discoverable only through the "unwritten," or common law.

3. Case Law and the Doctrine of Precedent[9]

a.   Structure of the Court System. On the federal and state levels there are hierarchical judicial systems in which some courts have jurisdiction, or control, over other courts. The typical court structure consists of three levels,[10] and it is important to understand what types of information are created at each level and where that information can be found.

Trial courts are courts of original jurisdiction that make determinations of law and of fact, with juries often making the determinations of fact. Documents prepared by the parties, called *pleadings* (complaint, answer, interrogatories, among others) and *motions*, are filed before, during, and after a trial; *exhibits* are submitted into evidence during the trial; and a *record* (or transcript) is made of the proceedings. Although in the past the pleadings, motions, exhibits, and records were usually only available directly from the court in which the litigation was conducted, some of these documents now are obtainable electronically from various governmental and commercial sources. After a trial, the trial court issues a judgment or decision and sometimes a written opinion; the opinions of trial courts are infrequently published, reported, or otherwise made generally available to the public.[11]

Intermediate appellate courts, sometimes called circuit courts or courts of appeal,[12] have authority over lower courts within a specified geographical area or jurisdiction.

---

[6] For general histories of American law, see LAWRENCE M. FRIEDMAN, A HISTORY OF AMERICAN LAW (3d ed. 2005); LAWRENCE M. FRIEDMAN, AMERICAN LAW IN THE 20TH CENTURY (2002); and KERMIT L. HALL, THE MAGIC MIRROR: LAW IN AMERICAN HISTORY (2d ed. 2008).

[7] See Chapter 22 of this book for a basic discussion of researching the law of the United Kingdom.

[8] JOHN HENRY MERRYMAN, THE CIVIL LAW TRADITION 23–25 (3d ed. 2007).

[9] Case law is discussed extensively in the following chapters of this book: Chapter 4, Court Reports; Chapter 5, Federal Court Reports; Chapter 6, State Court Reports and the National Reporter System; and Chapter 7, Digests for Court Reports.

[10] A chart included in Chapter 4, Section A depicts the typical court structure of both the federal judicial system and a state judicial system.

[11] Many legal researchers are surprised to learn that written opinions are not issued in all cases, and that only a small percentage of written opinions are published and reported. For a more complete discussion of this subject, see Chapter 4, Section A.

[12] Some states have no intermediate appellate courts; appeals go directly to the courts of last resort in these states. The titles used for different courts vary from state to state. For example, Indiana's circuit courts are trial courts; New York's highest court is the Court of Appeals and its supreme courts are trial courts. For

Appellate courts generally will not review factual determinations made by lower courts, but will review claimed errors of law that are reflected in the record created in the lower courts. Appellate courts accept written *briefs* (statements prepared by the counsel arguing the case) and frequently hear *oral arguments*. Some large law libraries collect copies of the briefs filed in appellate courts. Intermediate appellate courts often issue written opinions that are sometimes published; they may be found in law libraries and electronic sources. Many appellate courts have the discretion to determine on a case-by-case basis whether to publish opinions. Rules of court in each jurisdiction specify whether "unpublished" opinions can be cited as authority.

A court of last resort, typically called a supreme court, is the highest appellate court in a jurisdiction. State courts of last resort are the highest authorities on questions of state law, and the Supreme Court of the United States is the highest authority on questions of federal law. Many libraries make available in paper or electronic format copies of the briefs and records filed in the Supreme Court of the United States and in the court of last resort in the state in which they are located. Transcripts of the oral arguments in these courts also are available in some law libraries and on the Internet. Courts of last resort usually issue written opinions that are almost always published, collected by libraries, and made available electronically.

    b.   *Federal and State Jurisdiction.* There are some matters over which a state or federal court has exclusive jurisdiction and some matters over which a state court has concurrent jurisdiction with the federal courts. Federal courts can, in some instances, decide questions of state law; state courts can, in some instances, decide questions of federal law. For both the beginning law student and the experienced attorney, it can be difficult to determine which matters are questions of federal law, which are questions of state law, and which can be subjects of both. In researching any particular problem, legal information of various types may be needed from both state and federal sources.

    c.   *Precedent.* In the early history of English law, the custom developed of considering the decisions of courts to be *precedents* that would serve as examples, or authorities, for decisions in later cases with similar questions of law. Under what has come to be called the *doctrine of precedent,* the decision of a common law court not only settles a dispute between the parties involved but also sets a precedent to be followed in future cases.[13] According to an older, now discredited, theory, judges merely declared what had always been the law when they decided a case. It is now generally acknowledged that judges often create new law when applying precedent to current problems.

    The doctrine of precedent is closely related to three other concepts represented by the Latin terms *stare decisis, ratio decidendi,* and *dictum.*

    Stare decisis, literally "to stand on what has been decided," is the principle that the decision of a court is binding authority on the court that issued the decision and on lower courts in the same jurisdiction for the disposition of factually similar controversies. In

_____

detailed diagrams of federal and state court systems, see CATHERINE A. KITCHELL, BNA'S DIRECTORY OF FEDERAL COURTS, JUDGES, AND CLERKS (annual).

    [13] The bare skeleton of an appeal to precedent is easily stated: "The previous treatment of occurrence X in manner Y constitutes, *solely because of its historical pedigree,* a reason for treating X in manner Y if and when X again occurs." Frederick Schauer, *Precedent,* 39 STAN. L. REV. 571 (1987). For a discussion of the early development of the doctrine of precedent, see M. ETHAN KATSH, THE ELECTRONIC MEDIA AND THE TRANSFORMATION OF LAW 33–39 (1989).

the hierarchical federal and state court systems, therefore, the decisions of a trial court can control future decisions of that trial court, but they do not control other trial courts or appellate courts. Appellate courts can bind themselves and lower courts over which they have appellate jurisdiction, but appellate courts cannot bind other appellate courts at the same level.[14]

The *ratio decidendi* is the holding or the principle of law on which the case was decided. It is the *ratio decidendi* that sets the precedent and is binding on courts in the future. Unlike legislatures, American courts do not promulgate general propositions of law, nor do they respond to hypothetical questions.[15] Rather, courts decide actual cases and controversies, and the rules they announce are tied to specific fact situations. Therefore, the *ratio decidendi,* or rule of the case, must be considered in conjunction with the facts of the case to understand its full meaning.

In contrast, *dictum* (or *obiter dictum*) is language in an opinion that is not necessary to the decision. *Dictum* comes from the Latin verb *decire,* "to say," and refers to what is "said by the way," that is, that which is not essential to the holding of the court. Although language categorized as *dictum* is not binding on future courts, it might be persuasive. Yesterday's *dictum* may develop into tomorrow's doctrine.

It is important to distinguish the *ratio decidendi* of a case from *dictum*, although that can be a challenge. The determination of what is the *ratio decidendi,* and what is

---

[14] For the views of a former U.S. Supreme Court justice regarding the importance of *stare decisis,* see Lewis F. Powell, Jr., *Stare Decisis and Judicial Restraint,* 47 WASH. & LEE L. REV. 281 (1990). *See also* William N. Eskridge, Jr., *The Case of the Amorous Defendant: Criticizing Absolute Stare Decisis for Statutory Cases,* 88 MICH. L. REV. 2450 (1990); Lawrence C. Marshall, *Contempt of Congress: A Reply to the Critics of an Absolute Rule of Statutory Stare Decisis,* 88 MICH. L. REV. 2467 (1990); David K. Koehler, *Justice Souter's "Keep-What-You-Want-and-Throw-Away-the-Rest" Interpretation of Stare Decisis,* 42 BUFF. L. REV. 859 (1994); Amy L. Padden, *Overruling Decisions in the Supreme Court: The Role of a Decision's Vote, Age, and Subject Matter in the Application of Stare Decisis After* Payne v. Tennessee, 82 GEO. L.J. 1689 (1994); Robert C. Wigton, *What Does It Take to Overrule? An Analysis of Supreme Court Overrulings and the Doctrine of Stare Decisis,* 18 LEGAL STUD. F. 3 (1994). For an empirical study of why justices of the Supreme Court of the United States chose to alter precedent during a 47–year period, see SAUL BRENNER & HAROLD J. SPAETH, STARE INDECISIS: THE ALTERATION OF PRECEDENT ON THE SUPREME COURT, 1946–1992 (1995). For an article that argues that justices are not influenced by landmark precedents with which they disagree, see Jeffrey A. Segal & Harold J. Spaeth, *The Influence of* Stare Decisis *on the Votes of United States Supreme Court Justices,* 40 AM. J. POL. SCI. 971 (1996), which is a portion of an entire issue devoted to *stare decisis.* For the economic effect of *stare decisis,* see Thomas R. Lee, *Stare Decisis in Economic Perspective: An Economic Analysis of the Supreme Court's Doctrine of Precedent,* 78 N.C. L. Rev. 643 (2000).

For an extensive sociological inquiry into the importance of precedent, including the need for attention to computer technology, see SUSAN W. BRENNER, PRECEDENT INFLATION (1991); Susan W. Brenner, *Of Publication and Precedent: An Inquiry into the Ethnomethodology of Case Reporting in the American Legal System,* 39 DEPAUL L. REV. 461 (1990). *But see* Michael Wells, *The Unimportance of Precedent in the Law of Federal Courts,* 39 DEPAUL L. REV. 357 (1990). For an attempt to describe precedent and its applications, see Ruggero J. Aldisert, *Precedent: What It Is and What It Isn't; When Do We Kiss It and When Do We Kill It?,* 17 PEPP. L. REV. 605 (1990). *See also* Lawrence C. Marshall, *"Let Congress Do It": The Case for an Absolute Rule of Statutory Stare Decisis,* 88 MICH. L. REV. 177 (1989); Note, *Constitutional Stare Decisis,* 103 HARV. L. REV. 1344 (1990); Evan H. Caminker, *Why Must Inferior Courts Obey Superior Court Precedents?,* 46 STAN. L. REV. 817 (1994).

[15] Some state courts (but no federal courts) issue advisory opinions, which basically advise on what the law would be based on a hypothetical set of facts. Advisory opinions are typically only issued at the request of a state government official or entity, and then only in narrowly proscribed situations. *See* John P. McIver, *Advice on State Court Advisory Opinions,* 13 PERSP: TEACHING LEGAL RES. AND WRITING 98 (2005).

dictum, is a focus of much legal analysis and is often the critical point of legal argument.[16]

Courts have much leeway in interpreting cases put forth as binding precedent.[17] No two cases are exactly the same, and, on one or more points, every case can be distinguished from others. Generally, a case is considered binding if it shares the same significant facts with the case at issue and does not differ in any significant facts from the instant case. Furthermore, similar issues must be presented in the two cases, and the resolution of those issues must have been necessary to the decision in the previous case (otherwise, the words of the court would be *dictum*). Courts can reject cases put forth as binding authority by distinguishing the cases on their facts or issues, thus finding that the previous cases are different from the instant case in some significant way.[18] In some situations, a court can avoid being bound by a previous case by finding that the rule put forth in the previous case is no longer valid and overruling it.

The doctrine of precedent assumes that decisions of common law courts should be given consideration even if they are not binding. Accordingly, researchers often look to relevant decisions in other U.S. jurisdictions and even other common law countries. Cases that are not directly on point may contain principles or legal theories on which legal arguments can be based. Decisions that are not binding, either because they have different fact situations or because they are from another jurisdiction, can be persuasive because of the depth of analysis and quality of reasoning in the opinion. Among other factors that can determine the persuasiveness of a non-binding opinion are the location and position of the court that issued the opinion, the identity of the jurist writing the opinion, the agreement (or lack thereof) among individual members of the court (i.e., unanimous decisions versus split decisions), and subsequent judicial and academic treatment of the opinion.

Policy considerations supporting the doctrine of precedent include the resulting fairness, as it encourages similar cases to be treated similarly; the predictability and stability it encourages within the legal system; and its efficiency in terms of time and energy as it enables decision-makers to take advantage of previous efforts and prior wisdom.[19] Critics argue that reliance on precedent can result in a rigid and mechanical jurisprudence that can force us to treat unlike cases as if they were similar; that the doctrine of precedent can perpetuate outmoded rules; and that its inherently conservative nature can impede the law from being responsive to new social needs.[20]

---

[16] *See* Pierre N. Leval, *Judging Under the Constitution: Dicta About Dicta*, 81 N.Y.U. L. REV. 1249, 1256–58 (2006).

[17] In a chapter entitled "The Leeways of Precedent," Karl Llewellyn presented "a selection of [sixty-four] available impeccable precedent techniques" used by courts to follow, avoid, expand, or redirect precedent. KARL N. LLEWELLYN, THE COMMON LAW TRADITION: DECIDING APPEALS 77–91 (1960).

[18] *See generally* Kent Greenawalt, *Reflections on Holding and Dictum*, 39 J. LEGAL EDUC. 431 (1989). The practice of judges writing separately, generally in the hope of laying the groundwork for a reversal or to demonstrate why one rationale may be better than another, is becoming commonplace. For some observations on this trend, see Laura Krugman Ray, *The Justices Write Separately: Uses of the Concurrence by the Rehnquist Court*, 23 U.C. DAVIS L. REV. 777 (1990); and Ruth Bader Ginsburg, *Remarks on Writing Separately*, 65 WASH. L. REV. 133 (1990).

[19] See John Henry Merryman, *The Authority of Authority, supra* note 5, for a discussion of the benefits of following precedent.

[20] *See* Steven M. Barkan, *Deconstructing Legal Research: A Law Librarian's Commentary on Critical Legal Studies,* 79 LAW LIBR. J. 617 (1987).

Notwithstanding these criticisms, the doctrine of precedent remains the foundation upon which our models of legal research are constructed. The written opinions of courts, particularly appellate courts, are the stuff of legal argument and the major source of legal doctrine. Consequently, they are the primary, but certainly not the only, objects of legal research. Law libraries and legal electronic databases are filled with published court opinions, along with secondary sources and index tools to help researchers find, interpret, and update opinions that are relevant to particular fact patterns.

4.   Legislation and the Interpretation of Statutes[21]

a.   Legislation. A *statute,* sometimes referred to as legislation, is a positive statement of legal rules enacted by a legislature. In comparison, a *constitution* is the fundamental body of principles, most often written, by which a political body, such as a nation or state, governs itself. Because many of the basic concepts and techniques of statutory and constitutional research are similar, they can be discussed together at an introductory level. However, American constitutional law, both federal and state, is a pervasive and specialized subject; including it in a general discussion of legislation should not obscure either its importance or its uniqueness.

In English law, the king enacted the earliest statutes with the concurrence of his council; later, the role of statute-maker was assumed by Parliament. In the United States, statutes are enacted by the legislative branch and signed into law by the chief executive. Statutory law has become increasingly pervasive since the industrial revolution, when it became apparent that a jurisprudence based only on judicial decisions could not meet the needs of a growing, dynamic society. Situations developed in which answers were needed that were not found in court reports, or the answers found in court reports either no longer met current needs or resulted in actions that were considered unjust.

Statutes, and collections of statutes arranged by subject called *codes,* have become very important in common law systems; American law combines both statutory and case law. Statutes are used to create new areas of law; to fill gaps in the law; and to change court-made rules. However, unlike in civil law systems, in the American legal system there is no presumption that a statute will apply to every legal problem or that codes are comprehensive statements of the law.[22]

b.   Statutory Interpretation. Courts play predominant roles in interpreting and applying statutes and in extending the law to subjects not expressly covered by statutes. The legislature may state a general legal rule in the form of a statute, but it is the judiciary that interprets the general rule and applies it to specific cases. Under the doctrine of precedent, it is the statute as *interpreted by the courts* that is applied in the next case. In theory, if the legislature disagrees with the way a court has interpreted a statute, the legislature should revise the statute.[23]

---

[21] Constitutions and legislation are discussed in the following chapters of this book: Chapter 8, Constitutional Law and the Supreme Court of the United States; Chapter 9, Federal Legislation; Chapter 10, Federal Legislative Histories; Chapter 11, State and Municipal Legislation.

[22] Louisiana's legal system is mixed, with some elements of a civil law system dating from its time as a colony of France and Spain, and may present an exception to this general rule.

[23] GUIDO CALABRESI, A COMMON LAW FOR THE AGE OF STATUTES 31–34 (1982). *See also* William N. Eskridge, Jr., *Overriding Supreme Court Statutory Interpretation Decisions,* 101 YALE L.J. 331 (1991).

Statutory interpretation is an important part of legal research.[24] Researchers must not only find the statutes applicable to a problem, they must also find information that will help determine what the statutes mean and how they should be applied. After looking for the "plain meaning" of the words of a statute,[25] and applying traditional canons or principles of statutory interpretation to the text of the statute,[26] researchers resort to a number of approaches to statutory interpretation.

An important method of statutory interpretation is to look for judicial opinions that have construed the specific statute. The persuasiveness of interpretive opinions depends on the similarity of facts involved and on the courts issuing the opinions. Legislatures sometimes pass laws that are designed to reflect existing common law rules; in such situations judicial opinions that pre-date the statute are useful aids to interpretation.

Researchers often attempt to identify the legislature's purpose in passing a statute and the legislature's intended meaning for specific statutory provisions. To do this, researchers look at the *legislative history* of the statute—documents, such as the original bill and revisions thereto, revised versions of bills and legislative debates, hearings, reports, and other materials, created by the legislature while the statute was under consideration—for evidence of legislative purpose and intent.[27] Although controversy exists over their proper use,[28] legislative histories are often consulted by lawyers and judges and are frequently used in legal argument.

Researchers also search for cases from other jurisdictions that have interpreted similar statutes. Although these opinions are not binding authority, well-reasoned opinions from other courts can be very persuasive. This approach is consistent with the doctrine of precedent, under which the decisions of other common law courts may be considered, even if they are not binding.

5. Administrative Law[29]

The third major institutional source of law is the executive branch of government. The President of the United States and the governors of the states issue orders and create other documents with legal effect. Executive departments and offices, and administrative agencies, establishments, and corporations all create legal information.

---

[24] On statutory construction in general, see ANTONIN SCALIA & BRYAN A. GARNER, READING LAW: THE INTERPRETATION OF LEGAL TEXTS (2012); F. REED DICKERSON, THE INTERPRETATION AND APPLICATION OF STATUTES (1975); NORMAN J. SINGER, STATUTES AND STATUTORY CONSTRUCTION (6th ed. 2000); KENT GREENAWALT, LEGISLATION: STATUTORY INTERPRETATION: 20 QUESTIONS (1999); and WILLIAM N. ESKRIDGE, JR. ET AL., LEGISLATION AND STATUTORY CONSTRUCTION (2000). For a variety of views on the role of statutory construction, see *Symposium on Statutory Interpretation*, 53 SMU L. REV. 1 (2000).

[25] Some states have "plain meaning" statutes that attempt to limit courts in their interpretation of statutes that are unambiguous on their face. For an example, see OR. REV. STAT. § 174.010 *et seq.* (2007).

[26] Karl Llewellyn provided an extensive listing of canons of construction to demonstrate that, since legal arguments suggest that there can be only one correct meaning of a statute, there are two opposing canons on every point. KARL N. LLEWELLYN, *supra* note 17, at 521–35.

[27] The usual components of a legislative history are described in detail in Chapter 10.

[28] *See* Peter C. Schanck, *An Essay on the Role of Legislative Histories in Statutory Interpretation*, 80 LAW LIBR. J. 391, 414 (1988); Philip P. Frickey, *From the Big Sleep to the Big Heat: The Revival of Theory in Statutory Interpretation*, 77 MINN. L. REV. 241 (1992); James J. Brudney, *Congressional Commentary on Judicial Interpretations of Statutes: Idle Chatter or Telling Response?*, 93 MICH. L. REV. 1 (1994). *But see* J. Myron Jacobstein & Roy M. Mersky, *Congressional Intent and Legislative Histories: Analysis or Psychoanalysis?*, 82 LAW LIBR. J. 297 (1990). *See also* Chapter 10.

[29] Research in administrative law is discussed in Chapter 13.

Administrative agencies, which exist on the federal and state levels, are created by the legislative branch of government and are usually part of the executive branch. A number of independent agencies, establishments, and corporations exist within the executive branch but are not considered to be executive departments.[30] For the most part, federal agencies handle matters of federal law and state agencies handle matters of state law, but there is often interaction between federal and state agencies. Administrative agencies conduct activities that are in nature both legislative and adjudicative, as well as executive. Under the authority of a statute, these agencies often create and publish rules and regulations that further interpret a statute. Agencies may also make determinations of law and fact in controversies arising under the statute and, like courts, publish opinions.

Administrative law can be a very complex area to research. Not only will researchers need to find, interpret, and update the rules, regulations, and decisions created by the administrative agency, but they will also need to find, interpret, and update the legislation the agency is administering and judicial opinions that interpret those rules, administrative adjudications, and legislation.

B. THE MATERIALS OF LEGAL RESEARCH

Published legal resources can be divided into three broad categories: (1) primary sources or authorities;[31] (2) secondary sources; and (3) index, search, or finding tools. All of these "published" legal resources can appear in more than one format, including printed books, electronic databases, digital images, microforms, compact disks (CD-ROMs and DVDs), videos, and audiocassettes. Many resources contain more than one type of information and serve more than one function. For example, some electronic resources and looseleaf services include both primary authority and secondary materials; they are, at the same time, designed to be finding tools. An understanding of how legal materials are structured and organized (regardless of the media in which they are published) is necessary to effective legal research.

1. Primary Sources

As previously noted, primary sources are authoritative statements of legal rules issued by governmental bodies. They include a range of sources, such as opinions and rules of courts, constitutions, legislation, and administrative regulations and opinions. Because many primary sources are published in the order they are issued, with little or no indexing or other subject access, secondary sources and indexing tools are needed to identify and retrieve them.

---

[30] The Federal Communications Commission, the Interstate Commerce Commission, and the Securities and Exchange Commission are among the many independent federal establishments and corporations. The *United States Government Manual* contains a complete list of executive agencies, independent establishments, and government corporations. A wealth of information about and from all branches of the federal government is available at the Government Printing Office website, *FDSys*, http://www.gpo.gov/fdsys/.

[31] As noted earlier, the terms *authority* and *source* are interchangeable when referring to types of legal materials.

2. Secondary Sources[32]

Secondary sources are materials about the law that are used to explain, interpret, develop, locate, or update primary sources. The major types of secondary sources are treatises, restatements, looseleaf services, legislative histories, law reviews and other legal periodicals, legal encyclopedias, *American Law Reports* (*A.L.R.*) *annotations*, and legal dictionaries. Secondary sources can be interpretive and may contain textual analysis, doctrinal synthesis, and critical commentary of varying degrees of persuasiveness. Depending upon the reputation of the author or publisher, some secondary sources, such as restatements, certain scholarly treatises, and some journal articles, can be persuasive to a court.[33] In contrast, practice manuals and legal encyclopedias have little persuasive value but are useful for basic introductions to subjects, for concise or "black letter" statements of legal rules, and for practical advice. Secondary sources can be used as finding tools to locate other information. For example, cases cited in treatises, law review articles, and encyclopedias can lead to other cases.

3. Index, Search, and Finding Tools[34]

Index, search, and finding tools help locate or update primary and secondary sources. The major types of finding tools are digests (to locate cases discussing similar points of law), annotations in annotated statutes and codes,[35] citators, and legal periodical indexes. Index, search, and finding tools are *not* authority and should never be cited as such.

Looseleaf services and computer-assisted legal research (CALR) systems, such as *Westlaw* and *LexisNexis*, are among the most valuable finding tools. They must be distinguished from other finding tools because they contain the full text of primary authorities, as well as materials from secondary sources.

4. American Law Publishing

a. Proliferation of Materials. In the colonial period of American history, law books were extremely scarce and consisted mostly of English law reports. The most extensive law book collections numbered from 50 to 100 volumes.[36] As the country spread westward and the economy changed from agrarian to industrial, greater demands were

---

[32] Secondary sources are discussed in the following chapters of this book: Chapter 10, Federal Legislative Histories; Chapter 14, Topical Services; Chapter 16, Legal Encyclopedias; Chapter 17, American Law Reports; Chapter 18, Legal Periodicals and Indexes; Chapter 19, Treatises, Restatements, Uniform Laws, and Model Acts; and Chapter 20, Practice Materials and Other Resources.

[33] It should be noted, however, that the writings of legal scholars are generally not held in the same high levels of esteem in common law systems as in civil law systems. *See,* JOHN HENRY MERRYMAN, THE CIVIL LAW TRADITION, *supra* note 8, at 56–60.

[34] In this book, index, search, and finding tools are discussed in conjunction with the resources they are designed to locate. Two chapters, however, are devoted to specific finding tools: Chapter 7, Digests for Court Reports; and Chapter 15, Citators.

[35] Do not confuse annotated statutes, which have brief annotations, or "squibs," describing cases that interpret statutory provisions, and annotated reports, such as *A.L.R.*, which have lengthy interpretive annotations of cases.

[36] LAWRENCE M. FRIEDMAN, A HISTORY OF AMERICAN LAW 474–82 (3d ed. 2005); ALBERT J. HARNO, LEGAL EDUCATION IN THE UNITED STATES 19 (1953). For thorough discussions of early American law book publishing, see ERWIN C. SURRENCY, A HISTORY OF AMERICAN LAW PUBLISHING (1990); Jenni Parrish, *Law Books and Legal Publishing in America, 1760–1840*, 72 LAW LIBR. J. 355 (1979).

made upon courts and legislatures, and the body of American legal literature grew proportionately.[37]

Extraordinary growth has occurred in the quantity of primary legal materials. During the period from 1658 to 1896, American courts reported 500,000 decisions;[38] by 1990 there were 4,000,000 reported decisions. By 2000, the number exceeded 6,000,000. In 1950, 21,000 cases were published, and it is estimated that over 220,000 cases are now published annually. Congress and the state legislatures produce huge amounts of statutory law every year, and federal and state administrative agencies produce thousands of rulings and regulations. Many of these primary authorities are published in multiple sources. The quantities of secondary sources and other law-related materials have expanded greatly as well. The flood of legal publications has caused concern to the legal profession for over 100 years, but little has been done to stem the proliferation of legal materials.[39]

b. Official and Unofficial Publications. American legal resources, whether books, electronic databases, or other media, can be divided into those that are *official* and those that are *unofficial.* This distinction is important but often misunderstood. An official publication is one that has been mandated by statute or governmental rule. It might be produced directly by the government, or it might be produced by a commercial entity under contract to the government or by governmental license.

Unofficial publications of cases, statutes, and regulations are often more useful than official publications. Unofficial publications of primary authorities contain the same text as their official counterparts, but are published faster and typically include editorial features and secondary information that help interpret the primary sources, along with locating or finding tools. Unofficial publications from reputable publishers should carry the same authority as official publications; citation rules[40] often require both official and unofficial citations.

c. Law Publishers. Private publishers traditionally have dominated American law publishing. The decade of the 1990s began a period of mergers, acquisitions, and consolidation for the publishing industry, but many of the trade names under which resources were originally published have been retained. Although the law publishing industry is dominated by a relatively small number of large publishers, the advent of the Internet and the World Wide Web has led to a plethora of both public and private electronic publishing ventures of varying degrees of reliability, accuracy, and comprehensiveness.

The largest private publisher of legal information is the Thomson Reuters Corporation, which acquired the West Publishing Company and several other legal publishers formerly known as the West Group. Thomson Reuters produces the *National Reporter System* (the largest and most comprehensive collection of federal and state judicial opinions), the *American Digest System,* an electronic research service called

---

[37] For an indication of the growth in size of academic law libraries, see J. Myron Jacobstein & Roy M. Mersky, *An Analysis of Academic Law Library Growth Since 1907,* 75 LAW LIBR. J. 212 (1982); GLEN-PETER AHLERS, THE HISTORY OF THE LAW SCHOOL LIBRARY IN THE UNITED STATES: FROM LABORATORY TO CYBERSPACE (2002).

[38] 1 CENTURY DIGEST iii (1897).

[39] For a discussion of the problems of excessive reporting, see J. Myron Jacobstein, *Some Reflections on the Control of the Publication of Appellate Court Opinions,* 27 STAN. L. REV. 791 (1975).

[40] See Chapter 24 for a discussion of legal citation form.

Westlaw, annotated statutes, treatises, legal encyclopedias, and many other resources. The West Publishing Company, which developed its resources around a theory of comprehensive reporting, has played such an important role in legal publishing that some scholars claim West influenced the development of American law.[41] Among the trade names acquired by Thomson Reuters are: Bancroft Whitney; Banks Baldwin; Clark Boardman Callaghan; Foundation Press; Lawyers Cooperative Publishing; Thomson/West; West Publishing Company; and West Group.[42]

Other major commercial legal publishers, and some of the trade names under which they publish, include: West Academic (West Academic Publishing; Foundation Press; Gilbert);[43] Reed Elsevier (Anderson; Butterworths; Lexis Law Publishing; LexisNexis; Matthew–Bender; Shepard's); Wolters Kluwer Law & Business (Aspen, CCH); Bloomberg BNA (formerly Bureau of National Affairs).[44]

d.   *Changes in Resources.* The changing corporate structure of legal publishers is just one example of the change that legal researchers face. For example, you might find that a work that was once published as a hardbound book with annual supplements is now republished annually as a softbound volume; a looseleaf service is now available only as a web product; a database that was available in *Westlaw* is now available only in *Bloomberg Law*; a new source is loaded in a government website. Legal researchers must be aware not only of changes in the law but of changes in the tools used to find the law.

5.   Evaluating Legal Resources

When inspecting and evaluating legal resources, it is important to determine and understand the purposes the resources were designed to serve. An awareness of the functions, features, interrelationships, strengths, and weaknesses of resources, whether they are traditional paper resources or electronic resources, is valuable for effectively conducting legal research. Is the resource part of a set, or is it designed to be used with other resources? Does it have finding tools or special features, such as indexes and tables? Is the text searchable electronically? How is the resource updated, and when was it last updated? The credibility of the author, editor, publisher, or producer should be considered, together with the types of authority (primary and secondary) included and the potential persuasiveness of the authority. With the expansion of resources available on the World Wide Web, evaluating resources for accuracy, credibility, and currency is increasingly important.[45]

C. AN ESSENTIAL SKILL

Professional accrediting and licensing organizations have recognized that the ability to perform legal research is an important practice skill. In 1992, the report of a

---

[41] *See* GRANT GILMORE, THE AGES OF AMERICAN LAW 58–59 (1977); Steven M. Barkan, *Can Law Publishers Change the Law?*, LEGAL REFERENCE SERVICES Q., Fall-Winter 1991, at 29; Robert C. Berring, *Full-Text Databases and Legal Research: Backing into the Future*, 1 HIGH TECH. L.J. 27 (1986).

[42] To avoid confusion that might result from the various brand names that have been applied in recent years to Thomson Reuters products (West, West Group, Thomson/West, Thomson Reuters, etc.), this book identifies the publisher of these products as "West," unless otherwise noted.

[43] West Academic, with several imprints formerly part of the Thomson Reuters suite, became a stand-alone business in 2013.

[44] An extensive listing of law publishers and their corporate affiliations can be found at http://www.aall net.org/main-menu/Advocacy/vendorrelations/CRIV-Tools/vendors.html.

[45] Chapter 23 provides additional discussion of evaluating resources available on the Internet.

special task force of the American Bar Association on law schools and the legal profession stated that "[i]t can hardly be doubted that the ability to do legal research is one of the skills that any competent practitioner must possess."[46] That report also stated that "[i]n order to conduct legal research effectively, a lawyer should have a working knowledge of the nature of legal rules and legal institutions, the fundamental tools of legal research, and the process of devising and implementing a coherent and effective research design."[47]

During 2011 and 2012, the National Conference of Bar Examiners sponsored a detailed study to determine the relative importance to newly licensed lawyers of numerous skills, competencies, and areas of knowledge. The study indicated that 89% of the respondents performed legal research and that research methodology ranked fifth of 86 areas of knowledge identified as relevant to newly licensed lawyers.[48]

Furthermore, the ABA's *Model Rules of Professional Conduct* provides: "A lawyer shall provide competent representation to a client. Competent representation requires the legal knowledge, skill, thoroughness, and preparation reasonably necessary for the representation."[49]

Clearly, a lawyer must be able to research the law to provide competent representation. In addition to issues of professional responsibility, questions relating to competency in legal research may arise in legal malpractice actions in which an attorney is sued for failing to know "those plain and elementary principles of law which are commonly known by well-informed attorneys, and to discover the additional rules which, although not commonly known, may readily be found by standard research techniques."[50] Issues relating to an attorney's competence in legal research also have been raised in claims for malicious prosecution,[51] and in claimed violations of the Sixth Amendment right to effective assistance of counsel.[52]

The ability to use fundamental legal research tools and to implement an effective and efficient research plan must become part of every lawyer's training if she or he is to provide competent representation and uphold the standards of the legal profession.

---

[46] LEGAL EDUCATION AND PROFESSIONAL DEVELOPMENT: AN EDUCATIONAL CONTINUUM, REPORT OF THE TASK FORCE ON LAW SCHOOLS AND THE PROFESSION: NARROWING THE GAP 163 (1992). This is most often referred to as the "MacCrate Report" after its chair, Robert MacCrate.

[47] *Id.*

[48] Susan M. Case, *The NCBE Job Analysis: A Study of the Newly Licensed Lawyer*, 82 B. EXAM'R, Mar. 2013, at 52. Links to a summary of the report and the full report can be found on the NCBE website, http://www.ncbex.org/publications/ncbe-job-analysis/.

[49] MODEL RULES OF PROF'L CONDUCT, R. 1.1 (1983).

[50] Smith v. Lewis, 13 Cal. 3d 349, 530 P.2d 589, 118 Cal. Rptr. 621 (1975). In this malpractice case, the plaintiff received a judgment of $100,000 against the defendant lawyer in connection with his negligence in researching the applicable law.

[51] *See, e.g.,* Sheldon Appel Co. v. Albert & Oliker, 47 Cal. 3d 863, 765 P.2d 498, 254 Cal. Rptr. 336 (1989) (plaintiff in a malicious prosecution action unsuccessfully arguing, among other things, that lack of probable cause for an action may be established by showing that the former adversary's attorney failed to perform reasonable legal research before filing a claim).

[52] *See, e.g.,* People v. Ledesma, 729 P.2d 839 (Cal. 1987). *See also* Mary Whisner, *When Judges Scold Lawyers*, 96 LAW LIBR. J. 557 (2004).

Chapter 2

THE LEGAL RESEARCH PROCESS

A. INTRODUCTION*

Legal research is as much art as science; at times, it benefits from serendipity almost as much as from strategy. There are many ways to approach a legal research problem, and most often there is no single or best way to conduct legal research. Methods vary according to the nature of the problem and depend on the researcher's subject expertise and research skills. Whatever the method chosen to address a given problem, however, the wise researcher is open to using creativity in approaches and exploring new theories and areas of law in addition to using proven strategies throughout the research process.

This chapter presents several approaches to legal research that can be modified and applied to most problems and can be merged with various approaches to legal writing. The examples are resource neutral, in that they can be applied to research in books, electronic resources, or a combination of media. In the end, researchers must develop research and writing methods that are most effective for their needs, but the frameworks presented here for constructing a research plan can guide any legal research from the outset. These frameworks include three basic and indispensable components: reliance on as complete and accurate a statement of legal issues and facts as possible, the identification of appropriate legal resources, and grounding the research in the correct jurisdiction.

Strategies for solving legal research problems are shaped by the availability of research materials. Because researchers do not always have access to a comprehensive array of resources, it helps to know a range of resources useful for addressing a specific type of problem and the methods for accessing those resources. Further, resources do not always produce the expected or desired results, and researchers need to be prepared to pursue alternative research strategies to overcome the limitations of a particular resource or research method. Finally, regardless of one's level of expertise in a particular field of law, a lawyer encounters problems involving unfamiliar subjects.

The processes of legal research, legal analysis, and legal writing are closely related.[1] The legal research process includes continual analysis and evaluation of the information found. Legal research informs legal writing; legal writing is meaningless—or worse—without accurate content gained from the research process. Some researchers prefer to conduct most of their research before beginning to write. Others prefer to write as they conduct their research. Regardless, the ability to solve legal problems accurately and

---

* This chapter was revised by Susan Nevelow Mart, Associate Professor and Director of the Law Library, University of Colorado Law School.

[1] In this context, "legal writing" means any method of communicating research results, including briefs, memoranda, letters, etc. See Chapter 3 for an introduction to the forms and processes of legal writing.

efficiently is developed best by constructing and practicing a systematic approach to legal research.

B. RESEARCH METHODOLOGIES

This section presents two research methodologies that are useful for organizing any legal research project. While they are described separately, the following discussions assume you have to resolve a legal problem with defined limitations, such as one given you in a legal research class that provides all the necessary facts and may identify areas of law to be researched. It is important to remember that, when you are working on a real legal problem, you may need to determine additional facts by interviewing key parties, questioning the assigning attorney, or engaging in other investigative activities. Getting the assignment from the client or the assigning attorney—and clarifying facts, issues, expectations, and other information—is part of the research process. As you work through the steps below and throughout the research process, any missing facts or documents should be noted as part of a research outline or log.

1. The Reporter's Questions

Most researchers are familiar with the "reporter's questions": who, what, where, when, and how.[2] Because these concepts are familiar to the novice legal researcher, the reporter's questions provide a familiar construct for starting a research project and easily adapt to legal research problems. Many researchers find it convenient to organize their use of the reporter's questions by constructing a chart or graph.

a.   *Who?* Use this question to figure out who the key parties are and who you represent. Are any of these parties legal entities rather than individuals? If a party is, for example, a unit of the government, a corporation, a trust, or a partnership, it may make a crucial difference in your analysis and your research path. If a party is an individual, does it matter, in the context of your problem, what the status of that individual is? Is the individual a minor, a ward of the court, or an ex-felon? Although you will be finding primary authority that is both favorable and unfavorable to your client's position, keeping in mind "who" you represent will help you in your analysis of that authority. These questions help define your stance as an advocate or deal-maker, and will guide you in analyzing your research for the finished work product you will be drafting.

b.   *What?* Use this question to help think about and frame the legal issues you will be researching. When you initially review a legal problem that you have been given to work on, you must extract the salient information that will guide your research.

What are the facts and descriptive words that you need to think about in this research? Keep in mind that you may not know exactly which facts are legally significant until you have done some research, but start out by thinking about and listing the facts that you think are important. When you have those facts, think about the legal descriptive words for them that might help you locate the law you need. For example, in a case where there is a default on a loan secured by a deed of trust, you may also want to investigate cases involving mortgages or foreclosures. Do not take for granted that the

---

[2] The question "why" is intentionally omitted from this discussion.

facts you extract from your research problem are true or undisputed. Your analysis must take into account what the result might be if your facts are disputed or proven untrue.

What are the legal issues and descriptive words that you need to think about in this research? This is the time to extract the substantive legal theories from your problem and think about the legal concepts you might research. If your legal problem involves a broken contract, for example, you will want to review in your mind the relevant contract theories that might apply. Is there a valid contract? Will you need to look up consideration, or fraud in the inducement, or rescission? Is the contract for goods or for services? Is the contract written or oral? As a researcher, you need to think about both potential legal theories and the descriptive words that might help locate relevant law.

What are the recommended sources? Before you start researching, think about the best places to look. When the problem involves an unfamiliar area of the law, as most problems do for new researchers, the first thing you must do is get context from an overview of the subject in a treatise, practice guide, law review article, or encyclopedia entry. Every area of the law has its own resources, so you must find out what those resources are. Does the problem involve class actions? There are treatises that deal specifically with class actions that can give a brief overview of most of the legal problems that can arise from bringing or defending a class action. Consult the law library's catalog or ask a librarian. In some cases, where public policy issues are implicated, the websites of nonprofit or government groups can be extremely helpful. For example, if the problem you are researching involves policy questions about traumatic brain injuries in athletes, the National Conference of State Legislatures' database of each state's enacted and proposed laws on this subject would be one recommended source.[3]

For each legal problem you research, using recommended resources and getting context and an overview as a beginning step will make the research process efficient and less confusing.

    c.   *Where?* Use this question to think about jurisdiction. Most law school casebooks do not focus on jurisdiction, but to practicing lawyers, the court where a case was decided or the place where a statute was enacted are of great importance. Is the court where you are filing your pleading required to follow the holding in the case you have found, or is your case authority merely persuasive to that court? You must be able to make these distinctions about the primary authority you will be citing.

You must determine if your legal problem involves state or federal law. Does the problem implicate both state and federal law? Which circuit's law is applicable, if you are in federal court? Is it appropriate, for the problem you are researching, to bring in the case law of other circuits or other states? Is there a choice of law issue you might want to consider? These questions will also help you to choose the appropriate recommended resources. Even a wonderful law review article on your topic might not be worth your time if it doesn't discuss the law in your jurisdiction.[4]

---

[3] National Conference of State Legislatures, *Traumatic Brain Injury Legislation: States with Enacted and 2011 Filed Legislation Targeting Youth Sports-Related Concussions* (Sept. 2011), *http://www.ncsl.org/ ?tabid=18687.*

[4] Note that the very same article could be extremely helpful if your jurisdiction has not actually answered the legal question you are researching. Each different problem will require a different set of "best" resources.

d.   When? Time is a critical element in many legal research problems. If the problem you are researching, for example, involves a statute and the events that are in dispute took place in 2002, then you must look at what you have identified as the relevant statue and determine whether the statue has been amended since 2002 and, more importantly, if it had even been enacted as of that date. If the statute has been amended, then you must look at the version of the statute that was in effect in 2002. The amendment could completely change how, and even if, the statute applies. The time period in which the events took place may similarly affect whether a case decided after a certain time is relevant. Similarly, if the legal research problem you are researching involves regulations, you must be certain that those regulations were in effect in the relevant time period.

Finding out whether the primary law you have found is still good law is a critical step in legal research. The two best known citators for checking the validity of your cases and statutes are *KeyCite* from Thomson Reuters—Legal (West), and *Shepard's* from LexisNexis.[5] If you are using a citator to see if a case is still good law, both citators function by trying to link the researcher to every instance where a new case has cited the case you are KeyCiting or Shepardizing. Both offer methods for limiting the sometimes overwhelming results by jurisdiction, legal topic, time, document type, or depth of treatment. Because each system uses different search methodologies and algorithms, the results returned by each system can be, and often are, different.[6] Researchers with access to both citators may want to use both. Incomplete overlap in the two citation systems highlights the need for redundancy in using legal research resources: researchers need to ensure that each relevant case that is found using a citator is itself put through the citator system and, where necessary, fully researched in statutes and in relevant secondary sources.

One thing to take into account when starting a research project, in school and in practice, is time management. When is this project due? Does this project require exhaustive research, or are you only being asked for a quick answer? What else are you working on that might conflict with this task? Time management is critical in legal practice, and when you are learning how to formulate a research plan, determining the scope of your project and time available to perform the work is a best practice you should incorporate into every research plan. Keep in mind that legal research involves carefully reading and analyzing everything you find and is, by necessity, time consuming. Allow plenty of time for reflection.

"When am I done?" is a question that has no simple answer. Use a variety of legal research resources and update your primary law. Then, when you are finding references to the same cases, statutes, and legal theories in your research and are beginning to formulate responses to your issues, you are getting signals that your research has been effective and you can wrap up the process.

---

[5] Although *KeyCite* and *Shepard's* are the best established, other systems also offer citators. For example, *Bloomberg Law*'s citator is called *BCite*. *Fastcase*'s *Authority Check* searches for cases that cite a given case; its *Bad Law Bot* highlights cases that are no longer good law. *Casemaker*'s citator is called *CaseCheck+*. Citators are not limited to checking the validity of cases and statutes, although that is their most common use. Citators can also check the validity or history of regulations, agency decisions, patents, law reviews, briefs, and more. See Chapter 15 for a complete description of the use of citators.

[6] For a more detailed discussion of this problem, see Susan Nevelow Mart, *The Relevance of Results Generated by Human Indexing and Computer Algorithms: A Study of West's Headnotes and Key Numbers and Lexis's Headnotes and Topics*, 102 Law Libr. J. 221 (2010).

e. *How?* Does your research assignment have limitations on the use or availability of legal resources? Have you been requested to use certain specific materials, or been asked to start your research in books before going online? Make sure you understand, before you start, how the person who has assigned you the research problem wants you to accomplish it.

2. A General Approach to Legal Research

Another well-known organizational method for legal research is this general approach.[7] It can accommodate most problems and is broken down into four basic steps:

STEP 1. Identify and analyze the significant facts;

STEP 2. Formulate the legal issues to be researched;

STEP 3. Research the issues presented; and

STEP 4. Update.

Although the steps are discussed individually, each step is closely related to the others. Each step may involve multiple processes, as legal research is rarely a linear process. Research involves reviewing what has already been located, analyzing your findings, and, in light of the information discovered, revising and refining your work,

a.   *STEP 1: Identify and Analyze the Significant Facts.* The researcher's first task is to identify and analyze the facts of the problem. Some facts have legal significance; others do not. The process of legal research begins with compiling a descriptive statement of legally significant facts. It is often difficult for a beginner to identify significant facts and discard insignificant ones. Consequently, when researching a problem in an unfamiliar area of the law, it is usually best to err on the side of over-inclusion rather than exclusion. You may even want to keep two lists: one for facts you believe are legally significant and one for facts you believe are not legally significant. As you research and your view of the relations of the law and facts changes, you can adjust your lists.

Factual analysis is the first step in identifying the legal issues to research. Factual analysis also enables a researcher to locate access points to the available resources. Which volumes are relevant? Which subjects should be consulted in indexes and tables of contents? Which words should be used in an initial search of an electronic database? Which websites should be examined? An experienced researcher is able to identify issues and appropriate subjects. The novice researcher, who does not have the experience to examine a fact pattern and readily categorize it and formulate legal issues, needs to devote more time and attention to this activity.

Inexperienced legal researchers might skim over the facts and immediately begin researching. No productive research can be done outside a particular fact pattern. Most controversies are over facts, not law; and cases are most often distinguished on their facts. Rules stated by courts are tied to specific fact situations, and must be considered in relation to those facts. Because the facts of a legal problem control the direction of research, the investigation and analysis of facts must be incorporated into the research

---

[7] The general approach to legal research described here was conceptualized by Professor Ervin Pollack in the first and second editions of this book. *See* ERVIN H. POLLACK, FUNDAMENTALS OF LEGAL RESEARCH 13–20 (1956); ERVIN H. POLLACK, FUNDAMENTALS OF LEGAL RESEARCH 14–18 (2d ed. 1962).

process. Identifying relevant facts and writing them down in narrative form is usually a worthwhile investment of time and energy.

The TARP Rule. A useful technique is to analyze facts according to the following factors:

T—**Thing** or subject matter;

A—Cause of **action** or ground of defense;

R—**Relief** sought; and

P—**Persons** or **parties** involved in the problem.

Thing or subject matter. The place or property involved in a problem or controversy may be important. Thus, when a consumer is harmed after taking a prescription drug, the drug becomes an essential fact in the dispute.

Cause of action or ground of defense. Identify the claim that might be asserted or the defense that might be made. For example, the cause of action might involve a breach of contract, negligence, intentional infliction of emotional distress, or some other legal theory giving rise to litigation.

Relief sought. What is the purpose of the lawsuit? It might be a civil action in which the party bringing the suit is seeking monetary damages for an injury, or an action in which a party is asking the court to order another party to do a specific act or to refrain from doing a specific act. Alternatively, the litigation may be a criminal action brought by the state.

Persons or parties involved in the problem, and their functional and legal status and relationship to one other. The parties or persons might be individuals, or might be a group that is significant to the solution of the problem or the outcome of the lawsuit. Similarly, the relationship between the parties, such as exists between spouses or between employer and employee, might be of special importance.

b. *STEP 2: Formulate the Legal Issues to Be Researched.* This is the initial intellectual activity that presumes some knowledge of the relevant substantive law and, consequently, the point at which inexperienced legal researchers are most likely to have trouble. The goal is to initially classify or categorize the problem into a general topic, and then into increasingly specific subject areas, before beginning to hypothesize legal issues. For example, is this a matter of civil or criminal law? Does it involve federal or state law? Does the litigation involve contracts or torts, or both? If torts, is it a products liability or a negligence case? Problems are often not easily compartmentalized. Problems can fall into more than one category, and categories affect each other.

(1) Get an Overview. To assist in formulating issues, it is important to consult general secondary sources for an overview of relevant subject areas. These sources can include national legal encyclopedias, a state encyclopedia, treatises, looseleaf services, or one or more subject periodicals or journals. The best choice will vary with each different legal problem and resources available, but it is wise to start with the most general and work to the more detailed and specific. These secondary sources can provide valuable context and direct a researcher to issues and primary sources. Note any constitutional provisions, statutes, administrative regulations, and judicial and administrative opinions cited by these sources. At this preliminary stage of research, these secondary sources provide background information and help formulate issues.

Writing a clear, concise statement of each legal issue raised by the significant facts is an important and difficult task. Failure to frame all issues raised by a particular set of facts can result in incomplete and inadequate research. It is better, when framing the issues, for a novice to err on the side of formulating too many issues. Insignificant issues can always be eliminated after they have been thoroughly investigated, and overlapping issues can be consolidated.

(2) Create an Outline. Once statements of the issues have been drafted, they should be arranged in a logical pattern to form an outline. Logically related issues might be combined as sub-issues under a broader main issue. Issues that depend upon the outcome of other issues should be arranged accordingly. The outline should be expanded, modified, and revised as research progresses. Once a particular issue has been researched, it might be found to be too broad; the statement of the issue should then be narrowed. It might also be necessary at times to split an issue into two, or to divide an issue into sub-issues. Alternatively, an original issue might be deemed too narrow and unlikely to lead to any relevant information. In such instances, the issue should be broadened. Many times, during the process of research, it becomes apparent that issues not originally considered to be relevant are, in fact, relevant. Keeping notes of your research will help you identify the sources you looked at that relate to the newly relevant issue. The task of framing and reframing issues in light of new research is an ongoing one.

c.   STEP 3: Continue Researching the Issues Presented. After you analyze the facts and frame the probable issues, it is time to take the information you have found in your secondary sources and focus your research.

(1) Organize and Plan. Although serendipity can play an important role in legal research, good legal researchers, as a rule, are systematic, methodical, and organized, and they keep good records. Every researcher must develop a system for taking and organizing notes.

For each issue, decide which sources to use, which sources not to use, and the order for reviewing resources you think would be most helpful. A good practice would be to write down all sources to be consulted for each issue, even if sources are repeated. As relevant information is found, its source and relevance should be recorded, and the legal research outline accordingly expanded. Maintaining an accurate list of sources consulted, terms and topics checked, and updating steps taken prevents inefficient uses of time and omissions of crucial information.

Frequently, it is not possible to research each issue completely before moving on to the next issue. It is common to move back and forth among issues, revising and refining them. As a general practice, it is best to research each issue completely before moving to the next issue. The ongoing nature of legal research emphasizes the importance of good note-taking, record-keeping, and organization.

Any number of legal research leads may prove irrelevant to resolution of the issues. It is often tempting to include information in a written product that has taken many hours to develop but which is ultimately unnecessary for a proper analysis of the issues. Remember that irrelevant information detracts from, and often masks, analysis that is directly on point.

(2) Identify, Read, and Update All Relevant Constitutional Provisions, Statutes, and Administrative Regulations. Identifying and reading relevant constitutional

provisions, statutes, and administrative regulations provides the framework upon which the rest of the research is built. These primary sources can be identified in several ways:

- *Secondary Sources.* You have already consulted secondary sources to get an overview and context. These sources, such as treatises, practice guides, encyclopedias, looseleaf services, and law review articles, commonly cite relevant constitutional provisions, statutes, and administrative regulations. As you read secondary sources, you should make note of the citations of these relevant documents. Depending upon the scope of the inquiry, secondary sources that focus on the law of one state or on federal law may prove especially valuable. Electronic versions of many secondary sources are available in *Westlaw*, *LexisNexis*, and other services.

- *Statutory Compilations.* Statutory compilations almost always include tables of contents and indexes listing the subjects and topics covered by the statutes. Because relevant statutory provisions are often found in several places in compiled statutes, consult both the table of contents and the index.

- *Electronic Legal Research.* The full text of the *United States Code*, *Code of Federal Regulations*, *Federal Register*, and statutes of the states are available on the Internet free of charge and are also available in *Westlaw*, *LexisNexis*, and other fee-based sources.

It is not always easy to identify all relevant statutes at the beginning of a research project. Indexing problems sometimes make it difficult to match concepts with indexing terms. Sometimes, issues are too vague or underdeveloped to ensure that relevant statutes are identified. Accordingly, research involving relevant constitutional provisions, statutes, and administrative regulations should be continually undertaken and issues and strategies modified accordingly.

(3) Identify, Read, and Update All Relevant Case Law. After relevant constitutional provisions, statutes, and administrative regulations are identified and read, case law that interprets and applies those forms of enacted law, as well as other case law relevant to the fact situation, must be located.

Do not limit research to cases that support a particular position. A competent researcher anticipates both sides of an argument and identifies cases that result in contrary conclusions. In many situations, the same case can be interpreted to support both sides of an issue; the argument may involve the question of whether the holding is to be broadly or narrowly applied, or whether the facts of the cases can be distinguished. It is common, however, for sides to argue that entirely different lines of cases are controlling.

At this stage of research, the goal is to compile a comprehensive, chronological list of relevant opinions for each issue. Because no two cases are exactly alike, it is unlikely for a researcher to find cases with identical fact patterns to the situation at hand. The most relevant judicial opinions come from the same court or superior appellate courts in the jurisdiction in question, as they are the only cases that are potentially binding. Next in importance are judicial opinions, which might be persuasive, from other courts and jurisdictions dealing with similar facts, statutes, and issues. Even if binding, authoritative cases are located, persuasive authority from other jurisdictions might support an argument, particularly if the opinions are from well-known and respected judges. Reading cases chronologically can reveal background information that is not necessarily repeated in each case, show the development of the case law, and point to the "lead" case that is cited in other opinions.

Cases that interpret statutes can be identified in several ways:

- *Annotated Statutes and Codes.* Annotated statutes and codes list interpretive cases after each statutory provision.

- *Treatises and Looseleaf Services.* Treatises and looseleaf services, particularly if they involve the law of a state being researched or a federal law that is the topic of an inquiry, cite cases that interpret the statutes they discuss.

- *Citators.* Citators, such as *Shepard's* and *KeyCite*, can provide a list of cases that have cited the statute.

- *Computer-Assisted Legal Research (CALR).* Materials available in *Westlaw* and *LexisNexis* and in other electronic resources can be searched for cases that have cited a particular statute.

- *Other Sources.* A.L.R. annotations and legal encyclopedias often provide relevant case citations. Relevant cases providing statutory interpretation can also be identified with finding tools, such as digests, which contain a subject arrangement of abstracts of cases that can be accessed through a table of contents and a descriptive-word index.

Once a relevant case is identified, other cases on the same subject can be located through several techniques. These techniques include tracing the key numbers used in that case through West's digests or *Westlaw* to find other cases with the same key numbers; using *KeyCite*, *Shepard's*, and CALR systems as citators to find other citing cases; and consulting the tables of cases in treatises, looseleaf services, encyclopedias, and digests.

As each case is read and briefed, its full citation, parallel citations, judge and court issuing the opinion, date of the decision, relevant facts, holding, summary of the court's reasoning, key numbers assigned, and sources cited by the court should be recorded. Each case should be incorporated into the legal research outline.

(4) Refine the Search. After primary sources are identified, read, and organized, secondary sources can be used to refine the search and expand the argument. Invariably, new cases and lines of argument appear. Treatises, law review articles, and restatements of the law are not binding authority, but they can be persuasive and can provide ideas on how best to use the primary sources. If the problem involves a statute, the legislative history might suggest the legislature's intent in passing the act and the problem the law was intended to remedy. Historical, social, economic, and political information can put legal arguments in their proper context and support policy arguments.

d. STEP 4: Update. The importance of updating legal research warrants special attention. Law changes constantly. Legislatures pass new statutes and modify old ones. Each appellate court decision creates new law, refines the law, reaffirms the law, or changes the law; researchers must be aware of the most recent decisions on the subject they are researching. Research that is current today may be out of date tomorrow. Lawyers would all agree that failure to update legal research can be careless and negligent, and sometimes leads to disastrous results.

Citation services, such as *KeyCite* and *Shepard's*, should be used to update the status of cases, statutes, and regulations. Remember that the signals in *KeyCite* and *Shepard's* apply to a specific holding in a case; the researcher must check first to see if the signal applies to the portion of the case relevant to the research. Signals are sometimes different in *KeyCite* and *Shepard's*, so thorough and competent research requires the researcher to read the citing case and make his or her own decision as to the effect of the court's language. Electronic databases, such as *Westlaw* and *LexisNexis*, should be consulted, as well as pocket parts and supplements, looseleaf services, and advance sheets, to determine whether the authorities have been interpreted or modified, or whether new cases, statutes, or regulations have been published.

C. WHEN TO STOP

The question of when to stop researching is difficult. With experience, researchers develop insight into the point at which further legal research is unproductive. In many instances an obvious repetition of citations or absence of new information suggests that enough research has been done. However, there is no uniform rule on how extensive research should be, and knowing when to stop is a skill that only develops over time.

Occasionally, researching a problem in all conceivable sources is needless, unwarranted, or repetitious. It is possible to over-research a problem. All cases are not of equal importance; much information is redundant. Including too much information can obscure important points. Furthermore, many simple problems do not call for exhaustive research. Common sense and professional insight play significant roles in legal research.

In the final analysis, research skills are measured as much by the knowledge of what can be omitted as by which research materials are used and how they are used. The attorney's stock in trade is time; a skilled legal researcher knows how to use it wisely.[8]

D. A FEW FINAL WORDS

You will have noted that the two research approaches discussed in this chapter have similar components. Each is a method to ensure that you have considered important legal and factual elements in your research problem, identified resources that might be helpful, and ensured that your research is fully updated. You may take elements from either of these approaches in formulating a research plan for your particular research problem, or you may find or even make up a different approach. Remember that you must have an approach or methodology before starting your research. Never start your research without a plan.

Legal research is a process, not a road. There is rarely one straightforward way to accomplish the task. That means that, throughout your research, you will encounter tempting theories, concepts, and scenarios that might not be relevant to your problem. It is easy to get sidetracked. Take a moment from time to time to make sure you are still on track or that the question you are researching has not changed as a result of your

---

[8] For an in-depth discussion of when to stop researching, see Christina L. Kunz, *Terminating Research*, 2 PERSP.: TEACHING LEGAL RES. & WRITING 2 (1993). *See also* Mary Whisner, *How Do You Know When Research Is Good?*, 98 LAW LIBR. J. 721 (2006).

findings. Strategy and serendipity each has a role in legal research; make sure you manage them both.

Chapter 3

COMMUNICATING RESEARCH RESULTS THROUGH WRITING*

This chapter briefly describes the types and forms of legal writing, describes common organizational strategies, discusses the general process of legal writing, and lists selected sources.

A. INTRODUCTION

As observed in the previous chapter, the processes of legal research and legal writing are closely related. A written product is very often the goal of performing research, and the quality of research fundamentally affects the quality of writing. And of course, legal analysis is intertwined as well, for a researcher who does not understand what question to answer does not identify relevant sources, and a writer who does not think clearly cannot write clearly.

Because writing is so intimately connected with research, this chapter presents a broad overview of the types of and general process of legal writing. Complete coverage of the craft of legal writing is beyond the scope of this research book. For that, the reader is referred to the many excellent resources on the nuts and bolts of legal writing, as well as its theory and rhetoric. The end of the chapter includes a selective list.

Legal writing begins with research and analysis. A piece of legal writing must convince the reader that the writer understands the problem discussed; has identified the issues and sub-issues, the key facts, and the unknowns; has researched and analyzed the relevant law; and has considered the appropriate arguments and counterarguments. Above all, the writing must persuade the reader that the writer's conclusions are valid.

B. TYPES OF LEGAL WRITING

Lawyers (and other legal writers, from law students to judges) produce many different types of written work, for different audiences and different purposes. A fundamental distinction among the types is that between *objective* writing and *persuasive* writing. In objective or predictive writing, the author provides a neutral analysis of the law governing a certain situation and predicts the likely outcome. For example, a summer associate in a law firm might write an office memorandum to a supervising attorney addressing one issue facing a client, exploring possible legal claims and defenses, and predicting how a court would resolve them, whether favorably or unfavorably for the client. Persuasive writing, on the other hand, is analysis with an agenda. The writer's goal is to convince or persuade the reader to make a particular decision. For example, if the client is sued, then the attorney might prepare a motion for

---

* This chapter was revised by Mary A. Hotchkiss, Associate Dean for Students, University of Washington School of Law.

summary judgment with a memorandum of law that tries to convince the judge to rule for the client.

It is important to note that objective and persuasive analysis and writing are closely related. In an objective document, the writer analyzes the arguments of both sides to predict the outcome. In a persuasive document, the writer still needs to address and resolve the arguments of both sides—this time, to advocate one position and counter the opposing arguments. This is why Chapter 2 advised researchers not to limit their research to cases that support a particular position. Both objective and persuasive legal writing follow certain conventions, such as citing authority for statements of law.

C. FORMS OF LEGAL WRITING

1. Memoranda

Memoranda (or *memos*, for short) are generally written for an internal audience (a supervising attorney within a firm or agency or, in the case of a bench memorandum, a judge). They analyze a legal problem, presenting both sides objectively. An objective memo should provide the reader with a balanced analysis of key authorities governing a legal issue.

Suppose a firm is considering whether to take on a case. To evaluate chances of success and to advise the client about her options, the lawyers need to research the applicable law. A senior lawyer might assign to an associate or a summer clerk the task of researching and writing a memorandum that outlines the facts and summarizes the law in the area, looking at both sides of the issue. The memorandum should state the facts that are assumed and areas where further investigation would be important. The memorandum should cite cases and other legal authority, carefully working through the legal analysis. A sample outline appears below. (In some offices or for some projects, supervising attorneys prefer other formats.)

The senior attorney will use the memo to help make a decision. It will also go in a file as the basis of later work. Sometimes attorneys write memos to themselves—or to the file—with varying levels of formality, for just the same purposes.

[Illustration 3–1]

SAMPLE MEMORANDUM OUTLINE

To:

From:

Date:

Re: Subject line includes name of client, nature of matter or claim, and procedural status, if appropriate]

Question(s) Presented: Identifies the legal issue and summarizes the key facts relating to the disputed issue.

Brief Answer(s): Responds directly to the question presented and provides an objective summary of the analysis, indicating degree of certainty.

Statement of Facts: Includes the relevant facts, generally in chronological order. May also suggest unknown facts that could be important to the issue.

Discussion

a.   A thesis paragraph introduces the issues and predicts an outcome without analyzing the law.

b.   First issue (sample): Is a demonstrator vehicle used by the dealer's sales staff covered under Washington State's Lemon Law, which covers only "new motor vehicles"?

   i.   Authority (rule + support)

      1.   Discusses cases and explains how the rule has worked in them.

      2.   Includes cases that demonstrate what scenarios will and will not satisfy the rule.

   ii.   Rule application (may include counterarguments)

c.   Second issue

   i.   Authority (rule + support)

      1.   Discusses cases and explains how the rule has worked in them.

      2.   Includes cases that demonstrate what scenarios will and will not satisfy the rule.

   ii.   Rule application (may include counterarguments)

d.   Third issue [repeat, as needed]

Conclusion: Recaps conclusions and restates prediction of outcome. Conclusion should not introduce new material and should not simply repeat the brief answer(s).

2.   Client or Opinion Letters

Client or *opinion letters* are written for an outside audience (i.e., a client). Their goal is to explain the law in plain English. A well-written client letter should provide sufficient information and options for the client to make an informed decision.

Typically, a client letter begins with an opening paragraph that restates the client's question and provides a brief answer. Subsequent paragraphs review the relevant facts and explain the relevant law. Then the writer outlines various options available to the client. If needed, the letter may request additional information from the client. A closing paragraph summarizes the letter. The letter should ensure that the reader understands issues of attorney-client confidentiality. A warning to the client not to share the letter with other readers will preserve the confidentiality.

[Illustration 3–2]

SAMPLE CLIENT LETTER

Ross, Marsh & Foster
Attorneys at Law
123 Fourth Ave
Marysville, WA 98270

July 1, 2015

Ms. Becky Smith
P.O. Box 215
Marysville, WA 98270

Dear Ms. Smith:

I have researched the possibility that the dealer will be required to replace or repurchase your 2014 Ford Explorer. The failure of the car's power steering is considered a serious safety defect under the Washington State Lemon Law (Wash. Rev. Code § 19.118.010). In my opinion, we can make a strong argument that the dealer's actions to date do not meet either the manufacturer's warranty or the statutory warranty. While I cannot guarantee that a court will agree with this opinion, I am optimistic that a lawsuit would be successful if you wish to proceed.

Before I explain the law and your various options, I would like to review the facts. When you purchased the Explorer, it had been used as a dealer's demonstrator vehicle. It was still under the manufacturer's warranty.

[The text of other key facts, explanation of the law, and discussion of various remedies has been deleted.]

Please talk these options over with your family and friends and give me a call if you have any questions or concerns. Please note that you should not show this letter to them; keeping the letter between us preserves attorney-client confidentiality.

After you have had a chance to think over the options, please set up an appointment so I can help you decide which remedy to pursue. We need to make a decision no later than July 31, 2015, because there is a time limit by which we must initiate litigation.

Sincerely yours,

3.   Demand Letters

In a *demand letter*, a lawyer explains his or her client's position and requests that the recipient take some action (or risk being sued). These letters are moving along the continuum from objective towards persuasive writing. A demand letter by its nature requires a level, professional tone.

The general structure of a demand letter is an opening paragraph, introducing the dispute and relevant facts, followed by an explanation of the client's position. The letter should make a specific demand and delineate the consequences of noncompliance.

[Illustration 3–3]

SAMPLE DEMAND LETTER

Ross, Marsh & Foster
Attorneys at Law
123 Fourth Ave.
Marysville, WA 98270

August 8, 2015

Ford Motor Company
Customer Relationship Center
P.O. Box 6248
Dearborn, Michigan 48126

Certified Mail—Return Receipt Requested

Dear Customer Relationship Representative:

On September 9, 2014, Ms. Becky Smith purchased a 2014 Ford Explorer from Sheehy Ford in Marysville, Washington, for $27,090. Within three months, she started experiencing significant problems with the power steering. The dealer "fixed" the problem three times (November 2014, January 2015, and April 2015).

[Text with additional facts has been deleted.]

Failure of power steering on a vehicle is considered a serious safety defect under the Washington State Lemon Law (Wash. Rev. Code § 19.118.010). Based on the above facts, demand is hereby made that you refund the sum of $27,090 to Ms. Smith in full.

Please be advised that failure to comply with this request may subject you to the following remedies available under Washington law: actual damages; civil penalty up to twice the actual damages; and court costs and attorney's fees.

Sincerely yours,

4. Litigation Documents

Litigation documents are varied. For instance, a *complaint* initiates a case by alleging facts and asking for relief; an *answer* responds to the complaint (perhaps by denying the facts); a *motion for summary judgment* asks a court to rule on some or all of the legal issues in a case before trial, based only on affidavits and stipulated facts; a *memorandum of points and authorities* in support of a motion (also known as brief in support of a motion) presents legal arguments; and an *appellate brief* argues for the reversal or affirmance of a trial court decision. The goal of each of these documents is ultimately to convince a judge to rule in the client's favor.

It is beyond the scope of a legal research text to describe the formats and rhetorical standards for all of these documents. For now, let us simply emphasize that all of these documents depend upon sound research and analysis. In fact, if the claims in a complaint are not supported by existing law or by a non-frivolous argument for the extension or modification of existing law, then the attorney who signs the complaint may be liable for sanctions.[1]

5.   Transactional Documents

Transactional documents are documents that themselves have legal effect. They are termed "transactional" because they implement transactions. For example, *contracts* spell out the terms of a sale or other agreement—and potentially make a party liable if it breaches the contract; *leases* provide for the length of time something will be rented, the amount one party must pay the other, which party is responsible for repairs, and so on—and, again, a party can be liable if it does not abide by the terms of the document. In a sense, one could consider a lease to be a special type of contract—a contract for one party to rent property to another in exchange for payment. Other special types of contracts include employment contracts, licenses, and retainer agreements. *Wills*, *trusts*, and other estate planning tools are also considered transactional documents, even though the recipient of the property that is transferred might not be aware of the "transaction" until many years after the document is written.

6.   Academic Writing

Academic writing includes formal scholarship in treatises, monographs, and periodicals. Examples of this genre of legal writing can fall anywhere on the spectrum from objective to persuasive. Some treatise authors, for instance, take a very strong position on what the law should be, while others adopt a more descriptive approach.[2]

Scholarly legal writing tends to be heavily footnoted, citing some authority to support almost every proposition. The footnotes are a boon for researchers but contribute to the impression that these works are not ideal beach reading (although some law review articles, even densely footnoted ones, can be fascinating).

Traditionally, law reviews have used the term "article" only for articles written by professionals—generally professors, lawyers, and judges. Articles can discuss doctrinal law or more theoretical issues. Like treatises, they can be strongly opinionated or more objective. The pieces by students are typically (but not always) shorter than articles and are usually called "notes," "comments," or "recent developments." Many law reviews also have a section for book reviews.

While these traditional forms of writing still predominate in law reviews, recent decades have seen new forms included in law reviews. These include personal narratives, fictional narratives, and poetry.[3]

7.   Other Legal Writing

Other legal writing can include a wide array of materials aimed at lawyers and other legal researchers. Lawyers develop outlines, checklists, or guides in various areas, often to support a presentation for a continuing legal education (CLE) program. Lawyers also write manuals, handbooks, and deskbooks—materials aimed at practitioners.

---

[1] *See, e.g.*, FED. R. CIV. P. 11 and corresponding state rules. For a discussion of cases in which judges criticize attorneys for inadequate research, among other things, see Mary Whisner, *When Judges Scold Lawyers*, 96 LAW LIBR. J. 557 (2004).

[2] For a discussion of treatises, see Chapter 19.

[3] For a discussion of legal periodicals, see Chapter 18.

Others write opinion pieces, commentary, and editorials for legal newspapers and bar association publications. These works are less scholarly than law reviews and treatises. Some lawyers also write for publication in online media, such as firm websites and blogs.

8. Email

Email is widely used in law practice because of its convenience and speed. It can be used to set up meetings, exchange drafts (as attachments), and convey information. It can be used as a medium for some of the forms of legal writing discussed above—for example, internal memoranda or client letters. Here are a few observations about email in law practice.

First, email tends to be short. And even if the email message is not short, what the recipient chooses to read may be. When you write email, be aware that the recipient might read it on a BlackBerry, iPhone, or other mobile device with a small screen. Get to the point quickly.

Second, be aware that legal writing should maintain a professional tone, regardless of the medium. Although email between friends is generally very casual and informal, messages to lawyers, judges, and clients should not be.

Third, proofread email as you would proofread any other document. Be aware that some smartphones and other devices have very aggressive autocorrect features and might garble what you enter. Pay special attention to proper names (including case names) and legal terms.

D. COMMON ORGANIZATIONAL STRATEGIES FOR LEGAL WRITING

As discussed above, there are a number of common forms of legal writing: memoranda, client letters, briefs, and so on. Some organizational strategies serve writers well across the different forms. First, begin with threshold issues. For example, the question of liability will not matter if the court does not have jurisdiction over the dispute or the statute of limitations has run. The rules of dividing property upon divorce might not need to be explained if the parties' marriage was invalid.

Another common strategy is to discuss simple issues before complex issues. Often, these simple issues lay the groundwork for the more intricate issues. Using the example from above, in a divorce, the distribution of a jointly owned savings account is a much simpler issue than child custody.

Legal issues and arguments are often complex. A writer can help the reader by using rhetorical devices that serve as roadmaps and signposts. In a memorandum or brief, the "questions presented" section gives readers a roadmap to what follows. In a memorandum or brief, the subheadings or point headings serve as signposts to guide readers. In a client letter, the introductory paragraph serves as a roadmap and, depending on the length of the letter, subheadings provide additional pointers. Similarly, in a law review article, an introduction or abstract serves as a roadmap.

To guide the readers through their arguments, good legal writers use a thesis paragraph at the beginning of each complex issue to outline the sub-issues. Navigational headings at the beginning of each major section serve as signposts.

Note that the outline you use to organize your notes as you are researching does not bind you to that order when you write. Even though you research a particular issue first, you might choose to discuss it last (or not at all)—e.g., because another issue would be dispositive.

E. THE GENERAL PROCESS OF WRITING

1. How the Writing Project Shapes Research

A researcher can become more efficient by bearing in mind the written product he or she hopes to create. There are several ways in which the anticipated work product should shape the research.

a. *The writing project affects the length, depth, or breadth of the research.* What issues will be discussed? What sort of support will be needed for each? How thorough should the work be? For example, an article in a bar journal might say, "At least a dozen states have adopted laws allowing doctors to apologize to patients without the apology being introduced as evidence in a civil trial," and provide no specific citations, while a law review article would need citations to each state's code.

b. *The writing project affects the notes the researcher takes.* For example, if you are writing a brief in a jurisdiction that requires parallel citations to cases in an official and a regional reporter, the notes should include the parallel citations. If a writing project is going to take a semester instead of a day, you might take more thorough notes, writing down the dates that different sources were consulted to make it easier to bring everything up to date before the project is finalized.

c. *The writing project can affect the order of the research.* For instance, finding a clear, determinative answer to a jurisdictional question might obviate (or at least reduce) the need to research other questions.

d. *The writing project affects the types of sources consulted.* A seminar paper might be greatly enhanced by material from history and economics that would seldom be cited in a practice manual.

2. Organizational Devices

Effective organization and good note-taking aid research, analysis, and writing. Many devices exist for organizing the multitude of cases, statutes, regulations, and other authorities one needs for a major research and writing project. Some are low tech (e.g., drawing a grid on a legal pad, using separate legal pads, or creating separate documents for separate issues). Students with a technical bent might prefer to use software to help them organize their notes (e.g., creating an outline in a word processing program, with hypertext links to cases). While no one method works for everyone, it is important to have *some* method to keep track of the sources you have consulted and the index terms or searches you have tried, what you found, and how current the material was.[4]

---

[4] *See* Penny A. Hazelton et al., *Develop the Habit: Note-Taking in Legal Research*, 4 PERSP.: TEACHING LEGAL RES. & WRITING 48 (1996); Peter Jan Honigsberg, *Organizing the Fruits of Your Labor: The Honigsberg Grid*, 4 PERSP.: TEACHING LEGAL RES. & WRITING 9 (1996); Mary Whisner, *Managing a Research Assignment*, 9 PERSP.: TEACHING LEGAL RES. & WRITING 9 (2000). Many programs are available to help researchers manage notes and citations. For example, *Evernote* enables users to save notes, webpages, documents, and email messages in a searchable database. *Zotero* manages notes and formats citations. *See* PAPPAS LAW LIBRARY, BOSTON UNIVERSITY SCHOOL OF LAW, TOOLS FOR MAKING BLUEBOOK CITATIONS AND KEEPING TRACK OF RESEARCH, lawlibraryguides.bu.edu/content.php?pid=210292 & sid=1750902 (June 20, 2013); Julie Tausend, *Organizational Apps*, LAW TECH (Pepperdine University School of Law Information Services), Lawtech.pepperdine.edu/organizational-apps/ (June 17, 2013).

Researchers should always note the information that will be needed for correct citation form later. Research notes do not have to be in polished form, but these notes should record the critical elements: author, title, date, reporter citation, court, etc.[5]

a. *Structured Research Log.* Using a structured research log encourages researchers to think strategically about the research and writing process. For example, the few moments spent in preliminary analysis—writing down the primary issue, key facts, and words and phrases, and determining the jurisdiction and level of prior knowledge—rather than going online immediately, will save both time and money. The notes that document the relevant primary sources are critical to developing one's legal analysis. However, it is not enough to take notes: whatever note-taking method is adopted, researchers should routinely review their notes as a way to organize both their writing and their follow-up research. These routine reviews can also be used as time- and project-management tools. When working on a project, you need to set aside sufficient time for researching, drafting, additional research, revising, editing, verification, and proofreading. While there is no substitute for experience in determining the appropriate mix of research and writing time, using a research log helps even novice writers think through the process more strategically. Here is a sample research log template:

[Illustration 3–4]

SAMPLE RESEARCH LOG: LEMON LAW PROJECT

Preliminary Analysis—Identify the issue(s), key facts, words, and phrases for searching, jurisdiction, and assess your prior knowledge related to the project

Initial Issue Statement: When a car sold under warranty by a dealership has been repeatedly repaired, does the consumer have the right to demand that the dealership buy back or replace the car?

Key facts: Vehicle purchased in 2009 for $27,090. 12,000 miles on odometer; had been used as a dealership demonstrator. Still under manufacturer's warranty. Problems with power steering. Numerous unsuccessful repairs. Dealership beginning to ignore client's complaints.

Words and Phrases: Vehicle, Automobile, Warranty, Purchaser, Consumer, Consumer Protection, Defect, Lemon Law, Repair, Replace, Refund

Jurisdiction: Washington State

Knowledge Assessment: Took Contracts; class talked briefly about warranties and remedies. Know nothing specific about Lemon Law or Washington State consumer protection statutes

Project details—Date project is due; requester's name and contact information; estimate of time to spend on the project; sensitivity to client's needs and budget; format of final work product, etc.

---

[5] For a discussion of legal citation form, see Chapter 24.

General Plan—Notes from intake from assigning attorney: consult secondary sources for general overview and citation to relevant primary sources. To save time, use state-based practitioner materials when available. Then follow up, first examining relevant statutes in an annotated code and then examining relevant case law. Refine your analysis and update your authorities while you research.

    b.   Case Analysis Chart. Another organizational tool many researchers find effective during the analytical, prewriting stage is developing a case analysis chart. A case analysis chart allows the comparison of cases across categories of procedure, facts, and holdings. This helps the researcher see analogies and distinctions among cases and spot patterns of fact scenarios that satisfy or do not satisfy a legal rule. As an organizational tool, the case analysis chart assists researchers in condensing and tracking key information about a given group of cases.[6]

[Illustration 3–5]

SAMPLE CASE ANALYSIS CHART: LEMON LAW

Case Title and Citation	*Chrysler Motors v. Flowers,* 116 Wash. 2d 208	*Ford Motor Co. v. Barrett,* 115 Wash. 2d 556	*Meyers v. Volvo,* 852 A.2d 1221
Court & Date	WA Sup. Ct. 1991	WA Sup. Ct. 1990	Pa. Superior 2004
Procedural Posture	Review of Summary Judgment	Superior Ct affirmed arbitration board; State AGO intervened to defend statute	Review of Summary Judgment
Is vehicle covered under the statute?	Yes, if car is new or under 24,000-mile warranty limitation	Ford conceded defect but contested statute's constitutionality	Volvo qualifies as "new motor vehicle" under PA Automobile Lemon Law
Previously titled?	No	No	No
Warranty in effect?	Yes	Yes	Yes
Number of repairs?	Eight	unknown	Four
Sent to arbitration?	Yes	Yes	Not applicable under PA

    c.   Approaches to Organization. Effective legal writing must synthesize multiple authorities (and accurately cite them) to support its analysis. One common organizational tool is IRAC (Issue, Rule, Application, Conclusion). For each *issue and sub-issue,* the writer identifies the *rules of law* and any elements that must be met. Next, the writer *applies* the rule to the key facts, showing how these facts meet (or do not meet) the required elements. Finally, the writer states a *conclusion.* The writer also determines whether cases or authorities that go against her position can be distinguished.

---

[6] *See* Tracy McGaugh, *The Synthesis Chart: Swiss Army Knife of Legal Writing,* 9 Persp.: Teaching Legal Res. & Writing 80 (2001).

Although IRAC is a common tool, it is not the only one, nor is it always appropriate.[7] One expert on legal writing describes IRAC as a "form of deductive reasoning appropriate to an objective analysis in an office memorandum" and CRAC, "Conclusion, Rule, Application of the legal rule to facts, and Conclusion," as the paradigm appropriate for advocacy.[8] Another legal writing expert advocates using CRuPAC: "Conclusion, *Rule, Proof of Rule,* Application, and Conclusion."[9]

d.   Prewriting and Writing. There are many models for the drafting process. Most legal writers begin with prewriting during the initial research and analysis stage. Prewriting includes categorizing your research into sections and subsections. This step will be simplified if you outlined your issues as you were conducting your research, as recommended in Chapter 2. For instance, the Lemon Law problem has two basic issues: (1) Is a demonstrator vehicle used by the dealer sales staff covered under Washington State Lemon Law? and (2) Is the specific problem a substantial defect? During the prewriting stage, the writer might work on one issue at a time. Prewriting includes setting out a basic thesis statement, as well as outlining key points and inserting relevant citations or excerpts within the outline. The first draft provides the basic structure, in a rough, imperfect form. The draft should identify the primary audience and lay the foundation for the reader. Effective legal research and writing requires multiple drafts, to develop both content and organization. The rewriting process builds on the rough draft and subsequent drafts, focusing on content revision and the large-structure organization. The editing process reviews the document at the sentence level, and polishes the tone and style. The final step is careful proofreading.

e.   Conclusion. Whether a document is predictive or persuasive, it should: (1) be tailored to a specific audience and purpose; (2) include the relevant law and facts; (3) use coherent, single-issue paragraphs; (4) provide clear distinctions among issues and sub-issues; and (5) provide a complete analysis that answers the reader's questions. For in the end, the goal of legal writing is communicating research results to the reader. That is what matters most. The processes of research, analysis, and writing are highly interdependent; effective legal writing begins with careful legal research and sound analysis. This broad overview is designed only to introduce various forms and strategies for written communication. Mastering the art and craft of legal writing is a lifelong challenge.

F.   SELECTED LEGAL WRITING RESOURCES

a.   Linda H. Edwards, *Legal Writing: Process, Analysis, and Organization* (5th ed. 2010).

b.   Linda H. Edwards, *Legal Writing and Analysis* (3d ed. 2011).

c.   Bryan A. Garner, *The Elements of Legal Style* (2d ed. 2002).

d.   Bryan A. Garner, *The Redbook: A Manual on Legal Style* (2d ed. 2006).

---

[7] For a discussion of variations of the IRAC structure, see Mary Beth Beazley, *Point/Counterpoint: Use of IRAC-type Formulas—Desirable or Dangerous?*, SECOND DRAFT, Nov. 1995, at 1.

[8] CHARLES R. CALLEROS, LEGAL METHOD AND WRITING 355 (6th ed. 2011).

[9] RICHARD K. NEUMANN, JR., LEGAL REASONING AND LEGAL WRITING: STRUCTURE, STRATEGY, AND STYLE 100 (5th ed. 2005).

e.   Tom Goldstein & Jethro K. Lieberman, *The Lawyer's Guide to Writing Well* (2d ed. 2002).

f.   Margaret Z. Johns & Clayton S. Tanaka, *Professional Writing for Lawyers: Skills and Responsibilities* (2d ed. 2012).

g.   Terri LeClercq & Karin Mika, *Guide to Legal Writing Style* (5th ed. 2011).

h.   Diana V. Pratt, *Legal Writing: A Systematic Approach* (4th ed. 2004).

i.   Theresa J. Reid Rambo & Leann J. Pflaum, *Legal Writing by Design: A Guide to Great Briefs and Memos* (2d ed. 2013).

j.   Pamela Samuelson, *Good Legal Writing: Of Orwell and Window Panes*, 46 U. PITT. L. REV. 149 (1984).

k.   Wayne Schiess, *Better Legal Writing: 15 Topics for Advanced Legal Writers* (2005).

l.   Eugene Volokh, *Academic Legal Writing: Law Review Articles, Student Notes, Seminar Papers, and Getting on Law Review* (4th ed. 2010).

m.   Richard C. Wydick, *Plain English for Lawyers* (5th ed. 2005).

Chapter 4

COURT REPORTS AND THE NATIONAL REPORTER SYSTEM

The significant role of judicial opinions is a defining characteristic of the American legal system and the common law in general, as explained in Chapter 1, Section A. Consequently, locating, reading, analyzing, and applying judicial opinions are key elements in the legal research process. Opinions may be of several types (e.g., majority, concurring, or dissenting) and are issued from both federal and state courts. They may be available individually or in a collection, organized by subject or jurisdiction. Some are "official" while others are "unofficial." Parts of an opinion may contain "the law," while other parts may deal with procedural matters or even be no more than a judge's personal viewpoint on the issue at hand. Legal researchers must understand the document that contains the judicial opinion, even before reading the opinion itself; this knowledge is crucial to using judicial opinions properly.

This chapter discusses how judicial opinions are published and reported; the segments of a reported judicial opinion; the differences between official and unofficial reports; the elements of judicial reporting; the organization of court reports; the *National Reporter System*, which is the most widespread set of court reports; and abbreviations and citations for court reports. This information is the foundation for understanding judicial opinions.

A. JUDICIAL OPINIONS

1. Introduction

The doctrine of precedent, discussed in Chapter 1, Section A-3-c, has as its premise that courts are to adhere to judicial precedent. Reliance on precedent, as derived from prior judicial decisions, is the foundation of the common law. Lawyers and judges are expected to turn to established judicial authority and rules of law as the bases for formulating legal arguments and deciding cases. Understanding the structure and organization of "case law"—the aggregate of reported cases that form a body of jurisprudence—is integral to the legal research process and is necessary to understand research results. The editing, publishing, and distribution of judicial opinions have special characteristics in American law.

Judicial decisions are typically compiled and arranged according to one or more common characteristics such as geographic jurisdiction, issuing court, time period, or subject matter. Compilations of court decisions may be referred to as "reports" or "reporters"; the terms have become interchangeable in common usage.[1]

---

[1] For many years, informal convention held that the series of printed volumes or databases that compile judicial opinions were referred to as *reports* when the information was issued directly from the government

When a court makes a determination about the outcome of a case, it may issue an opinion in which it states the reasons for its decision.[2] Technically speaking, the *decision* of the court signifies the resolution of the case and is indicated by *Affirmed, Reversed, Remanded,* or similar words or phrases. The *opinion* provides the explanation for the decision. In common practice, the terms *opinion* and *decision,* and sometimes *case,* are used interchangeably.[3]

The first volume of court reports from an American state was published in 1789 in Connecticut.[4] Reports of the Supreme Court of the United States were first published officially, by the Court, in 1817, after having been produced by various court reporters since the Court's first term.[5] The numbers of published reports have increased dramatically since that time. More than 10,000,000 judicial opinions from U.S. jurisdictions are now in published form, and over 250,000 new American cases are reported each year from more than 600 courts. Most of these published opinions are from federal and state appellate courts.

Information technology has changed court reporting in fundamental ways. The development *LexisNexis* and *Westlaw,* both launched in the 1970s, brought a new format to court reporting, expanding access and speeding up distribution, but also creating issues of trustworthiness and completeness. Since then, new providers of electronic legal information have entered (and left) the marketplace, offering legal materials in a variety of formats. As this book is written in 2013, almost all electronic legal information providers have migrated their products to a web-based delivery system. The changes brought about by information technologies to court reporting, and legal information sources and research generally, will be covered throughout this book.

Do not be daunted by this tremendous body of case law and its many sources and formats. As Justice Holmes observed, "It is a great mistake to be frightened by the ever-increasing number of reports. The reports of a given jurisdiction in the course of a generation take up pretty much the whole body of law, and restate it from the present point of view. We could reconstruct the corpus from them if all that went before were burned."[6] Much of your research will involve more recent opinions, and excellent tools exist to aid in locating even the oldest cases. A major purpose of this text is to explain those tools.

---

and *reporters* when provided by a commercial entity. "In general, when a series is called simply 'Reports,' as *Oregon, Virginia,* or *Indiana Reports,* it is likely to be an official series." MILES O. PRICE & HARRY BITNER, EFFECTIVE LEGAL RESEARCH 116 (1953). For example, the official reports of the Maryland Court of Appeals (the highest/supreme court of the state) are the *Maryland Reports.* The *Atlantic Reporter* and the *Maryland Reporter* (an "offprint" of the *Atlantic Reporter,* containing decisions of Maryland courts only and retaining the *Atlantic Reporter* pagination) are issued by commercial publishers. The distinction between reports and reporters grows murkier by the year, as states cancel their own publishing programs and contract with commercial publishers to produce official publications.

    [2] *See* Section A-5 for an explanation of when a case is reported.

    [3] For a discussion of the difference between *decision of the court* and *opinion of the court,* see Rogers v. Hill, 289 U.S. 582, 587 (1933). *See also* Towley v. King Arthur Rings, Inc., 40 N.Y.2d 129, 351 N.E.2d 728, 386 N.Y.S.2d 80 (1976).

    [4] *See* app. D.

    [5] A description of the U.S. Supreme Court's publishing is found in Chapter 5, Section A-1, *infra.*

    [6] OLIVER WENDELL HOLMES, *The Path of the Law, in* COLLECTED LEGAL PAPERS 167, 169 (1920 & photo reprint 1985).

2. Sources of Judicial Opinions: The Court System

Each jurisdiction in the United States has its own system of court organization although, in general, the structures are very similar. [Illustration 4–1] There are two basic types of courts: trial courts and appellate courts. Trial courts are the courts in which the parties to a dispute appear, witnesses testify, and evidence is presented. In trial courts, questions of fact are resolved and rules of law are applied to the facts, resulting in a disposition of the case. Trial courts are sometimes referred to as courts of first instance, courts of first impression, or courts of original jurisdiction.

Ordinarily, cases decided by state trial courts are not reported. Only a few states, such as New York, Ohio, Pennsylvania, and Virginia, publish some trial court opinions, but those selected are few in number and represent only a very small portion of the total cases heard by the trial courts. In contrast, many opinions of trial courts at the federal level, especially including the federal district courts, are published.[7]

After the trial court proceeding is concluded, the losing party typically has a right to appeal the decision to an appellate court. Each state has a final appellate level court, a "court of last resort," which is usually called a supreme court. Forty states and Puerto Rico also have intermediate appellate courts.[8] Generally, the appellate court can only address claims that the law was identified or applied incorrectly, "errors of law"; appellate courts usually are required to adhere to the trial court's findings of fact. The appellate decision in a case is based on the trial court record, e.g., pre-trial proceedings, exhibits, and the trial transcript. Appellate courts do not hear new witnesses or decide questions of fact. In most states, only the appellate courts issue written opinions.

When a case is appealed to an appellate court, the parties to the trial submit written briefs that contain a summary of the facts and arguments on the relevant points of law. The appellate court may hear oral arguments by the attorneys. The court decides the case and, usually, issues an opinion in which it states the reasons for its decision. If the losing party before an intermediate appellate court believes the court's decision was wrong and its position is legally correct, the appellate court decision may be appealed, under certain conditions, to the court of last resort. Not all appellate court opinions are published (nor are all decisions accompanied by opinions), and publication procedures differ from state to state and in the federal courts.

3. Publication of Judicial Opinions

Judicial opinions are published, that is, released to the public, in a variety of ways. Generally, an opinion is first published as a *slip opinion*. Originally referring to the fact that the opinion was printed on an individual page of paper, a "slip," slip opinion has come to mean a single opinion, regardless of its number of pages or format, published almost as soon as it is issued by the court. It is increasingly common for print and electronic slip opinions to be released almost simultaneously. Usually, each slip opinion is paginated separately and includes no (or very few) editorial enhancements.

---

[7] Federal court reports are discussed in Chapter 5.

[8] For detailed information on the activities of state courts, see *Court Statistics Project*, produced jointly by the Conference of State Court Administrators and the National Center for State Courts, available at http://www.courtstatistics.org/. *See also* latest COUNCIL OF STATE GOVERNMENTS, THE BOOK OF THE STATES (1935–).

An advantage of slip opinions is that the court's decision and rationale in a particular case are quickly available. Disadvantages include that slip opinions may be withdrawn for editing and they most typically have no other indexing or finding points besides their date and the case's name and docket number. The ease of locating materials in electronic format has made finding slip opinions somewhat less complicated than with print slip opinions,[9] which are commonly arranged in binders by date with no other indexes or finding tools.

After the issuance of slip opinions, the most common method of publishing opinions in print is as *advance sheets*. Advance sheets are almost always softbound pamphlets that contain a number of recently decided cases, typically in chronological order by date of decision. Their pages are consecutively numbered from one pamphlet to the next and are published as quickly as they can be assembled after the decisions are issued. After publication of several advance sheets (typically three to five issues), the decisions are published in a hardbound volume that uses the same page numbers as the advance sheets. This process makes recent decisions easier to find and provides permanent citations to opinions. The features of the cases in the advance sheets are similar to those included in bound volumes, described below. Some jurisdictions do not publish advance sheets. Electronic sources distribute opinions as soon as they are received and processed, eliminating the need for advance sheets and bound volumes but generally retaining the page numbering of advance sheets and bound volumes for citation purposes.

The most extensive and widely known collection of judicial opinions is West's *National Reporter System*, which includes both advance sheets and bound volumes in print, and is available electronically in numerous sources. The *National Reporter System,* which began in 1879, comprises several publications, together with an extensive indexing system, that will be described in detail in the following chapters.

4.   Official and Unofficial Reports

The text of judicial opinions is not copyrightable.[10] Consequently, numerous sets of court reports, published by both governmental and commercial publishers, in both print and electronic formats, can be found in most jurisdictions. If a statute or court rule requires the publication of court reports, those reports are referred to as *official* reports. [Illustration 4–6] In some instances, the government itself publishes the official court reports. In others the government may contract with a private publisher to produce the official court reports. In either instance, the important characteristic is that the court reports are published by governmental authority. All other court reports are referred to as *unofficial* reports. Neither term necessarily reflects superior quality or accuracy because the text of the opinions reported in both should be identical. Unofficial publications often are more useful research tools because they typically have editorial enhancements and are available to the public much faster than official reports. [Illustrations 4–2 through 4–5] However, citation to official reports is required by most courts for most legal documents.[11]

---

[9] A listing of especially useful websites that provide slip opinions and other court opinions is provided in Chapter 23.

[10] Wheaton v. Peters, 33 U.S. (8 Pet.) 591 (1834). *See also* Banks v. Manchester, 128 U.S. 244 (1888).

[11] For a list of jurisdiction-specific citation rules and style guides, see BLUEBOOK tbl BT2.1, at 30.

5. Published and Unpublished Decisions

Many judges, lawyers, and legal scholars believe that far too many judicial opinions are published. They argue, for example, that many published decisions make no doctrinal clarifications or advancements. Although important to the parties, these cases add little (or nothing) to our understanding of the law. The tremendous growth in the number of available opinions has led to attempts to limit the number and use of cases that are published.

Some courts and legislatures have attempted to control the volume of judicial opinions by only officially publishing opinions that (1) enunciate a new rule of law or change or modify an existing rule; (2) apply an established rule of law to a new or significantly different fact situation; (3) involve a legal issue of continuing public interest; (4) criticize existing law; (5) resolve an apparent conflict of authority; or (6) contribute to the legal literature by collecting relevant case law or reciting legislative history.[12] Any opinions not meeting one or more of the criteria are referred to as "unpublished"—a term of art indicating that the court has designated a case as not for publication, even though it might be "published" in the sense of being widely distributed in print, on court websites, and in commercial online services. Some courts also have "non-citation" or "no-citation" rules that prohibit the citation to opinions not officially published or, sometimes, not specifically marked "For Publication." Some courts limit or remove the precedential value of unpublished opinions, or restrict or impose conditions on their use.[13]

Advocates for liberalizing or eliminating non-citation rules argue that unpublished opinions are widely available and are, in fact, relied on by lawyers and judges. Further, they contend that non-citation rules make it less likely that similar situations will be treated in a similar manner and the rules, therefore, work against the interests of justice. In their view, public policy favors elimination of the non-citation rules. Those favoring retention of the non-citation rules argue that the rules work well to limit the number of published opinions. They believe that the elimination of non-citation rules would increase the costs of legal research, create new professional obligations for lawyers, and increase the work of the courts.[14] The federal courts of appeals permit citation of unpublished opinions issued on or after January 1, 2007,[15] but several individual circuits still discourage the practice or limit the precedential weight of the unpublished opinions.

---

[12] The value of restricting the publication of appellate court opinions, often referred to as "selective publication," has caused considerable debate. For a historical survey, see J. Myron Jacobstein, *Some Reflections on the Control of the Publication of Appellate Court Opinions*, 27 STAN. L. REV. 791 (1975).

[13] For a survey of the various federal and state rules, see Melissa M. Serfass & Jessie Willace Cranford, *Federal and State Court Rules Governing Publication and Citation of Opinions: An Update*, 6 J. APP. PRAC. & PROCESS 349 (2004). For citations to federal and state cases, see Jason B. Binimow, Annotation, *Precedential Effect of Unpublished Opinions*, 105 A.L.R.5TH 499 (2003). (Although the Annotation was first published in 2003, the pocket part and the version in *Westlaw* have more recent cases.) *See, e.g.*, Wis. R. App. P. 809.23, (listing criteria for publishing opinions and limiting citation of unpublished opinions).

[14] For an introduction to the controversy, see Joseph L. Gerken, *A Librarian's Guide to Unpublished Judicial Opinions*, 96 LAW LIBR. J. 475 (2004). Although the title indicates it is for librarians, the article, presented in a question-and-answer format, is a very useful introduction for law students and lawyers as well. It includes an annotated bibliography of selected articles. For citations to many more articles, see Mary Whisner, *Unpublished Decisions: A Working Bibliography*, http://ssrn.com/abstract=2306184 (Aug. 5, 2013).

[15] FED. R. APP. P. 32.1

The increased availability of previously difficult to locate unpublished opinions makes this an important issue. Researchers must know the publication status of opinions, and should ascertain the rules of each court in their jurisdiction before citing unpublished opinions. Court rules are discussed in Chapter 12.

6.   The Organization of Court Reports

Court reports are typically published in both print and online versions. In almost every instance, the electronic version retains the print numbering system (volumes and pages, paragraph numbers, etc.), although there is a movement towards "format neutral" or "vendor neutral" citations that do not depend on print publications.[16] Generally, the individual decisions are arranged by the date they were issued by the court. Court reports may be organized in one or more of the following ways.

a.   By Issuing Court. The reports of a particular court are often published in a numbered series, such as the *Arizona Reports*, the *Illinois Appellate Court Reports*, or the *United States Tax Court Reports*. In some instances, the reports of several courts are published together. Most typically this happens when decisions of both a state's highest court and its intermediate appellate court are published in the same set; an example is the *California Reporter.*

b.   By Geography. West's *National Reporter* System, the best-known example of geographical reporting, publishes the opinions of geographically adjacent states in a single series. For example, the *North Western Reporter* includes cases from the appellate and supreme courts of Iowa, Michigan, Minnesota, Nebraska, North Dakota, South Dakota, and Wisconsin.[17]

c.   By Subject. Sets of specialized subject law reports contain cases dealing with a specific subject. Examples of these subject reports are *Federal Rules Decisions*, *Labor Law Reports*, and *United States Patents Quarterly*.

Many print court reports are part of an integrated series of research publications from the court reports' publisher that include indexes and locating tools and a current updating service. Electronic versions may or may not include separate research or updating components. Finding and using court reports will be covered in the following chapters.

B.   THE SEGMENTS OF COURT OPINIONS

An American court case typically includes the following segments. [Illustrations 4–2 and 4–3]

1.   Name

Cases generally are identified by the names of the parties involved. While most typically spoken of as the "name" of the case, other labels used include the "title," the "style," or the "caption" of the case. In legal writing, the method of referring to cases is controlled by citation and court rules, and usually is, in essence, an abbreviation of the full name. Examples include:

---

[16] *See, e.g.*, Peter W. Martin, *Neutral Citation, Court Web Sites, and Access to Authoritative Case Law*, 99 LAW LIBR. J. 329 (2007), and http://www.aallnet.org/main-menu/Advocacy/access/citation/neutralrules.

[17] The components of the *National Reporter System* are discussed in Chapters 5 and 6.

a.   *Carol Berry, Plaintiff v. Richard M. Green, Defendant.* This case would be referred to as *Berry v. Green.*

b.   *In re Berry.* This is the name of a judicial proceeding in which there are no adversarial parties. Examples include a bankruptcy case, a probate case, an adoption or guardianship matter, a contempt case, or a disbarment proceeding.

c.   *Ex parte Berry.* This case name is used to identify a special proceeding for the benefit of one party only.

d.   *State on the relation of Berry v. Green.* This would be referred to as *State ex rel. Berry v. Green.* A case with this kind of name involves extraordinary legal remedies, often based on a writ such as *mandamus,* prohibition, *quo warranto,* or *habeas corpus.*

e.   *State v. Berry.* This the name of a criminal proceeding, brought by the state government in its representative capacity as the party wronged by a criminal act. *People* or *Commonwealth* is used in some states instead of *State.* If the United States brings the suit, it is named *United States v. Berry.*

f.   *The Caledonia.* In maritime law, a suit may be brought against a ship, in which instance the name of the proceeding is the name of the ship.

g.   *United States v. 37 Photographs.* Cases involving the seizure of commodities refer to the commodity as a party.

The first listed name is that of the plaintiff or the party initiating the proceeding. The second name is that of the defendant. Usually, the case name remains the same if the case is appealed; the parties may be referred to as the appellant and the appellee. However, in some states the order of names is reversed on appeal and the appellant is listed first.

2. Citation

The citation to the case usually appears near the name of the case at the beginning of the decision. The citation is the unique identifier for a case, distinguishing the specific case from all others and allowing users to find the case in its published form. For print materials, the citation typically includes the volume number, title of the source (which is often the name of jurisdiction), the page on which the case is located, and the date the case was issued. For electronic materials, the citation may be the same as for the print publication or it may be numerical (e.g., a docket number or combination of date and document number).[18] In many instances, a case will be published in more than one set or database. In this situation, a publisher often includes "parallel citations" to other sources in which the case is published.

3. Docket Number

A docket number is the unique identification number assigned to a case by a court. Typically, the docket number includes the year the case was filed and then a sequential designation, e.g., No. 2002–1145. It is the primary means of identifying the case before

---

[18] There is a move towards a "format-neutral" or "universal" citation form that is changing the citation practices in several jurisdictions. *See* Michael Umberger, *Checking up on Court Citation Standards: How Neutral Citation Improves Public Access to Case Law*, 31 LEGAL REFERENCE SERVICES Q., nos. 3–4, 2012, at 312 (discussing development of neutral citation and listing states that have adopted neutral citation forms).

a decision is published, and often remains the number by which briefs and other records associated with the case are located.

4.   Date of Decision

This is the date on which the decision was released.

5.   Syllabus or Headnote

The syllabus or headnote is a brief summary of points of law in the case, usually accompanied by relevant facts bearing on each point of law. Courts that include a syllabus typically have only one; courts that use headnotes may have several for a single case. They are typically drafted by editors or reporters employed by the court, or by commercial publishers, although in a few states a syllabus or headnote may be prepared by the judge writing the decision.

The syllabus or headnotes are often useful in allowing the reader to grasp relatively quickly the legal issues discussed in the opinion and locate these issues in the case. In most instances, neither a syllabus nor a headnote should be relied upon as being "the law," and the entire case must be read.[19] Headnotes in particular often can be useful in finding other cases involving the same or similar points of law.[20] [Illustrations 4–2 and 4–4]

6.   Prefatory Statement

The prefatory statement explains the nature of the case, its disposition in the lower court, the name of the lower court and sometimes its judge, and the disposition of the case in the appellate court, e.g., *Affirmed* or *Reversed*. In many recent print versions, the prefatory statement is divided into two parts, "background" and "holding."

7.   Names of Counsel

The names of counsel for both parties to a suit precede the opinion of the court.

8.   Name of Judge

The name of the deciding judge or judges is immediately preceding the text of the opinion. If a judge concurred or dissented from the opinion, his or her name is included at the beginning or the end of the opinion.

9.   Opinion of the Court

The *opinion* of the court is the explanation of the court's decision. The decision is the conclusion or result in a controversy. In practice, the terms opinion and decision are used interchangeably. The court's opinion is often referred to as the *majority opinion*. It is written by one member of the court and represents the principles of law that a majority

---

[19] The Ohio Supreme Court has gone farther than most courts in giving a special status to the syllabus. Ohio's Supreme Court Rules for the Reporting of Opinions provide that "[t]he law stated in a Supreme Court opinion is contained within its syllabus (if one is provided), and its text, including footnotes." OHIO S. CT. REP. OP. R. 1(B)(1). "If there is disharmony between the syllabus of an opinion and its text or footnotes, the syllabus controls." OHIO S. CT. REP. OP. R. 1(B)(2).

[20] Syllabi and headnotes are discussed in more detail in Chapter 7.

of the judges has decided are operative in a given decision.[21] The majority opinion is the most common kind of judicial opinion.

There are, however, several other types of opinions. One or more members of the majority, while agreeing with the decision, may disagree with its reasoning; an opinion explaining the reasons for the disagreement is called a *concurring opinion*. One or more judges that disagree with the decision, referred to as a minority, may write a *dissent*, or *dissenting opinion*. An opinion in *accord* with the dissent is written by a dissenting judge when he or she agrees with the conclusions and results of the dissent, but disagrees with its reasoning. There may be more than one dissenting opinion in a case. Dissenting and concurring opinions are not the law; they are not binding as precedent and serve merely as persuasive authority. However, the majority opinion may later be overruled and a dissenting or concurring opinion might then be accepted as the new, correct statement of the law. A dissent or concurrence may be persuasive to a court in another jurisdiction.

On rare occasions, there is no majority of appellate judges that agrees to a single decision. When that happens, the decision and accompanying opinion with which the largest number of judges agrees is referred to as the *plurality opinion*. This opinion, and its decision, represents the outcome of the case.

A *per curiam opinion* is an opinion of the entire majority as distinguished from an opinion written by a specific judge. In some courts, e.g., New York Court of Appeals, a *per curiam* opinion may present a discussion of the issues in the case. In other courts, e.g., Supreme Court of the United States, this type of opinion may only give the conclusion without any reasoning.[22] A *memorandum opinion* is a very brief opinion by the entire court; it may simply consist of a statement of the court's holding. A *rescript opinion* is an appellate court's decision, typically unsigned, that is sent down to the trial court for a specific action. An *advisory opinion* is a nonbinding opinion rendered by a court at the request of the government or an interested party that indicates how the court would likely rule if the matter were to come before it. Not every court can issue an advisory opinion.

Obiter dictum (usually shortened to *dictum* or *dicta*) is an official, incidental comment made by a judge in the text of an opinion. The dictum is not necessary to the formulation of the decision and is not binding as precedent. The language of a dissent or concurrence is considered equivalent to dictum.

10. Decision, with Judgment or Decree

The decision is the conclusion, the actual disposition of the case by the court. A *decision* is noted by such terms as *Affirmed, Reversed, or Modified*. The decision is most often found at the end of the opinion, although a syllabus or headnote may also include this information. Often, the words *decision* and *judgment* are used synonymously.[23]

---

[21] As noted in Chapter 1, the *ratio decidendi* is the point in a case that determines the result. In other words, it is the basis of the decision that is stated in the opinion, explicitly or implicitly.

[22] For discussion of the decline in the use of the *per curiam* opinion by the Supreme Court of the United States, see Stephen L. Wasby et al., *The Per Curiam Opinion: Its Nature and Functions*, 76 JUDICATURE 29 (1992). *See also* Stephen L. Wasby et al., *The Supreme Court's Use of Per Curiam Dispositions: The Connection to Oral Argument*, 13 N. Ill. U. L. Rev. 1 (1992); Laura Krugman Ray, *The Road to* Bush v. Gore: *The History of the Supreme Court's Use of the Per Curiam Opinion*, 79 NEB. L. REV. 517 (2000).

[23] A decree, typically issued in equity or admiralty actions, announces the legal consequences of the facts as determined by the court.

C. ILLUSTRATIONS

[Illustration 4–1]

BASIC COURT STRUCTURE IN THE UNITED STATES

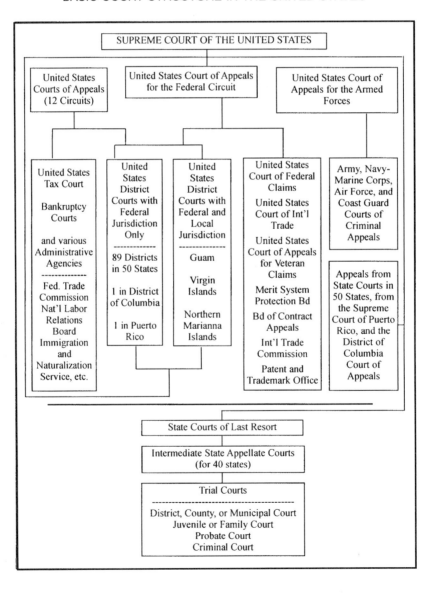

[Illustration 4-2]

FIRST PAGE OF A TYPICAL CASE AS REPORTED IN A SET OF OFFICIAL STATE COURT REPORTS (72 MASS. APP. CT. 288)

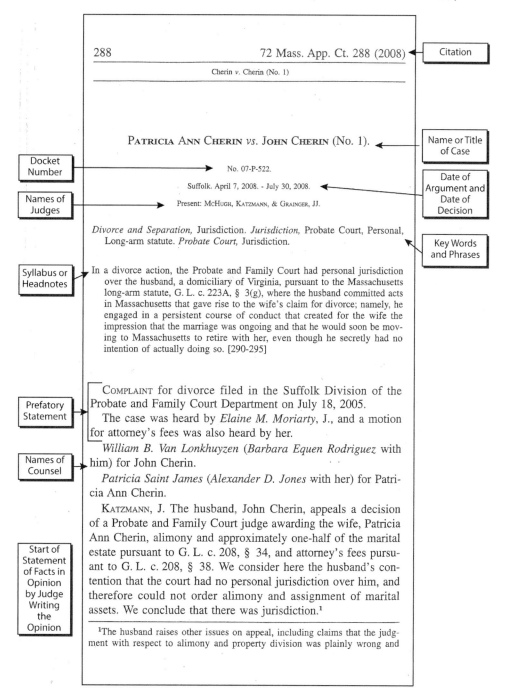

288　　　　　　　　　　72 Mass. App. Ct. 288 (2008)　　　◄── Citation

Cherin *v.* Cherin (No. 1)

PATRICIA ANN CHERIN *vs.* JOHN CHERIN (No. 1). ◄──　Name or Title of Case

Docket Number ──────► No. 07-P-522.

Suffolk. April 7, 2008. - July 30, 2008. ◄──　Date of Argument and Date of Decision

Names of Judges ──────► Present: McHUGH, KATZMANN, & GRAINGER, JJ.

Divorce and Separation, Jurisdiction. *Jurisdiction,* Probate Court, Personal, Long-arm statute. *Probate Court,* Jurisdiction. ◄── Key Words and Phrases

Syllabus or Headnotes ──► In a divorce action, the Probate and Family Court had personal jurisdiction over the husband, a domiciliary of Virginia, pursuant to the Massachusetts long-arm statute, G. L. c. 223A, § 3(g), where the husband committed acts in Massachusetts that gave rise to the wife's claim for divorce; namely, he engaged in a persistent course of conduct that created for the wife the impression that the marriage was ongoing and that he would soon be moving to Massachusetts to retire with her, even though he secretly had no intention of actually doing so. [290-295]

Prefatory Statement ──► COMPLAINT for divorce filed in the Suffolk Division of the Probate and Family Court Department on July 18, 2005.

The case was heard by *Elaine M. Moriarty,* J., and a motion for attorney's fees was also heard by her.

Names of Counsel ──► *William B. Van Lonkhuyzen (Barbara Equen Rodriguez* with him) for John Cherin.

Patricia Saint James (Alexander D. Jones with her) for Patricia Ann Cherin.

KATZMANN, J. The husband, John Cherin, appeals a decision of a Probate and Family Court judge awarding the wife, Patricia Ann Cherin, alimony and approximately one-half of the marital estate pursuant to G. L. c. 208, § 34, and attorney's fees pursuant to G. L. c. 208, § 38. We consider here the husband's contention that the court had no personal jurisdiction over him, and therefore could not order alimony and assignment of marital assets. We conclude that there was jurisdiction.[1]

Start of Statement of Facts in Opinion by Judge Writing the Opinion

[1]The husband raises other issues on appeal, including claims that the judgment with respect to alimony and property division was plainly wrong and

[Illustration 4–3]

LAST PAGE OF OPINION (7 MASS. APP. CT. 295)

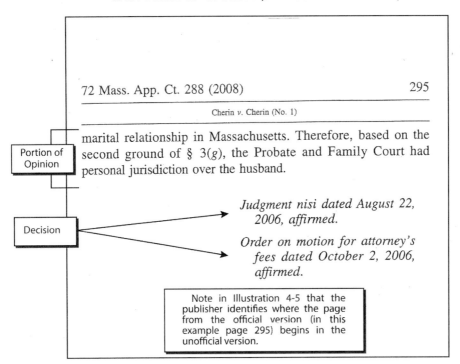

72 Mass. App. Ct. 288 (2008)   295

Cherin v. Cherin (No. 1)

Portion of Opinion

marital relationship in Massachusetts. Therefore, based on the second ground of § 3(*g*), the Probate and Family Court had personal jurisdiction over the husband.

Decision

Judgment nisi dated August 22, 2006, affirmed.

Order on motion for attorney's fees dated October 2, 2006, affirmed.

Note in Illustration 4-5 that the publisher identifies where the page from the official version (in this example page 295) begins in the unofficial version.

[Illustration 4–4]

FIRST PAGE OF A TYPICAL CASE AS REPORTED IN A SET OF UNOFFICIAL REPORTS (SAME CASE AS 72 MASS. APP. CT. 288)

684 Mass.　891 **NORTH EASTERN REPORTER, 2d SERIES**

72 Mass.App.Ct. 288

Patricia Ann CHERIN

v.

John CHERIN (No. 1).

No. 07–P–522.

Appeals Court of Massachusetts, Suffolk.

Argued April 7, 2008.

Decided July 30, 2008.

Background: In divorce action, the Probate and Family Court Department, Suffolk County, Elaine M. Moriarty, J., entered judgment awarding wife alimony, a portion of the marital estate, and attorney fees. Husband appealed, alleging that trial court lacked personal jurisdiction over him.

Holding: The Appeals Court, Katzmann, J., held that trial court had personal jurisdiction over husband under the long-arm statute.

Affirmed.

1. Courts ⬠12(2.35)

Husband committed acts in state that gave rise to the wife's claim for divorce, and thus trial court had personal jurisdiction over husband under the long-arm statute, even though husband was not domiciled in state on date of irretrievable breakdown of marriage, and the couple had been largely separated geographically before that time; husband engaged in a persistent course of conduct that created for the wife the impression that the marriage was ongoing and that he would soon be moving to state to retire with her, even though he secretly had no intention of actually doing so. M.G.L.A. c. 223A, § 3(g).

2. Divorce ⬠201

In order to issue a support obligation or property division as part of a divorce decree, a court must have in personam jurisdiction over the obligor spouse.

3. Courts ⬠12(2.1)

This is the same case as shown in Illustrations 4–2 & 4–3 as it appears in the *North Eastern Reporter 2d*, an unofficial set of court reports.

The editorial staff at West prepares the prefatory statement and headnotes to the left in this Illustration. Note that these headnotes are *not* the same as in the official *Massachusetts Appeals Court Reports*.

Although the material preceding the opinion of the court may vary in the unofficial hard copy reports and computer-retrievable versions from that in the official reports, the text of the opinion itself is identical. [See Illustration 4–5]

The difference between the official and unofficial reports, as well as other features of court reports, are discussed further in Chapters 5 and 6.

See Appendix D of this book for a list of states that have discontinued their official reports.

William B. VanLonkhuyzen, Boston (Barbara Equen Rodriguez with him) for John Cherin.

Patricia Saint James, Wellesley (Alexander D. Jones with her) for Patricia Ann Cherin.

Present: McHUGH, KATZMANN, & GRAINGER, JJ.

KATZMANN, J.

┃288┃The husband, John Cherin, appeals a decision of a Probate and Family Court judge awarding the wife, Patricia Ann Cherin, alimony and approximately one-half of the marital estate pursuant to G.L.

[Illustration 4–5]

LAST PAGE OF OPINION (891 N.E.2D 684, 689)

DOVNER v. EDELMAN   Mass. **689**
Cite as 891 N.E.2d 689 (Mass.App.Ct. 2008)

deception that made his June 30, 2005, e-mail, in which he revealed his true intent, so devastating,[10] ultimately giving rise to the irretrievable breakdown of the marriage and the wife's claim for divorce, alimony, and property settlement. See *Tatro v. Manor Care, Inc.,* 416 Mass. 763, 771, 625 N.E.2d 549 (1994) ("arising from" language in G.L. c. 223A, § 3[a], should be interpreted "broadly"). In short, the June 30, 2005, communication unmasked that the husband had engaged in a pattern of deception in Massachusetts during the previous years, and ultimately destroyed the wife's expectation of a continuing marital relationship in Massachusetts. Therefore, based on the second ground of § 3(g), the Probate and Family Court had personal jurisdiction over the husband.

Judgment nisi dated August 22, 2006, affirmed.

Order on motion for attorney's fees dated October 2, 2006, affirmed.

72 Mass.App.Ct. 904

David DOVNER & another[1]

v.

William EDELMAN.

07–P–1482

Appeals Court of Massachusetts.

Aug. 5, 2008.

Background: Motorists who were injured in accident with minor who had taken car for a joyride without owner's permission brought negligence action against car owner. The Superior Court entered summary judgment in favor of car owner, and motorists appealed.

> Compare this illustration with Illustration 4–3. Note that all of page 295 of the *Massachusetts Appeals Court Reports* (vol. 72) is contained on page 689 of the *North Eastern Reporter 2d* (vol. 891) and that the opinion in both sources is identical.

Car owner owed no duty to protect motorists who were injured in accident with minor who had taken owner's car for a joyride without owner's permission; owner had no special relationship with minor, who took spare car key from owner's house while there for lunch, and owner had no knowledge that minor was using the car.

2. Negligence ⟐220

In general, there is no duty to protect others from the criminal or wrongful activities of third persons.

3. Negligence ⟐220

A duty to protect others from the criminal or wrongful activities of third persons may arise where existing social values and customs impose such a duty.

4. Negligence ⟐220

A duty of reasonable care to protect against criminal acts may arise when special circumstances would suggest to a pru-

---

LaVallee v. Parrot–Ice Drink Prods. of Am., Inc., 193 F.Supp.2d 296, 300 (D.Mass.2002) ("it is well established that fraudulent misrepresentation is a sufficient basis for jurisdiction under § 3[c]").

10. Evidence of the wife's surprise can be found in a June 22, 2005, e-mail from her to the husband in which, after learning from

Chiara that the husband said he would have to move out of the Virginia marital home if she tried to move back in, she wrote to the husband that she was "hurt, very hurt, and then angry," and that she "had not expected this."

1. Susan Dovner.

[Illustration 4–6]

TYPICAL STATUTORY PROVISIONS FOR PUBLICATION OF COURT REPORTS

Excerpt from West's Ann. Calif. Gov't Code

§ 68902.　Publication of official reports.

Such opinions of the Supreme Court, of the courts of appeals, and of the appellate divisions of the superior courts as the Supreme Court may deem expedient shall be published in the official reports. The reports shall be published under the general supervision of the Supreme Court.

Excerpts from McKinney's Consol. Laws of N.Y. Ann. Judiciary Law

§ 430.　Law reporting bureau; state reporter

There is hereby created and established the law reporting bureau of the state of New York. The bureau shall be under the direction and control of a state reporter, who shall be appointed and be removable by the court of appeals by an order entered in its minutes. The state reporter shall be assisted by a first deputy state reporter and such other deputy state reporters and staff as may be necessary, all of whom shall be appointed and be removable by the court of appeals.

§ 431.　Causes to be reported

The law reporting bureau shall report every cause determined in the court of appeals and every cause determined in the appellate divisions of the supreme court, unless otherwise directed by the court deciding the cause; and, in addition, any cause determined in any other court which the reporter, with the approval of the court of appeals, considers worthy of being reported because of its usefulness as a precedent or its importance as a matter of public interest.

Excerpt from Vernon's Ann. Mo. Stat.

§ 477.231.　Designation of private publication as official reports

The supreme court may declare the published volumes of the decisions of the supreme court as the same are published by any person, firm or corporation, to be the official reports of the decisions of the supreme court, and the courts of appeals may jointly make a similar declaration with respect to published volumes of the opinions of the courts of appeals. Any publication so designated as the official reports may include both the opinions of the supreme court and the courts of appeals in the same volume.

D.　THE NATIONAL REPORTER SYSTEM

The *National Reporter System*, which began in 1879, is the largest and most comprehensive collection of state and federal cases in printed form. It consists of three main types of cases: (1) cases from state courts, (2) cases from federal courts, and (3) cases from special courts. There are also subject-based reporters that extract cases from the various *National Reporter System* units[24] and "off-prints," cases from a single state extracted from the geographically arranged regional reporters.

---

[24] *See* Appendix E for a chart showing coverage of the *National Reporter System*.

The development of the *National Reporter System* has had a profound impact on the method of finding judicial opinions and, some suggest, on the development of American law.[25] At the inception of the *National Reporter System*, the states and territories in existence at the time, the various federal circuit courts, and the Supreme Court of the United States all published court reports with varying features and arrangements; some of these publications had been in existence for almost a century. It was extremely difficult to find cases dealing with similar points of law, both within a single jurisdiction and across jurisdictions. The *National Reporter System*, in conjunction with West's topic and key number classification system (discussed in Chapter 7), brought organization to the disorder resulting from the rapid growth in published court reports by numerous sources. The *National Reporter System* continues to play an important role in legal research, although technological developments have made it possible for case law to be disseminated, stored, and retrieved in new ways.

The *National Reporter System* contains the full text of cases decided by the various state and federal courts. West adds editorial enhancements that facilitate research. These common features, discussed below, make it possible for researchers to find cases from all the states, as well as those decided in the federal courts, on the same or similar points of law.

When West receives opinions from the courts, its editors prepare headnotes and assign key numbers from its *American Digest System*. West publishes these cases first in advance sheets and then in bound volumes. The key numbers are the basis of the *National Reporter System*'s indexing method, described in Chapter 7. Bound volumes retain the same volume and page numbers as the advance sheets.[26]

In addition to the opinions and headnotes, the advance sheets and bound volumes of the *National Reporter System* include a synopsis of the case, a digest section containing headnotes and key numbers of the cases covered, a table of cases arranged by state, a table of statutes interpreted by cases covered (ceased at the start of 2000), a list of words and phrases defined in the cases reported, and a table showing cases that have cited the second edition of the American Bar Association's *Standards for Criminal Justice*. From time to time, the various units also include proposed changes to or newly approved versions of court rules.

The advance sheets to the reporters contain several current awareness features that are not incorporated into the bound volumes. For example, the state and regional reporters contain summaries of federal cases arising in each state covered by that reporter. "Judicial Highlights," contained in both the state and regional reporters, are features that briefly describe cases of special interest or significance.

---

[25] *See* Thomas A. Woxland, *"Forever Associated with the Practice of Law": The Early Years of the West Publishing Company*, LEGAL REFERENCE SERVICES Q., Spring 1985, at 115; Joe Morehead, *All Cases Great and Small: The West Publishing Company Saga*, 14 SERIALS LIBR., nos. 3–4, 1988, at 3. *See also* Robert C. Berring, *Full-Text Databases and Legal Research: Backing into the Future*, 1 HIGH TECH. L.J. 27, 29–38 (1986); Robert C. Berring, *Legal Research and Legal Concepts: Where Form Molds Substance*, 75 CALIF. L. REV. 15 (1987); Robert C. Berring, *Chaos, Cyberspace and Tradition: Legal Information Transmogrified*, 12 BERKELEY TECH. L.J. 189 (1997).

[26] Occasionally after a case has been published in an advance sheet, the judge who wrote the opinion might, for one reason or another, decide that it should not be published and recalls the opinion. In such instances, another case is published in the appendix of a subsequent advance sheet with the same pagination as the withdrawn case. By this means, the original pagination is preserved in the bound volume.

In addition to the federal, state, and regional reporters mentioned above, West also publishes specialized subject reporters such as the *Education Law Reporter*, *Social Security Reporting Service*, and *United States Merit Systems Protection Board Reporter*. Although the publisher does not consider these sets to be part of its *National Reporter System*, the sets often reprint cases contained in it and have finding aids that function as if part of it.

[Illustration 4–7]

MAP OF THE NATIONAL REPORTER SYSTEM® *
SHOWING THE STATES IN EACH REGIONAL REPORTER GROUP

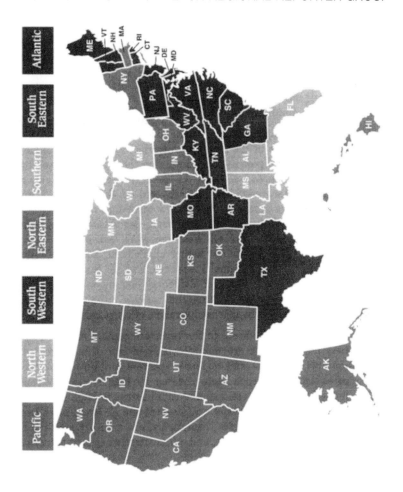

* The National Reporter System also includes:

Supreme Court Reporter	Federal Reporter
Federal Supplement	Federal Rules Decisions
West's Bankruptcy Reporter	New York Supplement
West's California Reporter	West's Illinois Decisions
West's Military Justice Reporter	Veterans Appeals Reporter
Federal Claims Reporter	Federal Appendix

E. CITATIONS TO COURT REPORTS

The purpose of a citation is to allow for the accurate and efficient location of the source being cited. Legal citation places a premium on conciseness, leading to a citation format with a generally standardized sequence of information that includes many abbreviations. The most widely used legal citation manual is *The Bluebook: A Uniform System of Citation* (19th ed. 2010), published by the editors of the *Columbia Law Review*, *Harvard Law Review*, *University of Pennsylvania Law Review*, and *Yale Law Journal*. A popular alternative to the *Bluebook* is the *ALWD Citation Manual* (4th ed. 2010), sponsored by the Association of Legal Writing Directors.[27]

Names of cases are abbreviated, generally with only one named plaintiff and one defendant regardless of the number of parties to the action. Further, the plaintiff and defendant names are shortened, usually resulting in only the last name of the parties being used. Chapter 24 covers this in depth.

Court reports are generally printed in numbered sets,[28] with the coverage of the set reflected in its title.[29] For example, the *Illinois Reports* are the opinions of the Illinois Supreme Court, the *United States Reports* are opinions of the Supreme Court of the United States, and the *Oil and Gas Reporter* prints opinions from all U.S. jurisdictions dealing with the law of oil and gas. In legal writing, it is customary, when referring to a court report, to give the name of the case and the date of the decision as part of its citation. But rather than a citation that would read, for example, [name of case] from [date] found in Volume 132 of the *Illinois Reports* starting at page 238, a legal citation for a court's opinion is given using a standard format and a standard abbreviation for the set of reports, e.g., [name of case], 132 Ill. 238 ([date]). Until the 1990s, citations to court reports, regardless of the actual format (print or electronic) of the court report, were based on the print citation to the bound volumes of decisions. Because the first databases containing court decisions were based on the printed volumes, citing an electronic version was originally the same as citing to a book. Even today, most cases are cited based on their print publication.

With the likelihood of multiple sources for a given decision—official and unofficial print reports, as well as electronic sources—citing with accuracy can be difficult, especially when quoting from a source requires a "pinpoint" cite to the page within the opinion where the quote appears. While the actual text of the decision should be identical in all sources, page numbers in print sources will vary because of editorial features like type size, font, and margins, among other reasons. Electronic sources may not have "pages" at all, just a continuous scroll of text or PDF images of the original opinion before it was prepared for publication. As a result, many unofficial sources developed a system of reporting cases referred to as "star pagination." Star pagination uses a symbol, most typically an asterisk (*) or a dagger (†), to indicate precisely the beginning of each page

---

[27] These two manuals are discussed and compared in Chapter 24.

[28] See Chapters 5 and 6 for details on the federal and state court reporting processes and the sources of court reports prior to their appearing in bound volumes

[29] The first American cases were often reported by private individuals and are cited to the name of that person. These volumes are often referred to as "nominative reporters." In Michigan, for example, the first volume of court reports was reported by Samuel T. Douglass and is cited as 1 Doug. The practice of citing to names or nominative reporters ceased in most jurisdictions during the middle of the nineteenth century.

in an official version of the decision. With star pagination, even those with access only to an unofficial version can determine an official citation with confidence.[30]

Citations to court reports must include the title of the specific source in which the decision appears, whether print or electronic. Titles are generally abbreviated following the basic rules in the *Bluebook* or the *ALWD Citation Manual*.

---

[30] With the trend toward official electronic sources and the development of format-neutral or universal citation formats, citations to electronic databases may no longer need to reflect the print sources. Jurisdiction-specific rules typically govern such citation, as noted in Section B-2, above. To enable researchers to find and give citations to slip opinions and unreported cases, both *Westlaw* and *LexisNexis* provide a standard format for citing recent cases and administrative decisions contained in their databases. These formats are called *Westlaw Cites* and *LEXIS Cites*, respectively.

Chapter 5

FEDERAL COURT REPORTS

Section 1 of Article III of the Constitution of the United States provides that "The judicial Power of the United States, shall be vested in one supreme Court, and in such inferior Courts as the Congress may from time to time ordain and establish." After the adoption of the Constitution in 1789, Congress organized the federal courts in several ways before settling on the current arrangement in 1880. Since that time, the federal court system has been arranged into three main levels: district courts (courts of original jurisdiction, or trial courts), courts of appeals (the circuit courts, the intermediate appellate courts); and the Supreme Court of the United States (the highest court).[1] Each level of court produces opinions that are published both in print and electronically.

A. UNITED STATES SUPREME COURT REPORTS

The Supreme Court of the United States deals with a small fraction of the total litigation of the federal court system. With certain exceptions, the Supreme Court selects only the cases it wishes to hear on appeal,[2] and these are relatively few in number. Because of the leading role played by the Supreme Court in our judicial system and the significance of its decisions in both federal and state jurisdictions, access to the Court's opinions is fundamental to legal research.

---

[1] Extensive information about the federal court system, including the jurisdiction of the district courts and the courts of appeals and links to individual court websites, is available at http://www.uscourts.gov. For a description of the federal court system, see DANIEL R. COQUILLETTE ET AL., 15 MOORE'S FEDERAL PRACTICE §§ 100–100.45 and Historical Appendix (3d ed.). *See also* ERWIN C. SURRENCY, HISTORY OF THE FEDERAL COURTS (1987); ADMINISTRATIVE OFFICE OF THE UNITED STATES COURTS, THE UNITED STATES COURTS: THEIR JURISDICTION AND WORK (1989) [hereinafter THE UNITED STATES COURTS]; ADMINISTRATIVE OFFICE OF THE UNITED STATES COURTS, UNDERSTANDING THE FEDERAL COURTS, http://www.uscourts.gov/uscourts/ EducationalResources/images/UFC03.pdf (2003). The Federal Judicial Center maintains a "History of the Federal Judiciary" at http://www.fjc.gov/history/home.nsf. This website provides the service record and biographical information for all judges who have served on the various federal courts since 1789. It also contains excellent information on the background of all the federal courts, along with other historical material.

This chapter covers sources for the decisions of Article III courts. It also lists reporters that publish opinions of some courts that are not established under Article III—e.g., bankruptcy courts, the United States Court of Military Appeals, and the United States Tax Court.

[2] The Court's jurisdiction is almost exclusively discretionary. Cases reach the Supreme Court either by writ of *certiorari* or by appeal and, in an extremely few instances, by original jurisdiction. For a brief discussion of the Court's jurisdiction, see 1 DAVID G. SAVAGE, GUIDE TO THE U.S. SUPREME COURT 334–39 (5th ed. 2010). For in-depth treatment, see STEPHEN M. SHAPIRO ET AL., SUPREME COURT PRACTICE (10th ed. 2013) [hereinafter SUPREME COURT PRACTICE].

[Illustration 5–1]

GEOGRAPHIC BOUNDARIES OF U.S. COURTS OF APPEALS AND DISTRICT COURTS

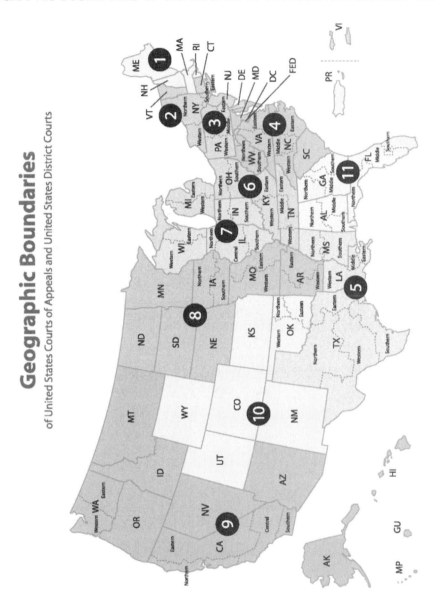

Geographic Boundaries
of United States Courts of Appeals and United States District Courts

All written opinions of the Supreme Court, including dissents and concurrences, are published in both official and unofficial print reports, and many are included in a variety of specialized print services.[3] Most of the Court's *per curiam* and memorandum opinions also are published in these sources. Electronic access to Supreme Court opinions is widespread, and the number of electronic resources continues to increase. Many sources,

---

[3] See *Where to Obtain Supreme Court Opinions* (Aug. 2009), issued by the Staff of the Supreme Court, for a list of sources for Court opinions, http://www.supremecourt.gov/opinions/obtainopinions.pdf. The list is not comprehensive. As of June 2014 it omits, for example, *Bloomberg Law, Google Scholar*, and *Fastcase*.

both print and electronic, are described in this chapter. The print *United States Reports* remains the official source for Supreme Court opinions, and print sources form the basis for most electronic resources.

1. Print Sources for Supreme Court Opinions

a. United States Reports. The *United States Reports* is the official version of cases decided by the Supreme Court. The first reports were prepared and published by private individuals with no official tie to the Court. In 1817, Congress authorized the Court to appoint a "reporter" with a salary. The first ninety volumes, covering decisions from 1790 through 1874, are cited by the name of the individual reporter, from Dallas through Wallace, who compiled the cases for publication. These volumes are referred to as nominative reports. There were seven of these early reporters, and each time a new reporter took over, the volume numbering began anew. Later, these nominative volumes were renumbered consecutively from 1 through 90. Commencing with volume 91 (1875), the name of the Reporter of Decisions of the Supreme Court was no longer used in citing reports.[4] The seven early reporters, with their abbreviations and volumes and years of coverage, are as follows:

Dallas (Dall.)	4 vol.	vol. 1–4	U.S.	(1789–1800)
Cranch (Cranch)	9 vol.	vol. 5–13	U.S.	(1801–1815)
Wheaton (Wheat.)	12 vol.	vol. 14–25	U.S.	(1816–1827)
Peters (Pet.)	16 vol.	vol. 26–41	U.S.	(1828–1842)
Howard (How.)	24 vol.	vol. 42–65	U.S.	(1843–1860)
Black (Black)	2 vol.	vol. 66–67	U.S.	(1861–1862)
Wallace (Wall.)	23 vol.	vol. 68–90	U.S.	(1863–1874)

The cases decided by the Supreme Court are officially printed and sold by the United States Government Printing Office and are issued in a sequence of publications. When the Court first announces its decision in a case, it releases a "bench opinion," which includes any concurring and dissenting opinions. Bench opinions are available in print and are distributed electronically by the subscription-based *Project Hermes* service. They are posted immediately on the Court's website. This is the text that is available within minutes of the Court's announcement of its decision. Bench opinions are replaced, often within hours, by the *slip opinion*.[5]

A *slip opinion* is a pamphlet that contains a single opinion, including all dissenting and concurring opinions and a syllabus and summary of facts prepared by the Reporter of Decisions. It is individually paginated. Several *slip opinions* are compiled together,

---

[4] 1 Dallas, although a volume of the *United States Reports*, contains only Pennsylvania cases. The other three volumes referred to as "Dallas" contain both Supreme Court of the United States and Pennsylvania cases. *See* Arthur John Keeffe, *Current Legal Literature: More Than You Want to Know About Supreme Court Reports*, 62 A.B.A. J. 1056, 1057 (1976). *See also* Craig Joyce, Wheaton v. Peters: *The Untold Story of the Early Reporters*, 1985 SUP. CT. HIST. SOC'Y Y.B. 35. For a description of these early reports and the early reporters, see MORRIS L. COHEN & SHARON HAMBY O'CONNOR, A GUIDE TO THE EARLY REPORTS OF THE SUPREME COURT OF THE UNITED STATES (1995). For a listing of the opinions by individual justices, see LINDA A. BLANDFORD & PATRICIA RUSSELL EVANS, SUPREME COURT OF THE UNITED STATES, 1789–1980: AN INDEX TO OPINIONS ARRANGED BY JUSTICE (1983). A 1994 supplement lists opinions of all justices from October 1980 through 1990.

[5] *Information About Opinions*, http://www.supremecourt.gov/opinions/info_opinions.aspx.

assigned permanent volume and page numbers, and published in an advance sheet pamphlet known as a *preliminary print*. Between issuance as a *slip opinion* and compilation into the *preliminary print*, the text of an opinion will be carefully reviewed and may be edited; an index will be added. It takes three to four years for the *preliminary print* to be issued, due in large part to the extensive editing and indexing processes involved. "[I]n the case of discrepancies between the slip opinion and preliminary print version of a case, the preliminary print controls."[6]

After several *preliminary print* pamphlets are published, they are combined ("cumulated") into a temporary bound volume that uses the now-permanent volume and page numbers of the *preliminary prints*. Three or four temporary bound volumes are issued per term.[7] [Illustrations 5–2 through 5–5] After one last editorial review, the final product—the bound, print *United States Reports* volumes—is available several years after the close of the term in which the opinions they contain were issued.[8] Due to the tardiness in publication and the editorial features in the unofficial reports discussed next, most researchers prefer the unofficial versions to the official *United States Reports*, even though citation rules require citing to the official version when available.

b.   *West's Supreme Court Reporter.* The *Supreme Court Reporter*, a unit of West's *National Reporter System*, reproduces the full text of the opinion or opinions for each U.S. Supreme Court case. The publisher also includes the many editorial features common to its other sets of law reports, e.g., a syllabus, and headnotes, topics, and key numbers (which form parts of West's legal classification and digesting system). Like other components of the *National Reporter System*, the *Supreme Court Reporter* is accompanied by a digest, the *Supreme Court Digest*, that provides subject and name access to Supreme Court cases and coordinates coverage with the entire *National Reporter System*.[9] Volume 1 of the *Supreme Court Reporter* corresponds with volume 106 (1882) of the official *United States Reports*. The *Supreme Court Reporter* does not reprint the cases reported in volumes 1 through 105 of the official reports. Volume and page citations to the official reports and the unofficial *Supreme Court Reporter* are different; star pagination in the *Supreme Court Reporter* allows for accurate citation to the official reports.

Advance sheets for the *Supreme Court Reporter* are issued twice a month while the Court is in session. Opinions in the advance sheets are compiled into temporary "interim" volumes while the bound *United States Reports* are in production. Once the official bound volumes are available, three bound, permanent volumes of the *Supreme Court Reporter* are printed, which replace the interim volumes.[10] The volume and page numbers used in the advance sheets and the interim volumes are the same as those in the later permanent volumes. Because the *Supreme Court Reporter* uses smaller type

---

[6] *Id.*

[7] The Supreme Court holds a "continuous annual Term commencing on the first Monday in October and ending on the day before the first Monday in October of the following year." SUP. CT. R. 3.

[8] "[I]n case of discrepancies between the preliminary print and the bound volume versions of a case, the bound volume controls." *Information About Opinions, supra,* note 5.

[9] These various features are discussed in Chapters 6 and 7.

[10] Through volume 79 of West's *Supreme Court Reporter*, the volumes of the *United States Reports* covering a term of the Court could be published in one volume of the West version. Commencing with the October 1959 term, West began publishing the opinions of a term in two books, e.g., volumes 80 and 80A. Commencing with the October 1985 term, coverage expanded to three books, e.g., volumes 106, 106A, and 106B, owing in great part to the growing numbers of concurring and dissenting opinions.

than is used in the official reports, resulting in more words per page, two or three volumes of official reports are contained in each single volume of West's *Supreme Court Reporter*. [Illustrations 5–6 and 5–7] *Supreme Court Reporter* advance sheets include other features designed to keep readers up to date on judicial developments from the Supreme Court and around the nation, including the text of Supreme Court Orders, federal court rules changes, and highlights of recent cases of interest.

Westlaw uses the *Supreme Court Reporter* as the basis for the SCT database.

c. *United States Supreme Court Reports, Lawyers' Edition*. The unofficial *United States Supreme Court Reports, Lawyers' Edition* (almost always referred to as "*Lawyers' Edition*") is published by LexisNexis (and was formerly published by Lawyers Cooperative Publishing Company). It is in two series. The first series, which covers 1 U.S. through 351 U.S. (1789–1956), has 100 volumes; the second, current, series, *L. Ed. 2d*, restarts numbering its volumes with volume 1 and continues its coverage of Supreme Court cases, uninterrupted, starting with 352 U.S. (1956).

The *Lawyers' Edition* reprints the opinions and syllabi of the *United States Reports*. These are supplemented with extensive editorial treatment given the cases by the publisher, including its own summary of each case and headnotes that precede the opinions. In addition, for selected cases, summaries are provided of the main arguments advanced in the attorneys' briefs submitted to the Court. Several annotations, which are articles or essays written by the publisher's editorial staff analyzing significant legal issues in a reported case, are included in an appendix to each bound volume.[11] These are very useful in gaining an understanding of the impact and meaning of the case. There is a digest, the *United States Supreme Court Reports, Lawyers' Edition Digest*, which provides subject and case name access.

Current opinions are published in advance sheets that are issued twice a month while the Court is in session. Advance sheets do not have annotations or summaries of briefs. The advance sheets contain a "Current Awareness Commentary" that notifies readers of some of the issues in cases accepted for review, discusses selected summary denials of review, and notes significant issues in some of the newest opinions that will be included in subsequent advance sheets. The volume number and pagination of the advance sheets are the same as in the subsequent bound volumes. Advance sheets are cumulated into interim bound volumes pending publication of the final, bound, official reports; at that time, the permanent *Lawyers' Edition* volume is published with star pagination to allow accurate citation to the official reports.

Information in the *Lawyers' Edition* is kept current by a set of paperbound volumes that are issued annually. These paperbound volumes include the Citator Service, the Later Case Service, and Corrections to the opinions. The Citator Service contains brief summaries of Supreme Court cases that significantly refer to (and often affect) Supreme Court cases published in other *Lawyers' Edition 2d* volumes. The Later Case Service provides references to cases that cite *Lawyers' Edition 2d* annotations. The Corrections, which are almost exclusively typographical in nature, document changes to opinions made by the Court. An annual Tables volume lists all the sections of the U.S. Constitution, the *U.S. Code*, the *Code of Federal Regulations*, and federal court rules that are cited in a meaningful way in Supreme Court cases. An annual *Quick Case Table*

---

[11] Annotations are also discussed in Chapter 17.

pamphlet contains an alphabetically arranged table of cases for all the Court's decisions, with citations to the *United States Reports*, the *Lawyers' Edition* (both series), and West's *Supreme Court Reporter*. It notes whether the case is included in an annotation in *Lawyers' Edition 2d* or any of the various *A.L.R.* series. A multivolume general index, also published as part of *Digest of United States Supreme Court Reports, Lawyers' Edition*,[12] provides a comprehensive topical index to cases decided by the Supreme Court. This index also includes a table of justices, statutory table, and an annotation history table. [Illustrations 5–8 and 5–9]

LexisNexis and *LexisNexis Advance* use the *Lawyers' Edition* as the basis for the USLED library.

d. *United States Law Week*. Rapid access to current U.S. Supreme Court cases is available through *United States Law Week*, a topical service published by Bloomberg BNA. The publisher receives slip opinions electronically on the day they are handed down, prints them, and promptly mails them to subscribers. Opinions also are posted to the *Law Week* website for immediate subscriber access. These Supreme Court cases have few added editorial features, but they do provide cases in print form within a week after they are released by the Court. For older cases, it is preferable to use one of the three other sets previously discussed because of their editorial enhancements and for proper citation.

United States Law Week in print consists of two looseleaf binders, containing "General Law Sections" and "Supreme Court Sections." The "General Law Sections" includes a summary and analysis of significant court opinions from lower federal courts and state courts. It also provides analysis of legal developments of interest to the professional.

The "Supreme Court Sections" binder begins with "Supreme Court Today," which contains summaries of cases recently filed and acted on by the Court, the Court's Journal of Proceedings, dockets, hearings schedules, and summaries of oral arguments from selected cases. The contents are indexed, and tables of cases and case status tables (i.e., when the case is scheduled for oral argument) are updated regularly. A separate section contains the full text of the Supreme Court's opinions from the most recent term. A topical index of pending cases is published at the beginning of the Court's term and is cumulated at frequent intervals as cases are decided, with a final cumulative index of dispositions published shortly after the Court's last session of the term. A supplemental electronic component provides both "near real time notice and text" of every Supreme Court action, including opinions. It also has a powerful, fully searchable archive. *United States Law Week* is an important source for researchers and attorneys who need fast access to a wide range of Supreme Court actions and information.

2. Electronic Sources for Supreme Court Opinions

Westlaw and *WestlawNext*, *LexisNexis and Lexis Advance*, *Bloomberg Law*, *Loislaw*, *United States Law Week*, *HeinOnline*, and *VersusLaw* (all fee-based services), and the Supreme Court website[13] and Cornell Law School's *Legal Information Institute* (*LII*),

---

[12] This source is discussed in Chapter 7.

[13] http://www.supremecourtus.gov/. The Court's official website also includes the oral argument calendar, court rules, schedules, visitor guides, and bar admission forms, among other important resources.

among others, provide electronic versions of the text of opinions of the Supreme Court of the United States.

Electronic access is available much faster than any of the print publications discussed above, with the exception of the bench opinions. The text of each opinion is transmitted electronically from the Court to information vendors almost simultaneously with the announcement of the decision from the bench. Cases frequently are available in these online sources within a day, and typically within a few hours, after being announced.

Contents of electronic services are updated much faster than the print resources. It is not unusual for the individual resources to be available in more than one library or database from a resource. For example, Supreme Court opinions are available in *Westlaw* in the SCT, ALLFEDS, and ALLCASES databases, and in many of the service's specialty databases. New databases and libraries are often added to an electronic resource, often causing the content of a given database or library to change. For these reasons, it is important to check the database or library coverage note the first time a resource is used.

Because content is added to electronic resources faster than it appears in print, some editing subsequent to electronic publication occurs to Supreme Court opinions. For example, when the official *United States Reports* are published, *Westlaw* and *LexisNexis* add star pagination to their online content to allow accurate citation to the official reports.

3.   In Chambers Opinions of the Supreme Court Justices

Each Supreme Court justice is assigned to supervise one or more federal judicial circuits; in that capacity, the Justice is referred to as the Circuit Justice. A major responsibility of the Circuit Justice is to handle "applications," or petitions, from parties to cases (federal or state) within his or her circuit.[14] These applications deal with matters of immediacy, which can range from counting ballots in elections to setting bail for accused criminals to stays of execution; the applications do not circulate through the entire Court. Most often, the applications are dealt with summarily, but occasionally the Circuit Justice will write an opinion explaining the action taken. An opinion resulting from an application is known as an *in chambers opinion*; unlike other types of opinions, the in chambers opinion does not circulate through the Court. Before the 1969 term, these in chambers opinions appeared only in *Lawyers' Edition* and West's *Supreme Court Reporter*. Starting with the 1969 Term, they appear in the official *United States Reports*.[15] *They are also included in United States Law Week* and the various electronic reporting services.

4.   Citing United States Supreme Court Cases

Standard citation practice calls for citing only to the *United States Reports* once a permanent citation is available from the *preliminary print* version, e.g., *Bush v. Gore*,

---

[14] *See* S. CT. R. 22.

[15] SUPREME COURT PRACTICE, *supra* note 2, at 873–74. *See also* Frederick Bernays Wiener, *Opinions of Justices Sitting in Chambers,* 49 LAW LIBR. J. 2 (1956); Marian Boner, *Index to Chambers Opinions of Supreme Court Justices,* 65 LAW LIBR. J. 213 (1972); CYNTHIA RAPP, A COLLECTION OF IN CHAMBERS OPINIONS BY THE JUSTICES OF THE SUPREME COURT OF THE UNITED STATES (2004–), which reproduces in chambers opinions beginning with those from 1925.

531 U.S. 98 (2000).[16] If the case is so recent that it is not yet in an official version, the practice is to cite to the *Supreme Court Reporter*, then to the *Lawyers' Edition*. For cases even more recent, the preferred cite is to *United States Law Week* (U.S.L.W.) or an electronic version distributed by *Westlaw* or *LexisNexis*.

The unofficial reporters, West's *Supreme Court Reporter* (S. Ct.) and *United States Supreme Court Reports, Lawyers' Edition* (L. Ed.), which have their own distinct pagination, also show the pagination of the *United States Reports* using the system of *star pagination* discussed in Chapter 4, Section E. Star pagination allows for an accurate citation to an official source from an unofficial source. Star pagination is available in *Westlaw* and *LexisNexis* databases and libraries for Supreme Court cases.

A *parallel citation* is the citation to more than one source in which a given case may be located. For example, *Bush v. Gore*, 531 U.S. 98, 121 S. Ct. 525, 148 L. Ed. 2d 388 (2000), includes parallel citations to the three bound Supreme Court opinion series. Providing *parallel citations* is sometimes a matter of courtesy, and it may be required by local citation practice or rules. Whenever citations are included in documents intended for use in a court proceeding, local court rules must be consulted to ensure conformance with local practice and requirements of citation form.[17]

When the only citation available is to West's *Supreme Court Reporter* or the *United States Supreme Court Reports, Lawyers' Edition*, the citation to the other two sets can be obtained by referring to:

- A citator (e.g., *Shepard's* in *LexisNexis*, *KeyCite* in *Westlaw*, or *BCite* in *Bloomberg Law*);[18]

- Viewing the full text of the opinion in an online service (e.g., *LexisNexis* or *Westlaw*) that includes parallel citations; and

- *Table of Cases* in one of the digests for federal cases.[19]

B. LOWER FEDERAL COURT REPORTS

The bulk of the work of the federal courts occurs in the federal district courts, which are trial courts with general jurisdiction, and in the United States courts of appeals, which review district court cases.[20] Each state and U.S. territory has one or more federal district courts. The appellate courts are divided into thirteen circuits—eleven numbered, geographically based circuits, plus the United States Court of Appeals for the Federal Circuit and the United States Court of Appeals for the District of Columbia Circuit. In addition, there are several federal courts with limited or specialized jurisdiction.

---

[16] *See* BLUEBOOK R. B4.1.3(i), at 10.

[17] *See, e.g.*, 11TH CIR. R. 28–1(k) ("Citations to decisions of the Supreme Court of the United States shall include both the United States Reports and the Supreme Court Reporter, where such citations exist."). ASS'N OF LEGAL WRITING DIR. & DARBY DICKERSON, ALWD CITATION MANUAL, App. 2 (4th ed. 2010) lists local court citation rules.

[18] Some libraries will have *Shepard's United States Citations: Cases* in print.

[19] Tables of cases and the *American Digest System* are discussed in Chapter 7; citators are discussed in Chapter 15.

[20] In addition to handling appeals from district courts, the courts of appeals also review actions of federal agencies. *See, e.g.*, 29 U.S.C. § 160(e)–(f) (2006) (giving courts of appeals jurisdiction to enforce or review orders of the National Labor Relations Board).

Only selected cases of the federal district courts are published. These opinions are reported unofficially only; there is no official source of opinions for the federal district courts. Unpublished opinions generally are available from the clerk of the court in which the case was heard.

All written opinions of the federal courts of appeals that are designated as being "for publication" are published in unofficial reports.[21] There is no official source of opinions for the federal courts of appeals. A large, and increasing, number of federal appellate court opinions that are not designated as being "for publication" are being published in unofficial sources including electronic legal research services, the *Federal Appendix* (a unit of West's *National Reporter System*), and other publications. Appellate court rules and local court rules should be consulted before citing to unpublished cases or relying on unpublished cases as authority.[22]

Opinions of federal courts with limited or specialized jurisdiction are selectively published. As noted below, some of these courts have official sources for these decisions.

1. Print Sources of Lower Federal Court Reports

No official reports are published for cases of the federal district courts and the United States courts of appeals.[23] Over a century ago, West Publishing Company, now Thomson Reuters, assumed the responsibility for publishing opinions from these courts, primarily through the federal units of its *National Reporter System*. Until the arrival of electronic legal research services, West's reporters, although unofficial, were the only comprehensive sources for accessing these opinions. The following print series, all part of the *National Reporter System*, publish lower federal court opinions. Most electronic research services now also provide access to these opinions, with databases and libraries generally based on the corresponding print series.

    a.   *Federal Cases.* Prior to 1880 (and the publication of federal cases in the *National Reporter System*), the opinions of the federal district courts and the circuit courts of appeals were privately published in many different sets of law reports.[24] In the mid-1890s, West reprinted these previously reported lower federal court opinions in one set of 31 volumes called *Federal Cases.* This set contains 18,313 opinions reported between 1789 and 1879, accompanied by brief notes (annotations) to the cases. Unlike most sets of court reports, in which the cases are arranged chronologically, the cases in this set are arranged alphabetically by case name and are numbered consecutively. Cases are cited by number. Volume 31 is the Digest volume; it includes tables printed on blue paper that cross-reference the citations of the original reports to *Federal Cases.*

---

    [21] *See, e.g.,* 5TH CIR. R. 47.5 Publication of Opinions:

47.5.1 Criteria for Publication. The publication of opinions that merely decide particular cases on the basis of well-settled principles of law imposes needless expense on the public and burdens on the legal profession. However, opinions that may in any way interest persons other than the parties to a case should be published. http://www.ca5.uscourts.gov/clerk/docs/frap2007.pdf.

    [22] See discussion of unpublished and nonprecedential decisions in Chapter 4, Section A-5.

    [23] For a few specialized lower federal courts, there are official reports, as described in this section.

    [24] One source notes that there were as many as 233 different sets of lower federal court decisions, published by different reporters and at different times, prior to 1880. MILES O. PRICE & HARRY BITNER, EFFECTIVE LEGAL RESEARCH: A PRACTICAL MANUAL OF LAW BOOKS AND THEIR USE 108 (1953).

  b. *Federal Reporter.* The *Federal Reporter* began in 1880 and includes all the features of the *National Reporter System.*[25] Today, it contains only officially published cases of the United States courts of appeals (formerly the U.S. circuit courts of appeals). However, over the years, the *Federal Reporter* published cases from other federal courts. It contained federal district court cases until 1932, when the *Federal Supplement* was created to publish district court cases. Cases from other federal courts that have since been abolished or reorganized also were included in the *Federal Reporter*, namely the United States Circuit Courts, Commerce Court of the United States, Temporary Emergency Court of Appeals, United States Emergency Court of Appeals, United States Court of Claims, and United States Court of Customs and Patents Appeals.[26]

  The *Federal Reporter* now comprises three series. The first series ended with Volume 300 in 1924. The second series, consisting of volumes 1 through 999, covers cases reported in 1924 and continued coverage into 1993. The third series began in the fall of 1993.[27]

  Only those opinions that are ordered by the federal courts of appeals to be published are included in the *Federal Reporter 2d* and *3d*. These are cases deemed by the courts to have "general precedential value."[28] Federal courts of appeals have local rules outlining the criteria to be used by judges when deciding whether to publish an opinion. Court of appeals opinions can be withdrawn before publication in the bound *Federal Reporter* volume; this is done with enough frequency that the advance sheets contain a table listing "Opinions Withdrawn from Bound Volume."

  c. *Federal Appendix.* This set, a part of the *National Reporter System*, reports the unpublished opinions of the U.S. courts of appeals, beginning in January 1, 2001. Opinions from the Fifth and Eleventh Circuits are not included. Each reported case in the *Federal Appendix* includes a caveat stating: "This case was not selected for publication in the Federal Reporter."

  The precedential value of an unpublished decision, and even the ability of parties to cite certain unpublished decisions, varies among the circuits. Although cases in the *Federal Appendix* may not have value as precedent, they might contain fact situations and applications of value to researchers, making their use desirable at times. Researchers should always check local court rules for guidance.

---

  [25] The uses of and features in the *National Reporter System* are discussed in Chapter 6.

  [26] Cases from the United States Court of Customs and Patents Appeals were reported in the *Federal Reporter*, beginning with volume 34 of the second series, until the court was abolished October 1, 1982. The function of that court, as well as that of the appellate division of the former United States Court of Claims, was transferred to the United States Court of Appeals for the Federal Circuit, whose cases are included in the *Federal Reporter*.

  [27] West provided little explanation about why a *Federal Reporter 3d* started after almost seventy years and 999 volumes of *Federal Reporter 2d*, other than saying only that it was "to avoid potential confusion that could arise from a four-digit case volume citation." Matthew Goldstein, *68 Years, 999 Volumes of F.2d End as New Era of F.3d Begins*, N.Y. L.J., Oct. 14, 1993, at 1. No change in format or coverage occurred in this new series. As other units in the *National Reporter System* have reached volume 999, they too have started a new numbering series commencing with volume 1. Given this practice, it is unlikely that any unit of the *National Reporter System* will ever have a volume 1000.

  [28] This recommendation first came from the Judicial Conference of the United States, the administrative governance body of the lower federal courts, as a means of assisting judges in controlling the rapidly increasing numbers of lower court decisions. ADMINISTRATIVE OFFICE OF THE UNITED STATES COURTS, JUDICIAL CONFERENCE REPORTS 1962–1964, at 11 (1964).

d.   Federal Supplement. This set began in 1932, to separate the growing number of federal district court and claims court cases from the appellate cases in the *Federal Reporter.* At the outset, the *Federal Supplement* included federal district court cases and United States Court of Claims cases (beginning with volume 182). Coverage of United States Court of Claims cases returned to the *Federal Reporter* in 1960 and remained there until the Court of Claims was abolished.

District courts are the general jurisdiction trial courts of the federal court system; therefore, the opinions reported in the *Federal Supplement* are exceptions to the general rule that only appellate court opinions are reported. It must be emphasized, however, that only a very small percentage of opinions from the cases heard in the federal district courts are reported in the *Federal Supplement.* The decision whether to publish is made by the judge writing the opinion. Some opinions from federal district courts that are not published in the print *Federal Supplement* may be printed in subject reporters or may be available electronically.

In addition to its federal district court coverage, the *Federal Supplement* reports cases from the United States Court of International Trade (since 1980); the United States Customs Court (from 1956 to 1980, when that court was replaced by the United States Court of International Trade); the Special Court under the Regional Rail Reorganization Act of 1973; and the Judicial Panel on Multidistrict Litigation (since its inception in 1969). The *Federal Supplement* includes volumes 1 through 999; *Federal Supplement 2d,* starting with volume 1, began in 1998. It is a part of the *National Reporter System.*

e.   Federal Rules Decisions (F.R.D.). This set, a part of the *National Reporter System,* began in 1939. It contains opinions of the federal district courts that construe the Federal Rules of Civil Procedure and, since 1946, cases interpreting the Federal Rules of Criminal Procedure. These opinions are not published in the *Federal Supplement.* In addition to judicial opinions, the *F.R.D.* also includes in-depth articles on various aspects of federal courts and federal procedure. A cumulative index to these articles is in every tenth *F.R.D.* volume, and a consolidated index for volumes 1 through 122 is in volume 122. The articles are also indexed in several legal periodical indexes and are included in *Westlaw*'s JLR database.

f.   Military Justice Reporter. This *National Reporter System* set, which began in 1975, is the successor to the *Decisions of the United States Court of Military Appeals* and the *Court-Martial Reports* (1951–1975), which were produced by other publishers. The *Military Justice Reporter* includes cases of the United States Court of Appeals for the Armed Forces[29] and the Courts of Criminal Appeals[30] of the Army, Navy–Marine Corps, Air Force, and Coast Guard.

g.   Bankruptcy Reporter. This set began in 1980 as a result of major changes in the bankruptcy laws, enacted in 1978,[31] that significantly increased the number of bankruptcy proceedings that reached the courts and the jurisdiction of those courts. The set reports opinions from the United States bankruptcy courts and Bankruptcy Appellate Panels and those cases from the federal district courts that deal with

---

[29] The name of this court was changed from the United States Court of Military Appeals, effective October 5, 1994.

[30] The name of these courts was changed from the Courts of Military Review, effective October 5, 1994.

[31] Bankruptcy Reform Act of 1978, Pub. L. No. 95–598, 92 Stat. 2549.

bankruptcy matters; these cases are no longer included in the *Federal Supplement.* The *Bankruptcy Reporter* has all the features of the other *National Reporter System* publications. The *Bankruptcy Reporter* also reprints bankruptcy opinions from the Supreme Court and the courts of appeals, retaining the pagination from the *Supreme Court Reporter* and *Federal Reporter 2d* and *3d.*

h.   *Federal Claims Reporter.* This set, which began in 1992, is a *National Reporter System* series covering the United States Court of Federal Claims, a trial-level federal court. In 1992, when the name of the United States Claims Court was changed to the United States Court of Federal Claims, the *United States Claims Court Reporter* (with volumes numbered 1 through 26) was renamed the *Federal Claims Reporter,* beginning with volume 27. This reporter also includes reprints from the *Federal Reporter 2d* and *3d* and the *Supreme Court Reporter* of those cases that have reviewed opinions of the United States Court of Federal Claims.[32]

i.   *Veterans Appeals Reporter.* Begun in October 1991, this *National Reporter System* set contains cases decided in the United States Court of Appeals for Veterans Claims[33] and cases of the United States Court of Appeals for the Federal Circuit and the Supreme Court, which hear appeals from the decisions of the Court of Appeals for Veterans Claims.

j.   *Reports of the United States Tax Court.* Washington, Government Printing Office, October 1942 to present. This officially published set began in 1970 with volume 1. The Tax Court hears cases between taxpayers and the Internal Revenue Service, with appeals going to the federal courts of appeals.[34]

k.   *Trade Cases Adjudged in the U.S. Court of Appeals for the Federal Circuit.* Washington, Government Printing Office, 1996 to present, with numbering beginning with volume 10. This set partially continues from volume 9 of *Cases Decided in the United States Court of Appeals for the Federal Circuit.* Washington, Government Printing Office, 1982–1991. An official publication of the Federal Circuit appellate court, this set now includes only cases dealing with tariffs, customs administration, and related matters.

l.   *United States Court of International Trade Reports.* Washington, Government Printing Office, 1980 to present. Formerly the United States Customs Court, the Court of International Trade hears civil cases dealing with the complex issues that arise under federal international trade statutes. Customs Court cases were reported volumes 1 through 85 of the *United States Customs Court Reports,* 1938–1980. Both series are official.

m.   *Topical Services.* Many lower federal court cases are reported in topical services, in both looseleaf format with related bound sets and electronically. For example, cases on employment discrimination are reported by Bloomberg BNA in the

---

[32] Prior to the publication of the *National Reporter System* sets, there was an officially published series for this court called *Cases Decided in the United States Court of Claims.* Its 231 volumes were published by the Government Printing Office, 1863–1982.

[33] This court was created by the Veterans' Judicial Review Act of 1988, Pub. L. No. 100–687, 102 Stat. 4105. *See* Laurence R. Helfer, *The Politics of Judicial Structure: Creating the United States Court of Veterans Appeals,* 25 CONN. L. REV. 155 (1992). For additional information about this court, see *Veterans Law Symposium,* 46 ME. L. REV. 1 (1994). The name of this court was changed from the Court of Veterans Appeals to the United States Court of Appeals for Veterans Claims in March 1999.

[34] Federal tax research is discussed in Chapter 26.

Labor Relations Reference Manual (looseleaf) and *Fair Employment Practice Cases* (bound set) and by Commerce Clearing House in *Employment Practices Decisions*.[35]

2.   Electronic Access

Major online legal research services—including *Westlaw*, *LexisNexis*, and *Bloomberg Law*—provide comprehensive, full-text coverage of published federal opinions, including those of the various specialized federal courts. These cases are made available electronically with ever-increasing speed, and always prior to publication in the print advance sheets. In addition, the services include many opinions found in topical looseleaf services but not designated by the courts for publications. Generally, the services note that status with a caution that the case may not be appropriate to rely on as authority. Most other commercial sources, such as *Loislaw*, *Fastcase*, *FindLaw*, and *VersusLaw*, offer electronic access to federal appellate court opinions, although the retrospective coverage is not as complete nor are the enhancements as extensive as those of *Westlaw* and *LexisNexis*.

By mid-1993, all federal courts of appeals were offering electronic access to their slip opinions through a variety of methods including their own websites. More recently, several websites have been created that provide access to federal court of appeals opinions. Excellent sources for links to these opinions are the *Legal Information Institute (LII)* of Cornell University Law School,[36] the *Court Locator* from the Administrative Office of the U.S. Courts,[37] and *Justia.com*.[38] *Google Scholar* provides access to a growing range of federal court opinions.[39] Federal court of appeals opinions may also be found on the *OpenJurist* site.[40] The opinions found using these, and similar sites, are typically from the mid-1990s forward, although most sites continue to add older materials to expand their coverage. Numerous district court opinions and the opinions from various specialized federal courts can often be located using these sites.

The United States Government Printing Office, through its *FDSys* program,[41] has begun a project to provide searchable electronic access to federal court opinions. Selected courts of appeals, district courts, and bankruptcy courts are available, with content beginning in April 2004.[42] The documents are authenticated—meaning that their content is protected from tampering—and the information is searchable and downloadable. It is expected that this project will be made permanent and its content expanded rapidly.

3.   Citing Lower Federal Court Cases

Because there are no official reports for the federal courts of appeals and the federal district courts, citations are to the three series of the *Federal Reporter*, to the two series

---

[35] Topical services are discussed in Chapter 14.

[36] http://www.law.cornell.edu/federal/opinions.html#other.

[37] http://www.uscourts.gov/court_locator.aspx.

[38] http://www.justia.com.

[39] http://scholar.google.com. Best results may come from using the advanced search option and limiting searches by court.

[40] http://openjurist.org/#practice.

[41] http://www.gpo.gov/fdsysinfo/aboutfdsys.htm.

[42] http://www.gpo.gov/fdsys/browse/collection.action?collectionCode=USCOURTS.

of *Federal Supplement,* to *Federal Appendix*, or to the specialized federal reporters, as appropriate.

Examples are:

> *United States v. One 1987 27 Foot Boston Whaler,* 808 F. Supp. 382 (D.N.J. 1992).
>
> *In re Bond,* 254 F.3d 669 (7th Cir. 2001).
>
> *Jones v. West*, 12 Vet. App. 383 (1999).

C. ILLUSTRATIONS

The case of *Solid Waste Agency of Northern Cook County v. United States Army Corps of Engineers* [531 U.S. 159, 121 S. Ct. 675, 148 L. Ed. 2d 576 (2001)] as it is published in:

5–2 to 5–5: Advance Sheets (Preliminary Print) of the United States Reports (Official)

5–6 to 5–7: Volume 121 of West's Reporter Interim Volume

5–8 to 5–9: Volume 148 of United States Supreme Court Reports, Lawyers' Edition, 2d Series (LexisNexis)

[Illustration 5–2]

SOLID WASTE AGENCY OF NORTHERN COOK COUNTY V. UNITED STATES ARMY CORPS OF ENGINEERS, AS REPORTED IN THE PRELIMINARY PRINT (ADVANCE SHEETS) OF THE UNITED STATES REPORTS, 531 U.S. 159 (2001)

OCTOBER TERM, 2000   159

Syllabus

SOLID WASTE AGENCY OF NORTHERN COOK COUNTY *v.* UNITED STATES ARMY CORPS OF ENGINEERS ET AL.

CERTIORARI TO THE UNITED STATES COURT OF APPEALS FOR THE SEVENTH CIRCUIT

No. 99–1178. Argued October 31, 2000—Decided January 9, 2001

Petitioner, a consortium of suburban Chicago municipalities, selected as a solid waste disposal site an abandoned sand and gravel pit with excavation trenches that had evolved into permanent and seasonal ponds. Because the operation called for filling in some of the ponds, petitioner contacted federal respondents, including the Army Corps of Engineers (Corps), to determine if a landfill permit was required under §404(a) of the Clean Water Act (CWA), which authorizes the Corps to issue permits allowing the discharge of dredged or fill material into "navigable waters." The CWA defines "navigable waters" as "the waters of the United States," 33 U. S. C. §1362(7), and the Corps' regulations define such waters to include intrastate waters, "the use, degradation or de-

> **This page is taken from the *Preliminary Print* (advance sheets) to the *United States Reports*.**
> **As is customary, indication is given to the court from which the case is being appealed.**
> **Note that the docket number, date of argument, and date of decision also are given.**

instant site pursuant to that Rule, the Corps refused to issue a §404(a) permit. When petitioner challenged the Corps' jurisdiction and the merits of the permit denial, the District Court granted respondents summary judgment on the jurisdictional issue. The Seventh Circuit held that Congress has authority under the Commerce Clause to regulate intrastate waters and that the Migratory Bird Rule is a reasonable interpretation of the CWA.

Held: Title 33 CFR §328.3(a)(3), as clarified and applied to petitioner's site pursuant to the Migratory Bird Rule, exceeds the authority granted to respondents under §404(a) of the CWA. Pp. 166–174.

  (a) In *United States* v. *Riverside Bayview Homes, Inc.,* 474 U. S. 121, this Court held that the Corps had §404(a) jurisdiction over wetlands adjacent to a navigable waterway, noting that the term "navigable" is of "limited import" and that Congress evidenced its intent to "regulate at least some waters that would not be deemed 'navigable' under [that term's] classical understanding," *id.,* at 133. But that holding was based in large measure upon Congress' unequivocal acquiescence to, and

[Illustration 5–3]

PAGE FROM 531 U.S. 159, 161

Cite as: 531 U. S. 159 (2001)   161

Syllabus

state activities that substantially affect interstate commerce, raise significant constitutional questions, yet there is nothing approaching a

---

Each case is preceded by a summary and syllabus prepared by the Reporter of Decisions. See also previous illustration.

Note the indication as to which justice wrote the majority opinion, which justices joined in the opinion, and which justices dissented. Note also how the names are given of the attorneys involved in the case before the Supreme Court of the United States.

---

ministrative deference. Pp. 172–174.

191 F. 3d 845, reversed.

REHNQUIST, C. J., delivered the opinion of the Court, in which O'CONNOR, SCALIA, KENNEDY, and THOMAS, JJ., joined. STEVENS, J., filed a dissenting opinion, in which SOUTER, GINSBURG, and BREYER, JJ., joined, *post*, p. 174.

Timothy S. Bishop argued the cause for petitioner. With him on the briefs were *Kaspar J. Stoffelmayr, Sharon Swingle,* and *George J. Mannina, Jr.*

Deputy Solicitor General Wallace argued the cause for respondents. With him on the brief for the federal respondents were *Solicitor General Waxman, Assistant Attorney General Schiffer, Malcolm L. Stewart,* and *John A. Bryson. Myron M. Cherry* filed a brief for respondents Village of Bartlett et al.*

---

*Briefs of *amici curiae* urging reversal were filed for the State of Alabama by *Bill Pryor,* Attorney General, *Alice Ann Byrne,* Assistant Attorney General, and *Jeffrey S. Sutton;* for the American Farm Bureau Federation et al. by *William G. Myers III;* for Arid Operations, Inc., by *Charles L. Kaiser;* for Cargill, Inc., by *Leslie G. Landau, Edgar B. Washburn,* and *David M. Ivester;* for the Cato Institute et al. by *Theodore M. Cooperstein, William H. Mellor, Clint Bolick, Scott G. Bullock, Timothy Lynch, Robert A. Levy,* and *Ronald D. Rotunda;* for the Center for the Original Intent of the Constitution by *Michael P. Farris* and *Scott W. Somerville;* for the Chamber of Commerce of the United States by *Robert R. Gasaway, Jeffrey B. Clark, Daryl Joseffer,* and *Robin S. Conrad;* for the Claremont Institute Center for Constitutional Jurisprudence by *Edwin Meese III;* for Defenders of Property Rights by *Nancie G. Marzulla;* for the National Association of Home Builders by *Thomas C. Jackson;* for the Nationwide

[Illustration 5–4]

PAGE FROM 531 U.S. 159, 162 (MAJORITY OPINION)

---

162   SOLID WASTE AGENCY OF NORTHERN COOK CTY.
v. ARMY CORPS OF ENGINEERS

Opinion of the Court

CHIEF JUSTICE REHNQUIST delivered the opinion of the Court.

Section 404(a) of the Clean Water Act (CWA or Act), 86 Stat. 884, as amended, 33 U. S. C. § 1344(a), regulates the discharge of dredged or fill material into "navigable waters." The United States Army Corps of Engineers (Corps) has interpreted § 404(a) to confer federal authority over an abandoned sand and gravel pit in northern Illinois which pro-

> This is the fourth page of the *Solid Waste Agency* case illustrating the start of the majority opinion. Note that if *amici curiae* briefs are filed in the case this information also is provided.

these waters, and, if so, whether Congress could exercise such authority consistent with the Commerce Clause, U. S. Const., Art. I, § 8, cl. 3. We answer the first question in the negative and therefore do not reach the second.

Petitioner, the Solid Waste Agency of Northern Cook County (SWANCC), is a consortium of 23 suburban Chicago

---

Public Projects Coalition et al. by *Lawrence R. Liebesman;* for the Pacific Legal Foundation et al. by *Anne M. Hayes* and *M. Reed Hopper;* for the Serrano Water District et al. by *Virginia S. Albrecht* and *Stephen J. Wenderoth;* for the Washington Legal Foundation et al. by *Mark A. Perry, Daniel J. Popeo,* and *Paul D. Kamenar;* for the U. S. Conference of Mayors et al. by *Richard Ruda* and *James I. Crowley;* and for James J. Wilson by *Steven A. Steinbach* and *Gerald A. Feffer.*

Briefs of *amici curiae* urging affirmance were filed for the State of California et al. by *Bill Lockyer,* Attorney General of California, *Richard M. Frank,* Chief Assistant Attorney General, *J. Matthew Rodriguez,* Senior Assistant Attorney General, *Dennis M. Eagan,* Supervising Deputy Attorney General, and *Joseph Barbieri,* Deputy Attorney General, and by the Attorneys General for their respective States as follows: *Thomas J. Miller* of Iowa, *Andrew Ketterer* of Maine, *John J. Farmer, Jr.,* of New Jersey, *W. A. Drew Edmondson* of Oklahoma, *Hardy Myers* of Oregon, *William H. Sorrell* of Vermont, and *Christine O. Gregoire* of Washington; for the Anti-Defamation League et al. by *Martin E. Karlinsky, Steven M. Freeman, Michael Lieberman,* and *Elliot M. Mincberg;* and for Environmental Defense et al. by *Louis R. Cohen* and *Michael Bean.*

Briefs of *amici curiae* were filed for the American Forest & Paper Association et al. by *Russell S. Frye;* for the Center for Individual Rights by *Michael E. Rosman;* for the National Stone Association by *Kurt E. Blase;* and for Dr. Gene Likens et al. by *Michael Bean.*

[Illustration 5–5]

PAGE FROM 531 U.S. 159, 174 (DISSENTING OPINION)

174   SOLID WASTE AGENCY OF NORTHERN COOK CTY.
v. ARMY CORPS OF ENGINEERS

STEVENS, J., dissenting

These are significant constitutional questions raised by respondents' application of their regulations, and yet we find nothing approaching a clear statement from Congress that it intended § 404(a) to reach an abandoned sand and gravel pit such as we have here. Permitting respondents to claim federal jurisdiction over ponds and mudflats falling within the "Migratory Bird Rule" would result in a significant impingement of the States' traditional and primary power over land and water use. See, e. g., Hess v. Port Authority Trans-Hudson Corporation, 513 U. S. 30, 44 (1994) ("[R]egulation of land use [is] a function traditionally performed by local governments"). Rather than expressing a desire to readjust the federal-state balance in this manner, Congress chose to "recognize, preserve, and protect the primary responsibil-

This is the last page of the majority opinion from the *Solid Waste Agency* case. The Supreme Court's decision was to *reverse* the Court of Appeals for the Seventh Circuit. Note that dissenting opinions immediately follow the majority opinion.

significant constitutional and federalism questions raised by respondents' interpretation, and therefore reject the request for administrative deference.[8]

We hold that 33 CFR § 328.3(a)(3) (1999), as clarified and applied to petitioner's balefill site pursuant to the "Migratory Bird Rule," 51 Fed. Reg. 41217 (1986), exceeds the authority granted to respondents under § 404(a) of the CWA. The judgment of the Court of Appeals for the Seventh Circuit is therefore

Reversed.

JUSTICE STEVENS, with whom JUSTICE SOUTER, JUSTICE GINSBURG, and JUSTICE BREYER join, dissenting.

In 1969, the Cuyahoga River in Cleveland, Ohio, coated with a slick of industrial waste, caught fire. Congress re-

---

[8] Because violations of the CWA carry criminal penalties, see 33 U. S. C. § 1319(c)(2), petitioner invokes the rule of lenity as another basis for rejecting the Corps' interpretation of the CWA. Brief for Petitioner 31–32. We need not address this alternative argument. See *United States* v. *Shabani*, 513 U. S. 10, 17 (1994).

[Illustration 5–6]

SOLID WASTE AGENCY OF NORTHERN COOK COUNTY V. UNITED STATES ARMY CORPS OF ENGINEERS, AS REPORTED IN 121 S. CT. 675 (2001) INTERIM VOLUME

SOLID WASTE AGENCY v. ARMY CORPS OF ENGINEERS   675
Cite as 121 S.Ct. 675 (2001)

[159]SOLID WASTE AGENCY
OF NORTHERN COOK
COUNTY, Petitioner,

v.

UNITED STATES ARMY CORPS
OF ENGINEERS, et al.
No. 99–1178.

Argued Oct. 31, 2000.

Decided Jan. 9, 2001.

Consortium of municipalities sued the United States Army Corps of Engineers, challenging Corps' exercise of jurisdiction over abandoned sand and gravel pit on which consortium planned to develop disposal site for nonhazardous solid waste and denial of a Clean Water Act (CWA) permit for that purpose. The United States District Court for the Northern District of Illinois, George W. Lindberg, J., 998 F.Supp. 946, granted summary judgment for Corps on jurisdictional issue, and con-

3. Game ⟝3.5

Navigable Waters ⟝38

Army Corps of Engineers' rule extending definition of "navigable waters" under Clean Water Act (CWA) to include intrastate waters used as habitat by migratory birds exceeded authority granted to Corps under CWA, and therefore, abandoned sand and gravel pit containing ponds used by migratory birds was not subject to Corps' jurisdiction under CWA. Federal Water Pollution Control Act Amendments of 1972, § 404(a), as amended, 33 U.S.C.A. § 1344(a); 33 C.F.R. § 328.3(a)(3).

4. Statutes ⟝219(6.1)

Army Corps of Engineers' rule extending definition of "navigable waters" under Clean Water Act (CWA) to include intrastate waters used as habitat by migratory birds which cross state lines was not entitled to *Chevron* deference; rule raised significant constitutional questions, such as whether Congress had never to regulate

This is the first page of the *Solid Waste Agency* case as it appears in West's *Supreme Court Reporter*, an unofficial set. The summary is prepared by the editors.

The seven numbered headnotes in this illustration were prepared by West's editorial staff. The significance of headnotes is discussed in Chapter 7.

under CWA to include intrastate waters used as habitat by migratory birds exceeded authority granted to Corps under CWA.

Reversed.

Justice Stevens filed dissenting opinion in which Justices Souter, Ginsburg, and Breyer joined.

1. Statutes ⟝217.4

Failed legislative proposals are a particularly dangerous ground on which to rest an interpretation of a prior statute.

2. Statutes ⟝220

For purposes of statutory interpretation, subsequent legislative history is less illuminating than contemporaneous evidence.

⟝330

Where an administrative interpretation of a statute invokes the outer limits of Congress' power, agency must establish a clear indication that Congress intended that result.

6. Administrative Law and Procedure ⟝330

Concern that agency interpretation of a statute exceeds limits of power granted by Congress is heightened where interpretation alters the federal-state framework by permitting federal encroachment upon a traditional state power.

7. Constitutional Law ⟝48(1)

Where an otherwise acceptable construction of a federal statute would raise

[Illustration 5–7]

PAGE FROM 121 S. CT. 675, 684 (2001) INTERIM VOLUME

---

684   121 SUPREME COURT REPORTER   531 U.S. 174

tion of their regulations, and yet we find nothing approaching a clear statement from Congress that it intended § 404(a) to reach an abandoned sand and gravel pit such as we have here. Permitting respondents to claim federal jurisdiction over ponds and mudflats falling within the "Migratory Bird Rule" would result in a significant impingement of the States' traditional and primary power over land and water use. See, e.g., Hess v. Port Authority Trans-Hudson Corporation, 513 U.S. 30, 44, 115 S.Ct. 394, 130 L.Ed.2d 245 (1994) ("[R]egulation of land use [is] a function traditionally performed by local governments"). Rather than expressing a desire to readjust the federal-state balance in this manner, Congress chose to "recognize, preserve, and protect the primary responsibilities and rights of States . . . to plan the development and use   of land

ed[175] to that dramatic event, and to others like it, by enacting the Federal Water Pollution Control Act (FWPCA) Amendments of 1972, 86 Stat. 817, as amended, 33 U.S.C. § 1251 et seq., commonly known as the Clean Water Act (Clean Water Act, CWA, or Act).[1] The Act proclaimed the ambitious goal of ending water pollution by 1985. § 1251(a). The Court's past interpretations of the CWA have been fully consistent with that goal. Although Congress' vision of zero pollution remains unfulfilled, its pursuit has unquestionably retarded the destruction of the aquatic environment. Our Nation's waters no longer burn. Today, however, the Court takes an unfortunate step that needlessly weakens our principal safeguard against toxic water.

It is fair to characterize the Clean Wa-

This is the last page of the majority opinion in the *Solid Waste Agency* case. All opinions in West's *Supreme Court Reporter* are identical to those in the official *United States Reports*. Only the editorial material preceding the majority opinion differs.

We hold that 33 CFR § 328.3(a)(3) (1999), as clarified and applied to petitioner's balefill site pursuant to the "Migratory Bird Rule," 51 Fed.Reg. 41217 (1986), exceeds the authority granted to respondents under § 404(a) of the CWA. The judgment of the Court of Appeals for the Seventh Circuit is therefore

Reversed.

Justice STEVENS, with whom Justice SOUTER, Justice GINSBURG, and Justice BREYER join, dissenting.

In 1969, the Cuyahoga River in Cleveland, Ohio, coated with a slick of industrial waste, caught fire. Congress respond-

assigned to the Army Corps of Engineers (Corps) the mission of regulating discharges into certain waters in order to protect their use as highways for the transportation of interstate and foreign commerce; the scope of the Corps' jurisdiction under the RHA accordingly extended only to waters that were "navigable." In the CWA, however, Congress broadened the Corps' mission to include the purpose of protecting the quality of our Nation's waters for esthetic, health, recreational, and environmental uses. The scope of its jurisdiction was therefore redefined to encompass all of "the waters of the United States, including the territorial seas." § 1362(7). That

8. Because violations of the CWA carry criminal penalties, see 33 U.S.C. § 1319(c)(2), petitioner invokes the rule of lenity as another basis for rejecting the Corps' interpretation of the CWA. Brief for Petitioner 31–32. We need not address this alternative argument.

See *United States v. Shabani*, 513 U.S. 10, 17, 115 S.Ct. 382, 130 L.Ed.2d 225 (1994).

1. See R. Adler, J. Landman, & D. Cameron, The Clean Water Act: 20 Years Later 5–10 (1993).

[Illustration 5–8]

SOLID WASTE AGENCY OF NORTHERN COOK COUNTY V. UNITED STATES ARMY CORPS OF ENGINEERS, AS REPORTED IN ADVANCE SHEETS OF 148 L. ED. 2D 576 (2001)

SOLID WASTE AGENCY OF NORTHERN COOK COUNTY, Petitioner

v

UNITED STATES ARMY CORPS OF ENGINEERS, et al.

⟶ 531 US —, 148 L Ed 2d 576, 121 S Ct —

[No. 99-1178]

Argued October 31, 2000. Decided January 9, 2001.

Decision: Clean Water Act provision (33 USCS § 1344(a)), requiring permit from Army Corps of Engineers for discharge of fill material into navigable waters, held not to extend to isolated, abandoned sand and gravel pit with seasonal ponds which provided migratory bird habitat.

SUMMARY ⟵

A consortium of suburban municipalities in northern Illinois selected as a solid waste disposal site an abandoned sand and gravel pit with excavation trenches that had evolved into permanent and seasonal ponds. These ponds were intrastate waters that were not adjacent to any bodies of open water. Because the operation called for filling in some of the ponds, the consortium contacted the Army Corps of Engineers (Corps) to determine if a landfill permit was required under § 404(a) of the Clean Water Act (CWA) (33 USCS § 1344(a)), which authorizes the Corps to issue permits allowing the discharge of dredged or fill material into "navigable waters." The CWA defines "navigable waters" as "the waters of the United States" (33 USCS § 1362(7))

This is the first page of the *Solid Waste Agency* case as it appears in an advance sheet of L. Ed. 2d. Formerly published by Lawyers Cooperative Publishing, this set is now published by LexisNexis. The Summary is prepared by the publisher's editorial staff. The omitted page numbers in the citations will be added when the case becomes part of the permanent bound volume.

Rule, the Corps refused to issue a § 404(a) permit. When the consortium brought suit in the United States District Court for the Northern District of Illinois to challenge the Corps' jurisdiction and the merits of the permit denial, the District Court granted the Corps summary judgment on the jurisdictional issue. The United States Court of Appeals for the Seventh Circuit, in affirming, held that (1) Congress had authority under the Federal Constitution's commerce clause (Art I, § 8, cl 3) to regulate intrastate

576

[Illustration 5-9]

PARTIAL PAGES FROM ADVANCE SHEETS OF 148 L. ED. 2D 576, 577 & 579 (2001)

⟶ **HEADNOTES**

Classified to United States Supreme Court Digest, Lawyers' Edition

Environmental Law § 30 — Clear Water Act — Corps of Engineers' jurisdiction — migratory bird rule

1a-1g. Section 404(a) of the Clean Water Act (CWA) (33 USCS § 1344(a)), which requires a permit from the Army Corps of Engineers for the discharge of dredged or fill material into navigable waters, does not extend to an abandoned sand and gravel pit with seasonal ponds which provides habitat for migratory birds, where such ponds are intrastate waters that are not adjacent to any bodies of open water, for (1) holding that such ponds fell under § 404(a) would assume that the use of the word "navigable" does not have any independent significance; (2) the Migratory Bird Rule, by which the Corps extends its jurisdiction over waters which "are or would be used as habitat by migratory birds esced to the Migratory Bird Rule; and (4) construing the CWA as supporting the Migratory Bird Rule would raise significant federal constitutional and federalism questions, as such a construction would result in significant impingement of the states' traditional and primary power over land and water use. (Stevens, Souter, Ginsburg, and Breyer, JJ., dissented from this holding.)

Environmental Law § 30 — Army Corps of Engineers — jurisdiction

2. While the Army Corps of Engineers' jurisdiction under § 404(a) of the Clean Water Act (33 USCS § 1344(a)) extends to wetlands that are adjacent to open water, the text of § 404(a) does not support an extension of jurisdiction where there is no nexus between the wetlands and navigable waters.

This illustration shows examples of headnotes (above, from page 577) in the *Solid Waste Agency* case in L. Ed. 2d as prepared by LexisNexis. Note that they differ from those in West's *Supreme Court Reporter*. "Research References" (below, from page 579) direct the user to related sources in other publications.

RESEARCH REFERENCES ⟵

61C Am Jur 2d, Pollution Control §§ 947 et seq.

33 USCS § 1344(a)

L Ed Digest, Environmental Law § 30; Statutes §§ 107, 112, 152, 156

L Ed Index, Clean Water Act

Annotations:

Supreme Court's views as to construction and application of Federal Water Pollution Control (Clean Water) Act (33 USCS §§ 1251-1376). 84 L Ed 2d 895.

What constitutes "discharge of dredged or fill materials" into navigable waters, so as to be subject to permit requirements under § 404(a) of Federal Water Pollution Control Act (33 USCS § 1344(a)). 72 ALR Fed 703

Criminal proceedings, under § 309(c)(1, 3) of the Federal Water Pollution Control Act (33 USCS § 1319(c)(1, 3), based on violation of § 301(a) of the Act (33 USCS § 1311(a)), prohibiting discharge of pollutants without a permit. 53 ALR Fed 481.

What are "navigable waters" subject to the provisions of the Federal Water Pollution Control Act, as amended (33 USCS §§ 1251 et seq.). 52 ALR Fed 788.

Chapter 6

STATE COURT REPORTS

This chapter discusses state court reports in both official and unofficial versions, and methods for citing state cases, including locating parallel citations.

A. OFFICIAL AND UNOFFICIAL STATE COURT REPORTS

The laws or court rules of the individual states specify the method of publishing state court reports. Case reports produced under or sanctioned by statutes or the state courts are called *official reports*. Private companies may also produce official court reports, often under contract with the state or as directed by the legislature or the courts. The private publications of cases that are not legislatively or court-endorsed are called *unofficial reports*, although they should be no less accurate than official reports. A court or its reporter of decisions may have the power to select the cases for publication in the official state reports. In the exercise of that power, some cases considered less important may be eliminated from the official reports.[1] The unofficial reports may duplicate the opinions in the official reports or may be the only source of publication.

Unofficial reports fall into two categories. The first consists of those sets that compete directly with the officially published state reports. These reports usually arrange the cases in chronological order and have more helpful editorial features and faster publication schedules than the official reports. In many states, an unofficial set is also a unit of West's *National Reporter System*, which is discussed in Chapter 4. The other category of unofficial reports is special or subject reports, discussed briefly in this chapter and in more detail in subsequent chapters.

1. Official State Court Reports

At one time, all states published their judicial opinions in bound volumes of reports, such as the *Michigan Reports*.[2] Those states having intermediate courts of appeals also may have separately bound sets of reports, such as the *Illinois Appellate Reports*.[3] In these publications, cases are published chronologically, by date of issuance for each case during a term of the court. Slip opinions or advance sheets are typically available prior

---

[1] See discussion of unpublished opinions in Chapter 4.

[2] For additional references to early law reporting in America, see 1–3 CHARLES EVANS, AMERICAN BIBLIOGRAPHY (1903); 4 ISAIAH THOMAS, HISTORY OF PRINTING IN AMERICA (2d ed. 1874); 1 CHARLES WARREN, HISTORY OF THE HARVARD LAW SCHOOL AND OF EARLY LEGAL CONDITIONS IN AMERICA 203–14 (1908); MARY R. CHAPMAN, BIBLIOGRAPHICAL INDEX TO THE STATE REPORTS PRIOR TO THE NATIONAL REPORTER SYSTEM (1977); GEORGE S. GROSSMAN, LEGAL RESEARCH: HISTORICAL FOUNDATIONS OF THE ELECTRONIC AGE 39–81 (1994); and Daniel R. Coquillette, *First Flower—The Earliest American Law Reports and the Extraordinary Josiah Quincy, Jr. (1744–1775)*, 30 SUFFOLK U. L. REV. 1 (1996).

[3] Most states have intermediate appellate courts. The exceptions are Delaware, Maine, Montana, Nevada, New Hampshire, Rhode Island, South Dakota, Vermont, West Virginia, and Wyoming. COUNCIL OF STATE GOVERNMENTS, THE BOOK OF THE STATES 250–51 (2013).

to the publication of official bound reports, and may be part of a subscription service to the bound reports.

The ease of publishing on the Internet has resulted in a remarkable growth in the availability of state case law in electronic form.[4] As of July 2013, almost every state offers some form of electronic case reporting. In some instances, such as Arkansas's Supreme Court and Court of Appeals, the electronic version of a state's court reports has been declared official and print publication has ended. In other states, the electronic version is provided as a convenience but is not designated as official. Some states do not provide guidance on whether the opinions published on state websites are official. It is important, however, to know the publication practice of the state in which you are practicing. In most instances, court rules will require citation to the state's official source of court reports.

Many websites, such as that of the National Center for State Courts, provide links to webpages and opinions of state courts.[5] These state sites are updated frequently as new court materials become available. State courts vary in the amount of information posted on their websites.

Twenty-one states have discontinued their direct publishing of print official state reports. Because the *National Reporter System* publishes the reports for all states, every state still has court reports available in print. States that have discontinued their own print court reports may designate the *National Reporter System* or an "offprint" (discussed below) or reports of another commercial publisher as their official reports[6] or they may only publish official reports electronically. Some states do not have a designated official set of reports. The unofficial print publications generally include advance sheets as part of the subscription and usually offer indexes and finding aids that make finding and using court reports easier.

In a general survey, such as this, it is not possible to present a detailed study of the reporting system for each state. State-specific legal research guides, available for most states, typically discuss a state's case law resources in depth.[7] State government websites, or websites for individual state courts, are also good sources for this information.

---

[4] Electronic publishing of official legal materials raises a number of questions regarding the authenticity, or trustworthiness, of the materials, as well as challenges in preserving electronic-only information. In order to provide a standardized approach to addressing these issues, the National Conference of Commissioners on Uniform State Laws approved the Uniform Electronic Legal Material Act (UELMA) in 2011, for introduction to the states. The prefatory note and comments to the UELMA includes a discussion of the issues and possible solutions. The UELMA, with its notes and comments, is available at UNIF. ELEC. LEGAL MATERIAL ACT, 7A, pt. 1, U.L.A. 122 (Supp. 2012), and http://uniformlaws.org/Act.aspx?title=Electronic%20 Legal%20Material%20Act. As of December 2013, UELMA had been enacted in California, Colorado, Connecticut, Hawaii, Minnesota, Nevada, North Dakota, and Oregon. Its progress can be tracked at http:// www.aallnet.org/Documents/Government-Relations/UELMA/uelmabilltrack2013.pdf or http://www.uniform laws.org/Act.aspx?title=Electronic%20Legal%20Material%20Act.

[5] http://www.ncsc.org/Information-and-Resources/Browse-by-State/State-Court-Websites.aspx. Cornell's *Legal Information Institute* (*LII*) provides links to state government legal resources on its website at http://www.law.cornell.edu/states/listing. *See also* STATE AND LOCAL GOVERNMENT ON THE NET, http:// www.statelocalgov.net/50states-courts.cfm.

[6] *See* Appendix D for a list of states that have discontinued their state reports and a table indicating the year of the first case decided for each state or territory. For a state-by-state guide to published court reports and how they interrelate with the *National Reporter System*, see KEITH WIESE, HEIN'S STATE REPORT CHECKLIST (2d rev. ed. 2000).

[7] A list of these state guides is published in Appendix B.

2.   The National Reporter System

The *National Reporter System* has, since its beginning, reported cases from each state's highest court. Although it now also reports cases from all state intermediate appellate courts, the inclusion of these cases began at different times. For example, Missouri appellate cases are included in the *South Western Reporter*, beginning with 93 Mo. App. (1902); Illinois appellate cases are contained in the *North Eastern Reporter*, beginning with 284 Ill. App. (1936).

The *National Reporter System* groups together cases from several adjoining states. The first of these geographical groupings was the *North Western Reporter*, which began in 1879. By 1887, an additional six groupings—*Pacific, North Eastern, Atlantic, South Western, Southern,* and *South Eastern*—in that order, had been added to make coverage nationwide. [Illustration 6–1] These seven units are often referred to as the "regional reporters," although the regions and the states in those regions are not always what might be expected. Oklahoma, for example, is in the *Pacific Reporter* and Michigan is in *North Western Reporter*. These early geographical groupings were based on the country's population and the states and territories in existence at the time the publications were created, and the expectation was that each regional unit would grow at approximately the same pace. This did not occur, but the regional groupings were not changed except when a new state was organized and its court reports needed to be added to one of the regional reporters. Today, each regional reporter contains several hundred volumes; all are in a second series, except *Atlantic, Pacific,* and *South Western*, which are in a third series.

Population growth did alter the coverage of two of the regional reporters. This occurred first in 1888 with the establishment of a separate reporter for New York, the *New York Supplement*. This reporter includes cases from the New York Court of Appeals, which is New Yorks court of last resort, as well as cases from the state's lower appellate courts. The only New York cases currently reported in the *North Eastern Reporter* are those of the New York Court of Appeals. In 1960, West began publishing the *California Reporter*. This series includes cases from the California Supreme Court and intermediate appellate courts. The intermediate appellate court cases from California are no longer in the *Pacific Reporter*, although California Supreme Court cases are still reported there. Both of these units of the *National Reporter System* are in their second series.

Often, it is impractical for attorneys to acquire a regional reporter when what they most need is access to cases from their state. Consequently, West publishes "offprint" reporters for individual states by reprinting a state's cases from a regional reporter and rebinding them under a new name, e.g., *Texas Cases, Missouri Decisions*. There are approximately 30 publications of this type. These offprints retain the volume number and pagination of the regional reporter. The exception to this is another *National Reporter System* unit, *Illinois Decisions*, in which each volume is paginated consecutively. Most states that no longer publish official state reports have adopted the regional reporter that covers their state, and the offprint version, as their official reports.

3. Other Sources of State Court Reports

Major online legal research services include all the cases found in the regional reporters.[8] In addition, they include other state cases, including cases decided before the start of the *National Reporter System*, some trial level cases, and appellate cases not selected for publication. Understanding the court of origin of an opinion, and therefore its precedential impact, is critical in legal research.[9] District courts and other trial level courts, for example, rarely create precedent. Court rules may limit or prohibit citation to cases that are "unpublished," a selection allowed to judges by court rule.[10] These cases are not gathered as systematically as are those of the primary content of the regional reporters: published appellate court opinions and all supreme court opinions. Researchers should check carefully for the coverage of any resource they consult.

For example, in *Westlaw,* the scope note in the ALLSTATES database includes a general statement that the

> database includes documents released for publication in West Regional Reporters, additional West reporters, and other publications . . ., "quick opinions" (cases available online prior to West advance sheets and which do not contain editorial enhancements), and opinions that are not scheduled to be reported by West, a Thomson business.[11]

The scope note also includes information that coverage of state cases begins with cases decided in 1658. Because cases decided well before the advent of the *National Reporter System* in 1879 were published in a variety of unofficial and official sources, the sources are generally described in the individual state's scope note.[12]

The scope note for *LexisNexis*'s state case law library notes that it "[c]ontains . . . selected trial and miscellaneous court decisions from all states." Coverage for an individual state is included in the scope note for that state. For instance, for Rhode Island the scope note states that the library includes "[s]elected unpublished decisions from 1980 for Superior [Court]."

Each legal research service provider aims for comprehensive case reporting, but despite their efforts, some cases will be missed in compiling a service. Occasionally, a case will appear in one system but not another. When it is critical to be exhaustive in your research, checking more than one service often turns up a case that would otherwise not be located.

---

[8] For example, *Bloomberg Law*, *LexisNexis*, and *Westlaw* all have nearly comprehensive coverage of all state decisions from colonial times to present.

[9] *See, e.g.,* Barbara Bintliff, *Mandatory v. Persuasive Case Authority*, 9 PERSP.: TEACHING LEGAL RES. & WRITING 83 (2001).

[10] Publication of court decisions is covered in Chapter 4 at Section A-5.

[11] The "quick opinions" are removed once an edited and editorially enhanced version is available, again changing the contents of the database.

[12] The *Westlaw.com* scope note for Connecticut state court coverage reads, "Additional cases have been obtained directly from the Superior Court of Connecticut for WESTLAW, although they are not scheduled to be reported by West, beginning February 9, 1979. Additional cases have been obtained directly from the Superior Court, Tax Session for WESTLAW, although they are not scheduled to be reported by West, beginning November 29, 1993. Additional selected cases have been obtained from the Superior Court, Housing Session, for WESTLAW, although they are not scheduled to be reported by West, beginning February 20, 1979."

All states maintain websites for state governmental agencies, and state court opinions are routinely included as part of the website's coverage of the judicial branch of government.[13] Many state governments are in a transitional period, moving their publication of court decisions and other primary legal materials from print to electronic formats. Each state is at a different stage in this process.

For example, some states only publish opinions electronically, while others maintain print and electronic formats that are completely duplicative. There is no uniformity among the states in the way in which their electronic court decisions are published; some states have scanned and made available all court decisions since statehood was gained, while others have only the most recent several years' worth of opinions. Furthermore, coverage of a given state's electronic court opinions may change over time, as older opinions are converted to electronic format and previously unpublished opinions are added to databases. Researchers must check coverage notes carefully.

Publication by the state of its judicial opinions does not mean that the opinions are official. The following notice provided on Minnesota's State Law Library website (which makes available appellate and supreme court decisions that are more than a few years old) is illustrative:

> **Please Note**: The slip opinions published on this website are subject to modification or correction by the court. The official opinions of the Minnesota appellate courts are those published by Thomson West in the *North Western Reporter* or *Minnesota Reporter*. Unpublished opinions of the court of appeals are not precedential and may not be cited except as provided by Minn. Stat. 480A.08, subd.3.[14]

Researchers must be aware of the status—official or unofficial—of the court decisions and other primary legal resources they are using. Citation rules may require reference to a particular source, for example. Researchers must also be aware of potential problems in researching in and citing to cases (and other primary materials) found in unsecured databases. There is no uniformity among the states in terms of whether their electronic court reports are official, and few states have made provisions for strong authentication measures to ensure trustworthiness of electronic legal materials.[15]

Several other online services also provide access to state case law. These include *Casemaker*, *Fastcase*, *Findlaw*, *Google Scholar*, and *Loislaw*. Thomson Reuters also publishes collections of state cases on CD-ROM.

In addition to the sources already mentioned, many state bar association journals, newsletters, and websites offer access to that state's court decisions. Specialty reporters, described in others chapters, selectively report state court decisions.

---

[13] *See* note 5, *supra*. Cornell's *Legal Information Institute* (*LII*) provides links to state government legal resources on its website, at http://www.law.cornell.edu/states/listing.

[14] http://www.lawlibrary.state.mn.us/archive/.

[15] The Uniform Electronic Legal Material Act, *supra* note 4, provides guidance to states for keeping electronic materials secure from tampering, as well as ensuring their permanent accessibility and preservation.

B. METHODS OF CITING STATE CASES

1. Name of Case

Generally, a citation should contain the name of the case followed by the citation to the case's location either in the official reports, if available, to the corresponding unit or units of the *National Reporter System*, or to both.[16] When both the official and unofficial citations are used, this is referred to as *parallel citation*. Generally, only the surname of the each party is given in the citation.

> Josephine RAVO, an Infant, by Her Father and Natural Guardian, Antonio RAVO, Respondent v. Sol ROGATNICK, Respondent, and Irwin L. Harris, Appellant

in a citation would be: *Ravo v. Rogatnick*.

2. Early State Reporters

Where the name of a reporter is used in citing an early state report, the preferred practice is to indicate the state in the parenthetical with the date. An example is:

> *Day v. Sweetser*, 2 Tyl. 283 (Vt. 1803).

3. Parallel Citations

When a case has been reported in an official state reporter and in a regional reporter, official court rules for the state may require a parallel citation. In such instances, the citation to the state report is given first, followed by the parallel citation to the appropriate regional reporter or reporters. The year the case was decided is then given in parentheses. Examples are:

> *Ravo v. Rogatnick*, 70 N.Y.2d 305, 514 N.E.2d 1104, 520 N.Y.S.2d 533 (1987).

> *Izazaga v. Superior Court*, 54 Cal. 3d 356, 815 P.2d 304, 285 Cal. Rptr. 231 (1991).

> *Commonwealth v. Jaime*, 433 Mass. 575, 745 N.E.2d 320 (2001).

When there is no official set of state reports or where there is no local court rule to the contrary, citation is given first to where the case is reported in the *National Reporter System*, followed by an indication of the court and year of decision in parenthesis. An example is:

> *Apex Towing Co. v. Tolin*, 41 S.W.3d 118 (Tex. 2001).

4. Finding Parallel Citations to State Court Opinions

Frequently, a researcher has only one citation to a case, either of the official state report or the *National Reporter System*, and needs to find the parallel citation. Parallel citations can be found:

---

[16] For state court documents, *The Bluebook: A Uniform System of Citation* requires parallel citations only for cases decided by courts of the state in which the documents are being submitted or if required by local court rules. The *ALWD Citation Manual* requires parallel citations if it is required by local court rules. However, courts do not necessarily follow either citation manual. It is essential, therefore, to check the appropriate court rules to determine proper citation form. Citation form is discussed further in Chapter 24.

- In a citator (e.g., *Shepard's* in *LexisNexis*, *KeyCite* in *Westlaw*, *BCite* in *Bloomberg Law*, or *Shepard's Citations* in print);

- When viewing the full text of the opinion in an online service (e.g., *Bloomberg Law*, *LexisNexis*, or *Westlaw*) that provides parallel citations. Often print volumes also include parallel citations as well;[17] or

- In a *Table of Cases* in a digest (state, regional, *Decennial*, or *General*).[18]

---

[17] As early as 1922, West provided "star pagination," or parallel pagination, from the texts of opinions in its *New York Supplement* to the corresponding pages in the official *New York Reports*. Star pagination allows the researcher to find "jump cites" or "pinpoint cites" to textual matter within the body of the case. Although this feature is still included for a few cases, the delay of most states in publishing their official reports, when coupled with West's speed in publishing the *National Reporter System*, often makes star pagination impossible in the print editions.

[18] See Chapter 7 for a discussion of West's digests.

Chapter 7

DIGESTS FOR COURT REPORTS

This chapter discusses digests, which traditionally have been one of the most important finding aids for locating judicial opinions. Digests are available in print and electronic formats, and offer an efficient and effective way to research case law. West is the most prominent producer of case law digests, and the focus of this chapter is on its digest system that works in conjunction with its *National Reporter System*.

A. DIGESTS IN GENERAL

Because our jurisprudential system is based on the precedent, it is essential for researchers to be able to locate earlier relevant case law to understand how courts have treated the problem at hand. Relevance may be determined in a number of ways, including similarities in the point of law under consideration and the factual situation. As has been noted, judicial opinions are published in court reports in chronological order. Without a method to locate cases by subject, retrieving cases with the same or similar points of law would be time consuming and difficult. Digests aid in finding relevant case law by organizing cases by subject and providing several ways to access the case law.

Digests are assembled following the release of a judicial decision. Editors, most typically working for commercial publishers, analyze the opinion and write brief descriptive abstracts of the various points of law in the opinion. These abstracts are typically referred to as *headnotes* or *digest paragraphs*. The headnotes are arranged by subject in a classification system created by the publisher. Taken together, these subject-arranged annotations are referred to as a digest of case law.

Digests vary in the types of cases they abstract and organize. Some include only cases from the courts of a single state (Texas or California), or from one court (U.S. Court of Trademark and Patent Appeals), or a system of courts (the federal courts); others include cases from a group of neighboring states (*Atlantic Digest*); and some include cases on only one broad subject (*Bankruptcy Digest*). One digest set is comprehensive, and includes cases from all state appellate and federal courts (the *Decennial Digests*).

Digests are finding aids that assist in locating cases by subject; they are, in effect, an index to case law. Digests have no legal authority and should never be cited as authority. Further, the text of the annotations or digest paragraphs should be used to locate relevant case law, but annotations should not be relied on for anything more than locating citations to cases. Digest paragraphs are necessarily brief and may not provide sufficient detail to allow a researcher to understand fully the reasoning for the court's decision or other factors that might have had an impact on the problem or its resolution. *In all instances, researchers should read the actual opinion from which the digest paragraph was developed.*

B. WEST'S KEY NUMBER DIGESTS

1. The Classification System

Soon after the *National Reporter System* began production in the late nineteenth century, West Publishing Company, as the publisher was then known, realized that users would require a way to locate cases by subject. To answer this need, West developed its own unique subject classification of law.[1]

West's classification system begins with an outline of the entirety of case law, referred to as the "seven main divisions of law": persons, property, contracts, torts, crimes, remedies, and government. More than 400 "topics" are then categorized into each division. [Illustration 7–1] The scope of each topic is clearly defined and an "analysis" organizes the topic into a series of discrete, highly specific concepts. Each concept is assigned a "key number." The amount of key numbers assigned within a topic varies from just a few to many hundreds, depending on the scope of the topic.

Editors determine the appropriate topic for each headnote or digest paragraph, and then the headnote or digest paragraph is assigned to a key numbered concept within that topic. In this manner, as the digest grows, cases dealing with highly specific concepts are gathered together, making it a straightforward proposition for the researcher to locate related cases. Over 500,000 new headnotes are written each year by West's editors.

The first West digest produced in this manner was the *Century Edition of the American Digest*, which covered cases from 1658 to 1896.[2] As West's opinion-reporting business expanded, the *Century Edition* was followed by a digest series commonly referred to as "the *Decennials*," the *American Digest System*, which is described by West as a "master index to all of the case law of our country," and a progression of more focused digests. These publications are discussed in more depth below.

2. The Key Number System

The process undertaken by West in developing its key number digests starts with receipt of an opinion directly from the court. That opinion is assigned to a West editor. Assume the editor receives the Illinois opinion for *Kasin v. Osco Drug, Inc.* The editor reads and analyzes the case and, in this instance, writes three headnotes, with each headnote representing a particular point of law addressed in the case. [Illustration 7–2]

In this example, an editor decides that one of the three headnotes derived from the *Kasin* case deals with "drugs." The editor consults the list of over 400 topics and assigns to the headnote the topic *Drugs and Narcotics*. The next step is the assignment of a particular key number or key numbers. The editor examines a detailed outline of subdivisions within the topic *Drugs and Narcotics*. This outline, discussed more fully in Section D-2 of this chapter, is referred to as the *Analysis*.

---

[1] West's was not the first digest. The West product was, in fact, built on the *United States Digest*, which was purchased from Little, Brown & Co. in 1888. For the history of digests, see ERWIN C. SURRENCY, A HISTORY OF AMERICAN LAW PUBLISHING 111–127 (1990).

[2] As explained in Section G below, the topical arrangement for this digest differs from all produced subsequently.

After consulting this outline, the editor determines that the headnote deals with manufacturers of drugs, a subject which corresponds to key number 18. The topic *Drugs and Narcotics*, therefore, receives key number 18. The same steps are followed for the other two digest paragraphs. One is assigned two topics: *Drugs and Narcotics*, key number 18, and *Physicians and Surgeons*, key number 15(8). The third digest paragraph is also classified under the topic *Drugs and Narcotics* and is assigned key number 19. After the editorial work is complete, the case, immediately preceded by the topics, key numbers, and digest paragraphs, is published in the appropriate unit or units of the *National Reporter System*. [Illustration 7–2] These topics, key numbers, and digest paragraphs are then incorporated into the appropriate sets of key number digests.

A set of brackets surrounding a number in the text of the published opinion, e.g., [3], indicates the language in the opinion that corresponds to the headnote. [Illustration 7–3] This enables a researcher interested in the point of law discussed in a particular headnote to go directly to that part of the case from which the headnote is derived. As indicated above, at times a headnote is classified to more than one topic. In such instances, all appropriate topics and key numbers are shown.[3]

3.   Common Features of West's Key Number Digests

West's key number digests have the following common features in addition to topics and key numbers:

a.   *Descriptive-Word Index* volume(s). This source is described in Section D-1.

b.   *Table of Cases* volume(s). This source is described in Section D-3.

c.   *Words and Phrases*. This is an alphabetical listing that contains words and phrases that have been judicially defined. These definitions are subsequently compiled in a multivolume set entitled *Words and Phrases*. It is discussed in Section M-1.

d.   *Supplements*. Digests are periodically updated by replacement volumes, pocket supplements, interim pamphlet supplements, and later bound volumes and advance sheets of the West reporters.

e.   *Numerical References to Topics*. The pocket supplements and recently published volumes of digests contain numerical references to topics that can be used in *Westlaw* searches for cases.

C.   KEY NUMBERS AND DIGEST PARAGRAPHS IN WESTLAW

Cases are searchable in *Westlaw* with the key number system. It is possible to search, for example, the topic *Drugs and Narcotics*, key number 18, and retrieve all cases classified under this point of law; to restrict the search to a particular period of time; or to add a specific search term, such as *manufacturer*, to the query. Hypertext links connect the headnotes and the related text in the opinion.[4] [Illustration 7–4]

In *Westlaw*, topics are converted to a numerical equivalent that corresponds to the alphabetically arranged topics used in the key number digests. [Illustration 7–1] The key number symbol is converted to the letter "k." [Illustration 7–4] Information

---

[3] For an article exploring the strengths and weaknesses of West's digests, see *Fritz Snyder, The West Digest System: The Ninth Circuit and the Montana Supreme Court*, 60 MONT. L. REV. 541 (1999).

[4] Electronic legal research is discussed in Chapter 23.

indicating *Westlaw*'s numerical equivalents to the West topic and key numbers is available online and in numerous print publications, including the more recent key number digest volumes.

The most recent innovation using the key number system in *Westlaw* is *KeySearch*. *KeySearch* is an electronic research tool that helps the user locate cases and secondary sources within a specific area of law. A researcher selects a legal issue from an organized hierarchy powered by the West key number system, and then *KeySearch* creates the query using relevant key numbers and their unique concepts. *KeySearch* includes approximately 10,000 legal issues that are used in running queries.

D. RESEARCH USING A STATE KEY NUMBER DIGEST

To demonstrate how to use a key number digest, we can focus on the use of a state digest. Because most features in a state key number digest are common to all key number digests, an understanding of the methods of using a state digest is transferable to the comprehensive and cumbersome-to-use *Decennial Digests* and *General Digests*, discussed in Section G of this chapter, and to the various specialized West digests. An understanding of the digest system also is extremely helpful in conducting *Westlaw* research.

West publishes a key number digest for almost every state.[5] A typical state key number digest consists of digest paragraphs for all reported appellate opinions of the state, including federal court opinions that arose in or were appealed from that jurisdiction. Some West state digests have special features unique to a particular state, such as references to law review articles from law schools in the state. [Illustration 7–6] Researchers should examine carefully the state digest available for their state and familiarize themselves with any special features.

Assume the following hypothetical problem, which will serve as the basis for discussion and most of the illustrations used later in this and other chapters of this book:

> Fran went to the doctor complaining of abdominal pain. The doctor correctly diagnosed the problem as acute gastritis and prescribed a relatively common medicine as treatment. Fran followed the directions for taking the drug provided by the pharmacist and the treating physician. Within a few days, Fran became ill and jaundiced. Shortly thereafter, Fran suffered complete liver failure requiring a transplant. All of these events occurred in Illinois. Who, if anyone, is liable for Fran's suffering?

Before beginning to research any legal problem, the researcher first must determine the important issues involved, and it might be necessary to conduct preliminary or background research in order to formulate the legal issues.[6] One issue might involve the duty, if any, of the pharmaceutical company that manufactured the drug to warn Fran of the adverse side effects of the drug. Other issues may relate to the potential liability of both the physician and pharmacist.

To find the law applicable to this situation, the researcher might begin by searching for appellate court opinions with the same or similar facts. If only case reporters were

---

[5] West publishes key number digests for every state except Delaware, Nevada, and Utah. A few states have digests available from other publishers.

[6] See Chapter 2 for a general approach to the research process.

available, it would be necessary to examine individually hundreds of volumes to determine if any cases were on point. If a relevant Illinois case could not be located, it then would be necessary to search for cases from other states. Because of their subject arrangement, digests reduce the laborious task of having to search for cases in court reports volume by volume.

In our earlier discussion, we explained how the West editors prepare topics, key numbers, and headnotes. With more than 400 topics and over 100,000 key numbers in use in West digests, learning how to find the appropriate topics and key numbers is very important for successful case finding. Four common methods are provided below for finding topics and key numbers. Once a topic and key number has been located, the research must be updated, as described at the end of this Section, to find the most recent cases on the topic.

1. The Descriptive-Word Method

A *Descriptive-Word Index* is a highly detailed, alphabetically arranged, subject index to the contents of the key number digests. This index is often the best starting point for research, unless a relevant case or the particular topic and key number is already known. It includes *catchwords* or descriptive words relating to the legal issues covered by the digests. A *Descriptive-Word Index,* often in several volumes, is a part of each key number digest.

Using the *Descriptive-Word Index* successfully requires analysis of the legal issues and often the ability to think in both broad and narrow terms and to shift perspective from the general to the specific. It might prove helpful at this point to review the *TARP Rule* discussed in Chapter 2 (Section B-2).

Let us examine the hypothetical problem presented previously to see how the *Descriptive-Word Index* to the *Illinois Digest 2d* is used to locate topics and key numbers for finding cases dealing with the liability of a manufacturer for making drugs that cause injury. When using this index, the first entry to consult should be a specific word or phrase relevant to the fact situation being researched.

In our fact situation, a specific word is *manufacturer.* An examination of this word in the *Descriptive-Word Index* to the *Illinois Digest 2d* reveals the following entry:

[Illustration 7–5]

MANUFACTURERS AND MANUFACTURING COMPANIES

DRUGS and medicine, civil liability.

Drugs & N 18

These references indicate that the topic *Drugs and Narcotics,* key number 18, contains digest paragraphs that address the legal issue being researched.

2. Analysis or Topic Method

As mentioned in Section B-1, over 400 topics are used in West's key number digests. Each topic is subdivided in outline form, setting forth the main headings and subdivisions to which key numbers are assigned. Instead of (or in addition to) using the *Descriptive-Word Index,* a researcher may browse the topics and their outlines to find relevant key numbers.

These outlines are published at the start of each topic in the various key number digests. Two preliminary sections, "Subjects Included" and "Subjects Excluded and Covered by Other Topics," are set forth immediately before the detailed outline. [Illustration 7–7] Reading this "scope note" is often helpful in determining if the research is being conducted in the proper topic. The topical outline that follows, which is the key number classification scheme for that topic, is titled the *Analysis*.

The *Analysis* sections under the topics *Drugs and Narcotics* and *Physicians and Surgeons* were used in establishing the key numbers for the headnotes in *Kasin v. Osco Drug, Inc.*, a case important in resolving our hypothetical problem. By carefully scanning the *Analysis*, a researcher often can see details in coverage that might not have come to mind in the initial assessment of a legal issue and, thus, identify the most specific key number (or additional key numbers) to use. Section lines, preceded by the key numbers, indicate the content of each key number under a topic. [Illustration 7–8]

Use of the *Analysis* method generally requires certainty that the topic selected is the appropriate one, as well as a thorough understanding of West's key number classification.[7] Use of this method is often most successful when combined with the *Descriptive-Word Index* method.

3. Table of Cases Method

Each key number digest includes, in one or more volumes, a *Table of Cases* that lists the parties to all cases included in the digest by both plaintiff and defendant name. The *Table of Cases* is arranged alphabetically. Each case listing includes the citation, the topics and key numbers under which the case has been digested, and any subsequent case history. For example, if the researcher has been told only that a case named *Kasin v. Osco Drug, Inc.* is relevant to the issue at hand, the *Table of Cases* provides both the citation to that case and the topics and key numbers assigned to that case. [Illustration 7–9] Once the pertinent topic and key numbers are identified, the *Analysis* can be consulted for other relevant key numbers.

4. Using Known Topics and Key Numbers

Citations to potentially relevant cases can be found in almost any legal source, e.g., a law review article, another case, a set of annotated statutes, a treatise, or an encyclopedia. Taking that citation, a researcher will typically go to the appropriate unit of the *National Reporter System* containing the text of the case. If the researcher reads the case and finds it germane, the next step in the research process is to note all topics and key numbers from that case that discuss the relevant point of law. The researcher can then go directly to any of West's key number digests and look under the same topics and key numbers to find additional case citations involving similar issues of law.

5. Updating West's Key Number Digests

Because digest paragraphs originate as headnotes in the advance sheets of the *National Reporter System*, updating research using the key number classification in

---

[7] *West's Analysis of American Law*, issued annually, reproduces the entire key number classification system in one softbound volume. It incorporates the latest changes and additions made to West's key number system. Near the front of each edition is a list of "Topics by Specialty." A researcher interested in environmental law, for instance, can quickly find half a dozen related topics, from Agriculture to Zoning and Planning, in addition to the obvious topic, Environmental Law.

print sources requires the researcher to consult the advance sheets of the relevant reporter. After locating an appropriate topic and key number in the bound volume of a digest, e.g., *Illinois Digest 2d*, the researcher must next check under the same topic and key number in the pocket supplement to that volume and in any interim pamphlets. A table, usually entitled *Closing with Cases Reported in*, is located in the front of the latest supplementation, typically on the back of the title page. This "closing table" indicates the last volume covered in each *National Reporter System* unit included in the digest.

For example, a closing table in *Illinois Digest 2d* includes references similar to the following:

Closing with Cases Reported in

Illinois Decisions ....254 Ill.Dec. 298

North Eastern Reporter, Second Series............................747 N.E. 2d 338

Supreme Court Reporter..212 S.Ct. 1752

Federal Reporter, Third Series..248 F. 3d 1186

Federal Supplement, Second Series...................................137 F.Supp.2d

Federal Rules Decisions..200 F.R.D. 51

Bankruptcy Reporter ....261 B.R. 321

Illinois Court of Claims...46 Ill.Ct.Cl.

After a researcher determines the extent of coverage of the digest, the next step is to check under this topic and key number in the digest section found in the *back* of any later bound volumes of reporters covering the jurisdiction being researched. The last step is to check the digest paragraphs found in the *front* of each advance sheet to these reporters. Only West's *Supreme Court Reporter* cumulates its digest paragraphs in the last advance sheet for a volume. A *Westlaw* topic and key number search for cases reported after the most recent available print resource would produce the most recent decisions.

E. KEY NUMBER DIGESTS FOR FEDERAL CASES

Whenever a researcher is aware that the research problem involves issues that would be decided in a federal court, research may be effectively conducted in a federal digest. Several key number digests are published for federal judicial opinions.

1. West's Federal Practice Digest, 4th and 5th

Currently, the latest digests for federal cases are *West's Federal Practice Digest, 4th* (with volumes published between 1999 and 2012) and *West's Federal Practice Digest 5th* (volumes published beginning in 2013).[8] These sets include digests of cases from 1984 to present for all federal courts.[9] Features include:

---

[8] As of April 2014, volumes in the new series covered only up to "Civil Rights" in the alphabetical list of topics.

[9] Publication of West's *Federal Practice Digest, 4th* began in 1989. No "bright line" exists as to its scope of coverage or of that of West's *Federal Practice Digest, 3rd*, which it continues. For example, some volumes of the 3rd series, issued in 1975 when this set began, covered cases through November 1975 and were never revised. These volumes contained pocket supplementation that included cases decided from December 1975 into 1983. Other volumes of the 3RD were revised at various times, the last issued in 1983. As new volumes of the 4TH were published, they incorporated the supplementation to the 3RD. This means that some volumes in

a.   Under each key number, cases are arranged by court and are listed in reverse chronological order. Cases decided by the Supreme Court of the United States are listed first, followed by cases from the courts of appeals and, finally, the district courts (arranged alphabetically by jurisdiction).

b.   The digest paragraphs include information as to whether a case has been *affirmed, reversed,* or *modified*.[10]

c.   Each topic and key number can be linked to its numerical equivalent in *Westlaw.*

2.   Earlier Federal Digests

Federal cases prior to 1984 are available in the following:

a.   *West's Federal Practice Digest, 3rd*, December 1975 to the beginning of *West's Federal Practice Digest, 4th.*

b.   *West's Federal Practice Digest, 2nd*, 1961–November 1975.

c.   *Modern Federal Practice Digest*, 1939–1960.

d.   *Federal Digest*, all federal cases prior to 1939.

3.   United States Supreme Court Digest

Because the Supreme Court of the United States plays such a significant role in the American legal system, a digest that contains only its cases can be extremely useful. West publishes a multivolume set, the *United States Supreme Court Digest,* which includes the Supreme Court digest paragraphs from the *American Digest System* and the various West federal digests.

F.   REGIONAL KEY NUMBER DIGESTS

Four sets of regional key number digests are published that correspond to four sets of the regional reporters of the *National Reporter System.* Other regional digests have ceased over time, presumably due to an inadequate subscription base. Regional digests are arranged under the topic and key number classification and include abstracts of all reported cases for each of the states in the region. The digest paragraphs under each key number are arranged alphabetically by the states included within the digest. The regional digests that continue to be published are:

Atlantic Digest, in two series

North Western Digest, in two series

Pacific Digest, in five series[11]

South Eastern Digest, in two series

---

the 4th contain cases from December 1975, while others have coverage commencing in 1983. Therefore, specifically for the period December 1975 through 1983, both the 3rd and 4th *must* be consulted to assure comprehensive coverage. For cases from 1984 forward, only the 4th must be consulted.

[10] As useful as this information is, you must still check for developments after the digest was published. Citators, extremely useful for this purpose, are covered in Chapter 15.

[11] Volumes in these series are not designated as 1st, 2d, etc. Rather, each series indicates the first volume of the *Pacific Reporter* or *Pacific Reporter 2d* included in the set.

G. DECENNIAL AND GENERAL DIGESTS

1. Comprehensive Nature

The *American Digest System* has as its core a massive set of materials in several units known as *Decennial Digests* and their companion volumes containing later information, the *General Digest*. These units contain every topic, key number, and digest paragraph ever assigned to cases reported by West. If research requires examining every case ever reported on a particular point of law, the only recourse in print is to use the *Decennial Digests*. Another way to think of this is as follows: if a key number digest paragraph is located in a state or federal digest or a specialized digest, that same digest paragraph also is contained in a volume of a *Decennial Digest* or the *General Digest*.

The process of developing a *Decennial Digest* unit begins with the publication of a volume of the *General Digest*. The *General Digest* is published in bound volumes, with a new volume issued approximately once a month. Each volume consists of *all* the headnotes taken from *all* the units of the *National Reporter System* for the period covered. These headnotes are arranged alphabetically by topic, and then under each topic numerically by key number.

If no further cumulation took place, digests of all the cases, arranged topically, would be in the bound volumes of the *General Digest*. Therefore, to find all the cases dealing with a particular topic, e.g., *Drugs and Narcotics*, it would be necessary to examine each one of hundreds of bound volumes. To avoid this problem, in 1906 West cumulated into one alphabetical arrangement all the topics and headnotes contained in all *General Digest* volumes from 1897 to 1906. This set is called the *First Decennial Digest*. By examining a volume of the *First Decennial* containing a particular topic and key number, all cases decided involving a particular point of law and decided during the period from 1897 to 1906 can be located.

This process of systematically cumulating a set of the *General Digest* into a new *Decennial* has taken place every ten years since 1897. Starting with the *Ninth Decennial*, the publisher began to issue the decennials in multiple parts, with each part covering a designated period of years. An advantage of this arrangement is that a researcher has fewer volumes of the *General Digest* to examine. The latest decennial published is the *Eleventh Decennial Digest, Part 3*, covering 2004 to 2007. A *General Digest, Twelfth Series* is underway, beginning with 2008.

Thus, given a topic and key number, one can start with the *First Decennial* and proceed through the *Eleventh, Part 3*, and the ongoing volumes in the *General Digest, Twelfth Series*, to locate all cases on a point of law under a particular topic and key number from 1897 to several weeks ago.[12]

Since each volume in the *General Digest* contains digest paragraphs covering only a short period of time, there may be as many as sixty volumes to search before they are cumulated and replaced by a new decennial. To avoid the necessity of examining a volume of the *General Digest* that does not include a particular key number, the

---

[12] In the decennials and the *General Digest*, cases are arranged hierarchically, beginning with those of the Supreme Court of the United States and followed by the lower federal courts, with the most recent case listed first in each grouping. Federal case headnotes are followed by headnotes for cases decided by state courts. These cases are arranged alphabetically by state and hierarchically by court, with the most recent case listed first in each grouping.

publisher includes a cumulative *Table of Key Numbers* in every volume of the *General Digest*. These tables indicate those volumes of the *General Digest* that contain cases assigned to a particular key number. The table is cumulative in ten-volume increments, and then starts a new cumulation. [Illustration 7–10]

2. *Century Edition*

It is possible to find all cases from 1658, the date of the first reported American case, as cases from 1658 to 1896 are digested in a publication entitled *Century Edition*. Because the *National Reporter System* did not exist during this period, the *Century Edition* does not contain key numbers. A different topical arrangement was used. For example, the topic *Drugs and Narcotics*, key number 18, in the decennials stands for *Civil Liability of Manufacturers*. In the *Century Edition*, *Drugs and Narcotics* 18 is listed under the heading of *Druggists*, and more specifically, under the sections *Persons Purchasing or Using Articles Sold or Dispensed* and *Actions for Damages*, which are digested under Section Numbers 8 and 9.[13]

3. Scope of Coverage

The sets in the *American Digest System* are:

Century Digest	1658–1896	50 vols.
First Decennial	1897–1906	25 vols.
Second Decennial	1907–1916	24 vols.
Third Decennial	1916–1926	29 vols.
Fourth Decennial	1926–1936	34 vols.
Fifth Decennial	1936–1946	52 vols.
Sixth Decennial	1946–1956	36 vols.
Seventh Decennial	1956–1966	38 vols.
Eighth Decennial	1966–1976	50 vols.
Ninth Decennial, Part 1	1976–1981	38 vols.
Ninth Decennial, Part 2	1981–1986	48 vols.
Tenth Decennial, Part 1	1986–1991	44 vols.
Tenth Decennial, Part 2	1991–1996	64 vols.
Eleventh Decennial, Part 1	1996–2001	64 vols.
Eleventh Decennial, Part 2	2001–2004	62 vols.
Eleventh Decennial, Part 3	2004–2007	62 vols.
General Digest, 12th Series	2008+	in progress

---

[13] In both the first and second decennials, cross-references are made from the decennial key numbers to the subject classification used in the *Century Edition*, with the cross-references in the second being more complete. If one locates a point of law in the *Century Edition*, key numbers for later cases on the same point of law can be located by consulting a pink reference table in volume 21 of the *First Decennial*.

H. KEEPING THE KEY NUMBER SYSTEM CURRENT

West keeps its key number system current with the changes and developments in law by adding new topics and by expanding or reclassifying existing topics. A researcher can retrieve all relevant cases under a current key number even though some of those cases may have been previously classified under a different key number. [Illustration 7–11]

1. Adding New Topics

When the original key number classification system was prepared in 1897, no provisions were made for cases dealing with damages resulting from a jet breaking the sound barrier or for the control and regulation of nuclear energy. Consequently, to cover these and other new areas of law, West occasionally adds new topics to its key number classification. Recently, for example, two new topics—*Child Custody* and *Child Support*—were added. These new topics collected the child custody and child support issues that were previously classified to three topics: *Divorce*, *Infants*, and *Parent and Child*. When a new topic is added, it is first published in the advance sheets to the *National Reporter System*.

2. Reclassifying and Expanding Topics

At times, key numbers are reclassified or revised in order to adapt to changing circumstances. For example, the topics *Bankruptcy* and *Federal Civil Procedure* were recently reclassified—i.e., existing key numbers were reassigned to new key numbers—in order to reflect changes in the federal laws governing these areas.

At other times, existing topics are expanded as additional issues emerge in the area over time. For example, until about forty years ago, all headnotes dealing with issues concerning liability of sellers of prescription drugs, an issue relevant to our research problem, received the topic *Druggists* and the key number 9. When reclassification or expansion occurs, key number translation tables, set forth near the start of the topic in the digest indicate new key numbers that replace old ones. [Illustration 7–12]

I. ILLUSTRATIONS: FINDING TOPICS AND KEY NUMBERS

[Illustration 7–1]

PAGE FROM ALPHABETICAL LIST OF DIGEST TOPICS USED IN KEY NUMBER SYSTEM

DIGEST TOPICS

See, also, Outline of the Law by Seven Main Divisions of Law
preceding this section.

The topic numbers shown below may be used in WESTLAW searches for cases
within the topic and within specified key numbers.

1	Abandoned and Lost Property	42	Assumpsit, Action of	79	Clerks of Courts
2	Abatement and Revival	43	Asylums	80	Clubs
		44	Attachment	81	Colleges and Universities
4	Abortion and Birth Control	45	Attorney and Client		
		46	Attorney General	82	Collision
5	Absentees	47	Auctions and Auctioneers	83	Commerce
6	Abstracts of Title			83H	Commodity Futures Trading Regulation
7	Accession	48	Audita Querela		
8	Accord and Satisfaction	48A	Automobiles	84	Common Lands
		48B	Aviation	85	Common Law
9	Account	49	Bail	88	Compounding
		50	Bailment		

> Over 400 topics are in the *American Digest System*. These topics
> are used in creating headnotes. See next illustration. This listing of
> digest topics is in the front of each volume of a key number digest.
> The numbers to the left of the topics can be used in accessing the
> topics on *Westlaw*. This is discussed in Section C.

	and Procedure	61	Breach of Marriage Promise		Protection
16	Admiralty			93	Contempt
17	Adoption	62	Breach of the Peace	95	Contracts
18	Adulteration	63	Bribery	96	Contribution
19	Adultery	64	Bridges	97	Conversion
20	Adverse Possession	65	Brokers	98	Convicts
21	Affidavits	66	Building and Loan Associations	99	Copyrights and Intellectual Property
23	Agriculture				
24	Aliens	67	Burglary		
25	Alteration of Instruments	68	Canals	100	Coroners
		69	Cancellation of Instruments	101	Corporations
26	Ambassadors and Consuls			102	Costs
		70	Carriers	103	Counterfeiting
27	Amicus Curiae	71	Cemeteries	104	Counties
28	Animals	72	Census	105	Court Commissioners
29	Annuities	73	Certiorari		
30	Appeal and Error	74	Champerty and Maintenance	106	Courts
31	Appearance			107	Covenant, Action of
33	Arbitration	75	Charities	108	Covenants
34	Armed Services	76	Chattel Mortgages	108A	Credit Reporting Agencies
35	Arrest	76A	Chemical Dependents		
36	Arson			110	Criminal Law
37	Assault and Battery	76H	Children Out-of-Wedlock	111	Crops
38	Assignments			113	Customs and Usages
40	Assistance, Writ of	77	Citizens	114	Customs Duties
41	Associations	78	Civil Rights	115	Damages

XV

[Illustration 7-2]

PAGE FROM KASIN V. OSCO DRUG, INC., 728 N.E.2D 77 (ILL.APP. 2000)

KASIN v. OSCO DRUG, INC.
Cite as 728 N.E.2d 77 (Ill.App. 2 Dist. 2000)

Ill. 77

granting summary judgment in favor of the State and we remand this cause for the defendant to receive a jury trial on his

> This is the first page of *Kasin v. Osco Drug, Inc.*, a case relevant to our research problem. Three headnotes were assigned to this case. Notice how each headnote has been assigned a topic or topics and a specific key number or key numbers.
>
> See next illustration.

concurring.

312 Ill.App.3d 823

245 Ill.Dec. 346

Clarence KASIN and Paul Kasin, Plaintiffs–Appellants,

v.

OSCO DRUG, INC., Defendant– Appellee.

No. 2–99–0356.

Appellate Court of Illinois, Second District.

April 12, 2000.

Pharmacy customer and his brother, whose kidney had been transplanted into the customer, sued the pharmacy for negligence, alleging that, in dispensing a prescription drug, the pharmacy had negligently advised the customer of the drug's side effects, including possible kidney failure. The Circuit Court, Lake County, John R. Goshgarian, J., granted summary judgment against the pharmacy, and plaintiffs appealed. The Appellate Court, Bowman, J., held that, by voluntarily undertaking to list some of a drug's side effects, a pharmacy did not assume a duty to list all possible side effects, so as to remove it from the protection of the learned intermediary doctrine.

Affirmed.

1. Drugs and Narcotics ⊜19

By voluntarily undertaking to list some of a drug's side effects, a pharmacy did not assume a duty to list all possible side effects, so as to remove it from the protection of the learned intermediary doctrine regarding side effects it did not list; side effects listed by the pharmacy constituted the extent of its undertaking.

2. Drugs and Narcotics ⊜18

Physicians and Surgeons ⊜15(8)

"Learned intermediary doctrine" provides that manufacturers of prescription drugs have a duty to warn prescribing physicians of a drug's known dangerous propensities and that physicians, in turn, using their medical judgment, have a duty to convey the warnings to their patients.

> See publication Words and Phrases for other judicial constructions and definitions.

3. Drugs and Narcotics ⊜18

Learned intermediary doctrine precludes the imposition of a duty upon drug manufacturers to warn patients directly of a drug's known dangerous propensities.

———

Charles A. Cohn, Erwin Cohn, Cohn & Cohn, Chicago, for Clarence Kasin and Paul Kasin.

Eric J. Parker, Ridge, Ridge & Lindsay, Waukegan, for Osco Drug Inc., Corp.

Presiding Justice BOWMAN delivered the opinion of the court:

Plaintiffs, Clarence and Paul Kasin, brought a negligence action in the circuit court of Lake County against defendants, Dr. James A. Gross and Osco Drug, Inc. (Osco). Subsequently, Dr. Gross was dismissed with prejudice. As to Osco, plaintiffs alleged that in dispensing the prescription drug Daypro Osco had negligently advised Clarence Kasin of the side effects of the drug when it failed to advise him "of symptoms to be aware of

[Illustration 7-3]

PAGE FROM 728 N.E.2D 77, 79 (ILL.APP. 2000)

KASIN v. OSCO DRUG, INC.   Ill. **79**
Cite as 728 N.E.2d 77 (Ill.App. 2 Dist. 2000)

tled to judgment as a matter of law. *Cramer v. Insurance Exchange Agency,* 174 Ill.2d 513, 530, 221 Ill.Dec. 473, 675 N.E.2d 897 (1996). The existence of a duty owed by the defendant to a plaintiff is a question of law to be determined on a motion for summary judgment. *Jacob v. Greve,* 2 Ill.Dec. 671, 673 Ill.Dec. 671, 673 court's review of a summary judgment *Mutual Insurance* App.3d 495, 502, N.E.2d 271 (1998).

[1-3] Plaintiffs first contend that Osco's voluntary undertaking to provide an information or a warning sheet with a prescription drug removed it from the protection of the "learned intermediary doctrine." The learned intermediary doctrine provides that manufacturers of prescription drugs have a duty to warn prescribing physicians of a drug's known dangerous propensities and that physicians, in turn, using their medical judgment, have a duty to convey the warnings to their patients. *Kirk v. Michael Reese Hospital & Medical Center,* 117 Ill.2d 507, 517, 111 Ill.Dec. 944, 513 N.E.2d 387 (1987). The doctrine precludes the imposition of a duty upon drug manufacturers to warn patients directly. *Kirk,* 117 Ill.2d at 519, 111 Ill.Dec. 944, 513 N.E.2d 387. The doctrine also has been applied to exempt pharmacies and pharmacists from giving warnings to patients. See *Fakhouri v. Taylor,* 248 Ill.App.3d 328, 187 Ill.Dec. 927, 618 N.E.2d 518 (1993); *Leesley v. West,* 165 Ill.App.3d 135, 116 Ill.Dec. 136, 518 N.E.2d 758 (1988).

Plaintiffs concede that absent Osco's voluntary undertaking it would have been shielded from liability by the learned intermediary doctrine but argue that because Osco voluntarily undertook to warn of some side effects of Daypro it was removed from the protection of the doctrine. Conversely, Osco maintains that pursuant to our supreme court's decision in *Frye v. Medicare–Glaser Corp.,* 153 Ill.2d 26, 178

Ill.Dec. 763, 605 N.E.2d 557 (1992), it was protected by the doctrine.

In *Frye* a pharmacist voluntarily undertook to affix to a prescription drug a label that might cause ... sued both the ... st under a vol... of liability. ... that neither macist had the ... us side effects ... ued that once they undertook to warn of dangerous side effects they undertook to warn of all potential dangers involved in taking the drug. The supreme court rejected plaintiff's argument and found that the defendants' liability depended upon the extent of their undertaking.

Osco asserts that the court in *Frye* determined that a pharmacist was still protected by the learned intermediary doctrine even though the pharmacist offered a warning to a consumer of a drug's dangerous propensities. To support this assertion Osco relies on a statement made by the *Frye* court, in *dicta.* The statement followed the court's rejection of the plaintiff's argument that the pharmacist's placement of a "drowsy eye" label on the prescription drug container might mislead a consumer into believing that drowsiness was the only side effect of the drug. The court stated:

> "In our opinion, consumers should principally look to their prescribing physician to convey the appropriate warnings regarding drugs, and it is the prescribing physician's duty to convey these warnings to patients." *Frye,* 153 Ill.2d at 34, 178 Ill.Dec. 763, 605 N.E.2d 557.

In so stating, the court made no reference to the learned intermediary doctrine. Given the context in which the statement was made, we are not persuaded that the statement indicated that the court had concluded that a pharmacist is protected by the learned intermediary doctrine even if the pharmacist voluntarily undertakes to warn a consumer of some side effects.

This is another page of Kasin v. Osco Drug, Inc. It illustrates how headnotes are developed. The bracketed numbers are inserted by the editors. Each section so bracketed has been condensed into a corresponding headnote for the point of law in each bracketed section.

See next illustration.

[Illustration 7–4]

SCREEN PRINT FROM WESTLAWNEXT SHOWING HEADNOTES

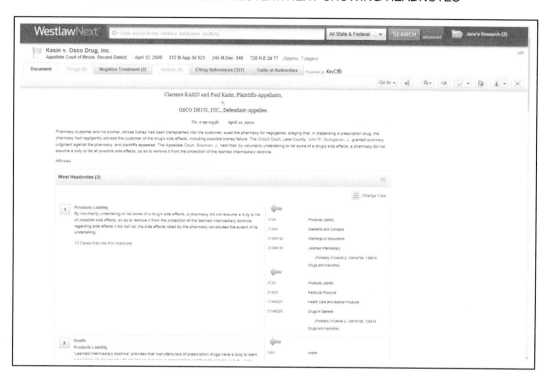

[Illustration 7–5]

PAGE FROM DESCRIPTIVE-WORD INDEX, ILLINOIS DIGEST 2D

MANHOLES　　　　　　　　　　　　　56 Ill D 2d—648

References are to Digest Topics and Key Numbers

MANHOLES—Cont'd
MUNICIPAL liability for injuries. Mun Corp 767, 783
　Pleading and proof. Mun Corp 816(10)
　Question for jury. Mun Corp 821(1, 13, 14, 19, 22)
　Unimproved street. Mun Corp 759(5)
OBSTRUCTION. Mun Corp 777
STREETS and highways—
　Injuries. Mun Corp 783
WATER company's liability for pedestrian's injury when
　manhole lid tilted. Waters 195

MANICURE PARLORS
WOMEN employees, operator permitting to massage
　male patrons' genitals, sufficiency of evidence.
　Nuis 86

MANIFEST

**MANUFACTURERS AND MANUFACTURING
COMPANIES—Cont'd**
BANKRUPTCY—
　Action of trespass against party at whose instigation
　　receiver was appointed where court had jurisdic-
　　tion. Bankr 114(1)
　Damages from petitioner on dismissal of petition.
　　Bankr 99
BANKRUPTCY laws, applicability. Bankr 72
BOUNTIES for manufacturing. Bounties 4, 7
BURDEN of proof on customer reworking manufactured
　goods in manufacturer's action for manufacture of
　goods. Bailm 31(1)
BYSTANDERS, injury from defective product, strict
　liability. Torts 14.1
CLAW hammer manufacturer, hammer defect, products

> This page illustrates how topics and key numbers can be located by using the
> *Descriptive-Word Index* to the *Illinois Digest 2d.* In this instance, we begin with a
> specific word in our fact situation, "manufacturer." Notice the major heading for
> "Manufacturers and Manufacturing Companies." Notice in the sub-entry "Drugs and
> medicine, civil liability" that we should consult "Drugs and Narcotics," Key Number 18.
>
> Many times, one will not find an index entry under the particular word or phrase
> chosen. In such instances, one should search in the *Descriptive-Word Index* under other
> appropriate words or phrases.

Defense or indemnification, liability policy. Insur-
　ance 435.24(6)
CONTRACTS—
　Certainty as to subject matter. Contracts 9(1)
　Construction. Contracts 201
　Implied contract to manufacture for United States.
　　U S 69(4)
　Mutuality of obligation. Contracts 10(2)

MANUAL DELIVERY
See this index Delivery

MANUAL POSSESSION
DEED, necessity that grantee have. Deeds 56(2)

MANUAL TRAINING
BOARD of Education's power to prescribe. Schools 55
COUNTY aid. Counties 153½

MANUAL TRAINING ROOM
WORKSHOP within Workmen's Compensation Act.
　Work Comp 140

MANUALS
SECURITIES, information as to issuer published in rec-
　ognized manual affecting validity of securities law
　exempting resales by brokers—
　Licens 18½(22)
　Statut 47

MANUFACTURERS AND MANUFACTURING
DRUGS, products liability, failure to warn patient.
　Drugs & N 20

**MANUFACTURERS AND MANUFACTURING
COMPANIES**
ACCOUNT, fiduciary relation between manufacturer and
　designer. Acct 4
　Evidence. Acct 18
　Theft of design. Acct 7
AIRCRAFT, liability of manufacturer. Aviation 13
ALLOWANCE in lieu of brokerage, manufacturer con-
　verting to direct selling. Trade Reg 915
ANIMAL food, liability not limited by privity of contract
　requirement. Neglig 27
ATTORNEY fees, paneling's noncompliance with city
　code concealed from hospital. Costs 172
AUTHORIZED dealer agreement, vertical restraints, rule
　of reason. Monop 17(1.3)
AUTOMOBILE, see this index Automobiles
BAILMENT, goods delivered for manufacture. Bailm
　14(2)

CONTRIBUTION, employer-buyer, strict liability. Con-
　trib 5(6)
CORN picker, injury complaint alleging defect—
　Neglig 111(2)
　Torts 26(1)
COSMETICS, intended for professional use, restraining
　sales to general public. Inj 89(1)
DANGEROUS products, tort liability. Torts 14.1
DEALERSHIP, cancellation, manufacturer selling direct-
　ly to end-users. Monop 28(7.4)
DISTRIBUTOR habitually negligent as driver, retention.
　Autos 197(7)
→ DRUGS and medicine, civil liability. Drugs & N 18
ELECTRIC vaporizer causing burns to infant—
　Burden of proof. Neglig 121.5
　Presumption. Neglig 121.3
　Question for jury. Neglig 136(17)
ELEVATOR of manufacturers as common carriers.
　Carr 235
EQUAL treatment, sales to competing buyers. Trade
　Reg 911
EVIDENCE in action against manufacturer of vaporizer,
　for breach of warranty—
　Neglig 121.3
　Sales 441(2)
EXCISE tax on manufacturers, see this index Excise
EXPLOSIVES. Explos 3, 8
　Illegal or negligent manufacture causing injuries. Ex-
　　plos 8
FOOD—
　Illegal manufacture. Food 13
　Implied warranty. Sales 255
GLASS coffee maker, injury on breaking, res ipsa loqui-
　tur doctrine. Neglig 121.3
GOVERNMENT contract, construction and operation.
　U S 70(1)

[Illustration 7–6]

PAGE FROM TOPIC, DRUGS AND NARCOTICS, ILLINOIS DIGEST 2D

23 Ill D 2d—1

DRUGS AND NARCOTICS

For other and later cases, see CHEMICAL DE-
PENDENTS

I. DRUGS AND DRUGGISTS IN GENERAL.

Research Notes

Application for use of new drug; practice under
Food, Drug and Cosmetic Law, see West's
Federal Practice Manual.

Library references

C.J.S. Drugs and Narcotics §§ 7 et seq., 10 et
seq., 27 et seq., 43 et seq., 72 et seq., 84 et
seq.

⟾2. Federal regulation.
See ⟾2.1.

⟾2.1. —— In general.
C.A.7 (Ill.) 2001. Statement in which manufacturers and marketers of over-the-counter and prescription strength forms of stomach acid reliever
ranitidine told consumer that he "could not" sub-

⟾15. —— Revocation or suspension.
Ill.App. 1 Dist. 2000. Actions of Department of
Professional Regulation in seeking either rehearing
or order directing State Pharmacy Board to reconsider its recommendation regarding penalty to be
imposed against licensed pharmacist who was subject of disciplinary proceeding, and remanding
matter, even if not authorized by statute, were not
prejudicial to pharmacist, and could not provide
basis for reversal, where Board confirmed its initial
recommendation on remand. S.H.A. 225 ILCS
85/35.8, 35.9; Ill.Admin. Code title 68,
§§ 1110.210(a)(8), 1110.240(g).—Wilson v. Illinois
Dept. of Professional Regulation, 250 Ill.Dec. 596,
739 N.E.2d 57, 317 Ill.App.3d 57.

Under Pharmacy Practice Act, Department of
Professional Regulation is authorized to request
that its Director take action contrary to a recommendation by State Pharmacy Board, as an incident to (1) Department's duty to effectuate the
purpose of the Pharmacy Act, and (2) its power to
discipline. S.H.A. 225 ILCS 85/11, 30(a), 35.10.—
Id.

Department of Professional Regulation acted

> When the topic and key number are known, sets of West digests
> can be consulted to locate cases with the same or similar points of
> law. It is good research practice to start with the most specific digest
> for your research problem, e.g., *Illinois Digest 2d*.
>
> Notice how digest paragraphs are reprinted as they originally
> appeared as headnotes in the reported cases. Notice also how
> citations are given after the digest paragraph to where the case is
> reported. West's state key number digests also often contain
> references to relevant law review articles from that state.

scription strength forms of stomach acid reliever
ranitidine indicated that two drugs were not the
same medications fell within exemption under Illinois Consumer Fraud and Deceptive Business
Practices Act (CFA) for actions specifically authorized by federal law, given that, for federal regulatory purposes, two products were different "drugs"
and manufacturers and marketers were thus authorized to say they were different "medications,"
even if statement was confusing as to laypersons.
Federal Food, Drug, and Cosmetic Act, § 1 et seq.,
21 U.S.C.A. § 301 et seq.; 21 C.F.R.
§§ 310.3(h)(4), 330.1(i); S.H.A. 815 I.L.C.S.
505/10b(1).—Bober v. Glaxo Wellcome PLC, 246
F.3d 934.

⟾8. —— Prescription drugs.
Law Rev. 1996. Rationalizing Product Liability
for Prescription Drugs: Implied Preemption, Federal Common Law, and Other Paths to Uniform
Pharmaceutical Safety Standards. David R. Geig-
er and Mark D. Rosen.—45 DePaul L. Rev. 395.

**⟾11. State and municipal regulation in gener-
al.**
Ill.App. 1 Dist. 2000. Purpose of Pharmacy
Practice Act is the protection of the public health,
safety, and welfare through regulation of the practice of pharmacy. S.H.A. 225 ILCS 85/1 et seq.—
Wilson v. Illinois Dept. of Professional Regulation,
250 Ill.Dec. 596, 739 N.E.2d 57, 317 Ill.App.3d 57.
Law Rev. 1996. Rationalizing Product Liability
for Prescription Drugs: Implied Preemption, Federal Common Law, and Other Paths to Uniform
Pharmaceutical Safety Standards. David R. Geig-
er and Mark D. Rosen.—45 DePaul L. Rev. 395.

Const.Amend. 14; S.H.A. 225 ILCS 85/11, 30(a),
35.10.—Id.

Sanction imposed by Director of Department of
Professional Regulation in disciplinary proceeding
brought against licensed pharmacist who had
pleaded guilty to federal felony charge of receipt of
misbranded drugs through interstate commerce,
under which pharmacist's license was revoked for
nine months, followed by 27 months of probation,
and license of pharmacy he owned and operated
was revoked, was not against manifest weight of
the evidence, and was not an abuse of discretion.
Federal Food, Drug, and Cosmetic Act, §§ 301(c),
303(a)(2), 21 U.S.C.A. §§ 331(c), 333(a)(2); S.H.A.
225 ILCS 85/11, 30(a), 35.10.—Id.

⟾18. —— Manufacturers.
Ill.App. 2 Dist. 2000. "Learned intermediary
doctrine" provides that manufacturers of prescription drugs have a duty to warn prescribing physicians of a drug's known dangerous propensities
and that physicians, in turn, using their medical
judgment, have a duty to convey the warnings to
their patients.—Kasin v. Osco Drug, Inc., 245 Ill.
Dec. 346, 728 N.E.2d 77, 312 Ill.App.3d 823.

Learned intermediary doctrine precludes the imposition of a duty upon drug manufacturers to
warn patients directly of a drug's known dangerous
propensities.—Id.
Law Rev. 1996. Defending the pill: Oral contraceptives and strict liability in Illinois. Craig T.
Liljestrand.—84 Ill.B.J. 364.
Law Rev. 1982. "Cause in fact" in tort law—A
philosophical and historical examination.—31 De
Paul L.Rev. 769.

[Illustration 7–7]

PAGE FROM ANALYSIS, DRUGS AND NARCOTICS, FROM A KEY NUMBER DIGEST

DRUGS AND NARCOTICS

⟶ SUBJECTS INCLUDED

Regulation of the manufacture, dispensing, and sale of medicines and other drugs and devices by pharmacists or others

Civil and criminal liabilities relating to drugs in general

Regulation of the sale, use, etc., of narcotics and hallucinogenic, depressant, and stimulant drugs

Violation of laws relating to such drugs and criminal liability and prosecution therefor

Searches, seizures, and forfeitures relating to such drugs

⟶ SUBJECTS EXCLUDED AND COVERED BY OTHER TOPICS

Commitment and treatment of addicts, see CHEMICAL DEPENDENTS

Insecticides and fungicides, see POISONS

Internal revenue acts generally, offenses and prosecutions under, see INTERNAL REVENUE

Poisons, regulations relating to, see POISONS

For detailed references to other topics, see Descriptive-Word Index

Analysis

I. DRUGS AND DRUGGISTS IN GENERAL, ☞1–40.

II. NARCOTICS AND DANGEROUS DRUGS, ☞41–198.
    (A) REGULATIONS, ☞41–60.
    (B) OFFENSES, ☞61–100.

I.

> This illustrates the "Analysis" method of locating topics and key numbers. If a researcher knows that a particular issue deals with *Drugs and Narcotics*, that topic can be consulted immediately in the appropriate volume or volumes of a West digest. After reading the "scope note" for information included, excluded, or covered elsewhere, the next step is to find a relevant key number.
> See next illustration.

[Illustration 7–8]

PAGE FROM ANALYSIS, DRUGS AND NARCOTICS, FROM A KEY NUMBER DIGEST

DRUGS & NARCOTICS   23 Ill D 2d—2

I. DRUGS AND DRUGGISTS IN GENERAL.—Continued.

 12. Registration, certificate, or license.
 12.1. —— In general.
 13. —— Necessity.
 14. —— Eligibility and right; licensing boards.
 15. —— Revocation or suspension.
 16. Conduct of business.
 17. Civil liability.
 17.1. —— In general.
 18. —— Manufacturers.
 19. —— Retailers or dispensers.
 20. Actions for damages.
 20.1. —— In general.
 21. —— Evidence.
 22. —— Questions for jury.
 23. Injunction.
 24. Penalties.
 25. Seizure and forfeiture.
 25.1. —— In general.
 26. —— Property subject and grounds.
 27. —— Proceedings.
 28. —— Evidence.
 29. Offenses.
 30. Criminal prosecutions.
 30.1. —— In general.
 31. —— Evidence and questions for jury.

II. NARCOTICS AND DANGEROUS DRUGS.

 (A) REGULATIONS.
 ⟐41. Nature and power to regulate.
 42. Statutes and other regulations in general.
 43. Validity of statutes.
 43.1. —— In general.
 44. —— Presumptions and inferences, provisions relating to.

> This is the second page from the *Analysis* in a key number digest. Note that the outline under "I. Drugs and Druggists In General" Includes the Civil liability of Manufacturers, Key Number 18. It is useful practice to browse the other listings in the outline for additional relevant key numbers.

 50. Civil liability.

 (B) OFFENSES.
 ⟐61. Nature and elements in general.
 62. Illegal possession.
 62.1. —— In general.
 63. —— Elements of offense in general.
 64. —— Knowledge and intent.
 65. —— Constructive possession.
 66. —— Substance and quantity possessed.

[Illustration 7–9]

PAGE FROM TABLE OF CASES, ILLINOIS DIGEST 2D

KARR;   55 Ill D 2d—30

References are to Digest Topics and Key Numbers

Karr; People v., IllApp 2 Dist, 25 IllDec 453, 386 NE2d 927, 68 IllApp3d 1040, habeas corpus gr US ex rel Karr v. Wolff, 556 FSupp 760, vac 732 F2d 615, on remand 1985 WL 2487.—Sent & Pun 537.

Karris; Ray v., CA7 (Ill), 780 F2d 636. –Sec Reg 60.40.

Kartholl, In re Marriage of, IllApp 2 Dist, 97 IllDec 347, 492 NE2d 1006, 143 IllApp3d 228.—Child C 120, 634, 637.

Kasbeer v. Kasbeer, IllApp 2 Dist, 159 NE2d 840, 22 IllApp2d 218.—Child C 7; Child S 24, 25, 60, 91, 556(1), 557(1).

Kasbeer; Kasbeer v., IllApp 2 Dist, 159 NE2d 840, 22 IllApp2d 218.—Child C 7; Child S 24, 25, 60, 91, 556(1), 557(1).

Kas' Estate, In re, IllApp 1 Dist, 303 NE2d 201, 14 IllApp3d 729.—Joint Adv 1.2(4), 1.15.

K., Ashley, In Interest of, IllApp 1 Dist, 156 IllDec 925, 571 NE2d 906, 212 IllApp3d 849. See Ashley K., In Interest of.

Kasin v. Osco Drug, Inc., IllApp 2 Dist, 245 IllDec 346, 728 NE2d 77, 312 IllApp3d 823.—Drugs & N 18, 19; Phys 15(8).

Kaspar v. Clinton-Jackson Corp., IllApp 1 Dist, 254 NE2d 826, 118 IllApp2d 364.—App & E 1004(1).

Kass v. Resurrection Medical Center, IllApp 1 Dist, 250 IllDec 194, 738 NE2d 158, 316 IllApp3d 1108, reh den. —App & E 1060.1(2.1); New Tr 27; Trial 125(1), 133.2, 133.3.

Kassnel; Adams v., IllApp 1 Dist, 148 NE2d 818, 16 IllApp2d 540.—Trade Reg 257.1.

Kautz v. Kautz, IllApp 1 Dist, 243 NE2d 426, 102 IllApp2d 165.—Child S 340.

Kautz; Kautz v., IllApp 1 Dist, 243 NE2d 426, 102 IllApp2d 165.—Child S 340.

Kavanaugh v. Ford Motor Co., CA7 (Ill), 353 F2d 710.— Trade Reg 871(2), 871(4).

Kavinsky; People v., IllApp 1 Dist, 47 IllDec 90, 414 NE2d 1206, 91 IllApp3d 784.—Sent & Pun 310.

Kavonius v. Industrial Com'n, IllApp 2 Dist, 247 IllDec 279, 731 NE2d 1287, 314 IllApp3d 166, reh den, appeal den 252 IllDec 78, 742 NE2d 328, 192 Ill2d 691.—Work Comp 1187, 1892.

Kawasaki Motors Mfg. Corp., USA; Boland v., IllApp 4 Dist, 243 IllDec 165, 722 NE2d 1234, 309 IllApp3d 645. —App & E 525(1), 970(2), 971(3); Death 21, 75; Evid 560; Pretrial Proc 14.1, 15, 39, 40, 45; Prod Liab 27, 40, 98; Trial 43, 252(2); Witn 267.

Kay v. Kay, IllApp 1 Dist, 318 NE2d 9, 22 IllApp3d 530.— Child C 7, 177, 178, 577, 638.

Kay; Kay v., IllApp 1 Dist, 318 NE2d 9, 22 IllApp3d 530. —Child C 7, 177, 178, 577, 638.

Kaznowski v. City of La Salle, IllApp 2 Dist, 43 NE2d 852, 316 IllApp 115.—App & E 1004(5).

K.B., In re, IllApp 4 Dist, 247 IllDec 866, 732 NE2d 1198, 314 IllApp3d 739.—Infants 156, 157, 158, 178, 180, 181, 196, 232, 247, 248.1, 252.

Kealey v. Carey's Estate, IllApp 1 Dist, 181 NE2d 197, 35 IllApp2d 61.—Theaters 6(36.1).

Kealey v. Kealey, IllApp 5 Dist, 33 IllDec 672, 397 NE2d 5, 77 IllApp3d 962.—Child S 140(2).

> When a researcher knows the name of a case that deals with a relevant point of law, key numbers assigned to that topic can be located by use of the Table of Cases volume(s). See, for example, the listing for *Kasin v. Osco Drug, Inc.* This same information is contained under *Osco Drug, Inc.; Kasin v.* Thus, a case can be located when either the plaintiff or defendant is known. Note also that parallel citations are provided.

Katris v. City of Waukegan, NDIll, 498 FSupp 48.—Civil R 206(2.1).

Katsigiannis; People v., IllApp 2 Dist, 122 IllDec 249, 526 NE2d 508, 171 IllApp3d 1090, 82 ALR4th 337.—Sent & Pun 55, 56, 60.

Katz v. Comdisco, Inc., NDIll, 117 FRD 403.—Sec Reg 154.1.

Katzenbach; Rini v., CA7 (Ill), 403 F2d 697.—Sent & Pun 349, 400.

Katzer v. Katzer, IllApp 1 Dist, 18 IllDec 852, 378 NE2d 316, 61 IllApp3d 299.—Child C 551, 553, 559, 567, 637, 921(1), 923(4).

Katzer; Katzer v., IllApp 1 Dist, 18 IllDec 852, 378 NE2d 316, 61 IllApp3d 299.—Child C 551, 553, 559, 567, 637, 921(1), 923(4).

Kauffman v. International Broth. of Elec. Workers, Local Union No. 461, NDIll, 124 FSupp2d 1127.—Fed Civ Proc 2497.1; Labor 16.1, 108.1, 109, 111, 112, 119.

Kauffman v. Kauffman, IllApp 4 Dist, 333 NE2d 695, 30 IllApp3d 159.—Child C 7, 67, 922(1), 922(2).

Kauffman; Kauffman v., IllApp 4 Dist, 333 NE2d 695, 30 IllApp3d 159.—Child C 7, 67, 922(1), 922(2).

Kauffman; People v., IllApp 4 Dist, 123 IllDec 182, 527 NE2d 645, 172 IllApp3d 1040, appeal den 128 IllDec 895, 535 NE2d 406, 123 Ill2d 563.—Sent & Pun 2037, 2038, 2041.

Kaufman; People v., IllApp 3 Dist, 23 IllDec 674, 384 NE2d 468, 67 IllApp3d 36.—Sent & Pun 31.

3355(1.10), 3355(2.1), 3382.1, 3385, 3420(12), 3423; Work Comp 1846, 1847, 1939.6, 1939.11(1), 2093.

Keathley; People v., IllApp 1 Dist, 248 NE2d 782, 109 IllApp2d 323.—Rob 24.10, 24.40.

Keating; People v., IllApp 2 Dist, 274 NE2d 362, 2 IllApp3d 884, supplemented 276 NE2d 350, 2 IllApp3d 884.—Drugs & N 45.1.

Keating; People v., IllApp 2 Dist, 191 IllDec 531, 624 NE2d 380, 252 IllApp3d 801.—Sent & Pun 85, 90.

Keaton v. Atchison, T. & S. F. Ry. Co., CA7 (Ill), 321 F2d 317.—Fed Cts 896.1.

Keck; People v., IllApp 3 Dist, 168 IllDec 892, 590 NE2d 529, 226 IllApp3d 937, appeal den 176 IllDec 811, 602 NE2d 465, 146 Ill2d 640.—Sent & Pun 2003, 2020, 2021.

Keck, Mahin & Cate, In re, NDIll, 253 BR 530.—Atty & C 26, 62; Bankr 2923, 3568(2), 3782, 3786; Fed Civ Proc 636; Fraud 3, 16; Judgm 634, 720.

Keefe; People ex rel. Legislative Commission on Low Income Housing v., Ill, 223 NE2d 144, 36 Ill2d 460.— Searches 75.

Keefer v. Keefer, IllApp 2 Dist, 245 NE2d 784, 107 IllApp2d 74.—Child C 176, 178, 187, 577, 638.

Keefer; Keefer v., IllApp 2 Dist, 245 NE2d 784, 107 IllApp2d 74.—Child C 176, 178, 187, 577, 638.

Keefer; U.S. v., CA7 (Ill), 464 F2d 1385, cert den 93 SCt 322, 409 US 983, 34 LEd2d 247.—Drugs & N 119.1.

Keehner; Luthy v., IllApp 3 Dist, 45 IllDec 509, 412 NE2d 1091, 90 IllApp3d 127.—Judgm 181(15.1).

For Later Case History Information, see KeyCite on WESTLAW

[Illustration 7–10]

PAGE FROM TABLE OF KEY NUMBERS FROM VOLUME 7, GENERAL DIGEST, 10TH SERIES

161]

DOWER AND CURTESY —Cont'd	DRUGS AND NARCOTICS —Cont'd	EASEMENTS—Cont'd	ELECTION OF REMEDIES —Cont'd
☞	☞	☞	☞
70.1—6	122—3	17(1)—4, 5, 6	5—2, 3, 4, 5, 6, 7
114—6	123.1—4	18(1)—1, 2, 3, 4, 5	7(1)—7
118—6	123.2—1, 2, 3, 4, 5, 6, 7	18(2)—2	9—3
	123.3—7	18(3)—1	14—4, 7
DRAINS	125.1—1, 6	22—1, 3, 6	15—2, 6, 7
☞	126—1, 2, 4, 6, 7	24—1, 4, 6, 7	
17—2	127—1, 4, 5	25—6	**ELECTIONS**
19—1, 2	128—2, 4, 5	26(1)—2, 4, 5, 6	☞
20—1	129.1—1, 2	26(2)—2, 6	1—3, 7
36(2)—6	130—2, 4, 5, 6	27—2, 7	3—4
36(6)—6	131—4, 5, 7	30(1)—1, 2, 3, 4, 6	5—3, 4, 5
45—4, 6	132—1, 2	30(2)—6	7—1
50—2	133—1, 2, 3, 4, 5, 6, 7	30(3)—2, 3	8.1—1, 2
52—4	182.3—6	32—2	9—7
57—1	183(1)—1	33—2	10—1, 4, 5, 6
70—2	183(2)—2, 3, 4, 5	36(1)—1, 2, 3, 4, 5, 6, 7	12(2.1)—3
71—6	183(3)—7	36(3)—1, 2, 3, 4, 5, 6, 7	12(3)—4
82(3)—2	183(4)—2	37—1, 7	12(6)—3, 4, 5, 6
82(5)—2	183(5)—2, 4, 5, 7	38—1, 2, 4, 5, 7	12(8)—3
	183(6)—2, 4, 5, 7	40—1, 2, 4	12(9.1)—3, 4, 7
DRUGS AND NARCOTICS	183.5—1	41—4, 5	12(10)—4, 5
☞	184(1)—2, 4, 5, 7	42—1, 4, 5, 6, 7	15—1
2.1—6, 7	184(2)—1, 4, 7	44(2)—1	21—2
3—6	184(6)—4, 5	48(4)—4, 5	22—3, 4
9—1, 5, 7	185(1)—7	48(6)—1, 2	24—2, 7
10—4, 5, 7	185(2)—2, 4	50—1, 7	27—1
11—2, 4, 5	185(3)—1, 2, 3, 4, 6	51—1, 4, 7	28—4
12.1—4, 5	185(4)—2, 4, 5, 7	53—1	29—3
15—4, 7	185(7)—2, 4	54—1, 2, 4, 5, 6	54—1
16—2	185(8)—4, 5, 7	57—4, 7	105—4, 5
17.1—1, 4, 5, 7	185.5—1, 4, 5, 6, 7	58(1)—4	108—3
18—1, 3, 4, 5, 7	185.10—1, 2, 4, 5, 6, 7	58(2)—4	114.1—6
19—4, 5	187(2)—2, 4, 6	58(3)—1, 4, 7	115—3
20.1—2, 3, 4, 5	188(1)—4	61(1)—4, 5	116—2
21—1, 2, 4		61(2)—1, 4, 5	

This table, which is cumulative in each volume of the *General Digest* through ten volumes and then starts a new cumulation, allows a researcher to determine which of the volumes contain a particular topic and key number.

The table in this illustration, cumulative for volumes 1-7, indicates that only five of the seven volumes need be consulted for cases dealing with *Drugs and Narcotics*, Key Number 18.

23—7			
41—7			
42—4, 5			
43.1—1, 2, 3,			
45.1—2			
46—2, 4, 6			
47—1, 6			
61—1, 2, 3, 4,			
62.1—2			
63—1, 2, 3, 4,			
64—1, 2, 3, 4,			
65—1, 2, 3, 4, 5, 6, 7	194.1—2, 4, 5, 7	☞	167—1
66—1, 2, 3, 4, 5, 7	195—1, 3, 4, 5, 6, 7	1—3, 4	172—1
67—1, 2, 4, 5, 6, 7	196—2, 3, 4, 5, 6, 7	3—4	177—2
68.1—7		7—3, 7	179—2
69—1, 2, 4, 5, 6	**EASEMENTS**	9(2)—3	186(1)—1
70—2	☞	9(3)—3	188—1
73.1—1, 2, 3, 4, 5, 6, 7	1—1, 2, 3, 4, 5, 6, 7	17—3	197—1
76—1, 2, 4, 5, 6, 7	2—6	19—4	208—2
78—2, 6, 7	3(1)—4, 5, 6	21—3	216.1—1, 4
102.1—1, 2, 4, 5	3(2)—4, 5	36—7	220—2
103—4, 5	5—1, 2, 3, 4, 5, 6, 7	62.1—3	227(1)—1, 4
104—2, 3, 4, 6	6—1, 2, 7	63—3	227(8)—1, 4
106—4, 5	7(0.5)—2, 4, 5	109—7	235—1
107—1, 2, 3, 4, 5, 6, 7	7(5)—3, 6	120(0.5)—3	236—1
108—1, 2, 3, 4, 5, 7	8(1)—1, 2, 4, 5, 6, 7	120(1)—3	239—4
109—1, 2, 3, 4, 5, 6, 7	8(2)—1, 2, 4, 5, 7	124—3	247—1
110.1—1, 2	8(4)—7	132—3	255—2
111—2, 3, 4, 5, 7	9(1)—3, 6		257—4, 5
112—1, 2, 6	10(1)—1	**ELECTION OF REMEDIES**	259—1
114—2, 4, 5, 7	12(1)—2, 3, 4, 5, 7	☞	260—1, 2
116—1, 2, 3, 4, 5, 6, 7	12(2)—2	1—2	262—1
117—1, 2, 3, 4, 5, 6, 7	12(3)—4, 5	2—2, 3	269—1, 4, 6
118—1, 2, 3, 4, 5, 6, 7	14(1)—1, 4, 5, 6, 7	3(1)—1, 2, 6	270—1, 4
119.1—1, 2, 3, 4, 5, 6, 7	15.1—2, 3, 4, 5, 6, 7	3(4)—2	271—1, 2, 4
120—2, 4, 5	16—4, 5, 7	4—3, 6	275—3

[Illustration 7–11]

PAGE FROM KEY NUMBER TRANSLATION TABLE IN A KEY NUMBER DIGEST

23 Ill D 2d—7   DRUGS & NARCOTICS

TABLE 2

KEY NUMBER TRANSLATION TABLE

DRUGS AND NARCOTICS TO PRIOR TOPICS

Drugs and Narcotics Key Number	Prior Topic and Key Number	Drugs and Narcotics Key Number	Prior Topic and Key Number
			Poisons ☜4, 9
1	Druggists ☜1, 5, 11	75	Poisons ☜4, 9
2.1–11	Druggists ☜2, 3, 5	76	Custom Duties ☜125;
12.1–15	Druggists ☜1–6		Druggists ☜12;
16	Druggists ☜5, 6		Internal Revenue ☜2401, 2447;
17.1–19	Druggists ☜8, 9		Poisons ☜4, 9
20.1–22	Druggists ☜9, 10	77	Customs Duties ☜125;
23	Druggists ☜2, 5		Druggists ☜12;
24–26	Druggists ☜2, 5, 11		Poisons ☜2, 4, 9
27, 28	Druggists ☜11	78	Poisons ☜2, 4, 9
29	Druggists ☜2, 3, 5, 12	101, 102.1	Druggists ☜12;
30.1, 31	Druggists ☜12		Poisons ☜2, 9
41	Druggists ☜2, 5;	103	Customs Duties ☜134;
	Physicians and Surgeons ☜10;		Internal Revenue ☜2433, 2441;
	Poisons ☜2, 4		Poisons ☜2, 4, 9
42	Druggists ☜2, 3, 5;	104	Poisons ☜4, 9
	Poisons ☜2, 4, 9	105	Internal Revenue ☜2433;
43.1	Druggists ☜2;		Poisons ☜4, 9
	Internal Revenue ☜2401;	106	Customs Duties ☜134;
	Poisons ☜2, 4		Internal Revenue ☜2446;
44	Poisons ☜2, 4, 9		Poisons ☜2, 4, 9
45.1	Druggists ☜2;	107	Customs Duties ☜134;
	Poisons ☜2–4, 9		Internal Revenue ☜2447

When a topic is expanded or reclassified in a key number digest, a Key Number Translation Table is printed immediately prior to the new topic. This illustration shows that Drugs and Narcotics, Key Numbers 17.1–19 were formerly covered by Druggists, Key Numbers 8 and 9. Frequently, the *Analysis* in earlier editions of digests can be consulted to see a more detailed breakdown of the original topic before it was expanded or reclassified.

Drugs and Narcotics Key Number	Prior Topic and Key Number	Drugs and Narcotics Key Number	Prior Topic and Key Number
	Poisons ☜4, 9	112	Internal Revenue ☜2449;
50	Druggists ☜9, 10;		Poisons ☜4, 9
	Poisons ☜4, 6	113, 114	Poisons ☜2, 4, 9
61	Druggists ☜2, 5, 12;	115.1	Customs Duties ☜134;
	Poisons ☜2, 4, 9		Internal Revenue ☜2449;
62.1	Poisons ☜2, 4, 9		Poisons ☜4, 9
63	Druggists ☜2;	116	Poisons ☜4, 9
	Poisons ☜4, 9	117	Druggists ☜2, 12;
64	Poisons ☜4, 9		Poisons ☜4, 9
65	Druggists ☜2;	118	Poisons ☜9
	Poisons ☜4, 9	119.1	Druggists ☜12;
66	Poisons ☜2, 4, 9		Poisons ☜9
67	Poisons ☜4, 9	120, 122	Poisons ☜9
68.1	Druggists ☜2, 12;	123	Customs Duties ☜134;
	Poisons ☜2, 4, 9		Druggists ☜12;
69, 70	Druggists ☜2;		Internal Revenue ☜2447, 2449;
	Poisons ☜4, 9		Poisons ☜4, 9
71	Poisons ☜2, 4, 9	124	Customs Duties ☜125, 134;
72	Poisons ☜4		Poisons ☜2, 9
73.1	Druggists ☜12;	125.1–127	Poisons ☜9
	Internal Revenue ☜2401;	128	Customs Duties ☜134;
	Poisons ☜2, 4, 9		Internal Revenue ☜2449;
74	Customs Duties ☜125, 134;		Poisons ☜9

[Illustration 7–12]

SCREEN PRINT FROM WESTLAWNEXT SHOWING A RECLASSIFIED TOPIC

J. OTHER SPECIALIZED WEST DIGESTS

1. *West's Bankruptcy Digest*

This key number digest includes cases from *West's Bankruptcy Reporter* and selected bankruptcy cases from *Federal Reporter 2d* and *3d* and West's *Supreme Court Reporter*.

2. *West's Military Justice Digest*

This key number digest includes cases from *West's Military Justice Reporter*.

3. *United States Federal Claims Digest*

This is a key number digest that includes cases from volumes 1 through 26 of the *United States Claims Court Reporter* and from volume 27 forward of the *Federal Claims Reporter*.

4. *West's Education Law Digest*

This publication provides key number digest paragraphs from all cases in the *National Reporter System* on topics relating to education law.

5. *West's Veterans Appeals Digest*

This is a key number digest that includes cases reported in the *Veterans Appeals Reporter*, and cases from the U.S. Court of Appeals for the Federal Circuit and the

Supreme Court of the United States that review those cases reported in the *Veterans Appeals Reporter*.

6. *United States Merit Systems Protection Board Digest*

This publication digests cases involving federal employees and the federal merit system. It uses a classification scheme different from the key number digests.

K. CHART ILLUSTRATING WEST GROUP'S KEY NUMBER DIGESTS

MASTER INDEX TO ALL CASE LAW	STATE COURT COVERAGE
American Digest System	**Individual State Digests**
Cases from: U.S. Supreme Court, all lower federal courts, all specialized federal courts, and all state courts	Coverage corresponds to regional digest in which state appears. Note: Some state digests are in a 2d, 3d, or 4th series. Published for all states except: Del. (Use: *Atlantic Digest*); Nev. and Utah (Use: *Pacific Digest*)
Use: Chronological Coverage	
*Century Digest 1658-1896	**Regional Reporter Digests**
First Dicennial 1896-1906	Cases from: The seven regional reporters, Calif. & N.Y., plus pre-reporter cases.
Second Dicennial 1907-1916	
Third Dicennial 1916-1926	Use as appropriate:
Fourth Dicennial 1926-1936	*Atlantic* (CT, DE, MD, ME, NH, NJ, PA, RI, VT, DC)
Fifth Dicennial 1936-1946	*1st* (to 1938)
Sixth Dicennial 1946-1956	*2d* (1938 to date)
Seventh Dicennial 1956-1966	*North Western* (IO, MI, MN, NE, ND, SD, WI)
Eighth Dicennial 1966-1976	*1st* (to 1941)
Ninth Dicennial (Part 1) 1976-1981	*2d* (1941 to date)
Ninth Dicennial (Part 2) 1981-1986	*Pacific* (AK, AZ, CA*, CO, HI, ID, KA, MT, NM, NV, OK, OR, UT, WA, WY)
Tenth Dicennial (Part 1) 1986-1991	1850-1931 (California & Pacific)
Tenth Dicennial (Part 2) 1991-1996	1-100 P.2d
Eleventh Dicennial (Part 1) 1996-2001	101-366 P.2d
Eleventh Dicennial (Part 2) 2001-2004	367-584 P.2d
Eleventh Dicennial (Part 3) 2004-2007	585-to date
General Digest (12th Series) 2008 + (in progress)	*South Eastern* (GA, NC, SC, VA, WV)
*The Century Digest indexes cases prior to the start of the National Reporter System. Therefore, digest coverage is more inclusive than reporter coverage.	*1st* (to 1934) *2d* (1934 to date)
	* * * * *

FEDERAL COURT COVERAGE	*North Eastern* (IL, ID, MA, NY, OH)
	    (to 1968)
	    CEASED PUBLICATION
	    Use: appropriate state digest

Complete Supreme Court coverage
 Cases from: *Supreme Court Reporter*
 Use: *U.S. Supreme Court Digest*
	Southern (AL, FL, LA, MS)
	    (to 1988)
	    CEASED PUBLICATION
	    Use: appropriate state digest

Complete Federal Court coverage
 Cases from: U.S. Supreme Court, all lower federal courts, and all specialized federal courts.
 Use: *Federal Practice Digest, 4th*
    (1984 to date)
 Federal Practice Digest, 3rd
    (Dec. 1975 to *Fed. Prac. Dig. 4th*)
 Federal Practice Digest, 2nd
    (1961 - Nov. 1975)
 Modern Federal Practice Digest
    (1939-1960)
 Federal Digest
	South Western
	    NOT PUBLISHED
	    Use: state digests for AR, KY, MO, TN, TX

	*Covers all Calif. courts to 1960 and only Cal. Sup. Ct. thereafter. For full coverage since 1960, use *California Digest* Series.

L. OTHER DIGESTS

Digests are not unique to West publications. Other publishers prepare digest volumes on a variety of topics, and researchers should become familiar with their format and features. Some of these digests are discussed below.

1. *Digest of United States Supreme Court Reports, Lawyers' Edition* **(LexisNexis; formerly published by Lawyers Cooperative Publishing Company)**

This is a multivolume digest, with annual pocket supplements, to all cases of the Supreme Court of the United States. The digest paragraphs used are collected from those published in the two editions of the *U.S. Supreme Court Reports, Lawyers' Edition.* This digest provides references to the publisher's other publications.

2. **Digests for Topical Reporters and Other Types of Publications**

Frequently, topical services (originally published in looseleaf format and now often online), multivolume treatises, and, on occasion, legal periodicals provide subject or alphabetically arranged abstracts of cases. At other times, materials are grouped under state or federal code sections. Still other digest volumes use a hybrid of these methods. Since digest volumes are useful finding aids for identifying similar materials, it is always useful to check sets for separate digest volumes and for case abstracts within these volumes.[14]

3. **A.L.R. Digests**

These publications are mentioned in Chapter 17, Section B-2.

4. **Digests for Federal Tax Materials**

See Chapter 26 for a discussion of tax research.

M. WORDS AND PHRASES AND POPULAR NAME TABLES

1. *Words and Phrases*

Sometimes a research problem involves the definition of certain words or phrases such as, for example, *learned intermediary doctrine,* which was derived from *Kasin v. Osco Drug, Inc.,* in our hypothetical problem. Courts frequently define the meaning of words and phrases to add clarity to their opinions.

Headnotes that contain judicial definitions are reprinted in West's *Words and Phrases,* a multivolume set containing approximately 600,000 alphabetically arranged judicial definitions of legal and non-legal terms. *Words and Phrases* is updated by annual cumulative pocket supplements, which are further supplemented by *Words and Phrases* tables in later bound volumes and advance sheets of the various units of the *National Reporter System.* Most of the key number digests also contain these tables. [See Illustration 7–13 for an example of a page from *Words and Phrases.* See also the second

---

[14] Topical services are discussed in Chapter 14. Note that the classification numbers from Bloomberg BNA digests can be searched in *Bloomberg Law* and in the Bloomberg BNA web product.

headnote in Illustration 7–2, which indicates that a judicial definition is derived from that headnote.]

Westlaw does not have an equivalent of the bound *Words and Phrases* set, but it can provide similar results with the use of the "wp" field. For example, searching for "wp(responsible)" in a case law database will retrieve cases whose headnotes discuss a definition of "responsible third parties," "responsible persons," and so on.[15]

2. Popular Name Tables

Some cases become better known by popular, and often descriptive, names rather than by their parties' names. For example, *Cruzan v. Director, Missouri Dept. of Health* is generally referred to as the "Right to Die Case." At other times, a group of cases may come to be known collectively by a popular name, such as the "Right to Counsel Cases." When only the popular name of a case or a group of cases is known, one can consult a table of cases by popular name to obtain citations to the actual case or cases.[16] Secondary sources are also useful for finding citations to, and discussions of, cases known by popular names.

N. A FEW TIPS FOR WORKING WITH KEY NUMBERS

West's key number system is a powerful tool, both in print and in *Westlaw*. And, like all tools, it is especially valuable in the hands of a skilled worker who understands its use.

1. Using the Key Number Outlines

The key number system is the same across all the jurisdictions the West digests and court reports cover, making it an especially powerful research tool. If a case about a landlord's liability for injuries due to a dangerous stairway is classified as key number 164 under the topic *Landlord and Tenant* in one state, a researcher can find cases from other states using that same topic and key number in the print digests. In *Westlaw*, one would search for 233k164, because 233 is the number associated with the topic *Landlord and Tenant*. In *Westlaw*, a researcher may also add words to a topic and key number search to further refine the results—for example searching for 233k164 and variants of the words "stair" or "steps."

A thorough researcher will skim the outline of key numbers to see whether there are any other potentially relevant numbers. Within *Landlord and Tenant*, key number 164, "Injuries to tenants or occupants," is part of a section headed "Injuries from Dangerous or Defective Condition." Looking a little farther, one sees key numbers 165 ("Injuries to employee of tenant"), 166 ("Injuries to property of tenant on premises"), 167 ("Injuries to third persons and their property"), 168 ("Contributory negligence"), and 169 "Actions for injuries from negligence"). Using some of those key numbers might well turn up more cases that are of interest to the researcher.

---

[15] This search works in either *Westlaw Classic* or *WestlawNext*. *Westlaw Classic* also has a database, WORDS-PHRASES, that provides a template for searching for definitions. Note that in this database, a document is a headnote, while in a case law database a document is a case. Since one case can have several headnotes discussing a definition, one often gets more documents (but not more cases) in WORDS-PHRASES than in ALLSTATES (Westlaw's database that includes cases from all states).

[16] The First through Sixth *Decennial Digests* had popular name tables. *Shepard's Acts and Cases by Popular Names* is another source.

Key numbers are arranged in a hierarchy, from broad to narrow, and individual key numbers may also be subdivided for added precision. Researchers using print digests may benefit from skimming only a subdivision of a key number. Searching for 233k164 in *Westlaw* will retrieve cases classified with key number 164, 164(1), 164(2), and so on, or an online researcher may choose to search just the subdivided key number, for instance, key number 164(4) ("Injuries due to unlighted passageways"), by specifying the narrower number in the search query.

2.   Federal and State Topics

Although the key number system is the same nationally, it is important to be aware that many procedural topics are classified differently depending on whether they are issues in the federal courts or are under state jurisdiction. For example, issues about the standard for a new trial in federal courts are classified under *Federal Civil Procedure*, key numbers 2365–77. Comparable issues in state court are in the topic *New Trial*. Venue for civil cases in state courts is treated in the topic *Venue*, but for civil cases in federal courts it is in the topic *Federal Courts*, key numbers 71–201. (Venue in criminal cases is treated within the topic *Criminal Law*, for both federal and state courts.)

The list of "Topics by Specialty" in *West's Analysis of American Law*[17] includes separate lists for federal civil procedure and state civil procedure. Some topics (e.g., *Evidence* and *Habeas Corpus*) are common to both. Some are only federal or only state.

3.   Procedural Questions

The key number system can be particularly useful in researching procedural questions, especially online. It is challenging to construct a good word search with common procedural terms (e.g., "juror," "evidence," "trial"). However, using a topic and key number—e.g., *New Trial*, key number 44(3) ("Consideration of matters not in evidence")—can help researchers find relevant cases quickly.

4.   Patents and Trademarks

Sometimes researchers want to be able to find cases adjudicating particular patents or trademarks. West lists these in digests (and in *Westlaw*):

a.   *Patents* key number 328 (291k328) lists adjudicated patents. In print digests, they are in numerical order.

b.   *Trademarks* key number 1800 (382Tk1800) lists adjudicated trademarks. In print digests, they are in alphabetical order.

7–13.   **Page From Volume of Words and Phrases**

---

[17] *See* note 7, *supra.*

[Illustration 7–13]

PAGE FROM VOLUME OF WORDS AND PHRASES

LEARNED INTERMEDIARY DEFENSE

24A W&P— 458

Minn.App. 2003. When the ultimate user, or an intermediary through whom the goods are supplied to the end user, knows or should know of the danger of the goods, the supplier is relieved of its duty to warn; this exception to the duty to warn is commonly called the "sophisticated user doctrine" or "learned intermediary defense."—Gray v. Badger Mining Corp., 664 N.W.2d 881, review granted, reversed 676 N.W.2d 268.—Prod Liab 14.

Nev. 1994. "Mass immunization" exception to "learned intermediary defense" applied in action against manufacturer of measles, mumps and rubella (MMR) vaccine administered by county health district; physician's advice to infant's mother that "it was time" for infant to receive vaccine was not type of "individualized medical judgment" contemplated by learned intermediary defense. (Per Springer, J., with one Justice concurring, Chief Justice concurring in results and two Justices concurring in part and dissenting in part.)—Allison v. Merck and Co., Inc., 878 P.2d 948, 110 Nev. 762.—Prod Liab 46.4.

Tex.App.–San Antonio 2001. Under the "learned intermediary defense" to a products liability action, a manufacturer may fulfill its duty to warn by proving that an adequate warning was given to an intermediary who would then pass the warning along to the user.—Coleman v. Cintas Sales Corp., 40 S.W.3d 544, rehearing denied, and review denied, appeal after remand 100 S.W.3d 384, review denied.—Prod Liab 14.

LEARNED INTERMEDIARY DOCTRINE

C.A.10 (Kan.) 2001. The "learned intermediary doctrine" under Kansas law states that once a manufacturer warns a doctor about a drug's inherent dangers, it has fulfilled its legal duty to provide a warning.—Wright ex rel. Trust Co. of Kansas v. Abbott Laboratories, Inc., 259 F.3d 1226.—Prod Liab 46.2.

C.A.5 (La.) 2002. Under the "learned intermediary doctrine" applied in Louisiana to products liability claims involving prescription drugs, a drug manufacturer discharges its duty to consumers by reasonably informing prescribing physicians of the dangers of harm from a drug. LSA–R.S. 9:2800.57.—Stahl v. Novartis Pharmaceuticals Corp., 283 F.3d 254, rehearing denied, certiorari denied 123 S.Ct. 111, 537 U.S. 824, 154 L.Ed.2d 34.—Prod Liab 46.2.

C.A.5 (La.) 1999. Under "learned intermediary doctrine," seller of medical product has obligation to inform physician of risks of that product.—Theriot v. Danek Medical, Inc., 168 F.3d 253.—Prod Liab 46.1.

C.A.5 (La.) 1999. Pedicle screw manufacturer's alleged failure to adequately test screws did not preclude summary judgment for seller pursuant to "learned intermediary doctrine" on claim under Louisiana Products Liability Act (LPLA) that seller failed to adequately warn plaintiff patient's treating physician of screw's potential side effects; physician testified that he was fully apprised of potential risks. LSA–R.S. 9:2800.52 et seq.—Theriot v. Danek Medical, Inc., 168 F.3d 253.—Prod Liab 46.1.

C.A.5 (La.) 1991. Under Louisiana's "learned intermediary doctrine," manufacturer has no duty to warn patient but need only warn patient's physician.—Willett v. Baxter Intern., Inc., 929 F.2d 1094.—Prod Liab 46.1.

C.A.5 (Miss.) 1992. Mississippi follows "learned intermediary doctrine," under which manufacturer's failure to warn patient of product's risk does not render product defective or unreasonably dangerous so long as manufacturer adequately warns learned intermediary.—Thomas v. Hoffman-La-Roche, Inc., 949 F.2d 806, rehearing denied 957 ~~F.2d 869, certiorari denied 112 S.Ct. 2304, 504 U.S.~~

> The paragraphs in *Words and Phrases* are essentially the same as the headnotes in the volumes of the *National Reporter System*. The pocket supplements and any supplemental pamphlets should always be checked.
>
> If a researcher needs to determine if other courts have defined a word or phrase, e.g., "learned intermediary doctrine," consulting *Words and Phrases* is a valuable time-saver.

excused from warning each patient who receives the drug; the doctor stands as a learned intermediary between the manufacturer and the ultimate consumer.—In re Norplant Contraceptive Products Litigation, 165 F.3d 374, rehearing denied.—Prod Liab 46.2.

C.A.4 (Va.) 1999. The "learned intermediary doctrine" provides an exception to the general rule imposing a duty on manufacturers to warn consumers about the risks of their products, and, for products requiring prescription or application by physicians, the doctrine holds that a manufacturer need only warn doctors and not consumers.—Talley v. Danek Medical, Inc., 179 F.3d 154.—Prod Liab 14.

C.A.10 (Wyo.) 2003. In applying the "learned intermediary doctrine" to an inadequate warning claim, a drug manufacturer has discharged its duty to consumers of its prescription drugs when it has reasonably informed prescribing physicians of the dangers of harm from such a drug; thus, a mere reference to an adverse effect is not necessarily an adequate warning.—Thom v. Bristol-Myers Squibb Co., 353 F.3d 848.—Prod Liab 46.2.

D.Conn. 1999. Under "learned intermediary doctrine" defense to products liability actions, adequate warnings to prescribing physicians obviate the need for manufacturers of prescription products to warn ultimate consumers directly. Restatement (Second) of Torts § 402A comment.—Vitanza v. Upjohn Co., 48 F.Supp.2d 124, question certified 214 F.3d 73, certified question answered 778 A.2d 829, 257 Conn. 365, answer to certified question conformed to 271 F.3d 89, affirmed 271 F.3d 89.—Prod Liab 46.1, 46.2.

N.D.Fla. 1998. Under Florida's "learned intermediary doctrine", manufacturers of prescription medical products have a duty only to warn physicians, rather than patients, of the risks associated

Chapter 8

CONSTITUTIONAL LAW AND THE
SUPREME COURT OF THE UNITED STATES

A constitution is the organic or fundamental law of a governmental entity. That is, the constitution is the document that sets out governmental structure, the rights and responsibilities of citizens, and the basic procedures by which the government acts. This is true of the federal constitution for the United States, as well as the state constitutions for each of the states;[1] it is also generally true for all countries of the world that have constitutions.

This chapter discusses researching U.S. constitutional law and the institution of the Supreme Court of the United States, as well as state constitutional law and the constitutions of other countries. The chapter does not include discussions of the reports of the opinions of the Supreme Court or the records and briefs of the Court; they are discussed in other chapters of this book.[2]

A. RESEARCHING THE U.S. CONSTITUTION AND CONSTITUTIONAL LAW

The Constitution of the United States is the highest law of the country.[3] It is embodied in the written document that was drafted at Philadelphia in the summer of 1787, plus the amendments that have since been added. Researching and proposing solutions to problems in constitutional law require reference to the document itself[4] and

---

[1] County and municipal charters can also be considered constitutions, being the fundamental documents for their respective government. More information can be found in Chapter 11, Section G. Indian tribes also have constitutions. *See* Chapter 25.

[2] Supreme Court opinions are discussed in Chapter 5 along with other federal court reports. Supreme Court records and briefs are discussed in Chapter 20.

[3] By the words of the Constitution itself, the "Constitution, and the Laws of the United States which shall be made in pursuance thereof; and all treaties made, or which shall be made, under the authority of the United States, shall be the supreme law of the land." U.S. CONST. art. VI, cl. 2. Referred to as the "supremacy clause," this language requires that federal laws and treaties must be consistent with the provisions of the Constitution. The judicial branch's role in the checks and balances established by the Constitution is to ensure that no acts of the other governmental branches become unreviewable. Chief Justice John Marshall noted that "[c]ertainly all those who have framed written constitutions contemplate them as forming the fundamental and paramount law of the nation, and consequently the theory of every such government must be, that an act of the legislature, repugnant to the constitution, is void." Marbury v. Madison, 5 U.S. 137, 177 (1803). Similarly, Justice Hugo Black clarified the status of treaties vis-à-vis the Constitution when he stated that "[t]he obvious and decisive answer to this, of course, is that no agreement with a foreign nation can confer power on the Congress, or on any other branch of Government, which is free from the restraints of the Constitution." Reid v. Covert, 354 U.S. 1, 16 (1957).

[4] The text of the Constitution and its amendments is readily available. In addition to being included with the official *United States Code* and the annotated federal codes (discussed in this section), it is typically included in sets of state annotated codes, as well as in constitutional law texts and casebooks, law dictionaries, and a multitude of Internet websites, e.g., U.S. CONSTITUTION, http://www.usconstitution.net/const.html;

consulting sources that assist in understanding its interpretation.[5] These sources can include interpretations of the Constitution by the Supreme Court of the United States as found in its reports of decisions, as well as interpretations by other courts, commentaries on the Constitution in treatises, monographs, legal periodicals, encyclopedias, and other secondary sources, and the records of the Constitutional Convention and documents contemporary to that period.

1.   Judicial Interpretations

a.   Annotated Editions of the U.S. Constitution

Some of the most useful sources for identifying citations to court decisions that interpret the Constitution are the various annotated editions of the Constitution. These publications provide case abstracts and citations, and often commentary, for cases interpreting each article, section, and clause of the Constitution and its amendments.

(1) *The Constitution of the United States of America: Analysis and Interpretation* (Centennial ed. 2014). This annotated, one-volume edition is prepared by the Congressional Research Service of the Library of Congress,[6] as authorized by a Joint Congressional Resolution.[7] This is often the preferred starting point for research on constitutional questions by scholars. The publication provides analysis and commentary for each article, section, and clause of the Constitution and its amendments. Important cases decided by the Supreme Court of the United States are discussed in the analysis, and citations to cases are given in the footnotes. [Illustrations 8–4 and 8–5] Frequently, the commentary quotes from the proceedings of the Constitutional Convention, opinions of dissenting justices, and other documents, to provide greater context and meaning to the analysis.

This volume, unlike the other works discussed below, does not attempt to cite or comment on all cases of the Supreme Court, but rather refers only to the more significant ones. It is the best place to begin researching proposed amendments, both those pending and ones not ratified. It has a detailed subject index and several useful tables, including:

- Acts of Congress held unconstitutional in whole or in part by the Supreme Court of the United States;

Cornell's *Legal Information Institute*, http://www.law.cornell.edu/constitution/; and the UNITED STATES SENATE, http://www.senate.gov/civics/constitution_item/constitution.htm.

[5] For an introduction to the various methods of constitutional interpretation, see, e.g., SOTIRIOS A. BARBER & JAMES E. FLEMING, CONSTITUTIONAL INTERPRETATION: THE BASIC QUESTIONS (2007). Two contrasting approaches to constitutional interpretation are explained by sitting justices. STEPHEN G. BREYER, ACTIVE LIBERTY: INTERPRETING OUR DEMOCRATIC CONSTITUTION (2005); ANTONIN SCALIA, A MATTER OF INTERPRETATION: FEDERAL COURTS AND THE LAW (1997). See also SHELLEY L. DOWLING, THE JURISPRUDENCE OF UNITED STATES CONSTITUTIONAL INTERPRETATION: AN ANNOTATED BIBLIOGRAPHY (2d ed. 2010), which provides annotated entries to more than 900 collections of documents, treatises, articles, electronic resources, and other items focusing on constitutional interpretation.

[6] THE CONSTITUTION OF THE UNITED STATES OF AMERICA: ANALYSIS AND INTERPRETATION, S. DOC. NO. 112–9 (2014), *available at* http://www.gpo.gov/fdsys/pkg/GPO-CONAN-REV-2014/pdf/GPO-CONAN-REV-2014.pdf, Earlier editions, beginning with the 1992 edition, are also available on *FDsys*. Cornell's *Legal Information Institute* offers a version of this with hyperlinks to the Supreme Court cases it cites, at http://www.law.cornell.edu/anncon/.

[7] 2 U.S.C. § 168 (2006). This Joint Resolution provides for a new edition every ten years with supplements to be issued biennially. The 2013 edition covers cases decided through June 26, 2013. The biennial supplement typically only updates the volume to within about a year of the date the supplement was issued.

- State constitutional and statutory provisions and municipal ordinances held unconstitutional or held to be preempted by federal law; and

- Supreme Court decisions overruled by subsequent Supreme Court decisions.

(2) *United States Code Annotated, Constitution of the United States Annotated* (Thomson West). This set is published as part of the *United States Code Annotated* (*U.S.C.A.*). Each article, section, and clause of the Constitution is annotated. Each annotation begins with *Library References* to relevant secondary sources and cross-references to pertinent sections in the *U.S.C.A.* Next are *Notes of Decisions*, which are digest paragraphs from all cases that have interpreted that constitutional provision or amendment. The publisher often provides a small index to the annotation itself, when there are enough cases noted to warrant further organization. [See Illustrations 8–1 through 8–3 for the method of locating a constitutional provision and the notes.]

These volumes are properly shelved at the beginning of the *U.S.C.A.* set. They are updated annually with pocket parts or supplementary pamphlets. A subject index to the Constitution is included at the end of the last volume of the set. An electronic version of the *U.S.C.A. Constitution of the United States Annotated* is available in *Westlaw.*

(3) *United States Code Service, Constitution* (LexisNexis). This is a separate unit of the *United States Code Service* (*U.S.C.S.*). It includes extensive references to articles, annotations, judicial opinions, and other resources that interpret provisions of the Constitution. These Constitution volumes are organized and updated in much the same way as those of the *U.S.C.A.* and are used in a similar manner, with the last volume containing a subject index. An electronic version of the *U.S.C.S., Constitution* set is available in *LexisNexis.*

b. *Digests of Federal Court Reports.* Digests of federal cases provide another way to access judicial interpretations of the Constitution.[8] See Chapter 7 for an explanation of case digests.

c. *Annotations.* Annotations on a variety of constitutional law topics can be found in *A.L.R. Federal* and the *U.S. Supreme Court Reports, Lawyers' Edition.*[9] *A.L.R.* is available in print and in *Westlaw* and *LexisNexis.*

d. *Online Research Services.* Case databases in *Westlaw, LexisNexis, Bloomberg Law*, and other computer-assisted legal research services can be searched using key terms from and citations to the Constitution to retrieve cases dealing with the specified constitutional language. Electronic legal research is discussed in Chapter 22.

e. *Citators. Shepard's* and *KeyCite* provide references to cases citing or construing the Constitution. Citators are discussed in Chapter 15.

f. *Compilations of Cases.* There are a number of works that compile selected cases of the U.S. Supreme Court. These are useful resources for identifying key or leading cases. While many of these works focus on a particular topic (Indian law, antitrust,

---

[8] State and regional digests contain digest paragraphs for federal cases arising within their jurisdictional coverage. State and regional digests also include information about state cases interpreting the federal constitution.

[9] *A.L.R., A.L.R.2d*, and *A.L.R.3d*, which predated *A.L.R. Fed.* also include annotations on federal topics, including constitutional law. The *American Law Reports* series are discussed in Chapter 17.

abortion, etc.), several of the general compilations include Donald E. Lively & Russell L. Weaver, *Contemporary Supreme Court Cases: Landmark Decisions since* Roe v. Wade (2006); Gary Hartman et al., *Landmark Supreme Court Cases* (2006); and Paul Finkelman & Melvin I. Urofsky, *Landmark Decisions of the United States Supreme Court* (2003).

2.   Secondary Sources: Commentaries on Constitutional Law

Constitutional case commentary by legal scholars is voluminous. Secondary sources, which are useful in gaining an understanding of context and an in-depth meaning of constitutional principles and interpretations, include monographs, treatises, encyclopedias, and periodical articles. Some of the most well-known sources are listed below.[10]

a.   The six-volume *Encyclopedia of the American Constitution*, edited by Leonard W. Levy & Kenneth L. Karst (2d ed. 2000) (Macmillan Publishing Co.) contains approximately 2,400 articles written by 237 authors, who include lawyers, historians, and political scientists. The articles contain both practical and theoretical perspectives, and deal with almost every aspect of constitutional law, beginning with the document's drafting. Many of the encyclopedia entries deal with individual cases. Some of the articles contain useful references to additional sources.

b.   Those interested in researching the twenty-seven amendments to the Constitution should consult *Constitutional Amendments, 1789 to date* (Kris E. Palmer ed., 2000) (Gale). This volume devotes a chapter to each amendment, analyzing the provision and providing context and arguments. A final chapter discusses failed amendments.

c.   While all law dictionaries provide definitions of terms bearing on constitutional law, the two-volume *Constitutional Law Dictionary*, by Ralph C. Chandler et al. (1985 and 1987) (ABC-CLIO) is intended specifically for this purpose. Volume 1 is subtitled *Individual Rights*, volume 2 *Governmental Powers*. Each volume contains a summary of approximately 300 cases organized in a subject-matter chapter format. This arrangement is followed by several hundred definitions. It is supplemented through the 1993 Supreme Court term.

d.   Highly regarded contemporary treatises on the subject of constitutional law are Laurence H. Tribe's *American Constitutional Law* (3d ed. 2000); the three-volume *Treatise on Constitutional Law: Substance and Procedure*, by Ronald D. Rotunda and John E. Nowak (3d ed. 2011); and the three-volume *Modern Constitutional Law*, by William J. Rich and Chester James Antieau (3d ed. 2011). Constitutional law casebooks[11] and legal periodicals[12] also provide analysis and interpretation of judicial decisions.

e.   *HeinOnline*'s World Constitutions Illustrated library includes hundreds of historic treatises, periodical articles, and other material on the United States

---

[10] Secondary sources are covered in Chapters 10, 14, 16, 17, 18, 19, and 20.

[11] A good example is KATHLEEN M. SULLIVAN & GERALD GUNTHER, CONSTITUTIONAL LAW (17th ed. 2010).

[12] Almost all legal periodicals publish articles on constitutional issues. Some, however, are devoted to these topics, such as the University of Minnesota's *Constitutional Commentary*, Seton Hall University's *Constitutional Law Journal, George Mason Civil Rights Law Journal, Harvard Civil Rights—Civil Liberties Law Review, Hastings Constitutional Law Quarterly*, University of Pennsylvania's *Journal of Constitutional Law, Texas Journal on Civil Liberties & Civil Rights*, and *William and Mary Bill of Rights Journal*. Legal periodicals are discussed in Chapter 18.

Constitution. A bibliography links to *WorldCat* records for books listed, to enable researchers to find the books in their local libraries.

3. Records of the Constitutional Convention and Other Historical Sources

In constitutional research, it is often important to determine the meaning of the document's words as used by those who drafted it. Therefore, researchers turn to sources that preceded the adoption of the Constitution, such as documents of the Continental Congress or the Articles of Confederation.[13]

Major historical sources can be located in the Library of Congress Legislative Reference Service's *Documents Illustrative of the Formation of the Union of the American States*.[14] Also useful is *Documentary History of the Constitution of the United States of America, 1786–1870*.[15] Indispensable are the essays of Madison, Jay, and Hamilton published as *The Federalist*.[16] Thurston Green's *The Language of the Constitution: A Sourcebook and Guide to the Ideas, Terms, and Vocabulary Used by the Framers of the United States Constitution* (1991) discusses the language used in drafting the Constitution. Major Internet collections include the Library of Congress's "Primary Documents in American History"[17] and "The Federalist Papers."[18]

Although the Constitutional Convention did not keep official records of its secret sessions, the most widely accepted source for insights into the debates is Max Farrand's three-volume (plus index) *Records of the Federal Convention of 1787* (1911).[19] For understanding the ratification process by the states, a valuable source is *Elliot's*

---

[13] *See, e.g.*, Morrison v. Olson, 487 U.S. 654, 674 (1988) (citing RECORDS OF THE FEDERAL CONVENTION OF 1787 (Max Farrand ed., 1966)); Welch v. Texas Dept. of Highways, 483 U.S. 468, 481 n.10 (1987) (citing ELLIOT'S DEBATES, 2d ed. 1861); Atascadero State Hosp. v. Scanlon, 473 U.S. 234, 271 (1985) (Brennan, J., dissenting) (citing DOCUMENTARY HISTORY OF THE RATIFICATION OF THE CONSTITUTION). Many of these sources, as well as other sources on the historical development of the Constitution, are available in *Westlaw* in the Legislative History–1776 (database identifier LH-1776) database.

[14] H.R. DOC. NO. 69–398 (Charles C. Tansill comp., 1927) (available in *HeinOnline*). *See also* SOL BLOOM, HISTORY OF THE FORMATION OF THE UNION UNDER THE CONSTITUTION (1941) (available in *HeinOnline*). For background on the Articles of Confederation, see William F. Swindler, *Our First Constitution: The Articles of Confederation*, 67 A.B.A. J. 166 (1961). For documents pertaining to the adoption of the Bill of Rights, see BERNARD SCHWARTZ, THE BILL OF RIGHTS: A DOCUMENTARY HISTORY (1971, 2 vols.), and THE COMPLETE BILL OF RIGHTS: THE DRAFTS, DEBATES, SOURCES, AND ORIGINS (Neil H. Cogan ed., 1997).

[15] (1894–1905; reprinted in 1965 by Johnson Reprint Corp. and available in *HeinOnline*).

[16] *The Federalist* has been published in many editions and is widely available on the Internet. *See, e.g.*, "The Federalist Papers," at the Library of Congress's *THOMAS* website. *THOMAS* is being replaced by *Congress.gov* in late 2014. (http://thomas.loc.gov/home/histdox/fedpapers.html). *See also* JAMES MADISON, THE PAPERS OF JAMES MADISON (Henry D. Gilpin ed., 1840).

[17] http://www.loc.gov/rr/program/bib/ourdocs/federalist.html.

[18] http://thomas.loc.gov/home/histdox/fedpapers.html.

[19] This is available in *HeinOnline* and through the Library of Congress's American Memory project at http://memory.loc.gov/ammem/amlaw/lwfr.html. *See also* JAMES H. HUTSON, SUPPLEMENT TO MAX FARRAND'S THE RECORDS OF THE FEDERAL CONVENTION OF 1787 (1987); WILBOURN E. BENTON, 1787: DRAFTING THE U.S. CONSTITUTION (1986) (2 vols.).

Debates.[20] The *Documentary History of the Ratification of the Constitution*[21] is the most comprehensive and up-to-date source of the history of the ratification of the U.S. Constitution.

The Founders' Constitution, edited by Philip B. Kurland and Ralph Lerner (1987)[22] is a five-volume set (print and online) that reproduces an extensive collection of documents that explain and discuss the text of the Constitution, from the Preamble through the Twelfth Amendment. The documents were written prior to or at the time the Constitution was drafted and debated. Volume 1 is arranged by theme and highlights the debate over the principles embodied in the Constitution, volumes 2 through 4 are arranged to correspond to the text of the Constitution, and volume 5 is devoted to the First through Twelfth Amendments.

Researchers seeking an extensive listing of secondary sources on the Constitution should consult Kermit L. Hall's *A Comprehensive Bibliography of American Constitutional and Legal History, 1896–1979.*[23] This five-volume set contains over 68,000 entries for books, journal articles, and doctoral dissertations. It is divided into seven chapters: general surveys and texts, institutions, constitutional doctrine, legal doctrine, biographical, chronological, and geographical.

B. ILLUSTRATIONS

The following illustrate an approach to researching this problem:

In a products liability case where suit was brought against a prescription drug manufacturer, *Abbot v. American Cyanamid Co.*, 844 F.2d 1108 (4th Cir. 1988), the issue related to defective design and failure to warn. Does federal law preempt state common law liability?

8–1. **Page from Volume Containing Index to Constitution: U.S.C.A.**

8–2. **Page from a Constitution Volume: U.S.C.A.**

8–3. **Page Showing Notes of Decisions from a Constitution Volume: U.S.C.A.**

8–4 to 8–5. **Pages from The Constitution of the United States of America**

---

[20] JONATHAN ELLIOT, THE DEBATES, RESOLUTIONS, AND OTHER PROCEEDINGS, IN CONVENTION, ON THE ADOPTION OF THE FEDERAL CONSTITUTION (1827). This set has appeared in many editions with different titles and somewhat different content, all known generally as *Elliot's Debates*. The most complete edition was published in five volumes in 1937. It is also available through the Library of Congress's *American Memory Project* at http://memory.loc.gov/ammem/amlaw/lwed.html and in *HeinOnline*.

[21] (Merrill Jensen et al. eds., 1976–). Twenty-six of a projected thirty volumes have been published. More information about the project is at http://www.wisconsinhistory.org/ratification/.

[22] Originally published by University of Chicago Press in 1987, it was reprinted, with permission, by the Liberty Fund in 2000). It is available at http://press-pubs.uchicago.edu/founders/tocs/toc.html.

[23] (1984). A two-volume supplement covers 1980 to 1987.

[Illustration 8–1]

PAGE FROM VOLUME CONTAINING INDEX TO CONSTITUTION: U.S.C.A.

INDEX

SUPREME LAW OF THE LAND
Generally, **U.S. Const. Art. VI cl. 2**

SURRENDER
See specific index headings

SUSPENSION
See specific index headings

TARIFFS
Customs Duties, generally, this index

TAXATION
Congress, levy, **U.S. Const. Art. I § 8, cl. 1**
Constitution of the United States, this index
Direct taxes, apportionment, **U.S. Const. Art. I § 2, cl. 3**
Elections, privileges and immunities, **U.S. Const. Am. XXIV**
Exports and Imports, this index
Indians, this index
Slavery, traffic, **U.S. Const. Art. I § 9, cl. 1**
Uniformity, **U.S. Const. Art. I § 8, cl. 1**

> The first step in researching a problem involving the United States Constitution is to look in the volume containing the index to the Constitution. For the problem under research, Article 6, Clause 2 should be examined.

TIME
See specific index headings

TONS AND TONNAGE
Ships and Shipping, this index

TRAFFICKING
Slavery, this index

TRAINING CAMPS
Bases, installations and reservations. Armed Forces, this index

TRANSPORTATION
Alcoholic Beverages, this index

TREASON
Constitution of the United States, this index
Extradition, **U.S. Const. Art. IV § 2, cl. 2**
Fines, penalties and forfeitures, **U.S. Const. Art. III § 3, cl. 2**
United States, impeachment, **U.S. Const. Art. II § 4**

TREASURY OF UNITED STATES
Coins and Coinage, generally, this index

TREATIES
Constitution of the United States, this index
Jurisdiction, **U.S. Const. Art. III § 2, cl. 1**
Powers and duties, **U.S. Const. Art. II § 2, cl. 2**

I–47

[Illustration 8−2]

PAGE FROM A CONSTITUTION VOLUME: U.S.C.A.

SUPREME LAW OF LAND   Art. 6

Restatement (Second) of Judgments § 28, Exceptions to the General Rule of Issue
Preclusion.

WESTLAW COMPUTER ASSISTED LEGAL RESEARCH

Westlaw supplements your legal research in many ways. Westlaw allows
you to
- update your research with the most current information
- expand your library with additional resources
- retrieve current, comprehensive history citing references to a case with
  KeyCite

For more information on using Westlaw to supplement your research, see the
Westlaw Electronic Research Guide, which follows the Explanation.

Clause 1. Debts Validated

All Debts contracted and Engagements entered into, before the
Adoption of this Constitution, shall be as valid against the United

This shows the text of the constitutional provision covering
federal supremacy in a Constitution volume of the *United States
Code Annotated*. Note the references to additional useful sources.
This set and the *United States Code Service* are kept current by
annual pocket supplements and subsequent pamphlets.

This Constitution, and the Laws of the United States which shall be
made in Pursuance thereof; and all Treaties made, or which shall be
made, under the Authority of the United States, shall be the supreme
Law of the Land; and the Judges in every State shall be bound
thereby, any Thing in the Constitution or Laws of any State to the
Contrary notwithstanding.

LAW REVIEW AND JOURNAL COMMENTARIES

Adjudication of federal causes of action in state court. Martin H. Redish and John
     E. Muench, 75 Mich.L.Rev. 311 (1976).
Adventures in federalism: some observations on the overlapping sphere of state
     and federal constitutional law. Jennifer Friesen, 3 Widener J.Pub.L. 25
     (1993).
Are the judicial safeguards of federalism the ultimate form of conservative judicial
     activism?. Saikrishna Prakash, 73 U.Colo.L.Rev. 1363 (2002).
Assault on Securities Act Section 12(2). Louis Loss, 105 Harv.L.Rev. 908 (1992).
Assuring federal facility compliance with the RCRA and other environmental
     statutes: An administrative proposal. Note, 28 Wm. & Mary L.Rev. 513
     (1987).
Automobile passive restraint claims post-Cipollone: An end to the federal preemp-
     tion defense. Comment, 46 Baylor L.Rev. 141 (1994).

466

[Illustration 8-3]

PAGE SHOWING NOTES OF DECISIONS FROM A CONSTITUTION VOLUME: U.S.C.A.

Art. VI cl. 2

SUPREME LAW OF LAND

Tender offers, securities regulation, miscellaneous laws or acts 410

Termination of employment, bankruptcy, miscellaneous laws or acts 328

Tort liability, state regulation of federal instrumentalities and property 167

Trade secrets, miscellaneous laws or acts 414

Transportation, miscellaneous laws or acts 415

Transportation, state regulation of federal instrumentalities and property 168

Treaties 41-90

Treaties as supreme generally 41

Treaties within clause 42, 43
    Generally 42
    Conventions 43

Trial by jury, courts and judicial procedure 268

Unemployment compensation, employment matters, miscellaneous laws or acts 356

Unemployment taxes, state taxation 227

Voting rights, miscellaneous laws or acts 419

War measures, courts and judicial procedure 269

War measures, miscellaneous laws or acts 420

War measures, state regulation of federal instrumentalities and property 170

Water rights, miscellaneous laws or acts 421

Water rights, state regulation of federal instrumentalities and property 171

Waterways safety, miscellaneous laws or acts 422

Weapons regulation, miscellaneous laws or acts 423

Welfare, miscellaneous laws or acts 397-400

Wills, trusts and estates, miscellaneous laws or acts 424

Wills, trusts and estates, state regulation of federal instrumentalities and property 172

> After the text of each clause of the Constitution are digest paragraphs of all cases that have interpreted the clause. These paragraphs are preceded by an index to these paragraphs.

Usury, miscellaneous laws or acts 417

Utilities, miscellaneous laws or acts 418

Utilities, state regulation of federal instrumentalities and property 169

Utility taxes, state taxation 228

matters, miscellaneous laws or acts 357

Wrongful death, miscellaneous laws or acts 425

Zoning, miscellaneous laws or acts 426

I. GENERALLY
Subdivision Index

Concurrent sovereignty of state and federal governments 10

Constitution as supreme 2, 3
    Generally 2
    Foreign relations and intercourse 3

Exhaustion of administrative remedies 13

Federal district courts, persons bound by supreme law 6

Foreign relations and intercourse, Constitution as supreme 3

International law 9

Persons bound by supreme law 5-8
    Generally 5
    Federal district courts 6
    State legislatures 7
    United States Supreme Court 8

Persons entitled to maintain action 12

Private rights of action 11

Purpose 1

State legislatures, persons bound by supreme law 7

States 4

United States Supreme Court, persons bound by supreme law 8

1. Purpose

The purpose of this clause was to avoid the disparities, confusions and conflicts that would follow if the federal government's general authority were subject to local controls. U. S. v. Allegheny County, Pa., U.S.Pa.1944, 64 S.Ct. 908, 322 U.S. 174, 88 L.Ed. 1209. States ⟐ 18.1; Constitutional Law ⟐ 1.1

This clause was intended to eliminate right of any state to regulate operations of federal government without its express consent. U. S. v. State Corp. Commission of Com. of Va., E.D.Va.1972, 345 F.Supp. 843, affirmed 93 S.Ct. 912, 409

[Illustration 8–4]

PAGE FROM THE CONSTITUTION OF THE UNITED STATES
OF AMERICA (LIBRARY OF CONGRESS)

PRIOR DEBTS, NATIONAL SUPREMACY, AND OATHS OF OFFICE

ARTICLE VI

Clause 1. All Debts contracted and Engagements entered into, before the Adoption of this Constitution, shall be as valid against the United States under this Constitution, as under the Confederation.

PRIOR DEBTS

There have been no interpretations of this clause.

Clause 2. This Constitution, and the Laws of the United States which shall be made in Pursuance thereof; and all Treaties made, or which shall be made, under the Authority of the United States, shall be the supreme Law of the Land; and the Judges in every State shall be bound thereby; any Thing in the Constitution or Laws of any State to the Contrary notwithstanding.

NATIONAL SUPREMACY

Marshall's Interpretation of the National Supremacy Clause

Although the Supreme Court had held, prior to Marshall's appointment to the Bench, that the Supremacy Clause rendered null and void a state constitutional or statutory provision which was in-

> This one-volume edition of the Constitution sets forth the full text of each Article, Section, and Clause of the Constitution and its Amendments. Analysis and commentary follow immediately, in smaller type.

which survived a century of vacillation under the doctrine of dual federalism. In the former case, he asserted broadly that "the States have no power, by taxation or otherwise, to retard, impede, burden, or in any manner control, the operations of the constitutional laws

---

[1] Ware v. Hylton, 3 U.S. (3 Dall.) 199 (1796).
[2] 17 U.S. (4 Wheat.) 316 (1819).
[3] 22 U.S. (9 Wheat.) 1 (1824).

959

[Illustration 8–5]

PAGE FROM THE CONSTITUTION OF THE UNITED STATES OF AMERICA (LIBRARY OF CONGRESS)

960   ART. VI—PRIOR DEBTS, SUPREMACY CLAUSE, ETC.

Cl. 2—Supremacy of the Constitution, Laws, and Treaties

enacted by Congress to carry into execution the powers vested in the general government. This is, we think, the unavoidable consequence of that supremacy which the Constitution has declared."[4] From this he concluded that a state tax upon notes issued by a branch of the Bank of the United States was void.

In *Gibbons v. Ogden*, the Court held that certain statutes of New York granting an exclusive right to use steam navigation on the waters of the State were null and void insofar as they applied to vessels licensed by the United States to engage in coastal trade. Said the Chief Justice: "In argument, however, it has been contended, that if a law passed by a State, in the exercise of its acknowledged sovereignty, comes into conflict with a law passed by Congress in pursuance of the Constitution, they affect the subject

> Analysis of the Supremacy Clause by the editors of the volume.
> Footnotes contain citations to cases mentioned in the analysis.

stitution, is produced by the declaration, that the Constitution is the supreme law. The appropriate application of that part of the clause which confers the same supremacy on laws and treaties, is to such acts of the State legislatures as do not transcend their powers, but though enacted in the execution of acknowledged State powers, interfere with, or are contrary to the laws of Congress, made in pursuance of the Constitution, or some treaty made under the authority of the United States. In every such case, the act of Congress, or the treaty, is supreme; and the law of the State, though enacted in the exercise of powers not controverted, must yield to it."[5]

Task of the Supreme Court Under the Clause: Preemption

In applying the Supremacy Clause to subjects which have been regulated by Congress, the primary task of the Court is to ascertain whether a challenged state law is compatible with the policy expressed in the federal statute. When Congress legislates with regard to a subject, the extent and nature of the legal consequences of the regulation are federal questions, the answers to which are to be derived from a consideration of the language and policy of the state. If Congress expressly provides for exclusive federal dominion or if it expressly provides for concurrent federal-state jurisdiction, the task of the Court is simplified, though, of course, there may still be doubtful areas in which interpretation will be necessary.

---

[4] 17 U.S. (4 Wheat.) 436 (1819).

[5] 22 U.S. (9 Wheat.) 210-211 (1824). *See* the Court's discussion of *Gibbons* in Douglas v. Seacoast Products, 431 U.S. 265, 274-279 (1977).

C. RESEARCHING THE SUPREME COURT OF THE UNITED STATES AND ITS JUSTICES

Most Supreme Court advocates, as well as law students and scholars writing papers, find it important to understand not only the Supreme Court's jurisprudence but also its members and even its history. It is critical to understand the institution of the Court itself as well as those who sit on its bench to predict the manner in which the Court will interpret the Constitution. As Justice Byron R. White observed, "[E]very time a new justice comes to the Supreme Court, it's a different court."[24]

There is a tremendous range of material, print and electronic, devoted to the Supreme Court, its practices and history, and its justices. Law school libraries, in particular, will have many more titles those listed here. This section describes only some of the best known and highly useful resources focusing on these topics.

1. Current Events and Reference Resources

a. The official website of the Supreme Court[25] contains useful information about the court, especially including biographies of current members, caseload information, court traditions, and a variety of sources important to briefing a case and preparing for a hearing. The website also contains Court rules, opinions since 1991, orders since 2003, *The Journal of the Supreme Court of the United States* since 1993, transcripts of oral arguments since 2000, dockets, and the current calendar.

b. *SCOTUS Blog* is a rich source of information, commentary, and analysis about the Court, especially for pending and recently decided cases.[26] The blog is written primarily by attorneys in private practice. It provides brief analyses, with extensive links, of cases and issues before the Court, news of Court activities, links to relevant blogs and websites, sources of Supreme Court opinions, statistics, judicial biographies, and other Court-related information.

c. *Preview of United States Supreme Court Cases*, an online subscription service published by the American Bar Association's Public Education Division, presents essays written by scholars about selected cases pending but not yet argued.[27] These essays provide excellent background and analysis of the cases that the Court subsequently will decide. *Preview* also has archived issues with analysis of cases from previous terms, briefs, and Court calendars.

d. Lawrence Baum, *The Supreme Court* (11th ed. 2013). This volume provides an introduction to the Court generally, with chapters focusing on the Court, the justices, cases, decision-making, policy outputs, and the Court's impact.

e. Lee Epstein, Jeffrey A. Segal, Harold J. Spaeth & Thomas G. Walker, *The Supreme Court Compendium: Data, Decisions, and Developments* (5th ed. 2012). This volume is filled with tables on such matters as trends in Supreme Court decision-

---

[24] *See* DENNIS J. HUTCHINSON, THE MAN WHO ONCE WAS WHIZZER WHITE: A PORTRAIT OF JUSTICE BYRON R. WHITE 467 (1998).

[25] http://www.supremecourt.gov.

[26] http://www.scotusblog.com.

[27] http://www.americanbar.org/publications/preview_home/alphabetical.html.

making, post-confirmation activities of the Court, and the political and legal environments in which the Court operates.

f.   Encyclopedia of the Supreme Court (Davis Schultz ed., 2005). This alphabetically arranged volume includes entries on famous cases, legal terms, and profiles of justices.

g.   The Oxford Companion to the Supreme Court of the United States (2d ed. Kermit L. Hall ed., 2005). This single-volume, encyclopedic compilation includes more than 400 alphabetically arranged summaries of important cases decided by the Court, legal terms and concepts, justices, important court personnel and practitioners.

h.   The Oyez Project at Chicago–Kent[28] is a multimedia archive devoted to the Supreme Court of the United States and its work. It aims to be a complete and authoritative source for all audio recorded in the Court since the installation of a recording system in October 1955. The Project also provides authoritative information on all justices and the Supreme Court building.

i.   David G. Savage, *Guide to the U.S. Supreme Court* (5th ed. 2010). The two-volume set provides an in-depth narrative overview of the workings and history of the Court.

j.   Richard Seamon et al., *The Supreme Court Sourcebook* (2013). This textbook presents a rich assortment of material about the Supreme Court and its justices. In addition to excerpts from books and articles, it also presents some materials from justices' personal papers showing the Court's internal processes (e.g., memos to justices about whether to grant *certiorari* in *Bowers v. Hardwick*, at 235–50, and Chief Justice Warren's conference notes, drafts, and other documents in *Miranda v. Arizona*, at 466, 491–509).

k.   Supreme Court of the United States: A Bibliography with Indexes (George H. Rutland ed., 2006).

l.   The Supreme Court, A to Z (Kenneth Jost ed., 5th ed. 2012). This single-volume work has brief entries on constitutional issues and individual justices. Arranged alphabetically, use of the volume is aided by an extensive index, a compilation of Court milestones and a selected bibliography.

m.   Supreme Court of the United States: A Bibliography with Indexes (George A. Rutland ed., 2006). This is a bibliography of print primary and secondary sources about the Court and individual justices.

n.   The Supreme Court Database.[29] The datasets provided in this site have been developed over more than twenty years, and have become the definitive source of empirical research on the Court. The site's goal is to include and classify every single vote by a Supreme Court justice in all argued cases; its coverage as of June 2014 begins with the 1946 term and concludes with the 2013 term. Data can be manipulated by subject, year, Court term, parties, votes, and a wide range of other criteria. There is no cost to access or use the data.

---

[28] http://www.oyez.org/.

[29] http://supremecourtdatabase.org.

2. Histories of the Court

The Supreme Court Historical Society website includes timelines, brief biographies of all Supreme Court justices, and more.[30] "Researching the Supreme Court of the United States: Available Resources for Commonly-Asked Questions"[31] contains significant guidance on historical research into a variety of Court-related areas.

The following is a brief selection of general histories that have been written of the Court.[32]

a.   Chester James Antieau, *Our Two Centuries of Law and Life 1775–1975: The Work of the Supreme Court and the Impact of Both Congress and the Presidents* (2001) (available in *HeinOnline*). The volume focuses on the interaction of Supreme Court decisions with presidential and congressional actions.

b.   Hampton L. Carson, *The Supreme Court of the United States: Its History* (1892) (available in *HeinOnline*). This classic work was written to commemorate the 100th anniversary of the Supreme Court.

c.   *The Oliver Wendell Holmes Devise: History of the Supreme Court of the United States* (Paul A. Freund & Stanley Katz eds., 1971–present). The most scholarly and comprehensive history of the Court, written by leading scholars; eleven of the projected fourteen volumes are available.

d.   Peter Irons, *A People's History of the Supreme Court* (2d ed. 2006). This volume provides an accessible history of the Court, focusing on the Court's most well-known decisions.

e.   *The Documentary History of the Supreme Court of the United States, 1789–1800* (Maeva Marcus & James R. Perry eds., 1895–2007) (available in *HeinOnline*). This eight-volume set gathers all original materials to reconstitute the record of the first eleven years of the Court.

f.   Jeffrey A. Segal, Harold J. Spaeth & Sara C. Benesh, *The Supreme Court in the American Legal System* (2005). This volume examines both the history of the Supreme Court and its relationship with lower courts.

g.   Robert Shnayerson, *The Illustrated History of the Supreme Court of the United States* (1986). Numerous portraits, photographs, and reproductions of historical documents are included in this introductory history of the Court.

The following journals focus on the history and work of the Court.

a.   The *Journal of Supreme Court History* (formerly *Yearbook of the Supreme Court Historical Society, 1976–1990*; Blackwell Publishing 1990–present). Published three times annually by the Supreme Court Historical Society, this journal provides in-depth articles on former justices and their Courts.

b.   *The Supreme Court Historical Society Quarterly* (1978–present). Published quarterly by the Supreme Court Historical Society, this pamphlet publishes current

---

[30] http://www.supremecourthistory.org.

[31] http://www.supremecourthistory.org/supremecourthistory/inc/schs_researching-the-court.pdf (2008).

[32] *HeinOnline*'s U.S. Supreme Court Library includes hundreds of books, most from the nineteenth and early twentieth centuries.

awareness articles about the Court and upcoming Society events, along with short articles focusing on the Court's history.

3. Case Selection and Decision-Making

Because the Supreme Court grants review to such a small percentage of the eligible cases, the Court's selection of cases has been a focus of much research. Similarly, the Court's decision-making process is the subject of a tremendous amount of scrutiny because of the potential impact of each case. The following works focus on the factors that influence Supreme Court case selection and decision-making.

   a.   Ryan C. Black & Ryan J. Owens, *The Solicitor General and the United States Supreme Court: Executive Branch Influence and Judicial Decisions* (2012).

   b.   *Supreme Court Decision Making: New Institutionalist Approaches* (Cornell W. Clayton & Harold Gillman eds., 1999).

   c.   Felix Frankfurter & James M. Landis, *The Business of the Supreme Court: A Study in the Federal Judicial System* (1928).

   d.   Lisa A. Kloppenberg, *Playing It Safe: How the Supreme Court Sidesteps Hard Cases and Stunts the Development of Law* (2001).

   e.   Richard L. Pacelle, *Decision Making by the Modern Supreme Court* (2011).

   f.   Bernard Schwartz, *Decision: How the Supreme Court Decides Cases* (1996).

   g.   *The Supreme Court in Conference, 1940–1985: The Private Discussions Behind Nearly 300 Supreme Court Decisions* (Del Dickson ed., 2001).

4. Biographies and Profiles of the Justices

Many works provide biographical information about the justices. The Federal Judicial Center's database, "Biographical Directory of Federal Judges, 1789–present,"[33] gives basic information about each justice's career, including dates of service, education, and professional work. The titles listed below, which provide much more information on individuals, are only a few of the many general biographical works on the Court. Biographies, and sometimes autobiographies, for almost all justices are also available.

   a.   *The Supreme Court and Its Justices* (Jesse H. Choper ed., 2001). A collection of essays from the *ABA Journal* about the Supreme Court and its members, including essays by Chief Justices Earl Warren and William H. Rehnquist and Justices Tom C. Clark and Lewis F. Powell, Jr.

   b.   Clare Cushman, *The Supreme Court Justices: Illustrated Biographies, 1789–2012* (3d ed. 2013).

   c.   Henry Flanders, *The Lives and Times of the Chief Justices of the Supreme Court of the United States* (T. & J.W. Johnson & Co. 1881, 2 vols.).

   d.   Leon Friedman & Fred L. Israel, *The Justices of the United States Supreme Court: Their Lives and Major Opinions* (1997, 5 vols.). Though becoming dated, this is perhaps the most comprehensive work on the topic for those covered. The multivolume set is organized by each justice's date of appointment to the Court. In addition to

---

[33] http://www.fjc.gov/public/home.nsf/hisj. The database enables searching by attributes such as party of nominating president, gender, and race. It includes entries for all Article III judges, not just justices.

providing detailed biographical information, the set includes a selected bibliography for each justice.

  e.   Timothy L. Hall, *Supreme Court Justices: A Biographical Dictionary* (2001). This volume also includes recommended readings for additional information on each justice.

  f.   *Biographical Encyclopedia of the Supreme Court: The Lives and Legal Philosophies of the Justices* (Melvin Urofsky ed., 2006). The volume provides profiles on every justice, accompanied by a brief bibliography and a list of noteworthy opinions.

5.   Confirmation Hearings for Justices

  The ideological and philosophical beliefs of a particular justice can be explored by examining transcripts of hearings held by the Senate Judiciary Committee during the confirmation process. The hearings are published by the Government Printing Office. They are distributed to depository libraries and are available selectively online via *FDSys, Westlaw, LexisNexis, HeinOnline,* and other services.

  Confirmation hearings are available in *HeinOnline*'s History of Supreme Court Nominations library and in Hein's print set, *The Supreme Court of the United States: Hearings and Reports on Successful and Unsuccessful Nominations of Supreme Court Justices by the Senate Judiciary Committee,* compiled by Tobe Liebert. Coverage begins with the 1916 nomination of Louis D. Brandeis (the year the confirmation hearings became public) and is updated as new justices are nominated.

  The Congressional Research Service has two publications with textual and statistical information on the nomination process: *Supreme Court Appointment Process: Roles of the President, Judiciary Committee, and Senate*[34] and *Supreme Court Nominations, 1789–2009: Actions by the Senate, the Judiciary Committee, and the President.*[35] In addition, another CRS report, Henry B. Hogue, *Supreme Court Nominations Not Confirmed, 1789–2007,*[36] gives information on unsuccessful nominations.

6.   Personal Papers of the Justices

  Sometimes, understanding the thinking of an individual justice about a particular decision can help researchers gain insight into the justice's views or influence on the Court generally. To aid this understanding, the personal papers of retired justices can become very important to researchers. These materials might be correspondence, records of an administrative nature, media reports, speeches, drafts of opinions and other case-related documents, and other items not part of the official record of a case.[37]

---

[34] RL 31989 (2010), *available at* http://www.fas.org/sgp/crs/misc/RL31989.pdf.

[35] RL 33225 (2009), *available at* http://assets.opencrs.com/rpts/RL33225_20090513.pdf.

[36] RL 31171 (2008), *available at* http://www.fas.org/sgp/crs/misc/RL31171.pdf.

[37] *See* Kathryn A. Watts, *Judges and Their Papers,* 88 N.Y.U. L. REV. 1665 (2013) (arguing that Congress should pass a law, similar to the Presidential Records Act, establishing federal judges' papers as public property and empowering the courts to make rules covering issues such as the timing of their release).

A number of sources for locating the personal papers of the justices are listed on the SCOTUSblog.[38] The Federal Judicial History Office's *Directory of Manuscript Collections Related to Federal Judges, 1789–1997*, compiled by Peter A. Wonders (1998), is very helpful.[39] A comprehensive, while dated, source of information about the location and accessibility of papers of the justices is Alexandra K. Wigdor, *The Personal Papers of the Supreme Court Justices: A Descriptive Guide* (1986).

D. STATE CONSTITUTIONS

Each U.S. state has its own constitution. A state's constitution is the highest legal authority for that state, except for matters controlled by federal law.[40]

All state constitutions have been amended, and many states have replaced an existing constitution with an entirely new one—sometimes more than once. Researching a state's constitutional law often involves reference to the current constitution and its amendments, any previous constitutions and amendments, historical documents related to constitutional drafting and adoption, and state and federal judicial opinions.[41] Further, a given provision of a state's constitution might not yet have been interpreted by the courts of that state; in such instances, it can be useful to research judicial interpretations of similar provisions in the constitutions of other states.

Judicial opinions interpreting provisions of a state's constitution can be located in ways similar to those for the U.S. Constitution discussed in Section A-1. These include consulting the case annotations accompanying the annotated version of the state constitution, state digests, computer-assisted legal research services, *A.L.R.* annotations, *Shepard's Citations*, and *KeyCite*. Likewise, treatises,[42] casebooks,[43] legal periodical articles,[44] and state legal encyclopedias (if any) can assist with constitutional interpretation. In addition, state-specific legal research guides typically discuss researching that state's constitution,[45] using the above-mentioned approaches as well as

---

[38] Ronald Collins, *Accessing the papers of Supreme Court Justices: Online & other resources*, SCOTUSBLOG (Aug. 22, 2013, 10:28 AM), http://www.scotusblog.com/2013/08/accessing-the-papers-of-supreme-court-justices-online-other-resources/.

[39] (1998), *available at* http://www.fjc.gov/public/pdf.nsf/lookup/judmsdir.pdf/$file/judmsdir.pdf.

[40] For an introduction to state constitutional law, see Mary Whisner, *Fifty More Constitutions*, 104 Law Libr. J. 331 (2012).

[41] For a listing of over 2,100 entries relating to the historical literature of state constitutions, see BERNARD D. REAMS, JR. & STUART D. YOAK, THE CONSTITUTIONS OF THE STATES: A STATE-BY-STATE GUIDE AND BIBLIOGRAPHY TO CURRENT SCHOLARLY RESEARCH (Oceana Publications 1987). This volume is also published as volume 5 of *Sources and Documents of United States Constitutions*, Second Series.

[42] The Oxford Commentaries on the State Constitutions of the United States, published by Oxford University Press, which updates the *Reference Guides to the State Constitutions of the United States* series by Greenwood Press, covers the development of each state's constitution. Content for each state is in a standardized format that facilitates comparative research. For each state, contents include an overview of the history and development of the state's constitution, the text of the state's constitution with a section-by-section analysis, a bibliographic essay, a table of cases, and an index. *See also* JAMES A. GARDNER, INTERPRETING STATE CONSTITUTIONS: A JURISPRUDENCE OF FUNCTION IN A FEDERAL SYSTEM (2005); G. ALAN TARR, UNDERSTANDING STATE CONSTITUTIONS (1998).

[43] *See, e.g.*, RANDY J. HOLLAND ET AL., STATE CONSTITUTIONAL LAW: THE MODERN EXPERIENCE (2010); ROBERT F. WILLIAMS, STATE CONSTITUTIONAL LAW: CASES AND MATERIALS (4th ed. 2006).

[44] Of note, since 1988 the *Rutgers Law Journal* has published an annual issue devoted to state constitutional law, including a section on "Developments in State Constitutional Law." The articles are published in issue 4 of each year's volume, and are available online at http://lawjournal.rutgers.edu/.

[45] See Appendix B for a listing of state-specific legal research guides.

offering individualized research strategies for that state and its available research resources.

1. Texts of State Constitutions

A reliable source for the text of a state constitution is the state code or revised statutes.[46] Annotated versions of state statutes commonly have at least one volume devoted to the state constitution. This constitution volume typically contains the current constitutional text, the text of previously adopted versions, case annotations, and research aids. State constitutions are available on state websites and other Internet sites.[47] Many states also publish an unannotated edition of their state constitution in pamphlet form.

Constitutions of the United States: National and State (1974–) is available in print and online[48]. The publication collects the texts of the constitutions of the United States and all U.S. states and territories. It is regularly updated.[49]

Robert L. Maddex, *State Constitutions of the United States* (2d ed. 2005), explains and compares the fifty state constitutions. It provides supplemental materials, including an overview of state constitutions, comparative tables, and information on "new rights" such as privacy and victim's rights and "special provisions" such as the environment and home rule.

2. Historical Sources

The process of adopting a new state constitution usually begins with the convening of a state constitutional convention. The records, journals, proceedings, and other documents from state constitutional conventions can provide valuable information about the intended meanings and interpretations given to state constitutions by their framers.

Prestatehood Legal Materials,[50] a two-volume set, is a state-by-state guide to the legal resources of each territory prior to its becoming a U.S. state. Constitutional convention documents and related resources figure prominently in the coverage. *Sources and Documents of United States Constitutions*,[51] compiled by William F. Swindler,

---

[46] State codes are discussed in Chapter 11.

[47] Cornell's *Legal Information Institute* maintains an up-to-date listing of direct links to state websites, "Constitutions, Statutes, and Codes," at http://www.law.cornell.edu/statutes.html. The NBER/Maryland State Constitutions Project includes a searchable database of current and previous state constitutions at http://www.stateconstitutions.umd.edu/index.aspx.

[48] Originally published by Oceana, this set's online content was migrated the *Oxford Constitutions of the World* site in September 2013.

[49] One method of locating comparative state constitutional provisions is through LEGIS. DRAFTING RESEARCH FUND, COLUM. UNIV., INDEX DIGEST OF STATE CONSTITUTIONS (2d ed. 1959) (available in *HeinOnline*), a companion to *Constitutions of the United States: National and State*. The *Index Digest* is arranged alphabetically by subject; each subject heading includes references to similar constitutional provisions of the states. Although this volume has been updated only through 1967, it can still be useful because many provisions of state constitutions do not change frequently. Columbia University's Legislative Drafting Research Fund issued two subject indexes to state constitutional law: 1980's *Fundamental Liberties and Rights: A Fifty State Index* as part of its *Constitutions of the United States: National and State*. This was followed in 1982 by *Laws, Legislatures, Legislative Procedure: A Fifty State Index*.

[50] PRESTATEHOOD LEGAL MATERIALS (Michael Chiorazzi & Marguerite Most eds., 2005).

[51] Oceana (1973–79, 11 vols. in 12 books). Volume 11, a bibliography, was added to this set in 1988. A second series began in 1982. Older, but still useful, titles for tracing the historical development of state constitutions are BENJAMIN PEARLEY POORE, CHARTERS AND CONSTITUTIONS (1878); FRANCIS NEWTON THORPE, FEDERAL AND STATE CONSTITUTIONS (1909); NEW YORK CONSTITUTIONAL CONVENTION COMMITTEE,

reprints in chronological order the major constitutional documents of each state. *State Constitutional Conventions, Commissions, and Amendments*, a microfiche collection published by ProQuest, covers the period from 1776 through 1988, and is the most comprehensive source of documents for all of the states.[52] (The last state to hold a constitutional convention was Rhode Island, which held a convention in 1986.[53])

E. FOREIGN CONSTITUTIONS

The most comprehensive source for the text of constitutions of foreign countries is *Constitutions of the Countries of the World* (Albert P. Blaustein & Gisbert H. Flanz eds., 1971–), available in print and electronically.[54] The constitutions for all countries of the world, together with sub-national and state constitutions, are included in English, with explanatory notes, extensive commentary, and annotated bibliographies. For countries where there is not an official English language version of the constitution, an English translation is provided. The introduction in Chapter 1 provides bibliographical references to previous compilations of constitutions. Supplements keep each constitution's text up to date.

A companion set is *Constitutions of Dependencies and Territories* (Philip Raworth ed., 1998–), available in print and online.[55] The entry for each entity contains the nation's constitutional provisions that define the relationship between the state and its dependencies and territories, as well as commentary and an annotated bibliography.

HeinOnline's World Constitutions Illustrated library includes most (if not all) nations' constitutions, in their original languages. It also includes a rich variety of historical and current commentary on the constitutions.

The Comparative Constitutions Project has created *Constitute*,[56] a website that provides the text of world constitutions with search features that enable users to find and compare text in different constitutions. For example, among the list of topics, you can select "Culture and Identity," then "Equality regardless of race," and see provisions from 137 constitutions. You can also filter by date and country.

Constitutions of the World, by Robert L. Maddex (3d ed. 2008) serves as a guide to the constitutions and constitutional histories of eighty nations, selected for their political

---

3 REPORTS: CONSTITUTIONS OF THE STATES AND UNITED STATES (1938). Although the Poore and Thorpe volumes are out of date, they are helpful for their parallel studies of state constitutions. The last item, although never brought up to date, is still useful for its index volume to the constitutions of all of the states as of its publication date. *See also* WALTER FAIRLEIGH, THE REVISION AND AMENDMENT OF STATE CONSTITUTIONS (1910); ALBERT LEE STURM, A BIBLIOGRAPHY ON STATE CONSTITUTIONS AND CONSTITUTIONAL REVISION, 1945–1975 (1975).

[52] Two printed bibliographies are provided with the set for access: CYNTHIA E. BROWNE, STATE CONSTITUTIONAL CONVENTIONS FROM INDEPENDENCE TO THE COMPLETION OF THE PRESENT UNION, 1776–1959: A BIBLIOGRAPHY (1973), and CONGRESSIONAL INFORMATION SERVICE, STATE CONSTITUTIONAL CONVENTIONS, 1959–1978: AN ANNOTATED BIBLIOGRAPHY (1981) (2 vols.).

[53] The Yale University Lillian Goldman Law Library's *Avalon Project* (http://avalon.law.yale.edu/default. asp) collects a wide range of documents related to law, history, politics, government, and other fields, beginning from ancient times. Many historical state constitutional documents are included in the collection, which can be searched by century. The University of Richmond's Constitution Finder (http://confinder.richmond.edu/circumscription.html) includes links to current and historical constitutions of many states.

[54] Originally published by Oceana, this set's online content migrated the *Oxford Constitutions of the World* site in September 2013.

[55] The online content is included in *Oxford Constitutions of the World.*

[56] https://www.constituteproject.org/

and constitutional importance. *Foreign Law Guide* (Marci Hoffman, general editor) (Brill Online) provides sources of English translations of full-text sources, including constitutions,[57] for almost all of the 192 member states of the United Nations, including some territories and dependencies.

The University of Bern's *International Constitutional Law (ICL) Project*[58] makes available the English texts of approximately ninety national constitutions. The site also provides background information about the countries for which it has constitutions, as well as for more than forty countries for which it does not have constitutions. Also provided are many useful links to other websites with information relevant to international and comparative constitutional law.

Another useful website is that of the Constitution Society, which provides the full text of many national constitutions, often with English translations.[59] The University of Richmond's Constitution Finder[60] links to sites with national constitutions, often in more than one language or edition.

---

[57] In some instances, documents in "accessible languages," primarily western European, are included.

[58] http://www.servat.unibe.ch/icl/.

[59] http://www.constitution.org/cons/natlcons.htm.

[60] http://confinder.richmond.edu/.

Chapter 9

FEDERAL LEGISLATION*

Article I, Section 8, of the United States Constitution enumerates the powers of Congress and provides the authority for Congress to make all laws necessary and proper for executing the enumerated powers, as well as other powers vested in Congress.

The Senate and the House of Representatives meet in two-year periods. Each year is a session, and the two-year period is known as a Congress. For example, the period in which Congress met from 2009 through 2010 is known as the 111th Congress.[1] Under the Constitution, Congress must meet at least once a year.[2]

This chapter discusses enacted federal legislation and sources for locating these materials. Chapter 10 discusses the various documents generated during the legislative process, the sources to use to locate these documents, and sources containing finding aids that help in locating them.

A. THE ENACTMENT OF FEDERAL LAWS

Before discussing the various ways federal legislation is published, a brief description of the legislative process is necessary.[3] At any time during a congressional session, representatives and senators can introduce legislation in their respective branch of Congress. When introduced, each proposed law is called a *bill* or a *joint resolution*.[4] The first bill in the House of Representatives in each Congress is labeled H.R. 1, with all subsequent bills numbered sequentially. Similarly, the first bill introduced in the Senate is labeled S. 1.

---

* This chapter was revised by Jane Thompson, Associate Director of Faculty Services and Research, William A. Wise Law Library, University of Colorado Law School.

[1] The 1st Congress took place over three calendar years, 1789 to 1791.

[2] U.S. CONST. art. I, § 4, cl. 2.

[3] For more detailed statements on the enactment of federal laws, see JOHN V. SULLIVAN, HOW OUR LAWS ARE MADE, H.R. DOC. NO. 110–49 (2007), *available at* http://thomas.loc.gov/home/lawsmade.toc.html [hereinafter HOW OUR LAWS ARE MADE]; ROBERT B. DOVE, ENACTMENT OF A LAW: PROCEDURAL STEPS IN THE LEGISLATIVE PROCESS, S. DOC. NO. 97–20 (1982). Updated, electronic versions of this publication in PDF and html format are available at http://thomas.loc.gov/home/enactment/enactlawtoc.html (1997). *See also* CONGRESSIONAL QUARTERLY, INC., GUIDE TO CONGRESS (6th ed. 2008) [hereinafter GUIDE TO CONGRESS]; ROBERT U. GOEHLERT & FENTON S. MARTIN, CONGRESS AND LAW-MAKING: RESEARCHING THE LEGISLATIVE PROCESS (2d ed. 1989).

[4] Most legislation is introduced as a *bill*. A *joint resolution* may also be used, but there is no practical difference between the two, and the two terms are used interchangeably. *Concurrent resolutions* are used for non-legislative matters that affect the operations of both houses. *Simple resolutions* are used for non-legislative matters concerning the operation of either house. Bills, joint resolutions, and concurrent resolutions are published in the UNITED STATES STATUTES AT LARGE; simple resolutions appear in the *Congressional Record*. HOW OUR LAWS ARE MADE, *supra* note 3, at 5–8.

After a bill passes the house in which it was introduced, it is sent to the other house for consideration.[5] If approved in identical form,[6] it is then sent to the president for signing. If the president signs it, the bill becomes a law. If the president vetoes a bill,[7] Congress can override the veto with a two-thirds vote in both houses of Congress.[8] Under the Constitution, a bill sent to the president also becomes law if the president does not either sign or veto it within ten days of receiving the bill.[9] Bills introduced but not passed during a specific Congress do not carry over to the next Congress. Sponsors who want the new Congress to consider the bill must submit it as a new bill; it will receive a new number in the new Congress.

After a bill becomes law, it is sent to the archivist, who is directed to publish all laws so received.[10] The archivist classifies each law as either a public law or a private law. A *public law* affects the nation as a whole or deals with individuals as a class, and relates to public matters. A *private law* benefits only a specific individual or individuals. Private laws deal primarily with matters relating to claims against the government or with matters of immigration and naturalization.[11]

Laws are numbered by their Congress and the sequence in which they are passed. Thus the first public law of the 113th Congress was Pub. L. No. 113–1. The first private law of that Congress was Priv. L. No. 113–1.

B. PUBLICATION OF FEDERAL LAWS

1. Recent Public Laws

The United States Government Printing Office issues the first official publication of a law in the form of a *slip law*. [Illustration 9–1] Each is separately published and may be one page or several hundred pages in length. Slip laws are available in all libraries that are depositories for U.S. government publications[12] and in other libraries that

---

[5] At this stage, a proposed piece of legislation ceases technically to be called a bill, but rather is an *act*, indicating it is an act of one body of Congress. However, it is still popularly referred to as a bill. Once a bill or joint resolution passes the house in which it was introduced, including changes made during floor action, it must be certified as accurate by either the Secretary of the Senate or the Clerk of the House of Representatives (depending upon the house in which it was passed). Once certified, this document (printed on blue paper) is known as an *engrossed bill*.

[6] Once a bill or joint resolution passes the Senate and House of Representatives in identical form, it is certified as an official copy by the chief officer of the house in which it originated and is signed by the Speaker of the House of Representatives and the Senate President *pro tempore*. Once the document is ready for the president's signature, it is known as an *enrolled bill* and is printed on parchment paper.

[7] For a list of presidential vetoes, see GREGORY HARNESS, PRESIDENTIAL VETOES, 1789–1988, S. PUB. 102–12 (1992); ZOE DAVIS, PRESIDENTIAL VETOES, 1989–2000, S. PUB. 107–10 (2001). The full text of each of the reports may be found at the Senate website at http://www.senate.gov/reference/reference_index_subjects/Vetoes_vrd.htm. In addition, the website tracks presidential vetoes since 2001.

[8] U.S. CONST. art. I, § 7, cl. 2.

[9] *Id.*

[10] 1 U.S.C. § 106(a); *See also* 44 U.S.C. §§ 709–711. Exec. Order No. 10530, ch. 47, CODIFICATION OF PRESIDENTIAL PROCLAMATIONS AND EXECUTIVE ORDERS 935, 936 (1989 comp.) (*available at* http://www.archives.gov/federal-register/codification/).

[11] For a complete discussion of private bills and laws, see GUIDE TO CONGRESS, *supra* note 3, at 614–15.

[12] There are approximately 1,200 depository libraries. To locate a federal depository library through the use of a clickable map or search box, see http://catalog.gpo.gov/fdlpdir/FDLPdir.jsp. Unless I'm hallucinating, I think there are other chapters in which you didn't insert a comma for a 4-digit number.

subscribe to these publications. Other sources commonly consulted for the text of recently enacted public laws are:

a. *FDsys* (formerly *GPO Access*).[13] The Government Printing Office's *Federal Digital System* (*FDsys*) website sets forth the text of all laws enacted beginning with the 104th Congress, 1995–1996. To guarantee official status and authenticity, public laws beginning with the 110th Congress are digitally signed and certified.

b. *Congress.gov*.[14] This electronic resource from the Library of Congress lists all public laws since the 93rd Congress. Each entry includes the bill number, its sponsor(s), committee action, and relevant report numbers. In addition, when available, *Congress.gov* provides access to the full text of proposed bills and a direct link to the full text of the public law from *FDsys*.

c. *United States Code Congressional and Administrative News.* This set, which began in 1941 with the 77th Congress, 1st Session, is published by West. During each session of Congress, West publishes monthly pamphlets that contain the full text of all public laws. Each monthly pamphlet contains a cumulative subject index and a cumulative Table of Laws Enacted. After each session of Congress, the pamphlets are reissued in bound volumes.

d. *United States Code Service, Advance Service.* LexisNexis publishes these monthly pamphlets, containing newly enacted public laws, in connection with the *United States Code Service*. This Advance Service contains a cumulative index arranged in alphabetical order.

e. *LexisNexis*, *Westlaw*, *Bloomberg Law*, and *Loislaw*.[15] These online services include the text of public laws.

f. *ProQuest Congressional* (formerly *LexisNexis Congressional*). *ProQuest Congressional* is an extensive web-based service offering access to a wealth of congressional documents and information, including that produced by Congressional Information Service, Inc. A basic subscription to this electronic resource provides access to the full text of public laws from 1988 to the present.

g. *Specialized Topical Services.* Publishers often provide the text of selected "important" public laws that relate to the subject covered by the topical service.[16]

2. United States Statutes at Large[17]

At the end of each session of Congress, all slip laws are published in numerical order as part of the set entitled *United States Statutes at Large*, which is commonly referred to as *Statutes at Large*. Public and private laws are in separate sections of the volumes. All laws enacted since 1789 are contained in the many volumes of this set. [Illustration 9–2]

The *United States Statutes at Large* was first published in 1846, beginning with the 29th Congress. Legislation enacted prior to that year was published as volumes 1

---

[13] http://www.gpo.gov/fdsys/browse/collection.action?collectionCode=PLAW.

[14] https://beta.congress.gov/. *Congress.gov* is replacing the *THOMAS* database in late 2014.

[15] Computer-assisted legal research services are discussed in Chapter 23.

[16] Looseleaf services are discussed in Chapter 14.

[17] *See* Chapter 21 for a discussion of treaties.

through 8 of the set; volumes 1 through 5 cover the public laws and volume 6 the private laws for the 1st through 28th Congresses (1789–1845), with volumes 7 and 8 devoted exclusively to treaties.[18]

The publication pattern for volumes 9 through 49 differs from that currently followed. Volume 9 covers the 29th–31st Congresses; volumes 10 through 12 cover two Congresses each (32nd–37th); and volumes 13 to 49 cover one Congress each (38th–74th). The current pattern of one numbered volume per session began in 1936 with the 75th Congress, 1st Session.[19]

It is important to keep in mind that the laws in *United States Statutes at Large* are arranged in chronological order rather than by subject. Because laws can be amended many years after they are first passed, amendments almost always appear in different volumes from the volume containing the law being amended. For example, a law passed in 1900 appears in volume 31 of *United States Statutes at Large*. If Congress amended that law in 1905, the amendment would appear in volume 34. Some laws have been amended many times. To obtain the full and current text of such a law, the *United States Statutes at Large* volume containing the original law must be examined, together with subsequent volumes in which amendments to that law appear.[20]

Each volume of *United States Statutes at Large* has its own subject index, and beginning in 1991, a popular name index as well. From 1957 through 1976, each volume contained tables listing previous public laws affected by the public laws published in that volume. Beginning with volume 33, marginal notes indicate House or Senate bill numbers, public law numbers, and dates of enactment. *United States Statutes at Large* also contains interstate compacts.[21] Regrettably, bound copies of *United States Statutes at Large* are approximately one Congress (or two years) behind in publication. When published, the *United States Statutes at Large* volume supersedes the slip laws for that volume.

Sources for the *United States Statutes at Large* are:

a.   *FDsys.* The Government Printing Office is collaborating with the Library of Congress to digitize retrospective volumes of the *Statutes at Large. FDsys* provides access to volumes published from 1951 to 2010 as of June, 2014.[22]

b.   A Century of Lawmaking for a New Nation: U.S. Congressional Documents and Debates, 1774–1875.[23] Part of the Library of Congress's American Memory project, *A Century of Lawmaking* contains 18 volumes of the *Statutes at Large* for the first 43 Congresses, 1789 through 1875.

---

[18] For a concise historical explanation of the development of *United States Statutes at Large*, its significance, and a complete bibliographic listing of the set, see CURT E. CONKLIN & FRANCIS ACLAND, AN HISTORICAL AND BIBLIOGRAPHIC INTRODUCTION TO THE UNITED STATES STATUTES AT LARGE (1992). *See also* LARRY M. BOYER, CHECKLIST OF UNITED STATES SESSION LAWS, 1789–1873 (1976).

[19] Although there is only one numbered volume per session, that volume is often published in two or more separate books. There are more physical books than volumes in the *Statutes at Large.*

[20] In practice, the *United States Code* and other subject-based versions of federal legislation make it unnecessary to consult multiple volumes of the *Statutes at Large. See* Section C.

[21] Interstate compacts are discussed in Chapter 11, Section F.

[22] http://www.gpo.gov/fdsys/browse/collection.action?collectionCode=STATUTE.

[23] http://memory.loc.gov/ammem/amlaw/lwsl.html.

    c.   HeinOnline's U.S. Statutes at Large collection provides access to the complete *Statutes at Large* (1789–2009) in PDF format.[24]

    d.   Westlaw. Westlaw provides the *Statutes at Large* for 1789 through 1972 in PDF format. The citations and titles of the laws are searchable, but not the contents of the PDFs.

    e.   United States Code Congressional and Administrative News (U.S.C.C.A.N.) and *United States Code Service Advance* pamphlets reprint public laws. The public laws in *U.S.C.C.A.N.* have the same pagination as in *Statutes at Large.*

3. Compilations of Laws

    When Congress amends a law, it must specifically indicate what law is being amended. For example, the Labor Management Relations Act of 1947 provided in Section 101 that "The National Labor Relations Act is hereby amended to read as follows." What followed, then, was the text of the amendments, resulting in new statutory language.[25] The new language became Section 1, Section 2, and so on of the National Labor Relations Act, replacing the previous text.

    For convenience in reading and understanding the law as amended, researchers often turn to unofficial compilations that merge the original text with all the amendments. These compilations are frequently available on the websites of the agencies that administer the laws. For example, the National Labor Relations Board posts the National Labor Relations Act,[26] the U.S. Citizenship and Immigration Services website includes the Immigration and Nationality Act,[27] and the Social Security Administration posts the Social Security Act, all as amended.[28] Commercial publishers often include statutory compilations with looseleaf services. Law students see them in statutory supplements to casebooks.[29] Researchers should remember that these compilations are unofficial and might be out of date.

C. CODIFICATION OF FEDERAL LAWS

    The chronological publication of congressional laws creates obvious problems determining the statutory provisions on any given subject. Therefore, the laws passed by Congress have been rearranged in a manner that accomplishes three objectives: (1) to collate the original law with all subsequent amendments, reflecting the deletion or addition of language made by those amendments; (2) to gather together all laws on the same subject or topic; and (3) to eliminate all repealed, superseded, or expired laws. This process is called *codification.*[30]

---

[24] http://heinonline.org.

[25] Labor Management Relations Act, 1947, ch. 114, § 101, 61 Stat. 136, 136.

[26] http://nlrb.gov/national-labor-relations-act.

[27] http://www.uscis.gov/portal/site/uscis; select "Laws."

[28] http://ssa.gov/OP_Home/ssact/comp-ssa.htm.

[29] *See, e.g.,* ROBERT A. GORMAN & MATTHEW W. FINKIN, 2012 STATUTORY APPENDIX AND CASE SUPPLEMENT 23 (2012) (supplementing ARCHIBALD COX ET AL., LABOR LAW: CASES AND MATERIALS (15th ed. 2011)) (reprinting National Labor Relations Act, showing Taft–Hartley amendments of 1947 in boldface type, the Landrum–Griffin amendments of 1959 in italics, and the 1974 amendments underscored).

[30] For a discussion of the process involved in codification, see Charles S. Zinn, *Revision of the United States Code,* 51 LAW LIBR. J. 388 (1958). For a discussion of the relationship between the *United States Code* and the *United States Statutes at Large,* see Mary Whisner, *The* United States Code, *Prima Facie Evidence,*

1.   United States Revised Statutes

By 1866, researching federal legislation had become quite difficult because *United States Statutes at Large* had no cumulating subject index. President Andrew Johnson, pursuant to congressional authorization, appointed a commission to address the problem. The commission began its work by extracting from the volumes of *United States Statutes at Large* all public laws that were still in force and were of a general and permanent nature. Next, it rewrote each public law and all its amendments into one document by incorporating amending language and removing deleted language. These updated laws were arranged topically into titles, and then further subdivided into chapters and sections. Title 14, for example, contained all legislation concerning the judiciary; Title 64 contained all legislation on bankruptcy. All titles were arranged in one volume, a subject index was prepared, and the volume was published as the *Revised Statutes of 1875,* the first codification of federal law.[31]

The entire *Revised Statutes of 1875* was introduced in Congress as a bill, which was passed and became a public law. Incorporated into the bill was language specifically repealing each previously enacted public law that had been incorporated into *Revised Statutes of 1875*.[32] Accordingly, the codification became positive law, legal evidence of the text of the law. Because *Revised Statutes of 1875* was positive law, it no longer was necessary to refer to the *United States Statutes at Large* for the authoritative text of federal legislation included in the *Revised Statutes.*

Unfortunately, the first publication of *Revised Statutes of 1875*, known as the first edition, was discovered to contain many inaccuracies and unauthorized changes.[33] In 1878, Congress authorized a second edition of *Revised Statutes*. This second edition included legislation passed since 1873, deleted sections that were repealed since 1873, and corrected the errors in the first edition. The second edition indicated changes to the text of the first edition through the use of brackets and italics.

It is important to note that Congress never enacted the second edition of *Revised Statutes* into positive law, and all changes indicated in it are only *prima facie* evidence of the law. Although several attempts were made to adopt a new codification, it was not until 1924 that Congress authorized the next publication of a codification of federal laws.[34]

2.   *United States Code (U.S.C.)*

a.   Background. Prior to 1926, the *Revised Statutes of 1875* and 24 subsequent volumes of *United States Statutes at Large* contained the positive law for federal

and Positive Law, 101 LAW LIBR. J. 545–56 (2009); Michael J. Lynch, *The U.S. Code, The Statutes at Large, and Some Peculiarities of Codification*, 16 LEGAL REFERENCE SERVICES Q., no. 1, 1997, at 69.

[31] This first codification is known as either the *Revised Statutes of 1873* (reflecting the last year of laws contained in the code), the *Revised Statutes of 1874* (reflecting the code's date of enactment), or the *Revised Statutes of 1875* (reflecting the publication date of the code). This chapter refers to the codification as "*Revised Statutes of 1875.*" *See* Ralph H. Dwan & Ernest R. Feidler, *The Federal Statutes—Their History and Use,* 22 MINN. L. REV. 1008, 1012–15 (1938) [hereinafter Dwan & Feidler].

[32] 32 REVISED STATUTES OF THE UNITED STATES, 1873–1874, Act of June 22, 1874, tit. LXXIV, §§ 5595–5601, at 1085 (1878).

[33] Dwan & Feidler, *supra* note 31, at 1014–15.

[34] For a discussion and bibliography of federal laws before 1926, see Erwin C. Surrency, *The Publication of Federal Laws: A Short History*, 79 LAW LIBR. J. 469 (1987).

legislation. In 1926, the *United States Code*, prepared under the auspices of special committees of the House and Senate, was published. This codification included all sections of *Revised Statutes of 1875* that had not been repealed as well as all public and general laws still in force that were included in the *United States Statutes at Large* volumes dated after 1873.

These laws were arranged into 50 titles and published as the *United States Code*, 1926 edition. Between 1927 and 1933, cumulated bound supplements were issued each year. In 1934, Congress issued a new edition of the *United States Code*, the 1934 edition, which incorporated the cumulated supplements to the 1926 edition. Subsequently, a new edition has been published every six years, with cumulative supplements issued during the intervening years. The *United States Code* is the "official" codification of federal public laws of a general and permanent nature that are in effect at the time of publication.

Unlike the *Revised Statutes of 1875*, the *United States Code* was never submitted to Congress and enacted into positive law in its entirety. Instead, beginning in 1947, Congress has enacted individual titles separately. To date, about half of the titles have been enacted into positive law.[35]

On December 18, 2010, President Barack Obama signed into law Pub. L. No. 111–314, "To enact certain laws relating to national and commercial space programs as Title 51, United States Code, National and Commercial Space Programs."[36] Titles 41 and 51 were enacted into positive law in the 111th Congress as part of a larger codification project now underway by the Office of Law Revision Counsel. Current positive law codification projects include existing titles 35 and 36, and proposed titles 52 (voting and elections), 53 (small business), 54 (National Park System), and 55 (environment).[37]

Thus, when using the *United States Code*, it is important to ascertain if the particular title has been enacted into positive law. Those titles not yet enacted are only *prima facie* evidence of the law. For these titles, should there be a conflict between the wording in the *United States Code* and the *United States Statutes at Large*, the latter will govern.[38]

   b.   *Features of United States Code.* The *United States Code* is typically abbreviated and referred to as *U.S.C.* In addition to the codified laws of the United States, the *U.S.C.*

---

[35] Titles enacted into positive law are 1, 3, 4, 5, 9, 10, 11, 13, 14, 17, 18, 23, 28, 31, 32, 35, 36, 37, 38, 39, 40, 41, 44, 46, 49, and 51. Title 10 eliminated Title 34; and the enactment of Title 31 repealed Title 6. A current list of titles reenacted as positive law can be found on the Office of Law Revision Counsel's website at http://uscode.house.gov/about/info.shtml. For a table listing the titles in the order of enactment, see Whisner, *supra* note 30, at 554.

[36] 124 Stat. 3328 (2010).

[37] See http://uscode.house.gov/codification/legislation.shtml for details of this project and bill status information.

[38] U.S.C. § 204(a) (2006) provides, "The matter set forth in the edition of the Code of Laws of the United States current at any time shall, together with the then current supplement, if any, establish *prima facie* the laws of the United States, general and permanent in their nature, in force on the day preceding the commencement of the session following the last session the legislation of which is included: *Provided, however,* That whenever titles of such Code shall have been enacted into positive law the text thereof shall be legal evidence of the laws therein contained, in all the courts of the United States, the several States, and the Territories and insular possessions of the United States." For examples of cases involving a conflict between the *U.S.C.* and the *Statutes at Large*, see Whisner, *supra* note 30, at 547–49.

and its supplements present a number of features that are useful in researching and using statutory provisions, including:

(1)   A historical note that lists *United States Statutes at Large* citations, public law numbers, date of original enactment, and any amendments at the end of each code section. [Illustrations 9–4 and 9–8]

(2)   A multivolume general index.

(3)   Historical notes that provide information on amendments or other public laws' effect on sections of the *United States Code*.

(4)   Cross-references to other sections of the *United States Code* that contain related matters or that refer to specific sections of the *U.S.C.*

(5)   A table of "Acts Cited by Popular Name," in which public laws are listed alphabetically by either the short titles assigned by Congress or by the names by which the laws have become known. Citations are provided to the *United States Code* and to *United States Statutes at Large.*

(6)   Volumes that include tables providing the following information:

> *(a)*   Table 1 indicates where titles of the *United States Code* that have been revised and renumbered since the 1926 edition appear within the current edition of the *U.S.C.*

> *(b)*   Table 2 provides references to the current edition of the *U.S.C.* from the *Revised Statutes of the United States of 1878.*

> *(c)*   Table 3 lists the public laws in *United States Statutes at Large* in chronological order and indicates where each section of a public law is contained in the current edition of the *United States Code.*

> *(d)*   Another table provides information on internal cross-references within the *United States Code.*

> *(e)*   Additional tables indicate where other materials, e.g., presidential executive orders, are referenced in the current edition of the *United States Code.*

The volumes containing tables are updated by the annual, cumulative bound supplements to the *United States Code.*

3.   Annotated Editions of the *United States Code*

The *United States Code* is printed and sold by the U.S. Government Printing Office; publication often is slow, particularly the issuance of supplements, which are seldom available until a year or more after the end of a session of Congress.

Furthermore, the meaning of a statute passed by a legislative body is not always clear, and a court must frequently interpret the language used in the statute. Because judicial opinions interpreting statutes are often sought, publishers have created annotated codes which provide digests of court opinions interpreting or deciding the constitutionality of specific code sections. Two annotated editions of the *United States Code* currently are published privately: *United States Code Annotated* (West) and *United States Code Service* (LexisNexis).

The annotated editions of the *United States Code* have many advantages over the official edition. These advantages include (1) updating of the entire set through publication of annual cumulative pocket supplements and, when necessary, recompiled volumes; (2) publication of pamphlets during the year updating the pocket supplements; (3) more detailed indexing [Illustration 9–3]; (4) inclusion of annotations of judicial opinions interpreting each *U.S.C.* section; (5) citations to the *Code of Federal Regulations;*[39] and (6) publication of each title in one or more smaller volumes, making them easier to use and carry than the *U.S.C.* volumes.

a. United States Code Annotated (U.S.C.A.). U.S.C.A., published by West, sets forth the text of legislation as it appears in the *United States Code.* Thus, it contains the same features that are listed in Section C-2 of this chapter. [Illustrations 9–5, 9–6, and 9–7]

Many enhancements have been included by the publisher to supplement those features found in the official version of the *United States Code.* Most important are the Notes of Decisions, which provide digests of cases that interpret a particular section of the *U.S.C.* These digests are popularly referred to as annotations. Notes of Decisions are organized under an alphabetical subject index that precedes the actual annotations.

Other features of the *U.S.C.A.* are as follows:

(1) References to other West publications and to topics and key numbers that can assist researchers in finding additional cases and other pertinent materials.

(2) The multivolume General Index, which is issued annually in paperback form. At the end of each title of the *U.S.C.A.* there is a separate index for that title.

(3) Supplementary pamphlets include those public laws enacted since the last supplementation of a title and that affect sections of that title. Public laws are classified to particular *U.S.C.* sections. The most recent Notes of Decisions also are included for sections that have been construed by the courts since the last pocket supplements were published.

(4) The "Popular Name Table for Acts of Congress" is published in two paperbound volumes. [Illustration 9–11] Listing is alphabetical by popular name, with references provided to both *United States Statutes at Large* and to the *U.S.C.* This popular name table is cumulatively updated by means of the pamphlets discussed in (3), above. Also, many titles of the *U.S.C.A.* contain tables entitled "Popular Name Acts," which provide an alphabetical listing of public laws within that title and references to sections of that specific title. If there is more than one volume, these tables are located in the first volume of the title.

The General Index to *U.S.C.A.* also includes, in the proper alphabetical location, the public law by popular name. Most frequently, the researcher is referred to the Popular Name Table for Acts of Congress in the last volume of *U.S.C.A.*'s General Index. Occasionally, a direct reference is given to a *U.S.C.* section.

(5) The *U.S.C.A.* contains many of the same tables contained in the *United States Code.* These tables are located in separate volumes and are updated by means of pocket and pamphlet supplementation as described above.

---

[39] This publication is discussed in Chapter 13.

b. *United States Code Service (U.S.C.S.).* This set is published by LexisNexis. Like *U.S.C.A.*, *U.S.C.S.* provides the same features found in the *United States Code*, e.g., historical notes and cross-references are set forth in a section entitled "History; Ancillary Laws and Directives," which follows each section of the *U.S.C.* [Illustrations 9–8 and 9–9]

U.S.C.S., unlike *U.S.C.A.*, follows the text of public laws as they appear in *United States Statutes at Large*. Therefore, if a title has not been enacted into positive law, the user of *U.S.C.S.* will have the authoritative language. If the editors of *U.S.C.S.* believe that clarification of the language of the public laws included in the set is necessary, they provide clarifying information through the use of brackets (inserting words or references) or explanatory notes.

U.S.C.S. provides, in its Interpretive Notes and Decisions, "pertinent" digests of judicial opinions and federal administrative agency decisions that interpret or construe a public law or a particular section of a public law.

An "analytical" index, which precedes the actual digest of cases and administrative decisions, enables users to focus their research. The Cumulative Later Case and Statutory Service pamphlets, issued three times a year, update the Interpretive Notes and Decisions between the release of annual pocket supplements.

Other features of the *U.S.C.S.* include:

(1) References to other publications, including those of LexisNexis, and to relevant law review articles. These references are set forth in a section entitled Research Guide.

(2) A multivolume General Index is kept current by a General Index Update pamphlet.

(3) The *Cumulative Later Case and Statutory Service* that indicates public laws enacted since the last supplementation of a specific title that affect sections of that title. This *Cumulative Later Case and Statutory Service* is issued three times a year.

(4) The Table of Acts by Popular Name is a table of enacted laws that are arranged alphabetically by popular name. Additionally, the popular name table provides references to *United States Statutes at Large* and to *U.S.C.S.* It is updated by the *United States Code Service Advance*, discussed in Section B-1-d. The General Index also includes the popular names of public laws.

(5) Additional tables similar to those as described for *U.S.C.* These tables are contained in separate volumes labeled as such and are updated by means of pocket and pamphlet supplementation as described above.

c. *Summary and Comparison: Annotated Editions of the United States Code.* Both *U.S.C.A.* and *U.S.C.S.* follow the same citation pattern as the official *United States Code*; a citation to the *United States Code* can be located in either of the two annotated sets.[40] As noted above, only certain titles of the *United States Code* have been enacted into positive law. The *U.S.C.A.* uses the text as it appears in the *United States Code*, while the *U.S.C.S.* follows the text as it appears in *United States Statutes at Large*. Thus, when

---

[40] For a discussion of these two sets, see Jeanne Benioff, *A Comparison of Annotated U.S. Codes*, LEGAL REFERENCE SERVICES Q., Spring 1982, at 37.

using *U.S.C.A.*, it may be necessary at times to check the text of *United States Statutes at Large* for those titles that are still only *prima facie* evidence of the law.

Both *U.S.C.A.* and *U.S.C.S.* contain digests of cases interpreting sections of the *United States Code*. Each set is updated by annual pocket supplements, periodic pamphlets, and, when necessary, by replacement volumes. Each version contains editorial materials that refer to other publications. The *U.S.C.A.* contains more annotations than the *U.S.C.S.* Both sets are easier to use, more current, and better indexed than the *United States Code*. However, when only the text of the *U.S.C.* is needed, it may be simpler to consult the official *United States Code*.[41] [See Illustrations 9–3 through 9–9, which show the use of various sets of the *U.S.C.*]

Both annotated codes include volumes containing the United States Constitution and various court rules.[42] In *U.S.C.A.* federal court rules are included in Title 28, but in *U.S.C.S.* they are published in separate volumes at the end of the set.

4. Access to the Code in Electronic Format

a.   LexisNexis. LexisNexis contains the *U.S.C.* as published in the *U.S.C.S.* Each section contains the full text of the law, a complete history of the *U.S.C.* section showing sources and derivations of the law (including any amendments), and a list of research references and interpretive notes. Each section is updated to include the new material in paper supplementation. Information regarding each section's currency is included. *ProQuest Congressional* also contains the text of the *U.S.C.*

b.   Westlaw. Westlaw contains the *U.S.C.* as published in the *U.S.C.A.* In addition, the USC database provides the unannotated version. A related materials directory in *Westlaw* enables the user to update the statutory section; to view historical notes, references, and tables; and to find notes of decisions. The USCA database contains the text of the *U.S.C.*, annotations, and a popular name table. The statutory section can be updated, and notes, references, and tables can be viewed by using the update feature.

c.   Loislaw and *Bloomberg Law* have unannotated versions of the *United States Code*.

d.   Internet Sources (free).

(1)   The *Legal Information Institute* at Cornell University has the full text of the latest edition of the *United States Code*.[43] An RSS feed for each title enables researchers to stay current.

(2)   *FDsys* contains the *United States Code*.[44]

(3)   U.S. House of Representatives, Office of the Law Revision Counsel, provides a website where the full text of individual titles of the *U.S.C.* can be downloaded or searched.[45] The website links to a Twitter feed reporting updates on the electronic *U.S.C.*

---

[41] The *Bluebook* requires citation to the *U.S.C.* "whenever possible." THE BLUEBOOK: A UNIFORM SYSTEM OF CITATION R. 12.3, at 114 (Columbia Law Review Ass'n et al. eds., 19th ed.2010).

[42] These subjects are discussed in Chapters 8 and 12.

[43] http://www.law.cornell.edu/uscode/.

[44] http://www.gpo.gov/fdsys/browse/collectionUScode.action?collectionCode=USCODE.

[45] http://uscode.house.gov/.

D. ILLUSTRATIONS

[Illustration 9–1]

SLIP LAW–106TH CONGRESS

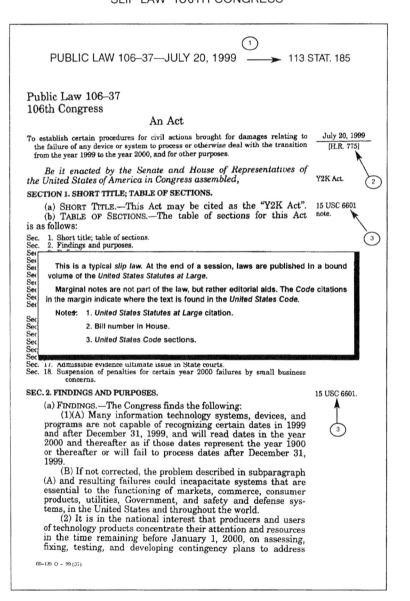

PUBLIC LAW 106–37—JULY 20, 1999 ⟶ 113 STAT. 185

Public Law 106–37
106th Congress

An Act

To establish certain procedures for civil actions brought for damages relating to the failure of any device or system to process or otherwise deal with the transition from the year 1999 to the year 2000, and for other purposes.

July 20, 1999
[H.R. 775]

Be it enacted by the Senate and House of Representatives of the United States of America in Congress assembled,

Y2K Act.

SECTION 1. SHORT TITLE; TABLE OF SECTIONS.

(a) SHORT TITLE.—This Act may be cited as the "Y2K Act".
(b) TABLE OF SECTIONS.—The table of sections for this Act is as follows:

15 USC 6601 note.

Sec. 1. Short title; table of sections.
Sec. 2. Findings and purposes.

> This is a typical *slip law*. At the end of a session, laws are published in a bound volume of the *United States Statutes at Large*.
>
> Marginal notes are not part of the law, but rather editorial aids. The *Code* citations in the margin indicate where the text is found in the *United States Code*.
>
> Notes: 1. *United States Statutes at Large* citation.
>
>   2. Bill number in House.
>
>   3. *United States Code* sections.

Sec. 17. Admissible evidence ultimate issue in State courts.
Sec. 18. Suspension of penalties for certain year 2000 failures by small business concerns.

SEC. 2. FINDINGS AND PURPOSES.

(a) FINDINGS.—The Congress finds the following:
    (1)(A) Many information technology systems, devices, and programs are not capable of recognizing certain dates in 1999 and after December 31, 1999, and will read dates in the year 2000 and thereafter as if those dates represent the year 1900 or thereafter or will fail to process dates after December 31, 1999.
    (B) If not corrected, the problem described in subparagraph (A) and resulting failures could incapacitate systems that are essential to the functioning of markets, commerce, consumer products, utilities, Government, and safety and defense systems, in the United States and throughout the world.
    (2) It is in the national interest that producers and users of technology products concentrate their attention and resources in the time remaining before January 1, 2000, on assessing, fixing, testing, and developing contingency plans to address

15 USC 6601.

69–139 O – 99 (37)

[Illustration 9–2]

PAGE FROM 106 UNITED STATES STATUTES AT LARGE

PUBLIC LAW 102-366—SEPT. 4, 1992   106 STAT. 1019

(2) within 180 days after the date of enactment of this Act, publish in the Federal Register final rules and regulations implementing this Act, and enter such contracts as are necessary to implement this Act and the amendments made by this Act.

SEC. 416. BUY AMERICA.

Section 102 of the Small Business Investment Act of 1958 (15 U.S.C. 1661) is amended by adding at the end the following: "It is the intention of the Congress that in the award of financial assistance under this Act, when practicable, priority be accorded to small business concerns which lease or purchase equipment and supplies which are produced in the United States and that small business concerns receiving such assistance be encouraged to continue to lease or purchase such equipment and supplies.".

15 USC 661.

SEC. 417. STUDIES AND REPORTS.

(a) SBA ANNUAL REPORT.—Section 308(g) of the Small Business Investment Act of 1958 (12 U.S.C. 687(g)) is amended by adding at the end the following new paragraph:

15 USC 687.

"(3) In its annual report for the year ending on December 31, 1993, and in each succeeding annual report made pursuant to section 10(a) of the Small Business Act, the Administration shall include a full and detailed description or account relating to—

"(A) the number of small business investment companies the Administration licensed, the number of licensees that have

> 15 U.S.C. § 661 was amended in 1992. Frequently, a single public law may simultaneously amend sections of various titles of the U.S.C.

"(B) the amount of government leverage that each licensee received in the previous year and the types of leverage instruments each licensee used;

"(C) for each type of financing instrument, the sizes, geographic locations, and other characteristics of the small business investment companies using them, including the extent to which the investment companies have used the leverage from each instrument to make small business loans, equity investments, or both; and

"(D) the frequency with which each type of investment instrument has been used in the current year and a comparison of the current year with previous years.".

(b) REPORT OF THE COMPTROLLER GENERAL.—Not later than 4 years after the date of enactment of this Act, the Comptroller General of the United States shall transmit to the Committees on Small Business of the House of Representatives and the Senate a report that reviews the Small Business Investment Company program (established under the Small Business Investment Act of 1958) for the 3-year period following the date of enactment of this Act, with respect to each item listed in section 308(g)(3) of the Small Business Investment Act of 1958, as amended by subsection (a).

15 USC 681 note.

SEC. 418. NO EFFECT ON SECURITIES LAWS.

Nothing in this Act (and no amendment made by this Act) shall be construed to affect the applicability of the securities laws, as that term is defined in section 3(a)(47) of the Securities Exchange Act of 1934, or any of the rules and regulations thereunder, or

15 USC 661 note.

[Illustration 9-3]

PAGES FROM VOLUME OF GENERAL INDEX TO THE U.S.C.A.

464   2001 GENERAL INDEX (Q-Z)

SMALL BUSINESS INVESTMENT COMPANIES AND PROGRAMS —Cont'd

Crimes and criminal procedure.
Bribery, 18 § 212, 213, 216.
Directors, 18 § 212, 216.
Embezzlement, 18 § 657.
Examiners, 18 § 212, 213, 1006.
False information, 18 § 1006, 1014.
Fines, penalties, and forfeitures.
 See within this heading, "Fines, penalties, and forfeitures."
Fraudulent actions or transactions, 18 § 1006
Funds, 18 § 657.
Gratuities, 18 § 212, 213.
Loans, 18 § 212, 213, 1014.
Officers and employees, 18 § 212, 216, 657, 1006.
Reports, 18 § 1006. 1014.
Securities, 18 § 657.
Date.
Period or duration. See within this heading, "Period or duration."
Debentures.
Borrowing operations, 15 § 683.
Development company debentures, 15 § 697.
Interest rate, 15 § 687i.
Pooling of debentures, 15 § 697b.
Sales, 15 § 697a.
→**Declaration of policy, 15 § 661.**
Default.
Pollution control facilities, 15 § 694-1.
Rentals by
15 § 69
Definitions.
Administra
Administra
Articles, 15
Bid bond, 1
Borrower, 1
Company, 1
Developmer
Generally, 15 § 662.
Issuer, 15 § 697f.
License, 15 § 662.
Licensee, 15 § 662.
Obligee, 15 § 694a.
Payment bond, 15 § 694a.
Performance bond, 15 § 694a.
Pollution control facilities, 15 § 694-1.
Prime contractor, 15 § 694a.
Principal, 15 § 694a.
Qualified contract, 15 § 694-1.
Qualified State or local development company, 15 § 697.
Small-business concern, 15 § 662.
Small business investment company, 15 § 662.
State, 15 § 662.
Subcontractor, 15 § 694a.
Surety, 15 § 694a.
Depository agents, 15 § 687.

SMALL BUSINESS INVESTMENT COMPANIES AND PROGRAMS —Cont'd

Design of pollution control facilities, 15 § 694-1.
Desist orders, 15 § 687a.
Development companies.
Development companies, defined, 15 § 662.
Loans to.
 Assistance, restrictions on, 15 § 697c.
 Authorization, 15 § 695.
 Debentures, 15 § 697 to 697b.
 Generally, 15 § 695 to 697c.
 Plant acquisition or construction, 15 § 696.
 Pooling of debentures, 15 § 697b.
 Private debenture sales, 15 § 697a.
Direct loans, 15 § 685.
Directors.
Removal and suspension, 15 § 687e.
Unlawful acts and omissions, 15 § 687f.
Direct provision of capital, 15 § 684.
Disadvantaged persons, companies financing, 15 § 681.
Disadvantage, financing disadvantage of businesses, 15 § 694-1.
Discretionary provisions.
Authority of Administration to guarantee, 15 § 692.

Documents, papers and books, 15 § 687a.
Duration.
Period or duration. See within this heading, "Period or duration."
Duties.
Powers and duties. See within this heading, "Powers and duties."
Embezzlement, 18 § 657.
Emergency preparedness functions of Administrator of SBA, 50 Appx § 2251 note.
Employees, 15 § 687f.
Enforcement of order, 15 § 687a.
Equity.
Capital, 15 § 684.
Equity Enhancement Act of 1992, 15 § 661 note.
Jurisdiction, 15 § 687c.
Escrow.
Authority of Administration, 15 § 692.

SMALL BUSINESS INVESTMENT COMPANIES AND PROGRAMS —Cont'd

Escrow —Cont'd
Requirements of Administration, 15 § 694-1.
Examinations and examiners, 15 § 687b; 18 § 212, 213, 1006.
Exchange.
Sale or transfer of property. See within this heading, "Sale or transfer of property."
Execution of subleases, 15 § 693.
Exemption from reporting requirements, 15 § 687g.
Expansion of plant, 15 § 696.
Expenses.
Costs and expenses. See within this heading, "Costs and expenses."
Extension of benefits, 15 § 687j.
Extension of long-term loans, 15 § 685.
Facilities.
Plant acquisition or construction, 15 § 696.
Pollution control facilities, 15 § 694-1.
Faith and credit, 15 § 697.
Federal Financing Bank, 15 § 687k.
Federal matters.
United States. See within this heading, "United States."
Fees.
Guarantees by Administration, 15 §
this
s."
f
thin
nnual

Financial matters.
Banks and financial institutions. See within this heading, "Banks and financial institutions."
Fiscal agents, 15 § 687.
Funds. See within this heading, "Funds."
Fines, penalties, and forfeitures.
Acceptance of loan or gratuity by examiner, 18 § 213.
Embezzlement, 18 § 657.
False entries, 18 § 1006.
False statement or report. 18 § 1014.
Generally, 15 § 687g.
Loan or gratuity to examiner, 18 § 212.
Operation and regulation of companies, 15 § 687.
Overvaluation of land, 18 § 1014.
Penalties and forfeitures, 15 § 687g.

FINDING A FEDERAL LAW

Problem: Find the section of the law dealing with the declaration of policy for investing in small businesses.

Step 1. Check the index to *U.S.C.*, *U.S.C.A.*, or *U.S.C.S.* This will indicate that this topic is covered in 15 U.S.C. § 661.

[Illustration 9–4]

PAGE FROM UNITED STATES CODE

Page 393   TITLE 15—COMMERCE AND TRADE   § 661

PART B—SURETY BOND GUARANTEES

Sec.
- 694a. Definitions.
- 694b. Surety bond guarantees.
- 694c. Revolving fund for surety bond guarantees.

SUBCHAPTER V—LOANS TO STATE AND LOCAL DEVELOPMENT COMPANIES

- 695. State development companies.
- 696. Loans for plant acquisition, construction, conversion and expansion.
- 697. Development company debentures.
- 697a. Private debenture sales.
- 697b. Pooling of debentures.
- 697c. Restrictions on development company assistance.
- 697d. Accredited Lenders Program.
- 697e. Premier Certified Lenders Program.
- 697f. Prepayment of development company debentures.
- 697g. Foreclosure and liquidation of loans.

SUBCHAPTER I—GENERAL PROVISIONS

§ 661. Congressional declaration of policy

It is declared to be the policy of the Congress and the purpose of this chapter to improve and stimulate the national economy in general and the small-business segment thereof in particular by establishing a program to stimulate and supplement the flow of private equity capital and long-term loan funds which small-business concerns need for the sound financing of their business operations and for their growth, expansion, and modernization, and which are not available in adequate supply: *Provided, however,* That this policy shall be carried out in such manner as to insure the maximum participation of private financing sources.

sistance under this chapter, when practicable, priority be accorded to small business concerns which lease or purchase equipment and supplies which are produced in the United States and that small business concerns receiving such assistance be encouraged to continue to lease or purchase such equipment and supplies."

SHORT TITLE OF 2004 AMENDMENT

Pub. L. 108–232, § 1, May 28, 2004, 118 Stat. 649, provided that:"'This Act [amending section 697e of this title] may be cited as the 'Premier Certified Lenders Program Improvement Act of 2004'."

SHORT TITLE OF 2001 AMENDMENT

Pub. L. 107–100, § 1, Dec. 21, 2001, 115 Stat. 965, provided that: "This Act [amending sections 636, 683, 687d, 687e, and 697 of this title, section 1833a of Title 12, Banks and Banking, and section 1014 of Title 18, Crimes and Criminal Procedure, and enacting provisions set out as notes under sections 636, 683, and 697 of this title] may be cited as the 'Small Business Investment Company Amendments Act of 2001'."

SHORT TITLE OF 2000 AMENDMENT

Pub. L. 106–554, § 1(a)(8) [§ 1(a)], Dec. 21, 2000, 114 Stat. 2763, 2763A–653, provided that: "This section [enacting part B of subchapter III of this chapter, amending section 683 of this title, section 109 of Title 11, Bankruptcy, and section 1464 of Title 12, Banks and Banking, and amending provisions set out as a note under section 631 of this title] may be cited as the 'New Markets Venture Capital Program Act of 2000'." •

Pub. L. 106–554, § 1(a)(9) [title III, § 301], Dec. 21, 2000, 114 Stat. 2763, 2763A–684, provided that: "This title [enacting section 697g of this title, amending sections 695 to 697 and 697e of this title, enacting provisions set out as a note under section 697g of this title, and repealing provisions set out as a note under section 697e of this title] may be cited as the 'Certified Development Company Program Improvements Act of 2000'."

Pub. L. 106–554, § 1(a)(9) [title IV, § 401], Dec. 21, 2000, 114 Stat. 2763, 2763A–690, provided that: "This title

> **Step 2.** Locate the title and section referred to in the index. Ordinarily, one would consult the latest edition of *U.S.C.* and its cumulative supplements, or one of the two annotated codes.
>
> This illustration shows how this law appears in the *U.S.C.*
>
> Note how at the end of § 661 (as is the case with all *U.S.C.* sections) citations are given to the section in the *United States Statutes at Large.* § 661 was first passed in 1958 and amended in 1992.

REFERENCES IN TEXT

This chapter, referred to in text, was in the original "this Act", meaning Pub. L. 85–699, which enacted this chapter, amended sections 77c, 77ddd, 80a–18, 633 and 636 of this title, and sections 217 [now 212], 218 [now 213], 221 [now 216], 657, 1006 and 1014 of Title 18, Crimes and Criminal Procedure, repealed section 352a of Title 12, Banks and Banking, and enacted notes set out under this section and section 352a of Title 12. Sections 212 and 213 of Title 18, as renumbered by Pub. L. 87–849, were subsequently repealed. For complete classification of this Act to the Code, see Short Title note set out below and Tables.

AMENDMENTS

1992—Pub. L. 102–366 inserted at end "It is the intention of the Congress that in the award of financial as-

SHORT TITLE OF 1992 AMENDMENT

Section 401 of title IV of Pub. L. 102–366 provided that: "This Act [probably means "This title", amending this section and sections 662, 682, 683, 685 to 687, 687b, and 687f of this title, enacting provisions set out as notes under this section and sections 681 and 687b of this title, and amending provisions set out as a note under section 631 of this title] may be cited as the 'Small Business Equity Enhancement Act of 1992'."

SHORT TITLE OF 1988 AMENDMENT

Pub. L. 100–590, title II, § 201, Nov. 3, 1988, 102 Stat. 3007, provided that: "This title [amending sections 694b and 694c of this title and enacting provisions set out as notes under section 694b of this title] may be cited as the 'Preferred Surety Bond Guarantee Program Act of 1988'."

[Illustration 9–5]

PAGE FROM TITLE 15 U.S.C.A. § 661

Ch. 14B   SMALL BUSINESS INVESTMENT   **15 § 661**

- update your research with the most current information
- expand your library with additional resources
- retrieve direct history, precedential history and parallel citations with the Insta-Cite service

For more information on using WESTLAW to supplement your research, see the WESTLAW Electronic Research Guide, which follows the Explanation

---

SUBCHAPTER I—GENERAL PROVISIONS

§ 661.   Congressional declaration of policy

It is declared to be the policy of the Congress and the purpose of this chapter to improve and stimulate the national economy in general and the small-business segment thereof in particular by establishing a program to stimulate and supplement the flow of private equity capital and long-term loan funds which small-business concerns need for the sound financing of their business operations and for their growth, expansion, and modernization, and which are not available in adequate supply: *Provided, however,* That this policy

This illustration and the next show references to the *United States Statutes at Large* and the historical notes summarizing the effect of the amendment on the original public law.

chapter shall be so administered that any financial assistance provided hereunder shall not result in a substantial increase of unemployment in any area of the country.

It is the intention of the Congress that in the award of financial assistance under this chapter, when practicable, priority be accorded to small business concerns which lease or purchase equipment and supplies which are produced in the United States and that small business concerns receiving such assistance be encouraged to continue to lease or purchase such equipment and supplies.

(Pub.L. 85–699, Title I, § 102, Aug. 21, 1958, 72 Stat. 689; Pub.L. 102–366, Title IV, § 416, Sept. 4, 1992, 106 Stat. 1019.)

HISTORICAL AND STATUTORY NOTES

Revision Notes and Legislative Reports

    1958 Acts. House Report No. 2060 and Conference Report No. 2492, see 1958 U.S. Code Cong. and Adm. News, p. 3678.

    1992 Acts. House Report No. 102–492 and Statement by President, see 1992 U.S. Code Cong. and Adm. News, p. 891.

References in Text

    This chapter, referred to in text, was in the original "this Act", meaning Pub.L. 85–699, which enacted this chapter, amended §§ 77c, 77ddd, 80a–18, 633 and 636 of this title, and §§ 217 [now 212], 218 [now 213], 221 [now 216], 657, 1006 and 1014 of Title 18, Crimes and Crimi-

[Illustration 9–6]

PAGE FROM TITLE 15 U.S.C.A. § 661

15 § 661   COMMERCE AND TRADE   Ch. 14B

nal Procedure, repealed § 352a of Title 12, Banks and Banking, and enacted notes set out under this section and § 352a of Title 12. For complete classification of this Act to the Code, see short title set out below and Tables.

Amendments

1992 Amendments. Pub.L. 102–366 inserted at end "It is the intention of the Congress that in the award of financial assistance under this chapter, when practicable, priority be accorded to small business concerns which lease or purchase equipment and supplies which are

681, 683, 684, and 686 of this title] may be cited as the 'Small Business Investment Act Amendments of 1972'."

1967 Amendments. Section 201 of Pub.L. 90–104, title II, Oct. 11, 1967, 81 Stat. 269, provided that: "This title [amending sections 681, 682, 683, 684, 686, 687, 687b, and 692 of this title] may be cited as the 'Small Business Investment Act Amendments of 1967'."

1966 Amendments. Section 1 of Pub.L. 89–779, Nov. 6, 1966, 80 Stat. 1359, provided: "That this Act [enacting sections 687e, 687f, 687g, and 687h of this title

These "Historical and Statutory Notes," continued from the prior illustration, show the intent of the 1992 amendments and the short title of the act.

supplies."

Short Title

1994 Amendments. Pub.L. 103–403, Title V, § 501, Oct. 22, 1994, 108 Stat. 4198, provided that: "This title [enacting section 697f of this title and provisions set out as a note under section 697f of this title] may be cited as the 'Small Business Prepayment Penalty Relief Act of 1994'."

1992 Amendments. Section 401 of Pub.L. 102–366 provided that: "This Act may be cited as the 'Small Business Equity Enhancement Act of 1992'." "This Act" probably refers to this title, meaning Title IV of Pub.L. 102–366, Sept. 4, 1992, 106 Stat. 1007, which amended this section and sections 662, 682, 683, 685, 686, 687, 687b, and 687l of this title, enacted provisions set out as notes under this section and sections 681 and 687b of this title, and amended provisions set out as notes under section 631 of this title. For complete classification of Pub.L. 102–366 to the Code, see Short Title of 1992 Amendments note set out under section 631 of this title and Tables.

1988 Amendments. Pub.L. 100–590, Title II, § 201, Nov. 3, 1988, 102 Stat. 3007, provided that: "This title [amending sections 694b and 694c of this title and enacting provisions set out as notes under section 694b of this title] may be cited as the 'Preferred Surety Bond Guarantee Program Act of 1988'."

1972 Amendments. Section 1 of Pub.L. 92–595, Oct. 27, 1972, 86 Stat. 1314, provided: "That this Act [enacting sections 687i and 687j of this title and amending sections 80a–18, 633, 636, 662,

may be cited as the 'Small Business Investment Act Amendments of 1966'."

1964 Amendments. Section 1 of Pub.L. 88–273, Feb. 28, 1964, 78 Stat. 146, provided: "That this Act [enacting section 687d and amending sections 682, 686, and 687 of this title] may be cited as the 'Small Business Investment Act Amendments of 1963'."

1961 Amendments. Section 1 of Pub.L. 87–341, Oct. 3, 1961, 75 Stat. 752, provided: "That this Act [enacting sections 687a, 687b, and 687c of this title, amending sections 633, 662, 681, 683 to 687, and 696 of this title, and enacting provisions set out as notes under sections 631 and 686 of this title] may be cited as the "Small Business Investment Act Amendments of 1961".

1960 Amendments. Section 1 of Pub.L. 86–502, June 11, 1960, 74 Stat. 196, provided: "That this Act [amending sections 662, 681, 682 and 684 of this title, and section 26–610 of the District of Columbia Code, 1973 edition] may be cited as the "Small Business Investment Act Amendments of 1960".

1958 Acts. Section 101 of Pub.L. 85–699 provided in part that: "This Act [enacting this chapter, amending sections 77c, 77ddd, 80a–18, 633 and 636 of this title, and sections 217 [now 212], 218 [now 213], 221 [now 216], 657, 1006 and 1014 of Title 18, Crimes and Criminal Procedure, repealing section 352a of Title 12, Banks and Banking, and enacting notes set out under this section and former section 352a of title 12] may be cited as the 'Small Business Investment Act of 1958'."

674

[Illustration 9–7]

PAGE FROM TITLE 15 U.S.C.A. § 661

Ch. 14B   SMALL BUSINESS INVESTMENT   15 § 662

Effect of Small Business Equity Enhancement Act of 1992 on Securities Laws

Section 418 of title IV of Pub.L. 102–366 provided that: "Nothing in this Act [probably means "this title", see Short Title of 1992 Amendment note above] (and no amendment made by this ~~Act] shall be construed to affect or limit~~

"Notwithstanding any law, rule, regulation or administrative moratorium, except as otherwise expressly provided in this Act [probably means "this title", see Short Title of 1992 Amendment note above], the Small Business Administration shall—

~~"(1) within 90 days after the date of~~

The important difference in the annotated sets of the *Code* is the digest of court cases after each section of the *Code*. These digests assist in interpreting the meaning of the *Code* section.

Also illustrated are other research aids available in *U.S.C.A.*

---

supersede or limit the jurisdiction of the Securities and Exchange Commission or the authority at any time conferred under the securities laws."

Regulations

Section 415 of title IV of Pub.L. 102–366 provided that:

"(2) within 180 days after the date of enactment of this Act, publish in the Federal Register final rules and regulations implementing this Act, and enter such contracts as are necessary to implement this Act and the amendments made by this Act."

LIBRARY REFERENCES ◄———

Administrative Law

Margin stock defined—
Credit by banks for the purpose of purchasing or carrying, see 12 CFR § 221.2.
Securities credit other than banks, brokers, or dealers, see 12 CFR § 207.2.
Programs, see West's Federal Practice Manual § 2062.
Small business investment companies, see 13 CFR § 107.20.

American Digest System

United States ☞53(8), 82.

Encyclopedias

C.J.S. United States §§ 70, 122.

NOTES OF DECISIONS ◄———

Private right of action   2
Purpose   1

———

1. Purpose

This chapter was passed for purpose of making loans available to those engaging in comparatively small enterprises who cannot obtain adequate borrowed funds through customary financial institutions. First Louisiana Inv. Corp. v. U. S., C.A.5 (La.) 1965, 351 F.2d 495.

Purpose of this chapter is to produce financing for small businesses for long term loans. Hernstadt v. Programs for Television, Inc., N.Y.City Ct.1962, 232 N.Y.S.2d 683, 36 Misc.2d 628.

2. Private right of action

There exists no private right of action under Small Business Investment Act. Hooven-Dayton Corp. v. Center City Mesbic, Inc., S.D.Ohio 1996, 918 F.Supp. 193.

§ 662. Definitions

As used in this chapter—

(1) the term "Administration" means the Small Business Administration;

675

[Illustration 9-8]

PAGE FROM TITLE 15 U.S.C.S. § 661

---

15 USCS § 661   COMMERCE AND TRADE

GENERAL PROVISIONS

§ 661. Congressional declaration of policy

It is declared to be the policy of the Congress and the purpose of this Act to improve and stimulate the national economy in general and the small-business segment thereof in particular by establishing a program to stimulate and supplement the flow of private equity capital and long-term loan funds which small-business concerns need for the sound financing of their business operations and for their growth, expansion, and modernization, and which are not available in adequate supply: Provided, however, That this policy shall be carried out in such manner as to insure the maximum participation of private financing sources.

It is the intention of the Congress that the provisions of this Act shall be so administered that any financial assistance provided hereunder shall not result in a substantial increase in unemployment in any area of the country. It is the intention of the Congress that in the award of financial assistance under this Act, when practicable, priority be accorded to small business concerns which lease or purchase equipment and supplies which are produced in the United States and that small business concerns receiving such assistance be encouraged to continue to lease or purchase such equipment and supplies.

(As amended Sept. 4, 1992, P. L. 102-366, Title IV, § 416, 106 Stat. 1019.)

HISTORY; ANCILLARY LAWS AND DIRECTIVES

Amendments:

1992. Act Sept. 4, 1992 added the sentence beginning "It is the intention of the Congress in the award . . .".

Short title:

Act Aug. 21, 1958, P. L. 85-699, Title I, § 101, 72 Stat. 689; April 5, 1999, P. L. 106-9, § 2(d)(3), 113 Stat. 18, provides: "This Act [15 USCS §§ 661 et seq. generally; for full classification, consult USCS Tables volumes] may be cited as the 'Small Business Investment Act of 1958'.".

Act Nov. 3, 1988, P. L. 100-590, Title II, § 201, 102 Stat. 3007, provides: "This title may be cited as the 'Preferred Surety Bond Guarantee Program Act of 1988'.".

Act Sept. 4, 1992, P. L. 102-366, Title IV, § 401, 106 Stat. 1007, provides: "This Act [title] may be cited as the 'Small Business Equity Enhancement Act of 1992'.". For full classification of such Title, consult USCS Tables volumes.

Act Oct. 22, 1994, P. L. 103-403, Title V, § 501, 108 Stat. 4198, provides: "This title may be

---

> This shows the text of 15 U.S.C.S. § 661, as amended, historical background relating to the law, and ancillary laws and directives. *U.S.C.S.* uses the text of the public law as it appears in the *United States Statutes at Large.*
>
> **See next illustration.**

---

the 'New Markets Venture Capital Program Act of 2000'.".

Act Dec. 21, 2000, P. L. 106-554, § 1(a)(9), 114 Stat. 2763 (enacting into law § 301 of Title III of H.R. 5667 (114 Stat. 2763A-__), as introduced on Dec. 15, 2000), provides: "This title [adding 15 USCS § 697g, and amending 15 USCS §§ 695, 696, 697, and 697e] may be cited as the 'Certified Development Company Program Improvements Act of 2000'.".

Act Dec. 21, 2000, P. L. 106-554, § 1(a)(9), 114 Stat. 2763 (enacting into law § 401 of Title IV of H.R. 5667 (114 Stat. 2763A-__), as introduced on Dec. 15, 2000), provides: "This title [amending 15 USCS §§ 662, 682, 683, and 687b] may be cited as the 'Small Business Investment Corrections Act of 2000'.".

Other provisions:

Implementation of the Small Business Equity Enhancement Act of 1992. Act Sept. 4, 1992, P. L. 102-366, Title IV, § 415, 106 Stat. 1018, provides:

"Notwithstanding any law, rule, regulation or administrative moratorium, except as otherwise expressly provided in this Act [Title IV of Act Sept. 4, 1992, P. L. 102-366; for full classification, consult USCS Tables volumes], the Small Business Administration shall—

"(1) within 90 days after the date of enactment of this Act, publish in the Federal Register proposed rules and regulations implementing this Act and the amendments made by this Act [Title IV of Act Sept. 4, 1992, P. L. 102-366; for full classification, consult USCS Tables volumes]; and

"(2) within 180 days after the date of enactment of this Act, publish in the Federal Register final rules and regulations implementing this Act [Title IV of Act Sept. 4, 1992, P. L. 102-366; for full classification, consult USCS Tables volumes], and enter such contracts as are necessary to implement this Act and the amendments made by this Act.".

Effect of Small Business Equity Enhancement Act of 1992 on securities laws. Act Sept. 4, 1992, P. L. 102-366, Title IV, § 418, 106 Stat. 1019, provides: "Nothing in this Act (and no

2

[Illustration 9–9]

PAGE FROM TITLE 15 U.S.C.S. § 661

SMALL BUSINESS INVESTMENT   **15 USCS § 662**

amendment made by this Act) [Title IV of Act Sept. 4. 1992, P. L. 102-366; for full classification, consult USCS Tables volumes] shall be construed to affect the applicability of the securities laws, as that term is defined in section 3(a)(47) of the Securities Exchange Act of 1934 [15 USCS § 78c(a)(47)], or any of the rules and regulations thereunder, or otherwise supersede or limit the jurisdiction of the Securities and Exchange Commission or the authority at any time conferred under the securities laws.''.

CODE OF FEDERAL REGULATIONS

This section is no longer cited as authority for:
13 CFR Part 116.

RESEARCH GUIDE

Federal Procedure:
10A Fed Proc L Ed, Economic Development §§ 27:181, 187, 190, 193–195, 198, 202, 213, 217, 219.

Am Jur:
17 Am Jur 2d, Consumer and Borrower Protection § 185.
69 Am Jur 2d, Securities Regulation—Federal (1993) §§ 107, 498.

INTERPRETIVE NOTES AND DECISIONS

Small Business Administration did not exceed its statutory authority by improper implementation of a standard operating procedure in action brought by businesses "graduated" from Small Business Administration's program in accordance with criteria established by regulation where regulation is not arbitrary, unreasonable, erroneous, or inconsistent exercise of power, despite argument that businesses were economically more viable than other program participants and more worthy of continued support. Roberts Constr. Co. v United States Small Business Admin. (1987, DC Colo) 657 F Supp 418.

Small business owner's claim against SBA and specialized small business investment company which financed it must fail, where owner claims company violated, and SBA failed to enforce, various regulations under Small Business Investment Act (15 USCS §§ 661 et seq.), because Act does not expressly create private right of action, and its language and legislative history intend enforcement to be undertaken solely by SBA. Hooven-Dayton Corp. v Center City Mesbic (1996, SD Ohio) 918 F Supp 193.

> **This illustrates the "Research Guide" and the annotations ("Interpretive Notes and Decisions"), which are editorial enhancements to the annotated sets of the Code. The pocket supplement should always be consulted for any additional amendments.**

(A) an investment by a venture capital firm, investment company (including a small business investment company) employee welfare benefit plan or pension plan, or trust, foundation, or endowment that is exempt from Federal income taxation—

(i) shall not cause a business concern to be deemed not independently owned and operated regardless of the allocation of control during the investment period under any investment agreement between the business concern and the entity making the investment;

(ii) shall be disregarded in determining whether a business concern satisfies size standards established pursuant to section 3(a)(2) of the Small Business Act [15 USCS § 632(a)(2)]; and

(iii) shall be disregarded in determining whether a small business concern is a smaller enterprise; and

(B) in determining whether a business concern satisfies net income standards established pursuant to section 3(a)(2) of the Small Business Act [15 USCS § 632(a)(2)], if the business concern is not required by law to pay Federal income taxes at the enterprise level, but is required to pass income through to the shareholders, partners, beneficiaries, or other equitable owners of the business concern, the net income of the business concern shall be determined by allowing a deduction in an amount equal to the sum of—

(i) if the business concern is not required by law to pay State (and local, if any) income taxes at the enterprise level, the net income (determined without regard to this subparagraph), multiplied by the marginal State income tax rate (or by the combined State and local income tax rates, as applicable) that would have applied if the business concern were a corporation; and

(ii) the net income (so determined) less any deduction for State (and local) income taxes calculated under clause (i), multiplied by the marginal Federal income tax rate that would have applied if the business concern were a corporation;

(6) [Unchanged]

(7) the term "license" means a license issued by the Administration as provided in section 301 [15 USCS § 681];

3

E. POPULAR NAMES FOR FEDERAL LAWS

Federal legislation is often referred to by its popular name, which may be a name given to a statute by the Congress or by the public or media. The popular name may describe the legislation (e.g., Gold Clause Act) or may refer to its authors (e.g., Taft-Hartley Act).[46]

Tables of popular names provide citations to acts when only the popular names are known. [Illustrations 9–10, 9–11, and 9–12] The following sources provide popular name tables:

- *U.S.C., U.S.C.A.,* and *U.S.C.S.* The popular names tables in each of these sets includes the public law citation (Stat.) and a general range where the law is codified. The *U.S.C.A.* Popular Name table additionally includes citations for each section of the law.

- Office of the Law Revision Counsel, *Popular Name Tool.*[47]

- Cornell's *Legal Information Institute, TOPN.*[48] This table includes links to where each section of an act is codified and to regulations authorized by each section.

- *Findlaw, United States Code Table of Popular Names.*[49]

- *Shepard's Acts and Cases by Popular Names* (print).

- *United States Code Congressional and Administrative News.* Since the 77th Congress, 2d Session, 1942, this source has included a table called "Popular Name Acts" for each session of Congress.

F. TABLES FOR FEDERAL LAWS

As noted, federal laws are first published in chronological order in the volumes of *United States Statutes at Large.* A particular law may cover one topic or may include matters on several different topics. Another law may amend one or several previous laws. Most are public laws of a general and permanent nature and are codified in the *U.S.C.*

Tables enable a researcher to trace each section of a law as it appears in *United States Statutes at Large* and to determine whether a particular section has been codified and, if so, its citation in the *U.S.C.* For example, assume a researcher is interested in Section 3(2) of Pub. L. No. 101–376. To ascertain this section's location in the *U.S.C.,* the researcher must consult the appropriate table of public laws. [Illustration 9–13]

From time to time, a particular title of *U.S.C.* is completely revised with entirely new section numbers. Tables permit researchers to translate citations from the old title to the section numbers in the revised title. [Illustration 9–14]

---

[46] *See* Renata E.B. Strause et al., *How Federal Statutes Are Named,* 105 LAW LIBR. J. 7 (2013). The authors created a database of federal statute popular names, arranged by title, date, and type (sponsor, description, honor, victim, etc.). *See also* Mary Whisner, *What's in a Statute Name?,* 97 LAW LIBR. J. 169 (2005).

[47] http://uscode.house.gov/popularnames/popularnames.htm.

[48] http://www.law.cornell.edu/topn/0.

[49] http://codes.lp.findlaw.com/uscodes/popularnames/index.html.

Each of the three previously described sets containing the *U.S.C.* includes one or more volumes with cross-reference tables that serve various purposes. These tables include the following:

- *Revised Title.* Revised Title tables indicate where sections of former titles of the *United States Code* that have been revised are now incorporated in the *U.S.C.*

- *Revised Statutes of 1878.* This table indicates the location of sections of *Revised Statutes* in the *U.S.C.*

- *United States Statutes at Large.* This table shows where public laws published in *United States Statutes at Large* are found in the *U.S.C.*

G. ILLUSTRATIONS: POPULAR NAMES AND TABLES

[Illustration 9–10]

PAGE FROM SHEPARD'S ACTS AND CASES BY POPULAR NAMES

FEDERAL AND STATE ACTS CITED BY POPULAR NAME   Rye

Rural Zoning Enabling Act (County)
Mich. Comp. Laws Ann., 125.201 et seq.

Rural/Downstate Health Act
Ill. Rev. Stat. 1991, Ch. 111 1/2, § 8051 et seq.

Rush Unsafe Buildings Law
N.Y. Local Laws 1973, Town of Rush, p. 2878

Russell Act (Business Licenses)
Ohio Laws Vol. 80, p. 129

Russell Amendment

Ryder Act (Revaluation of Property)
Wash. Rev. Code Ann., 84.41.010 et seq.

Rye Park Act
N.Y. Laws 1907, Ch. 711

> Frequently, a public law will become known by a popular name. When only the popular name is known, popular name tables enable the actual citations to be found. *See, e.g.,* Ryan White Comprehensive AIDS Resources Emergency Act of 1990.
>
> See next two illustrations.

Russian Friendship Treaty
Haw. Session Laws 1870, p. 83, June 19, 1869

Russian Roulette Act (Taxation)
Fla. Stat. Ann., 194.101

Rutgers, The State University Act
N.J. Stat. Ann., 18A:65-1 et seq.

Ryan Act (Drug Users)
Mich. Comp. Laws Ann., 335.201 et seq.

Ryan Act (Teacher Preparation and Licensing)
Cal. Education Code 1976, § 44200 et seq.

Ryan Liquor Control Act
N.Y. Alcoholic Beverage Control Law (Consol. Laws Ch. 3B) § 101b

Ryan Master Teacher Act
Cal. Education Code 1976, § 44490 et seq.

Ryan White Comprehensive AIDS Resources Emergency Act of 1990
Aug. 18, 1990, P.L. 101-381, 42 U.S. Code § 201 nt.
May 20, 1996, P.L. 104-146, 42 U.S. Code § 201 nt.

993

[Illustration 9–11]

PAGE FROM POPULAR NAME TABLE IN U.S.C.A. ANNUAL INDEX

1195   POPULAR NAME TABLE

Rural Local Broadcast Signal Act
  Pub.L. 106–113, Div. B, § 1000(a)(9) [Title II (§§ 2001, 2002], Nov. 29, 1999, 113 Stat. 1536,
    1501A–544 (47 § 338 note)

Rural Post-Roads Act
  See Federal Aid Acts

Rural Rehabilitation Corporation Trust Liquidation Act
  May 3, 1950, ch. 152, 64 Stat. 98 (7 § 1001 note; 40 §§ 440 to 444)

Rural Small Business Enhancement Act of 1990
  Pub.L. 101–574, Title III, Nov. 15, 1990, 104 Stat. 2827 (5 § 601 note; 15 §§ 631 note, 631b,
    636, 648, 653, 653 note, 654)

Rural Telecommunications Improvements Act of 1990
  Pub.L. 101–624, Title XXIII, Subtitle F, Nov. 28, 1990, 104 Stat. 4038 (7 §§ 901 notes, 918,
    924 to 928, 932, 935, 936, 939, 945, 946, 946 note, 948, 950)

Rural Telephone Cooperative Associations ERISA Amendments Act of 1991

**This is a typical page from the Popular Name Table in the Index volumes of *U.S.C.A.*
This example shows the findings for the same popular name in the previous illustration.**

Russell-Overton Amendment
  Sept. 16, 1940, ch. 720, § 9, 54 Stat. 892 (50 App. § 1158)

Ryan White CARE Act Amendments of 1996
  Pub.L. 104–146, May 20, 1996, 110 Stat. 1346 (5 § 4103 note; 42 §§ 201 note, 294n, 300d,
    300cc note, 300ff–11, 300ff–11 note, 300ff–12 to 300ff–18, 300ff–21 to 300ff–23,
    300ff–26, 300ff–27, 300ff–27a, 300ff–28 to 300ff–31, 300ff–33, 300ff–33 note, 300ff–34 to
    300ff–37, 300ff–47 to 300ff–49, 300ff–51, 300ff–52, 300ff–54, 300ff–55, 300ff–64,
    300ff–71, 300ff–74, 300ff–76 to 300ff–78, 300ff–84, 300ff–101, 300ff–111)
  Pub.L. 106–345, Title V, § 503(b), Oct. 20, 2000, 114 Stat. 1355 (42 § 300ff–22)

Ryan White CARE Act Amendments of 2000
  Pub.L. 106–345, Oct. 20, 2000, 114 Stat. 1319 (see Tables for classification)

Ryan White Comprehensive AIDS Resources Emergency Act of 1990
  Pub.L. 101–381, Aug. 18, 1990, 104 Stat 576 (42 §§ 201 note, 284a, 286, 287a, 287c–2, 289f,
    290aa–3a, 299c–5, 300x–4 note, 300ff, 300ff–1, 300ff–11, 300ff–11 note, 300ff–12 to
    300ff–18, 300ff–21 to 300ff–30, 300ff–41 to 300ff–46, 300ff–46 note, 300ff–47 to
    300ff–55, 300ff–61 to 300ff–67, 300ff–71 to 300ff–76, 300ff–80, 300ff–80 note, 300ff–81
    to 300ff–90, 300aaa to 300aaa–13)

SAA
  See Safety Appliance Acts

SAA
  See Suits in Admiralty Act

Sabbatino Amendment
  See Hickenlooper Amendment

Saccharin Study and Labeling Act
  Pub.L. 95–203, Nov. 23, 1977, 91 Stat. 1451 (21 §§ 301 note, 321, 343, 343a; 42 §§ 218 note,
    289/–1 note)
  Pub.L. 96–273, June 17, 1980, 94 Stat. 536 (21 § 348 note)
  Pub.L. 97–42, § 2, Aug. 14, 1981, 95 Stat. 946 (21 § 348 note)
  Pub.L. 98–22, § 2, Apr. 22, 1983, 97 Stat. 173 (21 § 348 note)
  Pub.L. 99–46, May 24, 1985, 99 Stat. 81 (21 § 348 note)
  Pub.L. 100–71, Title I, July 11, 1987, 101 Stat. 431 (21 § 348 note)
  Pub.L. 104–180, Title VI, § 602, Aug. 6, 1996, 110 Stat. 1594 (21 § 348 note)
  Pub.L. 106–554, § 1(a)(1) [Title V, § 517], Dec. 21, 2000, 114 Stat. 2763, 2763A–73 (21
    § 343a)

Saccharin Study and Labeling Act Amendment of 1981
  Pub.L. 97–42, Aug. 14, 1981, 95 Stat. 946 (21 §§ 301 note, 348 note)

Saccharin Study and Labeling Act Amendment of 1983
  Pub.L. 98–22, Apr. 22, 1983, 97 Stat. 173 (21 §§ 301 note, 348 note)

[Illustration 9–12]

PAGE FROM POPULAR NAME TABLE FROM TITLE 42, U.S.C.A.

POPULAR NAME ACTS

Popular Name	Sections
Rural Housing Amendments of 1983	1441 note, 1471, 1472, 1472 note, 1474, 1476, 1479 to 1487, 1490, 1490a, 1490a note, 1490c, 1490e to 1490g, 1490i to 1490o
Ryan White Comprehensive AIDS Resources Emergency Act of 1990	201 note, 284a, 286, 287a, 287c–2, 289f, 290aa–3a, 299c–5, 300x–4 note, 300ff, 300ff–1, 300ff–11 note, 300ff–11 to 300ff–18, 300ff–21 to 300ff–30, 300ff–41 to 300ff–46, 300ff–46 note, 300ff–47 to 300ff–49a, 300ff–50, 300ff–51 to 300ff–55, 300ff–61 to 300ff–67, 300ff–71 to 300ff–76, 300ff–80 note, 300ff–80 to 300ff–90

> This page from the Popular Name Table within Title 42 of the *U.S.C.A.* shows the findings for the same popular name in the two previous illustrations.

	300g to 300g–6, 300h to 300h–7, 300i, 300i–1, 300j to 300j–3, 300j–4 to 300j–9, 300j–11, 300j–21 to 300j–25
Safe Drinking Water Act Amendments of 1986	201 note, 300f, 300g–1 to 300g–6, 300g–6 notes, 300h to 300h–2, 300h–4 to 300h–7, 300i, 300i–1, 300j, 300j–1 note, 300j–1 to 300j–4, 300j–7, 300j–11, 6939b, 6979b
Safe Drinking Water Amendments of 1977	201 note, 300f, 300f notes, 300g–1, 300g–3, 300g–5, 300h, 300h–1, 300j to 300j–2, 300j–4, 300j–6, 300j–8, 300j–10, 7401 note, 7410, 7411, 7413, 7414, 7416, 7419, 7420, 7426, 7472 to 7475, 7478, 7479, 7502, 7502 notes, 7503, 7506, 7521, 7522, 7525, 7541, 7545, 7549, 7602, 7604, 7607, 7623 note, 7625a, 7626
SARA	See Superfund Amendments and Reauthorization Act of 1986
School Lunch Act	See National School Lunch Act
School Lunch and Child Nutrition Amendments of 1986	1751 note, 1752, 1755, (1758, 1760) and notes, 1761, 1762a,

[Illustration 9–13]

PAGE FROM TABLES VOLUME, U.S.C.S.

Pub. L.	Section	Stat. Page	USCS Title	Section	Status	Pub. L.	Section	Stat. Page	USCS Title	Section	Status
103 Stat			**STATUTES AT LARGE**								**101st Cong**
			1990 August—Cont'd						1990 August—Cont'd		
101-366—Cont'd						101-371		453	Spec.		Un-class.
	102(b)	431	38	prec. 4141	Added						
			38	4141	Added	101-372		454	Spec.		Un-class.
		435	38	4142	Added						
	102(c)	436	38	4107(e)(1)	Amd.	101-373		455	Spec.		Un-class.
	102(d)		58	prec. 4101	Amd.						
	103	437	38	4107(e)(5)	Amd.	101-374	1	656	42	201 nt.	New
	104		38	4141 nt.	New		2(a)		42	290aa-12(a)	Amd.
	201(a)(1)		38	620C	Added		2(b)(1)		42	290aa-12(d)	Rpld.
	201(a)(2)	438	38	prec. 601	Amd.		2(b)(2)		42	290aa-12(e)- (g)	Redes.
	201(b)		58	620C nt.	New					{(c), (e), (f)}	
	2*2(a)		38	5051	Amd.		2(b)(3)		42	290aa-12(c),	Added
	202(b)(1)		38	5053(a)	Amd.					(d)	
	202(b)(2)		38	5053(b)	Amd.		2(c)(1)		42	290aa-12(g)(1)	Amd.
	203(1)	439	38	4114(a)(3)(A)	Amd.		2(c)(2)		42	290aa-12(g)(3)	Amd.
	203(2)		38	4114(a)(3)(C)	Amd.		2(c)(3)	457		Appn.	Un-class.
	204		38	612A nt.	Amd.		2(d)			Spec.	Un-class.
	205(a)(1)		38	prec. 4351	Amd.		2(e)		42	290aa-12 nt.	New
			38	4351	Added		2(e)		42	290aa-2	Amd.
		440	38	4352	Added						
			38	4353	Added						
			38	4354	Added						

> This table lists all public laws and indicates where each section has been codified in the *U.S.C.* For example, Section 3(2) of Pub. L. 101–376 can be located in Title 5, § 7701 (j) in the *U.S.C.*, *U.S.C.A*, or *U.S.C.S.*

Pub. L.	Section	Stat. Page	USCS Title	Section	Status	Pub. L.	Section	Stat. Page	USCS Title	Section	Status
	205(c)(2)		38	5303(a)(1), (b)	Amd.						class.
	205(c)(3)		38	4304(1)(A), (2)						1990 August 17		
				(D), (5)	Amd.							
	206(a)		38	1784A	Added							
	206(b)	442	38	1434 nt.	New	101-376	1	461	5	7501 nt.	New
	206(c)		38	prec. 1770	Amd.		2(a)		5	7511	Amd.
	206(d)		5	552a nt.	New		2(b)	462	5	4303(e)	Amd.
	207		38	1622 nt.	New		2(c)		5	4303 nt.	New
	208(a)	443	38	1791(b)	Amd.		3(1)		5	7701(k)(1)(j)]	Redes.
	208(b)		38	1791 nt.	New		3(2)		5	7701(j)	Added
	209			Spec.	Un-class.		4	463	5	4303 nt.	New
101-367	1, 2	445		Spec.	Un-class.	101-377	1	464	16	430g-4	New
							2		16	430g-5	New
101-368	1	446	42	201 nt.	New		3	465	16	430g-6	New
	2(a)(1)		42	247b(j)(2)	Amd.		4		16	430g-7	New
	2(a)(2)		42	247b(k)(2)(A)-			5	466	16	430g-8	New
				(D)	Amd.		6	467	16	430g-9	New
	2(b)		42	247b(l)	Added		7		16	430g-10	New
	3(c)		42	247b(j)(2)	Amd.	101-378	Title I				
101-369	1	448	9	prec. 301	Amd.		101	468		Spec.	Un-class.
			9	301	Added		Title II				
			9	302	Added		201			Spec.	Un-class.
			9	303	Added						
		449	9	304	Added		202			Spec.	Un-class.
			9	305	Added						
			9	306	Added		203	469		Spec.	Un-class.
			9	307	Added						
	2	450	9	prec. 1	Amd.		204			Spec.	Un-class.
	3		9	301 nt.	New						
101-370	1	451	49				205(a)	470	16	1132 nt.	Amd.
			Appx.	1475(d)(4)	Added		205(b)			Spec.	Un-class.
	2		49				Title III				
			Appx.	1357(g)	Amd.		301(1)	471	43	1629c(d)(1)(A)	Amd.
	3	452	49				301(2)		43	1629c(d)(2)(B)	
			Appx.	1482 nt.	New					(i)((d)(2)(B)]	Redes.

400

[Illustration 9–14]

PAGE FROM TABLES VOLUME, U.S.C.S.

T 38   REVISED TITLES

TITLE 38—VETERANS' BENEFITS

[This title was enacted into law by Act Sept. 2, 1958, P. L. 85-857, § 1, 72 Stat. 1105. This table shows where sections of former Title 38 are incorporated in revised Title 38]

Title 38 Former Sections	Title 38 New Sections	Title 38 Former Sections	Title 38 New Sections
1–3	Omitted	16b	5203
4	214	16c	5204
5–9	Omitted	16d	5205
10	215	16e	5206
11	201, 210(b)	16f	5207
11a	101(1), 210(a), 210(b)	16g	5208
11a-1	Omitted	16h	601(4), 5209
11a-2	211(a)	16i	5210
11a-3	233	16j	Omitted
11b	5006	17	5220
11c–11d-1	Omitted	17a	5221
11e	214	17b	5222
11f	Omitted	17c	5223
11g	202	17d	5224
11h	3303	17e	5225
11i	5014	17f	5226
11j	233(1), (2)	17g	5227
11k	233(4)	17h	5228
11*l*	3204	17i	Omitted
12	Omitted	17j	210(c)

> When a title of the *U.S.C.* is revised with new section numbering, a table similar to this one is prepared and can be consulted in the Tables volumes of the various sets containing the *Code*.

13e	4206	34	902
13f	4207	35	Omitted
13g	4208	36	3102(b)
14	5101	37	101(4)
14a	5102	38	107(a)
14b	5103	39, 39a	505
14c	5104	41	3002
14d	5105	42–49	Omitted
14e	214	49a	3107
15	4101	50	3020
15a	4102	51–57	Omitted
15b	4103	58	See 3011
15c	4104	71–75	Omitted
15d	4105	76	111(a)–(c)
15e	4106	77	111(d)
15f	4107	91–95	Omitted
15g	4108	96	See 3021
15h	4109	97	Omitted
15i	4110	101	3402, 3403
15j	4111	102	3404
15k	4112	103	3405
15*l*	4113	104	Omitted
15m	4114	111	3404
15n	4115	112–115	Omitted
16	5201	121–124	Omitted
16a	5202	125	3301

92

H. FEDERAL LEGISLATION: RESEARCH PROCEDURE

1. Public Laws in Force

To determine whether any *U.S.C.* sections pertain to a given topic, the following procedures may be used:

a.   Index Method. Check first the general index to one of the sets of the *U.S.C.* Because both *U.S.C.A.* and *U.S.C.S.* have more current indexes, it is usually better to start with either of these sources rather than with the official *U.S.C.* The index will direct the researcher to the title under which the subject being researched will be found. Next, check the index to the individual title in either of the annotated editions. The individual title indexes may provide better guides to the subject matter of the title than the entries located in the general index.

b.   Topic or Analytic Method. If the researcher is familiar with a *U.S.C.* title that includes the topic under research (e.g., bankruptcy or copyright), it may be useful to obtain the volumes covering the title and consult the outline or table of contents preceding the relevant title. This table of contents sets forth headings for each section and, therefore, can narrow the research path.

c.   Definition Method. The general indexes of all three sets of the *U.S.C.* include a main entry, "Definitions." Under this main entry are sub-entries consisting of all terms defined within the *U.S.C.* This method may be a quick way to access particular provisions. For example, if the research involves labor relations and the researcher consults the Definitions entry in the General Index and the sub-entry *supervisor* to determine if *supervisor* is defined in the *U.S.C.,* the following relevant entries are noted:

Supervisor,

Labor management relations, 29 § 142

Federal employees, 5 § 7103

Federal Service, 5 § 7101 note, Ex. Ord. No. 11491

National Labor Relations Act, 29 § 152

Similar information is found in the *U.S.C.A.* and the *U.S.C.S.*

2. Public Laws No Longer in Force

If a researcher wants to find public laws that are no longer in force, the following indexes should be consulted:

a.   Middleton G. Beaman & A.K. McNamara, *Index Analysis of the Federal Statutes (General and Permanent Law), 1789–1873* (1911).

b.   Walter H. McClenon & Wilfred C. Gilbert, *Index to the Federal Statutes, 1874–1931* (1933).

To see the text of a codified law as it existed at an earlier time, superseded editions of the *U.S.C.* can be consulted. As noted above, the *U.S.C.* began in 1926 and, since 1934, has been published every six years, with annual cumulative supplements issued between editions. Many law libraries retain these superseded editions in print or have them in microform. *HeinOnline* provides electronic access to all earlier editions of the *U.S.C.* A microfiche collection of historical compilations of federal laws, *Hein's Early Federal Laws*

(1992), can be consulted to locate federal laws from the eighteenth and nineteenth centuries.

3.   Private, Temporary, and Local Laws

Occasionally, a researcher may need to locate a private, temporary, or local law that was never included in the *U.S.C.* These laws are contained in *United States Statutes at Large* and can be consulted if the date of enactment is known. If this date is not known, it becomes more difficult to locate such laws. The *Consolidated Index to the Statutes at Large of the United States of America from March 4, 1789 to March 3, 1903,* may be used to find laws within the period covered. After that period the volumes of *United States Statutes at Large* must be checked individually.

One of the volumes included in the *United States Code Service, Notes to Uncodified Laws and Treaties*, contains interpretive notes and decisions for laws that were not classified in the *U.S.C.* or that were classified in the *U.S.C.* but subsequently eliminated. The text of the law is not included.

4.   Shepard's and KeyCite

Shepard's (both in print as *Shepard's Federal Citations* and online in *LexisNexis*) can be used to determine the history and treatment of a federal statute. *KeyCite* in *Westlaw* can be used in much the same way, although there are some differences. Uncodified statutes and superseded code editions may be Shepardized in print, but not online in either *Shepard's* or *KeyCite*. *KeyCite* statute search results retrieve only section-level specific citations, as compared to the subsection-level specific citation results retrieved through *Shepard's*.[50]

---

[50] *Shepard's* and *KeyCite* are discussed in detail in Chapter 15 of this book.

Chapter 10

FEDERAL LEGISLATIVE HISTORIES AND LEGISLATIVE MATERIALS*

This chapter discusses federal legislative histories, including their sources and documents. It identifies the documents typically created during the legislative process, lists sources of previously compiled legislative histories, describes methods for identifying and locating the documents of a legislative history, and indicates methods for tracking the legislative process.[1]

A. LEGISLATIVE HISTORIES IN LEGAL RESEARCH

A law is the means by which a legislative body expresses its intent to declare, command, or prohibit some action. *Legislative history* is the term used to describe the documents generated by the legislature during the process of enacting legislation. One purpose of compiling a legislative history, therefore, is to gain an understanding of the considerations leading to the enactment of a law or the failure of a bill to become law. Also, researchers and interest groups may need to determine the current status of proposed legislation and locate documents generated during the progress of the legislation through Congress.

Courts and advocates often use legislative histories when interpreting statutes.[2] Differences of opinion exist as to the extent to which courts should use legislative histories.[3] An increasingly vocal group of federal judges led by Justice Antonin Scalia of the U.S. Supreme Court argues that legislative history has become an unreliable guide to congressional intent because lobbyists and congressional staff members so often distort it.[4] This conflict has led to a re-examination of legislative histories as a subject in

---

* This chapter was revised by Jane Thompson, Associate Director of Faculty Services and Research, William A. Wise Law Library, University of Colorado Law School.

[1] This chapter focuses exclusively on federal legislative histories. Chapter 11 discusses state legislative histories. Chapter 9 discusses the published sources of federal legislation.

[2] "But, while the clear meaning of statutory language is not to be ignored, 'words are inexact tools at best,' . . . and hence it is essential that we place the words of a statute in their proper context by resort to the legislative history." Tidewater Oil Co. v. United States, 409 U.S. 151, 157 (1972).

[3] *See, e.g.,* Schwegmann Bros. v. Calvert Distillers Corp., 341 U.S. 384, 395 (1951) (Justice Jackson in a concurring opinion indicating that "we should not go beyond Committee reports"), *reh'g denied*, 341 U.S. 956 (1951); National Small Shipments Traffic Conference, Inc. v. Civil Aeronautics Board, 618 F.2d 819, 828 (D.C. Cir. 1980) (court warns against the manufacture of legislative histories). *But see* Schwenke v. Sec'y of the Interior, 720 F.2d 571, 576 (9th Cir. 1983) (reversing the lower court for failure to consider legislative history of the statute in question). *See also Conference on Statutory Interpretation: The Role of Legislative History in Judicial Interpretation: A Discussion Between Judge Kenneth W. Starr and Judge Abner J. Mikva*, 1987 DUKE L.J. 361.

[4] *See* Antonin Scalia, A MATTER OF INTERPRETATION: FEDERAL COURTS AND THE LAW (1997); Charles Rothfeld, *Read Congress's Words, Not Its Mind, Judges Say*, N.Y. TIMES, Apr. 14, 1989, at B5, col. 3; Charles Tiefer, *The Reconceptualization of Legislative History in the Supreme Court*, 2000 WIS. L. REV. 205. *See also* Elizabeth A. Liess, Comment, *Censoring Legislative History: Justice Scalia on the Use of Legislative History in Statutory Interpretation*, 72 NEB. L. REV. 568 (1993); Arthur Stock, Note, *Justice Scalia's Use of Sources in*

law school legal research courses.[5] These controversies are more academic than practical, however, because the use of legislative histories is a well-established practice of contemporary litigation. Moreover, legislative materials have many uses in addition to arguing for a particular interpretation of a statute.[6]

Components of a legislative history are the documents produced by Congress in enacting a law. The language of a *bill* as introduced in Congress and subsequent amendments to it may explain the success or failure of the bill to become law. Reports of legislative committees to which the bill was assigned, hearings and debates on the bill, and other documents prepared in connection with the bill's progress through Congress may offer insight as to the purpose of the law or the meaning of specific language in the law. Ancillary documents, such as committee prints, Congressional Research Service Reports, presidential messages and signing statements, as well as blogs and podcasts produced by legislators and political parties, can provide useful information about the purposes of legislation.

B. DOCUMENTS RELEVANT TO FEDERAL LEGISLATIVE HISTORIES

Before compiling a federal legislative history, researchers should familiarize themselves with the types of documents that may be relevant to establishing intent. These documents are typically found on federal government websites, especially *Congress.gov* (the successor to *THOMAS*)[7] and *FDsys* (the successor to *GPO Access*); in

---

Statutory and Constitutional Interpretation: How Congress Always Loses, 1990 DUKE L.J. 160. For a recent study examining the U.S. Supreme Court's use of legislative history in cases interpreting federal statutes (1953–2006), see David S. Law & David Zaring, *Law Versus Ideology: The Supreme Court and the Use of Legislative History*, 51 WM. & MARY L. REV. 1653 (2010).

For discussions of the use, misuse, abuse, or appropriateness of legislative histories in judicial decision-making, see Anthony D'Amato, *Can Legislatures Constrain Judicial Interpretation of Statutes?*, 75 VA. L. REV. 561 (1989); GEORGE A. COSTELLO, SOURCES OF LEGISLATIVE HISTORY AS AIDS TO STATUTORY CONSTRUCTION (1989); Stephen Breyer, *On the Uses of Legislative History in Interpreting Statutes*, 65 S. Cal. L. REV. 845 (1992); William T. Mayton, *Law Among the Pleonasms: The Futility and Aconstitutionality of Legislative History in Statutory Interpretation*, 41 EMORY L.J. 113 (1992); W. David Slawson, *Legislative History and the Need to Bring Statutory Interpretation Under the Rule of Law*, 44 STAN. L. REV. 383 (1992); Jack Schwartz & Amanda Stakem Conn, *The Court of Appeals at the Cocktail Party: The Use and Misuse of Legislative History*, 54 MD. L. REV. 432 (1995); Edward Heath, *How Federal Judges Use Legislative History*, 25 J. LEGIS. 95 (1999); Bernard W. Bell, *R-E-S-P-E-C-T: Respecting Legislative Judgments in Interpretive Theory*, 78 N.C. L. Rev. 1253 (2000); Adrian Vermeule, *The Cycles of Statutory Interpretation*, 68 U. CHI. L. REV. 149 (2001); Paul E. McGreal, *A Constitutional Defense of Legislative History*, 13 WM. & MARY BILL RTS. J. 1267 (2005); JOSEPH L. GERKIN, WHAT GOOD IS LEGISLATIVE HISTORY? JUSTICE SCALIA IN THE FEDERAL COURTS OF APPEALS (2007); Anita S. Krishnakumar, *Statutory Interpretation in the Roberts Court's First Era*, 62 HASTINGS L.J. 221 (2010); James J. Brudney, *Confirmatory Legislative History*, 76 BROOK. L. REV. 901 (2011); Mark Tushnet, *Theory and Practice in Statutory Interpretation*, 43 TEX. TECH L. REV. 1185 (2011).

[5] *See, e.g.,* Peter C. Schanck, *An Essay on the Role of Legislative Histories in Statutory Interpretation*, 80 LAW LIBR. J. 391 (1988); J. Myron Jacobstein & Roy M. Mersky, *Congressional Intent and Legislative Histories: Analysis or Psychoanalysis?*, 82 LAW LIBR. J. 297 (1990); Peter C. Schanck, *Uses and Values of Legislative Histories: A Reply*, 82 LAW LIBR. J. 303 (1990); Peter C. Schanck, *The Only Game in Town: Contemporary Interpretive Theory, Statutory Construction, and Legislative Histories*, 82 LAW LIBR. J. 419 (1990). For references to additional sources regarding the uses of legislative histories, see Peter C. Schanck, *The Use of Legislative Histories in Statutory Interpretation: A Selected and Annotated Bibliography*, 13 LEGAL REFERENCE SERVICES Q., no. 1, 1993, at 5.

[6] *See* Mary Whisner, *Other Uses of Legislative History*, 105 LAW LIBR. J. 243 (2013).

[7] *THOMAS.gov* is being retired at the end of 2014. Until then, it is accessible at http://thomas.loc.gov/home/thomas.php.

federal depository libraries; and through commercial electronic sources (particularly *ProQuest*, *HeinOnline*, *Westlaw*, and *LexisNexis*).

1. Congressional Bills

A proposed piece of legislation is introduced as a bill or a joint resolution[8] in either the House of Representatives (where it is assigned an H.R. or H.J. Res. number) or the Senate (where it is assigned an S. or S.J. Res. number).[9] This number stays with the bill until either it is passed or the end of the Congress in which it was introduced. When a bill is amended, it usually is reprinted with the amending language; less frequently, the amendment or amendments are printed separately. A comparison of the language of the bill as introduced, its subsequent amendments, and the final language of the bill as passed (the public law) may reveal legislative intent because of the insertion or deletion of language.[10]

The bill that ultimately becomes law may have a different number from the bill that was the subject of committee hearings and reports. It may be necessary to look at language in more than one bill to trace legislative history.

The researcher should identify and obtain each of the following documents that exist in connection with the legislation being researched:

- The forms of the bill as first introduced in both the House and the Senate;

- Amended forms of the bill, from each house;

- The form of the bill as it was passed by each house (the engrossed version from each house);

- If the bill was sent to a conference committee, the bill as finalized in conference committee;

- If the bill was sent to conference committee, amended forms of the bill from the conference committee; and

- The final form of the bill, as it was passed in identical versions by both houses.[11]

2. Committee Reports

After a bill is introduced in either the House or the Senate, it is assigned to one or more committees that have jurisdiction over the bill's subject matter.[12] The committee's

---

[8] "While bills are used for purposes of general legislation, joint resolutions . . . are used to propose constitutional amendments and for a variety of special or subordinate purposes, such as continuing appropriations. Except for those proposing constitutional amendments, joint resolutions become law in the same manner as bills." JULIA TAYLOR, LEGISLATIVE HISTORY RESEARCH: A BASIC GUIDE 3 (2013), http://www.fas.org/sgp/crs/misc/R41865.pdf. The following discussion speaks of "bills" but applies equally to joint resolutions.

[9] *See* Chapter 9, Section A.

[10] United States v. St. Paul, M. & M. Ry. Co., 247 U.S. 310, 318 (1918). *See also* Donovan v. Hotel, Motel & Rest. Emps. & Bartenders Union, Local 19, 700 F.2d 539, 543 n.4 (9th Cir. 1983).

[11] This final form of the bill is called the enrolled version. The slip law (or public law) version can substitute for the enrolled version in compiling a legislative history. The slip law has the identical text as the enrolled version and is generally easier to locate.

[12] A bill's committee assignments may be located in two ways. First, the bill information page on the *Congress.gov* website includes a tab for "Committees," listing the committee assignment. In addition, CCH's

task is to consider the bill and decide whether to recommend its passage. If passage is not recommended or no action is taken during the Congress in which the bill was introduced, the bill "dies in committee." If the committee recommends passage, it does so in a written report that usually includes its recommended final form of the bill, indicating changes, if any, made in committee; an analysis of the intent and content of the proposed legislation; and the rationale behind the committee's recommendation.

When the house in which it was first introduced approves the bill, it is sent to the other house and again assigned to an appropriate committee or committees, where it receives similar consideration.[13] When both houses pass a bill but in different versions, a conference committee convenes to reconcile the different versions of the bill. The conference committee consists of a group of representatives and senators; the activities of the committee are restricted to reconciling differing language in the respective versions of the bill. The conference committee issues a conference committee report, which contains recommendations for reconciling the differences between the two bills and a statement explaining the effect of the actions. Both houses must then vote on the compromise bill.

Committee reports are considered among the most important documents in determining the legislative intent of Congress because they reflect the understanding of those members of Congress closely involved in studying the subject matter and drafting the proposed legislation.[14] [Illustration 10–1]

The researcher should, therefore, also identify and obtain each of the following documents that exist for the bill under consideration:

- The reports of the committees of both houses to which the bill was assigned.

- The report, if any, of the conference committee of the House and Senate. This report is usually issued as a House report.[15]

3. Committee Hearings

Hearings, which may be held by committees of the House and Senate, are generally of two types. The first type is a hearing held to investigate matters of general concern, such as AIDS or the use of steroids in athletics. *Investigative* hearings may or may not result in legislation. The second, more familiar type is a hearing related to proposed legislation. *Legislative* hearings are held after a bill is assigned to a congressional committee.

The primary function of legislative hearings is to provide committee members with information that may be useful in their consideration of the bill. Interested persons and experts on the subject matter of the bill may be invited or subpoenaed to express their

---

Congressional Index contains a list of all bills introduced in each Congress. This list includes all sponsors of the bill and the bill's initial committee assignments.

[13] After a bill passes one house, it is thereafter referred to as an *act*. An act only becomes a law if it successfully makes its way through the entire legislative process, as described in this chapter.

[14] GWENDOLYN B. FOLSOM, LEGISLATIVE HISTORY: RESEARCH FOR THE INTERPRETATION OF LAWS 33 (1972). *See also* Zuber v. Allen, 396 U.S. 168, 186 (1969); Stevenson v. J.C. Penney Co., 464 F. Supp. 945, 948–49 (N.D. Ill. 1979).

[15] Under the rules of Congress, the conference report is also to be printed as a Senate report. This requirement frequently is waived by the unanimous consent of the Senate. ROBERT B. DOVE, ENACTMENT OF A LAW: PROCEDURAL STEPS IN THE LEGISLATIVE PROCESS, S. DOC. NO. 97–20, at 25 (1982).

opinions or answer questions about the bill's purpose or effect; they may suggest changes or amendments to the bill. In most, but not all, instances, transcripts of the hearings are published. When published, a hearing document contains the transcript of testimony, the questions posed by committee members and the answers provided by witnesses, written statements and exhibits submitted by interested parties, and occasionally the text of the bill that is the subject of the hearing.

Hearings are not held on all legislation, nor are all transcripts of hearings published. Moreover, hearings that are pertinent to the intent of a public law may have been held during a session of Congress prior to the one in which the law was enacted. Also, hearings may have been conducted on other proposed legislation that contains provisions similar to those of the law being researched. Therefore, it is often useful to extend the search for hearings beyond a particular congressional session or to search for hearings on related legislation. This is especially true if no hearings were held or if hearings were not published for the legislation being researched.

Committee hearings are not the best evidence of legislative intent when they contain the testimony of outside witnesses, but they may offer clues as to which arguments were persuasive to legislators. Also, senators and representatives offer testimony, too, so hearings should be consulted when available. Hearings can be a rich source of background about the policies under consideration.

The researcher should identify and obtain each of the following documents, if they exist:

- Hearings held by the committees to which the bill was assigned;

- Hearings from previous congressional sessions concerning the subject matter of the bill being researched; and

- Hearings on related bills, or bills containing similar provisions, that may have been held in prior Congresses as well as the Congress in question.

4. Congressional Debates

Floor debate on a bill in the House or Senate can occur at almost any stage of the legislative process. Debate is usually scheduled after a bill has been reported out of the committee to which it was assigned.[16] During the debate, legislators may propose amendments, argue for and against the bill and its amendments, and discuss and explain ambiguous or controversial provisions. Some authorities suggest that floor statements of legislators on the substance of a bill under discussion should not be considered by courts as determinative of congressional intent.[17] Generally, courts give some weight to such statements, especially when made by the bill's sponsors, whose stated intention is to clarify or explain the bill's purpose.[18] Such statements are published in the

---

[16] As a practical matter, most bills receive little, if any, floor debate. House rules limit floor debate for most bills to 40 minutes. Senate rules require the body's consent to bring the bill to the floor at all. http://beta. congress.gov; click on "The Legislative Process," which contains video and text explanations for procedures on the "House Floor" and "Senate Floor."

[17] See, e.g., Oliver Wendell Holmes, Jr., The Theory of Legal Interpretation, 12 HARV. L. REV. 417, 419 (1899) ("We do not inquire what the legislature meant; we ask only what the statute means.").

[18] See S & E Contractors, Inc. v. United States, 406 U.S. 1, 13 n.9 (1972); Federal Energy Admin. v. Algonquin SNG, Inc., 426 U.S. 548, 564 (1976). But see Ohio v. U.S. Envtl. Prot. Agency, 997 F.2d 1520, 1532 (D.C. Cir. 1993). See generally Lori L. Outzs, A Principled Use of Congressional Floor Speeches in Statutory Interpretation, 28 COLUM. J.L. & SOC. PROBS. 297 (1995).

Congressional Record and are usually included as an integral part of legislative histories.[19] [Illustration 10–8]

5. Committee Prints

Committee prints are special studies about specific subjects prepared for congressional committees and their staffs. These publications may include bibliographies, analyses of similar bills on a subject, and excerpts from hearings. The researcher should identify and obtain those committee prints that may have some relation to the legislation under consideration.

6. Congressional Research Service (CRS) Reports

In 1914, Congress passed legislation to create the Legislative Reference Service; in 1970, it was renamed the Congressional Research Service (CRS).[20] CRS is a department within the Library of Congress charged with providing members of Congress and its committees with confidential, nonpartisan, legislative research and legal analysis. CRS experts examine major policy issues and generate reports and issue briefs, which provide background information for legislative proposals; these are referred to collectively as "CRS reports." The reports are usually brief, and many are updated versions of previous reports. A CRS report does not become public unless a member of Congress releases it. A few reports are posted on the websites of members of Congress or congressional committees (and the reports are occasionally published as committee prints). A majority of CRS reports can be located only through Internet collections and commercial services.

Reports of the Congressional Research Service are not evidence of legislative intent, but they can assist the legislative history researcher in understanding the policy issues that Congress is attempting to address through legislation.

7. Presidential or Executive Agency Documents

Occasionally, other documents are relevant to a legislative history, but because Congress does not produce them they are not—strictly speaking—sources of legislative intent. These documents may consist of presidential messages or reports and documents of federal agencies. The president of the United States—or members of an executive agency, who usually act through the president—often sends proposed legislation to Congress for consideration. Presidential messages or executive agency memoranda may

---

[19] The *Congressional Record* may not reflect what was actually said on the floor of either house of Congress, because members have the right to correct their remarks before publication. Studies have shown that this privilege is generally not abused, as the majority of revisions are syntactical or otherwise within the bounds of propriety. Prior to 1978, members of Congress were allowed to insert remarks into the *Congressional Record* that were not delivered on the floor of either house, without any indication that the remarks were extraneous. Effective March 1, 1978, Congress changed its rules to provide that statements in the *Congressional Record* that were not spoken on the floor of either house of Congress were to be preceded and followed with a round "bullet" symbol. If, however, any part of a statement was delivered orally, the entire statement was to appear without the symbol. 124 CONG. REC. 3852 (1978). Commencing with vol. 132, no. 115, of the *Congressional Record* (Sept. 8, 1986), the House of Representatives abolished the bullet symbol and substituted instead the use of a different style of typeface to indicate material inserted or appended. [Illustration 10–8] The Senate, however, has retained the bullet symbol to distinguish undelivered remarks. *See* Joe Morehead, *Into the Hopper: Congress and the Congressional Record: A Magical Mystery Tour*, 13 SERIALS LIBR. 59 (1987). *See also* Donald J. Dunn, *Letter to the Editor*, 14 GOV'T PUBLICATIONS REV. 113 (1987) (updating a part of Michelle M. Springer, *The Congressional Record: "Substantially a Verbatim Report"?*, 13 GOV'T PUBLICATIONS REV. 371 (1986)).

[20] http://www.loc.gov/crsinfo/.

accompany the proposal to Congress. These documents explain the purpose of, and describe the president's or agency's intent in, proposing the legislation.

After a bill passes Congress, it is sent to the president. If the president signs or vetoes the legislation, the president may add a signing statement or veto message incorporating the president's rationale for the action taken on the legislation.[21] Many signing statements take the form of general comments praising or expressing the purpose of an act of Congress. Problematic or controversial signing statements allege that portions of the legislation are unconstitutional, and these statements may express the president's intent not to enforce those provisions.[22] Some critics argue that the latter statements exceed the authority of the executive, which is either to enforce or veto legislation.[23]

In summary, the federal legislative history researcher needs to identify and obtain each of the following presidential or agency documents:

- Presidential or executive agency reports accompanying proposed legislation sent to Congress by the president; and

- Presidential signing statements[24] or veto messages.

8. Blogs and Podcasts

Both major parties, as well as individual legislators, lobbyists, think tanks, political action committees, and influential commentators, use blogs and podcasts to discuss

---

[21] The role of presidential signing statements in a legislative history is discussed in Frank B. Cross, *The Constitutional Legitimacy and Significance of Presidential "Signing Statements"*, 40 ADMIN. L. REV. 209 (1988); Marc N. Garber & Kurt A. Wimmer, *Presidential Signing Statements as Interpretations of Legislative Intent: An Executive Aggrandizement of Power*, 24 HARV. J. ON LEGIS. 363 (1987); Mark R. Killenbeck, *A Matter of Mere Approval? The Role of the President in the Creation of Legislative History*, 48 ARK. L. REV. 239 (1995); Laura McDonald, *The Interpretive Worth of Presidential Signing Statements: A New Form of Legislative History*, 38 FLA. ST. U. L. REV. 179 (2010).

In April 2006, a newspaper reporter created a stir by spotlighting the use of "objecting" signing statements during the George W. Bush administration. *See* Charlie Savage, *Bush Challenges Hundreds of Laws; President Cites Powers of His Office*, BOSTON GLOBE, Apr. 30, 2006, at A1. Savage's article was followed by the release of an American Bar Association task force report opposing the misuse of signing statements, and by subsequent ABA adoption of a new policy urging Congress to pass legislation providing for judicial review of presidential signing statements. *See* AM. BAR ASS'N, REPORT BY THE ABA TASK FORCE ON PRESIDENTIAL SIGNING STATEMENTS AND THE SEPARATION OF POWERS DOCTRINE (Aug. 2006), http://www. abanow.org/wordpress/wp-content/files_flutter/1273179616signstatereport.pdf.

In three recently completed sessions of Congress (2006–09), both houses introduced bills and resolutions targeting perceived misuse or abuse of presidential signing statements. *See* GEORGETOWN LAW LIBRARY, PRESIDENTIAL SIGNING STATEMENTS RESEARCH GUIDE, http://www.ll.georgetown.edu/guides/presidential signingstatements.cfm (bills). The controversy remains active.

[22] *See, e.g., Statement on Signing the USA PATRIOT Improvement and Reauthorization Act of 2005*, 42 WEEKLY COMP. PRES. DOC. 425–26 (Mar. 9, 2006) (asserting a constitutional right *not* to enforce new congressional oversight provisions in the USA PATRIOT Act reauthorization bill).

[23] For an overview of the recent controversy over signing statements and positions taken by critics and defenders of the practice, see Charlie Savage, *Introduction: The Last Word? The Constitutional Implications of Presidential Signing Statements*, 16 WM. & MARY BILL RTS. J. 1 (2007).

[24] There are excellent, web-based research guides on presidential signing statements. *See* LAW LIBRARY OF CONGRESS, PRESIDENTIAL SIGNING STATEMENTS, http://www.loc.gov/law/help/statements.php; GEORGETOWN LAW LIBRARY, PRESIDENTIAL SIGNING STATEMENTS RESEARCH GUIDE, http://www.ll.georgetown. edu/guides/presidentialsigningstatements.cfm. *See also* I-Wei Wang, *Schoolhouse Rock Is No Longer Enough: The Presidential Signing Statements Controversy and Its Implications for Library Professionals*, 100 LAW LIBR. J. 619 (2008) (review of historical and contemporary debate regarding presidential signing statements and advice on researching signing statements).

policy positions and to describe, comment upon, criticize, and support various legislative initiatives.[25] Blogs and podcasts can be revealing sources of information about the intent and meaning behind various legislative initiatives. Current senators' and representatives' blogs are linked from their profile pages on the House and Senate websites. Researchers may also use a web search engine such as *Google* or *Google Blogs* to locate blog entries on specific legislation. Podcasts may be easily found in the same manner or by using a podcast aggregator such as *iTunes*,[26] the largest single source of links to political podcasts.

C. CHART: DOCUMENTS OF FEDERAL LEGISLATIVE HISTORIES

The documents created during the legislative process that may be relevant to a federal legislative history are identified in the following chart.

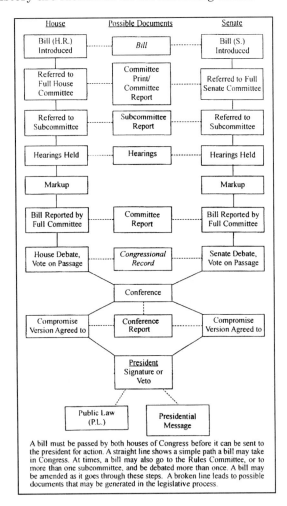

A bill must be passed by both houses of Congress before it can be sent to the president for action. A straight line shows a simple path a bill may take in Congress. At times, a bill may also go to the Rules Committee, or to more than one subcommittee, and be debated more than once. A bill may be amended as it goes through these steps. A broken line leads to possible documents that may be generated in the legislative process.

---

[25] For an example of a senator's blog, see Senator Harry Reid, SILVER STATE BLOG, http://reid.senate.gov/blog/.

[26] http://www.apple.com/itunes.

D. COMPILED FEDERAL LEGISLATIVE HISTORIES

Identifying and locating the documents that make up a legislative history can be time-consuming, so it is a boon to the researcher when someone has already compiled and published a legislative history on a particular act. The following information first describes lists of compiled legislative histories that can assist in locating relevant legislative documents, and then identifies sources of compiled legislative histories that reproduce the relevant documents.

1. Listings of Compiled Legislative Histories

The following sources indicate whether a compiled legislative history might exist for a specific law. These sources do not contain the text of the documents comprising a legislative history.

a. *Sources of Compiled Legislative Histories: A Bibliography of Government Documents, Periodical Articles, and Books.*[27] This resource, available in print and on *HeinOnline* in its U.S. Federal Legislative History Library, provides references to print and electronic sources that contain compiled legislative histories (either the full text of or citations to the legislative documents) for major laws. Coverage begins with the first Congress in 1789. Indexes provide access by publication title, by public law number, and by popular name of the statute.

b. *Union List of Legislative Histories.*[28] This publication, compiled by the Law Librarians' Society of Washington, D.C., Legislative Research Special Interest Section, provides information on compiled legislative histories commercially produced or compiled in-house by librarians in the Washington, D.C., area and held by the law libraries in that region. Supplemented in 2002, the list's coverage is from the 1st Congress (1789–1791) through the 107th Congress (2001–2002).

c. *Catalog of U.S. Government Publications* (formerly *Monthly Catalog of United States Government Publications*). This comprehensive index to publications of the federal government since 1976 includes information on legislative histories compiled by federal agencies.[29]

d. *Library catalogs.* Legislative histories from commercial and government sources—and even some locally produced histories—are included in library catalogs.

e. *Federal Legislative Histories: An Annotated Bibliography and Index to Officially Published Sources* (1994). Compiled by Bernard D. Reams, Jr., the 255 entries in this annotated bibliography cover congressional, executive agency, and special commission sources published from 1862 through 1990.

---

[27] NANCY P. JOHNSON, SOURCES OF COMPILED LEGISLATIVE HISTORIES: A BIBLIOGRAPHY OF GOVERNMENT DOCUMENTS, PERIODICAL ARTICLES, AND BOOKS (1979) (print version updated through 2007 supplement; *HeinOnline* version updated through 111th Cong., 2009–2010).

[28] LAW LIBRARIANS' SOCIETY OF WASHINGTON, D.C., UNION LIST OF LEGISLATIVE HISTORIES (7th ed. 2000 & Supp. 2002). *See also* KEVIN P. GRAY, LEGISLATIVE HISTORY UNION LIST OF THE CHICAGO ASSOCIATION OF LAW LIBRARIES (2001).

[29] The print version of this publication (*Monthly Catalog*) was discontinued in December 2004. It is now available electronically at the Government Printing Office website as the *Catalog of U.S. Government Publications (CGP),* http://catalog.gpo.gov. *Catalog* documents that are available on the Internet contain a hot link within the citation. "Legislative history" is a standard part of the subject heading for legislative histories, so the phrase makes a good search term.

2. Sources of Compiled Legislative Histories

The sources described below list, identify, or cite to documents that are generated as a bill travels through Congress and in many cases reproduce the documents themselves, in print, microform, or electronic format.

a. CIS/Index and *CIS Microfiche Library* (published by ProQuest). *CIS/Index* began in 1970 as a product of the Congressional Information Service and simplified the method of compiling a federal legislative history. *CIS/Index* provides monthly paper Index and Abstracts issues that cumulate in bound Annual volumes (titled Index, Abstracts, and Legislative Histories) to locate legislative history on bills, when some action has occurred after the bill's introduction. A companion microfiche set reproduces many of the documents needed to determine the intent of the public law. The components of the *CIS/Index* and *Microfiche Library* are described below.

(1) *CIS/Index.* The monthly *CIS/Index* Abstract pamphlet contains entries that briefly describe the format and scope of the hearings, reports, committee prints, and other congressional publications, such as House and Senate documents, included in the *Index.* The Abstract pamphlet is cumulated annually as the *CIS Annual/Abstracts.* An index provides access. [Illustration 3]

(2) *Legislative Histories of U.S. Public Laws.* From 1970 to 1983, each *CIS Annual* volume contained a section on legislative histories for public laws passed during the year. Starting in 1984, this section became a separate volume titled *Legislative Histories of U.S. Public Laws.* Each public law is listed and citations are given to the bill number, committee reports, hearings, *Congressional Record*, and other documents that may be relevant to a legislative history. Several indexes provide access.

The *Legislative Histories* volumes contain histories in two formats. For laws identified as major legislation, the citations to congressional committee publications also include the CIS abstracts. Additional citations are provided to all relevant bills and debates. [Illustration 10–2] Both formats provide citations to presidential signing statements or veto messages.

For laws not classified as major legislation, entries do not include the full abstracts but, instead, references to the abstracts, which the researcher can look up in other volumes.[30]

(3) *CIS Microfiche Library*, 1970 to present. For bills that have become public laws, this component provides a microfiche reprint of the bills, hearings, reports, committee prints, and congressional documents related to the enacted legislation.

b. ProQuest Congressional (formerly *LexisNexis Congressional*). This commercial service provides an electronic version of the *CIS/Index* and online access to some documents in the CIS microfiche collection.[31] *ProQuest Congressional* has the CIS

---

[30] Slip laws are discussed in Section E-1 of this chapter and in Section B-1 of Chapter 9.

[31] A basic subscription to *ProQuest Congressional* provides access to index/abstracts for documents, prints, reports, and published hearings, 1970 to present; legislative histories, 1969 to present; committee hearings, selected transcripts, and full text statements, 1988 to present; committee prints, selected full text, 1993–2004; committee reports full text, 1990 to present; House and Senate documents full text, 1995 to present; GAO report abstracts and PDFs, 2004 to present; *Congressional Record* daily edition, 1985 to present; bill texts and tracking, 1989 to present; public law texts, 1988 to present; *United States Code; Code of Federal Regulations*, 1981 to present; *Federal Register*, 1980 to present; campaign finance data, 1987 to present; key votes data, 1987 to present; member financial disclosures, profiles, and voting records; political news; hot bills

indexes and abstracts for committee hearings, reports, documents, and prints from 1970 to the present. It includes a legislative history search form and provides "abbreviated" legislative histories of public laws; coverage begins in 1969. From 1999 forward, *ProQuest Congressional* includes full legislative histories for all public laws. Laws enacted prior to 1969 do not have compiled histories, but *ProQuest Congressional* offers a "Search by Number" option that allows the user to search by bill number from the 6th Congress (1799–1801) to the present, and by public law number from the 57th Congress (1901–1903) to the present.

The *ProQuest (CIS)* print indexes, microfiche, and online products are the quickest and most efficient method of locating citations to, and the full text of, many of the documents that comprise a legislative history. The frequency of publication, thoroughness of the indexing, citation to all relevant documents, and the availability of full-text documents make *ProQuest (CIS)* products invaluable for legislative history research.

c.   *ProQuest Legislative Insight.*[32] This *ProQuest* electronic service provides searchable PDFs of more than 18,000 full-text legislative histories covering laws enacted from 1929 to the present. It includes updated versions of histories included in *ProQuest Congressional.*

d.   *LexisNexis. LexisNexis's* CIS Legislative Histories file provides a searchable, online equivalent to the *CIS Legislative Histories of U.S. Public Laws* index volumes from 1970 forward. *LexisNexis* also provides compiled legislative histories for selected banking, bankruptcy, environment, securities, and tax (1954–) statutes. The documents included vary with each legislative history.

e.   *United States Code Congressional and Administrative News (USCCAN).* In addition to the tables in the *United States Code Congressional and Administrative News* discussed below, *USCCAN* contains a finding aid list and the text of selected documents relevant to a federal legislative history.

USCCAN's legislative history section provides researchers with citations to all committee and conference reports, references to the dates of consideration and passage of the bill in both houses, and citations to any presidential signing statements. This information is found immediately before the reprints of selected committee reports and other documents. [Illustration 10–1] Prior to the 99th Congress (1985–1986), *USCCAN* usually printed only a House report or a Senate report. Since then, it has also included any statement that the president made upon signing the law. *USCCAN* has recently provided joint explanatory statements and statements by legislative leaders for laws that the editors view as major legislation. These statements often contain citations to the *Congressional Record.*

This set is published by Thomson Reuters and is issued in monthly pamphlets during each session of Congress. After each session, the monthly pamphlets are reissued

---

and hot topics; and committee rosters and schedules. Optional modules in *ProQuest Congressional* include *(1) Historical Indexes: the CIS U.S. Serial Set Index (1789–1969); U.S. Congressional Hearings Index* (1834–1969); *Unpublished House Committee Hearings Index* (1833–1972); *Unpublished Senate Committee Hearings Index* (1824–1984); *U.S. Congressional Committee Prints Index* (1830–1969); *U.S. Senate Executive Documents & Reports Index* (1817–1969), and (2) *U.S. Statutes at Large,* 1789 to present.

[32] http://cisupa.proquest.com/ws_display.asp?filter=Legislative%20Insight%20Overview.

in bound volumes. All public laws for each session are included; a separate volume sets forth legislative histories.

USCCAN is available in many law libraries and provides a simple method of obtaining one of the key documents of a legislative history, the committee report.

f.   *Westlaw*. *Westlaw*'s Legislative History—U.S. Code file in its U.S. Federal Materials library contains all legislative history published in *USCCAN* from 1948 through 1989. Beginning in January 1990, *Westlaw*'s Legislative History file contains the full text of all congressional reports, including those for bills that did not become law.

Westlaw contains compiled legislative histories prepared by the law firm of Arnold & Porter for major public laws. Examples of areas covered are pensions, environment, banking, bankruptcy, and securities. The documents included vary with each legislative history. *Westlaw* also offers legislative histories compiled by the U.S. Government Accountability Office (GAO) for most public laws enacted between 1921 and 1995 (Pub. L. No. 104–191).

g.   *LLSDC's Legislative Sourcebook*. The Law Librarians' Society of Washington, D.C., has created two excellent web-based guides to compiled legislative history in its *Legislative Sourcebook*: (1) *Legislative Histories of Selected U.S. Laws on the Internet*[33] (links to free sources), and (2) *Legislative Histories of U.S. Laws on the Internet: Commercial Sources*[34] (links to *HeinOnline, Westlaw,* and *LexisNexis*).

h.   *GAO Legislative History Collection*. This is an outstanding collection of legislative histories compiled by the U.S. Government Accountability Office (GAO), formerly known as the General Accounting Office. The GAO began compiling legislative histories for departmental use in 1921, and over the years it compiled over 20,000 histories in hard copy. In 1990, the GAO contracted with the Remac Information Corporation to create a microfiche collection of the entire set. Remac produced microfiche copies of about half of the set (67th through 96th Congresses; 1921–1980) then ceased. There was a very limited distribution of the microfiche set; the Congressional Research Service and the Law Library of Congress are the best sources of the microfiche. The GAO continued to compile legislative histories through the 104th Cong., 1st Sess. (1995) (Pub. L. No. 104–191). The entire collection is now available in *Westlaw*.

i.   *HeinOnline*'s U.S. Federal Legislative History Title Collection. This database in *HeinOnline*'s U.S. Federal Legislative History Library contains the full text of several hundred compiled legislative histories collected from many different sources, including individuals, law firms, and federal agencies. Also included is a well-known but out-of-print work by Eugene Nabors, *Legislative Reference Checklist: The Key to Legislative Histories from 1789–1903* (1982).

j.   *Public Laws, Legislative Histories* (CCH). From the 96th Congress through the 100th Congress (1979–1988), Commerce Clearing House issued this microfiche set, which made available the House and Senate bills as introduced; the reported House bills, Senate bills, or both; committee reports, conference reports, and committee prints; slip laws; and relevant legislative debate as reported in the *Congressional Record*. All

---

[33] http://www.llsdc.org/Leg-Hist/.

[34] http://www.llsdc.org/lh-of-us-laws-on-the-internet-commercial-sources.

enactments are indexed by subject, public law number, and bill number. This set includes a compiled legislative history for every public law.

  k. *U.S. Department of Justice Legislative Histories.*[35] Legislative histories, initially compiled by Department of Justice Library staff for internal use, are available on the agency's website. The collection covers 29 major laws enacted between the 41st Congress (1869–1871) and the 108th Congress (2003–2004).

  l. *Looseleaf Services, Treatises, and Other Compiled Legislative Histories.* Many looseleaf services and treatises dealing with specific areas of the law—e.g., securities, tax, and labor—may contain compiled legislative histories for laws related to their subject. Other publications may have as their sole purpose the compilation of a federal legislative history.

E. IDENTIFYING THE DOCUMENTS OF A LEGISLATIVE HISTORY

  If a compiled legislative history cannot be located or information is needed about a bill that has not been enacted as law, researchers will need to identify the materials that were created during the legislative process. To begin research, it is helpful to have either the public law number, or the *Statutes at Large* citation, or the bill number and session of Congress.

  The first step in this process is to create a list of documents related to the public law, the legislation that was not enacted, or the pending bill. The sources described below provide information, references, or citations to the documents typically generated during the legislative process.

1. Slip Laws and *United States Statutes at Large*

  Since 1975, a legislative summary at the end of each slip law (and law in *United States Statutes at Large*) provides: citations to the bill that became the public law; committee reports; dates of consideration and passage of the bill by both houses of Congress; and presidential statements, if any. The slip laws provide the volume number of the *Congressional Record* for dates of consideration and passage of the bill, but they do not provide page references. [Illustration 10–7]

  For the years 1963 to 1974, the references now found at the end of each slip law are listed in a Guide to Legislative History of Bills Enacted into Public Law in *United States Statutes at Large.*[36]

2. *United States Code Congressional and Administrative News* (USCCAN)

  The monthly pamphlets of *USCCAN* contain a Legislative History Table that provides information on bills that have become public laws. The tables are cumulated in the annual bound volume. These legislative history tables, which are arranged by public

---

[35] http://www.justice.gov/jmd/ls/legislative_histories/legislative-histories.html.

[36] References to presidential statements were first included in 1971 for the 91st Congress, 2nd Session.

  The bill numbers for laws enacted between 1903 and 1962 are included in *Statutes at Large.* Bill numbers for laws passed prior to 1903 can be located in EUGENE NABORS, LEGISLATIVE REFERENCE CHECKLIST: THE KEY TO LEGISLATIVE HISTORIES FROM 1789–1903 (1982) (available in *HeinOnline*'s U.S. Federal Legislative History Library).

law number, provide citations to *United States Statutes at Large,* bill number and committee reports, and references to dates of consideration and passage of the bill. The information provided for committee reports includes committee report numbers and abbreviated references to the committees of the House and Senate, and the conference committee, if any. For dates of consideration and passage of the bill, *USCCAN* references the volume of the *Congressional Record,* along with the dates when the House and Senate took these actions.

3. *Congressional Record*

This publication is discussed in detail later in this chapter; however, several features are highlighted here because of their usefulness for identifying documents that are part of federal legislative histories.

a.   *History of Bills and Resolutions.*[37] The *History of Bills and Resolutions* is a section of the bi-weekly index to the daily edition of the *Congressional Record.* This section is divided by chamber and arranged by bill number. It includes a brief digest of the legislation, the name of the sponsor, and the committee to which the legislation was referred. Also included are references to debates, committee reports, and dates of passage. Page references are provided to the daily *Congressional Record* where the activity is reported. [Illustration 10–5] Although this section covers only bills acted upon during the two weeks covered by the index, coverage for any bill so included is complete back to the date of the bill's introduction. A cumulative "History of Bills and Resolutions" for each session of Congress is a part of the annual Index to the bound set of the *Congressional Record.* The Government Printing Office's *FDsys* website provides access to this information under the category "History of Bills."

b.   *History of Bills Enacted into Public Law.* This table appears in the annual Daily Digest volume of the bound *Congressional Record.* It includes the same information as the *History of Bills and Resolutions,* except that it does not include entries for sponsors or debates. As its name states, this table only covers bills that have become public laws.

Both history tables in the *Congressional Record* provide citations to bill numbers. The history table in the biweekly index provides information on pending bills, bills that did not become public law, and bills that were enacted into public law.

4. *Congress.gov*

This website, maintained by the Library of Congress, contains all bills since 1973, searchable by word, phrase, or bill number. After a search, the results can be narrowed by selecting facets from a menu or by searching within the results. Each bill is displayed with several tabs offering summaries (prepared by the Congressional Research Service), text, actions, committees, and so on. The Actions tab links to detailed information about the bill's progress through Congress. From the "Overview" display, one can follow links to Congressional Budget Office cost estimates, and the bill's constitutional authority statement.[38]

---

[37] History of Bills, available via *FDsys,* at http://www.gpo.gov/fdsys/browse/collection.action?collection Code=HOB, provides the same information as the print version. The online coverage begins with volume 129 of the *Congressional Record,* in 1983. Coverage for the current session is updated daily.

[38] Since January 2011, a representative introducing a bill or resolution must present a "statement citing as specifically as practicable the power or powers granted to Congress in the Constitution to enact the bill or

5. *Congressional Index* (CCH)

This two-volume looseleaf service published by Commerce Clearing House is updated weekly while Congress is in session and for several weeks thereafter, until all public bills and resolutions sent to the president have been acted upon. New volumes are issued for each Congress. A number of tables and indexes provide information about and access to bills. Older volumes can be consulted to gather information on bills from 1937 forward, including bills that were not enacted. [Illustration 10–4]

6. House and Senate Calendars

The calendars chronicle the activity of bills as they travel through Congress. These calendars provide bill numbers and can be used to trace action on pending legislation, public laws, and bills that did not become law.

a. *Calendars of the United States House of Representatives and History of Legislation*.[39] This is the "calendar" of the House of Representatives, but it actually consists of five calendars to which House bills may be assigned. It is printed each day the House is in session. Although the title refers only to the House, it serves as an index to all legislation that has been reported by the committees and acted upon by either or both chambers. Senate resolutions not of interest to the House and special House reports are excluded.

The information in the calendars is cumulated at the end of each Congress. A subject index for both House and Senate legislation reported by a committee and acted upon by either or both of the chambers is printed in the calendars on the first legislative day of the week that the House is in session. It does not list hearings and debates comprehensively.

The section of the calendars entitled "History of Bills and Resolutions: Numerical Order of Bills and Resolutions Which Have Been Reported to or Considered by Either or Both Houses" divides the pending legislation by chamber and then again by the form of legislation. It provides the current status and legislative history of all activity on each piece of legislation on which some action has been taken. Information on hearings is not provided. Entries are arranged by bill or resolution number.

b. *Senate Calendar of Business*.[40] This calendar is less useful for tracing the current status of Senate legislation because it is not cumulative and has no index. However, a General Orders section covers all Senate legislation by bill number, title, and report number.

7. House and Senate Journals

The House and Senate journals, unlike the *Congressional Record,* are constitutionally mandated. Both journals are published at the end of each session; they have subject indexes and History of Bills and Resolutions sections. The *House Journal*

---

joint resolution." Rules of the House of Representatives R. XII, clause 7(c), *available at* http://clerk.house.gov/legislative/house-rules.pdf.

[39] The *House Calendar* from the 104th Congress (1995–1996) to the present is at http://www.gpo.gov/fdsys/browse/collection.action?collectionCode=CCAL.

[40] The *Senate Calendar* from the 104th Congress (1995–1996) to the present is at http://www.gpo.gov/fdsys/browse/collection.action?collectionCode=CCAL.

is available on the *FDsys* website.[41] Historical collections of both the House and Senate journals from 1789 to 1875 are available on the Library of Congress *American Memory: A Century of Lawmaking for a New Nation* website.[42]

8. Digest of Public General Bills and Resolutions

The *Digest of Public General Bills and Resolutions* was published by the Congressional Research Service of the Library of Congress from the 75th through the 101st Congresses (1937–1990). Accordingly, this resource is helpful for historical research. It can be found in federal depository libraries and purchased as part of the Law Library Microform Consortium (LLMC) Digital service. The *Digest* provides information on bills enacted into public law, bills that were pending, and bills not enacted as public laws. The *Digest*, issued annually in two volumes, is divided into three parts.

The first part summarizes the provisions of the legislation on which some action occurred after the bill was introduced. This part is further divided into "Public Laws" and "Other Measures Receiving Action." The "Public Laws" section includes digests and legislative histories of enacted laws. The "Other Measures" section discusses current bills with their legislative histories.

The second part includes digests of bills and resolutions where no action was taken after the measure was introduced and assigned to a committee. Indexes by sponsor and co-sponsor, short title, subject, and identical bills comprise the third part.

9. ProQuest Congressional Digital Collections

Researchers with access to one or more components of the *ProQuest Congressional* digital backfiles will find them extremely useful for identifying and retrieving legislative history materials.[43] The full text of the documents in these collections is fully searchable, making it possible to identify documents by bill number, public law number, *Statutes at Large* citation, title, subject, sponsor, witness, and many other descriptors.

10. Hearings

Not all hearings are published. Each congressional committee decides for itself whether to release a specific hearing,[44] and citations to hearings are not always included in the sources noted above or in compiled legislative histories. Finding citations to hearings can, therefore, take an additional step when compiling a legislative history. In addition to the sources listed in below in Section H-5, the following sources are useful in locating citations to hearings:

   a.   *Index of Congressional Committee Hearings (not confidential in character) prior to January 3, 1935, in the United States Senate Library.*

---

[41] The *House Journal* is at http://www.gpo.gov/fdsys/browse/collection.action?collectionCode=HJOURNAL; coverage is from 1992 through 1999. The *Senate Journal* is not available on the *FDsys* website.

[42] *See* http://memory.loc.gov/ammem/amlaw/lwhj.html (House) and http://memory.loc.gov/ammem/amlaw/lwsj.html (Senate).

[43] The components of the ProQuest Digital Collections are: *Congressional Hearings Digital Collection*; *Congressional Record Permanent Digital Collection*; *Congressional Research Digital Collection; Legislative Insight;* and *U.S. Serial Set Digital Collection.* These collections are also discussed in Section H of this chapter.

[44] The unpublished hearings are transferred to the National Archives and Records Administration (NARA) and remain closed for a period of between twenty and fifty years. *See* http://proquest.libguides.com/quick_start_hearings/unpublished.

b.   Cumulative Index of Congressional Committee Hearings (not confidential in character) from Seventy-Fourth Congress (January 3, 1935) through Eighty-Fifth Congress (January 3, 1959) in the United States Senate Library.

c.   Shelflist of Congressional Committee Hearings (not confidential in character) in the United States Senate Library from Eighty-Sixth Congress (January 7, 1959) through Ninety-First Congress (January 2, 1971).

d.   Congressional Hearings Calendar: An Index to Congressional Hearings by Date, Committee/Subcommittee, Chairman, and Title, 1985 to the present. The purpose of these compilations is to provide a means of identifying recently held hearings that may not yet be covered by document indexes. The *Calendar* index also provides different access points than does *CIS,* e.g., date of hearing, name of committee and subcommittee, and name of the chair presiding over the hearing. This is especially helpful for multi-part hearings, making only one look-up necessary.

e.   Monthly Catalog of United States Government Publications, published electronically as *Catalog of U.S. Government Publications (CGP).* This index provides references to hearings held on specific legislation. The paper version of this index was discontinued in December 2004; coverage in the electronic version goes back to 1976.[45]

11. Presidential Documents

Presidential messages and memoranda, including those related to pending legislation and bill signing or vetoes, are published in the electronic-only *Daily Compilation of Presidential Documents* (Jan. 20, 2009–), the *Weekly Compilation of Presidential Documents* (Aug. 2, 1965–Jan. 29, 2009), and the *Public Papers of the Presidents* (1929–). These resources are explained in Section H-9 below.

F.   ILLUSTRATIONS: IDENTIFYING DOCUMENTS

10–1.   Pages from 2010 USCCAN Legislative History Volume Showing
               Legislative History Listing for Pub. L. No. 111–296 and Senate
               Report No. 111–178

10–1 cont'd.   Pages from 2010 USCCAN Legislative History Volume Showing
               Presidential Signing Statement for S. 3307

10–2.   Page from 2010 CIS/Annual Legislative Histories Volume for Public
               Law 111–296

10–3.   Page from 2010 CIS/Index

10–4.   Page from House Status Table from Congressional Index (CCH)

10–5.   Page from 2010 Congressional Record Bi-Weekly Index

---

[45] http://catalog.gpo.gov/.

[Illustration 10–1]

PAGES FROM 2010 USCCAN LEGISLATIVE HISTORY VOLUME SHOWING
LEGISLATIVE HISTORY LISTING FOR PUB. L. NO. 111–296
AND SENATE REPORT NO. 111–178

HEALTHY, HUNGER–FREE KIDS ACT

PUBLIC LAW 111–296, see page 124 Stat. 3183

→ DATES OF CONSIDERATION AND PASSAGE

House: December 1, 2, 2010

Senate: August 5, 2010

Cong. Record Vol. 156 (2010)

→ **Senate Report (Agriculture, Nutrition, and Forestry Committee)
No. 111–178, May 5, 2010
[To accompany S. 3307]**

The Senate Report is set out below.

SENATE REPORT 111–178

[page 1]

The Committee on Agriculture, Nutrition, and Forestry, having considered an original bill (S. 3307) to reauthorize child nutrition programs, and for other purposes, having considered the same, reports favorably thereon without amendment and recommends that the bill do pass.

Legislative histories are included in a separate section or volume of *USCCAN*. This is the first page of the legislative history of Pub. L. No. 111-296. Notice how, at the top of the page, reference is made to committee reports and to the dates of consideration and passage.

While *USCCAN* is useful and widely available, it does not set forth the text of all documents of a legislative history. *USCCAN* reprints the House or Senate report and the conference report, if any. Since 1986, it includes the text of presidential signing statements. See next page of illustration.

PURPOSE OF THE LEGISLATION

The purpose of this legislation is to extend and improve the nation's policies and programs pertaining to child nutrition. Congress most recently addressed these programs comprehensively in the Child Nutrition and WIC Reauthorization Act of 2004 (P.L. 108–

1233

[Illustration 10–1 cont'd]

PAGES FROM 2010 USCCAN LEGISLATIVE HISTORY VOLUME
SHOWING PRESIDENTIAL SIGNING STATEMENT FOR S. 3307

HEALTHY, HUNGER–FREE KIDS ACT

PUBLIC LAW 111–296

For text of Act see page 124 Stat. 3183

⟶ **STATEMENT BY PRESIDENT OF THE UNITED STATES**

STATEMENT BY PRESIDENT BARACK OBAMA UPON SIGNING S. 3307

White House Press Release,
December 13, 2010

THE PRESIDENT: Hello, hello, hello! (**Applause.**) Thank you. Thank you very much. Thank you so much. Thank you, everybody. Please, please have a seat.

Good morning, everybody.

AUDIENCE: Good morning.

THE PRESIDENT: Well, I want to thank all the students and faculty and staff here at Tubman Elementary for hosting us today at your beautiful school. And we want to thank Principal Harry Hughes for doing outstanding work here. Thank you—give them all a big round of applause. (**Applause.**)

We are thrilled [...] Hungry–Free Kids Act—a bill that's [...] ur kids and to our country. But before [...] folks who are here, as well as a few wh [...] t role in getting this legislation passed.

> When the president signs a piece of legislation, the president may add a signing statement, such as this one, incorporating the reasons for signing the legislation.

On the stage we have Madam Speaker, Nancy Pelosi. (**Applause.**) Two outstanding senators, Blanche Lincoln and Tom Harkin, who worked so hard to get this done. (**Applause.**) Members of the House of Representatives Miller, DeLauro and Platts who all worked so hard to make this happen. (**Applause.**) We're grateful to you. And three of my outstanding members of my Cabinet who worked tirelessly on this issue, Secretary of Agriculture Tom Vilsack—it happens to be his birthday today. Happy birthday. (**Applause.**) Secretary Arne Duncan, our great Secretary of Education. (**Applause.**) And Secretary Kathleen Sebelius of Health and Human Services. (**Applause.**)

They couldn't be here today but they played a huge role in making this happen— Senator Harry Reid, the Majority Leader in the Senate; Senator Mike [*sic*] McConnell, the ranking Republican who helped facilitate the smooth passage of this bill; Senator Chambliss, who was the lead Republican; Republicans Hoyer, Clyburn and McCarthy all

S35

[Illustration 10–2]

PAGE FROM 2010 CIS/ANNUAL LEGISLATIVE HISTORIES VOLUME FOR PUBLIC LAW 111–296

Public Law 111-296
124 Stat. 3183

Healthy, Hunger-Free Kids Act of 2010

December 13, 2010

Public Law

1.1   Public Law 111-296, approved Dec. 13, 2010. (S. 3307)

(CIS10:PL111-296   84 p.)

"To reauthorize child nutrition programs, and for other purposes."

Amends the Richard B. Russell National School Lunch Act and other acts to extend through FY2015 and revise USDA child nutrition programs.

Authorizes performance awards for States' direct certification of children who receive other public assistance as eligible for free meals under school lunch and breakfast programs.

Directs USDA to establish programs of grants to States to expand the school breakfast program and to retain and support summer food service programs after the expiration of the start-up funding grants.

Expands the child and adult care food program afterschool meals program for at-risk children.

Revises the supplemental nutrition program for women, infants, and children (WIC), and makes breastfeeding support and promotion goals of the WIC program.

Authorizes grants to States for demonstration projects to reduce or eliminate childhood hunger.

Requires USDA to establish science-based nutrition standards for all foods sold in schools.

Authorizes an organic food pilot program to increase quantity of organic foods provided the school lunch program.

Authorizes a nutrition education and obesity prevention grant program to promote healthy food choices consistent with specified dietary guidelines.

P.L. 111-296 Reports

111th Congress

2.1   S. Rpt. 111-178 on S. 3307, "Healthy, Hunger-Free Kids Act of 2010," May 5, 2010.

(CIS10:S163-1   56 p.)
(Y1.1/5:111-178.)

Recommends passage of S. 3307, the Healthy, Hunger-Free Kids Act of 2010, to amend the Richard B. Russell National School Lunch Act and five other acts to extend and revise USDA child nutrition programs.

Includes provisions to:

a. Promote direct certification of children who receive other public assistance as eligible for free meals under school lunch and breakfast programs.

b. Extend and revise the Women, Infants and Children Program.

c. Update nutritional standards for school lunch and breakfast programs.

d. Revise management of child nutrition programs.

Includes additional and supplemental views (p. 54-55).

111th Congress, 2nd Session

Related Reports

111th Congress

2R.1   H. Rpt. 111-665 on H. Res. 1742, "Providing for Consideration of the Bill (S. 3307) To Reauthorize Child Nutrition Programs," Nov. 30, 2010.

(CIS10:H683-56   2 p.)
(Y1.1/8:111-665.)

Recommends adoption of H. Res. 1742, to provide for consideration of S. 3307, the Healthy, Hunger-Free Kids Act of 2010.

P.L. 111-296 Bills

111th Congress

ENACTED BILL

3.1   S. 3307, an original bill, as reported by the Senate Agriculture, Nutrition, and Forestry Committee May 5, 2010; as passed by the Senate Aug. 5, 2010.

COMPANION BILL

3.2   H.R. 5504 as introduced.

Related Bills

This page is from the *CIS Legislative Histories* volume for Pub. L. 111-296. CIS provides abstracts with full citations to the actual documents. The set is especially useful because it cites all relevant congressional documents for each public law.

P.L. 111-296 Debate

156 Congressional Record
111th Congress, 2nd Session - 2010

4.1   Aug. 5, Senate consideration and passage of S. 3307, p. S6832.

4.2   Dec. 1, House consideration and passage of H. Res. 1742, and consideration of S. 3307, p. H7767, H7778, H7814.

CIS INDEX Legislative Histories   411

[Illustration 10–3]

PAGE FROM 2010 CIS/INDEX

Index of Subjects and Names

Heim, Lori J.

see also Federal Hospital Insurance Trust Fund
see also Managed health care
see also Medicaid
see also Medicare
see also TRICARE
see also Workers' compensation
Health Insurance Industry Antitrust Enforcement Act
Health insurance cos anticompetitive measures, antitrust exemption repeal, S521-58
Health Insurance Industry Fair Competition Act
House consideration of legislation, committee rule, H683-6
Health Insurance Portability and Accountability Act
Health care system reform initiatives, PL111-148
Health info technology dev and use, patient privacy issues, S521-22.1
Health of workers
see Occupational health and safety
Health Professions and Nursing Education Coalition
DOL, HHS, Educ Dept, and related agencies programs, FY2011 approp, H181-83.2
Health Professions Education Partnerships Act
Mental retardation terminology use in Fed laws, revision, S433-1, PL111-256
Health Research and Health Services Amendments
Mental retardation terminology use i Fed laws, revision, PL111-256
Health Resources and Services Administration
Approp, FY2011, H181-44, S183-11
Health care access in rural areas, H161-29.1
Hurricane Katrina disaster response, HHS primary health care services assistance, GAO letter, J942-315
Infant hearing loss research, prevention, and treatment programs, FY2010-FY2015 authorization, PL111-337
see also National Health Service Corps
Healthcare Financial Management Association
Municipal bond industry status and impact on State and local govts, H371-21.2
Healthcare Leadership Council
Health info technology dev and use and economic stimulus package role, S431-8.1
HealthRisk Strategies
Hazardous chemicals, EPA regulatory measures implementation issues, S321-4.2
Healthy Families Act
Employees paid leave for illness, estab, H341-1
Employees paid leave for illness, estab, impact on workers access to paid sick leave, staff rpt, J842-11
Healthy, Hunger-Free Kids Act
Child nutrition programs, extension and revision, S163-1, PL111-296
House consideration of legislation, committee rule, H683-56

Heaney, Mark S.
Veterans caregivers assistance programs review, H761-24.2
Hearing aids
Telecommunications accessibility improvement measures estab, H361-13, H363-13, S263-30, PL111-260
Hearing and hearing disorders
Emergency alert systems, Fed, State, and private sector reform efforts review, H751-53.2
Health Resources and Services Admin programs, FY2011 approp, H181-44
Infant hearing loss research, prevention, and treatment programs, FY2010-FY2015 authorization, PL111-337
Military personnel hearing assessment requirement estab, H761-50
see also Deaf
see also Ear diseases and infections
see also Hearing aids
see also Noise
Hearing Loss Association
Emergency alert systems, Fed, State, and private sector reform efforts review, H751-53.2
Heart Disease Education, Analysis Research, and Treatment for Women Act
Women's cardiovascular disease educ, prevention and treatment programs estab, H363-33
Heart diseases
see Cardiovascular diseases
Heart Mountain Relocation Center

> In the 2010 *CIS/Index*, the Index of Subjects and Names, one can locate references under the title of Public Law No. 111-296, Healthy, Hunger-Free Kids Act.

Japanese Amers relocation and internment during WWII, Wyo relocation center inclusion in natl park system, feasibility study estab, H583-31, S311-21, S313-44
Heart of a Champion Foundation
School safety and bullying prevention strategies review, H341-13.1
Heart transplantation
see Medical implants and transplants
Heartland Consumers Power District
Economic recovery promotion measures estab, Reclamation Bur and Geological Survey project selection and funding review, H581-6.1
Heath, Max
Postal rate increase impact, H601-38.2
Heath, Richard
Internet domain name system top level domains expansion, proposal review, H521-52.1
Heating and cooling systems
Small business tax incentives and proposals review, H721-37.1
Heating oil
HHS low-income home energy assistance program, S431-1
HHS low-income home energy assistance program, fraudulent activities and oversight, GAO rpt, J942-350
Propane Educ and Research Council and Natl Oilheat Research Alliance ops, Fed oversight review, GAO rpt, J942-361

Heavy Duty Hybrid Vehicle Research, Development, and Demonstration Act
Hybrid electric heavy duty plug-in vehicle R&D, demonstration, and commercial application program estab, S313-89
Heber, Albert J.
Air pollution control, greenhouse gas emissions measurement programs, H701-49.2
Hebertson, Peter C.
Medicare managed health care program abusive sales and mktg practices and Fed, State, and private insurance co response, S361-22.1
Hecht, Kenneth
Child nutrition programs, issues review, S161-4.2
Heckl, Karsten
USMC V-22 aircraft program ops review, H601-50.1
Heddell, Gordon S.
Def Contract Audit Agency mismgmt and misconduct allegations, S481-54.1
DOD contract mgmt, efficacy review, H181-18.4
Nomination to be Inspector Gen, DOD, S201-26.7
Hedden, Bill
Grand Canyon Natl Park watershed pollution control efforts, uranium mining regulation estab, H581-16.2
Hederman, Rea, Jr.
Economic recovery promotion measures estab, impact on small business, H721-11.1
e Fund Adviser Registration Act
estment hedge funds, registration equirements estab, H371-16
y-Whyte, E. Tessa
ronic Traumatic Encephalopathy in Athletes: Progressive Tauopathy After Repetitive Head Injury", H521-66.2
Heenan, Bart
Small business research and experimentation tax credit extension and revision, H721-10.1
Heer, Jerome
Economic recovery promotion measures estab, State and local govts funds accountability and waste and fraud prevention efforts, H601-14.2
Heffernan, Patrick
"Forest Management Solutions for Mitigating Climate Change in the United States", H161-19.2
Hegarty, John F.
USPS financial status and ops consolidation efforts review, H601-40.3
USPS financial status and ops reform review, H601-1.2
USPS mail delivery and collection outsourcing issues, H601-32.3
Heidelbaugh, Heather S.
Pres 2008 election admin, issues review, H521-2.1
Height, Dorothy I.
US post office in DC, designation, PL111-310
Heim, Lori J.
DOL, HHS, Educ Dept, and related agencies programs, FY2011 approp, H181-83.2
Health care workforce shortages, mitigation proposals review, H721-8.1

[Illustration 10–4]

PAGE FROM HOUSE STATUS TABLE FROM CONGRESSIONAL INDEX (CCH)

→ Current Status of Senate Bills   **20,513**

See also Status at pages 20,101 and 21,001.

103   12-29-2010   For digest, see "Bills" and "Resolutions" Divisions.

Hrgs by Public Lands and Forests Subcom   .9/29/2010

S 3294

Hrgs by Public Lands Subcom 6/16/2010

S 3297

Introduced 5/4/2010
Ref to S Foreign Relations Com 5/4/2010
Ordered reptd w/amdts by S Foreign
   Relations Com 9/21/2010
Reptd w/amdts, S Rept 111-369, by Foreign
   Relations Com 12/15/2010

S 3302

Introduced 5/4/2010
Ref to S Commerce Com 5/4/2010
Hrgs by Commerce Com 5/19/2010
Ordered reptd w/amdts by Commerce Com . 6/9/2010
Reptd w/amdts, w/o written rept, by
   Commerce Com 11/29/2010
Reptd w/o amdts, S Rept 111-381, by
   Commerce, Science, and Transportation
   Com . . . .

Introduced . . . . .
Ref to S Energy and N
Hrgs by National Park
Ordered reptd w/amd

★ S 3304

Introduced 5/4/2010
Ref to S Commerce Com 5/4/2010
Hrgs by Communications Subcom 5/26/2010
Ordered reptd w/amdts by Commerce Com .7/15/2010
Reptd w/amdts, w/o written rept, by
   Commerce Com 8/3/2010
Amdts adopted (Voice) 8/5/2010
Passed by S (Voice) 8/5/2010
Held at desk by H 8/9/2010
Passed under suspension of rules by 2/3 vote
   (Voice) 9/28/2010
Signed by President 10/8/2010
Public Law 111-260 (124 Stat 2751) 10/8/2010
Reptd w/o amdts, S Rept 111-386, by
   Commerce Com 12/22/2010

S 3305

Introduced 5/4/2010
Ref to S Environment and Public Works Com . 5/4/2010
Hrgs by Environment and Public Works
   Com 6/9/2010
Ordered reptd w/amdts by Environment and
   Public Works Com 6/30/2010
Reptd w/amdts, S Rept 111-249, by
   Environment and Public Works Com 8/5/2010

★ S 3307

Introduced 5/5/2010
Ref to S 5/5/2010
Reptd w/o amdts, S Rept 111-178, by
   Agriculture Com 5/5/2010
Amdts adopted (Voice) 8/5/2010
Passed by S (Voice) 8/5/2010
Ref to H Education and Labor Com 8/9/2010
Ref to H Budget Com 8/9/2010
Rule granted allowing limited amdts (H Res
   1742) 11/30/2010
Motion to recommit rejected (200 to 221; H
   Leg 602) .12/2/2010
Passed by H (264 to 157; H Leg 603) 12/2/2010
Signed by President 12/13/2010
Public Law 111-296 (124 Stat 3183) 12/13/2010

S 3310

Introduced 5/5/2010
Ref to S Energy and Natural Resources Com . 5/5/2010
Hrgs by Public Lands Subcom 6/16/2010

This Status Table in the *Congressional Record Index (CCH)* for the 111th Congress lists all bills introduced during the Congress. Citations to committee reports and date references for hearings are also provided.

. . . . 5/5/2010
rces Com . 5/5/2010
. . . . . . .6/16/2010

and
. . . . . . .7/21/2010
Energy
. . . . . . .9/27/2010

S 3314

Introduced 5/5/2010
Ref to S Veterans' Affairs Com 5/5/2010
Hrgs by Veterans' Affairs Com 5/19/2010

S 3317

Introduced 5/5/2010
Ref to S Foreign Relations Com 5/5/2010
Hrgs by Foreign Relations Com 5/19/2010
Ordered reptd w/amdts by Foreign Relations
   Com 5/25/2010
Reptd w/amdts, S Rept 111-225, by Foreign
   Relations Com 7/19/2010

S 3325

Introduced 5/6/2010
Ref to S Veterans' Affairs Com 5/6/2010
Hrgs by Veterans' Affairs Com 5/19/2010
Ordered reptd w/amdts by Veterans' Affairs
   Com 8/5/2010
Reptd w/amdts, S Rept 111-286, by Veterans'
   Affairs Com 9/13/2010

Congressional Index—2009-2010   **S 3325**

[Illustraton 10–5]

PAGE FROM 2010 CONGRESSIONAL RECORD B-WEEKLY INDEX

SENATE BILLS   H.B. 7

S. 3295—Continued
    Mr. Casey, Mr. Begich, Ms. Mikulski, Mr. Sanders,
    Mr. Harkin, Mr. Rockefeller, Mrs. McCaskill, Mr.
    Menendez, Mrs. Shaheen, Mr. Lautenberg, Mrs.
    Feinstein, Mr. Tester, Mr. Baucus, Mr. Conrad,
    Mrs. Boxer, Mr. Akaka, Mr. Nelson of Florida,
    Mr. Levin, and Mr. Burris), S3006 [30AP]
Cosponsors added, S3037 [3MY], S3092 [4MY], S3165
    [5MY]
S. 3296—A bill to delay the implementation of certain
    final rules of the Environmental Protection Agency
    in States until accreditation classes are held in
    the States for a period of at least 1 year; to
    the Committee on Environment and Public Works.
    By Mr. INHOFE (for himself, Mr. Coburn, Mr.
    Vitter, Mr. Barrasso, Mr. Crapo, Mr. Alexander,
    Mr. Bond, Mr. Hatch, Mr. DeMint, Mr. Bunning,
    Mr. Brown of Massachusetts, Mr. Cornyn, Ms.
    Collins, Mr. Enzi, Mrs. Hutchison, Mr. Grassley,
    Mr. Risch, Mr. Brownback, Mr. Cochran, Mr.
    McConnell, Mr. Isakson, Mr. Wicker, Mr. Chambliss,
    Mr. Roberts, and Mr. Burr), S3091 [4MY]
Cosponsors added, S3165 [5MY]
S. 3297—A bill to update United States policy and
    authorities to help advance a genuine transition
    to democracy and to promote recovery in Zimbabwe;
    to the Committee on Foreign Relations.
    By Mr. FEINGOLD (for himself, Mr. Isakson, and
    Mr. Kerry), S3091 [4MY]
S. 3298—A bill to establish a pilot program to reduce
    the increasing prevalence of overweight/obesity
    among 0–5 year-olds in child care settings; to the
    Committee on Health, Education, Labor, and Pen-
    sions.
    By Mr. UDALL of [. . .] (for himself, Mr.
    Franken), S3091 [4MY]
S. 3299—A bill to a[. . .]
    Act of 2002 to al[. . .]
    by mail in Federa[. . .]
    on Rules and Admini[. . .]
    By Mr. WYDEN (for [. . .]
    Ms. Cantwell, Mr. [. . .]
    S3091 [4MY]
Text, S3096 [4MY]
Cosponsors added, S33[. . .]
S. 3300—A bill to est[. . .]
    program; to the Com[. . .]
    tion.
    By Mr. WYDEN (for himself, Mr. Kerry, Mr. Carper,
    Ms. Cantwell, Mr. Merkley, and Mrs. Gillibrand),
    S3091 [4MY]
Text, S3097 [4MY]
Cosponsors added, S3359 [6MY]
S. 3301—A bill to establish an Online Voter Registration
    grant program; to the Committee on Rules and
    Administration.
    By Mr. WYDEN (for himself and Mr. Kerry), S3091
    [4MY]
Text, S3098 [4MY]
S. 3302—A bill to amend title 49, United States Code,
    to establish new automobile safety standards, make
    better motor vehicle safety information available
    to the National Highway Traffic Safety Administra-
    tion and the public, and for other purposes; to
    the Committee on Commerce, Science, and Transpor-
    tation.
    By Mr. ROCKEFELLER (for himself, Mr. Pryor,
    Mrs. Boxer, Ms. Cantwell, Mr. Lautenberg, Ms.
    Klobuchar, Mr. Begich, and Mr. Udall of New
    Mexico), S3091 [4MY]
Cosponsors added, S3407 [7MY]
S. 3303—A bill to establish the Chimney Rock National
    Monument in the State of Colorado; to the Committee
    on Energy and Natural Resources.
    By Mr. BENNET (for himself and Mr. Udall of
    Colorado), S3091 [4MY]
S. 3304—A bill to increase the access of persons
    with disabilities to modern communications, and
    for other purposes; to the Committee on Commerce,
    Science, and Transportation.
    By Mr. PRYOR (for himself, Mr. Kerry, Mr. Conrad,
    and Mr. Dorgan), S3091 [4MY]

S. 3305—A bill to amend the Oil Pollution Act of
    1990 to require oil polluters to pay the full cost
    of oil spills, and for other purposes; to the Committee
    on Environment and Public Works.
    By Mr. MENENDEZ (for himself, Mr. Nelson of
    Florida, Mr. Lautenberg, Mr. Cardin, Mr. Schumer,
    Mr. Whitehouse, and Mr. Sanders), S3091 [4MY]
Cosponsors added, S3165 [5MY], S3359 [6MY], S3408
    [7MY]
S. 3306—A bill to amend the Internal Revenue Code
    of 1986 to require polluters to pay the full cost
    of oil spills, and for other purposes; to the Committee
    on Finance.
    By Mr. MENENDEZ (for himself, Mr. Nelson of
    Florida, Mr. Lautenberg, Mr. Cardin, Mr. Schumer,
    Mr. Whitehouse, and Mr. Sanders), S3091 [4MY]
Cosponsors added, S3165 [5MY], S3360 [6MY], S3408
    [7MY]
S. 3307—An original bill to reauthorize child nutrition
    programs, and for other purposes; from the Com-
    mittee on Agriculture, Nutrition, and Forestry.
    By Mrs. LINCOLN, S3164 [5MY]
    Reported (S. Rept. 111–178), S3162 [5MY]
S. 3308—A bill to suspend certain activities in the
    outer Continental Shelf until the date on which
    the joint investigation into the Deepwater Horizon
    incident in the Gulf of Mexico has been completed,
    and for other purposes; to the Committee on Energy
    and Natural Resources.
    By Mr. NELSON of Florida (for himself, Mr. Sanders,
    Mr. Reed, Mrs. Feinstein, and Mrs. Boxer), S3164
    [5MY]
S. 3309—A bill to amend the Internal Revenue Code

Legislative history information can be located using the History of Bills and Resolutions Table in the *Congressional Index*.

This table gives the history of all bills introduced into each session of Congress. It refers to all relevant documents, except hearings.

These tables are located in the bound annual index volumes of the *Congressional Record*, and in the bi-weekly index of unbound issues. H.B. in this illustration stands for History of Bills and Resolutions.

S. 3312—A bill to amend the Homeland Security Act
    of 2002 to authorize the Securing the Cities Initiative
    of the Department of Homeland Security, and for
    other purposes; to the Committee on Homeland
    Security and Governmental Affairs.
    By Mrs. GILLIBRAND, S3164 [5MY]
S. 3313—A bill to withdraw certain land located in
    Clark County, Nevada, from location, entry, and
    patent under the mining laws and disposition under
    all laws pertaining to mineral and geothermal leasing
    or mineral materials, and for other purposes; to
    the Committee on Energy and Natural Resources.
    By Mr. REID, S3164 [5MY]
Text, S3167 [5MY]
Cosponsors added, S3360 [6MY]
S. 3314—A bill to require the Secretary of Veterans
    Affairs and the Appalachian Regional Commission
    to carry out a program of outreach for veterans
    who reside in Appalachia, and for other purposes;
    to the Committee on Veterans' Affairs.
    By Mr. BROWN of Ohio, S3164 [5MY]
S. 3315—A bill to amend title XVIII of the Social
    Security Act to protect Medicare beneficiaries' access
    to home health services under the Medicare Program;
    to the Committee on Finance.
    By Ms. COLLINS (for herself and Mr. Feingold),
    S3164 [5MY]
S. 3316—A bill to provide for flexibility and improve-
    ments in elementary and secondary education, and
    for other purposes; to the Committee on Health,
    Education, Labor, and Pensions.
    By Ms. COLLINS (for herself and Mrs. Snowe),
    S3164 [5MY]
S. 3317—A bill to authorize appropriations for fiscal
    years 2010 through 2014 to promote long-term,

sustainable rebuilding and development in Haiti,
    and for other purposes; to the Committee on Foreign
    Relations.
    By Mr. KERRY (for himself, Mr. Corker, Mr. Cardin,
    and Mr. Durbin), S3164 [5MY]
S. 3318—A bill to amend title XVIII of the Social
    Security Act to eliminate contributing factors to
    disparities in breast cancer treatment through the
    development of a uniform set of consensus-based
    breast cancer treatment performance measures for
    a 6-year quality reporting system and value-based
    purchasing system under the Medicare Program;
    to the Committee on Finance.
    By Mrs. GILLIBRAND, S3164 [5MY]
S. 3319—A bill to amend the Internal Revenue Code
    of 1986 to provide recruitment and retention incen-
    tives for volunteer emergency service workers; to
    the Committee on Finance.
    By Ms. COLLINS (for herself and Mr. Dodd), S3164
    [5MY]
S. 3320—A bill to amend the Public Health Service
    Act to provide for a Pancreatic Cancer Initiative,
    and for other purposes; to the Committee on Health,
    Education, Labor, and Pensions.
    By Mr. WHITEHOUSE, S3358 [6MY]
S. 3321—A bill to establish an advisory committee
    to issue nonbinding governmentwide guidelines on
    making public information available on the Internet,
    to require publicly available Government information
    held by the executive branch to be made available
    on the Internet, to express the sense of Congress
    that publicly available information held by the legisla-
    [. . .] should be available
    [. . .] purposes; to the Committee
    [. . .] Governmental Affairs.
    [. . .]e Atomic Energy Act
    [. . .]ted States Nuclear Fuel
    [. . .] and for other purposes;
    [. . .]nment and Public Works.
    [. . .]imself, Ms. Murkowski,
    [. . .]MY]
    [. . .]anagement and oversight
    [. . .] for other purposes; to
    [. . .]d Security and Govern-
    By Mr. FEINGOLD (for himself and Mr. Coburn),
    S3358 [6MY]
S. 3324—A bill to amend the Internal Revenue Code
    of 1986 to extend the qualifying advanced energy
    project credit; to the Committee on Finance.
    By Mr. BROWN of Ohio (for himself, Mr. Schumer,
    Mr. Merkley, Mr. Casey, and Mrs. Hagan), S3358
    [6MY]
S. 3325—A bill to amend title 38, United States Code,
    to authorize the waiver of the collection of copay-
    ments for telehealth and telemedicine visits of vet-
    erans, and for other purposes; to the Committee
    on Veterans' Affairs.
    By Mr. BEGICH (for himself and Mr. Grassley),
    S3358 [6MY]
S. 3326—A bill to provide grants to States for low-
    income housing projects in lieu of low-income
    housing credits, and to amend the Internal Revenue
    Code of 1986 to allow a 5-year carryback of
    the low-income housing credit, and for other pur-
    poses; to the Committee on Finance.
    By Ms. CANTWELL (for herself, Mr. Kerry, and
    Mrs. Boxer), S3358 [6MY]
S. 3327—A bill to add joining a foreign terrorist organiza-
    tion or engaging in or supporting hostilities against
    the United States or its allies to the list of acts
    for which United States nationals would lose their
    nationality; to the Committee on the Judiciary.
    By Mr. LIEBERMAN (for himself and Mr. Brown
    of Massachusetts), S3358 [6MY]
S. 3328—A bill to examine and improve the child
    welfare workforce, and for other purposes; to the
    Committee on Finance.
    By Mrs. LINCOLN (for herself and Mrs. Landrieu),
    S3358 [6MY]

G. ILLUSTRATIONS: DOCUMENTS

[Illustration 10–6]

S.3307, 111TH CONGRESS, 2ND SESS, AS PRINTED IN CONGRESSIONAL RECORD

August 5, 2010 CONGRESSIONAL RECORD — SENATE **S6911**

SA 4595. Mr. REID (for Mr. NELSON, of Florida) proposed an amendment to amendment SA 4594 proposed by Mr. REID (for Mr. BAUCUS (for himself, Ms. LANDRIEU, and Mr. REID)) to the bill H.R. 5297, supra.

SA 4596. Mr. REID (for Mr. JOHANNS) proposed an amendment to amendment SA 4595 proposed by Mr. REID (for Mr. NELSON of Florida) to the amendment SA 4594 proposed by Mr. REID (for Mr. BAUCUS (for himself, Ms. LANDRIEU, and Mr. REID)) to the bill H.R. 5297, supra.

SA 4597. Mr. REID to the bill H.R. 5297,

SA 4598. Mr. REID to the bill H.R. 5297,

SA 4599. Mr. REID to the bill H.R. 5297,

SA 4600. Mr. REID to amendment SA 4 to the bill H.R. 5297,

SA 4601. Mr. REID to the amendment SA 4 to the amendment SA 4599 proposed by Mr. REID to the bill H.R. 5297, supra.

SA 4602. Mr. REID (for Mr. ROCKEFELLER) proposed an amendment to the bill S. 3729, to authorize the programs of the National Aeronautics and Space Administration for fiscal years 2011 through 2013, and for other purposes.

SA 4603. Mr. REID for Mr. PRYOR (for himself, Mr. ENSIGN, Mr. KERRY, and Mrs. HUTCHISON)) proposed an amendment to the bill S. 3304, to increase the access of persons with disabilities to modern communications, and for other purposes.

SA 4604. Mr. REID (for Mr. LEVIN (for himself and Mr. LUGAR)) proposed an amendment to the resolution S. Res. 322, expressing the sense of the Senate on religious minorities in Iraq.

SA 4605. Mr. REID (for Mr. LEVIN (for himself and Mr. LUGAR)) proposed an amendment to the resolution S. Res. 322, supra.

TEXT OF AMENDMENTS

SA 4588. Mrs. FEINSTEIN (for herself and Mr. BOND) proposed an amendment to the bill S. 3611, to authorize appropriations for fiscal year 2010 for intelligence and intelligence-related activities of the United States Government, the Community Management Account, and the Central Intelligence Agency Retirement and Disability System, and for other purposes; as follows:

On page 12, strike lines 3 through 9 and insert the following:

SEC. 106. BUDGETARY PROVISIONS.

The budgetary effects of this Act, for the purpose of complying with the Statutory Pay-As-You-Go-Act of 2010, shall be determined by reference to the latest statement titled "Budgetary Effects of PAYGO Legislation" for this Act, submitted for printing in the Congressional Record by the Chairman of the Senate Budget Committee, provided that such statement has been submitted prior to the vote on passage.

Beginning on page 88, strike line 20 and all that follows through page 89, lines 16 and insert the following:

(1) CONGRESSIONAL ARMED SERVICES COMMITTEES.—To the extent that the report required by subsection (a) addresses an element of the intelligence community within the Department of Defense, the Director of National Intelligence, in consultation with the Secretary of Defense, shall submit that portion of the report, and any associated material that is necessary to make that portion understandable, to the Committee on Armed Services of the Senate and the Committee on Armed Services of the House of Representatives. The Director of National Intelligence may authorize redactions of the report and any associated materials submitted pursuant to this paragraph, if such redactions are consistent with the protection of sensitive intelligence sources and methods.

(2) CONGRESSIONAL JUDICIARY COMMITTEES.—To the extent that the report required by subsection (a) addresses an ele-

[callout box:] From the indexes or tables shown in previous illustrations, the researcher should now have citations to (1) bill number, (2) reports, and (3) *Congressional Record*.

This illustration shows S.3307, 111th Congress, 2nd Sess., as printed in *Congressional Record*.

sistent with the protection of sensitive intelligence sources and methods.

Beginning on page 89, strike line 17 and all that follows through page 91, line 6.

Beginning on page 91, strike line 10 and all that follows through page 92, line 15.

On page 214, line 16, strike "committees" and insert "committees, the Committee on the Judiciary of the Senate, and the Committee on the Judiciary of the House of Representatives".

SA 4589. Mrs. LINCOLN (for herself and Mr. CHAMBLISS) proposed an amendment to the bill S. 3307, to reauthorize child nutrition programs, and for other purposes; as follows:

Strike all after the enacting clause and insert the following:

SECTION 1. SHORT TITLE; TABLE OF CONTENTS.

(a) SHORT TITLE.—This Act may be cited as the "Healthy, Hunger-Free Kids Act of 2010".

(b) TABLE OF CONTENTS.—The table of contents for this Act is as follows:

Sec. 1. Short title; table of contents.
Sec. 2. Definition of Secretary.

TITLE I—A PATH TO END CHILDHOOD HUNGER

Subtitle A—National School Lunch Program

Sec. 101. Improving direct certification.
Sec. 102. Categorical eligibility of foster children.
Sec. 103. Direct certification for children receiving Medicaid benefits.
Sec. 104. Eliminating individual applications through community eligibility.
Sec. 105. Grants for expansion of school breakfast programs.

Subtitle B—Summer Food Service Program

Sec. 111. Alignment of eligibility rules for public and private sponsors.
Sec. 112. Outreach to eligible families.
Sec. 113. Summer food service support grants.

Subtitle C—Child and Adult Care Food Program

Sec. 121. Simplifying area eligibility determinations in the child and adult care food program.
Sec. 122. Expansion of afterschool meals for at-risk children.

Subtitle D—Special Supplemental Nutrition Program for Women, Infants, and Children

Sec. 131. Certification periods.

Subtitle E—Miscellaneous

Sec. 141. Childhood hunger research.
Sec. 142. State childhood hunger challenge grants.
Sec. 143. Review of local policies on meal charges and provision of alternate meals.

TITLE II—REDUCING CHILDHOOD OBESITY AND IMPROVING THE DIETS OF CHILDREN

Subtitle A—National School Lunch Program

Sec. 201. Performance-based reimbursement rate increases for new meal patterns.
Sec. 202. Nutrition requirements for fluid milk.
Sec. 203. Water.
Sec. 204. Local school wellness policy imple-
ol lunch pricing.
n nonprogram foods
ools.
nd notification of
formance.
ndards for all foods
ool.
for the public on the
rition environment.
ilot program.
d Adult Care Food Program

Sec. 221. Nutrition and wellness goals for meals served through the child and adult care food program.
Sec. 222. Interagency coordination to promote health and wellness in child care licensing.
Sec. 223. Study on nutrition and wellness quality of child care settings.

Subtitle C—Special Supplemental Nutrition Program for Women, Infants, and Children

Sec. 231. Support for breastfeeding in the WIC Program.
Sec. 232. Review of available supplemental foods.

Subtitle D—Miscellaneous

Sec. 241. Nutrition education and obesity prevention grant program.
Sec. 242. Procurement and processing of food service products and commodities.
Sec. 243. Access to Local Foods: Farm to School Program.
Sec. 244. Research on strategies to promote the selection and consumption of healthy foods.

TITLE III—IMPROVING THE MANAGEMENT AND INTEGRITY OF CHILD NUTRITION PROGRAMS

Subtitle A—National School Lunch Program

Sec. 301. Privacy protection.
Sec. 302. Applicability of food safety program on entire school campus.
Sec. 303. Fines for violating program requirements.
Sec. 304. Independent review of applications.
Sec. 305. Program evaluation.
Sec. 306. Professional standards for school food service.
Sec. 307. Indirect costs.
Sec. 308. Ensuring safety of school meals.

Subtitle B—Summer Food Service Program

Sec. 321. Summer food service program permanent operating agreements.
Sec. 322. Summer food service program disqualification.

Subtitle C—Child and Adult Care Food Program

Sec. 331. Renewal of application materials and permanent operating agreements.
Sec. 332. State liability for payments to aggrieved child care institutions.
Sec. 333. Transmission of income information by sponsored family or group day care homes.
Sec. 334. Simplifying and enhancing administrative payments to sponsoring organizations.
Sec. 335. Child and adult care food program audit funding.

[Illustration 10–7]

PUBLIC LAW 111–296 AS PRINTED AS A SLIP LAW

PUBLIC LAW 111–296—DEC. 13, 2010   124 STAT. 3183

Public Law 111–296
111th Congress

An Act

To reauthorize child nutrition programs, and for other purposes.

Dec. 13, 2010
[S. 3307]

Be it enacted by the Senate and House of Representatives of the United States of America in Congress assembled,

Healthy, Hunger-Free Kids Act of 2010.

SECTION 1. SHORT TITLE; TABLE OF CONTENTS.

42 USC 1751 note.

(a) SHORT TITLE.—This Act may be cited as the "Healthy, Hunger-Free Kids Act of 2010".

(b) TABLE OF CONTENTS.—The table of contents for this Act is as follows:

Sec. 1. Short title; table of contents.
Sec. 2. Definition of Secretary.

Note how the slip law refers to (1) the date the bill became law and (2) the bill that became law. The text of the public law as it appears here can be compared to the introduced bill to determine legislative intent, if amendments were made.

Since 1975, a brief summary at the end of each slip law (3) provides references or citations to some documents that may be relevant to the legislative history of a public law.

Sec. 113. Summer food service support grants.

Subtitle C—Child and Adult Care Food Program

Sec. 121. Simplifying area eligibility determinations in the child and adult care food program.
Sec. 122. Expansion of afterschool meals for at-risk children.

Subtitle D—Special Supplemental Nutrition Program for Women, Infants, and Children

Sec. 131. Certification periods.

Subtitle E—Miscellaneous

Sec. 141. Childhood hunger research.
Sec. 142. State childhood hunger challenge grants.
Sec. 143. Review of local policies on meal charges and provision of alternate meals.

TITLE II—REDUCING CHILDHOOD OBESITY AND IMPROVING THE DIETS OF CHILDREN

Subtitle A—National School Lunch Program

Sec. 201. Performance-based reimbursement rate increases for new meal patterns.
Sec. 202. Nutrition requirements for fluid milk.
Sec. 203. Water.
Sec. 204. Local school wellness policy implementation.
Sec. 205. Equity in school lunch pricing.
Sec. 206. Revenue from nonprogram foods sold in schools.

[Illustration 10–7 cont'd]

PUBLIC LAW 111–296 AS PRINTED AS A SLIP LAW CONT'D

124 STAT. 3266   PUBLIC LAW 111–296—DEC. 13, 2010

42 USC 1751
note.

SEC. 445. EFFECTIVE DATE.

Except as otherwise specifically provided in this Act or any of the amendments made by this Act, this Act and the amendments made by this Act take effect on October 1, 2010.

Approved December 13, 2010.

LEGISLATIVE HISTORY—S. 3307:

SENATE REPORTS: No. 111–178 (Comm. on Agriculture, Nutrition, and Forestry).
CONGRESSIONAL RECORD, Vol. 156 (2010):
     Aug. 5, considered and passed Senate.
     Dec. 1, 2, considered and passed House.
DAILY COMPILATION OF PRESIDENTIAL DOCUMENTS (2010):
     Dec. 13, Presidential remarks.

[Illustration 10–8]

PAGE FROM DEBATES ON S.3307, 110TH CONGRESS, 2ND SESS., IN CONGRESSIONAL RECORD

S6832 CONGRESSIONAL RECORD — SENATE *August 5, 2010*

Mr. LEVIN. Is the Senator from Arizona suggesting we did not have a vote on hate crimes last year?

Mr. McCAIN. The Senator from Arizona is saying that the Senator from Michigan filled up the tree; did he not? Was the tree fille[...] chairman of the co[...]

Mr. LEVIN. It is [...] but that is not my[...] tion is whether we [...] crimes.

Mr. McCAIN. My [...] prevent the tree fro[...]

Mr. LEVIN. We [...] vote on hate crime[...] my answer.

The PRESIDING OFFICER. The Senator from Arkansas.

HEALTHY, HUNGER-FREE KIDS
ACT OF 2010

Mrs. LINCOLN. Madam President, I ask unanimous consent that the Sen-

ate proceed to the immediate consideration of Calendar No. 363, S. 3307, the Healthy, Hunger-Free Kids Act of 2010.

The PRESIDING OFFICER. The clerk will report the bill by title.

The assistant legislative clerk read [...]

[...] a third time, passed, and the motion to reconsider be laid upon the table; that any statements relating to the bill be printed in the RECORD, without intervening action or debate, and that the pay-go statement from Senator CONRAD be printed in the RECORD.

The PRESIDING OFFICER. Without objection, it is so ordered.

The amendment (No. 4589) was agreed to.

(The amendment is printed in today's RECORD under "Text of amendments.")

The bill (S. 3307), as amended, was ordered to be engrossed for a third reading, was read the third time, and [...]

[...] President, this is [...]dgetary Effects of [...] for S. 3307, as [...]

[...]ts of S. 3307 for the 5-[...]O Scorecard: net in-[...]814 million.

[...]cts of S. 3307 for the 10-year Statutory PAYGO Scorecard: net increase in the deficit of $2.189 billion.

Also submitted for the RECORD as part of this statement is a table prepared by the Congressional Budget Office, which provides additional information on the budgetary effects of this Act.

The table is as follows:

> The discussion of a pending bill by members of Congress may be useful in determining congressional intent. The researcher should ascertain whether such discussion occurred in either house of Congress.

ESTIMATE OF THE STATUTORY PAY-AS-YOU-GO EFFECTS FOR AN AMENDMENT IN THE NATURE OF A SUBSTITUTE TO S. 3307, REAUTHORIZING CHILD NUTRITION PROGRAMS (AS TRANSMITTED ON AUGUST 5, 2010—WEI10567)

[Millions of dollars, by fiscal year]

	2010	2011	2012	2013	2014	2015	2016	2017	2018	2019	2020	2010–2015	2010–2020
Net Increase or Decrease (−) in the On-Budget Deficit Relative to Current Law (as of August 5, 2010)													
Net Budgetary Impact	0	−51	−50	279	−5,108	−4,127	−2,484	−1,004	−165	265	259	−9,056	−12,184
Less:													
Previously Designated as Emergency Requirements [1]	0	0	0	0	−5,446	−4,424	−2,775	−1,290	−438	0	0	−9,870	−14,373
Statutory Pay-As-You-Go Impact	0	−51	−50	279	338	297	291	286	273	265	259	814	2,189
Net Increase or Decrease (−) in the On-Budget Deficit Relative to the Effects of H.R. 1586 as Amended by the Senate on August 5, 2010													
Net Budgetary Impact [2]	0	−51	−50	279	−2,138	297	291	286	273	265	259	−1,662	−287
Less:													
Previously Designated as Emergency Requirements [1]	0	0	0	0	−2,475	0	0	0	0	0	0	−2,476	−2,476
Statutory Pay-As-You-Go Impact	0	−51	−50	279	338	297	291	286	273	265	259	814	2,189

Note: Components may not sum to totals because of rounding.
[1] Savings in Title IV that would result from a change to the Supplemental Nutrition Assistance Program that was previously designated as emergency.
[2] If H.R. 1586 were to clear the Congress prior to this bill, the net deficit impact would change because some of the savings in Title IV of the child nutrition legislation that would result from a change to the Supplemental Nutrition Assistance Program are also included in H.R. 1586. Total savings would decline from $14.4 billion to about $2.5 billion over the 2010–2020 period. The net decrease in the deficit would be $1.7 billion over the 2010–2015 period and $287 million over the 2010–2020 period, if H.R. 1586 were to clear the Congress prior to this bill.
Source: Congressional Budget Office.

Mrs. LINCOLN. Madam President, for the past 2 weeks, I have come to the floor of the Senate to speak about the critical importance of passing child nutrition legislation before we adjourn for the August recess, and I want to say a very special thanks to all of my colleagues for their hard work on this initiative, their willingness to rise above partisan politics, regional differences, or anything else, to seize this opportunity. I am so pleased today to say we have seized this opportunity to make a historic investment in our children.

I started out my discussion here on the floor last week by saying all we would need to get this bill done was a mere 8 hours—a simple 8 hours to pass a bill that would improve the lives of millions of children across this country. With the assistance of my colleagues, we were able to accomplish this goal in much less time than that, and I want to thank my colleagues again for sending such a strong bipartisan message of support for child nutrition.

Before I go any further, I wish first to thank my good friend and the ranking member of our Agriculture Committee, Senator CHAMBLISS, for his tremendous assistance in crafting this

legislation and bringing us to this vote today. He is a wonderful partner in the Senate Committee on Agriculture, Nutrition, and Forestry, and he has been a true partner in this effort. I greatly appreciate all his work on this bill. We could not have gotten to this point, nor could we have passed this, without him. So I am grateful to him. I also add my thanks to his staff—Martha Scott Poindexter and Kate Coler. And, of course, all my thanks go out to my staff on the Agriculture Committee—Robert Holifield, Brian Baenig, Dan Christenson, Hillary Caron, Courtney Rowe, and Julie Anna Potts. They are the absolute best.

I also need to thank the administration—the President and First Lady, as well as Secretary Vilsack—for their incredible leadership on childhood nutrition. Their hands-on involvement, particularly in the last few days, has ensured that we will be able to accomplish this goal. I know this is an issue they all care very deeply and passionately about, and that is reflected in the many shared priorities between the Congress and the administration that are included in this bill.

I must say the presence of the First Lady, her compassion, her diligence, her tenacity in wanting to see some-

thing happen on behalf of the children of this country that was productive, was progressive, and that moved us forward past the benchmarks we had been at since 1973 have been amazing, and I am certainly grateful to her for all she has done.

With the passage of this bill, I am pleased we are bringing some fresh bipartisan air into the Senate. It goes to show that when you are willing to roll up your sleeves, work across the aisle in a collective and bipartisan manner, you truly do see results. That is what the American people elected us to do. That is what they expect and that is what this bill represents.

Most importantly, this bill is about our children, and about doing what is right for them and for their families. It is about connecting more children with the child nutrition programs which their families depend upon to make ends meet. It is about making sure they get the nutritious meals they deserve so they can succeed in the classroom and learn better. It is about making sure our schools and classrooms, our childcare settings are all places that promote good health and wellness, because we know that children who are healthier learn better and they also

H. OBTAINING THE DOCUMENTS OF A LEGISLATIVE HISTORY

Previous sections of this chapter discussed sources that allow a researcher to identify the existence of documents relevant to the legislative history of a specific law. This section describes where the full text of these documents can be located. As a general rule, most legislative history materials from the 1990s to the present can be found either on the Library of Congress's *Congress.gov* (replacing THOMAS in 2014) or on the GPO's *FDsys* website[46] (formerly *GPO Access*). [Illustration 10–9] These sites are the quickest way to access the documents needed for a legislative history. However, absent a compiled legislative history, locating older materials requires access to at least some of the resources listed below, whether in print or electronic format.

1. Public Laws

The following sources provide access to public laws as slip laws, or as published in bound session-law volumes of the *United States Statutes at Large*:

a. *THOMAS*[47]. This website has slip laws from 1973 to the present.

b. *FDsys* and GPO print edition. The U.S. Government Printing Office's *FDsys* website provides access to slip laws from 1995 to the present,[48] and to *U.S. Statutes at Large* volumes from vol. 65 (1951) forward.[49] The GPO's official print edition of the *U.S. Statutes at Large* began publication in 1789 and is available in most federal depository libraries.

c. *United States Code Congressional and Administrative News* (*USCCAN*). All public laws are printed in *USCCAN* in chronological order from 1941 to the present.

d. *Westlaw*. Slip laws are available from 1973 to the present in *Westlaw's* USCCAN database. *Westlaw* also provides the *U.S. Statutes at Large* volumes from 1789 through 1972.

e. *LexisNexis*. *LexisNexis* has slip laws from 1998 to the present.

f. *ProQuest Congressional*. A basic subscription provides access to slip laws from 1988 to the present. The *ProQuest Congressional* U.S. Statutes at Large collection offers comprehensive access to the *U.S. Statutes at Large,* in PDF format, from 1789.

g. *HeinOnline*. A complete set of the *U.S. Statutes at Large* is available in *HeinOnline's* United States Statutes at Large Library in PDF format.

h. *LLMC*.[50] The Law Library Microform Consortium, a nonprofit library cooperative, offers the complete backfile of the *U.S. Statutes at Large* in PDF format in *LLMC Digital* and on microfiche.

---

[46] http://www.gpo.gov/fdsys/.

[47] http://thomas.loc.gov/home/LegislativeData.php?&n=PublicLaws#. THOMAS is being replaced by Congress.gov in late 2014.

[48] http://www.gpo.gov/fdsys/browse/collection.action?collectionCode=PLAW.

[49] http://www.gpo.gov/fdsys/browse/collection.action?collectionCode=STATUTE. The retrospective coverage of *U.S. Statutes at Large* is almost complete as of June 2014; only the most recent volumes are missing, and new material is continually added.

[50] http://www.llmc.com/.

i.   *American Memory: A Century of Lawmaking for a New Nation*.[51] This Library of Congress historical website provides the first 18 volumes of the *U.S. Statutes at Large* (1789–1875), which may be browsed or searched.

2.   Public Bills

a.   *Current and recent bills*. The following electronic services provide the most timely access to recent congressional materials.

(1)   *FDsys*. This website of the U.S. Government Printing Office provides Congressional Bills,[52] a database containing all bills from the 103rd Congress (1993–1994) to the present. The database is updated daily when the House or Senate is in session.

(2)   *THOMAS*.[53] *THOMAS* provides the full text of bills beginning with the 101st Congress (1989–1990), summaries of all bills introduced in either the House or Senate beginning in 1973, and access to the Bill Summary & Status (BSS) section that provides links to everything about a bill except the full text. This section will provide links to full-text versions of the bill or public law, if available.

(3)   *Westlaw*. *Westlaw* provides the full text of all bills beginning with the 104th Congress (1995–1996). The bills from each Congress may be searched separately or combined.

(4)   *LexisNexis*. *LexisNexis* provides the full text of all bills beginning with the 101st Congress (1989–1990). The bills from each Congress may be searched separately or combined.

(5)   *ProQuest Congressional*. A basic subscription to this commercial service provides texts of bills beginning with the 101st Congress (1989–1990).

b.   *Historical research*.

(1)   *American Memory: A Century of Lawmaking for a New Nation*.[54] This Library of Congress website includes the text of House bills and resolutions from the 6th Congress (1799–1800) through the 42nd Congress (1871–1873); the text of Senate bills and resolutions from the 16th Congress (1819–1821) through the 42nd Congress (1871–1873); and the text of Senate joint resolutions from the 18th Congress (1824–1825) through the 42nd Congress (1871–1873).

(2)   *United States Congress Public Bills and Resolutions*. Bills from 1979 to 2000 (96th Congress through 106th Congress) are available in this microfiche set, distributed to depository libraries. Access is via the *Microfiche Users Guide/Bill Finding Aid.* [55]

(3)   *CIS Microfiche Library* (offered through ProQuest). Beginning coverage in 1970, *CIS* provides reprints of bills that have become public laws.

---

[51] http://memory.loc.gov/ammem/amlaw/lwsl.html.

[52] http://www.gpo.gov/fdsys/browse/collection.action?collectionCode=BILLS.

[53] http://thomas.loc.gov or http://www.thomas.gov. *THOMAS* links to the *FDsys* website to provide many documents in PDF format.

[54] http://memory.loc.gov/ammem/amlaw/lwhbsb.html.

[55] The researcher should be aware that the *Guide* may refer to a public bill or resolution that has not been provided in the microfiche set. Older print versions of bills are available on microfiche or microfilm through the Law Library of Congress (1789–) and certain federal depository libraries.

(4) *Public Laws—Legislative Histories on Microfiche.* From 1979 through 1988, Commerce Clearing House published reprints of bills in this collection.

(5) *GAO Legislative History Collection.* For selected legislation that has become public law, reprints of relevant bills and amendments are available on microfiche. This source and years of coverage is described above in Section D-2-h.

(6) *Congressional Record.* Occasionally, the text of a bill, especially if amended on the floor of either house during discussion or debate, may be printed in the *Congressional Record.*

(7) *Committee Reports.* Committee reports often reprint bills, as amended by committees, for those bills reported out of committee.[56]

3. House, Senate, and Conference Committee Reports

a. *Electronic Services.* The following services provide the most timely access to recent congressional materials.

(1) *FDsys.* This website's "Congressional Reports" page includes the full text of all committee reports issued by Congress beginning with the 104th Congress (1995–1996).

(2) *Congress.gov.* This website provides House and Senate committee reports, including conference and joint committee reports, from the 104th Congress to the present (1995–1996).

(3) *Westlaw* includes all committee reports printed in *USCCAN* since 1948. From 1990 to the present, *Westlaw* contains all committee reports, even for bills that did not become law.

(4) *LexisNexis* provides House and Senate reports for legislation since 1990.

(5) *ProQuest Congressional.* A basic subscription to this commercial service provides access to committee reports from 1990 to the present. A comprehensive collection is available in the *ProQuest U.S. Serial Set Digital Collection.*

(6) *Bloomberg Law* has committee prints beginning in 1995.

b. *United States Congressional Serial Set.* Committee reports are reprinted in the official print series and in the commercial microfiche set (CIS) from *ProQuest*. The *Serial Set* is available online in the *Readex U.S. Congressional Serial Set* from 1817 to 1980, and in the *ProQuest U.S. Serial Set Digital Collection* from 1789 to 1969 (Part I) and 1970 to the present (Part II).[57] The Library of Congress' *American Memory: A Century of Lawmaking for a New Nation* website offers free access to selected *Serial Set* volumes from the 23rd Congress (1833–1835) through the 64th Congress (1915–1917).

c. *Congressional Record.* This publication occasionally contains committee reports.

d. *CIS* (offered through *ProQuest*). Reports from 1970 to the present for bills that have become public law can be found in the *CIS Microfiche Library.*

---

[56] Committee reports reprinted in the *United States Code Congressional and Administrative News (USCCAN)* do not include the text of the bill, even if it was included in the original report.

[57] The *Serial Set* is discussed below in Section H-8.

  d. GAO Legislative Histories. Committee reports for bills that became public laws are available for selected laws.[58]

  f. Public Laws—Legislative Histories on Microfiche. This set from Commerce Clearing House (CCH) makes available Senate, House, and conference committee reports for public laws enacted during the 96th (1979–1980) through 100th Congresses (1987–1988).

  g. Looseleaf Services and Treatises. Committee reports for specialized areas of legal research may be reproduced for subscribers to these services.

4. Congressional Debates

  The *Congressional Record* is the primary source for the transcripts of debates and votes on legislation. (It also includes floor discussion of topics other than proposed legislation.) When using the *Congressional Record*, the researcher should be acquainted with its history and pattern of publication to allow for its most efficient use.

  a. Predecessors to the Congressional Record.[59] The predecessors to the *Congressional Record* are the *Annals of Congress,* 1789–1824 (1st to 18th Cong., 1st Sess.); the *Register of Debates,* 1824–1837 (18th Cong., 2nd Sess. to 25th Cong., 1st Sess.); and the *Congressional Globe,* 1837–1873 (25th Cong., 2nd Sess., to 42nd Cong., 2nd Sess.). The early volumes of the *Congressional Globe* contain abridged versions of the proceedings of Congress. The *Congressional Record* began in 1873 with the 43rd Cong., 1st Sess.

  b. Congressional Record Daily Edition. The *Congressional Record* is published daily while either chamber is in session. It consists of four sections: the proceedings of the House of Representatives and the Senate (including debates) in separate sections; the Extension of Remarks (reprints of articles, editorials, book reviews, and tributes); and, since the 80th Congress, the Daily Digest. The latter summarizes the day's proceedings, lists actions taken and laws signed by the president that day, and provides very useful committee information. [Illustrations 10–6 and 10–8]

  Each section of the daily *Congressional Record* is paginated consecutively during each session of Congress. Each page in each section is preceded by the following letter prefix: S–Senate, H–House, E–Extension of Remarks, and D–Daily Digest.

  An index to the *Congressional Record* is published every two weeks and provides access in a single alphabetical listing by subject, name of legislator, and title of legislation. These indexes are non-cumulative.

  c. Congressional Record Permanent Edition. A permanent, bound edition of the *Congressional Record* is published after the end of each session of Congress. Publication of paper and microfiche copies of these editions is behind schedule. The permanent edition is generally the most authoritative source for research.

---

  [58] This source and years of coverage are described above in Section D-2-h.

  [59] The predecessors to the CONGRESSIONAL RECORD are on the Library of Congress website, American Memory: A Century of Lawmaking for a New Nation, U.S. Congressional Documents and Debates, at http://memory.loc.gov/ammem/amlaw/.

The permanent edition renumbers all pages into one sequence rather than using the pagination of the daily edition that separately numbers Senate, House, Extension of Remarks, and Daily Digest.[60]

The permanent edition includes an index that is composed of two parts: an Index to the Proceedings, including materials in the Extensions of Remarks (arranged by name and subject) and a History of Bills and Resolutions (arranged by bill and resolution numbers). The Daily Digest section of each of the daily editions of the *Congressional Record* is cumulated in one volume of the permanent edition.

When citing to the *Congressional Record*, cite to the permanent edition if it is available. Because the page numbers in the daily and permanent (bound) edition are unrelated, the user must consult the indexes or run keyword searches in both to locate corresponding material. *HeinOnline* provides a helpful "Congressional Record Daily to Bound Locator" conversion tool for vol. 126 (1980) through the latest bound volume.

    d.   Electronic Sources. The following electronic sources provide current or retrospective access to the daily or permanent editions of the *Congressional Record*.

    (1)   *FDsys.* The *FDsys* website provides the *Congressional Record* (daily edition) beginning in 1994.[61] An index to the *Congressional Record* dates back to 1983.[62] The bound permanent edition of the *Congressional Record* is available only for 1999 to early 2002, as of June 2014.[63] On *FDsys*, the *Congressional Record Index*'s History of Bills and Resolutions is a separate collection that begins with the 98th Congress (1983–1984).[64]

    (2)   *Congress.gov.* This website contains the full text of the daily edition of the *Congressional Record* beginning with the 101st Congress (1989–90). The biweekly *Congressional Record Index* can be searched or browsed by keyword beginning with the 104th Congress (1995–96).[65]

    (3)   *American Memory: A Century of Lawmaking for a New Nation.* This Library of Congress website contains vol. 1 (1873) to vol. 3 (1875) of the *Congressional Record* permanent edition.[66]

    (4)   *Westlaw.* Coverage of the daily edition begins with the 99th Congress (1985–1986).

    (5)   *LexisNexis.* Coverage of the daily edition begins with the 99th Congress (1985–1986).

    (6)   *BloombergLaw.* Coverage includes the daily edition from 1989 to date; it also has the Daily Digest from 1939 to date.

    (7)   *ProQuest Congressional.* A basic subscription to this commercial service provides access to the *Congressional Record* daily edition beginning with the 99th Congress (1985–1986). The *ProQuest Congressional Record Permanent Digital Collection*

---

[60] The permanent edition does not contain the Extensions of Remarks from 1955 to 1968.

[61] http://www.gpo.gov/fdsys/browse/collection.action?collectionCode=CREC.

[62] http://www.gpo.gov/fdsys/browse/collection.action?collectionCode=CRI.

[63] http://www.gpo.gov/fdsys/browse/collection.action?collectionCode=CRECB.

[64] http://www.gpo.gov/fdsys/browse/collection.action?collectionCode=HOB.

[65] http://thomas.loc.gov/home/r110query.html.

[66] http://memory.loc.gov/ammem/amlaw/lwcr.html.

provides access to the *Congressional Record* from 1873 to the late 1990s, as of June 2014. It also includes the three predecessors to the *Congressional Record* (1789–1873).

(8)   *HeinOnline.* Coverage of the *Congressional Record* permanent edition in HeinOnline is from 1873 to 2008. Coverage of the daily edition begins in 1980.

(9)   *LLMC Digital (Law Library Microform Consortium).* Coverage of the *Congressional Record* permanent edition is from vol. 1 (1873) to vol. 4 (1876), and from vol. 136 (1990) to vol. 154 (2008).

5.   Hearings

Many federal depository libraries have individual hearing transcripts. In addition to the references provided above, the following resources may provide information useful for locating both published and unpublished hearings:

a.   *FDsys.*[67] All hearings released to the GPO from congressional committees are available in full text beginning with the 104th Congress (1995–1996).

b.   *Congressional Information Service (CIS)* (offered through *ProQuest*). CIS produces the full text of all available Senate and House hearings in microfiche, including appendices to the hearings, and publishes comprehensive indexes for locating hearings. Since 1970, CIS finding tools have provided citations to all Senate and House hearings.

(1)   *CIS U.S. Congressional Committee Hearings Index.* This index identifies published hearings from 1833 to 1969. An accompanying microfiche component provides the text of indexed hearings.

(2)   *CIS Index to Unpublished U.S. Senate Committee Hearings.* This index identifies unpublished Senate hearings from 1823 to 1984. The accompanying microfiche component provides the text.

(3)   *CIS Index to Unpublished U.S. House of Representatives Committee Hearings.* This index provides citations to unpublished hearings; an accompanying microfiche component reproduces the text. Coverage is from 1833 to 1972.

c.   *ProQuest Congressional.* A basic subscription to this commercial service provides access to selected congressional hearing transcripts and full text statements from 1988 to the present. The *ProQuest Congressional Hearings Digital Collection* includes full transcripts of both published and unpublished hearings, along with all related proceedings, such as oral statements, committee questions, and discussion, from 1824 to the present.

d.   *LexisNexis.* Commercial transcripts from *CQ Transcriptions*, *CQ Congressional Testimony*, the Federal Documents Clearing House (FDCH) *News Service Capitol Report*, the *Federal News Service*, and *National Narrowcast Network Transcripts* are included in *LexisNexis* from 1988 to the present. Coverage varies by source.

e.   *Westlaw.* Commercial transcripts from the FDCH, *CQ Roll Call*, and *CQ Transcriptions* are included from 1993 to the present. Coverage varies by source.

f.   *Bloomberg Law.* Official and commercial transcripts for selected hearings from 1995 are offered.

---

[67] http://www.gpo.gov/fdsys/browse/collection.action?collectionCode=CHRG.

    g. Websites of the U.S. House of Representatives[68] *and the U.S. Senate*[69] contain links to committee websites, which post hearings. The Law Librarians' Society of Washington, D.C. (LLSDC) maintains a web page of Quick Links to House and Senate Committee Hearings and Other Publications[70] in its *Legislative Sourcebook*. Also, individual hearings may be available in print through a federal depository library.

6. Committee Prints

    The following sources provide access to committee prints[71]:

    a. CIS US Congressional Committee Prints Index and microfiche component (offered through ProQuest). This multivolume index identifies committee prints from 1830 to 1969, and the microfiche component reprints the documents.

    b. CIS/Index (offered through ProQuest). From 1970 forward, the *CIS/Index* and *Abstracts* volumes identify committee prints; the CIS microfiche library provides reprints of the documents.

    c. United States Congressional Serial Set. If a committee print is designated as a House or Senate document[72] it becomes available as part of the official print *Serial Set*, or in the *CIS U.S. Serial Set Index* and corresponding microfiche.

    d. ProQuest Congressional. A basic subscription to this commercial service provides access to *selected*, full text committee prints from 1993 to 2004. The *ProQuest® Congressional Research Digital Collection* offers access to the full text of *all* committee prints from 1830 to the present.

    e. LexisNexis contains selected committee prints from August 1994 through December 22, 2003. It also provides an index to committee prints from 1830 to 1969.

    f. FDsys. All committee prints are available in full text beginning with the 104th Congress (1995–1996). Selected committee prints from the 94th Congress (1975–1976), the 102nd Congress (1991–1992), and the 103rd Congress (1993–1994) are also included.[73]

    g. Bloomberg Law has committee prints beginning in 1995.

7. Congressional Research Service (CRS) Reports

    The following sources provide access to CRS Reports:

    a. Electronic sources:

---

[68] From the House of Representatives home page, http://www.house.gov, click on the Committees link.

[69] From the Senate home page, http://www.senate.gov, click on the Committees link.

[70] http://www.llsdc.org/hearings-quick-links.

[71] Often, only a limited number of committee prints are printed for the use of committee members. Committee prints have recently become more available through the federal depository library program and online databases, though indexing is often incomplete. All committee prints from the 104th Congress (1995–1996) to the present are available in *FDsys* at http://www.gpo.gov/fdsys/browse/collection.action?collection Code=CPRT.

[72] Committee prints are produced by and for a particular committee. They are not considered a publication of the chamber of Congress in which the committee sits. For that reason, a committee print is not considered a "document" of the House or the Senate as a whole. A print will only rarely be designated a House or Senate document and included in the *Serial Set*, an official compilation of House and Senate publications. http://www.gpo.gov/help/index.html#about_congressional_committee_prints.htm.

[73] http://www.gpo.gov/fdsys/browse/collection.action?collectionCode=CPRT.

(1)   *Internet sites.* Free websites such as Federation of American Scientists,[74] *IP Mall* (University of New Hampshire School of Law, 1993–),[75] National Council for Science and the Environment (1990–),[76] and *University of North Texas Digital Library* (1990–)[77] provide searchable or topical access to selected CRS reports.

(2)   *Commercial services.* Penny Hill Press[78] (full coverage from 1995; selected coverage before 1995) and *CQ Roll Call*[79] (beginning coverage with 1993) provide comprehensive access to newer CRS reports. The *ProQuest Congressional Research Digital Collection* offers retrospective and current access to all CRS reports beginning in 1916, as well as committee prints from 1830.

b.   *Major Studies and Issue Briefs of the Congressional Research Service.* ProQuest offers access to this collection of CRS reports on microfilm (1916–) and microfiche (1991–); it originated as a product of University Publications of America (UPA). The print *Cumulative Index to CRS Reports, 1916–1989*, also available from ProQuest, indexes seventy-five years of the microfilm.

8.   The Serial Set

The *United States Congressional Serial Set*, published by the Government Printing Office, has been known by various titles since its inception in 1789 (e.g., *American State Papers*, 1789–1838). The *Serial Set* compiles a variety of works that Congress orders published. The most important for legislative history research are committee reports and the presidential messages related to specific legislation.[80] According to the latest publication schedule, the *Serial Set* is published about four years after the cover dates of the reports and documents it compiles.[81]

The following sources provide access to the *Serial Set*:

a.   *FDsys.* This website contains documents and reports from the *Serial Set* from the 100th Congress (1987–88) to the present.[82] *FDsys's* predecessor, *GPO Access*, provides a Numerical List of Documents and Reports published in volumes of the *Serial Set* from the 85th Congress (1957–1958) through the 109th Congress (2005–2006).[83]

b.   *CIS/ProQuest.* ProQuest publishes the *CIS US Serial Set Index,* covering 1789 to 1969, along with microfiche that provides the documents indexed. The *Index* features

---

[74] http://www.fas.org/sgp/crs/index.html.

[75] http://ipmall.info/

[76] http://www.cnie.org/nle/crs/.

[77] http://digital.library.unt.edu/explore/collections/CRSR/.

[78] http://www.pennyhill.com/.

[79] http://corporate.cqrollcall.com/?s=CRS.

[80] From the 84th through the 95th Congresses, House and Senate reports on public and private bills were available in bound volumes entitled "Miscellaneous Reports" by type of bill. Beginning with the 96th Congress, all reports are compiled and arranged in numerical sequence in bound volumes. Presidential messages can be found in the House and Senate Documents section of the *Serial Set.* Occasionally, a committee print may be classified as a House or Senate document and can be found in this set.

For a helpful discussion of the material that is included in the *Serial Set* (and was included in the past), see Richard J. McKinney, *An Overview of the U.S. Congressional Serial Set, in* LAW LIBRARIANS' SOCIETY OF WASHINGTON, D.C., LEGISLATIVE SOURCEBOOK, http://www.llsdc.org/serial-set-volumes-guide#Overview (Sept. 21, 2012).

[81] The publishing schedule can be found at http://www.gpoaccess.gov/serialset/schedule.html.

[82] http://www.gpo.gov/help/u.s._congressional_serial_set.htm.

[83] http://www.gpoaccess.gov/serialset/numerical.html.

a Numerical List of Documents and Reports, and references to the *Serial Set* volumes in which those items are published; an Index of Subjects and Keywords; an Index of Names and Organizations; and a four-volume Index by Reported Bill Numbers.

ProQuest also offers the *U.S. Serial Set Digital Collection*. When completed, it will be a comprehensive database of the full text of the *Serial Set* from 1789 to the present. The collection is complete through 1969, in Part I; content for Part II, beginning with 1970, is complete through 2003.

c.   *Readex*. Readex offers a digital product called *The U.S. Congressional Set, 1817–1994*. It is cross-searchable with all collections in Readex's *America's Historical Government Publications* collection (including *American State Papers*), to which larger university libraries may subscribe.

d.   *American Memory: A Century of Lawmaking for a New Nation*. This Library of Congress website offers free access to selected *Serial Set* volumes from the 23rd Congress (1833–35) through the 64th Congress (1915–17).[84]

9.   Presidential Documents

The messages and statements that the president issues when sending proposed legislation to Congress, or when signing or vetoing a bill, are available in the following sources.[85]

a.   *Daily* and *Weekly Compilation of Presidential Documents*. The *Daily Compilation of Presidential Documents* began as a web-based publication on January 20, 2009, the first day of Barack Obama's presidency. The *Daily* replaces the print *Weekly Compilation of Presidential Documents*, which was issued each Monday from August 2, 1965, through January 26, 2009.[86] Both titles consist of presidential documents released from the White House Press Secretary and published officially by the Office of the Federal Register, a component of the National Archives and Records Administration. Of particular importance to compilers of legislative histories are messages to Congress, veto messages, signing statements, and the list of acts approved by the president.

The *Weekly Compilation* contained an annual Index divided by Subject, Name, and Document Categories List. Prior to volume 31, number 1, January 9, 1995, every *Weekly* issue contained cumulative Subject and Name indexes for all prior issues of the current quarter. From 1995 to 2009 the *Weekly Compilation* issued separate quarterly indexes and no more cumulative indexes in each issue. A finding aid titled "Acts Approved by the President" was a recurring feature of the *Weekly Compilation*.

HeinOnline contains the complete backfile of the *Daily* and *Weekly Compilations* and delayed coverage of current issues of the *Daily Compilation*.[87] *Westlaw* publishes the full text of the *Daily Compilation* and the *Weekly Compilation* from 2000 to the present.

---

[84] http://memory.loc.gov/ammem/amlaw/lwss.html.

[85] Occasionally, presidential documents may be published as House or Senate documents. Agency memoranda are sometimes transmitted to Congress, along with an accompanying communication from the president proposing legislation, and thus may be inserted in congressional hearings or reports. Agency and White House websites post some agency memoranda; if not available there, the agency can be contacted directly. Agency memoranda are typically not available in depository collections.

[86] http://www.gpo.gov/fdsys/browse/collection.action?collectionCode=CPD.

[87] *See* Chapter 18, Section A-2-b, for a description of *HeinOnline*.

   b.   The *Compilation of Presidential Documents* is a web-only collection available in *FDsys* and published by the Office of the Federal Register.[88] It comprises the *Daily Compilation of Presidential Documents* and its predecessor, the *Weekly Compilation of Presidential Documents*, back to 1993.

   c.   *Public Papers of the Presidents.* This annual print series began with President Herbert Hoover's administration in 1929; it is being compiled contemporaneously and retrospectively by the Office of the Federal Register. Prior to 1977, *Public Papers* was an edited version of the *Weekly Compilation.* However, beginning with the administration of President Carter and continuing through the volume for 1988–89, the last year of President Reagan's administration, the set included all of the material printed in the *Weekly Compilation of Presidential Documents.* The papers of President Franklin Roosevelt are not part of this series; they are, however, published commercially.[89]

   The final volume for each year of an administration contains an index. A cumulative index for each administration is published commercially under the title *The Cumulated Indexes to the Public Papers of the Presidents of the United States.*[90]

   HeinOnline provides the full run of this title (1929–) in its U.S. Presidential Library. *FDsys's* coverage of the *Public Papers* starts in 1991.[91] Issues of the *Public Papers* and the *Weekly* and *Daily Compilations* are available in *LexisNexis* from March 24, 1979, through February 2, 2011.

   d.   *United States Code Congressional and Administrative News.* Since 1986, *USCCAN's* annual legislative history volumes reprint the text of presidential signing statements. The signing statements in *USCCAN* also are available through *Westlaw.* The *U.S. Statutes at Large* cites to signing statements in its "Legislative History" footnotes, but it does not reprint their texts.

   e.   The *American Presidency Project* website[92] of the University of California, Santa Barbara, offers a "Presidential Documents Archive" with the text of presidential signing statements from 1929 to the present. It also reprints most of the *Public Papers* series and the *Daily* and *Weekly Compilation of Presidential Documents* (1977 to the present).

   f.   *Additional Sources.* Presidential messages also can be found in the *Congressional Record,* the House and Senate *Journals,* and in the *Serial Set* (if considered a House or Senate document). The White House website has a collection of presidential speeches and remarks, and statements and press releases, some of which concern legislation.[93]

---

[88] http://www.gpo.gov/fdsys/browse/collection.action?collectionCode=CPD.

[89] THE PUBLIC PAPERS AND ADDRESSES OF FRANKLIN D. ROOSEVELT (1938–1950).

[90] This publication is discussed in Chapter 13, Section H-6-b.

[91] http://www.gpo.gov/fdsys/browse/collection.action?collectionCode=PPP.

[92] http://www.presidency.ucsb.edu/.

[93] http://www.whitehouse.gov/.

I.   ILLUSTRATIONS: SOURCES

10–9.   Browse GPO's Federal Digital System (FDSYS) Publications

[Illustration 10–9]

BROWSE GPO'S FEDERAL DIGITAL SYSTEM (FDSYS) PUBLICATIONS

J.   CHARTS: FINDING AIDS AND SOURCES FOR DOCUMENTS

These charts identify finding aids, documents, and some of the sources in which the documents may be located.

Finding Aids	Documents	Sources
Congressional Record (daily edition) Daily Digest and biweekly Index; Congressional Record (permanent edition) Index; Congressional Index (CCH); CIS/Index; slip laws; Statutes at Large; House and Senate Calendars; House and Senate Journals; USCCAN Table.	Public Bills and Resolutions	**Always:** United States Congress Public Bills and Resolutions; CIS Microfiche Library; Public Laws—Legislative Histories on Microfiche; Westlaw and LexisNexis; FDsys; Congress.gov; ProQuest Congressional (basic edition); American Memory. **Sometimes:** GAO Legislative History Collection; Congressional Record; Committee Reports.
Congressional Record (daily edition) Daily Digest and biweekly Index; Congressional Record (permanent edition) Index; Congressional Index (CCH); CIS/Index; slip laws; Statutes at Large; House and Senate Calendars; House and Senate Journals; USCCAN Table; CIS U.S. Serial Set Index; ProQuest Congressional Digital; Monthly Catalog.	Committee Reports	**Always:** CIS Microfiche Library; USCCAN (selected); Serial Set; Public Laws—Legislative Histories on Microfiche; FDSys; Congress.gov; Westlaw and LexisNexis; ProQuest Congressional Digital and ProQuest Congressional (basic edition); American Memory. **Sometimes:** GAO Legislative History Collection; topical services and treatises; Congressional Record.
Congressional Record (daily edition) and biweekly Index; Congressional Record (permanent edition) Index; Congressional Index (CCH); CIS/Index; House and Senate Calendars; slip laws; Statutes at Large; House and Senate Journals; USCCAN Table; ProQuest Congressional Digital; HeinOnline.	Debates	**Always:** Congressional Record; Public Laws—Legislative Histories on Microfiche; GAO Legislative History Collection; FDsys; Congress.gov; Westlaw and LexisNexis; ProQuest Congressional Digital and ProQuest Congressional (basic edition; HeinOnline; LLMC Digital; American Memory. **Sometimes:** topical services; USCCAN (citations).

CIS/Index; Congressional Index (CCH); CIS U.S. Congressional Committee Hearings Index; CIS Indexes to Unpublished US Senate and House Committee Hearings; ProQuest Congressional Digital; various Senate Indexes to Hearings; Congressional Hearings Calendar; Monthly Catalog.	Hearings	**Always:** CIS microfiche (various sets); ProQuest Congressional Digital and ProQuest Congressional (basic edition); LexisNexis and Westlaw; FDsys; Congressional Documents Online (Rutgers); committee websites. **Sometimes:** GAO Legislative History Collection; topical services; federal depository libraries.
CIS/Index; CIS US Congressional Committee Prints Index; CIS US Serial Set Index; Monthly Catalog; ProQuest Congressional.	Committee Prints	**Always:** CIS Microfiche; Public Laws—Legislative Histories on Microfiche; ProQuest Congressional (selected) and ProQuest Congressional Digital; LexisNexis (selected); FDsys; Congressional Documents Online (selected, Rutgers). **Sometimes:** Serial Set; topical services.
CIS/Index; slip laws; Statutes at Large; HeinOnline; USCCAN Index and Tables.	Presidential Documents	**Always:** Daily Compilation of Presidential Documents and Compilation of Presidential Documents (FDsys); Public Papers of the Presidents; LexisNexis and Westlaw; HeinOnline; USCCAN (executive orders and proclamations). **Sometimes:** Congressional Record; House and Senate Journals; Serial Set.

Document Type	Sources, with Dates of Coverage
Compiled Legislative Histories	**Current:** CIS Legislative Histories of U.S. Public Laws (print), 1984–, LexisNexis (online), 1970–; ProQuest Congressional (online), 1969–1998 (abbreviated), 1999– (full); ProQuest Legislative Insight (online), 1929–; LexisNexis tax legislative histories (online), 1954–; USCCAN (print), 1941–; Westlaw (online), 1948– (USCCAN, selective prior to 1990), 1974– (Arnold & Porter, selected); LLSDC's Legislative Sourcebook (web), Legislative Histories of Selected U.S. Laws; Commercial Legislative Histories of U.S. Laws on the Internet (coverage varies); HeinOnline, U.S. Federal Legislative History Title Collection, 1909– (selected). **Historical:** LexisNexis (selected subjects, coverage varies) Public Laws—Legislative Histories (microfiche), 1979–1988 (CCH) CIS Annual (print, legislative histories section of Abstracts volume), 1970–1983 Westlaw (online), 1921–1995 (GAO) GAO Legislative History Collection (microfiche), 1921–1980 U.S. Dept. of Justice (web), 1869–2004 (selected)
Public Laws	**Current:** FDsys (web), 1995– (slip laws); 1951– (Stat.); LexisNexis (online), 1988– (slip laws); ProQuest Congressional (online), 1988– (slip laws); Congress.gov (web), 1973– (slip laws); USCCAN (print), 1941–; Westlaw (online), 1789–1972 (Stat.), 1973– (USCCAN); ProQuest Congressional U.S. Statutes at Large (online), 1789–; HeinOnline, 1789–; LLMC (online and microfiche), 1789–; U.S. Statutes at Large (print), 1789–. **Historical:** American Memory: A Century of Lawmaking (web), Statutes at Large, 1789–1875.

Public Bills and Resolutions	**Current:** Westlaw (online), 1995–; FDsys (web), 1993– (text), 1983– (history of bills); LexisNexis (online), 1989–; ProQuest Congressional (online), 1989–; Congress.gov (web), 1989– (text), 1973– (summaries); CIS Microfiche Library, 1970– (if enacted). **Historical:** United States Congress Public Bills and Resolutions (microfiche), 1979–2000; Public Laws—Legislative Histories on Microfiche (CCH), 1979–1988 (if enacted); GAO Legislative History Collection (microfiche), 1921–1980 (if enacted); Congressional Record (print, microfiche), 1873– (selected); Law Library of Congress (microfiche), 1805–; American Memory: A Century of Lawmaking (web), House bills, 1799–1873, Senate bills, 1819–1873, Senate resolutions, 1824–1873.

Committee Reports	**Current:** FDsys (web), 1995–; Congress.gov (web), 1995–; Westlaw (online), 1990– (all), 1948– (selected, USCCAN); LexisNexis (online), 1990–; ProQuest Congressional (online), 1990–; ProQuest U.S. Serial Set Digital Collection: Pt. 2 (online), 1970–; CIS Microfiche Library, 1970–; USCCAN (print), 1948– (selected); U.S. Congressional Serial Set (print), 1817– **Historical:** Public Laws—Legislative Histories on Microfiche (CCH), 1979–1988; GAO Legislative Histories Collection (microfiche), 1921–1980; Readex U.S. Congressional Serial Set (online), 1817–1980; American Memory: A Century of Lawmaking (web), U.S. Serial Set, 1833–1917 (selected volumes); ProQuest U.S. Serial Set Digital Collection: Pt. 1 (online), 1789–1969; CIS U.S. Serial Set (ProQuest), 1789–1969 (microfiche); American State Papers (print), 1789–1838.

Debates	**Current:**
	FDsys (web), 1994– (daily ed.), 1999–2001 (permanent ed.), index, 1983–;
	Congress.gov (web), 1989– (daily ed.), keyword index, 1995–;
	LLMC Digital (online), 1990– (permanent ed.);
	Westlaw & LexisNexis (online), 1985– (daily ed.);
	ProQuest Congressional (online), 1985– (daily ed.);
	Congressional Record (print, microfilm/microfiche), 1873–;
	HeinOnline, 1789– (permanent ed.), 1980– (daily ed.);
	ProQuest Congressional Record Permanent Digital Collection (online), 1789–.
	Historical:
	LLMC Digital (online), 1873–1876 (permanent ed.);
	American Memory: A Century of Lawmaking (web), 1789–1875 (permanent ed.);
	Congressional Globe (print, CIS microfiche), 1833–1873;
	Register of Debates (print, CIS microfiche), 1824–1837;
	Annals of Congress (print, CIS microfiche), 1789–1824;
Hearings	**Current:**
	Congressional committee websites (coverage varies) (use LLSDC Quick Links) (web);
	FDsys (web), 1995–, 1985–1988 (Senate only);
	Westlaw (online), 1993– (selected), 1996– (full);
	ProQuest Congressional (online), 1988– (selected);
	LexisNexis (online), 1988– (selected);
	CIS Microfiche Library, 1970–;
	ProQuest Congressional Hearings Digital Collection (online), 1824– (all).
	Historical:
	Congressional Documents Online (web), 1960s–1998.

Committee Prints	**Current:** Committee web pages (selected, coverage varies); FDsys (web), 1995– (all), 1991–1992 (selected); LexisNexis (online), 1994–2003 (selected); ProQuest Congressional (online), 1993–2004 (selected); CIS Microfiche Library, 1970–; ProQuest Congressional Research Digital Collection (online), 1830–; U.S. Congressional Serial Set (print), 1817– (if H.R. Doc. or S. Doc.). **Historical:** Congressional Documents Online (web), 1960s–1998 (selected); American Memory: A Century of Lawmaking (web), 1833–1917 (selected volumes, if H.R. Doc. or S. Doc.); Readex The U.S. Congressional Serial Set (online), 1817–1980 (if H.R. Doc. or S. Doc.); CIS Serial Set (microfiche), 1789–1969 (if H.R. Doc. or S. Doc.); American State Papers (print and American Memory online), 1789–1838 (if H.R. Doc. or S. Doc.).
CRS Reports: Reports of the Legislative Reference Service (LRS, 1916–1969) and the Congressional Research Service (CRS, 1970–)	**Current and Historical:** OpenCRS.com (web); Federation of American Scientists (web); IP Mall, University of New Hampshire School of Law (web), 1993–; National Council for Science and the Environment (web), 1990–; U. North Texas Digital Library (web), 1990–; Penny Hill Press (online), 1995–, selected 1993–1994 and earlier. CQ Roll Call (online), 1993–; ProQuest Congressional Research Digital (online), 1916–; Major Studies and Issue Briefs of the Congressional Research Service (ProQuest), 1916– (microfilm) and 1991– (microfiche).

Presidential Documents (messages and statements)	**Current:** White House (web), 2009– (speeches, remarks, statements, and press releases); FDsys (web), 2009– (daily compilation), 1993– (compilation of presidential documents), 1991– (public papers). HeinOnline, 2009– (daily compilation), 1965–2009 (weekly compilation), 1931– (public papers); Westlaw (online), 1993–; USCCAN (print and Westlaw), 1986– (signing statements); LexisNexis (online), March 24, 1979 through February 2, 2011 (daily and weekly compilations, public papers); Public Papers of the Presidents (print), 1929–; The American Presidency Project, Presidential Documents Archive: Presidential Signing Statements, 1929–; U.S. Congressional Serial Set (print), 1817– (H.R. Doc. or S. Doc.). **Historical:** Weekly Compilation of Presidential Documents (print), 1965–2009; American Memory: A Century of Lawmaking (web), 1833–1917 (selected volumes, if H.R. Doc. or S. Doc.); Readex U.S. Congressional Serial Set (online), 1817–1980 (H.R. Doc. or S. Doc.); CIS Serial Set (microfiche), 1789–1969 (H.R. Doc. or S. Doc.).

K. TRACKING PENDING LEGISLATION

In addition to the sources previously described, the following online sources allow researchers to track the progress of pending legislation and, in most cases, identify documents generated during the bill's progress.

1. BILLCAST

BILLCAST, a product of State Net, provides a forecast report for public bills pending in the current Congress. The report gives a brief summary of the bill's purpose and predictions of its chance of passing in committee and on the floor. *BILLCAST* for the current Congress, as well as archival information back to the 99th Congress (1985–1986), is available in *LexisNexis*.

2. Bill Tracking Reports

a. *Congress.gov*. This Library of Congress website is one of the best resources for tracking the status of bills back to 1973. It can be searched in a variety of ways, such as by keyword, number, sponsor, and committee.

b. *Westlaw*. A bill tracking database contains summaries and status information relating to current federal legislation. Public bills are tracked through each step of the legislative process. An archive provides information back to 2005; some state material also is included.

c. *LexisNexis*. Daily bill tracking summaries cover the status of bills pending in both houses of the current Congress. Each summary contains a link to the bill text, synopsis of the bill, introduction date, committee referrals, and a complete legislative chronology, including references to the *Congressional Record*. An archive provides information back to 1989.

d. *CQ BillTrack* (*CQ.com*). Tracking legislative activity is a strong point of this CQ Roll Call service, which also provides email alerts to those following specific pending legislation.

e. *ProQuest Congressional*. A basic subscription to this commercial service tracks federal bills from 1989 forward.

f. *Congressional Index* (CCH). This looseleaf service, which is updated weekly, provides bill status information from 1941–1942 to the present.

g. *GovTrack.us*.[94] Civic Impulse, LLC, provides this free web tool to help the public track the status of federal legislation and votes in Congress. The site offers RSS feeds for bills introduced and laws enacted.

3. CQ Roll Call Materials

CQ Roll Call is a consolidation of three companies: Congressional Quarterly (CQ), Roll Call, and Capitol Advantage. For years CQ has been a prolific publisher of materials dealing with all branches of the federal government. Some publications particularly relevant to federal legislative histories are highlighted in this section.

a. *CQ Weekly* (formerly *Congressional Quarterly Weekly Report*). This magazine of congressional news contains summaries of major legislation and public policy issues. Although coverage is not comprehensive, *CQ Weekly* is valuable because of its extensive analysis and background discussion of laws and legislative issues. *CQ Weekly Online* provides access to back issues from 1983 to the present. It also offers continuous updating, customized email alerting, and full text searching. *CQ Weekly* is available in *Westlaw* from 2005 to the present.

b. *CQ Almanac*. Published at the end of each session of Congress, *CQ Almanac* provides information of permanent research value on congressional activity during that year. *CQ Almanac* provides an excellent narrative overview of the legislative history of major bills passed. It is a good starting point to determine whether a specific section of the bill became a part of the law. *CQ Almanac Online* provides access to volumes published from 1945 to the present.

---

[94] http://www.govtrack.us/.

c.   Congress and the Nation. This quadrennial publication began in 1964 as a project to cumulate and summarize information in individual *CQ Almanacs.* The publication currently evaluates and assesses the politics and legislation for the time period addressed. The *Congress and the Nation Series Online Edition* covers 1945 through 2008.

d.   CQ Today. This daily reporting service, available in print and online, provides information on legislation currently before Congress. It covers committee markups and hearings and floor activity. *CQ Today* is available in *Westlaw* from 2005 to the present.

e.   CQ.com. This online service includes the text of bills, committee reports, the *Congressional Record,* and testimony. Supplementary information includes selected references to articles discussing the legislation.

4.   Other Materials for Tracking Congress

OpenCongress[95] is a free nonprofit, nonpartisan website that incorporates government data, news coverage, blog posts, and public comments on what is happening in Congress. *OpenCongress* is a project of the Participatory Politics Foundation and the Sunlight Foundation.

National Journal[96] is a weekly magazine covering national politics and government. The company also publishes a newsletter called *National Journal Daily.* Both are available in *Westlaw* and by subscription through the *National Journal* website.

The Hill, a thrice-weekly newspaper covering Congress, offers a free Internet site.[97]

---

[95] http://www.opencongress.org/.

[96] http://nationaljournal.com/.

[97] http://thehill.com/.

Chapter 11

STATE AND MUNICIPAL LEGISLATION*

State and local governments enact legislation that regulates conduct within their jurisdictions. This chapter discusses tools for researching that legislation.[1]

State statutes are enacted, organized, and published in ways very similar to federal statutes. The differences that exist among the statutes of the states are mostly in terminology rather than substance. Each state has a state legislature, and, with the exception of Nebraska, each has an upper and lower house similar to the Senate and the House of Representatives of the United States Congress. In general, the legislative process for the passage of state laws is like that described for federal laws in Chapter 10.[2]

One respect in which state legislation differs from the federal model is that twenty-four states grant legislative power to the people. The *initiative process* enables citizens to propose and enact legislation via ballot measure. The *popular referendum* is a mechanism for the voters to accept or reject laws enacted by the legislature.[3]

A. SESSION LAWS

Each state publishes a series of bound volumes containing all of the laws passed during each session of its legislature. The generic name for these is *session laws*, although the published volumes in some states have other names, such as *acts (and resolves), statutes*, or *laws*. By whatever name they are published, these session laws include public laws (those that relate to the public as a whole), as well as private, temporary, local, and appropriation acts. State session laws are typically published chronologically in order of adoption, much like the *United States Statutes at Large*, and are issued in bound form after the legislative session is over.

---

* This chapter was revised by Bonnie Shucha, Assistant Director for Public Services, University of Wisconsin Law Library.

[1] For a discussion of federal legislation, see Chapter 9.

[2] Information about each state's legislature, including terminology, frequency of session, and so on, is available in *The Book of the States*, published annually by the Council of State Governments since 1935. The current and past editions of *The Book of the States* are available at http://knowledgecenter.csg.org/drupal/category/content-type/content-type-book-states.

[3] *See* Beth Williams, *Introduction to Researching Initiative and Referendum Law: General Strategies and Resources*, 26 LEGAL REFERENCE SERVICES Q., nos. 3–4, 2007, at 1. Williams's article introduces a special double issue of *Legal Reference Services Quarterly* (also published as a book, EXPLORING INITIATIVE AND REFERENDUM LAW: SELECTED STATE RESEARCH GUIDES (Beth Williams ed., 2007)) with articles about researching initiatives and referendums in twenty-three states (Alaska, Arizona, Arkansas, Colorado, Florida, Idaho, Illinois, Maine, Massachusetts, Michigan, Mississippi, Missouri, Montana, Nebraska, Nevada, North Dakota, Ohio, Oklahoma, Oregon, South Dakota, Utah, Washington, and Wyoming). For California, see Tobe Liebert, *Researching California Ballot Measures*, 90 LAW LIBR. J. 27 (1998). An updated version of Liebert's article is chapter 5 of DANIEL W. MARTIN, HENKE'S CALIFORNIA LAW GUIDE (8th ed. 2006).

1. Finding Session Laws

All states publish print session law volumes, but these are usually not available until well after the end of the legislative session. Therefore, most states also publish *slip* laws in pamphlet form soon after they are passed;[4] many also make them available electronically via their websites.[5] Recently enacted laws are also frequently published by private companies in advance sheets as part of a subscription to an annotated state code.[6] [Illustration 11–1]

Session laws for all fifty states are available electronically in *HeinOnline's* Session Laws Library, beginning with each state's inception. Laws are arranged by state, then by year. Keyword searching is also available by individual states or across all states.[7]

Westlaw, *LexisNexis*, and *Loislaw* also offer electronic state session laws from the late 1990s to the present. The years of coverage vary by state, with new laws added as they are published. In addition, *Westlaw* and *LexisNexis* have current and archival bills and bill tracking.[8]

B. CODIFICATION OF STATE LAWS

In addition to session laws, which are arranged chronologically, each state also produces a set of statutes that cumulates and organizes the session laws topically for ease of use (similar to the subject arrangement of the *United States Code*). [Illustration 11–2] The terms *revised*, *compiled*, *consolidated*, and *code* are often used to describe such sets of currently enforceable statutes. *Codification* is the act of gathering and organizing laws into a code.[9]

---

[4] The term *slip* refers to the fact the laws are printed individually on separate slips of paper before their inclusion in the bound session laws.

[5] The National Conference of State Legislatures offers a directory of the legislative content that each state makes available online at http://www.ncsl.org/?tabid=17173. In addition, the *Legislative Source Book* (http://www.llsdc.org/sourcebook) from the Law Librarians' Society of Washington, D.C., has a list of state legislatures, laws, and regulations. This list, which includes both web links and contact information, is at http://llsdc.memberclicks.net/state-legislation.

[6] For information about the availability of slip laws, advance legislative services, advance annotation services, and electronic versions of state documents, see WILLIAM H. MANZ, GUIDE TO STATE LEGISLATION, LEGISLATIVE HISTORY, AND ADMINISTRATIVE MATERIALS (7th ed. 2008) (AALL Publication Series, no. 61).

[7] In addition, William S. Hein & Co. publishes state session laws on microfiche in a collection entitled *Session Laws of American States and Territories*. Content begins in 1775 with the earliest states; actual years of coverage vary by state.

[8] *Bloomberg Law* has session laws for 19 states and the District of Columbia, generally beginning in the late 1990s.

[9] *See* BLACK'S LAW DICTIONARY 294 (9th ed. 2009) (defining codification as "the process of compiling, arranging, and systematizing the laws of a given jurisdiction, or of a discrete branch of the law, into an ordered code.").

The codes discussed here are *statutory codes* (like the *United States Code*); that is, they are compilations of statutes, generally statutes that had been enacted over many years. Statutory codes typically compile the statutes in a subject arrangement. For discussions of states' experience codifying statutes, see Dennis R. Bailey et al., Comment, *1975—A Code Odyssey: A Critical Analysis of the Alabama Recodification Process*, 10 CUMB. L. REV. 119 (1979); Diana S. Dowling, *The Creation of the Montana Code Annotated*, 40 MONT. L. REV. 1 (1979); Vincent C. Henderson, II, T*he Creation of the Arkansas Code of 1987 Annotated*, 11 U. ARK. LITTLE ROCK L.J. 21 (1988–1989); Terry A. McKenzie, *The Making of a New Code: The Official Code of Georgia Annotated: Recodification in Georgia*, 18 GA. ST. B.J., 102 (1982); Morell E. Mullins, *An Academic Perspective on Codification and the Arkansas Code of 1987 Annotated*, 11 U. ARK. LITTLE ROCK L.J. 285 (1988–1989); Marcia J. Oddi & Margaret C. Attridge, *The Indiana Code of 1971: Its Preparation, Passage and Implications*, 5 IND.

In some states, compilations of laws are published under official auspices; in others, by private publishers; and, in some states, there are both official and unofficial sets of codes. Some state codes have been enacted into positive law; others are only *prima facie* evidence of the law. In the latter case, positive law continues to be set forth in the volumes of the session laws.

Each state has a set of session laws and at least one current code. Whether session laws or code, the resource being used should be examined carefully to note its features, method of publication, and frequency and method of updating its contents. Because state codes contain public acts only, private, temporary, local, and appropriation acts are available exclusively in the session laws.

1. Features of State Codes

Every state code contains the currently (as of the date of publication) enforceable public laws of a general nature arranged by subject. [Illustration 11–2] The following features are common to many sets of state codes:

a. Historical Notes. Historical references, which follow the text of each statute, provide citations to the session laws from which the statute was derived. Since many states have had several codifications of laws over the years, citations are frequently given to a previous codification's version of the current law.

b. Annotations. At least one annotated code is published for each state and in some instances there are two, each by a different publisher. Some are very similar in appearance to *U.S.C.A.* or *U.S.C.S.* and include notes of decisions, citations to law review articles, legal encyclopedias, and other research aids, and cross-references to related

---

LEG. F. 1 (1971); R. Perry Sentell, Jr., *Codification and Consequences: The Georgian Motif*, 14 GA. L. REV. 737 (1980).

A different sense of "code" is used in civil law systems such as France and Germany, whose codes are aimed at comprehensive, systematic, simple coverage of the whole body of law, often reasoning from general principles. *See* Gunther A. Weiss, *The Enchantment of Codification in the Common-Law World*, 25 YALE J. INT'L L. 435, 454–70 (2000).

Common law systems rely on developing the law through precedent as well as by legislation. They generally do not have codes in the sense used in civil law countries. Louisiana is an exception, because of its history as a colony of France and Spain. *See, e.g.*, Weiss, at 499–501; GEORGE DARGO, JEFFERSON'S LOUISIANA: POLITICS AND THE CLASH OF LEGAL TRADITIONS (1975); John H. Tucker, Jr., *Tradition and Technique of Codification in the Modern World: The Louisiana Experience*, 25 LA. L. REV. 698 (1965). *See also* Shael Herman & David Hoskins, *Perspectives on Code Structure: Historical Experience, Modern Formats, and Policy Considerations*, 54 TUL. L. REV. 987 (1979) (discussing possible revision of Louisiana Civil Code of 1870); A.N. Yiannopoulos, *The Civil Codes of Louisiana*, 1 CIV. L. COMMENTS 1 (2008), *available at* http://www.law.tulane.edu/tlscenters/eason/index.aspx?id=12946.

Codification of existing common law rules has been proposed at different times in English and American history. *See* Weiss, at 471–527. *See also* Roscoe Pound, *Sources and Forms of Law III: The Imperative Element*, 22 NOTRE DAME LAW. 1, 61–81 (1946). In the nineteenth century, many states codified their procedural rules, which had formerly been based in common law. Particularly influential was New York's Code of Civil Procedure, enacted in 1848, often called the Field Code after its principal architect, David Dudley Field. *See* LAWRENCE M. FRIEDMAN, A HISTORY OF AMERICAN LAW 293–98 (3d ed. 2005). (For a discussion of a more recent codification in New York, see Barbara C. Salken, *To Codify or Not to Codify—That Is the Question: A Study of New York's Efforts to Enact an Evidence Code*, 58 BROOK. L. REV. 641 (1992).) Field also advocated codifying all of the common law. Some states, particularly in the West, adopted codes for certain subjects. For example, California adopted a civil code, a penal code, and a government code. *See* FRIEDMAN, at 302–04; *see also* Lewis Grossman, *Codification and the California Mentality*, 45 HASTINGS L.J. 617 (1994).

The Uniform Commercial Code was adopted in large part by all states in the mid-twentieth century (Louisiana, the last state, adopted most of the U.C.C. in 1974). FRIEDMAN, at 564. Comparative law scholars see the U.C.C. as similar to the style of codes in civil law countries. *See* Weiss, at 520–27.

code provisions. [Illustration 11–2] Some codes include pamphlet "advance annotation services" containing the latest topically arranged materials prior to their incorporation into the pocket supplements.

c.   *Constitutions.* Each state code contains the state constitution that is currently in effect, usually with annotations, as well as the text of previous constitutions.[10] The text of the Constitution of the United States, typically unannotated, is usually included as well.

d.   *Rules of Court.* State codes often contain the rules of court, which detail the procedural requirements for presenting matters before the various courts within the state.[11] Usually, a separate "rules" volume, issued annually, accompanies the print set.

e.   *Indexes.* All print sets of state codes contain a separate subject index for use in locating materials within the entire set. [Illustration 11–4] These indexes may provide the popular names of state acts if this information is not provided in a separate table. In addition, most of these sets also contain an index at the end of each subject grouping, or title, within the set.

f.   *Tables.* Each print state code has tables, usually in a separate volume, that cross-reference from session laws to code sections. [Illustration 11–3] Many also have tables that relate older state codifications to the current one and a table of popular names of state acts.

2.   Finding State Codes

When using the code in print, the researcher should consult the subject index to find applicable provisions. [Illustration 11–4] To ensure currency, the method of supplementation should be noted (e.g., revised replacement volumes, pocket supplements, bound cumulative supplements, or advance pamphlets), and any updated sources should be checked for the most recent enactments.

There are times when only the name of an act is known, be it the actual name or the popular name. Most print state codes index acts by name, either in a separate table or incorporated into the code's index. [Illustration 11–5][12]

Both *Westlaw* and *LexisNexis* include annotated current codes for all states, the District of Columbia, and the territories. They also include either an unannotated code or offer the ability to search just the text of the code, omitting annotations. These state statutory databases within *Westlaw* and *LexisNexis* can be searched individually or collectively for all states or browsed by table of contents. [Illustration 11–6] The most recently enacted legislation, commonly offered by means of an advance legislative service, is also available in *Westlaw* and *LexisNexis*. Several other commercial publishers, including *Bloomberg Law, Fastcase, Loislaw,* and *VersusLaw,* also provide access to state statutory codes.[13]

---

[10] Constitutions are discussed in Chapter 8.

[11] Court rules are discussed in Chapter 12.

[12] *Shepard's Acts and Cases by Popular Names* is also helpful for locating citations when only the name of the act is known. See Chapter 15 for additional discussion of *Shepard's.*

[13] These services are discussed in more detail in Chapter 23.

LexisNexis StateCapital is a powerful resource for researching state legislation.[14] The service provides access to state bills and bill tracking, codes, constitutions, proposed and enacted administrative regulations, newspapers of record, articles about legislative issues affecting the states, and legislature membership. Users can search for information about one state, any combination of states, or all states.

All fifty states make their state codes available online.[15] There are several sources that provide free and easy access to these state materials. *American Law Sources Online (ALSO!)*,[16] from LawSource, Inc., is a portal that provides links to sources of state and federal law that are freely available online. Content is organized geographically, with a separate page for each state containing links to session laws, codes, bills, judicial opinions, regulations, court rules, local legislation, and other legal information sources.

Public Library of Law,[17] powered by *Fastcase*, also offers links to state codes, regulations, court rules, and other legal information. It also features a collection of state and federal judicial opinions. Other portals to state legislation are Cornell's *Legal Information Institute*[18] and *FindLaw*.[19]

At times, a research problem involves an act that has been repealed or is no longer in force. To locate these superseded acts, consult either a version of the code that was in effect when the law was in force or the session laws volume that contains the text of the act as originally passed by the legislature.

Westlaw and *LexisNexis* offer superseded state codes from the 1990s to the present. *Fastcase* has superseded state codes for almost all states, generally starting between 2006 and 2008.

State Statutes: A Historical Archive in *HeinOnline* contains digitized volumes of annotated codes which were replaced by later volumes in sets that are currently published, as well as sets that are no longer published.[20]

"Superseded," as used in these collections, does not suggest that all laws in a replaced volume are inoperative, just that the code itself has been replaced by a later edition.

---

[14] *LexisNexis StateCapital* is not included in the standard law school *LexisNexis* service. It is a separate product available from LexisNexis.

[15] There is concern that the codes that states have made available online may not be accurate or authentic representations of the text of the law. In July 2011, the Uniform Law Commission approved the *Uniform Electronic Legal Material Act (UELMA), which requires that* official electronic legal material be authenticated, by providing a method to determine that it is unaltered; preserved, either in electronic or print form; and accessible, for use by the public on a permanent basis. *See* http://www.uniformlaws.org/shared/docs/electronic%20legal%20material/uelma_final_2011.pdf for UELMA's text and comments.

[16] http://www.lawsource.com/also/.

[17] http://www.plol.org.

[18] http://www.law.cornell.edu/statutes.html.

[19] http://www.findlaw.com/11stategov/.

[20] William S. Hein & Co. also sells superseded code volumes in microfiche.

C. ILLUSTRATIONS FOR STATE LEGISLATION

[Illustration 11–1]

PAGE FROM THE 2000 WASHINGTON LEGISLATIVE SERVICE (SESSION LAW)

Ch. 111　　　　　　　　　　REGULAR SESSION

COURTS—COURTS OF LIMITED JURISDICTION—
STATE–WIDE WARRANT PROCESSING

CHAPTER 111

S.H.B. No. 2799

AN ACT Relating to granting state-wide warrant jurisdiction to courts of limited jurisdiction; amending RCW 3.66.010, 3.66.060, 3.66.070, 3.46.030, 3.50.020, and 35.20.030; and creating new sections.

BE IT ENACTED BY THE LEGISLATURE OF THE STATE OF WASHINGTON:

NEW SECTION. **Sec. 1.** The administrator for the courts shall establish a pilot program for the efficient state-wide processing of warrants issued by courts of limited jurisdiction. The pilot program shall contain procedures and criteria for courts of limited jurisdiction to enter into agreements with other courts of limited jurisdiction throughout the state to process each other's warrants when the defendant is within the processing court's jurisdiction. The administrator for the courts shall establish a formula for allocating between the court processing the warrant and the court that issued the warrant any moneys collected and costs associated with the processing of warrants.

Sec. 2. RCW 3.66.010 and 1984 c 258 s 40 are each amended to read as follows:

(1) The justices of the peace elected in accordance with chapters 3.30 through 3.74 RCW are authorized to hold court as judges of the district court for the trial of all actions enumerated in chapters 3.30 through 3.74 RCW or assigned to the district court by law; to hear, try, and determine the same according to the law, and for that purpose where no special provision is otherwise made by law, such court shall be vested with all the necessary powers which are possessed by courts of record in this state; and all laws of a general nature shall apply to such district court as far as the same may be applicable and not inconsistent with the provisions of chapters 3.30 through 3.74 RCW. The district court shall, upon the demand of either party, impanel a jury to try any civil or criminal case in accordance with the provisions of chapter 12.12 RCW. No jury trial may be held in a proceeding involving a traffic infraction.

(2) A district court participating in the program established by the office of the administrator for the courts pursuant to section 1 of this act shall have jurisdiction to take recognizance, approve bail, and arraign defendants held within its jurisdiction on warrants issued by any other court of limited jurisdiction participating in the program.

Sec. 3. RCW 3.66.060 and 1984 c 258 s 44 are each amended to read as follows:

The district court shall have jurisdiction: (1) Concurrent with the superior court of all

> This is a 2000 session law from the state of Washington. The Act shown amends certain sections of the *Revised Code of Washington (RCW)* and adds new sections. The illustration is from West's *Washington Legislative Service*. After the end of a legislative session, all laws passed will be published in a bound volume of session laws. Public laws, such as this one, will also be incorporated into the state code. See Illustration 11-2.

Sec. 4. RCW 3.66.070 and 1991 c 290 s 2 are each amended to read as follows:

All criminal actions shall be brought in the district where the alleged violation occurred: PROVIDED, That (1) the prosecuting attorney may file felony cases in the district in which the county seat is located, (2) with the consent of the defendant criminal actions other than those arising out of violations of city ordinances may be brought in or transferred to the district in which the county seat is located, and (3) if the alleged violation relates to driving, or being in actual physical control of, a motor vehicle while under the influence of intoxicating

534　　　　Additions are indicated by underline; deletions by strikeout

[Illustration 11–2]

PAGE FROM THE 2002 POCKET SUPPLEMENT, REVISED
CODE OF WASHINGTON ANNOTATED (STATUTE)

COURTS OF LIMITED JURISDICTION   3.66.020

This Illustration is from the 2002 pocket supplement to West's *Revised Code of Washington Annotated*. Notice how the session law that was passed two years before (See Illustration 11-1) was incorporated into the state code. Notice also how a citation is given to the session law from which § 3.66.010 was codified.

Following the text of each session of a statute, citations are provided to: (1) "Historical and Statutory Notes"; (2) "Library References" that index articles from law reviews published in the state and references to encyclopedias, digests, and treatises; and (3) "Notes of Decisions" from all federal and state cases and Attorney General opinions that have cited and interpreted this section of the statute.

jury to try any civil or criminal case in accordance with the provisions of chapter 12.12 RCW. No jury trial may be held in a proceeding involving a traffic infraction.

(2) A district court participating in the program established by the office of the administrator for the courts pursuant to RCW 2.56.160 shall have jurisdiction to take recognizance, approve bail, and arraign defendants held within its jurisdiction on warrants issued by any other court of limited jurisdiction participating in the program.

[2000 c 111 § 2; 1984 c 258 § 40; 1979 ex.s. c 136 § 20; 1961 c 299 § 112.]

Historical and Statutory Notes ◄——————

2000 Legislation
Laws 2000, ch. 111, § 2, inserted the subsection numbering; and, added subsec. (2).

Library References ◄——————

Trials, verdicts, see Wash.Prac. vol. 4A, Orland, CRLJ 49.

Notes of Decisions ◄——————

Municipal court   7
Powers, generally   6

——————

4. Transfer of venue
Seastrom v. Konz (1976) 86 Wash.2d 377, [main volume] 544 P.2d 744.

6. Powers, generally
This section delineating general powers of district courts does not give district courts the power to appoint special prosecuting attorneys. Ladenburg v. Campbell (1990) 56 Wash.App. 701, 784 P.2d 1306.

7. Municipal court
RCWA 3.66.010 authorizing county district court judges to sit as municipal court judges did not permit district court judge to sit as municipal judge without mayoral appointment. Nollette v. Christianson (1990) 115 Wash.2d 594, 800 P.2d 359.

3.66.020. Civil jurisdiction

If the value of the claim or the amount at issue does not exceed fifty thousand dollars, exclusive of interest, costs, and attorneys' fees, the district

[Illustration 11-3]

PAGE FROM A TRANSFER TABLE IN THE WASHINGTON LEGISLATIVE SERVICE

TABLE 1—CUMULATIVE

REVISED CODE OF WASHINGTON—
AMENDMENTS, REPEALS,
ADDITIONS, ETC.

Listing the Chapters and Sections of the Revised Code of Washington and the Revised Code of Washington Annotated affected by the Laws of 2000, published in the 2000 Washington Legislative Service.

RCWA and RCW Sec.	Effect	2000 Chap.	Sec.
1.16.050	Amended	60	1
2.24.040	Amended	73	1
3.46.030	Amended	111	5
3.50.020	Amended	111	6
3.50.090	Amended	55	1
3.66.010	Amended	111	2
3.66.020	Amended	49	1
3.66.060	Amended	111	3
3.66.070	Amended	111	4
4.64.030	Amended	41	1
6.27	Section added	72	6
6.27.005	Amended	72	1

When only a citation to a state session law is available, a transfer table may be consulted to locate where a particular section of a session law is within the state's code. These tables are usually included in a volume of the state's code as well as in the back of the legislative service pamphlets. For example, this illustration shows that Chapter 111, Sec. 2 of the 2000 legislative session amended § 3.66.010 of the *RCW*.

Sometimes an individual session law will deal with several Different matters, as does Chapter 111. In these instances, notice how the session law is incorporated into several sections of the code.

9.94A.110	Reenacted and amended	75	8
9.94A.120	Reenacted and amended	28	5
		43	1
9.94A.130	Amended	28	9
9.94A.135	Amended	28	27

T1-1

[Illustration 11–4]

PAGE FROM AN INDEX VOLUME, REVISED CODE OF WASHINGTON ANNOTATED

DISTRICT

DISTRICT COURTS—Cont'd
Jurisdiction—Cont'd
  Personal jurisdiction, 3.66.040
  Postsentence, suspension or deferral,
    3.66.067, 3.66.068
  Small Claims Department, 12.40.010
    Failure to pay judgments, increase
      of amount, jurisdictional limits,
      12.40.105
  Time, when jurisdiction acquired,
    12.04.130
Jury, 3.66.010, 12.12.030
  Costs, 12.12.030
  Delivery of verdict, 12.12.080
  Discharge, 12.12.090
  Holiday, 2.28.110
  Inability to agree on verdict, 12.12.090
  Oaths and affirmations, 12.12.070
  Small Claims Department, appeal and
    review, 12.36.055
Juvenile delinquents and dependents,
  concurrent jurisdiction, 13.04.0301
Labor and employment, venue, 3.66.040
Leases, courtrooms and offices, 3.58.050
Legal parap...
  Departr
  12.36.05
Lights and l
Location, 3.3
  Districting
Magistrates,
Marriage sol
  3.66.110
Meetings, judges association, 3.70.020
Misdemeanors, jurisdiction, 3.66.060
Motions, transfer to proper district,
  3.66.050
Motor vehicle drivers licenses, suspen-
  sion and revocation, jurisdiction,
  3.66.060
Municipal Courts, generally, this index
Municipalities, this index
Names,
  Districting plans, 3.38.020
  Judges, 3.30.030
Nonresidents,
  Defendants, venue, 3.66.040
  Security for costs, 12.04.170
Notice,
  Arbitration and award, filing fees,
    3.62.070
  Commencement of actions, service of
    process, 12.04.010, 12.04.030
  Small Claims Department, appeal and
    review, 12.36.020
Numbers and numbering, judges,
  3.34.010, 3.34.020
  Additional positions, 3.34.025

DISTRICT COURTS—Cont'd
Oaths and affirmations,
  Administering, 3.54.020
  Judges, 2.28.060, 3.34.080
  Jury, 12.12.070
  Verification of pleadings, 12.08.070
Offenses. Crimes and offenses, general-
  ly, ante
Offices,
  Furnishing of, 3.58.050
  Location, 3.38.022
Open, when, 3.30.040
Orders, superior court appearance, inad-
  equate punishment, 3.66.065
Ordinances, violations, jurisdiction,
  3.66.060
Organization, 3.30.050
Parole and probation, application of law,
  interstate transfers, 3.66.140
Part time, judges, 3.34.040
Parties,
  Depositions, adverse parties, 12.16.060
  Refusal, 12.16.080
  Rebuttal testimony, adverse parties,
...
...s, general-

6.17.010

cting

Pleadings, 12.08.010 et seq.
  Accounts, 12.08.060
  Amendments, 12.08.090, 12.08.110
  Answers, 12.08.020
    Insufficient knowledge or informa-
      tion, 12.08.050
    Setoff and counterclaim, 12.08.120
  Complaints, 12.08.020
    Commencement of actions, service of
      process, 12.04.030
    Filing complaints, acquisition of ju-
      risdiction by court, 12.04.130
    Service, commencement of actions,
      12.04.010
  Continuance, amendment of pleadings,
    12.08.110
  Defective pleadings, 12.08.090
  Failure to state claim or defense, ob-
    jections, 12.08.090
  Forms, 12.08.040
  Instruments, 12.08.060
  Insufficient knowledge or information,
    answers or replies, 12.08.050
  Oaths and affirmations, verification of
    pleadings, 12.08.070
  Objections, 12.08.090

When attempting to locate a state statute by subject, the index to the state code should be consulted.

This Illustration shows how the Index to the *Revised Code of Washington* is used to locate the powers and duties of the district courts, the subject of Illustrations 11–1 through 11–3.

[Illustration 11–5]

PAGE FROM THE POPULAR NAME TABLE, WEST'S WISCONSIN STATUTES ANNOTATED

POPULAR NAME TABLE

Employment Peace Act, 111.01 et seq.
Enforcement of Foreign Judgments Act, 806.24
Evidence rules, 901.01 et seq.
Extradition, 976.03
Extradition of Prisoners as Witnesses Act, 976.01
Extradition of Witnesses in Criminal Actions Act, 976.02
Fair Dealership Law, 135.01 et seq.
Family Code, 765.001 et seq.
Federal Lien Registration Act, 779.97
Fiduciaries Act, 112.01
Food Regulation Law, 97.01 et seq.
Franchise Investment Law, 553.01 et seq.
Fraudulent Transfers Act, 242.01 et seq.
Fresh pursuit, Uniform Act on Close Pursuit, 976.04
Funds transfers, Uniform Commercial Code, 410.10
General Municipa[l] ... seq.
Hazardous Subst[ances] ... 100.37
Hazardous Waste ... 291.001 et se[q.]
Hospital Regulati[on] ... 50.32 et seq.
Housing Authorit[y] ...
Housing Authority for Elderly Persons Law, 66.1213
Huber Law, 303.08
Implied Consent Law, 343.305
Industrial Development Law, 59.57
Insurance, Consumer Act, 424.101 et seq.
Insurers Rehabilitation and Liquidation Act, 645.01 et seq.
Interstate agreement on qualification of educational personnel, 115.46 et seq.
Interstate Arbitration of Death Taxes Act, 72.35
Interstate Compact for Adult Offender Supervision, 304.16
Interstate Compact for Juveniles, 938.999
Interstate Compact for the Placement of Children, 48.99
Interstate Compact on Detainers, 976.05
Interstate Compact on Juveniles, 938.991
Interstate Compact on Mental Health, 51.75 et seq.
Interstate Compact on Placement of Children, 48.988
Interstate Family Support Act, 769.101 et seq.
Interstate Insurance Product Regulation Compact, 601.58

Investment securities, Uniform Commercial Code, 408.101 et seq.
Joint Obligations Act, 113.01 et seq.
Judicial Notice of Foreign Law Act, 902.02
Juvenile Justice Code, 938.01 et seq.
Lease of goods, Uniform Commercial Code, 411.101 et seq.
Letters of credit, Uniform Commercial Code, 405.101 et seq.
Limited Partnership Act, 179.01 et seq.
Living wills, 154.01 et seq.
Long Arm Statute, 801.05
Marital Property Act, 766.01 et seq.
Megans Law, 301.45
Mental Health Act, 51.001 et seq.
Metallic Mining Reclamation Act, 293.01 et seq.
Model Real Estate Time Share Act, [...]
[...]1 et seq.
[...], Safety Respon[...]et seq.
[...]429.101 et seq.
[...]Law, 344.22
[...]w, 342.01 et seq.
[...]de, 101.971 et [seq.]
Municipal Electric Company Act, 66.0825
Municipal Employment Relations Act, 111.70 et seq.
Municipal Law, 66.0101 et seq.
Navigable Waters Protection Law, 281.31
Negotiable instruments, Uniform Commercial Code, 403.102 et seq.
Nonprobate Transfers on Death Act, 705.10 et seq.
Nonprofit Association Act, 184.01 et seq.
Nonstock Corporation Law, 181.0103 et seq.
Notarial acts, 706.07
Oil Inspection Act, 168.01 et seq.
Open Meeting Law, 19.81 et seq.
Open Records Act, 19.31 et seq.
Organized Crime Control Act, 946.80 et seq.
Out of state parolee supervision, 304.13
Partnership Act, 178.01 et seq.
Photographic Copies of Business and Public Records as Evidence Act, 889.29
Police, Uniform Act on Close Pursuit, 976.04
Power of Attorney for Finances and Property Act, 244.01 et seq.
Principal and Income Act, 701.20

1598

Many state codes index acts by name, either in a separate table or incorporated into the code's index.

For example, if one knows that Wisconsin has enacted the Open Records Act, the citation to the act can be found by consulting the popular name table.

[Illustration 11–6]

SCREEN PRINT, WISCONSIN STATUTES–ANNOTATED, TABLE OF CONTENTS, WESTLAW CLASSIC

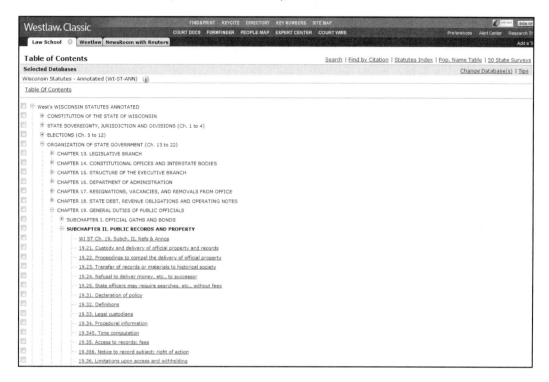

[Illustration 11-6 cont'd]

SCREEN PRINT, WISCONSIN STATUTES–ANNOTATED,
TABLE OF CONTENTS, WESTLAWNEXT

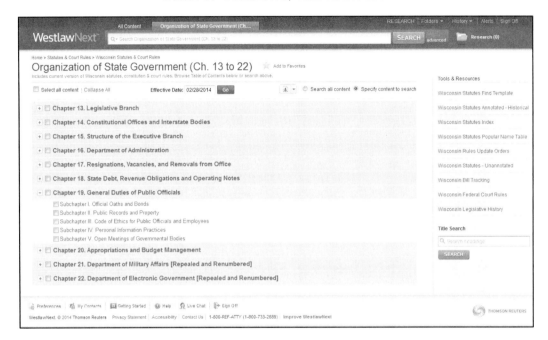

D. COMPARATIVE STATE STATUTORY RESEARCH

When a researcher wants to compare a particular law of one state with that of another or with similar laws of all states, searching each state code individually may be required. Unfortunately, state statutes are not organized in the same way, and their indexes might use different descriptive language. Therefore, it can be challenging to find substantially similar statutory provisions from different states by searching state codes or session laws.

Fortunately, several sources have pulled together state statutes on particular subjects. Some of those sources are described below.

1. Secondary Sources

Treatises, legal periodical articles, and other secondary sources are often good sources for multi-state comparisons of state laws. Especially helpful is *Subject Compilations of State Laws*,[21] a bibliography of articles, books, government documents, looseleaf services, court opinions, and websites that compare state laws on hundreds of subjects. Coverage begins with 1979. It is updated annually in print and quarterly in *HeinOnline*.[22]

---

[21] CHERYL RAE NYBERG & CAROL BOAST, SUBJECT COMPILATIONS OF STATE LAWS: AN ANNOTATED BIBLIOGRAPHY (1984–).

[22] *See also* JON S. SCHULTZ, STATUTES COMPARED: A U.S., CANADIAN, MULTINATIONAL RESEARCH GUIDE TO STATUTES BY SUBJECT (2d ed. 2001).

2. Fifty-State Surveys

The increasing availability of fifty-state surveys has vastly simplified comparative statutory research. These surveys compile the statutory, and oftentimes regulatory, provisions covering a designated topic for all fifty states. Both *Westlaw* and *LexisNexis* have fifty-state survey databases, which include charts comparing the laws of each state, the citation to the statute or regulation, and the subject matter and/or details about the laws.

Another source for fifty-state surveys is *National Survey of State Laws*.[23] This volume also offers charts that allow users to make basic state-by-state comparisons of current state laws for various legal topics. Content from *National Survey of State Laws* is available electronically in *Westlaw's* 50 State Surveys database.

Some surveys are available online. *Wex*, from Cornell's *Legal Information Institute*, offers links to state statutes in about forty broad subject categories (e.g., Commercial Law or Marriage).[24]

3. Topical Services

Many topical services provide citations to, abstracts of, or the full text of state statutes dealing with a specific subject. For example, Commerce Clearing House's *Inheritance, Estate and Gift Tax Reporter* includes separate volumes that set forth the text of state laws from all states on wills, trusts, and estates.[25]

4. Martindale-Hubbell Law Digest

For many years, this digest of state laws was a part of the *Martindale–Hubbell Law Directory* in print.[26] However, the publisher discontinued the set in 2010. Researchers may still find the 2010 and previous summaries useful. The *Law Digest* archive is in *LexisNexis*.

E. STATE LEGISLATIVE HISTORIES

Attempting to compile a legislative history for a state law in a manner similar to that described in Chapter 10 for federal laws is often difficult and, at times, is impossible. As a general rule, state legislatures do not publish their debates, committee reports, or transcripts of hearings held before legislative committees. Yet, the need for these sources is often just as great, because state laws can contain provisions that are vague or ambiguous and need clarification.[27]

The most accessible official documents are the state Senate and House journals. These journals usually contain only brief minutes of the proceedings and final votes on

---

[23] RICHARD A. LEITER, NATIONAL SURVEY OF STATE LAWS (6th ed. 2008).

[24] http://topics.law.cornell.edu/wex/state_statutes.

[25] Looseleaf services are discussed in Chapter 14.

[26] *Martindale–Hubbell* is discussed more fully in Chapter 20.

[27] To determine which state documents are available, see MANZ, *supra* n.6. For information on the legislative process for each state, see STATE LEGISLATIVE SOURCEBOOK: A RESOURCE GUIDE TO LEGISLATIVE INFORMATION IN THE FIFTY STATES (annual). Also useful is José R. Torres & Steve Windsor, *State Legislative Histories: A Select, Annotated Bibliography*, 85 LAW LIBR. J. 545 (1993), and Beth Williams, *Determining Legislative Intent in State Courts: Selected Methods and Sources*, 30 LEGAL REFERENCE SERVICES Q., no. 1–2, 2011, at 1.

legislation.[28] A few states may issue reports of a state law revision commission or the reports of special committees of the legislature for selected laws. If a state has an annotated code, the notes should be examined carefully to see if reference is made to documents of this type.

Westlaw's STATE–LH database contains legislative history materials for all states, including bill analyses, bill histories, committee reports, legislative journals, legislative transcripts, vote records, and governors' messages.

Local newspapers may also be useful sources for legislative history research. News stories, articles, interviews, and editorials written around the time that the legislation was proposed and enacted may help illustrate legislative intent.

Often, guidance for research in state legislative history is available in the state legal research guides listed in Appendix B of this book or from librarians with knowledge of sources within the state. Some states maintain "working documents" or copies of legislative history materials that are only available through a visit to the state's legislative library.[29] In many instances, however, extrinsic aids for determining legislative intent are not available, and one must rely on the language of the act by using the ordinary rules of statutory construction.[30]

F. INTERSTATE COMPACTS

The United States Constitution provides that "No State shall, without Consent of Congress . . . enter into any Agreement or Compact with another State. . . ."[31]

In an early interpretation of this clause, the Supreme Court of the United States held that the Constitution prohibited all agreements between states unless consented to by Congress.[32] However, in a subsequent case, the Court changed its position and held that congressional consent was not necessary for agreements or compacts that did not increase the political powers of the states or interfere with the supremacy of the United States.[33] Normally, however, interstate agreements or compacts are formally enacted by the legislatures of the states involved and are then submitted to Congress for its consent.[34]

---

[28] Maine and Pennsylvania, however, have legislative journals that record actual legislative debate and parallel the *Congressional Record* in form and content.

[29] Contact information for state legislative libraries appears in the Law Librarians' Society of Washington, D.C.'s *Legislative Source Book*, http://www.llsdc.org/state-leg/. The site also lists contact information for commercial sources for state legislative research.

[30] *See* NORMAN J. SINGER & J. D. SHAMBIE SINGER, STATUTES AND STATUTORY CONSTRUCTION (7th ed. 2007). Because this treatise's original author was J. G. Sutherland, many researchers still refer to it as "Sutherland," and in fact the *Westlaw* database identifier for it is SUTHERLAND. *See also* ANTONIN SCALIA & BRYAN A. GARNER, READING LAW: THE INTERPRETATION OF LEGAL TEXTS (2012).

[31] U.S. CONST. art. I, § 10, cl. 3.

[32] Holmes v. Jennison, 39 U.S. (14 Pet.) 540 (1840).

[33] Virginia v. Tennessee, 148 U.S. 503, 518 (1893). *See also* U. S. Steel Corp. v. Multistate Tax Comm'n, 434 U.S. 452 (1978).

[34] Interstate compacts do not have to be formally enacted by Congress. *See* THE CONSTITUTION OF THE UNITED STATES OF AMERICA: ANALYSIS AND INTERPRETATION 402–07 (1992 ed.) (annotation to art. 1, § 10, cl. 3). *See also* PAUL T. HARDY, INTERSTATE COMPACTS: THE TIES THAT BIND (1982); Kevin J. Heron, *The Interstate Compact in Transition: From Cooperative State Action to Congressionally Coerced Agreements*, 60 ST. JOHN'S L. REV. 1 (1985); Jill Elaine Hasday, *Interstate Compacts in a Democratic Society: The Problem of Permanency*, 49 FLA. L. REV. 1 (1997); Matthew Pincus, *When Should Interstate Compacts Require Congressional Consent?*, 42 COLUM. J.L. & SOC. PROBS. 511 (2009).

Until about 1900, most interstate compacts dealt with boundary disputes between states. Since then, compacts have more commonly been used to resolve, through cooperation, problems common to two or more states, such as flood or pollution control, or the establishment of a port authority.

1. Publication of Interstate Compacts

The texts of interstate agreements are set forth in the session laws of the enacting states and are usually included in the respective state codes as well. Since they involve agreements among the states involved, they also appear in the *United States Statutes at Large*.

The Council of State Governments' Interstate Compact Database indexes all active interstate compacts from more than 1,500 statutes.[35] Accompanying each compact is a PDF of the statutory language.

2. Locating Judicial Opinions on Interstate Compacts

a.   State Code Annotated Editions. Interstate compacts usually appear in the respective state codes. Consult the annotations for select opinions interpreting the compacts.

b.   Citators. KeyCite via *Westlaw* or *Shepard's* in print or online via *LexisNexis* can be used to locate opinions interpreting interstate compacts.

c.   Digests. Digests of cases involving interstate compacts are under topic *States*, key number 6, in *Westlaw* and the West print digests and under *States, Territories & Possessions* § 52 in *Digest of United States Supreme Court Reports, Lawyers' Edition*.

G. MUNICIPAL OR LOCAL GOVERNMENT LEGISLATION

Traditionally, the various forms of local government are known as *municipal corporations* or *municipalities*. Municipalities are instruments of the state and have only such powers as are granted to them by the state. These powers vary from state to state, and the constitution and statutes of the state in which the municipality is located must be examined to ascertain a municipality's scope of authority.[36]

1. Municipal Charters

In general, a municipality operates under a charter, which is the basic document setting forth its power. Usually the charter has been adopted by the voters of a municipality and is analogous to a state constitution. The form of publication varies and, in the larger cities, may include bound volumes.

2. Ordinances

Ordinances are the legislative enactments of local jurisdictions, as passed by their legislative body, e.g., the city council, county commissioners, or board of supervisors. Ordinances are to municipalities what session laws are to the federal and state governments. In larger cities, ordinances are first published in an official journal and

---

[35] http://apps.csg.org/ncic/.

[36] *See generally* Mary Whisner, *Enact Locally*, 102 LAW LIBR. J. 497 (2010).

may be separately published in *slip* form. In smaller communities, they are frequently published in the local newspaper.

3.   Codes

Municipal codes are codifications of ordinances. They generally contain only ordinances in force at the time of publication and are usually classified and arranged by subject. Many municipalities are now publishing their codes, ordinances, and charters online.[37] *American Law Sources Online* includes links to municipal and county codes, if available, for each state.[38]

Comparatively few municipal codes are published in print. Most often, these are for cities, rather than townships or counties, and may not be supplemented in a timely fashion. When municipal codes are not published in print or available electronically, it may be necessary to go to the seat of government and examine the ordinances on file there. The local public library may also maintain a copy of the code.

4.   Interpretations of Municipal Charters and Ordinances

Most municipal codes do not include annotations of opinions interpreting the charters and ordinances. The following sources are useful in obtaining judicial opinions for municipal legislation:

a.   *Treatises.* Both McQuillin's *The Law of Municipal Corporations*[39] and *Antieau on Local Government Law*[40] are useful in locating judicial opinions. *Ordinance Law Annotations*[41] summarizes cases construing local ordinances. Helpful in understanding and drafting ordinances are *Municipal Ordinances: Text and Forms*[42] and *Municipal Legal Forms with Commentary.*[43]

b.   *State Digests.* Judicial opinions interpreting ordinances or charters are included in state digests. The location of the appropriate West key numbers or paragraph numbers under which such opinions are abstracted can be located through the use of the index or topical outlines to the print digest.

---

[37] Most municipal ordinances on the Internet are made available through code publishing companies. These include American Legal Publishing, Code Publishing Company, General Code Publishers, LexisNexis Municipal Codes, Municipal Code Corporation, Quality Code Publishing, and Sterling Codifiers.

Some municipalities offer additional legislative documents online through *Legistar,* from the Municipal Code Corporation. *Legistar* is a legislative management software package that helps municipalities manage the flow of documents through the legislative process. These documents (ordinances, resolutions, reports, committee minutes, etc.) are then made available online. *See* http://www.municode.com/services/Legistar.aspx.

[38] http://www.lawsource.com/also/.

[39] EUGENE MCQUILLIN, THE LAW OF MUNICIPAL CORPORATIONS (3d ed. 1949–) (most volumes in the set have been reissued in the last several years) (available in *Westlaw*).

[40] SANDRA M. STEVENSON & CHESTER JAMES ANTIEAU, ANTIEAU ON LOCAL GOVERNMENT LAW (2d ed. 2012–) (available in *LexisNexis*).

[41] ORDINANCE LAW ANNOTATIONS: A COMPREHENSIVE DIGEST OF AMERICAN CASES THAT INTERPRET OR APPLY CITY AND COUNTY ORDINANCES (1982–) (available in *Westlaw*).

[42] BYRON S. MATTHEWS, THOMAS ALEXANDER MATTHEWS & JUDITH O'GALLAGHER, MUNICIPAL ORDINANCES: TEXT AND FORMS (4th ed. 2010) (available in *Westlaw*).

[43] RALPH J. MOORE, MUNICIPAL LEGAL FORMS WITH COMMENTARY (1999) (available in *Westlaw*).

Chapter 12

COURT RULES AND PROCEDURES

—————

This chapter describes the resources that provide and explain rules and procedures for the conduct of courts. Court rules control the operation of the courts and the conduct of the litigants appearing before them. They deal with the procedures for initiating and defending a case and for appealing cases to appellate courts. Court rules relate to matters such as the filing of complaints, assignment of cases, methods of appeal, and the proper means for making motions that are required during the many phases of litigation. Some rules are as basic as specifying the format that must be followed in preparing a document. Other rules establish time limitations that control whether a matter can proceed. In general, the purposes of court rules are to establish uniform procedures, provide parties to a lawsuit with information and instructions on matters pertaining to judicial proceedings, and aid the court in conducting its business. The sources covered in this chapter include legislation, rules promulgated by courts, judicial opinions construing these rules and legislation, and legal forms used in court proceedings.

Court rules from both federal and state courts are easily accessible online. Federal and state courts and/or bar associations usually post current electronic versions of the rules of court for their jurisdiction. Additionally, websites such as *LLRX.com*,[1] the *Public Library of Law*,[2] and the *Legal Information Institute* at Cornell University Law School[3] aggregate court rules. *LexisNexis*, *Westlaw*, and *Loislaw* provide access to court rules with additional editorial enhancements such as citations to cases and secondary sources.[4] Rules of court also are available in many print sources ranging from multivolume fully annotated sets to unannotated pamphlets.

A. FEDERAL COURT RULES: SOURCES, INTERPRETATIONS, ANALYSIS, AND FORMS

1. In General

The power of a court to promulgate court rules is found either in its inherent authority or in constitutional or statutory provisions. For example, Section 17 of the Judiciary Act of 1789 gave the federal courts the authority to promulgate rules relating to the orderly conduct of their business. Federal statutory language, found primarily in Title 28 of the *United States Code (U.S.C.)*, mandates some procedural requirements for the courts.

—————

[1] *LLRX.com* has aggregated most, if not all, rules of court that have been posted online. *See* http://www.llrx.com/courtrules.

[2] http://www.plol.org.

[3] http://www.law.cornell.edu.

[4] *Bloomberg Law* also includes federal and state court rules, but without annotations.

Federal court rules and procedures can be grouped into four categories: (1) rules of general application that are national in scope; (2) rules for specific federal courts, such as for the Supreme Court of the United States and the bankruptcy courts; (3) local rules for individual courts within the federal court system; and (4) statutory requirements found in Title 28 of the *United States Code.*

Four sets of rules of general application in the federal courts have been promulgated: the Federal Rules of Civil Procedure, effective September 16, 1938; the Federal Rules of Criminal Procedure, effective March 21, 1946; the Federal Rules of Appellate Procedure, effective July 1, 1968; and the Federal Rules of Evidence, effective July 1, 1975.

In addition, various federal courts have rules specific to their operations. For example, filing a motion in the U.S. Court of International Trade may involve a different process from filing a motion in the U.S. Court of Federal Claims. Local rules often add procedural requirements or limitations. For example, one federal district court may permit television cameras in the courtroom; another may not. Additionally, separate statutes, and judicial interpretations of these statutes, can control matters of court procedure.

Court rules often are available in both unannotated and annotated versions.

2.   **Unannotated Rules**

a.   Electronic Sources. As noted above, the rules of most federal courts have been posted online and are easily accessible either directly from a court's website or through an aggregating website such as *LLRX.com.* Commercial services such as *Westlaw* and *LexisNexis* provide access to the federal rules.

b.   United States Code. The Federal Rules of Criminal Procedure are in the Appendix to Title 18 of the *United States Code*; the Federal Rules of Civil Procedure, Appellate Procedure, and Evidence, as well as the rules for some of the specialized federal courts, are contained in the Appendix to Title 28 of the *U.S.C.* Other court rules accompany the particular *U.S.C.* title covering specific subjects, e.g., Bankruptcy, Title 11; Copyright, Title 17.

The *U.S.C.* also includes Judicial Conference Advisory Committee Notes with each set of court rules. These notes are provided by the committee that drafted the original rules and include notes by any subsequent committees that proposed changes to the rules. These notes can prove especially helpful in interpreting the meaning and intent of the rules.

Because of the delay in publishing the *U.S.C.*, other privately produced sources often are more useful, especially for recent rules changes.

c.   Federal Procedure, Lawyers' Edition (Thomson Reuters). This treatise includes several pamphlets with rules of general application and Advisory Committee notes, along with several other sets of specialized rules. Additional volumes contain the rules adopted by each of the circuit courts of appeals and the district courts within each circuit.

d.   Federal Rules Service (Thomson Reuters). This set, discussed in Section A-5-b of this chapter, contains a Finding Aids volume that includes the Federal Rules of Civil Procedure along with a cumulative table of cases construing these rules and a supplemental word index.

e. *Pamphlet Editions.*[5] Thomson Reuters publishes annually pamphlets that contain various federal rules and related statutory provisions. In addition, in connection with the state statutory compilations published by Thomson Reuters and LexisNexis, pamphlets are issued annually that contain the federal district court and appellate court rules for the corresponding courts in that state. The equivalent of print pamphlet editions is available in both *Westlaw* and *LexisNexis.*

f. *Reporters of Federal Cases.* When changes to major rules are proposed or adopted, they are published in the advance sheets to the *Supreme Court Reporter, Federal Reporter 3d, Federal Supplement 2d*, and *Federal Rules Decisions*. The advance sheets to the *U.S. Code Congressional and Administrative News* contain amendments to the rules for all courts. The bound *Federal Rules Decisions* also includes rule changes, preliminary drafts of proposed changes, proposed amendments, congressional acts concerning court rules, and the publisher's editorial comments.[6]

3. Annotated Rules

The most important sources for annotated versions of federal rules include:

a. *United States Code Service* (LexisNexis). The various court rules are in unnumbered volumes (usually shelved at the end of the set) entitled Court Rules. The text of each rule is set forth, followed by annotations of cases involving the rule. [Illustrations 12–1 and 12–2] The notes following the rules include comments from the Advisory Committee, as well as references to law review articles and appropriate sections of other publications by LexisNexis. This compilation of rules is especially useful for its historical references.

b. *United States Code Annotated* (Thomson Reuters). The annotated rules in this set correspond to the arrangement of the *United States Code* with rules following Titles 18 and 28. Each rule is followed by editorial annotations and Advisory Committee notes along with citations to law review articles and other secondary sources. [Illustrations 12–3 and 12–4]

c. *Digest of United States Supreme Court Reports, Lawyers' Edition* (LexisNexis). This set includes several Court Rules volumes containing the rules for all federal courts, the Advisory Committee notes, references to other publications, and annotations of cases decided by the Supreme Court of the United States that interpret the rules.

d. *Moore's Federal Rules Pamphlets* (Matthew Bender/LexisNexis). Published annually, these pamphlets contain the four sets of rules of general application, the rules for the Supreme Court of the United States, and a few selected statutory provisions. Excerpts from the Advisory Committee notes, annotations of leading cases, and references to the multivolume treatise, *Moore's Federal Practice*, also are provided. These pamphlets are also available in *Lexis.*

---

[5] Note that in law a "pamphlet" is simply a softbound work (*e.g.* a paperback) and is not necessarily the sort of flimsy leaflet that "pamphlet" connotes in ordinary life. For example, the 2013 Revised Edition of *Federal Civil Judicial Procedure and Rules* (Thomson Reuters) pamphlet is 1230 pages, plus a 138–page index. It includes the Federal Rules of Civil Procedure, Evidence, and Appellate Procedure, the Rules of the Supreme Court, excerpts from title 28 of the *U.S.C.*, and more.

[6] A discussion of the process for amending rules is on the United States Courts website, http://www.us courts.gov/RulesAndPolicies/rules/about-rulemaking.aspx. *See* Ellen J. Platt, *How to Research Federal Court Rule Amendments: An Explanation of the Process and a List of Sources*, 6 PERSP.: TEACHING LEGAL RES. & WRITING 115 (1998).

4. Statutory Provisions Relating to Court Procedure

Statutory provisions addressing court procedure are in various titles of the *U.S.C.* Perhaps the most notable are the venue and *habeas corpus* provisions in Title 28. These statutory provisions are referenced in treatises and often are in pamphlets that include the federal rules of general application.

5. Federal Rules Interpreted by the Courts

The meaning of the rules and their applicability to specific situations are frequently litigated. The following sources are useful for locating cases interpreting federal rules:

a. *Federal Rules Decisions* (Thomson Reuters). *Federal Rules Decisions (F.R.D.)* is a unit of the *National Reporter System* that contains cases of the federal district courts since 1939 that interpret the Federal Rules of Civil Procedure and cases since 1946 that interpret the Federal Rules of Criminal Procedure. These cases are not published in the *Federal Supplement*. Similar to other units of the *National Reporter System, F.R.D.* is issued in advance sheets and bound volumes, with headnotes that are classified in West's key number system. In addition to judicial opinions, the set also includes articles on various aspects of federal courts and federal procedure. A cumulative index to these articles is in every tenth volume, and a consolidated index for volumes 1 through 122 is in volume 122.

b. *Federal Rules Service* (Thomson Reuters). This set compiles and provides access to judicial opinions construing the Federal Rules of Civil Procedure and the Federal Rules of Appellate Procedure. It is composed of three sections:

(1) *Federal Rules Service* reporter provides edited versions of cases focusing exclusively on Federal Rules of Civil Procedure or Federal Rules of Appellate Procedure issues. The reporter is currently in its third series with coverage as follows:

First Series, 1939–1958

Second Series, 1958–1985

Third Series, 1985 to present

(2) *Federal Rules Digest*, 3d ed. This multivolume digest classifies all judicial opinions from April 1954 to present that appear in the *Federal Rules Service* reporter. Headnotes are organized using the publisher's Findex system of rule subdivisions, which enables a user to pinpoint a rule of interest and go directly to digest sections listing pertinent cases. Abstracts of cases from 1938 to 1954 are located in the four volumes of *Federal Rules Digest*, 2d ed.

(3) *Finding Aids* volume. This volume includes a word index to the Federal Rules of Civil Procedure and the Federal Rules of Appellate Procedure. The full text of the Federal Rules of Civil Procedure and the Federal Rules of Appellate Procedure is also set forth in the Finding Aids volume, together with an outline of the Findex system following each rule.

c. *Federal Rules of Evidence Service* (Thomson Reuters). This set provides edited versions of civil and criminal federal cases that have interpreted the Federal Rules of Evidence. The format is similar to that of the *Federal Rules Service* in that the set contains a case reporter (covering September 1975 to present), a digest, and a Finding Aids volume with the Findex feature.

6. Treatises

Many treatises pertain to the practice and procedure of the federal courts. Often, the text of each rule is followed by an analysis of that rule with citations to judicial opinions provided in the footnotes. The multivolume sets discussed below are useful in obtaining commentary on federal practice:

a. *Cyclopedia of Federal Procedure*, 3d ed. (Thomson Reuters) (*Westlaw*). This set is arranged by subject and provides extensive annotations on jurisdiction, pleading, trial practice and appellate procedure.

b. *Federal Procedure, Lawyers' Edition* (Thomson Reuters). Organized by subject, this set covers federal district and appellate courts in addition to the United States Supreme Court, specialized federal courts, and selected administrative agency adjudicatory bodies such as the Board of Veterans Appeals and the Board of Patent Appeals and Interferences.

c. Charles Alan Wright et al., *Federal Practice and Procedure*, 3d ed. (Thomson Reuters) (*Westlaw*) This text is the most frequently cited source on federal practice and procedure features sections on the Federal Rules of Criminal Procedure, Federal Rules of Civil Procedure, Federal Rules of Appellate Procedure, and Federal Rules of Evidence. The set is organized by rule number for ease of use. [Illustration 12–5]

d. *Moore's Federal Practice*, 3d ed. (Matthew Bender) (*LexisNexis*). Organized by rule number, this set covers both civil and criminal practice with detailed analysis of the Federal Rules of Civil Procedure, the Federal Rules of Criminal Procedure, the Federal Rules of Appellate Procedure, and Supreme Court Rules.

e. *Federal Litigation Guide* (Matthew Bender) (*LexisNexis*). This set, prepared by the firm of Jenner & Block, focuses on federal civil procedure and is organized by litigation stage from the filing of the complaint through trial and appeal.

f. *Orfield's Criminal Procedure Under the Federal Rules*, 2d ed. (Thomson West). Organized by rule number, this set focuses exclusively on criminal procedure and provides a discussion of each rule, including practical applications of the rule in federal courts and related criminal proceedings along with historical commentary of its drafting and development.

g. *Weinstein's Federal Evidence*, 2d ed. (Matthew Bender) (*LexisNexis*). Focused on the Federal Rules of Evidence and organized by rule number, this set provides in-depth analysis and historical coverage.

7. Form Books

Publications with model federal practice forms generally correlate the federal rules to the forms which they require. These forms contain terms, phrases, and other essential details needed by attorneys filing documents in federal courts and assist attorneys in complying with the federal rules. The resources discussed in this section are multivolume practice form books.[7]

---

[7] Form books are discussed in Chapter 20.

a. *Bender's Federal Practice Forms* (Matthew Bender) (*LexisNexis*). This publication cross-references to *Moore's Federal Practice*, 3d ed. and provides numerous forms covering civil and criminal federal practice.

b. *Nichols Cyclopedia of Federal Procedure Forms* (Thomson Reuters) (*Westlaw*). A companion to *Cyclopedia of Federal Procedure*, the forms are annotated and cover civil and criminal rules, as well as rules promulgated by certain administrative agencies.

c. *West's Federal Forms* (Thomson Reuters) (*Westlaw*). This set, covering both civil and criminal forms for use in the federal courts, is annotated and includes references to *Federal Practice and Procedure*, 3d ed.

d. *Federal Procedural Forms, Lawyers' Edition* (Thomson Reuters) (*Westlaw*). A companion to *Federal Procedure, Lawyers' Edition*, this set provides civil and criminal forms for use in all federal courts, as well as for adversary and rulemaking proceedings before administrative agencies.

8. Historical Sources

At times, it may be necessary to go beyond the text of the rules, the Advisory Committee notes, judicial interpretations, and secondary sources. The following sources are especially helpful in providing historical information about the federal rules:

a. *Records of the U.S. Judicial Conference: Committees on Rules of Practice and Procedures* (1935–1996) (ProQuest (formerly CIS)). This major microfiche compilation, updated periodically, gathers together the minutes and transcripts of meetings, deskbooks, correspondence, and comments of committees established by the Supreme Court of the United States to draft new rules of practice and procedure for the federal district and appellate courts. Three printed indexes provide access to the set: List of Documents, Index by Rule Topics, and Index by Names of Individuals and Organizations.[8]

b. *Drafting History of the Federal Rules of Criminal Procedure* (Madeleine Wilken & Nicholas Triffin comps., 1991) (William S. Hein & Co.) (*HeinOnline*). This seven-volume set provides the equivalent of a legislative history for the Federal Rules of Criminal Procedure. It includes a reproduction of the four-volume *Comments, Recommendations, and Suggestions Concerning the Proposed Rules of Criminal Procedure* originally used by the committee members. In addition, the set contains previously unpublished preliminary drafts, letters and Supreme Court memoranda, successive preliminary drafts of the Rules of Criminal Procedure, the Final Committee report, and final approved Federal Rules of Criminal Procedure.

c. *Federal Rules of Evidence: Legislative Histories and Related Documents* (James F. Bailey, II & Oscar M. Trelles, III, comps., 1980) (William S. Hein & Co.) (*HeinOnline*). This four-volume collection contains materials from the American Law Institute, the National Conference of Commissioners on Uniform State Laws, and the Judicial Conference of the United States, as well as congressional hearings and legislation relating to the Federal Rules of Evidence.

---

[8] The rules committees' reports to the Judicial Conference (1960–present) are available at http://www.uscourts.gov/RulesAndPolicies/rules/archives/reports-judicial-conference.aspx.

B. FEDERAL COURT RULES OF SPECIFIC APPLICABILITY, INCLUDING LOCAL RULES

The Supreme Court of the United States, federal courts of appeals, federal district courts, and various specialized courts have promulgated court rules. These rules apply only to the court adopting them and are mainly concerned with its operation. These include court-specific rules for filing motions and preparing briefs, as well as other rules dealing with the procedure of the court. The rules for the various federal courts are contained in the following publications:

1. Rules for the Supreme Court of the United States

The most widely used treatise for practice in the Supreme Court of the United States is Eugene Gressman et al., *Supreme Court Practice* (9th ed. 2007) (BNA Books) (*Bloomberg Law*). In addition to the Rules for the Supreme Court of the United States, topics covered include the Court's certiorari and appeal jurisdiction, when the Court's original jurisdiction can be invoked, other extraordinary writs, and compliance with the Court's precise rules.

The Rules for the Supreme Court of the United States are available on the Supreme Court's website[9] and in many other sources, including those listed above.

2. Rules for the Courts of Appeals

a. *Federal Procedure, Lawyers' Edition* (Thomson Reuters). This set includes pamphlets setting forth the rules for the various federal courts and specialized courts. Separate pamphlets are available for the first through the eleventh circuits. These pamphlets also include the rules adopted by the district courts within the circuit.

b. *Federal Local Court Rules*, 2d ed. (Thomson Reuters). This set contains the rules currently in force for all federal district courts and federal courts of appeals. The last volume contains the rules for the courts of appeals.

c. *U.S.C.A.* and *U.S.C.S.* Rules are included in the volumes following Title 18 and Title 28 in the *U.S.C.A.*, and are included in the Court Rules volumes at the end of the *U.S.C.S.*

d. *Digest of United States Supreme Court Reports, Lawyers' Edition* (LexisNexis). Rules are included in volumes at the end of this set.

e. Federal courts of appeals post their rules on their websites; they may also issue them in pamphlet form.[10]

3. Rules for the Federal District Courts

a. *Federal Procedure, Lawyers' Edition* (Thomson Reuters). This set includes pamphlets with the rules adopted by the district courts within the circuit.

b. *Federal Local Court Rules*, 2d ed. (Thomson Reuters). This set contains the rules currently in force for all federal district courts. Rules are arranged alphabetically

---

[9] http://www.supremecourt.gov/.

[10] Links to federal court websites are here: http://www.uscourts.gov/Court_Locator/CourtWebsites.aspx.

by state, and the volumes are updated as amendments and new rules are issued. [Illustration 12–6]

    c.   Federal district courts post their rules on their websites; they may also issue them in pamphlet form and post the rules to their websites. The United States Courts website includes links to all the district court rules.[11]

4.　Rules for the Specialized Federal Courts

    a.   *Federal Procedure, Lawyers' Edition* (Thomson Reuters). This set, discussed above in Section B-2-a, sets forth rules for the specialized courts, e.g., admiralty, bankruptcy, copyright, international trade, and tax.

    b.   *U.S.C.A.* and *U.S.C.S.* Rules for specialized courts, including the Court of Federal Claims, the Court of International Trade, Tax Court and Veterans Claims Court, are included in the volumes following Title 18 and Title 28 in the *U.S.C.A.*, and are included in the Court Rules volumes at the end of the *U.S.C.S.*

    c.   *Digest of United States Supreme Court Reports, Lawyers' Edition* (LexisNexis). Rules for specialized courts, including the Court of Federal Claims, the Court of International Trade, and Tax Court, are included in the volumes at the end of this set.

C.　COURT RULES FOR STATE COURTS

    The methods of publication of the rules of courts vary from state to state.[12] In most states, court rules are published in the state code, in separate rules pamphlets, or in the state case reports. Court rules for many state courts are available online on the state website, the state bar association website, or the court's own website. The *LLRX.com* website aggregates state court rules from the various sites where they have been posted. *Bloomberg Law*, *LexisNexis*, *Loislaw*, and *Westlaw* also provide access to state court rules, often with extensive annotations.

    Treatises on state civil and criminal practice are published for many states. They can be located using the catalog of a law library.

D.　CITATORS

    Electronic citation services, such as *KeyCite* and *Shepard's*, track citations of federal and state court rules.[13] In print, *Shepard's Federal Rules Citations* includes citations to the Federal Rules of Civil Procedure, Criminal Procedure, Appellate Procedure, and Evidence, as well as the rules of the U.S. Supreme Court, U.S. courts of appeals and district courts, and many specialized federal courts. *Shepard's United States Citations— Statutes* includes citations to federal court rules. The state units of *Shepard's* include citations to state and federal cases that have cited state court rules.

---

[11] Links to federal court websites are at http://www.uscourts.gov/Court_Locator/CourtWebsites.aspx.

[12] For a table of sources for state court rules for each state, the District of Columbia, and the territories of the United States, see Betsy Reidinger & Virginia Till Lemmon, *Sources of Rules of State Courts*, 82 LAW LIBR. J. 761 (1990). If one is available, also check the relevant state legal research manual. See Appendix B of this book for a listing of these state legal research guides.

[13] Citators are discussed in Chapter 15 of this book.

E. ILLUSTRATIONS

Problem: Assume that your research involves determining whether two or more criminal indictments can be tried together. See Illustrations 12–1 through 12–5. Assume further that you need to determine if the trial can be televised in the Northern District of Florida. See Illustration 12–6.

12–1 to 12–2.   Pages from a U.S.C.S. Rules Volume Containing Rule 13, Federal Rules of Criminal Procedure

12–3 to 12–4.   Pages from U.S.C.A. Title 18 Appendix Containing Rule 13, Federal rules of Criminal Procedure

12–5.   Page from C. Wright & A. Miller, Federal Practice and Procedure, Containing Rule 13, Federal Rules of Criminal Procedure

12–6.   Page from Federal Local Court Rules (Florida)

[Illustration 12–1]

PAGE FROM A U.S.C.S. RULES VOLUME CONTAINING RULE 13,
FEDERAL RULES OF CRIMINAL PROCEDURE

Rule 12.3 RULES OF CRIMINAL PROCEDURE

INTERPRETIVE NOTES AND DECISIONS

Rule's disclosure requirement does not unfairly interfere with constitutional right to compulsory process for obtaining witnesses; it does not prohibit compulsory process, but merely requires compliance with simple disclosure rules to guarantee that all parties will receive fair trial, and requirement is consistent with court's duty to ensure fair and orderly trial. United States v Seeright (1992, CA4 Md) 978 F2d 842, 36 Fed Rules Evid Serv 1399.

Government had no reason to make inquiries of particular law enforcement agencies regarding defendant's alleged cooperation with them where they were not listed among those defendant submitted pursuant to Rule 12.3. United States v Roach (1994, CA8 Ark) 28 F3d 729, 40 Fed Rules Evid Serv 1341.

Fact that rule refers only to belief, not to reasonableness, does not mean that reasonableness of belief is not element of defense; rule is procedural and elements of defense are found in federal common law dealing with substance of defense. United States v Burrows (1994, CA9 Cal) 36 F3d 875, 94 CDOS 7427, 94 Daily Journal DAR 13663.

Defendant is not entitled to raise in pretrial motion question whether government breached agreement with him if agreement provides defense to liability for crimes charged in indictment; resolution of that question requires trial of general issue and is not properly decided in pretrial motion. United States v Doe (1995, CA2 NY) 63 F3d 121, subsequent app (1996, CA2 Conn) 103 F3d 234, 25 Media L R 1211.

Rule 12.3(a)(1) of FRCrP is constitutional and must be complied with, even though alleged heroin importers asserting authorization defense challenge rule mandating pretrial notice of that defense on Fifth Amendment and Due Process grounds, because (1) there is nothing incriminatory about giving notice of defense to be offered at trial, (2) nothing is compelled since defendants are not under any compulsion to pursue defense, and (3) rule triggers discovery of witness names and addresses but grants defendants reciprocal discovery rights. United States v Abcasis (1992, ED NY) 785 F Supp 1113, request den (1992, ED NY) 811 F Supp 828, 37 Fed Rules Evid Serv 913.

Rule 13. Trial Together of Indictments or Informations

The court may order two or more indictments or informations or both to be tried together if the offenses, and the defendants if there is more than one, could

> After the text of the rule are historical notes from the Advisory Committee and cross-references and citations to related sources of the publisher, as well as to other secondary sources. For some rules, scholarly commentary is provided.

Other provisions:
Notes of Advisory Committee. This rule is substantially a restatement of existing law, 18 U.S.C. [former] § 557 (Indictments and presentments; joinder of charges); *Logan v United States*, 144 U.S. 263, 296, 12 S. Ct. 617, 36 L. Ed. 429; *Showalter v United States*, 260 F. 719 (C.C.A. 4th), cert. den., 250 U.S. 672, 40 S. Ct. 14, 63 L. Ed. 1200; *Hostetter v United States*, 16 F2d 921 (C.C.A. 8th); *Capone v United States*, 51 F.2d 609, 619–620 (C.C.A. 7th).

CROSS REFERENCES
Joinder of offenses and defendants, USCS Rules of Criminal Procedure, Rule 8.
Relief from prejudicial joinder, USCS Rules of Criminal Procedure, Rule 14.

RESEARCH GUIDE
Federal Procedure:
24 Moore's Federal Practice (Matthew Bender 3d ed.), Trial Together of Indictments or Informations §§ 613.01 et seq.
28 Moore's Federal Practice (Matthew Bender 3d ed.), Procedure for Misdemeanors or Petty Offenses § 658.20.
9 Fed Proc L Ed, Criminal Procedure §§ 22:571, 1000, 1008.
20 Fed Proc L Ed, Internal Revenue § 48:1375.

618

[Illustration 12-2]

PAGE OF ANNOTATIONS FOR RULE 13, U.S.C.S., FROM RULES VOLUME, FEDERAL RULES OF CRIMINAL PROCEDURE

RULES OF CRIMINAL PROCEDURE   **Rule 13, n 4**

Am Jur:

1 Am Jur 2d, Actions § 136, 137.

Forms:

7 Fed Procedural Forms L Ed, Criminal Procedure (1994) § 20:415.

Annotations:

Joinder of offenses under Rule 8(a), Federal Rules of Criminal Procedure. 39 ALR Fed 479.

What constitutes "series of acts or transactions" for purposes of Rule 8(b) of Federal Rules of Criminal Procedure, providing for joinder of defendants who are alleged to have participated in same series of acts or transactions.

> Following the explanatory notes and various references to related sources, annotations ("Interpretive Notes and Decisions") of cases are set forth that have interpreted the rule.

Texts:

Cook, Constitutional Rights of the Accused: Pretrial Rights.
Orfield, Criminal Procedure Under the Federal Rules.

Law Review Articles:

Procedure. 18 Litig 5, Spring 1992.

➤ INTERPRETIVE NOTES AND DECISIONS

1. Generally
2. Constitutionality
3. Relationship with other rules
4. —FRCrP 8
5. —FRCrP 14
6. Discretion of court
7. Offenses that could have been joined
8. —Prejudice
9. —Same or similar acts
10. —Connected acts or transactions
11. —Conspiracy and substantive offenses
12. —Separate offenses
13. —Consent of defendant
14. Defendants that could have been joined
15. —Same offense
16. —Common scheme
17. —Conspiracy and substantive offenses
18. Judgment and sentence
19. Appeal and review
20. —Harmless error

1. Generally

Indictments that are consolidated become, in legal effect, separate counts of one indictment. Dunaway v United States (1953) 92 US App DC 299, 205 F2d 23.

Identity of parties in both indictments is not prerequisite to consolidation. United States v Samuel Dunkel & Co. (1950, CA2 NY) 184 F2d 894, cert den (1951) 340 US 930, 95 L Ed 671, 71 S Ct 401.

Rule 13 is designed to promote economy and efficiency and to avoid multiplicity of trials where this can be achieved without substantial prejudice to

rights of defendants to fair trial. Daley v United States (1956, CA1 Mass) 231 F2d 123, 56-1 USTC ¶ 9405, 49 AFTR 392, cert den (1956) 351 US 964, 100 L Ed 1484, 76 S Ct 1028.

2. Constitutionality

Trial of defendant before one jury upon indictment for unlawful sale of narcotics in which 11 separate offenses are charged is not denial of due process of law. Brandenburg v Steele (1949, CA8 Mo) 177 F2d 279.

Joint trial of defendants charged with conspiracy does not violate standards of due process. United States v Keine (1971, CA10 Colo) 436 F2d 850, cert den (1971) 402 US 930, 28 L Ed 2d 864, 91 S Ct 1531.

3. Relationship with other rules

Where joinder of offenses is improper under Rules 8 and 13, relief from joinder should be granted under Rule 14 and failure to do so is not harmless error under Rule 52. United States v Graci (1974, CA3 Pa) 504 F2d 411.

Unless indictment has been transferred under Rule 21, court may not order indictment pending in another district consolidated with case pending in court's district. United States v Sklaroff (1971, SD Fla) 323 F Supp 296.

4. —FRCrP 8

Consolidation, on government's motion, of 3 separate indictments against 1 defendant, being of same or similar character is permissible under language of

619

[Illustration 12–3]

PAGE FROM U.S.C.A. TITLE 18 APPENDIX CONTAINING RULE 13, FEDERAL RULES OF CRIMINAL PROCEDURE

Rule 12.4   **RULES OF CRIMINAL PROCEDURE**

Research References

Forms

5 West's Federal Forms § 7502, Disclosure of Corporate Interests; Certif...

Like the set shown in Illustrations 12–1 and 12–2, this set sets forth the rule and then provides references to related sources of the publisher, as well as to various secondary sources.

WESTLAW ELECTRONIC RESEARCH

See Westlaw guide following the Explanation pages of this volume.

Notes of Decisions

Organizational victims   1

———

1. Organizational victims

Government's failure to disclose information regarding the organizational victims, under plain error standard of review, did not affect defendant's substantial rights in prosecution for passing counterfeit checks, where district judge had notice of organizational victims without disclosure statement since they were identified in superceding indictment. U.S. v. Henderson, C.A.8 (Mo.) 2006, 440 F.3d 453, rehearing and rehearing en banc denied, certiorari denied 127 S.Ct. 270, 166 L.Ed.2d 208. Criminal Law ☞ 1035(2)

Rule 13.   Joint Trial of Separate Cases

The court may order that separate cases be tried together as though brought in a single indictment or information if all offenses and all defendants could have been joined in a single indictment or information.

(As amended Apr. 29, 2002, eff. Dec. 1, 2002.)

ADVISORY COMMITTEE NOTES

1944 Adoption

This rule is substantially a restatement of existing law 18 U.S.C. § 557 (Indictments and presentments; joinder of charges); *Logan v. United States*, 144 U.S. 263, 296, 12 S.Ct. 617, 36 L.Ed. 429; *Showalter v. United States*, 4 Cir., 260 F. 719 certiorari denied, 250 U.S. 672, 40 S.Ct. 14, 63 L.Ed. 1200; *Hostetter v. United States*, 8 Cir., 16 F.2d 921; *Capone v. United States*, 7 Cir., 51 F.2d 609, 619, 620, C.C.A.7th.

2002 Amendments

The language of Rule 13 has been amended as part of the general restyling of the Criminal Rules to make them more easily understood and to make style and terminology consistent throughout the rules. These changes are intended to be stylistic only.

LIBRARY REFERENCES

American Digest System

Criminal Law ☞ 620, 622.
Key Number System Topic No. 110.

Corpus Juris Secundum

CJS Criminal Law § 803, Consolidation of Trials of Multiple Defendants Separately Charged.

608

[Illustration 12–4]

PAGE OF ANNOTATIONS FOR RULE 13 FROM U.S.C.A. TITLE 18 APPENDIX, FEDERAL RULES OF CRIMINAL PROCEDURE

Rule 13   **RULES OF CRIMINAL PROCEDURE**

Federal Procedure, Lawyers Edition § 22:1083, Relief from Prejudicial Joinder under Fed. R. Crim. P. 14(a).

Federal Procedure, Lawyers Edition § 22:2210, Consolidation Order under Fed. R. Crim. P. 13.

1A Wright & Miller: Federal Prac. & Proc. § 212, Several Offenses.

16A Wright & Miller: Federal Prac. & Proc. App. A, Orders of the Supreme Court of the United States Adopting and Amending the Appellate Rules.

19A Wright & Miller: Federal Prac. & Proc. App SUPR. CT. ORDERS, Orders of the Supreme Court of the United States Adopting and Amending Rules.

WESTLAW ELECTRONIC RESEARCH

See Westlaw guide following the Explanation pages of this volume.

Notes of Decisions

Generally 1

Abuse of discretion, discretion of court 8

Conspiracy and substantive offenses 10-14

     Generally 10

     Drug offenses 11

     Fraud 12

     Miscellaneous offenses 14

     Transportation in interstate commerce 13

L.Ed.2d 819. Criminal Law ⟐ 622.7(2); Criminal Law ⟐ 622.7(5)

Test as to whether separately indicted defendants may be jointly tried is whether they could have been jointly indicted. King v. U.S., C.A.1 (Mass.) 1966, 355 F.2d 700. Criminal Law ⟐ 622.6(1)

Single joint trial of several defendants may not be had at expense of defendant's right to fundamentally fair trial. U.S. v.

> Annotations ("Notes of Decisions") of cases interpreting the rule are set forth after explanatory notes, various references to related sources, and the outline of the "Notes of Decisions."

Drug offenses, conspiracy and substantive offenses 11

Duty of court 6

Fraud, conspiracy and substantive offenses 12

Identity of parties 17

Miscellaneous offenses, conspiracy and substantive offenses 14

Nature of consolidation process 4

Power of court 5

Purpose 3

Same or connected transactions 16

Similarity of consolidated charges 15

Time for motion 19

Transportation in interstate commerce, conspiracy and substantive offenses 13

Use of evidence against codefendant 18

Waiver 20

---

1. Generally

There is substantial public interest in joint trial of persons charged with committing same offense or with being accessory to its commission. U.S. v. Camacho, C.A.9 (Ariz.) 1976, 528 F.2d 464, certiorari denied 96 S.Ct. 2208, 425 U.S. 995, 48

N.D.III.1990, 754 F.Supp. 1101, enforcement granted in part, set aside in part 754 F.Supp. 1197, vacated in part on reconsideration 754 F.Supp. 1206, clarified 764 F.Supp. 1248, reconsideration denied 764 F.Supp. 1252. Criminal Law ⟐ 622.6(2)

Law generally favors joint trial for reasons of judicial economy and presentation of the whole of an alleged illegal operation at one time. U.S. v. Mandel, D.C.Md.1976, 415 F.Supp. 1033. Criminal Law ⟐ 620(1)

2. Construction with other rules

This rule has no relation to rule 8(a) of these rules providing that more than one offense may be included in one indictment, nor does phrase "single indictment" in this rule mean one sentence, or change effect of being indicted for three separate crimes whether in one indictment or separately. U.S. v. Koury, C.A.6 (Ohio) 1963, 319 F.2d 75.

This rule must be read with rule 8(b) of these rules authorizing two or more defendants to be charged in the same information, if they allegedly participated in

[Illustration 12-5]

PAGE FROM C. WRIGHT & A. MILLER, FEDERAL PRACTICE AND PROCEDURE, CONTAINING RULE 13, FEDERAL RULES OF CRIMINAL PROCEDURE

RULE 13. TRIAL TOGETHER OF INDICTMENTS OR INFORMATIONS

§ 215 History and Purpose of the Rule
§ 216 Trying Indictments or Informations Together

Text of Rule 13

The court may order that separate cases be tried together as though brought in a single indictment or information if all offenses and all defendants could have been joined in a single indictment or information.

As amended Apr. 29, 2002, eff. Dec. 1, 2002.

ADVISORY COMMITTEE NOTES

The Advisory Committee Notes to this rule and its amendments are set out in Appendix C of Volume 3C.

§ 215. History and Purpose of the Rule

Rule 13 was part of the original criminal rules, and at the time of adoption it reflected a restatement of existing law.[1] The pre-rules statute that governed this topic, which went back to 1853, permitted the joinder of charges in an indictment and the consolidation of indictments for trial.[2] The original drafters avoided using the term "consolidation" in the Rule as had been used in the statute, hoping to avoid any technical or ambiguous meanings connected with the words "consolidated" and "consolidation."[3] The phrase "tried together" is used instead, although courts continue to use

---

[Section 215]

[1] **Restatement of existing law**

[2] **Prior statute**

The statute, formerly 18 U.S.C.A. § 557 and now repealed,

295–296, 36 L.Ed. 429.

See generally Lester B. Orfield, Consolidation in Federal Criminal Procedure, 1961, 40 Or.L.Rev. 318.

provided: "When there are several charges against any person for the same act or transaction, or for two or more acts or transactions con-

whole may be joined in one indictment in separate counts; and if two or more indictments are found in such cases, the court may order them to be consolidated."

[3] **Term consolidation avoided**

Page from C. Wright & A. Miller, *Federal Practice and Procedure*, setting forth the text of the rule. Thereafter, the authors present commentary regarding the rule. Other treatises on the federal rules often do likewise.

554

[Illustration 12–6]

PAGE FROM FEDERAL LOCAL COURT RULES (FLORIDA)

FLORIDA (ND)   **Loc. R. 77.2**

magistrate judge conduct any or all proceedings in the case and order the entry of a final judgment. The notice shall state that the parties are free to withhold their consent without adverse substantive consequences.

(2) *Execution of Consent.* Any party who consents to trial of any or all of the civil case by a magistrate judge must execute a consent form and return it to the office of the clerk of the court within forty-five (45) days of the date of service of the notice. The form shall not be returned if the party does not consent. No magistrate judge, district judge, or other court official may attempt to coerce any party to consent to the reference of any matter to

> **Rule 77.1 of the Federal District Court, Northern District of Florida, pertains to television in the courtroom. The rules for each federal district court are contained in this set. When rules for a particular court are amended or added, the publisher supplies a new set of up-to-date rules for that court.**

shall be referred to the full-time magistrate judge assigned to the case, and notice thereof shall be made a part of the file, with copies furnished to the parties.

(B) Misdemeanor Cases.

(1) If the defendant consents to disposition of a misdemeanor or petty offense case by a magistrate judge or if consent is not required pursuant to 28 U.S.C. § 636(a), the magistrate judge shall proceed as provided in Fed. R. Crim. P. 58. If the defendant does not consent to disposition of the case by a magistrate judge in cases requiring such consent, the magistrate judge shall:

(a) If the prosecution is on a complaint charging a misdemeanor other than a petty offense, proceed as provided in Fed. R. Crim. P. 5(c) and 5.1.

(b) In all other cases, order the defendant to appear before a district judge for further proceedings on notice, fix appropriate conditions of release under 18 U.S.C. § 3142, and appoint counsel for eligible defendants under 18 U.S.C. § 3006A.

Adopted effective April 1, 1995. Amended effective October 1, 1999; July 15, 2005.

RULE 77.1 PHOTOGRAPHS; BROADCASTING OR TELEVISING

Except as provided in N.D. Fla. Loc. R. 77.2, the taking of photographs or the broadcasting or televising of judicial proceedings is prohibited, except that a judge may authorize:

(A) the use of electronic or photographic means for the presentation of evidence or for the perpetuation of a record; and

(B) the broadcasting, televising, recording, or photographing of investiture, ceremonial, naturalization, or other special proceedings.

In order to facilitate the enforcement of this rule, no photographic, broadcasting, television, sound or recording equipment of any kind, except that of court personnel or other employees of the United States on official business in the building, will be permitted in any part of any building where federal judicial proceedings of any kind are usually conducted or upon the exterior grounds thereof, unless such is done with the approval of one of the judges of this court.

Adopted effective April 1, 1995.

RULE 77.2 VIDEO OR TELEPHONE TRANSMISSIONS IN CIVIL CASES

(A) Hearings and Conferences. In the discretion of the judicial officer, conferences and hearings, including evidentiary hearings, may be held in civil cases by means of video or telephonic transmission from remote locations.

27

Chapter 13

ADMINISTRATIVE LAW*

This chapter explains the manner in which the rules, regulations, and adjudications of federal administrative agencies are published and the means of locating these materials. The chapter also discusses presidential documents and state administrative materials.

A. INTRODUCTION: FEDERAL ADMINISTRATIVE REGULATIONS AND DECISIONS

Administrative law has been defined as:

[T]he law concerning the powers and procedures of administrative agencies, including especially the law governing judicial review of administrative action. An administrative agency is a governmental authority, other than a court and other than a legislative body, which affects the rights of private parties through either adjudication, rulemaking, investigating, prosecuting, negotiating, settling, or informally acting. An administrative agency may be called a commission, board, authority, bureau, office, officer, administrator, department, corporation, administration, division, or agency.[1]

The power to issue regulations[2] and to adjudicate disputes is delegated to administrative bodies by Congress.[3] The increasing complexity of American society, especially industry and government, brought about a tremendous increase in the number of administrative agencies and the number of publications produced by them. "Federal agencies adjudicate far more disputes involving individual rights than do the federal courts. They create more binding rules of conduct than Congress. Agencies also administer in the broadest sense of that word. They investigate, enforce, cajole, politicize, spend, hire, fire, contract, collect information, and disseminate information."[4]

Ordinarily, Congress delegates to an administrative office or agency the power to issue rules and regulations; some offices and agencies are also delegated the power to

---

* This chapter was revised by Keith Ann Stiverson, Director of the Library, ITT Chicago–Kent College of Law.

[1] KENNETH CULP DAVIS, ADMINISTRATIVE LAW AND GOVERNMENT 6 (2d ed. 1975).

[2] Procedures that affect the rulemaking process and recent developments in rulemaking are explained in JEFFREY S. LUBBERS, A GUIDE TO FEDERAL AGENCY RULEMAKING (5th ed. 2012).

[3] For a discussion of congressional authority to delegate legislative power to agencies, see 1 JACOB A. STEIN ET AL., ADMINISTRATIVE LAW § 3.03 (LexisNexis). State and local governments also have administrative agencies, with their own regulations and adjudications. This chapter focuses on federal administrative agencies, but the state systems are similar.

[4] 1 RICHARD J. PIERCE, JR., ADMINISTRATIVE LAW TREATISE 2 (5th ed. 2010). For a recent study of the federal administrative system, see DAVID E. LEWIS & JENNIFER L. SELIN, ADMIN. CONF. OF THE UNITED STATES, SOURCEBOOK OF UNITED STATES EXECUTIVE AGENCIES 15 (2012), http://www.acus.gov/publication/sourcebook-united-states-executive-agencies.

hear and settle disputes arising under particular statutes. Some can enforce rules or adjudications, for example through fines, and have other powers. For instance, the National Labor Relations Board (NLRB) not only promulgates regulations, but is also authorized to adjudicate disputes between management and labor unions; the results of its adjudications are published in a format similar to court reports. The NLRB can also determine labor union representation questions and a host of related matters.

All federal administrative regulations are issued under authority delegated to the agency by a federal statute or by authority of a Presidential Executive Order.

Federal agencies may issue: rules and regulations; orders; licenses; advisory opinions; decisions; and guidance documents. A brief description of each follows:

1. Rules and regulations. Rules and regulations (the terms are often used interchangeably) are statements of general or particular applicability made by an agency and are designed to implement, interpret, or prescribe law or policy. Rules and regulations that were properly promulgated have the same practical legal effect as statutes.

2. Orders. An order describes the final disposition of an agency matter (other than rulemaking, but including licensing).

3. Licenses. Licenses include permits, certificates, or other forms of permission.

4. Advisory opinions. Advisory opinions contain agency advice regarding contemplated action; these opinions are not binding and serve only as authoritative interpretations of statutes and regulations.

5. Decisions. Quite a few federal agencies are empowered to adjudicate controversies arising out of the application of statutes and administrative rules and regulations. The results of these adjudications are issued as decisions of the agencies. Special boards of review, hearing examiners, or other officers perform the adjudication function.

6. Guidance documents explain an agency's interpretation of the law or approach to enforcement. They are not binding and yet shape the actions of regulated individuals and industries. Some agencies use this type of material extensively. For example, "the Centers for Medicare and Medicaid Services claims that it issues thousands of new or revised guidance documents annually, with 'perhaps most' of the 37,000 documents on its website constituting guidance documents."[5]

Federal agencies also act in many other ways in performing their missions. Consider these examples from just a fraction of federal agencies: the Food and Drug Administration informs professionals and the public about potentially dangerous medical devices; the Environmental Protection Agency investigates polluters; the Social Security Administration sends out checks to retirees; the Centers for Disease Control and Prevention monitors disease outbreaks; the Department of Veterans Affairs administers a network of hospitals; and the National Park Service manages the nation's parks. Legal researchers sometimes focus on agencies' production of documents with

---

[5] Jessica Mantel, *Procedural Safeguards for Agency Guidance: A Source of Legitimacy for the Administrative State*, 61 ADMIN. L. REV. 343, 353–54 (2009) (footnotes omitted). For more on guidance documents, see Mary Whisner, *Some Guidance About Federal Agencies and Guidance*, 105 LAW LIBR. J. 385, 389–94 (2013).

legal effect—notably regulations and decisions—but it is worth remembering that the administrative state includes activities as diverse as collecting taxes (Internal Revenue Service) and rescuing sailors from sinking vessels (Coast Guard). For information about the work of federal agencies, see the *United States Government Manual*, discussed in Section G-1.

B. HISTORICAL BACKGROUND: PUBLICATION OF FEDERAL REGULATIONS

Before 1936, no official source for publication of rules and regulations of federal agencies existed; nor, indeed, were such agencies required to make their rules and regulations available to the public. Accordingly, there was no easy way to determine if any proposed action was prohibited by a federal agency. In fact, in one well-known instance, a case, *Panama Refining Co. v. Ryan*,[6] reached the Supreme Court of the United States before the Attorney General realized that the action was based on a regulation that had been revoked prior to the time the original action had begun.[7]

In 1935, as a result of the *Panama Refining* case, Congress passed the Federal Register Act,[8] providing for the publication of the *Federal Register*. The *Federal Register* was first published in 1936. Any administrative rule or regulation that has general applicability and legal effect must be published in the *Federal Register*. The definition of a document that has "general applicability and legal effect" is:

> . . . [A]ny document issued under proper authority prescribing a penalty or course of conduct, conferring a right, privilege, authority, or immunity, or imposing an obligation, and relevant or applicable to the general public, members of a class, or persons in a locality, as distinguished from named individuals or organizations. . . .[9]

As a consequence, since 1936 the *Federal Register* has published, in chronological order, every regulation having general applicability and legal effect, and amendments thereto, promulgated by federal agencies that are authorized by Congress or the president to issue rules and regulations.[10]

Had the *Federal Register* continued year after year with no subject access, the ability to locate regulations would have been compromised and researchers would not have been much better off than they were before the *Panama Refining* case. Fortunately, in 1937, Congress amended the Federal Register Act[11] and provided for a systematic method to codify and provide subject access to these regulations. The *Code of Federal Regulations (C.F.R.)*, first published in 1938, bears the same relationship to the *Federal*

---

[6] Panama Refining Co. v. Ryan, 293 U.S. 388 (1935).

[7] *See* Note, *The Federal Register and the Code of Federal Regulations—A Reappraisal*, 80 HARV. L. REV. 439 (1966).

[8] Ch. 417, 49 Stat. 500 (1935) (codified as amended at 44 U.S.C. §§ 1501–1511).

[9] 1 C.F.R. § 1.1 (2011). It is often difficult to determine precisely which documents the government is required to publish in the *Federal Register*. For a discussion of this problem, see Randy S. Springer, Note, *Gatekeeping and the Federal Register: An Analysis of the Publication Requirement of Section 552(a)(1)(D) of the Administrative Procedure Act*, 41 ADMIN. L. REV. 533 (1989).

[10] For an entertaining (but informative) video introducing the *Federal Register*, see William Cuthbertson, *What Is the Federal Register?*, YOUTUBE (July 23, 2013), http://www.youtube.com/watch?v=jDIUrEmaDFE&list=PL335DAD254DA3A769.

[11] Ch. 369, 50 Stat. 304 (1937) (codified as amended at 44 U.S.C. § 1510 (2012)).

Register as the *United States Code* bears to *United States Statutes at Large*. Over the years, it has been published at different intervals and in different formats, but since 1968 the *C.F.R.* has been published annually, in quarterly installments.

Despite the fact that by 1937 a regular vehicle existed for the publication and compilation of agency rules and regulations, the process and procedures of agency rulemaking remained an enigma to the public. In 1946, Congress addressed this situation by passing the Administrative Procedure Act,[12] which granted the public the right to participate in the rulemaking process by requiring agencies to publish notice of their proposed rulemaking in the *Federal Register* and by giving the public the opportunity to comment on proposed regulations.

Subsequently, three additional laws were enacted to enhance the public's access to agency information. The Freedom of Information Act of 1966[13] requires that agencies publish in the *Federal Register* (1) descriptions of their organizations, including those agency employees from whom the public may obtain information; (2) rules of procedure and general applicability; and (3) policy statements and interpretations. The Government in the Sunshine Act of 1976[14] requires agencies to publish notices of most meetings in the *Federal Register*.

In 1980, Congress passed the Regulatory Flexibility Act,[15] which dictates that agencies publish in the *Federal Register*, each October and April, an agenda (known as a regulatory flexibility agenda or, more commonly, regulatory agenda or unified agenda), briefly detailing (1) the subject of any rule that the agency expects to propose or promulgate that would have a significant economic impact on a substantial number of small entities; (2) a summary of the rules being considered, their objectives, the legal basis for issuance; and (3) the name and telephone number of an agency official knowledgeable about the rule. *Regulations.gov* has a convenient list with links to each agency's regulatory agendas since fall 2007.[16]

C. SOURCES OF FEDERAL REGULATIONS

1. The *Federal Register*[17]

The *Federal Register* is published Monday through Friday (except on federal holidays), and its contents are required to be judicially noticed.[18] All issues in a given year constitute a single volume with consecutive pagination throughout the year. In recent years, most volumes of the *Federal Register* have exceeded 70,000 pages (the 2010 volume was more than 80,000 pages). In addition to chronologically published rules and regulations of federal agencies [Illustration 13–9], issues of the *Federal Register* contain the following features:

---

[12] Ch. 324, 60 Stat. 237 (1946) (codified as amended in scattered sections of 5 U.S.C.).

[13] Pub. L. No. 89–487, 80 Stat. 250 (1966) (codified as amended at 5 U.S.C. § 552 (2012)).

[14] Pub. L. No. 94–409, 90 Stat. 1241 (1976) (codified as amended at 5 U.S.C. §§ 551–552, 556–557; 5 U.S.C. app. § 10; 39 U.S.C. § 410 (2012)).

[15] Pub. L. No. 96–354, 94 Stat. 1164 (1980) (codified as amended at 5 U.S.C. §§ 601–612 (2012)).

[16] http://resources.regulations.gov/public/component/main?main=UnifiedAgenda.

[17] Additional information is provided in OFFICE OF THE FEDERAL REGISTER, THE FEDERAL REGISTER: WHAT IT IS AND HOW TO USE IT (1992); an online tutorial is at http://www.archives.gov/federal-register/tutorial.

[18] 44 U.S.C. § 1507 (2012).

     a.   Contents. At the front of each issue is a table of contents in which agencies are listed alphabetically. Under the name of each agency, the documents appearing in that issue are arranged by category, and page numbers are provided.

     b.   C.F.R. Parts Affected in This Issue. Discussed in Section E-1-b, below.

     c.   Presidential Documents. Discussed in Section H, below.

     d.   Proposed Rules. This section contains notices of proposed rules and regulations. Its purpose is to give interested persons an opportunity to participate in the rulemaking process prior to the adoption of final rules.

     e.   Notices. This section of the *Federal Register* contains documents other than rules or proposed rules that are of interest to the public, e.g., grant application deadlines and the filing of petitions and applications. Since 1996, notices of meetings, required by the Government in the Sunshine Act, are included in this section. Before 1996, those notices appeared in a separate section entitled "Sunshine Act Meetings."

     f.   Unified Agenda of Federal Regulations. See Section B, above.

     g.   Reader Aids. This section appears at the end of the *Federal Register* and lists telephone numbers for information and assistance, online resources, a parallel table of *Federal Register* pages for the month, a cumulative table of *C.F.R.* parts affected during the month, and a List of Public Laws, setting forth those bills from the current session of Congress that have recently become law. The Monday issue contains a C.F.R. Checklist of the current *C.F.R.* parts.

     h.   Special Sections. To accommodate the duplication and distribution needs of issuing agencies, some agency documents are published in separate sections near the end of each issue, rather than in the appropriate sections.

     i.   Electronic Access. In addition to the print and microfiche copies available from the federal government, an online version of the *Federal Register* on *FDsys* is published by authority of the Administrative Committee of the Federal Register. The electronic version is updated by 6:00 a.m. each day that the *Federal Register* is published, and includes both the text and graphics from Volume 59, Number 1 (January 2, 1994), to the present.[19] See also Subsection 4, below.

2.   The *Code of Federal Regulations* (C.F.R.)[20]

     The *Code of Federal Regulations* is the codification of the rules and regulations first published in the *Federal Register*, with all regulations and amendments that are currently in force brought together by subject. The *C.F.R.* is *prima facie* evidence of the text of the documents[21] and consists of fifty titles (similar, but not identical, to the arrangement of the *United States Code*). Titles are subdivided into chapters, subchapters, parts, and sections. Citation is by title and section, e.g., 42 C.F.R. § 405.501. [Illustrations 13–3 and 13–4] Each year, the volumes of *C.F.R.* are issued in a binding color different from the previous year's, making it easier to spot the current year on the shelf. The titles are updated on a quarterly basis according to the following schedule:

---

     [19] http://www.gpo.gov/fdsys/browse/collection.action?collectionCode=FR.

     [20] For a detailed history of the publication of the earlier editions of the *Code of Federal Regulations*, see ERVIN H. POLLACK, FUNDAMENTALS OF LEGAL RESEARCH 366–72 (3d ed. 1967).

     [21] 44 U.S.C. § 1510(e) (2012).

Title 1 through Title 16, as of January 1

Title 17 through Title 27, as of April 1

Title 28 through Title 41, as of July 1

Title 42 through Title 50, as of October 1

Therefore, at most times during the year, the "current" C.F.R. is a combination of volumes in this year's color and last year's color.

Each new volume contains the text of regulations then in force, incorporating those promulgated during the preceding twelve months, and deleting those that have been revoked. All regulations first published in the *Federal Register* and currently in force are rearranged by subject and agency in the fifty titles of the *C.F.R.* For example, the regulations issued by the Federal Communications Commission, and still in force, are in Title 47 and are updated through October 1.

In early 2007, West began publishing an unofficial but annotated version of certain volumes of the *C.F.R.* entitled *West's Code of Federal Regulations Annotated*, which supplements the text of the regulations with case summaries and other materials.

3.   Topical Services

Topical services, discussed in Chapter 14, may contain documents published in the *Federal Register* and the *Code of Federal Regulations*. These services often contain better indexes than the corresponding print government publications and have other features that are helpful to the researcher.

Consequently, when it is necessary to research administrative law, one approach is to determine whether a topical service covers the subject area being researched and to use that service as a starting point. Within the past few years, a number of specialized topical services have been published as online, web-based products, saving the expense of labor-intensive filing and presumably enabling the publisher to update the materials more easily. The topical approach, whether print or electronic, can be especially helpful in regulation-intensive areas of the law.

4.   Electronic Sources

The following sources provide federal regulations:

a.   The Government Printing Office's *FDsys* site includes the *Federal Register* in both authenticated PDF and text versions, 1994–present.[22] It has the annual edition of the *C.F.R.*, also in both authenticated PDF and text versions, 1996–present.[23] The *e-C.F.R.* is a current but unofficial edition of the *C.F.R.*; it is at www.ecfr.gov.

b.   *Bloomberg Law* includes the full run of the *Federal Register* (March 14, 1936–present) (with page images) and the current *C.F.R.*

c.   *HeinOnline* includes scanned PDF images of the *Federal Register* from 1936 to the present, and the *Code of Federal Regulations* from 1938 to the present (1992–1997 currently includes only Title 37). *HeinOnline* also includes presidential material.

---

[22] http://www.gpo.gov/fdsys/browse/collection.action?collectionCode=FR.

[23] http://www.gpo.gov/fdsys/browse/collectionCfr.action?collectionCode=CFR.

HeinOnline posts these documents to its site soon after they appear on the *FDsys* website.

  d. *LexisNexis* includes the *Federal Register* from July 1, 1980, to the present; it has the *Code of Federal Regulations* from 1981 to the present. The *C.F.R.* and *Federal Register* can be searched in a combined file.

  e. *ProQuest Congressional*, a separate database of legislative and regulatory information, includes the *Federal Register* from 1980 to the present and the *Code of Federal Regulations* from 1981 to the present.

  f. *Westlaw* includes the *Federal Register* from its beginning. The FR-OLD database includes 1936–1979; the FR database has 1980 to the present. *Westlaw* includes the current *C.F.R.* and archived versions back to 1984. *Westlaw's RegulationsPlus* enhances regulatory research by pulling together prior and current versions of regulatory information as well as annotations created by *Westlaw* editors.

  g. Other databases, such as *Loislaw* and *Fastcase*, also include the *Federal Register* and the *C.F.R.*

5. Other Sources

  Selected regulations are also published in the monthly pamphlet supplements to the *United States Code Congressional and Administrative News* (Thomson Reuters) and in the *United States Code Service, Advance Service* (LexisNexis).

D. FINDING FEDERAL REGULATIONS

  Because the *Federal Register* and the *Code of Federal Regulations* are the official sources for federal agency regulations, their use will be emphasized in this discussion over unofficial sources of federal regulations.

  Whether research is begun in the *Federal Register* or the *Code of Federal Regulations* depends upon the date of the regulation in question. If the regulation was issued recently, that is, later than the scope of coverage of the appropriate *Code of Federal Regulations* volume, research should begin in the *Federal Register*. If, however, the regulation was not recently enacted or amended or if the date of the amendment's enactment is not known, the starting point should be the *Code of Federal Regulations*. These two sources are accessed differently.

  It is useful to find the regulation in the *Federal Register* because for final rules of any economic significance, that is where the agency is required to explain that it considered alternatives to the rule and provide other relevant information. This analysis often discusses in great detail how the rule will be applied. Similarly, for proposed rules, the agency may include a discussion of why a rule is needed along with the proposed text. This discussion usually is more helpful than the text itself in understanding the rule.

1. Access to the *Federal Register*

  a. *Full-text searching.* Searching the full text of the *Federal Register*, using the sources listed above, is often the easiest way to find regulations. In searching, consider using agency names (if the agency is known) as well as keywords.

  b. *Federal Register Index.* This official index, a slim volume arranged alphabetically by agency, is issued every month. Each issue of the *Federal Register Index* cumulates that year's previous monthly indexes, and the December issue is the final index of the year. Because an issue of the *Index* is not distributed until several weeks after the month it covers, the contents of each issue of the *Federal Register* published after the last monthly *Index* must also be consulted. The *Index* and contents are not very detailed; at times, it may be difficult to find a regulation if one does not know the issuing agency.[24]

2. Access to the *Code of Federal Regulations*

 a. *Full-text searching.* Searching the full text of the *C.F.R.*, using the sources listed above, is often the easiest way to find regulations. In searching, consider using agency names (if the agency is known) as well as keywords.

 b. *Agency websites.* If the agency is known, quick access to the regulations is often found on its website.

 c. *C.F.R. Index and Finding Aids.* This single volume accompanies the *C.F.R.* and is revised annually.[25] It provides several access points to the *C.F.R.*

 (1) *Index.* This alphabetical index includes entries for both subjects and agency names. The subject terms used in the index are taken from the thesaurus developed by the Office of the Federal Register.[26] Use of this thesaurus ensures that, although different agencies may use different terms to describe the same concept, references to all of those terms will be gathered together under one subject heading. For example, one agency may use the word *compensation* in its regulations, while another might use *pay,* and yet a third, *salaries.* By using the thesaurus, references to all three of these regulations will appear in the index under the subject heading *Wages.*

 The *Index* provides references to the appropriate title of the *C.F.R.* and to the specific part within the title, but not to specific sections. [Illustration 13–1]

 (2) *Parallel Table of Authorities and Rules.* This table lists rulemaking authority for regulations codified in the *C.F.R.* [Illustration 13–2] If the researcher knows the citation to the law or presidential document that authorized the issuance of regulations, then using this table will lead to the relevant *C.F.R.* sections. The table also includes statutory citations which are noted as being interpreted or applied by regulations codified in the *C.F.R.* The citations are divided into four segments: *U.S.C.*, by title and section; *U.S. Statutes at Large*, by volume and page number; public law, by number; and presidential documents, by document number. Within each segment, citations are arranged in numerical order.

 (3) *List of Agency-Prepared Indexes Appearing in Individual C.F.R. Volumes.* This list enables the researcher to locate agency-prepared (and therefore, presumably more extensive) indexes published in various volumes of the *C.F.R.*

---

[24] The *CIS Federal Register Index*, published 1984–1998, provided comprehensive coverage for all issues of the *Federal Register*. It may remain useful for historical research.

[25] LexisNexis publishes the C.F.R. INDEX AND FINDING AIDS volume as a supplement to the UNITED STATES CODE SERVICE.

[26] The thesaurus is available online at http://www.archives.gov/federal-register/cfr/thesaurus.html.

3. Regulations No Longer in Force

It is often necessary to determine the regulations that were in force as of a particular date. If prior editions of the *C.F.R.* are available, one may simply consult the edition that was current on the appropriate date. Many libraries keep superseded editions of *C.F.R.* in print copy or in microform—and, as noted in Section C-4, above, several online sources include past editions.

One might also begin by locating the applicable subject matter in the current edition of *C.F.R.* Each *C.F.R.* section sets forth the date and *Federal Register* citation for the adoption of that section, and the same information for each subsequent amendment of that section. Researchers may therefore determine whether the present language of the section was in effect at the applicable time and may find the original language in the *Federal Register* if the section has been amended.

The following official publications also provide *C.F.R.* citations that allow one to find the precise text of regulations that were in force on any given date during the years covered. There are four separate compilations thus far: *Code of Federal Regulations List of Sections Affected: 1949–1963; 1964–1972; 1973–1985;* and *1986–2000.*[27] For changes after the last compilation, each volume of the *C.F.R.* contains a *List of C.F.R. Sections Affected* that appears at the end of the volume.

E. UPDATING REGULATIONS

After locating a regulation, further research is necessary to determine whether the regulation has been amended or revoked. If the regulation was amended or revoked or if a new regulation on the topic has been promulgated, the *Federal Register* contains the documentation. The sources described below aid in retrieving citations to the *Federal Register* where changes to regulations are published.

1. Sources

   a. *LSA: List of C.F.R. Sections Affected.*[28] This publication is issued monthly and includes finalized and proposed changes to regulations adopted since the latest publication of the *C.F.R.* The December issue cumulates all changes for Titles 1 through 16; the March issue contains all changes for Titles 17 through 27; the June issue lists changes for Titles 28 thorough 41; and the September issue indicates changes for Titles 42 through 50. [Illustration 13–5] For changes to regulations that have become final, the *LSA* is arranged by *C.F.R.* title and section and sets forth the nature of the changes, e.g., "revised," and provides page number references to the *Federal Register.* [Illustration 13–6] For proposed changes, the *LSA* is arranged by title and part with reference to the applicable *Federal Register* page numbers. [Illustration 13–7] A separate section of the *LSA* updates the *Parallel Table of Authorities and Rules.*

   b. *C.F.R. Parts Affected.* Each issue of the *Federal Register* contains a section near the front that lists *C.F.R. Parts Affected in This Issue.* However, this section is incorporated in the cumulative list in the Reader Aids section. The section in the front

---

[27] Searching by date for regulations no longer in effect in *FDsys* is possible using the "advanced search" function at http://www.gpo.gov/fdsys/search/advanced/advsearchpage.action. The compilations are available in *HeinOnline.*

[28] http://www.gpo.gov/fdsys/browse/collection.action?collectionCode=LSA&browsePath=LSAMONTHLY &isCollapsed=false&leafLevelBrowse=false&ycord=0.

of the *Federal Register* should be consulted if one must review each issue of the *Federal Register* to ascertain if a specific regulation has changed.

Each issue of the *Federal Register* also includes a list of *C.F.R. Parts Affected* in the Reader Aids section. The list is cumulative within the month of publication—e.g., a *Federal Register* issue on May 16 lists all changes from May 1 to May 16. [Illustration 13–10] The lists near the front of the issue and the list in the Reader Aids section give page number references to the *Federal Register*.

     c.   *Converting Page Number References to Specific Issues of the Federal Register.* If a particular regulation has been affected, a reference to the appropriate *Federal Register* is set forth in the *LSA* and/or the list of *C.F.R. Parts Affected*. This reference is to the page number of the *Federal Register* on which the amendment, proposed amendment, or removal appears. To find the issue of the *Federal Register* in which the change appears, use the conversion table in the *Federal Register Index* or the *LSA*, whichever is more current. [Illustration 13–8] If the page number does not appear in the *Index* or *LSA* conversion table, one must turn to the last issue of each month of the *Federal Register* published since the *Index* or the *LSA* and use the conversion tables in the Reader Aids section. [Illustration 13–10]

     d.   *Citators.* Online citators, such as *Shepard's* (*LexisNexis*) or *KeyCite* (*Westlaw*) will indicate federal cases concerning regulations.[29]

     e.   A federal government website, *Regulations.gov*, which became available in 2003, describes its role under the tag line: "Your Voice in Federal Decision-making." The site enables the public to find, view, and comment on federal regulatory actions online. The site purports to be the public's online source for U.S. government regulations from nearly 300 agencies.[30]

2. Research Methodology

The need to update regulations depends on the published source of the regulation in question. Updating in the various databases, including *LexisNexis*, *Westlaw*, and *FDsys*, can be done in a few keystrokes rather than a protracted search for all the print resources. The following steps should be followed if one is working only with print sources:

If the regulation was found in the *C.F.R.*, the researcher should first use the most current *LSA*. It is important to note the publication date on the cover of the *C.F.R.* volume in which the regulation was found to cover the appropriate time period. Because the *LSA* is issued monthly, a further check must be made in the cumulative *List of C.F.R. Parts Affected* in the *Federal Register* for any later changes. Therefore, note the coverage of the *LSA* used, and check the *List of C.F.R. Parts Affected* in the last issue of each subsequent month, including the current month, of the *Federal Register*.

If the regulation was found in the *Federal Register*, and if the latest issue of *LSA* is for a month *later* than the month of the issue of the *Federal Register* in which the regulation appears, first use the *LSA* that covers the period from the date of the issue of the *Federal Register* in which the regulation was found. Because the *LSA* is issued

---

[29] In print, *Shepard's Code of Federal Regulations Citations* performs this function. Citators are discussed in Chapter 15.

[30] http://www.regulations.gov/#!aboutPartners.

monthly, a further check must be made for any later changes in the cumulative list of *C.F.R. Parts Affected* in the *Federal Register*. Therefore, note the coverage of the particular *LSA* used, and check the list of *C.F.R. Parts Affected* in the last issue of each subsequent month, including the current month, of the *Federal Register*.

If the regulation was found in an issue of the *Federal Register* and if the latest *LSA* available is for a month *prior* to the month of the issue of the *Federal Register* in which the regulation appears, check the *List of C.F.R. Parts Affected* in the last issue of the month of the *Federal Register* in which the regulation was found and the *List of C.F.R. Parts Affected* in the last issue of each subsequent month, including the current month, of the *Federal Register*.

If the regulation appears in an issue of the *Federal Register* for the current month, check the *List of C.F.R. Parts Affected* in the last available issue of the current month's *Federal Register* to be as up-to-date as possible.

F. ILLUSTRATIONS: FEDERAL REGISTER AND CODE OF FEDERAL REGULATIONS

Problem: Find regulations pertaining to notice requirements under the labeling proceedings for alcoholic beverages.

13–1.	**Page from C.F.R. Index and Finding Aids volume**
13–2.	**Page from Parallel Table of Authorities and Rules, C.F.R. Index and Finding Aids volume**
13–3 to 13–4.	**Pages from Title 27 of C.F.R.**
13–5.	**Title page from LSA: List of C.F.R. Sections Affected pamphlet**
13–6 to 13–7.	**Pages from LSA: List of C.F.R. Sections Affected pamphlet**
13–8.	**Page from LSA's Table of Federal Register Issue Pages and Dates showing volume 71, Federal Register (2006)**
13–9.	**Page from volume 71, Federal Register**
13–10.	**Page from volume 71, Federal Register–List of C.F.R. Parts Affected**

[Illustration 13-1]

PAGE FROM C.F.R. INDEX AND FINDING AIDS VOLUME

CFR Index   **Alcohol and alcoholic beverages**

Conduct on Pentagon Reservation, 32   Commercial driver's license program,
  CFR 234   State compliance, 49 CFR 384
Drunk and drugged driving, 32 CFR 62b   Commercial driver's license standards,
Drug and alcohol abuse prevention, 34 CFR   requirements and penalties, 49 CFR
  86   383
Energy Department, human reliability   Controlled substances and alcohol use and
  program, 10 CFR 712   testing, 49 CFR 382
Federal and federally assisted alcohol and   Driving of commercial motor vehicles, 49
  drug abuse treatment programs,   CFR 392
  confidentiality of patient records, 42   Longer combination vehicles driver and
  CFR 2   driver instructor qualifications, 49
                                               CFR 301

Step 1:
   To research the problem presented in this section, consult the Index in the *CFR Index
and Finding Aids*. The reference is to Title 27, Part 13. See next illustration.

Pilots, flight instructors, and ground   Homeless Providers Grant and Per Diem
  instructors, 14 CFR 61   Program, 38 CFR 61
Certification and operations, domestic,   Medical benefits, 38 CFR 17
  flag, and supplemental operations,   State homes, grants to States for
  operating requirements, 14 CFR 121   construction or acquisition, 38 CFR
Commuter and on-demand operations and   59
  rules governing persons on board
  such aircraft, operating requirements,   **Alcohol and alcoholic beverages**
  14 CFR 135   *See also* Beer; Gasohol; Liquors; Wine
Federal employees' health and counseling   Alcohol beverage dealers, 27 CFR 31
  programs, 5 CFR 792   Alcohol, tax free distribution and use, 27
Federal Railroad Administration, railroad   CFR 22
  safety, alcohol and drug use control, 49   Alcoholic beverages
  CFR 219   Basic permit requirements under Federal
Federal Transit Administration, alcohol   Alcohol Administration Act, distilled
  misuse and prohibited drug use   spirits and wine nonindustrial use,
  prevention in transit operations, 49 CFR   distilled spirits bulk sales and
  655   bottling, 27 CFR 1
Highway safety programs   Commercial bribery, 27 CFR 10
  Alcohol-impaired driving prevention   Consignment sales, 27 CFR 11
    programs, incentive grant criteria, 23   Exclusive outlets, 27 CFR 8
    CFR 1313   Health warning statement, 27 CFR 16
  Motor vehicles operation—   Labeling proceedings, 27 CFR 13
    Intoxicated minors, 23 CFR 1210   Tied house, 27 CFR 6
    Intoxicated persons, 23 CFR 1225   Armed services military club and package
    Repeat intoxicated driver laws, 23 CFR   stores, 32 CFR 261
      1275   Customs and Border Protection Bureau
  National minimum drinking age, 23 CFR   Air commerce regulations, aircraft liquor
    1208   kits, 19 CFR 122
Marine safety   Drawback on customs duties, 19 CFR 191
  Marine investigation regulations, personnel Denatured alcohol and rum
    action, 46 CFR 5   Distribution and use, 27 CFR 20
  Operating a vessel while intoxicated, 33   Formulas, 27 CFR 21
    CFR 95   Distilled spirits, wine, and beer, imports, 27
Motor carrier safety   CFR 27

67

[Illustration 13-2]

PAGE FROM PARALLEL TABLE OF AUTHORITIES AND RULES, C.F.R. INDEX AND FINDING AIDS VOLUME

CFR Index

26 U.S.C. (1986 I.R.C.)—Continued	CFR
9034	11 Part 9034
9035	11 Part 9035
9036	11 Part 9036
9037	11 Part 9037
9038	11 Parts 201, 9038
9039	11 Parts 201, 9031—9039
9801	26 Part 54
9806	26 Part 54
9833	26 Part 54
27 U.S.C.	
202	27 Parts 6, 8, 10, 11
203—204	27 Part 1
203	27 Parts 26, 251, 252
204	27 Part 71
205	27 Parts 4—13, 16, 26, 179, 197, 251, 252
206	27 Part 1
211	27 Part 1

28 U.S.C.—Continued	CFR
	40 Part 23
	46 Part 502
2343—2344	40 Part 23
2401—2402	32 Part 536
2401 note	49 Part 229
2402	32 Part 842
2412	34 Part 21
2461	14 Part 13
	18 Part 385
	20 Parts 356, 702
	30 Parts 723, 845
	32 Part 269
	46 Part 506
	49 Part 224
2461 note	5 Parts 2634, 2636
	10 Parts 2, 13, 207, 218, 430, 501, 601, 820, 1013, 1017, 1050

Step 1a: An alternative method of finding regulations in the CFR.

There are times when the *U.S.C.* citation to the statute that delegated the authority to issue regulations is known. In such instances, the Parallel Table of Authorities and Rules in the CFR Index and Finding Aids volume can be used to locate citations to regulations in the *CFR*. For example, the statutory authorization for labeling proceedings for alcoholic beverages is found at 27 U.S.C. § 205.

	501, 503, 504, 506, 509—511, 513, 522—524, 527, 540—545, 547—553, 570—572, 600—603, 1216
	48 Part 2819
509	28 Parts 27, 36, 64, 80, 549, 551
510	28 Parts 27, 36, 549, 551
	48 Parts 2801—2810, 2812—2817, 2822, 2824, 2825, 2828—2835, 2845, 2852, 2870
513	32 Part 516
515—519	28 Parts 0, 17, 27
515	28 Parts 600—602
	32 Part 516
515—518	28 Part 9
524	28 Part 9
528	28 Part 45
530B	28 Part 77
534	28 Parts 16, 20
	32 Part 635
534 note	32 Part 637
543	28 Parts 600, 603
	32 Part 516
586	28 Part 58
1346	28 Part 543
	32 Parts 536, 842
1498	10 Part 782
1608	22 Part 93
1733	22 Part 131
1746	8 Part 3
	30 Part 870
	34 Part 690
1784	22 Part 92
1821—1825	28 Part 21
1821	22 Part 713
1823	32 Part 534
2112	5 Part 2429
	21 Parts 10, 12—16
	29 Parts 101, 2200

	594, 595, 597, 598
	33 Parts 27, 326
	34 Part 36
	40 Parts 19, 27
	45 Part 672
	49 Parts 107, 171, 209, 213, 214, 215—216, 217, 218, 220—225, 228, 230-241, 244, 1503
2671—2680	14 Part 1261
	22 Part 511
	28 Part 543
	32 Part 536
	38 Part 14
	39 Part 912
	43 Part 22
2671—2672	32 Part 842
2672	5 Part 177
	10 Parts 14, 1014
	13 Part 114
	14 Part 15
	15 Part 2
	20 Part 429
	22 Part 304
	24 Part 17
	28 Part 14
	29 Parts 15, 100
	31 Part 3
	32 Part 1280
	33 Part 25
	34 Part 35
	40 Part 1620
	45 Part 35
	46 Part 204
	49 Part 1
2674—2680	32 Part 842
2675	14 Part 15
2679	10 Part 14

812

[Illustration 13–3]

PAGE FROM TITLE 27 OF C.F.R.

Pt. 13

Julien, Sancerre, Santenay, Saumur, Savigny or Savigny-les-Beaunes, Tavel, Touraine, Volnay, Vosne-Romanee, Vouvray.

(c) *Italy:* Asti Spumante, Barbaresco, Barbera d'Alba, Barbera d'Asti, Bardolino, Barolo, Brunello di Montalcino, Dolcetto d'Alba, Frascati, Gattinara, Lacryma Christi, Nebbiolo d'Alba, Orvieto, Soave, Valpolicella, Vino Nobile de Montepulciano.

(d) *Portugal:* Dao, Oporto, Porto, or Vinho do Porto.

(e) *Spain:* Lagrima, Rioja.

PART 13—LABELING PROCEEDINGS

Subpart A—Scope and Construction of Regulations

Sec.
13.1   Scope of part.
13.2   Delegations of the Administrator.
13.3   Related regulations.

Subpart B—Definitions

13.11   Meaning of terms.

Subpart C—Applications

13.20   Forms prescribed.
13.21   Application for certificate.
13.22   Withdrawal of applications.
13.23   Notice of denial.
13.25   Appeal of qualification or denial.
13.26   Decision after appeal of qualification or denial.
13.27   Second appeal of qualification or denial.

13.45   Final decision after appeal.

Subpart E—Revocation by Operation of Law or Regulation

13.51   Revocation by operation of law or regulation.
13.52   Notice of revocation.
13.53   Appeal of notice of revocation.
13.54   Decision after appeal.

Subpart F—Miscellaneous

13.61   Publicity of information.
13.62   Third-party comment on certificates.
13.71   Informal conferences.

27 CFR Ch. I (4–1–06 Edition)

13.72   Effective dates of revocations.
13.73   Effect of revocation.
13.74   Surrender of certificates.
13.75   Evidence of receipt by TTB.
13.76   Service on applicant or certificate holder.
13.81   Representation before TTB.
13.91   Computation of time.
13.92   Extensions.

Subpart G—Appeals Concerning Other Agencies' Rules

13.101   Appeals concerning use of the term "organic."

AUTHORITY: 27 U.S.C. 205(e), 26 U.S.C. 5301 and 7805.

SOURCE: T.D. ATF–406, 64 FR 2129, Jan. 13, 1999, unless otherwise noted.

EDITORIAL NOTE: Nomenclature changes to part 13 appear by T.D. ATF–449, 66 FR 19085, Apr. 13, 2001.

Subpart A—Scope and Construction of Regulations

§ 13.1   Scope of part.

The regulations in this part govern the procedure and practice in connection with the issuance, denial, and revocation of certificates of label approval, certificates of exemption from label approval, and distinctive liquor bottle approvals under 27 U.S.C. 205(e) and 26 U.S.C. 5301. The regulations in this part also provide for appeal procedures when applications for label approval, exemptions from label approval, or distinctive liquor bottle approvals are denied. These regulations also cover appeals of certificate revocations and appeals concerning the use of the term "organic" on alcohol beverage labels. See § 13.101.

[T.D. ATF–406, 64 FR 2129, Jan. 13, 1999, as amended by T.D. ATF–483, 67 FR 62858, Oct. 8, 2002]

§ 13.2   Delegations of the Administrator.

The regulatory authorities of the Administrator contained in this part are delegated to appropriate TTB officers. These TTB officers are specified in TTB Order 1135.13, Delegation of the Administrator's Authorities in 27 CFR Part 13, Labeling Proceedings. You

---

Step 2:
  Refer to Title 27, Part 13 of the *CFR* as located using Step 1. After each part, a detailed list of sections is given. In this instance, Section 13.11 is relevant. Note how at the end of Subpart G the statutory authorization is noted. See next illustration for text of Section 13.11.

[Illustration 13–4]

PAGE FROM TITLE 27 OF C.F.R.

Alcohol and Tobacco Tax and Trade Bureau, Treasury §13.11

may obtain a copy of this order by accessing the TTB Web site (*http://www.ttb.gov*) or by mailing a request to the Alcohol and Tobacco Tax and Trade Bureau, National Revenue Center, 550 Main Street, Room 1516, Cincinnati, OH 45202.

[T.D. TTB–44, 71 FR 16924, Apr. 4, 2006]

§13.3 Related regulations.

The following regulations also relate to this part:

7 CFR Part 205—National Organic Program
27 CFR Part 1—Basic Permit Requirements Under the Federal Alcohol Administration Act, Nonindustrial Use of Distilled Spirits and Wine, Bulk Sales and Bottling of Distilled Spirits
27 CFR Part 4—Labeling and Advertising of Wine
27 CFR Part 5—Labeling and Advertising of

Act. The Federal Alcohol Administration Act.

Administrator. The Administrator, Alcohol and Tobacco Tax and Trade Bureau, Department of the Treasury, Washington, DC.

Applicant. The permittee or brewer whose name, address, and basic permit number, or plant registry number, appears on an unapproved Form 5100.31, application for a certificate of label approval, certificate of exemption from label approval, or distinctive liquor bottle approval.

Appropriate TTB officer. An officer or employee of the Alcohol and Tobacco Tax and Trade Bureau (TTB) authorized to perform any functions relating to the administration or enforcement of this part by TTB Order 1135.13, Delegation of the Administrator's Authori-

> **Step 2 cont'd:**
> This shows the text of Section 13.11 as it appears in Title 27 of the *CFR*.

27 CFR Part 16—Alcoholic Beverage Health Warning Statement
27 CFR Part 19—Distilled Spirits Plants
27 CFR Part 24—Wine
27 CFR Part 25—Beer
27 CFR Part 26—Liquors and Articles from Puerto Rico and the Virgin Islands
27 CFR Part 27—Importation of Distilled Spirits, Wines, and Beer
27 CFR Part 28—Exportation of Alcohol
27 CFR Part 71—Rules of Practice in Permit Proceedings

[T.D. ATF–483, 67 FR 62858, Oct. 8, 2002, as amended by T.D. TTB–8, 69 FR 3829, Jan. 27, 2004]

Subpart B—Definitions

§13.11 Meaning of terms.

Where used in this part and in forms prescribed under this part, where not otherwise distinctly expressed or manifestly incompatible with the intent thereof, terms shall have the meaning ascribed in this subpart. Words in the plural form shall include the singular, and vice versa, and words importing the masculine gender shall include the feminine. The terms "include" and "including" do not exclude things not enumerated that are in the same general class.

beer for sale.

Certificate holder. The permittee or brewer whose name, address, and basic permit number, or plant registry number, appears on an approved Form 5100.31, certificate of label approval, certificate of exemption from label approval, or distinctive liquor bottle approval.

Certificate of exemption from label approval. A certificate issued on Form 5100.31 which authorizes the bottling of wine or distilled spirits, under the condition that the product will under no circumstances be sold, offered for sale, shipped, delivered for shipment, or otherwise introduced by the applicant, directly or indirectly, into interstate or foreign commerce.

Certificate of label approval. A certificate issued on Form 5100.31 that authorizes the bottling or packing of wine, distilled spirits, or malt beverages, or the removal of bottled wine, distilled spirits, or malt beverages from customs custody for introduction into commerce, as long as the project bears labels identical to the labels affixed to the face of the certificate, or labels with changes authorized by the certificate.

279

208-103   D-10

[Illustration 13–5]

TITLE PAGE FROM LSA: LIST OF C.F.R. SECTIONS AFFECTED PAMPHLET

Code of Federal Regulations

LSA

List of CFR Sections Affected

November 2006

Title 1–16
Changes January 3, 2006
through November 30, 2006

Title 17–27
Changes April 1, 2006
through November 30, 2006

Title 28–41
Changes July 1, 2006
through November 30, 2006

Title 42–50
Changes October 1, 2006
through November 30, 2006

Step 3:
    Title 27 of the CFR is revised annually as of April 1. Hence, it must be ascertained if any changes have subsequently occurred. This is accomplished by using this list. It is issued monthly, with the December, March, June, and September issues consisting of an annual cumulation as indicated on the title page.

[Illustration 13–6]

PAGES FROM LSA: LIST OF C.F.R. SECTIONS AFFECTED PAMPHLET

NOVEMBER 2006   **75**

CHANGES APRIL 1, 2006 THROUGH NOVEMBER 30, 2006

5.4 Revised 16921
5.11 Amended 16921
5.22 (k)(1), (2) and (l)(2) amended
   16922
5.23 (a)(2) amended..........................16922
5.26 (b) amended 16922
5.28 Introductory text amended
   16922
5.32a Added; interim 42268
5.32b Added; interim 42268
5.33 (g) amended 16922
5.34 (a) amended 16922
5.35 (a) amended 16922

nated as (c)(12) through (22);
    new (c)(11) added 34527
9.157 (b) introductory text and
    (c)(13) through (18) revised;
    (b)(41) and (42) amended;
    (b)(43) added 34524
9.194 Added 33242
9.195 Added 40414
9.196 Added 40414
9.197 Added 40414
9.198 Added 40414
9.199 Added 40414
9.200 Added 40414

> **Step 4:**
> Note that section 13.11 of Title 27 has been amended. This addition was first printed at page 16924 of the 2006 *Federal Register*. This should be read for the text of the addition.

5.55 (a), (b) and (c) amended 16922
5.65 (a)(4), (5) and (g) amended
   16922
6.5 Revised 16922
6.6 (a) through (c)(3) amended 16922
6.11 Amended 16922
7.3 (a) amended; (b) revised 16922
7.5 Revised 16922
7.10 Amended 16923
7.20 (c)(1) amended.........................16923
7.22a Added; interim 42269
7.22b Added; interim 42269
7.23 (b) amended 16923
7.24 (g) amended 16923
7.25 (a)(1) amended.........................16923
7.29 (a)(4), (5) and (d) amended
   16923
7.31 (a), (b) and (c) amended 16923
7.41 (a) amended 16923
7.54 (a)(4) and (5) amended 16923
8.5 Revised 16923
8.6 (a) through (c)(3) amended 16923
8.11 Amended 16923
9.3 (a) amended 16923
9.11 Amended 16923
9.32 (a) revised 66455
9.46 (b) and (c) revised 34531
9.59 (c)(13) revised; (c)(14) through (19) redesignated as (c)(16) through (21); new (c)(14) and (15) added 34527
9.75 (b) introductory text and (c)(10) through (16) revised; (b)(40) and (41) amended; (b)(42) and (43) added 34524
9.139 (c)(9) and (10) revised; (c)(11) through (21) redesig-

10.5 Revised 16923
10.6 (a) through (c)(3) amended
   16924
10.11 Amended 16924
11.5 Revised 16924
11.6 (a) and (b) amended.................16924
11.11 Amended 16924
12.1 Amended 16924
12.3 (a) and (b) amended.................16924
12.31 Introductory text amended
   16924
13.2 Revised 16924
13.11 Amended 16924
13.20 (a) amended; (b) revised 16924
13.21 (a) and (b) amended 16925
13.22 Amended 16925
13.23 Amended 16925
13.25 (a) and (b) amended 16925
13.26 (a) and (b) amended 16925
13.27 (a), (b) and (c) amended 16925
13.41 Amended 16925
13.42 Amended 16925
13.43 (a) and (b) amended 16925
13.44 (a) and (b) amended 16925
13.45 (a) and (b) amended 16925
13.51 Amended 16925
13.52 Amended 16925
13.53 Amended 16925
13.54 (a) and (b) amended 16925
13.61 (a)(2), (b) and (d) amended
   16925
13.62 Amended 16925
13.71 (a) and (b) amended 16925
13.72 (b) amended 16925
13.74 Amended 16925
13.75 Heading amended 16925
13.76 (a) amended 16925

[Illustration 13–7]

PAGES FROM LSA: LIST OF C.F.R. SECTIONS AFFECTED PAMPHLET

88   **LSA—LIST OF CFR SECTIONS AFFECTED**

CHANGES APRIL 1, 2006 THROUGH NOVEMBER 30, 2006

TITLE 27 Chapter I—Con.

70.482 (a) introductory text and
  (d)(1)(i) amended 16963
70.483 Amended 16963
70.484 Amended 16963
70.485 (a) and (d)(1) amended...........16963
70.486 Amended 16963
70.504 (c)(2) amended.......................16963
70.506 Amended 16963
70.507 (g) amended 16963
70.602 (a) and (b)(1) introductory
  text amended...........................16963
70.606 Introductory text amended
 16963
70.608 Amended 16963
70.609 Amended 16963
70.701 (a)(1), (2), (c), (d)(1), (2)
  heading, (i)(A), (B), (iii)(B),
  (C), (D), (iv)(A), (B) and (C)
  amended..................................16963
70.702 (c) amended..........................16963
70.801 Amended 16963
70.802 (c) through (g) amended........16963
70.802 (g) amended 16964
70.803 (b)(1), (2), (c), (d) introductory text, (3), (e) heading, (1)
  through (5) introductory

71.63 Amended 16965
71.64 (a), (b) and (c) amended 16965
71.65 Amended 16965
71.70 Amended 16965
71.71 Amended 16965
71.72 Amended 16965
71.73 Amended 16965
71.75 Amended 16965
71.78 Amended 16965
71.79 (b) amended 16965
71.80 Amended 16965
71.85 Amended 16965
71.95 Amended 16965
71.96 Amended 16965
71.97 Amended 16965
71.98 Amended 16965
71.99 Amended 16965
71.100 Amended 16965
71.105 Amended 16965
71.106 Amended 16965
71.107—71.110 Undesignated cen-
  ter heading removed................16965
71.107 Amended 16965
71.107a Heading, (a) introductory
  text, (2) and (3) amended 16965
71.108 (a) and (b) amended..............16966

Step 5:
  The *LSA* should also be consulted to ascertain if proposed rules may be relevant.

71.25 Amended 16965
71.26 Amended 16965
71.27 Amended 16965
71.29 Amended 16965
71.31 Amended 16965
71.35 Amended 16965
71.36 Amended 16965
71.37 Amended 16965
71.38 Amended 16965
71.45 Amended 16965
71.46 Amended 16965
71.48 Introductory text amended
 16965
71.49 Amended 16965
71.49a Introductory text amend-
  ed...16965
71.49b Introductory text and (c)
  amended..................................16965
71.55 (a) amended...........................16965
71.57 Amended 16965
71.59 Amended 16965
71.60 (a), (b) and (c) amended 16965
71.61 Amended 16965
71.62 Amended 16965

71.118 Amended 16966
71.126 Amended 16966
71.129 Amended 16966

Chapter II—Bureau of Alcohol, Tobacco, Firearms, and Explosives, Department of Justice (Parts 400—699)

555.141 (a)(10) added 46101

Proposed Rules: ◄

4..42329, 54943
5..42329, 54943
7..42329, 54943
9 .....25795, 37870, 40458, 40465, 53612, 65432,
                      65437
40...62506
41...62506
44...62506
45...62506
555...46174

[Illustration 13–8]

PAGE FROM LSA'S TABLE OF FEDERAL REGISTER ISSUE PAGES AND DATES SHOWING VOLUME 71, FEDERAL REGISTER (2006)

TABLE OF FEDERAL REGISTER ISSUE PAGES AND DATES   125

2006

71 FR Page

1–230	Jan. 3
231–536	4
537–872	5
873–1387	6
1389–1471	9
1473–1681	10
1683–1914	11
1915–2133	12
2135–2451	13
2453–2855	17
2857–2989	18
2991–3203	19
3205–3407	20
3409–3752	23
3753–4032	24
4033–4230	25
4231–4449	26
4451–4804	27
4805–4973	30
4975–5153	31
5155–5578	Feb. 1
5579–5775	2
5777–5965	3
5967–6190	6
6191–6331	7
6333–6660	8
6661–6971	9
6973–7392	10

Pages	Date
15005–15320	27
15321–15556	28
15557–16013	29
16015–16192	30
16193–16476	31
16477–16689	Apr. 3
16691–16972	4
16973–17334	5
17335–17689	6
17691–17965	7
17967–18159	10
18161–18588	11
18589–19096	12
19097–19426	13
19427–19619	14
19621–19803	17
19805–19982	18
19983–20334	19
20335–20515	20
20517–20862	21
20863–23854	24
23855–24550	25
24551–24801	26
24803–25057	27
25058–25482	28
25483–25738	May 1
25739–25917	2
25919–26188	3
26189–26407	4
26409–26673	5
26675–26815	8

Step 6:

This table lists pages of the Federal Register and shows the date of the Federal Register in which the pages are located. Page 16924 is found in the April 4, 2006 Federal Register.

See next illustration.

Pages	Date
10411–10603	Mar. 1
10605–10830	2
10831–11133	3
11135–11286	6
11287–11504	7
11505–12117	8
12119–12276	9
12277–12612	10
12613–12989	13
12991–13241	14
13243–13523	15
13525–13735	16
13737–13921	17
13923–14087	20
14089–14353	21
14355–14628	22
14629–14793	23
14795–15003	24

Pages	Date
29757–30046	24
30047–30261	25
30263–30558	26
30559–30791	30
30793–31068	31
31069–31914	June 1
31915–32263	2
32265–32414	5
32415–32799	6
32801–33145	7
33147–33373	8
33375–33592	9
33593–33988	12
33989–34230	13
34231–34505	14
34507–34786	15
34787–35141	16
35143–35371	19

[Illustration 13–9]

PAGE FROM VOLUME 71, FEDERAL REGISTER

16924   Federal Register / Vol. 71, No. 64 / Tuesday, April 4, 2006 / Rules and Regulations

Street, Room 1516, Cincinnati, OH 45202.

§ 10.6   [Amended]

■ 34. Amend § 10.6 as follows:
■ a. In paragraph (a) remove the word "Director" each place it appears and add, in its place, the word "Administrator".
■ b. In paragraph (b), the heading of paragraph (c), and paragraphs (c)(1), (c)(2) and (c)(3), remove the reference to "ATF" each place it appears and add, in its place, a reference to "TTB".
■ 35. Amend § 10.11 as follows:
■ a. Remove the definitions of "Appropriate ATF officer" and "Director".
■ b. Add, in alphabetical order, definitions of "Administrator" and "Appropriate TTB officer" to read as

Bureau, Department of the Treasury, Washington, DC.
  Appropriate TTB officer. An officer or employee of the Alcohol and Tobacco Tax and Trade Bureau (TTB) authorized to perform any functions relating to the administration or enforcement of this part by TTB Order 1135.10, Delegation of the Administrator's Authorities in 27 CFR Part 10, Commercial Bribery.
  *   *   *   *   *

PART 11—CONSIGNMENT SALES

■ 36. The authority citation for part 11 continues to read as follows:
  Authority: 15 U.S.C. 49–50; 27 U.S.C. 202 and 205.

■ 37. Revise § 11.5 to read as follows:

§ 11.5   Delegations of the Administrator.

  Most of the regulatory authorities of the Administrator contained in this part are delegated to appropriate TTB officers. These TTB officers are specified in TTB Order 1135.11, Delegation of the Administrator's Authorities in 27 CFR Part 11, Consignment Sales. You may obtain a copy of this order by accessing the TTB Web site (*http://www.ttb.gov*) or by mailing a request to the Alcohol and Tobacco Tax and Trade Bureau, National Revenue Center, 550 Main Street, Room 1516, Cincinnati, OH 45202.

§ 11.6   [Amended]

■ 38. Amend § 11.6 as follows:
■ a. In paragraph (a) remove the word "Director" each place it appears and

add, in its place, the word "Administrator".
■ b. In paragraph (b) remove the reference to "ATF" each place it appears and add, in its place, a reference to "TTB".

■ 39. Amend § 11.11 as follows:
■ a. Remove the definitions of "Appropriate ATF officer" and "Director".
■ b. Add, in alphabetical order, definitions of "Administrator" and "Appropriate TTB officer" to read as follows:.

§ 11.11   Meaning of terms.

*   *   *   *   *

  Administrator. The Administrator, Alcohol and Tobacco Tax and Trade Bureau, Department of the Treasury, Washington, DC.

of the Administrator's Authorities in 27 CFR Part 11, Consignment Sales.
*   *   *   *   *

PART 12—FOREIGN NONGENERIC NAMES OF GEOGRAPHIC SIGNIFICANCE USED IN THE DESIGNATION OF WINES

■ 40. The authority citation for part 12 continues to read as follows:
  Authority: 27 U.S.C. 205.

§ 12.1   [Amended]

■ 41. Amend § 12.1 by removing the word "Director" and adding, in its place, the word "Administrator".

§ 12.3   [Amended]

■ 42. Amend § 12.3 as follows:
■ a. In paragraph (a) remove the word "Director" and add, in its place, the word "Administrator".
■ b. In paragraphs (a) and (b), remove the reference to "ATF" each place it appears and add, in its place, a reference to "TTB".

§ 12.31   [Amended]

■ 43. Amend the introductory text of § 12.31 by removing the word "Director" and adding, in its place, the word "Administrator".

PART 13—LABELING PROCEEDINGS

■ 44. The authority citation for part 13 continues to read as follows:
  Authority: 27 U.S.C. 205(e), 26 U.S.C. 5301 and 7805.

■ 45. Revise § 13.2 to read as follows:

§ 13.2   Delegations of the Administrator.

  The regulatory authorities of the Administrator contained in this part are delegated to appropriate TTB officers. These TTB officers are specified in TTB Order 1135.13, Delegation of the Administrator's Authorities in 27 CFR Part 13, Labeling Proceedings. You may obtain a copy of this order by accessing the TTB Web site (*http://www.ttb.gov*) or by mailing a request to the Alcohol and Tobacco Tax and Trade Bureau, National Revenue Center, 550 Main Street, Room 1516, Cincinnati, OH 45202.

■ 46. Amend § 13.11 as follows:
■ a. In the definition of "Applicant" remove the reference to "ATF F 5100.31" and add, in its place, a reference to "Form 5100.31".
■ b. Remove the definitions of

in its place, a reference to "Form 5100.31".
■ d. In the definitions of "Certificate holder," "Certificate of exemption from label approval," and "Certificate of label approval," remove the reference to "ATF F 5100.31" and add, in its place, a reference to "Form 5100.31".
■ e. In the definition of "Liquor bottle" remove the reference to "ATF" and add, in its place, a reference to "TTB".
■ f. Add, in alphabetical order, definitions of "Administrator", "Appropriate TTB officer", and "TTB" to read as follows:

§ 13.11   Meaning of terms.   ←
*   *   *   *   *

  Administrator. The Administrator, Alcohol and Tobacco Tax and Trade Bureau, Department of the Treasury, Washington, DC.
  Appropriate TTB officer. An officer or employee of the Alcohol and Tobacco Tax and Trade Bureau (TTB) authorized to perform any functions relating to the administration or enforcement of this part by TTB Order 1135.13, Delegation of the Administrator's Authorities in 27 CFR Part 13, Labeling Proceedings.
*   *   *   *   *

  TTB. The Alcohol and Tobacco Tax and Trade Bureau, Department of the Treasury, Washington, DC.

■ 47. Amend § 13.20 as follows:
■ a. In paragraph (a) remove the reference to "ATF" and add, in its place, a reference to "TTB".
■ b. Revise paragraph (b) to read as follows:

Step 7:
   This is the page from the *Federal Register* on which the revision to Section 13.11 is published.

[Illustration 13–10]

PAGE FROM VOLUME 71, FEDERAL REGISTER–LIST OF C.F.R. PARTS AFFECTED

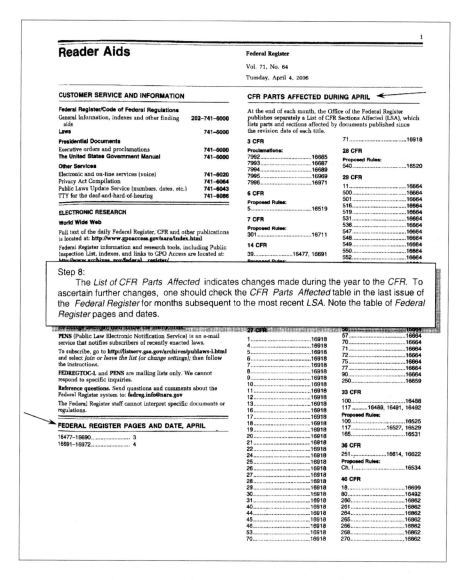

G. OTHER SOURCES OF INFORMATION ABOUT ADMINISTRATIVE AGENCIES

1. *The United States Government Manual*

This handbook, published by the Office of the Federal Register, is revised annually and contains general information about Congress and the federal judiciary.[31] The major

---

[31] The current edition of the *United States Government Manual* is available at http://usgovernmentmanual.gov. Editions, from 1995 through 2012, are at http://www.gpo.gov/fdsys/browse/collection.action?collectionCode=GOVMAN. *HeinOnline*, a fee-based service, has PDF images of this title from

emphasis of *The United States Government Manual* is on the executive branch and regulatory agencies. Each department and agency is concisely described, with citations to the enabling statute that created the department or agency. A description of functions and authority, names of government officials, and listings of major publications are provided.

The *Manual* includes several appendices. One appendix lists all abolished and transferred agencies, with an indication of what happened to the functions for which they had responsibility. For example, under *Civil Service Commission, U.S.*, it is noted that the agency has been re-designated as the *Merit Systems Protection Board* and its functions transferred to the *Board* and to the *Office of Personnel Management* by the Reorganization Plan No. 2 of 1978.

Other appendices list commonly used abbreviations and acronyms, and all agencies, in alphabetical order, that appear in the *C.F.R.* Separate indexes for name and agency/subject are provided.

2. *Federal Regulatory Directory*

The *Federal Regulatory Directory*[32] can be used to augment information contained in *The United States Government Manual*. Discussions of the topics of regulations and current issues involving federal administrative agencies, as well as extensive profiles of the largest and most important agencies, are included. Summary information on most other federal agencies is also provided.

3. *Federal Yellow Book* and *Federal Regional Yellow Book*

These titles, two in a series of directories that are updated semiannually, provide website information, email addresses, and telephone numbers for government officials.[33]

4. *USA.gov*

This federal government website[34] began several years ago as FirstGov.gov, and is a one-stop site for federal, state, and local government websites. There is an A to Z agency list on the home page, as well as links to state, local, and tribal government home pages.

H. PRESIDENTIAL DOCUMENTS

Most rules and regulations are the result of activities of federal agencies operating under powers delegated by Congress. The president also has the authority to issue documents that have legal effect. This authority is constitutional, statutory, or sometimes both. This section describes the types of presidential documents and the sources in which documentation of presidential activities may be found.

1935 to the present. For more on the *Government Manual* and its history, see Mary Whisner, *A Manual "to Inform Every Citizen,"* 99 LAW LIBR. J. 159 (2007).

[32] FEDERAL REGULATORY DIRECTORY (15th ed. 2013) (CQ Press).

[33] Published by Leadership Directories, Inc., these titles and the rest of the series are also available as a fee-based electronic database.

[34] http://www.usa.gov.

1. Proclamations and Executive Orders[35]

Proclamations and Executive Orders have been widely used by presidents to exercise their authority. Proclamations are generally addressed to the entire nation, and their content frequently relates to ceremonial or celebratory occasions. Executive Orders are generally used by the president to direct and govern the activities of government officials and agencies. [Illustration 13–11]

Proclamations and Executive Orders appear in both print and electronic form in the following titles:

a. The *Federal Register.*

b. The *Weekly Compilation of Presidential Documents* (the daily *Compilation* succeeded the *Weekly Compilation* in February 2009 and is available only online).

c. Title 3 of the *C.F.R.* and compilation volumes of Title 3.

d. *Public Papers of the Presidents* (until January 1989).

e. *United States Code Congressional and Administrative News,* Advance pamphlets.

f. *United States Code Service, Advance Service.*

g. *The American Presidency Project,* created in 1999, now includes nearly 100,000 documents related to the presidency.[36]

h. *LexisNexis* and *Westlaw. Westlaw* contains Executive Orders issued since 1936 and all other presidential documents from the *Federal Register* since 1984. *LexisNexis* contains presidential documents from 1980 to the present.

i. *HeinOnline* includes a Presidential Library with PDF images of the complete file of the *Compilation of Presidential Documents, Public Papers of the Presidents,* and a variety of other materials.

j. Proclamations also may be found in *United States Statutes at Large.*

k. The White House home page[37] contains all White House documents released during the current administration, including executive orders and presidential proclamations. [Illustration 13–12] In addition, the other electronic research sources described in Section C-4, above, contain presidential documents that are included in the *Federal Register* and the *C.F.R.*

---

[35] For detailed historical information, see HOUSE COMM. ON GOVERNMENT OPERATIONS, 85TH CONG., 1ST SESS., EXECUTIVE ORDERS AND PROCLAMATIONS: STUDY OF A USE OF PRESIDENTIAL POWERS (Comm. Print 1957); KENNETH R. MAYER, WITH THE STROKE OF A PEN: EXECUTIVE ORDERS AND PRESIDENTIAL POWER (2001). For additional historical detail, see Mary Woodward, *Executive Orders: A Journey,* 10 LEGAL REFERENCE SERVICES Q., no. 3, 1990, at 125.

To locate Executive Orders issued prior to the publication of the *Federal Register,* see NEW YORK CITY HISTORICAL RECORDS SURVEY, PRESIDENTIAL EXECUTIVE ORDERS, NUMBERED 1–8030, 1862–1938 (1944); NEW JERSEY HISTORICAL RECORDS SURVEY, LIST AND INDEX OF PRESIDENTIAL EXECUTIVE ORDERS: UNNUMBERED SERIES, 1789–1941 (1944).

[36] http://www.presidency.ucsb.edu/index.php.

[37] http://www.whitehouse.gov.

2.   Codification of Presidential Proclamations and Executive Orders

The Office of the Federal Register began publishing the *Codification of Presidential Proclamations and Executive Orders* in 1979, but suspended publication in 1995. Its purpose was to provide in one source proclamations and executive orders that have general applicability and continuing effect. This codification arranges all the previously published proclamations and executive orders still in force by subject. Amendments to the original documents are incorporated in the text.

The codification is arranged in fifty titles corresponding to those of the *Code of Federal Regulations*, and covers the period April 13, 1945, through January 20, 1989. A "Disposition Table" at the back of the volume lists all proclamations and executive orders issued with their amendments, and indicates their current status and chapter designations, where applicable. The codification was widely distributed, but is now out of print. It is available online.[38]

3.   Reorganization Plans

By the provisions of 5 U.S.C. §§ 901 through 912, the president is authorized to examine the organization of all agencies and make changes that provide for better management of the executive branch of the government. The president is authorized to submit proposed reorganization plans to both houses of Congress. Proposed reorganization plans are published in the *Congressional Record*. A reorganization plan becomes effective if the president accepts the joint resolution passed by the House and the Senate that approves the plan submitted by the president.

Reorganization plans are published, as approved, in the *Federal Register*, Title 3 of the *C.F.R.*, *United States Statutes at Large*, and *5 U.S.C.* Appendix. The *Congressional Record* is the best source for plans not approved by Congress.

4.   Other Presidential Documents

In addition to the documents discussed above, the president issues administrative orders, such as findings, determinations, and memoranda; executive agreements; and messages to Congress and signing statements. Administrative orders are published in the *Federal Register* and in Title 3 of the *Code of Federal Regulations*. The American Presidency Project contains an enormous amount of information, and has organized everything from inaugural addresses to signing statements on one website.[39]

5.   Presidential Nominations

A list of presidential nominations submitted to the Senate was provided at the end of each issue of the *Weekly Compilation of Presidential Documents* until it ceased publication at the end of January 2009; the daily *Compilation of Presidential Documents*, which is available only online, includes nominations as a separate list. The White House website lists nominations by name and by date.[40] Issues of the *Congressional Record*'s *Daily Digest* for the Senate contains the names of those nominated and those confirmed by the Senate.

---

[38] http://www.archives.gov/federal-register/codification.

[39] http://www.presidency.ucsb.edu/index.php.

[40] http://www.whitehouse.gov/briefing-room/nominations-and-appointments.

6. Compilations of Presidential Documents

The following sources provide comprehensive collections of presidential documents:

a.　Compilation of Presidential Documents (1965–present).　The *Weekly Compilation* was published every Monday, 1965 through January 2009. It contained statements, messages, and other presidential materials released by the White House during the preceding week. An index of contents is available at the beginning of each issue for documents included in that issue. Until 1995, each issue also contained a cumulative subject index and name index for the previous issues of the current quarter. An annual index is divided into names and subjects. From 1995 (volume 31, no. 1) until it ceased publication in 2009, the indexes were issued quarterly and distributed separately. Other finding aids include lists of laws approved by the president, nominations submitted to the Senate, and a checklist of White House releases. Beginning with the administration of President Obama, the compilation is an online daily publication.

The National Archives and Records Administration site available through *FDsys* contains the *Compilation of Presidential Documents* (weekly version, from 1993 through January 2009, as well as the current daily *Compilation*).[41]

b.　Public Papers of the Presidents.[42] The series starts with the administration of President Hoover. It is published annually in one or more volumes and includes a compilation of the presidents' messages to Congress, public speeches, news conferences, and public letters. The final volume for each year contains a cumulative index to the volumes published during the year. After all volumes for an administration are published, a commercial firm publishes a cumulative index for that president.[43] The papers of President Franklin Roosevelt and some of the earlier presidents, not part of the *Public Papers* series, have been published commercially.

Beginning with the 1977 volumes, which cover the first year of President Carter's administration, and continuing through the volume for 1988–89, the last year of President Reagan's administration, the set includes all of the material printed in the *Weekly Compilation of Presidential Documents*. Beginning in 1989, the first year of the administration of President George Herbert Walker Bush, Proclamations and Executive Orders are not included. Instead, a table refers the user to the appropriate issues of the *Federal Register* in which the documents are published.

c.　The American Presidency Project is the largest online compilation of presidential documents, with over 105,000 documents as of June, 2014.[44] It includes the contents of all *Public Papers of the Presidents*, all executive orders from 1826 to the present, all proclamations from 1789 to the present, the *Weekly Compilation of Presidential Documents* from 1977, and the current daily compilation. It also includes some obscure data, such as "Number of Requests of Congress in State of the Union

---

[41] http://www.gpo.gov/fdsys/browse/collection.action?collectionCode=CPD. It is also available on commercial research services, such as *LexisNexis* and *Westlaw*.

[42] Available from 1991 to the present, http://www.gpo.gov/fdsys/browse/collection.action?collectionCode=PPP.

[43] *The Cumulated Indexes to the Public Papers of the Presidents of the United States* has been produced by different publishers: KTO Press (1977–79), Krauss International Publications (1979–81), and Bernan Press (1995).

[44] http://www.presidency.ucsb.edu/index.php.

Addresses" and "List of Acknowledged Guests Sitting in House Galleries" during the State of the Union Address. There is an audio/video archive and links to all the presidential library websites.

    d.   Title 3 of the Code of Federal Regulations. Presidential documents required to be published in the *Federal Register* are compiled in Title 3 of the *C.F.R.* Before 1976, compilation volumes of Title 3 were published covering varied time periods. Since 1976, a compilation volume has been published annually. Unlike the other yearly codifications of agency regulations, each compilation of Title 3 is a unique source of presidential documents rather than an updated codification; therefore, each compilation of Title 3 is a permanent reference source.

7. Updating Presidential Documents

    Shepard's Code of Federal Regulations Citations, mentioned in Section E-1-d above, can be used to determine if a presidential proclamation, executive order, or reorganization plan has been changed in some manner. Presidential documents included in Title 3 of the *C.F.R.* can be updated using the *LSA* (see Section E-1-a).

I. ILLUSTRATIONS: PRESIDENTIAL DOCUMENTS

13–11.   **Example of Presidential Executive Order**
13–12.   **White House Website**

[Illustration 13–11]

SCREEN PRINT, EXAMPLE OF PRESIDENTIAL EXECUTIVE ORDER

[Illustration 13–12]

SCREEN PRINT, WHITE HOUSE WEBSITE

The White House home page, http://www.whitehouse.gov, includes links to presidential proclamations, Executive Orders, etc.

J.   FEDERAL ADMINISTRATIVE DECISIONS

1.   Agency Decisions

Many federal administrative agencies also serve an adjudicatory function and, in performing this function, issue decisions.[45] The Federal Communications Commission, for example, is authorized by statute to license radio and television stations. It also has the authority to enforce its regulations concerning the operations of these stations. When stations allegedly violate the terms of the statute or regulations, the Federal Communications Commission can hear charges and issue decisions.

---

[45] Many of the mysteries concerning administrative law courts are explained in Harold H. Bruff, *Specialized Courts in Administrative Law*, 43 ADMIN. L. REV. 329 (1991).

Decisions of administrative agencies are published not in the *Federal Register*, but in separate sources.[46] Decisions can be published in print or electronically by the U.S. Government Printing Office (*FDsys*), the agency itself,[47] and/or commercial publishers.

a.   *Government Publication of Decisions of Federal Administrative Agencies.* Print versions of some of these publications are available in law libraries and in public and university libraries that are official depositories of the U.S. Government Printing Office. The format, frequency, and method of publication vary from agency to agency. Generally, agency publications in print are issued infrequently and are poorly indexed. Some print sets include indexes and digests in the back of each volume. For other sets, separate indexes and digests are published. Some sets of federal administrative decisions have an advance sheet service. Increasingly, agency decisions are available from *FDsys* or from agency websites.

b.   *Commercial Publication of Decisions of Federal Administrative Agencies.* Commercial publishers sometimes republish agency decisions in topical services. Both electronic and print versions typically are organized into volumes of decisions, similar to volumes that contain court cases. Research services such as *LexisNexis* and *Westlaw* include agency decisions.[48]

2.   Judicial Review of Agency Decisions

After an agency has issued an administrative decision, it may be appealed to the federal courts. The decisions resulting from these appeals may be found by searching full-text databases of federal cases, using digests, or consulting secondary sources such as treatises and law review articles.

As noted elsewhere in this chapter, websites of government agencies often contain decisions, rules and regulations, and other documents pertinent to the agencies. Quite often in recent years, material is available on the agency website that is never published in print form.

K. STATE ADMINISTRATIVE REGULATIONS AND DECISIONS

Although comprehensive research in state administrative law is difficult due to the varied (and often inadequate) publication policies of the states, the proliferation of websites and electronic resources makes state administrative materials more widely available than they were in the past.[49] In addition, recent publications assist in locating print and electronic resources.[50]

---

[46] For a selected list of official federal administrative agency and executive materials, see THE BLUEBOOK: A UNIFORM SYSTEM OF CITATION 218–28 (19th ed. 2010).

[47] A University of Virginia website maintains a list of online agency sites at http://www2.lib.virginia.edu/govtinfo/fed_decisions_agency.html.

[48] Topical services are discussed in Chapter 14; electronic legal research is discussed in Chapter 23.

[49] Both *LexisNexis* and *Westlaw* contain a wide variety of state materials. Cornell's *Legal Information Institute* has a directory of the states that links to all the primary source materials that are available for each state, at http://www.law.cornell.edu/states/listing.html.

[50] *See, e.g.*, CHERYL RAE NYBERG, STATE ADMINISTRATIVE LAW BIBLIOGRAPHY: PRINT AND ELECTRONIC SOURCES (2000); WILLIAM H. MANZ, GUIDE TO STATE LEGISLATION, LEGISLATIVE HISTORY, AND ADMINISTRATIVE MATERIALS (AALL Publication Series, No. 61, 2008) (*HeinOnline*).

1. State Regulations

The regulations of state agencies are published in a variety of formats. In some states, administrative regulations are officially codified and published in sets similar to the *Code of Federal Regulations.* These may be supplemented by a publication similar to the *Federal Register.* In other states, each agency issues its own regulations, and research inquiries must be directed to the appropriate agency. State regulations are increasingly being made available at no charge through state websites, although commercial publishers continue to produce subscription publications or databases with regulations for some states.[51]

Recent surveys by the American Association of Law Libraries (AALL) reveal that print versions of state primary legal materials are being discontinued in favor of online publication, but that the new online versions are often not considered official. Further, many online publications, of regulations as well as of other legal materials, are not capable of being authenticated, which leaves the user without assurance of their accuracy or trustworthiness.[52] As more states adopt the Uniform Electronic Legal Material Act (UELMA), these issues will be addressed.[53]

2. State Administrative Decisions

Many state agencies also publish their decisions, most commonly those of entities such as unemployment compensation commissions, tax commissions, and public utility commissions. Like state regulations, state agency decisions are increasingly being posted on websites and added to commercial services such as *Westlaw* and *LexisNexis.*

3. Research in State Administrative Law

a.   Check the state code to determine if the state has an Administrative Procedure Act and if the method for publication of regulations is prescribed therein.

b.   Consult a state legal encyclopedia or state administrative law treatise if available.

c.   Consult a state legal research manual, if available.[54]

d.   Check electronic sources to determine if state regulations and agency decisions are available.

---

[51] An alphabetical list of state websites can be found on the main federal government website, http://www.usa.gov, and also through the Cornell *Legal Information Institute* site, http://www.law.cornell.edu.

[52] The AALL study, entitled *State-by-State Report on Authentication of Online Legal Resources* (March 2007), and its updates are published at http://aallnet.org/Documents/Government-Relations/authen_rprt.

[53] The text of the UELMA and other documents concerning this effort can be found at http://www.uniform laws.org/Act.aspx?title=Electronic%20Legal%20Material%20Act.

[54] Appendix B of this book provides a listing of state-specific guides to legal research.

Chapter 14

TOPICAL SERVICES

———

Topical services provide timely and up-to-date access to information in specific areas of law. These services typically bring together in one source various types of primary and secondary authority, as well as finding tools. Traditionally they have been called "looseleaf" services because they are published in binders rather than as bound books, so that superseded pages can easily be removed and new pages inserted.[1]

In recent years, the content of many looseleaf services has been made available electronically in full text on the Internet, directly from publishers and through *Bloomberg Law, LexisNexis, Westlaw,* and *Loislaw.* The electronic format allows levels of currency, access, and precise searching that are not available with print resources. Some services are now available only online and so are no longer "looseleaf" at all. Nonetheless, this chapter will frequently use the traditional designation of "looseleaf service,"[2] primarily in discussing print publications.

A. BENEFITS OF TOPICAL SERVICES

To research a problem in the law of taxation, for example, a researcher might need to locate not only relevant statutes and judicial opinions but also administrative regulations of the Internal Revenue Service and the Treasury Department, rulings of the Commissioner of Internal Revenue, news releases, technical information publications, and other agency documents. Topical services can provide access to many of these different types of sources. Most topical services aim to consolidate into one source the statutes, regulations, judicial opinions, agency decisions, and commentary on a particular legal topic and then facilitate access to this material, whether through printed detailed indexes and other finding aids or online full-text searching.

In some areas of law, such as taxation and other areas of administrative law, there is a need for frequent updating. Topical services can be updated much more quickly, both in print and online, with additional or replacement pages and new releases, than can other publications updated by pocket parts, supplemental pamphlets, or replacement volumes.

Most topical services include current awareness information, which can include news of proposed legislation, pending agency regulations, court and agency decisions, and even informed rumor. They also frequently contain forms, summaries of professional

---

[1] Many treatises by named authors are also published in binders. They are not looseleaf services because they do not have the range of constantly updated material contained in topical services. Treatises are discussed in Chapter 19.

[2] For a wide-ranging history of looseleaf services—including background on the legal profession, legal publishing, office technology, and the Industrial Revolution—see Howard T. Senzel, *Looseleafing the Flow: An Anecdotal History of One Technology for Updating,* 44 AM. J. LEGAL HIST. 115 (2000). A much briefer history is presented in Peyton Neal, *Loose-Leaf Reporting Services,* 62 LAW LIBR. J. 153 (1969).

meetings, calendars of forthcoming events, and other news relevant to researchers or practicing attorneys in the field.

Services published in a looseleaf format generally: (1) have new pages *interfiled* with existing materials; (2) come in *newsletter* format, with each issue added chronologically to a binder; or (3) use a combination of (1) and (2). Traditionally, looseleaf publications have had standardized publication schedules, typically weekly, biweekly, or monthly.

The electronic versions are available on the Internet directly from the publishers and also, in some cases, via electronic research services such as *LexisNexis* and *Westlaw*. Rather than requiring subscribers to file pages mailed by the publisher, electronic services are updated immediately when new materials are added, deleted, or changed. An electronic full-text version of a topical service is an efficient source for research in updated materials and offers precise searching capabilities.[3]

This chapter highlights only those features common to most topical services. Particular attention is given to representative publications of Commerce Clearing House (CCH) and the Bureau of National Affairs (Bloomberg BNA or BNA) because of the large number of topical services produced by these two companies.

The convenience, currency, frequency, and indexing of topical services often make them the best place to begin researching many types of legal problems. In some rapidly developing areas of the law, such as privacy, the environment, and consumer protection, a topical service may be the only extensive research tool available.[4]

The original topical services were looseleafs, and the print format for many topical services remains widely used. The contents and, to a great extent, the organization of electronic services reflect their print origin. The discussion below describes the major features of the print versions and the publications of the two major topical services publishers, with brief information about the publishers' electronic publications.

B. CHARACTERISTICS OF LOOSELEAF SERVICES

1. Interfiled Looseleafs in General

Most topical looseleaf services, in which new pages replace older pages, share these characteristics:

a. Full text of the statutes on the topic, often with significant legislative history;

b. Either full text or abstracts of relevant judicial opinions and administrative agency decisions;

c. Editorial commentary and explanatory notes;

d. Topical indexes;

---

[3] The best method for determining whether a particular publication is available in electronic format is to consult the publisher's website or print catalog. The content guides for *Westlaw, LexisNexis, Loislaw,* and *Bloomberg Law* indicate the looseleaf services available via that research service. Also helpful is the "Electronic Format Index" in *Legal Looseleafs in Print* (Arlene L. Eis comp. & ed.). This is an annual publication that lists approximately 3,600 titles by over 240 publishers. It includes information on the number of volumes in a looseleaf set, price, frequency, cost of supplementation, and Library of Congress classification number. It is arranged alphabetically by title and includes publisher, subject, and electronic format indexes.

[4] For assistance in identifying relevant topical services, see *Legal Looseleafs in Print, supra,* note 3.

    e.   Tables of cases and statutes;

    f.   Finding lists for statutes, cases, and administrative materials;

    g.   Indexes to current materials and cumulative indexes; and

    h.   Current reports summarizing recent developments.

2.   Newsletter Looseleafs in General

Most topical looseleaf services in the newsletter format, in which pamphlet updates are filed sequentially and chronologically, share these characteristics:

    a.   News and editorial comments of general interest;

    b.   Explanations of recent state and federal developments and recent developments in particular areas within the broad subject;

    c.   Text of, or excerpts from, major legislation, judicial opinions, administrative regulations, and agency decisions; and

    d.   Subject and table of cases indexes.

3.   Commerce Clearing House (CCH) Services

    a.   *Print Services.* Commerce Clearing House (CCH) publications are typically of the type in which pages are interfiled. Examples include the *Copyright Law Reporter*, *Federal Securities Law Reporter*, *Products Liability Reporter*, and *Trade Regulation Reporter*. CCH publications range from those that consist of one binder to those that consist of a dozen or more binders.

CCH publications begin with an introductory section that discusses the use and organization of the service. The importance of this section cannot be over-emphasized. A careful reading of it can save the researcher much time and frustration. Volumes are divided into sections by tab cards. These tabs offer quick access to major topic headings. Typically, there is a comprehensive Topical Index to the full service. In addition, some services have special indexes to specific topics or volumes. The quality of the indexing is generally quite high, as the publisher strives to provide as many access points as possible.

The indexes are made more useful by the unique, dual numbering system employed by the publisher. Under this system, in addition to regular pagination, a paragraph number is assigned to each topic area. Materials organized under one paragraph number may consist of as little as one textual paragraph or as many as fifty or more pages. This flexibility of format allows for frequent additions and deletions to the text without disrupting the indexing system. Research can begin by consulting one of the indexes, which will reference the appropriate paragraph numbers where relevant information can be found. In these services, page numbers often are used only as guides for filing new pages and removing old ones.

The volumes containing the CCH editorial commentary and explanations, various reference materials, laws and regulations, and forms are typically referred to as "compilation" volumes. Full text of new judicial opinions and agency rulings, often supplied as part of the looseleaf service, generally are placed in a separate volume or section from the compilation volume(s).

Each case or ruling is commonly assigned its own paragraph number that can be located in several ways. Most services have tables of cases, statutes, and administrative regulations. When a citation to a case, statute, or administrative regulation is available, research can begin by consulting the appropriate table and obtaining the paragraph number where the cited material is discussed. Special indexes cross-reference materials found under the paragraph numbers to materials concerning current developments.

Materials summarizing current developments are often included in bulletins that accompany new pages sent from the publisher; the bulletins may be weekly, monthly, quarterly, or on another schedule. These bulletins are usually retained as part of the service and can be valuable research tools themselves. [Illustrations 14–1 through 14–4]

Often, a CCH service that systematically reports judicial opinions or agency decisions is accompanied by a separate, bound reporter.[5] For example, CCH's widely used *Standard Federal Tax Reporter* includes a binder labeled "U.S. Tax Cases—Advance Sheets." These advance sheets are cumulated into bound volumes twice a year, with the "Advance Sheet" volume always containing only the most recent materials.

In general, the successful use of CCH looseleaf services requires that the researcher:

(1)   Locate the topic or topics being researched by consulting the Topical Index to the service.

(2)   Read carefully all materials under paragraph numbers referenced in the Topical Index. When abstracts of cases are available, citations to cases should be noted so that the full text can be read.

(3)   Consult the appropriate index or indexes to current materials.

b.   Electronic Services. CCH IntelliConnect provides access to full text primary and secondary materials in a wide range of subjects, including pensions, employment law, OSHA, health care law, corporate governance, mergers and acquisitions, intellectual property, government contracts, antitrust and trade regulation, and transportation law. It also contains federal and state tax materials, including codes, regulations, forms, IRS letter rulings, and current news. This new interface merges the resources formerly known as *CCH Internet Research Network*, *CCH Business and Finance Research Network*, and *CCH Tax Research Network*.

4.   Bloomberg BNA Services

a.   Print Services. Bloomberg BNA is another major publisher of looseleaf services (those formerly published by the Bureau of National Affairs). Bloomberg BNA's typical format consists of one or more three-ring binders in which periodic issues (or releases) are filed. Unlike CCH, the issues generally do not contain individual pages to be interfiled with existing text, but instead consist of pamphlets numbered sequentially and filed chronologically. Thus, there is no provision for revision of earlier issues. This format allows for the service to be issued quickly. Examples of these publications are *Antitrust*

---

[5] As noted in Chapter 5, federal district court opinions are reported selectively. Cases not officially reported sometimes are published in one or more subject looseleaf services, as well as in the *National Reporter System*'s *Federal Appendix*, computer-assisted legal research services, and on the Internet. Consequently, it is worthwhile to check the table of cases of looseleaf services for cases not reported in the *Federal Supplement*.

& *Trade Regulation Report*, *Securities Regulation & Law Report*, and *Patent, Trademark & Copyright Journal*.

Many differences exist among Bloomberg BNA's numerous publications and services. Some consist of several separate components, usually including a summary and analysis of major developments, the text of pertinent legislation, and the full text or abstracts of judicial opinions. Important speeches, government reports, book reviews, and bibliographies also may be included. Each of these components is generally filed behind its own tab divider. Examples of services providing this type of information are *United States Law Week*,[6] *Criminal Law Reporter*, and *Family Law Reporter*.

Some services include state law sections. The information in these is generally arranged by state, with the paragraph numbers that are used for subject-matter organization assigned uniformly to the same topic for each state. In some instances, *all-state* charts are published that provide state-by-state comparisons of specific legislation. [Illustration 14–5]

Bloomberg BNA services feature cumulative indexes that offer topical access to material. Consecutive pagination is used. Case tables are provided for each service. For some of its services, Bloomberg BNA periodically supplies special storage binders for old issues, so that the main volumes always contain current material. Regardless of whether the service is issued as a single newsletter or in several pamphlet-type components, it is intended to keep the researcher fully informed of developments in the subject area.

One of Bloomberg BNA's most comprehensive looseleaf services is its *Labor Relations Reporter*. This set, together with its *Environment Reporter* and *Occupational Safety & Health Reporter*, is arranged differently from most other BNA services. *Labor Relations Reporter* includes the following segments:

Labor Management Relations (federal)

Labor Arbitration and Dispute Settlements

Wages and Hours

Fair Employment Practices

State Labor Laws

Individual Employment Rights

Americans with Disabilities

These looseleaf volumes contain relevant statutes, regulations, and judicial opinions. Periodically, reports of court cases are removed from the looseleaf volumes and reprinted in bound volumes, e.g., *Labor Arbitration Reports* and *Wage and Hour Cases*. Each series has its own index and digest, in which the cases are classified according to Bloomberg BNA's own classification scheme.

The entire *Labor Relations Reporter* set is unified by a two-volume looseleaf "Master Index" and a two-volume looseleaf "Labor Relations Expediter." [Illustrations 14–6 through 14–9]

---

[6] *Law Week* is discussed in Chapter 5, Section A-1.

b. *Electronic Services.* Bloomberg BNA makes its many topical services available in an online subscription service[7] as well as in *Bloomberg Law.* Bloomberg BNA's electronic services, like its print services, can be grouped in several broad subject areas: corporate law and business; employee benefits; employment and labor law; environment, health and safety; health care; human resources; intellectual property; litigation; tax and accounting; and international materials.

C. ILLUSTRATIONS

ILLUSTRATIONS USING CCH PRODUCTS LIABILITY REPORTER

Problem: What constitutes adequate warning about the potential dangers of a product's design?

14–1.	**Page from Topical Index**
14–2 to 14–3.	**Pages from Compilation Volume**
14–4.	**Page from Cumulative Index**

---

[7] http://www.bna.com.

[Illustration 14–1]

PAGE FROM TOPICAL INDEX, CCH PRODUCTS LIABILITY REPORTER

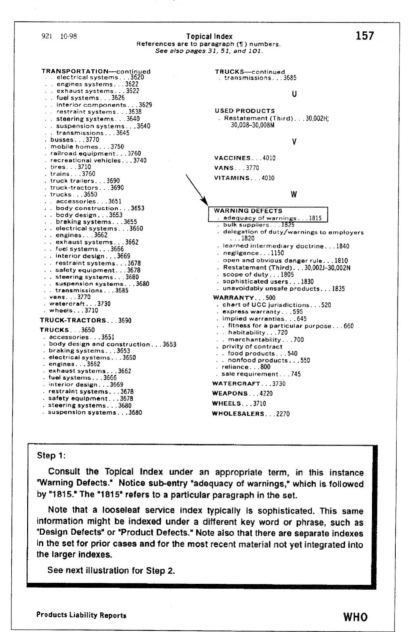

921 10-98

Topical Index 157

References are to paragraph (¶) numbers.
See also pages 31, 51, and 101.

TRANSPORTATION—continued
. . electrical systems. . .3620
. . engines systems. . .3622
. . exhaust systems. . .3522
. . fuel systems. . .3626
. . interior components. . .3629
. . restraint systems. . .3638
. . steering systems. . .3640
. . suspension systems. . .3640
. . transmissions. . .3645
. busses. . .3770
. mobile homes. . .3750
. railroad equipment. . .3760
. recreational vehicles. . .3740
. tires. . .3710
. trains. . .3760
. truck trailers. . .3690
. truck-tractors. . .3690
. trucks. . .3650
. . accessories. . .3651
. . body construction. . .3653
. . body design. . .3653
. . braking systems. . .3655
. . electrical systems. . .3650
. . engines. . .3662
. . exhaust systems. . .3662
. . fuel systems. . .3666
. . interior design. . .3669
. . restraint systems. . .3678
. . safety equipment. . .3678
. . steering systems. . .3680
. . suspension systems. . .3680
. . transmissions. . .3685
. . vans. . .3770
. . watercraft. . .3730
. . wheels. . .3710

TRUCK-TRACTORS. . .3690

TRUCKS. . .3650
. accessories. . .3651
. body design and construction. . .3653
. braking systems. . .3653
. electrical systems. . .3650
. engines. . .3662
. exhaust systems. . .3662
. fuel systems. . .3666
. interior design. . .3669
. restraint systems. . .3678
. safety equipment. . .3678
. steering systems. . .3680
. suspension systems. . .3680

TRUCKS—continued
. transmissions. . .3685

U

USED PRODUCTS
. Restatement (Third). . .30,002H;
30,008–30,008M

V

VACCINES. . .4010

VANS. . .3770

VITAMINS. . .4010

W

WARNING DEFECTS
. adequacy of warnings. . .1815
. bulk suppliers. . .1825
. delegation of duty/warnings to employers
. . .1820
. learned intermediary doctrine. . .1840
. negligence. . .1150
. open and obvious danger rule. . .1810
. Restatement (Third). . .30,002J–30,002N
. scope of duty. . .1805
. sophisticated users. . .1830
. unavoidably unsafe products. . .1835

WARRANTY. . .500
. chart of UCC jurisdictions. . .520
. express warranty. . .595
. implied warranties. . .645
. . fitness for a particular purpose. . .660
. . habitability. . .720
. . merchantability. . .700
. privity of contract
. . food products. . .540
. . nonfood products. . .550
. reliance. . .800
. sale requirement. . .745

WATERCRAFT. . .3730

WEAPONS. . .4220

WHEELS. . .3710

WHOLESALERS. . .2270

Products Liability Reports **WHO**

Step 1:

Consult the Topical Index under an appropriate term, in this instance "Warning Defects." Notice sub-entry "adequacy of warnings," which is followed by "1815." The "1815" refers to a particular paragraph in the set.

Note that a looseleaf service index typically is sophisticated. This same information might be indexed under a different key word or phrase, such as "Design Defects" or "Product Defects." Note also that there are separate indexes in the set for prior cases and for the most recent material not yet integrated into the larger indexes.

See next illustration for Step 2.

[Illustration 14–2]

PAGE FROM COMPILATION VOLUME, CCH PRODUCTS LIABILITY REPORTER

981 2-2001   Warning Defects   4221

¶ 1815 ADEQUACY OF WARNINGS

Once a duty to warn is established, which is generally a question of law, the adequacy or sufficiency of the warning must be established. The question of adequacy is most often a question of fact for the jury.

Under strict products liability, a product carrying an inadequate warning is defective because it is unreasonably dangerous to the user or consumer in the absence of an adequate warning. The adequacy of any warning is measured by what warning would be reasonable under the circumstances, which is technically a general negligence standard.

The content of a warning that would discharge a seller's responsibility to the user is one that, if followed, would render the product safe for users. Factors that must be considered by a jury include consumer expectations as to how the product operates, how complicated the product is, the severity and likelihood of harm to which the user will be subject if the product is not properly used, and whether a warning is feasible and likely to prevent injury.

To fulfill this duty, the manufacturer or supplier may be required to list specific dangers inherent in the product or in its use on the product's label or instruction manual. If the product must be used in a certain way to avoid injury, the instructions

---

Step 2:

Consult the paragraph number referred to in the Topical Index, i.e., "¶ 1815." Most CCH looseleaf services provide a brief discussion of the subject of the paragraph, in this instance "Adequacy of Warnings."

Following the general discussion under the paragraph number, there is frequently an alphabetical listing of "Annotations by Jurisdiction" or "Annotations by Topic."

See next illustration.

When a warning is given, the seller may reasonably assume that it will be read and heeded. A product bearing such a warning, which is safe for use if it is followed, is not in a defective condition, nor is it unreasonably dangerous.

Inadequacy of warning is treated under the *Restatement (Third) of Torts: Products Liability* § 2, Comment *i* (see ¶ 30,002J).

Hypersensitive or Idiosyncratic Users. Warnings by a product manufacturer or seller are not necessarily inadequate because they do not specifically warn an allergic user; it is generally sufficient to warn of known dangers. Some decisions have limited liability where there has not been an "appreciable" number of users suffering an adverse reaction. However, where the severity of the potential injury is great, even if the risk to the ordinary user is slight, a duty to warn may be imposed, and warnings may be inadequate based on failure to warn of a slight risk of severe injury. This topic is discussed by the *Restatement 3d* at Comment *k* (see § 30,002L).

Annotations to ¶ 1815 Appear by Jurisdiction Below, as Follows:

Alabama	.01	Colorado	.06
Alaska	.02	Connecticut	.07
Arizona	.03	Delaware	.08
Arkansas	.04	District of Columbia	.09
California	.05	Florida	.10

Products Liability Reports   **¶ 1815**

[Illustration 14–3]

PAGE FROM COMPILATION VOLUME, CCH PRODUCTS LIABILITY REPORTER

4222   **Strict Liability**   981 2-2001

.01 Alabama.—Whether a warning to a tester of a high-pressure vessel not to stand in front of a pipe stopper during a hydrostatic test adequately apprised the tester of the risk of injury and death presented by the mismatching of the jaws securing the stopper was a question of fact. The tester sustained a fatal head injury when the stopper became dislodged and shot off of one of the vessel's pipes during the test. [SJ]'

> *Hicks v. Commercial Union Ins. Co.* (AlaSCt 1994) PRODUCTS LIABILITY REPORTS ¶ 14,023, 652 So2d 211.

Manufacturer's warnings that were included on the labels, decals, instructions, and hang tag that accompanied a kerosene heater, as well as in the own[...]
ni[...]
an[...]
ha[...]
os[...]
tu[...]
pr[...]
from the purchaser's use of gasoline to fuel the heater. The purchaser had read the instructions and warnings before using the heater and failed to heed them. [SJ]

> *Yarbrough v. Sears, Roebuck & Co.* (AlaSCt 1993) PRODUCTS LIABILITY REPORTS ¶ 13,745, 628 So2d 478.

Warnings given by a manufacturer of a silicone breast implant understated the risks of the implant's rupturing during a surgical procedure.

> *Toole v. McClintock* (11thCir 1993) PRODUCTS LIABILITY REPORTS ¶ 13,606, 999 F2d 549; *2d opin* (11thCir 2000), *sub nom. Toole v. Baxter Healthcare Corp.*, PRODUCTS LIABILITY REPORTS ¶ 15,971.

Whether warnings by the manufacturer of a multipiece wheel assembly, which had propensity to explode when a tire was being inflated on it, were adequate was a jury question. A tire changer

died when he inflated a tire. The wheel assembly exploded, and he was struck by pieces of the wheel rim. The assembly parts were not imprinted with a warning and were not color-coded to prevent mismatching. The changer had no access to manuals or charts to insure that parts he was using were matching parts. [SJ]

> *Reynolds v. Bridgestone/Firestone, Inc.* (11thCir 1993) PRODUCTS LIABILITY REPORTS ¶ 13,477, 989 F2d 465.

Warnings on packages of cigarette lighters that the lighters should be kept out of the reach of, or away from, children were inadequate as a matter of law. An action was brought by the parents of a 4-year-old child who died in a fire she allegedly [...]
[...]
LIABILITY REPORTS ¶ 13,165, 597 So2d 1550.

In an action brought by the estate of a tractor owner who was killed when his tractor tipped over and landed on him, the warning supplied by the manufacturer in the owner's manual that the tractor should not be operated without a roll guard was inadequate as a matter of law. A jury question remained as to whether the danger of the tractor's rollover propensity was obviated by the manufacturer's warning.

> *Deere & Co. v. Grose* (AlaSCt 1991) PRODUCTS LIABILITY REPORTS ¶ 12,957, 586 So2d 196.

A manufacturer and a seller of a one-person motorcycle adequately warned of the dangers associated with carrying passengers on the vehicle as a matter of law. Thus, a 14-year-old passenger who disregarded the manufacturer's warnings could not recover damages for a leg injury he sustained while being driven on the motorcycle.

Starting with paragraph 1815.01 are digests of all cases, arranged alphabetically by state, dealing with "Adequacy of Warnings."

Be sure to read the relevant cases in their entirety. Notice how citations are given to both the CCH reporter and to the *National Reporter System.*

' [SJ] *indicates a post-1992 summary judgment ruling.*

¶ **1815.01**

[Illustration 14–4]

PAGE FROM CUMULATIVE INDEX, CCH PRODUCTS LIABILITY REPORTER

979   1-2001   **Cumulative Index to Prior Decisions**   **11,103**
                See also Cumulative Index to Current Decisions

From Compilation   **To Current Decisions**
Paragraph No.   **Paragraph No.**

1770	.05	Design defect claim involving assault rifle not allowed (CalCtApp)	15,872
	.14	Employer's addition of safety device to envelope machine (NDIll)	15,875
	.19	No evidence of laundry unit safety device's feasibility (GaCtApp)	15,938
	.36	Issue as to truck bunk bed's lack of safety device (EDPa) (applying Ohio law)	15,856
	.39	Jury issue as to truck bunk bed's lack of safety device (EDPa)	15,856
1780	.15	Jury properly instructed on defective design in cigarette case (IndCtApp)	15,846
	.49	Issue as to pesticide's unavoidably unsafe character (WashSCt) ans'g cert ques fr (9thCir)	15,931
1805	.07	No duty to warn of beer consumption levels' effects (DConn)	15,913
	.21	No heeding presumption for cigarette smoker who knew of dangers (DMd)	15,883
	.22	Snowblower maker has no continuing duty to warn remote purchasers (MasAppCt)	15,825
	.31	Recycling plant conveyor maker has warning duty as component supplier (2dCir) (applying NJ law)	15,881
	.33	Brush chipper maker's successor could have independent duty to warn (WDNY)	15,917
	.36	Jury issue as to truck bunk bed's lack of warnings (EDPa) (applying Ohio law)	15,856
	.36	Smoking dangers not common knowledge from 1950 to 1965 (6thCir)	15,857
	.36	Failure-to-warn instruction correct in air bag defect claim (6thCir)	15,898
	.39	Jury issue as to truck bunk bed's lack of warnings (EDPa)	15,856
	.41	Smoker's claims allowed based on pre-1964 conduct (DRI)	15,827
1810	.21	Cigarettes' dangers open and obvious, common knowledge (DMd)	15,883
	.33	Jury issue as to worker's actual knowledge of tire rim danger (NYAppDiv)	15,873
	.36	Firearms' dangers open and obvious in municipality's claim (OhioCtApp)	15,880
	.36	Dangers of cigarette smoking matter of common knowledge (6thCir)	15,899
	.39	SUV cargo area danger not open and obvious (EDPa)	15,912
1815	.09	No proof that hormone maker inadequately warned of birth defects (DDC)	15,921
	.14	Jury issue as to adequacy of envelope machine's warnings (NDIll)	15,875
	.19	Pickup truck manual adequately warned about air bag nondeployment (EDLa)	15,939
	.28	Propane gas seller adequately warned of odorant fade danger (8thCir)	15,945
	.31	Recycling plant conveyor maker provided adequate warnings (2dCir) (applying NJ law)	15,881
	.36	Failure-to-warn instruction correct in air bag defect claim (6thCir)	15,898
	.37	Issue as to adequacy of water sports vest's warnings (10thCir)	15,946
	.39	Jury issue as to pneumatic nail gun's adequacy of warnings (EDPa)	15,821
	.39	Jury issue on adequacy of SUV's warning on riding in cargo area (EDPa)	15,912
1830	.28	Propane gas seller has no duty to warn sophisticated users (8thCir)	15,945
	.37	Issue as to duty to warn experienced mechanic of lift's use (OklaCtCivApp)	15,936
1835	.09	Synthetic hormone deemed unavoidably unsafe product (DDC)	15,921

A researcher must determine if any relevant cases were decided after those appearing in the main (compilation) volume. This is accomplished by consulting the cross-reference tables that contain current materials.

Parties

2130	.05	Nuclear power worker's spouse could be foreseeable bystander (9thCir)	15,864
	.05	Firefighter's rule bars claim v. semiautomatic assault rifle maker (CalCtApp)	15,872
	.36	Municipality cannot bring claims against firearms makers (OhioCtApp)	15,880
2220	.11	Issue as to forklift assembler's liability as manufacturer (GaCtApp)	15,922
2230	.31	Recycling plant conveyor maker has warning duty as component supplier (2dCir) (applying NJ law)	15,881
	.45	Water pump maker not liable for finished spa's defects (TexCtApp)	15,887
2240	.26	Insufficient proof of workbridge maker's identity (8thCir)	15,862
	.33	Question as to market share liability of handgun makers (2dCir) ques cert to (NYCtApp)	15,882
	.36	Municipality must specify firearms makers, defects in claims (OhioCtApp)	15,880
	.37	Semi-tractor frame lift sufficiently identified (OklaCtCivApp)	15,936
2245	.33	Exceptions do not apply to brush chipper maker's successor (WDNY)	15,917
2260	.11	Pharmacist, pharmacy not subject to strict liability (GaCtApp)	15,851
	.47	Utility did not sell electricity that caused house fire (VtSCt)	15,914
	.49	Swimming pool trade association owes duty to consumers (WashCtApp)	15,894
	.51	Reconditioner could be liable for crane's new ladders (WisSCt)	15,876

Products Liability Reports

ILLUSTRATIONS USING BNA FAIR EMPLOYMENT PRACTICES (FEP) DIVISION OF LABOR RELATIONS REPORTER

Problem: Can attorneys' fees be collected for the work of paralegals and law clerks?

[Illustration 14–5]

PAGE FROM BNA LABOR RELATIONS REPORTER,
FAIR EMPLOYMENT PRACTICES ALL-STATES VOLUME

451:108   STATE FAIR EMPLOYMENT PRACTICE LAWS   No. 923

State Family Leave Laws/Rules Exceeding Federal FMLA Requirements

Comparison Chart — The chart that follows shows those states that have family related leave mandates in *excess* of those contained in the federal Family and Medical Leave Act. Footnotes indicate those states that provide such leave for public employees only and any separate maternity, parental, school, or adoption leave provisions.

The first three categories of the chart relate to a state's family medical leave act or rule. The fourth category relates only to a state's separate maternity, parental, school, or adoption leave provisions. When this benefit applies only to state employees, it is followed by a pound symbol (#).

STATE MANDATES BEYOND FMLA

STATE (# means public employees only)	Length of Leave (More than 12 weeks)	Minimum Number of Employees (Fewer than 50)	Employee's Qualification (Fewer)	Separate Maternity* Parental** School*** Adoption****
Alabama	none	none	none	yes* #
Alaska#	yes	yes	yes	none
Arizona	none	none	none	yes** #
Arkansas	none	none	none	yes* #
California	none	none	none	yes*/ **/ ***
Colorado#	yes	none	none	yes****
Connecticut	yes	none	yes	none

> Several looseleaf services include coverage for state laws. In some, comparison charts are published showing how different states have dealt with a particular issue through legislation, as is shown in this illustration. Occasionally, a chart will show where the laws on a topic for various states are located in the looseleaf service.

STATE				
Georgia	none	none	none	none
Hawaii	none	none	yes	yes*
Idaho	none	none	none	yes* #
Illinois	none	none	none	yes***/ ****#
Indiana	none	none	none	yes* #
Iowa	none	none	none	yes*
Kansas#	yes	none	none	none
Kentucky#	yes	none	none	yes****
Louisiana	none	none	none	yes*/ ***
Maine	none	yes	none	none

[Illustration 14–6]

PAGE FROM BNA MASTER INDEX TO LABOR RELATIONS REPORTER
CONTAINING FAIR EMPLOYMENT PRACTICES (FEP) OUTLINE OF CLASSIFICATIONS

D-I 116   FEP Cases OUTLINE OF CLASSIFICATIONS

▶ **108.81—Contd.**   ▶ **108.89 Attorneys and Attorneys' Fees**

.8155   —Against EEOC, etc.   [For attorneys and attorneys' fees in
.8157   —Depositions   the federal sector, see ▶ 110.8901 et seq.]
.8158   —Interrogatories   .8901   In general
.8160   —Records, documents, etc.   .8903   Appointment
            [For interrogatories, see   [For petition for attorney, see
            ▶ 108.8158.]   ▶ 108.6915.]
.8162   —Requests for admission   .8905   Disqualification
.8163   —Ex parte interviews; access to em- .8908   Paralegals and law clerks
            ployees and ex-employees   Fees
            [For cases prior to FEP Vol. 53.   .8911   —In general
            see ▶ 108.8151.]   .8912   —Factors in determining fees
        —Defenses   [For contingency fee cases after
.8165   ——In general   FEP Vol. 46, see ▶ 108.8920. For
            [For relevancy defense cases   incentive fees, including bonuses,
            after FEP Vol. 52, see   multipliers and upward adjust-
            ▶ 108.8170.]   ments of fees, see ▶ 108.8918. For
.8166   ——Privilege   delay in awarding fees, see
                                                        ▶ 108.8919.]
                                                    Discovery for purpose of determin-
                                                        ing fees
                                                    Purpose of award
Step 1:   Burden of proof
                                                    Contingency fees
   Consult the Outline of Classifications for Fair   [For cases before FEP Vol. 47,
Employment Practices (FEP) in the Master Index to   see ▶ 108.8912.]
BNA's Labor Relations Reporter. Note how 108.8908 Incentive fee (bonus, multiplier,
seems relevant to our research problem. Consult   upward adjustment of fees, etc.)
this paragraph number for digests of cases in the
Consolidated Digest and Index (CDI) in the Master   [For upward adjustment or mul-
Index. See next illustration.   tiplier due to delay in award after
                                                        FEP Vol. 30, see ▶ 108.8919.]
   Note: This search could have started in the   Delay in awarding fees
FEP-Master Index using a subject approach rather   [For cases prior to FEP Vol. 31,
than a classification approach.   see ▶ 108.8912 and ▶ 108.8918.]
                                                    Award; entitlement
                                                    In general
                                                        [Includes Equal Access to Justice
                                                        Act cases]
                                                    Discretion of court in awarding
                                                        fees
                                                    Discretion of court as to amount
                                                    Date of payment
                                                        [For time spent in litigating fee
.839   State FEP Acts   issue, see ▶ 108.8918.]
            [For cases prior to FEP Vol 53, see .8927   —Calculation of hours
            ▶ 108.831.]   .8928   —Allocation of liability, award
                                                        against attorneys
▶ **108.85 Sanctions**   .8932   —Award against EEOC, US
                                             .8933   —Award against state, local govern-
            [For sanctions in discovery proceedings,   ments
            see ▶ 108.8175. For attorneys' fees for dis- .8935   —Appeals, fees for
            covery proceedings, see ▶ 108.8937. For .8937   —Discovery proceedings, fees for
            sanctions for appeals, see ▶ 108.781.] .8938   —Time spent in litigating fee issue
.8501   In general   [For rate of payment, see
.8511   Fed.R.Civ.P. 11   ▶ 108.8926.]
                                             .8940   Prevailing party
                                             .8943   Interim award
▶ **108.87 Pattern-or-Practice Suits**   .8950   Recovery by employer, union
                                             .8960   1866 and 1871 Acts, availability of
            [For remedies, see ▶ 200.01 et seq.]   fees
.871   In general   .8965   Recovery by private non-profit corpo-
.873   Jurisdiction and procedure   ration
.875   Evidence   .8967   Third parties; intervenors

[Illustration 14–7]

PAGE FROM BNA MASTER INDEX TO LABOR RELATIONS REPORTER CONTAINING FAIR EMPLOYMENT PRACTICES (FEP) CUMULATIVE DIGEST AND INDEX (CDI)

A732   85 FEP Cases   Final CDI

▶ **108.871** (Contd.)
public interest in eliminating employment discrimination. —*Reid v. Lockheed Martin Aeronautics Co.* (DC NGa) 85 FEP Cases 602

▶ **108.8901**   Failure of unsuccessful former employee to oppose employer's bill of costs is not evidence of bad faith that would entitle employer to sanctions, since 28 U.S.C. §1920 states that costs will be allowed of course to prevailing party that files bill of costs, there is no dispute that employer is prevailing party, and unless former employee had reason to challenge reasonableness or amount of costs it would have been indication of bad faith, or at least indication that he intended to harass employer, for him to have challenged employer's bill of costs. —*Kron v. Moravia Central School District* (DC NNY) 85 FEP Cases 1414

Counsel representing female employee of CIA will not be permitted to attend federal district cou̶rt's in camera review of CIA director's cl̶
details co̶
and statut̶
in unclassi̶
ee's reque̶
and files, ̶
has been ̶
would per̶
vit. —*Til̶*
Cases 404̶

Attorne̶
client for ̶
negligent f̶
42 U.S.C̶
caused hi̶
those obta̶
cially esto̶
he would ̶
ages unde̶
despite co̶
position on matter throughout earlier action, where attorneys were not parties in that action, and issue of whether former client had claim under §1981 was never addressed on merits. —*Olmsted v. Emmanuel* (Fla DistCtApp) 85 FEP Cases 651

White former employee who recovered damages under Title VII but who was precluded from seeking additional damages under 42 U.S.C. §1981 because of his attorneys' negligent failure to raise §1981 as basis for relief in pretrial statement cannot show, for purpose of his malpractice action, that reasonable person could have found that he would have prevailed on §1981 claim but for attorneys' negligence, where he had alleged that he had been discharged

in retaliation for complaining to superiors about employment practices that discriminated against blacks, but federal court of appeals had ruled in earlier case that §1981 did not apply to claimant who did not allege that discrimination against him was due to his race. *Id.*

▶ **108.8908**   Lodestar amount of attorneys' fees of $1,096,412.60, which includes $25,920 for work of paralegals and externs, will not be reduced simply because it is larger than amount recovered by 11 employees who accepted offers of judgment, where each of them has received substantial recovery that is not just nuisance value settlement, some remain employed by employer and some have retained right to press forward with other claims, their attorneys performed well, and fees are not some large multiple of recovery. —*Kitchen v. TTX Co.* (DC NIll) 85 FEP Cases 96

▶ **108.8911**   Attorneys' fees were properly ̶ved that em̶
̶ for assisting̶
̶OC charges,̶
̶ld have been̶
̶ attendance̶
̶d Corp. (CA̶

̶n for award̶
̶nsidered un̶
̶t filed within̶
̶s required by̶
̶e that judg-̶
̶t of appeals̶
̶ not address̶
̶nctive relief,̶
̶aterials were̶
̶n-final judg-̶
̶s (DC NGa)̶

▶ **108.8912**   Federal dist. court properly awarded $150,837 in attorneys' fees to exemployee who prevailed on his ADA claim, where court found that his attorneys' lodestar value accurately reflected complexity and novelty of case, that ability and reputation of attorneys was accurately reflected in their customary billing rates, and that result obtained justified lodestar value. —*Giles v. General Electric Co.* (CA 5) 11 AD Cases 844

Federal district court properly awarded $150,837 in attorneys' fees to former employee who prevailed on his ADA claim, where his attorneys' lodestar value accurately reflected complexity and novelty of case, ability and reputation of attorneys was

Step 2:

Note how 108.8908 digests cases dealing with the question of awarding attorneys' fees to non-lawyers employed by attorneys.

The search must be updated by consulting any supplemental indexes.

Full texts of the digested cases are in the volumes entitled *Fair Employment Practices* (FEP) Cases. Note that the case is located in volume 85 of FEP Cases. This case is published first in the looseleaf "Cases" binder of the FEP volumes and later in a bound volume.

See next illustration.

[Illustration 14–8]

PAGE FROM A VOLUME OF BNA FAIR EMPLOYMENT PRACTICES CASES

Kitchen v. TTX Company   85 FEP Cases 97

non-attorney work such as photocopying, where attorney's presence at depositions was necessary for effective preparation of trial team and made her more effective in reviewing documents, her presence probably resulted in lower total fee request because her rate was lower than those of other attorneys, and counsel were reasonable in time spent on letter writing and non-attorney work; moreover, hours billed by employer's counsel, which do not include valuable and time consuming efforts by employer's in-house counsel, ex-

whose opinion was ultimately barred, where such compilation was reasonable in that it was gathered to assist expert in his attempt to establish that race played role in promotions within employer.

[9] Costs ▶ 108.901

Employees who accepted offers of judgment are entitled to award of $12,680 for creation of demonstrative exhibits, despite employer's contention that it did not know about

---

Step 3:

This is the start of the full text of the opinion referenced in the previous Illustration. Read the full text of digested cases located through indexes. In the problem given, only one case is relevant. Note how the publisher provides headnotes that enable the researcher to go directly to the point in the case being researched, in this instance headnote 7.

See next illustration.

▶ 108.8926

Hourly rate for employees' attorneys will be determined with reference to number of years of practice, their overall experience during those years, fees that other courts have set in past, observation of their performance, and evidence submitted pertaining to fees for other similar practitioners; one attorney who requested rate of $325 per hour is entitled to $295 per hour, another attorney who also sought $325 per hour will be awarded $240 per hour, and third attorney, who sought $190 per hour, will be awarded $185 per hour.

[7] Attorneys' fees 108.8908 ▶ 108.8912 108.8921

Lodestar amount of attorneys' fees of $1,096,412.60, which includes $25,920 for work of paralegals and externs, will not be reduced simply because it is larger than amount recovered by 11 employees who accepted offers of judgment, where each of them has received substantial recovery that is not just nuisance value settlement, some of them remain employed by employer and some have retained right to press forward with other claims, their attorneys performed well for them, and fees are not some large multiple of recovery.

[8] Costs ▶ 108.901

Costs associated with compilation of statistical data, which was performed by husband of one of employees' attorneys, are reimbursable, even though data were compiled for use in statistical analysis by employees' expert

penses, including taxi cab fares and some deposition transcripts, that their attorneys are unable to document, since attorneys have responsibility to account for their expenses.

H. Candace Gorman and Gregory X. Gorman (Law Office of H. Candace Gorman), Chicago, Ill., for plaintiffs.

John Yo-Hwan Lee (Ross & Hardies), Chicago, Ill., and Terrence C. Newby, Thomas P. Kane, and David M. Wilk (Oppenheimer, Wolff & Donnelly), St. Paul, Minn., for defendant.

Full Text of Opinion

WAYNE R. ANDERSON, District Judge.

This case is before the Court to resolve the petition for fees filed by H. Candice Gorman, Gregory X. Gorman and Catherine Caporusso, the attorneys for the plaintiffs in this action. Each of the eleven plaintiffs accepted a Rule 68 Offer of Judgment made to each of them by the defendant TTX Company, their employer. The parties submitted extensive briefs and the Court conducted a hearing over four days with respect to this issue. The petitioners requested $1,308,153 in attorneys' fees and $54,127.46 as reimbursement for expenses. We have concluded that the defendant should pay to them a total of $1,096,412.60 as fair and reasonable attorneys' fees and $51,357.66 as reimbursement for expenses.

[Illustration 14–9]

PAGE FROM A VOLUME OF BNA FAIR EMPLOYMENT PRACTICES CASES

85 FEP Cases 100   Kitchen v. TTX Company

(We note, parenthetically, that the hours billed by defense counsel to TTX exceeded the hours for which plaintiffs' attorneys have sought compensation, and the dollars paid to defense counsel exceed the amount requested by the plaintiffs' attorneys. Moreover, during the course of this lawsuit the Court observed that in-house counsel for TTX made extremely valuable and time consuming contributions to the defense of the case; none of this in-house counsel time was included in the billings made by defense counsel to TTX. Although these observations are certainly not decisive with respect to the Court's determination of the reasonableness of the request made by plaintiffs' attorneys, they are a very strong indicator that the time spent and the amount requested by the attorneys for the plaintiffs are well within the realm of reasonableness.)

[6] We have determined the hourly rate for all three attorneys with reference to the number of years they have practiced, their overall

is larger than the recovery and we determine that the total fee award is $1,059,260.60.

V. Costs

TTX challenges the bill of costs in several ways. TTX argues that the expenses associated with Christopher Ross' services should not be compensated. Second TTX argues that they should not have to pay for the demonstrative exhibits. Third, TTX argues that they should not have to pay for the expenses which plaintiffs' attorneys cannot document. Finally, TTX argues that, based on whether all plaintiffs are prevailing parties, it should only pay a pro rata share of the remaining expenses.

[8] Christopher Ross, H. Candice Gorman's husband, compiled statistical data for use by plaintiffs' expert Dr. Skoog. Dr. Skoog prepared a statistical analysis which attempted to establish that race played a role in promotions within TTX. Although the Magistrate Judge ultimately barred the use of Dr. Skoog's opin-

Bracketed numbers in the text of the opinion, in this example [7], identify the location that served as the topic of the headnote.

other similar practitioners. We determined that H. Candice Gorman is entitled to $295 per hour, Gregory X. Gorman is entitled to $240 per hour and Catherine Caporusso is entitled to $185 per hour. Multiplying the number of hours by the hourly rate results in a lodestar figure of $1,070,492.60. In addition, plaintiffs are entitled to the reasonable sum of $25,920 for the work of paralegals and externs. Therefore, the total fee lodestar is $1,096,412.60.

[7] Finally, we must determine whether the fee is reasonable given the degree of success obtained. We believe the fee is reasonable. There is no mechanical rule requiring that a reasonable attorneys' fee be no greater than the recovery. *Connolly v. National Sch. Bus Serv. Inc.*, 177 F.3d 593, 597 [80 FEP Cases 92] (7th Cir. 1998). We have considered the question of proportionality. All plaintiffs have received a substantial recovery. Furthermore, some of the plaintiffs remain employed by TTX and some have retained their rights to press forward with other claims. As we noted above, the offers of judgment do not represent nuisance value settlements, all plaintiffs prevailed and the plaintiffs' attorneys performed well for their clients. Finally, the argument for reducing the lodestar is most compelling if the fees are some large multiple of the recovery. *Id.* That is not the case here. Therefore, we will not reduce the lodestar simply because it

pensation for the services of Christopher Ross.

[9] TTX argues that it did not know about the demonstrative exhibits when it made the offers of judgment. TTX made the offers on the eve of trial. Plaintiffs were reasonably preparing for a jury trial by creating demonstrative exhibits for the jury. This is a reasonable practice and TTX has advanced no authority to suggest that the touchstone of awarding costs is whether defendant was aware of the expenditure. Therefore, we award plaintiffs $12,680 for the creation of demonstrative exhibits.

[10] TTX argues that plaintiffs should not be compensated for expenses which plaintiffs cannot document. We agree. Plaintiffs' attorneys have been unable to document several expenses including taxi cab fares and some deposition transcripts. Plaintiffs' attorneys have a responsibility to account for their expenses. Because they are unable to do so here, we grant defendant's objection and disallow $2,769.80 in expenses.

TTX's final argument is that plaintiffs should only be entitled to fees for the prevailing plaintiffs. Because we determined above that all plaintiffs prevailed in this action, we will not consider whether we would have divided the expenses on a pro rata basis. Plaintiffs' attorneys are entitled to all the reasonable fees.

Chapter 15

CITATORS*

Law is a discipline that looks both backward and forward. In advising clients, drafting agreements, arguing cases before a court, proposing legislation, and analyzing legal developments, lawyers refer to cases, statutes, regulations, and secondary sources. They rely upon those sources to reflect the law on a particular subject at a particular point in time. Lawyers may be interested in determining the sources of a particular law or legal theory; they look backward from a particular source to find earlier discussions of the same issue. Or researchers may wish to determine how an issue articulated in an authority has been addressed by subsequent authorities; attorneys look forward to see citations to the original authority in more recent materials. To find sources of a law or legal theory, lawyers look to the document at hand; they read citations and note footnote and bibliographic references. Lawyers consult citators, also called citation services, to determine how a particular legal authority has been used and interpreted by, "cited" by, other authority and if it has been followed or dismissed.

Citators identify where a specific source, the "cited authority," has been cited by another source, the "citing authority." A citator can also indicate the kind of treatment an authority has received. Citation services are not unique to the discipline of law. But, because our legal system is based on the doctrine of precedent—that is, we rely on judicial precedent to ensure similar outcomes—citation services play a more important role in legal research than they do in many other disciplines. The adverse consequences of citing to, and relying on, a judicial holding that has been criticized or overturned can be serious. Courts have little sympathy for attorneys who fail to ensure the continuing validity of the authorities they cite.[1] The use of legal citation services enables attorneys to ensure that the authorities they rely on continue to represent "good" law.

As law practice and legal scholarship become more interdisciplinary and more international, the sources used by attorneys and scholars to make legal arguments correspondingly expand. So, in addition to looking backward and forward, legal researchers increasingly look sideways—they seek to broaden their research across disciplines, jurisdictions, and audiences; more and more frequently, they may need to consult citation services or alternatives to those services outside traditional legal research resources.

This chapter focuses on the traditional and most widely used legal citation services—*Shepard's*, (in *LexisNexis* and print format) and *Westlaw's KeyCite* (as it exists in both the *Westlaw Classic* and the *WestlawNext* platforms)—but also examines other

---

* Jeanne F. Price, Associate Professor of Law and Director of the Law Library, William S. Boyd School of Law, University of Nevada, Las Vegas, revised this chapter.

[1] *See, e.g.*, McCarthy v. Oregon Freeze Dry, Inc., 976 P.2d 566, 567 (Or. App. 1999): "The trial court denied the motion, concluding that the mistake alleged—failure to 'Shepardize' a key case—was not excusable. Plaintiff appealed, we affirmed without opinion, and the Supreme Court eventually denied review." For more examples, see Mary Whisner, *When Judges Scold Lawyers*, 96 LAW LIBR. J. 557, 561–64 (2004).

legal citators and citation services outside the legal domain. The chapter concludes with a discussion of alternatives to citation services that may enable researchers to accomplish similar objectives but within a larger universe of information and using different metrics to measure impact and influence.

Legal researchers typically use a single citator service during the course of a research project and even throughout their careers. You should be aware, however, that the citators' differences in arrangement, searching, and coverage, as well as unique underlying software algorithms for searching each service, might result in differences in their results.[2] Some researchers on occasion use a second citator to double-check their results.

A. USES AND FUNCTIONS OF CITATORS

By identifying sources that have cited a particular authority, citation services serve two primary functions: (1) they enable researchers to assess the validity and strength of the cited authority, and (2) they provide a means of expanding research across jurisdictions and types of sources.

Citators indicate a case's *direct history*—that is, earlier and later proceedings in the same dispute. They also provide citations to cases and other sources that *cite* the case— authorities that might affect the case's precedential value or provide useful research leads.

B. EXAMPLE: USES AND FUNCTIONS OF CITATION SERVICES

The following example illustrates the use of a citator in effective legal research. Consider *City of Chicago v. Terminiello*, 79 N.E. 2d 39 (Ill. 1948), a case decided by the Illinois Supreme Court in 1948. [Illustration 15–1] That case's *prior* history includes two reported cases:

> — First, a decision by the Illinois Supreme Court in January 1947 (*City of Chicago v. Terminiello*, 71 N.E. 2d 2 (Ill. 1947))—in that case, the Illinois Supreme Court determined that it did not have jurisdiction absent a particular finding by the trial court); and

> — Second, a decision by an Illinois appellate court in June 1947 (*City of Chicago v. Terminiello*, 74 N.E. 2d 45 (Ill. App. Ct. 1947)).

The *subsequent* history of *City of Chicago v. Terminiello*, 79 N.E. 2d 39, the 1948 Illinois Supreme Court case, includes three reported decisions:

> — First, the decision by the United States Supreme Court in December 1948 to grant certiorari in the *Terminiello* case (*Terminiello v. City of Chicago*, 335 U.S. 890 (1948));

> — Second, a United States Supreme Court decision (*Terminiello v. City of Chicago*, 337 U.S. 1, 65 S. Ct. 894 (1949)) reversing the 1948 Illinois Supreme Court case; and

---

[2] *See, e.g.*, Susan Nevelow Mart, *The Relevance of Results Generated by Human Indexing and Computer Algorithms: A Study of West's Headnotes and Key Numbers and LexisNexis's Headnotes and Topics*, 102 LAW LIBR. J. 221 (2010).

— Third, the decision of the United States Supreme Court not to rehear the case (*Terminiello v. City of Chicago*, 337 U.S. 934 (1949)).

Citators provide references to the *direct* history of a case—its prior and subsequent history. By tracing a case as it moves through the judicial system—from intermediate court of appeals to court of last resort, and, perhaps, back again—researchers can determine whether the principles enumerated in any particular case were questioned or somehow devalued in later decisions.

Beyond a case's direct history, citators provide references to cases, administrative adjudications, law review articles, other secondary sources, and, in many instances, court documents (e.g., petitions, pleadings, motions, and briefs) that cite the case. To the extent that a particular case is relevant to a research question, authorities that cite that case may be equally, or sometimes more, relevant. Moreover, the nature and quantity of courts and the number and prestige of scholars that cite a particular judicial authority provide a researcher with some indication of the importance of that authority. If a case has been cited frequently (and favorably) by a variety of appellate courts, its influence is strong and it is probably important to cite to that case in any argument involving the issue it discusses. Judges, practitioners, and scholars all value comprehensive research; use of citation services is one way of ensuring thoroughness.

Similarly, for legislation, citators can provide information about prior versions of a statute, as well as subsequent legislative activities and judicial action that affect the validity of that statute. Materials that reference the statute—from legislative history materials to law review articles to cases and other statutes—will also be included in statute citators. Similarly, information provided by citators for regulatory materials may include historical information (i.e., regulatory documents that evidence the regulation's adoption and amendment) and references to cases, administrative documents, and secondary sources that cite the regulation.

Citators may also be used to find material that cites some secondary sources. For example, *KeyCite* (in *Westlaw*) and *Shepard's* (in *LexisNexis*) both show more than thirty cases and hundreds of secondary material citing William J. Brennan, Jr., *The Bill of Rights and the States: The Revival of State Constitutions as Guardians of Individual Rights*, 61 N.Y.U. L. REV. 535 (1986). Among secondary sources, law review articles are most comprehensively represented in citators, both as cited authorities and as citing references. Coverage of other secondary sources is more limited.[3]

C. HISTORY AND FORMATS OF CITATION SERVICES

Except for a few looseleaf services that provided citation information in specialized areas of law, prior to the late 1990s there existed only one comprehensive legal citation service: *Shepard's Citations*. From its beginnings in the late nineteenth century as a case citation service, *Shepard's Citations* evolved to include constitutions, statutes, administrative rules and regulations, administrative adjudications, court rules, law review articles, restatements, and individual patents. Jurisdictions covered in the print

---

[3] Note that online citators draw their citing references from material available in their related databases. For example, if *Nimmer on Copyright* (a treatise available on *LexisNexis*) cites a case, then *Shepard's* will list it as a citing reference for that case. *Westlaw*'s citator, *KeyCite* will not list it, because *Nimmer on Copyright* is not available in *Westlaw*. The reverse is true for a case cited in, say, *Patry on Copyright*, a treatise available in *Westlaw*.

versions of *Shepard's* included the United States, both federal and state, and Canada. In its print version, *Shepard's* was (and continues to be) published in several different units. Each unit of *Shepard's* provides similar information with respect to the different authorities it covers and retains the distinctive Shepard's organization, format, and system of notation.

The use of *Shepard's Citations* to update and verify legal authority became so established that lawyers commonly referred to that process as "Shepardizing."[4] In the 1980s, the company that produced *Shepard's Citations* licensed it for use in *LexisNexis* and *Westlaw*. The online data was no more current than the print product, but it was much more convenient to use. In the late 1990s, *Shepard's Citations* was acquired by Reed Elsevier, which also acquired *LexisNexis*. *Shepard's* is now available only in *LexisNexis*. In 1997, *Westlaw* introduced its own electronic citation service, *KeyCite*. With the introduction of *WestlawNext* in 2010, *KeyCite* was more completely integrated into the *Westlaw* research system. Although *KeyCite* functionality continues to exist within *WestlawNext*, *KeyCite* is less of a discrete component of *WestlawNext* than was the case with respect to *Westlaw*.

Shepard's and *KeyCite* continue to be the most comprehensive products available, in terms of jurisdictions and types of authorities covered. With the advent of other online legal research products, however, additional citation services have become available. *Loislaw*, *VersusLaw*, *Bloomberg Law*, *Casemaker*, and *FastCase*, each of which offers to subscribers a variety of primary authorities and, in some cases, secondary authorities, all have citation service components.[5] Their citators are not yet as well-developed and comprehensive as *Shepard's* or *KeyCite*.

The marriage of digital technology and citation services is a happy one. Tasks that were time consuming and tedious in print format have been made far easier in an electronic environment. The rapidity of updating, improved interface, graphical representation of concepts and chronology, and elimination of multiple sources all combine to make use of electronic citators far more efficient than use of the traditional print services. That said, attorneys might find themselves in situations without access to electronic resources. Furthermore, an understanding of the development and structure of the print version of *Shepard's* can provide insights into the use and functionality of online citators. The focus of this chapter is on the digital version of *Shepard's* and on *KeyCite*, and especially its iteration in *WestlawNext*, but descriptions and explanations of the print versions of *Shepard's* also are included, as are summary descriptions of other online citators and alternatives to citation services.

D. ELECTRONIC CITATORS: *SHEPARD'S* AND *KEYCITE*

There are many similarities in the features of the most widely used citators, *Shepard's* and *KeyCite*, as well as some differences. These are described below:

---

[4] The term "Shepardize" is a registered trademark of Reed Elsevier Properties, Inc.

[5] Researchers who find cases on *Google Scholar* may use the "How cited" function to find cases citing them. And *HeinOnline* offers links to citing articles from its articles and Supreme Court cases. Both processes are versions of a citator.

1.   Common Features

a.   Validating Authority and Finding Other Relevant Authority. Shepard's distinguishes between these functions by offering two options in the *Shepard's* interface in *lexis.com*—"*Shepard's* for Validation" or "*Shepard's* for Research." [Illustration 15–2] "*Shepard's* for Validation"—or what *LexisNexis* calls the "KWIC" view of citing references—includes, for cases, subsequent appellate history and only those citing references that have been assigned analytical notations. The same information is found in *Lexis Advance*. For example, for the U.S. Supreme Court case of *Terminiello v. City of Chicago*, 337 U.S. 1 (1949), "*Shepard's* for Validation" includes the case's subsequent history (the denial of rehearing by the United States Supreme Court at 337 U.S. 934) and more than 150 citing references that include some sort of analytical notation assigned by *Shepard's* that describes the court's treatment of the *Terminiello* case. [Illustration 15–3]

By contrast, "*Shepard's* for Research"—or what *LexisNexis* terms the "FULL" view of citing references—includes, for cases, references to all prior and subsequent history, all cases that refer to the cited source, whether they merit editorial annotation, annotations to statutes that cite the case, and secondary sources that cite the Shepardized case. So, for the *Terminiello* case, "*Shepard's* for Research" includes both prior and subsequent history for the Supreme Court case, as well as references to nearly 800 cases and more than 900 secondary sources (law review and bar journal articles, annotations, and treatises) that have cited the case. [Illustration 15–4]

Similarly, for statutes, "*Shepard's* for Validation" (the KWIC format) sets forth cases and administrative adjudications that have been assigned analytical notations. "*Shepard's* for Research" references all cases, administrative materials, and selected secondary sources and court documents that have cited the statute. [Illustration 15–5] Historical and legislative history information for statutes is made available in *LexisNexis* outside of *Shepard's* through the *Practitioner's Toolbox* link that appears when the text of the statute is viewed.

For regulations, "*Shepard's* for Validation" references administrative and other primary authorities that have been assigned analytical notations describing the treatment of the regulation, while "*Shepard's* for Research" includes citations to all primary authorities and selected secondary authorities and court documents that cite the regulation.

Westlaw similarly provides options to researchers in selecting the types of authorities retrieved upon a citation check. In *Westlaw Classic*, users may elect to limit the number and nature of citing references retrieved for any authority. A researcher may elect to limit *KeyCite* results to "history" or to retrieve all citing references. If the researcher's purpose is to ascertain the validity of a case, there is an additional option available. For cases, *KeyCite* provides (1) the "full" history of the case (which includes prior and subsequent history, as well as "negative" citing references—i.e., those references to which some sort of negative analytical comment is attached), (2) the case's direct (i.e., only prior and subsequent) history, portrayed in a graphical display, or (3) all citing references (cases, administrative materials, secondary sources, and court documents that cite the original case). [Illustration 15–6]

When a case is displayed in *WestlawNext*, tabs above the text of the case link to the history of the case (a graphical presentation of the decisions in the case itself in its different steps up and down the appellate ladder), negative treatment of the case (a list of all cases that have negatively referenced the cited case), and all citing references (including cases, secondary sources, and court documents). [Illustration 15–7]

For statutes, both *Westlaw Classic* and *WestlawNext* provide history and citing reference options. Looking at the history of a statute in *Westlaw Classic*, a user may review either (1) a list of actions and authorities that have affected a statute or (2) a graphical display that portrays the history of the statute over time. [Illustration 15–8] *WestlawNext's* history tab similarly provides both a list of legislative authorities and its version of a graphical display that resembles a timeline of the statute's history. [Illustration 15–9] In both resources, the "citing references" option includes citations to all cases and administrative materials, as well as selected secondary sources and court documents that cite the statute. [Illustration 15–10]

For regulations, *Westlaw Classic's* "history" option includes references to administrative materials that have finalized the administrative action or amended the regulations, while *WestlawNext's* history tab points to prior versions of the regulation. The "citing references" option in both *Westlaw Classic* and *WestlawNext* provides citations to primary authorities that have cited the regulation and to selected secondary sources and court documents.

    b.   Notation of Analytical Treatment and Assignment of Cautionary Signals. The fact that one authority cites an earlier authority often indicates that the citing authority recognizes the persuasiveness and rationale of the prior authority. However, not every citation to an authority is one of endorsement or approval. An authority may be criticized by a subsequent decision or secondary source; the prior authority may be distinguished from the case at hand; or the cited authority may be cited in a dissenting opinion (which, by implication, might indicate that the majority opinion did not agree with the holding or reasoning of the cited authority). In the most extreme case, one authority may cite another only to expressly overrule it. In determining the validity of a particular source, a researcher must be able to identify quickly those subsequent authorities that criticize or distinguish it. Both *Shepard's* and *KeyCite* provide substantive notations that indicate the nature of the treatment received by a cited authority.

Shepard's categorizes citing references and, for cases, denominates those references as including "cautionary," "questioned," "positive," or "neutral" analyses. [Illustration 15–11] A citing case that is categorized under the "cautionary" label has superseded, overruled, not followed, criticized, or distinguished the cited authority. Similarly, *KeyCite* groups some citing references under a "negative cases" or "negative treatment" label; negative cases include those that overturn, abrogate, supersede, recognize the reversal of, distinguish, criticize, or decline to extend the holding of the cited case. [Illustrations 15–6 and 15–12]

These analyses of subsequent authorities enable both *Shepard's* and *KeyCite* to assign substantive labels to cited primary authorities. Those labels provide some indication of the strength and validity of the cited source. *KeyCite* and *WestlawNext* assign labels to judicial decisions, selected administrative decisions, patents, statutes, and regulations. *Shepard's* assigns labels primarily to adjudications and selected administrative materials. *Westlaw* labels range from a red flag (indicating, for cases, that the authority is no longer "good" law with respect to at least one of the issues it discusses) to a green "C" (denoting that the case has neither direct history nor negative citing references). [Illustration 15–13] Similarly, *Shepard's* assigns symbols to authorities ranging from a red stop sign (an indication of "strong" negative treatment) to a green plus sign (a representation that the citing references have a positive impact on the validity of the cited case). [Illustration 15–14]

It is important to note that the symbols assigned to particular authorities by *Shepard's* and *KeyCite* are merely labels that reflect judgments made by editors about the strength of an authority. A diligent researcher will always investigate the subsequent treatment of any cited case. A red flag associated with a case or other authority does not mean that it cannot be cited. The authority may have been criticized for reasons or issues quite distinct from those for which it is cited. The assignment of negative symbols should be understood to be an indication that these authorities require more thorough exploration.

Another indication of the subjective nature of the symbols assigned by *Shepard's* and *KeyCite* is the fact that those two citation services often assign very different labels to the same authority. For example, a 1998 federal district court case, *Piacentini v. Levangie*, 998 F. Supp. 86 (D. Mass. 1998), is assigned a yellow cautionary flag by *KeyCite* (indicating some negative treatment) and a green plus sign by *Shepard's* (a representation that subsequent citing references have a positive impact on the authority of the case). Similarly, the United States Supreme Court case, *Miranda v. Arizona*, 384 U.S. 436 (1966), is assigned a red stop sign by *Shepard's* and a yellow cautionary flag by *KeyCite*. Again, researchers should not overemphasize the significance of symbols assigned by citators to particular authorities; there is no substitute for reading and analyzing an authority on which reliance is placed.[6]

    c.   *Sorting and Filtering Retrieved References.* As a method for finding other relevant sources, citation searches for a popular or well-known case or statute can yield an unworkable number of citing authorities. For example, there are more than 90,000 *Westlaw KeyCite* results for *Miranda v. Arizona*, and more than 17,000 results in *Shepard's* for Securities and Exchange Commission Rule 10b–5. The efficient use of a citation service requires that researchers use methods to narrow the results.

Both *Shepard's* and *KeyCite* provide mechanisms for limiting citing references; the nature of the limitations depends on the type of cited authority. In both services, citing references may be limited by date, jurisdiction, and type of authority. Both services also allow the user to impose a requirement that particular words or phrases appear in the full text of the citing reference. The *Shepard's* mechanism for limiting citing references is the "Focus" feature, which permits the user to restrict retrieved results, for cases as cited authorities, by analysis (positive or negative), citing reference source (e.g., concurring or dissenting opinion), and headnote. [Illustration 15–15] *Westlaw Classic* allows the user to limit the results retrieved by depth of treatment, and headnote topic discussed, while *WestlawNext* groups citing references by type of authority and then provides for narrowing of the results by the application of filters appropriate to each type of authority. [Illustrations 15–16 and 15–17]

For checking citations to cases, *Shepard's* and *KeyCite* both enable the user to limit citing references (at least cases as citing references) to those that address particular substantive legal issues discussed in the cited authority. *LexisNexis* and West headnotes are the vehicles that make this limitation possible. *Shepard's* allows researchers to limit

---

[6] *See* Kent C. Olson, *Waiving a Red Flag: Teaching Counterintuitiveness in Citator Use*, 9 PERSP.: TEACHING LEGAL RES. & WRITING 58.

citing references to those cases that discuss issues described in particular *LexisNexis* headnotes associated with the cited case (and, in a smaller number of cases, to issues described in other publishers' headnotes). Similarly, *KeyCite* can limit citing references to those authorities citing a case for the proposition described in specific West headnotes.

  d. Notification of New Citations. Having found a relevant authority, an attorney might want to be made aware of every newly issued authority that cites it. Both *Shepard's*, through its *Shepard's Alert* service, and *Westlaw*, through *KeyCite Alert*, allow researchers to set up automatic email notification services that inform the user whenever a particular authority is cited.

2. Differences and Distinctions

  a. Coverage of Cited Authorities and Citing References. The task of a citation service is a straightforward one: given an authority, identify other authorities or documents that make reference to it. *Shepard's*, the first legal citation service, was developed as a tool for updating case law. *Shepard's*, *KeyCite*, and other legal citation services now include other types of primary authority and secondary authority as well, and more types of authorities continue to be integrated into these services.

  Both *Shepard's* and *KeyCite* include law reviews as cited authorities, and both services are expanding the number of types of secondary sources and court documents retrieved as citing references. As *Shepard's* and *KeyCite* continue to develop, it is likely that more secondary sources, ranging from practitioner treatises to current awareness materials to news and business resources, will be incorporated into these citation services, both as cited authorities and as citing references. As more secondary sources are incorporated into *Shepard's* and *KeyCite*, the two services will become more distinctive, as each service provides access to different publishers' secondary sources. It will be increasingly important to check both citation services to ensure comprehensive results with respect to secondary sources and court documents.

  b. Classification of Search Results. As noted above, both *Shepard's* and *KeyCite* enable researchers to categorize or filter retrieved results according to various parameters. Date, jurisdiction and treatment (i.e., positive or negative) are limits common to both services.

  For judicial authority, both services allow researchers to restrict results to those cases that discuss particular substantive issues; this is accomplished by incorporating limits based on headnotes. Those headnotes, however, may refer to different topic classifications. *KeyCite* headnote references are to the West headnotes appearing in the *National Reporter System*, which incorporate the key number system. *Shepard's* headnote limitations are to the *LexisNexis* headnotes. Historically, *Shepard's* also had included limitations based on West headnotes, officially published headnotes, and, for United States Supreme Court cases, headnotes published in *United States Supreme Court Reports, Lawyers' Edition*. Some—but increasingly fewer—citation results in *Shepard's* continue to include references to West headnotes. For U.S. Supreme Court cases, *Shepard's* continues to incorporate headnotes from *United States Supreme Court Reports, Lawyers' Edition* (in addition to *LexisNexis* headnotes).

  Shepard's also allows researchers to limit results based on the treatment of the cited authority by the citing references. So, for example, filtered search results might include only those references in which the authority is cited in a dissenting or concurring opinion.

Westlaw also categorizes cases that are citing references according to a "depth of treatment" concept. [Illustration 15–18] Citing cases are labeled as either "examining" a cited authority (discussing the case in some depth, usually involving at least a printed page of discussion), "discussing" an authority (including an analysis of more than a paragraph, but less than a printed page), "citing" an authority (incorporating some brief—less than a paragraph long—discussion of the cited authority), or "mentioning" a cited reference (including the authority as one of several in a string citation). Citing cases that merely mention an authority probably are of far less utility to a researcher than authorities that discuss a case in depth. The depth of treatment limitation enables a researcher to retrieve cases that have actually considered the authority and analyzed it in varying degrees of depth.

c.   *Manipulation and Display of Results. Shepard's* and *KeyCite* retrieve citing references and display those results in different formats. *Shepard's* provides a summary of results at the beginning of the display, followed by direct history and then judicial authority, organized by jurisdiction and level of court. By default, both *Westlaw Classic* and *WestlawNext* organize judicial authorities that are "positive" citing references by depth of treatment categories. In *WestlawNext*, results may be reordered by date. Both services allow users to manipulate the results retrieved by applying filters; the order and appearance of those filtered results defaults, for judicial authorities, in *Shepard's*, to reverse chronological order, and, in *KeyCite*, to depth of treatment categories. As digital citation services continue to evolve and improve, we can expect that users will gain more flexibility in manipulating, sorting, and filtering results.

3.   Using Full-Text Databases as Citators

Almost any full-text database can be used as a citator. The researcher need only search for terms in the cited source's title or citation.[7] Although new types of cited and citing authorities continue to be added to the citation services, many authorities and sources are not included. Researchers wanting to find citing references in authorities that are not included in *Shepard's* or *KeyCite* can simply search for all or part of a citation within a *LexisNexis* or *Westlaw* database.

For example, *Westlaw's KeyCite* retrieves more than 300 secondary source citing references, not including law review articles, for 26 C.F.R. 1.213–1, an income tax regulation. Those secondary source citing references include practitioner-oriented materials, legal encyclopedias, treatises, and current awareness materials specific to taxation. On the other hand, Shepardizing 26 C.F.R. 1.213–1 in *LexisNexis* results in a smaller number of non-law review secondary sources (slightly more than 70). But the *LexisNexis* research database includes a large number of well-recognized practitioner-oriented publications in the tax area; those publications, however, are not currently among the citing references retrieved by *Shepard's*. A search for the term "1.213–1" within tax-specific secondary sources in *LexisNexis* will retrieve texts that cite that regulation. Indeed, searching for "1.213–1" within a single tax-specific database in *LexisNexis* (Tax Analysts Tax Publications) results in nearly 250 citing references. [Illustration 15–19]

Researchers should note that it is possible to run a citation check in a full-text database simply by searching for all or part of a citation within the documents in that

---

[7] See Chapter 23 for an additional discussion of the use of CALR services as citators.

database. The results may not be analyzed, organized, or displayed in an easily understood or convenient format, but the results should at least indicate how and in what documents a particular authority has been cited.

E. ILLUSTRATIONS: *SHEPARD'S* AND *KEYCITE*

[Illustration 15–1]

SCREEN PRINT FROM WESTLAWNEXT
SHOWING THE DIRECT HISTORY OF A CASE

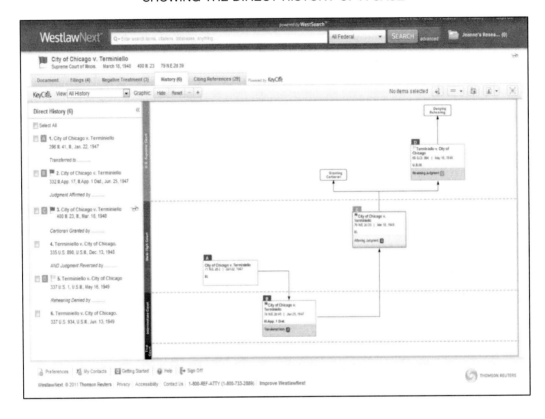

[Illustration 15–2]

SCREEN PRINT SHOWING SHEPARD'S APPELLATE HISTORY TAB

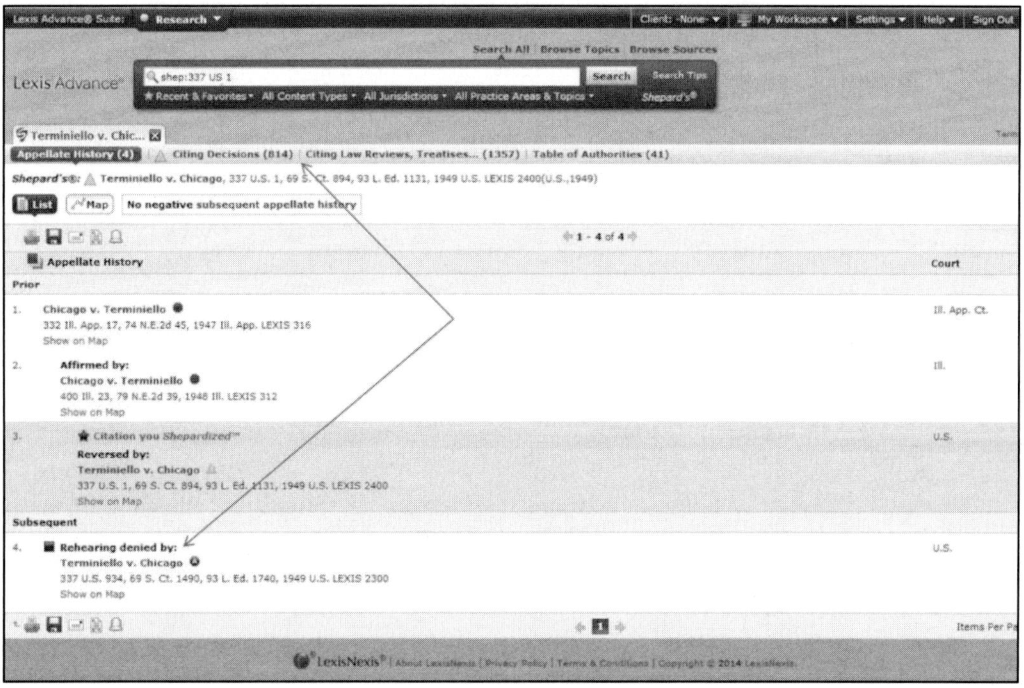

[Illustration 15–3]

SCREEN PRINT SHOWING SHEPARD'S RESULTS FOR CITING DECISIONS

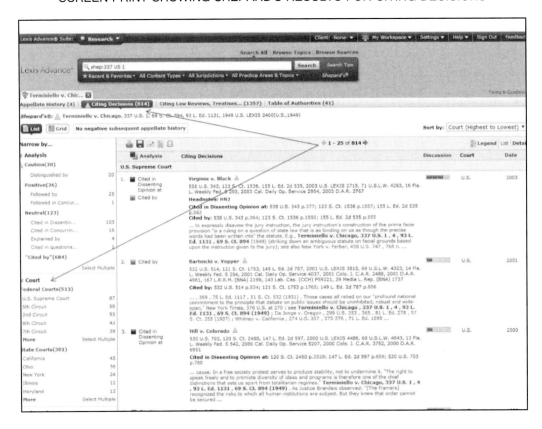

[Illustration 15–4]

SCREEN PRINT SHOWING SHEPARD'S CITING SECONDARY SOURCES

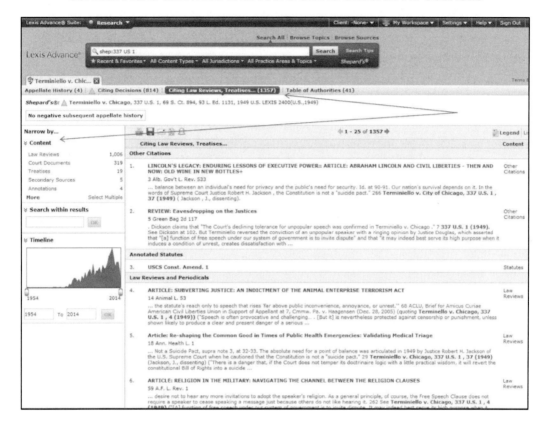

[Illustration 15–5]

SCREEN PRINT SHOWING SHEPARD'S REPORT FOR STATUTES

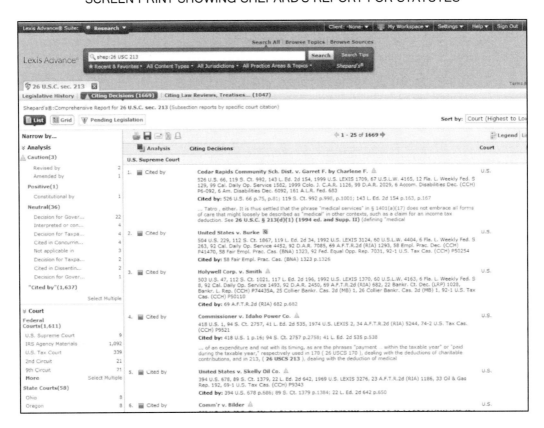

[Illustration 15–6

SCREEN PRINT SHOWING TRADITIONAL WESTLAW KEYCITEOPTIONS AVAILABLE FOR A CASE

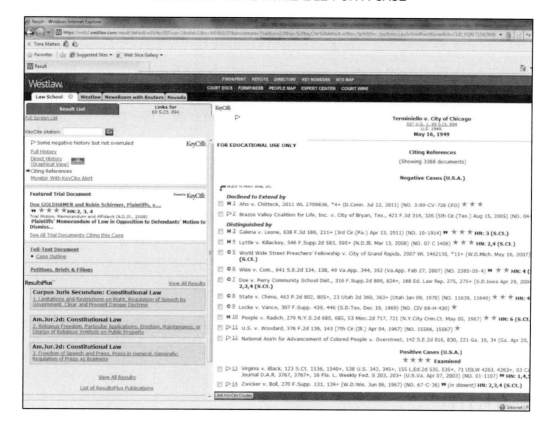

[Illustration 15–7]

SCREEN PRINT SHOWING WESTLAWNEXT
HISTORY AND CITATION OPTIONS FOR A CASE

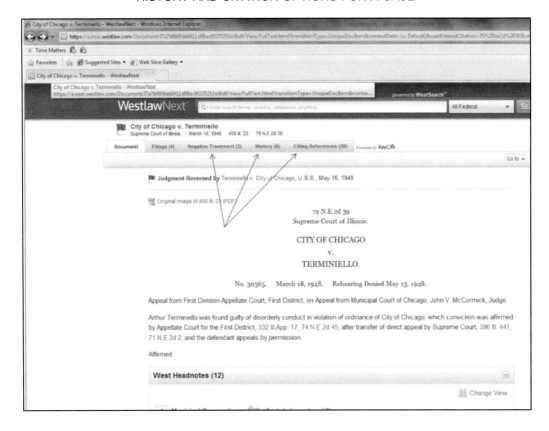

[Illustration 15–8]

SCREEN PRINT SHOWING TRADITIONAL WESTLAW GRAPHICAL DISPLAY OF A STATUTE'S HISTORY

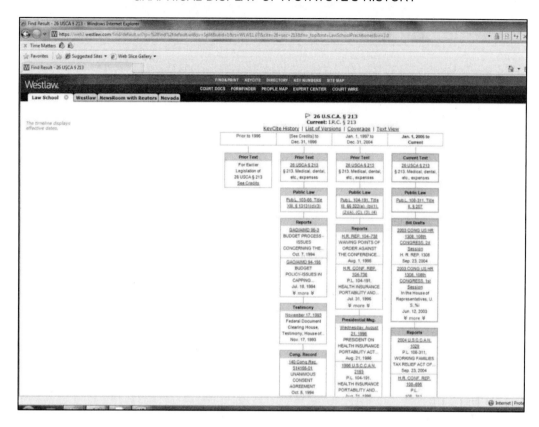

[Illustration 15-9]

SCREEN PRINT SHOWING WESTLAWNEXT'S TIMELINE OF A STATUTE'S HISTORY

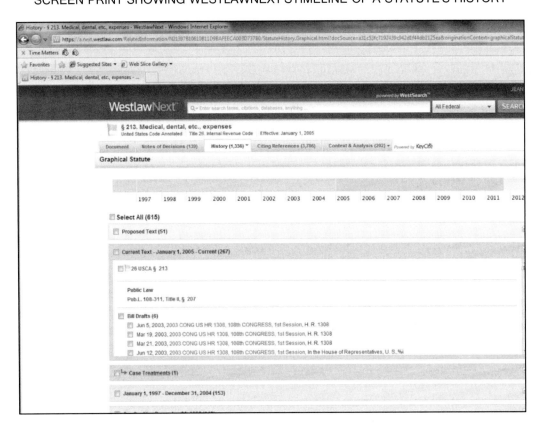

[Illustration 15–10]

SCREEN PRINT SHOWING WESTLAWNEXT'S CITING REFERENCES FOR A STATUTE

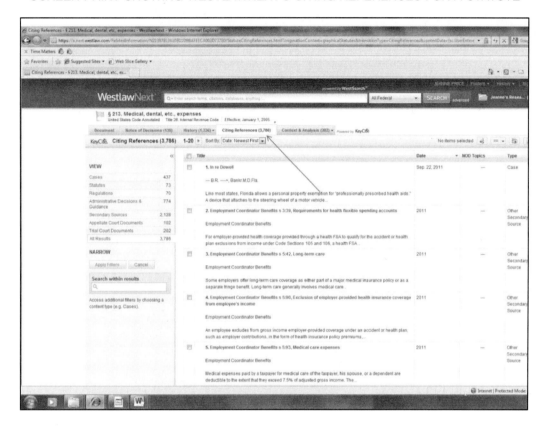

[Illustration 15–11]

SCREEN PRINT SHOWING SHEPARD'S "NARROW BY ANALYSIS" OPTIONS

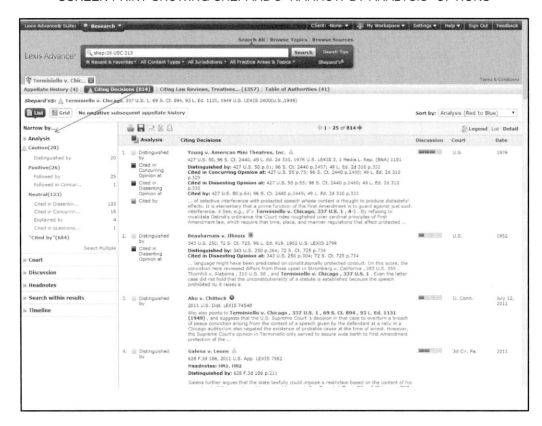

[Illustration 15–12]

SCREEN PRINT SHOWING WESTLAWNEXT
TABS FOR NEGATIVE TREATMENT AND CITING REFERENCES

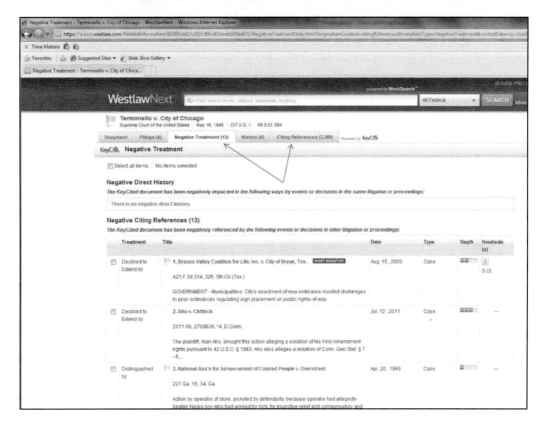

[Illustration 15–13]

SCREEN PRINT OF STATUS FLAGS IN KEYCITE

[Illustration 15-14]

SCREEN PRINT OF SHEPARD'S SIGNALS LEGEND

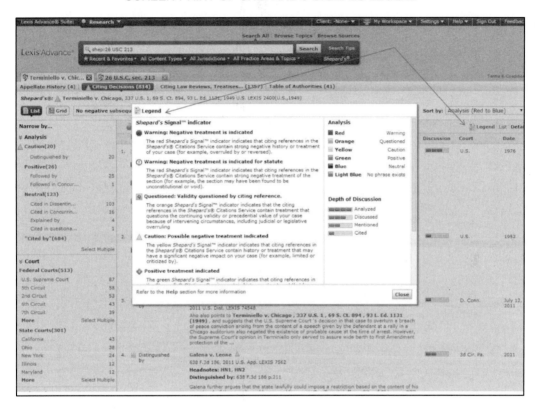

[Illustration 15–15]

SCREEN PRINT OF SHEPARD'S "NARROW BY" OPTION FACETS

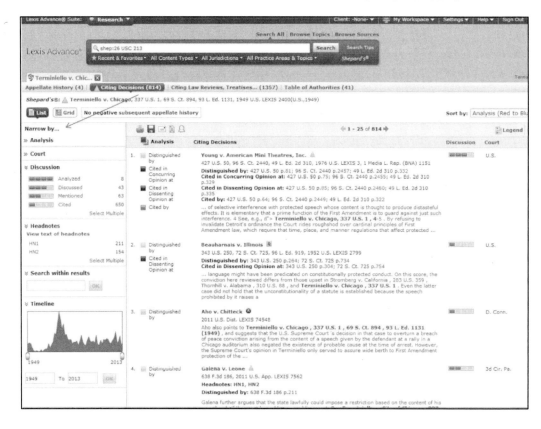

[Illustration 15–16]

SCREEN PRINT SHOWING TRADITIONAL WESTLAW KEYCITE LIMITS OPTIONS

[Illustration 15–17]

SCREEN PRINT SHOWING WESTLAWNEXT
FILTERS FOR CASES AS CITING REFERENCES

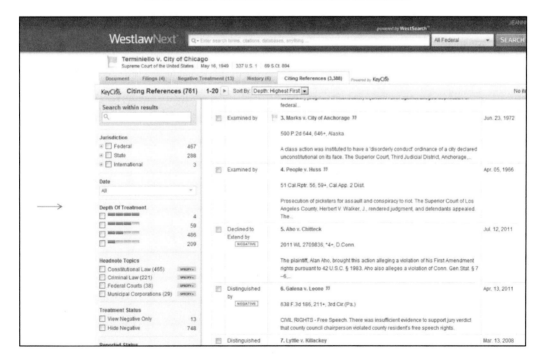

[Illustration 15–18]

SCREEN PRINT SHOWING WESTLAWNEXT DEPTH OF TREATMENT INDICATORS

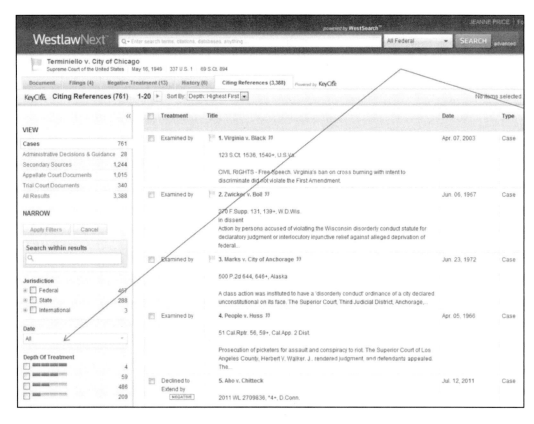

[Illustration 15–19]

SCREEN PRINT SHOWING RESULTS IN LEXISNEXIS SECONDARY SOURCE DATABASE

[Illustration 15–20]

SCREEN PRINT SHOWING "HOW CITED" RESULTS IN GOOGLE SCHOLAR

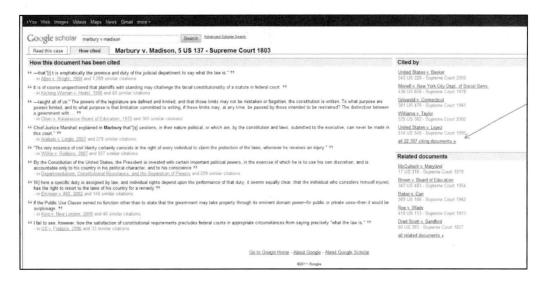

[Illustration 15–21]

SCREEN PRINT SHOWING CITING REFERENCES IN WEB OF KNOWLEDGE

[Illustration 15–22]

SCREEN PRINT SHOWING ABSTRACT VIEWS, FULL TEXT DOWNLOADS, AND CITATIONS IN SSRN

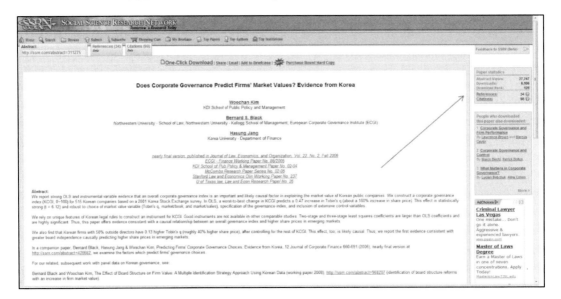

F. OTHER ONLINE LAW-RELATED CITATION SERVICES

As legal citation services, electronic *Shepard's* and *KeyCite* are unrivaled in their nearly comprehensive coverage of primary authority, the depth of their secondary sources, their currency, and their efficiency and ease of use. As alternatives to *LexisNexis* and *Westlaw* enter the market (usually at lower costs), the inclusion of citation services in those products is essential if they are to be competitive. Each of *VersusLaw*, *Loislaw*, *Bloomberg Law*, *Casemaker*, and *FastCase* include some sort of citator. The nature and number of citing references, as well as the authorities for which the citator is available, depend on the content of the resource. *HeinOnline*, a legal research database that includes the full text of law reviews as well as historical authorities, provides, for each law review article, a list of other articles in its database that cite to that original secondary authority.

Even *Google Scholar* includes a citator for cases and law review articles. For each case reproduced in *Google Scholar*, users may retrieve a list of cases and secondary sources in the *Google Scholar* database that cite the case. For example, using *Google Scholar*'s "how cited" feature for *Marbury v. Madison*, a United States Supreme Court case decided in 1803, more than 22,300 citing references are retrieved; those citing references include cases, books, law review articles, encyclopedias, and dictionaries. [Illustration 15–20] By way of contrast, *KeyCite* points to slightly more than 20,000 citing references and *Shepard's* to around 13,400.

Other citation services exist in specialized practice areas (usually in areas regulated by federal administrative agencies). These services may provide very useful alternatives to *Shepard's* and *KeyCite*. Subject-specific citators provide parallel citations to (usually practitioner-oriented) materials. They may also include esoteric administrative materials, as well as important and well-recognized secondary authorities, among citing references. Subject-specific citators allow for a variety of citation formats and provide access to a wide range of administrative and secondary authority as citing references.[8]

G. CITATORS IN PRINT: *SHEPARD'S* CITATIONS

Shepard's traditionally has been published in print in several different units. Some units collect resources by jurisdiction (e.g., *Shepard's Texas Citations, Shepard's Federal Citations*), some by reporter (e.g., *Southwestern Reporter Citations*), others by type of authority (e.g., *Shepard's Federal Rules Citations, Shepard's Law Review Citations*), and still others by subject matter (e.g., *Shepard's Bankruptcy Citations*). Each unit provides similar information about cited authorities and retains the distinctive *Shepard's* organization, format, and notation system. After a researcher has mastered *Shepard's* organization and notation system, use of the printed volumes of *Shepard's* is relatively straightforward, albeit time-consuming.

Previous editions of this text provided detail about the structure and use of *Shepard's* in print. That detail is unnecessary for the many researchers who have access to one or more online citators. If you are using a library that has *Shepard's* in print and does not provide access to an online citator, be certain to read the instructions printed at the front of each *Shepard's* volume and supplement. For questions concerning the *Shepard's* print edition, send email to helpcite@lexisnexis.com or telephone 1–800–899–6000, option 5.

H. CITATION SERVICES IN OTHER DISCIPLINES

Both law practice and legal scholarship are increasingly interdisciplinary and international in nature. Consequently, it is common to see citations in primary and especially secondary authority to other than traditional legal research resources. At the same time, more and more non-law publications are citing legal scholarship. Both *LexisNexis* and *Westlaw* have expanded the content of their online resources to include non-law publications, especially newspapers, magazines, and other popular periodicals, and sources related to business and industry.

Most of the non-law trade publications included in *LexisNexis* and *Westlaw* are more likely to be helpful to the practitioner than to the scholar. For example, *Westlaw* includes publications such as *Airport Business, Real Estate Observer*, and *Strategic Finance*. Similarly, publications like *Technology Business Journal, Consumer Reports and Health*, and *Manufacturing Engineer* are made available through *LexisNexis*. Although these publications are not currently retrieved as citing references, researchers could certainly determine, through fairly simple searches, whether particular legal authorities have been cited in them. There is no reason that these non-law materials might not eventually be included in *Shepard's* and *KeyCite* citing references. In fact, we can expect resources like *LexisNexis* and *Westlaw* to continue to expand their content with materials not traditionally included in the legal research process. And resources concentrating on disciplines other than law can be expected to include more traditional legal research materials. Citation services that make connections among these diverse research resources will become increasingly important and valuable.

LexisNexis and *Westlaw* have been less inclined to include scholarly or academic publications from other disciplines in their databases. Researchers who wish to

---

[8] For example, tax-specific citators are discussed in Chapter 26.

determine whether law-related secondary sources have been cited in certain non-law publications (primarily journals) may consult non-law scholarly citation services. The *Social Sciences Citation Index* has long served as a citation service for materials published in the social sciences. *Web of Knowledge*, the electronic resource that has evolved from the original print *Social Sciences Citation Index* and encompasses several other interdisciplinary research databases, now incorporates science, social science, and arts and humanities citation indexes. A relatively small number of law reviews have been incorporated into this index, and selected law review articles appear both as cited and citing references. *Web of Knowledge* is owned by Thomson Reuters, the parent company of *Westlaw*. Integrating *Westlaw's* citation services with those provided by *Web of Knowledge* seems like a natural next step in the evolution of citation services across disciplines. Interdisciplinary resources, such as *Web of Knowledge*, provide other means for expanding perspectives on issues and determining the influence of particular secondary authorities.

I. ALTERNATIVES TO CITATORS

Traditionally, scholars and courts have gauged the influence of law-related secondary authorities by considering the frequency and nature of citation. Law review articles that have been cited frequently and favorably by courts (especially appellate courts and courts of last resort) and other commentators gain a certain luster; their authors' repute and prestige are enhanced. The number of citations to a particular authority offered a quantifiable measure of influence that was not available for other uses of authority. Simply reading an authority, without citing to it, no matter how useful or influential the authority turned out to be, at least in a print environment, is not an activity that can be reliably measured.

Open access repositories of scholarship now exist in a variety of contexts. Individual academic institutions often maintain their own digital repositories of scholarship,[9] and both commercial and nonprofit entities have established repositories that collect scholarly works in a variety of subjects. The *Social Science Research Network* (http://ssrn.com/)—or as it is commonly known, *SSRN*—is among the most widely recognized of these online aggregators of scholarship.

The advent of new digital technologies and open access repositories has enabled the use of new metrics in assessing an article's influence. *SSRN* ranks articles posted in its repository on the basis of the number of (1) views of the abstract, (2) full text downloads, and (3) citations to the article in papers posted on *SSRN*.[10] Institutional repositories frequently provide similar data, allowing authors and readers to assess in a different way the impact of scholarship.

As digital resources and the technologies associated with them continue to improve, we can expect more sophistication in ranking mechanisms and more types of metrics that can be applied to assess the influence or importance of publications. In fact, *Google's*

---

[9] As an example, the Scholarly Commons (http://scholars.law.unlv.edu/) at the William S. Boyd School of Law, University of Nevada, Las Vegas, includes, among other materials, the full text of law faculty scholarship.

[10] *SSRN* began its tracking of citations by looking at papers whose references were in a bibliography at the end. Since almost all law papers cite sources in footnotes rather than bibliographies, citations for most law papers are greatly undercounted. *See* Michael C. Jensen, *SSRN's CiteReader Project Update*, SSRN BLOG (Apr. 26, 2011), http://ssrnblog.com/2011/04/26/ssrns-citereader-project-update/.

ranking mechanism relies to at least some extent on both the importance of a webpage (determined by the number and authority of other pages that link to it) and its popularity (assessed by the number of visits to a website).[11] In ordering the results retrieved upon a search, *Google* uses (among other metrics) citation analysis. Again, as ranking mechanisms continue to evolve, we can expect more complex combinations of metrics being used—much like *Google* uses to rank retrieved results—to assess the impact of particular scholarship.[12]

---

[11] *See* Sergey Brin & Lawrence Page, *The Anatomy of a Large-Scale Hypertextual Web Search Engine, in* SEVENTH INTERNATIONAL WORLD-WIDE WEB CONFERENCE (WWW 1998), APRIL 14–18, 1998, BRISBANE, AUSTRALIA (1998), *available at* http://ilpubs.stanford.edu:8090/361/.

[12] A number of articles analyze citations patterns in law. A good introduction to the field may be found in the articles in *Interpretation of Legal Citations: A Symposium Sponsored by the West Group*, 29 J. LEGAL STUD. 317–584 (2000).

Chapter 16

LEGAL ENCYCLOPEDIAS*

Previous chapters have focused on the primary sources of the law—judicial opinions, constitutions, statutes, and court rules—and various finding and verification aids for these sources—indexes, digests, citators, and other legal materials that enable a researcher to find both the source and status of the law. The amount of primary source materials has become so large that secondary sources play significant roles in identifying and explaining the law. This chapter and the next four chapters focus on secondary sources. These secondary sources consist of legal encyclopedias, periodicals, treatises, restatements, and other miscellaneous sets of law books.

An individual beginning a research project often lacks even the most basic knowledge necessary to identify and research the legal issues involved. At other times, a refresher in broad concepts is needed. Legal encyclopedias, discussed in this chapter, are very useful for objective background information and as sources of leads to other materials.

A. INTRODUCTION

Legal encyclopedias consist of entries written in narrative form and arranged alphabetically by subject, each containing footnote references to cases, statutes, and other sources. In most instances, the entries are not critical or evaluative. Instead, they simply state and explain general propositions of law, with introductory-level explanations. These features make legal encyclopedias popular and useful research tools. They are seldom useful as strong persuasive authority, but sometimes are cited for the broad overview they can offer.

In most research problems, it is necessary to go beyond general sources such as encyclopedias. An encyclopedia entry or the sources cited within it frequently will not fully address all aspects of the situation being researched; the facts of the problem at hand usually are distinguishable from those in the cited cases; or the case, statute, or regulation referred to by the encyclopedia may no longer be good law. In most instances, the cases and other sources cited must be read, analyzed, and updated with a citator. Statutory and regulatory sources must be checked to ascertain whether their rules apply in the particular jurisdiction being researched.

These criticisms should not detract from the appropriate purposes and functions of legal encyclopedias. These publications are excellent introductory guides to the law. They can be effective means to identify relevant issues, index terms, topics and key numbers, statutes, cases, and other sources. So long as their limitations are kept in mind

---

* This chapter was revised by Melissa J. Bernstein, Library Director & Professor of Law, S.J. Quinney Law Library, University of Utah.

and legal encyclopedias are not relied upon as the final authority for legal propositions, they can be valuable research tools.

B. CURRENT GENERAL ENCYCLOPEDIAS

1. *Corpus Juris Secundum (C.J.S.)*

Corpus Juris Secundum has been published by West (now Thomson Reuters) since 1936. Its entries include topics of both procedural and substantive law. It is available in print and in *Westlaw*. As its original subtitle indicated, *C.J.S.* was intended initially to be "a complete restatement of the entire American law as developed by all reported cases." Its coverage was almost exclusively of case law and it aimed at citing all reported cases in its footnotes. However, in the mid-1980s, West abandoned its attempt to cite every case and adopted a new approach reflecting a different scope of coverage for revised volumes—"a contemporary statement of American law as derived from reported cases and legislation." *C.J.S.* no longer attempts to refer to every case and now provides some discussion of federal and state statutory law.

In print, *C.J.S.* is a massive set, with over 160 volumes. (Because of expanding topics and new topics added over the years, some volume numbers include a letter; the volume numbers range from 1 to 101A.) *C.J.S.* supersedes its predecessor, *Corpus Juris.*[1] Over 400 broad topics, listed at the beginning of each volume, are covered as *C.J.S.* entries. Each entry is subdivided into many sections. Preceding each discussion of a point of law, i.e., one of the subdivision topics, is a brief summary of the prevailing rule of law. This "black letter"[2] statement is followed by text expounding upon that point of law. Footnote references are arranged hierarchically by federal court and then alphabetically by state. [Illustration 16–2] Newer volumes include "Research References" after the initial topic outline that cite to relevant subjects in *West's ALR Digest* and *ALR Index.*[3]

C.J.S. includes cross-references relating its titles and sections to the corresponding West key number digest, permitting easy entry into the *American Digest System.* West topics and key numbers and secondary authority sources are noted under "Research References," which precede each section's discussion in both the main volumes and in the annual cumulative pocket supplements.

C.J.S. has a multivolume, softbound General Index that is issued annually. Each volume also has a separate index to each of the topics contained in it. When a topic is covered in more than one book, the topic index is at the end of the last book that includes that topic, e.g., *Drugs and Narcotics* is covered in volumes 28 and 28A, and the index is in volume 28A. There is also a General Index Update pamphlet that covers replacement volumes published after the printing of the General Index. The index is available in *Westlaw.*

Research in *C.J.S.* is similar to that described in Chapter 7 for digests. *C.J.S.*'s General Index uses the familiar descriptive-word approach. A researcher might alternatively choose to begin research in the appropriate volume. For example, if one is

---

[1] Although *Corpus Juris Secundum* supersedes the text of *Corpus Juris,* occasionally the footnotes in *C.J.S.* refer to the earlier work.

[2] For a history of the term "black letter law," see JAMES E. CLAPP ET AL., LAWTALK: THE UNKNOWN STORIES BEHIND FAMILIAR LEGAL EXPRESSIONS 31 (2011).

[3] *American Law Reports (A.L.R.)* is discussed in Chapter 17.

interested in the subject of *products liability*, the index volumes can be bypassed and the search started immediately by consulting the volume that contains the topic *Products Liability*. If the researcher is not initially able to determine the broad topic of the law in which the issue is discussed, begin the research in the index volumes. At the beginning of each topic is an outline and classification for the organization of that topic. In *Westlaw*, researchers may browse the table of contents and drill down through subheadings. (It can also be searched full text.) Either in print or online, skimming the outlines offers an overview of a topic.

C.J.S. is updated in print by replacement volumes and annual cumulative pocket supplements. The pocket supplements may include rewritten text, citations to cases decided since the publication of the original volumes, and references to secondary sources. Replacement volumes are published when significant sections of the text require rewriting or when the pocket supplements become extensive and unwieldy. Each replacement volume contains a correlation table that relates sections in the older volume to the corresponding section in the replacement volume. Volumes covering the Internal Revenue Code are issued annually. Online, *C.J.S.* is updated quarterly.

2. *American Jurisprudence 2d (Am. Jur. 2d)*

American Jurisprudence 2d, originally published by the Lawyers Cooperative Publishing Company until West acquired that publisher, is a noncritical statement of substantive and procedural law, arranged under more than 430 topics that are divided into subtopics. In print, it contains over 130 volumes. (Because of expanding topics and new topics added over the years, some volume numbers, such as 67A and 67B, include a letter; the volume numbers range from 1 to 83.) It is available in both *Westlaw* and *LexisNexis*. *Am. Jur. 2d* supersedes the earlier edition, *American Jurisprudence*. The editorial philosophy consistently underlying *Am. Jur. 2d* is to set forth points of law, together with discussions of those legal subjects and citations to controlling cases that interpret and construe those points of law. Citations to the selected cases are set forth in footnotes.

Each entry in *Am. Jur. 2d* starts with an outline of the topic and is followed by "Research References." This section includes references to the corresponding West key number digest, as well as relevant *Westlaw* databases, primary authority, and *A.L.R.* and other *Am. Jur.* publications (discussed in Section B-3, below). "Research References" also appears in each subsection, again noting West topics and key numbers and *A.L.R.* citations. The publishers contrast *Am. Jur. 2d*, a source of the law in breadth, with *A.L.R.*, a source of the law in depth. The former is useful in obtaining a quick answer to a problem that may then be explored further in *A.L.R.*

The organization of *Am. Jur. 2d* is similar to that of *C.J.S. Am. Jur. 2d* has a multivolume, softbound index that is issued annually. The last volume of this index contains a popular name table. A separate index covering the contents of each volume is set forth at the end of each book. As with *C.J.S.*, when a topic is covered in more than one book, the topic index is at the end of the last book that includes that topic. There is also a General Index Update pamphlet that covers replacement volumes published after the printing of the General Index. Using either *LexisNexis* or *Westlaw*, researchers may browse the table of contents and drill down through subheadings. The index is not online. [Illustrations 16–3 and 16–4]

In print, *Am. Jur. 2d* is updated with annual pocket parts and revised volumes. When a volume is revised, the revision contains a "Correlation Table" relating subjects in previous editions to references in the current volume. In *Westlaw*, *Am. Jur. 2d* is updated quarterly; in *LexisNexis* it is updated annually.

Other features of *Am. Jur. 2d* include:

a. *Greater (as compared with C.J.S.) emphasis placed on statutory law, federal procedural rules, and uniform state laws.* Federal statutory law germane to a topic is noted, while state statutory law is covered in a more general way (without reference to the specific laws of each state). A separate annual volume, Table of Laws and Rules, relates the United States Constitution, the *United States Code Annotated*, the *United States Statutes at Large*, the *Code of Federal Regulations*, the Federal Rules of Civil Procedure, the Federal Rules of Criminal Procedure, the *United States Sentencing Commission Guidelines Manual*, the International Court of Justice decisions, and the *Restatement Third, Torts* to section discussions within *Am. Jur. 2d*. A "Table of Statutes and Rules Cited" in the back of each volume indicates citations to federal statutes and rules in that volume.

b. *Annual volumes focusing on the Internal Revenue Code.* This material is contained in the Federal Taxation volumes.

c. *New Topic Service.* The *American Jurisprudence 2d New Topic Service*, a looseleaf volume, covers (1) new topics of law that have developed after the printing of the main volumes and (2) substantial changes in the already published encyclopedic articles. For example, this service contains articles on "Limited Liability Companies" and "Real Estate Time Sharing." The general index to *Am. Jur. 2d* includes references to this service. An annual cumulative supplement updates the new topics and provides a table of statutes and rules cited. When new bound volumes are issued, these topics are incorporated into the full set and removed from the looseleaf binder.

3. *American Jurisprudence 2d*: Related Resources

After the substantive law of the problem under investigation is identified, multivolume sets related to *Am. Jur. 2d* can provide additional information needed to prepare a case for trial. These sets are:

a. *American Jurisprudence Proof of Facts, 1st, 2d,* and *3d.* Collectively, the three series exceed 140 volumes. The purpose of *Proof of Facts* is to provide a guide for lawyers in the organization and preparation of materials for trial and in the examination of witnesses. It is designed to assist lawyers in obtaining information from clients, taking depositions, writing briefs, and otherwise preparing for trial. Each article within *Proof of Facts* contains "Research References" that cite to relevant articles in both *Proof of Facts* and *Am. Jur. Trials*, the corresponding West key number digest, relevant *Westlaw* databases, primary authority, *A.L.R.* citations and other *Am. Jur.* publications, an article outline and index, and checklists and planning guides designed to assist in the establishment of the facts in issue. A multivolume, softbound index to the three series is published annually. There is also a General Index Update pamphlet that covers replacement volumes published after the printing of the General Index. The three series in the set are updated with annual pocket supplements, and by adding new volumes to the 3d series. It is available in *Westlaw* and as a CD-ROM product. The series is accompanied by a medical dictionary for attorneys, which is supplemented by pamphlets.

b.   American Jurisprudence Trials. This set is a treatise on trial practice. The first six volumes cover matters common to all types of trial practice. The remaining volumes, entitled *Model Trials*, deal with the handling of specific types of trials, e.g., personal injury, business-related, and criminal. Unlike *Am. Jur. 2d* and the other related sets, the publisher's editorial staff does not write *Trials*. Rather, an experienced trial lawyer authors each topic in the set. This set is accompanied by a separate softbound index and is updated by annual pocket supplements. It is available in *Westlaw*.

c.   American Jurisprudence Pleading and Practice Forms Annotated and *American Jurisprudence Legal Forms 2d*. These two sets contain forms useful in conducting trials and in other aspects of a lawyer's practice.[4]

4.   *West's Encyclopedia of American Law, 2d ed.*

This encyclopedia, published by Thomson Gale in 2005, is directed toward the non-lawyer. Consisting of 13 volumes and containing nearly 5,000 entries, *West's Encyclopedia of American Law 2d ed.* replaces *The Guide to American Law: Everyone's Legal Encyclopedia* (1983). Entries consist of terms, concepts, events, movements, cases, and persons significant to United States law. Included among the many entries are definitions, cross-references, sidebars, biographies, milestones in the law, graphics, tables, and bibliographies. "In Focus" pieces, accompanying some entries, provide additional facts, details, and arguments on particularly important or controversial issues. Sidebars highlight material in some entries. Volumes 1 through 10 each have their own index. Three appendix volumes contain relevant historical materials. Volume 11, Milestones in the Law, focuses on landmark U.S. Supreme Court cases such as *Brown v. Board of Education* and *Miranda v. Arizona*. Volume 12 contains select primary documents from various periods of history such as the Magna Carta, Stamp Act, Articles of Confederation, Missouri Compromise, and the Civil Rights era. Volume 13 contains a dictionary and an index to the set. An annual *American Law Yearbook*, updating the set, has been published since 1998. *West's Encyclopedia of American Law 2d* is available in *Gale Virtual Reference Library* (an online package marketed to college and public libraries).

C. ILLUSTRATIONS: ENCYCLOPEDIAS

Legal encyclopedias, such as *Corpus Juris Secundum* and *American Jurisprudence 2d*, can be useful tools to identify relevant issues, index terms and topics, key numbers, statutes, and cases.

Problem: Do prescription drug manufacturers have a duty to warn?

16–1.	**Page from Volume 28 of C.J.S. Showing Topic Outline: Drugs and Narcotics**
16–2.	**Page from Topic: Drugs and Narcotics § 124, 28 C.J.S. (2008)**
16–3.	**Page from an Am. Jur. 2d General Index volume Showing Topic: Products Liability**
16–4 and 16–4 cont'd.	**Pages from Topic: Products Liability § 1024, 63A Am. Jur. 2d**

---

[4] Form books are discussed in more detail in Chapter 20.

[Illustration 16–1]

PAGE FROM VOLUME 28 OF C.J.S. SHOWING TOPIC OUTLINE: DRUGS AND NARCOTICS

DRUGS AND NARCOTICS

§ 113	Generally
§ 114	To whom liability extends
§ 115	Causation requirement
§ 116	Strict liability
§ 117	—Exception where drug is unavoidably unsafe
§ 118	Preparation and testing of drugs

(2) Alternate Theories of Liability Where Manufacturer of Drug Cannot be Identified; Diethylstibestrol (DES) Cases

§ 119	Generally
§ 120	Alternative-liability theory
§ 121	Concert-of-action theory
§ 122	Enterprise or industry-wide liability
§ 123	Market-share liability

b. Warning of Dangers

§ 124	Generally
§ 125	Scope of duty to warn
§ 126	Failure to warn as proximate cause of injury
§ 127	To whom warnings must be provided
§ 128	—The learned-intermediary doctrine
§ 129	Adequacy of warnings
§ 130	—Rare reactions and individual hypersensitivity
§ 131	—Compliance with federal laws and regulations

> The most common method of locating relevant sections in *C.J.S.* is by consulting the annual General Index volumes. Sometimes, it may be easier to take a topical approach. In this instance, by consulting the Topic Outline for Drugs and Narcotics, it quickly becomes apparent that the matter under research is covered in §124.

c. Government Agencies and Government Compensation Programs

§ 132	Liability of governmental agencies generally
§ 133	Government compensation programs; The National Childhood Vaccine Injury Act of 1986

3. Actions for Damages; Injunction

a. In General

§ 134	Generally
§ 135	Effect of privity of contract between pharmacist and injured party
§ 136	Governing law
§ 137	—Preemption under the Federal Food, Drug, and Cosmetic Act
§ 138	—Preemption under the National Childhood Vaccine Injury Act of 1986

b. Defenses

§ 139	Generally
§ 140	Unavoidably unsafe product defense to strict liability
§ 141	Comparative negligence
§ 142	Assumption of risk; wrongful conduct
§ 143	Limitation of actions

c. Pleadings

§ 144	Generally
§ 145	Actions based upon alternative theories of liability

[Illustration 16–2]

PAGE FROM TOPIC: DRUGS AND NARCOTICS § 124, 28 C.J.S. (2008)

§ 123   Corpus Juris Secundum

keting for use by pregnant women.[15] Under such latter authority, a defendant will not be liable if it sold DES in a form unsuitable for use during pregnancy or establishes that its product was not marketed for pregnancy.[16]

Defendants in DES actions who are unable to exculpate themselves will become part of the DES market.[17] While a national market is used under some authority,[18] under other authority the rule is that the relevant market should be as narrowly defined as the evidence in a given case allows.[19]

Non-DES cases.

In cases involving other drugs and vaccines[20] and in cases in which the product causing injury is not specified,[21] courts have declined to adopt market-share liability theory. However it has been applied in others.[22] Market-share liability theory will not be extended to the manufacturers of a product which is not intrinsically defective for the purpose for which it was used.[23] A manufacturer's duty to plaintiffs who will use its drug or be injured by it does not extend to anyone who uses the type of drug manufactured by the manufacturer.[24]

b.   Warning of Dangers

§ 124   Generally ←

Research References

West's Key Number Digest, Health ⬥306, 308; Products Liability ⬥46.2

A drug manufacturer or wholesaler will be liable for injury to a user of the drug distributed by it if it fails to give an adequate warning of the dangers involved in its use.

Generally, a manufacturer or wholesaler of drugs is under a duty to give warning of the dangers incident to using the drugs it sells or distributes.[1] A manufacturer is under a duty to provide warn-

---

This illustration shows the start of a discussion of cases dealing with the duty of prescription drug manufacturers to warn. Preceding each discussion in a section is a brief summary, in bold type, of the prevailing rule of law, the so-called "black letter" law.

R.I.—Gorman v. Abbott Laboratories, 599 A.2d 1364 (R.I. 1991).

seller for injury or death allegedly caused by failure to warn regarding danger in use of vaccine or

[Illustration 16-3]

PAGE FROM AN AM. JUR. 2D GENERAL INDEX VOLUME
SHOWING TOPIC: PRODUCTS LIABILITY

AMERICAN JURISPRUDENCE 2d

PRODUCTS LIABILITY—*continued*
Warnings—*continued*
  drugs and medical supplies, **ProductsLi**
    § 279, 1067, 1133, 1138
  duty to warn, **ProductsLi § 1023 to**
    1070
  economic losses, **ProductsLi § 1818**
  employers, **ProductsLi § 1073, 1093**
  evidence
    generally, **ProductsLi § 1106 to 1141**
    absence of other accidents,
      ProductsLi § 1117
    adequacy of warning, questions of law
      and fact, **ProductsLi § 1109**
    advertising, **ProductsLi § 1126**
    burden of proof, **ProductsLi § 1106,**
      1127
    causation, generally, **ProductsLi**
      § 1127 to 1141
    documentary evidence, **ProductsLi**
      § 1124
    expert and opinion evidence,
      ProductsLi § 1111 to 1113
    foreseeability, questions of law and
      fact, **ProductsLi § 1107**
    governmental standards, **ProductsLi**
      § 1121, 1122
    industry standards, **ProductsLi**
      § 112
    instructi
      § 1110
    knowled
      law an
    knowled
    other i
    this group
    obviousness of danger, questions of
      law and fact, **ProductsLi § 1108**
    other accidents, **ProductsLi § 1114 to**
      1117
    presumption that warnings will be
      read and heeded, **ProductsLi**
      § 1128, 1129
    professional groups, notice to,
      ProductsLi § 1126
    questions of law and fact, **ProductsLi**
      § 1107 to 1109, 1130
    rebuttal of presumption that warnings
      will be read and heeded,
      ProductsLi § 1129
    recalls, **ProductsLi § 1125**
    strict liability, subsequent remedial
      measures, **ProductsLi § 1119**
    subsequent remedial measures,
      ProductsLi § 1114 to 1117
    substantial similarity, other accidents,
      ProductsLi § 1115
    ultimate issues, expert and opinion
      evidence, **ProductsLi § 1113**
  expert, manufacturer held to knowledge
    of, **ProductsLi § 1040**

PRODUCTS LIABILITY—*continued*
Warnings—*continued*
  expert and opinion evidence,
    ProductsLi § 1111 to 1113, 1727
  expression. Form and expression, below
    in this group
  FDA regulations, **ProductsLi § 1086,**
    1097
  foreseeability
    dissemination of warnings,
      ProductsLi § 1087
    knowledge of defendant, below in this
      group
    questions of law and fact, **ProductsLi**
      § 1107
  form and expression
    generally, **ProductsLi § 1075 to 1086**
    FDA regulations, compliance with,
      ProductsLi § 1086
    instructions for use, **ProductsLi**
      § 1076, 1077
    misleading or ambiguous language,
      ProductsLi § 1082
    readable and conspicuous language,
      ProductsLi § 1080
    reasonableness test, **ProductsLi**
      § 1078
    specificity, **ProductsLi § 1083**
    statutes, compliance with, **ProductsLi**

government contractor defense,
  ProductsLi § 1370 to 1372
inability to read warning, **ProductsLi**
  § 1135
inadequacy of, warranties, **ProductsLi**
  § 654
industry standards, **ProductsLi § 1123**
instructions for use, **ProductsLi § 1036**
  to 1038, 1076, 1077
instructions to jury, **ProductsLi § 1110**
intermediaries. Dissemination, above in
  this group
knowledgeable or sophisticated parties,
  ProductsLi § 1063 to 1065
knowledge of defendant
  generally, **ProductsLi § 1039 to 1053**
  allergies to product, **ProductsLi**
    § 1051
  alteration of product, **ProductsLi**
    § 1049
  expert, manufacturer held to knowl-
    edge of, **ProductsLi § 1040**
  foreseeability, generally, **ProductsLi**
    § 1045 to 1053
  intended or normal uses as foresee-
    able, **ProductsLi § 1046**

PRODUCTS LIABILITY—*continued*
Warnings—*continued*
  knowledge of defendant—*continued*
    misuse, **ProductsLi § 1048**
    nonmanufacturing suppliers,
      ProductsLi § 1042
    state of the art defense, **ProductsLi**
      § 1043, 1044
    testing and other investigations, duty
      to acquire knowledge through,
      ProductsLi § 1041
    third parties, acts of, **ProductsLi**
      § 1047
    unusually susceptible consumers,
      ProductsLi § 1050 to 1053
  knowledge or conduct of plaintiff or
    other instrumental party
    generally, **ProductsLi § 1054 to**
      1065, 1131 to 1141
    actual knowledge of danger,
      ProductsLi § 1061, 1062
    adequate warning would have altered
      conduct, evidence that, **ProductsLi**
      § 1137
    adequate warning would not have
      altered conduct, evidence that,
      ProductsLi § 1137, 1138
    children, open and obvious dangers,
      ProductsLi § 1059
    phisticated par-
    § 1063 to 1065
    ngers,
    6 to 1060
    ers generally
    known to, **ProductsLi § 1055**
    plaintiff or other party did not heed
      available warning, evidence that,
      ProductsLi § 1136
    plaintiff or other party did not read
      available warning, evidence that,
      ProductsLi § 1132 to 1135
    plaintiff or other party had knowledge
      of hazard, evidence that,
      ProductsLi § 1139, 1140
    plaintiff or other party had no knowl-
      edge of hazard, evidence that,
      ProductsLi § 1141
    plaintiff or other party read available
      warning, evidence that, **ProductsLi**
      § 1132
    prescriptions, **ProductsLi § 1133,**
      1138
    professionals as knowledgeable or
      sophisticated parties, **ProductsLi**
      § 1065
    proximate cause, actual knowledge of
      danger, **ProductsLi § 1062**
    questions of law and fact, **ProductsLi**
      § 1108
    workplace settings, plaintiff or other
      party did not read available warn-

> The annual General Index to *Am. Jur. 2d* will lead the researcher to where the topic bbeing researched is covered in *Am. Jur. 2d*.
>
> See next Illustration.

For assistance using this index call 1-800-328-4880

[Illustration 16–4]

PAGES FROM TOPIC: PRODUCTS LIABILITY § 1024, 63A AM. JUR. 2D

PRODUCTS LIABILITY   § 1024

the buyer or user is unaware of that information.[4]

The duty to warn adequately does not require the manufacturer to educa[...] [...]ing of inhere[...] [...]d user of the[...] [...]n the produc[...] [...]oduct leaves [...]icular hazard[...] [...]pends in par[...] [...]m the absenc[...] [...]rise a party [...]

> Notice that *Am. Jur. 2d* contains fewer footnotes than *C.J.S.,* even after the change in *C.J.S.'s* editorial philosophy. Also notice the reference to *A.L.R.,* where additional cases can be located. *Am. Jur. 2d* provides a useful way to find *A.L.R.* annotations.
>
> Note: Both *Am. Jur. 2d* and *C.J.S.* have annual pocket supplements. A researcher should always remember to check these supplements for references to later sources.

An [...] the circumstances.[9] A warning may be inadequate in factual content, the expression of facts, or in the method by which it is conveyed.[10]

§ 1024 Failure to warn may render product defective

Research References

West's Key Number Digest, Products Liability ⚏133, 392
Products Liability: Pacemakers, 23 A.L.R.6th 223
Products Liability: Liability of Manufacturer, Supplier, or Seller of Passenger or Freight Elevator, Hoist, or Elevator Component for Injury or Damage Resulting from Alleged Defect in Elevator or Component, 117 A.L.R.5th 267
Products Liability: Prudent Manufacturer Test, 86 A.L.R.5th 215
Products liability: Swimming pools and accessories, 65 A.L.R.5th 105
Products liability: failure to provide product warning or instruction in foreign language or to use universally accepted pictographs or symbols, 27 A.L.R. 5th 697
Products liability: lighters and lighter fluids, 14 A.L.R.5th 47
Products liability: application of strict liability doctrine to seller of used product, 9 A.L.R.5th 1
Products liability: roofs and roofing materials, 3 A.L.R.5th 851
Failure to warn as basis of liability under doctrine of strict liability in tort, 53 A.L.R.3d 239
Cause Of Action Under Strict Liability For Personal Injuries Or Property

---

[4]Glittenberg v. Doughboy Recreational Industries, 441 Mich. 379, 491 N.W.2d 208 (1992).

[5]Mackowick v. Westinghouse Elec. Corp., 525 Pa. 52, 575 A.2d 100 (1990).

[6]Balder v. Haley, 399 N.W.2d 77 (Minn. 1987).

[7]Humble Sand & Gravel, Inc. v. Gomez, 146 S.W.3d 170 (Tex. 2004).

[8]Collins v. Hyster Co., 174 Ill. App. 3d 972, 124 Ill. Dec. 483, 529 N.E.2d 303 (3d Dist. 1988).

[9]Wooderson v. Ortho Pharmaceutical Corp., 235 Kan. 387, 681 P.2d 1038 (1984); Terhune v. A. H. Robins Co., 90 Wash. 2d 9, 577 P.2d 975 (1978).

[10]Graham by Graham v. Wyeth Laboratories, a Div. of American Home Products Corp., 666 F. Supp. 1483 (D. Kan. 1987) (applying Kansas law).

As to the adequacy of warnings, generally, see §§ 1075 to 1086.

[Illustration 16–4 cont'd]

PAGES FROM TOPIC: PRODUCTS LIABILITY § 1024, 63A AM. JUR. 2D CONT'D

§ 1024   AMERICAN JURISPRUDENCE 2D

A manufacturer has a duty to warn with respect to latent dangerous characteristics of a product, even though there is no "defect" in the product itself.[1] A failure to warn of such a latent danger will, without more, cause the product to be unreasonably dangerous as marketed.[2] In such a case, a product, although faultlessly manufactured and designed, may be defective when placed in the consumers' hands without an adequate warning concerning the manner in which to use the product safely.[3] Conversely, a finding of failure to warn does not require a finding of defective design.[4]

§ 1025   Factors affecting existence of duty

Research References

West's Key Number Digest, Products Liability ⊙129, 133

Products liability: failure to provide product warning or instruction in foreign language or to use universally accepted pictographs or symbols, 27 A.L.R. 5th 697

Proof in Strict Products Liability Case That Product Was Misused, 109 Am. Jur. Proof of Facts 3d 183

Am. Jur. Pleading and Practice Forms, Products Liability § 87 (Instruction to

---

[Section 1024]

[1]Miles v. Olin Corp., 922 F.2d 1221, 32 Fed. R. Evid. Serv. 55 (5th Cir. 1991); Vitanza v. Upjohn Co., 257 Conn. 365, 778 A.2d 829 (2001); Streich v. Hilton-Davis, a Div. of Sterling Drug, Inc., 214 Mont. 44, 692 P.2d 440, 40 U.C.C. Rep. Serv. 109 (1984); Walton v. Avco Corp., 530 Pa. 568, 610 A.2d 454 (1992).

[2]Garside v. Osco Drug, Inc., 976 F.2d 77 (1st Cir. 1992) (applying Massachusetts law); Miles v. Olin Corp., 922 F.2d 1221, 32 Fed. R. Evid. Serv. 55 (5th Cir. 1991) (applying Louisiana law); Natural Gas Odorizing, Inc. v. Downs,

685 N.E.2d 155 (Ind. Ct. App. 1997); Swan v. I.P., Inc., 613 So. 2d 846 (Miss. 1993).

[3]Argubright v. Beech Aircraft Corp., 868 F.2d 764 (5th Cir. 1989) (applying Texas law); First Nat. Bank and Trust Corp. v. American Eurocopter Corp., 378 F.3d 682 (7th Cir. 2004) (applying Indiana law); Lorfano v. Dura Stone Steps, Inc., 569 A.2d 195, 11 U.C.C. Rep. Serv. 2d 39 (Me. 1990).

[4]Petree v. Victor Fluid Power, Inc., 831 F.2d 1191, 23 Fed. R. Evid. Serv. 1213, 8 Fed. R. Serv. 3d 1060 (3d Cir. 1987) (applying Pennsylvania law).

D. STATE ENCYCLOPEDIAS

Some states have legal encyclopedias devoted to their own laws, with most published by West. These are:

California Jurisprudence, 3d

Florida Jurisprudence, 2d

Georgia Jurisprudence

Indiana Law Encyclopedia

Maryland Law Encyclopedia

Michigan Civil Jurisprudence

New York Jurisprudence, 2d

Ohio Jurisprudence, 3d

Summary of Pennsylvania Jurisprudence, 2d

South Carolina Jurisprudence

Texas Jurisprudence, 3d

Some of these encyclopedias are modeled after *Am. Jur. 2d*, while others follow the format of *C.J.S.* Most of these encyclopedias are available in *Westlaw*, and some are available in *LexisNexis*. Some are also available in CD-ROM format.

Encyclopedias are available from other publishers for Illinois, Michigan, New Hampshire, Pennsylvania, Puerto Rico, Tennessee, and Virginia/West Virginia; they are available in *LexisNexis*.

E. SPECIFIC SUBJECT ENCYCLOPEDIAS

Several smaller legal encyclopedias that are national in scope focus on specific legal subjects. The four-volume *Encyclopedia of Crime and Justice* (Macmillan Reference USA 2002) (available in *Gale Virtual Reference Library*) contains almost 300 topical encyclopedic essays by named scholars covering a range of issues affecting criminal behavior and society's responses to it. The *Encyclopedia of the American Judicial System: Studies of the Principal Institutions and Processes of Law* (Charles Scribner's Sons 1987) is a three-volume work containing eighty-eight encyclopedic essays by named scholars that provide historical accounts and discussions of substantive law, institutions and personnel within the legal system, the judicial process, and constitutional law. The *Encyclopedia of the American Constitution*, 2d ed., is discussed in Chapter 8, Section A-2.

Also encyclopedic in nature is the four-volume *Great American Court Cases* (The Gale Group 1999), which profiles almost 800 judicial proceedings under the broad headings of Individual Liberties, Criminal Justice, Equal Protection and Family Law, and Business and Government. *Great American Lawyers: An Encyclopedia* (ABC-CLIO 2001) is a two-volume work that provides essays about the lives of 100 great American lawyer-litigators.

Chapter 17

AMERICAN LAW REPORTS (A.L.R.)*

The Lawyers Cooperative Publishing Company began producing the *American Law Reports* (*A.L.R.*) series in 1919;[1] the series is currently published by West.[2] *A.L.R.* is sometimes referred to as a "selective reporter" of appellate court opinions, meaning that its editors select and publish only what they believe to be the most significant judicial opinions—those that are representative of an important legal issue or that expand or change the law in some significant way. With these opinions, the editors provide lengthy *annotations*, which are encyclopedic essays that collect opinions germane to the particular point of law and then, using those cases, discuss and analyze that point of law in depth. It is the annotations, rather than the selectively reported opinions, that are most valuable to researchers. Identifying an *A.L.R.* annotation on point can save significant amounts of research time in identifying and synthesizing the issues and the law relevant to a problem. As is the case with legal encyclopedias, however, *A.L.R.* annotations are best viewed as introductory secondary sources and finding tools and are not as authoritative and persuasive as scholarly treatises or journal articles.

A. A.L.R., A.L.R. FED., AND A.L.R. INTERNATIONAL

Between five and ten separate annotations are published in each volume of *A.L.R.* The summary of contents of each volume lists the annotations within that volume. [Illustration 17–1]

1. American Law Reports Series

American Law Reports originally included cases and annotations on both federal and state law. Because of the increasing importance of federal case law, *A.L.R. Fed*, a new series covering only federal law topics, was launched in 1969. In 2005 the publisher added *A.L.R. International*, with annotations on international law topics.

---

* This chapter was revised by Melissa Bernstein, Library Director & Professor of Law, S.J. Quinney Law Library, University of Utah.

[1] The *American Law Reports* replaced the *Lawyers' Reports Annotated* (*L.R.A.*). For information about this set, three series collectively known as the *Trinity Series*, and other earlier sets of annotated reports, see ERVIN H. POLLACK, FUNDAMENTALS OF LEGAL RESEARCH 116–17 (3d ed. 1967).

[2] Lawyers Cooperative Publishing Company (and its related company, Bancroft Whitney Company) had its own system of research tools, known as the *Total Client Service Library*. In contrast to West's practice of comprehensive reporting, Lawyers Cooperative Publishing reported opinions selectively, on the theory that most judicial opinions did not merit reporting. In 1996, Thomson Corporation acquired Lawyers Cooperative Publishing, West Publishing Company, and several other legal publishers and established the West Group, thus bringing together two traditional law publishing competitors. In 2008, Thomson Corporation and Reuters Group PLC combined to form Thomson Reuters. For more on the contrasting historical philosophies of Lawyers Cooperative Publishing and West Publishing, see Steven M. Barkan, *Can Law Publishers Change the Law?*, LEGAL REFERENCE SERVICES Q., Fall-Wtr. 1991, at 29.

Within these titles are different series. For example, the original *A.L.R.*, published 1919–1948, ended with volume 175 and was followed by *A.L.R. 2d*, which was published 1948–1965.

Even the oldest volumes are still updated (see Section C). Many of the annotations in the old volumes have been superseded by more recent annotations. For example, a 1982 annotation about a doctor or psychotherapist's liability to prevent a suicide was superseded by one on the same topic in 2000.[3] Perhaps surprisingly, many old annotations have *not* been superseded. For example, an annotation about discrimination in the employment of schoolteachers and other public employees that was originally published in 1941 has not been superseded but instead has been updated with citations to newer cases.[4]

The nine series of *American Law Reports* are:

a.   *Sixth Series (A.L.R.6th), 2005–present.* This series covers constitutional and state topics and includes several enhancements. For example, the Sixth Series includes references to *West's A.L.R. Digest*, which has been reclassified to correspond to the West key number system, as well as legal encyclopedias *Am. Jur. 2d* and *C.J.S.*; suggested *Westlaw* databases; an expanded list of related annotations in all series of *A.L.R.*; jurisdictional tables of cited statutes and cases; and references to secondary sources, such as law reviews, treatises, and practice aids. It also includes the standard features contained in most *A.L.R.* series—illustrative cases, outlines, annotations, indexes, and references to other West publications. The illustrative cases reported in each volume follow all the annotations in that volume.

b.   *Fifth Series (A.L.R.5th), 1992–2005, 125 volumes.* This series covers state topics only and includes enhancements not found in some of the earlier series discussed below. The Fifth Series includes references to West digest key numbers as well as legal encyclopedias *Am. Jur. 2d* and *C.J.S.*; detailed electronic search queries; jurisdictional tables of cited statutes and cases; and references to secondary sources, such as law reviews, treatises, and practice aids. The standard features contained in most *A.L.R.* series can also be found—illustrative cases, outlines, annotations, indexes, and references to other West publications. The illustrative cases reported in each volume follow all the annotations in that volume.

c.   *Fourth Series (A.L.R.4th), 1980–1992, 90 volumes.* This set covers state topics only and contains the traditional *A.L.R.* series features, including illustrative cases, outlines, annotations, indexes, and references to related publications. The illustrative case immediately precedes the related annotation. The same enhancements included in *A.L.R.5th* and in *A.L.R. Fed. 2d* are added to the pocket supplements of *A.L.R.4th*. A separate paperback book, *Electronic Search Queries and West Digest Key Numbers for Annotations in ALR 4th*, contains the materials referenced in its title.

---

[3] Patricia C. Kussman, Annotation, *Liability of Doctor, Psychiatrist, or Psychologist for Failure to* Take *Steps to Prevent Patient's Suicide*, 81 A.L.R. 5TH 167 (2000), *superseding* James L. Rigelhaupt, Jr., *Annotation, Liability of Doctor, Psychiatrist, or Psychologist for Failure to Take Steps to Prevent Patient's Suicide*, 17 A.L.R. 4TH 1128 (1982).

[4] C.T.F., Annotation, *Discrimination Because of Race, Color, or Creed in Respect of Appointment, Duties, Compensation, Etc., of Schoolteachers or Other Public Officers or Employees*, 130 A.L.R. 1512 (1941). As of April 2014, the supplement in *Westlaw* already included several cases from 2014.

   d.   Third Series (A.L.R.3d), 1965–1980, 100 volumes. This series covers both state and federal topics for the period from 1965 to 1969. After *A.L.R. Fed.* began in 1969, coverage in *A.L.R.3d* was limited to state topics. It includes the traditional features found in the more recent *A.L.R.* series.

   e.   Second Series (A.L.R.2d), 1948–1965, 100 volumes. This series covers both state and federal topics and includes the standard features found in the later *A.L.R.* series.

   f.   First Series (A.L.R.), 1919–1948, 175 volumes. Coverage and features are the same as in *A.L.R.2d.*

   g.   Federal 2d Series (A.L.R. Fed. 2d), 2005–present. This series is broader in scope than *A.L.R. Fed.* In addition to federal topics, it includes international topics that are jurisdiction specific and affect only the United States. At the beginning of each volume is a list of subjects annotated in that volume. The illustrative cases reported in the volume follow all the annotations in that volume. This set includes references to *West's A.L.R. Digest* and *West's Key Number Digest*, as well as legal encyclopedias *Am. Jur. 2d* and *C.J.S.*; suggested *Westlaw* databases; an expanded list of related annotations in all series of *A.L.R.*; jurisdictional tables of cited statutes and cases; and references to secondary sources, such as law reviews, treatises, and practice aids. An annual four-volume pamphlet set, the *A.L.R. Federal Tables*, lists cases covered in *A.L.R. Fed.* and *A.L.R. Fed. 2d* and provides both a volume-by-volume listing of annotation titles and annotation history tables that indicate when annotations have been superseded or supplemented.

   h.   Federal (A.L.R. Fed.), 1969–2005, 200 volumes. This series discusses federal topics only and was developed because of the increasing amount and importance of federal case law. In volumes 1 to 110, the illustrative case immediately precedes the related annotation. Commencing with volume 111 (1993), the illustrative cases reported in the volume follow all the annotations in that volume. Beginning in 1996 when West took over publication, references to West's key number system and to West's other legal encyclopedia, *C.J.S.,* were included.[5] Also included are suggested electronic search queries; jurisdictional tables of cited statutes and cases; and references to secondary sources, such as law reviews, treatises, and practice aids. An annual four-volume pamphlet set, the *A.L.R. Federal Tables*, lists cases covered in *A.L.R. Fed.* and *A.L.R. Fed. 2d* and provides both a volume-by-volume listing of annotation titles and annotation history tables that indicate when annotations have been superseded or supplemented.

   i.   International (A.L.R. Int'l), 2010–present. The newest series of *A.L.R.* includes annotations covering a wide range of legal issues of global importance, regardless of whether the United States is affected. As of mid-2014, there were 8 volumes. At the beginning of each volume is a list of subjects annotated in that volume. The illustrative cases reported in the volume follow all the annotations in that volume. This set includes references to *West's A.L.R. Digest* and *West's Key Number Digest*, as well as legal encyclopedias *Am. Jur. 2d* and *C.J.S.*; suggested *Westlaw* databases; a list of related annotations in all series of *A.L.R.*; jurisdictional tables of cited statutes and cases; and references to secondary sources, such as law reviews, treatises, and practice aids.

------

   [5] Because *Am. Jur.* also was published by Lawyers Cooperative Publishing Company, the first series of *A.L.R.* included references to it. When West took over *Am. Jur. 2d*, it began including references to both of its legal encyclopedias, *Am. Jur. 2d* and *C.J.S.*

2.   A.L.R. Annotations in Electronic Format

A.L.R. annotations are available in *Westlaw* and *LexisNexis*. *Westlaw*'s ALR database includes the full text of annotations from all series of *A.L.R.* except *A.L.R. Int'l*, along with the *A.L.R. Index*. The database also features *electronic annotations* (*e-annos*), which are special annotations available online. These *e-annos* may be included in subsequent *A.L.R.* volumes. The *Westlaw* ALRDIGEST database includes the case headnotes from reported cases for annotations in all the *A.L.R.* series organized according to West key number topics. *A.L.R. International* is available in a separate database in *Westlaw* (ALR–INTL) that is not part of the standard *Westlaw* academic package.

The *LexisNexis* ALR database contains the full text of the annotations in all but the first series of *A.L.R.* and *A.L.R. International*.

Most of the *A.L.R.* series are available in two CD-ROM products entitled *A.L.R. in LawDesk*. The federal series contains all annotations published in *A.L.R. Fed.*, *A.L.R. Fed. 2d*, and *A.L.R.3d* dealing with federal matters. The other series contains all of *A.L.R.3d*, *4th*, *5th*, and *6th* (volumes 1–forward) and the *A.L.R. Index*. These products enable a user to "jump" directly to the articles and sections needed.

B.   FINDING A.L.R. ANNOTATIONS

Finding *A.L.R.* annotations and demonstrating their value is best evidenced with an example and illustrations. Recall the hypothetical problem set forth at the start of Chapter 7, Section D of this book and the reference to the *learned intermediary doctrine*.

In *Edwards v. Basel Pharmaceuticals*[6] the widow of a smoker who died of a nicotine-induced heart attack as a result of smoking cigarettes while wearing two nicotine patches brought a products liability action against the patch manufacturer. The publisher determined that the Oklahoma Supreme Court's decision [Illustration 17–2] was significant in any discussion of the duty of a drug manufacturer to warn customers of dangers associated with its products and the role of the "learned intermediary doctrine." Accordingly, an editor prepared a 140-page annotation entitled *Construction and Application of Learned-Intermediary Doctrine*. [Illustration 17–3]

In preparing this annotation, the editor researched the entire area of the law covered by the topic of the annotation, collected cases from all jurisdictions that related to the annotation, and wrote the annotation, incorporating the many editorial features common to the *A.L.R.* series. This annotation, as with all *A.L.R.* annotations, discusses all sides of the cases involving an issue; presents general principles of law derived from the cases; and gives exceptions to, and qualifications, distinctions, and applications of those principles. [Illustrations 17–4 through 17–7]

1.   Index Method

The first step in locating an *A.L.R.* annotation in print is to consult the multivolume, subject-arranged *A.L.R. Index*. This set indexes all annotations in all the *A.L.R.* series, including *A.L.R. Int'l* and *Westlaw*'s *A.L.R. electronic annotations*. It gives almost 300,000 direct references to the nearly 15,000 annotations in these series. A single-volume *ALR Table of Laws, Rules and Regulations*, part of the *A.L.R. Index*, provides

---

[6] Edwards v. Basel Pharmaceuticals, 933 P.2d 298 (Okla. 1997).

citations to every annotation in which these sources are mentioned. The *A.L.R. Index* is updated by annual pocket supplements; in the current set, these supplements cover *A.L.R.6th*, *A.L.R. Fed.*, *A.L.R. Fed. 2d*, *A.L.R. Int'l*, and *Westlaw's A.L.R. electronic annotations*.

A separate, annual, one-volume *A.L.R. Federal Quick Index* includes references to all annotations in *A.L.R. Fed.* and *A.L.R. Fed. 2d*. An annual one-volume *A.L.R. Quick Index* for *A.L.R.3d*, *4th*, *5th*, and *6th* reproduces the references found in the *A.L.R. Index*.

In our example above, one term to look up in the *A.L.R. Index* might be "products liability." [Illustration 17–8]

2. Digest Method

West's A.L.R. Digest covers all series of *A.L.R.*[7] *It is updated by pocket part or pamphlet supplement. These digests are classified into over 400 topics arranged alphabetically. Under each topic are digest paragraphs (headnotes) from cases reported in the entire A.L.R.* family with the exception of *A.L.R. Int'l*, along with a listing of the annotations that deal with the particular subject in question. [Illustration 17–9] [NEW]

3. Electronic Format Method

Annotations can be located through Boolean and natural language searches, together with the access mechanisms available for printed copies of *A.L.R.* In addition, annotations are retrieved automatically in *Westlaw* when one searches all federal cases or all state cases.[8] From a retrieved annotation, a researcher can go directly to a cited case, statute, related *A.L.R.* annotation, or other source by clicking its hypertext link. *Westlaw* updates the First Series annually; the remaining series are updated weekly by adding relevant new cases. *LexisNexis* updates its ALR database on a less regular schedule.

C. HOW A.L.R. IS KEPT CURRENT

1. Upkeep Service

Once an *A.L.R.* annotation is found, further steps must be taken to locate cases subsequent to those cited in the annotation. Over the years, the publisher has developed several different methods of updating its various *A.L.R.* series.

a. A.L.R.3d, 4th, 5th, 6th, Fed., Fed. 2d. Each volume of these series has an annual cumulative pocket supplement with later cases and other references. Abstracts of cases are related directly to the relevant sections of the annotation. Thorough researchers can also check volumes of *A.L.R.6th* and *A.L.R. Fed. 2d* published after the pocket parts were published to see whether their topics are covered. These series are supplemented weekly in *Westlaw* and less frequently in *LexisNexis*.

b. A.L.R. Int'l. A.L.R. Int'l is supplemented weekly in *Westlaw* and annually in print with a cumulative pocket supplement.

---

[7] *A.L.R.*'s previous publisher had a digest with its own outline system. After West acquired the sets, it reclassified the annotations to fit with its own key number system.

[8] Researchers should be aware that clicking through to an *A.L.R.* annotation from a "Results Plus" list could incur an additional charge if the ALR database is not included in the particular subscription package.

    c.   *A.L.R.2d.* This series is kept current with a multivolume *A.L.R.2d Later Case Service*, with each volume covering two to four volumes of the 100 volumes in *A.L.R.2d.* This *Later Case Service* provides digests of cases and then relates them directly to the relevant sections of the *A.L.R.2d* annotations. This set is updated with annual pocket supplements and occasional revised volumes. Thus, to update an *A.L.R.2d* annotation, both the bound *Later Case Service* and its supplement must be checked. *A.L.R. 2d* annotations are updated in *Westlaw* and *LexisNexis*.

    d.   *A.L.R. (First Series).* This series is kept current through a cumbersome eleven-volume set (ten hardbound volumes with a softbound supplement) entitled the *A.L.R. Blue Book of Supplemental Decisions.* Each volume lists citations to all cases on the same topic as the annotations during a span of years, but provides no discussion of the cases. *A.L.R.* annotations are updated in *Westlaw.*

2.   Superseding and Supplementing Annotations

    a.   *Superseding Annotations.* Frequently, a topic of law of an *A.L.R.* annotation is completely changed by later cases. For example, an annotation in an early volume of *A.L.R.* might show that there is little likelihood that one would be convicted of cruelty to animals. Subsequently, statutes are enacted, cases interpret those statutes, and the law changes. The editors may then decide to rewrite and publish in a later *A.L.R.* volume a *superseding* (replacement) annotation. Sometimes only a part of a previous annotation is superseded.

    b.   *Supplementing Annotations.* This method was used most frequently in *A.L.R.* and *A.L.R.2d.* In such instances, a new annotation was written that supplemented the original one. Therefore, for comprehensive coverage both annotations must be read together as if they are one annotation.

3.   Locating the Most Recent Annotations

    a.   *Annotation History Table.* Whenever a researcher has a citation to an *A.L.R. Annotation*, to avoid wasting time by reading an obsolete annotation or one not fully covering a topic, the researcher should always first check to see if an annotation has been *superseded* or *supplemented.* This is done by either checking the citation in the appropriate *A.L.R.* upkeep volume or using the Annotation History Table located in back of each volume of the *A.L.R. Index.* This table gives the history of annotations in all of the *A.L.R.* series. Its use is best shown with the excerpt below:

ANNOTATION HISTORY TABLE

12 ALR 111 Supplemented 37 ALR2d 453	13 ALR 17 Supplemented 39 ALR2d 782	13 ALR 1465 Superseded 3 ALR5th 370
12 ALR 333 Superseded 7 ALR2d 226	13 ALR 151 Superseded 46 ALR2d 1227	14 ALR 240 Superseded 51 ALR2d 331
12 ALR 596 Superseded 57 ALR2d 379	13 ALR 225 Superseded 13 ALR4th 1060	14 ALR 316 Superseded 11 ALR3d 1074

    This example indicates that 12 A.L.R. 111 and 37 A.L.R.2d 453 should be read together as if they are a single annotation, and then updated for later cases using the *A.L.R.2d Later Case Service* as previously described.

Suppose, however, that the researcher has found a citation to 82 A.L.R.2d 794, an annotation on cruelty to animals. By checking the Annotation History Table in the *A.L.R. Index*, it would be noted that this annotation is *superseded* as indicated below and that only the later annotation should be consulted:

ANNOTATION HISTORY TABLE

78 ALR2d 412	79 ALR2d 431	82 ALR2d 794
Superseded 69 ALR Fed 600	§ 29, 36 Superseded 46 ALR4th 1197	Superseded 6 ALR5th 733
	§ 35 Superseded 63 ALR4th 105	
78 ALR2d 429	§ 37 Superseded 54 ALR4th 574	82 ALR2d 1183
Superseded 98 ALR Fed 778		§ 3-5 Superseded 53 ALR4th 282
	79 ALR2d 990	63 ALR4th 221
78 ALR2d 446	Superseded 20 ALR3d 1127	
Superseded 25 ALR3d 383	38 ALR4th 200	82 ALR2d 1429
		Superseded 44 ALR4th 271
	79 ALR2d 1005	
	Superseded 54 ALR4th 391	

---

b. *A.L.R. Alerts.* Review *A.L.R. Alerts* for *A.L.R. 6th*, *A.L.R. Fed. 2d*, and *A.L.R. Int'l* on the *A.L.R.* website.[9]

c. *KeyCite. KeyCite*, available in *Westlaw*, provides electronic citation validation and verification services. Upon entering an *A.L.R.* citation into this service, the researcher retrieves citations to all supplementing or superseding annotations.

d. *Latest Case Service Hotline.* Each pocket supplement lists a toll-free number that can be used to obtain citations to any relevant cases decided since the last supplement.

D. UNITED STATES SUPREME COURT REPORTS, LAWYERS' EDITION

Chapter 5 discusses the *United States Supreme Court Reports, Lawyers' Edition*. It was pointed out that a significant aspect of this set is the *Annotations* that are provided for selected important cases. These *Annotations* are published in the bound volumes (but not the advance sheets) and are available exclusively in *LexisNexis*. Since the merger of Thomson Reuters and West Publishing in 1997, *Supreme Court Reports, Lawyers' Edition* annotations are no longer referenced in the *A.L.R. Digest* and *A.L.R. Index*.

E. ILLUSTRATIONS: LOCATING AND UPDATING A.L.R. ANNOTATIONS

---

[9] http://west.thomson.com/westlaw/litigator/alr/alerts/default.aspx.

[Illustration 17–1]

CONTENTS OF AN A.L.R.5TH VOLUME

Contents of This Volume

Near the front of each volume is the contents, which lists the annotations contained within. Following the contents are several pages containing "Subjects Annotated" in this volume, which is an alphabetical subject guide to the annotations in the volume.

xi

[Illustration 17–2]

START OF OPINION IN A.L.R.5TH

SUBJECT OF ANNOTATION

Beginning on page 1

Construction and application of learned-intermediary doctrine

Alpha EDWARDS, Personal Representative of the Estate of
John T. Edwards, Deceased,
Plaintiff-Appellant

v

BASEL PHARMACEUTICALS, a DIVISION OF CIBA-
GEIGY CORPORATION,
Defendant-Appellee

Supreme Court of Oklahoma
March 4, 1997

933 P2d 298, Prod Liab Rep (CCH) P 14894, 57

A case representative of the subject of each *A.L.R.* annotation in an *A.L.R.* volume is also reported in that same volume. When citing to an *A.L.R.* annotation, reference is to the annotation, not the representative case. Immediately preceding the first page of the case are digest paragraphs classified to the *ALR Digest*. This annotation is classified under Products Liability §§ 4, 100, and 104.

result of smoking cigarettes while wearing two nicotine patches brought products-liability action against patch manufacturer. The United States Court of Appeals for the Tenth Circuit certified question. The Supreme Court, Summers, V.C.J., held that compliance with Food and Drug Administration (FDA) warning requirements does not necessarily satisfy manufacturer's common-law duty to warn consumer.

Question answered.

793

[Illustration 17–3]

FIRST PAGE OF ANNOTATION, 57 A.L.R.5TH 1

57 ALR5th 1

CONSTRUCTION AND APPLICATION OF LEARNED-INTERMEDIARY DOCTRINE

by
Diane Schmauder Kane, J.D.

The learned-intermediary doctrine provides that the manufacturer or supplier of a prescription drug has no legal duty to warn a consumer of the dangerous propensities of its drug, as long as adequate warnings are provided to the prescribing physician. The doctrine has been extended to encompass medical devices and equipment that can be sold only through a physician or a physician's prescription. In certain cases, however, the courts have created exceptions to this doctrine and have ruled that the manufacturer or supplier has a duty to warn consumers directly of the risks associated with the use of its product. In Edwards v. Basel Pharmaceuticals, 933 P.2d 298, ~~Prod. Liab. Rep. (CCH) ¶ 14804, 57 A.L.R.5th 793 (Okl~~

This is the first page of the annotation in 57 A.L.R.5th 1. This prefatory paragraph, a feature that began with A.L.R.5th, briefly describes the subject of the annotation. For A.L.R.5th, the illustrative cases used with the annotations are published toward the back of the volume following all annotations in that volume. For the earlier *A.L.R.* series, the case immediately precedes the annotation.

ability, despite the fact that the manufacturer adequately may have warned the decedent's physician of the risks associated with its patch. This annotation collects and analyzes those cases in which the courts have discussed or applied the learned-intermediary doctrine in the context of a failure-to-warn claim brought against the manufacturer or supplier of a prescription drug, device, or product.

Edwards v. Basel Pharmaceuticals is fully reported at page 793, infra.

1

[Illustration 17–4]

FIRST PAGE OF OUTLINE TO ANNOTATION, 57 A.L.R.5TH 1

LEARNED-INTERMEDIARY DOCTRINE   57 ALR5th
57 ALR5th 1

TABLE OF CONTENTS

Research References

Index

Jurisdictional Table of Cited Statutes and Cases

ARTICLE OUTLINE

I. PRELIMINARY MATTERS

§ 1. Introduction
    [a] Scope
    [b] Related annotations

§ 2. Summary and comment
    [a] Generally
    [b] Practice pointers

II. APPLICABILITY OF DOCTRINE TO PARTICULAR PRODUCTS

§ 3. Prescription drugs other than contraceptives, smoking-cessation drugs, or investigational drugs

§ 4. Vaccines
    [a] Doctrine held applicable
    [b] Doctrine held inapplicable—mass-immunization exception

> This is the first page of a detailed outline of the annotation. It follows the prefatory paragraph shown in Illustration 17-3. Notice that while this annotation covers the point specific to the *Edwards* case, it covers numerous other issues as well. The outline enables a researcher to turn immediately to a section being researched and find relevant discussion and cases.

    [f] Norplant

§ 6. Medical devices designed for surgical implantation in the human body

§ 7. Blood and blood products

§ 8. Smoking-cessation drugs and products
    [a] Doctrine held applicable
    [b] Doctrine held inapplicable

§ 9. Investigational drugs

§ 10. Prescription drugs withdrawn from market

2

[Illustration 17–5]

PAGE SHOWING RESEARCH REFERENCES FOR ANNOTATION, 57 A.L.R.5TH 1

57 ALR5th   LEARNED-INTERMEDIARY DOCTRINE
           57 ALR5th 1

63 Am Jur 2d, Products Liability § 337

Practice Aids

9 Am Jur Pl & Pr Forms (Rev), Drugs and Controlled Substances, Forms
    53, 55

20A Am Jur Pl & Pr Forms (Rev), Products Liability, Forms 211–213, 215,
    219–222

7 Am Jur Proof of Facts 3d 1, Injuries from Drugs

7 Am Jur Proof of Facts 3d 225, Defective Design of Golf Cart

49 Am Jur Proof of Facts 2d 125, Teratogenic Drugs

47 Am Jur Proof of Facts 2d 227, Manufacturer's Failure to Warn
    Consumer of Allergenic Nature of Product

6 Am Jur Proof of Facts 2d 175, Manufacturer's Duty to Warn Ultimate
    User Directly of Product-Connected Danger

Digests and Indexes

ALR Digest, Drugs and Druggists § 2

ALR Digest, Products Liability §§ 100, 143

ALR Index, Drugs and Narcotics; Drugstores and Druggists; Food and
    Drug Administration; Food, Drug, and Cosmetic Act; Intermediaries;
    Manufacturers and Manufacturing; Medical Equipment and Supplies;
    Physicians and Surgeons; Prescription Drugs; Products Liability; Side
    ~~Effects; Vaccination and Vaccines; Warning~~

Following the outline, the *A.L.R.* annotations include "Research References" to other West publications, as well as to sources by other publishers. In earlier series, these references were in a box on the first page of the annotation.

RESEARCH SOURCES

The following are the research sources that were found to be helpful in compiling this annotation.

Encyclopedias

25 Am Jur 2d, Drugs and Controlled Substances §§ 239, 241

63 Am Jur 2d, Products Liability §§ 327, 337

28 CJS, Drugs and Narcotics §§ 61–65

Texts

Am Law Prod Liab 3d §§ 32:32–32:42, 89:1–89:9, 90:3–90:6

Law Review Articles

Marvinney, How Courts Interpret A Manufacturer's Communications to
    Consumers: The Learned Intermediary Doctrine, 47 Food and Drug
    L.J. 69

5

[Illustration 17–6]

LAST PAGE OF INDEX TO ANNOTATION, 57 A.L.R.5TH 1, AND START OF JURISDICTIONAL TABLE

---

57 ALR5th   LEARNED-INTERMEDIARY DOCTRINE
                        57 ALR5th 1

Vaccines, §§ 4, 12[b], 18, 20[a], 21[b], 24, 25[a], 30[a, c, d], 32

Venous thrombosis, § 21[a]

Ventilator, § 11[a]

Veterinarians and veterinary prescriptions, §§ 12, 20, 30[a]

Viral hepatitis, § 7

Vision and eyes, §§ 5[a], 11[b], 13, 16, 22[a], 23[a], 28, 33

Voluntary direct warning to consumer by manufacturer, § 31[c]

Weight-control drug, §§ 27[a], 28

Who is learned intermediary, §§ 17-20, 23[a]

Withdrawn from market, prescription drugs which have been, § 10

X-ray equipment and radiology, §§ 11[a], 14

Jurisdictional Table of Cited Statutes and Cases*

UNITED STATES

21 CFR § 130.45(e)(3). See § 31[b]
21 CFR § 201.105. See § 30[a]
21 CFR § 310.501. See § 5[a, b]
21 CFR § 310.502. See § 5[d]

A.L.R.5th annotations include a detailed index that can lead to specific points in the annotation. Note that Illustration 17-4 referenced § 8 of the annotation. See next illustration. If the researcher is interested in "who is a learned intermediary," reference would be to §§ 17-20, and 23[a] as shown above. Lengthy annotations in earlier series also contain as index.

The jurisdictional table, found in *A.L.R.5th*, provides citations to statutes and cases relevant to the annotation. This information is much more detailed than in earlier series.

(S.D.N.Y. 1993)—§ 29

Hill v. Searle Laboratories, a Div. of Searle Pharmaceuticals, Inc., 884 F.2d 1064, Prod. Liab. Rep. (CCH) ¶ 12250 (8th Cir. 1989)—§ 6

Hurley v. Lederle Laboratories Div. of American Cyanamid Co., 863 F.2d 1173 (5th Cir. 1988)—§ 22[b]

Reyes v Wyeth Laboratories, 498 F.2d 1264 (5th Cir. 1974)—§ 4[c]

---

* Statutes, rules, regulations, and constitutional provisions bearing on the subject of the annotation are included in this table only to the extent, and in the form, that they are reflected in the court opinions discussed in this annotation. The reader should consult the appropriate statutory or regulatory compilations to ascertain the current status of relevant statutes, rules, regulations, and constitutional provisions.

For federal cases involving state law, see state headings.

11

[Illustration 17–7]

PAGE FROM ANNOTATION, 57 A.L.R.5TH 1

§ 7   LEARNED-INTERMEDIARY DOCTRINE   57 ALR5th
                                  57 ALR5th 1

of a blood-clotting agent failed to adequately warn of the risks of contracting the AIDS virus from its product. The court explained simply that a
pharmaceutical manufacturer is required to warn physicians or other
medical personnel authorized to prescribe drugs by state law of all reasonably foreseeable risks associated with the use of the product.

In Doe v American Nat'l Red Cross (1994, DC Md) 866 F Supp 242

Notice how § 8 of the annotation discusses cases dealing with
prescription smoking-cessation medication. The jurisdictional table,
partially shown in Illustration 17-6, can be used to identify relevant
cases and statutes from any state. For example, under Oklahoma
the table indicates that *Edwards v. Basel Pharmaceuticals*, the
illustrative case chosen for this annotation, is discussed under
§§ 2[b]. 8[b], and 31[b].

§ 1 of an annotation gives its scope and then lists related
annotations.

ated with prescription drugs extends only to the attending physician, and
not to the patient.

§ 8. Smoking-cessation drugs and products

[a] Doctrine held applicable

In the following case involving a prescription smoking-cessation medication, the court held that the learned-intermediary doctrine was applicable
and that, therefore, the manufacturer of the product had no obligation to
warn the user directly of the side effects associated with its product.

A failure-to-warn claim brought against the manufacturer of Nicorette
tablets, a smoking-cessation medication, by the administratrix of the estate
of a participant in a smoking-cessation program was governed by the
learned-intermediary doctrine, concluded the court in Tracy v Merrell
Dow Pharmaceuticals, Inc. (1991) 58 **Ohio St 3d** 147, 569 NE2d 875,
CCH Prod Liab Rep ¶ 12950, reversing the judgment of the court below.
Prior to entering the smoking-cessation program, which was an investigational drug study, the decedent underwent a screening by a physician who
was participating in the study. The doctor physically examined the
decedent, finding no evidence of heart disease. The decedent did not,
however, tell the doctor about his heavy smoking habits or the fact that he
previously had been hospitalized for alcoholism. The decedent was given
a written agreement which included a warning against the use of alcohol
or other drugs while taking the Nicorette tablets, and the doctor warned

78

[Illustration 17–8]

PAGE FROM A.L.R. INDEX

ALR INDEX

PRODUCTS LIABILITY—Cont'd
Instructions to jury—Cont'd
    products liability case, **52 ALR3d
    101**
    fires, res ipsa loquitur as to cause of or
    liability for real-property fires, **21
    ALR4th 929**
Insurance
    generally, **45 ALR2d 994**
    causation of injury, insurance coverage
    as extending only to product-caused
    injury to person or other property, as
    distinguished from near product fail-
    ure, **91 ALR3d 921**
    clause excluding products liability
    from coverage of liability insurance
    policy, **54 ALR2d 518**
    completed operations, in this topic
    event triggering liability insurance
    coverage as occurring within period
    of time covered by liability insur-
    ance policy where injury or damage
    is delayed—modern cases, **14
    ALR5th 695**
    premises liability insurance, coverage
    of premises liability insurance
    extending to liability for injuries or
    damage caused by product sold or
    rented by insured and occurring
    away from insured premises, **62
    ALR3d 889**
    sistership clause of policy excepting
    from coverage cost of product recall
    or withdrawal of product from mar-
    ket, validity and construction of, **32
    ALR4th 630**
    workers' compensation, in this topic
Intermediaries
    learned-intermediary, construction and
    application of learned-intermediary
    doctrine, **57 ALR5th 1**
    warning, liability of manufacturer or
    seller as affected by failure of
    subsequent party in distribution
    chain to remedy or warn against
    defect of which he knew, **45
    ALR4th 777**
Intervening purchaser's knowledge of
    defects in or danger of article, or failure
    to inspect therefor, as affecting liability
    of manufacturer or dealer for personal

PRODUCTS LIABILITY—Cont'd
    injury or property damage to subsequent
    purchaser or other third person, **164
    ALR 371**
Joint tortfeasors, manufacturer and dealer
    or distributor as joint or concurrent
    tortfeasors, **97 ALR2d 811**
Judgment in action against seller or sup-
    plier of product as res judicata in action
    against manufacturer for injury from
    defective product, **34 ALR3d 518**
Jurisdiction
    admiralty, products liability claim as
    within admiralty jurisdiction, **7 ALR
    Fed 502**
    long-arm statutes, in this topic
    personal jurisdiction over nonresident
    manufacturer of component
    incorporated in another product, **69
    ALR4th 14**
Knowledge. Notice or knowledge, in this
    topic
Labor and employment
    contribution or indemnity, right of
    manufacturer or seller to contribu-
    tion or indemnity from user of prod-
    uct causing injury or damage to third
    person, and vice versa, **28 ALR3d
    943**
    conveyor belts, industrial accidents
    involving conveyor belts or systems,
    2 ALR4th 262
    food, employer's liability for injury
    caused by food or drink purchased
    by employee in plant facilities, **50
    ALR3d 505**
    hammer as simple tool within simple
    tool doctrine, **81 ALR2d 965**
    industrial presses, **8 ALR4th 70**
    spoliation of evidence, effect of spolia-
    tion of evidence in products liability
    action, **102 ALR5th 99**
    workers' compensation, in this topic
Lacquer reducer
    misuse, sufficiency of evidence to sup-
    port product misuse defense in
    products liability actions concerning
    paint, cleaners, or other chemicals,
    58 ALR4th 76, § 6(b), 18(c)

Consult POCKET PART for Later Annotations

668

[Illustration 17–9]

PAGE FROM WEST'S ALR DIGEST

☞ 221 PRODUCTS LIABILITY

Corp., 488 A.2d 716, 40 U.C.C. Rep. Serv. 836, 54 A.L.R.4th 561 (**R.I.** 1985).

Where permanent wave lotion itself was harmless to beauty operator, and fixative by itself was equally harmless, distributor could not have foreseen dermatitis which was caused by allergy to combination of lotion and fixative. Bennett v. Pilot Products Co., 120 **Utah** 474, 235 P.2d 525, 26 A.L.R.2d 958 (1951).

[Annotated at 26 A.L.R.2d 963]

☞ 222. Pesticides, herbicides, insecticides, fungicides, and rodenticides

Annotations:

Liability for injury consequent upon spraying or dusting of crop, 12 A.L.R.2d 436

☞ 223. Health care and medical products

☞ 224. —— In general

Anno

App
in to
radia

Application of rule of strict liability in tort to person or entity rendering medical services, 100 A.L.R.3d 1205

Federal pre-emption of state common-law products liability claims pertaining to drugs, medical devices, and other health-related items, 98 A.L.R. Fed. 124

☞ 225. —— Drugs in general

Annotations:

Liability of Name Brand Drug Manufacturer for Injury or Death Resulting from Use of Prescription Drug's Generic Equivalent, 56 A.L.R.6th 161

Liability of Prescription Drug Manufacturer for Drug User's Suicide or Attempted Suicide, 45 A.L.R.6th 385

Liability of hospital or medical practitioner under doctrine of strict liability in tort, or breach of warranty, for harm caused by drug, medical instrument, or similar device used in treating patient, 65 A.L.R.5th 357

Headnotes:

Under Texas law, "learned intermediary" doctrine excuses drug manufacturer from warning each patient who receives its product when manufacturer properly warns the prescribing physician of prod-

uct's dangers. Ackermann v. Wyeth Pharmaceuticals, 526 F.3d 203, 45 A.L.R.6th 801 (**5th Cir.** 2008).

[Annotated at 45 A.L.R.6th 385]

Under Texas law, "learned intermediary" doctrine is not an affirmative defense; rather, it delineates to whom defendant, usually a prescription drug manufacturer, owes duty to warn. Ackermann v. Wyeth Pharmaceuticals, 526 F.3d 203, 45 A.L.R.6th 801 (**5th Cir.** 2008).

[Annotated at 45 A.L.R.6th 385]

Under Texas law, patient who complains that prescription drug warning is inadequate must show, not just that the warning was inadequate, but that this alleged inadequacy caused her doctor to prescribe drug for her; if physician was aware of possible risks involved in use of drug but decided to use it anyway, or if proper warning would not have changed decision of treating physician to prescribe drug,

[Relevant information can be found in the digest under the topic and key number "Product Liability" 225. Notice the references to other sources, including annotations.]

Under Texas law, drug manufacturer's warning is adequate as matter of law, in prescription drug cases involving "learned intermediary" doctrine, where warning specifically mentions circumstances complained of. Ackermann v. Wyeth Pharmaceuticals, 526 F.3d 203, 45 A.L.R.6th 801 (**5th Cir.** 2008).

Even assuming that warning which drug manufacturer provided on package insert of risks of suicide associated with use of its antidepressant prescription drug was misleading, based on significant difference allegedly existing between manufacturer's quantification of suicide risk, as allegedly "occurring in 1/100 to 1/1000 patients," and actual risk of suicide known by drug manufacturer at time, manufacturer's allegedly inadequate warning was not producing cause of patient's death by suicide after he had taken this prescription drug, such that his widow could not recover on negligence or strict liability claims predicated on insufficiency of warning; evidence showed that treating physician would have prescribed drug, subject to same monitoring that he in fact performed, even if manufacturer had given alternate warning suggested by widow or "black box" warning. Ackermann v. Wyeth Pharmaceuticals, 526 F.3d 203, 45 A.L.R.6th 801 (**5th Cir.** 2008).

Chapter 18

LEGAL PERIODICALS AND INDEXES*

Legal periodicals can be extremely valuable secondary sources in legal research. Their value typically lies in the depth to which they analyze and criticize a particular topic and the extent of their footnote references to other sources. During the nineteenth century, legal periodicals greatly contributed to improving the image of the legal profession in America.[1] With the proliferation of legislation and judicial opinions, legal periodicals in the twenty-first century play an important role in keeping researchers current in developing areas of the law and in providing information on specialized areas of the law. The rapid growth of electronic legal research services makes them increasingly accessible.

The legal periodical is an important and useful secondary authority containing articles, frequently by specialists, on specific legal topics. The articles are either critical or expository in nature, and their scholarly interpretations are relied on frequently by American courts and lawyers.[2] Legal periodicals can be classified into five types of publications: (1) law reviews and specialized journals published by law schools or edited by law professors; (2) subject, special interest, and interdisciplinary journals published by commercial publishers; (3) bar association periodicals; (4) legal newspapers; and (5) legal newsletters.[3] A variety of specialized indexes provide access to these publications. The various types of legal periodicals and finding aids used in accessing the contents of these legal periodicals are the subjects of this chapter.

---

* This chapter was revised by Bonnie Shucha, Assistant Director for Public Services, University of Wisconsin Law Library.

[1] MAXWELL H. BLOOMFIELD, AMERICAN LAWYERS IN A CHANGING SOCIETY, 1776–1876, at 142–43 (1976). For a brief account of legal periodicals in nineteenth-century America, see LAWRENCE M. FRIEDMAN, A HISTORY OF AMERICAN LAW 481–82 (3d ed. 2005). Additional sources that deal with the early history of legal periodicals in the United States include Marion Brainerd, *Historical Sketch of American Legal Periodicals*, 14 LAW LIBR. J. 63 (1921), and Roscoe Pound, *Types of Legal Periodical*, 14 IOWA L. REV. 257 (1929). For an extensive history of law school reviews, see Michael I. Swygert & Jon W. Bruce, *The Historical Origin, Founding, and Early Development of Student-Edited Law Reviews*, 36 HASTINGS L.J. 739 (1985), and Michael L. Closen & Robert J. Dzielak, *The History and Influence of the Law Review Institution*, 30 AKRON L. REV. 15 (1996).

[2] *See, e.g.*, Whit D. Pierce & Anne E. Reuben, Empirical Study [Student Piece], *The Law Review Is Dead; Long Live the Law Review: A Closer Look at the Declining Judicial Citation of Legal Scholarship*, 45 WAKE FOREST L. REV. 1185 (2010) (finding citations to law reviews in judicial opinions, especially opinions using "first impression"—i.e., in cases that were likely to involve novel issues). Citation studies are an imperfect measure of how much journals are used. Lawyers and judges (or their clerks) could read articles for background and mine their footnotes for useful authority without ever citing the articles.

[3] For additional breakdowns of categories and for recommendations of titles that should be in a broad-based legal periodical collection, see Donald J. Dunn, Kim Dulin & Michelle Pearse, *Law, in* MAGAZINES FOR LIBRARIES 519 (Cheryl LaGuardia ed., 19th ed. 2010).

A. LEGAL PERIODICALS

1. Types of Legal Periodicals

    a. Law School Reviews/Journals. A periodical published by a law school most often is called a *review,* although *journal* is also widely used, e.g., *Harvard Law Review, Michigan Law Review, Yale Law Journal.* The two terms are used interchangeably. In the United States, student editors typically control the editorial policy and management of law reviews. Students forming the membership of law reviews are commonly chosen on the basis of their academic record, through a writing competition, or by a combination of the two. These students "on law review" write articles and edit each other's work, evaluate for potential publication the writings submitted by academics and practitioners, and then edit those pieces accepted for publication.

    The typical law review is published quarterly, although some are issued annually and others as often as eight times a year. The parent institution usually subsidizes the cost of publication and sells subscriptions at a modest price, most often to law libraries, alumni, and members of the bar within the jurisdiction where the review is published.

    These publications generally consist of two or more major sections. The first section contains articles on various topics, usually written by law professors and occasionally by practitioners, judges, or academics from other disciplines. These articles are typically lengthy and scholarly in nature; some have a substantial impact in changing the law or in charting the course for newly developing fields of law.[4] Frequently, a law review issue is devoted to a symposium on a particular subject[5] or contains an annual review of the work of a particular court.

    The second section, often called "Notes and Comments," is written by law students; the notes consist of critical analyses of recent judicial opinions or legislation, [Illustration 18–1] while the comments consist of surveys or critiques of selected subjects of contemporary importance. Many journals also publish book reviews written by legal scholars. These book reviews are critical, detailed expositions that frequently venture beyond an assessment of the book to include the reviewer's personal opinion about the issues raised in the book. These book reviews are frequently lengthy and extensively documented.

    Law reviews sometimes also contain "Commentary" sections.[6] These commentaries, which typically undergo little or no student editing and, therefore, can be published more quickly than other pieces, often set forth a scholar's position on a controversial topic. Commentaries are sometimes followed in the same or a subsequent issue with responses from other scholars challenging those views. Commentary sections are sometimes entitled "Essays" or "Correspondence."

---

    [4] *See, e.g.*, Samuel D. Warren & Louis D. Brandeis, *The Right to Privacy*, 4 HARV. L. REV. 193 (1890); William L. Prosser, *The Assault upon the Citadel (Strict Liability to the Consumer)*, 69 YALE L.J. 1099 (1960); Akhil Reed Amar, *The Bill of Rights as a Constitution*, 100 YALE L.J. 1131 (1991).

    [5] *See* Jean Stefancic, *The Law Review Symposium Issue: Community of Meaning or Re-inscription of Hierarchy?*, 63 U. COLO. L. REV. 651 (1992) (discussing symposium publishing) (this piece was itself part of a symposium issue: *Symposium on Legal Scholarship*, 63 U. COLO. L. REV. 521–781 (1992)).

    [6] For an example of this practice, see *Commentary*, 24 CONN. L. REV. 157 (1991), which contains seven brief articles.

Historically, law reviews were general in subject; today, only a law school's so-called "flagship" review or journal typically remains general in nature. "Secondary" reviews on specialized subjects, e.g., civil rights, constitutional law, dispute resolution, environmental law, international law, and taxation, or reviews that are interdisciplinary in nature, e.g., law and economics, law and society, and law and medicine, now predominate.[7]

Law school reviews have had a high degree of success in providing students with a meaningful research and writing experience,[8] while also serving as a forum for the contributions of the foremost legal scholars.[9] It is not uncommon for courts, including the United States Supreme Court, to cite or quote from law review articles as well as student notes and comments.[10]

Faculty-edited law reviews, sometimes subsidized by law schools, differ from student-edited law reviews in that they are "refereed," i.e., selection of an article for inclusion is based on peer review, often with those participating in the evaluative process not knowing the author of the piece—a so-called "blind" review.[11] Some of these highly respected journals include *The American Journal of Legal History* (Beasley School of Law, Temple University), *Journal of Legal Studies* (University of Chicago Law School), *Journal of Law and Economics* (University of Chicago Law School and University of Chicago Booth School of Business), and *Law and Society Review.* Some faculty-edited journals are sponsored by professional societies—e.g., *Law and History Review* (published for the American Society for Legal History by Cambridge University Press), *Law & Society Review* (published for the Law and Society Association by Wiley–Blackwell), *Journal of Empirical Legal Studies* (published for the Society for Empirical Legal Studies by Wiley–Blackwell).

---

[7] *See* Tracey E. George & Chris Guthrie, *Symposium: An Empirical Evaluation of Specialized Law Reviews*, 26 FLA. ST. U. L. REV. 813 (1999); Robert M. Lawless & Ira David, *The General Role Played by Specialty Law Journals: Empirical Evidence From Bankruptcy Scholarship*, 80 AM. BANKR. L.J. 523 (2006). A directory of law journals—including an option for selecting by subject specialty—is produced by the Washington & Lee Law Library: LAW JOURNALS: SUBMISSION AND RANKING, 2005–2012, http://lawlib.wlu.edu/LJ/ (last visited Dec. 15, 2013).

[8] For more on the value of student-edited law reviews, see James W. Harper, *Why Student-Run Law Reviews?*, 82 MINN. L. REV. 1261 (1997).

[9] *See,* e.g., Fred R. Shapiro, *The Most-Cited Law Review Articles*, 73 CALIF. L. REV. 1540 (1985); Fred R. Shapiro, *The Most-Cited Articles from The Yale Law Journal*, 100 YALE L.J. 1449 (1991). A book resulted from the first article: THE MOST-CITED LAW REVIEW ARTICLES (Fred R. Shapiro ed., 1987), which collected and reprinted the twenty-four law review articles that had been most cited in other law review articles. For later citation studies, see Fred R. Shapiro, *The Most-Cited Law Review Articles Revisited*, 71 CHI.–KENT L. REV. 751 (1996), and Fred R. Shapiro, *The Most-Cited Law Reviews*, 29 J. LEGAL STUD. 389 (2000). *See also* THE CANON OF AMERICAN LEGAL THOUGHT (David Kennedy & William W. Fisher III eds., 2006).

[10] For more on judicial citation of law reviews, see, e.g., Michelle M. Hamera & Jason A. Cantone, *Is Legal Scholarship out of Touch? An Empirical Analysis of the Use of Scholarship in Business Law Cases*, 19 U. MIAMI BUS. L. REV. 1 (2011) (finding steady use of scholarship by Delaware courts, especially in complex cases); Richard A. Mann, *The Use of Legal Periodicals by Courts and Journals*, 26 JURIMETRICS J. 400 (1986); Brent E. Newton, *Law Review Scholarship in the Eyes of the Twenty-First-Century Supreme Court Justices: An Empirical Analysis*, 4 DREXEL L. REV. 399 (2012) (analyzing citations by Supreme Court justices 2001–2011); Lee Petherbridge & David L. Schwartz, *An Empirical Assessment of the Supreme Court's Use of Legal Scholarship*, 106 NW. U. L. REV. 995, 1028 (2012) (studying sixty-one years of Supreme Court decisions and finding that "the Supreme Court not only often uses legal scholarship, but it also disproportionately uses scholarship when cases are either more important or more difficult to decide"); and Louis J. Sirico, Jr., *The Citing of Law Reviews by the Supreme Court: 1971–1999*, 75 IND. L.J. 1009 (2000).

[11] For more on the difference between student-edited and faculty-edited law reviews, see Richard A. Epstein, *Faculty-Edited Law Journals*, 70 CHI–KENT L. REV. 87 (1994).

Much has changed in the world of law review publishing in recent years. Notable is the proliferation of subject-oriented and interdisciplinary journals. In 1941, the number of reviews published by American law schools totaled fifty.[12] Today, students at approximately 200 American Bar Association-accredited law schools publish approximately 900 titles.[13] As authors want to publish their work in the most respected journals, a fair amount of literature is published that attempts to rate the law reviews.[14]

Another recent development is the movement for "open access" to legal scholarship. The effort to make the law more widely accessible has led to new publication models that offer scholarly content on the Internet at no charge.[15]

Although law reviews have numerous virtues, they are not without their critics.[16] The substance of the criticism is usually aimed at their pedantic style, excessive use of footnotes,[17] and similarity to each other. A classic criticism was voiced by Professor Fred Rodell in 1936: "There are two things wrong with almost all legal writing. One is its style. The other is its content. . . . The average law review writer is peculiarly able to say nothing with an air of great importance."[18] One member of Congress has even attacked law reviews as having an insidious influence on the Supreme Court of the United States.[19] In spite of these criticisms, law school law reviews serve as important vehicles for the publication of significant legal research, as valuable resources for references to additional sources of information, and as incisive and effective teaching tools.

     b.   Subject, Special Interest, and Interdisciplinary Legal Journals. As the literature of the law proliferates and reflects the growing complexity of society, it is more

---

[12] This number is derived from the listing of law reviews in FREDERICK C. HICKS, MATERIALS AND METHODS OF LEGAL RESEARCH 207–09 (3d rev. ed. 1942).

[13] John Doyle, *The Law Reviews: Do Their Paths of Glory Lead But to the Grave?*, 10 J. APP. PRAC. & PROCESS 179, 180 (2009). *See* Alena Wolotira, *From a Trickle to a Flood: A Case Study of the Current Index to Legal Periodicals to Examine the Swell of American Law Journals Published in the Last Fifty Years*, 31 LEGAL REFERENCE SERVICES Q. 150 (2012).

[14] *See, e.g., Chicago–Kent Law Review Faculty Scholarship Survey*, 65 CHI.–KENT L. REV. 195 (1989); Janet M. Gumm, *Chicago–Kent Law Review Faculty Scholarship Survey*, 66 CHI.–KENT L. REV. 509 (1990); and Colleen M. Cullen & S. Randall Kalberg, *Chicago–Kent Law Review Faculty Scholarship Survey*, 70 CHI.–KENT L. REV. 1445 (1995) (three Chicago–Kent studies ranking the leading law reviews based on frequency of citation, as well as the amount of scholarship by law school faculties in those leading reviews); Robert M. Jarvis & Phyllis Coleman, *Ranking Law Reviews: An Empirical Analysis Based on Author Prominence*, 39 ARIZ. L. REV. 15 (1997); Robert M. Jarvis & Phyllis Coleman, *Ranking Law Reviews by Author Prominence—Ten Years Later*, 99 LAW LIBR. J. 573 (2007) (two studies ranking student-edited law reviews based on the prominence of the lead article authors); John Doyle, *Ranking Legal Periodicals and Some Other Numeric Uses of the* Westlaw *and* Lexis *Legal Periodical Databases*, LEGAL REFERENCE SERVICES Q., No. 2/3, 2004, at 1 (examining the use of full-text periodical databases in *Westlaw* and *LexisNexis* for statistical analysis, particularly in ranking legal periodicals). *See* Kincaid C. Brown, *How Many Copies Are Enough? Using Citation Studies to Limit Journal Holdings*, 94 LAW LIBR. J. 301, 310–13 (2002) (compiling rankings from eighteen different lists).

[15] For a further discussion of open access article repositories, see Section A-2-e, below.

[16] *See, e.g.,* Fred Rodell, *Goodbye to Law Reviews*, 23 VA. L. REV. 38 (1936); Fred Rodell, *Goodbye to Law Reviews—Revisited*, 48 VA. L. REV. 279 (1962); Roger C. Cramton, *"The Most Remarkable Institution": The American Law Review*, 36 J. LEGAL EDUC. 1 (1986); James Lindgren, *Student Editing: Using Education to Move Beyond Struggle*, 70 CHI.–KENT L. REV. 95 (1994); Richard A. Posner, *The Future of the Student-Edited Law Review*, 47 STAN. L. REV. 1131 (1995); Harry T. Edwards, *The Growing Disjunction Between Legal Education and the Legal Profession*, 91 MICH. L. REV. 34 (1992).

[17] The current record, as of June 2014, is 4,824, established by Arnold S. Jacobs, *An Analysis of Section 16 of the Securities Act of 1934*, 32 N.Y.L. SCH. L. REV. 209 (1987).

[18] Rodell, *supra* note 16, at 38. As of December 2013 *HeinOnline* listed 254 articles citing this one—a good entry point to the decades of debate about the value of law reviews in legal education and the legal profession.

[19] 103 CONG. REC. 16, 159–62 (1957) (statement of Rep. Patman) (characterizing legal writing as "an organized form of lobbying").

difficult for lawyers to remain current with developments of the law and their own particular legal interests. Many legal periodicals now target particular subgroups within the legal profession. Law schools publish some of these subject- or audience-specific periodicals that are edited by students or faculty members and follow the format of the traditional law review. Nonprofit associations and commercial publishing companies publish others, in ever-increasing numbers. Another recent development is the publication of periodicals devoted to law and its interaction with other disciplines.

(1) Subject Journals. Journals devoted to one area of law vary in scope from the very practical to the very theoretical. *TAXES—The Tax Magazine* and *Trusts and Estates*, both published commercially, are examples of periodicals aimed primarily at practicing attorneys specializing in specific fields of law. These publications contain articles written by well-known practitioners interpreting the impact of recent legislation and judicial opinions. Many commercially published subject journals contain reviews of books within their subject area. *The American Journal of International Law* and *The American Journal of Comparative Law* are examples of periodicals published under the auspices of learned societies, while *Ecology Law Quarterly*, published at the University of California at Berkeley School of Law, and *The Review of Litigation*, published at the University of Texas School of Law, are typical of subject journals that are similar to traditional law school reviews.

(2) Special Interest Journals. These periodicals are aimed at those members of the legal community who have similar interests and serve as a means to encourage writing and research within the special area of interest. They include such journals as *The Journal of Catholic Legal Studies*, *The Judges' Journal*, *National Black Law Journal*, *Berkeley La Raza Law Journal*, *The Scribes Journal of Legal Writing*, and *Women Lawyers' Journal*.

(3) Interdisciplinary Journals. These interdisciplinary periodicals reflect the increasing emphasis many law schools and legal and non-legal scholars place on integrating the findings and methods of the social and behavioral sciences with the legal process. Perhaps the most distinguished of this group is *Journal of Law and Economics*, published by the faculty of the University of Chicago School of Law. Other representative titles are *Journal of Law & Politics*, *Law & Society Review*, *The Journal of Law and Religion*, *The Journal of Legal Medicine*, *Law & Psychology Review*, and *Yale Journal of Law & the Humanities*.

c.   *Bar Association Periodicals.* All states and the District of Columbia have bar associations.[20] In some states, membership is voluntary; in other states, those having what is called an *integrated bar*, membership is a prerequisite to practicing law within the state. Many counties and large cities also have their own local bar associations. Most national and state bar associations, sections within these associations, and many local and specialized bar groups publish periodicals. These publications vary in scope from such distinguished periodicals as the *ABA Journal* and *The Record of the Association of the Bar of the City of New York* to those that have only very brief notices about their organization's activities.

The primary purposes of bar association publications are to inform the membership of the association's activities, and to comment on pending and recent legislation and case

---

[20] For a complete list of bar associations, see the American Bar Association's *Bar Association Directories* website at http://www.americanbar.org/groups/bar_services/resources/bar_association_directories.html.

law. Articles in bar association publications tend to focus more on practical aspects of the law, with an emphasis on problem-solving, rather than on theoretical issues. These publications serve a different audience and perform a different function than do academic journals. Accordingly, when compared with law reviews, bar association publications generally have less theoretical value, but are more useful when researching subjects of current interest to practitioners. However, several publications from the American Bar Association have scholarly, footnoted articles and are comparable to law journals; these include *Business Lawyer* and *International Lawyer*.

    d.　Legal Newspapers. Legal newspapers can be national, state, or local in focus and are frequently available electronically as well as in print form.[21] Two weekly legal newspapers that are national in scope—*Legal Times* and *The National Law Journal*—began in 1978 and merged in 2009.[22] The *National Law Journal* contains articles and regular columns pertaining to a variety of issues that are valuable sources for fast-breaking legal developments. The monthly *The American Lawyer*, also national in scope, tends to focus on events at large firms. *Inside Counsel: Business Insights for Law Department Leaders* is an example of a monthly, national newspaper with a subject focus. *Lawyers USA* is a biweekly national newspaper that places special emphasis on the needs of the smaller law firm.

    Legal newspapers are published for many states. These are typically issued either weekly or monthly and concentrate on legal matters of particular importance in the state. They often contain articles of both state and national interest, synopses of cases, and reports of disciplinary proceedings. Examples include *The Connecticut Law Tribune*, *Massachusetts Lawyers Weekly*, *Wisconsin Law Journal*, and *The Texas Lawyer*.[23]

    The legal community within some large cities supports a newspaper devoted to the legal affairs of that metropolitan area. These local legal newspapers are generally published each business day, and primarily contain information on court calendars and dockets, changes in court rules, legal notices, news about recent changes in legislation and administrative rules, and stories about local judges and lawyers. Some of these larger publications, such as *New York Law Journal* and *The Los Angeles Daily Journal*, also publish reports of current judicial opinions and articles on various legal topics.

    e.　Legal Newsletters. As law has become more specialized, subject-matter newsletters by commercial publishers and law firms have flourished. One would be hard pressed to find a subject area of the law that is not served by at least one newsletter. These publications are typically issued weekly or monthly, consist of only a few pages, and focus on the most recent trends and developments in a particular area of the law. Rarely do they contain an index and even more rarely are they indexed by the major indexing publications. Their value lies in providing the practitioner with current

---

[21] A list of legal newspapers is available in the annual *Gale Directory of Publications and Broadcast Media*. One can also compile a list of legal newspapers using the online *Ulrich's Periodicals Directory*.

[22] The surviving newspaper is the *National Law Journal*, but the *Legal Times* name lives on in *BLT: The Blog of the Legal Times*, http://legaltimes.typepad.com/ and in its website, http://legaltimes.com (http://www.law.com/jsp/nlj/legaltimes/index.jsp).

[23] The *Legal Researcher's Desk Reference* (2012–2013) lists legal newspapers at 369; a separate list, at 375, indicates legal newspapers available in *LexisNexis* and *Westlaw*.

awareness information.[24] Many legal newsletters are available in one or more of *Bloomberg Law*, *LexisNexis*, or *Westlaw*.

2. Electronic Access to Full-Text Legal Periodicals

Vendors such as *Westlaw*, *LexisNexis*, and *HeinOnline* continue to expand their coverage of legal periodicals. An increasing amount of scholarly content is also freely available on the World Wide Web, both on journal websites and in repositories such as *SSRN* and *bepress*.

a.   *Westlaw*, *LexisNexis*, and *Bloomberg Law*. The complete text of many legal periodical articles is available in *Westlaw* and *LexisNexis*. This means that articles can be searched on both systems using Boolean logic or natural language searches. Since the legal periodical indexes described in the next section of this chapter cannot capture all the nuances of an article in the subject headings assigned to it, full-text electronic access greatly enhances one's ability to locate topics discussed within the articles.

One of the larger databases in *Westlaw* is Law Reviews, Texts & Bar Journals, which contains law reviews, bar journals, *American Law Reports*, legal texts and more. The Journals & Law Reviews database is a subset of the larger database. Each law review or journal title can also be searched separately in *Westlaw*.[25]

The largest legal periodicals database in *LexisNexis* is Law Reviews, CLE, Legal Journals & Periodicals, Combined. Subsets of this database, such as the US Law Reviews and Journals, Combined database are also available. Each law review or journal title can also be searched separately in *LexisNexis*.[26]

Today, the two electronic legal research vendors follow a similar philosophy as to how legal periodical articles are added to their services. From the beginning, it has been *LexisNexis*'s policy to add the complete full-text coverage of each title it carries. Although *Westlaw* currently also offers complete full-text coverage of each of its titles, this is a change from its initial selection policy; until 1994, only selected works of national interest were offered in full text. In both *Westlaw* and *LexisNexis*, dates of coverage for legal periodicals vary from the early 1980s to the most recent issue.

Although coverage is not comprehensive in either *Westlaw* or *LexisNexis*, both continue to add law reviews, journals, and related materials to their services. Coverage is by no means limited to traditional law reviews, as legal newspapers, bar journals, commercial legal periodicals, and newsletters are also included in the databases.

Bloomberg Law is a more recent entrant to the field. Its collection of law journals is not as wide and does not go back as far as those of *LexisNexis* and *Westlaw*, but it is growing. The articles, in PDF, are fully searchable.

---

[24] The best source for identifying commercial publications is the annual *Legal Newsletters in Print*, which lists titles published in the United States. Published by Infosources Publishing, it is available both in print and electronically. Many commercial newsletters are available via *Westlaw* and *LexisNexis*.

Increasingly, law firms are making their newsletters available via the Internet. Websites that aggregate content from some legal newsletters include *Lexology* (http://www.lexology.com) and *Mondaq* (http://www.mondaq.com/).

[25] A directory of *Westlaw* databases is at http://directory.westlaw.com/.

[26] A directory of *LexisNexis* databases is at http://w3.nexis.com/sources/.

Note that in both *Westlaw* and *LexisNexis* it is more time and cost efficient to search the smallest database that meets a researcher's needs. *See* Chapter 23 for further explanation.

b. *HeinOnline*. *HeinOnline* offers a range of electronic legal content, but it is best known for its Law Journal Library, which offers electronic access to legal periodicals dating back to the first issue of every title it carries. Much of the older content is not available through *Westlaw* or *LexisNexis*. *HeinOnline* includes almost 1,500 legal periodical titles, and all its content is available in the original page-image (PDF), which is especially useful for citation checking. The Law Journal Library also includes the *Index to Periodical Articles Related to Law*, which is discussed in Section E-10, and the *Index to Foreign Legal Periodicals*, which is discussed in Section D-1.

The *Law Journal Library* provides multiple searching capabilities. In addition to a citation search and a basic, full text keyword search, field search offers the ability to limit a search by a specific field (title, author, etc.), subject, date, and/or section (articles, comments, notes, etc.). *HeinOnline* also supports Boolean logic (and, or, not), proximity connectors, phrase searching and word truncation. Search results can be sorted by relevance, date, author, title or by number of times cited.

The journals included in the Law Journal Library are also indexed electronically by *Google Scholar*.[27] Links are provided to the full-text content in *HeinOnline* for users who have *HeinOnline* subscriptions.

c. *Index to Legal Periodicals Full Text (ILP)*. The *Index to Legal Periodicals*, which began in 1908, is a product of the H.W. Wilson Company. *ILP* indexes approximately 1,025 English language legal periodicals; full text is available for over 325 periodicals. *ILP* is covered in more detail in Section B of this chapter.

d. *Internet*. Increasingly, legal scholarship is being made available at no cost on the Internet. Many law schools are simultaneously publishing their journals electronically and in print. A few law reviews are published exclusively on the Internet, e.g., *Richmond Journal of Law & Technology*. This enables users to access these sources electronically without having to rely on costly electronic legal research services.

To bridge the gap between the slow-moving pace of traditional scholarship and the fast-paced world of electronic media, several law reviews have created online supplements to their regular print issues. These supplements typically contain very short commentaries on emerging legal issues.[28]

There are several portals to legal journal content available on the web, including law review directories from the *Max Planck Institute for International Law*[29] and *FindLaw*.[30]

e. *Repositories*. The desire to make the law more widely accessible, combined with the increasing price of journal subscriptions, has fueled the movement for "open access" to legal scholarship. Open access refers to the electronic publication of scholarly content that is made available at no charge without copyright constraints other than

---

[27] *Google Scholar* is discussed more in Section B-4.

[28] *See, e.g., Harvard Law Review Forum, Michigan Law Review's First Impressions, Northwestern University Law Review Colloquy, University of Pennsylvania Law Review's PENNumbra*, and *The Yale Law Journal Online*. For a more complete list of online law review supplements with submission guidelines, see Colin Miller, *Submission Guide for Online Law Review Supplements, Version 7.0* (July 22, 2013), at *SSRN*, http://ssrn.com/abstract=1410093.

[29] http://rzblx1.uni-regensburg.de/ezeit/index.phtml?bibid=MPIV & colors=3 & lang=en (select Law).

[30] http://stu.findlaw.com/journals/law-review.html.

attribution.[31] In 2008, Harvard Law School became the first law school to commit to a mandatory open access policy.[32]

Open access content is often distributed through digital scholarship repositories. Many universities have developed such repositories to collect, preserve, and disseminate the intellectual output of the institution. Other repositories are consortial, such as the *NELLCO Legal Scholarship Repository*.[33]

Many of these institutional repositories are built upon tools developed by the *Berkeley Electronic Press (bepress)*.[34] Founded by academics from the University of California at Berkeley in 1999, *bepress* is a private, for-profit corporation that offers a portfolio of products and services to improve scholarly communication.[35] In addition to institutional repositories, *bepress* also hosts several subject matter repositories. [Illustration 18–10] The *bepress* legal repository features approximately 45,000 papers from scholars and researchers at major national and international law departments, firms, and associations.[36] Anyone can download and read these papers at no cost. A free email alert service, which notifies subscribers of new content in specific subject areas, is also available.

The largest repository of legal scholarship is the *Social Science Research Network (SSRN)*, established in 1994. *SSRN* is a worldwide, for-profit collaborative effort devoted to the rapid dissemination of social science research.[37] *SSRN* is composed of a number of specialized research networks in the social sciences. One of these is the *Legal Scholarship Network (LSN)*. [Illustration 18–9] To date, more than 166,000 law-related papers and abstracts have been uploaded to *SSRN*.[38] Most of these are made available to readers at no cost.[39]

Researchers can locate *SSRN* papers by using the site's search tool, by browsing the eLibrary, or by searching *Google Scholar*.

SSRN also offers two types of email abstracting services. The first type, sponsored by individual universities, distributes abstracts of new papers published by the school's faculty. Universities pay *SSRN* to distribute this content; readers may subscribe and download papers at no cost. The other type of abstracting service, produced by *SSRN*,

---

[31] Paul George, *Members' Briefing: The Future Gate to Scholarly Legal Information*, AALL SPECTRUM (Apr. 2005). For more on the open access movement, see Michael W. Carroll, *The Movement for Open Access Law*, 10 LEWIS & CLARK L. REV. 741 (2006); Richard A. Danner, *Applying the Access Principle in Law: The Responsibilities of the Legal Scholar*, 35 INT'L J. LEGAL INFO. 355 (2007). The movement exists in most academic disciplines, not just law. *See, e.g.*, Peter Suber, *Open Access Overview* (revised Aug. 12, 2013), http://legacy.earlham.edu/~peters/fos/overview.htm.

[32] Press Release, Harvard Law School, Harvard Law Faculty Votes for "Open Access" to Scholarly Articles (May 7, 2008), http://www.law.harvard.edu/news/spotlight/faculty-research/hls-faculty-votes-for-% 27open-access% 27–to-articles.html.

[33] http://lsr.nellco.org/.

[34] http://www.bepress.com/.

[35] *bepress* also offers article submission and editorial management services and publishes several online journals.

[36] http://law.bepress.com/repository/.

[37] http://www.ssrn.com/.

[38] The primary motivation for many legal scholars to post their works to *SSRN* and *bepress* is to make their new works widely known as quickly as possible. Both services track the number of times papers are downloaded. *SSRN* makes these statistics public, whereas only authors can view them on *bepress*. There is no cost to scholars to upload papers in either *SSRN* or *bepress*.

[39] *SSRN* hosts some content provided by other organizations. There may be a fee to access this material.

selects papers and abstracts submitted to *SSRN* on particular subject areas and distributes them to subscribers.[40] There is a fee to subscribe to this service; however, many institutions purchase a site license for their users.

B. COMPREHENSIVE PERIODICAL INDEXES

The usefulness of legal periodicals depends almost entirely on the researcher's ability to find what articles have been written and where they have been published. When the full text is not available electronically, it is necessary to rely on indexes to legal periodical literature for this purpose. Even when the full text is searchable, indexes can often provide efficient, focused access.

1. *Jones & Chipman's Index to Legal Periodicals*

Jones & Chipman's Index to Legal Periodicals was the first index that attempted to provide a comprehensive and systematic index to English language legal periodicals. It is available electronically through *19th Century Masterfile*, a collection of indexes covering nineteenth-century periodicals and newspapers. This electronic edition of *Jones & Chipman's* indexes legal periodicals and related materials from America, England, Scotland, Ireland, and the English colonies from 1786 to 1922.

The coverage for the print edition of *Jones & Chipman's* is somewhat larger. It contains six volumes that index periodicals published from 1786 to 1937. The first three volumes, which cover the years 1786 to 1907, precede the more extensive *Index to Legal Periodicals* that began in 1908 and is discussed below. Therefore, these first three volumes of *Jones & Chipman's* should be consulted to locate articles prior to 1908.

2. *Index to Legal Periodicals (ILP)* and *Legal Source*

The *Index to Legal Periodicals* was begun in 1908 by the American Association of Law Libraries, and until 1980, it was the only extensive index of legal periodical articles. *ILP* was jointly managed by the AALL and the H.W. Wilson Company for many years until Wilson took over sole ownership and management. In 2011, Wilson merged with EBSCO Publishing.

ILP indexes English language legal periodicals published in the United States, Canada, Great Britain, Ireland, Australia, and New Zealand. Journals indexed must regularly publish legal articles of high quality and of permanent reference value.

There are three electronic *ILP* products: *Index to Legal Periodicals Full Text*, *Index to Legal Periodicals & Books*, and *Index to Legal Periodicals Retrospective*.

- *Index to Legal Periodicals Full Text* indexes 1,050 legal periodicals from 1982 to the present. Books are indexed beginning in 1994. Over 350 periodicals are also available in full text from 1994 to the present.

- *Index to Legal Periodicals & Books* presents the same indexing offered in *Index to Legal Periodicals Full Text*, but without links to full text articles. The same journals are covered. [Illustration 18–8]

- *Index to Legal Periodicals Retrospective* indexes almost 900 legal periodicals from 1908 to 1981.

---

[40] *SSRN* refers to these abstracts as "subject matter ejournals."

All three electronic *ILP* products became available on the *EBSCOhost* platform in 2012. In addition, EBSCO also released a new product called *Legal Source* in 2012 that combined the *ILP* content with content from EBSCO's *Legal Collection,* as well as new additional content. In total, the *Legal Source* database contains over 1,200 full text legal journals.

The print edition of *ILP* is issued monthly, with quarterly and annual cumulations.[41] From 1908 to 1993, the print edition is titled *Index to Legal Periodicals.* In 1994, when monographs were added to the index, the title was changed to *Index to Legal Periodicals & Books.*

There are four different access points to the print edition of *ILP*:

a.   *Subject and Author Index.* Authors and subjects are included in one index with complete citation information under each entry. [Illustration 18–1]

b.   *Table of Cases.* The table of cases lists the names of cases (for the time period covered by the issue or volume) that have had a note or comment written on them.

c.   *Table of Statutes.* The table of statutes lists statutes about which a periodical article or book has been written. [Illustration 18–2]

d.   *Book Review Index.* The book review index lists the author of books reviewed in the periodicals indexed by *ILP*. [Illustration 18–3]

3.   *Current Law Index (CLI), LegalTrac,* and *Legal Resource Index (LRI)*

These three indexes are produced by Gale Cengage Learning, with the American Association of Law Libraries (AALL) Committee on Indexing of Periodical Literature selecting the periodicals to be indexed. As described below, the three titles used for these indexes reflect their different formats and, in some instances, slightly different coverage.

The indexes include publications from the United States, Canada, the United Kingdom, Ireland, Australia, New Zealand, and the European Union. The publications are primarily English language, although some Canadian and Puerto Rican titles include articles in French or Spanish.

a.   *Current Law Index (CLI). Current Law Index* is a printed index issued monthly with quarterly and annual cumulations. It indexes over 1,500 academic reviews, bar association journals, specialty journals, and selected journals in allied disciplines. It covers the years 1980 to the present.

Each of the first seven volumes consists of a single book. Beginning with volume 8 (1987), *CLI* is published in two parts: Part A includes the subject index, while Part B includes an index by author/title and tables of cases and statutes. A four-volume cumulative subject index is available for the years 1991 to 1995.

CLI offers several different access points:

---

[41] It does not appear that the print edition of *ILP* will be affected by the merger with EBSCO, although this is not certain.

(1) *Subject Index.* The subject heading list organizes entries by subject, including personal and proper names that are the subject of articles. [Illustration 18–4]

(2) *Author/Title Index.* This section alphabetically lists the authors of articles and book reviews, and the titles of books reviewed, with full title and periodical citation.

(3) *Book Reviews.* Book reviews that appear in the periodicals covered by *CLI* are indexed under the author and title of the book and the author of the review.

(4) *Table of Cases.* Judicial opinions that are the subject of case notes are listed under the names of both plaintiff and defendant. [Illustration 18–5]

(5) *Table of Statutes.* This table lists statutes cited in articles, with references to official citation forms if different from popular names. [Illustration 18–6]

  b. LegalTrac. LegalTrac is Gale Cengage's electronic counterpart to *Current Law Index.* [Illustration 18–7] It includes all titles in *CLI* plus several major legal newspapers. Searches can be conducted in "Basic" or "Advanced" formats. A "Basic" search enables the researcher to search keywords from titles, authors, abstracts, and subjects. An "Advanced" search allows the user to limit the search by journal and date and to search within various database fields, such as author, title, and subject. *LegalTrac* supports Boolean logic, proximity connectors, phrase searching, and word truncation.

  LegalTrac is primarily an index, but it offers the full text of the articles from about 250 titles. Some articles are available in PDF.

  c. Legal Resource Index (LRI). Legal Resource Index is the name given to *LegalTrac* when it is made available through third-party vendors, such as *Westlaw* and *LexisNexis*. The indexing available in *LRI* is identical to that in *LegalTrac*, except that it includes a few additional years of coverage. Coverage for *LegalTrac* and *CLI* begins in 1980, whereas *LRI* extends back to 1977 for select publications.

4. *Google Scholar*

  Google Scholar indexes scholarly literature across many disciplines and sources, including articles, theses, books, and abstracts. It pulls together data from many major academic publishers and repositories worldwide, including both free sources (such as *SSRN*) and subscription sources (such as *HeinOnline*). It also indexes federal and state court opinions. The advanced search allows users to limit their search by author, publication, and date, and by jurisdiction when searching court opinions.

  The search results in *Google Scholar* include title, author and a short selection from the source, as well as the number of times that the source was cited. Results are listed in relevancy order weighing the full text of each document, where it was published, and who it was written by, as well as how often and how recently it has been cited in other scholarly literature.

Google Scholar includes links to the full text when available. Users affiliated with a university can set their preferences to link directly into their library's online subscriptions.[42] Email alerts are also available.[43]

5. *Directory of Open Access Journals (DOAJ)*

The *Directory of Open Access Journals*,[44] from the Lund University Libraries, indexes journals that use a funding model that does not charge readers or their institutions for access. The *DOAJ* covers open access scientific and scholarly journals from many disciplines, only including those that use a quality control system to guarantee the content.

As of December 2013, the *DOAJ* indexes 200 law-related open access journals from around the world. Many of these journals are not included in other legal periodical indexes.[45]

6. Current Awareness Publications

a. Current Index to Legal Periodicals (CILP). The *Current Index to Legal Periodicals* is produced weekly by the Marian Gould Gallagher Law Library of the University of Washington.[46] It indexes law journal articles approximately four to six weeks before they are indexed by commercial sources such as *Current Law Index* or *Index to Legal Periodicals & Books*. Articles are organized within 100 relevant subject headings, and complete tables of contents of all journals indexed are included. *CILP* is available both electronically and in print. Recent issues are available in *Westlaw*.

CILP also offers a customizable email service called *SmartCILP* that alerts users to new articles matching their individual research interests. It includes links to the full text article in *Westlaw* and *LexisNexis* when available.

b. In-House Law Library Publications. Many libraries, agencies, firms, and other groups of legal professionals publish their own in-house newsletters designed to alert users to the most recent articles in legal periodicals by reproducing their contents pages.

c. Current Law Journal Content from Washington and Lee University School of Law was a free service which indexed articles from over 1,350 law journals from 2000 through April 2011.[47] Although it ceased publication in May 2011, existing indexing will remain searchable.

7. Annual Legal Bibliography

Published by the Harvard Law Library from 1961 to 1981, this source indexed the books and articles the library received. Over 2,000 periodicals were covered.

---

[42] Online access to library subscriptions is usually restricted to patrons of that library. Patrons may need to log in with a library password, use a campus computer, or configure their browser to use a library proxy.

[43] For further discussion, see Alena Wolotira, *Googling the Law: Apprising Students of the Benefits and Flaws of Google as a Legal Research Tool*, 21 PERSP.: TEACHING LEGAL RES. & WRITING 33 (2012).

[44] http://www.doaj.org/.

[45] Edward T. Hart, *Indexing Open Access Law Journals . . . Or Maybe Not*, 38 INT'L J. LEGAL INFO. 19 (2010).

[46] http://lib.law.washington.edu/cilp/cilp.html.

[47] http://lawlib.wlu.edu/CLJC/.

C. ILLUSTRATIONS: LEGAL PERIODICALS AND INDEXES

[Illustration 18–1]

PAGE FROM SUBJECT AND AUTHOR INDEX, INDEX TO LEGAL PERIODICALS & BOOKS

SUBJECT AND AUTHOR INDEX   205

P5 Mr 2013

Information Calls Can Constitute Telemarketing J. Beck *Insidecounsel* V24 No253 P58 Ja 2013

Best Evidence Rule

The Best Evidence Rule Made Better: A Glimpse Into Georgia's New Evidence Code W. M. Wilson And R. L. Carlson *Georgia Bar Journal* V19 No1 P12 Ag 2013

Best Interests Of The Child (Law)

Best Interests Of Neonates: Time For A Fundamental Re-Think N. Bhatia And M. Bagàric *Journal Of Law & Medicine* V20 No4 P852 Je 2013

Best Interests Of The Child Versus Unfitness Of The Parent: Unraveling The Intertwinement V. Serrato *Massachusetts Law Review (01631411)* V94 No4 P142 Ja 2013

Child Protection Proceedings In The Childrens Court In Queensland: Therapeutic Opportunities Lost C. Tilbury*australian Journal Of Family Law* V27 No2 P170 Ag 2013

Commercial Surrogacy — Some Troubling Family Law Issues M. Keyes And R. Chisholm*australian Journal Of Family Law* V27 No2 P105 Ag 2013

Could The Bic-Q Be A Decision-Support Tool To Predict The Development Of Asylum-Seeking Children? A. E. Zijlstra, M. E. Kalverboer Et Al *International Journal Of Law & Psychiatry* V36 No2 P129 Mr 2013

Guardians Ad Litem: Should The Child's Best Interests Advocate Give More Credence To The Child's Best Wishes In Custody Cases? C. R. Mabry *American Journal Of Family Law* V27 No3 P172 Fall 2013

Modification Of Permanent Parenting Plans In Tennessee M. E. Moses *Tennessee Bar Journal* V49 No5 P27 My 2013

'People Out Of Place'? Advocates' Negotiations On Children's Participation In The Asylum Application Process In Sweden L. Ottosson And A. Lundberg*international Journal Of Law, Policy & The Family* V27 No2 P266 Ag 2013

Privacy Of Mental Health Records In Divorce And Custody Proceedings Siew-Ling Shea*tennessee Bar Journal* V49 No7 P21 Jl 2013

Science Friction In The Courts M. Kelly *Lawyer* V27 No28 P8 Jl 8 2013

The State And The "Psycho Ex-Wife": Parents' Rights, Children's Interests, And The First Amendment K. Kanavy*university Of Pennsylvania Law Review* V161 No4 P1081 Mr 2013

To Cut Or Not To Cut?: Addressing Proposals To Ban Circumcision Under Both A Parental Rights Theory And Child-Centered Perspective In The Specific Context Of Jewish And Muslim Infants A. E. Behrns *William & Mary Bill Of Rights Journal* V21 No3 P925 Mr 2013

Too Many Cooks In The Kitchen?: The Potential Concerns Of Finding More Parents And Fewer Legal Strangers In California's Recently-Proposed Multiple-Parents Bill E. A. Pfenson *Notre Dame Law Review* V88 No4 P2023 Ap 2013

Voiding Motherhood: North Carolina's Shortsighted Treatment Of Subject Matter Jurisdiction In Boseman V. Jarrell S. Birdsong *American University Journal Of Gender, Social Policy & The Law* V21 No1 P109 2013

Watt's Love Got To Do With It: Relocating The Best Interests Of Wyoming's Children In Custodial Parent Relocation Law S. M. Larson *Wyoming Law Review* V13 No1 P95 2013

Best Lawyers (Company)

Nolan, Thomsen & Villas, P.c. Congratulates *Michigan Bar Journal* V92 No1 P17 Ja 2013

Best Management Practices (Pollution Prevention)

The Clean Water Act And The Challenge Of Agricultural Pollution J. G. Laitos And H. Ruckriegle *Vermont Law Review* V37 No4 P1033 Summ 2013

Best Practices

Abuse Of Dominance In Technology- Enabled Markets: Established Standards Reconsidered? M. Rato And N. Petit *European Competition Journal* V9 No1 P1 Ap 2013

American College Of Bankruptcy--Best Practices Report: Formation, Function, And Obligations Of Equity Committees In Chapter 11 H. Lennox, D. J. Connolly Et Al *Annual Survey Of Bankruptcy Law* P105 2013

American College Of Bankruptcyintroduction To Best Practices Report: Formation, Function And Obligations Of Equity Committees In Chapter 11 H. Lennox And T. A. Wilson *Annual Survey Of Bankruptcy Law* P99 2013

Banker-Customer Relationship F. Mok And K. Tiah *Journal Of International Banking Law & Regulation* V28 No5 P55 2013

Battle Plan A. Post *Insidecounsel* V24 No260 P14 Ag 2013

Best Practices For Investigating And Prosecuting Child Abuse: Applying Lessons Learned From Delaware's Earl Bradley Case K. Ensslin And N. L. Phillips *Widener Law Review* V19 No1 P51 2013

Best Practices Report On Electronic Discovery (Esi) Issues In Bankruptcy Cases *Business Lawyer* V68 No4 P1113 Ag 2013

Beyond Public Health Emergency Legal Preparedness: Rethinking Best Practices J. A. Bernstein*journal Of Law, Medicine & Ethics* V41 P13 Spr 2013 Supplement

Creating The Best Practices In Dna Preservation: Recommended Practices And Procedures K. A. Dolan *Criminal Law Bulletin* V49 No2 P319 Mr/Ap 2013

Deconstructing Independent Directors M. Gutiérrez And M. Sáez*journal Of Corporate Law Studies* V13 No1 P63 Ap 2013

Failing To Protect Participants' Fundamental Rights In Drug Treatment Court M. P. Fullerton *Montana Law Review* V74 No2 P375 Summ 2013

Getting Connected D. L. Cohen*aba Journal* V99 No1 P30 Ja 2013

Investment Management Best Practices For Family Offices S. Campbell And D. Bailin *Trusts & Estates* V152 No8 P42 Ag 2013

Learning On The Wires: Byod, Embedded Systems, Wireless Technologies And Cybercrime B. Longo *Legal Information Management* V13 No2 P119 Je 2013

The Reappearing Judge S. S. Gensler And L. H. Rosenthal *Kansas Law Review* V61 No3 P849 2013

Social Licensing In The Construction Industry: Community And Government Interests R. E. Barreiro-Deymonna *Construction Law International* V8 No1 P22 Ap 2013

Sponsor's Comment *Lawyer* P8 Je 24 2013 Lawyer Management

Sustainable Public Procurement: Life-Cycle Costing In The New EU Directive Proposal D. Dragos And B. Neamtu*european Procurement & Public Private Partnership Law Review* V8 No1 P19 2013

Teaching For Tomorrow: Utilizing Technology To Implement The Reforms Of Maccrate, Carnegie, And Best Practices S. M. Johnson *Nebraska Law Review* V92 No1 P46 2013

Best Practices -- Congresses

Conference Recap C. Flahardy *Insidecounsel* V24 No258 P2 Je 2013

Best, Brendan G.

Putting Employees First *Michigan Bar Journal* V92 No5 P38 My 2013

Best, Nichole A.

Safeguarding Opportunities For America's Wounded Warriors: A Proposed Solution To Subcontracting Abuse In The Service-Disabled Veteran-Owned Small Business Program And The Veterans First Contracting Program *Public Contract Law Journal* V42 No2 P347 Wint 2013

Bestiality (Law)

R. V. B *Criminal Law Review* No7 P614 2013

Bestnet Europe Ltd. -- Trials, Litigation, Etc.

Keeping Secrets S. Turner *Intellectual Property Magazine* P74 Jl/Ag 2013

Beswick, Samuel

Two Spying Tales *New Zealand Law Journal* P213 Jl 2013

Beswick, Simon

The Happy Mediums N. Stanton *Lawyer (Online Edition)* P13 Jl 1 2013

Hot 100: Simon Beswick, Osborne Clarke *Lawyer (Online Edition)* P69 Ja 28 2013

Osborne Clarke Puts 13 Senior Fee Earners On Redundancy Consultation N. Stanton *Lawyer (Online Edition)* P2 My 15 2013

Osborne Clarke Rejigs German Management As Offices Continue Growth J. Harris *Lawyer (Online Edition)* P10 Jl 18 2013

Bet Tzedek Legal Services (Company)

Making Self-Help Work: Bet Tzedek's Conservatorship Clinic P. Bertenthal And J. Passman *Clearinghouse Review* V47 No1-2 P50 My-Je 2013

Beta (Finance)

"There Is No Alpha": Bounded Rationality In The Mutual Funds Market R. Bollen *Banking & Finance Law Review* V28 No2

[Illustration 18-2]

PAGE FROM TABLE OF STATUTES, INDEX TO LEGAL PERIODICALS & BOOKS

TABLE OF STATUTES   3103

Florida Law Review V65 No2 P443 Ap 2013
Jumpstart Our Business Startups (Jobs) Act. Pub. L. No. 112- 106, 126 Stat. 306 (2012)
    Computer & Internet Lawyer V30 No8 P17 Ag 2013
Jumpstart Our Business Startups Act.
    Business Lawyer V68 No3 P839 My 2013
Jumpstart Our Business Startups Act. Pub. L. No. 112-106, §§ 101-108, 126 Stat. 306, 307-13 (2012); 15 U.s.c.
    Cornell Law Review V98 No6 P1573 S 2013
Jumpstart Our Business Startups Act. H.r. 3606, 112Th Cong. § 201(A) (2012)
    Ohio State Law Journal V74 No2 P189 2013
Jumpstart Our Business Startups Act. Pub. L. No. 112-106 § 201(A) (1)
    Notre Dame Law Review V88 No3 P1457 F 2013
Jumpstart Our Business Startups Act. Pub. L. No. 112-106, 126 Stat. 306
    Massachusetts Law Review (01631411) V94 No4 P117 Ja 2013
Jumpstart Our Business Startups Act. Pub. L. No. 112-106, 126 Stat. 306 (2012)
    Notre Dame Law Review V88 No5 P2065 Je 2013
Jumpstart Our Business Startups Act. Pub. L. No. 112-106, 126 Stat. 306 (2012)
    Securities Regulation Law Journal V41 No3 P319 Fall 2013
Jumpstart Our Business Startups Act. Pub. L. No. 112-106, 126 Stat. 306 (2012)
    Cornell International Law Review V46 No2 P427 Spr 2013
Jumpstart Our Business Startups Act (Jobs Act).
    Practical Lawyer V59 No2 P15 Ap 2013
Jumpstart Our Business Startups Act (Jobs Act).
    Seattle University Law Review V36 No2 P999 Wint 2013
Jumpstart Our Business Startups Act (Jobs Act). Pub. L. No. 112-106, § 201, 126 Stat. 306, 313 (2012); 15 U.s.c.
    Fordham Law Review V81 No6 P3389 My 2013
Jumpstart Our Business Startups Act (Jobs Act). Pub. L. No. 112-106, §§ 301-305, 126 Stat. 306 (2012)
    Hofstra Law Review V41 No3 P777 Spr 2013
Jumpstart Our Business Startups Act Of 2012. Pub. L. No. 112-106, § 501, 126 Stat. 306, 325
    Indiana Law Journal V88 No1 P151 Wint 2013
Jury Selection And Service Act. 28 U.s.c.a. § 1861 Et Seq . (West 1994)
    Employee Relations Law Journal V39 No2 P3 Aut 2013
Juvenile Diversion Act.
    Michigan Bar Journal V92 No7 P70 Jl 2013
Kansas Restraint Of Trade Act. Kan. Stat. Ann. § 50-101 (West 2012)
    Washburn Law Journal V52 No2 P323 2013
Kansas-Nebraska Act Of 1854. 10 Stat. 277 (1854)
    Rutgers Law Journal V43 No3 P515 Fall/Wint 2013
Ku Klux Klan Act. 42 U.s.c. § 1983
    University Of Hawaii Law Review V35 No1 P51 Wint 2013
Labor Management Relations Act. 29 U.s.c. § 185(A) (2006)
    Boston College Law Review V54 No3 P1237 My 2013
Labor Management Relations Act (Lmra).
    Employee Relations Law Journal V39 No1 P88 Summ 2013
Labor Management Relations Act Of 1947. Pub. L. No. 80-101, 61 Stat. 136 (1948)
    Thomas Jefferson Law Review V35 No2 P229 Spr 2013
Labor-Management Relations Act. 29 U.s.c. § 157
    Washburn Law Journal V52 No3 P429 2013
Lacey Act. 16 U.s.c. §§ 3371-3376
    Houston Journal Of International Law V35 No2 P397 Spr 2013
Lacey Act. 16 Usc C 3371-3378
    Oil, Gas & Energy Quarterly V61 No3 P563 Mr 2013
Lanham (Trademark) Act. 15 U.s.c. §§ 15(A)(1), 15A(1), 15C(A) (2)(A) (2006)
    Trademark Reporter V103 No4 P913 Jl 2013
Lanham Act.
    Advocate (05154987) V56 No10 P32 O 2013
Lanham Act.
    Fordham Law Review V81 No5 P2987 Ap 2013
Lanham Act.
    Computer & Internet Lawyer V30 No5 P42 My 2013
Lanham Act. 15 U.s.c. § 1015 Et Seq
    Practical Lawyer V59 No3 P41 Je 2013

Lanham Act. 15 U.s.c. § 1051 (2006)
    Southern California Law Review V86 No4 P921 My 2013
Lanham Act. 15 U.s.c. § 1051 Et Seq. (2006)
    Idea: The Intellectual Property Law Review V53 No2 P131 2013
Lanham Act. 15 U.s.c. § 1051 Et Seq. (2006)
    Idea: The Intellectual Property Law Review V53 No2 P258 2013
Lanham Act. 15 U.s.c. § 1053 (1946)
    Cardozo Arts & Entertainment Law Journal V31 No2 P357 2013
Lanham Act. 15 U.s.c. § 1114(L)(A)
    Santa Clara Law Review V53 No1 P143 2013
Lanham Act. 15 U.s.c. § 1125(A)(1)(A) (2006)
    Ohio State Law Journal V74 No2 P241 2013
Lanham Act. 15 U.s.c. § 1127
    Utah Bar Journal V26 No2 P16 Mr/Ap 2013
Lanham Act. 15 U.s.c. § 127 (2006)
    Hastings Communications & Entertainment Law Journal (Comm/Ent) V35 No2 P247 Wint 2013
Lanham Act. 15 U.s.c. §§ 1052(A), 1125 (2006)
    Boston College Environmental Affairs Law Review V40 No1 P229 2013
Lanham Trademark Act. Ch. 540, 60 Stat. 427; 15 U.s.c. § 501 (C) (3) (2006)
    Boston College Law Review V54 No1 P243 Ja 2013
Lanham Trademark Act Of 1946. 15 U.s.c. §§ 1051-72, 1091-96, 1111-27 (2006)
    Washington Law Review V88 No2 P723 Je 2013
Leadership Against Hiv/Aids, Tuberculosis, And Malaria Act Of 2003 (Leadership Act). 22 U.s.c.a § 7631(A) (West 2008)
    Brooklyn Law Review V78 No3 P1131 Spr 2013
Leahy Smith America Invents Act (Aia).
    Journal Of The Patent & Trademark Office Society V95 No1 P3 2013
Leahy-Smith America Invents Act. Pub. L. No. 112-29; 125 Stat. 284 (2011)
    Richmond Journal Of Law & Technology V19 No2 P1 Wint 2013
Leahy-Smith America Invents Act. Pub. L. No. 112-29, 125 Stat. 284 (2011); 28 And 35 U.s.c.
    American University Law Review V62 No4 P1105 Ap 2013
Leahy-Smith America Invents Act. Pub. L. No. 112-29, 125 Stat 284 (2011); 35 U.s.c. § 102
    Southern Law Journal V23 No2 P249 Fall 2013
Leahy-Smith America Invents Act. Pub. L. No. 112-29, 125 Stat. 284 (2011); 35 U.s.c.
    Texas Intellectual Property Law Journal V21 No1 P63 2013
Leahy-Smith America Invents Act. H.r. 1249, 120Th Cong. (2011)
    Journal Of Law & Health V26 No2 P375 2013
Leahy-Smith America Invents Act. Pub. L. No. 112-29, § 3(C), 125 Stat 284 At 287 (2011)
    University Of Toronto Law Journal V63 No1 P126 Wint 2013
Leahy-Smith America Invents Act. Pub. L. No. 112-29, 125 Stat. 284
    University Of Colorado Law Review V84 No4 P1227 Fall 2013
Leahy-Smith America Invents Act. Pub. L. No. 112-29, 125 Stat. 284
    Journal Of The Patent & Trademark Office Society V95 No2 P124 2013
Leahy-Smith America Invents Act. Pub. L. No. 112-29, 125 Stat. 284 (2011)
    Florida Law Review V65 No2 P341 Ap 2013
Leahy-Smith America Invents Act. Pub. L. No. 112-29, 125 Stat. 284, S. 14 (2011)
    Canadian Business Law Journal V54 No1 P38 Je 2013
Leahy-Smith America Invents Act. Pub. L. No. 112-29,125 Stat. 284 (2011)
    Aipla Quarterly Journal V41 No1 P73 Wint 2013
Leahy-Smith America Invents Act. Pub. L. No. 112-29,125 Stat. 284 (2011)
    Journal Of The Patent & Trademark Office Society V95 No2 P223 2013
Leahy-Smith America Invents Act. Pub. L. No. 112-29, 125 Stat. 284 (2011); §§ 15, 28, 35, 42, And 51 U.s.c.
    Duke Law Journal V63 No1 P1 O 2013

[Illustration 18-3]

PAGE FROM BOOK REVIEWS, INDEX TO LEGAL PERIODICALS & BOOKS

BOOK REVIEWS   3131

*Bench & Bar of Minnesota*v70no2p26F 2013

Fatur, A. EU Competition Law And The Information And Communication Technology Network Industries. 2012
   International Journal of Law & Information Technology-
   v21no1p105-8Spr 2013L. Da Cenreggio Luciano
   International Journal of Law & Information Technology-
   v21no1p105-8Mr 2013L. D. C. Luciano

Faure, M. and Peeters, M. Climate Change Liability.2011
   *Carbon & Climate Law Review*v7no1p81-22013R. Verheyen

Feld, B. C. Kids, Cops, And Confessions.2012
   *California Lawyer*v33no6p32-3Je 2013B. Pesta

Fernandez, L. and others Shutting Down The Streets.2011
   New York University Journal of International Law & Politics
   v45no3p926-31Spr 2013A. Mehta

Field, S. and Colson, R. The Transformation Of Criminal Jus-
tice.2011
   *Criminal Law Review*no10p863-72013D. Giannoulopoulos

Finke, D. and others Reforming the European Union.2012
   New York University Journal of International Law & Politics
   v45no2p681-5Wint 2013G. R. Gaeda

Finkelstein, C. and others Targeted Killings.2012
   *European Journal of International Law*v24no2p72-9My
   2013R. Geiß

Finkelstein, C. and others Targeted Killings.2012
   *American Journal of International Law*v107no1p274-8Ja
   2013S. R. Ratner
   *European Journal of International Law*v24no2p722-9My
   2013R. Geiß
   *Journal of International Criminal Justice*v11no1p277-82Mr
   2013S. J. Barela
   *Texas Law Review*v91no4p925-38Mr 2013A. D. Sofaer

Finlay, J. The Community Of The College Of Justice.2012
   *Cambridge Law Journal*v72no2p448-51Jl 2013S. W. Stark
   *Journal of Legal History*v34no2p234-6Ag 2013J. D. Ford

Finnane, M. and Douglas, H. Indigenous Crime And Settler
Law.2012
   *Alternative Law Journal*v38no1p63-42013T. Anthony

Fisher, K. J. Moral accountability And International Criminal
Law.2012
   *Criminal Law Forum*v24no2p267-72Je 2013A. Kiyani

Fitz-Gibbon, K. and Flynn, A. A Second Chance For Justice.2013
   *Deakin Law Review*v18no1p207-102013V.Colvin

Fitzgerald, E. and others Commercial And Residential Service
Charges.2013
   *Conveyancer & Property Lawyer*no4p352-32013C. Bevan

Fleming, J. E. and McClain, L. C. Ordered Liberty.2013
   *Boston University Law Review*v93no4p1469-79Jl 2013M. C. Dorf
   *Constitutional Commentary*v28no3p383-406Spr 2013T. M. Mas-
   saro
   *Constitutional Commentary*v28no3p407-19Spr 2013K. I. Kersch
   *Constitutional Commentary*v28no3p421-33Spr 2013A. S. Greene
   *Constitutional Commentary*v28no3p435-49Spr 2013L. C. McClain

Fletcher, G. L. and others Life In The Law.2013
   *Utah Bar Journal*v26no4p40Jl/Ag 2013E. D. Crane

Florini, A. and others China Experiments.2012
   New York University Journal of International Law & Politics
   v45no2p685-9Wint 2013 Hank Zhou

Flowers, R. K. and Morgan, R. C. Ethics In The Practice Of Elder
Law.2013
   *Bench & Bar of Minnesota*v70no1p35Ja 2013

Floyd, R. E. and Grier, I. S. Personal Insolvency.1998
   *Journal of Business Law*no7p7652013J.Briggs

Flynn, A. and Fitz-Gibbon, K. A Second Chance For Justice.2013
   *Deakin Law Review*v18no1p207-102013V.Colvin

Flynn, J. Overdraft.2012
   *Colorado Lawyer*v42no5p147My 2013

Foltea, M. International Organizations In WTO Dispute Settlement.
2012
   *European Journal of Risk Regulation*v4no3p421-22013C. Maria
   Cantore

Fonseca, L. C. and de Carvalho, E. M. Semiotics Of International
Law .2011
   *International Journal of Speech, Language & the
   Law*v20no1p151-72013J. Jemielniak

Ford, R. T. Rights Gone Wrong.2011
   *Michigan Law Review*v111no6p903-29Ap 2013A. K. Chen

Forder, J. and others Principles Of Remedies.2012
   *Law Institute Journal: Official Organ of The Law Institute of Vic-
   toria* v87no8p72-3Ag 2013T. Ash Fleming

Forsyth, C. And Shetreet, S. The Culture Of Judicial Indepen-
dence.2012
   *Modern Law Review*v76no1p181-4Ja 2013L.Neudorf

Foster, C. E. Science And The Precautionary Principle In International Courts And Tribunals. 2012
   *European Journal of International Law*v24no3p971-4Ag
   2013O. Perez

Foster, C. E. Science And The Precautionary Principle In Interna-
tional Courts And Tribunals. 2011
   *Journal of Environmental Law*v25no2p336-7Jl 2013N. De
   Sadeleer

Francioni, F. and Ronzitti, N. War By Contract.2011
   *European Journal of International Law*v24no3p977-81Ag
   2013R. Müllerson *New York University Journal of International Law & Politics* v45no3p931-6Spr 2013H. M. Junker-
   man

Francis, T. B. and others So You Want To Be A Lawyer.2012
   *Wisconsin Lawyer*v86no4p48-9My 2013T. A. Golski

Francq, S. and others International Antitrust Litigation.2012
   *American Journal of Comparative Law*v61no2p461-6Spr
   2013D. Earl Childress III

Frank, C. Master And Servant Law.2010
   *Law & History Review*v31no4p892-4N 2013N. Landau

Frankel, S. and Lewis, M. K. International Economic Law And National Autonomy.2010
   New York University Journal of International Law & Politics
   v45no2p689-94Wint 2013T. M. Artaki

Frascogna, X. M. and others Entertainment Law For The General
Practitioner.2011
   *GPSolo*v30no2p58-9Mr/Ap 2013

Freedland, M. and Kountouris, N. The Legal Construction Of Personal Work Relations.2011
   *Industrial Law Journal*v42no2p199-201Jl 2013A. Carse

Freeman, M. and Smith, F. Law And Language.2013
   *Bench & Bar of Minnesota*v70no4p26Ap 2013
   *International Journal .of Speech, Language & the Law*v20no
   1p159-612013

Freund, J. C. and Azar, J. Anatomy Of A Mediation.2012
   *Colorado Lawyer*v42no5p95My 2013J. Livingston

Freund, J. C. and Azar, J. Anatomy Of A Mediation.2012
   *Dispute Resolution*v19no4p4-6Summ 2013J. Meyer

Friedland, P. Seeing Justice done.2012
   *Law & History Review*v31no4p894-5N 2013R. McGowen

Friedman, L. M. The Human Rights Culture.2011
   *Journal of Legal Education*v62no4p663-7My 2013M.Pinto

Friedman, L. M. and Grossman, J. L. Inside The Castle.2011
   *Michigan Law Review*v111no6p1001-20Ap 2013K. Abrams

Frischmann, B. M. Infrastructure.2012
   *University of Chicago Law Review*v80no3p1499-555Summ
   2013Y. Benkler

Fruehwald, E. S. Think Like A Lawyer.2013
   *Bench & Bar of Minnesota*v70no8p28S 2013

Fry, J. and others The Secretariat's Guide to ICC Arbitration.2012
   *International Construction Law Review*v30no1p125-32Ja 2013

Fung, W. K. and Hu, Y. Statistical DNA Forensics.2008
   *Law, Probability & Risk*v12no2p165Je 2013J. Won Lee

Fybel, R. D. and Darmer, M. K. National Security, Civil Liberties
And The War On Terror.2011
   *Federal Lawyer*v60no1p84-5Ja/F 2013L. Fisher

G

Galton, E. and Love, L. P. Stories Mediators Tell.2012
   *Cardozo Law Review*v34no6p2415-21Ag 2013W. Brazil

Gammeltoft-Hansen, T. Access To Asylum.2011
   *Leiden Journal of International Law*v26no1p234-8Mr 2013B.
   N. Ghráinne

Gani, M. and others Shooting To Kill.2012
   *Criminal Law Review*no5p444-62013B. Dickson

Garber, R. L. and Liebs, D. Summoned To The Roman Courts.2012
   *Law & History Review*v31no1p267-8F 2013C. Ando

Garcia, R. J. Marginal Workers.2012
   *Berkeley Journal of Employment & Labor Law*v34no1p155-

[Illustration 18-4]

PAGE FROM SUBJECT INDEX, CURRENT LAW INDEX

SUBJECT INDEX   EUROPEAN PARLIAMENT

ETHNOLOGICAL methods
Iran: an anthropologist engaging the human rights discourse and practice. by Reza Afshari
34 Human Rights Quarterly 507-545 May, 2012
ETHNOPSYCHIATRY *see*
Cultural psychiatry
ETHYLMETHYLBUTYLBARBITURIC acid *see*
Pentobarbital
ETHYLMETHYLBUTYLPYRIMIDINETRIONE *see*
Pentobarbital
ETSY Inc.
The torch slinger: General Counsel Etsy Sarah Feingold.(Interview) by Catherine Dunn
19 Corporate Counsel 94(1) August, 2012
ETTENBERG, Jodi
Legal nomad. (lawyer and blogger Jodi Ettenberg) (Interview) by Leslie A. Gordon
40 Student Lawyer 11(1) Jan, 2012
ETYMOLOGY
Lean on me - attorney, client, barrister, esquire, lawyer, solicitor, and versus.(history of words for those who practice law) by Bill C. Berger
41 Colorado Lawyer 77(4) Sept, 2012
EU *see*
European Union
EU Commission *see*
European Union. European Commission
EUCLIDEAN geometry
Numerical classification of curvilinear structures for the identification of pistol barrels. by Rachel S. Bolton-King, Martin Bencsik, J. Paul O. Evans, Clifton L. Smith, Derek F. Allsop, Jonathan D. Painter and Wayne M. Cranton
220 Forensic Science International 197(13) July 10, 2012
EUCLID'S Elements *see*
Euclidean geometry
EUGENICS
Compensating victims of forced sterilization: lessons from North Carolina. by Jennifer M. Klein
40 Journal of Law, Medicine & Ethics 422(5) Summer, 2012
Putting Buck v. Bell in scientific and historical context: a response to Victoria Nourse. (article in this issue, p. 101) (Supreme Mistakes) Buck v. Bell by Edward J. Larson
39 Pepperdine Law Review 119-128 Dec, 2011
Social Darwinism in Nazi family and inheritance law. by Ellis Washington
13 Rutgers Journal of Law & Religion 173-225 Fall, 2011
Narcissus at the gene pool.(human intervention in genetic destiny) by Ruth C. Stern
14 Quinnipiac Health Law Journal 225-249 Spring, 2011
see also
Birth control
Contraception
Family
Social problems
EURO area
''To look without understanding was their lot''. (sovereign default in the eurozone) (Editorial) by Panos Koutrakos
36 European Law Review 613-614 Oct, 2011
EURO (Currency)
U.S. tax implications of euro re-denomination.(Cover story) by Olivia Defoort, David Golden, Lee Holt and Karla Johnsen
66 Tax Notes International 945-952 June 4, 2012
U.S. tax implications of euro re-denomination. by Olivia Defoort, David Golden, Lee Holt and Karla Johnsen
135 Tax Notes 475-482 April 23, 2012
Tough break: would Greece's unilateral withdrawal from the euro be legal under EU law? by Paul Stanley
156 Solicitors Journal 21(1) Feb 28, 2012
Avoiding the euro debt trap. by Nick Young and Richard Holden
162 New Law Journal 211(2) Feb 10, 2012
The influence of the euro in reshaping global monetary governance: perceptions from financial elites in Brazil and China. by Miguel Otero-Iglesias
18 European Law Journal 122(21) Jan, 2012
Saving the euro: tensions with European treaty law in the European Union's efforts to protect the common currency. by Boris Ryvkin
45 Cornell International Law Journal 227-255 Wntr, 2012
see also
Eurocurrency market
EURO-CURRENCY market *see*
Eurocurrency market
EURO-DOLLAR market *see*
Eurocurrency market
EUROBOND market
Beneficial ownership a la Russe: the effect on Eurobonds and other business structures. by Kirill Vikulov
66 Tax Notes International 263-267 April 16, 2012
Russia sweetens pill for eurobond structures. by Alexei Kuznetsov
65 Tax Notes International 797-798 March 12, 2012

EUROCENTRISM
Shut your mouth when you're talking to me: silencing the idealist school of critical race theory through a culturalogical turn in jurisprudence. by Tommy J. Curry
3 Georgetown Journal of Law & Modern Critical Race Perspectives 1-38 Spring, 2011
EUROCURRENCY market
The tax consequences of dropping the euro.(Cover story) by Jeremiah Coder
65 Tax Notes International 407-410 Feb 6, 2012
see also
Euro (Currency)
Foreign exchange market
International banking
EURODOLLAR market *see*
Eurocurrency market
EUROMARKETS
EU constitutionalism in flux: is the eurozone crisis precipitating centralisation or diffusion? by Nicole Scicluna
18 European Law Journal 489(15) July, 2012
Breaking up is hard: euro divergence tax consequences. by Jeremiah Coder
134 Tax Notes 384-387 Jan 23, 2012
Holding on.(European governance on eurozone crisis) by Niamh Nic Shuibhne
36 European Law Review 767-768 Dec, 2011
Central bank collateral and the Lehman collapse. by Christian Hofmann
6 Capital Markets Law Journal 456-469 Oct, 2011
see also
Eurocurrency market
Financial markets
Sovereign debt market
EUROPEAN badger
Badgers and bovine tuberculosis: the relationship between law, policy and science.(United Kingdom) Badger Trust v. Welsh Ministers by Patrick Bishop
24 Journal of Environmental Law 145-154 Spring, 2012
EUROPEAN Commission *see*
European Union. European Commission
EUROPEAN Community. Commission of the European Communities *see*
European Union. European Commission
EUROPEAN Community. Council of Ministers *see*
European Union. Council of the European Union
EUROPEAN Community. European Commission *see*
European Union. European Commission
EUROPEAN Community. European Investment Bank *see*
European Union. European Investment Bank
EUROPEAN Community law
In principle ... interpretation or application - is the Court of Appeal right?(inconsistency in approach to what makes for a preliminary ruling reference between the Court of Appeal and the European Court of Justice)(United Kingdom) by Paul Lasok
162 New Law Journal 1120(2) Sept 7, 2012
How far can we go when using the English language for private law in the EU? by Ruth Sefton-Green
8 European Review of Contract Law 30(17) March, 2012
EU law in U.S. legal academia.(The European Union 20 Years After Maastricht: Transatlantic Perspectives Symposium) by Daniela Caruso
20 Tulane Journal of International and Comparative Law 175-201 Winter, 2012
Intersectional litigation and the structuring of a European interpretive community.(Symposium: The Changing Landscape of EU Constitutionalism) by Marco Dani
9 International Journal of Constitutional Law 714-736 July-Oct, 2011
The legal integration of the American continent: an invitation to legal science to build a new ius commune. by Juan Pablo Pampillo Balino
17 ILSA Journal of International & Comparative Law 517-553 Summer, 2011
see also
International law
EUROPEAN Community. Parliament *see*
European Union. European Parliament
EUROPEAN Community Research Council
The European Research Council as case study for agency design in the EU. by Herwig C.H. Hofmann
18 European Public Law 175-190 March, 2012
EUROPEAN cooperation
Multi-jurisdictional filing processes - towards further convergence?(European Union) by Emma Trogen
33 European Competition Law Review 237-240 May, 2012
From 'administrative cooperation' in the application of European Union law to 'administrative cooperation' in the protection of European rights and liberties. by Micaela Lottini
18 European Public Law 127-147 March, 2012
Article 8 TEU: towards a new generation of agreement with the neighbouring countries of the European Union?(Treaty on European Union) by Peter Van Elsuwege and Roman Petrov
36 European Law Review 688-703 Oct, 2011
see also
International cooperation
EUROPEAN Council *see*
European Union. European Council

EUROPEAN Court of First Instance *see*
European Union. General Court
EUROPEAN Court of Human Rights
British sovereignty and the European Court of Human Rights. by Ed Bates
128 Law Quarterly Review 382-411 July, 2012
The record of the House of Lords in Strasbourg. (United Kingdom, European Union) by Brice Dickson
128 Law Quarterly Review 354-381 July, 2012
La Cour europeenne des droits de l'homme: le chemin parcouru, les defis de demain.(Conference annuelle Claire-L'Heureux-Dube) by Francoise Tulkens
53 Les Cahiers de Droit 419(27) June, 2012
Presumed guilty: how the European Court handles criminal libel cases in violation of article 6(2) of the Convention for the Protection of Human Rights and Fundamental Freedoms. by Adam Berkaw
50 Columbia Journal of Transnational Law 774-804 Spring, 2012
The risks of ''continuing situation'' litigation in transitional political systems: lessons from the ECtHR for the Constitutional Court of Kosovo.(European Court of Human Rights) by David M. Palko
25 Harvard Human Rights Journal 183-217 Spring, 2012
Concentric democracy: resolving the incoherence in the European Court of Human Rights' case law on freedom of expression and freedom of association. by Stefan Sottiaux and Stefan Rummens
10 International Journal of Constitutional Law 106-126 Jan, 2012
Evolutions in non-discrimination law within the ECHR and the ESC systems: it takes two to tango in the Council of Europe.(European Court of Human Rights, European Social Charter)(Evolutions in Antidiscrimination Law in Europe and North America) by Samantha Besson
60 American Journal of Comparative Law 147-180 Wntr, 2012
Taking care of Strasbourg: the status of the European Convention on Human Rights and the case-law of the European Court of Human Rights in Kosovo's domestic legal system. by Fisnik Korenica and Dren Doli
32 Liverpool Law Review: A Journal of Contemporary Legal and Social Policy Issues 209-223 Dec, 2011
European Court of Human Rights: May 2010-April 2011. by Alastair Mowbray
17 European Public Law 605-631 Dec, 2011
The convergence of the European legal system in the treatment of third country nationals in Europe: the ECJ and ECtHR jurisprudence. by Sonia Morano-Foadi and Stelios Andreadakis
22 European Journal of International Law 1071-1088 Nov, 2011
The European Court of Human Rights' approach to the responsibility of member states in connection with acts of international organizations. by Cedric Ryngaert
60 International and Comparative Law Quarterly 997-1016 Oct, 2011
Shifting the balance achieved by the Abduction Convention: the contrasting approaches of the European Court of Human Rights and the European Court Justice. by Lara Walker and Paul R. Beaumont
7 Journal of Private International Law 231-249 August, 2011
(European) stars or (American) stripes: are the European Court of Human Rights' neutrality and the Supreme Court's wall of separation one and the same?(Religious Legal Theory) by Andrea Pin
85 St. John's Law Review 627-648 Spring, 2011
EUROPEAN Court of Justice *see*
European Union. Court of Justice of the European Communities
EUROPEAN currency unit *see*
Euro (Currency)
EUROPEAN Debt Crisis, 2008- *see*
Global Economic Crisis, 2008-
EUROPEAN Economic Community. Council of Ministers *see*
European Union. Council of the European Union
EUROPEAN federation
Legal order, legal pluralism, fundamental principles: Europe and its law in three concepts. by Giulio Itzcovich
18 European Law Journal 358(27) May, 2012
see also
Federalism
Regionalism (International organization)
EUROPEAN General Court *see*
European Union. General Court
EUROPEAN Investment Bank *see*
European Union. European Investment Bank
EUROPEAN Monetary System
To what extent has the EU banking regulation accomplished a single banking objective alongside the protection and inclusion of customers? by Eleni D. Nikolaou
27 Journal of International Banking Law and Regulation 144-152 March, 2012
EUROPEAN monetary union
The Stability, Coordination and Governance Treaty: principle, politics and pragmatism. by Paul Craig
37 European Law Review 231-248 June, 2012
EUROPEAN Parliament *see*
European Union. European Parliament

381

[Illustration 18–5]

PAGE FROM TABLE OF CASES, CURRENT LAW INDEX

R. v. Wills

2011 E.W.C.A. Crim. 1936 Manner of cross-examination - witnesses young female complainants - appellant charged with sexual activity with children - judge directing counsel not to challenge witnesses - whether appellant's cross-examination unfairly hindered.(United Kingdom)

Criminal Law Review 565-568 July, 2012

R. v. Wilson

2012 E.W.C.A. Crim. 386 Guilty plea in face of overwhelming evidence - whether sentencing judge entitled to withhold discount for guilty plea.(United Kingdom)

Criminal Law Review 560-562 July, 2012

RAAD van bestuur van het Uitvoeringsinstituut werknemersverzekeringen v. Akdas

Case C-485/07 (E.C.J. May 26, 2011) Portability of social benefits and reverse discrimination of EU citizens vis-a-vis Turkish nationals: comment of Akdas.

37 European Law Review 204-212 April, 2012

RABB, State v.

920 So. 2d 1175 (Fla. Dist. Ct. App. 2006) Something smells afoul: an analysis on the end of a district court split.

36 Nova Law Review 201-226 Fall, 2011

RABINOWITZ, United States v.

339 U.S. 56 (1950) Post-racialism and searches incident to arrest.(Race & Immigration Symposium)

44 Arizona State Law Journal 113-153 Spring, 2012

RABITO, LeBreton v.

714 So. 2d 1226 (La. 1998) An uncertain prescription - medical malpractice actions in Louisiana.

72 Louisiana Law Review 487-518 Wntr, 2012

RABOBANK International v. Jurong Technologies Industrial Corp.

2011 S.G.C.A. 48 (Sing. C.A.) Unfair preference in Singapore.

33 The Company Lawyer 222-224 July, 2012

RABONE v. Pennine Care National Health Service Foundation Trust

2012 U.K.S.C. 2 Leading from the front: human rights and tort law in Rabone and Reynolds.(United Kingdom, European Union)

128 Law Quarterly Review 323-327 July, 2012

Liability under the Human Rights Act 1998: the duty to protect life, indirect victims and damages.(United Kingdom)

71 Cambridge Law Journal 263-266 July, 2012

Damages for non-pecuniary loss re-visited.(United Kingdom)

33 Business Law Review (UK) 181-184 July, 2012

Wrongful death, human rights, and the Fatal Accidents Act.(United Kingdom)

128 Law Quarterly Review 327-331 July, 2012

The Supreme Court and the state's duty to protect vulnerable groups: the effect of Rabone.(United Kingdom)

2012 Scots Law Times 75-79 April 6, 2012

Protecting the vulnerable: why Rabone is a landmark human rights decision.(United Kingdom)

162 New Law Journal 446(2) March 30, 2012

A matter of life & death: why reforming archaic inquest laws is essential.(United Kingdom)

162 New Law Journal 321(1) March 2, 2012

RADISSON Hotels International, Inc. v. Majestic Towers, Inc.

488 F. Supp. 2d 953 (C.D. Cal. 2007) Lost future royalties: lessons from recent decisions.

31 Franchise Law Journal 150(8) Wntr, 2012

RADMACHER v. Granatino

2010 U.K.S.C. 42 The after-shock; pre-nuptial agreements: where are we now?(United Kingdom)

162 New Law Journal 796(2) June 15, 2012

Applicable law light.(United Kingdom)

42 Family Law 294-299 March, 2012

All's fair in love...? The approach of the court to enforcement of ante- & post-nuptial agreements.(United Kingdom)

162 New Law Journal 11(2) Jan 6, 2012

The first post-Radmacher decision: Z. v. Z. (no. 2). (United Kingdom)

42 Family Law 73-75 Jan, 2012

A prenup for Prince William and Kate? England inches toward twentieth century law of antenuptial agreements; how shall it enter the twenty-first?

23 Florida Journal of International Law 447-480 Dec, 2011

RAI v. Charity Commission

2012 E.W.H.C. 1111 (Ch.) Litigation and the pursuit of charitable purpose. (United Kingdom) (Editorial)

156 Solicitors Journal 13(1) June 12, 2012

RAILROAD Commission v. Texas Citizens for a Safe Future & Clean Water

2011 WL 836827 (Tex. Mar. 11, 2011) Texas versus Chevron: Texas administrative law on agency deference after Railroad Commission v. Texas Citizens.

74 Texas Bar Journal 984(5) Dec, 2011

RAINY Sky S.A. v. Kookmin Bank

2011 U.K.S.C. 50 Reviewing the approach to contractual interpretation. (United Kingdom)

156 Solicitors Journal 12(2) May 29, 2012

Absurdity and ambiguity - making sense of contractual construction. (United Kingdom)

71 Cambridge Law Journal 34-37 March, 2012

The role of "business common sense" in the construction of commercial contracts.(United Kingdom)

33 Business Law Review (UK) 32-33 Feb, 2012

Interpreting commercial contracts: a case of ambiguity?(United Kingdom)

Lloyds Maritime and Commercial Law Quarterly 26-29 Feb, 2012

Commercial purpose and business common sense in contractual interpretation.(United Kingdom)

23 King's Law Journal 94-100 Feb, 2012

RAJAMANNAN, Paulownia Plantations de Panama Corp. v.

793 N.W.2d 128 (Minn. 2009) Civil procedure: forum non conveniens - convenience or conniving? (Minnesota) (Case note)

38 William Mitchell Law Review 433-459 Fall, 2011

RAMBUS, Inc. v. FTC

522 F.3d 456 (D.C. Cir. 2008) Private and public approaches to patent hold-up in industry standard setting.(The Use and Abuse of Voluntary Standard-Setting Processes in a Post-Rambus World: Law, Economics, and Competition Policy) *57 Antitrust Bulletin 59(29) Spring, 2012*

Known unknowns: uncertainty and its implication for antitrust policy and enforcement in the standard-setting context.(The Use and Abuse of Voluntary Standard-Setting Processes in a Post-Rambus World: Law, Economics, and Competition Policy)

57 Antitrust Bulletin 89(28) Spring, 2012

Learning from Rambus - how to tame those troublesome trolls.(The Use and Abuse of Voluntary Standard-Setting Processes in a Post-Rambus World: Law, Economics, and Competition Policy)

57 Antitrust Bulletin 117(44) Spring, 2012

U.S. and E.U. antitrust enforcement efforts in the Rambus matter: a patent law perspective.

52 Idea 31-61 Wntr, 2012

Economic remedies for anticompetitive hold-up: the Rambus cases.

56 Antitrust Bulletin 583(26) Fall, 2011

RAMIREZ-PEYRO v. Holder

574 F.3d 893 (8th Cir. 2009) Protecting Mexican informants from themselves.(Case note)

42 University of Miami Inter-American Law Review 415-442 Wntr-Spring, 2011

RAMORA UK Ltd., In re

2011 E.W.H.C. 3959 (Ch.) Courts clarify priority of notices of intention to appoint administrators.(United Kingdom)

5 Corporate Rescue and Insolvency 101-102 June, 2012

RAMSEY Food Processing Pty., Fair Work Ombudsman v.

2011 F.C.A. 1176 (Austl. Fed. Ct.) Attempted inter-positioning of company fails. (Australia)

49 Law Society Journal 52(2) Dec, 2011

RAMSEY Winch, Inc. v. Henry

555 F.3d 1199 (10th Cir. 2009) Pro-gun property regulation: how the State of Oklahoma controls the property rights of employers through firearm legislation.

64 Oklahoma Law Review 81-110 Fall, 2011

RANDOLPH, Georgia v.

547 U.S. 103 (2006) Third-party consent to search: analyzing triangular relations.

19 Duke Journal of Gender Law & Policy 303(44) Spring, 2012

Georgia v. Randolph: implications, weaknesses, and suggestions for the future.

47 Criminal Law Bulletin 1224-1240 Nov-Dec, 2011

A parent's "apparent" authority: why intergenerational coresidence requires a reassessment of parental consent to search adult children's bedrooms.

21 Cornell Journal of Law and Public Policy 39-75 Fall, 2011

RANGEL, State v.

977 P.2d 379 (Or. 1999) Cyberstalking and free speech: rethinking the Rangel standard in the age of the Internet.(Oregon)

90 Oregon Law Review 303-333 Fall, 2011

RANKINE, Geary v.

2012 E.W.C.A. Civ. 555 Geary v. Rankine.(property interest)(United Kingdom)

42 Family Law 953-955 August, 2012

RANTSEV v. Cyprus

No. 25965/04 (Eur. Ct. H.R. Jan. 7, 2010) Dancing on the borders of article 4: human trafficking and the European Court of Human Rights in the Rantsev case.

30 Netherlands Quarterly of Human Rights 163-194 June, 2012

Obligations towards trafficking victims.

86 Australian Law Journal 166-169 March, 2012

RAPANOS v. United States

547 U.S. 715 (2006) "A stream would rise from Earth, and water the whole face of the ground": the ethical necessity for wetlands protection post-Rapanos.

26 Notre Dame Journal of Law, Ethics & Public Policy 621-644 Summer, 2012

Six years after Rapanos - what's changed? Answer: not much.(Special Institute on Federal Regulation of Cultural Resources, Wildlife, and Waters of the U.S.)

2012 Mineral Law Series: Rocky Mountain Mineral Law Foundation CH13(20) April 26, 2012

Toward a constitutional Chevron: lessons from Rapanos.

160 University of Pennsylvania Law Review 1479(47) April, 2012

Distinguishing water law from land use to protect water quality and navigate Rapanos.

24 Environmental Claims Journal 136-172 April-June, 2012

Rapanos guidance III: "waters" revisited.

42 Environmental Law Reporter 10118-10129 Feb, 2012

New federal guidance on identifying waters protected by the Clean Water Act.

40 Colorado Lawyer 65(7) Dec, 2011

The intended scope of Clean Water Act jurisdiction.

41 Environmental Law Reporter 11118-11126 Dec, 2011

'Enemy of the people': the need for Congress to pass the Clean Water Restoration Act. (New Directions in Environmental Law and Justice Symposium Edition)

6 Florida A&M University Law Review 257-297 Spring, 2011

RAPIDSHARE AG, Perfect 10, Inc. v.

No. 09-CV-2596 H (S.D. Cal. May 18, 2010) Off with the head? How eliminating search and index functionality reduces secondary liability in peer-to-peer file-sharing cases.

7 Washington Journal for Law, Technology & Arts 28-46 Summer, 2011

RAS Riunione Adriatica de Sicurta (The Front Comor), West Tankers, Inc. v.

2007 U.K.H.L. 4 Flaws in the system: the Brussels regulation. (United Kingdom, European Union)

162 New Law Journal 835(3) June 22, 2012

RASMUSSON v. SmithKline Beecham Corp.

413 F.3d 1318 (Fed. Cir. 2005) Enablement of utility: sound prediction for the United States?

27 Canadian Intellectual Property Review 371-383 Dec, 2011

RASUL v. Bush

542 U.S. 466 (2004) Defending the rule of law: reconceptualizing Guantanamo habeas attorneys.

44 Connecticut Law Review 617-673 Feb, 2012

RATTAN Specialties, Inc., Arroyo v.

117 D.P.R. 35 (1986) Asuntos controversiales del examen poligrafico dentro del sistema de derecho puertorriqueno.

51 Revista de Derecho Puertorriqueno 373-389 Jan-June, 2012

RAW v. Giradeau

2010 E.W.H.C. 3581 (Fam.) Raw v. Giradeau. (publicity) (United Kingdom)

41 Family Law 1337-1338 Dec, 2011

RAWLINGS, Marley v.

2012 E.W.C.A. Civ. 61 Marley v. Rawlings and another. (wills) (United Kingdom)

42 Family Law 403-405 April, 2012

Signed and sealed: even a simple administrative mistake in a will could lead to severe consequences for both practitioners and their clients. (United Kingdom) (Editorial)

156 Solicitors Journal 9(1) Feb 28, 2012

RAWLINS, People v.

884 N.E.2d 1019 (N.Y. 2008) The confrontation clause and expert testimony: recent developments in the Supreme Court and the New York State Court of Appeals.(Crawford and Beyond: Confrontation Clause Limitations on the Admissibility of Testimonial Hearsay Become "Curiouser and Curiouser", The End of the Beginning or the Beginning of the End?)

20 Journal of Law and Policy 457-484 Fall, 2012

RAWLINSON, Dothard v.

433 U.S. 321 (1977) Scaling the wall and running the mile: the role of physical-selection procedures in the disparate impact narrative.

160 University of Pennsylvania Law Review 1195(45) March, 2012

RAYBURN House Office Building Room 2113, United States v.

497 F.3d 654 (D.C. Cir. 2007) Reigning in the speech or debate clause to fight corruption in Congress post-Rayburn. (Third Annual Survey of the Ninth and Tenth Circuits) (Case note)

2012 Brigham Young University Law Review 493-508 April, 2012

RDR Books, Warner Brothers Entertainment v.

575 F. Supp. 2d 513 (S.D.N.Y. 2008) The problem of fictional facts: idea, expression, and copyright's balance between author incentive and public interest.

58 Journal of the Copyright Society of the U.S.A. 549-584 Summer, 2011

READY America, Inc., Original Creations, Inc. v.

No. 11 C 3453 (N.D. Ill. Oct. 5, 2011) Single sale through Web site insufficient to establish specific personal jurisdiction.

29 The Computer & Internet Lawyer 30(2) Jan, 2012

2039

[Illustration 18–6]

PAGE FROM TABLE OF STATUTES, CURRENT LAW INDEX

TABLE OF STATUTES DODD-FRANK WALL STREET REFORM AND

Culture of the future: adapting copyright law to accommodate fan-made derivative works in the twenty-first century.
24 Regent University Law Review 117-146 Fall, 2011

Navigating the nexus: DMCA anti-circumvention protection of computer software.(Digital Millennium Copyright Act of 1998)
43 Arizona State Law Journal 1081-1106 Fall, 2011

Stream capture: returning control of digital music to the users.
25 Harvard Journal of Law & Technology 159(19) Fall, 2011

Copyright infringement pushin': Google, YouTube, and Viacom fight for supremacy in the neighborhood that may be controlled by the DMCA's safe harbor provision.(Digital Millennium Copyright Act of 1998)
51 Idea 607-648 Fall, 2011

Legal constraints on the imagination in the virtual world of Second Life.
23 Intellectual Property Journal 327-353 Sept, 2011

Scary monsters: hybrids, mashups, and other illegitimate children.(Creativity and the Law)
86 Notre Dame Law Review 2133(24) Sept, 2011

Lord of the files: international secondary liability for Internet service providers.
68 Washington and Lee Law Review 1555-1588 Summer, 2011

The Copyright Office's protection of fair uses under the DMCA: why the rulemaking proceedings might be unsustainable and solutions for their survival.(Digital Millennium Copyright Act of 1998)
58 Journal of the Copyright Society of the U.S.A. 521-547 Summer, 2011

A matter of access: how bypassing DRM does not always violate the DMCA.(Digital Rights Management, Digital Millennium Copyright Act)
7 Washington Journal for Law, Technology & Arts 13-25 Summer, 2011

Strong wills, weak locks: consumer expectations and the DMCA anticircumvention regime. (Digital Millennium Copyright Act of 1998) (Technology: Transforming the Regulatory Endeavor)
26 Berkeley Technology Law Journal 1457-1487 Summer, 2011

ACTA fool or: how rights holders learned to stop worrying and love 512's subpoena provisions. (Anti-Counterfeiting Trade Agreement)
15 Marquette Intellectual Property Law Review 465(20) Summer, 2011

The bill of unintended consequences: the Combating Online Infringement and Counterfeit Act.
21 Journal of Art, Technology & Intellectual Property Law 283-322 Spring, 2011

Who owns a copy? The Ninth Circuit misses an opportunity to reaffirm the right to use and resell digital works.
2 Cybaris: An Intellectual Property Law Review 45-72 Spring, 2011

Viacom v. YouTube: an erroneous ruling based on the outmoded DMCA. (Digital Millennium Copyright Act of 1998)
31 Loyola of Los Angeles Entertainment Law Review 101-142 Spring, 2011

17 U.S.C. 512(c) Substantially perfect: the Southern District of New York's problematic rewrite of the DMCA's elements of notification.(Digital Millennium Copyright Act of 1998)
29 Cardozo Arts & Entertainment Law Journal 495-521 Summer, 2011

17 U.S.C. 1201 What the Digital Millennium Copyright Act can learn from medical marijuana: fixing the antitrafficking provisions by basing liability on the likelihood of harm.
35 The Columbia Journal of Law & the Arts 503-547 Summer, 2012

DIGITAL Performance Right in Sound Recordings Act of 1995

Again, from the top! The continuing pursuit of a general public performance right in sound recordings.
22 Albany Law Journal of Science & Technology 1-48 Spring, 2012

Stream capture: returning control of digital music to the users.
25 Harvard Journal of Law & Technology 159(19) Fall, 2011

DIGITAL Signatures Act of 2000 *see*
Electronic Signatures in Global and National Commerce Act of 2000

DISCOUNT Pricing Consumer Protection Act of 2011 (Draft)

Not with a bang, but a whimper: Congress's proposal to overturn the Supreme Court's Leegin decision with the Discount Pricing Consumer Protection Act of 2009.
18 Villanova Sports & Entertainment Law Journal 645-682 Fall, 2011

DISTRICT of Columbia. Business Organizations Code *see*
District of Columbia. Code Title 29 (Business Organizations) Enactment Act of 2010

DISTRICT of Columbia. Code Title 29 (Business Organizations) Enactment Act of 2010

New D.C. Business Organizations Code: major overhaul for better business climate. (part 2)
26 Washington Lawyer, The 30(7) Dec, 2011

DISTRICT of Columbia. Rules of Professional Conduct

Rule 4.2 Can we talk?(right to communication with an unrepresented person)
26 Washington Lawyer, The 10(2) May, 2012

DNA Analysis Backlog Elimination Act of 2000

Questions of time, Place, and Mo(o)re: personal property rights and continued seizure under the DNA Act.
92 Boston University Law Review 733-762 March, 2012

DO-NOT-TRACK Online Act of 2011 (Draft)

Do not track me online: the logistical struggles over the right "to be let alone" online.
22 Journal of Art, Technology & Intellectual Property Law 229-286 Fall, 2011

DODD-FRANK Wall Street Reform and Consumer Protection Act of 2010

Introducing "abusive": a new and improved standard for consumer protection.
100 California Law Review 1401-1443 Oct, 2012

Regulatory financial reform: impact of Dodd-Frank Act on it compliance.
38 Rutgers Computer & Technology Law Journal 254(23) Fall, 2012

The taxation of Dodd-Frank.(Tax Notes 40th Anniversary Issue)
136 Tax Notes 1411-1430 Sept 17, 2012

2012 mid-year securities enforcement update.
26 Insights: The Corporate & Securities Law Advisor 2(19) August, 2012

Informational failures in structured finance and Dodd-Frank's "improvements to the regulation of credit rating agencies".
17 Fordham Journal of Corporate & Financial Law 665-749 August, 2012

The future of the Dodd-Frank reforms hinges on political developments and the forcefulness of the US federal regulators.
86 Australian Law Journal 525-529 August, 2012

"The shape of things to come".(financial markets regulation)
26 Insights: The Corporate & Securities Law Advisor 46(5) August, 2012

Shareholders: the power is in their own hands.
33 The Company Lawyer 243-244 August, 2012

SEC adopts final rules implementing Dodd-Frank provisions on independence of compensation committees and their advisers.
26 Insights: The Corporate & Securities Law Advisor 2(7) July, 2012

Waiting for Volcker: JP Morgan's big loss further complicates the equation, as the long wait for a proprietary trading rule drags on.(former Federal Reserve Chairman Paul Volker, Volker rule passed as part of the Dodd Frank reforms)
19 Corporate Counsel 18(1) July, 2012

Fiduciary interest: regulation of the financial services sector after Dodd-Frank and the sovereign debt crisis.
50 Law Society Journal 16(3) July, 2012

Being responsive to stockholders and avoiding say-on-pay lawsuits - shareholder outreach and executive compensation disclosure.
25 Benefits Law Journal 65(8) Summer, 2012

Hide that syndicated junk in the closet! A case for credit risk retention in the CLO market.(collateralized loan obligations)
87 Chicago-Kent Law Review 935-963 Summer, 2012

Is extraterritorial jurisdiction still alive? Determining the scope of U.S. extraterritorial jurisdiction in securities cases in the aftermath of Morrison v. National Australia Bank.
37 North Carolina Journal of International Law and Commercial Regulation 1187-1238 Summer, 2012

Empty creditor syndrome and vivisepulture: preventing credit-default-swap holders from pushing companies into premature graves by refusing to negotiate restructurings.
62 Case Western Reserve Law Review 1285(29) Summer, 2012

Credit risk transfer governance: the good, the bad, and the savvy.
42 Seton Hall Law Review 1009-1080 Summer, 2012

Still floating: security-based swap agreements after Dodd-Frank.
42 Seton Hall Law Review 953-1008 Summer, 2012

The effect of the Dodd-Frank Act on arbitration agreements: a proposal for consumer choice.
12 Pepperdine Dispute Resolution Law Journal 503-524 Summer, 2012

Effects of the JOBS Act on marketing activities of private investment funds.(Jumpstart Our Business Startups Act)
26 Insights: The Corporate & Securities Law Advisor 33(11) June, 2012

Skirting Morrison.(state pension fund investment securities fraud protections limited after extraterritoriality of Securities Exchange Act denied)
32 California Lawyer 10(2) June, 2012

What you should know about the SEC whistleblower rules and program.
58 The Practical Lawyer 8(4) June, 2012

CFTC and SEC finalize a key piece of the Dodd-Frank Act registration requirements puzzle with the final entity definitions rules, but many pieces of the puzzle remain missing.
32 Futures & Derivatives Law Report 15(18) June, 2012

Administrative law as blood sport: policy erosion in a highly partisan age.
61 Duke Law Journal 1671(92) May, 2012

Controlling financial chaos: the power and limits of law.
2012 Wisconsin Law Review 815-840 May-June, 2012

SEC staff releases study on cross-border scope of private action under section 10(b).
26 Insights: The Corporate & Securities Law Advisor 16(3) May, 2012

What is a swap? Maybe (almost) everything? You gotta a problem with that?
32 Futures & Derivatives Law Report 1(4) May, 2012

Agents of change: the fiduciary duties of forwarding market professionals.
61 Duke Law Journal 1563(36) April, 2012

Corporate law and governance update.
28 Corporate Counsel's Quarterly 395-435 April, 2012

SEC reform after Dodd-Frank and the financial crisis.(Speech)
28 Corporate Counsel's Quarterly 385-394 April, 2012

Dodd-Frank checklist.
24 International Quarterly 269-276 April, 2012

Shareholder rights: an evolving story.
7 Capital Markets Law Journal 107-121 April, 2012

Liability holding companies.
59 UCLA Law Review 852-913 April, 2012

Derivatives clearinghouses and systemic risk: a bankruptcy and Dodd-Frank analysis.
64 Stanford Law Review 1079(30) April, 2012

The avalanche is coming: a user's guide to the CFTC's swap data reporting rules.(Commodity Futures Trading Commission)
32 Futures & Derivatives Law Report 1(14) April, 2012

Bankers, bureaucrats, and guardians: toward tripartism in financial services regulation.
37 The Journal of Corporation Law 621 Spring, 2012

Principles-based regulation and legislative congruence.
15 New York University Journal of Legislation and Public Policy 45-108 Spring, 2012

The refinancing crisis in commercial real estate: Dodd-Frank threatens to curtail CMBS lending. (commercial mortgage backed securities)
13 Transactions: The Tennessee Journal of Business Law 361-381 Spring, 2012

Assessing the impact of Wal-Mart Stores, Inc. v. Dukes on fair lending litigation.
21 Journal of Affordable Housing & Community Development Law 195(38) Spring, 2012

Promising to be prudent: a private law approach to mortgage loan regulation in common-interest communities.
19 George Mason Law Review 739-774 Spring, 2012

Give the start-ups a chance: innovation, the American economy and the argument for carving IP ABS and specifically patent abs out from 17 C.F.R. s. 229.1111 and 17 C.F.R. s. 230.193.(intellectual property, asset backed securities)
12 Wake Forest Journal of Business & Intellectual Property Law 339-363 Spring, 2012

Protecting investors in securitization transactions: does Dodd-Frank help, or hurt?(The 2011 Diane Sanger Memorial Lecture)
72 Louisiana Law Review 591-603 Spring, 2012

Thinking before rulemaking: why the SEC should think twice before imposing a uniform fiduciary standard on broker-dealers and investment advisers.
50 University of Louisville Law Review 491-526 Spring, 2012

Watering down the Volcker rule.(Cover story)
134 Tax Notes 1339-1345 March 12, 2012

What happens in London, stays in London: the long and "strong" arms of Dodd-Frank's extraterritorial provisions.
16 North Carolina Banking Institute 195(27) March, 2012

Debit card interchange fees and the Durbin Amendment's small bank exemption.
16 North Carolina Banking Institute 223(25) March, 2012

Demonstrating scienter in market manipulation claims under the Commodity Exchange Act: a checkered history and an uncertain future.
32 Futures & Derivatives Law Report 11(3) March, 2012

2125

[Illustration 18−7]

SCREEN PRINT SHOWING RESULTS VIEW, LEGALTRAC

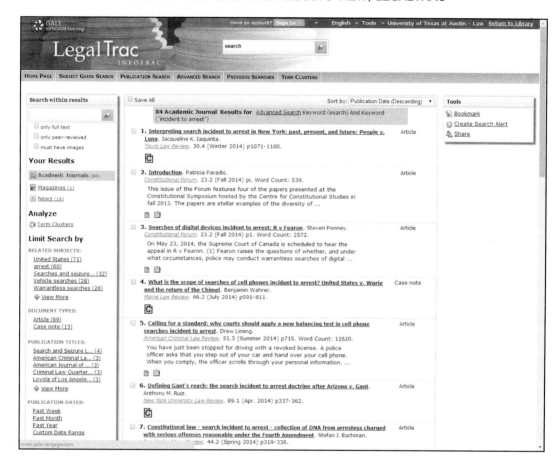

[Illustration 18–8]

SCREEN PRINT SHOWING RESULTS VIEW, INDEX TO LEGAL PERIODICALS AND BOOKS ONLINE

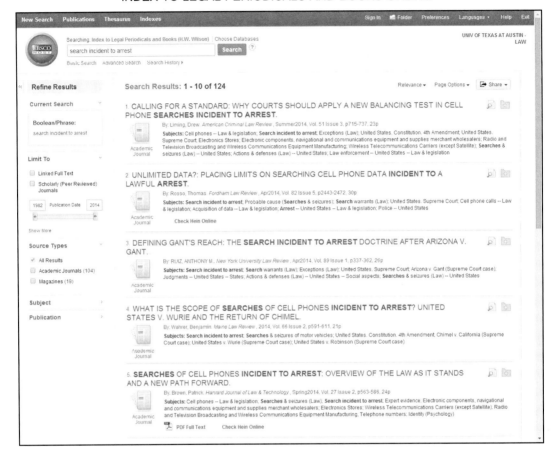

[Illustration 18-9]

SCREEN PRINT SHOWING SSRN LEGAL SCHOLARSHIP NETWORK

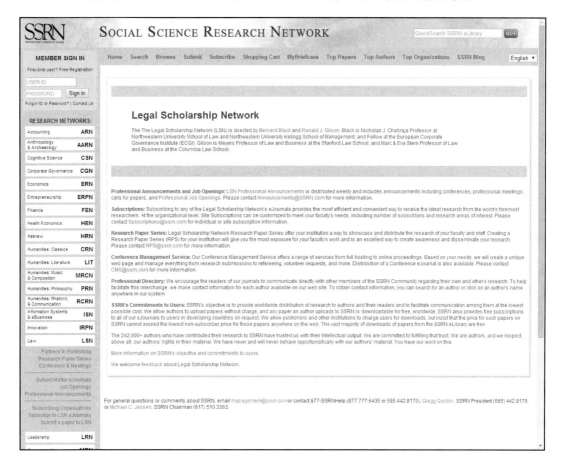

[Illustration 18–10]

SCREEN PRINT SHOWING BEPRESS DIGITAL COMMONS NETWORK LAW

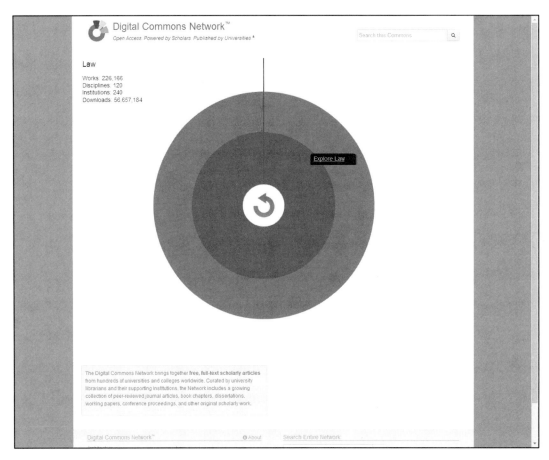

D. INDEXES TO FOREIGN PERIODICAL LITERATURE

Periodical indexes focusing on legal journals published in other countries are often useful in legal research.

1. *Index to Foreign Legal Periodicals*

The *Index to Foreign Legal Periodicals* (*IFLP*) began in 1960 and is produced by the American Association of Law Libraries. *IFLP* is a multilingual index to articles and book reviews appearing in approximately 470 legal journals published worldwide. It provides in-depth coverage of public and private international law, comparative and foreign law, and the law of all jurisdictions other than the United States, the United Kingdom, Canada, and Australia. *IFLP* also indexes reports, essay collections, and yearbooks.

IFLP is published quarterly with an annual cumulation by William S. Hein & Co. In addition, *IFLP* is available electronically from 1985 to the present via *HeinOnline*. Index entries are linked to the full text articles in *HeinOnline* when possible.

2. *Public International Law: A Current Bibliography of Books and Articles*

The *Public International Law* bibliography, compiled by the Max Planck Institute, indexes articles published on all aspects of public international law that are contained in over 1,400 journals, yearbooks, and commemorative compilations from 1975 to the present. Starting in 1990, it began indexing recently published monographs and collections of essays.

Each volume of the print edition consists of two issues which are published semiannually. *Public International Law* is also indexed electronically in Gale's *Academic OneFile* and *Google Scholar*.

3. *Index to Canadian Legal Periodical Literature*

The Canadian Association of Law Libraries began publishing the *Index to Canadian Legal Periodical Literature* in 1961 to provide access to the growing number of Canadian legal journals. Articles in Canadian legal periodicals discuss two systems of law, civil and common, in two languages, English and French.

The index, which is available exclusively in print, is arranged by both author and subject. A table of cases and book review index are included.

4. *Index to Canadian Legal Literature* (ICLL)

This index, which is published in association with the Canadian Association of Law Libraries, is available in print as part of Carswell's *Canadian Abridgement*. The *Index to Canadian Legal Literature* is a comprehensive index of Canadian legal articles, books, government publications, case comments, continuing legal education materials, etc., in English and French.

In addition to a consolidation volume covering 1985 to 2000, one cumulative supplement volume is published annually. Separate subject and author indexes are provided. *ICLL* is also available in *Westlaw* and *Westlaw Canada*.

5. *Legal Journals Index* (*LJI*) and *European Legal Journals Index* (*ELJI*)

Legal Journals Index indexes over 800 legal journals from the United Kingdom and Europe. Published by Legal Information Resources Ltd., *LJI* began in 1986. Beginning in 1993, journals devoted to European law were moved to a companion publication, *European Legal Journals Index*. Although both titles were discontinued in print in 1999, the content is still published electronically, once again combined as *Legal Journals Index*. *LJI* is available via *Westlaw*.

6. *Index to Indian Legal Periodicals*

Since 1963 the Indian Law Institute has published the *Index to Indian Legal Periodicals*. This resource indexes periodicals published in India (including yearbooks and other annuals) pertaining to law and related fields. It is issued semiannually with annual cumulations.

7. *Index to Legal Periodicals in Israel*

This index, published by the Bar–Ilan University Law Library, indexes Israeli legal periodicals and collections of essays. Two print volumes (available from William S. Hein & Co.) cover the years 1976 to 1996 and 1997 to 2002. The index is also available electronically from the Bar–Ilan University Libraries.[48]

E. INDEXES TO SPECIFIC SUBJECTS

Several indexes provide access to periodical articles on specific legal subjects:

1. *Index to Federal Tax Articles*

This print index, first published by Warren, Gorham & Lamont and now by Thomson Reuters, covers the literature on federal income, estate, and gift taxation contained in legal, tax, and economic journals, as well as non-periodical publications. Articles are indexed by subject and author.

Three volumes provide retrospective coverage from 1913 to 1974. Since then, there have been several multiyear cumulations. The most current cumulation covers 2005 to the present and is updated on a quarterly basis.[49]

2. *Federal Tax Articles*

This looseleaf reporter, published by Commerce Clearing House, Inc., contains summaries of articles on federal taxation (income, estate, gift, and excise) appearing in legal, accounting, business, and related periodicals. Proceedings and papers delivered at major tax institutes are also indexed.

Summaries are arranged by Internal Revenue Code section numbers. Separate author and subject indexes are also provided. Cumulative bound volumes, with coverage dating from 1954, are published periodically to make room for current materials in the looseleaf volume. The reporter is updated on a monthly basis.[50]

3. *ProQuest Criminal Justice*

ProQuest Criminal Justice (formerly *Criminal Justice Periodicals Index* or *CJPI*) covers U.S. and international scholarly journals on crime, its causes and impacts, legal and social implications, and litigation and crime trends. Full text and abstracts are provided for many titles.

The print edition of *CJPI* was published by University Microfilms International from 1972 to 1998. It features an author index and a subject index, which includes case names. *ProQuest Criminal Justice* is now available electronically from ProQuest from 1969 to the present.

4. *Criminal Justice Abstracts*

Criminal Justice Abstracts, by EBSCO Publishing, is an electronic index covering hundreds of journals from around the world on essential areas related to criminal justice

---

[48] http://law.biu.ac.il/en/node/785. Select "Index to Legal Periodicals in Israel." After selecting English (if you can't read Hebrew), use the pull-down menu to select the index.

[49] See Chapter 26 for more on federal tax research.

[50] See Chapter 26 for more on federal tax research.

and criminology. *Criminal Justice Abstracts with Full Text* is the full text counterpart of *Criminal Justice Abstracts*.

5. *National Criminal Justice Reference Service (NCJRS) Abstracts Database*

Established in 1972, the National Criminal Justice Reference Service (NCJRS)[51] is a federally funded resource offering justice and drug-related information to support research, policy, and program development worldwide. The *NCJRS Abstracts Database* contains summaries of more than 210,000 publications, reports, articles, and audiovisual products from the United States and around the world. The abstracts include the title, author, journal citation, and a summary of the document's contents.

6. *Kindex*

Subtitled *An Index to Legal Periodical Literature Concerning Children, Kindex* was published by the National Center for Criminal Justice until 2001. It covers the years 1965 to 2001, emphasizing practical information for those involved in the criminal justice system.

Kindex is available in print or electronically through *HeinOnline*. Access points include a subject index (called a "classification" index) and an author index.

7. *Legal Information Management Index*

Legal Information Management Index covers periodicals related to law librarianship, library management, online and manual research, and related topics. It is published by Legal Information Services.

The print edition began in 1984 and is issued bimonthly with an annual cumulation. It includes keyword, author, and review indexes. The index is also available electronically from Legal Information Services.

8. *Subject Compilations of State Laws*

Subject Compilations of State Laws is a bibliography of articles, books, government documents, looseleaf services, court opinions, and websites that compare state laws on hundreds of subjects.[52] Coverage begins with 1979. It is updated annually in print and quarterly in *HeinOnline*.

9. *Annuals and Surveys Appearing in Legal Periodicals: An Annotated Listing*

This looseleaf volume indexes surveys appearing in law reviews, bar association journals, and annuals. It is divided into three sections: state surveys, federal court surveys, and subject-specific surveys. Published by William S. Hein & Co., it first appeared in 1987, was revised in 1995 and again in 2009 and has annual supplements.

---

[51] https://www.ncjrs.gov/.

[52] For more information on *Subject Compilations of State Laws*, see Chapter 11.

10. *Index to Periodical Articles Related to Law*

The *Index to Periodical Articles Related to Law* reflected the contributions of other disciplines to the study of law. It included legal articles of research value that appeared in periodicals not covered by the *Index to Legal Periodicals & Books*, *Legal Resource Index*, or the *Index to Foreign Legal Periodicals*.

This index, published by Glanville Publishers from 1958 to 2005, was issued quarterly and cumulated annually. Citations are arranged by subject and author. It is available both in print and in *HeinOnline*.

11. Non-Legal Periodical Indexes

Since law affects many other disciplines, it is sometimes necessary to turn to comprehensive indexes that are non-legal in nature to locate general information or to examine legal issues from a non-legal perspective. There are many indexes of this type— for example, *Business Periodicals Index*, *Humanities Index*, *Reader's Guide to Periodical Literature* (which covers popular magazines), and *Social Science Index*. *PAIS International*, published by Public Affairs Information Service, Inc., focuses on economics and public affairs and includes several law reviews and government publications in its coverage.

Gale Cengage Learning, publisher of *Current Law Index*, *LegalTrac*, and *Legal Resource Index*, also publishes a number of non-legal indexes, including *Academic OneFile* (which covers scholarly publications from numerous disciplines) and *General OneFile* (an index somewhat comparable to *Reader's Guide*).

F. OTHER SOURCES

References to legal periodical articles are frequently found in other sources. Many annotated state codes and the annotated editions of the *United States Code* cite relevant articles. Most West digests cite, under the topic and key number, to some pertinent law review articles. Similarly, many other West sources, including both national legal encyclopedias, provide references to legal periodical articles.

In addition, citators enable the researcher to locate articles *cited by* courts and other legal periodical articles, as well as articles that *cite to* cases, constitutions, statutes, and rules.[53] This is most easily accomplished through the use of the electronic citators, *Shepard's*, available via *LexisNexis*, and *KeyCite*, available via *Westlaw*.

Several print-based *Shepard's* citators also index law reviews; however, coverage may not be as extensive as in the electronic citators. *Shepard's Law Review Citations*, with coverage beginning in 1957, provides citations for legal periodicals that have been cited in published reports of the state and federal courts and other law reviews.

Federal Law Citations in Selected Law Reviews lists each time certain nationally recognized law reviews[54] cite to a case in the *U.S. Reports*, *Federal Reporter*, *Federal Cases*, *Federal Supplement*, *Federal Rules Decisions*, *Bankruptcy Reporter*, and other lower federal court reporters. It also notes each time any of these reviews cites the U.S.

---

[53] Citators are discussed in Chapter 15.

[54] Note that the electronic *Shepard's* in *LexisNexis* indexes substantially more law reviews, approximately 600.

Constitution, any edition of the *United States Code*, or the various federal court rules. Coverage is for articles published since 1973.

The individual state citators provide citations to cases, statutes, constitutions, and court rules that have been cited in the law reviews and bar journals of the state unit being used or by select nationally recognized law reviews. In addition, some of the specialized *Shepard's* citators, e.g., *Federal Tax Citations*, have limited citations to articles.

Chapter 19

TREATISES, RESTATEMENTS,
UNIFORM LAWS, AND MODEL ACTS*

This chapter discusses two frequently used categories of secondary sources: legal treatises and restatements of the law. Also discussed are two secondary sources that are intended to provide guidance on the drafting and interpretation of statutes: uniform laws and model acts.

A. TREATISES: IN GENERAL

Legal treatises are an important category of secondary authority of law. Treatises are extensive expositions by legal experts on case law and legislation pertaining to a particular doctrinal subject and published in book form.[1] Legal treatises, therefore, include a wide variety of types of publications, ranging from multivolume works and textbooks to shorter monographs. Treatises are typically able to treat a subject in greater depth than a legal encyclopedia; treatises are usually less speculative than journal articles.

Legal scholars wrote the first treatises during the period of the early development of the common law. Because few judicial opinions were available as precedent during the formative stages of our legal system, writers such as Lord Coke and William Blackstone played significant roles in the development of the law through their thoughtful, detailed commentaries. The growth of the law resulted in an ever-increasing number of law reports, and treatises organized and synthesized diffuse principles of case law. One commentator has noted that treatises were first written because of the lack of precedents and then because of their overabundance.[2]

During the eighteenth and early nineteenth centuries in the United States, treatises on English law were an integral part of an American lawyer's library. Gradually, American lawyers and legal scholars, such as James Kent and Joseph Story, began publishing treatises devoted entirely to American law.[3] By the twenty-first century, thousands of law books are being published annually on almost every legal topic

---

* This chapter was revised by Melissa Bernstein, Library Director & Professor of Law, S.J. Quinney Law Library, University of Utah.

[1] Even this most basic definition is subject to some qualification, as many treatises published in book form are also available in electronic format.

[2] GEORGE PATON, A TEXTBOOK OF JURISPRUDENCE 264 (4th ed. 1972). *See* A.W.B. Simpson, *The Rise and Fall of the Legal Treatise: Legal Principles and the Forms of Legal Literature*, 48 U. CHI. L. REV. 632 (1981). For two articles that rank the contributions of scholars to the legal literature, particularly treatises and legal periodical articles, see Fred R. Shapiro, *The Most-Cited Legal Books Published Since 1978*, 29 J. LEGAL STUD. 397 (2000), and Fred R. Shapiro, *The Most-Cited Legal Scholars*, 29 J. LEGAL STUD. 409 (2000).

[3] For a discussion of the development and influence of treatises on American law, see LAWRENCE M. FRIEDMAN, A HISTORY OF AMERICAN LAW 476–81 (3d ed. 2005). *See also* Erwin C. Surrency, *The Beginnings of American Legal Literature*, 31 AM. J. LEGAL HIST. 207 (1987).

imaginable. The American system of federalism has resulted in a flourishing market for books on federal law, state law generally, and the laws of specific states.

1. The Nature of Treatises

Treatises can be broadly classified into four types: (1) treatises that are critical, interpretive, or expository; (2) law student texts; (3) practitioner-oriented works; and (4) law for the general public. In most instances, however, particular treatises do not fall neatly into such a classification, and they may include some features of all types. Regardless of how scholarly the work, a careful researcher would not rely on a treatise without verifying the relevance and accuracy of the underlying authorities.

a.   Critical, Interpretive, or Expository Treatises. Treatises in this category generally examine an area of law in depth, although they vary in the extent to which they critique, interpret, and explain the law. Some constructively criticize rules of law as presently interpreted by the courts. They might include historical analyses to show that certain rules once had different meanings or interpretations than those presently given by the courts. The author may include an examination of the policy reasons for one or more such rules. Some treatises do not attempt to evaluate rules in relation to underlying policy, but rather attempt to explain the terminology and meaning of the rules as they exist. In these treatises, emphasis is placed upon understanding the law and not upon proposing what the law should be. Some treatises exist primarily as substitutes for digests and are principally used as case finders. These treatises typically consist of survey-type essay paragraphs arranged under conventional subject headings with numerous footnote citations. Usually minimal analysis and synthesis of conflicting cases are the most a researcher can expect to find in them. [Illustrations 19–1 and 19–2]

b.   Student Textbooks. Student textbooks or hornbooks are typically elementary treatments that include more limited critical and interpretive discussions than those found in full treatises. In fact, the term "hornbook law"[4] is commonly used to refer to basic doctrinal principles of law. [Illustration 19–3] Student texts are useful as case finders because their references are usually selective and limited to landmark cases. Major publishers of student texts include West Academic, Foundation Press (now a subsidiary of West Academic), Matthew Bender (LexisNexis), and Wolters Kluwer Law & Business.

Student texts include hefty, footnoted works by law professors (e.g., *Law of Federal Courts*, in West's Hornbook Series[5]), smaller paperbacks (e.g., *Torts in a Nutshell*[6] or *Acing Contracts*[7]), and lengthy, detailed outlines (e.g., *Property*, in the Emanuel Law Outlines series[8]). Some works are more useful in research and others are more useful to reinforce what was covered in class.

---

[4] A hornbook is a basic or rudimentary primer on a given subject. For the derivation of the terms *hornbook* and *hornbook law*, see JAMES E. CLAPP ET AL., LAWTALK: THE UNKNOWN STORIES BEHIND FAMILIAR LEGAL EXPRESSIONS 125 (2011). "Hornbook Series" is a registered trademark of West Academic Publishing used for its one-volume texts on legal subjects.

[5] CHARLES ALAN WRIGHT & MARY KAY KANE, LAW OF FEDERAL COURTS (7th ed. 2011).

[6] EDWARD J. KIONKA, TORTS IN A NUTSHELL (5th ed. 2010).

[7] SUZANNE DARROW-KLEINHAUS, ACING CONTRACTS: A CHECKLIST APPROACH TO CONTRACTS LAW (2010).

[8] STEVEN EMANUEL, PROPERTY (7th ed. 2010).

c.   *Practitioner-Oriented Books.* In recent years, the number of continuing education programs for lawyers has increased significantly. For example, the American Bar Association, the American Law Institute, the Practising Law Institute (PLI), and state bar associations hold seminars and symposia on many contemporary subjects that are directed toward practicing lawyers and intended to keep them updated on new developments in law. Many states have their own continuing legal education institutes. It is quite common for such institutes to publish handbooks in conjunction with their programs.

These volumes, as well as a rapidly increasing number of practice-oriented books by commercial publishers, usually furnish analyses of the law, practical guidance, forms, checklists, and other time-saving aids. These publications often deal with business transactions, personal injuries, commercial and corporate practice, probate practice, trial practice, and other subjects of primary interest to practicing attorneys. West, for example, publishes a *Practitioner Treatise Series.*

d.   *Law for the General Public.* So-called "self-help" books are intended to help the public conduct some legal affairs, e.g., preparation of a will, without the aid of an attorney.[9] Nolo, of Berkeley, California, is the leading publisher of books of this genre. Oxford University Press's *Legal Almanac Series* attempts to describe basic legal issues in simple language. The American Civil Liberties Union has also published numerous titles targeted for the lay audience.[10]

Well-written and carefully researched books aimed at non-lawyers can be useful for law students and lawyers in several ways. First, such a book can provide a quick, easy-to-read introduction to an unfamiliar area. Second, these works offer models for writing clearly about legal issues, an important skill for lawyers who need to communicate with their clients. Third, lawyers who are familiar with these works may find it helpful to recommend them to their clients, not because they will answer all of the clients' questions but because they will help the clients understand the law and the legal system.

2.   The Structure of Treatises

Treatises typically contain the following elements:

a.   *Table of Contents.* The table of contents sets forth the topical divisions of the treatise, which is usually arranged by chapters and subdivisions.

b.   *Tables of Authorities.* Most treatises include a table of cases that lists the cases discussed by the author and provides page number references. Depending on the subject covered, many treatises also have a table of statutes or court rules (e.g., Federal Rules of Evidence or Model Rules of Professional Conduct).

---

[9] AMBER HEWETT & DIANE MURLEY, LAW FOR THE LAYPERSON: AN ANNOTATED BIBLIOGRAPHY OF SELF-HELP LAW BOOKS (3d ed. 2006), is a good source for identifying works, although it is dated. In library catalogs, using "popular works" in a search will retrieve works aimed at non-lawyers. For example, *The Copyright Handbook: What Every Writer Needs to Know* is cataloged with the subject heading "Copyright-United States-Popular works."

[10] See https://nyupress.org/series.aspx?seriesId=62 for descriptions of the more than 50 self-help books produced by the ACLU and published by New York University Press. Lawhelp.org offers a national directory of websites with legal information for non-lawyers (http://www.lawhelp.org/find-help)—e.g., http://www.peoples-law.org/ (Maryland), http://texaslawhelp.org/ (Texas), http://www.washingtonlawhelp.org/ (Washington State), http://www.badgerlaw.net/ (Wisconsin).

c.   Contents. The bulk of the treatise is its discussion of the law, generally broken into chapters and often sections and subsections. The text is supported with citations to authority.

d.   Appendixes. Many treatises include appendixes with supplemental material such as statutes, legislative history, or forms.

e.   Index. An index, setting forth the topics, subtopics, and descriptive words, all arranged alphabetically, and with cross-references among index entries, is typically the last feature found in a treatise. [Illustration 19–1]

f.   Supplementation. Some treatises are updated and supplemented by pocket parts for insertion in the back of the volume or by separate pamphlets. Other treatises take the form of looseleaf volumes, which allow the removal and replacement of obsolete material.[11] Updated materials indicate recent statutory and case developments. Some treatises are published in softbound volumes so they can be updated and replaced annually (or more often).

3.   Locating Treatises

The starting point for determining whether a library has treatises on a subject or treatises by a specific author is its public catalog. Almost all libraries have electronic catalogs that enable a researcher to locate materials by author, title, and subject, and typically enable users to access information by any word or combination of words in the bibliographic record for that item. Most law libraries use the classification system and subject headings established by the Library of Congress, allowing for the use of the same subject headings and classification numbers in the catalogs of many libraries. An often-useful keyword search for a treatise is to combine a subject with the word "treatise."

OCLC WorldCat, a database that includes millions of records of information resources held in libraries around the world, is a very useful resource for locating treatises.[12] Librarians also may have access to an array of other sources, both print and electronic, that can assist in locating materials. If an item is identified that is not available in your library, it might be possible to obtain that item through interlibrary loan.

Research guides can be very helpful in locating treatises—and often in identifying those that are well respected in their fields. A research guide prepared for one's own library is useful, of course, because it identifies resources that are available there. But research guides prepared for other libraries are also useful because so many resources—including standard treatises and online resources—are common to many libraries. Cornell Law Library offers a search engine that searches legal research guides.[13]

Georgetown Law Library maintains a series of "Treatise Finders"[14] listing treatises in different areas of law. Icons indicate whether a work is a "preeminent treatise" or a study aid and whether it is in *Westlaw* or *LexisNexis.* For example, the Treatise Finder

---

[11] Note that a treatise published in a binder is not the same as a looseleaf service. Looseleaf services are discussed in Chapter 14.

[12] http://www.worldcat.org.

[13] http://www.lawschool.cornell.edu/library/WhatWeDo/ResearchGuides/Legal-Research-Engine-results. cfm.

[14] http://www.law.georgetown.edu/library/research/treatise-finders/.

for intellectual property[15] indicates that *Chisum on Patents* is a preeminent treatise and is in *LexisNexis* and that *Copyright: Examples and Explanations* is a study aid.

Other resources for identifying treatises on a particular subject or by a specific author include:

a.   Kendall F. Svengalis, *Legal Information Buyer's Guide & Reference Manual* (New England LawPress 2011). This book provides, among other valuable information, a history of legal publishing, information on maintaining a law library (including costs), and ways to evaluate legal materials. In addition to discussing statutes, reporters, digests, legal encyclopedias, and other major legal research tools, this *Guide* provides an annotated listing of legal treatises under approximately sixty subject categories. A separate section contains a practitioner's guide to legal publications by state.

b.   *IndexMaster. IndexMaster* is a web-based subscription service that permits keyword, title, author, and publisher searching of the table of contents and indexes of over 7,000 legal treatises and practice materials.

c.   *Law Books and Serials in Print.* This annual publication by Bowker contains over 40,000 titles of legal books, serials, and multimedia publications. A brief descriptive annotation is given for each title.

d.   *Law Books in Print. Law Books in Print* was a bibliographic listing of law books in the English language from around the world. It began in 1957 and ended in 1997 with the five-volume eighth edition (coverage was through 1996). It contained separate indexes for author/title, publisher, and subject.

e.   *Indexes Covering Treatises.* In 1994, the *Index to Legal Periodicals (ILP)* added books to the scope of its coverage. Approximately 1,400 book titles are included in each issue of *ILP*. Entries are listed under main entry (author or title) and under subject at the end of the subject entries for articles. *PAIS International* indexes some law-related titles as well, including government publications. The *Index to Canadian Legal Literature*, which began in 1987, is a comprehensive index to Canadian periodical, monographic, and book review literature on law.

f.   *Books in Print.* Also useful in locating treatises and other books about law is Bowker's annual *Books in Print. Bowker's Global Books in Print*, the electronic version of this resource, is updated daily and contains books about to be published, as far as six months in advance.

g.   *Historical Research.* Several resources can help researchers identify treatises from the past. This can be useful for legal history projects. It can also prove useful for researching some current issues—for instance, to interpret a provision of a state constitution that was adopted in 1889, a judge or lawyer might read contemporary constitutional law treatises to learn what the understanding of "police power" was at that time. Historical research resources include:

(1)   *Making of Modern Law: Legal Treatises 1800–1926.* This database is produced by Gale Cengage Learning. It contains the full text of approximately 22,000 works on United States and British law published from 1800 through 1926. It includes treatises,

---

[15] http://www.law.georgetown.edu/library/research/treatise-finders/intellectualproperty.cfm (last visited Dec. 16, 2013).

casebooks, local practice manuals, form books, works for lay readers, pamphlets, letters, speeches, and other documents.

(2) *Rise of American Law, Digital Archive of 19th and 20th Century Legal Texts.* This electronic collection of legal resources from West covers the period from 1840 to 1970. It provides access to over 1,700 out-of-print volumes in PDF format, including multivolume sets and multiple editions. Searching is by keyword, author, or title.

(3) *Bibliography of Early American Law (BEAL).* This six-volume set, compiled by Morris L. Cohen and published in 1998 by William S. Hein & Co., covers the period from the beginnings of American history up to and including 1860. The over 14,000 items in the set include treatises, bibliographies, commentaries, digests, lectures, polemics, biographies, civil and criminal trials, and numerous other important documents of this period. Eight indexes provide multiple points of access to the set. *BEAL* is also available in *HeinOnline* and in CD-ROM.[16]

(4) *A Catalogue of the Law Collection of New York University with Selected Annotations* (Julius Marke ed., 1953). This is an excellent source for older treatises and includes book review annotations. It is available in *HeinOnline*.

(5) *Law Books Recommended for Libraries.* In the 1960s, the Association of American Law Schools (AALS) undertook a large scale Library Studies Project designed to identify all published treatises and rate their importance to a law school library collection.[17] Arranged under forty-six subjects and titled *Law Books Recommended for Libraries*, these lists were published separately in six notebook volumes from 1967 to 1970, with supplements issued for forty-two of these subjects from 1974 to 1976. Actual coverage of titles extended only to approximately 1970. The project was discontinued after 1976. This set is available in *HeinOnline*.

(6) *Recommended Publications for Legal Research* (Mary F. Miller ed.), published by William S. Hein & Co., began under different editors, Oscar J. Miller and Mortimer D. Schwartz, as an effort to fill the gap left by the cessation of the AALS Library Studies Project. A separate volume for each year dating back to 1970 was prepared, and each year a new volume is issued covering titles published during the previous year. This publication uses the A, B, and C ratings employed in the AALS project. It is available in *HeinOnline*.[18]

(7) *Catalog of Current Law Titles.* This source, published by William S. Hein & Co., began in 1984 as *National Legal Bibliography* and was renamed *Catalog of Current Law Titles* in 1989. The title ceased publication in July 1998. It lists by subject and jurisdiction titles cataloged by over 60 law libraries around the country. A separate section lists those titles cataloged by at least one-fourth of those libraries. A cumulative supplement was issued annually.

---

[16] *See* Mary Whisner, *"That Most Congenial Lawyer/Bibliographer,"* 104 LAW LIBR. J. 135 (2012) (discussing *BEAL*).

[17] Titles were rated A, B, or C. "A" indicated that the title was "recommended for inclusion in the basic minimum collection." "B" indicated that the title was appropriate for "a library which is in the intermediate phase of development and is progressing toward support of a research program and an enriched curriculum which includes seminar offerings." "C" indicated that the title was "recommended for larger libraries with research collections of such quality and scope that they will support original scholarship in considerable depth."

[18] As of June 2014, the most recent edition online is 2012.

B. TREATISES: RESEARCH PROCEDURE

1. Case Method

If the name of a leading case on point is known, the table of cases of an appropriate treatise will lead to a discussion of the subject matter, along with additional cases on point.

2. Index Method

Consult the subject index in the back of the book if the name of a case is not known or if the research relates to a particular aspect of a subject. Select an appropriate descriptive word or legal topic to use the index. References will direct the researcher to the text of the publication.

3. Topic Method

The topic method can be used through the table of contents; however, its effectiveness in locating pertinent text depends on the researcher's understanding of how the author organized the subject.

4. Definition Method

The index or a separate glossary to the treatise may list words and phrases that are defined and explained in the text.

5. Full-Text Searching (Electronic Versions)

Electronic access enables a researcher to search the full text of the work and use strategies unavailable in the print versions. Often it is possible to link, through hypertext, to and from sections in the treatise and to sources cited by that treatise. Note that most online editions also include tables of contents, which can enhance access online, just as they do in print.

C. ILLUSTRATIONS: TREATISES

Problem: Does the "learned intermediary doctrine" provide any protections for manufacturers of prescription drug products?

19–1.   Page from Index to Frumer & Friedman, Products Liability
19–2.   Page from Frumer & Friedman, Products Liability
19–3.   Page from Dobbs, The Law of Torts

[Illustration 19–1]

PAGE FROM INDEX TO FRUMER & FRIEDMAN, PRODUCTS LIABILITY*

DRUG P   **INDEX**   I-58

[References are to Sections and Appendices.]

DRUG PRODUCTS—Cont.

Overpromotion of product (See subhead: Warnings, duty to provide)

Packaging requirements under Poison Prevention Packaging Act (See POISON PREVENTION PACKAGING ACT)

Penicillin (See ANTIBIOTICS)

Pharmacist's liability

    Generally . . . 50.03[1]

    Causation in negligent prescription cases . . . 50.05[2]

    Generic drugs, substitution of . . . . . . 50.03[2][b]

    Instructions on prescription, error in . . 50.03[2][b]

    Patient's condition, pharmacist's knowledge of . . . 50.03[3]

    Physician's error in prescription, pharmacist's duty in regard to . . . 50.03[2][b]

    Restatement (Third) of Torts . . . . . . 50.07[5]

    Standard of care . . . 50.03[2][a]

    Strict liability . . . 5.11; 50.03[4]

    Substitution of ingredients in prescription . . . 50.03[2][b]

    Warn, duty to . . . 12.06[6][d]; 50.03[3]

    Warranty, breach of . . . 50.03[5]

DRUG PRODUCTS—Cont.

Restatement (Third) of Torts—Cont.

    Design defects . . . 50.07[3]

    Learned intermediary doctrine . . . . . . 50.07[4]

    Manufacturing defects . . . 50.07[2]

    Pharmacist's liability . . . 50.07[5]

    Risk/utility test . . . 50.07[3]

    Warnings . . . 50.07[4]

Risk/utility test . . . 50.07[3]

Sampling in product testing, role of . . . . . 95.07[2]

Sealed containers (See POISON PREVENTION PACKAGING ACT)

Strict liability

    Generally . . . 8.07[4], [5]

    Distributor's liability . . . 50.04[3]

    Non-applicability of . . . 10.01[2]

    Pharmacist's liability . . . 5.11; 50.03[4]

    Restatement (Second) of Torts . . . . . 8.07[4], [5]

    Restatement (Third) of Torts . . . . . . 50.07[2]

    Substantial risk as factor . . . 8.07[5]

    Unavoidably unsafe drugs . . . 12.01[4]; 55.02[1][c]

To locate a reference to discussion in a treatise, such as Frumer & Friedman, *Products Liability*, of the issue presented in the problem, consult the index.

    . . . 50.05[5]

Privity requirement (See subhead: Warranty actions)

Product Liability Fairness Act, text of AppA.06

Proximate cause (See subhead: Causation, proof of)

Publicly available information . . . 55.07[5][c]

Punitive damages

    Manufacturers of prescription drugs, against . . . 50.08

    Pharmacist, substitution of drugs by . . 50.03[2][b]

Recalls

    Generally . . . 12.06[6][h]; 57.02[3]

    Punitive damages in cases of manufacturer's failure to conduct . . . 50.08

Report of Committee on Commerce, Science and Transportation, text of . . . AppA.06

Restatement (Third) of Torts

    Generally . . . 50.07[1]

Testimony of prescribing physician on causation . . . 50.05[5]

Tetracycline (See ANTIBIOTICS)

Thalidomide (See THALIDOMIDE)

Tobacco as drug, FDA's attempt to regulate . . . 56.02[8]

Unavoidably unsafe drugs

    Generally . . . 8.07[4], [5]; 12.01[4]

    Restatement (Second) of Torts, Comment k of . . . 8.07[4], [5]

    Strict liability . . . 8.07[4], [5]; 12.01[4]; 55.02[1][c]

Vaccines (See VACCINES)

Warnings, duty to provide

    Generally . . . 12.01[4]; 50.04[1], [2]

    Adequacy of warnings . . . 12.03[1][b]; 50.04[4]

    Bystanders, duty to warn . . . 12.06[2]

    Contraceptives, actions involving

    → Learned intermediary doctrine . . . 12.06[6][c], [d], [g][ii]; 50.04[2]

(Matthew Bender & Co., Inc.)   (Rel.88–7/01 Pub.560)

[Illustration 19–2]

PAGE FROM FRUMER & FRIEDMAN, PRODUCTS LIABILITY[*]

§ 50.04[2] PRODUCTS LIABILITY 50–28

[2]—Who Should Be Warned?

In prescription drug cases, the "nearly universal" rule, which is called the learned intermediary doctrine,[9] is that manufacturers have a duty to warn the physicians, dentists and other health care professionals who prescribe drugs for patients. *See* § 12.08 *above*, for an extensive discussion of this doctrine.

Nevertheless, as also discussed in § 12.08 *above*, in a few states, two specific exceptions to the learned intermediary doctrine have developed. One situation involves mass-immunization with vaccines, where vaccines are administered to everyone, without a balancing of risks as to a specific patient.[10] In a few states, the second exception applies where patients have chosen to utilize a specific type of prescription drug, or prescription device, for birth

[9] **The learned intermediary doctrine is nearly universal.** *See, e.g.*:

Arkansas	Hill v. Searle Laboratories, Div. of Searle Pharmaceuticals, Inc., 686 F. Supp. 720, 726 (E.D. Ark. 1988), *aff'd in part and rev'd in part on other grounds*, 884 F.2d 1064, 1070–1072 (8th Cir. 1989), applying Arkansas law ("nearly universal rule"); West v. Searle & Co., 305 Ark. 33, 42, 806 S.W.2d 608, 613 (1991) ("almost universally applied exception").
West Virginia	Pumphrey v. C.R. Bard, Inc., 906 F. Supp. 334, 337 (N.D. W.Va. 1995) (Frumer & Friedman cited; "nearly universal").

> Note that the index leads to a relevant discussion of the issue under research. A typical treatise, such as this one, contains text and then footnote references to cases and other pertinent materials. If supplementation is provided, this material should be consulted for later material.

Iowa	Brazzell v. U.S., 788 F.2d 1352, 1358 (8th Cir. 1986) (swine flu vaccine).
Kansas	Graham v. Wyeth Laboratories, Div. of American Home Prods. Corp., 666 F. Supp. 1483, 1498 (D. Kan. 1987) (DPT vaccine).
Montana	Davis v. Wyeth Laboratories, Inc., 399 F.2d 121, 131 (9th Cir. 1968) (Frumer and Fried cited; Type III Sabin oral polio vaccine).
Nevada	Allison v. Merck & Co., 110 Nev. 762, 776, 878 P.2d 948, 958 (1994) (measles, mumps, rubella vaccine, MMR II).
Oklahoma	Cunningham v. Charles Pfizer & Co., Inc., 532 P.2d 1377, 1381–1382 (Okla. 1974) (Sabin oral polio vaccine).
Pennsylvania	Mazur v. Merck & Co., 964 F.2d 1348, 1357–1360 (3d Cir.), *cert. denied*, 506 U.S. 974, 113 S. Ct. 463, 121 L. Ed. 2d 371 (1992) (measles, mumps, rubella vaccine, MMR II).
Texas	Reyes v. Wyeth Laboratories, 498 F.2d 1264, 1277 (5th Cir.), *cert. denied*, 419 U.S. 1096, 95 S. Ct. 687, 42 L. Ed. 2d 688 (1974) (Sabin oral polio vaccine).

(Matthew Bender & Co., Inc.) (Rel.84-4/00 Pub.560)

[Illustration 19–3]

PAGE FROM DOBBS, THE LAW OF TORTS

warning could be brighter or bigger does not in itself show that it is inadequate.[18]

English-only warnings. Children, illiterate adults, and adults who read only or mainly a foreign language cannot be warned by an English-only label. In a California case, an aspirin manufacturer targeted Spanish-speaking groups with its Spanish advertising, but its aspirin contained no Spanish warnings that aspirin could cause small children severe neurological damage, blindness, spastic quadriplegia and mental retardation. The court thought that the legislature, by affirmatively requiring warnings in English, negatively implied that no others could be required.[19] A few other cases have gone the other way, considering

> This page is from a treatise written primarily for law students. This particular title is part of the West *Hornbook Series*. Note the footnote references to court cases and secondary sources. Not shown in this illustration are suggested *Westlaw* queries that can be used to research this issue electronically.

altogether and makes federal law the only law on point. The federal statute requiring warnings on cigarette packages is like this. It preempts state tort law that would require a more adequate warning.[21] In broader perspective, the question is whether tort obligations should be decided exclusively by administrative regulations or statutes where they exist.[22]

§ 365. Prescription Drugs, Medical Device Warnings

Prescription drugs, medical devices. Courts almost always hold that a prescription drug manufacturer's warning to the doctor who prescribes a drug is sufficient to warn the doctor's patient as well. If the doctor fails to inform the patient of the risks, the patient has a claim against the doctor, but not against the manufacturer of the drug.[1] This is usually referred to as the learned intermediary doctrine, and it is usually

will ignite leaves or grass, but the only warning was burried in the 100-page owner's manual); cf. Payne v. Soft Sheen Prods., Inc., 486 A.2d 712, 58 A.L.R.4th 15 (D.C. 1985) (chemicals for hair treatment in multiple steps provided warning of burns only at the end of the instructions, after the instructions had guided operator through each step).

18. See General Motors Corp. v. Saenz, 873 S.W.2d 353 (Tex.1993).

19. Ramirez v. Plough, Inc., 6 Cal.4th 539, 25 Cal.Rptr.2d 97, 863 P.2d 167 (1993).

20. Hubbard–Hall Chem. Co. v. Silverman, 340 F.2d 402 (1st Cir.1965) (suggesting skull and crossbones on deadly poison used by agricultural workers); Campos v. Firestone Tire & Rubber Co., 98 N.J. 198, 485 A.2d 305 (1984) ("In view of the unskilled or semi-skilled nature of the work and the existence of many in the work force

who do not read English, warnings in the form of symbols might have been appropriate"). See Marjorie A. Caner, Annotation, Products Liability: Failure to Provide Product Warning or Instruction in Foreign Language or to Use Universally Accepted Pictographs or Symbols, 27 A.L.R.5th 697 (1995).

21. Cipollone v. Liggett Group, Inc., 505 U.S. 504, 112 S.Ct. 2608, 120 L.Ed.2d 407 (1992).

22. See § 373.

§ 365

1. E.g., Stone v. Smith, Kline & French Labs., 447 So.2d 1301 (Ala.1984); Humes v. Clinton, 246 Kan. 590, 792 P.2d 1032 (1990) Restatement of Products Liability § 6 (d). Although the doctor is not chronologically an intermediary between pharmacist and patient, the doctor is the final and

D. RESTATEMENTS OF THE LAW

In the early part of the twentieth century, prominent American judges, lawyers, and law professors became concerned about two aspects of case law: its growing uncertainty and undue complexity. As a result, in 1923, they founded the American Law Institute (ALI) to address these issues.[19] The objectives of the ALI focused on reducing the number of legal publications that had to be consulted by the bench and bar, simplifying case law by a clear, systematic restatement of it, and diminishing the flow of judicial decisions. The founders feared that the increasing mass of unorganized judicial opinions threatened to break down the common law system of expressing and developing law.[20]

To remedy these problems, the ALI undertook to produce clear and precise restatements of the existing common law that would have "authority greater than that now accorded to any legal treatise, an authority more nearly on a par with that accorded the decisions of the courts."[21]

This was accomplished by eminent legal scholars engaged as reporters for the various subjects to be restated. Each reporter prepared tentative drafts of the particular restatement. These drafts were then submitted to and approved by the members of the ALI. Often, many tentative drafts, with the work extending over many years, were prepared before final agreement was reached and a restatement adopted.

Between 1923 and 1944, restatements were adopted for the law of agency, conflict of laws, contracts, judgments, property, restitution, security, torts, and trusts. Since 1957, a second series of restatements has been adopted for agency, conflict of laws, contracts, foreign relations law (there was no first series of this restatement), judgments, property (landlord & tenant and donative transfers), torts, and trusts.

In 1986, a third series of restatements began with issuance of *Restatement (Third) of the Foreign Relations Law of the United States*. Since 1986, restatements have been adopted for agency, economic torts and related wrongs, employment law, the law governing lawyers, property (mortgages), property (servitudes), property (wills and other donative transfers), suretyship and guaranty, torts (apportionment of liability, liability for physical and emotional harm, and products liability), trusts (prudent investor rule), unfair competition, and the U.S. law of international commercial arbitration. In addition, tentative drafts of additional topics for both the second and third series continue to be issued, likely resulting in additional restatements in the future.[22]

---

[19] This discussion of the restatements is drawn from the following sources: (1) William Draper Lewis, *History of the American Law Institute and the First Restatement of the Law, in* AM. LAW INST., RESTATEMENT IN THE COURTS 1–23 (permanent ed. 1945); (2) HERBERT F. GOODRICH & PAUL A. WOLKIN, THE STORY OF THE AMERICAN LAW INSTITUTE, 1923–1961 (1961); (3) AM. LAW INST., THE AMERICAN LAW INSTITUTE 50TH ANNIVERSARY (1973) [hereinafter ALI 50TH ANNIVERSARY]; (4) AM. LAW INST., THE AMERICAN LAW INSTITUTE SEVENTY-FIFTH ANNIVERSARY, 1923–1998 (1998); and (5) AM. LAW INST., ANNUAL REPORTS. *See also The American Law Institute Restatement of the Law and Codifications, in* 3 PIMSLEUR'S CHECKLISTS OF BASIC AMERICAN LEGAL PUBLICATIONS § V (Marcia S. Zubrow ed. & comp., looseleaf) (AALL Publication Series, No. 4).

[20] Lewis, *supra* note 19, at 1.

[21] *Report of the Committee on the Establishment of a Permanent Organization for the Improvement of the Law Proposing the Establishment of the American Law Institute, in* ALI 50TH ANNIVERSARY, *supra* note 19, at 34.

[22] ALI has begun work on a fourth restatement of foreign relations law. For a list of past and present ALI projects, see http://www.ali.org/doc/past_present_ALIprojects.pdf. This list is updated periodically. A listing of current projects can be found at http://www.ali.org/index.cfm?fuseaction=projects.currentprojects.

ALI publishes *Principles of the Law*: recommendations for change in areas of the law thought to need reform. These projects have included corporate governance, family dissolution, and transnational civil procedure.[23] Current projects include *Principles of Election Law: Resolution of Election Disputes*, *Principles of Government Ethics*, *Principles of the Law of Charitable Nonprofit Organizations*, and *Principles of the Law of Liability Insurance*.

The status of the revision of specific restatements and information pertaining to proposed new restatements can be ascertained from the latest *ALI Annual Reports*, and from its quarterly newsletter, *The ALI Reporter*. ALI's website[24] includes the status of its publications along with a variety of other useful information.

Early on Harlan Fiske Stone recommended that state legislatures be required to approve the restatements, not as formal legislative enactments, but as aids and guides to the judiciary so that they will feel free to follow "the collective scholarship and expert knowledge of our profession."[25] This proposal, however, was not adopted by the ALI membership. Nevertheless, many courts give greater authority to the restatements than that accorded to treatises and other secondary sources. In many instances, the restatements are accorded an authority nearly equal that of decided cases.[26]

The first series of the restatements reflected the desire of the ALI's founders that the restatements be admired and adopted by the courts. To this end they deliberately omitted the reporters' citations and references to the tentative drafts upon which the restatement rules were based.

With publication of the second series of the restatements, ALI abandoned the idea of the restatements serving as a substitute for the codification of existing common law. The Second and Third Series sometimes indicate a new trend in the common law and attempt to state what a new rule will or should be.[27] This change in policy is also reflected in the appearance of citations to judicial opinions and to the notes of the reporters. Appendices contain citations to, and brief synopses of, all cases that have cited the restatements. It should be noted that a new restatement on the same topic as an existing one does not supersede the older version. Some courts, in fact, continue to cite earlier restatements.

The frequency with which the restatements are cited by the courts suggests their value and importance to legal research.[28] Restatements not only provide statements of the rules of common law, which are operative in a great number of states, but also are valuable sources for finding cases on point.

Moreover, a comparison of the texts of the restatements and state case law reveals that there are surprisingly few deviations from the common law that are expressed in

---

[23] http://ali.org/index.cfm?fuseaction=about.instituteprojects.

[24] http://www.ali.org.

[25] Alpheus Thomas Mason, *Harlan Fiske Stone Assays Social Justice, 1912–1923*, 99 U. PA. L. REV. 887, 915 (1951) (quoting from a speech given by Stone).

[26] For a discussion of the precedential authority of the restatements, see James F. Byrne, *Reevaluation of the Restatements as a Source of Law in Arizona*, 15 ARIZ. L. REV. 1021, 1023–26 (1973).

[27] *Id.*

[28] Courts have cited restatements and *Principles of the Law* 191,000 times through June 2013. AM. LAW INST., THE AMERICAN LAW INSTITUTE ANNUAL REPORT 2012/2013, at 12, *available at* http://www.ali.org/doc/ALI_annual-report-2013.pdf.

the restatements. It has been suggested, therefore, that there is in fact a common law that transcends state lines and prevails throughout the nation.[29] However, courts may at times inaccurately and confusingly state legal rules. Thus, another objective of the restatements is to assist courts in stating doctrinal rules of law more clearly.

1. Features of the Restatements

The various restatements are typically divided broadly into chapters, and further subdivided into narrower titles, and then into numbered discrete sections. Each section begins with a "black letter" (**boldface**)[30] restatement of the law, followed by comments that contain hypothetical illustrations. Reporters' notes are set forth at the end of each section.[31] [Illustrations 19–5 through 19–8] These notes serve as a history of the section and will, if applicable, include the text of the section or sections of earlier restatements that are replaced by this later section.

The second and third series of the restatements also have:

a. *Tables.* These list citations to judicial opinions, statutes, and other authorities referenced in the restatement.

b. *Conversion or Parallel Tables.* These enable a user to locate a section in a tentative draft or prior restatement series within the text in the final restatement.

c. *Cross-references.* These give references to West's key number system and to *A.L.R.* annotations.

2. Indexes

a. *Restatements, First Series.* A one-volume index to all restatements in the first series has been published. Each restatement also has its own subject index.

b. *Restatements, Second Series* and *Third Series.* Some of the older restatements have their own subject index in each volume, covering only the materials in that volume. More recent restatements contain an index in the last volume of the restatement or in a separate volume. [Illustration 19–4] There is no comprehensive index to all restatements.

3. Restatements Cited by Courts

Researchers often want to find cases citing a restatement section. Appendix volumes list cases with brief annotations.[32] The appendix volumes are updated with pocket parts or separate annual cumulative supplements. A semiannual pamphlet entitled *Interim Case Citations* updates all of the restatements' appendix volumes. New appendix volumes are published periodically.

---

[29] Herbert F. Goodrich, *Restatement and Codification, in* DAVID DUDLEY FIELD: CENTENARY ESSAYS CELEBRATING ONE HUNDRED YEARS OF LEGAL REFORM 241–50 (Allison Reppy ed., 1949).

[30] For a history of the term "black letter law," see JAMES E. CLAPP ET AL., LAWTALK: THE UNKNOWN STORIES BEHIND FAMILIAR LEGAL EXPRESSIONS 31 (2011).

[31] For the first three *Restatements (Second)*, agency, torts, and trusts, the reporters' notes are in the appendix volumes accompanying these subjects.

[32] A separate set, *Restatements in the Courts*, was issued first as a permanent edition covering 1932 to 1944 and then updated with bound supplements covering from 1945 to 1975. These annotations were subsequently recompiled and added to the individual appendix volumes of the current restatements.

4. Electronic Access to Restatements

Restatements are available in *Westlaw* and *LexisNexis*. The first series of most restatements is not available in *LexisNexis,* where the text is searchable separately from case citations. *Westlaw* includes drafts of restatements. Both *Westlaw* and *LexisNexis* include the various *Principles of the Law.*

5. Citators for Restatements

Both *Shepard's* (in *LexisNexis*) and *KeyCite* (in *Westlaw*) include citations to the restatements. [Illustration 19–9] A print set, *Shepard's Restatement of the Law Citations*, is devoted entirely to the restatements.

6. Restatements in the American Law Institute Archive

HeinOnline's American Law Institute Library contains ALI's annual reports, proceedings, and more, beginning with ALI's founding in 1923. William S. Hein & Co. publishes a comparable set in microfiche.

E. ILLUSTRATIONS: RESTATEMENT (THIRD) OF TORTS: PRODUCTS LIABILITY

Problem: Does the "learned intermediary doctrine" provide any protections for manufacturers of prescription drugs?

19–4:   **Page from Index to Restatement (Third) of Torts: Products Liability**

19–5 to 19–8:   **Pages from Restatement (Third) of Torts: Products Liability § 6**

19–9:   **Screenshot from Shepard's Restatement of the Law Citations on Lexis Advance**

[Illustration 19–4]

PAGE FROM INDEX TO RESTATEMENT (THIRD) OF TORTS: PRODUCTS LIABILITY

INDEX

LATENCY PERIOD OF HARM
Causation and proportional liability, § 15 Com. *c*; § 15 RN to Com. *c*

LAUNDROMAT
Bailment as commercial distribution, dryers, § 20 Com. *f*

LEARNED INTERMEDIARY RULE
Generally, § 6 Com. *b*; § 6 RN to Com. *b*; § 6 RN to Com. *d*

LEASES
Financing. See Finance Lessors
One who otherwise distributes a product, § 20(b); § 20 Com. *c*; § 20 RN to Com.
    c
One who sells or otherwise distributes, defined, § 20(b)
Used product sellers' or distributors' liability for defective used products, short-term
    product leases, § 8 Com. *j*; § 20 RN to Com. *c*

LESSORS
One who otherwise distributes a product, lessor as, § 20(b); § 20 Com. *c*; § 20 RN
    to Com. *c*

> In multivolume sets of Restatement 2d and 3d, an index is sometimes in each volume and only covers the topics addressed by that volume; for some sets the index is in the last volume for that subject. Once the appropriate volume is located, typically by reference to the Table of Contents, that volume's index can be used to locate relevant material. In the problem being researched, a likely subject heading to consult is "learned intermediary doctrine" or "learned intermediary rule."
>
> See the next four illustrations for examples of how the restatements are arranged.

LIVESTOCK
"Product," tangible personal property as, § 19 Com. *b*; § 19 RN to Com. *b*

LIVING ANIMALS
"Product," tangible personal property as, § 19 Com. *b*; § 19 RN to Com. *b*

LONGEVITY
Omission of reasonable alternative rendering product not reasonably safe, § 2 Com.
    f

LOSS OF EARNINGS
Plaintiff's person, resulting from harm to, § 21 Com. *b*

LUMBER
"Product," tangible personal property as, § 19 Com. *b*; § 19 RN to Com. *b*

M

MAINTENANCE SERVICES
Successor liability for harm caused by successor's own post-sale failure to warn,
    § 13; § 13 Com. *b*;

MAINTENANCE
Omission of reasonable alternative rendering product not reasonably safe, § 2 Com.
    f
Services, distinguished from, § 19 Com. *f*

MALFUNCTION
Doctrine, § 3 RN 1 to Com. *b*

MALFUNCTIONS
Economic loss from harm to product itself, § 21 Com. *d*; § 21 RN to Com. *d*

[Illustration 19–5]

PAGE FROM RESTATEMENT (THIRD) OF TORTS: PRODUCTS LIABILITY § 6

§ 5   PRODUCTS LIABILITY   Ch. 1

ing a partial summary judgment motion to bar claims against a defendant that manufactured a component because genuine issue of material fact existed as to whether defendant was involved in the design); Koonce v. Quaker Safety Prods. & Mfg. Co., 798 F.2d 700 (5th Cir.1986) (applying Texas law).

A component-part manufacturer that does not substantially participate in the integration of the product is not liable under Subsection (b). Courts frequently absolve the compo-

v. Marquess & Nell, Inc. 675 A.2d 620, 627 (N.J.1996); Depre v. Power Climber, Inc., 635 N.E.2d 542, 544 (Ill.App.1994); Noonan v. Texaco, Inc. 713 P.2d 160, 164 (Wyo.1986). These decisions are consistent with the thrust of Subsection (b). In all of the cited cases, the component supplier did not substantially participate in the design of the integrated product and thus would not be subject to liability. Courts appear to be using the concept of lack of "control" as a shorthand method of expressing the

A restatement's "black letter" rule immediately follows the section number.

the integrated product. See e.g., Trevino v. Yamaha Motor Corp., 882 F.2d 182, 184–185, 186 (5th Cir.1989); Artiglio v. General Electric Co., 71 Cal.Rptr.2d 817 (Cal.App.1998); Zaza

seller that does not substantially participate in the integration of the component into the design of the product has no control over the decisionmaking process that brought about the defective product.

§ 6. Liability of Commercial Seller or Distributor for Harm Caused by Defective Prescription Drugs and Medical Devices

(a) A manufacturer of a prescription drug or medical device who sells or otherwise distributes a defective drug or medical device is subject to liability for harm to persons caused by the defect. A prescription drug or medical device is one that may be legally sold or otherwise distributed only pursuant to a health-care provider's prescription.

(b) For purposes of liability under Subsection (a), a prescription drug or medical device is defective if at the time of sale or other distribution the drug or medical device:

(1) contains a manufacturing defect as defined in § 2(a); or

(2) is not reasonably safe due to defective design as defined in Subsection (c); or

(3) is not reasonably safe due to inadequate instructions or warnings as defined in Subsection (d).

144

[Illustration 19–6]

PAGE FROM RESTATEMENT (THIRD) OF TORTS: PRODUCTS LIABILITY § 6

Ch. 1   LIABILITY BASED ON TIME-OF-SALE DEFECTS   § 6

(c) A prescription drug or medical device is not reasonably safe due to defective design if the foreseeable risks of harm posed by the drug or medical device are sufficiently great in relation to its foreseeable therapeutic benefits that reasonable health-care providers, knowing of such foreseeable risks and therapeutic benefits, would not prescribe the drug or medical device for any class of patients.

(d) A prescription drug or medical device is not reasonably safe due to inadequate instructions or warnings if reasonable instructions or warnings regarding foreseeable risks of harm are not provided to:

(1) prescribing and other health-care providers who are in a position to reduce the risks of harm in accordance with the instructions or warnings; or

(2) the patient when the manufacturer knows or has reason to know that health-care providers will not be in a position to reduce the risks of harm in accordance with the instructions or warnings.

(e) A retail seller or other distributor of a prescrip

> Following the "black letter" rule is a Comment section explaining the purpose of the rule.

(1) at the time of sale or other distribution the drug or medical device contains a manufacturing defect as defined in § 2(a); or

(2) at or before the time of sale or other distribution of the drug or medical device the retail seller or other distributor fails to exercise reasonable care and such failure causes harm to persons.

Comment:

a. *History.* Subsections (b)(1) and (d)(1) state the traditional rules that drug and medical-device manufacturers are liable only when their products contain manufacturing defects or are sold without adequate instructions and warnings to prescribing and other health-care providers. Until recently, courts refused to impose liability based on defective designs of drugs and medical devices sold only by prescription. However, consistent with recent trends in the case law, two limited exceptions from these traditional rules are generally recognized. Subsection (d)(2) sets forth situations when a prescription-drug or medical-device manufacturer is required to warn the patient directly of risks associated with consumption or use of its product. And

145

[Illustration 19–7]

PAGE FROM RESTATEMENT (THIRD) OF TORTS: PRODUCTS LIABILITY § 6

§ 6   PRODUCTS LIABILITY   Ch. 1

Illustration:

1. ABC Pharmaceuticals manufactures and distributes D, a prescription drug intended to prolong pregnancy and thus to reduce the risks associated with premature birth. Patricia, six months pregnant with a history of irregular heart beats, was given D during a hospital stay in connection with her pregnancy. As a result, she suffered heart failure and required open-heart surgery. In Patricia's action against ABC, her expert testifies that, notwithstanding FDA approval of D five years prior to Patricia's taking the drug, credible studies published two years prior to Patricia's taking the drug concluded that D does not prolong pregnancy for any class of patients. Notwithstanding a finding by the trier of fact that ABC gave adequate warnings to the prescribing physician regarding the serious risks of heart failure in patients with a history of irregular heart beats, the trier of fact can find that reasonably informed health-care providers would not prescribe D for any class of patients, thus rendering ABC subject to liability.

g. Foreseeability of risks of harm in prescription drug and medical device cases. Duties concerning the design and marketing of prescription drugs and medical devices arise only with respect to risks of harm that are reasonably foreseeable at the time of sale. Imposing liability for unforeseeable risks can create inappropriate disincentives

Frequently, the Comment section includes hypothetical examples.

risks, insuring against losses due to unknowable risks would be problematic. Drug and medical device manufacturers have the responsibility to perform reasonable testing prior to marketing a product and to discover risks and risk-avoidance measures that such testing would reveal. See § 2, Comments *a* and *m*.

Illustrations:

2. DEF Pharmaceuticals, Inc., manufactures and distributes prescription drugs. Seven years ago DEF, after years of research and testing, received permission from the FDA to market X, a drug prescribed for the treatment of low-grade infections. Three years later, Jim, age 12, began taking X on his physician's prescription for a recurring respiratory-tract infection. Jim took X for approximately one year. Two years after Jim had stopped taking X, medical research discovered that X causes loss of vision in adolescents. Prior to this discovery DEF had not warned of this risk. Jim has begun to manifest symptoms of the sort caused by the drug. No evidence suggests that DEF's testing of X was substandard, or that any reasonable drug company should have

150

[Illustration 19–8]

PAGE FROM RESTATEMENT (THIRD) OF TORTS: PRODUCTS LIABILITY § 6

§ 6   PRODUCTS LIABILITY   Ch. 1

patients suffering injury for whom the pamphlets would have been effective in avoiding risks of usage.

REPORTERS' NOTE

Comment b. Rationale. Courts have advanced a number of reasons for exclusive reliance on the learned intermediary rule. See, e.g., West v. Searle & Co., 806 S.W.2d 608, 613–14 (Ark.1991) (provider is best assessor of relevant risks and benefits); Brown v. Superior Court, 751 P.2d 470, 478–79 (Cal.1988) (concern that increased liability would drive prices of drugs too high and make them less available); Lacy v. G.D. Searle & Co., 567 A.2d 398 (Del.1989); In re Certified Questions, 358 N.W.2d 873, 883 (Mich.1984) (Boyle, J., dissenting) (in some cases directly warning patient

Merck & Co. v. Kidd, 242 F.2d 592 (6th Cir.) (applying Tennessee law), cert. denied, 355 U.S. 814, 78 S.Ct. 15, 2 L.Ed.2d 31 (1957); Abbott Labs. v. Lapp, 78 F.2d 170 (7th Cir.1935); Hruska v. Parke, Davis & Co., 6 F.2d 536 (8th Cir.1925); Randall v. Goodrich-Gamble Co., 70 N.W.2d 261 (Minn.1955). Comment k to § 402A of the Restatement, Second, of Torts reflects this rule: "The seller of [prescription drugs], *with the qualification that they are properly prepared* and marketed, is not to be held to strict liability for unfortunate consequences attending their use" (empha-

> The Reporter's Notes contain information pertaining to the development of the restatement and include references to cases and secondary authorities. These Notes are in the Appendix volumes for the Restatements (Second) of Agency, Torts, and Trusts. For all other Restatements 2d and for all Restatements 3d, these Notes are at the end of each section of the restatement.

Federal Food and Drug Administration (FDA) regulates vaccine manufacturers.... The regulations are quite detailed in their setting of standards for safety, effectiveness and adequate labelling."); Gravis v. Parke-Davis & Co., 502 S.W.2d 863, 870 (Tex.App.1973) ("[The] entire system of drug distribution in America is set up so as to place the responsibility ... upon professional people"). For a useful discussion of the rule and its underlying rationale, see T. Schwartz, Consumer-Directed Prescription Drug Advertising and the Learned Intermediary Rule, 46 Food Drug Cosm. L.J. 829, 830–31 (1991).

Comment c. Manufacturers' liability for manufacturing defects. Prescription drug manufacturers are strictly liable for harm caused by manufacturing defects. See, e.g.,

ball, 77 A. 405 (Me.1910); Burgess v. Sims Drug Co., 86 N.W. 307 (Iowa 1901).

Comment d. Manufacturers' liability for failure adequately to instruct or warn prescribing and other health-care providers. The traditional rule, often referred to as the "learned intermediary rule," holds that manufacturers of prescription drugs discharge their duty of care to patients by warning the health-care providers who prescribe and use the drugs to treat them. See, e.g., DeLuryea v. Winthrop Labs., 697 F.2d 222, 228–29 (8th Cir.1983); Werner v. Upjohn Co., 628 F.2d 848, 858 (4th Cir.1980), cert. denied, 449 U.S. 1080, 101 S.Ct. 862, 66 L.Ed.2d 804 (1981); Lindsay v. Ortho Pharm. Corp., 637 F.2d 87, 91 (2d Cir.1980) (applying New York law). Accord, Salmon v. Parke, Davis

152

[Illustration 19-9]

PAGE/SCREENSHOT FROM SHEPARD'S RESTATEMENT OF THE LAW CITATIONS

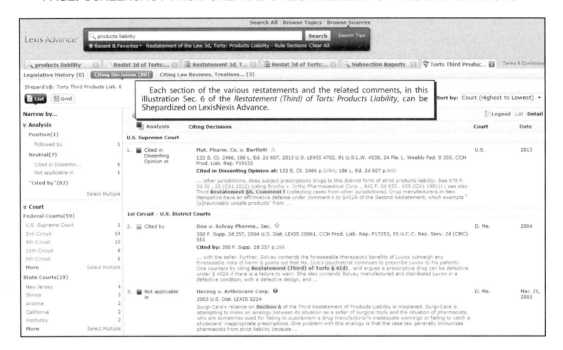

F. UNIFORM LAWS AND MODEL ACTS

1. Uniform Laws

The same law reform movement that led to the creation of the restatements also focused on statutory law and the need, in many instances, for uniform statutes among the states. Toward this goal, the American Bar Association passed a resolution recommending that each state and the District of Columbia[33] adopt a law providing for the appointment of commissioners to confer with commissioners of other states on the subject of uniformity in legislation on certain subjects. In 1892 the National Conference of Commissioners on Uniform State Laws was organized (it is now referred to as the Uniform Law Commission). By 1912 each state had passed such a law. According to the organization's constitution, its object is to "promote uniformity in state law on all subjects where uniformity is desirable and practical."[34]

A draft of a proposed law is designated as a *uniform law*, and adoption in its entirety is urged, when its purpose is to establish the same law among all the states. A *model act* is one whose purposes can be achieved even if the act is not adopted in its entirety by

---

[33] Commissioners now include representatives from the Commonwealth of Puerto Rico and the U.S. Virgin Islands.

[34] This document is published annually in the HANDBOOK OF THE NATIONAL CONFERENCE OF COMMISSIONERS ON UNIFORM STATE LAWS AND PROCEEDINGS OF THE ANNUAL MEETING. For a more detailed discussion of the National Conference, see WALTER P. ARMSTRONG, A CENTURY OF SERVICE: A CENTENNIAL HISTORY OF THE NATIONAL CONFERENCE OF COMMISSIONERS ON UNIFORM STATE LAWS (1991); Richard E. Coulson, *The National Conference of Commissioners on Uniform State Laws and the Control of Law-Making— A Historical Essay*, 16 OKLA. CITY U. L. REV. 295 (1991).

every state; model acts are intended to serve as guidelines, and individual sections can be adopted or adapted by states, as desired. The Conference meets once a year and considers drafts of proposed laws. When a uniform law is approved, the duty of the commissioners is to try to persuade their state legislatures to adopt it.[35] Of course, adoption by the Conference has no legal effect; only subsequent enactment by state legislatures can achieve this result. The Conference has produced over 200 acts; perhaps the most notable example is the Uniform Commercial Code.

Laws approved by the Uniform Law Commission are published in the following forms:

a.   On the Conference's website (see the discussion in 3-a).

b.   In the annual *Handbook* of the National Conference. There is some delay in the publication of this title.

c.   In *Uniform Laws Annotated, Master Edition.* This multivolume set, published by Thomson Reuters and available in *Westlaw*, contains approximately 200 uniform laws. A law must have been adopted by at least one state to be included in this set. [Illustrations 19–10 to 19–12] Volumes are revised periodically and pocket supplements and annual pamphlets are issued.

Each section of a uniform law is typically followed by an Official Comment of the Commissioners. In most cases, this is followed by references to law review articles, related West digest topics and key numbers, and *Corpus Juris Secundum* sections. In recently revised volumes and the supplementation, *Westlaw* references also are provided. Each volume contains a detailed index to the laws it contains, and indexes may also be found at the end of the volume in which a particular act ends. Tables in both the bound volumes and the supplements list the states that have adopted each uniform law. [Illustration 19–15]

d.   National Conference of Commissioners on Uniform State Laws—Archive Publications, a library in *HeinOnline*, contains thousands of documents, including transcripts of meetings and successive drafts of uniform laws up to and including the uniform laws as adopted. William S. Hein & Co. also publishes a comparable set in microfiche.

2.   Other Sources of Model Legislation

Many other organizations (and some individuals) propose model legislation. The American Law Institute[36] has drafted the influential Model Penal Code.[37] The Uniform Law Commission and the ALI worked jointly on the Uniform Commercial Code. The American Bar Association has also proposed legislation (e.g., the Model Business Corporation Act[38]). Some professional associations or advocacy groups propose model

---

[35] The commissioners do not have an obligation to advocate for the adoption of model acts. Despite the organization's efforts, some uniform laws are adopted by only a handful of states.

[36] Documents pertaining to the uniform laws and model acts with which the ALI has been associated are contained in the *American Law Institute Archive Publications* described in Section D-6.

[37] *See* AM. LAW INST., MODEL PENAL CODE: OFFICIAL DRAFT AND EXPLANATORY NOTES (1985).

[38] *See* COMM. ON CORP. LAWS, AM. B. ASS'N, MODEL BUSINESS CORPORATION ACT: OFFICIAL TEXT WITH OFFICIAL COMMENTS AND STATUTORY CROSS-REFERENCES, REVISED THROUGH DECEMBER 2010 (2011); COMM. ON CORP. LAWS, AM. B. ASS'N, MODEL BUSINESS CORPORATION ACT ANNOTATED: MODEL BUSINESS CORPORATION ACT WITH OFFICIAL COMMENT AND REPORTER'S ANNOTATIONS (2008).

legislation in their areas of interest. The American Legislative Exchange Council (ALEC), an organization of conservative legislators and businesspeople, proposes model legislation on a wide variety of topics.[39]

3. Locating Information About Uniform Laws and Model Acts

a.   The National Conference on Uniform State Laws website.[40] This is an excellent source for learning about all of the organization's activities. It details the legislative status of, and information on, uniform acts (listed alphabetically and searchable by title and keyword), ongoing drafting projects, and topics under discussion.

b.   Handbook of the National Conference of Commissioners on Uniform State Laws. This annual publication includes discussions of pending legislation, as well as the texts of all uniform laws adopted during that year. Through this *Handbook* a researcher can locate a uniform law, even if it has not been adopted by any state. A complete list of acts approved by the National Conference appears each year in the *Handbook*'s appendices. Charts are included that show which states have adopted specific uniform laws and model acts, and the dates of adoption. There is some delay in the publication of this title.

c.   Directory of Uniform Acts and Codes. This annual pamphlet, published as part of the *Uniform Laws Annotated, Master Edition*, indicates the volume of the *Master Edition* in which a particular law is published. [Illustration 19–13] This directory also includes a state-by-state listing of uniform laws adopted by each state [Illustration 19–14], a list of the Commissioners by state, and a brief subject index to all acts in the set.

d.   Legal Periodical Articles. Articles about uniform laws and other model legislation can be found by checking the major indexes to legal periodicals: *Index to Legal Periodicals* (ILP), *Current Law Index* (CLI), *LegalTrac*, and *Legal Resource Index* (LRI).

G. ILLUSTRATIONS: UNIFORM LAWS

19–10 to 19–12. Pages from Uniform Laws Annotated, Master Edition, Volume 9, Part II

19–13.   Page from Uniform Laws Annotated, Directory of Uniform Acts and Codes

19–14.   Page from Uniform Laws Annotated, Directory of Uniform Acts and Codes, Table of Jurisdictions Listing Uniform Acts Adopted

19–15.   Page from Uniform Laws Annotated, Master Edition, Volume 9, Part II, Table of Jurisdictions Adopting the Uniform Controlled Substances Act

---

[39] *See* Mary Whisner, *There Oughta Be a Law—A Model Law*, 106 LAW LIBR. J. 125 (2014).

[40] http://uniformlaws.org.

[Illustration 19–10]

PAGES FROM UNIFORM LAWS ANNOTATED, MASTER EDITION, VOLUME 9, PART II

CONTROLLED SUBSTANCES (1994) ←   § 101

[ARTICLE] 7

MISCELLANEOUS

Westlaw Computer Assisted Legal Research

Westlaw
  • u
  • e
  • r   se

This is the first page of the Uniform Controlled Substances Act (1994). This Act, which may have relevance to the research problem presented in Sections C and E, is an example of a typical uniform law drafted by the Uniform Law Commission (ULC; also referred to as the National Conference of Commissioners on Uniform State Laws (NCCUSL)).

For more   Westlaw
Electronic Research Guide, which follows the Preface.

[ARTICLE] 1

DEFINITIONS

Action in Adopting Jurisdictions

Because of the numerous variations resulting from the frequent amendments made to the corresponding sections of text of this Act by the adopting jurisdictions, it is not feasible to note the differences between the official text of this Act and the counterpart texts in the adopting jurisdictions.

§ 101. Definitions

As used in this [Act]:

15

[Illustration 19–11]

PAGES FROM UNIFORM LAWS ANNOTATED, MASTER EDITION, VOLUME 9, PART II

CONTROLLED SUBSTANCES (1994)   § 401

    (ii) [50] kilograms or more, but less than [100] kilograms, the person is guilty of a crime and upon conviction [may] [must] be imprisoned for not less than [ ] nor more than [ ] and fined not less than [ ];

    (iii) [100] kilograms or more, the person is guilty of a crime and upon conviction [may] [must] be imprisoned for not less than [ ] nor more than [ ] and fined not less than [ ].]

  (h) Except as authorized by law, a person may not knowingly or intentionally possess piperidine with intent to manufacture a controlled substance, or knowingly or intentionally possess piperidine knowing, or having reasonable cause to believe, that the piperidine will be used to manufacture a controlled substance contrary to this [Act]. A person who violates this subsection is guilty of a crime and upon conviction may be imprisoned for not more than [ ], fined not more than [ ], or both.

  [(i) Except as provided in subsection (j), with respect to an individual who is found to have violated subsection (g), adjudication of guilt or imposition of sentence may not be suspended, deferred, or withheld, nor is the individual eligible for parole before serving the mandatory term of imprisonment prescribed by this section.]

  (j) Notwithstanding any other provision of this [Act], the defendant or the attorney for the State may request the sentencing court to reduce or suspend the[   ]d
wh[After each section of a uniform law, the official Comment of the   ]f
a p[Commissioners is given explaining that section.   ]y
an opportunity to be heard in reference to the request. Upon good cause shown, the request may be filed and heard in camera. The judge hearing the motion may reduce or suspend the sentence if the judge finds that the assistance rendered was substantial.

Comment

  Except for Section 406, which contains a specific reference to a misdemeanor, criminal penalties throughout the Act are referred to by language "is guilty of a crime and upon conviction may be imprisoned for not more than [ ], fined not more than [ ], or both." States that have a criminal penalty classification system should replace this language with references to their classified penalties, e.g., "is guilty of a class [ ] felony." Actual penalties are not included because it is felt that such a designation is purely a state decision. The penalties imposed under the federal act are found at 21 U.S.C. 841, and additional federal penalties were created by the Anti–Drug Abuse Act of 1986, Public Law 99–570. The criminal penalties in subsection (a) are classified based on the penalties in the federal act, 21 U.S.C.
841(b) as amended by the Anti–Drug Abuse Act of 1986, Public Law 99–570, § 1002 (the "Narcotics Penalties and Enforcement Act of 1986"). In subsection (a)(1) there are no references to amounts of mixtures or substances containing the proscribed controlled substances, and the adopting State should insert amounts appropriate for that State. A reference to an amount is contained in subsection (a)(1)(vii) with respect to marijuana to allow a State that includes this provision to distinguish this provision from subsection (a)(5). Subsections (b), (d), and (e) are based on Florida Statutes Section 893.135. Subsection (c) is based on the offense in the federal act with respect to piperidine, added in 1978 and found in 21 U.S.C. 841(d).

[Illustration 19–12]

PAGES FROM UNIFORM LAWS ANNOTATED, MASTER EDITION, VOLUME 9, PART II

§ 302   CONTROLLED SUBSTANCES (1994)

(2) a common or contract carrier or warehouseman, or an employee thereof, whose possession of any controlled substance is in the usual course of business or employment; and

(3) an ultimate user or a person in possession of a controlled substance pursuant to a lawful order of a practitioner or in lawful possession of a substance included in Schedule V.

(d) The [appropriate person or agency] by rule may waive the requirement for registration of certain manufacturers, distributors, or dispensers upon finding it consistent with the public health and safety.

(e) A separate registration is required for each principal place of business or professional practice where the applicant manufactures, distributes, or dispenses controlled substances.

(f) The [appropriate person or agency] may inspect the establishment of a registrant or applicant for registration in accordance with rules adopted by the [appropriate person or agency].

Comment

This section requires any person who engages in, or intends to engage in, manufacturing, distributing, or dispensing of

designed to eliminate many sources of diversion, both actual and potential.

Common and contract carriers, ware-

At the end of each section of a uniform law, references are given to additional research aids. Also, annotations are provided to all court cases citing the section. The supplementation should always be checked for later information.

stances, the State will know who is responsible for a substance and who is dealing in these substances. The registration requirements imposed by this section are

In addition, the annual registration requirement will be a form of check on persons authorized to deal in controlled substances.

Library References

Controlled Substances ☞10.
Westlaw Topic No. 96H.

Notes of Decisions

Generally   1
Corporations   4
Exempt persons   8
Federal action and requirements   3
Part-time pharmacist   6
Purpose of law   2
Residents and nonresidents   5
State officers   9
Status of unregistered persons and entities   7

Ultimate user exemption   10

---

1. Generally

When viewed in the context of the Controlled Substances Act as a whole, the right to possess drugs incident to professional use is dependent on compliance with the Act's registration requirement. State v. Mann, R.I.1978, 382 A.2d 1319, 119 R.I. 720. Controlled Substances ☞ 41

92

[Illustration 19–13]

PAGE FROM UNIFORM LAWS ANNOTATED, DIRECTORY OF UNIFORM ACTS AND CODES

DIRECTORY OF UNIFORM ACTS

Title of Act	Uniform Laws Annotated Volume	Page
Adoption Act (1994)	9, Pt. IA	11
Adoption Act (1969)	9, Pt. IA	133
Child Abduction Prevention Act	9, Pt. IA	Pocket Part
Child Custody Jurisdiction Act	9, Pt. IA	261
Child Custody Jurisdiction and Enforcement Act	9, Pt. IA	649
Civil Liability for Support Act	9, Pt. IB	1
Gifts to Minors Act (1966)	8A	297
Gifts to Minors Act (1956)	8A	299
Interstate Family Support Act (2001)	9, Pt. IB	159
Interstate Family Support Act (1996)	9, Pt. IB	281
Interstate Family Support Act (1992)	9, Pt. IB	469
Juvenile Court Act	9A	1
Parentage Act (2000)	9B	295
Parentage Act (1973)	9B	377
Paternity Act	9C	1
Putative and Unknown Fathers Act	9C	59
Reciprocal Enforcement of Support Act (1968)	9C	81
Reciprocal Enforcement of Support Act (1950)	9C	273
Revised Abortion Act	9, Pt. IA	1
Status of Children of Assisted Conception	9C	363
Transfers to Minors Act	8C	1
Civil Liability for Support Act	9, Pt. IB	1
Class Actions [Act] [Rule] (Model)	12	93
Code of Military Justice	11	197
Collaborative Law Act	7, Pt. IB	Pocket Part
Collateral Consequences of Conviction Act	11	Pocket Part

This table lists all uniform laws contained in the set and shows in which volume the text of the uniform law can be located. The uniform laws are also available on the NCCUSL website at http://www.uniformlawcommission.com/Acts.aspx. This website arranges the acts alphabetically, by subject matter, and by state.

Common Trust Fund Act	7, Pt. II	180
Community Property, Disposition of Community Property Rights at Death Act	8A	213
Comparative Fault Act	12	121
Computer Information Transactions Act	7, Pt. II	199
Condominium Act	7, Pt. II	485
Conflict of Law-Limitations Act	12	155
Conservation Easement Act	12	165
Construction Lien Act	7, Pt. III	1
Consumer Credit Code (1974)	7, Pt. III	88
Consumer Credit Code (1968)	7, Pt. III	285
Consumer Leases Act	7A, Pt. I	1
Consumer Sales Practices Act	7A, Pt. I	69
Contribution Among Tortfeasors Act	12	193
Controlled Substances Act (1994)	9, Pts. II, III, IV, V	1
Controlled Substances Act (1990)	9, Pt. V	781
Controlled Substances Act (1970)	9, Pt. V	853
Conveyances, Fraudulent Conveyance Act	7A, Pt. II	1
Correction or Clarification of Defamation Act	12	315
Corrections, Sentencing and Corrections Act (Model)	10	325
Crime Victims Reparations Act	11	61
Crimes and criminals, Attendance of Witnesses from Without the State in Criminal Proceedings, Act to Secure	11	1
Crime Victims Reparations Act	11	61

[Illustration 19–14]

PAGE FROM UNIFORM LAWS ANNOTATED, DIRECTORY OF UNIFORM ACTS AND CODES, TABLE OF JURISDICTIONS LISTING UNIFORM ACTS ADOPTED

TABLE OF JURISDICTIONS LISTING UNIFORM ACTS ADOPTED

———

List of jurisdictions, in alphabetical order, listing the Uniform Acts or Codes adopted by that particular jurisdiction, and where each may be found in Uniform Laws Annotated, Master Edition.

Each Uniform Act or Code in the Master Edition contains a Table showing the statutory citations of each of the adopting jurisdictions.

———

ALABAMA

Title of Act	Uniform Laws Annotated Volume	Page
Adult Guardianship and Protective Proceedings Jurisdiction Act	8A	Pocket Part
Anatomical Gift Act (2006)	8A	Pocket Part
Anatomical Gift Act (1968)	8A	69
Athlete Agents Act (2000)	7, Pt. IB	53
Attendance of Witnesses From Without a State in Criminal Proceedings, Act to Secure	11	1
Certification of Questions of Law Act (1967)	12	61
Child Abduction Prevention Act Jurisdiction and Enforcement Act	9, Pt. IA	Pocket Part
Child Custody Jurisdiction and Enforcement Act	9, Pt. IA	649
Commercial Code [1]	1 to 3B	
Common Trust Fund Act	7, Pt. II	180
Condominium Act	7, Pt. II	485
Conservation Easement Act	12	165
Controlled Substances Act (1994)	9, Pts. II, III, IV, V	1
Controlled Substances Act (1990)	9, Pt. V	781
Controlled Substances Act (1970)	9, Pt. V	853
Criminal Extradition Act	11	63

This table lists all uniform laws contained in the set and shows in which volume the text of the uniform law can be located. The uniform laws are also available on the NCCUSL website at http://www.nccusl.org/nccusl/uniformacts.asp. This website arranges the acts alphabetically, by subject matter, and by state.

Environmental Covenants Act	13, Pt. I	Pocket Part
Estate Tax Apportionment Act (2003)	8A	Pocket Part
Federal Lien Registration Act	7A, Pt. I	328
Fiduciaries Act	7A, Pt. I	364
Foreign-Country Money Judgments Recognition Act	13, Pt. II	Pocket Part
Fraudulent Transfer Act	7A, Pt. II	2
Guardianship and Protective Proceedings Act (1982)	8A	429
Health-Care Decisions Act	9, Pt. IB	83
Interstate Depositions and Discovery Act	13, Pt. II	Pocket Part
Interstate Enforcement of Domestic–Violence Protection Orders Act	9, Pt. IB	133
Interstate Family Support Act (1996)	9, Pt. IB	281
Limited Liability Company Act (1996)	6B	545
Limited Partnership Act (2001)	6A	325

11

[Illustration 19-15]

PAGE FROM UNIFORM LAWS ANNOTATED, MASTER EDITION, VOLUME 9,
PART II, TABLE OF JURISDICTIONS ADOPTING THE UNIFORM
CONTROLLED SUBSTANCES ACT

UNIFORM LAWS ANNOTATED

UNIFORM CONTROLLED SUBSTANCES ACT (1994)

1994 ACT

(Last amended or revised in 1994)

*The National Conference of Commissioners on Uniform State Laws
changed the designation of the Controlled Substances Acts (1990)(1994)
from Uniform to Model as approved by the Executive Committee on July
11, 2006.*

*See, also, the Uniform Controlled Substances Acts (1990) and (1970),
in Vol. 9, Pt. V Uniform Laws Annotated, Master Edition or ULA
Database on Westlaw.*

**Table of Jurisdictions Wherein Either the 1970, 1990, or 1994 Versions
of the Act or a Combination Thereof Has Been Adopted** [1]

Jurisdiction	Laws	Effective Date	Statutory Citation
Alabama	1971, No. 140	9–16–1971 *	Code 1975, §§ 20–2–1 to 20–2–190.
Alaska	1982, c. 45	1–1–1983	AS 11.71.010 to 11.71.900, 17.30.010 to 17.30.900.
Arizona	1979, c. 103	7–1–1980	A.R.S. §§ 36–2501 to 36–2553.
Arkansas [2]	1971, No. 590	4–7–1971	A.C.A. §§ 5–64–101 to 5–64–608.
California	1972, c. 1407	3–7–1973	West's Ann.Cal. Health & Safety Code, §§ 11000 to 11657.
Colorado			18–18–
Connecti			
Delawar			
District			8–901.01 to
Florida			65.
Georgia	1974, p. 221	7–1–1974	O.C.G.A. §§ 16–13–20 to 16–13–56.
Hawaii	1972, c. 10	1–1–1973	HRS §§ 329–1 to 329–128.
Idaho	1971, c. 215	5–1–1971	I.C. §§ 37–2701 to 37–2751.
Illinois	1971, P.A. 77–757	8–16–1971	S.H.A. 720 ILCS 570/100 to 570/603.
Indiana	1976, P.L. 148	7–1–1977	West's A.I.C. 35–48–1–1 to 35–48–7–15.
Iowa	1971, c. 148	7–1–1971	I.C.A. §§ 124.101 to 124.602.
Kansas	1972, c. 234	7–1–1972	K.S.A. 65–4101 to 65–4166.
Kentucky	1972, c. 226	7–1–1972	KRS 218A.010 to 218A.993.
Louisiana	1972, No. 634	7–26–1972	LSA–R.S. 40:961 to 40:995.
Maine	1975, c. 499	5–1–1976	17–A M.R.S.A. §§ 1101 to 1118.
	1941, c. 251	4–16–1941	22 M.R.S.A. §§ 2383, 2383–A, 2383–B.
Maryland	2002, c. 26	10–1–2002	Criminal Law, §§ 5–101 to 5–1101.
Massachusetts	1971, c. 1071	7–1–1972	M.G.L.A. c. 94C, §§ 1 to 48.
Michigan	1978, No. 368	9–30–1978	M.C.L.A. §§ 333.7101 to 333.7545.
Minnesota	1971, c. 937	6–18–1971	M.S.A. §§ 152.01 to 152.20.
Mississippi	1971, c. 521	4–16–1971	Code 1972, §§ 41–29–101 to 41–29–185.
Missouri	1971, H.B. No. 69	9–28–1971	V.A.M.S. §§ 195.010 to 195.320.
Montana	1973, c. 412	7–1–1973	MCA 50–32–101 to 50–32–405.

> A table, preceding the start of each uniform law, indicates
> the jurisdictions that have adopted the Act, its effective date,
> and where it can be located in the state's code and session
> laws.

Chapter 20

PRACTICE MATERIALS AND OTHER RESOURCES*

This chapter covers a variety of resources that do not readily fit into any of the categories discussed in previous chapters. These resources include general legal reference sources, form books, jury instructions, law dictionaries and listings of legal abbreviations, directories, collections of quotations, court records and briefs, and attorney general opinions. The final section of this chapter discusses researching the subject of legal ethics.

A. GENERAL LEGAL REFERENCE SOURCES

Often researchers need information that is not strictly legal, such as statistics, maps, information on state and federal agencies, interest and annuity tables, abbreviations, and addresses and telephone numbers for various groups and organizations. At other times, quick reference may be needed to the U.S. Constitution, the *Model Rules of Professional Conduct*, biographies, bibliographies, and succinct discussions of legal concepts and legal issues. Although no single resource can respond to all legal ready-reference needs, those described below collectively fill the most frequent needs.

a. American Jurisprudence 2d Desk Book (Thomson Reuters). This volume, with pocket supplements, consists of four parts: historical documents, international agreements, and organizations; federal government and agencies; national statistics; and research and practice aids. It includes such items as federal agency organization charts, population statistics, medical diagrams, compound interest and annuity tables, and tables of weights and measures.[1]

b. Arlene L. Eis, Legal Researcher's Desk Reference (Infosources Publishing, biennial). This volume includes addresses and phone numbers for agencies, elected officials, clerks, U.S. attorneys, law publishers, and other law-related organizations, plus state court structure charts, legal research bibliographies, state information and statistics, and tables of economic information. Subscribers to the print edition also have access to an electronic version.

c. Law and Legal Information Directory (Steven Wasserman et al. eds., Gale Cengage Learning, annual). This volume provides descriptions and contact information for institutions, services, and facilities in the law and legal information industry

---

* This chapter was revised by Jane O'Connell, Deputy Director, Tarlton Law Library, Jamail Center for Legal Research, University of Texas School of Law.

[1] The *American Jurisprudence 2d Desk Book* is a component of the *American Jurisprudence 2d* (*Am. Jur. 2d*) legal encyclopedia. Other related components include *American Jurisprudence Proof of Facts* and *American Jurisprudence Trials*, discussed in Chapter 16, and *American Jurisprudence Legal Forms* and *American Jurisprudence Pleading and Practice Forms Annotated*, discussed later in this chapter.

412 PRACTICE MATERIALS AND OTHER RESOURCES CH. 20

including bar associations, federal courts, law schools, scholarships and grants, legal periodicals, lawyer referral services, legal aid offices, and public defender offices.

d. *The Lawyer's Almanac* (Aspen Publishers, annual). This volume contains four main sections: (1) The Legal Profession, which provides information on the nation's 700 largest law firms, mandatory continuing legal education (CLE) requirements in the fifty states, bar exam statistics, state bar associations, and ABA leadership; (2) The Judiciary, which includes contact information for federal courts and state supreme courts along with federal litigation statistics; (3) Government Departments and Agencies, which includes contact information for federal agencies and state attorneys general along with where to request vital records for each state; and (4) Commonly Used Abbreviations.

e. *Oxford Companion to American Law* (Kermit Hall ed., 2002). With 500 entries ranging from broad topics such as environmental law to specific cases such as *Palsgraf v. Long Island Railroad Co.*, this volume aims to provide a contextual overview of American law.

f. Dana Shilling, *Lawyer's Desk Book* (Aspen Publishers, annual). This volume contains topical discussions on such matters as business planning and litigation, contract and property law, financial and credit law, personal planning, tax issues, civil litigation, criminal law, and law office issues.

B. FORMS

Drafting legal documents such as wills, trusts, and leases is an essential part of law practice. Form books and software provide sample legal documents that can be tailored to specific situations. Today, it is common for practitioners to store electronically documents that have been created for subsequent revision and reuse. Most of the resources described below are available in both print and electronic formats.

1. General Forms

General form books provide forms for all aspects of legal practice and are typically multivolume sets. They are often annotated with references to cases that have favorably construed provisions contained in the form. Editorial comment also is frequently included. Examples of general form books are:

a. *American Jurisprudence Legal Forms, 2d* (Thomson Reuters) (available in *Westlaw*). This set includes more than 22,000 legal forms organized into 268 topical chapters. Arranged alphabetically by topic, each chapter contains form drafting guides, notes on use, and sample forms. Two separate volumes, *Federal Tax Guide to Legal Forms*, serve as a companion to the larger set.

b. *American Jurisprudence Pleading and Practice Forms Annotated* (Thomson Reuters) (available in *Westlaw*). This set contains more than 43,000 state and federal forms. Arranged alphabetically by topic, the set provides research references in addition to forms for notices, complaints, petitions, declarations, answers, counterclaims, cross-complaints, interrogatories, motions, affidavits, orders, jury instructions, findings of fact, and judgments.

c. *Nichols Cyclopedia of Legal Forms, Annotated* (Thomson Reuters) (available in *Westlaw*). This set of transactional forms covers over 230 topics of law, arranged alphabetically and ranging from abandonment and abstracts of title to workers' compensation and zoning. Each subject area contains an overview of the topic, tax implications, drafting checklists, and references to other publications along with forms.

d. Jacob Rabkin & Mark H. Johnson, *Current Legal Forms with Tax Analysis* (Matthew Bender LexisNexis) (available in *LexisNexis*). This set provides transactional forms for corporate, commercial, employment, family/estate planning, and real estate matters. It does not cover criminal law or litigation. Each chapter includes a tax background, a practice background, drafting guidelines, and forms.

e. *West's Legal Forms, 3d, 4th,* and *5th eds.* (Thomson Reuters) (available in *Westlaw*). This set is organized into twelve major topics: Agents and Independent Contractors, Alternative Dispute Resolution, Business Organizations with Tax Analysis, Commercial Transactions, Debtor and Creditor Relations, Domestic Relations with Tax Analysis, Elder Law, Employment, Estate Planning with Tax Analysis, Intellectual Property, Real Estate Transactions, and Retirement Plans with Tax Analysis. Additionally, the set offers a section of specialized forms such as computer contracts, franchise agreements, and nonprofit organizations. The set is currently being revised, resulting in some volumes being part of the third edition and others being part of the fourth or fifth editions.

2. Federal Forms

Some form books are created specifically for practice in the federal courts. Examples of federal forms are:

a. *Bender's Federal Practice Forms* (LexisNexis Matthew Bender) (available in *LexisNexis*). This set, a companion to the treatise *Moore's Federal Practice*, provides a complete range of litigation forms needed for practice in any federal court. Twelve volumes cover civil proceedings in federal district courts, from initial complaint through trials and post-trial motions and provide relevant forms. Two volumes cover criminal prosecutions in the federal district courts. Additional volumes provide forms for civil and criminal appeals to the United States courts of appeals, and proceedings in the U.S. Supreme Court.

b. *West's Federal Forms* (Thomson Reuters) (available in *Westlaw*). A companion to the treatise Wright & Miller's *Federal Practice and Procedure* (often called "Wright and Miller," after its first two authors), this set provides procedural forms for civil and criminal matters arranged by the particular federal court to which they pertain. In addition to the United States Supreme Court, courts of appeals and district courts, bankruptcy and admiralty courts also are covered.

c. *Federal Procedural Forms, Lawyers' Edition* (Thomson Reuters) (available in *Westlaw*). A companion to *Federal Procedure, Lawyers' Edition*, this set is arranged by topic, and provides guidance for drafting forms for use before federal courts and—notably—administrative agencies.

3. Subject Form Books

Many form books are devoted to a particular subject or to a particular phase of the litigation process. Examples of subject forms are:

a. *National*

(1) *Bender's Forms of Discovery* (LexisNexis Matthew Bender) (available in *LexisNexis*). This set provides sample interrogatories under more than 200 categories,

from accountants and advertising to x-rays and zoning. Additional volumes focus on discovery under the Federal Rules of Civil Procedure and state rules and provide charts comparing the discovery rules of the fifty states with the federal discovery rules.

(2) *Fletcher Corporation Forms, Annotated, 4th and 5th eds.* (Clark Boardman Callaghan Thomson Reuters) (available in *Westlaw*). This set, cross-referenced to the treatise *Fletcher Cyclopedia Corporations*, is divided into thirty-two categories that cover various areas of corporate law, such as pre-incorporation contracts, bylaws, organization of corporation, corporate financing, directors and meetings, consolidations and mergers, and rolling stock agreements. The set is currently being revised resulting in some volumes being part of the fifth edition and others being part of the fourth edition.

(3) F. Lee Bailey & Kenneth J. Fishman, *Complete Manual of Criminal Forms, 3d ed.* (Clark Boardman Callaghan Thomson Reuters) (available in *Westlaw*). The set contains over 1,000 federal and state criminal forms covering criminal matters from pre-trial proceedings through the trial to post-trial proceedings.

(4) Michael L.M. Jordan, *Drafting Wills & Trust Agreements, 4th ed.* (Clark Boardman Callaghan Thomson Reuters). This set provides forms for drafting will or trust agreements with a focus on estate planning, federal tax law, and various state laws relevant to estate planning.

b. State. There are also many state-specific form books focused on local practice. These are published both by commercial publishers and by state bar associations. They contain the same features as the form books discussed above, but are designed for local use and, therefore, may be more useful for the practitioner. Examples of state-specific form books include:

(1) *California Legal Forms: Transaction Guide* (Matthew Bender LexisNexis) (available in *LexisNexis*). This set provides California-specific, transactional forms for business and nonprofit organizations, real estate transactions, commercial transactions, wills and trusts, contracts and obligations, and personal transactions

(2) *West's Texas Forms, 3d ed.* (Thomson Reuters) (available in *Westlaw*). This set is organized into ten major topics: Creditors Remedies and Debtors Rights, Administrative Practice, Business Litigation Minerals, Oil and Gas, Business Entities, Civil Trial and Appellate Practice, Estate Planning, Administration of Decedents Estates, Real Property, and Family Law. Each topic features legal summaries in addition to numerous forms.

4. Other Sources of Forms

a. Forms in Treatises. Many treatises include forms, either integrated into the text or in separate volumes.

b. State Codes. Some state codes include both substantive and procedural forms. Within a particular state code, consult the general index under Forms.

c. Internet. A wide variety of websites provide legal forms. The providers include federal agencies (such as the Internal Revenue Service and the Copyright Office), state agencies, courts, public service organizations, law schools, and commercial vendors. General forms on the Internet may or may not accurately reflect the law of a specific jurisdiction.

C. JURY INSTRUCTIONS;
VERDICT AND SETTLEMENT AWARDS

1. Jury Instructions

Before a jury begins deliberations, the judge instructs it on the applicable law. Attorneys often have the opportunity to submit proposed instructions to the judge, tailoring these instructions to the evidence and theory of the case. It is at the judge's discretion whether to use these instructions, modify them, use his or her own instructions, or use instructions from other sources.

Many publications contain "pattern" or "model" jury instructions. Some of these are prepared for use with particular subjects such as antitrust, torts, employment discrimination, or medical malpractice. Some are designed for use in specific states or specific federal courts. The Federal Judicial Center, the Judicial Conference of the United States, and committees of the various circuits often are instrumental in preparing federal circuit instructions. These instructions are published in pamphlet form and often are available on a court's website.[2] Two commercially published sets that contain extensive collections of instructions for use in the federal courts, together with commentary and case references, are:

a.   Kevin F. O'Malley et al., *Federal Jury Practice and Instructions: Civil and Criminal, 5th and 6th eds.* (Thomson Reuters) (available in *Westlaw*). This set provides instructions for federal civil and criminal trials including instructions for specific federal crimes and types of civil actions governed by federal law. The pattern or model jury instructions promulgated by a number of federal circuits are also included. The set is currently being revised, resulting in some volumes being part of the fifth edition and others being part of the sixth edition.

b.   John S. Siffert, *Modern Federal Jury Instructions* (Matthew Bender LexisNexis) (available in *LexisNexis*). Both civil and criminal instructions are provided along with commentary, case references, and frequent citations to the "pattern" or "model" jury instructions of a number of federal circuits.

2. Verdict and Settlement Awards

Legal researchers often seek information about the amount of damages that might be awarded in a particular type of case. This information can influence an attorney's decision whether to accept a case, go to trial, or settle. For state-specific information, the National Association of State Jury Verdict Publishers' website[3] provides links to various regional publications focused on verdicts and settlement awards. *Westlaw* and *LexisNexis* also have extensive verdict and settlement databases that can be searched by specific jurisdiction. The following publications provide general information about jury verdicts and settlements:

a.   *Personal Injury Valuation Handbooks* (Jury Verdicts Thomson Reuters) (available in *Westlaw*). This nine-volume set is arranged by type of injury, recovery probabilities, and psychological factors affecting verdicts. Each report focuses on a

---

[2] For example, both civil and criminal jury instructions are available on the website of the United States Court of Appeals for the Fifth Circuit, http://www.lb5.uscourts.gov/juryinstructions/.

[3] http://www.juryverdicts.com.

specific injury or liability and provides comparable case summaries, distribution of settlements and awards, and award medians, means, and probability ranges for recent years.

      b.   *What's It Worth: A Guide to Current Personal Injury Awards and Settlements* (Matthew Bender LexisNexis). This publication contains summaries of decisions and settlements during the previous three years. Arrangement is by specific type of injury and then alphabetically by state. *LexisNexis* has files with this title preceded by state postal abbreviations (e.g., "AK—What's It Worth? A Guide to Personal Injury Awards and Settlements").

D.   LAW DICTIONARIES

      Law dictionaries provide definitions of legal terms derived from a variety of sources, including learned treatises and judicial opinions. Some legal dictionaries provide references that trace the etymology of the word or phrase being defined. It is important to read the introductory matter of the dictionary being consulted to understand the sources and methods used to develop its definitions.[4]

      The multivolume set *Words and Phrases,* discussed in Chapter 7, Section M, includes digests from judicial opinions in which a word or phrase has been judicially interpreted. *Words and Phrases* can also be used as a dictionary, but because it is limited to the definitions of words as set forth in judicial opinions, it is not a comprehensive dictionary of legal terms.

      Several law dictionaries currently are available on the Internet and are easily searchable. The Legal Information Institute's website at Cornell University Law School includes *Wex,* an electronic dictionary.[5] Commercial publishers such as Law.com,[6] Nolo,[7] and Findlaw.com[8] also provide their own online legal dictionaries. The websites of many law school libraries provide links to a variety of reference materials, including online legal dictionaries.

      Described below are some of the more commonly used American and British law dictionaries. The commercially published dictionaries are more thorough and more authoritative than the dictionaries available free on the web.

1.   American Law Dictionaries

      a.   *Ballentine's Law Dictionary, with Pronunciations* (3d ed. 1969) (Lawyers Cooperative Publishing Company) (available in *LexisNexis*). This volume contains over 40,000 definitions of legal terms and often provides citations to *A.L.R. Annotations, American Jurisprudence 2d,* and relevant case law.

      b.   *Black's Law Dictionary* (Brian A. Garner ed., 9th ed. 2009) (Thomson Reuters) (available in *Westlaw*). *Black's* is the most widely used of all law dictionaries and contains over 45,000 definitions. Individual entries may contain references to statutes,

---

      [4] *See* ANTONIN SCALIA & BRYAN A. GARNER, *A Note on the Use of Dictionaries, in* READING LAW: THE INTERPRETATION OF LEGAL TEXTS 415 (2012) (discussing legal and English dictionaries, with a chronological table of dictionaries helpful for determining usage).

      [5] http://topics.law.cornell.edu/wex.

      [6] http://dictionary.law.com/.

      [7] http://www.nolo.com/dictionary/.

      [8] http://dictionary.findlaw.com/.

West key numbers, and *Corpus Juris Secondum*. An abridged, paperback version (2010) and a third pocket edition (2006) are also available, as is an iPad app.[9] The tenth edition of *Black's* will be published in 2014.

    c. *Bouvier's Law Dictionary and Concise Encyclopedia* (8th ed., 3d rev. 1914) (West Publishing Company; reprinted by William S. Hein & Co., 1984) (available in *HeinOnline*).[10] Although outdated, this is a particularly scholarly work. Many of its definitions are encyclopedic in nature, and it remains useful for many historical terms. The first edition was published in 1837. In addition to the 1914 edition, *HeinOnline* includes editions from 1839, 1848, 1871, 1883, and 1897.[11]

    d. Gerry W. Beyer, *Modern Dictionary for the Legal Profession* (4th ed. 2008) (William S. Hein & Co.). This work, containing more than 10,000 terms, focuses on modern terminology and includes slang and colloquialisms.

    e. William C. Burton, *Burton's Legal Thesaurus* (4th ed. 2006) (McGraw Hill). This volume includes words in legal contexts, words used by the legal community, and words used in legal communications. It includes "associated concepts" and translations of many foreign words and phrases.

    f. Susan Ellis Wild, *Webster's New World Law Dictionary* (2006) (Wiley). This volume contains definitions of more than 4,000 legal terms, common abbreviations, foreign words and phrases, and the United States Constitution.

    g. Bryan A. Garner, *Garner's Dictionary of Legal Usage* (3d ed. 2011) (Oxford University Press). Containing definitions, spelling rules, and grammar guidelines, this volume provides clear and persuasive guidance on many usage questions.

    h. *The Law Dictionary* (7th ed. 1997) (Anderson Publishing Company) (available in *LexisNexis*). Containing over 5,000 legal terms, this volume is a condensed dictionary including a Table of Abbreviations. The version in *LexisNexis* is updated annually, according to the information screen.

    i. Daniel Oran, *Oran's Dictionary of the Law* (4th ed. 2008) (Thomson/Delmar Learning). This dictionary is written for a wide audience with concise, accessible definitions. A brief introduction to legal research is also included.

    j. *The Wolters Kluwer Bouvier Law Dictionary* (Stephen Michael Sheppard ed., 2011). Derived from the nineteenth century classic law dictionary, this work offers updated definitions. It is available in a compact edition, desk edition, and mobile apps.

2. British Law Dictionaries

    a. *A Dictionary of Law* (Elizabeth A. Martin & Jonathan Law eds., 7th ed. 2009) (Oxford University Press). This volume includes over 4,200 entries that define the major terms, concepts, processes, and the organization of the English legal system and provides citations to relevant case law.

---

[9] For a discussion of the online and iPad versions, see Mary Whisner, *Books on My Desk*, 104 LAW LIBR. J. 597, 603–04 (2012).

[10] *HeinOnline* has a large collection of law dictionaries from the eighteenth and nineteenth centuries, in the library called "Spinelli's Law Library Reference Shelf."

[11] *See* Mary Whisner, *Dictionaries Make Strange Bedfellows, in* LANGUAGE AND THE LAW: PROCEEDINGS OF A CONFERENCE, Dec. 6–8, 2001, at 93 (Marlyn Robinson ed., 2003), *available at* http://ssrn.com/abstract= 1344744 (discussing John Bouvier, the development of the dictionary, and its current use).

b.   *Jowitt's Dictionary of English Law* (Daniel Greenberg ed., 3d ed. 2010) (Sweet & Maxwell). This set aims to provide a comprehensive lexicon of English law and includes the historical context of words, citations to relevant cases and statutes, and cross-references to *Stroud's Judicial Dictionary of Words and Phrases*. European terms are also included insofar as they form part of the law of England and Wales.

c.   James Penner, *The Law Student's Dictionary* (13th ed. 2008) (Oxford University Press). This source includes entries on core student topics.

d.   *Osborn's Concise Law Dictionary* (Mick Woodley ed., 12th ed. 2013) (Sweet & Maxwell). This volume includes technical terms and phrases in both English and European law; extensive references for further research; and a Table of Law Reports, Journals, and Abbreviations.

e.   *Stroud's Judicial Dictionary of Words and Phrases* (Daniel Greenberg & Alexandra Millbrook eds., 8th ed. 2012 & 2013 supp.) (Sweet & Maxwell). This multivolume set includes historic, archaic, and obscure legal terms and expressions, along with numerous case citations and references to statutes.

3.   Special Law Dictionaries

A number of bilingual and multilingual law dictionaries are available, such as English–Spanish, English–Portuguese, English–Japanese, and English–French–German. A dictionary that explains the use of Latin terminology in a broader context is Russ VerSteeg, *Essential Latin for Lawyers* (Carolina Academic Press 1990). Some legal dictionaries are devoted to specific subjects, such as labor law, family law, environmental law, and taxation. Listed below are several subject-specific legal dictionaries:

a.   James R. Fox, *Dictionary of International & Comparative Law* (3d ed. 2003) (Oxford University Press).

b.   Bryan A. Garner, *A Handbook of Family Law Terms* (West 2001).

c.   Bryan A. Garner, *A Handbook of Criminal Law Terms* (West 2000).

d.   James J. King, *The Environmental Dictionary and Regulatory Cross-Reference* (3d ed. 1995) (Wiley).

e.   John P Grant and J. Craig Barker, *Parry & Grant Encyclopaedic Dictionary of International Law* (3d ed. 2009) (Oxford University Press).

f.   Robert Sellers Smith, *West's Tax Dictionary* (West, annual).

g.   Richard A. Westin, *WG & L Tax Dictionary* (Warren, Gorham & Lamont, biennial).

E.   LEGAL ABBREVIATIONS

Many legal dictionaries and books about legal research contain tables of abbreviations. The following resources also are especially useful in determining the meaning of legal abbreviations:

1.   Mary Miles Prince, *Prince's Bieber Dictionary of Legal Abbreviations* (6th ed. 2009) (William S. Hein & Co.). (The 5th ed. is available in *LexisNexis*.) This volume is divided into two parts. The first part sets forth the abbreviation followed by the word or words represented. The second part sets forth the word or words followed by the abbreviation.

2. Mary Miles Prince, *Prince's Dictionary of Legal Citations* (7th ed. 2006) (William S. Hein & Co.). This volume provides examples of statutes, reporters, and legal periodicals in *Bluebook* form.

3. Donald Raistrick, *Index to Legal Citations and Abbreviations* (3d ed. 2008) (Sweet & Maxwell). This publication focuses on the legal literature of the United Kingdom, the Commonwealth, Europe, and the United States and includes over 34,000 legal abbreviations.

4. *World Dictionary of Legal Abbreviations* (Igor I. Kavass & Mary Miles Prince, eds., 1991) (William S. Hein & Co.). Includes abbreviations and acronyms from many jurisdictions in many languages (English, Bulgarian, French, German, Hebrew, Italian, Japanese, Korean, Portuguese, and Spanish). Volume 4 provides abbreviations by subjects, such as environment, maritime, military, and taxation.

F. LAW DIRECTORIES

Law directories are useful for locating information about lawyers, law firms, courts, and administrative agencies. Law directories vary in their scope of coverage. Some directories attempt to list all lawyers; others are limited to a region, state, municipality, or practice specialty.

Many law directories are available online, where they can be updated more frequently than an annual printed publication. In addition, the websites of organizations such as state bar associations may provide access to databases, which often give current contact information and may provide biographical information about members. Moreover, websites for individual attorneys and law firms often provide the information that used to be found only in directories (name, address, bar admission), and much more (photographs, descriptions of practices, and so on).

The wealth of information available online has resulted in a dramatic shift in the publication of law directories, including the elimination of some print publications. Other publishers of print directories also provide electronic versions of the directory.

1. General Directories

a. *Martindale–Hubbell Law Directory* (Martindale–Hubbell, annual) (available in *LexisNexis* with the name LexisNexis Law Directory). *Martindale–Hubbell Law Directory*, an extensive directory of lawyers, law firms, and other related information, traces its roots to *The Martindale Directory*, first published in 1868. For decades, the print version of *Martindale–Hubbell Law Directory* was the most important law directory in the United States. The free electronic availability of its content through its website, http://www.martindale.com, and the related website, http://www.lawyers.com, has dramatically reduced the use of the print multivolume set. Numerous law libraries have ended their subscriptions to the print edition and now rely upon electronic resources.

The print set is composed of the United States Lawyer volumes, which included Practice Profiles and Professional Biographies arranged alphabetically by state. All lawyers admitted to the bar of any jurisdiction were eligible for a general listing in the Practice Profiles at no charge. The Professional Biographies are not comprehensive because inclusion in this section requires payment. Ratings obtained through confidential inquiries made to members of the bar also are given. These ratings attempt to evaluate legal ability and provide general recommendations.

The *Martindale–Hubbell International Law Directory* covers Europe, Asia, Australasia, the Middle East, Africa, North America, the Caribbean, and Central and South America and includes Professional Biographies.

b. *West Legal Directory.* Comprising more than a million profiles, this online directory contains profiles of law firms, a listing of branch offices, and biographical records of lawyers from the United States, Puerto Rico, the Virgin Islands, Canada, England, and Europe. *West Legal Directory can be accessed in Westlaw or FindLaw*[12] *and can be purchased on CD-ROM.* All attorneys are offered a free basic listing that includes name, firm name, contact information, areas of practice, bar admissions, and law school. For a fee, attorneys can include an expanded listing. A related service in *Westlaw*, PROFILER–WLD, provides biographical information and links to pleadings, filings, and briefs.

c. *Avvo.* Founded in 2006, *Avvo* (http://www.avvo.com) combines basic directory information with ratings and biographical information. *Avvo* starts by harvesting names and addresses from bar associations. Lawyers can claim their profiles (without charge) and add details about their practices, and clients and other lawyers can comment on lawyers. Ratings are based on years in practice, industry recognition (e.g., bar association awards), disciplinary history, and peer assessments. (Client ratings show on the profile but don't affect the overall rating.) *Avvo* currently has full coverage for just over half the states; the remaining states have incomplete coverage.[13]

d. *Justia Lawyers. Justia* provides a national directory of lawyers. Individuals may claim their profiles and add information without charge. (They may also claim their profiles and hide them from public view.) Some profiles provide extensive biographical information, including links to firms' websites. Other profiles have little more than name, address, and years in practice. Cornell's *Legal Information Institute* is associated with *Justia Lawyers.*[14]

e. *Who's Who in American Law* (Marquis Who's Who, biennial). This compilation contains biographical information on approximately 20,000 attorneys selected for their prominence as judges, educators, or practitioners. No claim is made to comprehensiveness in any area of the profession. The format is similar to that used in other Marquis *Who's Who* publications.

f. *Chambers USA: America's Leading Lawyers for Business* (Chambers & Partners, annual). This volume gives national rankings by practice areas and then alphabetically by state. Firms and individual lawyers are ranked based on their work and interviews with clients and industry experts. The volume also includes a firm index and lawyer index. A section of the *Chambers & Partners* website, http://www.chambers andpartners.com/, provides access to some of the information found in the print edition.

g. *Chambers Global: The World's Leading Lawyers* (Chambers & Partners, annual). This volume is organized alphabetically by country and only covers firms and lawyers engaged in global areas of practice. It provides a firm index and leading lawyers index. A section of the *Chambers & Partners* website, http://www.chambersandpartners. com/Global, provides access to some of the information found in the print edition.

---

[12] http://lawyers.findlaw.com/.

[13] *See Current State Coverage—Attorney Directory*, http://www.avvo.com/support/current_states.

[14] From *LII*'s directory, http://lawyers.law.cornell.edu/, the FAQ leads to *Justia*'s directory.

h. Martindale–Hubbell Canadian Law Directory (Martindale–Hubbell, annual). This one-volume directory, in a format similar to its American counterpart, is a guide to Canada's legal profession. The Canadian *Martindale–Hubbell* website, http://www. martindale-hubbell.ca/, and associated Canadian Lawyers website, http://www. canadian-lawyers.ca/, provides access to some of the information found in the print edition.

i. The American Bar including Lawyers of the world (Forster–Long, Inc., annual). These are annual biographical directories of prestigious United States and foreign lawyers. An individual attorney index, firm name and location index, and practice areas index are also included to aid users.

A paperback reference handbook provides an abridged version of the main set, and includes firm name, members, location, and contact information, including website and attorney email addresses when provided. Additionally, the *American Bar* website (http:// americanbar.com/)[15] provides access to some of the information found in the print edition.

j. Other International Directories. Many other companies publish directories that can be used to locate attorneys in particular countries. Among these directories are *The Canadian Law List* (Canada Law Book), *Chambers UK: The UK Leading Lawyers* (Chambers & Partners, annual), *The International Law List* (L. Corper–Mordaunt & Co.), and *Waterlow's Solicitors' & Barristers' Directory* (Waterlow).

2. State and Regional Directories

Directories of the attorneys practicing within a specific state also are available. Legal Directories Publishing Co., publishes directories for more than twenty states. These directories list attorneys by county and city, and also contain some biographical data. The website provides attorney, firm, and mediator listings.[16] In addition to print resources, many state bar organizations now make membership information available online.

3. Judicial Directories and Biographies

a. Directories

(1) *BNA's Directory of State and Federal Courts, Judges, and Clerks* (Bloomberg BNA, annual). This volume provides federal court information along with court information for each state in alphabetical order. For each court system, a flow chart of the court system is provided along with contact information for each individual court.

(2) *Federal-State Court Directory* (CQ Press, annual). This volume includes contact information for all federal courts, bankruptcy trustees, federal administrative law

---

[15] This website is owned by Forster–Long, Inc., the company that publishes *The American Bar* and *The American Bench.* It is not connected with the American Bar Association, whose website is http://americanbar. org.

[16] http://www.legaldirectories.com. The online directory includes all states, but lists only lawyers who have a membership in one of the twenty-one states for which the company has a directory. For example, searching for lawyers in California (for which the company does not have a directory) turned up lawyers who had "out of state listings" in Florida, Indiana, and Pennsylvania (states for which the company does publish directories).

judges, and state bar associations. For each state court system, a flow chart of the court system is provided along with limited contact information.

(3) *Judicial Staff Directory* (CQ Press, annual). This volume provides information on the court structure for the federal and state courts along with contact information for each court. A flow chart of the Department of Justice along with contact information for its various branches, a chart correlating counties and all cities with population over 1,500 with their federal circuit and district courts, an index of Article III judges, biographies for key judicial personnel, and an index to individuals are added features of the volume. An electronic version is available for a subscription fee.

(4) *United States Courts Court Locator* (Administrative Office of the U.S. Courts) (http://www.uscourts.gov/Court_Locator.aspx). This website provides links to contact court clerks (referred to as information clerks, an administrative function, to distinguish the position from that of from law clerks, who perform legal research and writing for an individual judge) and administrative offices for all federal courts.

b.   *Biographical Directories*

(1)   *Current*

(a)   *The Almanac of the Federal Judiciary* (Aspen Law & Business, biennial updates) (available in *Westlaw*). This is the most thorough source for biographical information on federal judges. In addition to the basic data found in other sources, such as address, education, and work experience, this directory includes descriptions of judges' noteworthy rulings and media coverage along with lawyers' anonymous evaluations of the judges' ability and temperament.

(b)   *The American Bench: Judges of the Nation* (Forster–Long, Inc., annual). This directory has biographical information about more than 18,000 judges at all levels of federal, state, and local courts with jurisdictional, structural, and geographical facts about the courts. Biographical information about state judges is organized alphabetically by state. An alphabetical name index and a gender ratio summary also are included.

(c)   *Biographical Directory of Federal Judges, 1789–present* (http://www.fjc.gov/history/home.nsf/page/judges.html). This database from the Federal Judicial Center covers all Article III judges throughout history. Searches can be limited to sitting judges. It is also possible to search by many other factors, including race, gender, nominating president, and confirmation date.

(c)   *Judicial Profiles* (ALM Media Properties) (available in *LexisNexis*). This database provides information about state and federal judges in California, Florida, Georgia, New Jersey, New York, Pennsylvania, and Texas. It has basic contact information for everyone and biographical information for some.

(2)   *Historical*

(a)   *Biographical Directory of the Federal Judiciary* (Bernan, 2001). The print volume covers 1789 to 2000 and includes the legislative history of each court, including its creation, addition of judgeships, and abolishment if applicable. Sections cover the Supreme Court, the circuit courts of appeals, the district courts, and courts of special jurisdiction. There are lists of every judge to serve on a specific court. A separate section provides biographical information for each of the judges. The texts of landmark legislation also are included.

Biographical Directory of Federal Judges, 1789–present, discussed above, is the online counterpart to this print source.

   (b)   Iris J. Wildman & Mark J. Handler, *Federal Judges and Justices: A Current Listing of Nominations, Confirmations, Elevations, Resignations, Retirements* (Fred B. Rothman & Co., 1987–2001). This source is a compilation of judicial nominations, confirmations, resignations, and retirement. It is divided by Congress from the 99th Congress (1985–1986) to the 107th Congress (2001–2002). Although the directory ceased publication in 2001, it contains useful information on judges that is not as easily found elsewhere.

4.   Academic Directories

The Association of American Law Schools compiles the *AALS Directory of Law Teachers* to serve the academic legal community. This annual volume provides addresses and phone numbers and biographical information about law school faculty, as well as a listing of faculty members arranged by teaching specialty. *HeinOnline* has every edition of this, 1922–2012.[17] No edition was prepared for 2013, but a new edition is expected in 2014.

The American Association of Law Libraries' *AALL Directory and Handbook* lists member law libraries in the United States and Canada, arranged geographically, and the law librarians employed by the member law libraries. A separate alphabetical list of law library personnel also is included. This directory can be accessed by AALL members from the AALL website.[18]

5.   Specialty Directories

Some directories list only attorneys specializing in particular areas of the law. Examples of these directories are *Lawyer's Register International by Specialties and Fields of Law* (Lawyer's Register), *Directory of Corporate Counsel* (Aspen) (available in *LexisNexis*), and Martindale–Hubbell's *International Arbitration and Dispute Resolution Directory*.

G.   LEGAL QUOTATIONS

A number of sources collect and index law-related quotations.[19] Examples include:

1.   Christopher A. Anzalone, *Encyclopedia of Supreme Court Quotations* (M.E. Sharpe, Inc., 2000). Quotations are grouped into thirteen broad themes (e.g., The Givers of Law, The Enforcers, The Least Dangerous Branch).

---

[17] The 2006–2007 edition is in *Westlaw* but is not being updated.

[18] http://www.aallnet.org.

[19] General interest quotation collections may be useful to legal writers as well.

2. Eugene C. Gerhart, *Quote It Completely! World Reference Guide to More Than 5,500 Memorable Quotations from Law and Literature* (William S. Hein & Co., 1998) (available in *HeinOnline*). This is a combined and enlarged edition of two separate collections: *Quote It!*, 1969; and *Quote It II*, 1988. Quotations are arranged by subject, with separate author and word indexes.

3. Simon James & Chantal Stebbings, *A Dictionary of Legal Quotations* (Macmillan Publishing Company, 1987). This volume is arranged under 160 subjects and includes indexes of authors, sources, and significant words.

4. Tony Lyons, *The Quotable Lawyer* (Lyons Press, 2002).

5. M. Frances McNamara, *2,000 Classic Legal Quotations* (Aqueduct Books, 1967; reprinted by Lawyers Cooperative Publishing in 1992). Quotations are arranged by subject; a general index also is included.

6. *The New Lawyer's Wit and Wisdom: Quotations on the Legal Profession, In Brief* (Bruce Nash & Allan Zullo eds., 2001) (Running Press). This volume contains quotations and brief anecdotes organized into 23 topical categories.

7. *Respectfully Quoted: A Dictionary of Quotations Requested from the Congressional Research Service* (Suzy Platt ed., Library of Congress 1989) (available as a searchable database at http://www.bartleby.com/73/). This volume contains 2,100 quotations, a significant number of which are law-related, gathered in response to congressional inquiries to the Congressional Research Service for quotations.

8. Fred R. Shapiro, *The Oxford Dictionary of American Legal Quotations* (Oxford University Press 1993). The most scholarly of the quotation books, this source contains more than 3,500 quotations by Americans about law or by non-Americans about United States law. It is arranged alphabetically by subject and chronologically within each subject. The volume also includes cross-references and author and keyword indexes.

9. David S. Shrager & Elizabeth Frost–Knappman, *The Quotable Lawyer* (rev. ed. 1998) (Checkmark Books). This volume contains more than 3,000 quotations arranged under 157 major subject headings. Author and subject indexes are included.

10. Margaret Graham Tebo, *Shakespeare for Lawyers: A Practical Guide to Quoting the Bard* (American Bar Association, 2010). Over 100 legal-related quotes from Shakespeare's plays and sonnets are analyzed in this volume.

11. Thomas Vesper, *Uncle Anthony's Unabridged Analogies, 3d: Quotes, Proverbs, Blessings & Toasts for Lawyers, Lecturers & Laypeople* (3d ed. 2012) (Thomson Reuters).

H. BRIEFS, RECORDS, AND ORAL ARGUMENTS

After a trial court or an intermediate court of appeals decides a case, the case may be appealed to a higher court. If the higher court considers the appeal, attorneys for each side submit written briefs in which they set forth the reasons why the appellate court should either affirm or reverse the lower court's decision. These briefs contain discussion and analysis of the law along with citation to authority supporting legal arguments. *Amicus curiae* ("friend of the court") briefs also may be filed by groups or individuals not parties to the case, but supporting one side or the other. Such *amicus curiae* briefs often are filed in cases before state supreme courts and the Supreme Court of the United States.

When available, the record of the trial court typically is submitted with the brief. This record usually contains the preliminary motions and pleadings in the case, transcripts of examination and cross-examination of witnesses, instructions to the jury, the opinion of the lower court, and various other exhibits.[20]

Briefs and records potentially can provide attorneys involved in similar cases with a great deal of information, together with a sense of what arguments have or have not succeeded with an appellate court. Oral arguments reveal the focus of the attorneys and judges during the in-court presentations.[21]

1. Supreme Court of the United States[22]

a. Records and Briefs. The more recent the case, the more likely it is that briefs will be available free on the web. Merits briefs since the October 2003 Term are available on the American Bar Association's site.[23] *FindLaw* provides petitioner, respondent, and *amicus* briefs from the October 1999 term to the October 2007 term at no charge.[24] All briefs filed by the Solicitor General on behalf of the government since the October 1998 term and selected briefs since 1982 are available on the Department of Justice's website.[25] Often organizations involved in Supreme Court cases post their own briefs.[26]

A small number of libraries receive print copies of briefs and records submitted to the Supreme Court of the United States. Most law school libraries and some large bar association libraries have these briefs and records available in microform or in electronic format. *Records and Briefs of the United States Supreme Court*, a microfiche collection, provides coverage of all argued cases since 1832 and non-argued cases since 1984. *CIS US Supreme Court Records & Briefs*, another microfiche collection, includes all argued cases since 1897 and, since 1975, all non-argued cases in which one or more justices wrote a dissent from the *per curiam* decision to deny review. Summaries of some attorneys' briefs are included in the *United States Supreme Court Reports, Lawyers' Edition*.

LexisNexis has briefs on the merits filed with the Supreme Court beginning in January 1979, with selective coverage prior to that date. Certiorari briefs in civil cases are available beginning with the October 1999 term. In *Westlaw*, the merits briefs are available beginning in 1930 and petitions for writ of certiorari are available beginning in 1985.

Gale Cengage Learning's *The Making of Modern Law: U.S. Supreme Court Records and Briefs, 1832–1978* offers electronic access to historical Supreme Court briefs. This database is searchable by keyword, docket number, party name, or citation to the Court's

---

[20] Whether or not a case has been appealed, researchers may be interested in the pleadings, motions, and orders in the trial court. *See* Section H-4.

[21] Although somewhat outdated, a good starting point to locate library collections with briefs, records, and oral arguments is MICHAEL WHITEMAN & PETER SCOTT CAMPBELL, A UNION LIST OF APPELLATE RECORDS AND BRIEFS: FEDERAL AND STATE (Fred B. Rothman & Co. 1999).

[22] For more on researching the Supreme Court, see Chapter 8.

[23] http://www.americanbar.org/publications/preview_home.html.

[24] http://supreme.lp.findlaw.com/supreme_court/briefs/index.html.

[25] http://www.justice.gov/osg/briefs/.

[26] *See, e.g.*, AMERICAN PSYCHOLOGICAL ASSOCIATION, *APA Amicus Briefs by Issue*, http://www.apa.org/about/offices/ogc/amicus/index-issues.aspx; AMERICAN CIVIL LIBERTIES UNION, http://www.aclu.org (search for "brief"); U.S. CHAMBER OF COMMERCE, NATIONAL CHAMBER LITIGATION CENTER, http://www.chamberlitigation.com/.

opinion in *U.S. Reports, Supreme Court Reporter*, or *United States Supreme Court Reports, Lawyers' Edition*.

    b.   Oral Arguments

    (1) *Audiotapes.* Oral arguments presented before the Supreme Court have been recorded since 1955. These tapes are available for a fee from the National Archives.[27]

    (2) *The Oyez Project.* This website is a U.S. Supreme Court multimedia database, providing digital audio of Supreme Court oral arguments.[28] The site's aim is to create a complete and authoritative archive of Supreme Court audio from October 1955, when the Court began recording its proceedings, through the most recent term. The site also includes biographical information on all Supreme Court justices and a virtual tour of the Supreme Court.

    (3) *Transcripts.* Starting with the 1952 term, transcripts of oral arguments are available from Congressional Information Service, Inc. in a microfiche set entitled *Oral Arguments of the U.S. Supreme Court.* Beginning with the October 2000 term, transcripts of oral arguments are available on the Supreme Court's website.[29] Beginning with the October 2006 term, the Court makes transcripts available on the same day the argument is heard by the Court. *LexisNexis* has transcripts of oral arguments from the October 1979 term, and *Westlaw* has transcripts of oral arguments from the October 1990 term.

    c.   Landmark Briefs and Arguments of the Supreme Court of the United States: Constitutional Law. This series, published by LexisNexis, covers cases from 1793 forward. The period 1793 to 1974 consists of 81 volumes. Annual supplements published since 1974 average approximately eight volumes each year. The series is now over 350 volumes. As the title indicates, coverage is selective.

2.   Federal Courts of Appeals

    All circuits provide access to appellate briefs via *PACER*.[30] Coverage varies dramatically by circuit, with some circuits providing only the fairly recent documents and others providing access back to 1998. *Westlaw* has selected federal court of appeals briefs from 1972. *LexisNexis* has selected federal court of appeals briefs since 2000. *Bloomberg Law*, which harvests content from PACER, has extensive coverage.

---

    [27] Until late 1993, audiotapes were not available until three years after the oral arguments, could be used only for educational or instructional purposes, and could not be copied and disseminated. However, the Supreme Court's policy changed following publication of MAY IT PLEASE THE COURT: THE MOST SIGNIFICANT ORAL ARGUMENTS MADE BEFORE THE SUPREME COURT SINCE 1955 (Peter Irons & Stephanie Guitton eds., 1993). This publication consists of a 370–page book and six 100–minute cassettes, which include twenty-three edited live recordings of oral arguments, with a voice-over narration by Irons. Publication of these materials created a furor, with charges levied by the Supreme Court that Irons violated contractual arrangements by duplicating and disseminating the tapes. *See, e.g.,* Tony Mauro, *Tapes Project Sparks Clash: Supreme Court to Legal Scholar: Keep Oral Arguments to Yourself,* LEGAL TIMES, Aug. 16, 1993, at 1; Maro Robbins, *"May It Please the Court" Doesn't Please the Court,* NAT'L L.J., Oct. 11, 1993, at 47. The result, however, was to cause the Supreme Court to change its policy and make the tapes readily and immediately available to the public through the National Archives. *See* Linda Greenhouse, *Supreme Court Eases Restrictions on Use of Tapes of Its Arguments,* N.Y. TIMES, Nov. 3, 1993, at A22, col. 1.

    [28] http://www.oyez.org.

    [29] http://www.supremecourtus.gov.

    [30] *PACER, Public Access to Court Electronic Records* (http://www.pacer.gov), is an electronic public access service that allows users to obtain case and docket information from federal appellate, district, and bankruptcy courts.

Additionally, a small number of law libraries receive print copies of briefs and records filed with the federal court of appeals for the circuit in which they are located.

3. State Courts

Many state courts are now providing electronic access to their briefs. For example, the Texas Supreme Court provides online access to briefs going back to 2001.[31] *LexisNexis* provides selected state court briefs since 2000, while *Westlaw* provides briefs since 1990. The dates of coverage vary by state.

Some law libraries also receive print copies of briefs and records from state courts. There are also a number of microfiche sets that provide access to the briefs for specific states. The dates of coverage vary by state and court. It is often best to contact the court directly or a major law library in the specific state to provide guidance on accessing state court records.

4. Dockets and Pleadings

Most courts now maintain their dockets online and allow or require litigants to file pleadings online. Some courts make all or part of this information available to the public. For federal courts (other than the Supreme Court), the official source for pleadings and dockets is *PACER*. Many documents may be found on *RECAP*, a crowdsourcing project where *PACER* users upload *PACER* documents.[32] *Justia* presents selected dockets—but not the underlying filings—on its website.[33] *Bloomberg Law* includes dockets and filings for federal cases from *PACER*. It also has coverage of state dockets and—for some courts—the related documents. *Westlaw* has pleadings databases for state and federal cases.[34]

I. ATTORNEY GENERAL OPINIONS

Attorneys general serve as legal advisors to the executive branch of government. The opinions of an attorney general usually relate to the interpretation of statutes or legal problems. Some attorneys general limit their advice and will not render opinions regarding the constitutionality of proposed legislation.

This advice is often provided as an official written opinion.[35] While formal opinions, written and signed by an attorney general, are official statements of an executive officer, issued pursuant to his or her authority, the opinions are merely advisory rather than mandatory orders. The recommendations and conclusions set forth in these opinions are persuasive and are often followed by executive officers. These opinions also may influence judicial deliberations.

---

[31] http://www.supreme.courts.state.tx.us/ebriefs/ebriefs.asp.

[32] https://www.recapthelaw.org/.

[33] http://dockets.justia.com/.

[34] *See* Sabrina I. Pacifici & Margaret Berkland, *LLRX Court Rules, Forms and Dockets*, http://www.llrx.com/courtrules (database updated Jan. 2011).

[35] For additional information on the role of attorneys general, see Scott M. Matheson, Jr., *Constitutional Status and Role of the State Attorney General*, 6 U. FLA. J.L. & PUB. POL'Y 1 (1993); STATE ATTORNEYS GENERAL: POWERS AND RESPONSIBILITIES (Lynne M. Ross ed., 1990) (prepared by the National Association of Attorneys General); UNITED STATES DEP'T OF JUSTICE, 200TH ANNIVERSARY OF THE OFFICE OF THE ATTORNEY GENERAL (1989) (Attorney General of the United States); Peter E. Heiser, Jr., *The Opinion Writing Function of Attorneys General*, 18 IDAHO L. REV. 9 (1982); and William N. Thompson, *Transmission or Resistance: Opinions of State Attorneys General and the Impact of the Supreme Court*, 9 VAL. U. L. REV. 55 (1974).

1. Opinions of the Attorneys General of the United States

Official Opinions of the Attorneys General of the United States compiles all attorney general opinions published between 1791 and 1982 in forty-three volumes. This publication is available in many law libraries and also in PDF format in *HeinOnline*. Since 1980, opinions of the attorneys general are included in the annual publication, *Opinions of the Office of Legal Counsel.*

A selection of 104 United States attorney general opinions is contained in H. Jefferson Powell, *The Constitution and the Attorneys General* (1999). These opinions were selected for their enduring significance. This volume also contains a listing of all U.S. attorneys general from 1791 to 1999.

The opinions of the attorneys general are available in *LexisNexis* and *Westlaw*. The *United States Code Annotated* and the *United States Code Service* include digests of U.S. attorneys general opinions in their annotations.

2. Opinions of the Office of Legal Counsel

The U.S. attorney general's Office of Legal Counsel has the duties of preparing formal opinions of the attorney general, rendering informal opinions to the various federal agencies, assisting the attorney general in the performance of his or her function as adviser to the president, and rendering opinions to the attorney general and the various organizational units of the U.S. Department of Justice.[36]

Opinions of the Office of Legal Counsel began as an annual publication in 1977[37] and includes the opinions written by various attorneys in the office on matters referred to that office for response, as well as formal attorneys general opinions. Only a small portion of the Office of Legal Counsel's opinions are actually published because the addressee of the opinion must agree to publication. But there are exceptions. Some opinions are requested through the Freedom of Information Act—and "OLC sometimes releases requested records as a matter of discretion, even if they fall within the scope of a FOIA exemption or have not been the subject of a FOIA request."[38] Documents that have not been officially published may be available in the office's FOIA Reading Room.[39]

The opinions are first published in a softbound preliminary print and are subject to revision until the hardbound volume is issued. Like the opinions of the attorney general, the opinions of the Office of Legal Counsel are merely advisory statements and are not mandatory orders.

Opinions of the Office of Legal Counsel is available in *HeinOnline*. Researchers seeking more recent opinions should consult the Department of Justice's website, which provides published opinions issued since 1992 and selected opinions from 1934 to 1977.[40] Published opinions also are available in *LexisNexis* and *Westlaw*.

---

[36] The functions of the Office of Legal Counsel are described in 28 C.F.R. § .25 (2013).

[37] Volume 19–20 was the last book in the series distributed through the Federal Depository Library Program. Later volumes (as well as the earlier ones) are available from William S. Hein & Co.

[38] OLC FOIA Reading Room, http://www.justice.gov/olc/olc-foia1.htm (last visited Dec. 19, 2013).

[39] *Id.* The collection includes many memoranda prepared in response to legal issues from the war on terror.

[40] http://www.usdoj.gov/olc/opinions.htm.

In 2013, the office began publication of a new series, *Supplemental Opinions of the Office of Legal Counsel (Op. O.L.C. Supp.)* (Nathan A. Forrester ed.), making public the opinions of the O.L.C. (and its predecessors) from 1933 to 1976.[41] Many of the opinions will be of interest to legal historians and historians—for instance opinions on the removal of Japanese aliens and citizens from Hawaii to the mainland (1942), the naval blockade of Cuba (1961), and presidential pardon or legislative pardon of the president (1974).

3.   Opinions of State Attorneys General

Almost every state publishes the opinions of its attorney general. A checklist of published opinions of state attorneys general is included in *Pimsleur's Checklists of Basic American Legal Publications* (Marcia S. Zubrow ed., William S. Hein & Co., looseleaf). *BNA's Directory of State Administrative Codes and Registers* (Judith A. Miller & Kamla J. King comps., 2d ed. 1995) includes an appendix detailing the availability of opinions of attorneys general, including those of U.S. territories and of the District of Columbia's corporation counsel.

References to state attorney general opinions are included in many annotated state codes. *Westlaw* and *LexisNexis* also contain opinions of state attorneys general. Coverage varies by state, often with selective coverage beginning as early as the 1940s or as late as the 1970s.

Increasingly, state attorney general opinions are available online at the website of the state attorney general's office. The National Association of Attorneys General website provides links to websites of state attorneys general.[42] While not all of these websites contain the full text of the opinions, many have added this information and some state attorneys general websites provide greater coverage than *LexisNexis* or *Westlaw.*

J.   RESEARCHING LEGAL ETHICS

Norms of conduct developed by the American Bar Association have influenced the conduct of lawyers since the *Canons of Professional Ethics* was first adopted in 1908. In 1969, the *Model Code of Professional Responsibility* replaced the *Canons.* In 1983, the *Model Rules of Professional Conduct* was promulgated, and it is the *Model Rules* that are intended to constitute the national standard of conduct for attorneys.[43] The *Model Rules* and their related comments have been amended numerous times.

While the ABA promulgates the model codes and rules, each state must decide whether to adopt those norms or some variation of them as its standard. Although over three-fourths of the states have adopted the *Model Rules,* some states have adopted only portions of them; other states continue to follow the *Model Code*; and still others, such as California, have their own set of rules.

The ABA also has promulgated rules of conduct for the judiciary, beginning with the *Canons of Judicial Ethics* in 1924. In 1972, the *Model Code of Judicial Conduct* was

---

[41] Volume 1 is available at in the OLC FOIA Reading Room, *supra* note 38.

[42] http://www.naag.org/current-attorneys-general.php.

[43] For information pertaining to the development of the MODEL RULES, see CTR. FOR PROF. RESPONSIBILITY, AM. B. ASS'N, A LEGISLATIVE HISTORY: THE DEVELOPMENT OF THE ABA MODEL RULES OF PROFESSIONAL CONDUCT, 1982–1988 (2d ed., 1999). Can't you just cite to ABA?

promulgated. In 1990, it was replaced with an updated version. The current version was adopted in 2007. As with the *Model Rules*, it is up to each state to determine its own rules of judicial conduct.

The American Bar Association provides electronic access to the *Model Rules* and the *Model Code of Judicial Conduct*.[44] Annotated print versions, *Annotated Model Rules of Professional Conduct* (7th ed. 2011) and *Annotated Model Code of Judicial Conduct* (2d ed. 2011), also are available. Some states include their rules of professional and judicial conduct in their compiled statutes. The websites of many state bar organizations provide electronic access to these rules.

Enforcement of these rules and the power to discipline lawyers and judges is the responsibility of the state legislature or the highest court in the state; the ABA, as a voluntary association, has no authority over these matters. The procedure for disciplining lawyers varies from state to state. The rules governing discipline can be located by consulting the indexes of the state codes. Disciplinary actions frequently are reported in state legal newspapers and in bar association journals.

1. Opinions on Legal Ethics

The American Bar Association has a Standing Committee on Ethics and Professional Responsibility, which is charged with interpreting the ABA's codes of conduct and recommending appropriate amendments and clarifications. Lawyers and judges can request an opinion from the committee about the propriety of a proposed action.

These opinions were traditionally published in *Opinions on Professional Ethics* (1967), *Informal Ethics Opinions* (1975), *Formal and Informal Ethics Opinions* (1984), and a looseleaf service that ended publication in 2008, *Recent Ethics Opinions*. The American Bar Association's Standing Committee on Ethics and Professional Responsibility provides free online access to only the most recent opinions.[45] New opinions are also published in the *ABA Journal*. ABA ethics opinions are also available in *Westlaw* and *LexisNexis*.

Most state bar associations have committees similar to the ABA Standing Committee. The opinions of these committees, along with other information on professional responsibility, can be located in the following sources:

a.   ABA/BNA Lawyer's Manual on Professional Conduct (BNA) (available in *Bloomberg BNA* and in *Bloomberg Law*). A joint project of the American Bar Association and Bloomberg BNA, this multivolume set is the most comprehensive source for a wide range of materials dealing with the legal profession. It includes judicial opinions involving lawyer discipline and the text of state ethics opinions.

b.   National Reporter on Legal Ethics and Professional Responsibility (University Publications of America). This multivolume service includes the full text of both court cases on legal ethics and ethics opinions from state and local bar associations. This publication is available in *LexisNexis*.

---

[44] http://www.americanbar.org/groups/professional_responsibility/publications.html.

[45] http://www.americanbar.org/groups/professional_responsibility/publications/ethics_opinions/complimentary_index.html.

c. *State and Local Bar Journals.* These publications often print recently issued opinions of state and local ethics committees.

d. *State Ethics Sources on the Internet.* Many state bar associations have published their ethics codes and opinions online or provide links to websites that provide this information.

LexisNexis has an ethics library, which includes state case law relevant to ethical issues, ethics rules from each state, and related ABA publications on professional responsibility. *Westlaw* also has an ethics library containing state case law relevant to ethical issues, ethics rules from each state, and ethics opinions for select states.

2. Shepard's Professional and Judicial Conduct Citations

This citator covers citations to judicial opinions from state and federal courts and to secondary sources that have cited the various codes of conduct and the ABA's formal and informal opinions.

Chapter 21

PUBLIC INTERNATIONAL LAW*

This chapter deals with research in the field known as public international law—the law governing relations among sovereign states and other actors on the international scene. In today's globalized world, an understanding of how to conduct research in international law is essential. Moreover, international law forms part of the law of the United States.[1]

All the main sources of international law are covered: international agreements (treaties), customary international law, general principles of law, adjudications, and commentary by leading writers. The chapter also discusses research on international organizations, focusing on two of the most important organizations, the United Nations and the European Union. The concluding section covers research on a substantive area of international law: international protection of human rights.

A. INTRODUCTION

1. International Law in United States Law

International law is part of our law, and must be ascertained and administered by the courts of justice of appropriate jurisdiction as often as questions of right depending upon it are duly presented for their determination.[2]

International law and international agreements of the United States are law of the United States and supreme over the law of the several States. Cases arising under international law or international agreements of the United States are within the Judicial Power of the United States, and subject to Constitutional and statutory limitations and requirements of justiciability, are within the jurisdiction of the federal courts.[3]

---

* Jonathan Pratter, Foreign and International Law Librarian, Tarlton Law Library, Jamail Center for Legal Research, University of Texas School of Law, revised this chapter.

[1] This chapter does not address some related areas: *foreign law* (the law of countries other than one's own), *comparative law* (the study that compares the laws or legal systems of two or more jurisdictions), and *private international law* (another term for international conflict of laws, which deals with jurisdictional matters in disputes between private individuals and entities arising in an international context). Research books for these topics (as well as for public international law) include GEO. WASH. INT'L INT'L L. REV., GUIDE TO INTERNATIONAL LEGAL RESEARCH (2013) (published by LexisNexis and available in *LexisNexis*) (includes information on foreign law as well as international law); MARCI HOFFMAN & MARY RUMSEY, INTERNATIONAL AND FOREIGN LEGAL RESEARCH: A COURSEBOOK (2d ed. 2012); MARCI B. HOFFMAN & ROBERT C. BERRING, INTERNATIONAL LEGAL RESEARCH IN A NUTSHELL (2008); ANTHONY S. WINER ET AL., INTERNATIONAL LAW LEGAL RESEARCH (2013).

[2] The Paquete Habana, 175 U.S. 677, 700 (1900).

[3] RESTATEMENT (THIRD) OF THE LAW, THE FOREIGN RELATIONS LAW OF THE UNITED STATES § 111(1)–(2) (1987) [hereinafter FOREIGN RELATIONS RESTATEMENT 3D].

These two quotations, one classic and one contemporary, accurately state the relation between international law and the law of the United States.[4] The Supremacy Clause of the Constitution declares:

> This Constitution, and the Laws of the United States which shall be made in Pursuance thereof, *and all Treaties made, or which shall be made, under the Authority of the United States,* shall be the supreme Law of the Land; and the Judges in every State shall be bound thereby, any Thing in the Constitution or Laws of any State to the Contrary notwithstanding.[5]

To give practical impact to these broad statements of law, consider the fact that since 1988, an agreement for the sale of goods, the most common of all commercial transactions, between a seller in the United States and a buyer in any of seventy-five other countries will be governed by an international agreement, the United Nations Convention on Contracts for the International Sale of Goods,[6] unless the parties provide otherwise. In an increasingly globalized world, lawyers practicing anywhere should consider an understanding of international law and its research methods to be fundamental.

2.   Definition of International Law

"International law . . . consists of rules and principles of general application dealing with the conduct of states and of international organizations and with their relations *inter se,* as well as with some of their relations with persons, whether natural or juridical."[7] Two points arise from this definition. First, the focus is on legal relations among sovereign states. For this reason, the subject is sometimes known as the law of nations, and sometimes as *public* international law. The latter term is often contrasted with *private* international law, or as more commonly known in the United States, the conflict of laws. Private international law concerns legal relations between and among persons where the law of more than one nation may be involved.

The second point to be made about the definition of international law is that sovereign states are not the only actors involved. Obviously, international organizations, such as the United Nations or the Organization of American States, are not nations. But their structure, powers, and activities are a significant topic of international law. Moreover, the individual is by no means excluded from participation, although exactly how persons (either natural or legal) participate in international law is not well settled. Nevertheless, it is clear that a topic like the protection of human rights in international law is centrally concerned with the position of the individual.

---

[4] Elucidating the precise fit between international law and the domestic law of the United States would require adding nuance to these statements. At least four questions have to be asked: (1) Does international law prevail over the Constitution?; (2) Is customary international law part of federal common law or state common law?; (3) If customary international law is part of federal law, are states obligated by it?; (4) Do federal statutes (or action by the executive) trump customary international law or an earlier international agreement (treaty)? For answers, see DAVID J. BEDERMAN, INTERNATIONAL LAW FRAMEWORKS 159–66 (3d ed. 2010).

[5] U.S. CONST. art. VI, § 2 (emphasis added).

[6] Apr. 11, 1980, 1489 U.N.T.S. 3, *reprinted in* 19 I.L.M. 671 (1980).

[7] FOREIGN RELATIONS RESTATEMENT 3D, *supra* note 3, § 101.

3. The Sources of International Law

International law lacks formal mechanisms for making law, an obvious characteristic of a national legal system. There is no duly constituted legislature, executive, or judiciary, although more or less distant analogs of each of these can be found. In the absence of such mechanisms, the question of where international law comes from has to receive much attention.

Article 38(1) of the Statute of the International Court of Justice[8] is considered to be an authoritative statement of the sources of international law. Article 38(1) provides:

> The Court, whose function is to decide in accordance with international law such disputes as are submitted to it, shall apply:

> (a) international conventions, whether general or particular, establishing rules expressly recognized by the contesting states;

> (b) international custom, as evidence of a general practice accepted as law;

> (c) the general principles of law recognized by civilized nations;

> (d) . . . judicial decisions and the teachings of the most highly qualified publicists of the various nations, as subsidiary means for the determination of rules of law.

We can then identify five broad categories of sources:

a. *International Conventions.* These conventions include treaties and other international agreements of all kinds. (Convention, as used here, is a synonym for agreement.) The category includes bilateral agreements (between two parties) and multilateral agreements (having three or more parties).

b. *Customary International Law.* Rules that arise out of the general and consistent practice of states acting out of a sense of legal obligation (referred to as state practice) are referred to as *customary international law.*

c. *General Principles of Law.* Examples of such general principles "common to the major legal systems" (to use the contemporary formulation) include the doctrine of laches or the passage of time as a bar to a claim, principles of due process in the administration of justice, and the doctrine of *res judicata.*[9]

d. *Judicial Decisions.* This category includes the decisions of both international tribunals and national courts when the latter deal with questions of international law. International tribunals range from the International Court of Justice to an ad hoc arbitral panel constituted to resolve a particular international dispute.

e. *Writings of International Law Scholars.* This phrase is the modern substitute for the archaic language found in Article 38 ("teachings of the most highly qualified publicists"). This category covers treatises and textbooks of leading scholars, the draft conventions and reports of the International Law Commission of the United Nations (formed for the purpose of encouraging the progressive development of international law

---

[8] 59 Stat. 1055 (1945), T.S. No. 993.

[9] *See generally* BIN CHENG, GENERAL PRINCIPLES OF LAW AS APPLIED BY INTERNATIONAL COURTS AND TRIBUNALS (1994).

and its codification),[10] and the reports and resolutions of such non-governmental groups as the American Society of International Law, the International Law Association, and the Institut de Droit International.

Lawyers and scholars often use the term secondary sources to describe such materials because they are commentaries on or discussion of the law rather than primary sources of law. This description is consistent with the usage of Article 38(1), which calls such materials subsidiary means. Judicial decisions, primary sources in U.S. law, are, under Article 38(1), subsidiary means.[11]

4. Impact of the Internet and the World Wide Web

The advent of the Internet has not altered the sources of international law.[12] However, the vast and constantly expanding amount of information available electronically has had a profound effect on *research* on international law. Consider research on state practice as an example. Many national governments, and their foreign ministries in particular, maintain websites. These websites publish official statements of position on a host of issues, in speeches and in other statements by high officials, in press releases, in programmatic documents, and in other announcements and notices. It is often possible to assemble evidence of state practice of national governments simply by consulting official webpages.

Information published on the Internet achieves the widest possible dissemination in the shortest time imaginable. Documentation that once was difficult or impossible to access is now readily available. Examples are manifold. Documents of the United Nations are now freely accessible on the World Wide Web.[13] This is a revolutionary development. The European Commission maintains a freely accessible web portal devoted to European Union law.[14] Reliable texts of significant international agreements can often be located simply by typing their names into a search engine such as *Google*.

One useful web-based resource is called *EISIL*,[15] which stands for Electronic Information System for International Law. It is sponsored by the American Society of International Law (ASIL). *EISIL* is best described as a moderated portal or gateway to international legal information on the World Wide Web. Because *EISIL* is moderated, the content is verified and checked for accuracy, so the researcher can have confidence that the sources listed are reliable.

Also of use as a complement to *EISIL* is the *ASIL Guide to Electronic Resources for International Law*,[16] which covers in a narrative fashion several fields of current interest (e.g., human rights, international environmental law, and international criminal law).

---

[10] *See generally* the Commission's website, http://www.un.org/law/ilc/.

[11] To avoid confusion, the reader should note that in discussions of researching international law the word sources can have two different senses. The first sense refers to the formal sources of international law as described in Article 38(1). The other sense refers to published sources, i.e., the publications and other resources described in this chapter that make up the documentation of international law.

[12] For an ambitious contrasting view, see John King Gamble, *New Information Technologies and the Sources of International Law: Convergence, Divergence, Obsolescence and / or Transformation*, 41 GERMAN Y.B. INT'L L. 170 (1998).

[13] http://www.un.org.

[14] http://europa.eu/eu-law/index_en.htm.

[15] http://www.eisil.org.

[16] http://www.asil.org/erghome.cfm.

An innovative and creative use of the World Wide Web for the free dissemination of information about international law is the *Audiovisual Library of International Law*, produced by the United Nations.[17] It has three components: (1) the Historical Archives, containing documents on the adoption of significant international legal instruments; (2) the Lecture Series, containing video lectures on various international legal topics given by leading scholars in the field; and (3) the Research Library, containing a broad array of links to international legal resources available for free on the World Wide Web.

The *International Law Library* of the World Legal Information Institute (WorldLII) is self-described as "the most comprehensive free access international law research infrastructure on the Internet."[18] The International Courts and Tribunals Collection contains over 30,000 decisions from various judicial and quasi-judicial fora ranging from the Caribbean Court of Justice to the U.N. Human Rights Committee. The International Treaties Collection consists of twenty-seven different treaty databases containing over 35,000 documents.

Several blogs in English on international law are worthy of note: *Opinio Juris*,[19] *IntLawGrrls*,[20] *EJIL: Talk!*,[21] and *International Law Prof Blog*.[22] Developments in international law take place constantly all over the world. Blogs function as excellent sources of news and comment on these developments.

B. INTERNATIONAL AGREEMENTS: UNITED STATES SOURCES

1. Introduction[23]

A *treaty* is "an international agreement concluded between States in written form and governed by international law . . . whatever its particular designation."[24] Any number of terms can be used to refer to international agreements, e.g., treaty, convention, protocol, covenant, charter, statute, act, declaration, concordat, exchange of notes, agreed minute, memorandum of agreement, and memorandum of understanding. The definition given above makes the important point that the terminology describing a particular international agreement does not affect its legal status as an agreement binding in international law.

The subject of treaties is complicated in the United States by the frequent use made of the *executive agreement.* Under the Constitution, the president has the "Power, by and with the Advice and Consent of the Senate, to make Treaties, provided two thirds of the Senators present concur. . . ."[25] But this formal treaty-making power does not exhaust

---

[17] http://www.un.org/law/avl/. The department responsible is the Codification Division of the Office of Legal Affairs in the U.N. Secretariat.

[18] http://www.worldlii.org/int/special/ihl/.

[19] http://www.opiniojuris.org. This blog was founded by U.S. law professors, with contributors from around the world.

[20] http://intlawgrrls.blogspot.com. As the name indicates, the contributors to this blog are women active in international law.

[21] http://www.ejiltalk.org. This is the blog of the *European Journal of International Law.*

[22] http://lawprofessors.typepad.com/international_law. Edited by an international team of law professors, this blog is part of the larger Law Professor Blogs Network.

[23] *See generally* Jonathan Pratter, *Treaty Research Basics*, 89 LAW LIBR. J. 407 (1997).

[24] Vienna Convention on the Law of Treaties, May 23, 1969, art. 2(1)(a), 1155 U.N.T.S. 331.

[25] U.S. CONST. art. II, § 2.

the federal government's authority to negotiate international agreements. In fact, there are far more executive agreements in force between the United States and other countries than there are treaties.[26] The difference between the two kinds of agreement is a subject for the substantive course in international law.[27] For our purposes, it is enough to know that both treaties and executive agreements constitute binding international agreements of the United States.[28]

2. Current Sources

a.   T.I.A.S. and U.S.T. Since 1945, the State Department has published the international agreements of the United States in pamphlets called *Treaties and Other International Acts Series (T.I.A.S.)*. Since 1950, the State Department has published the agreements that first appear in *T.I.A.S.* in a series of bound volumes, *United States Treaties and Other International Agreements (U.S.T.)*. *U.S.T.* currently consists of thirty-five volumes; each volume may have as many as five or six separately bound parts. Volume 35, part 6, the most recently issued as of this writing, ends with *T.I.A.S.* 11059, an agreement concluded in 1984. The publication of *T.I.A.S.* is also several years behind. By statute, both *U.S.T.* and *T.I.A.S.* are authoritative sources for the text of agreements published there.[29] Both *T.I.A.S.* and *U.S.T.* are available in *HeinOnline* in the Treaties and Agreements Library.

Beginning with agreements from 2002, the numbering of *T.I.A.S.* has changed. Formerly, agreements were numbered consecutively in the order in which they were published. Now, each agreement receives a number based upon the date in which it entered into force. For example, the Memorandum of Understanding on Defense Cooperation between the U.S. and the Netherlands, which entered into force on February 12, 2004, received the designation *T.I.A.S.* 04–0212.

T.I.A.S. and *U.S.T.* are supposed to be current, but there are serious delays in their publication. This section will describe strategies for finding more recent international agreements of the United States that have not been published in *T.I.A.S.* or *U.S.T.*[30]

b.   Internet. Given the lengthy time lag in the publication of the official treaty series, finding a substitute source for more recent U.S. international agreements is essential.

Fortunately, the Office of Treaty Affairs in the Office of the Legal Adviser of the State Department has started to make the effort to publish *T.I.A.S.* online at the website of the Office of Treaty Affairs.[31]

In 2004, the statute 1 U.S.C. § 112a was amended to add subsection (d):

---

[26] *See* John C. Yoo, *Laws as Treaties?: The Constitutionality of Congressional-Executive Agreements*, 99 MICH. L. REV. 757, 765–68 (2001).

[27] *See generally* SEAN D. MURPHY, PRINCIPLES OF INTERNATIONAL LAW 208–10 (2006).

[28] *See* CONGRESSIONAL RESEARCH SERVICE, LIBRARY OF CONGRESS, TREATIES AND OTHER INTERNATIONAL AGREEMENTS: THE ROLE OF THE UNITED STATES SENATE, S. PRT. NO. 106–71, 77 (2001) (providing a thorough treatment of United States treaty practice). This document is available online in full text at http://www.au.af.mil/au/awc/awcgate/congress/treaties_senate_role.pdf.

[29] http://www.state.gov/s/l/treaty.

[30] It is possible that *U.S.T.* has ceased publication altogether. However, the State Department has not confirmed this.

[31] http://www.state.gov/s/l/treaty/tias/index.htm. In December 2013, the menu listed treaties from 1996 to 2013.

The Secretary of State shall make publicly available through the Internet website of the Department of State each treaty or international agreement proposed to be published in the compilation entitled "United States Treaties and Other International Agreements" not later than 180 days after the date on which the treaty or agreement enters into force.

Thus recent international agreements of the U.S. can now be found on the State Department's website.[32]

Some U.S. government agencies post collections of international agreements related to their work on their websites. Among the most consulted websites are the Office of the United States Trade Representative (trade agreements[33]), Department of Commerce Trade Compliance Center (bilateral investment treaties[34]), Internal Revenue Service (income tax treaties[35]), Federal Trade Commission (international antitrust and consumer protection cooperation agreements[36]), and the State Department (private international law[37] and arms control treaties and agreements[38]).

c.   *Westlaw, LexisNexis, and other commercial online sources. Westlaw* and *LexisNexis* provide relatively easy access to U.S. international agreements. Both systems combine recent and historical documents in one file. In *Westlaw*, the database identifier is USTREATIES. In *LexisNexis*, a similar database called U.S. Treaties in Lexis will be found under "Area of Law—By Topic—International Law." In addition, a commercial online collection called *Treaties and International Agreements Online* is available.[39]

d.   *Other Collections of U.S. Treaties.* William S. Hein & Co. publishes treaties in two formats: *HeinOnline*'s Treaties and Agreements Library (online) and *Hein's United States Treaties and Other International Agreements: Current Service* (microfiche). Oceana Publications produces *Consolidated Treaties & International Agreements: Current Document Service.*[40]

e.   *U.S.C., U.S.C.A., U.S.C.S., and Federal Register.* There might be a tendency to think that U.S. international agreements would be found in the official *U.S.C.*, the *Federal Register*, or in the annotated federal codes. In general, that is *not* true. *U.S.C.* does not include treaties, nor does *U.S.C.A. U.S.C.S.* has an unnumbered volume entitled International Agreements containing the text of forty miscellaneous multilateral agreements to which the U.S. is a party. Case notes and references to secondary sources are appended to some agreements. Another volume of *U.S.C.S.* entitled Annotations to Uncodified Laws and Treaties contains case notes to Native American treaties and to an additional group of miscellaneous bilateral international agreements. The *Federal Register* rarely publishes U.S. international agreements.

---

[32] http://www.state.gov/s/l/treaty/tias/index.htm.

[33] http://www.ustr.gov/trade-agreements.

[34] http://tcc.export.gov/Trade_Agreements/Bilateral_Investment_Treaties/index.asp.

[35] http://www.irs.gov/businesses/international/article/0,,id=96739,00.html. (Note the double comma in the URL.)

[36] http://www.ftc.gov/oia/agreements.shtm.

[37] http://www.state.gov/s/l/c3452.htm.

[38] http://www.state.gov/t/avc/trty/index.htm.

[39] *See* http://www.oceanalaw.com for more information.

[40] (Oceana Publications 1990–). As of June 2014, the most recent volume published is volume 5 from 2011.

Research for the text of U.S. international agreements *should not* begin with any of these sources. On the other hand, they *should* be consulted in order to find implementing legislation and judicial interpretation, as noted below in Section B-7.

3. Earlier Publications

a. *United States Statutes at Large.* International agreements of the United States were published in *United States Statutes at Large* from volume 8 through volume 64 (1949). Volume 8 includes agreements entered into between 1776 and 1845. Beginning with volume 47, executive agreements were included. Volume 64, part 3 (1950–1951), contains an index of all the agreements in *United States Statutes at Large.*

b. *T.S. and E.A.S.* The current pamphlet series, *T.I.A.S.*, was preceded by the *Treaty Series (T.S.)* and the *Executive Agreement Series (E.A.S.).* The *Treaty Series* reached pamphlet number 994 and the *Executive Agreement Series* went to pamphlet number 506, for a total of 1500. Thus, *T.I.A.S.* begins at 1501.[41]

c. *Bevans.* A useful collection published by the State Department is *Treaties and Other International Agreements of the United States of America, 1776–1949* (Charles I. Bevans comp., 1968–1976) known as Bevans. This series collects, in thirteen volumes, the international agreements of the United States up to the beginning of *U.S.T.* Multilateral treaties are arranged chronologically in volumes 1 through 4. Bilateral treaties are arranged alphabetically by the name of the other country in volumes 5 through 12. Volume 13 is a general index. Two other collections published by the State Department are also known by the names of their respective compilers: *Treaties, Conventions, International Acts, Protocols, and Agreements Between the United States of America and Other Powers* (William M. Malloy comp., 1910–1938) (Malloy), and *Treaties and Other International Acts of the United States of America (Hunter Miller ed., 1931–1948)* (Miller). For most purposes, Bevans supersedes both of the earlier collections. In Table 4, Treaty Sources, Unofficial treaty sources, the *Bluebook* allows citation to Bevans. All three compilations are available in *HeinOnline.*

4. United States Treaties in Congressional Documents

a. *Senate Treaty Documents and Senate Executive Reports.* When seeking the Senate's advice and consent on a proposed treaty, the president submits a message to the Senate with the text of the agreement annexed. The proposed treaty is referred to the Committee on Foreign Relations for hearings and a recommendation to the full Senate. Until the 97th Congress (1981–1982), the Senate printed the proposed treaty under the name *Senate Executive Document* with a letter designation. Beginning with the 97th Congress, the printed treaties are called *Treaty Documents* and receive a number, the first part of which indicates the Congress that considered the treaty. For example, the message from the president transmitting the Treaty with Russia on Measures for Further Reduction and Limitation of Strategic Offensive Arms, signed in April 2010, is the *Senate Treaty Document* designated 111–5.

The Committee on Foreign Relations then makes its recommendation to the full Senate in a report printed in the numbered series of *Senate Executive Reports.* For

---

[41] For detailed information on these series and on the bibliography of the early publication of United States international agreements, see 1 HUNTER MILLER, TREATIES AND OTHER INTERNATIONAL ACTS OF THE UNITED STATES OF AMERICA 35–138 (1931).

example, the Committee's report of October 2010 favorably reporting the above arms reduction treaty with Russia is *Senate Executive Report* 111–6. Again, the first part of the number reflects the Congress that considered the treaty.

Researchers should note the significance of these congressional Treaty Documents. The message of transmittal from the president in the *Treaty Document* series always includes the text of the agreement in an annex, as well as the letter of submittal from the Secretary of State to the president, which itself often contains a detailed article-by-article analysis of the agreement. The report of the Senate Foreign Relations Committee in the *Executive Report* series has the Committee's analysis of the agreement, discussion of needed implementing legislation, and a statement of minority views, as the case may be, along with other useful information. Given the delay in the standard official publication of U.S. international agreements, these congressional Treaty Documents often furnish the sole official source of publication for purposes of citation.[42]

Moreover, in the case of agreements that have generated disagreement or controversy in the Senate, the Foreign Relations Committee often appends statements of "conditions," "declarations," "understandings," or "provisos" to its recommendation of advice and consent to the full Senate. If the full Senate gives its advice and consent to ratification subject to these conditions, important consequences for the correct understanding of the treaty text and of the legal obligations it imposes will follow, at least from the point of view of the United States. The committee report in the *Executive Report* series is often the only place to find the text of these appended statements, although they are sometimes in the *Congressional Record* where the Senate's vote on advice and consent to ratification is published.

Treaty Documents and *Executive Reports* beginning with the 104th Congress (1995–1996) are available from the United States Government Printing Office website.[43] In addition, Treaty Documents beginning with the 99th Congress (1985–1986), are available in the *Federal Digital System* (*FDsys*), also produced by the Government Printing Office.[44] Treaty Documents are also in *HeinOnline* in the Treaties and Agreements Library.

Christian L. Wiktor, *Treaties Submitted to the United States Senate: Legislative History, 1989–2004* (2006) (Martinus Nijhoff) compiles the information on Senate treaty consideration. It is organized chronologically. Each entry begins with the title of the agreement and then gives the references to the relevant Treaty Document, committee hearing, and *Executive Report*. Information on advice and consent by the full Senate as found in the *Congressional Record* is also given.

b.   Pending Treaties. Treaties submitted to the Senate for advice and consent can be held over from year to year. Some international agreements remain pending in the Senate for a long time. For example, the Vienna Convention on the Law of Treaties,[45] one of the more significant international agreements of the modern era, was submitted

---

[42] *See* BLUEBOOK R. 21.4.5(a)(i) (allowing citation to Senate *Treaty Documents* for the text of agreements not found in *U.S.T.*, *Stat.*, *T.I.A.S.*, *T.S.*, or *E.A.S.*).

[43] http://www.gpoaccess.gov/serialset/cdocuments/index.html   and   http://www.gpoaccess.gov/serialset/creports/index.html.

[44] http://www.gpo.gov/fdsys/browse/collection.action?collectionCode=CDOC.

[45] 1155 U.N.T.S. 331 (1969).

as *Executive Document L* during the 92nd Congress, 1st Session (1971). It has remained pending before the Senate Committee on Foreign Relations, without action, ever since.

The U.S. Senate Committee on Foreign Relations maintains on its website a list of treaties pending before the committee.[46] Volume 1 (Senate) of the *Congressional Index* has a "Treaties" tab that is useful for tracking treaties pending in the Senate.

5.   Other Publications

   a.   Christian L. Wiktor, *Unperfected Treaties of the United States, 1776–1976* (1976) This multivolume set is an annotated collection of treaties to which the United States was a signatory, but which never went into force.

   b.   *Extradition Laws and Treaties of the United States* (Igor I. Kavass & Adolph Sprudzs eds., 1979–) (available in *HeinOnline*'s Immigration Law and Policy in the U.S. library). This looseleaf set contains extradition treaties currently in force between the United States and other countries, arranged alphabetically by the name of the other country. Additional volumes in this set reprint U.S. agreements concerning international judicial assistance in criminal matters.

   c.   *Indian Affairs: Laws and Treaties*[47] (Charles J. Kappler ed., 1903–1941).[48] Volume 2 contains treaties made by the United States with Indian tribes between 1778 and 1883. Volume 7 of *United States Statutes at Large* also includes a compilation of Indian treaties. Treaties concluded with Indian tribes before the independence of the United States are in *Early American Indian Documents: Treaties and Law, 1607–1789* (Alden T. Vaughn ed., U.P.A. 1979–1989).

   d.   *Tax Treaties.* This looseleaf published by CCH provides comprehensive coverage with annotations and background material of the income and estate tax treaties of the United States currently in force and of those pending ratification. It is available in *IntelliConnect*, as part of the International Tax Treaty Expert Library.

6.   Finding United States International Agreements and Verifying Their Status

Locating international agreements requires skills and sources that resemble those used in researching other legal materials, but which differ from them as well. As is the case for other primary sources of law, after locating the text of an international agreement, the current status of that document must be verified.

Multilateral agreements do not come into force as soon as they are negotiated. A minimum number of countries must agree to join a multilateral treaty before it goes into effect; this may take years. Moreover, only those countries that agree to become parties to a multilateral agreement are bound by it, thus making it essential to know what the "states party" are. States may accede to (join) a multilateral treaty long after it is first negotiated. As a final complication, states may denounce (terminate) their participation

---

[46] http://foreign.senate.gov/treaties/. See also the Treaties Pending in the Senate page on the State Department website, http://www.state.gov/s/l/treaty/pending/index.htm.

[47] See Chapter 25, Native American Tribal Law, for additional information.

[48] This is available in *HeinOnline* in the Treaties and Agreements Library and in the Oklahoma State University Library Electronic Publishing Center, http://digital.library.okstate.edu/kappler/index.htm. It was reprinted under the title *Indian Treaties* (1972) (Interland Publishing). *See also* EARLY RECOGNIZED TREATIES WITH AMERICAN INDIAN NATIONS, http://earlytreaties.unl.edu.

in either a multilateral or bilateral agreement at some time after becoming a party. Obviously, the process of verification is crucial. The finding tools noted in this section refer to the location of the text of international agreements. They also provide critical additional information for verifying current status.

a. *Treaties in Force.*[49] *Treaties in Force* is published by the State Department. It is divided into bilateral and multilateral sections. The bilateral section is organized alphabetically by the name of the other country and subdivided by subject matter; the multilateral section is organized alphabetically by subject matter and chronologically within each subject heading.

Each entry begins with the name of the agreement, followed by the place and date it was concluded, the date it entered into force (if multilateral, the date of entry into force in general and for the United States in particular), the citation (with parallel citations), a list of the other states party to the agreement (if multilateral), and brief notes regarding such points as whether a state entered a reservation or declaration to a multilateral agreement.

Treaties in Force can answer several questions: (1) what international agreements are currently in place between the United States and a particular country or on a particular subject; (2) is a particular international agreement in force for the United States; (3) where can the text of the agreement be found; and (d) what other countries are parties to a multilateral agreement.

The current edition of *Treaties in Force* in PDF is now part of the Treaty Affairs section of the State Department's website.[50] [Illustration 21–1] In fact, the web is now the chief mode of publication of *Treaties in Force*. The introductory text says:

> The electronic edition of *Treaties in Force* may be updated periodically throughout the year on the Treaty Affairs webpage. . . . The print edition of *Treaties in Force* is published annually in limited quantities to meet the needs of certain users who are unable to consult the online version. Because the print edition is updated only annually, the electronic edition will, in most cases, better reflect the current status of U.S. treaties and international agreements.

Sometimes *Treaties in Force* does not provide all information needed. For example, when an agreement has not been published in *T.I.A.S.* or *U.S.T.*, there may be no citation, merely the unhelpful indication "TIAS ___." When the U.S. or another party has entered a declaration or reservation to a multilateral agreement, this will be noted, but the text is not reproduced. When all else fails, the researcher should use the information and follow the instructions found at the Contact Information page in the Treaty Affairs section of the State Department's website.[51]

b. *Treaty Actions.* The Treaty Affairs section of the State Department's website also has a page called Treaty Actions, which updates *Treaties in Force*.[52]

---

[49] The full title of this annual publication is *Treaties in Force: A List of Treaties and Other International Agreements in Force on January 1, 20__*. It has been published since 1944.

[50] http://www.state.gov/s/l/treaty/tif/index.htm.

[51] http://www.state.gov/s/l/treaty/contact. Experience has shown that the more the researcher knows about the question she has, the more helpful the Treaty Affairs Office is likely to be.

[52] http://www.state.gov/s/l/treaty/c3428.htm.

    c. *Kavass's Guide to the United States Treaties in Force* (Igor I. Kavass ed., 1983–) (available in *HeinOnline*). This commercial publication contains essentially the same information as that found in *Treaties in Force*. However, as it is more heavily indexed, it can be used to find references to agreements that might be hard to locate in *Treaties in Force*. For example, it contains lists of agreements newly added to the current *Treaties in Force*, as well as of agreements removed from *Treaties in Force* since the previous year.

    d. *United States Treaty Index* (Igor I. Kavass ed., 1982–). This is a commercial index of international agreements of the United States entered into from 1776 through 2004. The set consists of a "master guide" in numerical order, a chronological guide, a country index, a subject index, and a "geographical subject index."

    e. *Kavass's Current Treaty Index* (Igor I. Kavass & Adolf Sprudz eds., 1982–) (available in *HeinOnline*. This is a semiannual supplement to the *United States Treaty Index*.

    The three commercial publications mentioned above (c, d, and e) contain useful information, but their organization can be confusing, often making them cumbersome and difficult to use. Researchers may find it easier to start with *Treaties in Force*, and then turn to the commercial publications for additional information.

7.   Implementation and Judicial Interpretation of United States Treaties

    a. *U.S.C., U.S.C.A., U.S.C.S., C.F.R.,* and *Federal Register*. Often, the terms of a U.S. international agreement require implementing legislation in order to become effective as part of U.S. law. For example, the Convention on the Recognition and Enforcement of Foreign Arbitral Awards[53] is implemented in chapter 2 of the Federal Arbitration Act.[54] When an agency is charged with carrying out various responsibilities of the United States under a treaty and its implementing legislation, there are implementing administrative regulations as well. For example, under the UNESCO Convention on the Means of Prohibiting and Preventing the Illicit Import, Export and Transfer of Ownership of Cultural Property[55] and its implementing legislation,[56] the U.S. Customs Service issues regulations to restrict the import of various kinds of cultural property. These regulations are first published in the *Federal Register* and later summarized in a list at 19 C.F.R. § 12.104g. When researching a U.S. international agreement, check for federal legislation and administrative regulations on point.

    b. *Judicial Decisions*. Several approaches are useful for cases decided under and interpreting U.S. international agreements.

    (1)   Use a full-text database of federal cases (e.g., in *Westlaw* or *LexisNexis*). Courts typically identify international agreements by name, though with some variation. Therefore, search queries can be formulated using significant words from the formal and popular name of the agreement, e.g., *(convention +3 contracts +3 "international sale of goods")* or *cisg*.

---

[53] 21 U.S.T. 2517, 330 U.N.T.S. 38.

[54] 9 U.S.C. §§ 201–08 (2012).

[55] 823 U.N.T.S. 231.

[56] Convention on Cultural Property Implementation Act, 19 U.S.C. §§ 2601–13 (2012).

(2)   The West key number digests include a topic, "Treaties," that collects cases involving the interpretation and application of U.S. international agreements.

(3)   *U.S.C.S.* includes a volume entitled *Uncodified: Notes to Uncodified Laws and Treaties*, which collects case notes to various multilateral, bilateral, and Indian treaties of the United States.

C. INTERNATIONAL AGREEMENTS: ADDITIONAL SOURCES

1. General Treaty Collections

a.   United Nations Treaty Series (U.N.T.S.). Under Article 102 of the United Nations Charter, every member of the United Nations is required to register its international agreements with the Secretariat, which, in turn, is required to publish them. Compulsory registration and publication are intended in part to prevent secret diplomacy. Begun in 1946, *U.N.T.S.* now has over 2,400 volumes and contains many thousands of agreements, both bilateral and multilateral. However, like *U.S.T.*, *U.N.T.S.* is slow to publish. Its index volumes likewise run behind and are difficult to use. The researcher should note that the formal title by which libraries catalog this source is *Treaty Series (United Nations).*

Agreements published in *U.N.T.S.* are now available on the *United Nations Treaty Collection* website.[57] Text is presented in an image format as the document appears in *U.N.T.S.* While this image format ensures authenticity, it is often difficult to determine the volume and page number of *U.N.T.S.* Searching by *U.N.T.S.* citation is possible, but not easy. This is something of a drawback when using *U.N.T.S.* online. *U.N.T.S.* is also available in *HeinOnline* in a fully searchable version. It can also be found on the *World Legal Information Institute (WorldLII)* website.[58]

The *United Nations Treaty Collection* website has a file of certified true copies of the multilateral treaties deposited with the Secretary-General.[59]

For more information on the registration and publication of international agreements by the United Nations, see the *Treaty Handbook* (2002) prepared by the Treaty Section of the United Nations Office of Legal Affairs.[60]

b.   League of Nations Treaty Series (L.N.T.S.). This predecessor of *U.N.T.S.* was published under the auspices of the League of Nations. In 205 volumes covering the period 1920 to 1946, *L.N.T.S.* published the treaties registered with the Secretariat of the League. The set is often cataloged under the title *Treaty Series (League of Nations)*. *L.N.T.S.* is now included in the *United Nations Treaty Collection* website.[61]

c.   Consolidated Treaty Series (C.T.S.) (1969–1981) (Oceana Publications). This series, 243 volumes covering the period 1648 to 1919, is valuable for locating the text of historically important international agreements.

---

[57] http://treaties.un.org.

[58] http://www.worldlii.org/int/special/treaties/.

[59] http://treaties.un.org/pages/CTCs.aspx.

[60] The *Treaty Handbook* is available in PDF on the *United Nations Treaty Collection* website, http://treaties.un.org/doc/source/publications/THB/English.pdf.

[61] http://treaties.un.org/pages/LONOnline.aspx.

Note that the three treaty series mentioned here (*C.T.S., L.N.T.S.,* and *U.N.T.S.*) cover a continuous period from 1648 to the present.

2. Other Treaty Collections

a. Council of Europe Treaty Series (C.E.T.S). The Council of Europe, an international organization of forty-seven European nations, has as one of its main purposes the drafting and sponsoring of multilateral agreements on subjects of mutual interest. The most significant treaty sponsored by the Council of Europe is the Convention for the Protection of Human Rights and Fundamental Freedoms.[62] The Council of Europe's treaties are first published as individual documents in the *Council of Europe Treaty Series.*[63]

Today, the clearly superior method for researching Council of Europe agreements is on the World Wide Web, using the Council of Europe's conventions website.[64]

b. International Legal Materials (I.L.M.). Published since 1962 by the American Society of International Law, *I.L.M.* is likely the best source for recent international documents of significance, including international agreements. A distinguished editorial board makes the selection. Published six times a year, *I.L.M.* contains many other kinds of documents, e.g., judicial decisions, arbitral awards, and the documents of international organizations. *I.L.M.* is available in both *Westlaw* and *LexisNexis*, and (with a delay) in *HeinOnline.*

c. O.A.S. Treaty Series. Like the Council of Europe, the Organization of American States drafts and sponsors multilateral agreements of mutual interest to member states. These are published in the *O.A.S. Treaty Series.* Its formal title, under which it is cataloged in libraries, is *Treaty Series (Organization of American States).* It continues the now-discontinued *Pan-American Treaty Series.*

Multilateral international agreements sponsored by the O.A.S. can now be conveniently consulted on the O.A.S. website.[65] They are organized both by year and by subject. Status information can also be found.

d. National Treaty Series. Like the United States, many other countries publish their international agreements in a special series. Examples are the *United Kingdom Treaty Series, Canada Treaty Series,* and *Recueil des Traités et Accords de la France.*

The *United Kingdom Treaty Series* is technically a subset of documents called "command papers." The *Treaty Series* command papers are now available as PDF documents from January 1997 forward at the website of the Foreign & Commonwealth Office.[66] In addition, the Foreign and Commonwealth Office now has a database called UK Treaties Online that includes information on over 14,000 treaties involving the UK for the period 1892 to 1996.[67] This includes links to the full text in PDF of the command papers published in the *United Kingdom Treaty Series.* The Australian government

---

[62] C.E.T.S. No. 5, 213 U.N.T.S. 221.

[63] The former title was *European Treaty Series (E.T.S.).* They have also been collected and republished (through 1998) in the seven volumes of *European Conventions and Agreements* (1971–2000) (Council of Europe).

[64] http://conventions.coe.int/.

[65] http://www.oas.org/DIL/treaties.htm.

[66] http://www.fco.gov.uk/en/publications-and-documents/treaty-command-papers-ems/.

[67] http://www.fco.gov.uk/en/publications-and-documents/treaties/uk-treaties-online/.

makes available an online source of its international agreements, the *Australian Treaties Library*.[68] This is a comprehensive database of all international agreements to which Australia is a party, and which are published in hard copy in the *Australian Treaty Series*. France now has a good database of its international agreements, both bilateral and multilateral, called *Base Pacte*.[69] The *Irish Treaty Series* is now online from 2002.[70] The Swiss Foreign Ministry maintains a database of Switzerland's international agreements called *Datenbank Staatsverträge*.[71] The Canadian government maintains a database concerning its international agreements called *Canada Treaty Information*.[72] Rather than the full text of agreements, it provides citations to *Canada Treaty Series* and other sources, in addition to full status information.

Countries that have official gazettes (this generally does not include the common law jurisdictions) will as a general practice publish international agreements of any significance in the official gazette. An excellent example is Germany, which devotes an entire part of its official gazette to the publication of international agreements—the *Bundesgesetzblatt, Teil II*.

e.   Subject Compilations. Many publishers, both governmental and commercial, have compiled collections of international agreements. These collections can be very useful because they bring together documents that otherwise are scattered in several sources. There are too many of these collections to list comprehensively here, but some leading recent examples are:

- Richard Plender, *Basic Documents on International Migration Law* (3d ed. 2007) (Martinus Nijhoff);

- *Collection of International Instruments and Legal Texts Concerning Refugees and Others of Concern to UNHCR* (2007);[73]

- *Copyright and Related Rights: Laws and Treaties* (1987–) (World Intellectual Property Organization);

- Adam Roberts & Richard Guelf, *Documents on the Laws of War* (3d ed. 2000) (Oxford University Press);

- *Industrial Property Laws and Treaties* (1976–) (World Intellectual Property Organization);

- *International Criminal Law: A Collection of International and European Instruments* (Christine Van den Wyngaert ed., 2005) (Martinus Mijhoff); and

- *International Environmental Law: Multilateral Treaties* (W.E. Burhenne ed., 1974–) (Kluwer Law International).

f.   Historical Collections. There are many collections of international agreements, both bilateral and multilateral, that are now chiefly of historical interest. To locate these,

---

[68] http://www.austlii.edu.au/au/other/dfat.

[69] http://www.doc.diplomatie.fr/pacte/index.html.

[70] https://www.dfa.ie/our-role-policies/international-priorities/international-law/find-a-treaty/.

[71] http://www.eda.admin.ch/eda/de/home/topics/intla/intrea/dbstv.html.

[72] http://www.accord-treaty.gc.ca/.

[73] This collection, produced by the United Nations High Commissioner for Refugees, is available at http://www.unhcr.org/publ/PUBL/455c460b2.html.

refer to Peter Macalister-Smith & Joachim Schwietzke, *Treaties, Treaty Collections and Documents on Foreign Affairs: From Sun King Suppilulima I to the Hague Peace Conferences of 1899 & 1907: An Annotated Bibliography* (2002) (Arbeitsgemeinschaft für Juristisches Bibliotheks-und Dokumentationswesen). Also of use is Columbia Law Library's *Guide to Researching Historical Treaties*.[74]

3.   International Agreements on the Internet

a.   Agreements Sponsored by International Organizations. Several international organizations maintain excellent websites with collections of international agreements for which they are responsible. Some examples are:

- Council of Europe;[75]

- Hague Conference on Private International Law;[76]

- International Atomic Energy Agency (IAEA);[77]

- International Committee of the Red Cross;[78]

- International Institute for the Unification of Private Law (UNIDROIT);[79]

- International Labor Organization (ILO) (NORMLEX);[80]

- Organization of American States (OAS);[81]

- United Nations Commission on International Trade Law (UNCITRAL);[82]

- United Nations Educational, Scientific and Cultural Organization (UNESCO);[83]

- United Nations Environment Programme (ECOLEX);[84]

- United Nations High Commissioner for Human Rights (UNHCHR);[85] and

- World Intellectual Property Organization (WIPO).[86]

b.   WorldLII International Treaties Collection.[87] This online resource of the World Legal Information Institute (WorldLII) aggregates a wide range of treaty collections maintained both by WorldLII and by other legal information institutes. The researcher will find the full text in PDF of the *United Nations Treaty Series*, as well as several national or regional treaty collections.

---

[74] http://www.law.columbia.edu/library/Research_Guides/internat_law/hist_treaties.

[75] http://conventions.coe.int.

[76] http://www.hcch.net/index_en.php?act=conventions.listing.

[77] http://www.iaea.org/Publications/Documents/Conventions/index.html.

[78] https://www.icrc.org/ihl.

[79] http://www.unidroit.org/english/conventions/c-main.htm.

[80] http://www.unidroit.org/library/overview (follow "Retification of ILO Conventions" link).

[81] http://www.oas.org/juridico/english/treaties.html.

[82] http://www.uncitral.org/uncitral/en/uncitral_texts.html.

[83] http://portal.unesco.org/en/ev.php-URL_ID=12025 & URL_DO=DO_TOPIC & URL_SECTION=-471.html.

[84] http://www.ecolex.org/start.php.

[85] http://www2.ohchr.org/english/law/index.htm.

[86] http://www.wipo.int/treaties/en/.

[87] http://www.worldlii.org/int/special/treaties/.

   c.   Treaty Secretariats. Many important international agreements provide for the establishment of secretariats to deal with administrative matters related to the operation of the agreement. Two examples are the Secretariat of the Convention on International Trade in Endangered Species of Wild Fauna and Flora[88] and the Secretariat of the Convention on Biological Diversity.[89] The secretariats' tasks include organizing periodic meetings of the states party to the agreement, preparing reports and technical studies, and distributing public information about the operation of the agreement. In addition, the secretariats often produce excellent websites for the use of the public. These websites invariably include a text of the agreement and related documents, along with much other current and relevant information.

   d.   Other Internet Sources. Creative use of Internet search engines will locate a multitude of websites reproducing various international agreements. Subjects covered run the range of topics in international law, e.g., international trade, the environment, disarmament, and humanitarian law. A word of caution is in order. The accuracy and authority of texts reproduced on Internet websites vary significantly from site to site. It is dangerous to rely, without verifying their accuracy, on texts retrieved from unofficial Internet sites. Texts available in official sources, either print or electronic, should be preferred. The Internet often does make available texts of international agreements not available elsewhere, however.

   e.   LexisNexis and *Westlaw. LexisNexis* has a variety of files containing international agreements. They are most easily found in *lexis.com* under "Area of Law–By Topic," then under "International Law-Treaties and International Agreements." These files are of varying degrees of usefulness. At the positive end of the spectrum is Tax Analysts Worldwide Tax Treaties. At the negative end is a file of European Community treaties that is obsolete. *Westlaw* has several collections of international agreements. The best way to find them in *Westlaw Classic* is to search the directory using the term "treaties." The *Westlaw* databases also vary in quality.

   Availability of international agreements on both *Lexis Advance* and *WestlawNext* is limited. This is expected to change as both systems continue to enhance their international content. *Lexis Advance* has a file named U.S. Treaties on Lexis that contains international agreements of the U.S. as found in such sources as *U.S.T., T.I.A.S.,* and *Bevans.* Similarly, WestlawNext has a database named United States Treaties and Other International Agreements that derives from *T.I.A.S.* and, for older agreements, *the United States Statutes at Large.*

4.   Finding and Updating International Agreements (When the United States May Not Be a Party)

   In addition to the finding tools mentioned in Section B-6, several sources can help in locating international agreements and determining their current status, regardless of whether the United States is a party. A convenient online source for quick consultation is *Frequently-Cited Treaties and Other International Instruments,*[90] prepared by the University of Minnesota Law Library, which covers seventy multilateral agreements.

---

[88] http://www.cites.org.

[89] http://www.cbd.int/.

[90] http://library.law.umn.edu/researchguides/most-cited.html.

    a.   *FLARE Index to Treaties.*[91] This is an online index to over 1,500 multilateral international agreements. The results display includes several parallel citations to hardbound sources of the agreement in question, as well as links to versions of the agreement available on the World Wide Web.

    b.   *Multilateral Treaties Deposited with the Secretary-General.* This resource from the United Nations tracks the status of more than 500 international agreements drafted under the auspices of the United Nations and League of Nations for which the Secretary-General performs depository functions. The preferred source for consulting this resource is the *United Nations Treaty Collection* website, where it is updated frequently.[92] The entry for each treaty gives complete information regarding the states party to the treaty and the relevant dates. This is one of the few sources that publish the text of various declarations and reservations entered by states at the time of becoming a party to an international agreement.

    c.   *Multilateral Treaties: Index and Current Status* (M.J. Bowman & D.J. Harris eds., 1984) (Butterworth) This useful but now dated volume provides information on about 1,000 treaties. Each entry sets out the date of conclusion, citations to the location of the text in multiple sources, date of entry into force, states party to the treaty, and states signatory. A notes section describes the agreement and makes reference to related documents. A supplement updates the volume to January 1, 1994.

    d.   *Multilateral Treaty Calendar, 1648–1995.*[93] This is a chronological listing of over 6,000 agreements in over a hundred sources. Each entry gives the full name of the agreement in English and French, date of conclusion, original parties, multiple citations, and notes. Several appendices and an extensive index are provided.

    c.   *World Treaty Index.*[94] This resource is self-described as "an electronic treaty database spanning the 20th century." It contains citations to several thousand bilateral and multilateral agreements entered into between 1945 and 1999. When complete, the *World Treaty Index* online will supersede its hardbound predecessor.[95]

5. Travaux Préparatoires

    The French phrase "travaux préparatoires" describes the documents making up the drafting history or negotiating history of an international agreement. Travaux préparatoires can play an important role in treaty interpretation.[96]

---

[91] http://193.62.18.232/dbtw-wpd/textbase/treatysearch.htm.

[92] http://treaties.un.org/pages/ParticipationStatus.aspx.

[93] CHRISTIAN L. WIKTOR (Martinus Nijhoff 1998).

[94] http://www.worldtreatyindex.com.

[95] WORLD TREATY INDEX (Peter H. Rohn ed., 2d ed. 1983).

[96] For detailed information on how to do research on travaux préparatoires, see Jonathan Pratter, *Update: À la Recherche des Travaux Préparatoires: An Approach to Researching the Drafting History of International Agreements,* http://www.nyulawglobal.org/globalex/Travaux_Preparatoires1.htm (Nov.–Dec. 2012).

D. CUSTOMARY INTERNATIONAL LAW

1. Introduction[97]

Article 38 of the Statute of the International Court of Justice speaks of "international custom, as evidence of a general practice accepted as law." Several questions arise from this formulation. The first must be: *Whose* custom? Many actors have roles to play in the creation of international law. However, when it comes to the creation of a binding norm of customary international law, it is usually *state* practice that counts. The next question must be: *What* is international custom? The text of Article 38 gives the germ of an answer: "a general practice accepted as law." Customary international law, then, has a dual character. It derives (1) from the general practice of states and other subjects of international law that are (2) acting from a sense of legal obligation.

The definition of international custom simply pushes the difficulty back a step. Now the question becomes: *How* does the researcher go about establishing the existence of something that by definition is unwritten and the evidence of which might be found in any number of sources?

A leading scholarly work on this question[98] has a chapter titled "Phenomenology of State Practice." Here the author draws up a catalog of possibilities, including:

- Diplomatic correspondence;
- Advice of the legal advisor to the foreign ministry (in the case of the U.S., the State Department);
- General statements of policy on international legal questions;
- Parliamentary practice (e.g., statements or documents from the Senate Committee on Foreign Relations);
- National legislation on international legal questions;
- Administrative practice on international legal questions; and
- Decisions of national courts on international legal questions.

The search for evidence of state practice as an element of customary international law must go forward on several fronts. Note that national legislation, administrative practice, and judicial decisions are included in the list. This means that the researcher can use research methods described elsewhere in this book as methods for discovery of state practice in international law. Despite the difficulties, some well-established sources are available with which the researcher can begin the process.

It is also apparent from the list that actions and statements by government officials, especially those charged with responsibility in foreign relations, carry substantial weight as components of state practice. This means that it is essential to observe what foreign

---

[97] *See generally*, INT'L L. ASS'N, COMM. ON FORMATION OF CUSTOMARY (GEN.) INT'L L., FINAL REPORT OF THE COMMITTEE: STATEMENT OF PRINCIPLES APPLICABLE TO THE FORMATION OF GENERAL CUSTOMARY INTERNATIONAL LAW (2000). A good guide is Silke Sahl, *Researching Customary International Law, State Practice and the Pronouncements of States Regarding International Law,* http://www.nyulawglobal.org/globalex/customary_international_law.htm.

[98] Luigi Ferrari Bravo, *Méthodes de Recherche de la Coutume Internationale dans la Pratique des États*, 192 (1985 III) RECUEIL DES COURS 233 (1986).

ministries around the world do and say. Today, this kind of research is greatly facilitated by the fact that foreign ministries have good websites, which they use to disseminate information about the policies and positions of their governments on the full range of international issues. For example, on the home page of Japan's Ministry of Foreign Affairs,[99] the researcher finds under the heading "Foreign Policy" a set of thirty links to information on international issues, everything from Agriculture to Women's Issues.

A good collection of web links to foreign ministries around the world is maintained by the United States Institute of Peace.[100]

An ambitious effort to establish detailed rules of customary international *humanitarian* law, based on a close analysis of state practice and including the study of many national military manuals, has been carried out under the auspices of the International Committee of the Red Cross (ICRC).[101]

2.   Digests of Practice: United States Publications

Digests of practice bring together references and quotations from a huge array of sources and organize them according to the main topics of public international law. Usually a digest focuses on the practice of a particular nation. The United States government traditionally has done a good job of publishing digests of international law or digests of practice in international law. The first of these was published in 1877.[102] The digests produced in the United States (under the auspices of the State Department) draw their material from a broad range of U.S. source documents. These digests are frequently referred to by the name of the preparer.

   a.   *A Digest of the International Law of the United States Taken from Documents Issued by Presidents and Secretaries of State, and from Decisions of Federal Courts and Opinions of Attorneys-General* (Francis Wharton ed., 1886). Wharton's digest, in three volumes, was the first to adopt a subject arrangement according to the main topics of international law.

   b.   *A Digest of International Law as Embodied in Diplomatic Discussions, Treaties and Other International Agreements, International Awards, the Decisions of Municipal Courts, and the Writings of Jurists* . . . (John B. Moore comp., 1906). Moore's digest, in eight volumes, sets the pattern for its successors and supersedes Wharton's (above).

   c.   *Digest of International Law* (Green H. Hackworth comp., 1940–1944) (available in *HeinOnline*). Hackworth's digest, in eight volumes, covers the period from 1906 to 1939.

   d.   *Digest of International Law* (Marjorie M. Whiteman comp., 1963–1975) (available in *HeinOnline*). Whiteman's consists of fourteen volumes plus an index volume.

---

[99] http://www.mofa.go.jp.

[100]   http://www.usip.org/publications/foreign-affairs-ministries-web.

[101]   CUSTOMARY INTERNATIONAL HUMANITARIAN LAW (Jean-Marie Henckaerts & Louise Doswald Beck eds., 2005). An updated version is available at no cost on the ICRC's website, https://www.icrc.org/customary-ihl/eng/docs/v1.

[102]   JOHN L. CADWALADER, DIGEST OF THE PUBLISHED OPINIONS OF THE ATTORNEYS-GENERAL, AND OF THE LEADING DECISIONS OF THE FEDERAL COURTS, WITH REFERENCE TO INTERNATIONAL LAW, TREATIES AND KINDRED SUBJECTS (U.S.G.P.O. 1877).

e.   Updating the U.S. Digests. In 1974, the State Department began a new project of preparing an annual *Digest of United States Practice in International Law.* Eight volumes covering the period 1973 to 1980 are followed by a three-volume set for the years 1981 to 1988. After a long delay, annual volumes for 2000 to 2009 have been published as well as a volume for 1989 to 1990. Finally, two volumes covering the period 1991 to 1999 were published.[103] It is expected that future volumes will be published in a timely fashion. Cumulative indexes for 1973 to 1980 and for 1989 to 2008 have been issued.

The *Digest*, along with supplementary documentation, is available in PDF in the State Department's website.[104] The online *Digest* publishes the full text of documents excerpted that would otherwise be difficult to find in hardbound or electronic format.

Since 1959 (volume 53), the *American Journal of International Law* has published in each quarterly issue a section entitled "Contemporary Practice of the United States Relating to International Law."

3.   Digests of Practice From Other Countries

Digests relating to the practice of other countries in international law are available. Some leading examples are given here.

a.   British Practice. A British Digest of International Law (Clive Parry ed., 1967–) (Stevens & Sons). This was to be a major project in two phases. Five volumes of the first phase, covering the years 1860 to 1914, were published, but nothing has appeared since 1967. Fortunately, other publications provide significant coverage, notably the *British Yearbook of International Law* (1920–), which includes a section entitled "United Kingdom Materials on International Law." Further, Oxford University Press has published a CD-ROM titled *United Kingdom Materials on International Law: 1975–2001* (Geoffrey Marston ed., 2004).

b.   Répertoire de la Pratique Française en Matière de Droit International Publique (Alexandre C. Kiss ed., 1962–1972) (C.N.R.S.). This digest of practice from France can be supplemented with the sections of the *Annuaire Français de Droit International* (CNRS Editions 1956–) entitled "Pratique Française du Droit International" and "Chronologie des Faits Internationaux d'Intérêt Juridique."

c.   Yearbooks. Yearbooks of international law can prove very useful because they typically contain sections documenting state practice for the country in which they are published. See Section G-4, below.

4.   Additional Sources Documenting State Practice

a.   Foreign Relations of the United States (1861) (available in *HeinOnline*). This multivolume series prepared by the State Department constitutes the official record of the foreign policy and diplomacy of the United States.

---

[103]   The *Digest* for the recent years is published by the International Law Institute under an agreement with the State Department, which produces the content. Oxford University Press now participates, too. Cambridge University Press has published two volumes of *United States Practice in International Law*, covering the years 1999–2001 and 2002–2004.

[104]   http://www.state.gov/s/l/c8183.htm.

b.   *American Foreign Policy: Current Documents* (1959–) (U.S.G.P.O.)[105] This is an annual series prepared by the State Department. The last volume published was for 1990. Each volume is organized into topical and regional chapters. These collections published by the government can be supplemented with these series: *Documents on American Foreign Relations* (1939–1970) (Council on Foreign Relations), *The United States in World Affairs* (1931–1971) (Council on Foreign Relations), and *American Foreign Relations* (1971–1978) (New York University Press).

c.   *British and Foreign State Papers* (1841–1977) (H.M.S.O.) (available in *HeinOnline*). The British equivalent of *Foreign Relations of the United States*, this series covers the period 1812 to 1968. For the period after 1945, *Documents on British Policy Overseas* (1984–2002) (H.M.S.O.) provides supplemental coverage, as does *Documents on International Affairs* (1929–1973) (Oxford Univ. Press) for the period 1928 to 1963.

d.   *United Nations Legislative Series.* This is the title for a group of materials published by the United Nations containing national legislation and other elements of state practice in areas of interest to the United Nations. The series includes *Laws Concerning Nationality*; *Laws and Regulations Regarding Diplomatic and Consular Privileges and Immunities*; *Legislative Texts and Treaty Provisions Concerning the Legal Status, Privileges and Immunities of International Organizations*; *Legislative Texts and Treaty Provisions Concerning the Utilization of International Rivers for Purposes Other than Navigation*; *Materials on Succession of States*; *National Legislation and Treaties Relating to the Territorial Sea, the Contiguous Zone, the Continental Shelf, the High Seas, and to Fishing and Conservation of the Living Resources of the Sea*; *Materials on Succession of States in Respect of Matters other than Treaties*; *National Legislation and Treaties Relating to the Law of the Sea*; *Materials on Jurisdictional Immunities of States and Their Property*; and *National Laws and Regulations on the Prevention and Suppression of International Terrorism*.

e.   *Bibliography. Sources of State Practice in International Law* (1841–1977) (available in *HeinOnline*) documents treaty collections, diplomatic documents, international law yearbooks, and digests of state practice for fourteen jurisdictions. There is also a chapter on "Multi-Jurisdictional Collections by Subject."

E. GENERAL PRINCIPLES OF LAW

General principles of law, the third main source set out in Article 38 of the Statute of the International Court of Justice, present some of the same kinds of difficulties as those encountered in researching customary international law: there is no authoritative collection of general principles. The evidence for the existence of a general principle of law must be developed from a variety of authorities. Some of these may be primary sources, but general principles are more likely discovered through authoritative secondary sources, such as leading treatises. These will cite the primary sources relied upon for the existence and application of a particular general principle of law.

A conceptual difficulty has to be resolved before research can begin. Does this source have to do with general principles of law as found in *national* legal systems, or does it refer to general principles that are peculiar to *international* law? There is substantial

---

[105]   *See generally* the online guide, *U.S. Foreign Policy: Information Resources*, produced by the Lehman Social Sciences Library of Columbia University, http://library.columbia.edu/subject-guides/social-sciences/foreign.html.

overlap, for example, where ideas such as good faith in the performance of agreements or the duty to compensate for causing harm are concerned. There is some disagreement, but the prevailing opinion is that "general principles of law" refers to those general principles common to the major *domestic* legal systems. Therefore, the phrase "general principles of law" has to be distinguished from another one, "general principles of *international* law"; the latter are principles derived from customary international law.[106]

Given the emphasis on domestic law, some understanding of *comparative* law, the comparative study of national legal systems, is important. Fortunately, there exists a wealth of information on international law discussing general principles of law applied in the international arena.[107]

F. ADJUDICATIONS

States may settle their differences in a variety of peaceful ways, ranging from diplomatic negotiation to compulsory submission of a dispute to the World Court,[108] with such mechanisms as conciliation, mediation, and binding arbitration in between.[109] Article 38 of the Statute of the International Court of Justice accepts "judicial decisions" as a "subsidiary means for the determination of rules of law." The phrase "subsidiary means" does not capture the true significance of the work of various judicial fora in the contemporary development of international law. Here the phrase "judicial decisions" includes decisions of international arbitral tribunals and decisions of national courts on international legal questions.

This section focuses on the leading sources for decisions of the main international tribunals.[110] It then discusses the ways of finding domestic judicial decisions dealing with questions of international law.

1. International Court of Justice

The International Court of Justice (I.C.J.) is the principal judicial organ of the United Nations. It was founded in 1945 at the same time as the United Nations. The governing instrument of the Court is the Statute of the International Court of Justice, which is an international agreement.[111] The seat of the Court is the Peace Palace at The Hague, Netherlands. The Court is composed of fifteen judges elected by the General

---

[106] *See generally* FOREIGN RELATIONS RESTATEMENT 3D, *supra* note 3, § 102 cmt. 1, reporter's note 7; IAN BROWNLIE, PRINCIPLES OF PUBLIC INTERNATIONAL LAW 16–19 (7th ed. 2008); Giorgio Gaja, *General Principles of Law, in* MAX PLANCK ENCYCLOPEDIA OF PUBLIC INTERNATIONAL LAW (online ed.) (article updated Mar. 2007).

[107] In addition to the references already noted, see generally BIN CHENG, GENERAL PRINCIPLES OF LAW AS APPLIED BY INTERNATIONAL COURTS AND TRIBUNALS (1953); Arnold D. McNair, *The General Principles of Law Recognized by Civilized Nations,* 33 BRIT. Y.B. INT'L L. 1 (1957). *See also* Michael D. Nolan & Frédéric Gilles Sourgens, *Issues of Proof of General Principles of Law in International Arbitration,* 3 WORLD ARB. & MEDIATION REV. 505 (2009).

[108] This is the informal name of the International Court of Justice and of its predecessor, the Permanent Court of International Justice.

[109] *See generally* J.G. MERRILLS, INTERNATIONAL DISPUTE SETTLEMENT (5th ed. 2011); JOHN G. COLLIER & VAUGHAN LOWE, THE SETTLEMENT OF DISPUTES IN INTERNATIONAL LAW: INSTITUTIONS AND PROCEDURES (1999).

[110] *See generally* RUTH MACKENZIE, CESARE P.R. ROMANO, YUVAL SHANY & PHILIPPE SANDS, MANUAL ON INTERNATIONAL COURTS AND TRIBUNALS (2d ed. 2010). *See also* PROJECT ON INTERNATIONAL COURTS AND TRIBUNALS, http://www.pict-pcti.org/.

[111] 59 Stat. 1055, 3 Bevans 1179 (1945). *See* THE STATUTE OF THE INTERNATIONAL COURT OF JUSTICE: A COMMENTARY (Andreas Zimmermann et al. eds., 2006).

Assembly and Security Council of the United Nations. Only states may be parties to a proceeding before the I.C.J. The I.C.J. takes jurisdiction of a dispute either by agreement of the parties, or because the parties have made a declaration under Article 36(2) of the Statute of the International Court of Justice that they accept the "compulsory jurisdiction" of the Court in any legal dispute involving a state that has made the same declaration. In addition to its jurisdiction in contentious cases, the Court is authorized to issue advisory opinions on legal questions to the General Assembly and Security Council. The judgments of the I.C.J. are the single most significant component of the source of international law known as judicial decisions. The publications of the I.C.J., and related materials, are described below.

a. *Reports of Judgments, Advisory Opinions, and Orders.* Along with other documents, the final decisions (judgments on the merits) of the Court are published in this series. The text of a final judgment, including separate and dissenting opinions, may extend to several hundred pages. English and French texts are printed together on facing pages. Decisions are first published individually; then the collected decisions for each year are published together in a single volume.

b. *Pleadings, Oral Arguments, Documents.* Volumes in this series are published after the end of a case, sometimes years after the judgment. They contain the pleadings, memorials (briefs), record of oral proceedings, and other documents, such as maps, that may be submitted to the Court. For each case, several volumes may be published.

c. *Acts and Documents Concerning the Organization of the Court.* This is a single volume that was updated in 2007. It is a useful place to find the United Nations Charter and the Statute and Rules of the Court.

d. *Yearbook.* This annual publication has chapters on the organization of the Court and its work during the year and useful biographies of the judges.

e. *Bibliography of the International Court of Justice.* Each year the Registry of the Court issues this bibliography listing works relating to the Court.

f. *International Court of Justice Website.* The website of the Court[112] vastly improves timely access to the Court's documentation, including its judgments and associated documents. [Illustration 21–2] Under "Decisions" are links to documentation relating to all cases in the Court since its inception in 1945. This documentation includes pleadings that otherwise would not be published until long after a case has been decided.

In *Pulp Mills on the River Uruguay (Argentina v. Uruguay)*, for example, the I.C.J. handed down its judgment on the merits in April 2010. Within hours the full text of the judgment and all dissenting and separate opinions were loaded on the I.C.J. website in PDF in both English and French. In the past, it would take months for the judgment in hardbound version to reach libraries. Further, ever since the case was first brought in 2006, the Court has posted important related documents, including the application (complaint), the memorials (briefs), and even verbatim transcripts of oral argument. These documents would not have appeared for years in the series *Pleadings, Oral Arguments, Documents.*

---

[112]   http://www.icj-cij.org.

g. *Secondary Literature.* Secondary literature concerning the Court is extensive. It can be researched using the subject heading "International Court of Justice" in library catalogs and journal indexes.[113]

2. Permanent Court of International Justice

The predecessor to the I.C.J. was the Permanent Court of International Justice (P.C.I.J.), established under the League of Nations. It heard cases from 1922 to early 1940 and was dissolved in 1946 when the I.C.J. was inaugurated. Many decisions of the P.C.I.J. continue to be of significance in international law. The publications of the P.C.I.J. were issued in series much like those of the I.C.J.

Series A. *Collection of Judgments* (up to 1930)

Series B. *Collection of Advisory Opinions* (up to 1930)

Series A/B. *Judgments, Orders and Advisory Opinions* (after 1930)

Series C. *Acts and Documents Relating to Judgments and Advisory Opinions* (up to 1930)/*Pleadings, Oral Statements and Documents* (after 1930)

Series D. *Acts and Documents Concerning the Organization of the Court*

Series E. *Annual Reports*

Series F. *Indexes*

The judgments of the P.C.I.J. are also available in *World Court Reports: A Collection of the Judgments, Orders and Opinions of the Permanent Court of International Justice* (Manley O. Hudson ed., Carnegie Endowment for International Peace 1934–1943). The complete set of P.C.I.J. documentation set out above is now available in PDF format on the I.C.J. website.

3. Digests of I.C.J. and P.C.I.J. Decisions

The use of the digests noted below facilitates research by providing detailed references and extensive excerpts from those parts of often very lengthy I.C.J. and P.C.I.J. judgments dealing with particular points of international law.

- *The Case Law of the International Court* (Edvard Hambro ed., 1952–1976) (A.W. Sijthoff);

- Rainer Hofmann et al., *World Court Digest* (1993–) (Springer);[114] and

- *A Digest of the Decisions of the International Court* (Krystyna Marek ed., 1974–1978) (Martinus Nijhoff)

---

[113] General works in English concerning the I.C.J. include REGISTRY OF THE INTERNATIONAL COURT OF JUSTICE, LA COUR INTERNATIONALE DE JUSTICE/THE INTERNATIONAL COURT OF JUSTICE (2006) (richly illustrated book, in French and English, prepared for the court's 60th anniversary), TERRY D. GILL, ROSENNE'S THE WORLD COURT: WHAT IT IS AND HOW IT WORKS (6th ed. 2003), SHABTAI ROSENNE, THE LAW AND PRACTICE OF THE INTERNATIONAL COURT, 1920–2005 (4th ed. 2006), MOHAMED SAMEH M. AMR, THE ROLE OF THE INTERNATIONAL COURT OF JUSTICE AS THE PRINCIPAL JUDICIAL ORGAN OF THE UNITED NATIONS (2003), and HOWARD N. MEYER, THE WORLD COURT IN ACTION: JUDGING AMONG THE NATIONS (2002).

[114] Before 1993, the title was *Digest of the Decisions of the International Court of Justice.* Earlier volumes in the series deal with the P.C.I.J.

4.   International Criminal Tribunal for the Former Yugoslavia[115]

The Tribunal was established in 1993 by United Nations Security Council Resolution 827. The Tribunal sits in The Hague, The Netherlands. The mandate of the Tribunal is to prosecute persons responsible for serious violations of international humanitarian law (including war crimes and genocide) committed in the territory of the former Yugoslavia since 1991.

To date, the Tribunal has produced much important documentation as a result of its work, including many judgments. The full text of the Tribunal's judgments is available on the Tribunal's website.[116] In addition, there is a separate database of all public documents in the Tribunal's cases.[117]

Volumes of the official series, *Judicial Reports*, have been published by Martinus Nijhoff for 1994 to 1999.

5.   International Criminal Court

The Rome Statute of the International Criminal Court of 1998,[118] an international agreement, establishes the International Criminal Court. The Court, seated at The Hague, has jurisdiction to try cases charging the most serious crimes of concern to the international community: genocide, crimes against humanity, war crimes, and aggression.

The best way to follow the activities of the Court and to gain access to its documentation is through its website.[119] As of November 2013, twenty cases were underway, arising out of eight "situations." To go to the case documentation, click the link "Situations and Cases." The documentation for each case is divided into two main categories: public court records and transcripts. The former include the filings of the parties, while the latter are the verbatim transcripts of hearings. Also available from the Court's website is a separate database called Legal Tools, containing over 40,000 documents of many types dealing with all aspects of international criminal law.[120]

---

[115]   A similar court, the International Criminal Tribunal for Rwanda, has also produced important decisions, which can be found at the Court's website, http://www.ictr.org. An official series, REPORTS OF ORDERS, DECISIONS AND JUDGMENTS (2000–), is published by Bruylant.

[116]   http://www.icty.org/sections/TheCases/JudgementList.

[117]   http://icr.icty.org/default.aspx.

[118]   2197 U.N.T.S. 90, 37 I.L.M. 999 (1998).

[119]   http://www.icc-cpi.int.

[120]   http://www.legal-tools.org/. A quasi-international criminal court worthy of note is the Special Court for Sierra Leone. Three cases have been completed and a fourth is under way as of June 2014. Trial chamber judgments on the merits have been rendered in two cases. Substantial documentation is available through the Court's website, http://www.rscsl.org/. Click on "Cases." *See also* CYRIL LAUCCI, DIGEST OF JURISPRUDENCE OF THE SPECIAL COURT FOR SIERRA LEONE, 2003–2005 (2007). Another international court worthy of mention is the International Tribunal for the Law of the Sea. The seat of the Tribunal is Hamburg, Germany. Although the Tribunal has heard only twenty-two cases as of June 2014, it is a significant component of the dispute resolution framework set up in the United Nations Convention on the Law of the Sea, Dec. 10, 1982, 1833 U.N.T.S. 3. Judgments and other documents produced in the Tribunal's cases are posted on the Tribunal's website, http://www.itlos.org. The official publication, published by Kluwer, is REPORTS OF JUDGMENTS, ADVISORY OPINIONS AND ORDERS (2000–).

6. Permanent Court of Arbitration

The Permanent Court of Arbitration (P.C.A.) was established in 1899, making it the first global institution for the adjudication of international disputes. Despite its name, it is not a court, but rather an institution that sponsors ad hoc international arbitrations. The P.C.A. is composed of a secretariat called the International Bureau, which maintains a roster of arbitrators who may be named to arbitral panels. Today, the best way to follow the work of the P.C.A. is through its website.[121] In recent years, the P.C.A. has become more active, in part because it has begun to administer investor-state arbitrations and other disputes between states and private parties. Cases from the early days of the P.C.A. are compiled in *The Hague Court Reports* (James B. Scott ed., 1929–1936) and *The Hague Arbitration Cases* (George G. Wilson comp., 1915).

7. International Arbitrations: Collections and Digests of Decisions

Finding published decisions of international arbitral tribunals is notoriously troublesome. Several circumstances contribute to this situation. Most international arbitrations are ad hoc. The tribunal is constituted to resolve the particular dispute, and there is no sponsoring institution to deal with publication. It has fallen to scholars working in their private capacity to prepare collections and digests. The result is that the documentation in this field is widely scattered.

The difficulties of finding international arbitral decisions should not discourage the researcher. The sources noted below and in the following section make the task less frustrating.[122]

a. Reports of International Arbitral Awards (R.I.A.A.).[123] Published by the United Nations, this is probably the leading current source for the text of *selected* international arbitral awards. Volume 30 (the latest published as of December 2013) includes a cumulative table of cases. The complete series of *R.I.A.A.* is available on the U.N.'s website[124] and in *HeinOnline.*

b. International Law Reports (1932–).[125] Because it contains the reports of many kinds of international adjudications, this series, published by Cambridge University Press, could be mentioned under any of several headings. It appears here because it is particularly valuable for its publication of substantial extracts from arbitral decisions difficult to find elsewhere.[126]

c. International Legal Materials (I.L.M.).[127] Significant arbitral awards often are published first in *I.L.M.*

---

[121]   http://www.pca-cpa.org/. Click on "Cases" for a list of cases heard or pending under the auspices of the P.C.A. The full text of awards in completed cases is often available.

[122]   Two collections of arbitral decisions, both in French, also deserve mention: A. DE LAPRADELLE & N. POLITIS, RECUEIL DES ARBITRAGES INTERNATIONAUX (Pedone 1905–1954); HENRI LA FONTAINE, PASICRISIE INTERNATIONALE: HISTOIRE DOCUMENTAIRE DES ARBITRAGES INTERNATIONAUX (Stämpfli 1902, reprinted in 1997 by Kluwer).

[123]   (United Nations 1948–).

[124]   http://www.un.org/law/riaa.

[125]   Until 1949, the title was *Annual Digest and Reports of Public International Cases*.

[126]   *International Law Reports* are now commercially available online from *Justis* (a legal research service in the UK).

[127]   See the main discussion of *I.L.M.* at Section C-2-b.

d.   John Bassett Moore, *History and Digest of the International Arbitrations to Which the United States Has Been a Party* (1898). The United States has long been an active participant in the process of international arbitration. In fact, a leading commentator notes that "[m]odern arbitration begins with the Jay Treaty of 1794 between the United States and Great Britain. . . ."[128] In many cases, the government would publish the results of the early arbitrations in which the United States participated, but those books are very difficult to find today. Therefore, Moore's *History and Digest* in six volumes continues to be a valuable source for reports of arbitrations of the United States from the late eighteenth to the end of the nineteenth century. It is available in *HeinOnline* and *Google Books*.

e.   *International Adjudications: Ancient and Modern: History and Documents* (John Bassett Moore ed., 1929–1936). This ambitious project was never completed, but six volumes were issued.

f.   *Iran–United States Claims Tribunal Reports* (1983–). Following the resolution of the Iran hostage crisis in late 1980, an arbitral tribunal was established to decide outstanding claims between United States citizens and companies and the government of Iran. Although the bulk of its work has been completed, a few cases remain on the docket as of June 2014. Decisions are reported in this series from Cambridge University Press, in *Westlaw,* and on the Tribunal's website.[129]

g.   *Investment Arbitrations.* Disputes between foreign investors and host states are often settled by arbitration. These arbitrations have substantial jurisprudential and practical significance, but finding arbitral awards and associated documents can be difficult. A selection of awards made under the auspices of the International Centre for the Settlement of Investment Disputes (ICSID) can be found on the Centre's website[130] and in the hard copy *ICSID Reports* (1993–).[131] Similar awards made under Chapter 11 of the North American Free Trade Agreement are on the websites of the U.S. State Department,[132] of Canada's Department of Foreign Affairs and International Trade,[133] and of Mexico's Secretaría de Economía.[134]

A valuable development in this field is the *Investment Treaty Arbitration*, or *ITA*, website, sponsored by the University of Victoria (Canada) Faculty of Law.[135] A wealth of primary-source documents is available on the site. These documents would otherwise be either unknown or impossible to find.

---

[128]   IAN BROWNLIE, PRINCIPLES OF PUBLIC INTERNATIONAL LAW 702 (7th ed. 2008). The arbitrations under the Jay Treaty concerned both boundaries and claims for compensation following the Revolutionary War.

[129]   http://www.iusct.org/index-english.html. *See also* CHRISTOPHER R. DRAHOZAL & CHRISTOPHER S. GIBSON, THE IRAN–U.S. CLAIMS TRIBUNAL AT 25: THE CASES EVERYONE NEEDS TO KNOW FOR INVESTOR-STATE AND INTERNATIONAL ARBITRATION (Oxford University Press 2007).

[130]   http://icsid.worldbank.org. Click "Cases," then "Search Online Decisions and Awards."

[131]   *See also* RICHARD HAPP & NOAH RUBINS, DIGEST OF ICSID AWARDS AND DECISIONS, 2003–2007 (2009).

[132]   http://www.state.gov/s/l/c3439.htm.

[133]   http://www.international.gc.ca/trade-agreements-accords-commerciaux/disp-diff/nafta.aspx?lang=en.

[134]   http://www.economia.gob.mx/comunidad-negocios/comercio-exterior/solucion-controversias.

[135]   http://italaw.com.

The United Nations Conference on Trade and Development (UNCTAD) offers a similar service called *Database of Treaty-Based Investor–State Dispute Settlement Cases*.[136] A commercial service called *Investment Claims* is available from Oxford University Press.[137]

8. Finding Tools for International Arbitrations

Research in international arbitration would be much more difficult without the use of the finding tools noted in this section.

a. *Survey of International Arbitrations, 1794–1989* (3d ed. 1990) (Martinus Nijhoff). This book covers approximately 600 international disputes that resulted in agreements to arbitrate, although in some cases awards were never rendered. The one-page entries for each case give all the critical information, including the names of the parties; a brief description of the dispute; a note on the agreement to arbitrate and its location, if available; and notes on the disposition, with citations to the text of the award if it is published.

b. *Repertory of International Arbitral Jurisprudence.* (Vincent Coussirat-Coustère & Pierre M. Eisemann eds., 1989–1991) (Martinus Nijhoff). This is a comprehensive collection of excerpts from hundreds of arbitral decisions organized according to a detailed outline of international law. Each extract refers to a table of awards where the researcher will find essential information about the decision, including a citation to the publication of the full text.[138] In three volumes, the *Repertory* covers the period from 1794 through 1988.

9. International Law in U.S. Courts

Searching for cases in United States courts on questions of international law is similar to searching for U.S. cases on any other topic. For example, the West digests have two topics, "International Law" and "Treaties," that collect cases on several points of international law as applied in the courts of the United States. The first topic is useful for such questions as the sources of international law and its relation to United States law, territorial sovereignty, foreign sovereign immunity, the act of state doctrine, and extraterritoriality. The second topic deals with the negotiation, operation, and interpretation of international agreements in United States law. Another topic on point in a specialized area is "Ambassadors and Consuls."

A series of the *American Law Reports—A.L.R. International*—publishes "global cases," which includes cases from U.S. courts on issues of international interest. For example, the annotation titled *Recovery of Paintings and Other Artworks Lost During World War II–Global Cases*, 4 A.L.R. Int'l 287 (2011), cites and discusses cases and legislation from France, Germany, Russia, Switzerland, the United Kingdom, and the United States.

---

[136]   http://investmentpolicyhub.unctad.org/IIA/CountryBits/223#iiaInnerMenu.

[137]   http://www.investmentclaims.com/index.html. *See also* the *KluwerArbitration* online service, http://www.kluwerarbitration.com/CommonUI/BITs-countries.aspx.

[138]   The researcher should be aware that sometimes the text of arbitral awards is never published in completely unabridged form. Instead, for example, lengthy extracts are published in one of the leading journals of international law.

In this area of research, the benefits of using online systems such as *Westlaw* and *LexisNexis* cannot be overstated. Cases in a United States court raising a question of international law might arise in almost any field of law. Significant cases having international legal implications could start life as a suit on a bill of lading[139] or promissory note.[140] Obviously, the digests do not deal adequately with this possibility. A well-designed search in *Westlaw* or *LexisNexis* is an indispensable step in the research process when looking for cases with an international legal component.

Currently under development by the American Society of International Law is a free database called *i.lex*,[141] described as "the legal research system for international law in U.S. courts." The database contains select U.S. court cases on a broad range of issues in international law. There are drop down menus for topic, jurisdiction, treaty, and statute. *i.lex* is still under development as of January 2014.

International Law Cases, published since 1971 by Oceana Publications, is now in a fourth series. As a general matter, it reprints cases already available elsewhere.[142]

10. International Law in National Courts of Other Countries

Domestic courts in other countries also decide cases involving issues of public international law. Finding these decisions is to a large extent a matter of researching *foreign law*. For common law jurisdictions such as the United Kingdom and Canada, which are well-represented in *Westlaw*, *LexisNexis*, and the web, the difficulty is not so great. Outside the leading common law jurisdictions, this research presents greater challenges. A good approach is to consult the digests of practice in international law discussed in Sections D-2 and D-3. The digests include summaries of judicial decisions.

Ideally, every country would be as well-served as Germany. There, the Max Planck Institute for Comparative Public Law and International Law publishes annual online installments of *Deutsche Rechtsprechung in Völkerrechtlichen Fragen (German Judicial Decisions on Questions of International Law)*.[143] This covers the years 1986 to 2001. Beginning with 2003, judicial decisions are included in the annual online installments of *Völkerrechtliche Praxis der Bundesrepublik Deutschland (German Practice in International Law)*,[144] which is reprinted from the journal of the Institute, the *Zeitschrift für Ausländisches Öffentliches Recht und Völkerrecht*.

Oxford University Press now produces the online service titled *Oxford Reports on International Law*.[145] One of the modules in this service is *Oxford Reports on International Law in Domestic Courts*, which has international law cases from national courts of about seventy jurisdictions. While that is a good number of countries, several

---

[139]   *See, e.g.*, Banco Nacional de Cuba v. Sabbatino, 376 U.S. 398 (1964) (act of state doctrine).

[140]   *See, e.g.*, Gau Shan Co., Ltd. v. Bankers Trust Co., 956 F.2d 1349 (6th Cir. 1992) (injunction against suit in a foreign court and international comity).

[141]   http://ilex.asil.org/.

[142]   *See also* COMMONWEALTH INTERNATIONAL LAW CASES (1974–95) (Oceana Publications).

[143]   http://www.mpil.de/ww/en/pub/research/details/publications/institute/rspr.cfm.

[144]   http://www.mpil.de/ww/en/pub/research/details/publications/institute/prax.cfm. For the years 1961 to 1985, the researcher can consult the hard copy DECISIONS OF GERMAN COURTS RELATING TO PUBLIC INTERNATIONAL LAW (Springer 1978–1989).

[145]   http://www.oxfordlawreports.com.

are represented by only one or two cases, and several important jurisdictions are not present at all.

G. SECONDARY SOURCES

Article 38 of the Statute of the International Court of Justice expressly acknowledges secondary sources ("the teachings of the most highly qualified publicists") as means for the "determination of rules of law."[146] A strong argument can be made that the researcher in international law, especially the beginner, should start work with a good secondary source, such as a leading textbook, because the beginner has not yet learned which are the significant primary sources of law for a specific question. A good secondary source refers to, cites, and analyzes crucial primary sources as part of the discussion of an issue. Therefore, a good secondary source can efficiently orient and give direction to research. The secondary literature of international law is massive and expanding rapidly. Moreover, it is multilingual. This section can give only an overview of available resources, with indications of specific titles that are particularly useful to researchers who are getting underway in their work.

1. Treatises and Textbooks

a. A good treatise (meaning a major, comprehensive work) on general international law, and usually having chapters on some subtopics (known as the "special part" of international law) is an indispensable starting point for research.[147] A textbook (meaning a less comprehensive work) is almost as good for starters. Treatises and textbooks on both the general part and special branches of international law are found by consulting the appropriate subject headings in the law library catalog. A caveat is in order here: a search on the subject "international law" may return thousands of hits. Limiting by date, language, or keyword will be necessary. In libraries using the Library of Congress classification system, browse international law in KZ.[148]

There is space here to mention only some of the better recent works on general public international law. In English, we may cite *Brownlie's Principles of Public International Law* by James Crawford (8th ed. 2012), *International Law* by Antonio Cassese (2d ed. 2005), *International Law* (Malcolm D. Evans ed., 3d ed. 2010), and *International Law* by Malcolm N. Shaw (6th ed. 2008). A classic in English is *Oppenheim's International Law: Vol. 1: Peace* (Robert Jennings & Arthur Watts eds., 9th ed. 1992). An older work, recommended for researchers in the U.S., is Charles Cheney Hyde's *International Law: Chiefly as Interpreted and Applied by the United States* (2d ed. 1945). International law scholars in the U.S. have not recently produced a major treatise on general public international law. On the other hand, there are good recent introductions, such as *Public International Law in a Nutshell* by Thomas Buergenthal and Sean Murphy (4th ed. 2007) or *International Law* by Mark Janis (6th ed. 2012).

Doing research in international law necessarily means going beyond English, if possible. Recent works in other languages that can be recommended include *Droit International Public* by Nguyen Quoc Dinh et al. (8th ed. 2009), *Droit International*

---

[146]   See the discussion in Section A-3.

[147]   The multivolume treatise is more frequent in languages other than English. Good examples are CHARLES ROUSSEAU, DROIT INTERNATIONAL PUBLIC (Sirey 1970–1983) and GEORG DAHM, JOST DELBRÜCK & RÜDIGER WOLFRUM, VÖLKERRECHT (W. de Gruyter 2d ed. 1989–).

[148]   It was preceded by the JX classification, where older materials may still be found.

Public by Jean Combacau and Serge Sur (9th ed. 2010), *Völkerrecht* by Wolfgang Vitzthum (general editor) (5th ed. 2010), *Völkerrecht: ein Studienbuch* by Knut Ipsen (general editor) (5th ed. 2004), and *Derecho Internacional: Curso General* by Antonio Remiro Brotóns et al. (2010).

b. *Restatement of the Law Third, The Foreign Relations Law of the United States.* This restatement, published in 1987, is likely the secondary source in the United States that can claim the greatest influence and authority in the field of international law. Its black-letter rules provide a clear and concise statement of the contemporary view of the leading international law scholars in the United States on a wide range of issues, both in general public international law and in the foreign relations law of the U.S. The comments and reporter's notes add background and depth. The American Law Institute has begun work on a *Restatement Fourth* for foreign relations.[149]

c. *Collected Courses of the Hague Academy of International Law.* Every summer, the Hague Academy of International Law offers a series of advanced courses on both public and private international law. This extensive series of collected monographs (often book-length essays devoted to a particular subject) is usually known by its title in French, *Recueil des Cours*. Not all contributions are in English (the other official language is French), but many are, and they are valuable secondary sources on current aspects of international law. Several volumes are published each year, along with indexes that appear at irregular intervals. The entire series, published in print by Martinus Nijhoff since 1925, is now available in both *Martinus Nijhoff Online* and *HeinOnline*.

2. Dictionaries and Encyclopedias

a. *Max Planck Encyclopedia of Public International Law.* This comprehensive encyclopedia is now available online from Oxford University Press.[150] Editorial responsibility lies with the Max Planck Institute for Comparative Public Law and International Law in Heidelberg, Germany. Over 1,200 articles have been published online. For most purposes, the earlier *Encyclopedia of Public International Law* (published 1992–2003) is now superseded.

b. *Parry and Grant Encyclopaedic Dictionary of International Law* (John P. Grant & J. Craig Barker eds., 2d ed. 2004). This dictionary of international law is accurate and useful.

c. James R. Fox, *Dictionary of International and Comparative Law* (3d ed. 2003).

3. Journals

Over ninety journals devoted to international law are currently published. Leading examples are the *Harvard International Law Journal*, *Columbia Journal of Transnational Law*, and *Texas International Law Journal*. The most important journal of international law in the United States is the *American Journal of International Law*, published by the American Society of International Law. Of course, many outstanding international law journals are published outside the United States. The leading example

---

[149] *See* http://www.ali.org/index.cfm?fuseaction=projects.proj_ip & projectid=28 (last visited Jan. 10, 2014).

[150] http://www.mpepil.com.

in English is the *International and Comparative Law Quarterly*, published by the British Institute of International and Comparative Law.

Quite possibly the most prestigious journals of international law are not published in English. (As already noted, international law is a field in which a working knowledge of more than one language is valuable.) Candidates for the position include the *Journal du Droit International* and the *Zeitschrift für Ausländisches Öffentliches Recht und Völkerrecht*.

4. Yearbooks[151]

A yearbook of international law is an annual publication, generally sponsored and edited by a national association of international law, a university institute of international law, or an editorial committee of international law scholars from one country. Unfortunately, no yearbook of international law is produced in the United States. The usual format of a yearbook begins with lead articles followed by shorter notes and book reviews. Almost every yearbook has sections covering developments in international law in the courts of the country and in the practices of the government. These sections make yearbooks very useful for keeping up with the latest developments as surveyed by leading scholars. There are roughly twenty-five yearbooks from various countries. Some examples in English are *Australian Year Book of International Law*, *Canadian Yearbook of International Law*, *German Yearbook of International Law*, *Italian Yearbook of International Law*, *Japanese Yearbook of International Law*, and *Netherlands Yearbook of International Law*. There are also some regional yearbooks, such as the *African Yearbook of International Law*, the *Asian Yearbook of International Law*, and the *Baltic Yearbook of International Law*. Most of these (and many other international law journals) are in *HeinOnline*.

5. Indexes and Bibliographies

The standard periodical indexes in law, *LegalTrac* and *Index to Legal Periodicals & Books,* are satisfactory resources for locating articles on international law published in the United States. In addition, they capture a fair percentage of articles on international law published in British law reviews. However, a substantial amount of writing on international law *in English* is done in sources published in Europe, Asia, and other parts of the world not covered by these indexes. In-depth research requires the use of additional resources.

Public International Law: A Current Bibliography of Books and Articles (1975–) is the only source that can make a claim to broad, transnational coverage. It is prepared at the Max Planck Institute for Comparative Public Law and International Law in Heidelberg, Germany. References are entered under thirty-three topics of international law. The hardbound bibliography is supposed to be published twice a year. A free online version of the references in the bibliography is available at the website of the Institute.[152] Another valuable resource is the *Index to Foreign Legal Periodicals* (1964–), which covers dozens of journals, other serials, and selected books in public international law. Finally, note that the festschrift, or celebratory book in honor of a person or institution, plays an important role in the secondary literature of international law. Help in navigating

---

[151]   *See also* Section D-3-c.

[152]   http://www.mpil.de/ww/de/pub/bibliothek/recherche/aufsatzdokumentation/pil.cfm.

through the many festschrifts in international law will be found in the book *Public International Law: Concordance of the Festschriften*, by Peter Macalister-Smith and Joachim Schwietzke (2006).

H. DOCUMENTS OF INTERNATIONAL ORGANIZATIONS

1. Introduction[153]

The term *international organization* refers to an association of states established by a treaty. The organization pursues the common aims of its member states as set out in the founding treaty. An international organization has a legal personality separate from its member states, and the founding treaty provides for decision-making and administrative structures to allow the organization to carry out its work. *Universal* international organizations, such as the United Nations, have wide-ranging purposes; membership is open to any state. Conversely, there are international organizations devoted to special purposes, e.g., the World Health Organization, or to particular regions of the world, e.g., the Organization of American States. The organizations addressed in this section are sometimes known as international *governmental* organizations (IGOs) to distinguish them from international *non-governmental* organizations (NGOs), such as Amnesty International or Greenpeace.

For our purposes, the significance of international organizations lies in the fact that they produce documents of great interest in international law. The constitutions and laws of international organizations, and their methods of deliberation and modes of action, are themselves part of the study of international law. Moreover, the substantive issues addressed by international organizations are at the forefront of contemporary international law.

Even experienced researchers have difficulty with the documents of international organizations for several reasons. First, a surprisingly large number of international organizations exist. Within the United Nations system alone, there are twenty affiliated international organizations, known collectively as *specialized agencies*, each autonomous, with its own founding treaty and membership. Next, each IGO has its own publishing program and method of organizing its documents. Then, there may be deficiencies in distribution. Finally, libraries sometimes inconsistently organize collections and have different means of providing access. Thus, it can be hard to find a particular document of a particular international organization.

An accurate citation that includes the name of the document or a clear indication of its subject matter, the document symbol or number assigned by the organization, and the date the document was issued are especially helpful in international organization documents research.[154]

---

[153]   *See generally* JAN KLABBERS, AN INTRODUCTION TO INTERNATIONAL INSTITUTIONAL LAW (2d ed. 2009); C.F. AMERASINGHE, PRINCIPLES OF THE INSTITUTIONAL LAW OF INTERNATIONAL ORGANIZATIONS (2d ed. 2005); JOSÉ E. ALVAREZ, INTERNATIONAL ORGANIZATIONS AS LAW-MAKERS (2005); PHILIPPE SANDS, PIERRE KLEIN, BOWETT'S LAW OF INTERNATIONAL INSTITUTIONS (6th ed. 2009). *See also* the journal *International Organizations Law Review*, published by Martinus Nijhoff, 2004–.

[154]   See INTERNATIONAL INFORMATION: DOCUMENTS, PUBLICATIONS, AND ELECTRONIC INFORMATION OF INTERNATIONAL GOVERNMENTAL ORGANIZATIONS (Peter I. Hajnal ed., 2d ed. 1997) for a good overview of issues concerning the use of documents produced by international organizations.

2.   United Nations

a.   Introduction. The United Nations (U.N.) carries out its work through a complex organizational structure. The wide range of U.N. concerns has led to the establishment of an equally wide range of commissions, committees, and conferences. The key to understanding United Nations documentation is to understand both the organization of the U.N. and its operation. Most U.N. documentation is the product of the U.N.'s official work, and documents are identified with the particular body within the U.N. structure that produced them. Those unfamiliar with the U.N. should consult the UN at a Glance section of the U.N. website[155] or one of several good print sources.[156]

Researchers can follow developments at the U.N. at the *UN News Centre*,[157] the website of the U.N. News Service. It has numerous news stories about the full range of U.N. activities, as well as U.N. press releases, and links to multimedia reports.

b.   United Nations Charter. The Charter is the constitutive document of the United Nations, as well as a binding international agreement that is acknowledged to state fundamental principles of international law. The text of the Charter can be found in many places, including the United Nations website[158] and numerous print sources.[159] There are excellent recent commentaries on the Charter in English[160] and French.[161] The other article-by-article commentary in English is outdated but still of some use.[162]

c.   United Nations Document Symbols. The United Nations uses a system of document symbols, based on the issuing body, to identify and organize its documentation. Each document symbol identifies the source of that document within the U.N. hierarchy of organization and provides additional information about the document. An example illustrates the system. A typical symbol is A/CN.9/728/Add.1. The forward slash is a distinguishing characteristic in all U.N. document symbols. This example is the first addendum (Add.1) to document number 728 issued by the United Nations Commission on International Trade Law (CN.9), a body established by the General Assembly (A).

The salient components of the system of United Nations document symbols are:

---

[155]   http://www.un.org/aboutun/index.html. The U.N. website also has a useful organization chart, at http://www.un.org/aboutun/chart.html.

[156]   *E.g.,* UNITED NATIONS DEP'T OF PUB. INFO., THE UNITED NATIONS TODAY (2008); THE OXFORD HANDBOOK OF THE UNITED NATIONS (Thomas G. Weiss & Sam Daws eds., 2007); JOHN A. MOORE & JERRY PUBANTZ, ENCYCLOPEDIA OF THE UNITED NATIONS AND INTERNATIONAL AGREEMENTS (2008); EDMUND JAN OSMAŃCZYK & ANTHONY MANGO, ENCYCLOPEDIA OF THE UNITED NATIONS AND INTERNATIONAL AGREEMENTS (3d ed. 2003); GUIDE TO UNITED NATIONS ORGANIZATION, DOCUMENTATION & PUBLISHING FOR STUDENTS, RESEARCHERS, LIBRARIANS (1978); INTRODUCTION TO INTERNATIONAL ORGANIZATIONS (Lyonette Louis-Jacques & Jeanne S. Korman eds., Oceana Publications 1996).

[157]   http://www.un.org/News.

[158]   http://www.un.org/aboutun/charter/index.html.

[159]   *E.g.,* BASIC DOCUMENTS IN INTERNATIONAL LAW (Ian Brownlie ed., 6th ed. 2009); YEARBOOK OF THE UNITED NATIONS (1947–).Documentary supplements to casebooks on international law generally include the Charter as well.

[160]   THE CHARTER OF THE UNITED NATIONS: A COMMENTARY (Bruno Simma ed., 2d ed. 2002).

[161]   JEAN-PIERRE COT & ALAIN PELLET, LA CHARTE DES NATIONS UNIES: COMMENTAIRE ARTICLE PAR ARTICLE (3d ed. 2005).

[162]   LELAND M. GOODRICH ET AL., CHARTER OF THE UNITED NATIONS: COMMENTARY AND DOCUMENTS (3d ed. 1969).

(1) *Leading elements,* denoting the four major United Nations organs that use the system (the International Court of Justice does not):

A/–	General Assembly
E/–	Economic and Social Council
S/–	Security Council
ST/–	Secretariat

(2) *Special leading symbols* have been created for other bodies. Some important examples are:

CCPR/–	Human Rights Committee (under the International Covenant on Civil and Political Rights)
CERD/–	International Convention on the Elimination of All Forms of Racial Discrimination
TD/–	United Nations Conference on Trade and Development (UNCTAD)
UNEP/–	United Nations Environment Programme

(3)   Elements denoting the *subsidiary organ*:

–/AC./–	Ad hoc committee
–/C./–	Standing or main sessional committee
–/CN./–	Commission
–/CONF./–	Conference
–/WG./–	Working Group

(4)   Elements denoting the *nature of the document*:

–/PV. . .	Verbatim records of meetings ("procès verbaux")
–/RES/–	Preliminary text of adopted resolutions
–/SR. . .	Summary records of meetings

(5)   Elements indicating a *change in an earlier document*:

–/Add. . . .	Addendum
–/Corr. . . .	Corrigendum
–/Rev. . . .	Revision

(6)   Elements indicating *distribution*:

–/L. . .	Limited
–/R. . .	Restricted

A good description of the system can be found on the website of the U.N.'s Dag Hammarskjöld Library.[163]

---

[163]   http://www.un.org/Depts/dhl/resguide/symbol.htm. *See also United Nations Documentation: Research Guide,* http://www.un.org/Depts/dhl/resguide. For detailed information on document symbols, see DAG HAMMARSKJÖLD LIBRARY, UNITED NATIONS DOCUMENT SERIES SYMBOLS, 1946–1996 (1998).

d.   United Nations Working Documents and Official Records. U.N. bodies produce vast amounts of documents relating to their work. The majority of these documents are working documents known as masthead documents because the header of each document contains the U.N. logo along with the symbol of the main issuing body in a large font.

A substantial number of U.N. documents are termed *official records.* The main organs of the United Nations—the General Assembly, the Security Council, the Secretariat, and the Economic and Social Council—issue official records. Both masthead documents and official records are issued with a document symbol as described above. Official records come out in both *provisional* and *final* form. In provisional form, official records are published individually on plain white paper. Official records are later collected together and republished in bound form, with tan paper covers for the General Assembly, yellow for the Security Council, and light blue for the Economic and Social Council. In final form, official records contain meeting records, annexes, and supplements. Note that significant working documents often reappear in the annexes to the official records.

A collection of U.N. documents is available on microfiche from Readex/Newsbank. Many law-related U.N. documents are available in *HeinOnline*'s United Nations Law Collection.

e.   Documents of the International Law Commission. The International Law Commission was established in the early days of the U.N. for the purpose of "the promotion of the progressive development of international law and its codification."[164] Its U.N. document symbol is A/CN.4/. The Commission pursues its purposes by carrying out studies of a wide range of issues in international law. Several of these studies have had concrete results in the development of international law. To give just one example, the Commission's work on draft articles on the law of treaties preceded the convening of the conference that adopted the Vienna Convention on the Law of Treaties.[165]

Much of the documentation of the Commission's work is available online on the U.N.'s website.[166] Useful access points to this documentation on the Commission webpage are the Research Guide page, the Analytical Guide to the Work of the International Law Commission, and the collection of the Commission's *Yearbooks.* Other U.N. bodies devoted to consideration of issues of international law include the Sixth Committee of the General Assembly and the United Nations Commission on International Trade Law (UNCITRAL).[167]

f.   Publications for Sale. The United Nations has an active publishing program through which it offers for sale a wide array of publications. This includes subscriptions to working documents and official records. Many titles in the fields of international relations, population issues, environmental policy, international trade and economics, and statistics are also available. These publications receive a sales number, such as

---

[164]   Statute of the International Law Commission, G.A. Res. 174 (II), U.N. Doc. A/519 (Nov. 21, 1947).

[165]   May 23, 1969, 1155 U.N.T.S. 331.

[166]   http://www.un.org/law/ilc/.

[167]   UNCITRAL makes available many documents related to all aspects of its work on its website, http://www.uncitral.org.

11.III.Q.1, which is used only for ordering and should not be confused with the document symbol.[168]

> g.   *Tools for Researching United Nations Documents.*

(1)   *ODS.*[169] The recommended starting point for researching U.N. documentation is *ODS*, the Official Document System of the United Nations. Coverage on *ODS* for recent years is excellent and it is fairly good back to 1993. New documents are added continuously and retrospective additions to the database are planned. Search options include document symbol and full text; a simplified search interface is available,[170] but it is not preferable to the standard *ODS* site.

(2)   *UNBISnet.*[171] The free online index to U.N. documentation published since 1979 is called *UNBISnet*. It doubles as the online catalog of the Dag Hammarskjöld Library in New York and the U.N. library in Geneva. Subject and keyword searching, as well as searching by document symbol, are possible. Records often link to the full text of indexed documents. *UNBISnet* practically supersedes the hardbound indexes. For research before 1979, it will be necessary to use *UNDEX* (1970–1978) and *United Nations Document Index* (1950–1973), both published by the U.N. These hardbound indexes are succeeded by *UNDOC: Current Index* for 1979 to 1996, and for 1998 to 2007 by the *United Nations Documents Index*.

(3)   *UN-I-QUE.*[172] This is another documents research database provided by the Dag Hammarskjöld Library. It focuses on U.N. documents of a recurring nature. For example, the researcher learns that the United Nations Conference on Disarmament publishes its annual report in the General Assembly Official Records, Supplement No. 27. Similarly, the report of the Conference of the Parties to the United Nations Framework Convention on Climate Change is issued under the symbol FCCC/CP/[year].

(4)   *UN Pulse.*[173] This is a blog that provides alerts of selected, just-released U.N. online information: major reports, publications, and documents. It is produced by the Dag Hammarskjöld Library.

(5)   *United Nations website.*[174] This is the main gateway to the U.N. It provides a variety of access points, including links to the webpages of each of the main bodies. There are also subject sectors: Peace & Security, Economic and Social Development, Human Rights, Humanitarian Affairs, and International Law. The U.N. website also provides access to U.N. documents,[175] but it should be used together with *ODS* for this purpose.

(6)   *Yearbook of the United Nations.* The *Yearbook* (1947–) describes the activities of both the U.N. and its specialized agencies. It is organized in broad subject categories, such as Political and Security Questions, Regional Questions, and Economic and Social Questions. Under each subtopic, the action of U.N. organs is summarized and important

---

[168]   The United Nations publications catalog is available at http://unp.un.org.

[169]   http://documents.un.org.

[170]   http://www.un.org/en/documents/ods/.

[171]   http://unbisnet.un.org.

[172]   http://lib-unique.un.org/DPI/DHL/unique.nsf?Open.

[173]   http://un-library.tumblr.com/.

[174]   http://www.un.org/en/index.shtml.

[175]   The Documents page of the U.N. website, http://www.un.org/en/documents/index.shtml, provides centralized access.

resolutions are reproduced. Particularly valuable are the references (by document symbol) to U.N. documents relating to the points discussed. All of the *Yearbooks* are now available on the U.N.'s website.[176]

(7) *Index to Proceedings of the General Assembly, Index to Proceedings of the Security Council,* and *Index to Proceedings of the Economic and Social Council.* These indexes are valuable resources that should be consulted for comprehensive research.

h.   Secondary Sources. The secondary literature on the U.N. and its work is enormous. Researchers should use both the library catalog and journal indexes for law and related disciplines. *PAIS International*, an index of public policy and political science literature, is very useful. Two good sources for starting research on the law of the U.N. are: *Law and Practice of the United Nations: Documents and Commentary*, by Simon Chesterman et al. (2008) and *Max Planck Yearbook of United Nations Law* (1998–).

3.   European Union

a.   Introduction. The European Union (E.U.) is an international economic and political federation composed of twenty-eight European countries: Austria, Belgium, Bulgaria, Croatia, Cyprus, the Czech Republic, Denmark, Estonia, Finland, France, Germany, Greece, Hungary, Ireland, Italy, Latvia, Lithuania, Luxembourg, Malta, The Netherlands, Poland, Portugal, Romania, Slovakia, Slovenia, Spain, Sweden, and the United Kingdom.[177] The main seat of E.U. institutions is Brussels. It also has a presence in Luxembourg (where the European Court of Justice sits) and Strasbourg (where the European Parliament holds some of its meetings). The E.U. is sometimes called a *supranational* organization because it has authority under the treaties that establish it to make law binding on the member states.[178]

A source of confusion is the similarity between the names of the E.U. and of the Council of Europe, a different organization set up to defend human rights and parliamentary democracy.[179] The Council of Europe is responsible, among other things, for the administration of the European Convention for the Protection of Human Rights and Fundamental Freedoms.[180] The European Court of Human Rights is an arm of the Council of Europe, *not* of the E.U.[181]

Again, the importance of the European Union for our purposes is, first, that it holds great law-making power that affects not only the member states, but may also have an impact on third states, such as the U.S., and, second, that it produces many documents

---

[176]   http://unyearbook.un.org.

[177]   Iceland, Montenegro, Serbia, the former Yugoslav Republic of Macedonia, and Turkey are candidates for membership as of June 2014. *See generally* http://europa.eu/about-eu/index_en.htm for information about the E.U.

[178]   The name of the European Union has changed several times since its inception. It began in 1957 as the European Economic Community, which was one of a trio of organizations, the others being the European Coal and Steel Community and the European Atomic Energy Community. These combined in 1967 to form the European Communities, which then consolidated into the European Community. The Maastricht Treaty of 1993 changed the name to the European Union.

[179]   The Council of Europe website (http://hub.coe.int/) gives information about the organization's purpose and activities and includes a useful explanation of the differences between the E.U. and the Council at http://www.coe.int/aboutCoe/index.asp?page=nepasconfondre&l=en.

[180]   C.E.T.S. No. 5.

[181]   See Section I-2 of this chapter for detailed discussion of European human rights research.

important to the study of the E.U. itself and of subjects with which the E.U. is concerned.[182]

The E.U. carries out its work through five main institutions: European Council, Council of Ministers, Commission, European Parliament, and Court of Justice. Of lesser importance for legal research are the Court of Auditors, Economic and Social Committee, and the Committee of the Regions. Understanding the institutional structure and law-making process of the E.U. will make research easier. For this purpose, a leading treatise on the law and institutions of the E.U. is indispensable.[183]

b.   *EUR-Lex.* The *EUR-Lex* website,[184] provides free access to European Union law. It should be the starting point for European Union legal research. *EUR-Lex* includes the following kinds of legal information, which are considered in more detail below:

- Founding treaties and other treaties relating to the establishment and functioning of the European Union;

- *Official Journal of the European Union;*

- Legislation in force;

- Preparatory acts; and

- Case law.

c.   *Founding Treaties and Other Treaties.* The European Union is based on a group of what are called founding treaties. Chief among these are the Treaty Establishing the European Community and the Treaty on European Union. An important amending agreement, the Treaty of Lisbon, entered into force in December 2009. Under it the new name of the Treaty Establishing the European Community is the Treaty on the Functioning of the European Union. The founding treaties and amending treaties, together with the accession treaties, are found on *EUR-Lex* under the "Treaties" link.[185]

d.   *Official Journal of the European Union.* The *Official Journal* is the central gazette of E.U. legal information. The *Official Journal* is published every business day in all European Union member languages.[186] The *Official Journal* has more than one part. Most important are the L series (containing final legislative acts, such as directives, regulations, decisions, opinions, and recommendations) and the C series (containing information and notices, proposals for legislation, European Parliament resolutions, opinions of the Economic and Social Committee, and excerpts from the judgments of the Court of Justice). Every issue of the *Official Journal* is numbered separately. Knowing

---

[182]   The EU Bookshop on the Web, http://bookshop.europa.eu, makes available a broad spectrum of EU publications, many of which are downloadable in PDF for free.

[183]   *See, e.g.*, ALAN DASHWOOD ET AL., WYATT AND DASHWOOD'S EUROPEAN UNION LAW (6th ed. 2011); P.S.R.F. MATHIJSEN, A GUIDE TO EUROPEAN UNION LAW (10th ed. 2010); TREVOR C. HARTLEY, THE FOUNDATIONS OF EUROPEAN UNION LAW: AN INTRODUCTION TO THE CONSTITUTIONAL AND ADMINISTRATIVE LAW OF THE EUROPEAN UNION (7th ed. 2010); DAMIAN CHALMERS ET AL., EUROPEAN UNION LAW: TEXT AND MATERIALS (2d ed. 2010).

[184]   http://eur-lex.europa.eu/en/index.htm.

[185]   These are the versions as published in the *Official Journal*. Consolidated versions of the Treaty on European Union and the Treaty on the Functioning of the European Union are found in O.J. C83 (2010), as posted on *EUR-Lex*.

[186]   The *Official Journal* was not published in English before 1973. An *Official Journal Special Edition* (1972–1973) published translations of EC law enacted before the United Kingdom and Ireland became members.

the relevant part and number is essential to locating a particular document within the *Official Journal*. A typical reference would be O.J. L146/10 (2011). This refers to issue 146 of the L series for 2011, page 10.

The *Official Journal* is no longer widely distributed in print. It is available online in full text PDF from January 1985 on *EUR-Lex*.[187] Libraries that hold the *Official Journal* in their collections now receive it in CD-ROM format. Before that, the *Official Journal* was distributed in microfiche.

e.   Legislation in Force. The European Union legislates using various kinds of enactments. These include directives, regulations, and decisions, among others. These appear first in the *Official Journal*. There is no code or compilation of European Union Law currently in force. The closest such source is the database of Legislation in force as found in *EUR-Lex*. Legislation in force can be searched by type of enactment, by search term in the title and full text, or by date. More recent legislation is produced in PDF as published in the *Official Journal*. Earlier legislation is in HTML with a full reference to the *Official Journal*. Searching is also possible using the classified scheme in the Directory of Community legislation in force as available in *EUR-Lex*.

f.   Preparatory Acts. Proposals for European Union legislation originate with the European Commission. *EUR-Lex* calls these Preparatory acts. However, in practice, these documents are usually called COM documents (COM=Commission). For example, the "Joint Proposal for a Council Regulation concerning restrictive measures in view of the situation in Syria" is COM(2011)266. Before *EUR-Lex*, COM documents were difficult to find. *EUR-Lex* now has COM documents in full text from January 1999.

Not all COM documents are proposals for legislation. For example, COM(2011)144 is titled "WHITE PAPER—Roadmap to a Single European Transport Area—Towards a competitive and resource efficient transport system." This type of COM document is also available on *EUR-Lex* in the Preparatory acts sector.

g.   Case Law. The European Court of Justice (E.C.J.) is one of the most important institutions of the European Union. Its decisions have far-reaching significance for the development of European Union law. The name of the official reporter for the E.C.J. is *Reports of Cases Before the Court*. The informal name is *European Court Reports* and the usual citation is *E.C.R.* The official reports appear late. The solution to this delay is to use the respected commercially published reporter *Common Market Law Reports* (*C.M.L.R.*),[188] which appears in weekly advance sheets.

Judgments of the E.C.J. are available on *EUR-Lex*. However, it appears that the court's own website[189] is preferable because it has better coverage of cases going back to June 1997.

The European Court of First Instance was established in 1989. The Treaty of Lisbon renamed it the General Court in 2009. It has initial jurisdiction over, *inter alia*, a number of types of direct actions brought by individuals and member states. Appeals on points

---

[187]   For some years before 1998, coverage is spotty.

[188]   (Sweet & Maxwell 1962–). There is a companion series called C.M.L.R. ANTITRUST REPORTS (Sweet & Maxwell 1991–).

[189]   http://curia.europa.eu/jcms/jcms/j_6/.

of law go to the E.C.J. Judgments of the General Court are also reported in *Reports of Cases Before the Court (E.C.R.).*

h. *PreLex.*[190] This is the European Commission's database for tracking decision-making in the European Union institutions regarding Commission proposals. It has links to relevant documents, including enacted legislation.

i. *Legislative Observatory (European Parliament).*[191] This is a database for tracking the progress of European Union legislation as it makes its way through the European Parliament. It has links to relevant documents, including enacted legislation.

j. *Europa.*[192] *Europa* is called the "Gateway to the European Union." It is the main web portal to European Union information. There are links to the websites of all European Union institutions. There are over thirty links to webpages on various topics relating to European Union activities. Use *EUR-Lex* in conjunction with *Europa* for the broadest and deepest access to European Union legal and other information online for free.

k. *Westlaw* and *LexisNexis.* Both *Westlaw* and *LexisNexis* have databases of European Union law. Both services provide access to the text of the E.U. treaties and legislation, and to decisions of the European Court of Justice. For most purposes, the free access to E.U. legal materials provided by *EUR-Lex* remains the preferred source. There may be occasions, however, when *Westlaw* or *LexisNexis* has material not available on *EUR-Lex.*

l. *Secondary Sources.* A mass of secondary literature is published about the European Union, much of it dealing specifically with legal issues. A large amount of literature on the E.U. also is available from the perspective of political science and international relations. The more recent Library of Congress subject headings for general works on the E.U. include "European Union," "Europe—Economic integration," "European Union countries—Politics and government," and "European Federation." Works on E.U. law in general receive the subject heading "Law—European Union countries." The subject subheading used in the last example can be used to narrow a search to specific fields of law, e.g., "Antitrust law—European Union countries."

Journal articles on European Union law can appear in virtually any law review published in the United States and Britain, as well as the rest of Europe. Therefore, research in the standard journal indexes will prove fruitful. Several English-language journals are devoted to E.U. law: *Common Market Law Review,*[193] *European Law Review,*[194] *Columbia Journal of European Law,*[195] and *European Law Journal.*[196] A journal from the perspective of political science is *Journal of Common Market Studies.*[197]

---

[190] http://ec.europa.eu/prelex/apcnet.cfm?CL=en.

[191] http://www.europarl.europa.eu/oeil/.

[192] http://europa.eu/index_en.htm.

[193] (Martinus Nijhoff 1963–).

[194] (Sweet & Maxwell 1975–).

[195] (Columbia Law School 1994–).

[196] (Blackwell 1995–).

[197] (Blackwell 1962–).

Annual publications of note are the *Yearbook of European Law*[198] and the *Cambridge Yearbook of European Legal Studies*.[199]

I.   INTERNATIONAL PROTECTION OF HUMAN RIGHTS

So far in this chapter, we have presented a general methodology for researching international law. In this section, we turn to a substantive field of international law, one that has consistently gained in significance as we enter further into the twenty-first century. This is the field known as the international legal protection of human rights.

The idea of fundamental human dignity is as old as civilization itself and is common to all cultures and religions. However, it was not until the Age of the Enlightenment in the late seventeenth century, and even more strongly in the eighteenth century, that the idea of individual *rights* became a central concept of our *political* vocabulary. While there are several candidates for the honor, we can refer to two documents of the late eighteenth century as canonical expressions of the concept of individual rights: the U.S. Declaration of Independence[200] and the French Declaration of the Rights of Man and Citizen.[201]

It was not until after the horrors of the Second World War that the idea of the protection of human rights in international law gained traction. The main obstacle had been the entrenched doctrine of domestic jurisdiction, according to which the way a state treated its own citizens was not a matter for the intervention of international law. Thanks mainly to the momentum gained from the founding of the United Nations, the doctrine gave way to the belief that the violation of human rights by a state against its own citizens was indeed a matter of concern for the international community and for international law.[202]

The human rights protections under international law are impressive. There will be space here to consider only the broad outline of their structure. We will consider the three major international systems of human rights protection: the United Nations system, the European system, and the Inter-American system.[203] We also will touch on developments in Africa and Asia, and on the indispensable work carried out by the international non-governmental organizations (NGOs).[204] The focus will always be on the ways and means of conducting research; the substantive descriptions will provide a backdrop to research method.

---

[198]   (Oxford University Press 1982–).

[199]   (Hart 1999–).

[200]   Declaration of Independence para. 2 (U.S. 1776) ("[A]ll men are created equal. . . . [T]hey are endowed, by their Creator, with certain unalienable rights. . . .").

[201]   Declaration of the Rights of Man and Citizen (Fr. 1789) ("Men are born and remain free and equal in rights."), *reprinted in* THE FRENCH REVOLUTION AND HUMAN RIGHTS: A BRIEF DOCUMENTARY HISTORY 77–79 (Lynn Hunt ed., 1996).

[202]   For an interesting interpretation of the historical development, see MICHELINE R. ISHAY, THE HISTORY OF HUMAN RIGHTS: FROM ANCIENT TIMES TO THE GLOBALIZATION ERA (2004).

[203]   A comprehensive collection of materials on the regional systems is DINAH SHELTON, REGIONAL PROTECTION OF HUMAN RIGHTS (2008).

[204]   The other approach to take would be *thematic*, meaning keyed to the full range of substantive rights, rather than to the systems of protection. For example, we could look at researching the right of self-determination, the rights of indigenous peoples and minorities, the rights of persons with disabilities, the rights of migrants, of refugees, or of children, labor rights, torture, the death penalty, and so on. Unfortunately, there is no room here to explore the thematic approach more fully.

1.   The United Nations System[205]

The United Nations Charter mentions human rights seven times. Significantly, the phrase occurs in both the preamble[206] and in article 1.[207] As one of its first major actions, the United Nations Economic and Social Council established the Commission on Human Rights in 1946. The Commission began immediately to draft the Universal Declaration of Human Rights, which was adopted by a resolution of the General Assembly.[208] From these beginnings, the United Nations has, over the course of sixty years, created an elaborate framework for human rights protection. The Office of the U.N. High Commissioner for Human Rights has prepared a good online collection of mostly United Nations human rights instruments.[209]

In the United Nations human rights system, the first step in the correct approach to doing research is to divide the system into its two main functional components: the Charter-based bodies and the treaty-based bodies. These two main elements are bridged by the Office of the United Nations High Commissioner for Human Rights, which is a department of the United Nations Secretariat.

   a.   Charter-Based Bodies. In 2006, the General Assembly established the Human Rights Council.[210] This was a fundamental change in the United Nations human rights system. The Council replaced the Commission on Human Rights, which was a dependency of the Economic and Social Council, rather than the General Assembly. The Commission had come under criticism for being politicized and ineffective and for having members who were guilty of serious human rights violations.[211]

The new Human Rights Council has forty-seven seats. Each member state must be elected individually by a majority of the General Assembly. Member states are required to uphold the highest standards of human rights. A two-thirds majority of the General Assembly may suspend a member if it commits serious abuses of human rights.

The Human Rights Council sits in Geneva, Switzerland. It holds at least three sessions a year for a total of at least ten weeks. It may and does also hold special sessions.

The Council's U.N. document symbol is A/HRC/-. For example, document A/HRC/17/26, dated May 2011, is the twenty-sixth document of the Council's seventeenth session, and is titled "Report of the Special Rapporteur on violence against women, its causes and consequences."

The Council is assisted in its work by the Advisory Committee made up of eighteen human rights experts who serve independently in their personal capacities. The role of the Advisory Committee is to provide expertise to the Human Rights Council, focusing on studies and research-based advice. The Advisory Committee replaces the old Sub-

---

[205]   A recent introduction is JULIE A. MERTUS, THE UNITED NATIONS AND HUMAN RIGHTS: A GUIDE FOR A NEW ERA (2d ed. 2009).

[206]   "We the peoples of the United Nations determined . . . to reaffirm faith in fundamental human rights. . . ."

[207]   "The purposes of the United Nations are . . . to achieve international co-operation . . . in promoting and encouraging respect for human rights."

[208]   G.A. Res. 217A (III), U.N. Doc. A/810 (Dec. 12, 1948).

[209]   http://www2.ohchr.org/english/law.

[210]   G.A. Res. 60/251, U.N. Doc. A/RES/60/251 (Mar. 15, 2006).

[211]   *See, e.g.,* Eric Heinze, *Even-Handedness and the Politics of Human Rights*, 21 HARV. HUM. RTS. J. 7, 41 (2008).

Commission on the Promotion and Protection of Human Rights. The U.N. document symbol for the Advisory Committee is A/HRC/AC/-.

In establishing the Human Rights Council, the General Assembly mandated that it "undertake a universal periodic review . . . of the fulfillment by each state of its human rights obligations and commitments . . . such a mechanism shall complement and not duplicate the work of treaty bodies."[212] The Universal Periodic Review (UPR) is carried out by the Working Group on the Universal Periodic Review, which is composed of all forty-seven member states of the Council. The document symbol of the working group is A/HRC/WG.6/. There is a "troika" of three rapporteurs who facilitate each review and help with the drafting of the final report. The Council adopted a calendar that sets up a four-year cycle for the UPR, which means that each member of the U.N. will be reviewed every four years. The second cycle began in 2012. The best way to follow the progress of the UPR and to find the reports is at the website of the High Commissioner for Human Rights.[213] You should also search the document symbol of the working group on the *ODS* system.

The Human Rights Council decided to continue some of the working methods developed under the old Commission. Much important work is carried out using what are called special procedures. Two of these are called country mandates and thematic mandates. As of May 2011, there are eight country mandates and thirty-three thematic mandates in place. Follow work on both country and thematic mandates on the High Commissioner's website[214] and on the *ODS* system.

The Council's mechanism for making individualized complaints is known formally as the Complaint Procedure. It is meant "to address consistent patterns of gross and reliably attested violations of all human rights and all fundamental freedoms occurring in any part of the world and under any circumstances." Communications under the Complaint Procedure must come from victims or from "persons, including non-governmental organizations, acting in good faith . . . and claiming to have direct and reliable knowledge of the violations concerned." The Complaint Procedure operates through two working groups. Note that the Complaint Procedure is *confidential*, which means that it produces no public documents. More information is available on the High Commissioner's website.[215]

b.   Treaty-Based Mechanisms. The nine core international human rights agreements in the United Nations system are:

- International Covenant on Civil and Political Rights;[216]

- International Covenant on Economic, Social and Cultural Rights;[217]

---

[212]   G.A. Res. 60/251, U.N. Doc. A/RES/60/251 (Mar. 15, 2006).

[213]   http://www.ohchr.org/EN/HRBodies/UPR/Pages/UPRMain.aspx.

[214]   http://www.ohchr.org/EN/HRBodies/SP/Pages/Countries.aspx and http://www.ohchr.org/EN/HRBodies/SP/Pages/Themes.aspx.

[215]   http://www2.ohchr.org/english/bodies/chr/complaints.htm.

[216]   Dec. 16, 1966, 999 U.N.T.S. 171. (Also cited to G.A. Res. 2200A (XXI), U.N. GAOR, 21st Sess., Supp. No. 16, at 52, U.N. Doc. A/6316 (1966).) *See generally* MANFRED NOWAK, U.N. COVENANT ON CIVIL AND POLITICAL RIGHTS: CCPR COMMENTARY (N.P. Engel 2d ed. 2005).

[217]   Dec. 16, 1966, 993 U.N.T.S. 3. (Also cited G.A. Res. 2200A (XXI), U.N. GAOR, 21st Sess., Supp. No. 16, at 49, U.N. Doc. A/6316 (1966).)

- International Convention on the Elimination of All Forms of Racial Discrimination;[218]

- Convention on the Elimination of All Forms of Discrimination against Women;[219]

- Convention against Torture and Other Cruel, Inhuman or Degrading Treatment or Punishment;[220]

- Convention on the Rights of the Child;[221]

- International Convention on the Protection of the Rights of All Migrant Workers and Members of their Families;[222]

- Convention on the Rights of Persons with Disabilities;[223] and

- International Convention for the Protection of All Persons from Enforced Disappearances.[224]

The human rights treaty bodies are committees of independent experts that monitor the implementation of the U.N. human rights treaties.[225] The committees meet in Geneva or New York and have from one to three sessions a year.

One of the main tasks of the committees is the consideration of state party reports. Every state party to any of the U.N. core agreements is under an obligation to submit regular reports to the respective monitoring committee. This system of monitoring by means of obligatory state reporting is common to the core treaties. Guidelines on the form and content of state reports under six of the core treaties have been compiled.[226] This document includes harmonized guidelines on state reporting under the treaties.

A state's first report is due usually one year after it becomes a party; later reports are due according to the requirements of each agreement (usually every four or five years). Also, the treaty committees may receive information on the human rights situation in a state party from other sources, including non-governmental human rights organizations (NGOs), U.N. agencies, or other international organizations. The treaty

---

[218]   Dec. 21, 1965, 660 U.N.T.S. 195. (Also cited G.A. Res. 2106 (XX), U.N. GAOR, 20th Sess., Supp. No. 14, U.N. Doc. A/6014 (1965).)

[219]   Dec. 18, 1979, 1249 U.N.T.S. 13. (Also cited G.A. Res. 34/180, U.N. GAOR, 34th Sess., Supp. No. 46, at 193, U.N. Doc. A/34/46 (1981).)

[220]   Dec. 10, 1984, 1465 U.N.T.S. 85. (Also cited G.A. Res. 39/46, U.N. GAOR, Supp. No. 51, U.N. Doc. A/39/51 (1984).)

[221]   Nov. 20, 1989, 1577 U.N.T.S. 3. (Also cited G.A. Res. 44/25, U.N. GAOR, 44th Sess., Supp. No. 49, U.N. Doc. A/44/49 (1989).)

[222]   G.A. Res. 45/158, U.N. GAOR, 45th Sess., Supp. No. 49A, at 262, U.N. Doc. A/45/49 (1990), 2220 U.N.T.S. 3.

[223]   G.A. Res. 61/106, U.N. GAOR, 61st Sess., Supp. No. 49 (vol. I), at 65, U.N. Doc. A/61/49 (2006), 46 I.L.M. 443.

[224]   G.A. Res. 61/177, U.N. GAOR, 61st Sess., Supp. No. 49 (vol. I), at 408, U.N. Doc. A/61/49 (2006).

[225]   The name of a committee generally coincides with the name of the agreement for which it is responsible: Human Rights Committee (HRC) for the International Covenant on Civil and Political Rights; Committee on Economic, Social and Cultural Rights (CESCR); Committee on the Elimination of All Forms of Racial Discrimination (CERD); Committee on the Elimination of All Forms of Discrimination against Women (CEDAW); Committee against Torture (CAT); Committee on the Rights of the Child (CRC); and Committee on the Rights of Persons with Disabilities (CRPD). Also, the U.N. document symbol for a committee coincides with the name of the agreement: CCPR/- for the HRC, E/C.12/- for the CESCR, CAT/- for the CAT, CEDAW/- for CEDAW, CERD/- for CERD, CRC/- for CRC, and CRPD/- for CRPD.

[226]   U.N. Doc. HRI/GEN/2/Rev.6.

committee examines the state report and then publishes its concerns, criticisms, and recommendations in a document called Concluding Observations.

Every core treaty committee drafts interpretations of provisions of the agreement that it monitors. These are called general comments. (They are sometimes referred to as general recommendations.) The Human Rights Committee has adopted thirty-one general comments. For example, there is General Comment No. 29, States of Emergency (Article 4).[227] The general comments of six treaty committees have been compiled as of 2008 in U.N. document HRI/GEN/1/Rev.9.

Five of the treaty bodies (HRC, CEDAW, CERD, CAT, and CRPD) have the authority to receive individual communications (complaints) alleging specific violations of an agreement by a state party. The state must have agreed to participate in the individual complaints procedure, either by joining an optional protocol or by making a declaration according to the terms of the treaty.

The individual communication initiates a proceeding in the relevant committee that bears a resemblance to judicial procedure. The resemblance is limited because, although the committee has the authority to make findings of fact and conclusions of law about specific violations, it has no firm enforcement power. If the committee concludes that there has been a violation, the committee issues its conclusions in the form of views. The state party is invited to supply information on the steps it has taken to give effect to the committee's views on the appropriate remedy. In case a state's remedial action is inadequate, there is the possibility of a follow-up procedure.[228]

Significantly for research purposes, the texts of final committee decisions on individual communications are posted on the website of the Office of the United Nations High Commissioner for Human Rights. These decisions make up what is referred to as the committee's jurisprudence.

c.   Website of the Office of the U.N. High Commissioner for Human Rights. Today, research on the United Nations human rights system should begin with the website of the Office of the United Nations High Commissioner for Human Rights (OHCHR).[229] [Illustration 21–3] In fact, the OHCHR website marks a major advance in United Nations human rights research. By clicking on the link for "Human Rights Bodies," it is possible to do research that tracks the bipartite functional structure of the United Nations human rights system that has been sketched here.

A large amount of essential documentation is available on the website. For example, under Treaty Bodies there is a link to "Treaty body document search." The researcher can then select the desired agreement and type of document. Types of documents that can be located include:

- State party reports;

- Concluding observations of the committee;

- General comments by the committee;

---

[227]   U.N. Doc. CCPR/C/21/Rev.1/Add.11 (August 2001).

[228]   See the detailed overview of the individual communications procedure on the website of the Office of the United Nations High Commissioner for Human Rights, http://www2.ohchr.org/english/bodies/petitions/index.htm.

[229]   http://www.ohchr.org/.

- Jurisprudence (decisions on individual communications);

- Summary records of committee meetings; and

- Sessional or annual reports of the committee to the General Assembly.

The same kind of research is possible for all of the core treaty bodies. Similarly, in-depth research is possible for the Charter-based bodies. If a desired document is not available on the OHCHR website, the researcher can turn to the Official Documents System of the United Nations, as described in Section H-2-c.

Researchers doing advanced work can consult another free database called the Universal Human Rights Index of United Nations Documents,[230] which is also administered by the OHCHR. This database does not go back very far in time, but it has the great advantage of allowing searching by keyword and state on the concluding observations of the treaty bodies, plus reports of special procedures mandate holders. Thus, for example, a search on "torture" with United States of America produces documents from the Committee Against Torture, the Human Rights Committee, the Special Rapporteur on Torture and other Cruel, Inhuman and Degrading Treatment or Punishment, and the Special Rapporteur on the Promotion and Protection of Human Rights and Fundamental Freedoms while Countering Terrorism.

It is important to note that human rights are referred to in the United Nations as a "cross-cutting priority." This means that human rights are supposed to be taken into account in virtually everything the United Nations does and so could be taken up by any of the United Nations organs or programs. Therefore, human rights research in the United Nations system requires application of the general principles of United Nations research covered in Section H-2 of this chapter.

2. The European System

The heart of the European system of human rights protection is the Convention for the Protection of Human Rights and Fundamental Freedoms,[231] usually called the European Convention on Human Rights. Adopted in 1950 under the auspices of the Council of Europe,[232] it was the first international human rights instrument in the form of a legally binding treaty. All forty-seven states that are members of the Council of Europe are also parties to the Convention. All states of Europe, including Russia and Turkey, are covered.

The Convention creates the European Court of Human Rights, which sits in Strasbourg, France. In terms of the number of cases it has decided, the range of issues it has dealt with, and the amount of commentary devoted to it, this is the most important

---

[230] http://uhri.ohchr.org/.

[231] C.E.T.S. No. 5, 213 U.N.T.S. 221. The U.N.T.S. citation is to the Convention in its original form. However, the Convention has been amended and altered several times by protocol. To locate an authoritative current version of the Convention, the Council of Europe's treaty website is recommended: http://conventions. coe.int/Treaty/en/Treaties/Html/005.htm. The negotiating history of the Convention has been published in eight volumes. COUNCIL OF EUROPE, COLLECTED EDITION OF THE "TRAVAUX PRÉPARATOIRES" OF THE EUROPEAN CONVENTION ON HUMAN RIGHTS (1975–1985).

[232] Note that the Council of Europe is a completely different international organization from the European Union. It is true that fundamental rights have a significant place in European Union law, but in the field of human rights in Europe the Council of Europe plays the leading role.

court in the world in the field of human rights. All states party to the Convention must accept the jurisdiction of the court to decide cases involving individual complaints.

Since its founding, the court has delivered more than 10,000 judgments. Judgments are published selectively in the official reports of the court. From 1996 these are titled simply *Reports of Judgments and Decisions*. Up to 1996 (volume 338), the title was *Publications of the European Court of Human Rights. Series A: Judgments and Decisions*. An unofficial commercial set of reports, published by Sweet & Maxwell since 1979, is titled *European Human Rights Reports*. At one time there was a *Series B: Pleadings, Oral Arguments and Documents*. This ceased publication in 1995, with volume 104.

Until 1998, there was a subsidiary body called the European Commission on Human Rights. It performed a screening function for the court, which is now carried out by the court itself. Selected decisions of the Commission were published in a series titled *Decisions and Reports* (1975–1998).

Today, research on the European Court of Human Rights should begin with its website,[233] and specifically with the database of the case law of the court, which is called *HUDOC*. Full text searching is possible, as is searching by the name of applicant, name of respondent state, application number, or relevant article of the Convention. Search results can be sorted in various ways, including by relevance and by date.

Both *Westlaw* and *LexisNexis* can be used to search the case law of the court. The *Westlaw* database (HER–RPT) derives from the *European Human Rights Reports*. In *LexisNexis*, the file is called Human Rights Cases. Confusingly, it is located with the databases for the European Union. Equally confusingly, the file contains material from a variety of human rights organs besides the European Court of Human Rights.

The secondary literature on the European Convention on Human Rights and the European Court of Human Rights is enormous. The leading treatise in English is *Jacobs, White, and Ovey: The European Convention on Human Rights*, by Robin White et al. (5th ed. 2010). Another standard treatise is *Harris, O'Boyle and Warbrick: Law of the European Convention on Human Rights*, by D.J. Harris et al. (2d ed. 2009). The leading journal in English is *European Human Rights Law Review* (1996–). A useful subject heading for use in library catalogs is "Human Rights—Europe." A valuable reference source is the *Yearbook of the European Convention on Human Rights* (1960–).

The European Convention on Human Rights by no means exhausts the human rights work of the Council of Europe. Other human rights treaties and organs are:

- European Social Charter;[234]

- European Social Charter (revised);[235]

- European Convention for the Prevention of Torture and Inhuman or Degrading Treatment or Punishment;[236]

---

[233]   http://www.echr.coe.int/.

[234]   Oct. 18, 1961, C.E.T.S. No. 35, 529 U.N.T.S. 89

[235]   May 3, 1996, C.E.T.S. No. 163. *See* http://www.coe.int/T/DGHL/Monitoring/SocialCharter/.

[236]   Nov. 26, 1987, C.E.T.S. No. 126, 27 I.L.M. 1152. See official documents and a database of information at http://www.cpt.coe.int/en/.

- Framework Convention for the Protection of National Minorities;[237]

- European Charter for Regional or Minority Languages;[238]

- Convention for the Protection of Human Rights and Dignity of the Human Being with Regard to the Application of Biology and Medicine (Convention on Human Rights and Biomedicine);[239]

- Commissioner for Human Rights;[240] and

- European Commission Against Racism and Intolerance.[241]

The European Union also makes the protection of human rights a high-profile issue. The Charter of Fundamental Rights of the European Union is binding law.[242] The *Europa* website for the Commission's Directorate-General Justice has a good page on the operation of the Charter.[243] The Commission publishes an annual report on the application of the Charter.[244]

The Charter of Fundamental Rights applies to action by the E.U. within the E.U., but human rights are an important element of E.U. external relations, too. The researcher can begin work on the external aspect of the E.U.'s promotion of human rights by using the *Europa* website.[245]

The European Union Agency for Fundamental Rights was established in 2007.[246] Its main activities are to give advice to the E.U. institutions and member states, to gather information and do research and analysis, and to cooperate with civil society while raising awareness of fundamental rights in the E.U. The best way to follow the Agency's work is through its website.[247]

Another European entity that devotes substantial attention to human rights is the Organization for Security and Co-operation in Europe (OSCE).[248] The OSCE focuses on Eastern Europe, South-Eastern Europe (the Balkans), the Caucasus, and Central Asia. The OSCE's main field of action is international peace and security in these regions.[249] However, the OSCE has also established an Office for Democratic Institutions and

---

[237]   Feb. 1, 1995, C.E.T.S. No. 157, 34 I.L.M. 351. *See* http://www.coe.int/t/dghl/monitoring/minorities/default_en.asp. *See also* THE RIGHTS OF MINORITIES IN EUROPE: A COMMENTARY ON THE EUROPEAN FRAMEWORK CONVENTION FOR THE PROTECTION OF NATIONAL MINORITIES (Marc Weller ed., Oxford University Press 2005).

[238]   Nov. 5, 1992, C.E.T.S. No. 148. *See* http://www.coe.int/t/dg4/education/minlang/Default_en.asp.

[239]   April 4, 1997, C.E.T.S. No. 164. See the Bioethics page of the Council of Europe website at http://www.coe.int/t/dg3/healthbioethic/default_en.asp.

[240]   See the large amount of information, including official documents, on the Commissioner's page of the Council of Europe website at http://www.coe.int/en/web/commissioner/home.

[241]   http://www.coe.int/ecri.

[242]   The citation for the official text of the Charter is O.J. C83/389 (2010). *See* HUMAN RIGHTS IN EUROPE: COMMENTARY ON THE CHARTER OF FUNDAMENTAL RIGHTS OF THE EUROPEAN UNION (William B.T. Mock ed., 2010).

[243]   http://ec.europa.eu/justice/fundamental-rights/index_en.htm.

[244]   The 2010 report is COM (2011) 160 final.

[245]   http://europa.eu/legislation_summaries/human_rights/human_rights_in_third_countries/index_en.htm.

[246]   O.J. L53/1 (2007).

[247]   http://fra.europa.eu.

[248]   http://www.osce.org/.

[249]   The OSCE speaks of the "politico-military dimension."

Human Rights (ODIHR), based in Warsaw, Poland. The best way to begin research on OSCE/ODIHR human rights activities is to go to the ODIHR website.[250] Note should also be made of the OSCE's High Commissioner on National Minorities,[251] its Special Representative and Co-ordinator on Combating Trafficking in Human Beings,[252] and its Representative on Freedom of the Media.[253]

3. The Inter-American System

Like the European system, the Inter-American system is regional. However, in structure it resembles the United Nations system because it has both an O.A.S. Charter-based body and a treaty-based body. The Charter-based body is the Inter-American Commission on Human Rights.[254] The treaty-based body is the Inter-American Court of Human Rights.[255]

The first key document is the American Declaration of the Rights and Duties of Man.[256] Adopted in May 1948, it predates the Universal Declaration of Human Rights by several months. The key human rights agreement is the American Convention on Human Rights.[257] The Convention has two important supplementary agreements: the Additional Protocol to the American Convention on Human Rights in the Area of Economic, Social and Cultural Rights ("Protocol of San Salvador")[258] and the Protocol to the American Convention on Human Rights to Abolish the Death Penalty.[259]

The Commission has a wide scope of activity. It is authorized to receive individual complaints charging violations of both the American Declaration and the American Convention. The Commission also carries out country studies and thematic reports. Unfortunately, individual Commission documents can be difficult to find. Therefore, it is recommended that researchers go first to the Commission's website. There, they will find a range of documentation, including the Commission's annual reports, which in turn contain links to Commission decisions on individual petitions presented during the reporting year. There is also a separate link to Commission decisions on individual petitions published by year. The thematic country studies will be found under the link "Special Reports." Links to webpages of the various rapporteurs on special human rights issues within the Inter-American system are listed under "Rapporteurships." For example, there is a Rapporteurship on the Rights of Afro-Descendants and against Racial Discrimination.

---

[250] http://www.osce.org/odihr/.

[251] http://www.osce.org/hcnm/.

[252] http://www.osce.org/cthb/.

[253] http://www.osce.org/fom.

[254] http://www.cidh.org/.

[255] http://www.corteidh.or.cr/.

[256] Formally the American Declaration is cited as Res. XXX, Final Act of the Ninth International Conference of American States, Bogotá, Colombia, Mar. 30–May 2, 1948. This document is almost impossible to find. Therefore, it is recommended that the citation include a "reprinted in" element referring to the O.A.S. publication prepared by the Inter-American Commission, BASIC DOCUMENTS PERTAINING TO HUMAN RIGHTS IN THE INTER-AMERICAN SYSTEM (2010). The O.A.S. document symbol is OEA/Ser. L/V/I.4 rev.13. The publication is available in HTML format at http://www.cidh.org/basicos/english/basic.toc.htm.

[257] Nov. 22, 1969, O.A.S.T.S. No. 36, 1144 U.N.T.S. 123. It should be noted that the U.S. is not a party to the American Convention.

[258] Nov. 17, 1988, O.A.S.T.S. No. 69, 28 I.L.M. 161.

[259] Aug. 28, 1991, O.A.S.T.S. No. 73, 29 I.L.M. 1447.

The Inter-American Court of Human Rights is a true judicial body, comparable to its European counterpart, although it has does not have the same caseload. The court exercises both contentious and advisory jurisdiction. It sits in San José, Costa Rica.

Currently, the court publishes its work in four official series. The most important of these are *Series A-Judgments and Opinions*[260] *and Series C-Decisions and Judgments*. Editorial work and the requirement of translation delay publication in final form. Fortunately, the jurisprudence of the court is available comprehensively on the court's website. The website has both a Spanish and an English version, although recent decisions may be available only in Spanish. The court also issues its *Annual Report of the Inter-American Court of Human Rights*, although it is not as comprehensive as the Commission's annual report. These are available from 1980 to the present on the court's website.[261]

Also to be consulted is the *Inter-American Yearbook on Human Rights*, published by the O.A.S. General Secretariat since 1973, although this appears several years behind.

Unfortunately, the secondary literature (books) in English on the Inter-American human rights system is somewhat sparse. Recent works are *The Inter-American Court of Human Rights: Case Law and Commentary*, by Laurence Burgorgue-Larsen and Amaya Úbeda de Torres (2011) and *The Practice and Procedure of the Inter-American Court of Human Rights*, by Jo M. Pasqualucci (2d ed. 2012). Two standard, but now somewhat dated, treatments are *The Inter-American System of Human Rights*, edited by David J. Harris and Stephen Livingstone (1998) and *The Inter-American Human Rights System*, by J. Scott Davidson (1997). A recent work on a specialized topic is *Provisional Measures in the Case Law of the Inter-American Court of Human Rights*, by Clara Burbano Herrera (2010).

The Inter-American human rights system includes several other specialized agreements:

- Inter-American Convention to Prevent and Punish Torture;[262]

- Inter-American Convention on Forced Disappearance of Persons;[263]

- Inter-American Convention on the Prevention, Punishment and Eradication of Violence Against Women;[264] and

- Inter-American Convention on the Elimination of all Forms of Discrimination against Persons with Disabilities.[265]

Other organizations under the O.A.S. umbrella that address human rights include:

- Inter-American Commission of Women;[266]

---

[260]   This is a confusing title. Series A actually publishes the *advisory opinions* of the court.

[261]   https://www.cidh.oas.org/annual.eng.htm.

[262]   Dec. 9, 1985, O.A.S.T.S. No. 67, 25 I.L.M. 519.

[263]   June 9, 1994, O.A.S. doc. OEA/Ser.P, AG/doc. 3114/94 rev.1, 33 I.L.M. 1529.

[264]   June 9, 1994, O.A.S. doc. OEA/Ser.P, AG/doc. 3115/94 rev.2, 33 I.L.M. 1534.

[265]   June 7, 1999, O.A.S. A.G. Res. 1608, 29th Sess., O.A.S. doc. OEA/Ser. AG/doc. 3826/99.

[266]   http://www.oas.org/en/cim/.

- Inter-American Children's Institute;[267] and

- Inter-American Institute of Human Rights.[268]

4. Developments in Africa

The central document for African human rights is the African Charter on Human and Peoples' Rights,[269] adopted under the auspices of the Organization of African Unity (O.A.U.). Related instruments are the Convention Governing the Specific Aspects of Refugee Problems in Africa,[270] the African Charter on the Rights and Welfare of the Child,[271] and the Protocol to the African Charter on the Rights of Women in Africa.[272]

The key body established by the African Charter is the African Commission on Human and Peoples' Rights, established in 1998.[273] The Commission has a protective mandate, which it carries out by exercising its authority to hear individual communications alleging specific violations of the African Charter. The Commission also has a promotional mandate that it carries out by considering and critiquing states' reports on their adherence to the African Charter. The Commission also acts through its special mechanisms, which include special rapporteurs and working groups, as well as missions to examine the human rights situation in particular countries. The Commission also adopts resolutions concerning significant human rights issues.

Research on the Commission's work can begin with its website.[274] There the researcher will find various Commission documents, including the Commission's concluding observations on state reports, the Commission's Activity Reports, and reports produced by the special mechanisms, as well as the text of Commission decisions on individual complaints ("communications"). The other valuable web resource is the University of Minnesota Human Rights Library. It has a page devoted to the Commission[275] that includes final communiqués from the Commission's sessions,

---

[267]   http://www.iin.oea.org/default_ingles.htm.

[268]   http://www.iidh.ed.cr/default_eng.htm. The Institute has an active publishing program. A good number of its publications are freely available in PDF on the Institute's website.

[269]   June 27, 1981, 1520 U.N.T.S. 217.

[270]   Sept. 10, 1969, 1001 U.N.T.S. 45, 8 I.L.M. 1288.

[271]   July 11, 1990, O.A.U. Doc. CAB/LEG/24.9/49, at http://www1.umn.edu/humanrts/africa/afchild. htm. See also the website of the African Committee of Experts on the Rights and Welfare of the Child, at http://www.au.int/en/content/african-charter-rights-and-welfare-child.

[272]   July 11, 2003, http://www1.umn.edu/humanrts/africa/protocol-women2003.html.

[273]   The court's website, http://www.african-court.org/en/, includes lists of pending and decided cases as well as basic documents. Although the court did not decide any cases in its first decade, nineteen finalized decisions were posted as of January 2014.

The African Union (A.U.) succeeded the O.A.U. in 2002. The judicial organ of the A.U. was to be the African Court of Justice. A proposal to merge the two courts into one, to be called the African Court of Justice and Human Rights, was embodied in a protocol that will become effective after fifteen member states ratify it. As of January 2014, this had not yet happened. The status list with ratifying states is available at: http://www.africancourtcoalition.org/index.php?option=com_content&view=article&id=87:ratification-status-protocol-on-the-statute-of-the-african-court-of-justice-and-human-rights&catid=7:african-union&Itemid=12. The protocol is available at http://www.au.int/en/sites/default/files/PROTOCOL_STATUTE_AFRICAN_ COURT_JUSTICE_AND_HUMAN_RIGHTS.pdf.

[274]   http://www.achpr.org.

[275]   http://www1.umn.edu/humanrts/africa/comission.html.

Commission resolutions, and a good number of Commission decisions on individual communications.[276]

Recommended secondary sources are *International Human Rights Law in Africa* by Frans Viljoen (2d ed. 2012) and *The African Charter on Human and Peoples' Rights: the System in Practice, 1986–2006*, edited by Malcolm Evans and Rachel Murray (2d ed. 2008). To find more, use the subject heading "Human rights—Africa" in the library catalog. Journals of note are *African Human Rights Law Journal* (2001–), *East African Journal of Peace and Human Rights* (1993–), and *South African Journal on Human Rights* (1985–).

5.   Developments in the Asia-Pacific Region

The Association of Southeast Asian Nations (ASEAN) adopted the ASEAN Human Rights Declaration (AHRD) in December 2012.[277] The ASEAN Intergovernmental Commission on Human Rights (AICHR) is an organ of ASEAN with a mandate to promote and protect human rights, but it does not have the mandate to hear individual grievances. ASEAN also has created a Commission for the Promotion and Protection of the Rights of Women and Children.[278]

6.   Human Rights NGOs, Country Reports, and Secondary Sources

Non-governmental organizations (NGOs) are private associations of like-minded people that act on the international scene. NGOs are sometimes referred to as the main component of international civil society. Human rights NGOs play an important role. They report in detail on human rights abuses around the world, they advocate for victims, they keep human rights issues in the public eye, and they assist and often criticize the performance of the official international human rights bodies. Two outstanding examples of human rights NGOs are Amnesty International[279] and Human Rights Watch.[280] There are many more.[281]

Both Amnesty International and Human Rights Watch publish annual reports on the human rights situation internationally and in virtually every country in the world. These are often called country reports. They are available both in print and online.[282] In addition, the U.S. State Department is required to submit to Congress annual human rights country reports. These are most easily consulted at the State Department's

---

[276]   http://www1.umn.edu/humanrts/africa/comcases/comcases.html. *See also* the African Human Rights Case Law Analyser, http://caselaw.ihrda.org/.

[277]   The AHRD and related documents are available at http://aichr.org/documents/.

[278]   http://www.asean.org/communities/asean-socio-cultural-community/category/acwc.

[279]   http://www.amnesty.org.

[280]   http://www.hrw.org.

[281]   *See, e.g.*, the link collections of the University of Minnesota Human Rights Library (http://www1.umn.edu/humanrts/links/ngolinks.html) and the Derechos NGO (http://www.derechos.net/links/ngo/all.html). *See also* MEIKLEJOHN CIV. LIBERTIES INST., HUMAN RIGHTS ORGANIZATIONS AND PERIODICALS DIRECTORY 2008–2009 (13th ed. 2008).

[282]   The formal titles are *Amnesty International Annual Report* and *Human Rights Watch World Report*. The URLs for the reports change, but the reports are easily findable from the home pages of both organizations.

website.[283] The State Department also submits annual reports on religious freedom,[284] trafficking in persons,[285] and advancing freedom and democracy.[286]

Both Amnesty International and Human Rights Watch maintain extensive online libraries of their publications, usually available in full text without charge.

The secondary literature is massive. An efficient solution is to use the Library of Congress subject heading "Human rights." This heading can be subdivided by country, e.g., "Human rights—Colombia." As well, thematic searching is possible using Library of Congress subject headings or keyword searches, e.g., "Children's rights," "Detention of persons," "Disappeared persons," "Fair trial," "Freedom of expression," "Freedom of religion," "Political prisoners," and so on.

HuriSearch is a search engine that searches over 5,000 human rights websites.[287] Although it has some shortcomings, such as an inability to limit by date or to display the most recent information first, *HuriSearch* is very useful.

The *Human Rights Web Archive*[288] is an initiative of the Columbia University Libraries and Columbia's Center for Human Rights Documentation and Research, in cooperation with the Archive-It service of the Internet Archive. Its purpose is to preserve access to human rights websites and webpages that would otherwise disappear. The archive is fully searchable.

HumanRights.Gov[289] is a portal to international human rights information from the U.S. government. There are sectors for human rights reporting by the U.S. government, as discussed above, for news on U.S. action in the field of human rights, for links to U.S. government agencies that deal with human rights, for hot topics, and for references, with links to human rights treaties and conventions available on the World Wide Web.

Many journals are devoted to international human rights, either generally or focusing on a particular aspect; in library catalogs they can be found with the subject heading "Human rights—Periodicals." Some of the more significant or interesting human rights journals in English are:

- *Asia-Pacific Journal on Human Rights and the Law;*

- *East European Human Rights Review;*

- *Harvard Human Rights Journal;*

- *Human Rights Law Journal: HRLJ;*

- *Human Rights Law Review;*

- *Human Rights Quarterly;*

- *International Review of the Red Cross;*

---

[283]   http://www.state.gov/g/drl/rls/hrrpt/. The hardbound version can be found in collections of U.S. government documents, but it is published late.

[284]   http://www.state.gov/g/drl/rls/irf.

[285]   http://www.state.gov/g/tip/rls/tiprpt.

[286]   http://www.state.gov/g/drl/rls/afdr/.

[287]   http://www.hurisearch.org.

[288]   http://library.columbia.edu/indiv/humanrights/hrwa.html.

[289]   http://www.humanrights.gov.

- *Journal of Human Rights;*

- *Muslim World Journal of Human Rights;*

- *Netherlands Quarterly of Human Rights;*

- *Religion and Human Rights: An International Journal;*

- *Security and Human Rights; and*

- *Yale Human Rights and Development Law Journal.*

In addition, many general international law journals publish articles on human rights.

J. ILLUSTRATIONS

21–1.   **Pages from the Multilateral Section of Treaties in Force as Found on State Department Website**

21–2.   **Judgment of the International Court of Justice as Posted on the Court's Website**

21–3.   **Website of the United National High Commissioner for Human Rights**

[Illustration 21–1]

PAGES FROM THE MULTILATERAL SECTION OF TREATIES
IN FORCE AS FOUND ON STATE DEPARTMENT WEBSITE

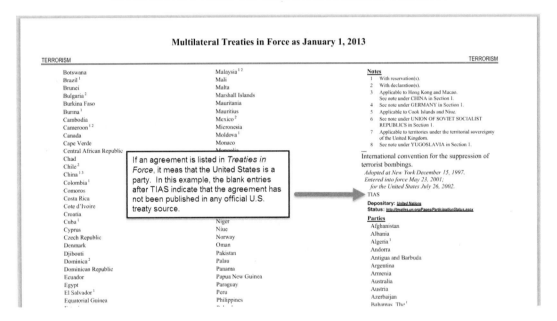

[Illustration 21–2]

JUDGMENT OF THE INTERNATIONAL COURT OF JUSTICE AS POSTED ON THE COURT'S WEBSITE

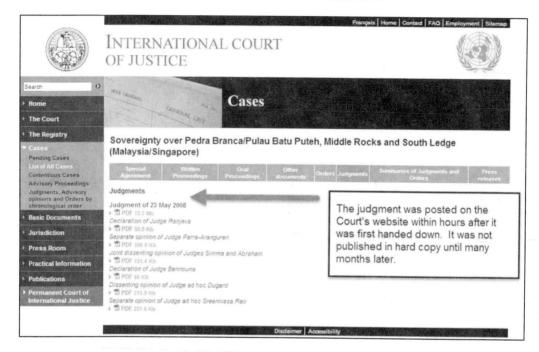

[Illustration 21–3]

WEBSITE OF THE UNITED NATIONAL HIGH COMMISSIONER FOR HUMAN RIGHTS

Chapter 22

RESEARCHING THE LAW OF THE UNITED KINGDOM*

The United Kingdom of Great Britain and Northern Ireland comprises four countries and three distinct legal systems. The countries, England, Wales, Scotland, and Northern Ireland, all share the same head of state, the Monarch. The existence of three legal systems is the result of arrangements made when the states unified (Wales with the 1535 Laws in Wales Act, Scotland with the 1707 Act of Union, and Northern Ireland in 1921 with the Government of Ireland Act).

Scotland and Northern Ireland have retained separate legal systems, evidenced by their different court structures, different legal professions, and, as a result of recent changes, different legislative bodies. Wales has some variances from England, but for the purposes of this chapter Wales is largely incorporated into the discussion of English legal research. The 1997 devolution[1] referendums changed the degree to which Scotland and, to a lesser extent, Wales are able to govern independently of the United Kingdom Parliament. As a result of the referendums and subsequent legislation, both Scotland and Wales now have their own legislative bodies with varying amounts of devolved authority.[2] The National Assembly for Wales and the Scottish Parliament opened in 1999. However, the U.K. Parliament in London, frequently referred to as "Westminster," continues to legislate on a variety of matters affecting the regions and all matters affecting the nation as a whole.

Following the 1998 "Good Friday" agreement,[3] the Northern Ireland Assembly, a multiparty legislative body, was established to legislate over certain matters specific to that country. Disagreement between representatives of the Unionists and the Nationalists led to the suspension of the Assembly in October 2002. Following the acceptance of the St. Andrews Agreement and the successful Assembly elections in early 2007, full power was restored to the Assembly in May 2007.[4] In light of the recent history of Northern Ireland, it is difficult to assess the long-term prospects for the Assembly. The result of these relatively recent constitutional changes is a United Kingdom that resembles a federal system of government, and a legal research methodology not unfamiliar to researchers in the United States.

---

* Stephen E. Young, Senior Reference Librarian, Judge Kathryn J. DuFour Law Library, Catholic University School of Law wrote this chapter.

[1] Devolution is "[t]he delegation by the central government to a regional authority of legislative or executive functions (or both) relating to domestic issues within the region." A DICTIONARY OF LAW 140 (Jonathan Law & Elizabeth A. Martin eds., 7th ed. 2013).

[2] The process of devolution is explored in NOREEN BURROWS, DEVOLUTION (2000).

[3] *Agreement Reached in the Multi-Party Negotiations*, Apr. 10, 1998, 37 I.L.M. 751 (1998) [hereinafter Good Friday Agreement].

[4] http://niassembly.gov.uk/.

A. ENGLISH LAW

The sources of English law can be divided into four main categories: statutes and treaties, case law, custom and convention, and the laws of the European Union.[5] Perhaps the most fundamental difference between English law and the law of the United States is the lack of a written constitution. However, it would be incorrect to assume that a constitution does not exist. The reality is that all of the sources described above comprise the country's constitution, albeit unwritten. Constitutional law is, therefore, a melting pot of legislation enacted by Parliament, decisions rendered by the courts of law, various customs and conventions that must be adhered to, and laws imposed on member countries by the European Union.

B. ENGLISH PRIMARY LEGISLATION

1. The Parliamentary Process

Parliament is a bicameral legislative body consisting of the House of Commons and the House of Lords. The House of Commons comprises 650 elected Members of Parliament. The House of Lords, recently a subject of reform, comprises eighty-eight hereditary peers (elected and appointed), 676 life peers, and twenty-five bishops. Some of the most useful sources of authoritative and up-to-date information on the Houses of Parliament are the *House of Commons Factsheets*. These are published on the Parliament website by the House of Commons Information Office and cover a variety of topics, including the workings of committees, the passage of legislation, and even the history of the House of Commons building.[6]

Bills are introduced into either the House of Commons or the House of Lords. Three classes of bills exist: public bills, which affect the general public; private bills, which affect either an individual or a company; and hybrid bills, which combine elements of public and private bills. Public bills introduced by a minister are referred to as *government bills*; those introduced by backbenchers[7] are referred to as *private members' bills*. Government bills usually survive the parliamentary process; only ten percent of private members' bills make it through both houses.

Copies of bills are printed by The Stationery Office[8] and are made available on the Parliament website shortly after their initial reading.[9] Once introduced, bills must then undergo a second reading (where floor debate may occur), a committee (in the Commons it will usually be a public bill committee named after the bill), a report, and a third reading. The bill is then referred to the second house, where it is again considered and, if approved, sent back to the originating house for final approval. If approved, the bill

---

[5] GARY SLAPPER & DAVID KELLY, THE ENGLISH LEGAL SYSTEM (9th ed. 2009).

[6] http://www.parliament.uk/about/how/guides/factsheets/.

[7] Members of Parliament who do not hold ministerial or shadow ministerial office are known as "backbenchers." They are so called because they sit on the back benches of the House of Commons.

[8] The publishing arm of Her Majesty's Stationery Office (H.M.S.O.) was privatized in 1996; publishing is now handled by The Stationery Office (T.S.O.). H.M.S.O. is now part of the National Archives and is responsible for administering Crown copyright and publication contracts for legislation and other official materials. http://www.tso.co.uk/about-tso/faqs. The T.S.O. Parliamentary & Legal Bookshop is at http://www.tsoshop.co.uk/parliament/.

[9] http://services.parliament.uk/bills/.

then receives the Royal Assent[10] and becomes an act of Parliament. Amendments are usually made after the second reading, in committee, or after being referred to the second house for approval. A bill will fail if it does not pass through all these stages before the end of the parliamentary session. If, however, the bill is introduced in two successive sessions and is approved by the House of Commons, but not by the House of Lords, the bill may still become an act of Parliament.[11]

Citations to bills include the initials of the house in which the bill had its initial reading, the session of Parliament, and the bill number. A bill receives a new number when it undergoes substantial changes and when it is referred to the second chamber of Parliament. *The Weekly Information Bulletin of the House of Commons* is the most complete source for tracking amendments and bill numbers and for determining where in the parliamentary process the bill is at any given moment in time.

Debate and proceedings concerning legislation also can be traced through the parliamentary process by using *The Official Report of Debates* ("*Hansard*"). *The Weekly Information Bulletin* and *Hansard* are available in full text on the Parliament website and are updated daily.[12] Major pieces of legislation are often accompanied by a research paper prepared by the House of Commons Library. These documents, available through the Parliament website, can provide valuable insights into the origins and purpose of the bill.

2. Acts of Parliament

Acts passed by Parliament are classified as either "private and local" or "public and general" acts.[13] Once they receive the Royal Assent, they are published individually by T.S.O. in a format known as the Queen's Printer's Copy. Full text copies are made available on the *Legislation* website on the day of publication.[14] The public acts, together with any General Synod Measures,[15] have been published in annual volumes since 1831, originally as *The Public General Acts and Measures* and now titled *Public General Acts and General Synod Measures*. The last volume for each year contains an index and tables listing the acts alphabetically and chronologically. In addition, this last volume also contains tables that show *derivations and destinations* of the consolidated acts and the effect of each statute upon earlier measures.[16]

---

[10] The Royal Assent is equivalent to the presidential signature on an act of Congress; however, the Royal Assent has not been refused since 1707.

[11] An example is the Financial Services and Markets Bill 1998–99. A full discussion of the progress of a bill through Parliament is available in *Factsheet L1, The Parliamentary Stages of a Government Bill*, at http://www.parliament.uk/documents/commons-information-office/l01.pdf.

[12] http://www.parliament.uk/business/publications.

[13] A more comprehensive treatment of acts of Parliament is available in DONALD GIFFORD, HOW TO UNDERSTAND AN ACT OF PARLIAMENT (1996).

[14] www.legislation.gov.uk [hereinafter the *Legislation* website].

[15] The legislation of the Church of England, referred to as "measures" and passed by its General Synod, are presented to Parliament for its approval by resolution before forwarding to the sovereign for General Assent. *See* http://www.churchofengland.org/about-us/structure/churchlawlegis/legislation.aspx. The Measures of the General Synod approved in this manner have the same force and effect as an Act of Parliament. Church of England Assembly (Powers) Act 1919, 9 and 10 Geo. 5, c. 76.

[16] Measures are akin to acts passed by the Congress of the United States.

3. Compilations of Statutes

England has no official codification of all enactments of Parliament comparable to the *United States Code*. There is, however, current interest in codifying particular branches of the law, such as criminal law and family law. For this purpose, and to make recommendations for reform of various areas of the law, Parliament created the Law Commission for England and Wales in 1965.[17] In addition, from time to time Parliament passes a consolidated statute in which relevant acts and amendments thereto are consolidated into one act. A number of official and commercial compilations of statutes also are available to the researcher.

a.   The Legislation Website.[18] This is the official revised edition of the primary legislation of the United Kingdom. It takes over from its predecessor, The United Kingdom *Statute Law Database*. The *Legislation* website is the official collection of all acts in force, as amended. It contains all acts since 1235 in effect and incorporates all amendments that add to or change the language of the original act.

b.   Halsbury's Statutes of England & Wales, 4th ed. (1985 & Supp.). This commercially published set is a compilation of statutes in force arranged by subject, and is considered the principal print source of primary legislation in England and Wales. [Illustration 22–1] Valuable features include the liberal use of annotations and the frequency of revisions that reflect recent changes in legislation. Annotations follow each section of an act and provide references to several kinds of information, including administrative regulations passed under the authority of the act and cases interpreting language used in the act. The fourth edition of this set has the following components:

(1) *The 50 volumes of the main set.* Volumes are reissued from time to time to reflect amendments and incorporate additions.

(2) *Cumulative Supplement.* This volume is issued annually and compiles changes and additions to material in the main volumes. [Illustration 22–2]

(3) *Consolidated Index volume.* This volume is issued annually. It contains a general subject index to the entire set and an alphabetical and chronological table of statutes.

(4) *Noter-up service.* This looseleaf volume, used together with the *Cumulative Supplement*, updates the main set to within a few weeks of the most recent legislation.

(5) *Current Statutes Service binders.* These looseleaf volumes (lettered A through F) contain the full, annotated text of new acts that have not yet been incorporated into the main set. [Illustration 22–3]

(6) *Destination Tables and Consolidated Table of Cases volumes.* These are the most recent additions to the set and provide useful information on the treatment and history of a statute.

(7) *Statutes Citator volume.* This is another recent addition to the set and serves to record changes to statutes by subsequent statutes.

c.   Current Law Statutes Service. This unofficial set, published by Sweet & Maxwell, prints the full text of all public and private acts once they have received the

---

[17] http://www.justice.gov.uk/lawcommission/index.htm.

[18] http://www.legislation.gov.uk.

Royal Assent. The acts first appear in booklet format one month after publication by T.S.O. and are filed in the Service File. Later, annotated versions of the acts for the current year are cumulated and published in annual volumes. The set includes a table of statutes dating back to 1700 and a table of parliamentary debates dating back to 1950.

4. In Force Legislation

An act of Parliament may not necessarily become law, even though it has received the Royal Assent and has not been repealed. Acts of Parliament, either in whole or in part, are required to be "in force" before they are considered part of the law of the land. Therefore, an essential component of English legislative research is determining whether the act, either in whole or in part, is currently "in force" (i.e., carries with it the force of law).

Most acts contain a commencement provision that states when the act comes into force. This provision is usually found near the end of the act alongside the short title and extent information (i.e., indicating whether sections of the act do not apply to Scotland or Northern Ireland); it is possible, however, for commencement information to be spread throughout an act (thereby making research challenging). Section 4 of the Interpretation Act 1978 (c. 30) states that a commencement provision may provide a date, either a fixed date or a date after an elapsed period of time (most commonly two months), on which either the whole act or designated sections of the act come into force. Or the provision may provide for a Minister of the Crown to determine when the act, or sections of it, should be brought into force (this is done through a piece of delegated legislation known as a "commencement order").[19] If an act does not provide a commencement provision, it is assumed that the entire act comes into force on the date of the Royal Assent. Such assumptions are usually only necessary in the case of short or uncomplicated acts.

Determining whether an act or part of an act has been brought into force can be as simple as examining the commencement provision of the original act. There are other sources, however, that not only provide information on whether the act is yet in force but also whether it remains in force. Among these, the most widely used is the companion volume to *Halsbury's Statutes of England & Wales*, 4th ed., appropriately entitled *Is It In Force?* This single volume outlines the commencement status, section by section, of all acts passed in the last twenty-five years. The twenty-five-year cut-off date can present some difficulties to the researcher needing to know whether a section of an older act has commenced, but most questions regarding the commencement of legislation can be answered using this source. An annual publication like *Is It In Force?* also has another limitation: very recent action is not included. To span this gap, the researcher must consult the *Statutes Citator* volume of *Halsbury's Statutes*.

The *Legislation* website provides the researcher with a new alternative to *Halsbury's*. The site contains commencement, repeal, and amendment information for acts.

5. Early English Statutes

Early English laws were published in many editions; the following statutory compilations are the most likely to be found in a law library in the United States.

---

[19] See Section C for a discussion of delegated legislation.

a.   *Statutes of the Realm.* Printed in twelve folio (tall) volumes, this set reproduces statutes enacted in the period 1225–1713. Published by the Record Commissioners, this set is considered the authoritative source for pre-1714 legislation (excluding the period of the Commonwealth). Some early statutes are reproduced in their original Latin or Norman French in addition to the English translation.

b.   *Statutes at Large.* This series provides coverage of legislation for the period 1225–1869. The title is a generic term for a number of compilations of the early statutes. The original compilation is entitled *The Whole Volume of Statutes at Large* (1587); however, a number of additional compilations share the same generic title. Arguably the most used compilation, by Danby Pickering, is *Statutes at Large from Magna Charta, to the End of the Eleventh Parliament of Great Britain, Anno 1761* [continued to 1806] (1807). This compilation is commonly referred to as "Pickering's Statutes." Another frequently cited compilation is the nine-volume set published by Owen Ruffhead between 1763 and 1765.[20]

c.   *Acts and Ordinances of the Interregnum, 1642–1660*

This is a three-volume integration of the laws enacted during the English Civil War (1642–1651) and the Interregnum.[21] The third volume of this set includes a Chronological Table of Acts and Ordinances; an Index to Subjects; and an Index of Names, Places, and Things.

7.   Electronic Access to English Statutes

The formation of The Stationery Office in 1996 not only led to an overhaul of the way in which official print material was made available, but also began the process of making official government widely available on the World Wide Web.

Very soon after the creation of T.S.O., legislative documents, including official, full-text versions of parliamentary bills and acts of Parliament, appeared online. Over the past few years, websites, such as parliament.uk,[22] have developed rapidly and now publish a wide variety of legislative material, including debates from both houses of Parliament, reports from committees, bill-tracking information, bills, acts, and other parliamentary documents. Although the Parliament website provides extensive coverage of the workings of Parliament and thus serves as an indispensable tool in tracking legislation, it does not provide the text of acts. The full text of acts can be located on the *Legislation* website.[23]

The most recent development in the area of online access to statutory information was the late 2006 release of the aforementioned *U.K. Statute Law Database*, which was incorporated into the *Legislation* site in 2008. The site is now maintained by the National Archives and provides free access to most types of legislation, both primary and secondary. The legislation is offered in revised form, meaning that it incorporates any amendments made to it by subsequent legislation. The database includes legislation

---

[20] A more complete discussion of the early statute compilations is available in WILLIAM HOLDSWORTH, 11 A HISTORY OF ENGLISH LAW 287 (1938).

[21] The Interregnum is the interval between the end of the reign of Charles I and the beginning of the reign of his successor, Charles II. During this period, the country was governed without a monarch.

[22] http://www.parliament.uk/.

[23] *See supra* note 14.

dating back to 1267's Statute of Marlborough, the oldest statute containing provisions still in force.

The following services, all but one of which are fee-based, also provide access to valuable legislative material:[24]

a.   *LexisNexis. LexisNexis* has a file of U.K. statutes with the full, amended text of all public general acts that are currently in force. Legislation that has been recently enacted but is not yet in force is also included.

b.   *Westlaw. Westlaw* has developed a useful database of in-force English primary legislation. *Westlaw* provides coverage of current and historic legislation. The Law In Force coverage for statutes begins in 1267 and is consolidated through the current year.

c.   *BAILII.* In 2000, the British and Irish Legal Information Institute (BAILII) began offering a free database designed to provide hypertext-linked, full-text versions of primary legislation and case law for the United Kingdom.[25] The legislative content for this database is obtained from the National Archives and is therefore essentially identical to the material found on the *Legislation* website.

d.   *Justis.* This is a database containing all acts of Parliament for England, Wales, and Scotland dating back to 1235.[26]

e.   *HeinOnline.* This service provides subscribers with access to the *Statutes of the Realm* (1235–1713) in PDF format.

8.   Citation of English Statutes

Prior to 1963, English statutes were cited by name, regnal year (the year of the sovereign's reign when the statute was passed), and chapter (the text of the statute)— e.g., National Services Act, 11 & 12 Geo. 6, c. 64. In this example, the act was passed during the parliamentary session that spanned the eleventh and twelfth years of the reign of King George VI. It should be noted that a parliamentary session usually begins in November and concludes either the following autumn, or earlier in an election year. The regnal year citation form requires that the year of passage of a statute be determined. As all legal writing on English law prior to 1963 cited to regnal year, a table of regnal years is set forth below for convenience.

The Acts of Parliament Numbering and Citation Act 1962, which came into force in 1963, changed this form of citation. Under provisions of this statute, citation to an act is to the short name of the act and calendar year in which it was passed—e.g., The Football Spectators Act 1999. Since 1898, each act of Parliament includes a section indicating the title by which it is to be cited.

---

[24] Throughout this chapter, references to *Westlaw* and *LexisNexis* refer to the content available through U.S. subscriptions to these services. It should be noted that separate U.K. subscriptions may contain different content.

[25] http://www.bailii.org.

[26] http://www.justis.com/titles/titles.html.

TABLE OF REGNAL YEARS

Sovereign	Reign Began
William I	Oct. 14, 1066
William II	Sept. 26, 1087
Henry I	Aug. 5, 1100
Stephen	Dec. 26, 1135
Henry II	Dec. 19, 1154
Richard I	Sept. 3, 1189
John	May 27, 1199
Henry III	Oct. 28, 1216
Edward I	Nov. 20, 1272
Edward II	July 8, 1307
Edward III	Jan. 25, 1327
Richard II	June 22, 1377
Henry IV	Sept. 30, 1399
Henry V	Mar. 21, 1413
Henry VI	Sept. 1, 1422
Edward IV	Mar. 4, 1461
Edward V	Apr. 9, 1483
Richard III	June 26, 1483
Henry VII	Aug. 22, 1485
Henry VIII	Apr. 22, 1509
Edward VI	Jan. 28, 1547
Mary	July 6, 1553
Elizabeth I	Nov. 17, 1558
James I	Mar. 24, 1603
Charles I	Mar. 27, 1625
The Commonwealth	Jan. 30, 1649
Charles II	May 29, 1660
James II	Feb. 6, 1685
William & Mary	Feb. 13, 1689
Anne	Mar. 8, 1702
George I	Aug. 1, 1714
George II	June 11, 1727
George III	Oct. 25, 1760
George IV	Jan. 29, 1820
William IV	June 26, 1830
Victoria	June 20, 1837
Edward VII	Jan. 22, 1901
George V	May 6, 1910
Edward VIII	Jan. 20, 1936
George VI	Dec. 11, 1936
Elizabeth II	Feb. 6, 1952

C. ENGLISH SECONDARY LEGISLATION

The term *secondary legislation*, sometimes known as *delegated legislation*, is the body of law referred to as administrative law in the United States. The Statutory Instruments (formerly called Statutory Rules and Orders) made[27] by Ministers of the Crown are the English equivalent of the rules and regulations published in the United States in the *Federal Register* and compiled in the *Code of Federal Regulations*. Statutory Instruments are orders, rules, and regulations promulgated by the Ministers under authority delegated to them by Parliament. Bylaws made by local governmental or other authorities exercising power conferred upon them by Parliament also are included in this body of material.

1. Publication of Statutory Instruments

Statutory Instrument (or SI) is a generic term derived from the Statutory Instruments Act 1946,[28] applicable to four types of delegated legislation: orders, rules, regulations, and bylaws.[29] The use of Statutory Instruments has grown rapidly, reflecting the increasing complexity of society.[30] Prior to the middle of the nineteenth century, relatively few pieces of secondary legislation were promulgated. Typically, T.S.O., on any given weekday, publishes numerous SIs, and over the past decade between 1,600 and 2,900 are brought into force each year. Each SI is assigned a number based on the order in which it is passed in the calendar year, (e.g., SI 2011/1068 is the 1,068th SI made in 2011). A letter may appear in parenthesis after the citation indicating a particular subseries of SI. The main subseries are C (commencement orders); L (legal matters, e.g., court rules); and W (Welsh only).

a. Statutory Instruments. SIs are made available online and in full text on the *Legislation* website.[31] SIs are also often listed in the major legal periodicals, e.g., *Solicitor's Journal* and *New Law Journal*. The full text of SIs appears in unannotated, annual bound volumes published by H.M.S.O., entitled simply *Statutory Instruments* (this set dates back to 1946).

b. Halsbury's Statutory Instruments. Although this set is selective in providing the full text of delegated legislation, it does at least offer a summary of all SIs currently in force. SIs are selected for full text inclusion based on their relative importance to the legal community. This multivolume work is arranged alphabetically by subject-based titles and contains, in addition to the twenty-two base volumes (nine of which are reissued annually), a Consolidated Index and Alphabetical List of Statutory Instruments volume, an E.C. Legislation Implementation volume, and a looseleaf service binder. The looseleaf binder contains useful tables (list of authorizing statutes, chronological list of SIs, commencement orders), an annual supplement to the base volumes, a monthly survey with an accompanying key to the base volumes, and the full text of selected new SIs arranged in numerical order.

---

[27] The word "made" is a term of art used to describe the creation or promulgation of delegated legislation.

[28] Statutory Instruments Act, 9 & 10 Geo. 6, c. 36 (1946).

[29] Prior to 1948 (when the act came into force), SIs were referred to as S.R. & O.s (Statutory Rules and Orders); prior to 1894, orders and proclamations were cited by their title and date.

[30] PETER CLINCH, USING A LAW LIBRARY: A STUDENT'S GUIDE TO LEGAL RESEARCH SKILLS 71 (2d ed. 2001).

[31] http://www.legislation.gov.uk.

Halsbury's Statutory Instruments is useful in tracing delegated legislation on a particular subject; the set can also be used to trace SIs by their title and even their citation (although the *Legislation* website may prove to be more convenient for this type of search). Each SI is annotated with case citations, and an overview of the relevant SIs is provided at the beginning of each title. Each title also contains a complete list of the SIs that have been summarized and a list of SIs no longer in force, e.g., those that have been repealed or superseded. New volumes are published periodically and may not be indexed until the following annual index.

2. Electronic Access to Statutory Instruments

Since 2008, the most convenient way to locate individual SIs is the *Legislation* website, which now contains the full text of individual SIs promulgated since 1987 (explanatory memorandums are available for early 2004 to present).[32] A search engine is available on the website. Welsh and Scottish SIs are also available on this site. Secondary legislation for Northern Ireland is discussed in Section N.

  a. LexisNexis. The *LexisNexis* Library of UK materials contains the full, amended text of all public general SIs currently in force. It is updated weekly.

  b. Westlaw. Westlaw coverage for SIs begins with 1948 and is kept relatively up-to-date. In addition to the in force SIs, a separate database contains historical versions of certain SIs beginning with 1992.

  c. BAILII. Coverage of SIs corresponds to the coverage on the official *Legislation* site.

  d. Justis. This fee-based service provides coverage of secondary legislation from 1671 to the present.[33]

3. The National Assembly for Wales

The National Assembly for Wales, located in the principality's capital, Cardiff, came into existence on July 1, 1999. Although the Assembly was not initially granted powers under the Government of Wales Act 1998 to make primary legislation, it has been granted limited primary law-making authority under the Government of Wales Act 2006; these powers were recently expanded following a referendum on March 3, 2011.[34]

The Assembly comprises sixty elected members. It is led by the Presiding Officer, who is elected by Assembly members, and an Assembly Commission currently comprised of four other Assembly members. The proceedings of the Assembly, including background information and documents presented to the Assembly, are available on the National Assembly of Wales website.[35] Legislation made by the Assembly, in the form of Statutory Instruments, Assembly Measures, or Legislative Competence Orders, is published by the National Archives on the *Legislation* site.[36] All documents produced by or on behalf of the Assembly are available in English and Welsh. Welsh SIs are identified by a parenthetical reference to Wales in the title and number of the citation—e.g., SI

---

[32] *Id.*

[33] http://www.justis.com/titles/uk_statutory_instruments.html.

[34] For a more complete discussion of the Assembly's powers, see http://www.assemblywales.org.

[35] *Id.*

[36] http://www.legislation.gov.uk/browse/wales.

2000/1079 (W. 72) The Homelessness (Wales) Regulations 2000. *Westlaw* and *LexisNexis* provide coverage of legislation made by the National Assembly.

D. ENGLISH CASE LAW

1. English Court Organization

The modern organization of the English court system began with The Judicature Act 1873 and continued into the twentieth century with subsequent Parliamentary legislation, such as the Courts Act of 1971, and the handover of the administration of the courts to The Court Service in 1995.[37] Recent changes include the passage of the Constitutional Reform Act of 2005 and the creation of a new United Kingdom Supreme Court.[38]

a.   Supreme Court. This body serves as the final court of appeal for the United Kingdom in civil cases and the final court of appeal for criminal cases from England, Wales, and Northern Ireland. The Court began hearing cases in October 2009.

b.   Court of Appeal. This court has two divisions: civil and criminal. It hears appeals from the High Court of Justice and certain other inferior courts.

c.   High Court of Justice. This court now consists of three divisions: Queen's Bench Division (including the Admiralty Court and Commercial Court), Chancery Division, and Family Division.[39] In practice, each division acts as a separate court.

d.   Crown Court. This court was created by the Courts Act 1971. It is a criminal court with general jurisdiction. As the main criminal court of England, it tries serious criminal cases and hears appeals from the Magistrates' Courts.

e.   County Courts. There are 216 County Courts. These courts have broad first-instance civil jurisdiction.

f.   Magistrates' Courts. The Magistrates' Courts play a significant role in the criminal courts structure. These courts handle the majority of minor criminal cases and some "either way" cases (criminal cases in which a "hybrid" offense has occurred).

2. Development of English Court Reports

The history of court reporting in England dates back to the thirteenth century.[40] The reporting of English cases can be divided into three distinct periods.

---

[37] The Court Service merged with the Magistrates' Courts Service on April 1, 2005, forming Her Majesty's Courts Service. This, in turn, merged with the Tribunals Service on April 1, 2011, to form Her Majesty's Courts and Tribunals Service.

[38] http://www.supremecourt.gov.uk.

[39] Prior to the enactment of the Courts Act 1971, the High Court of Justice consisted of Queen's Bench Division; Probate, Divorce, and Admiralty Division; and Chancery Division.

[40] For a detailed treatment of the development of English court reporting, see RICHARD WARD, WALKER & WALKER'S ENGLISH LEGAL SYSTEM (10th ed. 2008). *See also* John H. Baker, *Dr. Thomas Fastoff and the History of Law Reporting,* 45 CAMBRIDGE L.J. 84 (1986); WILLIAM SEARLE HOLDSWORTH, SOURCES AND LITERATURE OF ENGLISH LAW (1925). Law students who think reading old English cases is a useless exercise should read David V. Stivison, *The Practical Uses of Legal History,* 33 PRAC. LAW. 27 (1987). The author discusses how some of these old cases can be useful in the modern practice of law.

a. Year Books, 1272–1537. The *Year Books*, originally written in Law French,[41] are the first available law reports. Their purpose and function are still disputed by legal historians, although it is widely believed that their original purpose was more educational than practical. Cases from the *Year Books* are still cited on occasion, but the *Year Books* are now largely used for historical research. The Selden Society has reprinted most of the *Year Books*, together with English translations.[42] *HeinOnline* also provides access to many of the Selden Society publications, including reprints of the *Year Books*.

b. Nominate Reports, 1537–1865. During the period from 1535 to 1865, there was no officially recognized system of court reporting. Any reporter could publish court reports, and although commentators argue over the exact number that were published, what we do know with some certainty is that many of them covered the same period of time and the same courts with varying degrees of accuracy.[43] It has been customary to refer to these reports by the names of the reporters—hence their generic name, *nominate reports*. Many of the cases reported in the various nominate reports have been reprinted in the following sets.

(1) *The English Reports, Full Reprint.* This is a reprint of the nominate reports and some *Year Books*, with coverage of reports from 1220 to 1865. When there were competing sets of reports, the editors included only the set they deemed most accurate. There are 176 volumes in this set, including a two-volume Table of Cases and a separate wall chart that lists all the nominate reports with reference to their location in the *Full Reprint*. This set is more widely available in American law libraries than many of the individual nominate reports and is considered the standard source for pre-1865 English cases. The entire set, together with accompanying charts and indexes, is available in *HeinOnline*.

(2) *The Revised Reports.* The *Revised Reports* are in 149 volumes and cover the period 1785 to 1865. Although this set largely duplicates *The English Reports, Full Reprint*, its value lies in the contributions of its editor, Sir Frederick Pollock, a distinguished legal scholar. Pollock not only selected cases, he also edited and combined cases to provide a more accurate reflection of the law.

(3) *The All England Law Reports Reprint.* This set covers selected cases from 1558 to 1935. The cases, arranged in thirty-six volumes, are chosen from the nominate reports and *The Law Times Reports* (a Victorian weekly periodical that selectively published reports of cases). Those cases selected were deemed to be of most use to the legal profession at the time of publication.

c. The Law Reports, 1865 to present. As a result of the inconsistent and overlapping nature of many of the nominate reports, the Incorporated Council of Law Reporting for England and Wales was formed in 1865. The Incorporated Council is a registered charity consisting of members nominated by the Inns of Court and by the General Counsel of the bar. As such, it has quasi-official status. Shortly after formation,

---

[41] Law French refers to "[t]he corrupted form of the Norman French language that arose in England in the centuries after William the Conqueror invaded England in 1066 and that was used for several centuries as the primary language of the English legal system." BRIAN A. GARNER, BLACK'S LAW DICTIONARY 964 (9th ed. 2009).

[42] http://www.selden-society.qmw.ac.uk/.

[43] The most useful treatments of the nominate reports are Van Vechten Veeder, *The English Reports 1292–1865*, 15 HARV. L. REV. 1 (1901), and Van Vechten Veeder, *The English Reports 1292–1865 II*, 15 HARV. L. REV. 109 (1901).

the Council began publication of *The Law Reports*. This series, discussed more fully below, has become the preeminent series of court reports in England and Wales and is available electronically in both *LexisNexis* and *Westlaw*.

3. Modern Law Reports

English cases decided since 1865 can be found in the following:

a. *The Law Reports*. This set reports selected decisions since 1865; it includes decisions of permanent significance of the Supreme Court (prior to 2009, the decisions were from the House of Lords), the Judicial Committee of the Privy Council, the Court of Appeal, and the High Court of Justice. In addition to the opinions of the judges, it also includes the legal arguments presented to the courts. Although originally published in eleven different series, *The Law Reports* are now published in four series: (1) *Appeal Cases* (includes decisions of the Supreme Court and of the Judicial Committee of the Privy Council), (2) *Queen's Bench*, (3) *Chancery*, and (4) *Family Division*. Decisions of the Court of Appeal are published in the last three series.

b. *The Weekly Law Reports*. This set is also published by the Incorporated Council of Law Reporting and includes many cases that will ultimately be published in *The Law Reports*. It is issued first in weekly pamphlets and then in annual bound volumes. *The Weekly Law Reports* also include cases not intended for publication in *The Law Reports*. These cases appear in the first of the three volumes published each year. Arguments of counsel are not included in *The Weekly Law Reports*.

c. *The All England Law Reports and Other Sets of Reports*. Although the Incorporated Council of Law Reporting assumed responsibility for systematizing court reporting, there is no prohibition on private reporting and many such sets are published. The most important of the private reports is *The All England Law Reports*. This set began in 1936 and incorporated both *The Law Journal Reports* and *The Times Law Reports* (reports of cases published in *The Times* newspaper). *The All England Law Reports* includes the decisions of the Supreme Court, Court of Appeal, High Court of Justice, and courts of special jurisdiction. The opinions are released in advance sheets and then in bound volumes. [Illustration 22–4] A great number of cases are reported only in either the daily newspapers or in professional journals. Accordingly, it is not uncommon to see citations to *The Times* or *The Law Society Gazette*.

4. Electronic Access to English Cases

a. *LexisNexis*. *LexisNexis* includes a library of English cases dating back to 1558, including all cases decided after 1865 and reported in *The All England Law Reports*, *The Law Reports*, *Lloyd's Law Reports* (a reporter for maritime and commercial cases), and a number of specialized reporters. Otherwise unreported decisions may also be available in *LexisNexis*.

b. *Westlaw*. Included in *Westlaw*'s U.K. materials is a database of case reports, including *The Law Reports* and *The Weekly Law Reports* dating back to 1865. Westlaw also provides some limited coverage of cases from 1220 to 1865.

c. *BAILII*. The British and Irish Legal Information Institute's website includes High Court of Justice, Court of Appeal, and Supreme Court/House of Lords decisions dating back to 1996.[44] Select decisions from earlier dates are also available. The companion website, *CommonLII* provides full text access to *The English Reports* (1220–1873).[45]

    d.   Additional Electronic Resources. Judgments from the Supreme Court are made available in full text on the Court's website within hours of the decision being rendered. Among the many commercial databases providing access to case law, *Justis* has one of the more complete collections, including access to *The English Reports, The Law Reports, The Times Law Reports,* and a number of specialist reporters.[46] *HeinOnline* provides a searchable full-text version of *The English Reports, Full Reprint.*

5.   Citation of English Cases

    Many American legal researchers are uncomfortable researching English case law due to a lack of familiarity with English case citation rules. Some general rules that apply to English case law research are set forth below.[47]

    a.   Cites include the year in brackets when it is essential to finding the case (e.g., [1969] 1 All E.R. 210) and the year in parenthesis when the volume numbering is sequential from year to year. All of *The Law Reports* series and many of the other major reports adopt the bracketed style of citation.

    b.   When citing English cases, the names of the parties are in italics, the "v" is not in italics, and the "v" is not followed by a period.

    c.   In the United States, the government is identified in the style of the case by the terms "State," "Commonwealth," or "United States." In the United Kingdom, by contrast, the government (i.e., The Crown) is usually identified by the letter "R." (The R indicates Regina or Rex, depending on whether a queen or king is reigning at the time the action is brought.) Cases involving the Crown are thus cited as R. v defendant.

    d.   Civil case names are said orally as Smith *and* Jones rather than Smith *versus* Jones, although they are cited in the written form as *Smith* v *Jones.* Criminal case names are referred to orally as the Crown *against* Williams, not *versus*; citation would take the form *R.* v *Williams.* Most case indexes use the initial letter R. instead of spelling out Regina or Rex

    e.   Some of the more common reporter abbreviations include:[48]

AC:Law Reports Appeal Cases [2001] AC 53

QB:Law Reports Queens Bench Division [2001] 1 QB 53

Ch:Law Reports Chancery Division [2001] 1 Ch 53

Fam:Law Reports Family Division [2001] Fam 53

All ER:All England Law Reports [2001] 2 All ER 53

---

[44] http://www.baillii.org.

[45] http://www.supremecourt.gov.uk/decided-cases/index.html.

[46] http://www.justis.com/titles/titles.html.

[47] For more complete information on citing legal materials from the U.K., see DEREK FRENCH, HOW TO CITE LEGAL AUTHORITIES (2002).

[48] A fairly comprehensive index of abbreviations and citations is described in Section G-3 of this chapter.

ER:English Reports, Full Reprint (1802) 3 Bos. & Pul. 116, 127 ER 62[49]

JP:Justice of the Peace Reports (2001) 165 JP 53

f.   Beginning in 2001, the Court of Appeal and parts of the High Court adopted a format-neutral citation system, which cites to the case name, year, case number, court, and paragraph number.[50] A Practice Direction issued in 2002 by the Lord Chief Justice further extended the format-neutral citation system to all parts of the High Court.[51]

E. DIGESTS AND ENCYCLOPEDIAS

1. Digests

The Digest: Annotated British, Commonwealth and European Cases.[52] This is a comprehensive digest of over 500,000 English cases reported from the earliest times to the present. It also includes cases from the courts of Scotland, Ireland, Canada, and other countries of the British Commonwealth and South Africa. Cases of only historical interest are excluded from the publication. *The Digest* is arranged topically and has a detailed outline at the beginning of each major subject area and an index at the end of each volume. Cases on a particular aspect of a general topic are grouped in chronological order and assigned case numbers.

The Digest has an annotated index that provides subsequent citation information. Each case annotation is followed by notes of subsequent citing cases, if any, indicating whether the annotated case has been approved, followed, distinguished, overruled, or otherwise mentioned. Under each section or subsection of *The Digest*, cross-references and references to pertinent statutes and to *Halsbury's Laws of England & Wales*, 5th ed. (described below) are given. There is a three-volume Consolidated Table of Cases and a two-volume Consolidated Index. *The Digest* is updated with reissue volumes, annual cumulative supplements, and quarterly surveys (i.e., updates).

2. Encyclopedias

The premier English encyclopedia for both statutory and case law is *Halsbury's Laws of England*, 5th ed.[53] The 5th ed. began publication in 2008 and is currently in the process of replacing the fourth edition.

Halsbury's Laws of England, consisting of over eighty volumes, is alphabetically arranged by topic. Each topic is subdivided into parts, sections, subsections, and paragraphs, with appropriate footnote references to cases, statutes, and statutory instruments. An annual cumulative supplement, an Annual Abridgment volume, and

---

[49] Note that citations to *The English Reports, Full Reprint* should also include a full reference to the original nominate report.

[50] An example is as follows: *Smith* v *Jones* W [2004] EWHC 1001 (Ch) [5]–[7]. The parties are Smith and Jones and the case is from Wales (W). This was the 1001th judgment from the England and Wales High Court in 2004, from the Chancery Division (Ch). [5]–[7] is a paragraph reference. See OSCOLA 2006: THE OXFORD STANDARD FOR CITATION OF LEGAL AUTHORITIES, https://www.law.ox.ac.uk/published/oscola/oscola_2006.pdf for a more complete citation system for English legal authorities.

[51] http://www.hmcourts-service.gov.uk/cms/816.htm.

[52] Prior to 1981, this set was entitled *The English and Empire Digest.*

[53] This set should not be confused with *Halsbury's Statutes of England & Wales*, the collection of legislation described in Section B-3.

two Current Service looseleaf volumes containing a noter-up service and monthly reviews update the set. [Illustration 22–5]

3.   *Current Law*

Current Law, dating from 1947, provides a digest of English law. It is arranged topically and, under each topic, sets forth annotations of cases, statutes, statutory instruments, and recent books and periodical articles. The publications consist of:

   a.   Current Law Monthly Digest. This is a monthly pamphlet advance sheet service that includes a number of useful case, statute, and statutory instrument tables.

   b.   Current Law Year Book. This annual cumulation includes, among other information, a cumulative subject index, table of cases, tables of statutory instruments and instruments affected, and digests of unreported cases.

   c.   Master Volume. The *Current Law Year Books* were consolidated into a 1947–51 volume; since then, a five-year cumulative *Year Book* entitled the *Master Volume* is published every five years.

   d.   Current Law Citators. These volumes are discussed in Section F.

Elements of the *Current Law* suite of publications also form part of *Current Legal Information (CLI)*, an electronic service from Sweet & Maxwell which also includes *Legal Journals Index*.

F.   CITATORS/NOTING UP

No English legal resources correspond exactly to American citators like *Shepard's* and *KeyCite*. There are, however, several methods of updating materials and obtaining later citations or, to use the correct term, *noting up,* cases or statutes.[54]

1.   Statutes

Citators for statutes are arranged chronologically. As a general rule, citations are given to each subsequent statute that amends or repeals the cited statute, and to each case that cites the statute. The primary resource for determining the status of legislation is the *Legislation* website, described in Section B. This site provides status information for statutes dating back to 1267. Additional citators for statutes are contained in the resources described below:

   a.   Chronological Tables of the Statutes. This publication consists of a detailed status table of all English statutes giving their status section by section. The researcher can tell whether a particular part of a statute of interest has been repealed, amended, or otherwise modified (but not what cites to it).

   b.   Current Law Statute Citator. These volumes update legislation between specified dates, while paperback volumes bring the set up to date. Citations to cases construing legislation are included. Statutory instruments have also been included in this set since 1993. The content from these publications is part of the *CLI* suite of databases.

---

[54] For a more detailed description of this topic, see Stephen Young, *"Shepardizing" English Law*, 90 LAW LIBR. J. 209 (1998).

c.   The All England Law Reports, Consolidated Tables and Index. The Tables volumes contain an extensive listing of statutes considered, with citations to cases in *The All England Law Reports.*

2.   Cases

a.   The Digest. This publication works both as a tool for finding cases by subject and as a citator. When there are later cases of note, the digest summary of the main case is followed immediately by an annotations paragraph citing to later cases that consider or cite to the main case.

b.   Current Law Case Citator. A variety of volumes are used in conjunction with each other to cover the period from 1947 to the present. References set forth the citation to the main case and to the paragraph of the *Current Law Year Book* containing annotations of later cases on point. The content from these publications is available electronically as part of the *CLI* suite of databases.

c.   The All England Law Reports, Consolidated Tables and Index. This set contains a cumulative table of cases reported and considered. Cases are listed alphabetically with each case followed by citations to later cases reported in *The All England Law Reports.*

d.   The Index to The Law Reports. The Index to The Law Reports (popularly known as the "Red" and "Pink" indexes) provides a table of Cases Judicially Considered and a table of Statutes Judicially Considered. Despite their official title, the "Red" and "Pink" indexes do much more than merely index cases to *The Law Reports.* Also included are references to cases reported in *Industrial Cases, Lloyd's Law Reports, Road Traffic Reports, Tax Cases, Criminal Appeal Reports, Local Government Reports,* and *The All England Law Reports.* The advance sheets to *The Weekly Law Reports* also include lists of cases judicially considered.

G.   REFERENCE TOOLS

1.   Court Rules

The *Civil Procedure Rules* are published biennially in the traditional "White Book" (formerly known as *Supreme Court Practice*) and are available, together with Practice Directions and recent updates, on the Ministry of Justice website.[55] The *Criminal Procedure Rules* are also available from the Ministry of Justice website.[56]

2.   Directories

Waterlow's Solicitors' and Barristers' Directory is an extensive directory, published annually, that is arranged by geographical location (London first), name of individual, and name of firm. Areas of specialization for law firms are provided. After the listings for solicitors are entries for barristers by chambers (London followed by the provinces) and by name. This is the *Martindale–Hubbell* of Britain. A limited version of *Waterlow's*

---

[55] http://www.justice.gov.uk/guidance/courts-and-tribunals/courts/procedure-rules/civil/index.htm.

[56] http://www.justice.gov.uk/guidance/courts-and-tribunals/courts/procedure-rules/criminal/index.htm.

is also available online.[57] The Law Society also provides a web-based directory for locating solicitors in England and Wales.[58]

3.   Abbreviations

The *Cardiff Index to Legal Abbreviations* is a relatively recent addition to the growing list of web-based legal reference sources.[59] This resource is particularly useful and has quickly become an indispensable tool for all legal researchers. The *Index to Legal Citations and Abbreviations* (4th ed. 2013), by Donald Raistrick, is the most comprehensive print listing of abbreviations used in English legal research. It is often referred to as "Raistrick's." An additional resource is the *Oxford Standard for the Citation of Legal Authorities*, which is commonly used in academic legal writing in the United Kingdom and is analogous to the *Bluebook* in American legal research.[60]

4.   Words and Phrases

A number of the standard English legal publications include definitions of words and phrases. Many of these publications are discussed in the preceding sections. Several other sources exclusively treat judicial interpretations of words and phrases.

a.   *Stroud's Judicial Dictionary of Words and Phrases* (8th ed. 2012). This three-volume publication includes not only definitions but also references to cases and statutes from which they are derived. It is kept current by annual supplements.

b.   *Words and Phrases Legally Defined* (4th ed. 2007). A revision of Burrow's *Words and Phrases Judicially Defined*, this work has been expanded to include treatise and statutory, as well as judicial, definitions. A cumulative supplement is published annually.

5.   Internet Resources

The nature of Internet resources is such that it is difficult to provide a listing that contains both authoritative and stable websites. The following selective list includes only those websites that have stood the test of time and have provided reliable, authoritative information.

a.   *Lawlinks*.[61] Compiled by the library staff at the University of Kent at Canterbury, this is one of the most extensive legal portals for the U.K. Information is organized by type of material and by jurisdiction. This website is regularly updated and logically arranged.

b.   *Official Documents*.[62] The Stationery Office administers this useful compilation of links to official documents including Command Papers and House of Commons Papers. The material can be accessed by document title, date of publication, or category of material.

---

[57] http://www.waterlowlegal.com/.

[58] http://www.lawsociety.org.uk/choosingandusing/findasolicitor.law.

[59] http://www.legalabbrevs.cardiff.ac.uk/.

[60] A free PDF is available at http://www.law.ox.ac.uk/publications/oscola.php.

[61] http://www.kent.ac.uk/lawlinks/.

[62] http://www.official-documents.gov.uk/.

c.   *BAILII.*[63] The British and Irish Legal Information Institute has created one of the most comprehensive databases of legislation and judgments for the various jurisdictions within the United Kingdom.

H. SCOTLAND

Scotland has been a member country of the United Kingdom since the 1707 Act of Union. The country has retained its own legal system and since 1998 has been granted a certain amount of home rule.[64] The origins and sources of Scottish law are different from those associated with English law. A heavy reliance on the Civil and Roman law tradition encouraged the development of a different legal system and, therefore, a different system of legal research.[65] In recent years the establishment of a new Scottish Parliament has dramatically changed the constitutional status of Scotland and its role as a member of the United Kingdom.[66]

I.   SCOTTISH PRIMARY LEGISLATION

1.   The Scottish Parliament

Since July 1, 1999, when the Scottish Parliament assumed its powers granted under The Scotland Act 1998, primary legislation affecting Scotland has been issued either by the U.K. Parliament in London or the Scottish Parliament sitting in Edinburgh.[67] Certain matters are "reserved" by the U.K. Parliament, i.e., deemed to be outside of the legislative competence of the Scottish Parliament. Other matters are "devolved" to the Scottish Parliament, i.e., deemed to be within the legislative competence of the Scottish Parliament. Reserved matters include the U.K. constitution, foreign policy, national security, fiscal policy, international trade policy, nuclear safety, certain areas of social security and employment policy, and certain areas of health policy. Devolved matters include education, local government, housing, tourism, civil and criminal law, emergency services, economic development, agriculture, and sports.

2.   Sources of Scottish Legislation

The source for Scottish primary legislation depends on which legislative body is responsible for producing the legislation. Acts of the U.K. Parliament extending to Scotland are available in the sources discussed in Section B. The extent section of U.K. acts, usually located toward the end of the act, details the geographical extent of the act; however, it is presumed that the act extends nationwide unless the extent section indicates otherwise.

For those matters that reside within the scope of Scotland's devolved legislative powers, the source of primary legislation is the Scottish Parliament.

---

[63] http://www.bailii.org/.

[64] The Scotland Act 1998, c. 46.

[65] DAVID M. WALKER, THE SCOTTISH LEGAL SYSTEM: AN INTRODUCTION TO THE STUDY OF SCOTS LAW (8th ed. rev. 2001).

[66] For a more complete discussion of the impact of devolution on the Scottish legal system, see CHRIS HIMSWORTH & CHRISTINE M. O'NEIL, SCOTLAND'S CONSTITUTION: LAW AND PRACTICE (2d ed. 2009). In a 2014 referendum, Scottish voters chose to remain in the United Kingdom. Steven Erlanger & Adam Cowell, *Scots Reject Independence from Britain*, N.Y. TIMES, Sept. 19, 2014, at A1.

[67] The determination as to which areas are governed by which legislative body is outlined in sections 29 and 30 and schedules 4 and 5 of the act.

3.   The Scottish Parliamentary Process

The passage of legislation through the Scottish Parliament differs from the process followed in the U.K. Parliament (see Section B-1). The Scottish Parliament website provides researchers with comprehensive information concerning the workings of this institution.[68] Because the Scottish Parliament is a unicameral body with 129 members, the passage of a bill in Scotland is understandably less complex than the corresponding process in the Parliament at London.

The passage of a bill through the Scottish Parliament entails three stages. Stage 1 involves the deliberation on the principles of the bill by a lead committee. At this stage, a determination is made as to whether the scope and purpose of the bill is acceptable. This determination is then reported to a plenary session of Parliament. Parliament, in plenary session, debates and votes on the principles of the bill. The details of the bill are discussed in Stage 2. In Stage 2, the bill is assigned to one or more committees of Parliament. At this stage, amendments to the bill can be made. Stage 3, held in plenary session, is the final debate and voting stage. Once again, amendments can be made; however, there are strict guidelines concerning the extent of amendments at this stage. The *Official Report* includes transcripts of committee discussions and floor debates from plenary sessions.[69] The passage of a bill can be tracked using the *Bills* section of the Scottish Parliament website.[70]

4.   Acts of the Scottish Parliament

Acts passed by the Scottish Parliament ("ASP") can be located using the following sources.

a.   The Legislation Website. This website contains full text versions of ASPs from 2000 to the present.[71]

b.   Print Versions. Full text versions of ASPs can be located in sessional volumes published by T.S.O. and in *Current Law Statutes*. In addition, selected ASPs are reproduced in the *Parliament House Book*, a five-volume looseleaf set published by W. Green & Son Ltd.

c.   Additional Online Resources. A complete run of ASPs in full text is available on *BAILII*. In addition, a series of *Westlaw* databases contain Scottish law, including one database containing legislation specifically or primarily affecting Scotland (UKSCO–ST). This database includes acts of both the U.K. government and the Scottish Parliament. Other databases in this series include Scottish legislation in force since 1706 (UKSCO–LIF), a Scottish legislative locator (UKSCO–LEGISLOC), and Scottish delegated legislation (UKSCO–SI). *LexisNexis* provides coverage of Scottish legislation in its SCOLEG file.

J.   SCOTTISH SECONDARY LEGISLATION

Delegated or secondary legislation comprises the body of law often referred to in the United States as administrative law. In Scotland, this law takes the form of either

---

[68] http://www.scottish.parliament.uk/parliamentarybusiness/official-report.aspx.

[69] http://www.scottish.parliament.uk/business/officialReports/index.htm.

[70] http://www.scottish.parliament.uk/parliamentarybusiness/bills.aspx.

[71] http://www.legislation.gov.uk.

Statutory Instruments made under powers granted by a U.K. act, or a Scottish Statutory Instrument (SSI) made under powers granted by an act of the Scottish Parliament. Devolution, therefore, created not only two levels of primary legislation for the region, but also two levels of secondary legislation. Delegated legislation made under powers not devolved to the Scottish Parliament continues to originate in London. Such delegated legislation can be most easily located by using the resources described in Section C.

The Scottish government (formerly the Scottish Executive) carries out Scottish delegated legislation under powers granted by acts of the Scottish Parliament. The Scottish government currently comprises the First Minister, six Cabinet Secretaries and fifteen ministers appointed by the First Minister, the Lord Advocate, and the Solicitor General. The Scottish government can make delegated legislation only on matters that are within its devolved competence as defined by section 54 of The Scotland Act 1998. Prior to coming into force, the majority of SSIs are reviewed by the Scottish Parliament.

SSIs are cited by their title and are assigned a sequential number according to the chronological order in which the Queen's Printer of Scotland receives the SSIs. For example, The Smoke Control Areas (Exempt Fireplaces) (Scotland) Order 2001 SSI 2001/16 is to the 16th Scottish Statutory Instrument made in 2001.

    a.   *The Legislation Website.*[72] SSIs become available on the *Legislation* website either instantaneously or within twenty-four hours of their print publication. Draft SSIs also are made available at this website.

    b.   *Print Versions.* The Queen's Printer for Scotland publishes print versions of SSIs, in both individual and cumulative bound versions. The *Parliament House Book* publishes select SSIs following the authorizing ASP.

    c.   *Additional Online Resources. Westlaw* includes SSIs in the UKSCO–SI database, together with U.K. statutory instruments affecting Scotland. *BAILII* also provides the full text of all SSIs in its Scotland database.[73] *LexisNexis* provides coverage of Scottish delegated legislation in its SCOLEG file.

K. SCOTTISH CASE LAW

1. The Scottish Court System

The Scottish court system comprises the following institutions for civil and criminal law:

    a.   *Civil*

(1) The Sheriff Court is the inferior court and, consequently, handles most civil cases. There are forty-nine Sheriff Courts in six regional Sheriffdoms, headed by a Sheriff Principal; each county in Scotland is in the jurisdiction of at least one Sheriff Court. Appeals are made to the Sheriff Principal.

(2) The Court of Session, which is both a court of first instance and a court of appeal, is divided into the Inner House (the court of appeal) and the Outer House (the court of first instance, or The Lords Ordinary). The Inner House, which is divided further into First and Second Divisions of equal authority, functions solely as an appeal court.

---

[72] *Id.*

[73] http://www.bailii.org/scot/legis/num_reg/.

(3)   The United Kingdom Supreme Court is the court of first instance for certain actions, but generally is the court of appeal for cases appealed from the Court of Session.

b.   Criminal

(1)   Justice of the Peace Courts. This court of first instance is presided over by justices of the peace and magistrates.

(2)   The Sheriff Courts (see above).

(3)   The High Court of Justiciary. This court functions as a court of first instance and a court of appeal. Criminal actions are not appealed to the Supreme Court; however, the European Court of Justice can review them.

2.   Modern Scottish Reporters

a.   Session Cases, 1821 to present. Published since 1957 by the Scottish Council of Law Reporting (SCLR), this reporter includes civil matters from Scotland appealed to the Supreme Court, criminal cases in the Court of Justiciary, and civil cases heard in the Court of Session. This reporter is considered official for citation purposes.[74] In the first eighty-five years of publication, the *Session Cases* appeared as five nominate series: Shaw (1821–1838); Dunlop (1838–1862); Macpherson (1862–1873); Rettie (1873–1898); and Fraser (1898–1906). From 1906 to 1957, the Faculty of Advocates published *Session Cases* until SCLR began publishing it. *Session Cases* reports cases from three courts, and each volume contains three separate page-number sequences corresponding to the different courts being reported. The Justiciary cases may be bound separately from the rest of the series. Citation form to an opinion within the set varies depending on whether a volume from a nominate series is being cited and on which court issued the opinion.

b.   Scots Law Times, 1893 to present. Coverage includes the Sheriff Courts, Court of Session, the High Court of Justiciary, and the House of Lords/Supreme Court. Cases from various other courts (see below) are also reported. The series is published weekly and cumulates annually. Each volume is divided into two sections: Notes and Reports. The Reports section sets forth reports from recent decisions of the courts listed above and is consecutively paged. The Notes section includes articles, news, and Acts of Sederunt.[75] Also included in this section are reports of cases from the following courts: Sheriff Court Reports (beginning in 1922); Scottish Land Court Reports (beginning in 1964), and Land Tribunals for Scotland Reports (beginning in 1971); Poor Law Reports (1932–1941); and Lyon Court Reports (1950–1959, 1966, and 1977).

c.   Scottish Civil Law Reports, 1987 to present. This publication reports cases from the Court of Session and the Sheriff Courts.

d.   Scottish Criminal Case Reports, 1981 to present. Coverage includes cases from the Sheriff Courts and the High Court of Justiciary.

3.   Older Scottish Reporters

a.   Practicks. Often these are the only reports available for very old cases (approximately 1469 to 1754). These volumes, frequently setting forth only rough notes

---

[74] *See* Court of Session Practice Note No. 5 of 2004, *available at* http://www.scotcourts.gov.uk/session/practicenotes/pn05_2004.pdf.

[75] Acts of Sederunt govern procedure in the Scottish civil courts. The equivalent rules for Scottish criminal courts are known as Acts of Adjournal.

of cases, are known by the name of the jurist responsible for the material. The most well-known are Balfour, Spotiswoode, and Hope. These have been reprinted by the Stair Society.

b.   *Private Reports.* Twenty-two private reports were published in the seventeenth and eighteenth centuries covering material from the Court of Session (1621–1833). Ten private reports cover the early Scottish cases decided in the House of Lords (1707–1865). Ten private reports also cover the early Justiciary (criminal) cases (1819–1916).

c.   *The Faculty Collection.* This set was published in three series: the old series (1752–1808); the new series (1808–1825); and the Octavo series (1825–1841). This set was the official reporter for the Court of Session for the periods indicated. The Octavo series is also known by the name Faculty Decisions.

d.   *Other Reports.* Other reporter sets include *The Scottish Jurist* (1829–1873), *Scottish Law Reporter* (1865–1924), and *Scottish Law Review and Sheriff Court Reports* (1885–1963).

e.   *Collections.* Two major collections of early reports are Kames & Woodhouselee, *Decisions of the Court of Session* (five volumes covering 1540 to 1796), and Morison, *Decisions, Court of Session in the Form of a Dictionary* (thirty-eight volumes covering 1540 to 1808). A five-volume supplement by Brown and an additional *Synopsis* by Morison add material omitted from the original work. Morison contains some reports dated before 1540 taken from the *Practicks.* A more recently published collection of older reports is *Scots Revised Reports* (forty-five volumes covering Scottish decisions prior to 1873).

4.   Electronic Access to Scottish Cases

a.   *Scottish Courts Website.* Beginning in 1998 opinions from the Court of Session, the High Court of Justiciary, and the Sheriff Courts are available in the Scottish Courts website.[76]

b.   *BAILII.* Scottish decisions since 1998 are available in *BAILII.* Coverage includes material from the Court of Session, the High Court of Justiciary, and the Sheriff Courts. The information on the *BAILII* site is sourced from the Scottish Courts website and is therefore identical.

c.   *Westlaw. Westlaw* covers cases reported in the *Scots Law Times* since 1893 and *Session Cases* since 1898.

d.   *LexisNexis.* Coverage includes *Session Cases* from 1930, *Scottish Criminal Case Reports* from January 1981, and *Scottish Civil Law Reports* from February 1986.

e.   *Justis.* In collaboration with the Scottish Council of Law Reporting, *Justis* has made available in PDF format *Session Cases* dating back to 1873. The database includes access to the earlier nominate series of *Session Cases.* This is a fee-based service.

5.   Digests and Indexes to Scottish Cases

a.   *Green's Weekly Digest.* The cases digested in *Green's* later appear in *Scots Law Times.*

---

[76] http://www.scotcourts.gov.uk/opinionsApp/index.asp?txt=False.

    b.   *The Faculty of Advocates' Digest.* This digest was published from 1868 to 1922 and supplemented through 1990.

    c.   *The Scots Digest.* Coverage varies depending on the court, but generally is from 1800 to 1944.

    d.   *Current Law*, 1948 to present. A separate Scottish edition ceased publication in 1991. Scottish cases are now incorporated, albeit in a separate section, into the monthly digests.

    e.   *The Digest.* This is the same tool used to locate English (and Commonwealth) case law. For a more complete description, see Section E-1.

L. NORTHERN IRELAND

The province of Northern Ireland was formed when the Government of Ireland Act 1920 divided Ireland into two regions. The act called for the creation of two separate parliaments, one in Dublin (to govern the 26 southern counties) and one in Belfast (to govern the six counties in the north loyal to Britain). In 1921, the Anglo-Irish Treaty was signed, thereby creating the Irish Free State and leading to the eventual creation of the Republic of Ireland in 1949. Since 1921 the responsibility for governing Northern Ireland has varied. At times, the province has experienced home rule; at other times, it has fallen under direct rule from the U.K. Parliament in London. To research Northern Ireland materials, an understanding of the history of the constitutional basis of the province is necessary.[77]

Northern Ireland experienced home rule in the period between 1921, when the Government of Ireland Act 1920 created the province, and 1972, when the British government declared an end to home rule and instituted direct rule from Westminster. During this period, the Northern Ireland Parliament ("Stormont")[78] operated as a devolved legislative body; it was perceived as a body more representative of the Protestants' interests than the Catholics'. The escalation of violence in the province during the late 1960s and early 1970s resulted in the suspension of home rule and the vesting of wide discretionary powers in the Secretary of State for Northern Ireland under direct rule. In 1974, a second attempt at devolution was made with the creation of the first Northern Ireland Assembly. This Assembly lasted only five months, although in that time it did manage to pass a number of measures. Direct rule of the province resumed in the summer of 1974 as a result of increased sectarian violence.

During the 1980s and 1990s, continued negotiations between the British government and various parties attempted to bring an end to the violence and establish a system of home rule. The breakthrough occurred in 1998 with the signing of the Good Friday Agreement.[79] This document formed the basis for the style of devolution currently experienced in Northern Ireland. Included within the agreement is a provision for a democratically elected legislative body for Northern Ireland. The Northern Ireland (Elections) Act 1998 lays out the process for electing the Assembly members, while the Northern Ireland Act 1998 provides for the peaceful transfer of functions to the new

---

[77] For a concise discussion of researching legal materials in Northern Ireland, see Heather Semple, *Researching the Law of Northern Ireland*, 8 LEGAL INFO. MGMT. 283 (2008).

[78] Stormont is the popular name given to Parliament Buildings on the Stormont Estate near Belfast.

[79] Good Friday Agreement, *supra* note 3.

Northern Ireland Assembly. In December 1999, the Assembly was eventually granted the devolved powers. Since 1999 the Northern Ireland Assembly has been suspended on a number of occasions, the longest period of suspension being almost five years. However, recent times appear to hold out the promise of a less turbulent future for the Assembly and for the province in general.

M. NORTHERN IRELAND PRIMARY LEGISLATION

1. The Northern Ireland Assembly

The powers conferred on the Northern Ireland Assembly include the power to adopt primary legislation for the province. However, the Northern Ireland Act 1998 clearly distinguishes between matters within the legislative competence of the Assembly and matters outside of its competence, and therefore leaves legislation subject to judicial review.[80] Drawing distinctions between transferred, entrenched, excepted, and reserved matters, the Northern Ireland Act 1998 defines the scope of the Assembly's powers. Entrenched matters include the Human Rights Act 1998, the European Communities Act 1972, and other basic constitutional documents outlined in section 7 of the act. The Assembly cannot amend these documents. Excepted matters are defined in section 6 as matters that are outside the legislative competence of the Assembly, and are listed in schedule 2 of the Northern Ireland Act 1998. Reserved matters are matters that are within the legislative competence of the Assembly, but can only be acted upon with the consent of the Secretary of State for Northern Ireland. Reserved matters are outlined in schedule 3. All other matters are considered transferred matters and are deemed within the legislative competence of the Assembly.

The Northern Ireland Assembly website provides researchers with access to a variety of information, including general information concerning the body, a calendar of events, and services for tracking legislation (primary and secondary) through the Assembly.[81] Bills can be tracked through the various legislative stages and accessed in full text; committee reports are also available. Transcripts of floor debates can be found using the *Official Report*, a daily Hansard publication. The legislative process adopted by the Assembly is very similar in practice to the one described above for the Scottish Parliament. As with acts passed by other legislative bodies in the United Kingdom, the acts of the Northern Ireland Assembly are published by the H.M.S.O. on behalf of the Government Printer for Northern Ireland and are, therefore, not located on the Assembly's website.[82]

2. Forms of Legislation for Northern Ireland

a.   The various forms of legislation for Northern Ireland are a direct result of the complex history of the province. Prior to 1999, Northern Ireland was subject to the following:

(1) *Acts of the Northern Ireland Parliament ("Stormont")*, 1921–1972. These acts are available in the *Statutes Revised Northern Ireland 2d*. This multivolume looseleaf set includes all legislation in force in the province, except U.K. legislation, up to 1981.

---

[80] The Northern Ireland Act 1998, c. 47.

[81] http://www.ni-assembly.gov.uk/.

[82] http://www.legislation.gov.uk.

(2) *Acts of the U.K. Parliament Extending to Northern Ireland and Orders in Council*, 1972–1973. Acts of the U.K. Parliament extending to Northern Ireland can be located in sources traditionally used to locate acts of Parliament (see Section B-2 for a description of these traditional sources). The Orders in Council passed for the province, although considered a form of delegated legislation, are made available in the *Statutes Revised Northern Ireland 2d* and in session volumes in *Northern Ireland Statutes*.

(3) *Measures of the Northern Ireland Assembly*, January 1974–May 1974. The few measures passed by the first Northern Ireland Assembly in its five-month existence are made available in the *Statutes Revised Northern Ireland 2d*.

(4) *Acts of the U.K. Parliament and Orders in Council*, June 1974–1999. Availability of this material is the same as described in (2) above; however, recent legislation is also available on the *Legislation* website.

b   Since 1999, primary legislation for Northern Ireland has included:

(1) *Legislation promulgated by the new Northern Ireland Assembly.* Acts of the new Northern Ireland Assembly are published on the *Legislation* website and by T.S.O. in hard copy.

(2) *Acts of the U.K. government Extending to Northern Ireland.* Acts of the U.K. government that extend to Northern Ireland can be located in the traditional U.K. primary legislation sources described above. Acts of the U.K. government that apply primarily or exclusively to Northern Ireland can be located on the *Legislation* website.

(3) *Orders in Council made for the province by the U.K. government.* Orders in Council are a form of secondary legislation considered primary legislation for Northern Ireland. They have been promulgated since the first period of direct rule in 1972; since 1998, their use has been limited to periods when the Assembly has been suspended. U.K. Orders in Council, made by and with the advice of the Privy Council, are published in full text on the *Legislation* website.

BAILII provides coverage of Orders in Council and Statutes of the New Northern Ireland Assembly. *LexisNexis* and *Westlaw* do not provide coverage of Northern Ireland Assembly legislation.

N. NORTHERN IRELAND SECONDARY LEGISLATION

The publication of delegated legislation for Northern Ireland is as complex as publication of Northern Ireland's primary legislation. Since 1998, delegated legislation for the province has taken any one of three forms. It has been issued as (1) U.K. statutory instruments extending to Northern Ireland, (2) U.K. statutory instruments made primarily or exclusively for Northern Ireland, or (3) statutory rules made under the authority of an act of the Northern Ireland Assembly.

1.   United Kingdom Statutory Instruments

U.K. statutory instruments extending to Northern Ireland can be located using the online resources described above, i.e., *LexisNexis*, *Westlaw*, *BAILII,* and the *Legislation* website. U.K. statutory instruments made primarily or exclusively for Northern Ireland are also located on the *Legislation* website.

2. Northern Ireland Statutory Rules

Delegated legislation made for Northern Ireland takes the form of statutory rules. The Northern Ireland Assembly details on its website the processes by which a statutory rule becomes law. Statutory rules presented to the Assembly are subject to affirmative resolution, confirmatory resolution, or negative resolution. Once a rule becomes law, it is posted on the *Legislation* website, together with statutory rules passed by the U.K. Parliament. *BAILII* includes a section for Northern Ireland Statutory Rules for the period 2001 to the present. *LexisNexis* and *Westlaw* do not provide access to Northern Ireland statutory rules.

O. NORTHERN IRELAND CASE LAW

1. The Northern Ireland Court System

Fortunately, the complexities associated with performing legislative research in the province are not carried over into case law. The court system of Northern Ireland is very similar to the court system in England and Wales. A simplified outline of the system follows.

- The United Kingdom Supreme Court is the final court of appeal for Northern Ireland;

- The Court of Appeal handles both civil and criminal appeals;

- The High Court of Justice, comprising the Queen's Bench, Family, and Chancery divisions, handles civil matters;

- The Crown Court handles serious criminal matters; and

- The inferior courts are the County Courts (seven divisions) and the Magistrates' Courts (twenty-one districts).

2. Northern Ireland Reporters

a.   The Northern Ireland Law Reports (NILR), 1925 to present. Issued in quarterly installments by LexisNexis, this reporter covers cases in the High Court of Justice and the Court of Appeal in Northern Ireland. Since 1970, reports of cases on appeal to the House of Lords (now the Supreme Court) are also included. This publication is cited as: case name [year] NI page number. Prior to 1925, Northern Ireland cases were reported in *Irish Reports*, alongside cases from the Irish Free State.

b.   Northern Ireland Judgements Bulletin (NIJB), 1972 to present. This publication is also published twice a year by LexisNexis. It includes reports of civil judgments from the High Court of Justice and the Court of Appeal. It also includes material not always available in *NILR*. This publication is cited as: case name [year] vol. NIJB page number.

c.   Northern Ireland Legal Quarterly, 1936 to present. This journal contains notes on decisions, rather than the full text of decisions. It is published by the Law Faculty at Queen's University, Belfast.

3.   Electronic Access to Northern Ireland Cases

a.   Northern Ireland Court and Tribunals Service Website.[83] This website provides the text of judgments from the Court of Appeal and the High Court dating back to 1999. It is also a useful website for information concerning the Northern Ireland courts and their business.

b.   BAILII. The British and Irish Legal Information Institute website has full text coverage of Court of Appeal, High Court of Justice, and Crown Court decisions since 1999.

c.   LexisNexis. This service provides coverage of reported Northern Ireland cases since 1945 and unreported cases since 1984. *Westlaw* does not provide coverage of either Northern Ireland case law or legislation exclusive to Northern Ireland.

4.   Digests and Indexes to Northern Ireland Cases

Index to Cases Decided in the Courts of Northern Ireland and Reported During the Period 1921–1970. This set is supplemented through 1975. It provides an index to Northern Ireland case materials, and also acts as a citator service for legislation, both primary and delegated.

P. ILLUSTRATIONS

Problem: Does the statute outlawing the "making" of indecent photographs of children include downloading photos taken by others?

22–1.	**Page from Halsbury's Statutes of England & Wales, 4th ed., Volume 12**
22–2.	**Page from Halsbury's Statutes of England & Wales, 4th ed., Cumulative Supplement**
22–3.	**Page from Halsbury's Statutes of England & Wales, 4th ed., Current Statutes Service**
22–4.	**Page from R v Bowden [2000] 2 All ER 418**
22–5.	**Paragraph 365 from Halsbury's Laws of England, 4th ed., Volume 11(1)**

---

[83] http://www.courtsni.gov.uk.

[Illustration 22–1]

PAGE FROM HALSBURY'S STATUTES OF ENGLAND & WALES, 4TH ED., VOLUME 12

---

6 Enactment of same provisions for Northern Ireland

An Order in Council under paragraph 1(1)(b) of Schedule 1 to the Northern Ireland Act 1974 (legislation for Northern Ireland in the interim period) which contains a statement that it operates only so as to make for Northern Ireland provision corresponding to this Act—

(a) shall not be subject to paragraph 1(4) and (5) of that Schedule (affirmative resolution of both Houses of Parliament); but

(b) shall be subject to annulment by resolution of either House.

NOTES

Order in Council . . . which contains a statement, etc. The power to make Orders in Council is exercisable by statutory instrument; see the Statutory Instruments Act 1946, s 1(1), Vol 41, title Statutes.

Subject to annulment. For provisions as to annulment of statutory instruments in pursuance of a resolution of either House of Parliament, see the Statutory Instruments Act 1946, ss 5(1), 7(1), Vol 41, title Statutes.

Northern Ireland Act 1974, Sch 1, para 1. See Vol 31, title Northern Ireland (Pt 2).

---

7 Short title, commencement and extent

(1) This Act may be cited as the Theft Act 1978.

(2) This Act shall come into force at the expiration of three months beginning with the date on which it is passed.

(3) This Act except section 5(3), shall not extend to Scotland; and except for that subsection, and subject also to section 6, it shall not extend to Northern Ireland.

NOTE

Three months beginning, etc. "Month" means a calendar month; see the Interpretation Act 1978, s 5, Sch 1, Vol 41, title Statutes. In calculating this period, the date (ie 20 July 1978) on which the Act was passed (ie received the Royal Assent) is reckoned; see *Hare v Gocher* [1962] 2 QB 641,

> The full text of the *Protection of Children Act 1978* is reproduced along with notes referring to commencement, regulations, and other statutes.

PROTECTION OF CHILDREN ACT 1978

(1978 c 37)

ARRANGEMENT OF SECTIONS

An Act to prevent the exploitation of children by making indecent photographs of them; and to penalise the distribution, showing and advertisement of such indecent photographs

[20 July 1978]

[Illustration 22-2]

PAGE FROM HALSBURY'S STATUTES OF ENGLAND & WALES, 4TH ED., CUMULATIVE SUPPLEMENT

VOLUME 12 (1997 Reissue)   HALSBURY'S STATUTES (4TH EDN) SUPPLEMENT

PAGE   **Criminal Law Act 1977 (c 45)** — *continued*

the Water Act 1989, s 190(3), Sch 27, Pt I; the Opticians Act 1989, s 37(4), Sch 2; and the Water Consolidation (Consequential Provisions) Act 1991, s 3(1), Sch 3, Pt I."

"Sch 5: para 1(1)(a), (2)(c) repealed by the Customs and Excise Management Act 1979, s 177(3), Sch 6, Pt I; para 1(1)(b), (c), (1A), (3) amend certain entries relating to penalties in the Misuse of Drugs Act 1971, Sch 4, Vol 28, title Medicine and Pharmacy (Pt 2), which have been further affected by the Criminal Justice Act 1982, Vol 27, title Magistrates; para 1(2)(a), (b) repealed by the Magistrates' Courts Act 1980, s 154, Sch 9; para 2 repealed in part by the Criminal Justice Act 1988, s 170(2), Sch 16, remainder repealed by the Road Traffic (Consequential Provisions) Act 1988, s 3(1), Sch 1, Pt I."

"Sch 6, which increased fines for certain summary offences, was superseded by the Criminal Justice Act 1982, Vol 27, title Magistrates; much of this Schedule has, however, been repealed by the following enactments: the Nurses, Midwives and Health Visitors Act 1979, s 23(5), Sch 8; the Merchant Shipping Act 1979, s 50(4), Sch 7; the Child Care Act 1980, s 89, Sch 6; the Residential Homes Act 1980, s 11(5), Sch 2; the Housing Act 1980, ss 145, 152, Sch 23, paras 6(2), 8(2); the Highways Act 1980, s 343(3), Sch 25; the Wildlife and Countryside Act 1981, s 73, Sch 17, Pt II; the Mental Health Act 1983, s 148(3), Sch 6; the Telecommunications Act 1984, s 109(6), Sch 7, Pt IV; the Registered Homes Act 1984, s 57(2), Sch 2, and Part Pt T

> This volume is arranged according to the volume and page number of the base volumes. This supplement indicates that the original act has been amended by the *Sexual Offenses (Protected Material) Act of 1997.*

(Consequential Provisions) Act 1988, s 3(1), Sch 1, Pt I; the Water Act 1989, s 190(3), Sch 27, Pt I; the Water Consolidation (Consequential Provisions) Act 1991, s 3(1), Sch 3, Pt I; the Education Act 1993, s 307(1), (3), Sch 19, para 68, Sch 21, Pt I; the Criminal Procedure (Consequential Provisions) Act 1995, ss 4, 6(1), Schs 3, 5; the Police Act 1996, s 103(3), Sch 9, Pt I; and the Housing Grants, Construction and Regeneration Act 1996, s 147, Sch 3, Pt II."

692   **Schedules 1–12**

Schedule 12 amended by Powers of Criminal Courts (Sentencing) Act 2000, s 165(4), Sch 12, Pt I, Vol 12, title Criminal Law.

Theft Act 1978 (c 31)

701   **Section 1**

Deception.   See also *R v Rai* [2000] 1 Cr App R 242.

Protection of Children Act 1978 (c 37) ◄———

706   *Prohibition on cross-examination in person of protected witnesses.*   The Youth Justice and Criminal Evidence Act 1999, s 35, applies to any offence under this Act; see s 35(3) thereof, Vol 17, title Evidence.

706   **Section 1**

Sub-s (1): It is an offence. An offence under this section, including an offence of conspiring, attempting or inciting another to commit such an offence, is a "sexual offence" for the purposes of the Sexual Offences (Protected Material) Act 1997; see s 2 of, and Schedule, paras 5–8 to, the 1997 Act, Vol 12, title Criminal Law.

---

710   **Halsbury's Statutes Enquiry Bureau 020 7400 2518**

[Illustration 22–3]

PAGE FROM HALSBURY'S STATUTES OF ENGLAND & WALES, 4TH ED., CURRENT STATUTES SERVICE

SEXUAL OFFENCES (PROTECTED MATERIAL) ACT 1997

(1997 c 39)

Preliminary Note

This Act, which received Royal Assent on 21 March 1997 and comes into force on a day to be appointed under s 11(2), regulates access by the defendant and others to victim statements and certain other material disclosed by the prosecutor in connection with proceedings relating to the sexual and other offences specified in the Schedule.

S 1 principally defines "protected material", in relation to proceedings for a sexual offence, as a copy (in whatever form) of statements relating to that or any other offence made by any victim of the offence, a photograph or pseudo-photograph of any such victim, or a report of a medical examination of the physical condition of any such victim, which is given by the prosecutor to any person under the Act.

S 2 defines other expressions used in the Act, including the expression "proceedings in relation to a sexual offence".

S 3 requires a prosecutor to disclose such material by giving a copy of it to the defendant's legal representative, if he has one and where the representative gives the prosecutor the undertaking required by s 4, or by giving a copy of it to the "appropriate person" for the purposes of s 5, in order for that person to show the

> The full text of the *Sexual Offenses (Protected Material) Act* is reproduced together with notes. This act will be incorporated into base volume 12 when the volume is reissued.

material or make a copy of it.

S 5 defines the "appropriate person" as a prison governor or officer in charge of a police station (or their nominee), and requires that person to give the defendant access to the protected material under the same conditions as are specified in s 4. Provision is also made for the prosecutor to give a copy of protected material to another person at the defendant's request.

S 6 provides for the further disclosure of material by the prosecutor where the defendant's legal representative ceases to act as such or dies, or where a previously undefended defendant becomes represented.

S 7 makes similar provision for the disclosure of material by the Criminal Cases Review Committee.

S 8 creates offences in connection with the unauthorised disclosure or possession of protected material.

S 9 modifies or amends certain other enactments; s 10 makes financial provision; and s 11 gives the short title, commencement and extent of the Act.

ARRANGEMENT OF SECTIONS

Introductory

[Illustration 22-4]

PAGE FROM R V BOWDEN [2000] 2 ALL ER 418

| 418 | All England Law Reports | [2000] 2 All ER |

R v Bowden

a

COURT OF APPEAL, CRIMINAL DIVISION

OTTON LJ, SMITH AND COLLINS JJ

2 SEPTEMBER, 10 NOVEMBER 1999

b

Criminal law – Indecent photographs or pseudo-photographs of children – Making indecent photographs of children – Whether offence encompassing downloading or printing out of computer data – Protection of Children Act 1978, ss 1(1)(a), 7.

c

The appellant, B, downloaded indecent photographs of young boys from the Internet, and either printed them out or stored them on his computer disks. He was charged, inter alia, with 12 counts of having 'made an indecent photograph' of children contrary to s 1(1)(a)[a] of the Protection of Children Act 1978. Under s 7[b] of that Act, the term 'indecent photograph' included a copy of such a photograph, and references to 'a photograph' included data stored on a computer disk which was capable of conversion into a photograph. Although B initially pleaded not

d

> The defendant in this case was charged with "making" indecent photographs of children. This case cites extensively to the 1978 act. See Illustration 22-1.

Held – The offence of making an indecent photograph of a child contrary to s 1(1)(a) of the 1978 Act was not confined to original photographs. Rather, by virtue of s 7 of that Act, it also applied to negatives, copies of photographs and data stored on computer disks. Thus a person who downloaded images onto a disk or printed them off was making them within the meaning of s 1(1)(a) of the 1978 Act. That Act was concerned not only with the original creation of images, but also with their proliferation. Photographs or pseudo-photographs found on the Internet could have originated from outside the United Kingdom, and downloading or printing them within the jurisdiction created new material that might not have hitherto existed therein. Accordingly, the appeal would be dismissed (see p 423 *e* to *h* and p 424 *e*, post).

f

g

Notes

For offences concerning indecent photographs of children, see 11(1) *Halsbury's Laws* (4th edn reissue) paras 365–366.

h

For the Protection of Children Act 1978, ss 1, 7, see 12 *Halsbury's Statutes* (4th edn) (1997 reissue) 706, 711.

Cases referred to in judgment

Pepper (Inspector of Taxes) v Hart [1993] 1 All ER 42, [1993] AC 593, [1992] 3 WLR 1032, HL.

R v Fellows, R v Arnold [1997] 2 All ER 548, CA.

j

a   Section 1, so far as material, is set out at p 420 *h* to p 421 *a*, post
b   Section 7, so far as material, is set out at p 421 *b* to *d*, post

[Illustration 22–5]

PARAGRAPH 365 FROM HALSBURY'S LAWS
OF ENGLAND, 4TH ED., VOLUME 11(1)

Para 364	*Vol 11(1): Criminal Law, Evidence and Procedure*	282

as the contrary is shown by evidence given on behalf of the same or any other party[6].

1 For the meaning of 'play' see para 362 note 3 ante.
2 'Script' in relation to the performance of a play, means the text of the play, whether expressed in words or in musical or other notation, together with any stage or other directions for its performance, whether contained in a single document or not: Theatres Act 1968 s 9 (2).
3 Ie under ibid s 2 (as amended) (see para 362 ante) or s 6 (public performance of a play provoking a breach of the peace: see THEATRES vol 45 para 956).
4 A police officer of or above the rank of superintendent, who has reasonable grounds for suspecting that any such offence has been committed by any person in respect of the performance of a play, or that the performance of a play is to be given and that any such offence is likely to be committed by a person in respect of it, may make a written order in relation to that person and that performance: ibid

> This encyclopedic tool outlines the law relating to a particular topic. In this section are references to the relevant acts and commentary on their interpretation.

s 10 (3). Any person who without reasonable excuse fails to comply with any such requirement is liable on summary conviction to a fine not exceeding level 3 on the standard scale: s 10 (4) (amended by the Criminal Justice 1982 ss 38, 46). For the meaning of 'the standard scale' see para 808 post.
5 Theatres Act 1968 ss 9 (1) (a), 10 (5) (amended by the Public Order Act 1986 s 40 (3), Sch 3).
6 Theatres Act 1968 ss 9 (1) (b), 10 (5).

(iii) Indecent Photographs of Children

365. Taking and distributing indecent photographs of children. It is an offence for a person[1]:
(1) to take[2], or permit to be taken, any indecent[3] photograph[4] of a child[5]; or
(2) to distribute[6] or show such indecent photographs; or
(3) to have in his possession such indecent photographs, with a view to their being distributed or shown by himself or others; or
(4) to publish or cause to be published any advertisement likely to be understood as conveying that the advertiser distributes or shows such indecent photographs, or intends to do so[7].
Proceedings for any such offence may not be instituted except by or with the consent of the Director of Public Prosecutions[8]. A person guilty of any such offence is liable on conviction on indictment to imprisonment for a term not exceeding three years or a fine, or to both, or on summary conviction to imprisonment for a term not exceeding six months or a fine not exceeding the prescribed sum, or to both[9].
Where a person is charged with an offence under heads (2) or (3) above, it is a defence for him to prove (a) that he had a legitimate reason for distributing or showing the photographs or, as the case may be, having them in his possession; or (b) that he had not himself seen the photographs and did not know, nor had any cause to suspect, them to be indecent[10].

1 Where a body corporate is guilty of an offence under the Protection of Children Act 1978 and it is proved that the offence occurred with the consent or connivance of, or was attributable to any neglect on the part of, any director, manager, secretary or other officer of the body, or any person who was purporting to act in any such capacity, he, as well as the body corporate, is deemed to be guilty of that offence and is liable to be proceeded against and punished accordingly: s 3 (1). Where the affairs of a body corporate are managed by its members, s 3 (1) applies in relation to the acts and defaults of a member in connection with his functions of management as if he were a director of the body corporate: s 3 (2).

Chapter 23

ELECTRONIC LEGAL RESEARCH*

Legal information is published in a variety of formats: print, electronic, and microform. A generation ago, print was the most common format, with electronic tools supplementing print research. Now many researchers do almost all of their research online. *Westlaw* and *LexisNexis*—the two dominant, national commercial legal information services—provide access to a wide variety of primary and secondary legal databases, along with news, business, public records, and other non-legal databases. Other electronic research products and services provide access to different collections of materials—either broad-based, covering many jurisdictions and topics, or focused on specialized topics. A wide range of legal materials are available free on websites sponsored by government agencies, nonprofit organizations, and others. Although particular resources are discussed throughout this book, this chapter discusses issues that arise in using and evaluating electronic resources more generally.

A. INTRODUCTION: THE INTERFACE OF TECHNOLOGY AND LEGAL INFORMATION

The technology of legal research has changed dramatically in the last thirty-seven years. The first edition of this textbook to discuss electronic tools was in 1977, when a chapter called "Computers and Microforms in Legal Research" introduced the concepts of full-text databases and Boolean searching.[1] At that time, coverage was much more limited than what today's researchers take for granted. For example, *LexisNexis* (then called *LEXIS*) provided coverage of Supreme Court cases from 1938 forward. It did not provide information for all states. The only topical libraries were for Delaware corporation law, federal tax law, and securities law. There was no mention of law reviews, treatises, or international materials.[2] *Westlaw* at that time was even more limited: it did not contain the full text of opinions, but provided only headnotes, key numbers, and topic headings. Its contents were available for an even shorter time period than in *LexisNexis*: federal courts from 1961 and state courts from 1967.[3]

Over the years, the content available online has grown dramatically. *LexisNexis* and *Westlaw*, the providers that were fairly new in 1977, now have hundreds of databases with millions of documents. And they offer multiple platforms and ways of searching, including *Westlaw Classic, WestlawNext, Lexis.com* and *Lexis Advance*. Further, within each platform there are multiple ways to navigate and search: e.g., browsing tables of

---

* This chapter was revised by George H. Pike, Director, Pritzker Legal Research Center, and Senior Lecturer Northwestern University School of Law.

[1] J. MYRON JACOBSTEIN & ROY M. MERSKY, FUNDAMENTALS OF LEGAL RESEARCH 456–62 (1977).

[2] *Id.* at 463–64.

[3] *Id.* at 465.

contents, Boolean searching, and natural language searching.[4] While *LexisNexis* and *Westlaw* still enjoy a large share of the legal research market, they have been joined by many other commercial providers. Moreover, researchers may now find legal materials on hundreds of free websites, hosted by government agencies, universities, nonprofit organizations, law firms, and businesses.

Meanwhile, researchers have changed too. Legal researchers who read prior editions of this textbook in the 1970s, 1980s, and even 1990s generally had little or no experience with online searching before they were introduced to *LexisNexis* and *Westlaw*. But many of the people learning how to do legal research now are digital natives. It may surprise someone starting law school in 2014 or 2015 to learn that *Wikipedia* has been around only since 2001[5] and *Google's* search engine was still being tested until late 1999,[6] because, as recent as *Wikipedia* and *Google* are, they were already available for those students to use when researching reports in middle school and high school. And new law students today also have had experience using many commercial databases— as well as free websites—in college.

In 1977, the authors' tasks included introducing the concept of "searching machine-readable data bases online"[7] and summarizing what was available in *LexisNexis* and *Westlaw*. Now researchers assume that content will be digitized and searchable and, in fact, the major research systems have so much material online—and coverage changes so quickly—that attempting to list what is on which system would be a waste of time. Search features and interfaces change frequently, as well. Therefore, this chapter will offer an overview of electronic legal research, along with some observations and tips for becoming effective users of the rich legal information sources now available online.

One important lesson for legal researchers—both beginners and those with years of experience—is to learn and stay current with whatever research systems are used. In law schools, it is typical for librarians or representatives of *LexisNexis*, *Westlaw*, and perhaps other companies to offer training sessions. Law firms, courts, and government agencies also regularly have training opportunities. The systems are easy enough to use that it might be tempting to skip the training and conduct research by trial and error. After all, typing in a few words and hitting Enter *does* generally lead to results—and maybe even relevant results. But training will help researchers become efficient searchers, able to find exactly what they need with less floundering and more precision. When time is a valuable commodity (either because it is being billed or because there just isn't enough of it to get everything done), hours saved from fruitless, inefficient searching make the training pay off.

Effective researchers also take time to use their systems' help screens, search templates, advanced search features, toll-free assistance services, and online chat. A researcher's guess about how to construct a search might be good—or it might be far off

---

[4] Each system also offers an app for use on iPhone or iPad and a mobile site for researchers using other devices. Each system also has a product it markets to colleges and universities: *LexisNexis Academic* and *WestlawNext Campus Research*.

[5] Wikimedia Foundation, *Our Projects*, https://wikimediafoundation.org/wiki/Our_projects (visited Dec. 2, 2013).

[6] Peter H. Lewis, *State of the Art: Searching for Less, Not More*, N.Y. TIMES, Sept. 30, 1999, at G1 (describing *Gurunet* and *Google*).

[7] Jacobstein & Mersky, *supra* note 1, at 458.

track. Advice from the system experts can save time, money, and frustration. Using these resources will pay off with better results in less time.

B. THE WESTLAW AND LEXISNEXIS SERVICES

The two most widely used electronic legal research services are *Westlaw*, owned by Thomson Reuters, and *LexisNexis*, a product of Reed Elsevier.[8] Today both services serve as comprehensive and sophisticated sources of legal information, providing primary source materials (including cases, statutes, and regulations) and secondary sources (such as legal periodicals and treatises). Both services also have been expanding their holdings of non-legal resources, now providing current and archived news, public records, and corporate and business information among many other offerings. Materials provided by *Westlaw* and *LexisNexis* are constantly undergoing expansion and refinement.[9]

The content of *Westlaw* and *LexisNexis* databases is determined by licensing agreements. Both systems have wide and deep coverage of primary legal materials produced by governments (which generally do not assert a copyright and typically cooperate with the online providers). They both have licensed the content of most student-edited law reviews and the journals published by the American Bar Association. The most apparent difference in their coverage is in commercially published treatises and practice materials. Notably, *Westlaw* includes treatises and other material published by Thomson Reuters (formerly West Publishing) and *LexisNexis* includes treatises and other material published by LexisNexis (including Matthew Bender titles); both also offer access to services from other information vendors. A vendor may eliminate or restrict information in *Westlaw* or *LexisNexis* when licensing costs reduce the profitability of placing material in an online environment, when a vendor enters into an exclusive arrangement with a different service provider, or when a vendor develops its own online product.[10] The educational contract between a law school and *Westlaw*, *LexisNexis*, or other database vendor may have additional restrictions on individual databases, due to cost, privacy, or other concerns.

Although a particular research resource or title may appear in *Westlaw* or *LexisNexis*, it is critical to the research process to determine the scope of the materials that actually are available online. For example, when legal information vendors introduce a new resource, they typically do not provide a complete retrospective file of the collection. Sometimes only selected content from the resource may be provided. A researcher should evaluate very carefully the scope and content of any database before relying on that database's contents for legal research. Database directories or menu screens provide instructions for determining the content of a file.

---

[8] An ABA survey asked lawyers in private practice which fee-based online service they used most often for legal research. The leading products were *WestlawNext* (28.1%), *Westlaw* (25.7%), *Lexis* (24.1%), and *Lexis Advance* (5.2%). Those four responses total 83.1%. 2013 AMERICAN BAR ASSOCIATION LEGAL TECHNOLOGY SURVEY REPORT V-45 (Joshua Poje ed., 2013) [hereinafter ABA TECH SURVEY].

[9] The size of these services is vast. For example, as of June 2014, *LexisNexis* contained over 45,000 legal, news, and business sources with billions of searchable documents. *Westlaw* offers similarly extensive content, also reporting billions of pages of content.

[10] For example, in 2013 Bloomberg BNA stopped licensing BNA newsletters and other BNA content to *LexisNexis* and *Westlaw*. They are now available only on the *Bloomberg BNA* web product and in *Bloomberg Law*.

1. Subscriptions and Availability

It is very common for United States law schools to subscribe to both *LexisNexis* and *Westlaw*. The typical educational contract provides access (for educational purposes) to most available content, including all federal and state primary sources, international and foreign law resources, hundreds of journals and treatises, and a wide range of practice-related materials, subject-specific collections, and non-law sources.

Many law firms, courts, and government agencies subscribe to one or both systems. It is common for these subscribers to opt for selected content only. For example, a small firm handling family law and estate planning might choose to subscribe to state materials from its home state, a specialized collection of estate planning materials, and *American Law Reports*. Another firm might choose federal statutes and cases, law reviews, and a labor and employment collection. These firms would still have access to other materials but would have to pay a premium for using them. Some solo practitioners and small firms do not subscribe to *LexisNexis* or *Westlaw* at all, and rely on using the systems at a local county or law school library. The libraries' licenses for this sort of public access are often limited—generally providing only their own state's materials.

Both *LexisNexis* and *Westlaw* offer a variety of pricing options. Most organizations negotiate a flat monthly rate for unlimited usage, but some organizations pay based on time used or number of searches run.[11] In plans that charge by time or by search (or a combination), the services typically charge more for the use of very large databases (e.g., a database with all state cases will be more expensive to search than a database with, say, Massachusetts cases). Some private practitioners pass along their online research costs to clients, whether at cost, with a mark-up, or discounted because an attorney's time spent researching is also being billed. Billing for online costs is more common in large firms than in small firms.[12]

2. Interfaces

Each of the two major systems offers two platforms. The older platforms are *Westlaw Classic* and *Lexis.com*. Using these platforms, a researcher generally navigates through menus or tabs to locate an appropriate database or file (e.g., a database of California cases or a database combining all law reviews on the system) and then constructs a search. The newer platforms are *WestlawNext* and *Lexis Advance*. These platforms allow a researcher to search first and then filter results by various criteria (e.g., selecting cases, then limiting by jurisdiction and date). The newer platforms also offer ways to manage results, such as highlighting passages and saving documents in folders for later reference. [Illustrations 23–1 to 23–4]

3. Searching

Each system offers various search options. The simplest is retrieving a document with a known citation or pulling up a case by using a template (e.g., with parties' names). Boolean searching (called "terms and connectors" searching in *Westlaw*) enables the

---

[11] *See* ABA TECH SURVEY, *supra* note 8, at V-40 (72.6% of respondents reported using a negotiated flat rate. Almost 15% did not know what fee structure they had!).

[12] *See id.* at V-41 (44.4% of respondents in solo practices and 36.4% of those in firms with 2–9 lawyers do not bill clients for online legal research; only 13% of respondents in firms of 100–499 and 9.3% of those in firms of 500 or more do not bill clients for online legal research).

researcher to specify words and phrases that must appear in a document in a certain relation by using simple terms like "and," "or," and "within" (e.g., the document must contain "*A and B,*" or "*C or D,*" or "*E within five words of F*"). Both systems allow users to require specified words or phrases to appear in particular parts of documents. (*Westlaw* calls these parts "fields" and *LexisNexis* calls them "segments.") Thus you can search for all cases in which "e.p.a." or "environmental protection agency" appears as a party, or for law review articles where "richard" is within two words of "posner" in the author field/segment.

Natural language searching allows a user to search by entering words or phrases (or even a question) in the search box without using Boolean search terms. The system's algorithms take the place of the Boolean terms and a results list is returned that matches the terms (or most of them), and ranks the results by a determination of relevancy based on relationships among the words and the distinctiveness of the terms. Boolean searching and natural language searching are both powerful, but in different ways. Boolean searching is especially useful when you want to have control over the precision of the search (for instance, if you want to be sure you have found all of the cases where "prior judgment of the supreme court" appears with "habeas corpus" or all of the articles with "global warming" in the title). Natural language searching can be easier to use when broader concepts need to be searched or a larger list of results is desired.

The newer platforms—*Lexis Advance* and *WestlawNext*—default to a type of natural language searching, but it is still possible to use Boolean operators and take advantage of field or segment limitations to make a more precise search.

4. Handling Results

Both systems offer options in viewing results—e.g., the researcher can specify that the results be a list of citations, the full text of a document, or a portion of the document that contains the search terms. The systems also offer ways to filter results by searching for additional terms within the original results list. Hyperlinks enable a researcher to go from one retrieved document to the documents it cites. Citators provide links to citing references.[13]

Users may read material online or print it out, email, or download it. *Lexis Advance* and *WestlawNext* also enable users to highlight, add notes, and save documents to folders.

5. Alerts

To support ongoing research, both companies provide alert services that notify a researcher of new cases, statutes, or other developments. An alert is a search query that the system automatically runs in a specified database on a periodic basis. The alert identifies any new documents that have been added to the database since the last alert search—or indicates that no new documents have been added. The researcher can program the alert to send an email notification, print the results, or save the results for later review.

Both services provide RSS alerts to commercial subscribers.

---

[13] *See* Chapter 15.

C. ILLUSTRATIONS: WESTLAW AND LEXISNEXIS

23–1.   **Screen Print, Westlaw Classic Directory and Main Page**
23–2.   **Screen Print, WestlawNext Main Page**
23–3.   **Screen Print, Lexis.com Directory and Main Page**
23–4.   **Screen Print, Lexis Advance Main Page**

[Illustration 23–1]

SCREEN PRINT, WESTLAW CLASSIC DIRECTORY AND MAIN PAGE

[Illustration 23–2]

SCREEN PRINT, WESTLAWNEXT MAIN PAGE

[Illustration 23–3]

SCREEN PRINT, LEXIS.COM DIRECTORY AND MAIN PAGE

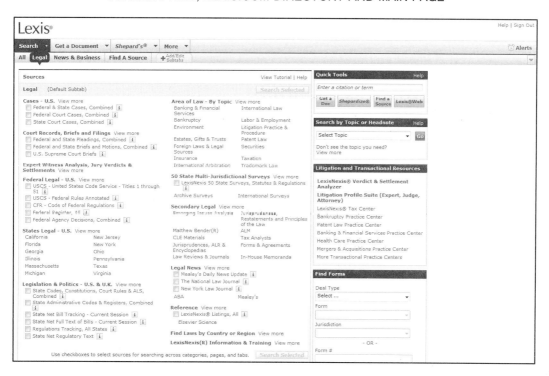

[Illustration 23–4]

SCREEN PRINT, LEXIS ADVANCE MAIN PAGE

D. OTHER ONLINE LEGAL INFORMATION SOURCES

Many other companies besides *LexisNexis* and *Westlaw* provide electronic access to primary and secondary legal information and related resources. Some of the content duplicates what is available in *LexisNexis* and *Westlaw*; other content is unique to the system.

Starting in the late 1980s, legal publishers began to publish secondary authority, and later, primary authority, on CD-ROMs. The cost of these CD-ROM products was often less than online access, eliminating researchers' concerns regarding the costly per minute charges of *Westlaw* and *LexisNexis,* as they were then priced, while still providing hyperlinking ability. The CD-ROM format, however, clearly limited the amount of data that could be stored and the CDs themselves required continual updating. Most legal publishers turned to the Internet as the preferred vehicle for providing access to electronic legal research resources. Using the World Wide Web and web browser software, legal publishers now provide fast access and an easier updating process than possible with CD-ROMs. Bloomberg BNA (formerly the Bureau of National Affairs), for example, now offers most of its publications in full text through its own proprietary web interface, with email alerts for their newsletters;[14] CCH from Wolters Kluwer offers its

---

[14] Bloomberg BNA content is also available on *Bloomberg Law.*

looseleaf services via the web; and Matthew Bender provides many of its popular treatises, like *Nimmer on Copyright,* on the web through *Matthew Bender Online.*[15]

There are two primary methods used to limit database access to licensed users: (1) individual passwords, and (2) Internet Protocol (IP) address authentication. For password-controlled access, individual passwords are issued to authorized users by the database vendor, such as in the cases of *Westlaw* and *LexisNexis.* For IP authentication, the vendor's server accepts search requests from researchers using computers with an IP address that is within a pre-approved range, such as desktops or laptops on a law school or law firm network. Websites using IP authentication may not be accessible from home or offsite locations.

1. Commercial Web-Based Services and Providers

Among the more popular commercial providers of web-based legal information are:[16]

a. Bloomberg BNA, http://www.bna.com. Bloomberg BNA (formerly the Bureau of National Affairs) is a major publisher of looseleaf services and topical newsletters, now available online. The major collections include Antitrust and Trade, Bankruptcy, Criminal Law, Employment Discrimination, Environmental Law, Family Law, Health and Medical Law, Intellectual Property, International Trade, Labor Law, Securities Regulation, and Taxation. *U.S. Law Week* provides news, in-depth analysis, and full-text opinions of the U.S. Supreme Court, information about and selected opinions of lower federal courts and state decisions, and legal developments generally. BNA provides full text access to the content of its looseleaf services. Some collections have an email service to provide daily or weekly highlights to users.

b. Bloomberg Law, http://www.bloomberg.com. Bloomberg has been a long-time provider of business, financial, and media information, but *Bloomberg Law* is a relatively new entrant into the electronic legal information marketplace. *Bloomberg Law*'s primary products are its subject-specific *Law Reports*, which are comprehensive analyses of legal and regulatory developments in a wide variety of topical areas. *Law Reports* are published periodically, often weekly or monthly. Bloomberg's acquisition of the Bureau of National Affairs in 2011 enabled *Bloomberg Law* to expand its content with BNA's high-quality newsletters and treatises. *Bloomberg Law* also delivers legal news, court dockets and filings, regulatory information, court opinions, company and biographical information, and other legal content. *Bloomberg Law* is available via individual passwords and dedicated terminals within law school, law firm, and corporate law department libraries.

c. Casemaker, http://www.casemaker.us and CasemakerX, http://www.case makerx.com. These related services provide access to a wide collection of state and federal legal research resources. *Casemaker* works with a consortium of state bar associations to provide access to current and archived state and federal case law, statutes, court rules, and regulations, plus additional state content including attorney

---

[15] See Chapter 14 for a discussion of BNA and CCH looseleaf services and Chapter 19 for a discussion of treatises.

[16] This is a selective list of commercial, web-based databases to which most academic law libraries and many larger law firm and corporate libraries subscribe, including both full-text databases and bibliographic databases. There are many specialty databases and pay-as-you-go services that are available through the web as well. Check with your law library for information about what subscription services are available to you, or go online to the particular service's home page for subscription information.

general opinions, ethics opinions, and jury instructions. Members of bar associations that participate in the *Casemaker* consortium have free access to these resources. *CasemakerX* provides access to the *Casemaker* databases to law students. *CasemakerX* provides an additional social networking service that allows students to connect with other students as well as attorney members of the *Casemaker* consortium by setting up *Facebook*-style profiles.

    d.   IntelliConnect from CCH, http://intelliconnect.cch.com. IntelliConnect from CCH offers web-based research services in the tax, accounting, and business practice areas. Resources include electronic editions of CCH and Wolters Kluwer full text looseleaf services and treaties in the tax and accounting areas; a business and finance network with corporate, securities, banking, trade regulation, and other business-related information; and a computer and Internet online network with treatises on Internet and e-commerce law. The *Tax and Accounting* product contains primary and secondary sources for both federal and state tax systems, including the full text of CCH's *Standard Federal Tax Reporter*, state tax guides, IRS publications, and other materials.

    e.   Fastcase, http://fastcase.com. Fastcase is an economically priced legal research service available directly by subscription and in some states through the state bar association. The search engine provides for keyword and natural language searching. Cases can be retrieved by citation, and there is an authority check function. The depth and breadth of the database is expanding.

    f.   HeinOnline, http://www.heinonline.org. HeinOnline is a rapidly expanding collection of primary and secondary source libraries. Its initial and most used library is its Law Journal Library, which contains full text law review and journal articles from most U.S. published law reviews. Journal coverage generally goes much further back in time than in *LexisNexis* or *Westlaw*, often back to the publication's inception. However, *HeinOnline* is sometimes limited in the speed with which it can provide journal content; some journals embargo (that is, they forbid publication of) their most recent content for six months to a year.

    HeinOnline also has collections of treaties, the *Federal Register* and *Code of Federal Regulations*, Supreme Court and attorney general opinions, selected legislative histories, *U.S. Statutes at Large* and state session laws, and a growing collection of classic legal treatises. *HeinOnline* is rapidly expanding its coverage of international and foreign materials, including English reports, international yearbooks, decisions of international tribunals, and some international and foreign law journals.

    Most of the documents in *HeinOnline* are available as PDFs of the original printed documents and are searchable in full text. This is particularly helpful in providing pagination and other information for citation purposes.

    g.   Index to Legal Periodicals and Books (ILP), http://www.ebscohost.com/wilson. Wilson's *Index to Legal Periodicals & Books (ILP,* now a service of *EBSCO)* is a bibliographic index to law reviews, bar association and journal publications, and government publications. An enhanced *ILP* subscription provides access to selected full text articles.[17] EBSCO/H.W. Wilson also provides the *Index to Legal Periodicals*

---

[17] See Chapter 18 for more discussion of law journals and journal indexes.

Retrospective: 1908–1981, which is the only online bibliographic index to journal articles published prior to 1980.

h.   *Legal Source, http://www.ebscohost.com/academic/legal-source. Legal Source* is a new product resulting from the merger of EBSCO and H.W. Wilson, introduced in 2012. *Legal Source* provides full text coverage of scholarly legal journals from the U.S., Canada, the U.K., Ireland, Australia, and New Zealand, along with detailed indexing of other legal journals, legal books and monographs, law reviews, yearbooks, statutes, bar association publications, university publications, and government publications.

i.   *LegalTrac, http://www.infotrac.galegroup.com. LegalTrac* is a bibliographic database that indexes law reviews, bar journals, and legal newspapers, from 1980 to the present. For some journals—particularly for more recent years—it also provides the full text or PDFs of articles.

j.   *LLMC Digital, http://www.llmc-digital.org. LLMC* (Law Library Microform Consortium) *Digital* is an online collection of state and federal primary materials, including an extensive collection of federal agency documents, early American state and federal case law and statutory compilations, territorial legal materials, and selected Anglo-American and foreign legal materials. Many of the documents are searchable and are presented as scanned images of document pages.

k.   *Loislaw, http://www.loislaw.com. Loislaw*, product of Wolters Kluwer, is an alternative to *Westlaw* and *LexisNexis. Loislaw* provides searchable, full text access to federal and state primary law, including appellate court opinions, statutes, regulations, constitutions, administrative law, and court rules. Case law dates back to 1899 for the U.S. Supreme Court, 1950 for federal appellate courts, and 1921 for district courts. Boolean searching and proximity connectors can be used. *Loislaw* also provides searchable, full text access to personal and corporate public records, libraries of Wolters Kluwer and CCH treatises and legal forms, and bar publications for selected states.

l.   *The Making of Modern Law, Legal Treatises, http://gdc.gale.com/. The Making of Modern Law* (*MOML*) is an archival collection of over 21,000 eighteenth, nineteenth, and early twentieth century legal treatises, casebooks, practice manuals, forms, letters and speeches, and other documents that have been scanned from library collections in the U.S. and England. Documents are available in PDF format. Full-text searching of the collection is available, or ninety-nine different subject areas can be browsed. In addition to historical treatises, other *MOML* collections are: Supreme Court Records and Briefs from 1832 to 1978; Primary Sources 1620–1926, featuring colonial and early state records, state codes and city charters and other primary source documents; Primary Sources II, 1763–1970, featuring legal and social history from the colonial era through the Cold War and Vietnam; and Trials, a collection of treatises about trials, trial transcripts, and related material from 1600 to 1926.

m.   *Matthew Bender Online, http://bender.lexisnexis.com.* Matthew Bender, a company owned by LexisNexis, is a publisher of multivolume treatises in a number of subject areas. *Matthew Bender Online* provides full text electronic access to those treatises. The service is broken down into subject-based libraries, including civil procedure, elder law, federal litigation, intellectual property law, labor and employment, and securities.

n.   *ProQuest Congressional, Serial Set, and others, http://proquest.libguides. com/cong_guides.* ProQuest offers several different databases containing current and archival federal legislative resources. The base product, *ProQuest Congressional*, provides searching, abstracts and indexing of congressional hearings, reports, and other documents since 1789. Additional databases, such as the *Serial Set*, provide full text PDF congressional documents, and *ProQuest Legislative Insight* provides full text legislative histories for most federal laws enacting since 1929. ProQuest resources also provide access to Congressional Research Service publications, the *Congressional Record*, and statistical data.

o.   *Rise of American Law, http://legalsolutions.thomsonreuters.com/law-products/Other/Rise-of-American-Law/p/100006646.* This collection of legal treatises and other resources from Thomson Reuters covers the period from 1820 to 1970. Access is provided to over 1,700 out-of-print volumes, including multivolume sets and multiple editions. Documents are in PDF format. Searching is by keyword, author, or title; the collection is available as either a web-based product or on DVD-ROM.

p.   *VersusLaw, http://www.versuslaw.com. VersusLaw* is a research service focusing on federal and state appellate opinions. United States Supreme Court cases are available from 1900, while most federal appellate court cases are available since 1930. *VersusLaw* has begun to add case law from the federal district courts. State appellate decisions date back to the 1920s to 1950s for most states. The company is expanding its collections to include statutes and regulations. *VersusLaw* uses Boolean searching or natural language searching, and provides links from its website to law school and law-related websites, legal forms, and state websites.

2.   Other Sources of Web-Based Legal Information

Other sources of Internet legal information include blogs, podcasts, wikis, and "open access" journal archives.

Blogs are maintained by individuals or groups and usually consist of commentary on a particular topic.[18] They are often enhanced with links to related web documents or articles, graphics, or audio files. Many blogs invite interested readers to respond to particular blog entries, often leading to an ongoing discussion of the issue raised in the original entry and its in-depth analysis. In addition to providing secondary content, a well-run blog, like many "traditional" secondary sources, can be an effective research tool through the publication of links or citations to primary sources, news articles, and other relevant materials.

Many legal blogs[19] are from the same scholars, policymakers, and attorneys who write many of the better secondary sources. It should be remembered, however, that blogs are secondary sources and should be carefully reviewed for authenticity and authority. Also, while many blogs are created, far fewer are maintained, so care should be taken to archive (online or in print) any blog material being relied on for your research.

Podcasts are similar to blogs in that they provide a forum for commentators and organizations to offer streaming or downloadable audio discussions on topics of interest.

[18] Many personal blogs will not focus on a particular topic, allowing the blogger to address whatever topic he or she wishes.

[19] The term "blawg" has been used to refer to blogs dealing with legal issues. Directories of legal blogs can be found at *Justia's BlawgSearch*, at http://blawgsearch.justia.com; *Law Professor Blogs*, at http://www.lawprofessorblogs.com; and *Blawg: Legal Blogs*, at http://www.blawg.com.

"Open access" journal archives and repositories are websites that provide a forum for authors to publish their work directly on the web instead of (or increasingly in addition to) publishing through a traditional law journal or commercial publisher.[20] *The Legal Scholarship Network* of the *Social Science Research Network (SSRN)*[21] and the *Berkeley Electronic Press (bepress)*[22] publish articles from identified legal scholars and named researchers from other disciplines.

A "wiki" is a website created around a particular subject or project, with the content contributed by a number of authorized users. *Wikipedia*[23] is the most prominent example. *Wikipedia* is an online encyclopedia that covers virtually any subject imaginable. The content, however, is written by unknown individuals who have—or purport to have—knowledge of a particular subject. While *Wikipedia* has a reputation for general accuracy, the absence of identifying information about its authors limits *Wikipedia's* credibility as an authoritative source.[24]

E. LEGAL RESEARCH ON THE INTERNET[25]

1. Introduction

The Internet is technically a global collection of computers and networks that uses a series of standardized communication protocols to exchange information. As a communications platform, the Internet offers a number of specific tools for exchanging information, including email, chat, and instant messaging; peer-to-peer and other forms of file exchange; and, most important for legal research purposes, the World Wide Web.[26] The World Wide Web (or just "the web") uses hyperlinks to provide almost seamless access to documents that are otherwise scattered among disconnected computer servers. The web makes the Internet user-friendly and simplifies sharing information.

---

[20] See Chapter 18 for a discussion of law reviews and other legal scholarship.

[21] http://www.ssrn.com/lsn/index.html. The *Social Science Research Network* also maintains open source repositories for other disciplines, including economics, marketing, management, politics, entrepreneurship, social and environmental impact, literature and classics, and philosophy. The main directory of repositories can be found at http://www.ssrn.com.

[22] http://www.bepress.com.

[23] http://www.wikipedia.org.

[24] A number of court decisions have cited to *Wikipedia* articles. However, this is usually in support of noncritical factual points and is often only a "see" or "see also" reference. *See* Phillips v. Pembroke Real Estate, Inc., 459 F.3d 128, 133 (1st Cir. 2006). Some *Wikipedia* articles will cite to references in support of the points in the *Wikipedia* article. Those references can and should be checked for authority and may be cited if they prove to be an independently authoritative source.

[25] The Internet itself has become a new specialty in the practice of law. If you are interested in legal issues involving the Internet, see GEORGE B. DELTA & JEFFREY H. MATSUURA, LAW OF THE INTERNET (1998–); JANINE HILLER, INTERNET LAW AND POLICY (2002); PIKE & FISCHER: INTERNET LAW & REGULATION (1999 to date); F. LAWRENCE STREET, LAW OF THE INTERNET (2001); KENT D. STUCKEY, INTERNET AND ONLINE LAW (2000–).

[26] It is common for researchers to use the phrase "the Internet" interchangeably with "the web," i.e., "I found the case on the Internet"—referring to a case found on a court's website. (See, *e.g.*, CAROLE A. LEVITT & MARK E ROSCH, FIND INFO LIKE A PRO: MINING THE INTERNET'S PUBLICLY AVAILABLE RESOURCES FOR INVESTIGATIVE RESEARCH (2010), in which all of the content focuses on various websites.) This chapter will use the phrases, "the web" or "the World Wide Web," unless specifically referring to the broader Internet network or one of the other communication tools.

Using the web, researchers can access a massive body of information on almost any subject. Over 785 million distinct websites,[27] containing billions of individual webpages, documents, and media files, are maintained by individuals, for-profit and not-for-profit organizations, governmental units, and educational institutions. The web can be a powerful tool that supplements traditional sources of legal research and increases the researcher's chances of locating needed information. The web provides users with access to a seemingly continuously growing body of information. And the web provides information not available in print or through traditional online services such as *Westlaw* and *LexisNexis*. For example, some legal materials, such as city or county ordinances, are only publicly accessible through the web.[28]

While many high-quality Internet sources are available free of charge, a growing number are fee-based, either by subscription or as pay-as-you-go services.

? Navigating the World Wide Web

a. *Website Addresses or Uniform Resource Locators.* Every webpage has a unique address, or Uniform Resource Locator, commonly known as a URL, which permits direct access to that particular webpage. A URL is comprised of the domain name, indicating the website's sponsor, and the nature of the sponsoring organization. For example, the address for the website of the Legal Information Institute at Cornell University Law School is:

http://www.law.cornell.edu

Each element of the address stands for the following:

http=hypertext transfer protocol, an abbreviation that serves as a signal notifying the Internet that you want to retrieve the website specified by the URL that follows

://=a separator between the transfer protocol and the URL

The phrase "http://" often precedes a website address although, as web browsers have become more sophisticated, including "http://" in the address is no longer necessary.[29] The http:// signal instructs the computer to look for the website address on the Internet, and allows links to other websites ("hypertexts") that complement or expand upon the information available at the initial website.

www=indicates the location of the sought-after resource as being on the World Wide Web

law=a URL subdivision identifying the server(s) hosting the website, here Cornell University's law school. In this example, law is a "subdomain." Not every URL has a subdomain, in which case the domain itself will host the website.

---

[27] Netcraft, *November 2013 Web Server Survey*, http://news.netcraft.com/archives/2013/11/01/november-2013-web-server-survey.html (visited Dec. 4, 2103).

[28] *See, e.g.*, http://www.municode.com (providing access to local ordinances published by Municode).

[29] Some websites require a high degree of secured access, including the use of passwords and encryption. Commercial databases and online banking and other financial services websites are examples. These websites often use the prefix "https" to identify them as "secured" websites utilizing a secured and encrypted http connection. Prefixes such as "ftp" (for "file transfer protocol") specify a different sort of access.

cornell=the website's sponsoring institution (the "domain")

edu=an indicator that the sponsoring institution is an educational institution (the "top-level domain")

URLs might be divided into components with a forward slash (/) separating them. The components of a URL direct the computer to the exact location of a specific webpage on a server. For example, http://www.law.pitt.edu/library/legal/index.php brings the user to a specific library webpage containing an index of legal websites on the University of Pittsburgh School of Law's server.

Note that in the Cornell and Pitt examples the top-level domain, ".edu," identifies an educational institution. At the beginning of the public use of the web, other types of organizational indicators in website addresses included ".org" for nonprofit organizations and associations, ".gov" for federal and (now) state government agencies, ".com" for commercial entities, ".mil" for military sites, and ".net" for computer-related organizations or communications networks. Due to the explosion of ".com" website addresses, additional new Internet suffixes have been created: ".info" for general information, ".biz" for business, ".name" for individuals, ".pro" for professionals, ".museum" for museums, ".coop" for business cooperatives, and ".aero" for the aviation industry. Researchers may also find website addresses with a national designation; for example, "gov.au" indicates the government-sponsored site is located in Australia, "amazon.de" indicates the Amazon.com site based in Germany (Deutschland).[30]

b.   *Search Engines.* A search engine is a type of web service that examines its database of webpages for specific search terms. A massive database of webpages is created and updated regularly by the search engine, using a computer-indexing program known as a crawler or spider that continuously investigates the web and follows its links to identify new pages to add to the database.

Each search engine explores its own database of webpages; the engines do not perform a search of the entire web.[31] Every search engine uses its own rules for finding, organizing, and delivering the webpages upon receiving a query. While search engines differ in some elements, they also have many similarities. All search engines contain a textbox for typing search terms. All search engines compare the search terms to the language used in various webpages, and they give users a list of webpages that contain those specified words or phrases. Search engines are often the starting point for research when the URL for a particular resource is not known.

---

[30] In the summer of 2011, the Internet Corporation for Assigned Names and Numbers (ICANN) voted to allow almost completely unrestricted naming of top-level domains, which will allow the use of almost any word, proper name, or brand, including the use of non-Latin characters, as the top-level domain. Because purchasing an unrestricted domain requires a substantial fee ($185,000, plus $25,000 annual renewal), unrestricted domains will likely be used primarily by large corporations with particularly famous brands or identifications.

[31] Even the most powerful search engines can reach only a portion of the billions of webpages on the Internet. In addition, there is a "deep" or "invisible" part of the web that is not accessible by general search engines. Webpages that are not locatable by search engines may include (1) websites lacking static URLs, (2) password-protected pages, and (3) collections of information contained within a database. (The search engine may locate the database but not the content contained in the database.) The unavailable information in the deep web may be critically important to legal researchers, who must understand the contents and limitations of any database or search engine on which they rely and ensure that their research includes all appropriate information sources.

A wide variety of search engines are available. *Google*[32] claims to have the web's largest webpage database and has emerged as the most dominant search engine.[33] Some of the other top-ranked search engines are *Yahoo*,[34] *Bing*,[35] and *Ask*.[36] Many of the better search engines provide advanced searching capability and may allow sophisticated Boolean searching. Others use natural language algorithms to automatically generate a suitable query, similar to the natural language search engines available on *Westlaw* and *LexisNexis*. Researchers should be aware that each search engine uses different algorithms for finding and organizing retrieved material. Some search engines allow websites to pay for more prominent placement on search engine retrieval lists.

Justia.com includes a specialty search engine for legal information.[37] CALI (the Center for Computer-Assisted Legal Instruction) provides a searchable database of law school websites, which often contain reports from research centers, study or research guides, faculty publications, and a variety of useful legal publications.[38] Another way to search the web is by using a metasearch tool, which takes a query and submits it to several search engines simultaneously. *Zoo* (formerly *Metacrawler*)[39] and *Dogpile*[40] are among the most well-known metasearch tools; they search as many as seven or eight popular search engines at once, including *Google*, *Yahoo*, and *Bing*. While metasearch tools are useful because they link several search engines together, they also may slow considerably the time required for search, and do not allow use of an individual search engine's advanced search capabilities.

c. *Search Directories.* Search directories differ from search engines in that directories organize information by category. Searchers can browse the categories in several ways, from broad, general groupings down to very specific topics. General, web-wide directories have largely been supplanted by search engines, but directories that focus on specific subjects remain a very popular tool for locating information within that subject.

A number of legal directories are available from both commercial and nonprofit sources. Among the commercial directories are *FindLaw for Legal Professionals*,[41] *Justia.com*,[42] *Hieros Gamos*,[43] *AllLaw.com*,[44] and *Lawsonline.com*.[45] Many law schools

---

[32] http://www.google.com.

[33] In October 2013, 66.9% of searches done in the U.S. were done on *Google*. Microsoft's search engine, *Bing*, was second, with 18.1% of searches; and *Yahoo* was third, with 11.1%. Danny Goodwin, *Google Fails to Gain Search Market Share, Bing Steals From Yahoo*, SEARCH ENGINE WATCH (Nov. 14, 2013), http://search enginewatch.com/article/2307115/Google–Fails-to-Gain–Search–Market–Share–Bing–Steals–From–Yahoo (visited Dec. 4, 2013).

[34] http://www.yahoo.com.

[35] http://www.bing.com.

[36] Formerly *Ask Jeeves,* at http://www.ask.com.

[37] From http://justia.com, click on Search Justia, then choose Legal Web.

[38] http://www.cali.org/search/lawschools.

[39] http://www.zoo.com/.

[40] http://www.dogpile.com/.

[41] http://www.findlaw.com. *FindLaw* and *FindLaw for Legal Professionals* (http://lp.findlaw.com) are owned by Thomson Reuters. The *FindLaw* site is oriented toward consumers and the general public, whereas *FindLaw for Legal Professionals* is oriented toward lawyers, law students, paralegals, etc.

[42] http://www.justia.com.

[43] http://www.hg.org.

[44] http://www.alllaw.com.

[45] http://www.lawsonline.com.

and law libraries provide legal directories as well. Among the oldest and most prominent are the *Legal Information Institute*,[46] at Cornell University Law School, and *WashLaw: Legal Research on the Web*,[47] from Washburn University School of Law.

d.   *Search Strategies*.[48] Because of the huge volume of content being indexed by the major search engines, locating information on the Internet is both easier and more complex than in *LexisNexis* or *Westlaw*. Basic web searching is generally done by typing a word or words, often referred to as keywords, in the search box. Entering a single word will return results containing that word. Search queries of multiple words presume a Boolean "AND" connector between the words. The search engine algorithms generally present results containing the terms as a phrase first, followed by the terms in close proximity, followed by terms occurring anywhere within the page, followed by occurrences of one of the terms.[49]

Google also allows use of quotation marks (" ") for specific phrases, truncation and wildcards (using an asterisk (*) in place of a letter or at the end of the word), synonym searching (using a tilde (~) prior to the search term), and segment searching by title (intitle:), URL (inurl:), and website (site:).[50] *Google's* Advanced Search page[51] allows even more sophisticated searching. You can search both individual terms and phrases and exclude words (similar to the Boolean "NOT" command). The Advanced Search feature also allows searching by language, file format (such as PDF files only), date, number of occurrences of your search term, and domain name.

3.   Legal Research on the Internet

As good as *Google* and the other search engines are, they cannot change one fundamental reality of doing legal research on the World Wide Web: the web works best when searching for specific information. It is not as useful when trying to gather comprehensive information on a subject. That is, the web is an effective (and free) tool for finding a copy of the U.S. Supreme Court's *Roe v. Wade* decision or the text of proposed legislation concerning abortion. It is less effective for performing comprehensive legal research on abortion law. The web and other Internet tools supplement, but do not replace, the other print and electronic research skills outlined in this book.

Part of this reality is the nature of the web. While *LexisNexis* and *Westlaw* are now available via the web, they remain dedicated research services, and their content is controlled by their respective parent companies. Reed Elsevier and Thomson Reuters,

---

[46] http://www.law.cornell.edu.

[47] http://www.washlaw.com.

[48] Many guides and tutorials on the Internet identify techniques essential to good information retrieval. Some excellent examples are *Bare Bones 101: A Basic Tutorial on Searching the Web*, published by the Beaufort Library at the University of South Carolina and found online at http://www.sc.edu/beaufort/library/pages/bones/bones.shtml, and the University of California at Berkeley's *Finding Information on the Internet: A Tutorial*, at http://www.lib.berkeley.edu/TeachingLib/Guides/Internet/FindInfo.html.

[49] Because of the billions of search pages that are indexed, it is not uncommon for a multi-word search to return thousands to millions of results. For example, a search for "George Pike" (without quotes) returned 29,800,000 results. The proprietary algorithms used by the search engines are intended to return the most likely relevant searches first, becoming less likely relevant as the results continue. While *Google* will report the total number of results, it presents only the first 1,000 hits.

[50] Information about these and other Google search techniques can be found through *Google's Web Search Guides*, available online at http://www.google.com/support.

[51] To get there from the main search page, click Settings, then choose Advanced Search.

respectively, devote tremendous resources to ensuring their databases are current, accurate, and relevant. On the other hand, the millions of websites available through the World Wide Web are created, owned, or controlled by millions of different entities. Each entity decides for itself what content to make available. That content may be current or outdated, it may be neutral in viewpoint or biased; it is sometimes almost impossible to tell. Web crawlers or spiders may or may not locate relevant websites. There are very few individual website owners that have the ability or time to aggregate or combine information from separate websites or filter out substantive analysis from incidental material, as *LexisNexis* or *Westlaw* do. Web search results can be extremely useful, irrelevant, incomplete, or downright misleading. Researchers are cautioned to evaluate web search results carefully.[52]

The other reality has to do with ownership. Materials that are written, organized, edited, updated, and published by commercial services are rarely made available at no cost on the web because of the expense involved in their creation and their producers' desire to keep their businesses profitable. They are often copyrighted, further limiting their usage. The web can provide the bare text of federal or state statutes, but it will not have the extremely useful annotated state codes with their notes of decisions and other value-added content. The web may offer access to federal and state court decisions, but does not provide the West digests' topic and key number system, or the topical databases for finding cases like in *LexisNexis*. The web will have some academic law journal articles from selected journals, but it will not have comprehensive law review collections or *LegalTrac* or other comprehensive bibliographic indexes. Legal research on the web is limited in the depth and breadth of materials available and the extent to which those materials can enhance the research process.

4.   Relying on Internet Sources

In discussing the traditional approach to law and its research methods, the legal scholar Karl Llewellyn once cautioned about the "threat of the available" and the "threat from apparent simplicity."[53] The former is the tendency to use the most readily available material, then make the mistake of assuming that is all that there is to see instead of researching further. The latter is the need to render things simple.

Llewellyn's observations preceded the development of the web by over half a century, but they remain very apt. The sheer volume of information available on the web is both its strongest asset and its greatest liability. The ease of web searching can lead to a false sense of confidence in search results—Llewellyn's threat from apparent simplicity. And the volume of information can make it exceedingly easy to find *some* relevant information—the threat of the available—but very difficult to locate *all* relevant material. Legal research often requires the researcher to search beyond the level of *some* information to adequately address the complexity of modern legal issues.

---

[52] For example, a *Google* search for "abortion law cases" (without quotes) returned 13,700,000 hits. Most of the first twenty hits were news articles, articles from advocacy groups and bloggers, and *Wikipedia* entries, with one link to *Roe v. Wade*. Changing the search to "abortion law cases" (with quotes) yielded 356,000 total hits, including one substantive journal article, but otherwise the results were primarily news articles and advocacy group materials. With some digging, several sources were found that had links to a few major court decisions. (Searches conducted on July 28, 2014)

[53] KARL N. LLEWELLYN, *Legal Tradition and Social Science Method—A Realist's Critique, in* JURISPRUDENCE: REALISM IN THEORY AND PRACTICE 77, 82–84 (1962) (reprinting essay from 1931).

Even when a researcher locates potentially valuable information, the next hurdle is to determine whether the information can be relied upon. The traditional legal research resources described in this book have long and distinguished pedigrees. Even if the court decisions published in West's case reporters and statutes published in annotated codes are "unofficial," researchers generally do not hesitate to rely on them because long experience has shown them to be authoritative and credible. Legal researchers have a similar level of comfort using established treatises, law review articles, legal encyclopedias, and similar secondary tools.

The legal publishing industry has a track record of producing authoritative, accurate, and reliable products.[54] However, reliability can be much more difficult to determine with Internet resources. The World Wide Web itself is only about twenty years old as a practical research source. Its youth does not give it the track record of a long-standing legal publisher such as West, BNA, or LexisNexis. The Internet is very fluid, with content coming and going quite rapidly. It is a global and comparatively inexpensive means of publishing, available to anyone with a computer and some rudimentary skills, which results in a lot of questionable, unverifiable, and potentially misleading information sources among its billions of webpages. But legal researchers must have reliable information; their clients' lives and property depend on it. Assuring the reliability of an information source is an indispensable part of the legal research process.

Confirming that a particular Internet source can be used with confidence depends on a mix of factors, including the following:

a.   *How was the website found?* Was its URL available on an established directory or portal, perhaps offered by a bar association or law library? Was it referred to by a credible source—an article, book, report, other website, a faculty member or attorney, etc.? In general, websites referred to from credible sources will themselves be credible.

b.   *Is the source of the information credible?* The legal research world is fortunate that its most important research materials are primary resources—statutes, cases, regulations—that come directly from federal and state government institutions. The federal government and most states provide a great deal of primary legal information on government websites. That makes online access easy and ubiquitous. Researchers can generally confirm that electronic information comes from a government source because of the .gov as the top-level domain in the URL. Generally, subject to its trustworthiness (discussed below) a .gov source is credible.

The more information you know about the source provider, the more confidence you can have in determining the accuracy and reliability of the information. Websites of well established commercial content providers, such as the *New York Times, Harvard Law Review, Dun and Bradstreet*, the United Nations, or most academic institutions (with a top-level domain of .edu), will have that history and can be relied on. If the website provides contact information for its source, you may be able to find more information on how the information was compiled. On the other hand, websites with no contact information or no clear author or creator, or with a cryptic name like "Society for Americans" may warrant further investigation. A tilde (~) in a URL often indicates a personal website, and a top-level domain of .org typically denotes an advocacy or not-for-

---

[54] For a discussion of the user community's trust in established publications, see Mary Whisner, Bouvier's, Black's, *and Tinkerbell*, 92 LAW LIBR. J. 99 (2000).

profit organization. This information can help you understand the identity of the source provider.

With secondary materials, the best indicator of authority is the reputation of the content author or provider. An obvious first step in verifying the authority of web content is to determine if the author or provider is identified. This is not automatic; some websites do not indicate the author or source of their content. It may be helpful to check the website's "About" information for authorship, find a means of contacting the provider (usually done by email), or identify a corporate affiliation and use the corporation's reputation as a guide.

An important way to assess the credibility of a particular website is to confirm the information it presents through another source. For example, has the website been cited by reliable authors for its content? If the website reproduces a resource like statutes, does the text conform to the official version? If a research report is available online, has the report been cataloged by a research library or relied on in subsequent research? There are as many ways to confirm the information as there are sources of information to begin with. This is not only an essential part of the web information verification process but also a good research practice.

Another indication of credibility is whether the website asserts copyright to its work. Claiming copyright means that the author or creator claims ownership of the information, and can also indicate that the information author or creator accepts ownership and responsibility for the information.

c.   Is there an obvious bias to the website? Websites expressing a particular viewpoint may be developed by political parties, public interest groups, policy think-tanks, educational centers and institutes, and individuals with axes to grind. Bias should not rule out the use of a website; the information may be sound, the statistics might be useful, and the viewpoint may support your client's interests. You need to be aware of the bias, however, before basing your conclusions or your case on the information. Can you verify the information using another source? What is the purpose of the website—public service, news, political action, advertising or marketing, education? Who is the content creator and what is its reputation? These types of factors will weigh heavily in your decision to use information from a website with a clear bias.

d.   Is the information itself a correct representation of what it purports to be? Another question to ask is whether the information is trustworthy. That is, is the content you see on the website the same content that was placed there by the content creator, or has there been some change to the content, whether malicious, intentional, or unintentional? Print statutes obtained from the state legislature, for example, are generally considered trustworthy, and online statutes on the legislature's website should be too. In fact, users should be able to consider as trustworthy those primary sources obtained directly from the government institution that produced the source. Unfortunately, this is not always the case, neither with statutes, nor with cases, executive orders, or other online material. Many government entities do not provide a means of assuring their online primary materials are unaltered, which leaves users with no assurance that the information is accurate and trustworthy.[55] Legal researchers must

---

[55] To be considered "authentic" the source must be verifiable as "complete and unaltered" when compared with the original text. A recent study by the American Association of Law Libraries determined that many of the "official" online legal sources have not been verified as "authentic." STATE BY STATE REPORT ON

take care to determine whether the online primary materials they consult have some means of verifying their accuracy, or authenticity.

   e.   Is the version you are using current? Another critical element to evaluate is whether the information is current. As noted, websites come and go, and they add and delete information all the time by processes invisible to researchers. Websites may have been abandoned by their developers, or updating may be slowed by any number of factors. Even governmental primary source materials should be checked for currency. For example, the "official" version of the *Code of Federal Regulations*, as published in the Government Printing Office's website,[56] is no more current than the print version. The presence of a "last modified" or "last updated" notation on a particular website is helpful, but it does not end the inquiry. Researchers must ensure the currency of their resources, which may require emailing or a phone call to the resource provider or a visit to a law library.

   f.   Does the website function smoothly and do links take you to the intended site? Is the website well organized? Is the text well written, using standard grammar, punctuation, and usage? Is it easy to navigate? Do its links work and do they take you to credible sources? Does it provide a site map or clear navigational links? A recognized or reputable institution tends to take care of its website and presents a useful resource. Less-established groups may have websites that do not function well or present a professional or credible appearance.

   Websites are notoriously impermanent. Even when the information provider is stable, like a university or a government institution, a website redesign can remove documents or change their URLs so dramatically that they can no longer be located or accessed. Studies have found that a high percentage of URLs cited in court opinions and law review articles are invalid within a couple of years.[57] Wise researchers will capture or print out online information if it is important to their work.

5. Noteworthy Legal and Law-Related Websites

   Staying up to date with the web's ever-growing resources is an overwhelming task for even the most industrious legal researcher. Current awareness websites, including

---

AUTHENTICATION OF ONLINE LEGAL RESOURCES (American Association of Law Libraries 2007), available online at http://www.aallnet.org/aallwash/authen_rprt/AuthenFinalReport.pdf. This situation suggests verifying the online source against an official source at some point in the research process. The Uniform Electronic Legal Material Act (UELMA), promulgated by the Uniform Law Commission in 2011, seeks to address the issue of authenticity of governmental electronic legal material. http://www.uniformlaws.org/shared/docs/electronic%20legal%20material/uelma_final_2011.pdf

   [56] http://www.gpo.gov/fdsys/browse/collectionCfr.action?collectionCode=CFR.

   [57] For discussions of the problem of "link rot," see, e.g., Tina S. Ching, *The Next Generation of Legal Citations: A Survey of Internet Citations in the Opinions of the Washington Supreme Court and Washington Appellate Courts, 1999–2005*, 9 J. APP. PRAC. & PROCESS 387 (2007); Helane E. Davis, *Keeping Validity in Cite: Web Resources Cited in Select Washington Law Reviews, 2001–03*, 98 LAW LIBR. J. 639 (2006); Susan Lyons, *Persistent Identification of Electronic Documents and the Future of Footnotes*, 97 LAW LIBR. J. 681 (2005); Sarah Rhodes, *Breaking Down Link Rot: The Chesapeake Project Legal Information Archive's Examination of URL Stability*, 102 LAW LIBR. J. 581 (2010); Mary Rumsey, *Runaway Train: Problems of Permanence, Accessibility, and Stability in the Use of Web Sources in Law Review Citations*, 94 LAW LIBR. J. 27 (2002); Arturo Torres, *Is Link Rot Destroying Stare Decisis as We Know It? The Internet-Citation Practice of the Texas Appellate Courts*, 13 J. APP. PRAC. & PROCESS 269 (2012); Jonathan Zittrain et al., *Perma: Scoping and Addressing the Problem of Link and Reference Rot in Legal Citations* (Harv. Pub. L. Working Paper No. 13–42, 2013), *available at* http://papers.ssrn.com/sol3/papers.cfm?abstract_id=2329161.

LLRX: The Law Librarians' Resource Exchange[58] and *Inter Alia: Tom Mighell's Technology Blog*,[59] can assist researchers in learning about and evaluating Internet sources. Useful law and law-related cyber-research print resources include Craig B. Simonsen and Christian R. Anderson, *Computer-Aided Legal Research on the Internet* (2d ed. 2005); Carole A. Levitt and Mark E. Rosch, *The Cybersleuth's Guide to the Internet: Conducting Effective Investigative and Legal Research on the Web* (9th ed. 2008); and Peggy Garvin, *United States Government Internet Manual, 2008* (5th ed. 2008).

There is a substantial and continuing proliferation of legal information websites. Many sites are sponsored by academic institutions, notably law schools and their libraries, nonprofit organizations, and government agencies. These sites provide content and links to other websites that support their programs. However, there also are several excellent websites of a comprehensive nature that are not affiliated with any educational institution. Major legal research websites of note include:

a. *Search Portals*[60]

(1) *FindLaw for Legal Professionals, http://lp.findlaw.com. FindLaw for Legal Professionals* is a comprehensive website providing access to case law, codes and statutes, law reviews, legal organizations, and specific legal subjects, including constitutional, intellectual property, and labor law, along with access to foreign and international resources. It claims to be the most heavily visited free legal portal. *FindLaw* is owned by Thomson Reuters, the parent company of *Westlaw*. *FindLaw* content generally does not come directly from *Westlaw* (e.g., court decisions on *FindLaw* are generally text or PDF versions of slip opinions, not scans or text from *Westlaw*.)

(2) *FirstGov, http://www.firstgov.gov.* This site is the U.S. government's portal to government information on the web. The site includes an A-to-Z directory of government agency websites and a search engine that examines over 2.7 million government webpages. This is a great starting place for locating information originating from the federal government.

(3) *Hieros Gamos, http://www.hg.org. Hieros Gamos* is one of the oldest and most comprehensive legal websites, boasting more than two million links. International in scope, it is organized under a very detailed index of topics and sources.

(4) *Justia, http://www.justia.com. Justia* is a well-organized site with a search engine that has options for searching the site, the content of other legal information websites, legal blogs, and legal podcasts. *Justia*'s directory is organized both by topical legal practice area and by legal research source. Direct links to many federal resources are available through *Justia*, including federal appellate and Supreme Court decisions, the United States Constitution, the *U.S. Code*, the *C.F.R.*, and some state content.

(5) *Guide to Law Online, http://www.loc.gov/law/public/law-guide.html.* This directory from the Law Library of Congress focuses on sites that offer the full texts of laws, regulations, and court decisions, along with commentary from lawyers writing

---

[58] http://www.llrx.com.

[59] http://www.inter-alia.net.

[60] A portal, sometimes referred to as a directory, is generally defined as a website that serves primarily as a point of access to other web information. Portals will often be little more than collections of hyperlinks to other content providers, usually organized by category and subcategory.

primarily for other lawyers. It also contains a comprehensive directory of foreign law sites arranged by country.

(6)   *Legal Information Institute, http://www.law.cornell.edu.* Provided by Cornell University Law School, this was one of the first comprehensive legal information sites on the web. It is organized by type of information and subject area as well as jurisdiction.

(7)   *State and Local Government on the Net, http://www.statelocalgov.net.* This is an excellent directory of official state and local governmental websites organized by jurisdiction and topic.

(8)   *WashLaw: Legal Research on the Web, http://www.washlaw.edu.* Washburn University's School of Law has been a leader in providing access to legal information. The site features a basic alphabetical arrangement by topic and by jurisdiction that makes it easy to navigate.

b.   *Government Sources*

(1)   *Administrative Office of U.S. Courts,* http://www.uscourts.gov. This is the central site for accessing information about all United States federal courts, including the Supreme Court, federal circuit courts, district courts, and bankruptcy and other special courts. Links are provided for individual court websites, which will provide access to current and archived opinions (generally going back to the mid-1990s); dockets; court rules, forms, policies and procedures; and judicial directories and other contact information.

(2)   *FedStats,* http://www.fedstats.gov. This site provides a gateway to statistical information from over 100 federal agencies, including the U.S. Census Bureau, Bureau of Labor Statistics, and Bureau of Justice Statistics. The links are arranged by agency, topic, or geographic location.

(3)   *FDsys: The Federal Digital System,* http://www.gpo.gov/fdsys/. Produced by the U.S. Government Printing office, *FDSys* provides official electronic versions of the *Federal Register* (updated daily), the *List of Sections Affected (LSA)*, and the *Code of Federal Regulations (C.F.R.).* There is also a version of the *C.F.R.* called the *e-CFR*, which, while unofficial, is updated daily. This site provides links to the official version of the *United States Code, Statutes at Large,* and presidential materials.

(4)   *Office of the Law Revision Council, United States Code,* http://uscode.house.gov. The Law Revision Council of the U.S. House of Representatives prepares and publishes the *U.S.C.* This version is fully searchable with Boolean and proximity connectors. It is usually the most current version available of the *U.S. Code.* A related set of classification tables at http://uscode.house.gov/classification/tables.shtml allows the researcher to update the online version of the *U.S. Code* by providing tables of current public law numbers and sections that affect *U.S. Code* sections.

(5)   *Office of the President,* http://www.whitehouse.gov. This resource includes presidential executive orders and proclamations, speeches, and press conference transcripts. It also includes a topical list of subjects such as budget management, health care, and national security, with links to related documents in each topic.

(6)   *Public Access to Court Electronic Records,* http://pacer.login.uscourts.gov. Known as *PACER,* this site provides access to dockets from most federal district, bankruptcy, and appellate courts. Dockets are accessed by jurisdiction, then by party

name or docket number; some PDF copies of pleadings, orders, and opinions that often are not available on the general court websites or other websites are provided.

(7) *THOMAS: Legislative Information on the Internet,* http://thomas.loc.gov (scheduled to be replaced by *Congress.gov,* http://beta.congress.gov, in late 2014). *THOMAS,* from the Library of Congress, should be any researcher's first stop for federal legislative information. Researchers can access current and archived bills with bill tracking, current and archived public laws, committee reports, the *Congressional Record,* and major documents such as the Constitution, Bill of Rights, and Declaration of Independence. *THOMAS* also provides links to other legislative sites, including the U.S. House and Senate webpages, which in turn link to individual Senators' and Representatives' websites, committee sites containing legislative hearings and business sessions, and party caucus sites.

c.   Other Sources

There are several open access websites that provide access to federal court decisions, including *Public.Resource.Org,*[61] *Justia.com,*[62] and the *Public Library of Law.*[63] The coverage of these websites varies, both in the courts from which decisions are offered and the dates of available decisions. Some of these websites feature search engines and browse-able directories, and have additional resources like state court decisions.

Other sources of legal information include:

(1) *Google Scholar—Law,* http://scholar.google.com. *Google Scholar* provides access to legal scholarship and court opinions from various websites, including the open access websites mentioned above, and additional content that is scanned by *Google.* Coverage is extensive. Journal articles include those published and posted to the web from a variety of open access, publisher, and individual author websites.[64]

(2) Law Librarians' Society of Washington, D.C., *Legislative Sourcebook,* http://www.llsdc.org/sourcebook. The *Legislative Sourcebook* is a portal to legislative information from a number of government and non-governmental sources. Included are links to selected legislative histories, government documents, related regulatory filings, and articles on conducting legislative research.

(3) *Municode.com,* http://www.municode.com. Municipal Code Corporation publishes print and online codes for several cities. Its online library has links to all of the online codes that it publishes, arranged by state and then city.

(4) *National Center for State Courts,* http://www.ncsc.org. This is a valuable source for finding information on courts, including coverage of juries and caseloads, statistics, and extensive links to state court sites.

(5) *OYEZ,* http://www.oyez.org/oyez/frontpage. *OYEZ* is a nonprofit service that provides a wide variety of material about the U.S. Supreme Court, including streaming audio and transcription of current and historical oral arguments.

---

[61] www.public.resource.org.

[62] www.justia.com.

[63] http://www.plol.org.

[64] *See* Alena Wolotira, *Googling the Law: Apprising Students of the Benefits and Flaws of Google as a Research Tool,* 21 PERSP.: TEACHING LEGAL RES. & WRITING 33 (2012)

d.   *Topical Websites*

(1) *American Bar Association (ABA),* http://www.americanbar.org. This site provides a variety of information about the ABA, its activities, and its publications. It also provides access to briefs for current U.S. Supreme Court cases. Individual ABA section websites often include extensive resources related to specific areas of law, although most limit access to members only.

(2) *Blawg.com,* http://www.blawg.com. This site provides a comprehensive directory of legal and law-related blogs, podcasts, and RSS feeds.

(3) *Jurist: Legal News and Research,* http://www.jurist.org/. *Jurist* is a legal news and real-time legal research service that tracks important legal news stories and annotates them with documents, commentary, and links to other resources.

(4) *LLRX, http://www.llrx.com. LLRX* primarily consists of articles and pathfinders written by law firm and academic librarians. It is notable for its comprehensive directory of online court rules.

(5) *Search Systems Public Record Database,* http://www.searchsystems.net. *Search Systems* provides links to over 1,700 free "public record" databases. Many of the databases are genealogical in nature or provide names and addresses of contact persons for found records, rather than the providing access to the records themselves. National records are in alphabetical order; state records are organized by state.

(6) *SEC Filings and Forms (EDGAR),* http://www.sec.gov/edgar.shtml. *EDGAR* provides access to financial and other filings for publicly traded companies in the U.S. It is searchable by company name, most recent filings, or full text.

(7) *Social Science Research Network,* http://www.ssrn.com and *Legal Scholarship Network,* http://www.ssrn.com/lsn/index.html. *SSRN* focuses on publishing scholarly papers and abstracts in all disciplines. This can include pre-publication works, working papers, and peer-reviewed materials. The *Legal Scholarship Network* includes dozens of eJournals on different topics.

(8) *Wex,* http://topics.law.cornell.edu/wex. *Wex* is a collaboratively created, public-access law dictionary and encyclopedia. It is sponsored and hosted by the Legal Information Institute at Cornell Law School.

(9) *Zimmerman's Research Guide: An Online Encyclopedia for Legal Researchers,* http://law.lexisnexis.com/infopro/zimmermans/. This is a comprehensive guide to web and Internet resources, print resources, or telephone contact information broken down into several hundred subjects and jurisdictions. The encyclopedia can be searched by keyword, or the researcher can browse through the entries. Many entries have "see also" references to direct the researcher to related information.

6.   Citation to Internet Resources[65]

The *Bluebook* "requires the use and citation of traditional printed sources . . . unless there is a digital copy of the source available that is authenticated, official, *or* an exact copy of the printed source. . . ."[66] If the source can be cited as if to an original print source and is considered official and authentic, it can be cited using traditional *Bluebook* rules

---

[65] *See also* Chapter 24.

[66] THE BLUEBOOK: A UNIFORM SYSTEM OF CITATION R. 18.2, at 165 (emphasis added).

without any additional URL requirement. This recent revision is intended to address the use of online access as an equivalent to, and increasingly as a replacement for, print publications. If the print source is obscure or "practically unavailable," then the URL should be appended to the citation. An "available at" reference with the URL is also appropriate in order to improve access to the resource.

Internet citations may be used for sources that do not exist in a traditional printed format. The information should include the "clearest path of access to the cited reference"[67] and include title, pagination and publication information, along with author, when available, followed by the URL.

URLs can be a challenging part of a web citation. The *Bluebook* requires that the URL "should point readers directly to the source cited rather than to an intervening page of links."[68] While this will often be straightforward,[69] some URLs can be long and full of nontextual characters. In this case, the researcher should cite to the most practical URL that leads closest to the specific document, then describe the step(s) needed to locate the document.

Author, title, case name, code section, date, and similar items generally follow *Bluebook* standards as much as possible. When citing a source from the Internet as a parallel citation, use the author, title, case name, docket number, date, pagination, etc., of the original printed source, then use the comment *"available at"* and provide the URL. If authorship of a specific item is not clearly stated, then the title alone may be used or the item may be described. Pinpoint citation to a specific page can be done if the document itself is paginated, e.g., for PDF documents that preserve pagination. Paragraph numbers may be used only if used by the source document. Screen numbers or other software-based numbers should not be used.

Court decisions provide a particular challenge because many web-published case decisions may not contain traditional West reporter citations (e.g., to "F.2d", "F. Supp.", "A.2d", etc.).[70] The *Bluebook* makes it clear that if the case is available in print, or through *LexisNexis* or *Westlaw*, then that citation should be provided, with a parallel citation to the Internet. If the case is not available in print or through *LexisNexis* or *Westlaw* (as may often be the case for very recent decisions, trial court decisions, or interim court orders), the closest standard for citing the case would be as an unreported case or slip opinion (*Bluebook* Rule 10.8.1(b)) that uses the case name, docket number, court and date, with an *"available at"* reference to the Internet source.

If a document obtained from the web provides a specific publication date, then that date should be used (year only) in the citation. If no date is provided, the date should be the date on which you last visited the website. The current edition of the *Bluebook* allows using a website's "last modified" or "last updated" date if the site is stable or not updated regularly.

---

[67] *Id.* R. 18.2.2, at 166.

[68] *Id.* R. 18.2.2(d), at 168.

[69] For example, "http://jurist.org/forum/2006/01/patriot-games-terrorism-law-and.php," locates a specific page on the *Jurist* website for a comment by Professor Susan Herman on the USA Patriot Act.

[70] The open access federal court decisions discussed in Section E-5-c often provide the West reporter citation for the particular decision. However, the decisions are not PDF documents from West reporters and generally do not have the pagination needed for pinpoint citations. Decisions found on court websites have the court's docket number but generally do not provide the West reporter citation.

Chapter 24

LEGAL CITATION FORM*

Citation form in all legal writing requires uniformity and consistency for two fundamental reasons. First, individuals relying on legal research need to be able to accurately and efficiently locate and verify referenced information. Second, a uniform system of citation provides the reader with information concerning the manner in which the source supports the text for which it is cited.[1]

This chapter offers an overview of basic legal citation form. The chapter refers to the 19th edition of *The Bluebook: A Uniform System of Citation*, which is the most commonly accepted form of legal citation. Additionally, the chapter includes a discussion of the 4th edition of the *ALWD Citation Manual: A Professional System of Citation*, an alternative citation manual that has gained acceptance primarily in the academic legal community. Finally, the chapter considers citation to electronic information, as well as neutral citation standards for citing legal information without relying on one format or publisher. Throughout the chapter, examples are used to illustrate the various citation systems.

A. THE BLUEBOOK: A UNIFORM SYSTEM OF CITATION

1. Historical Development of *The Bluebook: A Uniform System of Citation*

Citation form developed along with the growth of the common law case reporting system. Its development reflected the legal system's dependency on case law under the concept of *stare decisis* and the use of precedent.[2] With the development of American legal education during the nineteenth century, law students founded law reviews to provide outlets for their own writing as well as professors' work.[3]

---

* This chapter was revised by Pat Newcombe, Associate Dean for Library and Information Resources, Western New England University School of Law Library.

[1] For further discussion of the reasons for citation rules, see Mary Whisner, *The Dreaded* Bluebook, 100 LAW LIBR. J. 393, 395–96 (2008).

[2] For an excellent historical summary of citation form, see Byron D. Cooper, *Anglo-American Legal Citation: Historical Development and Library Implications*, 75 LAW LIBR. J. 3 (1982). For a general discussion of the advent of the footnote in scholarly writing, see ANTHONY GRAFTON, THE FOOTNOTE: A CURIOUS HISTORY (1997).

[3] *See* Michael I. Swygert & Jon W. Bruce, *The Historical Origins, Founding, and Early Development of Student-Edited Law Reviews*, 36 HASTINGS L.J. 739, 778 (1985). After short-lived student publications at Albany and Columbia, *id.* at 764–69, a group of students began publishing the *Harvard Law Review* in 1887. *Id.* at 773. "In a twenty year period following the founding of the *Harvard Law Review*, five of the nation's then most prestigious law schools—Yale (1891), Pennsylvania (1896), Columbia (1901), Michigan (1902), and Northwestern (1906)—modeled legal periodicals after the Harvard prototype. During the next two decades, the law review tide swept the country as many other law schools started and nurtured student-edited periodicals." *Id.* at 779.

In 1926, the law review editorial boards of Harvard, Yale, Columbia, and the University of Pennsylvania produced the first edition of *A Uniform System of Citation*. At the time, the costs associated with typesetting detailed footnotes were greater than the costs of typesetting the text of the article. By developing a consistent shorthand expression for citation form, these early law review editors were able to reduce both typesetting costs and the space required for footnotes.[4]

Over time, *The Bluebook: A Uniform System of Citation*, now in its 19th edition,[5] became the most widely used standard for legal citation form.[6] Typically, gaining a detailed and accurate understanding of the *Bluebook* rules was one of a law student's rites of passage into the legal profession.

2. The Rules of *The Bluebook: A Uniform System of Citation*

The *Bluebook* is a lengthy (511 pages), complex, and self-proclaimed definitive guide to legal citation form.[7] The *Bluebook* serves two functions: it acts as a guide to citation form and as a style manual for legal publication. Its periodic revisions, including rule changes, are a frequent source of frustration for those attempting to conform their citation practices to those in the latest edition of the *Bluebook*.[8]

The most recent edition of the *Bluebook* is organized into three major parts. The first part is the Bluepages, printed on light blue paper, directly after the Introduction.

---

[4] Cooper, *supra* note 2, at 21. A precursor was the *Yale Law Journal*'s in-house pamphlet, *Abbreviations and Form of Citation* (1921). *See* Fred Shapiro, Letter to the Editor, *Who Wrote the* Bluebook?, N.Y. TIMES, Nov. 27, 2013 (Book Review), at 6. With the 15th edition, the editors added "The Bluebook" to the title to reflect the manual's nickname derived from its traditional blue cover.

[5] As noted in the Preface to this text, A full citation to the *Bluebook* in a footnote would be:
THE BLUEBOOK: A UNIFORM SYSTEM OF CITATION R. 1.4(e), at 50 (Columbia Law Review Ass'n et al. eds., 19th ed. 2010). Because this is cumbersome for a book that so often cites the *Bluebook*, we usually shorten *Bluebook* references to: BLUEBOOK R. 1.4(e), at 50. References to editions other than the most recent will be designated by edition number.

[6] Some jurisdictions and several law reviews, working on a belief that their individual jurisdictional citation needs were not adequately addressed by the *Bluebook*, have developed alternative citation manuals. One example is the manual produced by the *University of Chicago Law Review* and the *University of Chicago Law Forum*. *See* U. Chi. L. Rev. & U. Chi. Legal F., *The University of Chicago Manual of Legal Citation*, 53 U. CHI. L. REV. 1353 (1986). This manual was subsequently published in 1989 (its first and only edition) by Lawyers Cooperative Publishing, Bancroft–Whitney Company, and Mead Data Central, Inc., as a 63–page pamphlet with a maroon cover, hence its common name, the *Maroon Book*. Rather than being a complete guide to citation form, like that provided by the *Bluebook*, the *Maroon Book* offered a guiding philosophy of citation form, emphasizing editorial discretion rather than consistent uniform citation form. It never gained wide acceptance and failed perhaps because it overreached its goal of being flexible, leaving the reader without clear guidance. Melissa H. Weresh, *The* ALWD Citation Manual: *A Coup De Grace*, 23 U. ARK. LITTLE ROCK L. REV. 775, 781–82 (2001).

[7] *See* BLUEBOOK at 1 (characterizing work as "the definitive style guide for legal citation in the United States"). For a restatement of the rules set out in the 19th edition of the *Bluebook*, see ALAN L. DWORSKY, USER'S GUIDE TO THE BLUEBOOK (2010). For a discussion and illustration of the rules of the *Bluebook*, see LINDA J. BARRIS, UNDERSTANDING AND MASTERING THE BLUEBOOK: A GUIDE FOR STUDENTS AND PRACTITIONERS (2d ed. 2011). For a learning tool for citation form, see, e.g., TRACY L. MCGAUGH & CHRISTINE HURT, INTERACTIVE CITATION WORKBOOK FOR THE BLUEBOOK: A UNIFORM SYSTEM OF CITATION (2011 ed.); Peter W. Martin, *Introduction to Basic Legal Citation* (LII 2010 ed.), http://www.law.cornell.edu/citation/. The Center for Computer-Assisted Legal Instruction (CALI) also provides computer-based programs offering self-directed instruction in the use of the *Bluebook* at http://www.cali.org.

[8] For reviews and reaction to the 19th edition of the *Bluebook*, see Richard A. Posner, *The* Bluebook Blues, 120 YALE L.J. 850 (2011); Stephen M. Darrow & Jonathan J. Darrow, *Beating the* Bluebook Blues: *A Response to Judge Posner*, 109 MICH. L. REV. FIRST IMPRESSIONS 92 (2011), http://www.michiganlawreview.org/firstimpressions/vol109/Darrow & Darrow.pdf; and Cathy Roberts, *The Dark Side of the* Bluebook, UTAH B.J., May/June 2011, at 22.

The Bluepages provide basic legal citation guidance suitable for the requirements of first-year law students, law clerks, and legal practitioners. This forty-nine-page section is designed as a practical guide to the most common citation forms used in non-academic legal documents. Examples provided in the Bluepages are printed using the ordinary typeface conventions typically used in legal practice. A useful feature is the Bluepages Tips, which appear throughout the Bluepages; they offer helpful explanations and provide references to the complete rules if more specificity is required. The tips are printed in darker blue to draw the reader's attention. This section also includes a table of suggested abbreviations for words commonly found in the titles of court documents and a table listing jurisdiction-specific citation rules and style guides.

The second part, printed on white paper, is the main body of the *Bluebook*. This section provides the detailed rules of citation and style needed to meet the complex and nuanced requirements of law review writing. Rules 1 through 9 provide general standards, and rules 10 through 21 provide rules for citations to various types of authority, such as cases, statutes, books, periodicals, and foreign and international materials. Examples provided throughout this part are printed using typeface conventions standard in law journal footnotes.

The third part of the *Bluebook*, printed on white paper with a blue border, provides tables that are organized by U. S. federal and state jurisdictions and that list the abbreviations for each jurisdiction's primary source materials. This section also has similar information for foreign jurisdictions and intergovernmental organizations, and abbreviations lists for words found in case names and court names, geographical terms, periodicals, services, and other frequently cited items.

The organizational structure and a variety of finding tools help users locate material and properly use the rules set out in the *Bluebook*. The inside front cover and first page provide a basic outline, with examples, of commonly used citations in the format used in law review footnotes. The last page and inside back cover provide the same examples of commonly used citations in the form used by practitioners in legal memoranda and court documents. The examples in both front and back covers are accompanied by references to the rule(s) involved, which detail finer points and subtleties. There is a comprehensive table of contents, and a detailed index at the end of the *Bluebook* provides direct access by subject to specific aspects of citation form.

The *Bluebook* is available on the Internet as *The Bluebook Online*.[9] Subscribers to the online version can access the full content of the *Bluebook* with full-text and advanced searching capabilities, and make and share notes and bookmarks. Even without a subscription, researchers who access the website can consult the Blue Tips, where the editors provide guidance on subjects covered by the *Bluebook*. These tips are regularly updated and searchable. The *Bluebook* is also available as an app for iPad.[10]

a.   *Style and Typeface.* Bluepages B1 and Rule 2 deal with typeface conventions and style issues. The *Bluebook* serves both the more pragmatic concerns of practitioners preparing legal briefs and memoranda and the more formal legal publication needs of

---

[9] https://www.legalbluebook.com/.

[10] The underlying app is *Rulebook*. Users can purchase court rules or the *Bluebook* to use with the app. *See* Rulebook, http://www.readyreferenceapps.com/. For comparisons of the formats, see Mary Whisner, Bluebook *Technologies*, http://www.llrx.com/features/bluebooktechnologies.htm (Sept. 18, 2012); *see also* Mary Whisner, *Books on My Desk*, 104 LAW LIBR. J. 597, 599–600 (2012).

law reviews. The most common typeface conventions are outlined in the Bluepages.[11] A more complex collection of typeface conventions, including ordinary roman type, italics, and large and small capitals, is detailed in the alternative rules applicable for law reviews, found in the body of the *Bluebook*. If the Bluepages do not cover a particular authority, practitioners can turn to the body of the *Bluebook* for guidance. The practitioner must then remember to convert the typeface in the rule examples and tables into the format for practitioners in accordance with Bluepages Rule B1.

The *Bluebook* identifies jurisdiction-specific court rules and manuals on local citation practice.[12] In addition to the *Bluebook*, many legal publications use style manuals designed for the social sciences, arts and humanities, or federal government publications to supplement the *Bluebook* rules.[13]

b.   Differences Between Editions. The preface to the 19th edition provides a discussion of the changes from the 18th edition. This feature is a welcome aid in highlighting revisions between editions. In addition, users should be aware that minute alterations to rules and tables may be made between printings of the same edition. The most current edition of the *Bluebook* should always be used unless a court or publication has expressly adopted a different version.

c.   Priority Within Citations: Citation Structure. Bluebook Rules 10 through 18 are ordered according to the perceived influence of the legal authority cited—e.g., citation to primary sources is discussed before citation of secondary authority, and citation of books is covered before citation of newspaper articles.[14] Each rule begins with a basic example. Within the rules for particular types of sources, individual rules are ordered according to the information conveyed within the citation, i.e., information set forth first in the citation is addressed by the first rule.

This pattern can be applied to the most frequent type of citation: cases. The elements of a case citation, moving from left to right, are:

- Case name;

- Volume number of the reporter;

- Abbreviated name of the reporter;

- Page number on which the opinion begins (and other pages included in the citation);

---

[11] The Bluepages offer practitioners the choice of underscoring or italics. The option of underscoring is a holdover from the days when practitioners' documents were prepared on typewriters. Now that word processing programs make it easy to italicize, experts advise against using underscoring. *See, e.g.,* BRYAN A. GARNER, THE REDBOOK: A MANUAL ON LEGAL STYLE R. 3.2, at 79 (3d ed. 2013); MATTHEW BUTTERICK, TYPOGRAPHY FOR LAWYERS: ESSENTIAL TOOLS FOR POLISHED & PERSUASIVE DOCUMENTS 79 (2010) ("[U]nless you're using a typewriter, fulfill your *Bluebook* destiny by italicizing, not underlining.").

[12] BLUEBOOK tbl. BT2, at 30–51.

[13] Manuals commonly used for this purpose are THE CHICAGO MANUAL OF STYLE (16th ed. 2010), KATE L. TURABIAN ET AL., A MANUAL FOR WRITERS OF RESEARCH PAPERS, THESES, AND DISSERTATIONS: CHICAGO STYLE FOR STUDENTS AND RESEARCHERS (8th ed. 2013), and U.S. GOV'T PRINTING OFFICE, STYLE MANUAL: AN OFFICIAL GUIDE TO THE FORM AND STYLE OF FEDERAL GOVERNMENT PRINTING (30th ed. 2008), *available at* http://www.gpo.gov/fdsys/pkg/GPO–STYLEMANUAL–2008/content-detail.html.

[14] Notice how Rules 1.3 and 1.4 relate to the order of information within a signal (*e.g., accord, see, see also, cf.*), moving from primary to secondary sources of legal information, while the ordering of the signals themselves moves from direct support of a legal proposition to contradictory sources of legal information.

- Abbreviated name of the court, including its geographic jurisdiction (if not apparent from the name of the reporter);

- Date or year of decision (give exact date of decision for unreported cases or slip opinions);

- Parenthetical information regarding the case;

- Prior and subsequent case histories;

- Special or unique citation forms; and

- Citation ends with a period.

Or, as is illustrated by this example:

Windsor v. United States, 699 F.3d 169 (2d Cir. 2012) (applying intermediate scrutiny to Defense of Marriage Act), *aff'd*, 133 S. Ct. 2675 (2013).[15]

Look at the elements of this citation and the sequence of rules in the *Bluebook* following the basic citation form set out at Rule 10.1. Note that all citation examples provided in this chapter are in the format used by practitioners, not in the format used for law reviews. Therefore, relevant Bluepages rules are provided in addition to the rules found in the white pages of the *Bluebook*.

Windsor v. United States	case name	Rule 10.2/B4.1.1
699 F.3d 169	reporter information	Rule 10.3/B4.1.2
(2d Cir. 2012)	court and date	Rule 10.4–10.5/B4.1.3
(applying intermediate scrutiny to Defense of Marriage Act)	parenthetical information	Rule 10.6/B4.1.5
aff'd, 133 S. Ct. 2675 (2013).	subsequent history	Rule 10.7/B4.1.6

3. Additional Aids for Using the *Bluebook*

Several tools can assist in applying *Bluebook* citation rules to documents:

a. Many online research services—including *LexisNexis* and *Westlaw*—offer the option to highlight text and "copy with cite" or "copy with reference." The citations copied generally comply with *Bluebook* rules. Sometimes they don't, however, and users should be alert to possible deviations; for example, *LexisNexis* and *Westlaw* both include parallel citations to cases that the *Bluebook* doesn't require.

b. *West CiteAdvisor* (available through, but licensed separately from, *Westlaw*) identifies citations in a document and suggests the correct citation format, with citation style options including the *Bluebook*, *ALWD Citation Manual*, and local rules.[16]

---

[15] The format for law review footnotes would be the same other than having the case name in ordinary roman type. BLUEBOOK R. 2.1(a), at 63.

[16] For a description, see Mary Susan Lucas, TOP TOOL FOR APPELLATE ADVOCACY CLASS: WEST CITEADVISOR, Charlotte Law Libr. News, Sept. 3, 2013, http://charlottelawlibrary.wordpress.com/2013/09/03/west-citeadvisor-top-tool-for-appellate-advocacy-class/.

c. *Prince's Dictionary of Legal Citations*[17] provides an alphabetical list of names of legal resources and other materials abbreviated according to *Bluebook* rules.

d. *Zotero*[18] (a free application), and *EndNote*[19] and *RefWorks*[20] (licensed services) can be used to put citations into *Bluebook* format. Many university libraries purchase campus-wide licenses for *EndNote* or *Refworks*.[21]

e. *CiteGenie*[22] converts citations copied from *LexisNexis*, *Westlaw*, or other sources into proper *Bluebook* form (or selected other styles).

f. *Citeus Legalus*,[23] a website that bills itself "the legal citation generator for lazy law students," creates *Bluebook* citations from information that the user enters manually (a slow process) or, for some type of materials, imports from *EndNote* or *Refworks*.

Sometimes, even after reading the various *Bluebook* rules and cross-references, a writer is still stumped about how to cite a work. As comprehensive as the *Bluebook* seems, there are some ambiguities and, occasionally, missing genres. One way to resolve the issue is simply to find an example in a law review citing the work in question, and use the format those editors used. Searching the four law reviews that produce the *Bluebook* is preferable, because you can assume that those editors know the *Bluebook* better than anyone, but most law reviews use the *Bluebook* as their style manual so finding any reference to the work can be helpful. For example, if a writer wanted to cite *Brown v. Board of Education of Topeka, Kansas* in a footnote and wasn't sure whether or how to abbreviate "Board" or "Education" or whether to include "of Topeka, Kansas," a quick search could find a 2012 article in the *Harvard Law Review* citing the case as "Brown v. Bd. of Educ., 347 U.S. 483 (1954)."[24]

---

[17] MARY MILES PRINCE, PRINCE'S DICTIONARY OF LEGAL CITATIONS (8th ed. 2011).

[18] http://www.zotero.org. Zotero is free for up to 300 MB of data. Users who store many documents may purchase additional storage.

[19] http://endnote.com/.

[20] http://www.refworks.com/.

[21] For comparisons of these and other citation management tools, see UNIV. LIBRARIES, UNIV. OF WASH., CITATIONS AND WRITING, http://guides.lib.washington.edu/citations (updated Jan. 8, 2014). For discussion of *Zotero* and other tools applied to legal materials, see PAPPAS LAW LIBRARY, BOSTON UNIVERSITY SCH. OF LAW, TOOLS FOR MAKING BLUEBOOK CITATIONS AND KEEPING TRACK OF RESEARCH, http://lawlibraryguides.bu.edu/content.php?pid=210292 & sid=1750902 (updated Jan. 18, 2014).

[22] http://www.citegenie.com. A ninety-day trial is free.

[23] http://citeuslegalus.com/.

[24] Of course, a famous Supreme Court case is only one sort of source to look up. This technique works well for treaties, government reports, and other materials that are not as familiar as cases. To make searching easier, one can set up the four journals—*Columbia Law Review, Harvard Law Review, University of Pennsylvania Law Review*, and *Yale Law Journal*—as favorites in *LexisNexis* and *Westlaw*. Looking at the model citation in print or PDF is helpful because *LexisNexis* and *Westlaw* versions of journal articles do not necessarily show all the formatting. For example, LARGE AND SMALL CAPS might be converted to LARGE CAPS or *italics* might show up as ordinary roman.

B. ALWD CITATION MANUAL:
A PROFESSIONAL SYSTEM OF CITATION

1. Historical Development of the *ALWD Citation Manual: A Professional System of Citation*

The *ALWD Citation Manual: A Professional System of Citation*[25] was designed to remedy some of the perceived complexities of the *Bluebook* and make teaching and using citations easier. The *ALWD Citation Manual* contains one system for all legal documents, making no distinction between law review articles and other types of legal writing.

One of the catalysts to the development of the *ALWD Citation Manual* was the 16th edition of the *Bluebook*, in which the editors substantially altered the meaning of citation signals. Citation signals (currently described in Rule 1) are used to introduce a citation and indicate to the reader the manner in which an authority supports or contradicts an assertion. The most significant modification in the 16th edition of the *Bluebook* concerned the frequently used "see" signal, and changed its meaning from indirect support to direct support of the proposition being made. The new meaning created confusion among legal writers who had used learned and used previous versions of the *Bluebook*, and created a strong likelihood that an author's use of authority would be misinterpreted if introduced by a "see" signal.

The 16th edition's signal changes drew a strongly negative response from the legal community.[26] This was compounded by longstanding general dissatisfaction with *Bluebook* rules, which were essentially citation rules imposed on practitioners and academicians by students at elite law schools without input from interested constituencies. The concern in the legal community about changes in the meaning of citation signals was so strong and, coupled with the already-existing dissatisfaction about *Bluebook* practices, that the Association of American Law Schools (AALS) passed a plenary resolution at the 1997 Annual Meeting to formally request that the editors of the *Bluebook* reinstate the introductory signals definitions from the 15th edition.[27] The resolution also advocated that law reviews continue to use the 15th edition's introductory signal rules.[28]

The Association of Legal Writing Directors (ALWD), encouraged by the AALS resolution, published their citation guide, which was written by legal educators. ALWD's goals were to develop a more user-friendly citation style and a better and more effective teaching tool, and not alter citation rules radically.[29] The intended result was a system

---

[25] ASS'N OF LEGAL WRITING DIRECTORS & DARBY DICKERSON, ALWD CITATION MANUAL: A PROFESSIONAL SYSTEM OF CITATION (4th ed. 2010) [hereinafter ALWD CITATION MANUAL]. Many people refer to it simply as "ALWD" (pronounced ALL-wood or ALL-wid). All references to the *ALWD Citation Manual* in this chapter are to the 4th edition. A fifth edition, with a new author (Coleen M. Barger) and a new title (*ALWD Guide to Legal Citation*), will be published in early 2014. http://www.alwd.org/publications/citation-manual/.

[26] Darby Dickerson, *An Un-Uniform System of Citation: Surviving with the New* Bluebook, 26 STETSON L. REV. 53, 56–57 (1996).

[27] Darby Dickerson, *Seeing Blue: Ten Notable Changes in the New* Bluebook, 6 SCRIBES J. LEGAL WRITING 75 (1996–1997) (outlining the action taken by the Association of American Law Schools).

[28] Not surprisingly, the *Bluebook* editors restored the introductory signal rules from the 15th edition in the 17th edition, with minor changes.

[29] Steven D. Jamar, *The* ALWD Citation Manual—*A Professional System of Citation for the Law*, 8 PERSP.: TEACHING LEGAL RES. & WRITING 65, 66 (2000).

that addressed specific deficiencies while retaining those rules that functioned well,[30] and presenting it in a more pleasing, accessible format.[31] The *AWLD Citation Manual* simplified some of the *Bluebook's* rules, making them easier to find, interpret, and apply. The first edition of the *ALWD Citation Manual* was published in March 2000.

2. Organization, Format, and Features of the ALWD Citation Manual

  a. *Organization.* The *ALWD Citation Manual* is organized into seven parts.

- Part 1 contains introductory material explaining the importance and purpose of legal citation, the organization of the manual, the role of local citation rules, and instructions on how to change default settings on a word processing program so that citations are not affected.

- Part 2 (Rules 1–11), "Citation Basics," contains rules applicable to citation of all types of authority, and includes coverage of typefaces, abbreviations, spelling, capitalization, footnotes, and endnotes.

- Part 3 (Rules 12–37) discusses citation formats for primary and secondary authorities in print.

- Part 4 (Rules 38–42) sets forth the rules regarding citation formats for electronic materials.

- Part 5 (Rules 43–46) details the incorporation of citations into documents.

- Part 6 (Rules 47–49) addresses quotations.

- Part 7 is comprised of a variety of appendices that provide information on state and federal primary sources, local court citation rules, abbreviations, and federal taxation materials. This Part includes a sample of a legal memorandum that demonstrates correct usage and placement of legal citations in a document.[32]

  b. *Format.* The *ALWD Citation Manual*, at 661 pages, is longer than the *Bluebook*. Its pages are larger and easier to read, with larger type. Spacing rules are clearly illustrated by colored icons (▲). (The *Bluebook* uses a dot (·) for this purpose.) The *ALWD Citation Manual* uses color changes in the text to emphasize points and clarify distinctions, and is written in a tabular style that highlights every aspect of each rule.

  c. *Features.* A useful feature in the *ALWD Citation Manual* is the "Sidebar," which provides supplementary information on specific rules to help users avoid common problems. The *ALWD Citation Manual* also contains "Fast Formats" at the beginning of most chapters. These give examples of citation to the specific sources (e.g., cases, statutes, treatises, and legal periodicals) covered by the chapter. The Fast Formats are comparable to the *Bluebook's* Quick Reference feature inside the front and back covers.

---

[30] Darby Dickerson, *It's Time for a New Citation System*, SCRIVENER, Summer 1998, at 2. For example, authors of the ALWD CITATION MANUAL note that present word processing capabilities have removed the archaic differentiation the *Bluebook* made between law review articles and legal and court memoranda. Furthermore, they recognize there is no valid rationale to use different typeface styles for footnote text versus main text or to make distinctions between citations in textual sentences and citations in footnotes. *Id.*

[31] Suzanne E. Rowe, *The* Bluebook *Blues: AWLD Introduces a Superior Citation Reference Book for Lawyers*, OR. ST. B. BULL., June 2004, at 31.

[32] The *ALWD Manual* "provides limited guidance" for foreign and international sources, other than treaties to which the U.S. is a party. ALWD CITATION MANUAL, *supra* note 25, at 4.

Although the *ALWD Citation Manual* provides a wider range of examples of proper citation format, they are placed throughout the book; the researcher must locate the correct rule in the manual to find the appropriate example. The *Bluebook's* citation examples, while more limited in number, are more readily accessed inside the book's covers.

A website supplements the *ALWD Citation Manual* with updates to the text, frequently asked questions, any necessary clarifications, and the text's appendices.[33]

3.   Rules of the *ALWD Citation Manual*[34]

The *ALWD Citation Manual* incorporates customary forms of citation, and many commentators observe that it simplifies the rules and achieves more consistency.[35] While the citation rules in the *ALWD Citation Manual* and the *Bluebook* overlap substantially, they are not identical.[36] Among the various simplifications outlined in the *ALWD Citation Manual*, two are most noteworthy. First is the provision of one consistent body of rules for all types of legal writing, regardless of where the citation appears. This eliminates confusion and complexity when using distinct citation methods for law review footnotes, the text of law review articles, and practitioners' memoranda and briefs, as the *Bluebook* does.

The second notable simplification in the *ALWD Citation Manual* involves the elimination of the use of large and small capitals in citations.[37] There are only two type systems required in the *ALWD Citation Manual*: italics and regular type.[38]

The *ALWD Citation Manual* rules for citing cases have some minor differences from the *Bluebook*. For example, the *ALWD Citation Manual* permits, but does not require, abbreviations within case names, unlike the *Bluebook*, which requires abbreviations. Some of the abbreviations in the *ALWD Citation* Manual also deviate from the *Bluebook's* abbreviations. The *ALWD Citation Manual* requires that when a state case is cited, the citation must include available information about departments, districts, or divisions that decided the case. The *Bluebook* generally does not require this information. Another difference in case citation is that the *ALWD Citation Manual* drops the abbreviation "Ct." in parentheticals within state appellate court citations.

While the editors of the *ALWD Citation Manual* made some modifications to citation form, these modifications are relatively marginal to the basic design of legal citation. The *ALWD Citation Manual* was prepared largely as a restatement of citation,[39] and was not intended to deviate substantially from conventional form. Rather, changes were made only to promote consistency or to add flexibility on matters that do not affect the

---

[33] See website at http://www.alwd.org/publications/citation-manual/.

[34] For a learning tool to citation form, see TRACY L. MCGAUGH & CHRISTINE HURT, INTERACTIVE CITATION WORKBOOK FOR ALWD CITATION MANUAL (2011 ed.). The Center for Computer-Assisted Legal Instruction also provides interactive computer-based programs in using the *ALWD Citation Manual* at http://www.cali.org.

[35] Andrea Kaufman, *Uncomplicating the Citation Process*, 87 ILL. B.J. 675, 675 (1999) (book review).

[36] Section C of this chapter provides a comparison of selected *ALWD Citation Manual* (4th edition) and the *Bluebook* (19th edition) rules.

[37] The *Bluebook* uses large and small capitals in its rules for law reviews, but notes that some law reviews replace them with ordinary roman type. BLUEBOOK R. 2.1, at 62. Even one of the four journals that produce the *Bluebook*—the *Columbia Law Review*—uses ordinary roman instead of large and small capitals.

[38] Underlining may be substituted for italics under either manual's rules.

[39] Darby Dickerson, *Professionalizing Legal Citation: The* ALWD Citation Manual, FED. LAW., Nov./Dec. 2000, at 20, 22.

reader's ability to locate or interpret the cited material. Most practitioners and judges are unlikely to notice whether the *ALWD Citation Manual* or the *Bluebook* was used to prepare a specific citation or document.[40]

A chart comparing citations in *Bluebook* format and *ALWD* format is available on ALWD's website.[41]

4.   The Future of the *ALWD Citation Manual*

Although other competitors to the *Bluebook* have failed to gain wide acceptance, the *ALWD Citation Manual* may have had the best chance to do so at its outset. The *ALWD Citation Manual* was produced by a national organization with members in almost every law school, many of whom had input into the manual's drafting. The *ALWD Citation Manual* was widely known as soon as it was published. Further, the ALWD manual did not radically depart from the *Bluebook's* rules, and was designed as much as a teaching tool as a citation manual. The *ALWD Citation Manual* was integrated into many first year law school writing curricula when the text was first published.

However, the editors of the *Bluebook* made improvements beginning with the 18th edition that responded to many of the criticisms leveled against it. It remains the standard legal citation authority. The *ALWD Citation Manual* has declined in popularity and is now required at a minority of law schools.[42] Most jurisdictions do not specify either the *Bluebook* or the *ALWD Citation Manual*.[43]

C.   CITATION TO ELECTRONIC RESOURCES

The *Bluebook* and the *ALWD Citation Manual* continue a preference for citation to print sources and generally require print whenever possible.[44]

---

[40] Jennifer L. Cordle, ALWD Citation Manual: *A Grammar Guide to the Language of Legal Citation*, 26 U. ARK. LITTLE ROCK. L. REV. 573 (2004).

[41] http://www.alwd.org/publications/comparison-chart/.

[42] *Compare* ASS'N OF LEGAL WRITING DIRS. & LEGAL WRITING INST., REPORT OF THE ANNUAL LEGAL WRITING SURVEY 18 (2013), *available at* http://www.alwd.org/wp-content/uploads/2013/08/2013–Survey–Report-final.pdf (reporting that 140, or 74%, of respondent legal writing programs planned to teach only the *Bluebook* in 2013–2014) *with* ASS'N OF LEGAL WRITING DIRS. & LEGAL WRITING INST., 2004 SURVEY RESULTS 14, *available at* http://www.alwd.org/wp-content/uploads/2013/02/2004–survey-results.pdf (reporting that 89 programs planned to teach only the *Bluebook* in 2003–04).

[43] For example, the rules of the U.S. Supreme Court set forth requirements for nearly every aspect of documents submitted to the Court, from size of paper used to font size for footnotes, yet do not articulate a requirement for citation form. According to ALWD, the jurisdictions that have officially adopted the *Bluebook* are the U.S. Court of Appeals for the Eleventh Circuit, U.S. Court of Appeals for the Armed Services, U.S. District Court for the District of Delaware, U.S. District Court for the District of Montana, U.S. Bankruptcy Court for the District of Montana, and the state courts of Alabama, California, Delaware, Florida, Idaho, Indiana, New Mexico, North Carolina, Texas, Washington, and Wisconsin. Most jurisdictions do not specify which citation form to follow. Of the sixteen court systems that have adopted the *Bluebook* as an acceptable citation guide, five also accept the *ALWD Citation Manual*. According to ALWD, these jurisdictions are the U.S. Court of Appeals for the Eleventh Circuit, U.S. District Court for the District of Montana, U.S. Bankruptcy Court for the District of Montana, and the state courts of Alabama and Idaho. *See* ALWD CITATION MANUAL, app. 2.

[44] *Bluebook* Rule 18.2 instructs that traditional print sources are required when available, unless there is a digital copy of the source available that is authenticated, official, or an exact copy of the print source, such as provided by a document in .pdf format. In this case, citation can be made as if to the original print source, without any URL information appended. One author speculates that citing to commercial databases may make retrieval onerous for some judges who may be unskilled in their use. DEBORAH E. BOUCHOUX, CITE-CHECKER: YOUR GUIDE TO USING THE BLUEBOOK 68 (3d ed. 2011).

1. Citation to *Westlaw* and *LexisNexis*

LexisNexis and *Westlaw* databases (and many other online services) may include documents, most notably cases, which are not available in print or in other sources. Typically, the services assign their own unique identifiers to such documents as soon as they are posted.[45] Writers who use either the *Bluebook* or the *ALWD Citation Manual* may cite to documents using these unique identifiers, as specified for different types of publications in the respective manuals. Further, researchers may add an electronic source as either a parallel citation (*Bluebook* Rule 18.2.3) or a parenthetical (*ALWD Citation Manual* Rule 12.12) if it will provide easier access to the information.

2. Citation to Information on the Internet

The *Bluebook* and the *ALWD Citation Manual* recognize that electronic information from a variety of sources will be cited in legal writing, including that available on the freely accessible Internet. Both style manuals have specific rules for citing to Internet sources. The *Bluebook* (Rule 18.2) provides that, when a source does not exist in a traditional print format or the print source cannot be located or is so obscure that it is practically unavailable, direct citation to the Internet is allowed without an explanatory phrase. When a source is available in a print but increased accessibility to the source will be provided by parallel citation to its Internet location, the citation must include the explanatory phrase "*available at*" before the URL. The ALWD manual covers general citation to information on the Internet (Rule 40), with specific instructions for case citations (Rule 12.15).

D. NEUTRAL CITATION

Courts, legislatures, and government officials and agencies, at all levels of government and in all jurisdictions, are changing their publication practices to accommodate both print and electronic publication of legal materials. Major companies continue to produce subscription databases like *Westlaw*, *LexisNexis*, and *Bloomberg Law* but increasing numbers of providers—government, for-profit, and nonprofit—also post legal information online. Governmental entities are releasing legal publications directly to the public, sometimes retaining a corresponding print publication and sometimes eliminating the print and offering the electronic version only; these electronic publications are increasingly being designated as official, making them a preferred (or required) source for legal citation. No longer do the traditional publishers control the legal information market. Legal documents available in only one format or from only one vendor are becoming rare. But multiple sources of the same legal material have led to a citation quandary: how should electronic sources available from a variety of vendors or institutions be properly cited?

Traditional citation rules, with their strong print preference, seemed to hamper the use of electronic resources in legal research and writing. By the end of the twentieth century, the rules for citing primary sources in electronic formats had not kept pace with the greatly enhanced access to online legal materials. In response, the American Association of Law Libraries (AALL) and the American Bar Association (ABA) each

---

[45] The *Bluebook* offers examples citing cases available in *LexisNexis*, *Westlaw*, *Bloomberg Law*, and *Loislaw*. *See* BLUEBOOK R. 18.3.1, at 171; *see also* R. B4.1.4, at 11 (*LexisNexis* and *Westlaw*) only.

developed a system of "neutral" citation style, aimed at adapting legal citation rules to the changing publication world.[46]

Neutral citation[47] refers to a citation that is medium neutral (that it, it is applicable to print or electronic formats) and vendor neutral (meaning that the citation does not require vendor-specific information such as the title of a case reporter). Citation to a specific case or statute, for example, would be identical whether the researcher located the document in print, in *Westlaw* or *LexisNexis* or some other subscription database, or on the Internet. Citations are assigned by the court, legislature, or other governmental entity that created the document, and are immediately available when the document is released. An effective neutral citation system for legal materials facilitates precise, pinpoint citations to material, regardless of format.

Proponents of neutral citation systems encourage citation to an electronic version of a source, regardless of the availability of the information in print. Nineteen state court systems have adopted some form of neutral citation.[48] The pace of reform has been slow,[49] despite no reports that the switch to neutral citation has proven costly or burdensome to attorneys or the government.[50]

---

[46] AALL published the first edition of its UNIVERSAL CITATION GUIDE (*UCG*) in 1999, with rules that covered cases, statutes, constitutions, and administrative regulations. CITATION FORMATS COMM., AM. ASS'N OF LAW LIBRARIES, UNIVERSAL CITATION GUIDE (1999). The second edition was published in 2004, providing formats for law reviews, court rules, and administrative decisions. CITATION FORMATS COMM., AM. ASS'N OF LAW LIBRARIES, UNIVERSAL CITATION GUIDE (2d ed. 2004). A third edition is expected in mid-2014. *See also* SPECIAL COMMITTEE ON CITATION ISSUES, AM. BAR ASS'N, REPORT AND RECOMMENDATION (May 23, 1996) (approved by the ABA House of Delegates on Aug. 6, 1996). In February 2003, the ABA House of Delegates passed the Universal Citation Facilitation resolution reaffirming its commitment to universal citation.

[47] Some other terms used to refer to the concept of neutral citation include medium-neutral, universal citation form, and public domain citation form

[48] The states which have adopted some version of neutral citation are Arizona, Arkansas, Colorado, Florida, Illinois, Louisiana, Maine, Mississippi, Montana, New Mexico, North Dakota, Ohio, Oklahoma, Pennsylvania, South Dakota, Utah, Vermont, Wisconsin, and Wyoming. Other U.S. jurisdictions with neutral citation rules include Puerto Rico, the United States Court of Appeals for the Sixth Circuit, and federal district courts in South Dakota and New Hampshire. For additional discussion, see Michael Umberger, *Checking up on Court Citation Standards: How Neutral Citation Improves Public Access to Case Law*, 31 LEGAL REFERENCE SERVICES Q. 312 (2012); Ian Gallacher, *Cite Unseen: How Neutral Citation and America's Law Schools Can Cure Our Strange Devotion to Bibliographical Orthodoxy and the Constriction of Open and Equal Access to the Law*, 70 ALB. L. REV. 491, 528 (2007); Peter W. Martin, *Neutral Citation, Court Web Sites, and Access to Authoritative Case Law*, 99 LAW LIBR. J. 329, 348 (2007); AM. ASS'N OF LAW LIBRARIES, VENDOR-NEUTRAL CITATION RULES ADOPTED BY AMERICAN JURISDICTIONS, http://www.aallnet.org/main-menu/Advocacy/access/citation/neutralrules (links to rules for states adopting vendor-neutral citation rules as of December 2007).

[49] An advocacy group favoring universal citation came together with a conference in 2011. *See* http://UniversalCitation.org. A recent white paper reaffirms AALL's strong support for universal citation in regards to court opinions, and encourages adoption by courts throughout the country. Carol Billings et al., *Universal Citation and the American Association of Law Libraries: A White Paper*, 103 LAW LIBR. J. 331 (2011). Neutral citation also has support from several online providers of legal information, including the *Legal Information Institute*, *Justia*, and *Fastcase*. *See, e.g.*, Courtney Minick, *Universal Citation for State Codes*, VOXPOPULII (Sept. 1, 2011, 7:51 AM), http://blog.law.cornell.edu/voxpop/2011/09/01/universal-citation-for-state-codes/.

[50] The Conference of Chief Justices report notes that those court systems that are adding sequential opinion numbers or paragraph numbers state that no additional costs are associated with this process. CONFERENCE OF CHIEF JUSTICES, REPORT OF THE COMMITTEE ON OPINIONS CITATION (National Center for State Courts 1999), http://ccj.ncsc.org/~/media/microsites/files/ccj/web%20documents/reportofthecommitteeonopinionscitations.ashx.

The basic citation form for neutral citation of court opinions, according to both the *Bluebook*[51] and the *ALWD Citation Manual*,[52] has the following components: case name, year of decision, the state's two-character postal code, the court abbreviation (unless it is the state's highest court), and the sequential number of the decision. (The *Bluebook* also requires the addition of a "U" at the end of the number if the decision is unpublished.) There is much variation among adopting states concerning spacing and punctuation in neutral citations, so writers of legal documents must follow any local rules.

---

[51] The *Bluebook's* coverage of public domain citation, the term it uses for neutral citation, is in Rule 10.3.3.

[52] The *ALWD Citation Manual* covers neutral citation in Rule 12.16. Appendix 2 can assist in determining whether a particular court requires neutral citation.

Chapter 25

NATIVE AMERICAN TRIBAL LAW*

This chapter discusses research on the law of American Indian tribes. Tribal law defines the governance of tribes themselves and is distinct from the subject known as American Indian law,[1] which deals with the legal relationship between tribes and the United States federal system.[2]

Native American tribes are sovereign entities that self-govern and have the power to legislate, regulate, police, and adjudicate. Because each tribe is an autonomous governmental unit, tribal law is unique to each Indian nation. As with other governments, tribal governments generally enjoy sovereign immunity.

The primary law of tribes may include treaties or agreements with the United States government, constitutions, codes, statutes and ordinances, compacts, administrative rules and regulations, and court decisions. Tribes also may adhere to orally transmitted, non-written, customary law.

A. IDENTIFYING TRIBES AND TRIBAL OFFICIALS

Native American political groups claim an inherent right of self-government that predates the formation of the United States government. Under federal law this sovereignty is acknowledged, with evolving legal limitations, through the establishment of a government-to-government relationship between the United States and the Native American political entity.

Federal recognition of this relationship is today extended to more than 566 historically distinct Indian tribes, bands, Pueblos, or Alaska native villages that exercise governmental authority.

Tribes may exist outside the umbrella of federal recognition, but the first tribal law research question is whether a tribe has been acknowledged as standing in a government-to-government relationship with the United States. Researchers must be aware that during various phases of federal Indian policy, the government-to-government relationship between some tribes and the federal government was unilaterally terminated by congressional mandate. When policy again changed, recognition for most of these tribes was "restored" or "reaffirmed." These terms may be encountered when conducting tribal research and a tribe's legal and jurisdictional history may be affected by gaps in recognition or a past period of termination.

---

* This chapter was written by Nancy Carol Carter, Professor of Law (retired), University of San Diego.

[1] The terms "American Indian" and "Native American" are used interchangeably in this chapter.

[2] For guidance on researching Indian law, see DAVID SELDEN & MONICA MARTENS, BASIC INDIAN LAW RESEARCH TIPS—PART I: FEDERAL INDIAN LAW, http://www.narf.org/nill/bulletins/lawreviews/articles/colorado LawyerArticle-fed.pdf (2008); GALLAGHER LAW LIBRARY, UNIV. OF WASH. SCH. OF LAW, INDIAN & TRIBAL LAW RESEARCH, https://lib.law.washington.edu/content/guides/indian (last updated Jan. 14, 2014); M. Christian Clark, *Analytical Research Guide to Federal Indian Tax Law*, 105 LAW LIBR. J. 505 (2013).

1. Federal Acknowledgement Process

Federal recognition, or acknowledgement, is a watershed legal determination affecting rights, immunities, privileges, and obligations and the tribes' ability to function as a government within the federal system. Services delivered by the Bureau of Indian Affairs (BIA) and other federal agencies, as well as limitations on the reach of state governments into tribal affairs, are conditioned upon federal recognition.

Historically, tribes were recognized on an ad hoc basis through BIA determinations, special acts of Congress, federal court decisions, or executive actions. Under a 1994 law, tribes may be recognized by act of Congress, a decision of a United States court, or through the BIA administrative process.

In 1978, a new administrative process, the Federal Acknowledgment Project, was created to streamline and regularize the handling of petitions for recognition sent to the BIA. Mandatory criteria for federal recognition were enumerated. Despite these reforms and subsequent efforts to speed up the evaluations, there is a surfeit of unprocessed petitions for tribal recognition and continuing dissatisfaction with an acknowledgement process that can take from two to ten or more years (and in one instance more than two decades). The work is slowed by meager staffing and the extensive historical, genealogical, and anthropological research required to properly evaluate petitions. The Government Accountability Office issued a 2005 report on the timeliness of the tribal recognition process,[3] finding that the process had improved but predicting that it would take years to clear the backlog of petitions.

Title 25 of the *Code of Federal Regulations* is dedicated to Indian matters, and Part 83 establishes the current Bureau of Indian Affairs "Procedures for Establishing that an American Indian Group Exists as a Tribe."[4] Revisions in the procedures have added specificity to the administrative rules, particularly in regard to the mandatory criteria for acknowledgement and establishing processing deadlines. Tribes seeking acknowledgement must show (1) identification as an American Indian entity on a substantially continuous basis since 1900; (2) a predominant portion of the petitioning group comprises a distinct community that has existed from historical times to the present; (3) the petitioner has maintained political influence or authority over its members as an autonomous entity from historical times; (4) copies of the group's governing document and membership criteria or a statement describing governance and membership; (5) evidence that the petitioner's membership descended from a historical Indian tribe or combined tribes that functioned as a single autonomous political entity; (6) that the membership of the petitioning group are not members of an acknowledged North American Indian tribe; and (7) the petitioner and its members are not subject to congressional legislation expressly terminating or forbidding a relationship with the federal government.[5]

---

[3] U.S. GOV'T ACCOUNTABILITY OFFICE, GAO-05-347T, INDIAN ISSUES: TIMELINESS OF THE TRIBAL RECOGNITION PROCESS HAS IMPROVED, BUT IT WILL TAKE YEARS TO CLEAR THE EXISTING BACKLOG OF PETITIONS (2005).

[4] 25 C.F.R. Part 83 was substantially revised in 1994. The Department of the Interior adopted new internal procedures in 2000. 65 Fed. Reg. 7052 (Feb. 11, 2000).

[5] 25 C.F.R. § 83.7 (2013).

2.   Petitions for Tribal Acknowledgement

The Bureau of Indian Affairs, Office of Federal Acknowledgement[6] website [Illustration 25–1] provides links to the *Code of Federal Regulations* procedures for petitioning for recognition, sample forms, lists of petitioners by state, and the very valuable "Status Summary of Acknowledgement Cases." The site links to the list of recognized tribes.

3.   Identifying Recognized Tribes

Indian Entities Recognized and Eligible to Receive Services From the United States Bureau of Indian Affairs[7] [Illustration 25–2] is the definitive listing of tribes acknowledged to be standing in a government-to-government relationship with the United States.

The Bureau of Indian Affairs did not begin publishing lists of recognized tribes until the 1970s, and then the updates were irregular. The agency is now mandated by Congress[8] to publish an annual list in the *Federal Register*.

Tribes are listed alphabetically by the name of the tribe, with Alaska Native villages in a separate alphabetical listing. The 1993 publication of the list[9] was accompanied by an informative text that explained problems with earlier lists and gave information on the inclusion of Alaska Native villages. Several tribes have changed their names in recent years. The BIA lists the former name of the tribe along with the new name to aid in identification, but after a few years, the older name is deleted.

Many websites reproduce the official BIA list of recognized tribes, but may not post the most current version. The National Congress of the American Indian[10] and the Tribal Law and Policy Institute[11] are reliable. The *500 Nations* website has a listing of tribes by state showing which tribes are federally recognized and which are not.[12]

4.   Guides to Tribal Traditions, Governments, and Officials

A number of general encyclopedias, guides, and directories provide information about the tribal traditions that help to shape Native American governments and justice systems and to locate tribal government offices, courts, and tribal officials.

a.   Encyclopedia of Native American Legal Tradition (Bruce Elliott Johansen ed., 1998) (Greenwood Press). This collection has entries of varying length and depth covering major Indian law cases and federal laws, along with profiles of leaders and institutions. It is included here for the entries shedding light on underlying traditions that affect choices about tribal governmental structure and justice systems, such as "Harmony Ethic, Cherokee" and "Upland Yuman Political and Legal Traditions."

---

[6] http://www.bia.gov/WhoWeAre/AS-IA/OFA/.

[7] 79 Fed. Reg. 4748 (January 29, 2014). The current list is also linked from the Bureau of Indian Affairs website at http://www.bia.gov/DocumentLibrary/index.htm.

[8] Pub. L. No. 103–454, 108 Stat. 4791 (1994) (codified at 25 U.S.C. § 479a (2006)).

[9] 58 Fed. Reg. 54,364 (Oct. 21, 1993).

[10] http://www.ncai.org/tribal-directory.

[11] http://www.tribal-institute.org/lists/nations.htm.

[12] http://500nations.com/tribes/Tribes_State-by-State.asp.

b. *Federally Recognized Indian Tribes.*[13] The National Congress of American Indians website lists tribes by BIA service areas and alphabetically. Each listing includes the executive officer, basic contact information, and links to tribal websites, when available. Entries also indicate whether a tribe is federally or state recognized.

c. *Gale Encyclopedia of Native American Tribes* (Laurie Edwards ed., 3d ed. 2012) (available as an e-book). This is a general information source for the cultural and historical background of eighty tribes within the United States and Canada. Legal and governmental commentary finds its way into the "current tribal issues" discussion. Each of the five volumes covers a different geographical region.

d. *Tribal Leaders Directory.*[14] This excellent list from the BIA is more current than most other sources. It lists tribal information by the BIA regional service area in which the tribe is located. Each entry includes the tribal name, executive officer, address, telephone and fax numbers, and email and website addresses (when available). The entries are indexed by the state in which the tribe is located and alphabetically by the name of the tribe. Tribal names may not appear in the alphabetical list as normally written. For example, Arctic Village Council appears under the letter "V," while Confederated Tribes of the Umatilla Indian Reservation appears under "U," [Illustration 25–3] and Native Village of Stevens is in the "S" listings.

e. *Tribal Court Directory.*[15] A service of the Tribal Law and Policy Institute's Tribal Court Clearinghouse, this is an online alphabetical list of tribal web links. While the links go directly to the tribe's court page, once directed to the website one can navigate to other tribal information such as history and traditions, government organization, leadership, contact information, business enterprises, and schools and services.

f. *United States Tribal Courts Directory*, by April Schwartz and Mary Jo B. Hunter (4th ed. 2011) (earlier editions available in *HeinOnline*). Tribal court contact information is organized by state, with added background information for some listings.

5. State Recognition of Indian Tribes

The United States Constitution makes Indian affairs an exclusive province of the federal government, but about forty percent of states offer some form of recognition to tribes, increasingly with a formalized recognition process. State recognition may be sought by tribes petitioning for federal acknowledgement or by tribes that have been denied or not attempted the federal process. State recognition is accomplished by legislative act, administrative process, or gubernatorial action. The legal consequence of state tribal recognition generally is minimal, but it is argued that recognition facilitates a mutually beneficial interaction between tribal and state governments and represents an important exercise of federalism.[16]

---

[13] National Congress of American Indians, http://www.ncai.org/tribal-directory.

[14] It is updated twice a year. The current copy is posted at http://www.bia.gov/WhoWeAre/BIA/OIS/Tribal GovernmentServices/TribalDirectory/index.htm.

[15] http://www.tribal-institute.org/lists/justice.htm.

[16] For types of state recognition, criteria employed, lists of state-recognized tribes, and an argument in favor of increased state recognition, see Alexa Koenig, *Federalism and the State Recognition of Native American Tribes: A Survey of State-Recognized Tribes and State Recognition Processes Across the United States*, 48 SANTA CLARA L. REV. 79 (2007).

The website of the National Congress of the American Indian includes a list of state-recognized tribes under the "Tribal Directory" tab.[17] Another listing by state, with tribal contact information, is found on the *500 Nations* website.[18]

B. PRIMARY SOURCES OF TRIBAL LAW

The primary sources of a tribe's law are similar to those of a state, but also may include treaties and agreements between the tribe and the federal government, executive orders specific to the tribe, and unique intergovernmental agreements, such as the tribal-state compacts required by the Indian Gaming Regulatory Act.[19]

1. Tribal Constitutions and Laws

Researching tribal law was once extremely difficult, but access to tribal constitutions, codes, and ordinances has dramatically improved in the Internet age. Tribal governments are not required to make tribal legal information available to the public at large. However, with economic development, particularly gaming on reservations, tribes find it advantageous to update their laws and make them transparent. The Navajo Nation was one of the first tribes to publish and sell a tribal code.[20] Only a handful of other tribes[21] publish a hard copy of their primary law, while a few tribes continue to closely hold their legal information.

An emergent model tribal code movement speaks to the growing complexity of tribal legal issues and law-making. The National Indian Justice Center is the source of several model codes. Tribal legislators can find model codes for business, commerce, juvenile justice, sex offenders, solid waste management, and other topics.

a.   Tribal Law Gateway.[22] Through its Access to Tribal Law Project, the National Indian Law Library (NILL) at the Native American Rights Fund [Illustration 25–4] has accumulated the largest collection of tribal codes and constitutions in the United States. More than 315 tribes have added their codes and constitutions to the collection. Many of the full-text documents are available online. The *Tribal Law Gateway: Codes* provides information and links to tribal codes and constitutions held by NILL and available online. Additionally, NILL may be contacted by any researcher seeking tribal documents.

b.   Tribal Laws and Codes.[23] This site, part of the Tribal Court Clearinghouse: A Project of the Tribal Law and Policy Institute, combines various sources for long lists of links to tribal laws and codes. Preceding these lists, there are links to tribal court practice and law enforcement materials under the heading "Tribal Legal Code Resource Series."

---

[17] http://www.ncai.org/tribal-directory.

[18] http://500nations.com/tribes/Tribes_States.asp.

[19] Pub. L. No. 100–497, 102 Stat. 2467 (1988) (codified at 25 U.S.C. §§ 2701–2721 (2012)).

[20] Currently available as *Navajo Nation Code Annotated*, vols. 1–4 (Thomson/West 2005, supplemented through 2009). This is in *Westlaw* (NAVAJO-TC), but is not included in most academic contracts.

[21] The Cherokee Nation, Jicarilla Apache Nation, and Mille Lacs Band are among those that publish a code.

[22] http://www.narf.org/nill/.

[23] http://www.tribal-institute.org.

c.   The Native American Constitution and Law Digitization Project.[24] This straightforward website, a project of the University of Oklahoma Law Library in cooperation with the National Indian Law Library, links to tribal codes, constitutions, and various other primary and secondary sources of Indian law. Original Indian Reorganization Era documents, including tribal corporate charters from the 1930s and 1940s are linked.[25]

d.   HeinOnline's American Indian Law Collection. This collection, released in October 2011, now has more than 900 unique titles and more than 900,000 pages dedicated to American Indian Law. It includes the Indian Reorganization Era tribal charters and constitutions from the 1930s and 1940s.

e.   Library of Congress American Indian Constitutions and Legal Materials.[26] This online collection includes many tribal constitutions and codes from the 1930s and 1940s as well as a variety of materials—mostly for tribes in the southern United States—from the nineteenth century.

2.   Treaties and Agreements

Treaty-making with Native American tribes extends back to the earliest colonial presence on this continent. The United States entered into treaties with tribes until 1871, when Congress ended the practice. Subsequently, tribes and the federal government negotiated "agreements." Treaties and agreements are a source of primary law for the tribes involved. Many documentary and online collections include treaties, but the following are the most authoritative sources.

a.   United States Statutes at Large, 1789–present; volumes 1 through 18 are online as part of the American Memory project.[27] This is the official source of Indian treaty texts. All the relevant volumes for this research are digitized. Volume 7 is a compilation of Indian treaties entered into from 1778 through 1845. The treaties are in chronological order and are indexed by tribal name. After volumes 7 and 8 (the first compilations of Indian and non-Indian treaties), texts of treaties were regularly published in a separate section at the back of each *Statutes* volume. Indian treaties are intermingled with all others. They are indexed within each volume by tribal name and also listed under the index headings "Indian Affairs," "Indian Treaties," or "Indian Department." Volume 16 of the *Statutes* carries the last substantial number of Indian treaties, although stray treaty texts show up in later volumes, as they were found and published.

b.   Indian Affairs. Laws and Treaties, vols. 1–5, edited by Charles J. Kappler and published by the Government Printing Office, 1904–1941,[28] and *Kappler's Indian Affairs: Laws and Treaties,* compiled by the U.S. Department of the Interior and numbered as vols. 6–7 (published by G.P.O. in 1979). The five original and two supplementary volumes have been fully digitized by Oklahoma State University

---

[24] http://thorpe.ou.edu.

[25] The documents from the 1930s and 1940s are also available from other sources including *LexisNexis* and the Library of Congress's *American Indian Constitutions and Legal Materials* digital collection, http://www.loc.gov/law/help/american-indian-consts/us-ne-atlantic.php.

[26] http://memory.loc.gov/ammem/amlaw/lwsllink.html.

[27] http://memory.loc.gov/ammem/amlaw/wsl.html.

[28] The original five *Kappler* volumes also were issued as part of the *United States Congressional Serial Set* as numbers: 4623 and 4624 (first edition of vols. 1–2), 4253 and 4254 (second edition of vols. 1–2), 6166 (vol. 3), 8849 (vol. 4), and 10458 (vol. 5).

Library.[29] They are also available in *HeinOnline*, *LexisNexis*, and *LLMC Digital*. This classic work offers a chronologically arranged compilation of treaties, statutes, executive actions, and miscellaneous information on Indian affairs from 1778 through 1938. All volumes have extensive tables of contents and indexes. Volume 1 has a turn-of-the-century listing of over 275 tribes and bands. Volume 2 is the best available compilation of Indian treaties and has been separately reprinted.[30] The index to volume 2 doubles as a guide to the name and number of treaties signed by various tribes [Illustration 25–5], although the careful researcher must note that *Kappler* did not separate out individual tribal names from confederated groups. Volumes 3 through 5 update the first two volumes, including a few additional treaties. Throughout the set, the texts of unratified treaties are included. Numerous miscellaneous inclusions increase the usefulness of the *Kappler* set, including population figures and tribal finances. Contents pages list the special features of each volume.

The two supplemental volumes compiled by the Department of the Interior provide a thirty-year update to *Kappler's* original work, extending coverage through 1970. Unlike the original, the update does not claim to be comprehensive in coverage. It includes statutes, administrative provisions, and orders and presidential proclamations relating specifically to Indians. Volume 7 has Tables of Statutes Affected that list amendments, repeals, and other changes dating back to *Kappler's* original collection of statutes through 1970. Treaty research can be updated by using the list of appropriations bills in fulfillment of treaty obligations. The second volume has a detailed index.

c.   *Documents of American Indian Diplomacy: Treaties, Agreements, and Conventions, 1775–1979* (Vine Deloria, Jr. & Raymond J. DeMallie eds., 1999) (Oklahoma University Press). A comprehensive two-volume collection of Indian diplomatic documents that includes all identified treaty texts, whether ratified or currently in force, and the infamously "lost" treaties of California. Treaties concluded with Indian tribes by the Republic of Texas and the Confederate States of America are included, along with agreements between and among tribes. Treaties are listed chronologically. The two oversized volumes are continuously paged, with an index at the end of the second volume.

d.   *Early American Indian Documents: Treaties and Laws, 1607–1789* (Alden T. Vaughan gen. ed., 1979–2004) (Univ. Pubs. of America). This scholarly, multivolume series aims to comprehensively collect documents and treaties from the first 200 years of colonial life in what is now the United States. It includes treaties not found in *Kappler*. With the first entries of a 1629 deed and a 1654 treaty between Swedes and Indians in the Pennsylvania area, the researcher is alerted to the rarity of the inclusions. This source may be used to trace the earliest tribal legal dealings.

3.   Presidential Proclamations and Executive Orders

Presidential proclamations and executive orders are potential sources of primary tribal law because almost every U.S. president has been a powerful maker of Indian law and policy. Numerous tribal statutes and policies are based on presidential actions; it is not unusual for those researching tribal law issues to find themselves working with these documents. After 1871, when Congress ended treaty-making with Indian tribes,

---

[29] http://digital.library.okstate.edu/Kappler/.

[30] *Indian Treaties 1778–1883* (1972) (Interland Pub.).

executive agreements and presidential decrees affected the disposition of millions of acres of Indian land. Proclamations and orders may speak to legal issues involving reservation land, original and modified reservation boundaries, the reserved rights of tribes on a reservation, and the jurisdictional powers of a state over aspects of Indian life on a reservation. Research into early executive orders and proclamations can be complicated by the lack of a consistent numbering scheme and scattered publication. Since 1936, newly issued proclamations and orders have been consistently published in the *Federal Register* and collected in Title 3 of the *Code of Federal Regulations*. The more recent digitization of sources, including the *CIS Index to Presidential Executive Orders and Proclamations,* resolve many problems of locating these presidential papers.[31]

4. Intergovernmental Agreements

Tribes may add to their base of primary law by entering into agreements or compacts with states, counties, or other political entities. Intergovernmental agreements may speak to taxation, education, water, law enforcement, gaming, or many other subjects. Locating such agreements for research purposes can be very difficult, unless one of the parties is required to provide public notice of the terms. While once impossible to find, gaming compacts now can be found on the website of the National Indian Gaming Commission.[32] In addition, some states, counties, and tribes also post gaming compacts online.[33] New or amended gaming compacts do not take effect until the notice of their approval is published in the *Federal Register*, as required by the tribal-state gaming compact process.[34] The National Indian Law Library, the National Congress of American Indians, and the Tribal Court Clearinghouse have selected intergovernmental agreements posted on their websites.

5. Tribal Courts

a. Structure of Tribal Courts. The traditional justice systems of most Native American tribes were shattered or radically altered by the changing circumstances of colonization. The process of rebuilding tribal justice systems is still evolving, as some tribes amalgamate traditional dispute resolution and restorative peacemaker practices with the mainstream court systems established on reservations by the Bureau of Indian Affairs.[35]

About 330 tribal courts were operating across the United States in 2010.[36] These courts are of three types: (1) Courts of Indian Offenses, which were established in the nineteenth century and originally staffed by the BIA when reservation law and order became a concern (also called "CFR courts" because their authority and operational rules are specified by the Bureau of Indian Affairs in the *Code of Federal Regulations*);[37] (2) traditional courts applying customary law and often relying on oral traditions; and (3)

---

[31] Presidential sources are discussed in Chapter 13.

[32] http://www.nigc.gov/Reading_Room/Compacts.aspx.

[33] *See, e.g.,* https://gaming.az.gov/law-compacts/tribal-state-compacts (Arizona); http://www.cgcc.ca.gov/?pageID=compacts (California); https://www.sni.org/government/nys-gaming-compact/ (Seneca Nation).

[34] 25 C.F.R. § 293.15 (2013).

[35] *See, e.g.,* Gloria Valencia-Weber, *Tribal Courts: Custom and Innovative Law*, 24 N.M. L. REV. 225 (1994); Angela R. Riley, *Good (Native) Governance*, 107 COLUM. L. REV. 1049 (2007).

[36] KIMBERLY A. COBB & TRACEY G. MULLINS, BUREAU OF JUSTICE ASSISTANCE, TRIBAL PROBATION: AN OVERVIEW FOR TRIBAL COURT JUDGES 3 (2010).

[37] Tribes with a Court of Indian Offenses are listed at 25 C.F.R. § 11.100 (2013).

tribal courts established after the Indian Reorganization Act of 1934,[38] which encouraged tribes to strengthen self-government by adopting written constitutions and codes of law and reframing tribal governments on the United States model of legislative, executive, and judicial branches.

Tribal courts organized after 1934 are the most common type. These courts function very similarly to municipal or state courts, but with federally imposed jurisdictional limitations[39] and power restrictions. For example, until very recently, tribal courts were not allowed to impose a sentence longer than one year. Congress approved a transformative expansion of tribal court powers in the Tribal Law and Order Act of 2010.[40] This law aims to enhance tribal abilities to reduce crime rates by enlarging the powers of tribal courts in criminal matters.[41] Tribal courts are empowered to try felony crimes and to impose sentences of up to three years. To assume these new powers, a tribal court will have to meet certain standards of training and guarantee counsel for indigent defendants.[42]

Special offices in the Department of the Interior[43] and the Department of Justice[44] work with tribal governments to strengthen their courts and are sources of information on Indian country justice. In the 1970s, federal funding was stepped up for facilities and equipment, training of judges and support personnel, and other institution building. In recent years, gaming revenue has given some tribes the means to further enhance and professionalize their tribal courts. Tribal court judges and advocates may be legally trained or laypersons. Tribes establish individual rules about who is authorized to appear in their tribal court.

b.   Tribal Court Decisions. Tribal court orders and opinions are flowing at a more rapid rate than at any time in the past, and more of this tribal court output is being published. A few tribes issue their own court reports, including the *Mvskoke Law Reporter: The Decisions of the Muscogee (Creek) Nation* and *West's Mashantucket Pequot Reporter.* While these dedicated reporters have the advantage of providing more of an

---

[38] Pub. L. No. 73–383, 48 Stat. 984 (codified as 25 U.S.C. § 479 (2006)).

[39] The Major Crimes Act of 1885 (18 U.S.C. § 1153 (2012)) granted federal courts exclusive jurisdiction over certain crimes on Indian land. The criminal jurisdiction of tribal courts was circumscribed by a Supreme Court decision. Tribal court jurisdiction reaches only crimes committed by tribal members residing on the reservation or doing business there. Oliphant v. Suquamish Tribe, 435 U.S. 191 (1978). Tribal courts have broader civil jurisdiction (generally over Indians and non-Indians who reside on the reservation or do business there).

[40] Pub. L. No. 111–211, tit. II, 124 Stat. 2258, 2261 (2010) (codified in scattered sections of 25 U.S.C.).

[41] Under prior law, felony charges were referred to federal prosecutors who were thought to be bringing only about fifty percent of the cases to court. Reservations with high crime rates have long been frustrated by the lack of deterrence in the system. The National Congress of American Indians editorialized that the Tribal Law and Order Act of 2010 will help tribes curb violence against women on reservations and bring down a high crime rate. "President Obama Signs Historic Tribal Law & Order Act Into Law," http://www.ncai.org/news/articles/2010/07/29/president-obama-signs-historic-tribal-law-order-act-into-law.

[42] The Tribal Law and Order Act created the Indian Law and Order Commission (http://www.aisc.ucla.edu/iloc/), an independent advisory group, *See* INDIAN LAW & ORDER COMM'N, A ROADMAP TO MAKING NATIVE AMERICA SAFER: REPORT TO THE PRESIDENT & CONGRESS OF THE UNITED STATES (2013), *available at* http://www.aisc.ucla.edu/iloc/report/index.html.

[43] The Bureau of Indian Affairs provides an Office of Justice Services that works to build and enhance justice systems in Indian country, http://www.bia.gov/WhoWeAre/BIA/OJS/index.htm. There is also a Division of Tribal Government Services, http://www.bia.gov/WhatWeDo/ServiceOverview/TribalGov/index.htm.

[44] The Department of Justice's Office of Tribal Justice website links to legal issues on reservations, reports, information on new and proposed legislation and administrative rules, and grants and funding information, http//www.justice.gov/otj/.

individual tribal court's rulings, they are unlikely to be widely available. Researchers necessarily look to the selected case reporting available through an established tribal court looseleaf reporter and on websites and databases. Each provider reports cases from a slightly different list of tribal courts, so it can be worthwhile to repeat the same search in different sources.

(1) *Indian Law Reporter* (looseleaf). The first and longtime standard reporter of tribal court decisions, this service, which has been published by the American Indian Lawyer Training Program since 1974, also reports selected tribal court opinions and selected cases from federal and state courts. [Illustration 25–6] Case summaries are always printed; the opinions are reproduced in full or edited versions, depending on importance. The set includes a table of cases. Administrative rules and proceedings, news, commentary, and announcements are also published along with the monthly case updates. An annual subject index is provided.

Because the looseleaf service does not offer its own cumulative topical index, the National Indian Law Library has created and regularly updates an index of the tribal court decisions.[45]

(2) *LexisNexis*. "Native American Law" is found in "Area of Law—By Topic" in *LexisNexis*. It includes decisions from about thirty tribes. Coverage is uneven; for example, included are cases from the Coushatta Tribe of Louisiana for 2000–2001 only and cases from the Puyallup Tribe (Washington State) from 1982–present.[46]

(3) *Tribal Court Decisions*.[47] The Tribal Court Clearinghouse of the Tribal Law and Policy Institute offers two approaches to finding tribal court decisions from its website. A word search can be done in a database of over 2,800 opinions from twenty-two courts, and direct links are provided to tribal court websites that post court decisions. From the same website, there are links to many other useful sites, making this a good starting place for tribal law research.

(4) *VersusLaw*.[48] This service is free to law school students and faculty and reasonably priced for others. One of its "libraries" of data is *Tribal Courts*. Word searches can be run on the opinions of one or more of the twenty-two tribal courts covered.

(5) *West's American Tribal Law Reporter*. Thirteen tribal courts submit opinions to this specialized reporter, including the Cherokee Nation of Oklahoma, the Ho-Chunk Nation, the Hopi Tribe of Arizona, and the Navajo Nation. Publication was initiated in 1997, and each volume has a table of cases at the front (arranged both by jurisdiction and alphabetically). Researchers can benefit from the value-added aspects of a West product, such as headnotes and key number searching.

---

[45] http://www.narf.org/nill/ilr/.

[46] The Native American Law library in *LexisNexis* also includes treaties, executive orders and presidential proclamations, *Lexis Law Directory* listings, Native American Solicitor's Opinions, Department of Interior Board of Indian Appeals Decisions, Indian gaming information, and the essential treatise in the field, *Cohen's Handbook of Federal Indian Law*.

[47] Tribal Law and Policy Institute, http://www.tribal-institute.org/lists/decision.htm.

[48] http://www.versuslaw.com/.

(6)   *Westlaw.* "Native American Law" is found under the Topical Practice Areas in *Westlaw.* Westlaw provides database access to its *Tribal Law Reporter*, but this service is not part of the standard academic contract.[49]

c.   *Jurisdictional Reach of Tribal Courts.* Scholars debate the way in which tribal court judgments should be received by state courts[50] and have called for a federal mandate to create a uniform approach,[51] but the matter remains the domain of individual states and tribes with an occasional federal interjection.

With three sovereign governments interacting, jurisdictional complications and frictions arise among tribes, states, and the federal government. The underlying policy issues are explored in depth in a report entitled *Building on Common Ground: A National Agenda to Reduce Jurisdictional Disputes Between Tribal, State, and Federal Courts.*[52] Determining tribal court jurisdiction and the reach of a tribal court judgment requires research that takes into account Public Law 280[53] and the ways in which shifting federal Indian policy has changed the rules over time.

Cohen's Handbook of Federal Indian Law (Nell Jessup Newton ed. 2012) (available in *LexisNexis*), a comprehensive Indian law treatise, provides an informed backdrop on jurisdictional issues, including the import of Public Law 280. Further jurisdictional research must be specific to the state and tribe in question and may require tracing the legal relationship of the tribe and federal government.

Full Faith and Credit. In 1994, Oklahoma adopted a reciprocal rule, extending full faith and credit to the judgments of all Oklahoma tribal courts that extend full faith and credit to the judgments of Oklahoma courts.[54] While the Full Faith and Credit Clause of the United States Constitution requires every state to respect and enforce the judgments of other states, there is no single mandate to guide state courts in handling tribal court

---

[49] *Westlaw* also has a collection of Native American Treaties, reports the decisions of the Department of the Interior Board of Indian Appeals, and has gaming updates and news.

[50] William V. Vetter, *Of Tribal Courts and "Territories": Is Full Faith and Credit Required?*, 23 CAL. W. L. REV. 219 (1987); Robert Laurence, *Full Faith and Credit in Tribal Courts: An Essay on Tribal Sovereignty, Cross-Boundary Reciprocity and the Unlikely Case of* Eberhard v. Eberhard, 28 N.M. L. REV. 19 (1998); JAMES G. FARRAR, NAT'L CTR. FOR STATE COURTS, MODEL COURT DEVELOPMENT PROJECT: FULL FAITH AND CREDIT FOR INDIAN COURT JUDGMENTS: FINAL REPORT (1982).

[51] Davis S. Clark, *State Court Recognition of Tribal Court Judgments: Securing the Blessing of Civilization*, 23 OKLA. CITY U. L. REV. 353 (1998); Stacy L. Leeds, *Cross-Jurisdictional Recognition and Enforcement of Judgments: A Tribal Court Perspective*, 76 N.D. L. REV. 311 (2000).

[52] This is a report with recommendations sponsored by the State Justice Institute, Conference of Chief Justices, Native American Tribal Courts Committee of the National Conference of Special Court Judges of the American Bar Association, the National American Indian Court Judges Association, and the National Center for State Courts. This report is posted on the Tribal Court Clearinghouse website under the "State Law" tab. http://www.tribal-institute.org. *See also* http://walkingoncommonground.org ("Resources for promoting and facilitating tribal-state-federal collaborations").

[53] Public Law 280 (Pub. L. No. 83–280, 67 Stat. 589 (codified as 18 U.S.C § 1162, 28 U.S.C. § 1360 (2012)) was enacted during a time when the federal government was attempting to terminate its special relationship with tribal governments and its legal responsibilities in Indian country. Without tribal consultation, Congress extended state jurisdiction over Indian lands in six states; other states were later allowed to assume similar jurisdiction. States later were allowed to make a retrocession of jurisdiction back to the federal government. Public Law 280 continues to complicate jurisdictional determinations.

[54] Okla. Dist. Ct. R. 30, "Standard for Recognition of Judicial Proceedings in Tribal Faith and Credit").

judgments and orders, although federal legislation has occasionally included a full faith and credit provision, directed to state and tribal courts.[55]

Doctrine of Comity. Some states are looking to comity, the doctrine allowing enforcement of foreign judgments in domestic courts, as a legal theory for the enforcement of tribal judgments. Other states are focused on practical outcomes rather than theoretical underpinnings. North Dakota, South Dakota, and Wisconsin are among the states working with tribes to reach agreements. Minnesota worked on the issue for years with a joint task force of tribal judges and state judges. Legislative analysts prepared *American Indians, Indian Tribes, and State Government,*[56] a guidebook discussing major issues between tribes and state governments, including criminal and civil jurisdiction, gaming, liquor regulation, taxation, human services, and education. Full of maps and statistics, this remarkable document could serve as a model for any state seeking to make informed policy decisions.

C. SECONDARY SOURCES OF TRIBAL LAW

There is a growing literature of tribal law. Much of the writing in the field is of a practical nature intended to serve tribal leaders, judges and tribal court administrators, and advocates. A rich array of reports, bench books, best practice guides, and similar works are available, often in an online, freely downloadable format. At the same time, greater numbers of academic writers are devoting attention to the intricacies of the field. And finally, practitioners are converting lessons learned into useful practice books for other lawyers. This section spotlights a few standard secondary sources in the field and offers an illustrative selection of newer practice materials. In the past, tribal law researchers had little chance of finding books devoted to a single topic within tribal law, such as employment or criminal procedure. That is changing rapidly and today well worth a searching for secondary materials directly on point.

1. Books

a. *American Indian Tribal Law*, by Matthew L. M. Fletcher (Wolters Kluwer). Published in 2011, this innovative work is intended to be used as a student textbook. It is the first casebook on tribal laws and court decisions, and is an ambitious effort to draw legal themes and understanding from the law promulgated by tribes. Tribal law researchers will find useful discussions of custom and justice traditions and in-depth treatments of tribal government structures and political processes. The chapter on regulatory and administrative law fills what is otherwise something of a void (tribes may publish administrative rules and regulations, but reports of administrative hearings and procedures are rare). Nuts-and-bolts topics like jurisdiction, contract disputes, and tort claims all find a place in this 800–page book. There is a table of cases, and a more generous index than found in the standard casebook.

b. *Arguing with Tradition: The Language of Law in Hopi Tribal Court*, by Justin B. Richland (2008) (Univ. of Chicago Press). This short book is much more than a linguistic study: it probes the social, cultural, and very practical outcomes of accommodating a foreign and adversarial legal system within tribal life. The ways in

---

[55] Such a provision was included in the Violence Against Women Act, Pub. L. No. 103–322, tit. IV, 108 Stat. 1902 (1994) (codified as 18 U.S.C. § 2265(a) (2006)), and the Child Support Orders Act, Pub. L. No. 103–383, 108 Stat. 4063 (codified as 28 U.S.C. § 1738B (2006)).

[56] The February 2014 edition is available at http://www.house.leg.state.mn.us/hrd/pubs/indiangb.pdf.

which the system is tested and sometimes tempered by the tribal legal heritage (and vice versa) provides an invaluable insight, especially for non-tribal members who have no experience of reservation life.

c.   *Cohen's Handbook of Federal Indian Law* (Nell Jessup Newton ed., 2012) (available in *LexisNexis*). Despite staking out federal Indian law as a focus, this essential treatise has much to offer the tribal law researcher. It is an ideal starting place when researching specialty areas such as Indian gaming, the Indian Child Welfare Act, civil rights under tribal authority, water rights, taxation, and numerous other topics. There are full discussions of tribal governments and tribal membership, and the meaning of "tribe," "Indian country," and "tribal law." In addition to a scholarly explanation, researchers will find abundant references to supporting primary sources.

d.   *Indian Land Cessions in the United States*, compiled by Charles Royce (1901).[57] This classic work documents in statistical detail and with maps the lands that tribes gave up to the federal government over a period of more than one hundred years. In neat columns, full information is recorded: the date of the land cession, where or how it was executed, the *Statutes at Large* reference (if cession was by treaty), the tribe giving up the land, a description of the land, a column for "historical data and remarks," and two map references.

2.   Practice Materials

a.   *Labor and Employment Law in Indian Country*, by Kaighn Smith, Jr. (2011) (Native American Rights Fund). Labor and employment lawyers found that much of their learned legal responses were inapplicable in Indian country when casinos and other enterprises begin to bring hundreds of workers onto reservations. Likewise, tribal leaders who had never managed large numbers of employees were confronted with new challenges. This new work, called "groundbreaking" by the Native American Rights Fund, is intended to guide lawyers and tribal leaders alike.

b.   *The Indian Child Welfare Act Handbook: A Legal Guide to the Custody and Adoption of Native American Children*, by B. J. Jones et al. (2d ed. 2008) (American Bar Association). Few legal areas so completely bring together tribal courts and state courts than implementation of the ICWA, which gives tribal governments exclusive jurisdiction over custody and adoption cases for children living on the reservation or under the legal protection of the tribe. Concurrent jurisdiction and a strong voice are also awarded to tribes when the Native American child does not reside on the reservation.

c.   *Indian Gaming and Tribal Sovereignty: The Casino Compromise*, by Steven Andrew Light and Kathryn R. L. Rand (2005) (Univ. Press of Kansas). While not strictly a practice book, this well-reviewed contribution to the burgeoning literature of Indian gaming addresses the key tribal law questions in regard to hosting gambling operations on the reservation.

d.   *Indian Tribal Court Handbook*.[58] Originally prepared by the State Bar of New Mexico and now updated by the staff of the *Tribal Law Journal*, this work offers information on the twenty-three tribal courts in New Mexico and is provided to "take

---

[57] http://memory.loc.gov/ammem/amlaw/lwss-ilc.html; also available in *HeinOnline* and published in the *United States Congressional Serial Set*, No. 4015.

[58] http://tlj.unm.edu/handbook/index.php.

some of the mystery out of practicing in tribal courts." Other tribes and states have similar publications or put practice guidelines on their tribal court websites.

  e.   Tribal Criminal Law and Procedure, by Carrie E. Garrow and Sarah Deer (2004) (Altamira Press). This textbook is part of the Tribal Legal Studies Series. The usual topics in this kind of work are discussed (e.g., jurisdiction, elements of crimes, criminal intent), but this book also compares criminal law in Anglo-American and Native societies, discusses traditional ways of viewing criminal acts, and includes case discussions and documentation from tribal courts in each of the chapters.

3. Blogs, Periodicals, and Websites

  The most tentative or simplistic online search will produce a plethora of information on tribal law and individual tribal governments and courts. The following is a select sample of resources that have been tested for usefulness. For solid research information, some of the best sites are at law school libraries (these include the following universities: Arizona, Arizona State, Idaho, Kansas, Montana, New Mexico, Oklahoma, Oklahoma City, Tulsa, and Washington).

  a.   American Indian Law Review.[59] While federal Indian law predominates in coverage, there are articles useful to tribal law researchers in this University of Oklahoma publication.

  b.   Indian Law Resource Center.[60] The Center is a nonprofit and advocacy organization that provides legal assistance to Indian and Alaska Native nations. Its website has a tremendous amount of news and information sources.

  c.   Indian Nations Archive: How to Build a Tribal Legal History, by Nancy Carol Carter.[61] A step-by-step, online research guide for identifying and procuring the documents comprising a tribal legal history.

  d.   National Congress of American Indians.[62] This website is full of information on legislation, policy, news, and events. The group has the strongest online presence in terms of policy information.

  e.   National Indian Court Judges Association (NAICJA).[63] NAICJA's mission is to strengthen and enhance tribal justice systems. The site advances education, information sharing, and advocacy and provides legislative updates, news, and new publications.

  f.   National Indian Law Library.[64] This is the essential website for tribal law researchers. In addition to a superior collection of legal information, it offers research guides and a news blog with developments in the Indian law field.

  g.   Tribal Court Clearinghouse.[65] This is a comprehensive website with resources for American Indian and Alaska Native nations, American Indian and Alaska Native people, tribal justice systems, victims' services providers, tribal service providers, and

---

[59] http://adams.law.ou.edu/ailr/.

[60] http://www.indianlaw.org/.

[61] http://www.narf.org/nill/legalhistory/archives.html.

[62] http://www.ncai.org/.

[63] http://www.naicja.org/.

[64] http://www.narf.org/nill/.

[65] http://www.tribal-institute.org/.

others involved in the improvement of justice in Indian country. It is maintained by the Tribal Law and Policy Institute.

  h. Tribal Law Journal.[66] Hosted at the University of New Mexico, this online journal aims to "promote indigenous self-determination by facilitating discussion of the internal law of the world's indigenous nations." The cleanly designed site offers quick access to articles, tribal resources, and legal updates.

  i. Turtle Talk.[67] Hosted at Michigan State University, this is a lively blog on Native American law and policy. It is a good source for thoughtful discussion and legal developments.

D. ILLUSTRATIONS

25–1. **Screen Print from Office of Federal Acknowledgement Website**

25–2. **Indian Entities Recognized and Eligible to Receive Services From the United States Bureau of Indian Affairs found at 79 Fed. Reg. 4748 (January 29, 2014)**

25–3. **Page from the Bureau of Indian Affairs 2013 Fall/Winter Tribal Leaders Directory**

25–4. **Screen Print from the National Indian Law Library Website**

25–5. **Index Page from Indian Affairs. Laws and Treaties, vol. 2 (1904)**

25–6. **Page from Indian Law Reporter**

---

[66] http://tlj.unm.edu.

[67] http://turtletalk.wordpress.com/.

[Illustration 25-1]

SCREEN PRINT FROM OFFICE OF FEDERAL ACKNOWLEDGEMENT WEBSITE

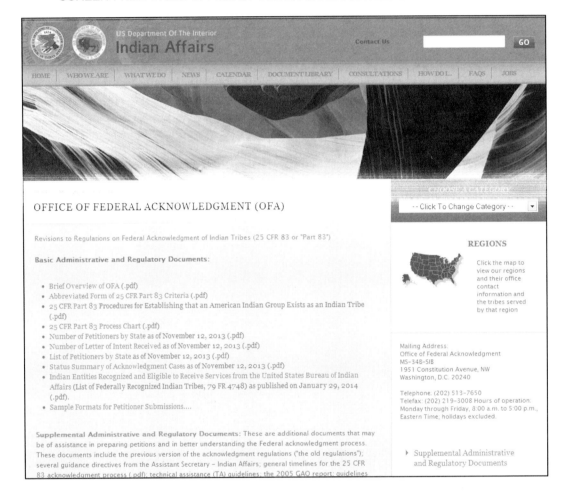

[Illustration 25-2]

INDIAN ENTITIES RECOGNIZED AND ELIGIBLE TO RECEIVE SERVICES FROM THE UNITED STATES BUREAU OF INDIAN AFFAIRS FOUND AT 79 FED. REG. 4748 (JANUARY 29, 2014)

4748 Federal Register / Vol. 79, No. 19 / Wednesday, January 29, 2014 / Notices

Respondents: Owners and operators of small passenger vessels.

Frequency: Annually and on occasion.

Burden Estimate: The estimated burden has increased from 379,784 hours to 399,420 hours a year due to an increase in the estimated annual number of respondents.

2. *Title:* Plan Approval and Records for Subdivision and Stability Regulations—Title 46 CFR Subchapter S.

OMB Control Number: 1625–0064.

Summary: The regulations require owners, operators, or masters of certain inspected vessels to obtain and/or post various documents as part of the Coast Guard commercial vessel safety program.

Need: Title 46 U.S.C. 3306 authorizes the Coast Guard to prescribe rules for the safety of certain vessels. Title 46 CFR Subchapter S contains the rules regarding subdivision and stability.

Forms: N/A.

Respondents: Owners, operators, or masters of vessels.

Frequency: On occasion.

Burden Estimate: The estimated burden has decreased from 13,624 hours to 10,639 hours a year due to a decrease

in the average annual number of respondents.

Dated: January 23, 2014.

R.E. Day,
Rear Admiral, U.S. Coast Guard, Assistant Commandant for Command, Control, Communications, Computers and Information Technology.

[FR Doc. 2014–01726 Filed 1–28–14; 8:45 am]

BILLING CODE 9110–04–P

DEPARTMENT OF THE INTERIOR

Fish and Wildlife Service

[FWS–R1–ES–2014–N017; FXES11130100000–145–FF01E00000]

Endangered Species; Issuance of Permits

AGENCY: Fish and Wildlife Service, Interior.

ACTION: Notice of issuance of permits.

SUMMARY: We, the U.S. Fish and Wildlife Service, have issued the following permits to conduct certain activities with endangered species under the authority of the Endangered Species Act, as amended (Act).

ADDRESSES: Program Manager for Restoration and Endangered Species Classification, Ecological Services, U.S. Fish and Wildlife Service, Pacific Regional Office, 911 NE. 11th Avenue, Portland, OR 97232–4181.

FOR FURTHER INFORMATION CONTACT: Colleen Henson, Fish and Wildlife Biologist, at the above address or by telephone (503–231–6131) or fax (503–231–6243).

SUPPLEMENTARY INFORMATION: We have issued the following permits to conduct activities with endangered species in response to recovery and interstate commerce permit applications we received under the authority of section 10 of the Act (16 U.S.C. 1531 *et seq.*). These permits were issued between July 1 and December 31, 2013. Each permit listed below was issued only after we determined that it was applied for in good faith; that granting the permit would not be to the disadvantage of the listed species; that the proposed activities were for scientific research or would benefit the recovery or the enhancement of survival of the species, and that the terms and conditions of the permit were consistent with the purposes and policy set forth in the Act.

Applicant	Permit No.	Date issued	Date expires
Bonneville Power Administration	037151	07/31/2013	06/30/2014
Bureau of Land Management	005901	12/09/2013	10/14/2016
Directorate of Public Works, U.S. Army	043638	09/30/2013	12/18/2015
Ha, Renee Robinette	09155B	10/31/2013	10/30/2016
Hammond, Paul C	212061	07/03/2013	05/25/2017
Hawaii Volcanoes National Park	018078	07/03/2013	06/27/2016
Hoku'akua, LLC	07458B	11/18/2013	11/17/2018
Lomnicky, Gregg A	103595	08/29/2013	08/28/2017
NOAA/NMFS Pacific Islands Fisheries Science Center	72088A	07/15/2013	12/31/2017
Rock, Dennis F	99618A	08/29/2013	03/12/2014
U.S. Geological Survey	08551B	07/15/2013	12/31/2016
USDA Forest Service	010354	07/08/2013	05/23/2017
USDA Forest Service, Institute of Pacific Islands Forestry	06459B	11/18/2013	11/17/2017

Availability of Documents

Documents and other information submitted with these applications are available for review, subject to the requirements of the Privacy Act and Freedom of Information Act, by any party who submits a written request for a copy of such documents (see **FOR FURTHER INFORMATION CONTACT**).

Authority

We provide this notice under the authority of section 10 of the Act (16 U.S.C. 1531 *et seq.*).

Dated: January 22, 2014.

Richard Hannan,
Acting Regional Director, Pacific Region, U.S. Fish and Wildlife Service.

[FR Doc. 2014–01717 Filed 1–28–14; 8:45 am]

BILLING CODE 4310–55–P

DEPARTMENT OF THE INTERIOR

Bureau of Indian Affairs

[145A2100DD/A0T500000.000000/AAK3000000]

Indian Entities Recognized and Eligible To Receive Services From the United States Bureau of Indian Affairs

AGENCY: Bureau of Indian Affairs, Interior.

ACTION: Notice.

SUMMARY: This notice publishes the current list of 566 tribal entities recognized and eligible for funding and services from the Bureau of Indian Affairs by virtue of their status as Indian tribes. The list is updated from the notice published on May 6, 2013 (78 FR 26384).

FOR FURTHER INFORMATION CONTACT: Gail Veney, Bureau of Indian Affairs, Division of Tribal Government Services, Mail Stop 4513–MIB, 1849 C Street NW., Washington, DC 20240. Telephone number: (202) 513–7641.

SUPPLEMENTARY INFORMATION: This notice is published pursuant to Section 104 of the Act of November 2, 1994 (Pub. L. 103–454; 108 Stat. 4791, 4792),

[Illustration 25-3]

PAGE FROM THE BUREAU OF INDIAN AFFAIRS 2013 FALL/WINTER TRIBAL LEADERS DIRECTORY

Index - Tribal Entities

Tribe	BIA Regional Office	Agency	State	Section 2 - Page No.
Circle Native Community	Alaska	Fairbanks Agency	AK	5
Citizen Potawatomi Nation, Oklahoma	Southern Plains	Southern Plains Regional Office	OK	77
Cloverdale Rancheria of Pomo Indians of California	Pacific	Central California Agency	CA	64
Cocopah Tribe of Arizona	Western	Fort Yuma Agency	AZ	88
Coeur D'Alene Tribe	Northwest	Coeur d'Alene Tribe BIA Agency	ID	54
Cold Springs Rancheria of Mono Indians of California	Pacific	Central California Agency	CA	64
Colorado River Indian Tribe	Western	Colorado River Agency	AZ	88
Comanche Nation, Oklahoma	Southern Plains	Anadarko Agency	OK	77
Confederated Salish & Kootenai Tribes of the Flathead Reservation	Northwest	Flathead Agency	MT	54
Confederated Tribes and Bands of the Yakama Nation	Northwest	Yakama Agency	WA	54
Confederated Tribes of Coos, Lower Umpqua and Siuslaw Indians	Northwest	Siletz Agency	OR	54
Confederated Tribes of Siletz Indians of Oregon	Northwest	Siletz Agency	OR	54
Confederated Tribes of the Chehalis Reservation	Northwest	Olympic Peninsula Agency	WA	54
Confederated Tribes of the Colville Reservation	Northwest	Colville Agency	WA	54
Confederated Tribes of the Goshute Reservation, Nevada and Utah	Western	Eastern Nevada Agency	UT	88
Confederated Tribes of the Grand Ronde Community of Oregon	Northwest	Siletz Agency	OR	55
Confederated Tribes of the Umatilla Indian Reservation	Northwest	Umatilla Agency	OR	55
Confederated Tribes of the Warm Springs Reservation of Oregon	Northwest	Warm Springs Agency	OR	55
Coquille Indian Tribe	Northwest	Siletz Agency	OR	55
Cortina Indian Rancheria of Wintun Indians of California	Pacific	Central California Agency	CA	64
Coushatta Tribe of Louisiana	Eastern	Eastern Regional Office	LA	32
Cow Creek Band of Umpqua Tribe of Indians	Northwest	Siletz Agency	OR	55
Cowlitz Indian Tribe	Northwest	Olympic Peninsula Agency	WA	55

[Illustration 25–4]

SCREEN PRINT FROM THE NATIONAL INDIAN LAW LIBRARY WEBSITE

News Bulletins   Library Catalog   Research By Topic   Tribal Law   Research Help   About NILL

National Indian Law Library

Home | Search | NARF

The **National Indian Law Library (NILL)** of the **Native American Rights Fund (NARF)** was founded in 1972 as a public law library devoted to federal Indian and tribal law. NILL serves the public by developing and making accessible a unique and valuable collection of Indian law resources and assisting people with their Indian law-related information needs.

JUSTICE THROUGH KNOWLEDGE!

Resources at NILL:

Stay Abreast of Current Events with Indian Law News Bulletins

- Including federal and state courts, legislation, regulations, news, and law reviews
- Available on our blog, by RSS feed, or email.
- Updated evey week or two.

Access Tribal Laws at the Tribal Law Gateway

- More than 300 tribes participating.
- More than 100 tribal codes available.
- Search across the entire collection of laws.
- Find tribal codes, court opinions, and other legal materials by tribe.

Use Online Research Guides and the Catalog of NILL's Unique Print Collection to Research Indian Law

- Includes hard-to-find materials like older case materials filed from the 1970s through the early 1990s.
- Search the collection of Indian Law Bulletins to find cases and news related to Indian Law.

Get Research Help by Email or Phone

If you need assistance with your Indian Law research, the staff at the National Indian Law Library are available to help. Research questions can be submitted through the online form (*Ask NILL*) or by phone.

Donate

NILL is not tax-supported and relies on generous people like you. By donating, you help ensure that the library continues to provide free resources, expand its collections, and pursue innovative digital initiatives. Your gift, no matter what size, shows your support for what we do.

Hours and Location

Please call for an appointment
(303) 447-8760
1522 Broadway, Boulder, CO 80302
Monday-Friday

[Illustration 25–5]

INDEX PAGE FROM INDIAN AFFAIRS. LAWS AND TREATIES, VOL. 2 (1904)

[Illustration 25–6]

PAGE FROM INDIAN LAW REPORTER

INDIAN LAW REPORTER

A PUBLICATION OF THE AMERICAN INDIAN LAWYER TRAINING PROGRAM, INC.

February 2013   *Celebrating 40 Years of Service*   Volume 40, No. 2

Month in Brief

UNITED STATES COURTS OF APPEALS

NINTH CIRCUIT

Environmental Regulation

In an action asserting that the Interior Secretary and the Bureau of Land Management (BLM) violated the National Environmental Policy Act, the Federal Land Policy and Management Act, and the Department's regulations by permitting the intervenor-defendant-appellees to restart uranium mining operations at the Arizona 1 Mine in 2009 after a 17-year hiatus under a plan that BLM approved in 1988, the U.S. Court of Appeals for the Ninth Circuit affirms the district court's grant of summary judgment in favor of appellees on all issues including BLM's invocation of the categorical exclusion for issuance of a gravel permit. **Center for Biological Diversity, et al. v. Salazar, et al.**, No. 11-17843, **40 Indian L. Rep. 2017** (9th Cir., Feb. 4, 2013).

TENTH CIRCUIT

Criminal Jurisdiction and Procedure

The U.S. Court of Appeals for the Tenth Circuit affirms the conviction of the defendant-appellant for embezzling or converting funds from the Northern Arapahoe Tribe's Department of Social Services (DSS). **United States v. Addison**, No. 11-8105, **40 Indian L. Rep. 2022** (10th Cir., Feb. 26, 2013).

FEDERAL CIRCUIT

Claims against United States
Leases and Leasing

In an action in which the appellant asserted a regulatory takings claim when the Bureau of Indian affairs removed a bridge that the appellant used to access a portion of property he leased from the Colorado River Indian Tribes, the U.S. Court of Appeals for the Federal Circuit affirms the U.S. Court of Federal Claims, holding that the appellant's regulatory takings claim never ripened and that the appellant had no cognizable property interest. **McGuire v. United States**, No. 2012-5073, **40 Indian L. Rep. 2025** (Fed. Cir., Feb. 20, 2013).

UNITED STATES DISTRICT COURTS

DISTRICT OF ARIZONA

Employment: Preference for Indians

In an action by the Equal Employment Opportunity Commission against Peabody Western Coal Company and the Navajo Nation and the U.S. Department of the Interior asserting that Title VII of the Civil Rights Act of 1964 applies to prohibit discrimination based on tribal affiliation as it relates to lease agreements containing a Navajo preference in hiring provision, the U.S. District Court for the District of Arizona concludes that the preference does not constitute unlawful national origin discrimination but is a political classification and thus not within the scope of Title VII, and grants the Interior Department's motion for summary judgment as to Peabody's third-party complaint and the Navajo Nation's renewed motion to dismiss or the Nation's motion for summary judgment on the merits of the Navajo Tribal Preference in Employment. **Equal Employment Opportunity Commission v. Peabody Western Coal Company, et al.**, No. 2:01-cv-01050 JWS, **40 Indian L. Rep. 3021** (D. Ariz., Oct. 18, 2012).

DISTRICT OF COLORADO

Civil Jurisdiction and Procedure
Environmental Regulation: National Environmental Policy Act
Leases and Leasing
Sovereignty: Sovereign Immunity; Tribal

The U.S. District Court for the District of Colorado applies the public rights exception to traditional joinder rules involving sovereign immunity and denies the respondent-intervenor Navajo Nation's motion to dismiss an action challenging the expansion of strip mining under the National Environmental Policy Act. **Diné Citizens Against Ruining Our Environment, et al. v. U.S. Office of Surface Mining Reclamation and Enforcement, et al.**, Civil Action No. 12-cv-1275-AP, **40 Indian L. Rep. 3025** (D. Colo., Jan. 4, 2013).

DISTRICT OF IDAHO

Tribal Courts: Jurisdiction; Exhaustion of Tribal Remedies
Tribal Law: Tribal Codes; Zoning

The U.S. District Court for the District of Idaho grants the Shoshone-Bannock Land Use Policy Commission's motions to dismiss an action challenging the Commission's zoning authority

40 ILR 5

Chapter 26

FEDERAL TAX RESEARCH*

This chapter discusses primary and secondary sources of federal tax law and provides information about research materials containing these items. The chapter also suggests methods for evaluating and updating results.

A. INTRODUCTION

Many researchers erroneously believe federal tax research has little or nothing in common with traditional legal research methods. In fact, researchers can solve problems involving federal taxation using techniques mastered in a basic legal research course and often can use traditional materials.[1] Many library collections include sources (e.g., topical services, including many which are in a looseleaf format) dealing solely with federal taxation. Because those tax-specific sources are more comprehensive and cover topics more thoroughly than do general legal research sources, they are better suited for tax research. Whether shelved together in a "tax alcove," dispersed throughout the collection, or accessed online, tax-specific materials are no more difficult to locate or use than are traditional research tools.

This chapter focuses on general tax research principles. So many items are available that a library may lack a source described in this chapter, contain materials omitted here, or include particular materials in a different format (e.g., CD-ROM or DVD). Because the publishing industry continues to consolidate and many formerly independent publishers are now commonly owned, researchers should not be surprised if a publication described in this chapter is renamed, merged into another, or its publication is ceased altogether. Researchers who understand basic tax research techniques will be able to adapt to these changes.

Tax researchers have available to them an assortment of topical services and specialized online sources that compile and analyze different authorities, such as the Internal Revenue Code, regulations and other administrative pronouncements, and judicial decisions. This chapter often includes internal cross-references from one section to another with a simple parenthetical—e.g., "(Section R)"—that guides readers to other publications directly related to the source under discussion.

Federal taxation involves an administrative agency in addition to Congress and the courts,[2] and it may have international implications. An individual who masters tax

---

* This chapter was revised by Gail Levin Richmond, Professor of Law, Nova Southeastern University Law Center. An expanded version is separately published under the title FEDERAL TAX RESEARCH: GUIDE TO MATERIALS AND TECHNIQUES (9th ed. 2014) (Foundation Press).

[1] This chapter mentions traditional legal research tools, but does not discuss them in detail. If the library lacks a tax-oriented tool, researchers should consult traditional materials. References to the appropriate chapters in this book assist in locating such materials.

[2] Administrative law research is discussed in Chapter 13. The URLs for government-sponsored websites referred to in this chapter appear at the end of Section R.

research techniques can transfer those research skills to problems involving areas as disparate as antitrust law, environmental law, and military law. And, because many areas of law have tax implications, acquiring basic tax research skills is a worthwhile endeavor regardless of the focus of your practice.

B. RESEARCH METHODOLOGY

Tax research follows general legal research procedures. Using a set of facts presented in a problem, researchers must ascertain the issues raised by these facts and determine whether any additional facts might be relevant. To resolve the issues, they must locate governing statutory language and sources that interpret that language. Legislative history, administrative pronouncements, and judicial decisions are three sources for guidance in interpreting the statute. Judicial decisions are also important in assessing the validity of any administrative pronouncements. Although most decisions relate to interpretation, courts may also hear constitutional challenges to a statute or to an administrative interpretation. If foreign source income or noncitizens are involved, research must also include applicable treaties.

Researchers who are familiar with the subject matter involved can often locate these items without resort to any secondary authority other than a citator. Those who lack such familiarity should proceed in an entirely different manner. They would begin with secondary materials, which will help them determine which Code sections are involved and will explain the underlying issues. Topical services, treatises, and periodical articles are useful for this purpose.

When researching a tax problem, the researcher must determine which types of authority are relevant, what degree of deference each item of authority will receive, and whether the authority's importance might be affected by pending legislative, administrative, or judicial action.[3]

C. CONSTITUTION

The Constitution contains several specific provisions for taxation. These include the apportionment clauses (Article I, section 2, clause 3, and Article I, section 9, clause 4), the origination clause (Article I, section 7, clause 1), the uniformity clause (Article 1, section 8, clause 1), and the export clause (Article I, section 9, clause 5). Because the income tax is specifically authorized by the Constitution's sixteenth amendment, it avoids an earlier holding that it was a direct tax subject to apportionment based on population.[4] The estate and gift taxes, on the other hand, are indirect taxes subject only to the requirement that they be uniform throughout the United States.

Because substantive tax research rarely involves the Constitution, tax-oriented research tools focusing on the Constitution are limited. In fact, the tax-oriented citators published by CCH and RIA (Section J) do not include the Constitution as cited material. Constitutional research can be performed using digests or annotated constitutions.[5]

---

[3] For useful video tutorials on the different types of tax authority, see *Tax Research: Understanding Sources of Tax Law*, http://www.cchgroup.com/webapp/wcs/stores/servlet/content_LP_learntaxlaw. The tutorials are also available in PDF format.

[4] Pollock v. Farmers' Loan & Trust Co., 158 U.S. 601 (1895); *cf.* Springer v. United States, 102 U.S. 586 (1881), concluding the Civil War income tax was indirect.

[5] *United States Code Annotated* and *United States Code Service* include annotated constitutions. *See* Chapter 8.

Alternatively, online subscription services (Section R) may be searched, using either a specific constitutional provision or a common term (e.g., due process). The *Standard Federal Tax Reporter* volume 1 (Section K) includes materials on litigation involving constitutional claims. Because constitutional litigation often involves provisions that do not specifically mention taxation, treatises and other secondary materials are an important part of initial constitutional tax research.[6]

D. STATUTES

United States Code Title 26, more commonly referred to as the Internal Revenue Code of 1986, contains the vast majority of statutes covering income, estate and gift, excise, and employment taxes. Throughout this chapter these materials are referred to as the Code. References to the two previous Codes—1939 and 1954—include the year.[7] The Code has numerous subdivisions, including subtitle, chapter, and subchapter. Researchers must keep these in mind, as many Code provisions apply only for purposes of particular subdivisions.

Some tax-related provisions are set forth outside the Internal Revenue Code. These include provisions codified in other *U.S.C.* titles and uncodified provisions. For example, many rules affecting retirement benefits appear in Title 29. Statutory relief rules in the employee/independent contractor area have been amended several times but have never been codified.[8]

1. Locating Tax Legislation

In researching a tax problem, the time frame involved is quite important. If, for example, the research involves a contemplated transaction, current statutory provisions are certainly important. If the current language is of recent vintage, research into its meaning might include any repealed or amended statute it replaced. And, because tax provisions change frequently, researchers ignore pending legislation at their peril. A bill changing the tax consequences of a proposed transaction might be enacted before a client negotiates a binding contract.[9] Finally, some provisions have specific sunset dates, which

---

[6] For a discussion of tax litigation involving constitutional claims, see JASPER L. CUMMINGS, JR., THE SUPREME COURT, FEDERAL TAXATION, AND THE CONSTITUTION (2013); 1 BORIS I. BITTKER & LAWRENCE LOKKEN, FEDERAL TAXATION OF INCOME, ESTATES AND GIFTS ch. 1 (3d ed. 1999 & most recent Cum. Supp.)

[7] Before 1939, tax statutes were reenacted in their entirety, or with necessary changes, on a regular basis. Because many current provisions can be traced back to the 1939 Code or even earlier—I.R.C. § 263, for example, contains language taken almost verbatim from § 117 of the 1864 Act, 13 Stat. 282—cross-references to these earlier materials are extremely useful. Section D-1-c discusses materials used to trace statutory language.

[8] Revenue Act of 1978, Pub. L. No. 95–600, § 530, 92 Stat. 2763, 2885, *extended indefinitely by* Tax Equity and Fiscal Responsibility Act of 1982, Pub. L. No. 97–248, § 269(c), 96 Stat. 324, 552, *and amended by* Small Business Job Protection Act of 1996, Pub. L. No. 104–188, § 1122, 110 Stat. 1755, 1766, *and by* Pension Protection Act of 2006, Pub. L. No. 109–280, § 864, 120 Stat. 780, 1024. Bills to repeal so-called section 530 relief are introduced on a regular basis.

[9] Effective dates for new legislation frequently precede the actual enactment date. However, transactions subject to binding contracts on an act's effective date are often exempted. In other cases, transactions that occur after a statute is enacted may be disqualified because the contract was entered into before the enactment. *See, e.g.,* Gulf Opportunity Zone Act of 2005, Pub. L. No. 109–135, § 405(a)(1), 119 Stat. 2577, 2634. Polone v. Comm'r, 505 F.3d 966 (9th Cir. 2007), *cert. denied,* 552 U.S. 1280 (2008), illustrates how a change in the law can affect a transaction spanning several years.

usually appear within the Code.[10] When working with Code provisions, researchers must avoid confusing enactment date, effective date, and sunset date.

The following sections discuss sources containing the text of relevant legislation. Legislative histories (Section E) may also be useful.

a.   *Current Code—Codifications.* The print version of *U.S.C.* is published every six years, supplemented by annual cumulative supplements. Both are available online in *FDsys* (Section R). If new legislation is enacted, commercially produced versions will initially be more current than the government publications.

Several publishers produce annual versions of the Internal Revenue Code.[11] Those publishing in a looseleaf format regularly integrate new material into the codification volumes. Publishers of bound volumes may use supplements for new matter or may not supplement at all during the year. Online services (Section R) insert new material directly into the relevant database. *Standard Federal Tax Reporter (SFTR)*[12] and *United States Tax Reporter (USTR)*[13] are topical services that include the Code; both are discussed in Section K. In addition to their print versions, both are included in subscription-based electronic services.

b.   *Individual Revenue Acts.* Acts are first published as slip laws and then bound in Public Law number order into the appropriate volume of *United States Statutes at Large.* Although the text of recent statutes is integrated into statutory codifications, the slip law version of an act remains valuable. Slip laws include effective dates and congressional instructions to the IRS. Codifications omit this information or reproduce it in relatively small print, making it easy to miss.

Online services, both government and commercial, are the best sources for the text of recent laws. *FDsys* includes slip laws enacted since the 104th Congress (1995 to date). *FDsys* also includes a *Statutes at Large* collection. It is not as current as the slip laws collection; in March 2014, it included laws enacted from 1951 to 2010. The Library of Congress website (*Congress.gov*)[14] includes information about laws enacted since 1973

---

[10] If a Code section does not include a sunset date, researchers can check the *List of Expiring Federal Tax Provisions* in the Publications section of the Congressional Joint Committee on Taxation (JCT) website, https:// www.jct.gov/. This document is updated annually and currently covers through 2024 (but no current sections expire after 2021). The JCT list is in expiration year order, and then by Code section within that year; IntelliConnect includes an Expiring Provisions Chart in Code section order. See Section E-1 for more information on the Joint Committee on Taxation.

[11] Codifications not limited to tax, such as *United States Code, United States Code Annotated,* and *United States Code Service,* are discussed in Chapter 9.

[12] *Standard Federal Tax Reporter* includes all federal taxes in its two Code volumes but covers only income and employment taxes in the remainder of the set. CCH also publishes *Federal Estate and Gift Tax Reporter* and *Federal Excise Tax Reporter.* Because their formats resemble that of *SFTR*, this chapter includes few separate references to those services. The Code provisions also appear in each service's compilation volumes.

[13] All federal taxes are covered in the two *United States Tax Reporter* Code volumes, but this service is otherwise limited to income and employment taxes. Because *USTR—Estate & Gift Taxes* and *USTR—Excise Taxes* cover their respective subject matters in a similar format, they are rarely referenced separately in this chapter. The Code provisions also appear in each service's compilation volumes.

[14] *Congress.gov* has replaced most of *thomas.loc.gov*; the replacement should be complete by the end of 2014.

(full-text for laws enacted since 1993). Researchers can also locate individual acts in various non-tax services[15] and in subscription-based electronic services.

The IRS-produced *Cumulative Bulletin* (Section O) previously included revenue acts, but it ceased publishing this material after the *Cumulative Bulletin* for 2003. *The Internal Revenue Acts of the United States: 1909–1950; 1950–1972; 1973–* (Section O) also includes individual acts; it is available in print and in *HeinOnline* (Section R). It does not cover every act since 1973.

c.   Tools for Tracing Amended and Repealed Code Sections. Many Code sections have been amended numerous times since their original enactment. Other sections have been repealed or allowed to sunset. The materials a researcher uses are affected by which of three tasks are being undertaken: (1) obtaining a cross-reference to the section number used in an earlier Code; (2) finding different versions of a particular Code section or finding a repealed Code section; or (3) determining when a particular section has been amended and possibly locating the statute that amended it. The materials listed below provide citations to amended sections and legislation that has been repealed altogether. Some of these services include excerpts or full text of the relevant legislation.

Code cross-reference tables provide section cross-references between the 1939 and 1954 Codes. [Illustration 26–1] Although these tables are useful, limitations apply. First, Congress changed section numbers (generally by inserting new subsections and moving old ones) after enacting the 1954 Code and again in the 1986 Code. Because cross-reference tables may not reflect these changes, researchers should determine when each provision was assigned its current section number. The section number in effect when the table was compiled must be consulted. A second limitation is also important. These tables reflect their compilers' opinions as to the appropriate cross-references. Different publishers' tables may yield different results.

The government publishes these tables in *United States Statutes at Large* (Appendix in volume 68A following text of the 1954 Code). It also publishes Joint Committee on Taxation, *Derivations of Code Sections of the Internal Revenue Codes of 1939 and 1954* (JCS–1–92), Jan. 21, 1992.[16] Three print topical services (Section K) include cross-reference tables. They are *Standard Federal Tax Reporter* (Code volume I) (also available online in IntelliConnect); Rabkin & Johnson, *Federal Income, Gift and Estate Taxation* (volume 7B); and Mertens, *Law of Federal Income Taxation—Code* (1954–58 Code volume) (1954 to 1939 Codes only). Several services that compile primary source materials (Section O) also include cross-reference tables. They are *Cumulative Changes* (1954 Code volume I); *Barton's Federal Tax Laws Correlated* (looseleaf volume); *Seidman's Legislative History of Federal Income and Excess Profits Tax Laws* (1939–53 volume II); and *Tax Management Primary Sources*.

Provisions that predate the 1939 Code can be traced using *Barton's*, *Seidman's*, or the Joint Committee on Taxation report listed above. There are also tables in *United States Statutes at Large* (Appendix in volume 53 (pt. 1) following text of the 1939 Code).

In addition to providing cross-references between the 1939 and 1954 Codes, three of the sources listed in the previous subsection include text from the relevant statutes.

---

[15] Sources such as *U.S. Code Congressional and Administrative News (USCCAN)* and *United States Code Service, Advance Service*, are discussed in Chapters 9 and 10.

[16] http://www.jct.gov/s-1-92.pdf.

These are *Cumulative Changes*, *Barton's*, and *Seidman's*.[17] *Barton's* and *Seidman's* are out of print; they are included in *HeinOnline* (Section R). *Cumulative Changes* has not been updated since 2010.

Instead of searching for a particular Code section and its prior versions, researchers may need to determine which Code sections have been amended recently. *Checkpoint* (Section R) includes tables of Code sections amended for each Congress. There is a separate table for each Public Law rather than a cumulative table for each Congress. *USCCAN*, which is discussed in Chapter 9, publishes a table in Code section order for each session of Congress.

[Illustration 26–1]

EXCERPT FROM 1939–1954 CROSS REFERENCE TABLE
STANDARD FEDERAL TAX REPORTER CODE VOLUME I

46	442
47(a)	443, 6011(a)
47(c)	443
47(e)	443
47(g)	443
48(a)	441, 7701(a)(23)

This version of the *SFTR* table appears in the *CCH Tax Research NetWork.*
The 1939 Code sections are on the left; the 1954 Code sections are on the right.

d. Pending and Potential Legislation. Even before a bill is introduced, taxpayers may receive hints that it is on the horizon. In presidential election years, for example, party platforms include potential legislative agendas. Presidential budget messages may also serve this function. Items of this nature are covered in newsletters (Section N) and in general interest newspapers.

Researchers can track pending legislation online or by using print sources. Online services (Section R) are usually the best means for following pending bills. *Congress.gov* is one such source. In addition, both *Lexis Advance* and *WestlawNext* provide bill-tracking services. Online tax-oriented services, such as *Checkpoint and IntelliConnect,* also cover pending legislation.

Although topical services (Section K) and newsletters cover pending legislation, only *Daily Tax Report* (Bloomberg BNA) lists a significant number of bills introduced in the current Congress. Its descriptions of most items are relatively brief; subscribers to Bloomberg BNA's *TaxCore* service or *Bloomberg Law* can access full text documents cited in the newsletter. Topical services are generally less valuable than newsletters; they typically cover only major bills and are likely to provide less detailed information.

---

[17] *Eldridge, The United States Internal Revenue Tax System* (Section O), provides annotated text for revenue acts through 1894. It can be used if *Seidman's* is unavailable, but it does not contain as much information.

2. Citators for Statutes

Citators indicate if a federal court considered a statute's constitutionality. Citators are discussed in Section J.

E. LEGISLATIVE HISTORIES

1. Overview[18]

The process for enacting tax legislation is virtually identical to that followed in the enactment of any federal law.[19] Because there are many steps and groups involved, the number of documents comprising the history of a major tax statute is likely to be large.

The House Committee on Ways and Means and the Senate Committee on Finance have primary jurisdiction over revenue bills. Each committee (or subcommittees thereof) may hold hearings, which will be published, and may issue a committee report when a bill is reported out of committee.[20] If House and Senate versions differ, a Conference Committee meets to resolve these differences. This group may generate its own report, which explains the resolution of those differences.

Five members each from Ways and Means and from Finance sit on a separate Joint Committee on Taxation (JCT).[21] While proposals and reports may emanate from this committee, it is not charged with drafting legislation and its reports lack the interpretive significance of those issued by the Ways and Means and Finance Committees.[22] In addition to studies for use in the hearings or drafting process, the JCT's staff publishes a post-enactment *General Explanation* (the "*Bluebook*" or "*Blue Book*"), which describes changes in the tax laws made by the just-adjourned Congress. The staff published no *General Explanations* between the one for the 1986 Act and 1996.[23]

Bills reported out by committee are debated on the floor of the appropriate house. Although Senate rules permit more extensive debate and floor amendments than do House procedures, each chamber can change the bill. Discussion of the bill during any congressional debate appears in the *Congressional Record*.

---

[18] See Chapter 10 for more information about federal legislative history.

[19] With one constitutional limitation—revenue-raising bills must originate in the House of Representatives (U.S. CONST. art. I, § 7)—the enactment process follows that described in Chapters 9 and 10.

[20] Committee reports can include explanatory language omitted from the act itself. *See, e.g.*, H.R. REP. NO. 104–737, 104TH CONG., 2D SESS. 301 (1996): "The House bill provides that the exclusion from gross income only applies to damages received on account of a personal physical injury or physical sickness. If an action has its origin in a physical injury or physical sickness, then all damages (other than punitive damages) that flow therefrom are treated as payments received on account of physical injury or physical sickness whether or not the recipient of the damages is the injured party. For example, damages (other than punitive damages) received by an individual on account of a claim for loss of consortium due to the physical injury or physical sickness of such individual's spouse are excludable from gross income." The IRS has cited this language in response to taxpayer requests for rulings. *See, e.g.*, Priv. Ltr. Rul. 2001–21–031 (May 25, 2001).

[21] I.R.C. §§ 8001–8023. The Committee is charged with investigating the operation and effects of the tax system, its administration, and means of simplifying it. *Id.* § 8022. The Joint Committee also reviews tax refunds exceeding $2,000,000. *Id.* § 6405.

[22] *See, e.g.*, United States v. Woods, 134 S. Ct. 557 (2013).

[23] Beginning in 2001, the *General Explanation* has been published at the end of each Congress, not at the end of each session or after the enactment of a specific revenue act. The *General Explanations* beginning with one for the Tax Reform Act of 1969 are available at https://www.jct.gov/publications.html (search for "general explanations" and year of Congress).

Bills die when a Congress's second session ends. Members work under extreme time pressure to complete major tax legislation by that date. Under these circumstances, a conference report's version of a bill may contain errors, which Congress passes along with the rest of the bill. If both houses agree, a Concurrent Resolution can be used to make necessary changes before the act is enrolled for submission to the president. If they cannot agree, or they find the errors too late, a technical corrections bill is inevitable.[24]

The president can sign or veto an act in its entirety (or allow it to become law without signing it); Congress can override a veto by a two-thirds vote of each house. After an act becomes law, the interpretive process begins. If no Treasury regulations are available, researchers may consult legislative history materials to ascertain congressional intent. Even after regulations are issued, they may use legislative history materials to challenge a regulation's validity.[25] Legislative history includes testimony at hearings, committee reports, and floor debate. It also includes presidential messages, statements of sponsors, and reports by the Joint Committee staff. Courts and agencies vary in the degree of weight accorded to legislative history materials.[26]

2. Locating Committee Reports

Major tax legislation may involve at least three committee reports. The Conference Committee issues a report in addition to those already issued by the relevant House and Senate committees. These reports are numbered sequentially by Congress, not by committee, and use the issuing house's initials as an identifier.[27] The Conference Committee report is issued as a House report. Note that the House and Senate reports are often issued with respect to different bill numbers because similar bills may be progressing simultaneously through both chambers. Not every act is sufficiently important (or involves sufficient inter-chamber differences) to require all three reports; some acts have no reports.

a.   Citations to Committee Reports. A citation to a committee report enables researchers to easily locate its text in one of the services discussed in the next paragraph or in the library's print or microform collection. Online services, such as *Congress.gov*

---

[24] For example, H.R. Con. Res. 528, 108th Cong., 2d Sess. (2004), removed language relating to access to tax returns from the Consolidated Appropriations Act, 2005. H.R. Con. Res. 395, 99th Cong., 2d Sess. (1986), failed to pass, thus leaving flaws in the 1986 Act. Technical corrections provisions often appear as titles within acts passed for other purposes.

[25] *See, e.g.,* United States v. Nesline, 590 F. Supp. 884 (D. Md. 1984) (invalidating a regulation that varied from the plain language of the statute and had no support in the committee reports); *cf.* Tutor-Saliba Corp. v. Comm'r, 115 T.C. 1 (2000) (holding that a regulation comported with congressional intent). In Ashburn v. United States, 740 F.2d 843 (11th Cir. 1984), the court referred to committee reports and to congressional debates as evidence of the meaning of a phrase in the Equal Access to Justice Act. *See also* Comm'r v. Engle, 464 U.S. 206 (1984) (citing to testimony at hearings, floor debates, and committee reports to assist in interpreting I.R.C. § 613A). The Supreme Court has become less receptive to using legislative history in interpreting statutes. *See* Mayo Found. for Med. Educ. & Research v. United States, 131 S. Ct. 704 (2011) (Treasury regulations issued following notice and comment are likely to enjoy so-called *Chevron* deference).

[26] The Treasury Department and IRS cite to legislative history in administrative documents. *See, e.g.,* T.D. 9194, 70 Fed. Reg. 18920, 18924 (2005) (a House report); Rev. Rul. 2006–1, 2006–2 I.R.B. 262, 263–64 (Senate floor amendment and other legislative history items).

[27] The House Ways and Means Committee report for the Safe, Accountable, Flexible, Efficient Transportation Equity Act: A Legacy for Users (SAFETEA-LU), Pub. L. No. 109–59, 119 Stat. 1144, is H.R. REP. NO. 109–12, 109TH CONG., 1ST SESS. (2005). The Senate Finance report for the same act is S. REP. NO. 109–53, 109TH CONG., 1ST SESS. (2005). The Conference Committee report is H.R. REP. NO. 109–203, 109TH CONG., 1ST SESS. (2005). Although this act's primary focus was on transportation issues, it included several tax provisions.

and *ProQuest Congressional* [Illustration 26–2], provide both citations and links to the documents themselves.

Several tax-oriented print services provide citations to committee reports. *Barton's Federal Tax Laws Correlated* (Section O) covers legislation through 1969.[28] The print version of the *Standard Federal Tax Reporter—Citator* (Section J) includes citations to 1986 Code reports printed in the *Cumulative Bulletin*. Citations appear in Code section order in the Finding Lists section. *TaxCite*, published in 1995 by the ABA Section of Taxation in conjunction with student editors from three law reviews, provides this information for commonly cited statutes enacted between 1913 and 1993.

b. *Text of Committee Reports.* Government websites and online commercial services (Section R) provide text of recent committee reports. Two topical services provide limited coverage: *Standard Federal Tax Reporter* and *United States Tax Reporter*. A third topical service, Rabkin & Johnson, *Federal Income, Gift and Estate Taxation*, covers only the 1954 Code. Topical services are discussed in Section K.

Several collections of primary source materials (Section O) provide at least partial texts of relevant committee reports, but many of them are no longer being updated. They are *Cumulative Bulletin* (1913–2003)[29]; *Tax Management Primary Sources* (1969–2003); *Seidman's Legislative History of Federal Income and Excess Profits Tax Laws* (1863–1953); and *The Internal Revenue Acts of the United States: 1909–1950; 1950–1972; 1973–*.

The Internal Revenue Acts of the United States volumes provide full text with original pagination for all materials. *Seidman's*, which includes at least partial texts, should be consulted for material dated before 1909; it does not cover estate and gift taxes.

3. Locating Other Documents

a. *General Explanation and Other Staff Documents.* The *General Explanation* issued by the staff of the Joint Committee on Taxation is not an official committee report. As such, it is not covered by materials giving citations to committee reports. The same is true for other Joint Committee staff reports and for reports of subcommittees of legislative committees. These reports are published as committee prints. Joint Committee on Taxation documents are available on the Joint Committee's website, on other online services (Section R), in microform collections (Section P), and in many libraries.

b. *Hearings.* Transcripts of hearings can be located in print or in microform in most large libraries. In addition, their full text or excerpts from their full text appears in three series discussed in Section O: *The Internal Revenue Acts of the United States:*

---

[28] The government itself occasionally prepares citations to legislative history materials. *See, e.g.*, J. COMM. ON TAXATION, LISTING OF SELECTED FEDERAL TAX LEGISLATION REPRINTED IN THE IRS CUMULATIVE BULLETIN, 1913–1990 (JCS–19–91) (1991), *available at* https://www.jct.gov/publications.html?func=startdown &id=3338.

[29] Committee reports for 1913 through 1938 appear in 1939–1 (pt. 2) C.B. With the exception of the 1954 Code, for which none are included, committee reports for most other acts appeared in the *Cumulative Bulletins* as they were issued. William S. Hein & Co. has issued a one-volume work, *Internal Revenue Code of 1954: Congressional Committee Reports* (1982) (reprinting a publication by the Senate Finance Committee covering the 1954 Code's history). In addition, Professor Bernard Reams has compiled a multivolume work containing texts of committee reports, hearings, and debates. This set is available from Hein as part of *The Internal Revenue Acts of the United States* series (Section O).

1909–1950; 1950–1972; 1973– (full text); *Tax Management Primary Sources* (excerpts) (1969–2003); and *Seidman's Legislative History of Federal Income and Excess Profits Tax Laws* (excerpts) (1863–1953).

Hearings transcripts are also available online (Section R). The *ProQuest Congressional* service [Illustration 26–2] provides citations to hearings and links to the actual testimony. If a committee releases a hearings transcript to the Government Printing Office, it will be available in *FDsys*. The relevant House and Senate committee websites also include hearings transcripts; the Senate Finance Committee's online Library is particularly useful for this purpose.

[Illustration 26–2]

PARTIAL LEGISLATIVE HISTORY FOR
PUB. L. NO. 109–222 FROM PROQUEST CONGRESSIONAL

Reports

109 -1 Congress Session - November 17, 2005

"Tax Relief Extension Reconciliation Act of 2005"

Committee:	Committee on Ways and Means. House
Bill Number:	109 H.R. 4297
Congressional Publication:	H.rp.109-304
CIS Number:	2005-H783-7
Length:	99 p.
Sudoc:	Y1.1/8:109-304

109 -1 Congress Session - December 07, 2005

"Providing for Consideration of H.R. 4297, Tax Relief Extension Reconciliation Act of 2005"

Committee:	Committee on Rules. House
Bill Number:	109 H.Res. 588
Congressional Publication:	H.rp.109-330
CIS Number:	2005-H683-100
Length:	13 p.
Sudoc:	Y1.1/8:109-330

109 -2 Congress Session - May 09, 2006

"Tax Increase Prevention and Reconciliation Act of 2005"

This service provides text of *Congressional Record* and PDF versions of committee reports. Note how the act's name changed from Tax Relief Extension Reconciliation Act to Tax Increase Prevention and Reconciliation Act.

c.   Floor Statements. Floor statements include sponsors' speeches at a bill's introduction and presidential messages accompanying an administration bill. In addition, questions and answers and other statements made during floor debate may illuminate the meaning of an act provision.

The *Congressional Record* includes full text of floor statements. It is available in *FDsys*, beginning with volume 140 (1994 to date) and on *Congress.gov* (1995 to date). Citations and links to full text can also be obtained from an online service such as *ProQuest Congressional* [Illustration 26–2]. Researchers can locate partial text for older material in *Tax Management Primary Sources* (1969–2003) and *Seidman's Legislative History of Federal Income and Excess Profits Tax Laws* (1863–1953). Researchers can use *Barton's Federal Tax Laws Correlated* as a shortcut for citations to material appearing from 1953 through 1969. These sources are discussed in Section O.

d.   Agency Reports. In addition to reports issued by congressional committees, reports issued by other agencies (both legislative and executive branch) may influence the enactment of tax legislation. Relevant agencies include Congressional Research Service, Congressional Budget Office, Treasury Inspector General for Tax Administration, and National Taxpayer Advocate Service. With the exception of the Congressional Research Service, these materials can be accessed through each agency's website. CRS materials that have been disclosed are available in sites such as *HeinOnline, IntelliConnect*, and *ProQuest Congressional*.

F. TREATIES

Although United States citizens residing in another country pay United States income tax on both domestic and foreign-source income, they may also be subject to taxation in the foreign country of residence. Congress has enacted several mechanisms to mitigate the resulting double taxation. These include foreign tax credits, deductions for foreign taxes, and exclusions for certain foreign source income.[30] Treaties between the United States and other countries are another means of preventing double taxation or other harsh tax consequences.[31]

In determining what authority governs a transaction, neither a treaty nor a statute automatically receives preferential treatment by virtue of its status. Article VI, clause 2, of the Constitution includes both statutes and treaties as the "supreme Law of the Land." However, Congress can decide that treaty provisions will override Code rules governing income earned (or property transferred) abroad by a United States citizen or resident or transactions undertaken in this country by a foreign national.[32] In addition, treaties can be overruled by a later statute, a later treaty, or treaty termination.

Treaties are considered by the Senate Foreign Relations Committee and then by the Senate as a whole. Unlike bills, treaties do not die if the Senate fails to ratify them before the end of a session of Congress.

There are several important dates to note in doing treaty research. The first is the date on which the treaty is signed. The second is the date on which it is ratified by the

---

[30] I.R.C. §§ 27, 164(a), 911, 912 & 2014.

[31] Treaty research is discussed in greater detail in Chapter 21.

[32] *See* I.R.C. §§ 894(a) & 7852(d). Disclosure requirements apply to taxpayers who claim that a tax treaty overrules or modifies an internal revenue law. *See* I.R.C. § 6114; Treas. Reg. § 301.6114–1; IRS Form 8833.

Senate. The third is the date on which the countries exchange instruments of ratification. The fourth is the date (or dates) on which treaty provisions become effective. The different dates are also relevant to any protocols and other items that amend the treaty.

1. Locating Treaties and Their Histories

Once a treaty goes into force, it is added to the State Department's *Treaties and Other International Acts Series* (*T.I.A.S.*). *T.I.A.S.* is the treaty equivalent of *Statutes at Large*; the treaty document equivalent of *United States Code* is *United States Treaties and Other International Agreements* (*U.S.T.*). Because the print official treaty publications have not been updated for many years, a researcher should use other sources to obtain the text of recent treaties.

Although tax treaties and their revising protocols and supplements are published in various places, several tax-oriented resources cover tax treaties. In addition to the services below, researchers can find tax treaties in online subscription services (e.g., *Lexis Advance* and *WestlawNext*) and on government websites.[33]

- Tax Analysts publications (*OneDisc Premium DVD;* online *Worldwide Tax Treaties Service*);

- Thomson Reuters publications (print and online *Federal Tax Coordinator 2d*, *Checkpoint*, and *WestlawNext*);

- *Legislative History of United States Tax Conventions* (Roberts & Holland Collection) (William S. Hein & Co.) (print topical service and *HeinOnline*) (updated by William Manz);

- *CCH Tax Treaties* (print topical service and *IntelliConnect*);

- Rhoades & Langer, *U.S. International Taxation and Tax Treaties* (Matthew Bender) (print topical service, CD-ROM, and *Lexis Advance*); and

- BNA *Tax Management-Foreign Income* (print topical service and online) (Section K).

In addition to treaty texts, these services may also include Senate Executive Reports and Treasury Department Technical Explanations prepared for the Senate.

2. Citators for Tax Treaties

Treaties are not formally covered by citators. Topical services (Section K), CD-ROMs and DVDs (Section Q), and online services (Section R) are the best current sources for locating administrative and judicial rulings involving treaties.

---

[33] Researchers using government sites to search for treaty documents may have to use *FDsys*, the IRS website, *and* the Treasury Department of Tax Policy website because no one site includes all relevant information. The IRS site includes treaty texts and revenue rulings and chief counsel documents related to treaties. The Treasury site includes recent treaties (including protocols, notes, and memoranda of understanding) and Treasury Technical Explanations. *FDsys* provides access to hearings, committee reports, and floor debate. For a non-subscription source providing citations to older treaty documents and administrative guidance, see JOINT COMMITTEE ON TAXATION, LISTING OF SELECTED INTERNATIONAL TAX CONVENTIONS AND OTHER AGREEMENTS REPRINTED IN THE IRS CUMULATIVE BULLETIN, 1913–1990 (JCS–20–91), Dec. 31, 1991. This document is available in the Publications section of the JCT website.

G. TREASURY REGULATIONS

Researchers may need to locate a current regulation and one or more prior versions. They may also need to determine if a regulation is about to be proposed or may wish to read the explanatory preambles that accompany Treasury regulations. Finally, they may need to determine whether a regulation has been challenged in court. In carrying out these tasks, researchers must understand how tax regulations are numbered, where they are published, and how much deference a court will accord them.

1. Overview

a. Authority for Regulations. I.R.C. § 7805(a) authorizes the Secretary of the Treasury to "prescribe all needful rules and regulations for the enforcement" of the tax statutes.[34] General authority regulations issued pursuant to this authorization are often referred to as interpretive (or interpretative). In contrast, there are so-called legislative regulations, issued for Code sections in which Congress has included a specific grant of authority, allowing IRS experts to write rules for highly technical areas.[35] When a regulation is issued or proposed, the transmittal includes a paragraph indicating the Treasury's authority for issuing the regulation, either a specific I.R.C. section (specific authority) or I.R.C. § 7805 (general authority). Before the Supreme Court issued its opinion in *Mayo Foundation for Medical Education and Research v. United States*,[36] it was commonly believed that courts gave more deference to specific-authority regulations than they gave general-authority regulations. The *Mayo* decision eliminated that distinction.

b. Types of Regulations. Regulations, whether general authority or specific authority, are categorized as proposed, temporary, or final. Only final regulations that have gone through notice and comment procedures are likely to receive *Chevron* deference. Proposed regulations are issued with project numbers and are published in the *Federal Register*. Temporary and final regulations are issued as Treasury Decisions (T.D.) and are published in both the *Federal Register* and the *Code of Federal Regulations* (*C.F.R.*). Tax regulations appear as title 26 of *C.F.R.* A citation to Treas. Reg. is equivalent to a citation to 26 C.F.R.

c. Regulations Numbering System. Most regulations consist of three segments, showing the part of title 26 the regulation falls in, the Code section involved, and the order of that regulation among those relating to that Code section. Thus Treas. Reg. § 1.106–1 is the first regulation for I.R.C. § 106 in Part 1 (the income tax) of 26 C.F.R. Regulations are not always numbered in chronological order; the IRS may reserve a regulations number for later issue and issue a regulation with a higher number.

d. Regulations Citation Format. The type of regulation is apparent from its citation form. A proposed regulation includes "Prop." (e.g., Prop. Treas. Reg. § 1.801–4(g)); a temporary regulation includes a "T" (e.g., Treas. Reg. § 1.71–1T or Temp. Treas.

---

[34] Regulations are formulated by the IRS and approved by Treasury Department personnel. *See* 26 C.F.R. § 601.601(a)(1).

[35] For example, I.R.C. § 42(n) provides: "The Secretary shall prescribe such regulations as may be necessary or appropriate to carry out the purposes of this section. . . ."

[36] 131 S. Ct. 704 (2011). Chevron U.S.A. Inc. v. Natural Res. Def. Council, Inc., 467 U.S. 837 (1984), gives more deference to the agency's interpretation than did Nat'l Muffler Dealers Ass'n, Inc. v. United States, 440 U.S. 472 (1979).

Reg. § 1.71–1T); a final regulation has no special identifier (e.g., Treas. Reg. § 1.106–1). These designations are used for both general-authority and specific-authority regulations.

    e. Preambles. When the government publishes a proposed, temporary, or final regulation, it accompanies the regulation's text with a preamble explaining the reason for the regulation. The preamble to a final regulation includes information about public comments and the government's consideration of those comments in the regulation's final version. The preamble also includes information about a variety of miscellaneous matters, such as the regulation's burden on small business. In addition to attacking the substance of the regulation, taxpayers may attack its validity based on the government's failure to include all the information required by such sources as the Administrative Procedure Act or Executive Orders 12866 and 13563.

2. Locating Final and Temporary Regulations

    Because final and temporary regulations are numbered based on the underlying Code section, they are easy to locate in a tax service or in the *C.F.R.* itself. The print version of 26 C.F.R., which includes temporary and final regulations, is published annually, as of each April 1. The *FDsys Code of Federal Regulations* collection follows the same updating schedule. The government's *e-CFR* site includes an up-to-date, albeit unofficial, version of *C.F.R.*

    Standard Federal Tax Reporter and *United States Tax Reporter* include Treasury regulations in Code section order, in their compilation volumes. These topical services are available in print and online. Other online services (Section R), including *Checkpoint*, *IntelliConnect*, *WestlawNext*, and *Lexis Advance*, provide easy access to the language of regulations.

3. Locating Proposed Regulations and Regulations Under Development

    The various drafts of proposed regulations, as well as any accompanying memoranda, may become relevant if the meaning of the regulation is disputed or litigated.[37] Project numbers for proposed regulations (e.g., REG–122813–11) do not reflect the underlying Code section, and the proposed regulations do not appear in the *C.F.R.* Many topical services include proposed regulations along with final and temporary regulations. Services that publish proposed regulations in a separate volume usually include a Code section cross-reference table. Using online services (Section R), researchers can easily locate a proposed regulation by searching for the Code section, project number, or subject matter.

    Because Congress enacts new statutes and amends old ones frequently, many Code sections lack regulations. Others have regulations that do not reflect current law. The Treasury Department and IRS issue an annual regulatory plan (*Priority Guidance Plan*) indicating projects that should yield regulations or other guidance during the coming

---

[37] *Compare* Jewett v. Comm'r, 455 U.S. 305, 313–14 (1982), *with* Sidell v. Comm'r, 225 F.3d 103, 110–11 (1st Cir. 2000), Armco, Inc. v. Comm'r, 87 T.C. 865 (1986), *and* Deluxe Check Printers, Inc. v. United States, 5 Cl. Ct. 498 (1984).

year.[38] The Treasury Department listing in the *Unified Agenda of Regulatory and Deregulatory Actions* provides extensive information about the status of pending items.[39]

4. Locating Prior Regulations

Prior regulatory language may be relevant for evaluating recent changes or determining the tax consequences of a completed transaction. It is also relevant when researchers are tracing the history of a statute and its interpretation by the IRS. Prior language can be obtained from *Mertens, Law of Federal Income Taxation—Regulations* (Section K) (1954–1985 material); and *Cumulative Changes* (Section O) (libraries are more likely to have the 1954 and 1986 Code versions than the 1939 Code version).

Researchers who have T.D. citations for a regulation or its amendment can locate the T.D.s in the *Federal Register*. If a 1954 Code regulation was originally published before 1960, it was republished that year in T.D. 6498, 6500, or 6516. The *C.F.R.* and the *United States Code Annotated* service omit the original publication in their history notes; *Cumulative Changes* omits the 1960 T.D.s; the *Mertens* bound volumes cite only the most recent change in a regulation.

Although most research projects involve regulations promulgated for 1986 or 1954 Code sections, researchers may occasionally need to find a regulation issued for a 1939 Code section. Regulations for all three Codes appear in the IRS *Cumulative Bulletin* and *Internal Revenue Bulletin*, *C.F.R.*, or *Federal Register* for the year of the regulation's promulgation.

5. Locating Preambles

Because preambles accompany the regulation when it is issued, they are published with the regulation in the *Federal Register*. Preambles do not appear in the *C.F.R.* Topical services that include regulations, such as *Standard Federal Tax Reporter* and *United States Tax Reporter*, also include one or more volumes of preambles. These are separate from the volumes that include the text of the regulations. Topical services are discussed in Section K.

6. Assessing a Regulation's Validity

Regulations rarely keep pace with congressional activity. When a Code section changes, existing regulations (including proposed regulations) may no longer be valid. If a regulation appears to contradict statutory language, researchers should check the date of issue of the most recent T.D. (or project number for proposed regulations) to determine if it predates amendments to the relevant Code section.

If an existing regulation affects a transaction, it is important to determine if courts have upheld or invalidated that regulation. The Treasury Department is not bound by adverse decisions in any tribunal other than the Supreme Court. As a result, it will not withdraw a regulation merely because one or more lower courts invalidate it.[40]

---

[38] *Priority Guidance Plans* since 1999 are available at http://www.irs.gov/uac/Priority–Guidance–Plan.

[39] The *Unified Agenda* for all federal agencies is at http://www.reginfo.gov/public/do/eAgendaMain. Items are categorized by status (e.g., proposed rule stage). The IRS is one of many subsidiary agencies covered by the Treasury Department's listing.

[40] The IRS response to the "equitable innocent spouse" decisions represents an unusual outcome for this type of litigation. Although the Tax Court held that Treas. Reg. § 1.6015–5(b)(1) was invalid in the context of I.R.C. § 6015(f), all three appellate courts that issued opinions upheld the regulation. Lantz v. Comm'r, 607

Researchers should use a citator indicating judicial action to determine the outcome of challenges to a regulation's validity. The *Shepard's* and *KeyCite* citators are better for this purpose than their CCH and RIA counterparts. *Shepard's* and *KeyCite* use the regulation section as the cited material; the other two citators use the T.D. number. The latter may give misleading results, as a single T.D. often involves several regulations for a single Code section or regulations for more than one Code section. Citators are discussed further in Section J.

H. INTERNAL REVENUE SERVICE PRONOUNCEMENTS

1. Types of IRS Pronouncements

There are several methods of categorizing IRS pronouncements. One method looks to the means of publication. The IRS officially publishes several pronouncements, most notably revenue rulings, revenue procedures, notices, and announcements, in the weekly *Internal Revenue Bulletin (I.R.B.)* and the semiannual *Cumulative Bulletin (C.B.)*.[41] Other items, including private letter rulings, technical advice memoranda, other chief counsel advice, and actions on decisions, are not published officially but are available to the public. Most documents in this group are currently released because of Freedom of Information Act (FOIA) litigation.

Another method of categorization involves a document's initial audience. Revenue rulings and other items published in the *I.R.B.* and *C.B.* are directed to all taxpayers and their representatives. Private letter rulings, on the other hand, are directed to a specific taxpayer; the IRS makes them available to other readers after deleting identifying material. Still other documents are written for government personnel. Although many of these, such as technical advice memoranda, are publicly available, the IRS resists releasing some other internal documents. In part because of privacy concerns, there are extensive deletions in most released documents.

A third method relates to the item's use as authority. The IRS binds itself to follow guidance published in the *I.R.B.* and *C.B.* in its dealings with taxpayers whose situations are substantially the same. Although it does not bind itself with respect to items released because of FOIA litigation, taxpayers can rely on several of those items in disputing their liability for the substantial understatement of income tax penalty.[42]

2. Officially Published IRS Pronouncements

    a.   *Revenue Rulings (Rev. Rul.).* The IRS issues rulings that apply the law to particular factual situations taxpayers have presented. Rulings fall into two categories: revenue rulings and private letter rulings. If the IRS determines a ruling to be of general interest, it publishes it in the *I.R.B.* as a revenue ruling.[43] Newsletters (Section N) and

---

F.3d 479 (7th Cir. 2010); Mannella v. Comm'r, 631 F.3d 115 (3d Cir. 2011); Jones v. Comm'r, 642 F.3d 459 (4th Cir. 2011). Despite these victories, the IRS ultimately conceded the issue and announced it would stop applying the two-year statute of limitations to equitable innocent spouse claims. Notice 2011–70, 2011–32 I.R.B. 135. If the IRS had not taken this step, Congress might have enacted legislation that negated the regulation.

    [41] For more information about the *I.R.B.* and the *C.B.*, see Section O.

    [42] Treas. Reg. § 1.6662–4(d) lists the items that can be relied on in making a claim that the taxpayer had "substantial authority."

    [43] The IRS occasionally issues a revenue ruling to indicate it will not follow an adverse appellate court decision. *See, e.g.*, Rev. Rul. 95–74, 1995–2 C.B. 36. Since 1993, it has primarily used nonacquiescences for this purpose.

online services (Section R) may report on a ruling several weeks before the ruling appears in the *I.R.B.* Subscribers to the free IRS GuideWire service receive advance email notification of rulings.

Although a revenue ruling is not as authoritative as a Treasury regulation, any taxpayer whose circumstances are substantially the same as those described in the ruling can rely upon it.[44] Subject to the limitations in I.R.C. § 7805(b), rulings can apply retroactively unless their text indicates otherwise. [See Illustration 26–3 for an excerpt from a revenue ruling.]

[Illustration 26–3]

EXCERPT FROM REV. RUL. 2010–4, 2010–4 I.R.B. 309

Rev. Rul. 2010–4

PURPOSE

This revenue ruling provides guidance on whether a tax return preparer is liable for criminal and civil penalties under Internal Revenue Code sections 7216 and 6713 when the tax return preparer discloses or uses tax return information under the circumstances described below.

ISSUES

(1) Is a tax return preparer liable for penalties under sections 7216 and 6713 when the tax return preparer uses tax return information to contact taxpayers to inform them of changes in tax law that could affect the taxpayers' income tax liability reported in tax returns previously prepared or processed by the tax return preparer?

(2) Is a tax return preparer, who is lawfully engaged in the practice of law or accountancy, liable for penalties under sec-

FACTS

Tax Return Preparers A, B, C, D, and E prepared individual and corporate income tax returns for 2008 and several other past years and expect to prepare 2009 income tax returns in the upcoming 2010 filing season.

Prompted by legislation passed by the Congress in 2009 authorizing net operating losses for 2008 to be carried back up to five years, Tax Return Preparer A reviews income tax returns and other tax return information of taxpayers whose income tax returns A has prepared or processed, even if A has not been engaged to prepare the taxpayers' most recent returns, in order to determine which taxpayer clients may be able to benefit from the expanded carryback rules. Following this review, A contacts the affected taxpayers to inform them of the change, advise them with regard to whether an amended return or returns can be filed for years affected by the change, and offer A's tax return preparation ser-

Tax Return Preparer C engages Third-party Service Provider X to publish both paper and electronic monthly newsletters containing educational tax information, tax tips, tax law updates, and direct solicitation for C's tax return preparation business. C discloses to X the names and mailing addresses of taxpayers whose tax returns C has prepared or processed who have not provided C with an email address, and X prints those addresses onto the paper newsletters it publishes for C. X provides C with the completed newsletters in paper and electronic format, and C then distributes them to C's tax return preparation clients, using a list that contains the tax return information authorized by § 301.7216–2(n), including taxpayer names, addresses and e-mail addresses.

Tax Return Preparer D has in the past periodically published and delivered to D's tax return preparation clients newsletters containing general educational tax information, tax tips, tax law updates, and direct solicitations for D's tax return prepa-

The IRS issues relatively few revenue rulings but large numbers of private letter rulings. Although they are not precedential, the latter illustrate IRS thinking.

The IRS numbers revenue rulings chronologically.[45] Ruling numbers do not indicate which Code section is involved. The IRS began issuing numbered revenue rulings in 1953 and adopted the current numbering system in 1954. Earlier revenue rulings, with different names were also published in the *Bulletins*.

Revenue rulings indicate the Code and regulations sections involved. Commonly used divisions of the text include Issue, Facts, Law, Analysis (or a combined Law and Analysis segment), Holding, and Effective Date. An Effect on Other Documents division

---

[44] *See* Rauenhorst v. Comm'r, 119 T.C. 157 (2002). On occasion, the IRS has issued an adverse revenue ruling based on facts encountered in an audit or refund claim and then attempted to assert that ruling as authority when that particular taxpayer litigates. *See* Niles v. United States, 710 F.2d 1391, 1393 (9th Cir. 1983) (discussing Rev. Rul. 79–427, 1979–2 C.B. 120); AMP Inc. v. United States, 185 F.3d 1333, 1338–39 (Fed. Cir. 1999) (discussing Rev. Rul. 91–21, 1991–1 C.B. 112).

[45] Rev. Rul. 2014–1 denotes the first revenue ruling issued in 2014; Rev. Rul. 99–1, the first revenue ruling issued in 1999. The IRS used two digits to indicate the year until 2000. Each week's rulings are numbered sequentially, generally in Code section order. The number of rulings varies from year to year. The IRS issued more than 700 in 1955; it released only 27 in 2013.

appears if the current ruling revokes, modifies, obsoletes, or otherwise affects a prior holding. Rulings also include information about the IRS official who drafted them.

b.   Revenue Procedures (Rev. Proc.) and Procedural Rules. Revenue procedures are published statements of IRS practices and procedures, numbered chronologically since 1955, and published in the *I.R.B.* (and, until recently, the *C.B.*) Procedures of general applicability may be added to the IRS Statement of Procedural Rules and published in the *C.F.R.*

Ten regularly issued revenue procedures are particularly important. For example, the first one issued each year (e.g., Rev. Proc. 2014–1) establishes procedures for obtaining letter rulings, determination letters, and closing agreements under the jurisdiction of chief counsel. It also includes a sample ruling request form and a schedule of user fees. The second revenue procedure each year deals with requests for technical advice, discussed in Section H-3, from chief counsel's office. The third, which is supplemented during the year, contains a cumulative list of areas in which the IRS will not grant rulings.

Revenue procedures include several subdivisions, which vary in number based on the procedure's scope and complexity. The following subdivisions are commonly used: Purpose, Background, Scope, Effect on Other Documents, and Effective Date. Drafting information also appears.

c.   Notices, Announcements, and Other Items. The IRS issues notices to provide guidance before revenue rulings and regulations are available. Notices can describe future regulations in a manner that will pass muster under I.R.C. § 7805(b) rules on retroactivity. Notices are numbered by year; their number does not indicate the Code section involved. Notices appear in both the *I.R.B.* and *C.B.*

Announcements appear in the *I.R.B.* but did not appear in the *C.B.* until 1998. They alert taxpayers to time-sensitive information and to corrections in previously published guidance. Announcements are numbered by year; their number does not indicate the Code section involved.

The *Bulletins* also contain disbarment notices and IRS acquiescences (and nonacquiescences) in unfavorable court decisions.[46] Non-IRS material includes Treasury regulations and proposed regulations.

Instructions accompanying tax return forms and explanatory booklets are published on a regular basis. However, they contain few, if any, citations to authority and do not indicate if the IRS position has been disputed. Further, even if they are misleading, taxpayers who rely on them cannot cite them as authority against a contrary IRS position.[47] These items do not appear in the *I.R.B.* or *C.B.* They are available in the IRS website.

---

[46] The IRS announced a policy change effective in 1991 and began including acquiescence notices for all courts beginning with 1993–1 C.B. Previously, it included this information only for Tax Court regular decisions. Prior to 1998, some miscellaneous items printed in the *I.R.B.* were omitted from the *C.B.*

[47] *See* Osborne v. Comm'r, 97–2 U.S.T.C. ¶ 50,524, 79 A.F.T.R.2d 97–3011 (6th Cir. 1997). *See also* T.A.M. 83–50–008 (involving IRS refusal to allow a taxpayer to claim reliance on a portion of the *Internal Revenue Manual* or on the 1982 version of IRS Publication 544). *But see* Gehl Co. v. Comm'r, 795 F.2d 1324 (7th Cir. 1986). The government decision not to seek *certiorari* in *Gehl* is explained in A.O.D. 1988–02.

3.   Publicly Released Pronouncements

The items below are useful in determining IRS positions on relevant issues; some constitute authority for avoiding the I.R.C. § 6662 penalty for substantial underpayment of taxes ("substantial understatement").[48] Unless otherwise indicated, they use a common numbering system (e.g., 2011–18–014). The first digits indicate the year, and the next two the week, of release; the final numbers indicate the item number for that week. Unless the identifying letters are added (e.g., P.L.R.), readers will not know the type of document being cited. Note that electronic services may omit periods or dashes (e.g., PLR 201413003 or TAM 201409010). The IRS website also omits the dashes.

These and other IRS guidance documents have been released because of FOIA litigation.[49] The public has access to them, generally subject to the disclosure limitations in I.R.C. § 6610, which are supposed to prevent taxpayer-identifying information from being made public and which exempt advance pricing agreements and closing agreements from disclosure. The IRS is not bound by these items in its dealings with taxpayers as a group.[50] Researchers can request release of IRS background documents, including IRS-taxpayer correspondence with regard to a particular ruling. The cost of such items can be substantial.[51]

   a.   Private Letter Rulings (P.L.R.; PLR; Ltr. Rul.; Priv. Ltr. Rul.). Private letter rulings, prepared in response to a taxpayer's inquiry about a proposed transaction, illustrate IRS policy and often indicate areas where future guidance in the form of a revenue ruling is likely. The requesting taxpayer receives a private letter ruling approximately three months before its release to the public. As a result, the actual week of release in the citation is later than that shown in the taxpayer's letter.[52]

   b.   Technical Advice Memoranda (T.A.M.; TAM; Tech. Adv. Mem.). Technical advice memoranda are issued by the IRS national office in response to IRS requests arising out of tax return examinations. While private letter rulings focus on proposed transactions, technical advice memoranda discuss transactions that have already taken place.

---

[48] I.R.C. § 6662 imposes a penalty on taxpayers for a "substantial understatement" of tax (as defined) but exempts understatements when the taxpayer has "substantial authority for such treatment." I.R.C. § 6662(d)(1), (2). Some pronouncements can be used as "substantial authority" for the taxpayer's position.

[49] Freedom of Information Act, 5 U.S.C. § 552, litigation led to the release of letter rulings and technical advice memoranda issued after October 31, 1976, and to the enactment of I.R.C. § 6110. *See* Tax Analysts & Advocates v. IRS, 405 F. Supp. 1065 (D.D.C. 1975). Letter rulings have been released as issued since mid-March 1977. I.R.C. § 6110(h) authorizes inspection of documents issued after July 4, 1967. Additional Tax Analysts lawsuits led to the release of other IRS documents, including G.C.M.s, A.O.D.s, F.S.A.s, and tax-exemption denials and revocations.

[50] *But see* Ogiony v. Comm'r, 617 F.2d 14, 17–18 (2d Cir. 1980) (Oakes, J., concurring). Although noting that they had no precedential value, courts have cited letter rulings as evidence of IRS inconsistent interpretation. *See* Rowan Cos., Inc. v. United States, 452 U.S. 247, 261 n.17 (1981). In United States v. Quality Stores, Inc., 2014 WL 1168968 (2014), the Supreme Court cited a technical advice memorandum in its discussion of IRS treatment of supplemental unemployment benefits.

[51] *See* I.R.C. § 6110. The IRS imposes a search fee and a per-page fee for the effort in deleting identifying and other confidential information from background documents. Rev. Proc. 2012–31, 2012–33 I.R.B. 256.

[52] Determination letters are similar to letter rulings. Directors of IRS operating divisions issue determination letters only if they can be based on clearly established rules that apply to the issues presented. Otherwise, the national office is the appropriate venue to issue a determination letter. Letter rulings generally involve proposed transactions; determination letters, completed transactions. The first revenue procedure issued each year indicates the subject-matter jurisdiction for rulings and determination letters within the IRS.

c.   Actions on Decisions (A.O.D.; AOD; action on decision; action on dec.). A.O.D.s indicate the reasoning behind the Service's recommendation whether to appeal an adverse decision by a trial or appellate court and whether to acquiesce in that decision.[53] A.O.D.s are numbered sequentially by year (e.g., A.O.D. 2011–01); the numbering provides no information about the underlying case name or issue.

d.   General Counsel Memoranda (G.C.M.; GCM; Gen. Couns. Mem.).[54] These memoranda from the Office of Chief Counsel indicate the reasoning and authority used in revenue rulings, private letter rulings, and technical advice memoranda. IRS personnel use them as guides in formulating positions.

G.C.M.s are numbered sequentially (e.g., G.C.M. 39890). The numbering system does not indicate the year of issue, the relevant Code section, or the document about which they supply information. Since 1997, G.C.M.s have been issued only to revoke previously issued items.

e.   Internal Revenue Manual (I.R.M., IRM). A tax problem may require knowledge of IRS operating policies. The *Internal Revenue Manual (I.R.M.)* is the best source of information about topics such as which IRS office is responsible for various types of guidance, the examining process, or procedures for dealing with rewards to informants. The *I.R.M.* has its own numbering system based on topics.

f.   Chief Counsel Advice (C.C.A.; CCA).[55] These documents provide individual taxpayer information to IRS field or service center employees. [Illustration 26–4] *C.C.A.* may respond to a field office query or may provide information about a taxpayer (such as a taxpayer's request to change accounting method being denied). Field service advice (F.S.A; FSA), service center advice (S.C.A; SCA), and other types of chief counsel advice, are classified and issued as *C.C.A.*

---

[53] The IRS originally issued notices of acquiescence and nonacquiescence only for Tax Court regular decisions. Beginning with 1993–1 C.B., it now issues these notices for decisions by other courts as well. A.O.D.s were never limited to Tax Court decisions.

[54] Do not confuse current G.C.M.s with revenue rulings issued before 1953, which were also called G.C.M.s. *See* Table 1.

[55] These documents are classified as IRS Legal Memoranda (ILM; I.L.M.) in Tax Analysts publications; the IRS and most other services use the Chief Counsel Advice (CCA; C.C.A.) designation. The IRS website combines private letter rulings, technical advice memoranda, and other chief counsel advice in the IRS Written Determinations part of the *Electronic Reading Room's* Non-precedential Rulings & Advice section. *See also* I.R.M. pt. 33.

[Illustration 26–4]

EXCERPT FROM CHIEF COUNSEL ADVICE 2011–05–036

ID: CCA_2011010614475243   **Number: 201105036**
                                        Release Date: 2/4/2011
Office:

UILC: 7216.20-00

From:
Sent: Thursday, January 06, 2011 2:47:54 PM
To:
Cc:
Subject: RE: 7216 Presentations

Hi

Yes, the taxpayer would not need to sign the consent prior to signing the return, because the consent is not being obtained in the context of solicitation of additional services. If the tax return preparer were to obtain a consent for purposes of soliciting other services (e.g., financial planning services), then the taxpayer would need to sign the consent prior to the preparer's presentation of the completed return to the taxpayer for signature.

Chief counsel advice ranges from the relatively informal, illustrated here, to lengthy responses and citations to authority. CCA 2011–05–036 can be located using the IRS website's search function [Illustration 25–6] or an online subscription service.

g.   Other IRS Items. The IRS website's *Electronic Reading Room*[56] divides IRS materials into five categories, some of which are discussed in the preceding paragraphs:

- Published Tax Guidance (*I.R.B.* items);

- Non-precedential Rulings & Advice (chief counsel items, legal advice issued by associate chief counsel and field attorneys, and legal advice issued to program managers);

- Admin Manuals & Instructions (*I.R.M.*, chief counsel notices, and other directives to IRS personnel);

- Program Plans & Reports (including the *Priority Guidance Plan* and reports by the Treasury Inspector General for Tax Administration (TIGTA)); and

- Training & Reference Materials (including audit techniques guides).

4.   Unreleased Documents

Closing agreements memorialize the resolution of specific IRS-taxpayer disputes. Advance pricing agreements are made between taxpayers and the IRS regarding income allocation between commonly controlled entities. They are important for companies that segment their operations between countries with different tax rates. I.R.C. § 6110(b)(1)(B) exempts closing agreements and advance pricing agreements from

---

[56] http://www.irs.gov/uac/Electronic–Reading–Room.

disclosure to the public. In limited instances, the IRS has forced exempt organizations to allow publication of a closing agreement.

5.   Locating IRS Pronouncements

a.   I.R.B. and C.B. Items—Citations and Texts. Unlike regulations, IRS rulings and other *I.R.B.* items do not carry numbers that correspond to the Code sections they discuss. As a result, online commercial services (Section R) are the best sources for finding these items; each database can be searched by topic, Code or regulations section, or prior ruling.

Four topical services that are discussed in Section K can be used to locate and read summaries of relevant items: *Standard Federal Tax Reporter*; *United States Tax Reporter* [Illustration 26–5]; *Federal Tax Coordinator 2d*; and Mertens, *Law of Federal Income Taxation* (does not print text of notices and announcements). Two others, *Rabkin & Johnson, Federal Income, Gift and Estate Taxation*, and *Tax Management Portfolios*, can be used to locate citations. Online versions of the topical services provide hyperlinks to full-text documents.[57]

[Illustration 26–5]

EXCERPT FROM UNITED STATES TAX REPORTER

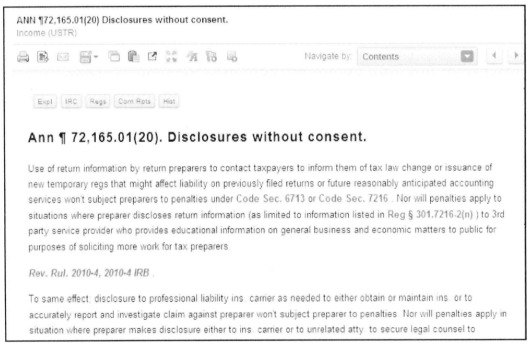

Revenue Ruling 2010-4 [Illustration 26–3] could be located using annotations in a topical service such as *United States Tax Reporter*, where it appears in ¶ 72,165.01(20). The excerpt above is from the *Checkpoint* version of *USTR*. Note how *USTR* uses the Code section number, § 7216, in its paragraph numbering system.

---

[57] A topical service's electronic version generally links to the text of IRS rulings even if its print version does not include rulings texts.

b.   Forms and Publications. The IRS website carries IRS publications and forms and accompanying instructions. Researchers can search for these items by number or topic, or can use the website's Advanced Search feature to search by word or phrase.

c.   Other IRS Documents. The IRS releases letter rulings and other documents on a weekly basis. It makes them available in its *Electronic Reading Room.* In most cases, it presents them in numerical order or in Uniform Issue List order, which reflects the underlying Code section but not subsection. [Illustration 26–6] Because neither format is user-friendly, researchers generally prefer other methods for locating these documents. Other sources include citators (Section J) and online commercial services (Section R). Researchers can also use online versions of newsletters (Section N) to keep apprised of the most recent items.

[Illustration 26–6]

SCREEN PRINT FROM IRS WEBSITE

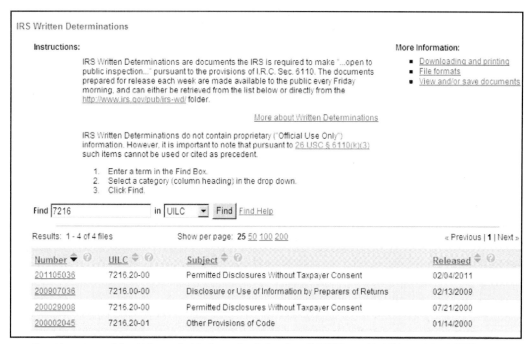

Researchers can search for chief counsel advice by number, Uniform Issue List (UILC), or subject. This search located CCA 2011–05–036. [Illustration 26–4] Note that the IRS does not use hyphens in its numbering system for private letter rulings, technical advice memoranda, or other chief counsel advice.

6.   Citators for IRS Materials

The IRS reviews revenue rulings and procedures for continued relevance. In appropriate cases, it modifies or revokes an item or declares it obsolete. In addition, some rulings have been subjected to judicial scrutiny. The status of these items is best determined from citators (Section J) and online services (Section R).

I.   JUDICIAL REPORTS

1.   Court Organization

Four federal courts serve as trial courts for most tax disputes: district courts; the Court of Federal Claims; the Tax Court; and bankruptcy courts.

a.   United States District Courts. Because federal district courts are courts of general jurisdiction, their judges rarely develop as high a level of expertise on tax law questions as do judges of the Tax Court or even of the Court of Federal Claims. Taxpayers must pay the amount in dispute and sue for a refund before litigating in district court, the only tribunal where a jury trial is available.

b.   United States Court of Federal Claims. Although the Court of Federal Claims does not hear tax cases exclusively, its caseload includes a greater percentage of such cases than that of the average federal district court. As in the district court, a taxpayer must first pay the disputed amount before bringing suit. Prior to October 1, 1982, this court was named the United States Court of Claims. Trials were conducted by a trial judge (formerly called a commissioner). Trial judges' decisions were reviewed by Court of Claims judges; only the Supreme Court had jurisdiction over appeals from Court of Claims decisions. Between October 1, 1982, and October 29, 1992, this court was named the United States Claims Court.

c.   United States Tax Court. Because Tax Court judges hear only tax cases, their expertise is substantially greater than that of judges in the other trial courts. Tax Court cases are tried by one judge, who submits an opinion to the chief judge for consideration. The chief judge can allow the decision to stand or refer it to the full court for review. The published decision indicates if it has been reviewed; concurring and dissenting opinions, if any, are included. In some instances, special trial judges hear disputes and issue opinions.

Two types of Tax Court opinions can be cited as precedent: the Government Printing Office prints opinions presenting important legal issues (regular opinions); other publishers print both regular opinions and opinions applying well-established legal issues to factual disputes (memorandum opinions).[58] A taxpayer can sue in the Tax Court without paying the amount in dispute prior to litigating. Taxpayers also had this privilege in the Tax Court's predecessor, the Board of Tax Appeals.

d.   United States Bankruptcy Court. In addition to deciding priority of liens and related matters, United States bankruptcy courts may also issue substantive tax rulings.[59] Most bankruptcy court decisions are reviewed by district court judges or by Bankruptcy Appellate Panels; some are reviewed directly by federal courts of appeals.[60]

e.   Appellate Review. When research uncovers conflicting decisions at the trial court level, those decisions should be traced to the appellate court level. If no appeals

---

[58] The Tax Court also has a Small Cases division that taxpayers can elect to use for disputes of $50,000 or less. Decisions in such cases cannot be appealed and cannot be used as precedents. I.R.C. § 7463. Decisions were not generally available until the Tax Court began publicly releasing them in January 2001. Booth v. Comm'r, T.C. Summ. Op. 2001–1 (Jan. 3, 2001), was the first such opinion released.

[59] *See, e.g.,* United States v. Yellin (*In re* Weinstein), 251 B.R. 174 (B.A.P. 1st Cir. 2000), *aff'g In re* Weinstein, 237 B.R. 4 (Bankr. D. Mass. 1999).

[60] 28 U.S.C. § 158.

have been taken, the Tax Court's specialized knowledge may cause greater weight to be accorded to its decisions than to decisions from the other trial courts.[61] In addition, if a court has ruled against the government and the IRS has issued a notice of acquiescence, the precedential value of the decision is enhanced.[62]

Decisions of federal district courts and the Tax Court are appealed to the court of appeals for the taxpayer's geographical residence[63] and from there to the Supreme Court. Decisions of the Court of Federal Claims are appealed to the United States Court of Appeals for the Federal Circuit. Because the Supreme Court reviews so few court of appeals decisions, filing in the Court of Federal Claims offers a forum-shopping opportunity to taxpayers living in circuits where appellate court decisions involving similar issues are adverse.[64]

2. Locating Decisions

Researchers can compile a preliminary reading list of decisions involving a particular statute, treaty, regulation, or ruling by using the citators discussed in Section J or the topical services discussed in Section K.

The texts of federal court decisions involving taxation appear in these sets:[65]

• Supreme Court (1796 to date): *United States Reports (U.S.)* (official); *United States Supreme Court Reports, Lawyers' Edition (L. Ed.; L. Ed. 2d)* (1796 to date); *Supreme Court Reporter (S. Ct.)* (1882 to date); *American Federal Tax Reports* (1796 to date); *U.S. Tax Cases* (1913 to date);

• Courts of Appeals (1880 to date): *Federal Reporter (F.; F.2d; F.3d)* (1880 to date); *American Federal Tax Reports* (1880 to date); *U.S. Tax Cases* (1915 to date). Unpublished opinions may be included in the *Federal Appendix (F. App'x)* reporter service (2001 to date);

• District Courts (1882 to date): *Federal Supplement (F. Supp.; F. Supp. 2d)* (1932 to date); *Federal Reporter* (from 1882 to 1932); *American Federal Tax Reports* (1882 to date); *U.S. Tax Cases* (1915 to date);

• Court of Federal Claims (1863 to date): *U.S. Court of Claims Reports (Ct. Cl.)* (official) (from 1884 to October 1, 1982); *Federal Reporter* (from 1929 to 1932; from 1960 to October 1, 1982); *Federal Supplement* (between 1932 and 1960); *United States Claims Court Reporter (Cl. Ct.)* (from October 1, 1982, to October 29, 1992); *United States Court of Federal Claims Reporter (Fed. Cl.)* (October 30, 1992, to date); *American Federal Tax Reports* (1876 to date); *U.S. Tax Cases* (1924 to date);

• Tax Court (1942 to date): *Tax Court of the United States Reports; United States Tax Court Reports (T.C.)* (official) (1942 to date); *CCH Tax Court Reporter* (regular and

---

[61] *But see* Baizer v. Comm'r, 204 F.3d 1231, 1233 (9th Cir. 2000) ("Although a presumption exists that the tax court correctly applied the law, no special deference is given to the tax court's decisions.").

[62] Always check if the IRS issued an A.O.D. (Section H) giving its rationale for appealing or acquiescing.

[63] From 1924 to 1926, decisions of the Board of Tax Appeals (the Tax Court's predecessor) were appealed to a district court. Revenue Act of 1924, ch. 234, § 900(g), 43 Stat. 253, 337; Revenue Act of 1926, ch. 27, § 1001(a), 44 Stat. 9, 109.

[64] Ginsburg v. United States, 184 Ct. Cl. 444, 449, 396 F.2d 983, 986 (1968), discusses this phenomenon in the court's predecessor, the Court of Claims.

[65] Relevant dates of coverage are indicated for each court and case reporter service. Case reporter services are discussed in Chapter 5.

memorandum opinions) (1942 to date); *RIA Tax Court Reports* (formerly *P-H*) (1942 to date); *RIA Tax Court Memorandum Decisions* (formerly *P-H*) (1942 to date). The Tax Court website includes an opinion search feature; [Illustration 26–7]

• Board of Tax Appeals (from 1924 to 1942; memorandum opinions from 1928 to 1942): *Board of Tax Appeals Reports (B.T.A.)* (official) (from 1924 to 1942); *P-H B.T.A. Memorandum Decisions* (from 1928 to 1942); and

• Bankruptcy Courts (1979 to date): *West's Bankruptcy Reporter (B.R.)* (1979 to date); *American Federal Tax Reports* (1979 to date); *U.S. Tax Cases* (1979 to date).

These decisions may also be found online (Section R), in microform (Section P) and in CD-ROM or DVD format (Section Q).

[Illustration 26–7]

SCREEN PRINT FROM TAX COURT WEBSITE OPINIONS SEARCH SCREEN

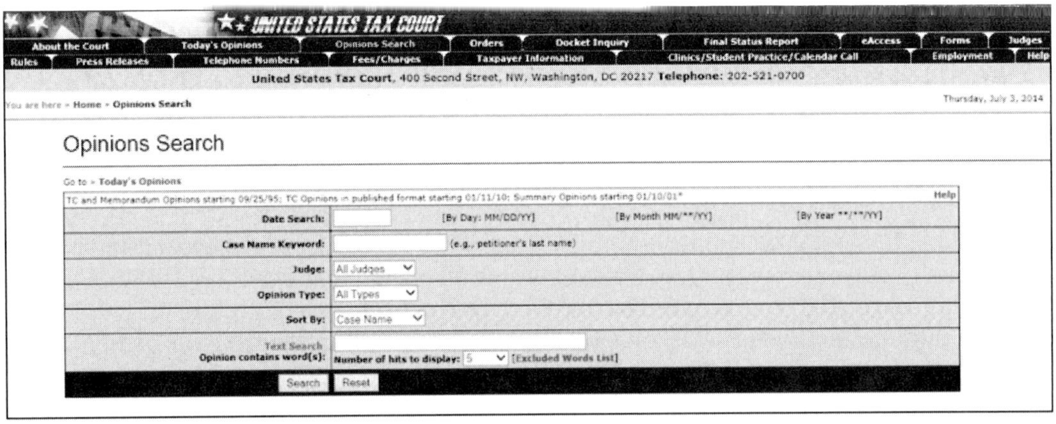

The Opinions Search function is relatively easy to use but offers fewer search options than do subscription services. In addition, it does not provide access to opinions issued before September 25, 1995 (regular and memorandum opinions) or January 1, 2001 (summary opinions).

3. Tax-Oriented Case Reporter Services

Most of the sets listed above are published by the Government Printing Office or by Thomson Reuters (West) and are used similarly for tax and non-tax research. The sets published by RIA and CCH differ enough from the others to warrant further discussion. The discussion below covers print (e.g., looseleaf) versions of these services. Researchers can also access these reporter services and related topical services in their publishers' tax-oriented online services (*Checkpoint* and *IntelliConnect*).

a. *American Federal Tax Reports (A.F.T.R.) and U.S. Tax Cases (U.S.T.C.).* The use of these sets can be coordinated with the use of each publisher's topical reporting service, *A.F.T.R.* with *United States Tax Reporter* and *U.S.T.C.* with *Standard Federal Tax Reporter*. Each service publishes decisions from all courts except the Tax Court, and each may include "unpublished" decisions omitted from *Federal Supplement* and *Federal Reporter*.[66] Decisions initially appear in an *Advance Sheets* volume of the related

---

[66] The earliest volumes of this service print all Supreme Court decisions and those lower court decisions of "genuine precedent value. . . ." *Foreword* to 1 U.S.T.C. (1938). When CCH began issuing two volumes per year, it expanded coverage to all decisions.

looseleaf reporting service. As a result, recent decisions are available in print on a weekly basis although each service occasionally prints decisions before the other does.

These very recently decided cases also appear in the listings of new material in the services' update volumes (*Recent Developments* for *United States Tax Reporter*; *New Matters* for *Standard Federal Tax Reporter*). The listings appear in Code section order and are cross-referenced to discussions in the services' compilation volumes. As a result, a recent case can be located when the Code section involved is known but not the taxpayer's name, and researchers can immediately find a discussion of the topic involved in the compilation volumes. The daily newsletters (Section N), which are probably the only more current print source of these cases, print only partial texts and lack a weekly index.

When using these reporter services, note the reference method being used. *U.S.T.C.* uses paragraph numbers for cross-references to the Advance Sheets and bound volumes (e.g., 2011–1 U.S.T.C. ¶ 50,436). RIA cites decisions in the *A.F.T.R.* Advance Sheets and bound volumes by page number (e.g., 107 A.F.T.R.2d 2011–519). The services sometimes differ in their captions for bankruptcy cases.[67] Captions may also differ for non-bankruptcy cases involving a decedent's estate. A reporter service might name the decedent or the personal representative. The citator related to each case reporter service is likely to use the naming convention used in the case reporter.

The bound volumes include all types of tax cases—income, estate and gift, and excise; the individual *Advance Sheets* volumes do not. The different types of cases appear in *Advance Sheets* sections accompanying each publisher's topical service for the particular area of tax law.

    b.   *Tax Court Reports. CCH Tax Court Reporter* has three binders. Volume 1 contains memorandum decisions and volume 2 contains regular decisions. Volume 3 contains case digests and information about pending litigation. Volume 1 has an alphabetical Table of Decisions, while volume 2 provides cross-references from the reporter service to CCH case numbers. Updating is weekly.

4.   Pending Litigation, Briefs, and Petitions

The method for determining whether appeals have been filed, or locating briefs and petitions, is affected by whether the researcher is currently reading a case or is doing follow-up research on a case that was read previously. For example, a researcher who has just finished reading a decision in *WestlawNext* might click on a link entitled Filings to access this information immediately.

For researchers doing follow-up research, either the *United States Tax Reporter Tables* volume or the *Standard Federal Tax Reporter New Matters* volume can be used to determine if appeals have been filed in recent tax cases. *United States Tax Reporter* has an alphabetical Table of Cases in which appeals are noted; the *SFTR* version is the current year's Case Table.

Researchers who know the taxpayer's name or the docket number can also obtain information about pending Tax Court cases by consulting the court's website.

---

[67] *Compare In re* Guardian Trust Company, 99–2 U.S.T.C. ¶ 50,819 (Bankr. S.D. Miss. 1999), *with* Henderson v. United States, 84 A.F.T.R.2d 99–5940 (Bankr. S.D. Miss. 1999). The *CCH Citator* lists the case as Guardian Trust Company; *RIA Citator 2nd* lists it as Henderson, Derek.

Because the IRS often indicates its recommendation about appealing adverse decisions in actions on decisions and in acquiescence and nonacquiescence notices (Section H), these documents should be consulted before deciding if appeals are likely in cases of interest.

5.   Citators for Decisions

There are four citators commonly used for judging the relative authority of any tax decision. They are *Shepard's Citations (Lexis Advance)*; *KeyCite (WestlawNext)*; *RIA Citator 2nd (Checkpoint* and *WestlawNext)*; *Standard Federal Tax Reporter—Citator (IntelliConnect)*. Many libraries offer access to all of them. All four are discussed in Section J.

In addition, the IRS website AOD section indicates IRS action with regard to cases it has lost. This information is also available, and easier to locate, in subscription-based online services (Section R). Subscription-based services cover AODs issued earlier than those included in the IRS *Electronic Reading Room*.

J.   CITATORS

Several web-based citators can be used to judge whether a particular statute, regulation, ruling, or judicial decision was criticized, approved, or otherwise commented upon in a more recent proceeding. The material being evaluated is referred to as the *cited* item; any later material that refers to it is a *citing* item. The four services are *Shepard's Citations*, West's *KeyCite*, *RIA Citator 2nd*,[68] and *Standard Federal Tax Reporter—Citator*.[69] With the exception of *KeyCite*, these services are also available in print versions. This chapter discusses the online versions, which are much easier to use and more up to date. [See Illustrations 26–8 through 26–11 for partial lists of citations to Lantz v. Commissioner, 607 F.3d 479 (7th Cir. 2010).]

Both *Shepard's* and *KeyCite* provide citations to secondary source material. Researchers can use each to determine if an article has cited a judicial decision and vice versa. When citing judicial decisions, these citators use headnote numbers to indicate issues, but each uses its own headnote numbering system. These citators also indicate whether the later item followed or disagreed with the earlier item.

RIA also indicates headnote numbers and how the citing item treated the cited item. Although *RIA* and *KeyCite* have a common owner, *RIA* uses its own headnote numbering system. Unlike *Shepard's* and *KeyCite*, *RIA* does not provide citations for secondary material. In addition, it does not provide citations for the Constitution or statutes.

CCH uses fewer citing cases than do the others. As was true for *RIA*, it does not provide citations for articles, the Constitution, or statutes. Although *CCH* indicates if a later decision cited an earlier one, it does not indicate if the later item agreed with the earlier item.

---

[68] The first series of the *RIA Citator* is available only in print. That series was initially published by Prentice–Hall.

[69] Other online citators exist but are not discussed here because they are not as widely used as these four. One such citator, *BCite*, the citator in *Bloomberg Law*, has the advantage of linking to *Bloomberg BNA* materials.

[Illustration 26-8]

SCREEN PRINT FROM SHEPARD'S CITATOR

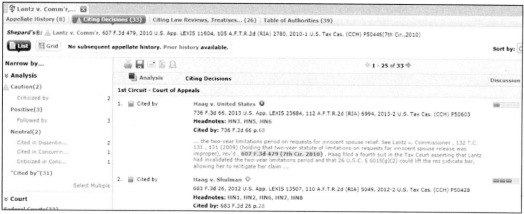

Researchers can narrow their results by type of citing material, by treatment (e.g., positive or negative), by court, by headnotes, and by several other factors.

[Illustration 26-9]

SCREEN PRINT FROM RIA CITATOR 2ND

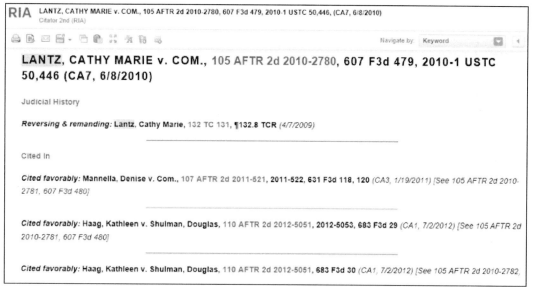

This excerpt is from *Checkpoint*; the *RIA Citator* is also available in *WestlawNext*.

[Illustration 26–10]

SCREEN PRINT FROM STANDARD FEDERAL TAX REPORTER—CITATOR

Federal Tax Citator, Lantz, Cathy M.

Lantz, Cathy M.

ANNOTATED AT ... 2014FED¶35,192.023, ¶35,192.25, ¶35,192.455

• **CA-7**-- (rev'g and rem'g TC) 2010-1 USTC ¶50,446 , 607 F3d 479

Haag CA-1, 2013-2 USTC ¶50,603 , 736 F3d 66

Karam CA-6, 2012-2 USTC ¶50,655 , 504 FedAppx 416

Haag CA-1, 2012-2 USTC ¶50,420 , 693 F3d 26

Jones CA-4, 2011-1 USTC ¶50,436 , 642 F3d 459

Manella CA-3, 2011-1 USTC ¶50,159 , 631 F3d 115

Popowski DC-SC, 2012-2 USTC ¶50,718

Goodrich Corporation DC-NC, 2012-1 USTC ¶50,159 , 406 FSupp2d 445

Haag TC, Dec. 59,812(M) , 107 TCM 1063 , TC Memo 2014-11

Cutler TC, Dec. 59,529(M) , 105 TCM 1704 , TC Memo 2013-119

This excerpt is from *IntelliConnect*. This citator includes references to CCH topical service annotations relevant to the *Lantz* decision.

[Illustration 26–11]

SCREEN PRINT FROM KEYCITE RESULTS IN WESTLAWNEXT

Lantz v. C.I.R.
United States Court of Appeals, Seventh Circuit.   June 8, 2010   607 F.3d 479   105 A.F.T.R.2d 2010-2780   2010-1 USTC P 50, 446   *(Approx. 9)*

| Document | Filings (9) | Negative Treatment (2) | History (2) | Citing References (132) | Table of Authorities | Powered by KeyCite |

Cases (28)

Administrative Decisions & Guidance (3)

Secondary Sources (57)

Declined to Extend by Hall v. C.I.R., U.S.Tax Ct., Septe

Appellate Court Documents (30)

Original Image of 607 F.3d 479 (PDF)

Trial Court Documents (14)

United States Court of Appeals,
Seventh Circuit.

Cathy Marie LANTZ, Petitioner–Appellee,

v.

COMMISSIONER of INTERNAL REVENUE, Respondent–Appellant.

No. 09–3345.   Argued April 9, 2010.   Decided June 8, 2010.

The researcher can select later material for reading from the menus at the top of the search results screen.

K. TOPICAL SERVICES

It may be necessary to consult explanatory materials early in the research effort, perhaps even before reading the relevant statutes. The texts described in this chapter often provide insight into the problem being researched, and their liberal use of citations is a useful introduction to the relevant cases and administrative pronouncements. Each is updated at frequent intervals, and most have at least one related newsletter (Section N).

The topical services described in this section are updated more frequently than legal encyclopedias or treatises.[70] Most of them take a subject matter approach, but two of the best-known services are arranged in Code section order.

Before using a topical service, researchers should become familiar with the service's format for designating materials. Cross-references to updating items use that format. This is particularly important when using the print versions of the services described in subsections 1 and 2. Each service is also available from at least one online provider; the online versions provide hyperlinks to updating material.

1. Code Section Arrangement

The *Standard Federal Tax Reporter*[71] (*SFTR*) (CCH) and the *United States Tax Reporter*[72] (*USTR*) (RIA) topical services take essentially the same approach. Compilation volumes provide the full texts of Code sections and Treasury regulations along with editorial explanations. An annotation section lists cases and rulings for each Code section. Users wanting ready access to the text of the law while they are reading explanations of it will appreciate this format.

Because of the arrangement described above, however, problems involving multiple Code sections do not receive comprehensive discussion in the Code compilations. Although the publishers supplement these services with newsletters and other aids, Code-based services are not the best tools for learning about a particular topic. Researchers who are unfamiliar with a particular area may find it easier to begin research in a topical service that is arranged by subject matter.

Although each service is arranged in Code section order, all materials are assigned paragraph numbers; a "paragraph" can be the size of a traditional paragraph or several pages long. *USTR* uses the Code section numbers in its paragraph numbering system; *SFTR* does not. Each service generally cross-references between paragraph numbers, not between page numbers. New developments are indexed according to the paragraph in the main compilation to which they relate, i.e., in Code section order. Both services provide information about pending litigation, proposed regulations, and other matters of interest to researchers.

---

[70] See Chapters 14, 16, and 19 for further discussion of these research tools. The annotated law reports discussed in Chapter 17 also provide textual material. Researchers doing historical research should check the *HeinOnline* Taxation & Economic Reform in America library and the *Making of Modern Law* treatise collection.

[71] Related titles are: *Standard Federal Tax Reporter* (income tax); *Federal Estate and Gift Tax Reporter*; *Federal Excise Tax Reporter*.

[72] Related titles are: *United States Tax Reporter—Income Taxes*; *United States Tax Reporter—Estate & Gift Taxes*; *United States Tax Reporter—Excise Taxes*. RIA also publishes a subject matter format service (*Federal Tax Coordinator 2d*).

Libraries often carry both *SFTR* and *USTR* in print and subscribe to the online versions. Users eventually develop a preference for one or the other. As each service's annotations are editorially selected, use of both can reduce the risk of missing a valuable annotation although it may substantially increase research time. The extra material obtained is unlikely to justify the additional time involved.

These services contain the following features. In addition, each has a variety of other useful tables and finding lists.

a.   *Code Volumes.* These volumes print, in Code section order, all provisions involving income, gift and estate, employment, and excise taxes and procedural provisions. *SFTR* contains tables that cross-reference between the 1939 and 1954 Codes. [Illustration 26–1] These tables appear in Code volume I in the print version and in the Code Finding Lists section in *IntelliConnect*.

b.   *Compilation Volumes.* These volumes contain, in Code section order, the full text of the Code, excerpts from congressional committee reports, proposed, temporary, and final regulations, and digest-annotations to judicial decisions, revenue rulings, and other IRS guidance. These volumes make up the largest part of each set. [Illustration 26–5]

c.   *Updating Volumes.* Recent material is indexed in the *New Matters* volume (*SFTR*) or *Recent* Developments volume (*USTR*). These materials are arranged according to the paragraph numbers used in the compilation volumes, making it easy to find recent rulings and decisions in any area of interest. The updating volumes print full text of recent IRS materials.

d.   *Advance Sheets Volumes.* These volumes contain the texts of income tax decisions rendered by courts other than the Tax Court. Decisions involving estate and gift taxes or excise taxes appear in the CCH and RIA services covering those topics. Court decisions covering all taxes are later issued in hardbound volumes as part of the *U.S.T.C.* and *A.F.T.R.* reporter services discussed in Section K. *SFTR* includes preambles to proposed regulations in the *Advance Sheets* volume; *USTR* has a separate *Proposed Regulation Preambles* volume.

e.   *Citator Volumes.* The CCH and RIA citators, which cover both judicial decisions and IRS materials, are discussed in Section J. The RIA citator is more comprehensive than its CCH counterpart.

2. Subject Matter Arrangement—Multiple Topics

The sets described in this section cover a wide range of topics, using a subject matter arrangement. Most of them include tables indicating where researchers can find discussion of judicial decisions and other primary source material. These services also have topical indexes.[73]

a.   *Federal Tax Coordinator 2d (RIA).* This weekly service contains excellent discussions of most areas of taxation, with minimal coverage of employment taxes. Discussions in each chapter of the text volumes include liberal use of citations, cross-references to topics of potential relevance discussed in other chapters, and analysis of as yet unresolved matters.

---

[73] *Tax Management Portfolios* have excellent Code and topical indexes, but lack case and rulings tables.

Each chapter has the following arrangement: a Detailed Reference Table for topics included; discussion of each topic, with extensive footnotes; and text of Code and regulations sections applicable to the chapters being discussed. Topics in each chapter are further subdivided into "paragraphs."

The service has an extensive Topical Index and cross-reference tables showing discussions of primary source material. A variety of practice aids, such as sample client letters and annuity tables, are also included.

Volumes 20 and 20A contain the texts of United States tax treaties and lists of signatory countries, in addition to textual material dealing with the treaties. Volumes 27 and 27A contain proposed regulations reproduced in the order in which they were issued, along with preambles and *Federal Register* citations.

b.   Bloomberg BNA Tax Management Portfolios. Bloomberg BNA issues three series of *Tax Management Portfolios*: *U.S. Income*; *Foreign Income*; and *Estates, Gifts, and Trusts.* Each series is subdivided into several wirebound *Portfolios* that cover narrow areas of tax law in great depth.[74]

Each *Portfolio* has three sections: (1) Detailed Analysis; (2) Worksheets—checklists, forms that can be used as models in drafting documents, and texts of relevant congressional and IRS materials; and (3) Bibliography—citations to regulations, legislative history, court decisions, IRS materials, books, and articles. Bloomberg BNA updates the *Portfolios* with Changes & Analysis sheets, or completely revises them, as warranted by new developments.

There are several methods for locating relevant *Portfolios*. The print *Portfolio Index* includes the Classification Guides, lists of *Portfolios* in each series arranged by major category (e.g., Real Estate), and a more detailed Key Word Index (Master Index). Each series also has an index covering the worksheets (Working Papers Index). A Code section index covers all series. IRS forms and publications are cross-referenced numerically to appropriate *Portfolios*. The *Portfolios* can be searched on either *Bloomberg Law* or *Bloomberg BNA*'s web product.

The *Portfolio* indexes refer to the *Portfolio* number and outline heading numbers in the print and online *Portfolios*. [Illustration 26–12]

---

[74] Subdivisions are so narrow that several *Portfolios* may cover a single Code section; for example, *Portfolios* 370, 389, 397, 506, 513, and 813 cover I.R.C. § 22. The index indicates the primary *Portfolio(s)* for each Code section with a "Main discussion" designation.

[Illustration 26–12]

SCREEN PRINT FROM TAX MANAGEMENT U.S. INCOME PORTFOLIOS INDEX

U.S. Income Portfolios Index

Go To: A B C D E F G H I J K L M N O P Q R S T U V W X Y Z

Click on ⊞ to expand a heading

    COLLATERALIZED MORTGAGE OBLIGATIONS (CMOs). *See* MORTGAGE-BACKED SECURITIES

⊟ **COLLECTIBLES**

Capital gains tax rate, TM 562.V.F.2.a(1)

Depreciation, ineligibility for, TM 531.III.D.3.b

IRA investment restrictions, TM 367.V.C

New markets credit, limit for qualified active low-income community businesses,

Partnership interest sales or exchanges, TM 716.IV.A.4; TM 716.II.A.2.c(2)

Qualified plan investment restrictions, TM 377.III.C

COLLECTION APPEALS PROGRAM (CAP). *See* TAX COLLECTION APPEALS

COLLECTION OF INCOME EXPENSES. *See generally* PRODUCTION OF INCOME EXPENSES

The online *Portfolios* index cites to volumes by text section rather than by page number.

The online *Portfolios* index cites to volumes by text section rather than by page number.

    c.   Mertens, Law of Federal Income Taxation (Clark Boardman Callaghan). The original *Mertens* service contained five sets of volumes: treatise, rulings, Code, Code commentary, and regulations. Although only the treatise and rulings materials have been continued in their original format, the archival Code and regulations materials are useful for 1954 Code research.

    (1)   Treatise. The treatise volumes closely resemble general encyclopedias such as *Am. Jur. 2d* and *C.J.S.* in format.[75] Discussion includes historical background and extensive footnoting.

    Tables volumes contain tables indicating where primary source materials are discussed. IRS materials include items printed in the *Cumulative Bulletin* and letter rulings.

    The Index volume contains a detailed subject matter index. Treatise materials are supplemented monthly; supplements are cumulated semiannually.

    (2)   Code. Each Code volume contains all income tax provisions enacted or amended during a particular time period (one or more years). Textual notations (diamond shapes and brackets) indicate additions and deletions. A historical note indicates act, section, and effective date and can be used to reconstruct the prior language. The subject matter index in a print volume cross-references each topic to applicable Code sections. This material covers only the 1954 Code.

    (3)   Code Commentary. The Code Commentary volumes initially provided useful short explanations of statutory provisions and cross-references to the discussions in the

---

[75] Encyclopedias are discussed in Chapter 16. Within each encyclopedia, discussions of taxation appear in separate volumes and are quite accessible.

treatise materials. More recent items are limited to references to statutory changes or to recent cases and rulings for the particular Code section.

(4) Regulations. Regulations materials have undergone change since the mid-1990s. In a separate service, but using the Mertens name, the publisher currently issues an annual softbound set of regulations in force (volumes 1 through 6) and proposed regulations (volume 7). Regulations appear in Code section order, and there is a subject-matter index. New material is issued throughout the year and filed in a *Current Developments and Status Table* binder. The service also includes looseleaf volumes containing the preambles to proposed, temporary, and final regulations.

Many libraries also contain hardbound volumes that include the texts and preambles of all income tax regulations issued or amended during a particular time period (two or more years). Publication is made in Code section order. Textual notations indicate deletions, additions, and other changes in amended regulations. Historical notes permit the determination of the regulation's prior wording. These volumes are no longer being updated.

(5) Rulings. These volumes contain the texts of revenue rulings and procedures. Each volume covers a particular time period and includes rulings in numerical order, followed by procedures in numerical order. *Mertens* adds current items monthly.

d. *Rabkin & Johnson, Federal Income, Gift and Estate Taxation (Matthew Bender).* The discussions in this service's treatise volumes do not purport to cover all types of authority. Letter rulings are rarely discussed or cited as authority "[b]ecause they lack precedential value."[76] New Matter pages appear near the beginning of each volume in text section number order.

Some libraries carry volumes that are no longer being updated; these cover legislative history and regulations for the 1954 Code.

3. Subject Matter Arrangement—Limited Scope

Various publishers issue textual materials discussing a limited number of Code sections, such as those covering S corporations. These texts are particularly useful for research involving complex topics. Researchers can find texts on almost any topic, from tax problems of the elderly to taxation of inventories. Although these materials are periodically supplemented, their updating is rarely as frequent as that for the topical services covered in subsections 1 and 2.

L. LEGAL PERIODICALS

Commentary on particular tax problems appears in various legal periodicals, several of which focus on taxation.[77] This group includes such offerings as *Journal of Taxation*, *Tax Lawyer*, *TAXES—The Tax Magazine*, and *Tax Law Review*. Many publications adopt a narrower focus within taxation, e.g., *Real Estate Taxation*.

---

[76] 1A RABKIN & JOHNSON, FEDERAL INCOME, GIFT AND ESTATE TAXATION § G 1.03[6], at G–11. This service is also available in *Lexis Advance*.

[77] While not technically periodicals, annual institutes, such as those given at New York University (taxation) and the University of Miami (estate planning), are extraordinarily useful sources of information, have their own excellent indexes, and are covered in several periodical indexes.

Researchers can obtain lists of articles online using both the tax-focused sources described below and more general sources. The latter group includes *Index to Legal Periodicals and Books*, *Current Law Index* (and its parallel products, *LegalTrac* and *Legal Resource Index*), *HeinOnline*, *Google Scholar*, and *Social Science Research Network* (*SSRN*). These services are discussed in Chapter 18.

1.　*Federal Tax Articles* (CCH)

This monthly looseleaf reporter contains summaries of articles on federal taxes appearing in legal, accounting, business, and related periodicals. Each month's contents appear in Code section order; each item receives a paragraph cross-reference number. [Illustration 26–13] Items receive new paragraph numbers when they are cumulated.

There are topic and author indexes. Multiyear volumes cover materials since 1954; a looseleaf volume contains the most recent material. Coverage in recent volumes is not as extensive as it was in earlier years.

[Illustration 26–13]

EXCERPT FROM FEDERAL TAX ARTICLES

593 1-2012   6573

¶ 8881 Shared Responsibility for Employers Regarding Health Coverage (Code Sec. 4980H)

2011 Article Summaries

¶8881.02 Mapping the Road to 2014; A Look at How Employers Are Viewing the Prospect of Health Insurance Exchanges - Including Some Outside-the-Box Ideas. Kathleen Koster. 9 Employee Benefit Adviser 6, Jun 1, 2011, p 4.

Explains that employers and insurance companies are not yet ready to step up to bat with the prospect of health insurance exchanges in the very near future. Notes

¶8881.04 American Health Insurance Exchanges under the Patient Protection and Affordable Care Act: An Overview and a Primer. Alden J Bianchi. Tax Management Compensation Journal, Oct 7, 2011.

Introduces the health insurance coverage provisions as enacted by the two legislative acts known as the Affordable Care Act. Supplies information on the health insur-

2.　*Index to Federal Tax Articles* (Warren, Gorham & Lamont)

This multivolume work covers the literature on federal income, gift, and estate taxation contained in legal, specialized tax, accounting, and economics journals and in non-periodical publications.

Coverage begins with 1913, making this an important tool for locating discussions of pre-1954 Code developments. Current material appears in the cumulative supplement volume. There are separate topical and author listings but no Code section index. The most recent entry appears first in each listing of articles. [Illustration 26–14]

[Illustration 26–14]

EXCERPT FROM INDEX TO FEDERAL TAX ARTICLES

INDEX TO FEDERAL TAX ARTICLES: *Topical Index*

Listed Transactions (See Reportable Transactions)

Litigation (See also Court of Claims; Courts; District Court; Procedure; Tax Court; Supreme Court)

    Making Plaintiffs Whole: A Tax Problem of Interest, William E. Foster, 64 Oklahoma Law Review No. 3, 325 (2012)

    A Dip in the Hot Tub: Concurrent Evidence Techniques for Expert Witnesses in Tax Court Cases, Michael R. Devitt, 117 Journal of Taxation No. 4, 213 (2012)

Litigation Expenses (See Attorneys; Business Expenses;

Loans—*Cont'd*

Mortgages—*Cont'd*

    Avoiding Insult to Injury: Extending and Expanding Cancellation of Indebtedness Income Tax Exemptions to Homeowners, Dustin A. Zacks, 66 Arkansas Law Review No. 1, 317 (2013)

    Partnership and Partner Penalties, William Pfeifer and Ken Milani, 90 Practical Tax Strategies No. 2, 61 (2013)

    Reforming the Taxation of Retirement Income, Richard L. Kaplan, 32 Virginia Tax Review No. 2, 327 (2012)

3. Tax Management Portfolios (Bloomberg BNA)

The Bibliography section of each *Portfolio* contains articles listings, arranged by year of publication. The *Portfolios* are discussed further in Section K.

4. Mertens, *Law of Federal Income Taxation* (Clark Boardman Callaghan)

Mertens lists current articles by topic in the Recent Tax Articles section of its monthly *Developments & Highlights* newsletter; the articles listings are not cumulated over time. Although Mertens is an income tax service, the lists include articles on estate planning. Mertens is discussed further in Section K.

5. *Tax Policy in the United States: A Selective Bibliography with Annotations* (1960–84)

Published by the Vanderbilt Law School Library in cooperation with the ABA Section of Taxation, this looseleaf covers articles, books, and government documents dealing with tax policy. Each item is explained briefly. There are author and subject indexes.

6. *WG & L Tax Journal Digest* (Warren, Gorham & Lamont)

Previously published as the *Journal of Taxation Digest*, an annual volume covers articles published in the *Journal of Taxation* and several other Warren, Gorham & Lamont publications. Coverage begins with 1977, and the titles covered have varied over time. The digests are arranged by topic; cross-references are given to relevant articles digested under other topical headings.

M. FORM BOOKS

Form books and checklists are useful aids in drafting documents, particularly if tax consequences will be determined by the drafter's choice of language. Authors often cite primary authority. Many form books are available online and in CD-ROM or DVD format; users can download and customize forms for their clients' needs. Numerous titles are available from LexisNexis and Thomson Reuters. In addition, several topical services include sample forms and client letters. The IRS occasionally publishes prototype language in revenue procedures and notices.

N. NEWSLETTERS

Researchers in any area must update their findings or risk citing obsolete sources. When the research involves taxation, the odds of change are higher than in most fields and the number of sources to be consulted may appear endless.

Newsletters are convenient tools for keeping up with changes in the law. While they are no substitute for updating with a citator or the new matter section of a topical service, they offer the opportunity for a leisurely review of changes occurring during a predetermined time period. The two newsletter described in this section are not tied to topical services. Other newsletters are included in a subscription to a topical service.

1. *Daily Tax Report* (Bloomberg BNA) (print and online)

This newsletter, published five times each week, provides extensive coverage of current developments in tax law.[78] Each issue includes a section describing congressional activity, including bills passed and introduced, committee hearings, and committee reports.

The *Daily Tax Report* prints full texts or digests of judicial decisions, IRS documents, and Treasury regulations. Subscribers can access full text documents online using Tax Management's *TaxCore* or *Bloomberg Law*.

2. *Tax Notes* (Tax Analysts) (print and online)

This weekly newsletter contains a comprehensive collection of recent tax-oriented material. *Tax Notes* includes information about regulations (including public comments), rulings, and judicial opinions. It also includes information about pending legislation and treaties. [Illustration 26–15] Each issue of *Tax Notes* includes substantive articles.

Full text information, such as statements at hearings on legislation and regulations, texts of tax articles, and IRS materials are included in Tax Analysts' online *Federal Research Library*. Document cross-references allow researchers to retrieve the full text documents mentioned in *Tax Notes*. Tax Analysts also publishes a DVD service (Section Q) covering both primary and secondary source material in addition to its web-based federal and international services.[79] Tax Analysts publications are also available in Lexis Advance.

---

[78] Bloomberg BNA also publishes a weekly newsletter, *Tax Management Weekly Report*, as well as a number of reports on specialized tax topics.

[79] In addition to *Tax Notes* (weekly, focused on federal tax), Tax Analysts also publishes *Tax Notes Today* (daily), *State Tax Notes Magazine* (weekly), *State Tax Today* (daily), *Tax Notes International Magazine* (weekly), and *Tax Analysts Worldwide Tax Daily*. Like *Tax Notes*, these newsletters are in *Lexis Advance* as well as in Tax Analysts' own online service.

EXCERPT FROM TAX NOTES (TAX ANALYSTS)

GUIDANCE
tax notes

Deadline Extended for Joining Voluntary Disclosure Initiative

By Joseph DiSciullo — jdisciul@tax.org

The IRS decided that the potential for disruption on the East Coast from Hurricane Irene was sufficient to push back the deadline for offshore voluntary disclosure initiative (OVDI) requests until September 9 (*Doc 2011-18360, 2011 TNT 167-45*).

The success of the initial offshore voluntary disclosure program, which closed on October 15, 2009, demonstrated the value of a uniform penalty structure for taxpayers who came forward voluntarily and reported their previously undisclosed foreign accounts and assets, the IRS said. The popularity of the program also spawned the 2011 OVDI for which the original deadline was August 31.

Non-Bank Trustees, Custodians

The IRS recently announced a list of entities previously approved to act as non-bank trustees and non-bank custodians under reg. section 1.408-2(e) (Announcement 2011-59, 2011-37 IRB 1, *Doc 2011-18452, 2011 TNT 169-6*).

As explained in the announcement, Archer medical savings accounts (MSAs) established under section 220, health savings accounts described in section 223, custodial accounts of retirement plans qualified under section 401, custodial accounts described in section 403(b)(7), trust or custodial accounts of IRAs established under sections 408 and 408A (Roth IRAs), Coverdell education savings accounts described in section 530, and custodial accounts of eligible deferred compensation plans described in section 457(b) won't be tax exempt if the account's trustee or custodian isn't a bank (as defined in section 408(n), and in the case of Archer

Tax Notes includes news items in addition to coverage of primary source materials. Note the references to full text sources in this article from September 5, 2011.

O. COLLECTIONS OF PRIMARY SOURCE MATERIALS

The materials described below, which are referred to at various points in this chapter, print several types of material necessary for tax research. Except as indicated in the following paragraphs, these sets contain no textual discussion of the materials presented.

1. *Internal Revenue Bulletin; Cumulative Bulletin; Bulletin Index-Digest System*

The first two of these IRS-generated series contain the text of almost every officially published non-judicial primary authority. Until it ceased publication, the *Bulletin Index-Digest System (Index-Digest)* was useful for accessing material in the other two series. The primary source materials printed in these volumes are also available in microform (Section P), CD-ROM and DVD (Section Q), and online services (Section R). The IRS website includes *Internal Revenue Bulletins* in both PDF (1996 to date) and HTML (mid-2003 to date) formats. *HeinOnline* includes the *Cumulative Bulletin* in PDF format, beginning with the first volume and ending in 2008, *Internal Revenue Bulletins* (since 2009), and the *Bulletin Index-Digest System*.

a. *Internal Revenue Bulletin (I.R.B.).* The weekly *I.R.B.* is divided into four parts. Part I prints all revenue rulings and final regulations issued during the week. Part II covers treaties, although this section rarely includes any documents. Part III contains notices and revenue procedures, while Part IV, "Items of General Interest," is varied in content. Its coverage ranges from disbarment notices to announcements of proposed regulations. *Federal Register* dates and comment deadlines are provided in addition to the preambles and text of proposed regulations. The *Bulletin* also indicates IRS acquiescence or nonacquiescence in judicial decisions decided against its position.

Although the *I.R.B.* has Finding Lists, citators (Section J) are a better means for locating and evaluating IRS material. Every issue contains a Numerical Finding List for each type of item, listing each in numerical order; these Finding Lists lack any tie-in to Code sections. The Finding List of Current Actions on Previously Published Items indicates IRS, but not judicial, action. The subject matter indexes are subdivided by type of tax but also lack Code section information; they are not cumulated from year to year. Researchers can search for *I.R.B.* items using the IRS website search tool, but searching in subscription-based services is easier. Because of its index format, the *I.R.B.* is best used to locate material for which citations are already available or as a tool for staying abreast of recent IRS and Treasury developments.

The *I.R.B.* ceased print publication with issue 2012–32. It is available in PDF and HTML on the IRS website. The *Federal Tax Coordinator* (Section K) reproduces it in print.

    b. *Cumulative Bulletin (C.B.).* From 1919 through 2008, the *I.R.B.s* were cumulated and republished in a hardbound volume, the *Cumulative Bulletin*. The *C.B.* format through 1997 follows that of the weekly *I.R.B.* with three exceptions.[80] First, major tax legislation and related committee reports generally appeared in a third volume rather than in the two semiannual volumes.[81] Second, only disbarment notices and proposed regulations appeared from Part IV. Finally, rulings appeared in the *C.B.* in semiannual Code section order instead of in numerical order. Beginning in 1998, the *C.B.* reprinted the *I.R.B.* verbatim without sorting items into Code section order. Researchers who have only an *I.R.B.* citation for pre-1998 material must obtain a separate *C.B.* page citation.

The 1998 and later *C.B.* provide Code section references to included items in a table, Code Sections Affected by Current Actions; the tables are not cumulated over multiple years. The *C.B.* indexes are also difficult to use, particularly in comparison to indexes created for topical services.

Cumulative Bulletin volumes initially were given Arabic numerals (1919–1921); the IRS adopted a Roman numeral system in 1922. From 1937 through 2008, volumes numbered by year (e.g., 1937–1). There have been two volumes annually (with occasional extra volumes for extensive legislative history material) since 1920; the –1, –2 numbering system for each year began in 1922. The *C.B.'s* format differed slightly from the above description until the 1974–2 volume. Proposed regulations, which appear as a separate category, were added in the 1981–1 volume.

    c. *Bulletin Index-Digest System.* The IRS issued the *Index-Digest* in four services: Income Tax, Estate and Gift Tax, Employment Tax, and Excise Tax until 1994. The *Index-Digest* provided *I.R.B.* or *C.B.* citations for revenue rulings and procedures, Supreme Court and adverse Tax Court decisions, Public Laws, Treasury Decisions, and treaties. In addition, it digested the rulings, procedures, and court decisions. The digests

---

[80] Although the *C.B.* included preambles, it omitted drafting information before 1998.

[81] Committee reports for 1913 through 1938 appear in 1939–1 (pt. 2) C.B. Committee reports for the 1954 Code's enactment never appeared in the *C.B.* After 2003, major legislation was no longer published in Part II of the *C.B.*

of IRS materials were arranged by topic. Researchers who did not know the underlying Code section number could still use these digests effectively. Because the *Index-Digest* is no longer current, it is best used for pre-1994 research.

2. *Tax Management Primary Sources* (Bureau of National Affairs)

Primary Sources is an excellent tool for deriving the legislative history of existing Code sections. It also covers the Employee Retirement Income Security Act (ERISA). It is no longer being updated, so its usefulness is limited to material appearing in 2003 and earlier.

This service includes extensive legislative history excerpts for selected Code sections. The sections chosen for inclusion in the historical binders are traced back to their original 1954 Code versions[82]; all changes are presented. [Illustration 26–16] Materials presented for each Code section include presidential messages, committee reports, Treasury Department testimony at hearings, and discussion printed in *Congressional Record*.

The legislative histories are published in five series, each of which covers several years. Within each series, material appears in Code section order. Each Series contains a Master Table of Contents in Code section order. *Primary Sources* began its coverage with Code sections affected by the Tax Reform Act of 1969 (with limited 1954 Act coverage).

[Illustration 26–16]

EXCERPT FROM BNA TAX MANAGEMENT PRIMARY SOURCES

IV-26   §168 [1981] pg.(i)

SEC. 168 – ACCELERATED COST RECOVERY SYSTEM

Table of Contents

Page

STATUTE — [As Added by the Economic Recovery Tax Act of 1981
(P.L. 97-34)] .... §168 [1981] pg. 1

LEGISLATIVE HISTORY

    Background
        97th Congress, 1st Sess. (H.R. 3849)
            Treasury Dept. Tech. Explanation of H.R. 3849 .... §168 [1981] pg. 28

    House of Representatives
        Ways and Means Committee
            Committee Hearings
                Statement of Donald Regan, Sec'y of Treasury .... §168 [1981] pg. 34
            Committee Report .... §168 [1981] pg. 35

    Senate
        Finance Committee
            Committee Hearings
                Statement of Donald Regan, Sec'y of Treasury .... §168 [1981] pg. 43
            Committee Press Releases
                No. 81-19 (June 24, 1981) .... §168 [1981] pg. 44
                No. 81-21 (June 26, 1981) .... §168 [1981] pg. 45
            Committee Report .... §168 [1981] pg. 46
        Senate Discussion
            Vol. 127 Cong. Rec. (July 20, 1981) .... §168 [1981] pg. 55
            Vol. 127 Cong. Rec. (July 23, 1981) .... §168 [1981] pg. 58

---

[82] Series 1 also includes the 1939 Code version for each section covered.

3. *Cumulative Changes* (Research Institute of America)

This multivolume looseleaf service allows researchers to track changes in the Code and Treasury regulations. There are series for the 1939, 1954, and 1986 Codes and regulations. Many libraries lack the 1939 Code series.

The Code and regulations materials appear separately, arranged in Code section order. The 1954 series contains parallel citation tables for the 1939 and 1954 Codes. Each quarterly update covers a limited group of changes, and RIA no longer advertises this service. It is best used for 1954 and early 1986 Code changes.

    a. Internal Revenue Code. A chart for each Code section indicates its original effective date. The chart includes the Public Law number, section, enactment and effective dates of each amendment, and the act section prescribing the effective date. The chart is particularly useful because it covers Code section subdivisions (subsections, paragraphs and even smaller subdivisions). It does not include *Statutes at Large* citations. The tables' format changed slightly in the mid-1990s; citations for effective dates are printed instead of the dates themselves. [Illustration 26–17]

The pages following each chart reproduced each version (except the most recent one) since the provision's original introduction in the relevant Code.

    b. Treasury Regulations. Tables of amendments cover all regulations sections for each tax (i.e., income tax, estate tax, etc.); individual sections do not have their own charts. The table indicates the original and all amending T.D. numbers and filing dates and provides a *C.B.* or *I.R.B.* citation. Cross-references to *United States Tax Reporter* are also given. A Table of Amending TDs, in T.D. number order, indicates the purpose, date, and *C.B.* or *I.R.B.* citation for each regulation issued under each Code.[83]

The 1954 and 1986 series tables list oddly numbered (e.g., not using the normal prefix designations) regulations last rather than in Code section order. The 1954 series includes tables for regulations that have been redesignated or replaced.

Immediately following the tables, the editors print prior versions of each regulation. Older materials note changes in italics and use footnotes to indicate stricken language; recent materials do not use this format. *Cumulative Changes* includes the T.D. number and the dates of approval and filing for each version.

---

[83] Although T.D. 6500, a 1960 republication of existing income tax regulations is not formally included, the 1954 *Cumulative Changes* does list the original pre-1960 T.D. A cautionary note warns the user to remember that pre-1960 regulations were republished in T.D. 6500. T.D. 6498 (procedure and administration) and T.D. 6516 (withholding tax) receive similar treatment. These T.D.s do not appear in the *C.B.*

[Illustration 26–17]

EXCERPT FROM CUMULATIVE CHANGES

3-2000   **Sec. 51. Amount of Credit**   § 51—p. 3

[See definitions preceding chart on page 1 of this section.]

SEC. 51 '86 I.R.C.	SUBSECTIONS					
	(f)—(h)	(i)(1)	(i)(2)	(i)(3)	(j)	(k)
Pub. Law 99-514, 10-22-86				Added by 1701(c) 1701(e)* Note 1		Redesig. 1878(f)(1) 1881* Note 1
AMENDING ACTS						
Pub Law 103-66, 8-10-93		13302(d) 13303* 8-10-93				

Public Law	Law Sec.	IRC Sec.	Eff. Date
P.L. 104-188	1201(a)	51(a)	1201(g)*
	1201(c)(1)	51(a)	1201(g)*
	1201(f)	51(c)(1)	1201(g)*
	1201(d)	51(c)(4)	1201(g)*
	1201(b)	51(d)	1201(g)*
	1201(e)(1)	51(g)	1201(g)*
	1201(c)	51(i)(3)	1201(g)*
	1201(e)(5)	51(j) Heading	1201(g)*
P.L. 105-34	603(b)(2)	51(d)(2)(A)	
	603(c)(2)	51(d)(9)-(11) Redes (10)-(12)	
	603(d)(2)	51(i)(3)	
P.L. 105-277	1002(a)	51(c)(4)(B)	1002(b)
	4006(c)(1)	51(d)(6)(B)(i)	
P.L. 106-170	505(a)	51(c)(4)(B)	505(c)
	505(b)	51(i)(2)	505(c)

Note the change in format for more recent amendments to the Code. As of December 2010, the table for section 51 continued through P.L. 108-311.

4. *Barton's Federal Tax Laws Correlated* (Federal Tax Press, Inc.)

The six volumes of this set trace income, estate, and gift tax provisions from the Revenue Act of 1913[84] through the Tax Reform Act of 1969. *Barton's* is no longer available in print; it is available in *HeinOnline* (Section R).

The five hardbound volumes reproduce in Code or act section order the text of the various tax acts through 1952. Because the acts are lined up in several columns on each page, researchers can read across a page and see every enacted version of a particular section for the period that volume covers.[85] Whenever possible, *Barton's* uses different typefaces to highlight changes.

The first two volumes provide a citation to *Statutes at Large* for each act. Volume 1 includes case annotations, and each volume includes a subject matter index. The volumes following the 1939 Code include tables indicating amending acts and effective

---

[84] The original Second Edition (vol. 1) also contained the text of the income tax laws from 1861 through 1909. This section was omitted in the Reproduced Second Edition. *HeinOnline* includes the Reproduced Second Edition.

[85] Volume 1 covers 1913–24; volume 2 covers 1926–38; volume 3 covers 1939–43; volume 4 covers 1944–49; volume 5 covers 1950–52.

dates for 1939 Code sections. Volume 5 has a retrospective table cross-referencing sections to pages in the four previous volumes.

The sixth volume does not print the text of Code sections. Instead it consists of Tables that provide citations to primary sources where desired material appears. Tables A through D are in Code section order; Table E is in Public Law number order.

Table A provides the history of the 1954 Act. It indicates *Statutes at Large* page; House, Senate, and Conference report page (official and *U.S. Code Congressional & Administrative News*); 1939 Code counterpart; Revenue Act where the provision originated; and relevant pages in volumes 1 through 5. Table C is similar to Table A, but it covers the 1939 Code. It gives the 1954 Code section; the origin of the 1939 Code provision; and cross-references to volumes 1 through 5.

Table B covers amendments to the 1954 Code. For each section it provides Public Law number, section, and enactment date; *Statutes at Large* citation; House, Senate, and Conference report numbers and location in the *C.B.*; comment (e.g., revision, amendment); and effective date information. Table D is the same as Table B, but it covers post-1953 changes to the 1939 Code.

Table E provides citations to legislative history for all acts from 1953 through 1969. Table E provides the following information provided for each act: Public Law number; date of enactment; congressional session; *Statutes at Large*, *C.B.*, and *USCCAN* citations for the act; congressional sessions, dates, and *Cumulative Bulletin* and *USCCAN* citations for House, Senate, and Conference report numbers; and *Congressional Record* citations for floor debate. Acts are not cited by popular name.

5. *Seidman's Legislative History of Federal Income and Excess Profits Tax Laws*[86] (Prentice-Hall)

Although *Seidman's* coverage stops in 1953, it remains useful for determining the legislative history of provisions that originated in the 1939 Code or even earlier.[87] This series follows each act in reverse chronological order, presenting the text of Code sections, followed by relevant committee reports and citations to hearings[88] and *Congressional Record*.[89] Because *Seidman's* uses different type styles, researchers can easily determine where in Congress a particular provision originated or was deleted. [Illustration 26–18]

---

[86] The two 1939–53 volumes include both taxes. Separate volumes for the income tax (1861–1938) and the excess profits tax (1917–47) were used for the earlier materials.

[87] I.R.C. § 263, for example, contains language taken almost verbatim from the 1864 Act, § 117. *See* 13 Stat. 282.

[88] *Seidman's* cites relevant page numbers in the hearings and indicates appearances by Treasury representatives.

[89] *Seidman's* cites to relevant pages and reproduces the text itself in some instances.

[Illustration 26–18]

EXCERPT FROM SEIDMAN'S LEGISLATIVE HISTORY OF FEDERAL INCOME TAX LAWS

```
for key to statute type]                1934 ACT                         381

SEC. 164 DIFFERENT TAXABLE YEARS.                                        Sec.
                                                                         164


        If the taxable year of a beneficiary is different from that of the estate or trust, the amount which he is required, under section
162 (b), to include in computing his net income, shall be based upon the income of the estate or trust for any taxable year of the estate
or trust (whether beginning on, before, or after January 1, 1934) ending within his taxable year.


                                        Committee Reports

        Report—Ways and Means         necessary in view of the policy adopted in section
Committee (73d Cong. 2d Sess., H. Rept.  1 to add additional language to provide for cases
704).—Section 164. Different taxable years: The  where the estate or trust has a taxable year
present law requires a beneficiary of an estate or  beginning in 1933 and ending in 1934 (p.32)
trust to include in his income amounts allowed as       Report—Senate Finance Committee
a deduction to the estate or trust under section  (73d Cong., 2d Sess., S. Rept. 558).—Same as
162 (b).  In order to continue this policy, it is  Ways and Means Committee Report. (p.40)

SEC. 166 REVOCABLE TRUSTS.                                               Sec.
                                                                         166


        Where at any time (96) <during the taxable year>the power to revest in the grantor title to any part of the corpus of the
trust is vested—
```

Seidman's prints proposed sections that were not enacted along with relevant history explaining their omission. Such information can aid in interpreting those provisions Congress actually adopted. Although its coverage has great breadth, *Seidman's* does not print every Code section. It omits provisions with no legislative history, items lacking substantial interpretative significance, and provisions the editor considered long outmoded. *Seidman's* does not cover gift, estate, or excise taxes.

Seidman's has three indexes and a Code cross-reference table. The Code section index lists each section by act and assigns it a key number. The same key number is assigned to corresponding sections in subsequent acts. The key number index indicates every act, by section number and page in the text, where the item involved appears. A subject index lists key numbers by topic. Volume II of the 1939–53 set contains a table cross-referencing 1953 and 1954 Code sections covered in *Seidman's*. *Seidman's* is available in *HeinOnline* (Section R).

6.   *The Internal Revenue Acts of the United States: 1909–1950; 1950–1972; 1973–* (William S. Hein & Co.)

a.   Original Series. This set, edited by Bernard D. Reams, Jr., provides the most comprehensive legislative histories of all materials discussed in this section. In addition to each congressional version of revenue bills, the 144 original volumes (1909–50) contain the full texts of hearings, committee reports, Treasury studies, and regulations. Official pagination is retained for relevant documents. In addition to income and excise taxes, this set includes estate and gift, social security, railroad retirement, and unemployment taxes. This set is available in print and microfiche. The original and later series are also available in *HeinOnline* (Section R).[90]

---

[90] *HeinOnline* includes additional legislative history compilations; some were prepared by law firms and others by the federal government.

An Index volume contains several indexes that researchers can use in locating relevant materials. [Illustration 26–19] The longest index, which is chronological, lists each act and every item comprising its legislative history. A volume reference is given for each item. Other indexes cover Miscellaneous Subjects, such as hearings on items that did not result in legislation; Treasury studies; Joint Committee reports; regulations; congressional reports; congressional documents; bill numbers; and hearings. Unfortunately, there is neither a Code section nor a subject matter index.

[Illustration 26–19]

EXCERPT FROM THE INTERNAL REVENUE ACTS OF THE UNITED STATES

```
                        REVENUE ACT OF 1916

                                                              Volume

 BILL IN ITS VARIOUS FORMS
      Passed Senate, 64th Cong., 1st session
      H.R. 16763. In the House of Representatives.
      September 6, 1916. Ordered to be printed
      with the amendments of the Senate numbered ....................................  61

 SLIP LAW
      Public No. 271, 64th Cong., (H.R. 16763),
      an act to increase the revenue, and for
      other purposes. Approved September 8, 1916
      39 Stat. 756 ....................................  91

 REPORTS
      To increase the revenue, and for other
      purposes, report, H.Rpt. 64-922, July 5, 1916 ....................................  93
```

Full-text materials appear by type of document rather than by the act involved. All hearings are printed together, as are all bills, laws (accompanied by committee reports), studies, and regulations. Researchers must access several volumes to assemble all materials for a particular law or provision. This is by no means a substantial drawback to using this set; assembling the same materials from elsewhere in a library (assuming they are all available) would be far more difficult. Nevertheless, it is easier to use this service online than in print.

b.   *Subsequent Series.* Professor Reams subsequently compiled materials to extend this set's coverage to later years. The later volumes are similar to the 1909–50 materials, although hearings receive less attention.

The 1954 volumes include committee reports, hearings, debates, and the final act. Revenue bills and Treasury studies do not appear. Because the IRS *Cumulative Bulletins* do not cover the 1954 Act, these materials are particularly valuable. A two-volume update published in 1993 includes fifty House and Senate bills missing from the original volumes.

Additional sets compiled by Professor Reams cover legislative histories for 1950–51, 1953–72, 1969, 1971, 1975, 1976, 1980, 1984, 1985 (Balanced Budget), 1986, 1987 (Balanced Budget), 1988, 1990, and 1993 acts. Several other sets, covering the Balanced Budget Act of 1997, the Taxpayer Relief Act of 1997, the Economic Growth and Tax Relief Reconciliation Act of 2001, the Tax Relief, Unemployment Insurance Reauthorization, and Job Creation Act of 2010, the Foreign Account Tax Compliance Act, the American Taxpayer Relief Act of 2012, and the Alternative Minimum Tax, were edited by William Manz. *HeinOnline* (Section R) includes these sets and also includes legislative history materials compiled by government agencies and by law firms.

7. **Eldridge,** *The United States Internal Revenue Tax System* **(William S. Hein & Co.)**

This reprint of early legislative materials is a useful complement to *Internal Revenue Acts of the United States*, discussed in the immediately preceding paragraphs. It includes texts of revenue acts passed through 1894. The author provides extensive textual material, annotations, and descriptive history for the various acts. This book is also available in the *Making of Modern Law: Legal Treatises 1800–1926* database (Chapter 23) and in *HeinOnline* (Section R).

P. MICROFORMS

As primary and secondary sources proliferate, many libraries seek alternatives to bound volumes. Microforms provide one option for expanding the collection within space limitations. In addition, libraries may sometimes obtain out-of-print materials only in microform.

An important caveat is in order. Many publishers that previously offered products in microform format have switched to CD-ROM, DVD, and online services, all of which are easier to navigate. As a result, their microform materials may no longer be current; they do remain valuable for historical research. For example, the *Tax Analysts Microfiche Database* provided access to primary sources and selected commentary. It included full texts of *Tax Notes* and other Tax Analysts publications in addition to primary source materials. Tax Analysts' print publications provided document numbers that facilitated access to the *Microfiche Database*. Tax Analysts now publishes this material on DVD and online instead of in microfiche.

A library may also have government publications in microform. These include *Congressional Record*, *Federal Register*, *Code of Federal Regulations*, IRS *Cumulative Bulletins*, and Tax Court and Supreme Court case reporter services. The microform collection may also include briefs filed with the United States Supreme Court.

Publishers offering legislative histories in microform include ProQuest and William S. Hein & Co. Some libraries may own BNA's *Tax Management Primary Sources-Series I* (Section O) in ultrafiche.

Q. CD-ROMS AND DVDS

Compact discs store significant amounts of information yet require little storage space. Thus, they offer another means for libraries to maintain large amounts of data in a small area. In many areas of research, CD-ROM and DVD have supplanted microform as an alternative to print materials. Unfortunately, unless a disc is networked, only one researcher can use it at a time. In addition, even a DVD has less capacity than a web-based service. Web-based services allow more than one simultaneous user, have space for significantly more material, and are often updated on a daily basis. As a result, they are likely to supplant both CD-ROM and DVD.

The Tax Analysts *OneDisc Premium* (quarterly or monthly DVD) includes a full array of legislative, administrative and judicial primary source materials. Commerce Clearing House and LexisNexis also offer some tax materials on CD-ROM.

R. ONLINE LEGAL RESEARCH

Online legal research systems have several useful features. First, they bring the research materials together in one readily accessible location. Libraries with tax alcoves require several rows of shelving to house relevant information; libraries without this arrangement may shelve relevant items on several floors. An online system requires only a computer with Internet access.

In addition to primary and secondary source material, Internet sites may provide tax-oriented information through email, blogs, and online discussion groups.

More important than the time saved in gathering the material is the ability to do searches that are virtually impossible to accomplish using print materials. Because the service responds to queries based on words appearing or not appearing in its database, an online system can be used to compile a list of all opinions by a particular judge. Likewise, the computer can quickly locate all decisions rendered in 2014, at every court level, involving the medical expense deduction. Although CD-ROM and DVD searches can yield similar results, an online service generally includes far more material than does a single disc.

A variety of services is available on the Internet. Some commercial services include tax materials in a general database. Others focus exclusively on tax materials. Sites that can be accessed without a fee vary in their coverage; they may include data from multiple sources or focus on a single type of information. Many of these sites provide online links to relevant materials rather than including the material itself in their databases.

Materials available online are usually available in print, often from the publisher that makes them available online. Coverage dates for each format may vary, which can affect a researcher's choice of format. Coverage for a source may begin at a later date online than it does in print. This is particularly likely for government websites.

1. Online Commercial Services—General Focus

Although they do not focus on tax, three commercial services, *WestlawNext*, *Lexis Advance*, and *HeinOnline*, have extensive tax or tax-relevant databases.[91] Although these services have vast databases, researchers may not have access to all of them, or may have access only by paying an additional fee. Before using any commercial service, researchers should ascertain which sources are available under the terms of the relevant contract.

a.   WestlawNext and Lexis Advance. These services frequently expand the number of sources and time periods covered. They also delete sources, generally substituting others. Such changes often reflect the parent companies' acquisitions of other publishers.

These services differ slightly in their coverage and in their interfaces. Both allow researchers to specify particular words that must appear or be absent in a document; if the words must be in a desired proximity, that limitation may be specified as well. For example, they can be used to locate decisions with the word "damages" within five words of the term "personal injury," or for decisions with the word "damages" that do not have

---

[91] Chapter 23 includes extensive coverage of these and other electronic resources. In some instances (e.g., finding law review articles), *WestlawNext* and *Lexis Advance* searches should not be limited to law reviews focusing on tax.

the phrase "personal injury." Searches can be limited to particular types of authority (e.g., only Tax Court) or to particular dates.

(1) *WestlawNext. WestlawNext* allows researchers to select Practice Areas, one of which is Tax. The Tax option provides access to an array of primary and secondary source material. These materials can also be accessed separately through individual files (e.g., judicial decisions or IRS material). Researchers can also search in combined files. Secondary source files cover tax-oriented law reviews, topical services, newsletters, and various materials published by Research Institute of America, and Warren, Gorham & Lamont. *WestlawNext* includes *RIA Citator 2nd* and West's *KeyCite*. [Illustration 26–20]

(2) *Lexis Advance. Lexis Advance* lets researchers select Browse Topics or Browse Sources options. If the researcher selects Tax as the topic area, the Browse Sources link shows only tax materials. As was true for *WestlawNext, Lexis Advance* gives a researcher access to an array of primary and secondary source materials. These materials can be accessed separately through individual files (e.g., statutes or regulations). Researchers can also search in combined files. Secondary source files cover tax-oriented law reviews, topical services, newsletters, and various materials published by Matthew Bender, Tax Analysts, and other publishers. *Shepard's Citations* is part of *Lexis Advance*. [Illustration 26–21]

The *Lexis Advance* interface is scheduled for revision during 2014. Although its layout may change, the material included is likely to remain much the same.

b. *HeinOnline. HeinOnline's* libraries include many tax periodicals, IRS *Cumulative Bulletins* and post-2008 *Internal Revenue Bulletins*, and Board of Tax Appeals and Tax Court regular opinions. Its Taxation & Economic Reform in America library includes a wealth of tax legislative history materials and older treatises.

[Illustration 26–20]

SCREEN PRINT FROM WESTLAWNEXT

WestlawNext™   Q ▾ Search Tax

Home

Tax   ☆ Add to Favorites

Search all Tax content above or navigate to specific content below.

☐ Select all content

☐ **Cases**

       U.S. Courts of Appeals

       U.S. District Courts

       U.S. Court of Federal Claims

       U.S. Tax Court

☐ **Statutes & Court Rules**

   Tax Statutes & Court Rules

     Internal Revenue Code

     U.S. Tax Court Rules

☐ **Regulations**

   Tax Regulations

     Treasury Regulations

☐ **Administrative Decisions & Guidance**

This screen print shows part of the *WestlawNext* tax database contents.

[Illustration 26–21]

SCREEN PRINT FROM LEXIS ADVANCE

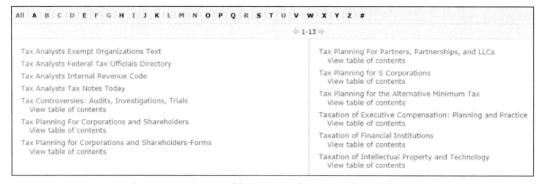

This screen print shows part of the *Lexis Advance* federal tax database contents.

2. Online Subscription Services—Tax Focus

The services listed below provide access to a variety of primary and secondary source materials.

a. IntelliConnect (Commerce Clearing House/Wolters Kluwer). IntelliConnect includes the Code, committee reports, regulations, treaties, IRS materials (including items such as letter rulings and the *Internal Revenue Manual*), and judicial decisions. The service includes *Standard Federal Tax Reporter*, CCH newsletters and journals, the CCH citator, and various practice aids. The service does not include *Federal Tax Articles*. [Illustration 26–22]

b. Checkpoint (Thomson Reuters). Many of the primary source and RIA secondary source materials included in *WestlawNext* are also included in *Checkpoint*. This service includes the Code, committee reports, regulations, treaties, IRS materials, judicial decisions, *Federal Tax Coordinator 2d*, *United States Tax Reporter*, and the *RIA Citator 2nd*. [Illustration 26–23]

c. Tax Analysts. Materials from Tax Analysts are included in *Lexis Advance*. Tax Analysts also offers its own subscription-based service, *Federal Research Library*. This service includes the Code, regulations, IRS materials, and judicial decisions. Tax Analysts also offers a web-based treaty service and web-based access to its newsletters.

d. Bloomberg Law's Tax Practice Center (Bloomberg BNA). The Tax Practice Center gives access to virtually every type of primary source material. Bloomberg BNA also offers *TaxCore*, which has links from the web-based *Daily Tax Report*. Available sources include the Code, committee reports, testimony at hearings, regulations, IRS materials, and judicial decisions. Other Bloomberg BNA offerings are *Portfolios Plus*, a web-based version of its *Tax Management Portfolios*, and several Bloomberg BNA newsletters.

[Illustration 26–22]

SCREEN PRINT FROM INTELLICONNECT

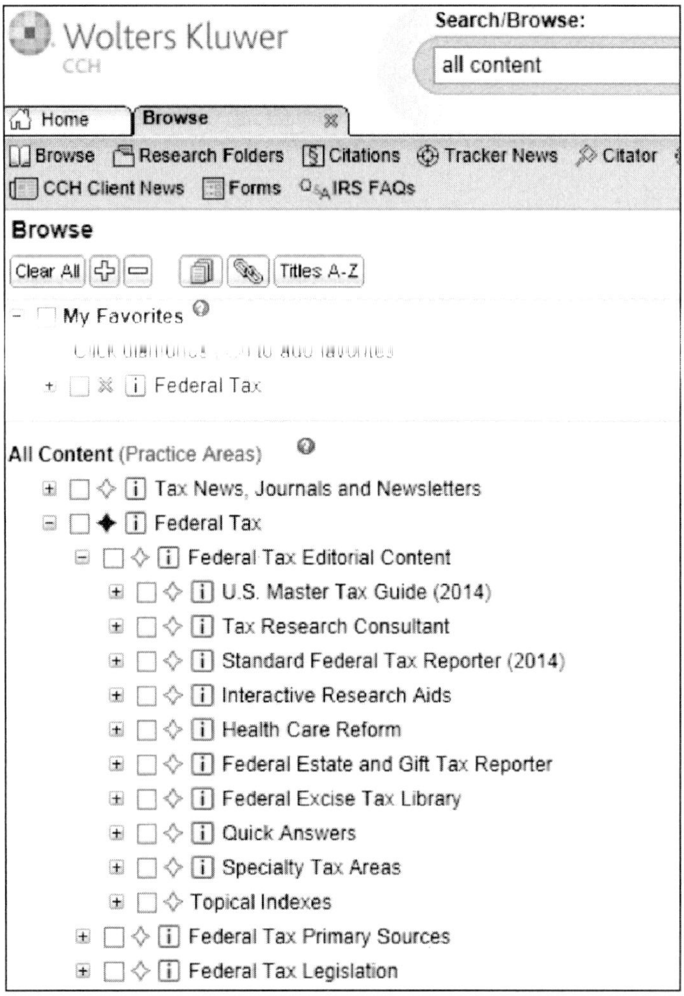

This screen print shows part of the *IntelliConnect* database contents.

[Illustration 26–23]

SCREEN PRINT FROM CHECKPOINT

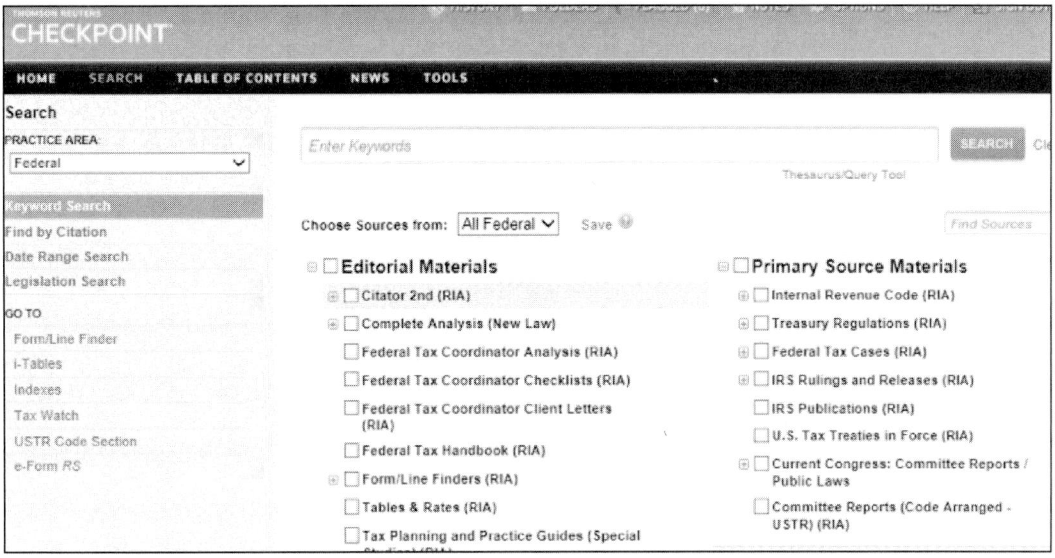

This screen print shows part of the *Checkpoint* database contents.

3.   Other Internet Services

There are a variety of useful websites available for tax research. Some provide primary source material directly; others provide hyperlinks to other websites; some sites perform both functions. Unfortunately, websites may change address or cease to exist altogether. A search engine will provide links for sites with new addresses.

Subsections a through d list several of these sites.

a.   Federal Government Sites. Many government sites also link to each other. The URL for each site appears, in alphabetical order by category, in Table 1.

(1)   Legislative Branch Sites:

- Library of Congress (*congress.gov*, superseding *THOMAS*)—users can find texts of bills, note the progress of bills in Congress, and access *Congressional Record* and committee reports.

- House Ways & Means Committee, Senate Finance Committee, Joint Committee on Taxation, and Congressional Budget Office—the first two sites provide information about committee activities, including hearings transcripts; the JCT site provides full text access to reports on proposed and enacted legislation. The Congressional Budget Office provides analysis that Congress can use in making budgetary decisions.

(2)   Executive Branch Sites:

- Internal Revenue Service—includes text of tax forms and publications, *Internal Revenue Bulletins*, the *Internal Revenue Manual*, treaties, and IRS releases that are not included in the *I.R.B.* It provides links to *United States Code*, *Code of Federal Regulations*, *Federal Register*, and additional treaty documents. This site could be better organized; location of the material is not intuitively obvious. For example, to reach many IRS rulings, researchers must first click on the Freedom of Information Act link and then click on the *Electronic Reading Room* link. The Taxpayer Advocate Service is an independent office within the IRS; the National Taxpayer Advocate annually reports to Congress on the most important problems facing taxpayers.

- Treasury Department—the Office of Tax Policy page provides text for tax treaty materials; the Office of Tax Analysis page includes analytical reports on tax policy issues. The Treasury Inspector General for Tax Administration (TIGTA) site analyzes IRS performance in carrying out internal revenue laws.

- *e-CFR*—provides current text of government regulations arranged in *C.F.R.* section order. This site includes material that has not yet appeared in the annual *C.F.R.* update.

- *Reginfo.gov*—*Unified Agenda of Regulatory and Deregulatory Actions* lists pending Treasury regulations projects.

- *Regulations.gov*—provides access to comments on regulations projects; it also includes the *Unified Agenda*.

- White House Home Page—provides text of presidential speeches, including bill-signing messages.

(3) Judicial Branch Site:

- United States Tax Court Home Page—provides text of regular, memorandum, and summary opinions. This site can be searched by judge, date, taxpayer name, or words and phrases.

(4) Government Printing Office Site:

- *Federal Digital System (FDsys)*—provides text of, or links to, documents generated by all branches of the federal government. *FDsys* includes past versions of the Code and regulations.

Table 1

Government Website URLs

Entity	URL
Legislative Branch	
Congressional Budget Office	http://cbo.gov
House Ways and Means Committee	http://waysandmeans.house.gov
Joint Committee on Taxation	http://jct.gov
Library of Congress congress.gov and THOMAS	http://beta.congress.gov
	http://thomas.loc.gov
Senate Finance Committee	http://finance.senate.gov

Executive Branch

e-CFR	http://www.ecfr.gov
Internal Revenue Service	http://www.irs.gov
National Taxpayer Advocate	http://www.taxpayeradvocate.irs.gov/Media-Resources/National-Taxpayer-Advocate-Bio
Regulations.gov	http://www.regulations.gov/
Reginfo.gov	http://www.reginfo.gov/public/
Treasury Department	http://www.treasury.gov/Pages/default.aspx
Treasury Department Office of Tax Analysis	http://www.treasury.gov/about/organizational-structure/offices/Pages/Office-of-Tax-Analysis.aspx
Treasury Department Office of Tax Policy	http://www.treasury.gov/about/organizational-structure/offices/Pages/Tax-Policy.aspx
Treasury Inspector General for Tax Administration	http://www.treasury.gov/tigta/
White House	http://www.whitehouse.gov

Judicial Branch

United States Tax Court	http://www.ustaxcourt.gov

Government Printing Office Site *Federal Digital* http://www.gpo.gov/fdsys/
System (FDsys)

b.   Other Sites Covering Primary Sources. These sites provide access to a variety of primary and secondary source materials, often by links to other sites.

- Cornell Law School's *Legal Information Institute* (http://www.law.cornell.edu/); and

- Washburn University School of Law, *WashLaw: Legal Research on the Web* (http://www.washlaw.edu)

c.   Organization Sites. The reports and other tax-related studies published by these groups provide useful data and proposals for the tax system.

- American Bar Association Section of Taxation (http://www.americanbar.org/groups/taxation.html);

- American Tax Policy Institute (http://www.americantaxpolicyinstitute.org/);

- Cato Institute (http://www.cato.org/);

- Citizens for Tax Justice (http://www.ctj.org/); and

- Tax Policy Center (http://www.taxpolicycenter.org/index.cfm).

d.   Blogs. Blogs provide links to primary and secondary source materials, to other blogs, or to policy group websites.

- *MauledAgain* (http://mauledagain.blogspot.com/), by James Edward Maule;

- *A Taxing Matter* (http://ataxingmatter.blogs.com/tax/), by Linda M. Beale; and

- *TaxProf Blog* (http://taxprof.typepad.com/), by Paul L. Caron. Resources page (http://taxprof.typepad.com/taxprof_blog/resources.html) includes a listing of many other tax blogs.

Appendix A

TABLE OF LEGAL ABBREVIATIONS*

Even the legal scholar may occasionally encounter an abbreviation whose complete title is difficult to identify. In such instances, researchers may have to consult a specialized source such as William H. Bryson's *Dictionary of Sigla and Abbreviations to and in Law Books Before 1607* (Buffalo: William S. Hein & Co. 1996); Mary Miles Prince's *Bieber's Dictionary of Legal Abbreviations* (Hein 5th ed. 2001—also on *LexisNexis* in the BIEBLA database); *World Dictionary of Legal Abbreviations,* edited by Igor I. Kavass and Mary Miles Prince (Hein 1991, 4 vols., looseleaf format and irregularly updated—vol. 3 Appx. A includes Bryson's *Dictionary of Sigla*); or Donald Raistrick's *Index to Legal Citations and Abbreviations* (London: Bowker–Saur 2d ed. 1993). Researchers may also need to check Colin Fong and Alan Edward's *Australian and New Zealand Legal Abbreviations* (Sydney: Australian Law Librarians Group, NSW Division 2d ed. 1995).[1] One of the largest listings of periodical abbreviations, including legal periodicals, is *Periodical Title Abbreviations* (Detroit: Thomson Gale 17th ed. 2007). Finally, among the many abbreviations lists on the internet, the most notable list may be the *Cardiff Index to Legal Abbreviations.*[2]

As primary and secondary legal materials continue to proliferate each year, it is extremely difficult to include in one place all their abbreviations and titles. Appendix A is restricted primarily to the English language periodicals, court reports, and looseleaf services that one could expect to find in a large American law library as of December 31, 2008. In addition, Appendix A includes many esoteric and historical citations. This appendix is not presumed to be authoritative in any official sense, but to reflect past and current usage by editors and publishers of English language legal materials. Superseded titles have been retained because they are never out-of-date as possible citations.

This table uses a strictly alphabetical arrangement. The entries for the abbreviation are to be read letter-by-letter and the ampersand is to be read as the word "and."

A

a.	Atlantic Reporter	A. & E.	Adolphus & Ellis Queen's Bench (Eng.)
A.	Same	A. & E.Ann. Cas.	American & English Annotated Cases
a2d	Same, Second Series	A. & E.Anno.	Same
A.2d	Same		

---

* Daniel W. Martin, Director of the Law Library and Professor of Law, Loyola Law School, Los Angeles, revised and updated this appendix with the assistance of Adriana Dulic, 2001 graduate of Pepperdine University School of Law, and Frank Park, 2008 graduate of Loyola Law School.

[1] http://www.nzlla.org.nz/documents/anzla2ded.pdf.

[2] http://www.legalabbrevs.cardiff.ac.uk/index.jsp.

A. & E.Cas.	Same
A. & E.Corp. Cas.	American & English Corporation Cases
A. & E.Corp. Cas. (N.S.)	Same, New Series
A. & E.Enc. L. & Pr.	American & English Encyclopedia of Law and Practice
A. & E.Ency.	American & English Encyclopedia of Law
A. & E.Ency. Law	Same
A. & E.P. & P.	American & English Pleading and Practice
A. & E.R.Cas.	American & English Railroad Cases
A. & E.R.Cas. (N.S.)	Same, New Series
A. & E.R.R. Cas.	American & English Railroad Cases
A. & E.R.R. Cas. (N.S.)	Same, New Series
AB	American Bankruptcy Reports
	Assembly Bill (CA)
A.B.	Anonymous Reports at end of Benloe, or Bendloe (Eng.)
A.B.A. Canon	American Bar Association Canons of Judicial Ethics
A.B.A. Code	American Bar Association Code of Professional Responsibility
A.B.A. Code, DR	American Bar Association Code of Professional Responsibility (Disciplinary Rules)
A.B.A. Code, EC	American Bar Association Code of Professional Responsibility (Ethical Considerations)
A.B.A.J.	American Bar Association Journal
A.B.A.Rep.	American Bar Association Reports
A.B.A.Sect. Ins.N. & C. L.Proc.	American Bar Association Section of Insurance, Negligence and Compensation Law Proceedings
Abb	Abbott's United States Circuit and District Court Reports
Abb.	Same
Abbadm	Abbott's Admiralty (U.S.)
Abb.Adm.	Same
Abb.App.Dec.	Abbott's Appeal Decisions (NY)
Abb.Dec.	Abbott's Decisions (NY)
Abb.Dict.	Abbott's Dictionary

Abb.N.Cas.	Abbott's New Cases (NY)
Abb.Prac.	Abbott's Practice (NY)
Abb.Prac. N.S.	Same, New Series
Abb.R.P.S.	Abbott's Real Property Statutes (WA)
A.B.C.Newsl.	International Association of Accident Boards and Commissions Newsletter
AbD	Abbott's Court of Appeals Decisions (NY)
A'Beck.Res. Judgm.	A'Beckett's Reserved Judgments (Vict.)
A.B.F.Researc h Reptr.	American Bar Foundation Research Reporter
A.B.F.Res.J.	American Bar Foundation Research Journal
AbN.	Abstracts, Treasury Decisions, New Series
ABn	American Bankruptcy Reports, New Series
Abogada Int'l	Abogada Internacional
AbPn	Abbott's Practice Reports, New Series
Abr	Halsbury's Abridgment
Abs.	Abstracts, Treasury Decisions
	Ohio Law Abstract
Abstr.Crim. & Pen.	Abstracts on Criminology and Penology
AC	American Annotated Cases
A.C.	Advance California Reports
	Appeal Cases (Can.)
	Law Reports Appeal Cases (Eng.)
ACA	Assembly Constitutional Amendment (CA)
A.C.A.	Advance California Appellate Reports
Acad.Pol.Sci. Proc.	Academy of Political Science Proceedings
Acct. for L. Firms	Accounting for Law Firms
A.C.L.U.Leg. Action Bull.	American Civil Liberties Union Legislative Action Bulletin
ACR	Assembly Concurrent Resolution (CA)
A.C.R.	American Criminal Reports
Act.	Acton Prize Cases, Privy Council (Eng.)
Acta Cancelariae	English Chancery Reports
Acta Crim.	Acta Criminologica
Acta Jur.	Acta Juridica
Acton	Acton Prize Cases, Privy Council (Eng.)

ACTR	Australian Capital Territory Reports
ad	Appellate Division Reports (NY)
AD	American Decisions
A.D.	Same
ad2d	Appellate Division Reports, Second Series (NY)
Adams	Adams (ME)
	Adams (NH)
Ad. & El.	Adolphus & Ellis, Queen's Bench (Eng.)
Ad. & El. (N.S.)	Same, New Series
ADC	U.S. Court of Appeals for the District of Columbia Reports
adcbna	American with Disabilities Cases (BNA)
ADCBNA	Same
Ad.Ct.Dig.	Administrative Court Digest
Add.	Addison's Reports (PA)
Add.Eccl.Rep.	Addams' Ecclesiastical Reports (Eng.)
addison	Addison Reports (PA)
Add.Penn.	Addison (PA)
Add.Rep.	Same
Adel.L.Rev.	Adelaide Law Review
Ad.L.	Pike and Fischer, Administrative Law
Ad.L.2d	Same, Second Series
Ad.L.Bull.	Administrative Law Bulletin
Ad.L.News	Administrative Law News
Ad.L.Newsl.	Administrative Law Newsletter
Ad.L.Rev.	Administrative Law Review
Adm. & Ecc.	Admiralty & Ecclesiastical (Eng.)
Adm. C.	California Administrative Code
Admin. L.J.	Administrative Law Journal
Admin.L.J. Am.U.	Administrative Law Journal of the American University
Admin.L.Rev.	Administrative Law Review
Adm Rules	Rules Regulating Admission to Practice Law in California
ADRLJ	Arbitration and Dispute Resolution Law Journal
Advocates' Q.	Advocates' Quarterly
advsheets	Massachusetts Advance Sheets
A/E Legal Newsl.	A/E Legal Newsletter

AELE Legal Liab.Rep.	AELE Legal Liability Reporter
A.F.L.Rev.	Air Force Law Review
Afr. J. Int'l L.	African Journal of International Law
Afr.L.Dig.	African Law Digest
Afr.L.R.	African Law Reports
Afr.L.R., Mal.Ser.	African Law Reports, Malawi Series
Afr.L.R., Sierre L.Ser.	African Law Reports, Sierra Leone Series
Afr.L.Stud.	African Law Studies
aftr	American Federal Tax Reports
AFTR	Same
aftr2d	Same, Second Series
AFTR2d	Same
Agric. C.	Agricultural Code (renamed Food and Agricultural Code) (CA)
Agric.Dec.	Agriculture Decisions
Agric.L.J.	Agriculture Law Journal
A.I.D.	Accident/Injury/Damages
AIDS L. Rep.	AIDS Law Reporter
AIDS L.Rev. Q.	AIDS Law Review Quarterly
AIDS Litigation Rep.	AIDS Litigation Reporter
aik	Aiken's Reports (VT)
Aik.	Same
A.I.L.C.	American International Law Cases 1783–1968
Air & Space L.	Air and Space Law
Air L.	Air Law
Air L.Rev.	Air Law Review
AJ	Assembly Daily Journal (CA)
AJB	Assembly Joint Resolution (CA)
AkA	Arkansas Appellate Reports
A.K.Marsh.	A.K. Marshall (KY)
Akron L.Rev.	Akron Law Review
Akron Tax J.	Akron Tax Journal
ala	Alabama Reporter
Ala.	Alabama Appellate Reports
alaapp	Alabama Appellate Court Reports
Ala.App.	Alabama Court of Appeals
Ala.Law.	Alabama Lawyer
Ala.L.J.	Alabama Law Journal
Ala.L.Rev.	Alabama Law Review
Ala.Sel.Cas.	Alabama Select Cases
alaska	Alaska Reports
Alaska	Same
Alaska B.Brief	Alaska Bar Brief

Alaska B.J.	Alaska Bar Journal
Alaska L.J.	Alaska Law Journal
Alaska L.Rev.	Alaska Law Review
Ala.St.B. Found.Bull.	Alabama State Bar Foundation Bulletin
Alb	Albany Law Review
Albany L.Rev.	Same
Alb.L.J.	Albany Law Journal
Alb.L.J.Sci. & Tech.	Albany Law Journal of Science and Technology
Alb.L.Rev.	Albany Law Review
Albuquerque B.J.	Albuquerque Bar Journal
Alc. & N.	Alcock & Napier, King's Bench (Ir.)
Alcohol. Treat.Q.	Alcoholism Treatment Quarterly
Alc.Reg.Cas.	Alcock Registry Cases (Ir.)
Ald.	Alden's Condensed Reports (PA)
Aleyn	Aleyn, King's Bench (Eng.)
AlF	Alaska Federal Reports
A.L.I.	American Law Institute
ALI–ABA CLE Rev.	American Law Institute–American Bar Association–Continuing Legal Education Review
Alison Pr.	Alison Practice (Scot.)
ALJ	Australian Law Journal
ALJR	Australian Law Journal Reports
Allen	Allen's Reports (MA)
Allen N.B.	Allen (N.B.)
All E.R.	All England Law Reports
All ER (EC)	All England Law Reports European Cases
All India Crim.Dec.	All India Criminal Decisions
All India Rptr.	All India Reporter
Allinson	Allinson, Pa. Superior District Courts
All N.L.R.	All Nigeria Law Reports
All Pak.Leg. Dec.	All Pakistan Legal Decisions
Alr	American Law Reports
ALR	Australian Law Reports
A.L.R.	American Law Reports
Alr(2d)	Same, Second Series
A.L.R.2d	Same
A.L.R.3d	Same, Third Series
A.L.R.4th	Same, Fourth Series
A.L.R.5th	Same, Fifth Series
A.L.Rec.	American Law Record

A.L.Reg. (N.S.)	American Law Register, New Series
A.L.Reg. (O.S.)	Same, Old Series
A.L.R.Fed.	American Law Reports Federal
Alta.	Alberta Law Reports
Alta.L.	Alberta Law
Alta.L.Q.	Alberta Law Quarterly
Alta.L.Rev.	Alberta Law Review
Am.Acad. Matri.Law. J.	American Academy of Matrimonial Lawyers Journal
Am. & E. Corp.Cas.	American & English Corporation Cases
Am. & E. Corp.Cas. (N.S.)	Same, New Series
Am. & Eng. Ann.Cas.	American & English Annotated Cases
Am. & Eng. Eq.D.	American & English Decisions in Equity
Am. & Eng. Pat.Cas.	American & English Patent Cases
Am. & E.R. Cas.	American & English Railroad Cases
Am. & E.R. Cas. (N.S.)	Same, New Series
A.M. & O.	Armstrong, Macartney & Ogle Nisi Prius (Ir.)
Amb.	Ambler, Chancery (Eng.)
Am.Bankr. L.J.	American Bankruptcy Law Journal
Am.Bankr. Reg.	American Bankruptcy Register
Am.Bankr. Rep.	American Bankruptcy Reports
Am.Bankr. Rev.	American Bankruptcy Review
Am.B.Found. Res.J.	American Bar Foundation Research Journal
Am.B.News	American Bar News
Am.B.R. (N.S.)	American Bankruptcy Reports, New Series
Am.Bus.L.J.	American Business Law Journal
amc	American Maritime Cases
A.M.C.	Same
Am.Corp.Cas.	American Corporation Cases
Am.Cr.	American Criminal Reports
Am.Crim. L.Q.	American Criminal Law Quarterly
Am.Crim. L.Rev.	American Criminal Law Review
amdd	Americans with Disabilities Decisions (LCP)
Am.Dec.	American Decisions

Am.Elect. Cas.	American Electrical Cases
Ames	Ames (MN)
	Ames (RI)
Ames K. & B.	Ames, Knowles & Bradley (RI)
Am.Fed.Tax R.	American Federal Tax Reports
Am.Fed.Tax R.2d	Same, Second Series
Am.For.L. Ass'n Newsl.	American Foreign Law Association Newsletter
Am.Hist.Rev.	American Historical Review
Amicus	Amicus (South Bend, IN)
	Amicus (Thousand Oaks, CA)
Am.Indian L.Rev.	American Indian Law Review
Am. Ind.J.	American Indian Journal
Am.Ind.L. Newsl.	American Indian Law Newsletter
Am.Insolv. Rep.	American Insolvency Reports
Am.J.Comp. L.	American Journal of Comparative Law
Am.J.Crim. L.	American Journal of Criminal Law
Am.J.Fam. L.	American Journal of Family Law
Am.J.For.Psych.	American Journal of Forensic Psychiatry
Am.J.Int'l Arb.	American Journal of International Arbitration
Am.J.Int'l L.	American Journal of International Law
Am.J.Juris.	American Journal of Jurisprudence
Am.J.L. & Med.	American Journal of Law and Medicine
Am.J.Legal Hist.	American Journal of Legal History
Am.J.Police Sci.	American Journal of Police Science
Am.J.Tax Pol'y	American Journal of Tax Policy
Am.J.Trial Advoc.	American Journal of Trial Advocacy
Am.Jur.	American Jurisprudence
	American Jurist
Am.Jur.2d	American Jurisprudence, Second Series
Am.Lab.Leg. Rev.	American Labor Legislation Review
Am.Law.	American Lawyer
Am.Law Rec.	American Law Record (OH)
Am.Law Reg.	American Law Register
Am.L.Ins.	American Law Institute
Am.L.J.	American Law Journal (OH)
	American Law Journal (PA)

Am.L.J. (N.S.)	Same, New Series
Am.L.Mag.	American Law Magazine
Am.L.Rec.	American Law Record (OH)
Am.L.Reg.	American Law Register
Am.L.Reg. (N.S.)	Same, New Series
Am.L.Reg. (O.S.)	Same, Old Series
Am.L.Rev.	American Law Review
Am.L.Sch. Rev.	American Law School Review
Am. L. T.	American Law Times United States Courts
Am.L.T. Bankr.	American Law Times Bankruptcy Reports
Am.Mar.Cas.	American Maritime Cases
Am.Negl.Cas.	American Negligence Cases
Am.Negl.Rep.	American Negligence Reports
Am.Notary	American Notary
Am.Pol.Sci. Rev.	American Political Science Review
Am.Prob.	American Probate Reports
Am.Prob. (N.S.)	Same, New Series
Am.Pr.Rep.	American Practice Reports (DC)
Am.R.	American Reports
Am.Railw. Cas.	American Railway Cases (Smith & Bates)
Am.R. & Corp.	American Railroad Corporation
Am.Rep.	American Reports
Am.R.Rep.	American Railway Reports
Am.Ry.Rep.	American Railway Reports
Am.Soc'y Int'l L.Proc.	American Society of International Law Proceedings
Am.St.R.	American State Reports
Am.St.R.D.	American Street Railway Decisions
Am.St.Rep.	American State Reports
Am.Trial Law.J.	American Trial Lawyers Journal
Am.Trial Law.L.J.	American Trial Lawyers Law Journal
Am.Tr.M. Cas.	American Trademark Cases (Cox)
Am.U.Intra. L.Rev.	American University Intramural Law Review
Am.U.J. Gender & L.	American University Journal of Gender and the Law
Am.U.J.Int'l L. & Pol'y	American University Journal of International Law and Policy
Am.U.L.Rev.	American University Law Review

AN	Abbott's New Cases	anp	Anthon's Nisi Prius Cases
An.B.	Anonymous Reports at end of Benloe, or Bendloe (Eng.)	anp2	Same, Second Series
		Anst.	Ansthruther, Exchequer (Eng.)
AnC	New York Annotated Cases		
And.	Anderson, Common Pleas (Eng.)	Anth.N.P.	Anthon's Nisi Prius (NY)
		Antitrust Bull.	Antitrust Bulletin
Anderson 2d; 3d	Anderson Uniform Commercial Code (2d and 3d ed.)	Antitrust L. & Econ.Rev.	Antitrust Law and Economics Review
		Antitrust L.J.	Antitrust Law Journal
Anderson Legal Forms 2d	Anderson Legal Forms (2d ed.)	Antitrust L.Sym.	Antitrust Law Symposium
Anderson P.P. Forms 2d	Anderson Pleading and Practice Forms (2d ed.)	AntNP	Anthon's Nisi Prius Cases(NY)
		AntNP2d	Same, Second Series
		AOA	Anderson's Ohio Appellate Unreported Decisions
Andr.	Andrews, King's Bench (Eng.)		
Ang.	Angell (RI)	A.O.C.Newsl.	Administrative Office of the Courts Newsletter
Ang. & Dur.	Angell & Durfee (RI)		
Anglo–Am.L. Rev.	Anglo–American Law Review	ApDC	Court of Appeals for District of Columbia
Animal Rights L.Rep.	Animal Rights Law Reporter	APLA Q.J.	American Patent Law Association Quarterly Journal
Ann.	Annaly's Hardwicke King's Bench (Eng.)	App.	Appleton (ME)
Annals	Annals of the American Academy of Political and Social Science		California District Courts of Appeal
		App.Cas.	Law Reports, Appeal Cases (Eng.)
Annals Air & Space	Annals of Air and Space Law	App.Cas.2d	Same, Second Series
Annaly	Annaly's Hardwicke King's Bench (Eng.)	App.Court Ad.Rev.	Appellate Court Administration Review
Ann.Cas.	American Annotated Cases	appdc	Appeal Cases (DC)
Ann.Dig.	Annual Digest and Reports of International Law Cases	App.D.C.	Same
		App.Div.	Appellate Division (NY)
Ann.Indus. Prop.L.	Annual of Industrial Property Law	App.Div.2d	Same, Second Series
		App.N.Z.	Appeal Reports (N.Z.)
Ann.Leg. Forms Mag.	Annotated Legal Forms Magazine	App.R.N.Z.	Same, Second Series
Ann.L.Reg. U.S.	Annual Law Register of the United States	App.Rep.Ont.	Ontario Appeal Reports
		A.P.R.	Atlantic Provinces Reports
Ann.Rev.Int'l Aff.	Annual Review of International Affairs	AR	American Reports
		A.R.	Alberta Reports
Ann.Surv. Afr.L.	Annual Survey of African Law	Arb.J.	Arbitration Journal
		Arb.J. (N.S.)	Same, New Series
Ann.Surv. Am.L.	Annual Survey of American Law	Arb.J. (O.S.)	Same, Old Series
		Arb.L.Dig.	Arbitration Law: A Digest of Court Decisions
Ann.Surv. Banking L.	Annual Survey of Banking Law		
		A.R.C.	American Ruling Cases
Ann.Surv. Colo.L.	Annual Survey of Colorado Law	Archer	Archer (FL)
		Archer & H.	Archer & Hogue (FL)
Ann.Surv. Commonw. L.	Annual Survey of Commonwealth Law	Argus L.R.	Argus Law Reports (Austl.)
		ariz	Arizona Reports
Ann.Surv. Ind.L.	Annual Survey of Indian Law	Ariz.	Same
		arizadvrep	Arizona Advance Reports
Ann.Surv. S.Afr.L.	Annual Survey of South African Law	arizapp	Arizona Appeals Reports
Ann.Tax Cas.	Annotated Tax Cases		

Ariz.App.	Same
Ariz.B.J.	Arizona Bar Journal
Ariz.J.Int'l & Comp.L.	Arizona Journal of International and Comparative Law
Ariz.Law.	Arizona Lawyer
Ariz.L.Rev.	Arizona Law Review
Ariz.St.L.J.	Arizona State Law Journal
ark	Arkansas Reports
Ark.	Same
arkapp	Arkansas Court of Appeals Reports
Ark.Just.	Arkley's Justiciary (Scot.)
Ark.L.J.	Arkansas Law Journal
Ark.Law.	Arkansas Lawyer
Ark.Law.Q.	Arkansas Lawyer Quarterly
Ark.L.Rev.	Arkansas Law Review
A.R.M.	Appeals & Review Memorandum Committee (I.R.B.)
Armour	Queen's Bench, Manitoba Tempere Wood, by Armour
Arms.Con. Elec.	Armstrong's Contested Elections (NY)
Army Law.	Army Lawyer
Arn.	Arnold, Common Pleas (Eng.)
Arn. & H.	Arnold & Hodges, Queen's Bench (Eng.)
Arnold	Arnold, Common Pleas (Eng.)
A.R.R.	Appeals & Review Recommendation (I.R.B.)
Art.	Article
Art & L.	Art and the Law
AS	American State Reports
	Annual Survey of American Law
A.S.A.Newsl.	Association for the Study of Abortion Newsletter
Ashm.	Ashmead (PA)
Asian Comp.L.Rev.	Asian Comparative Law Review
Asian Pac. Comm.Law.	Asian Pacific Commercial Lawyer
ASILS Int'l L.J.	Association of Student International Law Society's International Law Journal
Aspin.	Aspinall's Maritime Cases (Eng.)
A.S.R.	American State Reports
Ass'n Trial Law.Am. Newsl.	Association of Trial Lawyers of America Newsletter
At	Atlantic Reporter
A.T.	Alcohol Tax Unit (I.R.B.)

Ateneo L.J.	Ateneo Law Journal
Atk.	Atkyns, Chancery (Eng.)
Atl.	Atlantic Reporter
A.T.L.A.J.	American Trial Lawyers Association Journal
ATLA L.J.	Journal of the Association of Trial Lawyers of America
Atom.Energy L.J.	Atomic Energy Law Journal
Att'y Gen.	Attorney General
Att'y Gen.L.J.	Attorney General's Law Journal
Att'y Gen.Rep.	United States Attorneys General's Reports
Atwater	Atwater (MN)
Auckland U.L.Rev.	Auckland University Law Review
Aust.Jur.	Australian Jurist
Austl. & N.Z. J.Crim.	Australian and New Zealand Journal of Criminology
Austl.Argus L.R.	Australian Argus Law Reports
Austl.Bankr. Cas.	Australian Bankruptcy Cases
Austl.Bus. L.Rev.	Australian Business Law Review
Austl.Com.J.	Australian Commercial Journal
Austl.Convey. & Sol.J.	Australian Conveyancer and Solicitors Journal
Austl.Current L.Rev.	Australian Current Law Review
Austl.J.For. Sci.	Australian Journal of Forensic Sciences
Austl.J.L. Soc'y	Australian Journal of Law and Society
Austl.Jr.	Australian Jurist
Austl.L.J.	Australian Law Journal
Austl.L.J. Rep.	Australian Law Journal Reports
Aust.L.T.	Australian Law Times
Austl.L. Times	Australian Law Times
Austl.Law.	Australian Lawyer
Austl.Tax	Australian Tax Decisions
Austl.Tax Rev.	Australian Tax Review
Austl.Y.B. Int'l L.	Australian Yearbook of International Law
Austr.C.L.R.	Commonwealth Law Reports, Australia
Auto.Cas.	Automobile Cases
Auto.Cas.2d	Same, Second Series
Auto.L.Rep.	Automobile Law Reporter (CCH)
Av.Cas.	Aviation Cases
Av.L.Rep.	Aviation Law Reporter (CCH)

AVMA	AVMA Medical & Legal Journal
Az	Arizona Reports

AzA	Arizona Court of Appeals Reports

B

B.	Weekly Law Bulletin
Bac.Abr.	Bacon's Abridgment (Eng.)
Bag. & Har.	Bagley & Harman (CA)
Bagl.	Bagley (CA)
Bagl. & H.	Bagley & Harman (CA)
Bail Ct.Cas.	Lowndes & Maxwell, Bail Court Cases (Eng.)
Baild	Baildon's Select Cases in Chancery (Eng.)
Bail.Eq.	Bailey's Equity (SC)
Bailey	Bailey's Law (SC)
BAJI	California Jury Instructions, Civil (7th rev. ed.)
Bal.Ann. Codes	Ballinger's Annotated Codes & Statutes (WA)
Bal.Pay't Rep.	Balance of Payments Reports (CCH)
baldw	Baldwin's United States Circuit Court Reports
Baldw.	Baldwin (U.S.)
Balf.Pr.	Balfour's Practice (Scot.)
Ball & B.	Ball & Beatty, Chancery (Ir.)
Ballantine	Ballantine & Sterling, California Corporation Laws (4th ed.)
Balt.L.T.	Baltimore Law Transcript
bamsl	Bankruptcy Reporter by Bar Association of Metropolitan St. Louis
bana	Banning & Arden's Patent Cases
B. & A.	Barnewall & Alderson, King's Bench (Eng.)
Ban. & A.	Banning & Arden, Patent Cases (U.S.)
B. & Ad.	Barnewall & Adolphus, King's Bench (Eng.)
B. & Ald.	Barnewall & Alderson, King's Bench (Eng.)
B. & Arn.	Barron & Arnold, Election Cases (Eng.)
B. & Aust.	Barron & Austin Election Cases (Eng.)
B. & B.	Ball & Beatty's Chancery (Ir.)
	Broderip & Bingham, Common Pleas (Eng.)

B. & C.	Barnewall & Cresswell's King's Bench (Eng.)
B. & C.R.	Reports of Bankruptcy & Companies Winding up Cases (Eng.)
B. & D.	Benloe & Dalison, Common Pleas (Eng.)
B. & F.	Broderip & Freemantle's Ecclesiastical (Eng.)
B. & H.Cr. Cas.	Bennet & Heard's Criminal Cases (Eng.)
B. & H.Crim. Cas.	Same
B. & Macn.	Brown & Macnamara, Railway Cases (Eng.)
B. & P.	Bosanquet & Puller, Common Pleas (Eng.)
B & PC	Business and Professions Code (CA)
B. & P.N.R.	Bosanquet & Puller's New Reports (Eng.)
B. & S.	Best & Smith, Queen's Bench (Eng.)
Bank. & Ins.R.	Bankruptcy & Insolvency Reports (Eng.)
Bank C	Banking Code (CA)
Bank.Cas.	Banking Cases
Bank.Ct.Rep.	Bankrupt Court Reports
Banking L.J.	Banking Law Journal
Banking L. Rev.	Banking Law Review
Bankr.B.Bull.	Bankruptcy Bar Bulletin
Bankr.Dev.J.	Bankruptcy Developments Journal
Bankr.L.Rep.	Bankruptcy Law Reporter (CCH)
Bankr.Reg.	National Bankruptcy Register (NY)
Banks	Banks (KS)
Bann.	Bannister's Common Pleas (Eng.)
Bann. & A.	Banning & Arden, Patent Cases (U.S.)
Bann. & Ard.	Same
Bar	Barbour's Supreme Court Reports (NY)
Bar. & Arn.	Barron & Arnold, Election Cases (Eng.)

Bar. & Aust.	Barron & Austin, Election Cases (Eng.)
Barb.	Barber (AR)
	Barbour (NY)
Barb.Ch.	Barbour's Chancery (NY)
Barber	Barber (NY)
Barn.	Barnardiston, King's Bench (Eng.)
Barn. & Ad.	Barnewall & Adolphus, King's Bench (Eng.)
Barn. & Ald.	Barnewall & Alderson, King's Bench (Eng.)
Barn. & C.	Barnewall & Cresswell, King's Bench (Eng.)
Barn. & Cress.	Same
Barn.Ch.	Barnardiston, Chancery (Eng.)
Barnes	Barnes, Practice Cases (Eng.)
Barnes' Notes	Barnes' Notes (Eng.)
Barnet	Barnet, Common Pleas (Eng.)
Barr	Barr (PA)
Barr.Ch.Pr.	Barroll, Chancery Practice (MD)
Bar Regs	Rules and Regulations of State Bar
Barrister	Barrister (Chicago)
	Barrister (Coral Gables, FL)
	Barrister (Davis, CA)
	Barrister (Fort Lauderdale, FL)
	Barrister (Toronto)
Barr.MSS.	Barradall, Manuscript Reports (VA)
Bart.Elec. Cas.	Bartlett's Election Cases
Bates Ch.	Bates, Chancery (DE)
Batty	Batty, King's Bench (Ir.)
Baxt.	Baxter (TN)
baxttn	Same
Bay	Bay (MO)
	Bay (SC)
Baylor L.Rev.	Baylor Law Review
B.Bull.	Bar Bulletin
B.C.	British Columbia
bca	Board of Contract Appeals Decisions (U.S.)
B.C.Branch Lec.	Canadian Bar Association, British Columbia Branch Meeting Program Reports
B.C.C.	Bail Court Cases (Eng.)
bcd	Bankruptcy Court Decisions
BCD	Same
B.C.Envtl. Aff.L.Rev.	Boston College Environmental Affairs Law Review

BCh	Barbour's Chancery Reports (NY)
B.C.Indus. & Com.L.Rev.	Boston College Industrial and Commercial Law Review
B.C.Int'l & Comp.L.J.	Boston College International and Comparative Law Journal
B.C. Int'l & Comp. L. Rev.	Boston College International and Comparative Law Review
BCLC	Butterworths Company Law Cases
B.C.L. Notes	British Columbia Law Notes
B.C.L.Rev.	Boston College Law Review
bcr	Bankruptcy Court Reporter (CO)
BCR	Same
B.C. Third World L.J.	Boston College Third World Law Journal
B.D. & O.	Blackham, Dundas & Osborne, Nisi Prius (Ir.)
Beale	Beale, The Conflict of Laws
Beasl.	Beasley (NJ)
Beav.	Beavan, Rolls Court (Eng.)
Beav. & W. Ry.Cas.	Beavan & Walford's Railway & Canal Cases (Eng.)
Beav.R. & C.Cas.	Beavan, Railway & Canal Cases (Eng.)
Beaw.Lex Mer.	Beawes Lex Mercatoria (Eng.)
Bee	Bee's (U.S.)
Bee Adm.	Bee's Admiralty, United States District Court (SC)
Bee C.C.R.	Bee's Crown Cases Reserved (Eng.)
Behav.Sci. & L.	Behavioral Sciences and the Law
Belg.Rev.Int'l L.	Belgian Review of International Law
Bell.	Bellewe, King's Bench (Eng.)
Bell App.Cas.	Bell's Appeal Cases, House of Lords (Scot.)
Bell Cas.	Bell's Cases (Scot.)
Bell.Cas.t.H. VIII	Bellewe, King's Bench, tempore Henry VIII (Eng.)
Bell.Cas.t.R. II	Same, tempore Richard II (Eng.)
Bell C.C.	Bell's Crown Cases Reserved (Eng.)
Bell Comm.	Bell's Commentaries (Eng.)
Bell Cr.C.	Bell's Crown Cases Reserved (Eng.)
Bellewe (Eng.)	Bellewe, King's Bench
Bell H.L.	Bell's Appeal Cases, House of Lords (Scot.)
Bell P.C.	Bell's Parliament Cases (Scot.)

Bell Sc.Cas.	Bell's Scotch Court of Sessions Cases
Bell Ses.Cas.	Same
ben	Benedict's District Court Reporter
Ben.	Same
Ben. & H.L.C.	Bennett & Heard, Leading Criminal Cases (Eng.)
Bendl.	Bendloe's English Common Pleas
Bened.	Benedict (U.S. District Court)
Benl.	Benloe's Common Pleas (Eng.)
	Benloe's King's Bench (Eng.)
Benl. & D.	Benloe & Dalison, Common Pleas (Eng.)
Benl. & Dal.	Same
Benl.K.B.	Benloe's King's Bench (Eng.)
Benl.Old	Benloe, Old English Common Pleas
Benn.	Bennett (CA)
	Bennett (Dakota)
	Bennett (MO)
Bent.	Bentley's Chancery (Ir.)
Berkeley Women's L.J.	Berkeley Women's Law Journal
Berry	Berry (MO)
Bev Hills BJ	Beverly Hills Bar Journal
B.Exam.	Bar Examiner
B.Exam.J.	Bar Examination Journal
bibb	Bibb (KY)
Bibb	Same
Bibl.Cott.	Cotton Manuscripts
B.I.C.I.L. Newsl.	British Institute of International and Comparative Law Newsletter
Bick.	Bicknell (NV)
Bick. & H.	Bicknell & Hawley (NV)
Big.Ov.Cas.	Bigelow's Overruled Cases
B.I.L.C.	British International Law Cases
Bill Rights J.	Bill of Rights Journal
Bill Rights Rev.	Bill of Rights Review
Bin	Binney's Reports (PA)
Bing.	Bingham, New Cases, Common Pleas (Eng.)
binn	Binney's Reports (PA)
Binn.	Same
biss	Bissell's U.S. Circuit Court Reports
Biss.	Same

Bitt.Rep. in Ch.	Bittleson's Reports, Queen's Bench (Eng.)
Bitt.W. & P.	Bittleson, Wise & Parnell Practice Cases (Eng.)
Bk.	Black (U.S.)
Bl.	William Blackstone's King's Bench (Eng.)
Bla.	Same
black	Black's U.S. Supreme Court Reporter
Black	Black (IN)
	Black (U.S.)
	Blackford's Reports (IN)
Black.	William Blackstone's King's Bench (Eng.)
Black.Cond.	Blackwell's Condensed Reports (IL)
Black.Cond. Rep.	Same
Black.D. & O.	Blackham, Dandas & Osborne, Nisi Prius (Ir.)
blackf	Blackford's Reports (IN)
Blackf.	Blackford (IN)
Black.H.	Henry Blackstone's Common Pleas (Eng.)
Black.Jus.	Blackerby's Justices' Cases (Eng.)
Black L.J.	Black Law Journal
Blackst.R.	William Blackstone's King's Bench (Eng.)
Blackw.Cond.	Blackwell's Condensed Reports (IL)
Bla.H.	Henry Blackstone's Common Pleas (Eng.)
Blair Co.	Blair County Law Reports (PA)
Blake	Blake (MT)
Blake & H.	Blake & Hedge (MT)
Bland	Bland's Chancery Reports (MD)
blandch	Same
blatch	Blatchford's U.S. Circuit Court Reports
Blatchf.	Blatchford (U.S.)
Blatchf. & H.	Blatchford & Howland (U.S. District Court)
Blatchf.Prize Cas.	Blatchford's Prize Cases (U.S.)
Bla.W.	William Blackstone's King's Bench (Eng.)
B.Leader	Bar Leader
Bleckley	Bleckley (GA)
blh	Blatchford & Howland (U.S. District Court)

Bl.H.	Henry Blackstone's Common Pleas (Eng.)	bpc	Blatchford's Prize Cases
Bli.	Bligh, House of Lords (Eng.)	br	Bankruptcy Reporter
Bli. (N.S.)	Same, New Series	BR	Same
Bligh	Same		Brooklyn Law Review
Bligh (N.S.)	Same, New Series	B.R. (Army)	Board of Review (Army)
Bliss	Bliss, Delaware County Reports (PA)	Bract.	Bracton De Legibus et Consuetudinibus Angliae (Eng.)
BLR	Building Law Reports	Bracton L.J.	Bracton Law Journal
BLRev	Business Law Review	Bradb	Bradbury's Pleading and Practice Reports (NY)
Blue Sky L.Rep.	Blue Sky Law Reporter (CCH)	Bradf	Bradford's Surrogate Court Reports (NY)
Bluett	Bluett's Isle of Man Cases	Bradf.	Bradford (IA)
Bl.W.	William Blackstone's King's Bench (Eng.)	Bradf.Surr.	Bradford's Surrogate Court (NY)
BMLR	Butterworths Medico–Legal Reports	Bradl.	Bradley (RI)
B.Mon.	Ben Monroe (KY)	Bradw.	Bradwell (IL)
BNA	Bureau of National Affairs	Brady (Bailey) (5th ed.)	Brady on Bank Checks (5th ed.) (Bailey)
BNA Banking Rep.	BNA's Banking Report	Brame	Brame (MS)
BNA Sec.Reg.	Securities Regulation & Law Report	Branch	Branch (FL)
Bogert	Bogert, The Law of Trusts and Trustees (2d ed.)	Br. & B.	Broderip & Bingham, Common Pleas (Eng.)
Bombay L.J.	Bombay Law Journal	Br. & Col.	British & Colonial Prize Cases
bond	Bond's U.S. Circuit Court Reports	Br. & F.Ecc.	Broderick & Freemantle's Ecclesiastical Cases (Eng.)
Bond	Same	Br. & Gold.	Browndow & Goldesborough's Common Pleas (Eng.)
Book of Judg.	Book of Judgments (Eng.)	Br. & L.	Brownlow & Lushington's Admiralty Cases (Eng.)
Boor.	Booraem (CA)	Br. & Lush.	Same
Bos	Bosworth's Reports (NY)	Brantly	Brantly (MD)
Bos.	Bosworth, Superior Court (NY)	Bray	Brayton's Reports (VT)
Bos. & P.	Bosanquet & Puller, Common Pleas (Eng.)	Brayt.	Brayton (VT)
Bos. & P. N.R.	Same	brayton	Same
Bos. & Pul.	Same	B.R.C.	British Ruling Cases
Bos.Pol.Rep.	Boston Police Reports	brcc	Brunner's Collected Cases
Bost.L.R.	Boston Law Reporter	Br.Eccl.	Brown's Ecclesiastical (Eng.)
Boston B.J.	Boston Bar Journal	Breese	Breese's Reports(IL)
Bosw.	Boswell (Scot.)	Breese App.	Breese Appendix
	Bosworth, Superior Court (NY)	breeseappx	Same, Appendix (IL)
Bott Poor Law Cas.	Bott's Poor Laws Settlement Cases (Eng.)	Brev.	Brevard (SC)
Bott's Set. Cas.	Same	Brew.	Brewer (MD)
Bould.	Bouldin (AL)		Brewster (PA)
Bouv.	Bouvier Law Dictionary	Brews.	Brewster (PA)
Bov.Pat.Cas.	Bovill's Patent Cases	Bridg.	J. Bridgmore, Common Pleas (Eng.)
Boy	Boyce's Reports (DE)	Bridgeport L.Rev.	Bridgeport Law Review
Boyce	Boyce (DE)	Bridg.J.	Sir J. Bridgman, Common Pleas (Eng.)
boycede	Same		

Bridg.O.	Sir Orlando Bridgman, Common Pleas (Eng.)
Brief/Case (S.F. Bar)	Brief/Case (San Francisco Bar Law Review)
Brightly	Brightly (PA)
Brightly El.Cas.	Brightly's Leading Election Cases (PA)
Brisb.	Brisbin (MN)
Brit.Cr.Cas.	British Crown Cases
Brit.J.Ad.L.	British Journal of Administrative Law
Brit.J. Criminol.	British Journal of Criminology
Brit.J.Law & Soc'y	British Journal of Law and Society
Brit.Prac. Int'l	British Practice in International Law
Brit.Ship.L.	British Shipping Laws (Stevens)
Brit.Tax Rev.	British Tax Review
Brit.Y.B.Int'l L.	British Year Book of International Law
B.R.–J.C. (Army)	Board of Review and Judicial Council of the Army
Br.N.C.	Brooke's New Cases, King's Bench (Eng.)
Br.N.Cas.	Same
Bro. & F.	Broderick & Freemantle's Ecclesiastical (Eng.)
Bro. & Fr.	Same
Bro. & Lush.	Browning & Lushington's Admiralty (Eng.)
Brock.	Brockenbrough (U.S.)
Brock. & Hol.Cas.	Brockenbrough & Holmes' Cases (VA)
Brock.Cas.	Brockenbrough's Cases (VA)
Brod. & F. Ecc.Cas.	Broderick & Freemantle's Ecclesiastical Cases (Eng.)
Brod. & Fr. Ecc.Cas.	Same
Brodix Am. & El.Pat.Cas.	Brodix's American & English Patent Cases
Bro.Just.	Brown's Justiciary (Scot.)
Brook Abr.	Brook's Abridgment (Eng.)
Brook. Barrister	Brooklyn Barrister
Brook.J.Int'l L.	Brooklyn Journal of International Law
Brook.L.Rev.	Brooklyn Law Review
Brook N.Cas.	Brook's New Cases, King's Bench (Eng.)
Brooks	Brooks (MI)
Brown	Brown (MS)
	Brown (MO)
	Brown (NE)

Brown A. & R.	Brown's United States District Court Admiralty & Revenue Cases
Brown Adm.	Brown's Admiralty (U.S.)
Brown. & L.	Browning & Lushington, Admiralty (Eng.)
Brown & MacN.	Brown & MacNamara, Railway Cases (Eng.)
Brown & R.	Brown & Rader (MO)
Brown Ch.	Brown's Chancery (Eng.)
Brown Dict.	Brown's Law Dictionary
Browne	Browne (MA)
	Browne, Common Pleas (PA)
Browne & G.	Browne & Gray (MA)
Browne & H.	Browne & Hemingway (MS)
Browne Bank Cas.	Browne's National Bank Cases
Brown Ecc.	Brown's Ecclesiastical (Eng.)
brownes	Browne's Reports (PA)
Brownl. & G.	Brownlow & Goldesborough, Common Pleas (Eng.)
Brown N.P.	Brown's Nisi Prius (MI)
Brown Parl. Cas.	Brown's House of Lords Cases (Eng.)
Brown P.C.	Same
brownsadm	Brown's U.S. Admiralty Reports
Bruce	Bruce (Scot.)
Brunn.Coll. Cas.	Brunner's Collected Cases (U.S.)
BRW	Bankruptcy Reporter (West)
bstockton	B. Stockton's New Jersey Equity Reports
Bt.	Benedict (U.S.)
bta	Board of Tax Appeals (U.S.)
B.T.A.	Same
btr	Brief Times Reporter (CO)
BTR	British Tax Review
BTW	United States Board of Tax Appeals Reports
Buck	Buck (MT)
	Buck, Bankrupt Cases (Eng.)
Buck.	Bucknill's Cooke's Cases of Practice, Common Pleas (Eng.)
Buck.Dec.	Buckner's Decisions (in Freeman's Chancery Reports) (MS)
Buf	Buffalo Law Review
Buff.L.Rev.	Same
B.U.Int'l L.J.	Boston University International Law Journal
B.U.J.Tax L.	Boston University Journal of Tax Law

Bull.	Weekly Law Bulletin
Bull.Am. Acad.Psych. & L.	Bulletin of the American Academy of Psychiatry and the Law
Bull.Can. Welfare L.	Bulletin of Canadian Welfare Law
Bull.Copyright Soc'y	Bulletin of the Copyright Society of the United States of America
Bull.Czech.L.	Bulletin of Czechoslovak Law
Buller N.P.	Buller's Nisi Prius (Eng.)
Bull.Int'l Fiscal Doc.	Bulletin for International Fiscal Documentation
Bull.Legal Devel.	Bulletin of Legal Developments
Bull.L.Science & Tech.	Bulletin of Law, Science and Technology
Bull.Waseda U.Inst. Comp.L.	Bulletin, Waseda University Institute of Comparative Law
B.U.L.Rev.	Boston University Law Review
Bulstr.	Bulstrode, King's Bench (Eng.)
Bunb.	Bunbury, Exchequer (Eng.)
B.U.Pub.Int. L.J.	Boston University Public Interest Law Journal
Bur	Burnett's Reports (WI)
Burf.	Burford (OK)
Burgess	Burgess (OH)
Burk	Burk (VA)
Burlesque Rep.	Skillman's New York Police Reports

Burnett	Burnett (OR)
	Burnett (WI)
Burr.	Burrow, King's Bench (Eng.)
Burr.S.Cases	Burrow's Settlement Cases (Eng.)
Burr.t.M.	Burrow's Reports, tempore Mansfield (Eng.)
Bus. & L.	Business and Law
Bus. & Prof. C.	Business and Professions Code (CA)
Busb.Eq.	Busbee, Equity (NC)
Busb.L.	Busbee, Law (NC)
Bush	Bush (KY)
Bus.Law.	Business Lawyer
Bus.L.J.	Business Law Journal
Bus.L.Rev.	Business Law Review (Eng.)
	Business Law Review (U.S.)
Bus.Reg.L. Rep.	Business Regulation Law Report
Buxton	Buxton (NC)
B–W Cal Civ Prac	Bancroft–Whitney California Civil Practice
B.W.C.C.	Butterworths Workmen's Compensation Cases (Eng.)
B.Y.U.J.L. & Educ.	Brigham Young University Journal of Law and Education
BYU J.Pub.L.	Brigham Young University Journal of Public Law
B.Y.U.L.Rev.	Brigham Young University Law Review

C

c	California Reports
C.	Same
	Cowen (NY)
c2d	California Reports, Second
C.2d	Same
c3d	Same, Third
C.3d	Same
c4th	Same, Fourth
C.4th	Same
ca	California Appellate Reports
C.A.	Same
[ ] C.A.	Recueils de Jurisprudence du Quebec, Cour d'appel. 1970
ca2d	California Appellate Reports, Second
C.A.2d	Same

ca2ds	California Appellate Reports, Supplement, Second
C.A.2d Supp.	Same
ca3d	California Appellate Reports, Third
C.A.3d	Same
ca3ds	California Appellate Reports, Supplement, Third
C.A.3d Supp.	Same
ca4bcr	Fourth Circuit and District of Columbia Bankruptcy Court Reporter
CA4S	California Appellate Reports, Fourth Series, Supplement
ca4th	California Appellate Reports, Fourth
ca4ths	California Appellate Reports, Supplement, Fourth

C.A.A.	Civil Aeronautics Authority Reports
C.A.B.	Civil Aeronautics Board Reports
Cab. & E.	Cababe & Ellis, Queen's Bench (Eng.)
CACJ	California Attorneys for Criminal Justice Forum
cad	Customs Appeals Decisions (by number)
C.A.D.	Same
Cahiers	Les Cahiers de Droit
Cai.	Caines' Reports (NY)
Cai.Cas.	Caines' Cases
CaiCs	Caines' Cases (NY)
Cai.R.	Caines' Reports
Cal	California Law Review
Cal.	California Supreme Court Reports
	California Reports
Cal.2d	Same, Second Series
Cal.3d	Same, Third Series
Cal 4th	Same, Fourth Series
Cal. Adm. Code	California Administrative Code
Cal.App.	California Appellate Reports
Cal.App.2d	Same, Second Series
Cal.App.3d	Same, Third Series
Cal.App.4th	Same, Fourth Series
Cal.App.Dec.	California Appellate Decisions
Cal Code Reg	California Code of Regulations
calcompcas	California Compensation Cases
Cal. Comp. Cases	Same
Cal. Const.	California Constitution
Calcutta W.N.	Calcutta Weekly Notes
Cald.	Caldecott's Magistrate's and Settlement Cases (Eng.)
	Caldwell (WV)
Cal.Dec.	California Decisions
Cald.J.P.	Caldecott's Magistrate's and Settlement Cases (Eng.)
Cald.M.Cas.	Same
Cald.Mag. Cas.	Same
Cald.S.C.	Same
Cald.Sett. Cas.	Same
Cal. Forms	California Legal Forms
Cal.Ind.Acci.De c.	California Industrial Accidents Decisions
CALJIC	California Jury Instructions, Criminal
Cal.Jur.	California Jurisprudence
Cal.Jur.2d	Same, Second Edition
Cal.Jur.3d	Same, Third Edition
Call	Call (VA)
Cal. Law.	California Lawyer
Cal.Leg.Rec.	California Legal Record
Cal LR	California Law Review
Cal.L.Rev.	Same
Cal.Prac.	California Practice
Cal. P.U.C.	Decisions of California Public Utilities Commission
Cal Real Prop J	California Real Property Journal
Cal.Reg.L. Rep.	California Regulatory Law Reporter
calrptr	West's California Reporter
Cal Rptr	Same
calrptr2d	Same, Second Series
Cal.Rptr.2d	Same
Cal. Rules of Court	California Rules of Court
Cal.St.B.J.	California State Bar Journal
Calthr.	Calthrop, King's Bench (Eng.)
Cal Trial LJ	California Trial Law Journal
calunrep	California Unreported Cases
Cal Unrep	Same
Cal.Unrep. Cas.	Same
Cal Western Int LJ	California Western International Law Journal
Cal Western LR	California Western Law Review
Cal. Western L. Rev.	Same
Cal.W.Int'l L.J.	California Western International Law Journal
Cal.W.L.Rev.	California Western Law Review
Cam.	Cameron's Privy Council Decisions
Cam. & N.	Cameron & Norwood's Conference Reports (NC)
Cambrian L.Rev.	Cambrian Law Review
Cambridge L.J.	Cambridge Law Journal
Cam.Cas.	Cameron's Cases (Can.)
Cameron	Cameron's Supreme Court Cases
Cameron Pr.	Cameron's Practice (Can.)
Camp	Camp (ND)
Campaign L.Rep.	Campaign Law Reporter
Campb.	Campbell (NE)
	Campbell's Nisi Prius (Eng.)
Campb.L.G.	Campbell's Legal Gazette (PA)

Campbell L.Rev.	Campbell Law Review
Can.App.Cas.	Canadian Appeal Cases
Can.B.A.J.	Canadian Bar Association Journal
Can.Bankr. Ann.	Canadian Bankruptcy Reports Annotated
Can.Bankr. Ann. (N.S.)	Same, New Series
Can.B.Ass'n Y.B.	Canadian Bar Association: Year Book
Can.B.J.	Canadian Bar Journal
Can.B.R.	Canadian Bar Review
Can.B.Rev.	Same
Can.Bus.L.J.	Canadian Business Law Journal
Can.Com.L. Rev.	Canadian Communications Law Review
Can.Communit y L.J.	Canadian Community Law Journal
Can.Com.R.	Canadian Commercial Law Reports
Can.Cr.Cas.	Canadian Criminal Cases
Can.Crim.	Criminal Reports (Can.)
Can.Crim. Cas. (N.S.)	Canadian Criminal Cases, New Series
Can.Crim. Cas.Ann.	Canadian Criminal Cases Annotated
C. & A.	Cooke & Alcock, King's Bench and Exchequer (Ir.)
C. & C.	Case and Comment
	Colemand & Caines' Cases (NY)
C. & D.	Corbett & Daniel's Election Cases (Eng.)
	Crawford & Dix's Abridged Cases (Ir.)
C. & D.A.C.	Crawford & Dix's Abridged Cases (Ir.)
C. & D.C.C.	Crawford & Dix's Circuit Cases (Ir.)
	Crawford & Dix's Criminal Cases (Ir.)
C. & E.	Cababe & Ellis, Queen's Bench (Eng.)
C. & F.	Clark & Finelly, House of Lords (Eng.)
C. & J.	Crompton & Jervis, Exchequer (Eng.)
C. & K.	Carrington & Kirwan, Nisi Prius (Eng.)
C. & L.	Connor & Lawson's Chancery (Ir.)
C. & L.C.C.	Caines & Leigh, Crown Cases (Eng.)

C. & M.	Carrington & Marshman's Nisi Prius (Eng.)
	Crompton & Meeson's Exchequer (Eng.)
C. & Marsh.	Carrington & Marshman's Nisi Prius (Eng.)
C. & N.	Cameron & Norwood's North Carolina Conference
C. & P.	Carrington & Payne's Nisi Prius (Eng.)
	Craig & Phillips, Chancery (Eng.)
C. & R.	Cockburn & Rowe's Election Cases
C. & S.	Clarke & Scully's Drainage Cases (Ont.)
Cane & L.	Cane & Leigh's Crown Cases Reserved (Eng.)
Can.Env.L.Ne ws	Canadian Environmental Law News
Can.Exch.	Canadian Exchequer
Can.Green Bag	Canadian Green Bag
Can.Human Rights Rep.	Canadian Human Rights Reporter
Can.Hum. Rts.Advocate	Canadian Human Rights Advocate
Can. J. Admin. L. & Prac.	Canadian Journal of Administrative Law & Practice
Can.J.Correctio n	Canadian Journal of Correction
Can.J.Crim & Corr.	Canadian Journal of Criminology and Corrections
Can.J.Fam.L.	Canadian Journal of Family Law
Can. J. L. & Juris.	Canadian Journal of Law and Jurisprudence
Can.Lab.	Canadian Labour
Can.Law.	Canadian Lawyer
Can.Legal Stud.	Canadian Legal Studies
Can.L.J.	Canadian Law Journal
Can.L.J. (N.S.)	Same, New Series
Can.L.R.B.R.	Canadian Labour Relations Board Reports
Can.L.Rev.	Canadian Law Review
Can.L.T. Occ.N.	Canadian Law Times Occasional Notes
Can.L.Times	Canadian Law Times
Can.Mun.J.	Canadian Municipal Journal
Can.Native L.Rep.	Canadian Native Law Reporter
Can.Oil & Gas	Canadian Oil and Gas (Butterworths)

Can.Pub.Ad.	Canadian Public Administration
Can.R.Cas.	Canadian Railway Cases
Can.Ry.Cas.	Same
Can.S.C.	Canada Supreme Court
Can.S.Ct.	Canada Supreme Court Reports
Can.Tax App. Bd.	Canada Tax Appeal Board Cases
Can.Tax Cas. Ann.	Canada Tax Cases Annotated
Can.Tax Found.Rep. Proc.Tax Conf.	Canadian Tax Foundation Report of Proceedings of the Tax Conference
Can.Tax J.	Canadian Tax Journal
Can.Tax News	Canadian Tax News
Can.-U.S.L.J.	Canada–United States Law Journal
Can.Wel.	Canadian Welfare
Can.Y.B.Int'l L.	Canadian Yearbook of International Law
Cap.U.L.Rev.	Capital University Law Review
CaR	California Reporter
CaR2d	Same, Second Series
CaR3d	Same, Third Series
Car. & K.	Carrington & Kirwan, Nisi Prius (Eng.)
Car. & P.	Carrington & Payne, Nisi Prius (Eng.)
Cardozo Arts & Entertainme nt L.J.	Cardozo Arts & Entertainment Law Journal
Cardozo L.Rev.	Cardozo Law Review
Car.H. & A.	Carrow, Hamerton & Allen, New Sessions Cases (Eng.)
carlrepos	Carolina Law Repository (NC)
Carolina L.J.	Carolina Law Journal
Carolina L.Repos.	Carolina Law Repository
Carp.	Carpenter (CA)
Carp.P.C.	Carpmael, Patent Cases (Eng.)
Caribbean L.J.	Caribbean Law Journal
Caribbean L.Libr.	Caribbean Law Librarian
Cart.B.N.A.	Cartwright's Constitutional Cases (Can.)
Carter	Carter (IN)
	Carter, Common Pleas (Eng.)
Carth.	Carthew, King's Bench (Eng.)
Cartwr.Cas.	Cartwright's Cases (Can.)
Cary	Cary Chancery (Eng.)

cas	California Appellate Reports, Supplement
Cas.C.L.	Cases in Crown Law (Eng.)
Case & Com.	Case & Comment
Case W.Res. J.Int'l L.	Case Western Reserve Journal of International Law
Case W.Res. L.Rev.	Case Western Reserve Law Review
Casey	Casey (PA)
Cass.Prac. Cas.	Cassels' Practice Cases (Can.)
Cass.S.C.	Cassels' Supreme Court Decisions
Cas.Tak. & Adj. Cases	Taken and Adjudged (Report in Chancery, First Edition) (Eng.)
Cas.t.Hardw.	Cases tempore Hardwicke, King's Bench (Eng.)
Cas.t.Holt	Cases tempore Holt, King's Bench (Eng.)
Cas.t.King	Cases tempore King, Chancery (Eng.)
Cas.t.Northingt on	Cases tempore Northington, Chancery Reports (Eng.)
Cas.t.Talb.	Cases tempore Talbot, Chancery (Eng.)
Cas.t.Wm. III	Cases tempore William III (Eng.)
C.A. Supp.	California Appellate Reports, Supplement
CaU	California Unreported Cases
Cates	Cates (TN)
Cath.Law.	Catholic Lawyer
Cath.U.L.Rev.	Catholic University of America Law Review
cb	Cumulative Bulletin (IRS)
C.B.	Same
	Manning, Granger & Scott, Common Bench (Eng.)
C.B. (N.S.)	Manning, Granger & Scott, Common Bench (New Series) (Eng.)
CBA Rec.	Chicago Bar Association Record
cbc	Collier Bankruptcy Cases
C.B.C.	Same
cbc2d	Same, Second Series
C.B.R.	Canadian Bankruptcy Reports
CC	Civil Code, United States Circuit Court
C.C.	Ohio Circuit Court Reports
C.C.A.	Circuit Court of Appeals (U.S.)
CCA	Court of Customs and Patent Appeals Reports (Customs)

C.C.C.	Canadian Criminal Cases
Ccf	Federal Contract Cases
CCF	Same
CCH	Commerce Clearing House
CCH Atomic En.L.Rep.	Atomic Energy Law Reporter (CCH)
cchblr	Bankruptcy Law Reporter (CCH)
CCH Comm. Mkt.Rep.	Common Market Reporter (CCH)
cchepd	Employment Practices Decisions (CCH)
CCH Fed.Federal Banking L.Rep.	Banking Law Reporter (CCH)
CCH Fed.Sec. L.Rep.	Federal Securities Law Reporter (CCH)
cchfslr	Federal Securities Law Reporter (CCH)
CCH Inh.Est. & Gift Tax Rep.	Inheritance, Estate, and Gift Tax Reporter (CCH)
CCH Lab. Arb.Awards	Labor Arbitration Awards (CCH)
CCH Lab.Cas.	Labor Cases (CCH)
CCH Lab.L. Rep.	Labor Law Reporter (CCH)
cchlc	Labor Cases (CCH)
cchnlrb	National Labor Relations Board Decisions (CCH)
cchoshd	Occupational Safety and Health Decisions (CCH)
cchplr	Products Liability Reports (CCH)
CCH Stand. Fed.Tax Rep.	Standard Federal Tax Reporter (CCH)
CCH State Tax Cas.Rep.	State Tax Cases Reporter (CCH)
CCH State Tax Rev.	State Tax Review (CCH)
CCH Tax Ct.Mem.	Tax Court Memorandum Decisions (CCH)
CCH Tax Ct.Rep.	Tax Court Reporter (CCH)
cchtc	Trade Cases (CCH)
cchuir	Unemployment Insurance Reporter (CCH)
CCL	Court of Claims Reports
C.C.L.T.	Canadian Cases on the Law of Torts
C.C. (N.S.)	Ohio Circuit Court Reports, New Series
CCP	Code of Civil Procedure
ccpa	Court of Customs and Patent Appeals

C.C.P.A.	Same
C.C.Supp.	City Court Reports Supplement (NY)
CD	Decisions of the Commissioner of Patents
C.D.	Commissioner's Decisions, United States Patent Office
	Ohio Circuit Decisions
	United States Customs Court Decisions
cdos	California Daily Opinion Service
CEB	Continuing Education of the Bar (CA)
C.E.Gr.	C.E. Greene's Equity (NJ)
C.E.Greene	Same
Cent.Dig.	Century Digest
Centr.L.J.	Central Law Journal
Cert Rules	State Bar Program for Certifying Legal Specialists
Ceylon L.Rev.	Ceylon Law Review
C.F.R.	Code of Federal Regulations
Ch.	Law Reports, Chancery (Eng.)
	Chapter
Cha.App.	English Law Reports, Chancery Appeal Cases
Chamb.Rep.	Chancery Chambers (Ont.)
Chand	Chandler's Reports (WI)
Chandl.	Chandler (NH)
	Chandler (WI)
Chaney	Chaney (MI)
Charley Pr.Cas.	Charley's Practice Cases (Eng.)
Charlt.	R.M. Charlton (GA)
	T.U.P. Charlton (GA)
chase	Chase (U.S. District Court)
Chase	Same
Ch.Cal.	Calendar of Proceedings in Chancery (Eng.)
Ch.Cas.	Cases in Chancery (Eng.)
Ch.Chamb.	Chancery Chambers (Upper Can.)
Ch.Col.Op.	Chalmers' Colonial Opinions
Ch.D.	Law Reports, Chancery Division (Eng.)
Ch.D.2d	Same, Second Series
Chest.Co.	Chester County (PA)
Chev.Ch.	Cheves' Chancery (SC)
Chev.Eq.	Same
Cheves	Cheves' Law (SC)
Chi.B.Record	Chicago Bar Record
Chicago L.B.	Chicago Law Bulletin
Chicago L.J.	Chicago Law Journal

Chicago L.Rec.	Chicago Law Record	Cin.Mun.Dec.	Cincinnati Municipal Decisions
Chicano–Latino L.Rev.	Chicano–Latino Law Review	Cin.R.	Cincinnati Superior Court Reporter
Chicano LR	Chicano Law Review	Cin.S.C.R.	Same
Chicano L.Rev.	Same	Cin.S.C.Rep.	Same
Chic.L.T.	Chicago Law Times	Cir	Connecticut Circuit Court Reports
Chi.-Kent L.Rev.	Chicago–Kent Law Review	Cir.Ct.Dec.	Circuit Court Decisions (OH)
Chi.Leg.N.	Chicago Legal News	Cir. DC	U.S. Court of Appeals, District of Columbia Circuit
China L.Rev.	China Law Review	Cir. Fed.	U.S. Court of Appeals, Federal Circuit
Chin.L. & Gov't	Chinese Law and Government	Cir.(number)	United States Court of Appeals, United States District Court Circuit (number)
Chip.	Chipman (N.Bruns.) Chipman (VT)		
ChipD	D. Chipman's Reports (VT)	cit	U.S. Court of International Trade
ChipN	N. Chipman's Reports (VT)		
Chit.	Chitty's Bail Court (Eng.)	CIT	Same
Chit.B.C.	Same	City Ct.R.	City Court Reports (NY)
Chitt.	Same	City Ct.R. Supp.	Same, Supplement
Chitty's L.J.	Chitty's Law Journal		
ChL	University of Chicago Law Review	City Hall Rec.	City Hall Recorder (NY)
		City Hall Rep.	City Hall Reporter, Lomas (NY)
Choyce Cas.Ch.	Choyce's Cases in Chancery (Eng.)	Civ. & Mil. L.J.	Civil and Military Law Journal
Ch.Prec.	Precedents in Chancery	Civ. C.	Civil Code (CA)
Ch.R.	Upper Canada Chambers Reports	Civ.Just.Q.	Civil Justice Quarterly
		Civ.Lib.	Civil Liberty
Ch.Rep.	Chancery Reports (Eng.)	Civ.Lib.Dock.	Civil Liberties Docket
	Chancery Reports (Ir.)	Civ.Lib.Rev.	Civil Liberties Review
Ch.R.M.	R.M. Charlton (GA)	Civ.Lib.Rptr.	Civil Liberties Reporter
Chr.Rep.	Chamber Reports (Upper Can.)	Civ.Litigation Rep.	Civil Litigation Reporter (CEB)
Chr.Rob.	Christopher Robinson's Admiralty (Eng.)	civprocns	Civil Procedure Reports, New Series (NY)
ChS	Chancery Sentinel Reports	Civ.Proc.R.	Civil Procedure Reports (NY)
ChS(2)	Same, No. 2	Civ.Rights Dig.	Civil Rights Digest
Ch.Sent.	Chancery Sentinel (NY)	C.J.	Corpus Juris
Ch.T.U.P.	T.U.P. Charlton (GA)	C.J.Ann.	Corpus Juris Annotations
Chy.Chrs.	Upper Canada Chancery Chambers Reports	CJQ	Civil Justice Quarterly
		C.J.S.	Corpus Juris Secundum
C.I.L.C.	Commonwealth International Law Cases	CLA	University of California at Los Angeles Law Review
C.I.L.J.S.A.	Comparative and International Law Journal of Southern Africa	C.L.A.I.T.	Constitutions and Laws of the American Indian Tribes (Scholarly Resources)
Cin.B.Ass'n J.	Cincinnati Bar Association Journal	Cl. & F.	Clark & Finnelly, House of Lords (Eng.)
Cincinnati Law Bull.	Weekly Law Bulletin (OH)	Clark	Clark (AL) Clark (PA)
Cinc.L.Bul.	Cincinnati Law Bulletin		
Cinc.Sup.Ct. Rep.	Cincinnati Superior Court Reporter	Clark & F.	Clark & Finnelly, House of Lords (Eng.)
Cin.Law Bull.	Weekly Law Bulletin (OH)		
Cin.L.Rev.	Cincinnati Law Review		

Clark & F. (N.S.)	Same, New Series	C.L.L.C.	Canadian Labour Law Cases
Clark App.	Clark, Appeals Cases House of Lords (Eng.)	C.L.L.R.	Canadian Labor Law Reports (CCH)
Clark Col.Law	Clark Colonial Law	CLP	Computer Law and Practice
Clarke	Clarke (IA)	CLQ	Cornell Law Quarterly
	Clarke (MI)	C.L.R.	Common Law Reports (Eng.)
	Clarke's Chancery Reports (NY)		Commonwealth Law Reports (Austl.)
Clarke & S. Dr.Cas.	Clarke & Scully's Drainage Cases (Ont.)		Cyprus Law Reports
		C.L.Rec.	Cleveland Law Record
Clarke Ch.	Clarke, Chancery (NY)	C.L.Reg.	Cleveland Law Register
C.L.A.S.	Criminal Law Audio Series	C.L.Rep.	Cleveland Law Reporter
Class Act. Rep.	Class Action Reports	C.L. Rev.	California Law Review
Clayt.	Clayton's Reports York Assizes (Eng.)	CLSR	Computer Law and Security Report
ClC	Claims Court Reporter	C.L.S.R.	Computer Law Service Reporter
C.L.Chambers	Chambers' Common Law (Upper Can.)	CLU J.	Chartered Life Underwriter Journal
clct	Claims Court Reporter	C.L.W.	Commercial Laws of the World (Oceana)
ClCt	Same		
	United States Claims Court and United States Court of Federal Claims	CLY	Current Law Yearbook
		C.M. & R.	Crompton, Meeson & Roscoe, Exchequer (Eng.)
Clearinghouse Rev.	Clearinghouse Review	C.M.A.R.	Canadian Court Martial Appeal Reports
C. Leg. Rec.	California Legal Record	CMLR	Common Market Law Reports
CLE J. & Reg.	Continuing Legal Education Journal and Register	C.M.R.	Court–Martial Reports
Clemens	Clemens (KS)	C.M.R. (Air Force)	Court–Martial Reports of the Judge Advocate General of the Air Force
Clev.Bar Ass'n J.	Cleveland Bar Association Journal		
Cleve.Law R.	Cleveland Law Reporter (OH)	CoA	Colorado Court of Appeals Reports
Cleve.Law Rec.	Cleveland Law Record (OH)	Cobb	Cobb (AL)
Cleve.Law Reg.	Cleveland Law Register (OH)		Cobb (GA)
Cleve.L.Rec.	Cleveland Law Record (OH)	CoCai	Coleman and Caines' Cases (NY)
Cleve.L.Reg.	Cleveland Law Register (OH)	Cochr.	Cochran (Nova Scotia)
Cleve.L.Rep.	Cleveland Law Reporter (OH)		Cochrane (ND)
Clev.Mar.L. Rev.	Cleveland Marshall Law Review	Cockb. & R.	Cockburn & Rowe's Election Cases (Eng.)
Clev.St.L. Rev.	Cleveland State Law Review	Cocke	Cocke (AL)
cliff	Clifford's U.S. Circuit Court Reports		Cocke (FL)
Cliff.	Same	CoCs	Coleman's Cases
Clif.South.El. Cas.	Clifford, Southwick Election Cases	Co.Ct.Cas.	County Court Cases (Eng.)
		Co.Ct.Ch.	County Court Chronicle (Eng.)
C.L.J.	California Law Journal	Co.Ct.Rep.	Pennsylvania County Court Reports
	Cambridge Law Journal	Code Am.	Code Amendments (CA)
C.L.J. & Lit. Rev.	California Law Journal and Literary Review	coderep	Code Reporter (NY)
		Code Rep.	Same
Clk's Mag.	Clerk's Magazine (London)	Code Rep. (N.S.)	Same, New Series
	Clerk's Magazine (RI)		
	Clerk's Magazine (Upper Can.)	CodR	Code Reporter (NY)

CodRn	Same, New Series	Colum.J.Gende	Columbia Journal of Gender
Cof	Coffey's Probate Decisions	r & L.	and Law
Coff.Prob.	Coffey's Probate (CA)	Colum.J.Int'l	Columbia Journal of
Co.Inst.	Coke's Institutes (Eng.)	Aff.	International Affairs
Coke	Coke, King's Bench (Eng.)	Colum.J.L. &	Columbia Journal of Law and
Col	Colorado Supreme Court	Arts	the Arts
	Reports	Colum.J.L. &	Columbia Journal of Law and
Col.	Coleman (AL)	Soc.Probs.	Social Problems
Col. & C.Cas.	Coleman & Caine's Cases	Colum.J.	Columbia Journal of
	(NY)	Transnat'l L.	Transnational Law
Col.Cas.	Coleman's Cases (NY)	Colum.L.Rev.	Columbia Law Review
Cold.	Coldwell (TN)	Colum. Soc'y	Columbia Society of
coldtn	Same	Int'l L.Bull.	International Law Bulletin
Coldw.	Same	Colum.Survey	Columbia Survey of Human
Cole	Cole (AL)	Human	Rights Law
	Cole (LA)	Rights L.	
Cole. & Cai.	Coleman & Caines' Cases	Colum.-VLA	Columbia Volunteer Lawyers
Cas.		J.L. & Arts	for the Arts Journal of Law
Cole.Cas.	Coleman's Cases		& the Arts
Col.Int'l Dr.	Colioque International de	Com. & L.	Communications and the Law
Comp.	Droit Compare	Com. & Mun.	Commercial & Municipal Law
Co.Litt.	Coke on Littleton (Eng.)	L.Rep.	Reporter
Coll.	Collyer's Chancery (Eng.)	Co.Mass.Pr.	Colby Massachusetts Practice
Coll. & E. Bank	Collier's & Eaton's American	Comb.	Comberbach, King's Bench
	Bankruptcy Reports		(Eng.)
Colles	Colles Cases in Parliament	Com.B.	Manning, Granger & Scott,
	(Eng.)		Common Bench (Eng.)
Coll.L.Bull.	College Law Bulletin	Com. C.	Commercial Code (CA)
Coll.L.Dig.	College Law Digest	Com.Cas.	Commercial Cases Since 1895
Col.L.Rev.	Columbia Law Review		(Eng.)
colo	Colorado Reports	Com.Dec.	Commissioners' Decisions
Colo.	Same		(Patent)
coloapp	Colorado Appeals Reports	Com.L.	Commercial Law (Can.)
Colo.App.	Same	Com.L.J.	Commercial Law Journal
colobcr	Colorado Bankruptcy Court	Com. L. Rep.	Commercial Law Report
	Reporter	Comm.B.	Manning, Granger & Scott,
Colo.J. Int'l	Colorado Journal of		Common Bench (Eng.)
Envtl.L. &	International	Comm.Cause	Common Cause
Pol'y	Environmental Law and	Comm.Mkt.L.R	Common Market Law Reports
	Policy	.	
Colo.Law.	Colorado Lawyer	Commodity	Commodity Futures Law
Colo.Law Rep.	Colorado Law Reporter	Futures	Reporter (CCH)
Colombo L.Rev.	Colombo Law Review (Ceylon)	L.Rep.	
Colonial Law.	Colonial Lawyer	Common Mkt.	Common Market Law Review
Colq.	Colquit (Modern) (Eng.)	L.Rev.	
Coltm.	Coltman Registration Appeal	Community	Community Property Journal
	Cases (Eng.)	Prop.J.	
Colum.Bus.L.	Columbia Business Law	Commw.Arb.	Commonwealth Arbitration
Rev.	Review		Reports
Colum.Hum.	Columbia Human Rights Law	Commw.L.R.	Commonwealth Law Reports
Rts.L.Rev.	Review	Comparisons in	Comparisons in Law and
Colum.J.	Columbia Journal of	L. &	Monetary Comments
Envtl.L.	Environmental Law	Monet.Com.	
		Comp.Dec.	United States Comptroller of
			Treasury Decisions

Comp.Gen.	United States Comptroller General Decisions
Comp.Jurid. Rev.	Comparative Juridical Review
Comp.Lab.L.J.	Comparative Labor Law Journal
Comp Lawyer	Company Lawyer
Compleat Law.	Compleat Lawyer
Comp.L.J.	Company Law Journal
Com.P.Reptr.	Common Pleas Reporter (Scranton, PA)
Comptr. Treas.Dec.	United States Comptroller of Treasury Decisions
Computer L. & Prac.	Computer Law & Practice
Computer L. & Tax	Computer Law and Tax Report
Computer L.J.	Computer Law Journal
Computers & L.	Computers and Law
Comst.	Comstock, Appeals (NY)
Comyns	Comyn's King's Bench and Common Pleas (Eng.)
Comyns Dig.	Comyn's Digest (Eng.)
Con.B.J.	Connecticut Bar Journal
Condee	Condee, California Probate Court Practice (2d ed.)
Condit.Sale— Chat.Mort. Rep.	Conditional Sale—Chattel Mortgage (CCH)
conf	North Carolina Conference Reports
Conf.	Same
ConfR	Conference by Cameron and Norwood (NC)
Conf.Teach. Int'l L.	Conference of Teachers of International Law
Cong.Dig.	Congressional Digest
Cong.Rec.	Congressional Record (U.S.)
conn	Connecticut Reports
Conn.	Same
connapp	Connecticut Appellate Reports
Conn.B.J.	Connecticut Bar Journal
conncir	Connecticut Circuit Reports
Conn.Cir.Ct.	Same
Conn.J.Int'l L.	Connecticut Journal of International Law
Conn.L.Rev.	Connecticut Law Review
connoly	Connoly's Surrogate's Court Reporter (NY)
Conn.Prob. L.J.	Connecticut Probate Law Journal
Connsupp	Connecticut Supplement
Conn.Supp.	Same

Conn.Surr.	Connolly's Surrogate (NY)
Conov.	Conover (WI)
Const.Afr.State s	Constitutions of African States (Oceana)
Const. Commentary	Constitutional Commentary
Const.Dep. & Sp.Sov.	Constitutions of Dependencies and Special Sovereignties
Const. Nations	Constitutions of Nations (Nijhoff)
Const.Rep.	Constitutional Reports (SC)
Const.Rev.	Constitutional Review
Const.World	Constitutions of the Countries of the World (Oceana)
Consumer Fin.L.Q. Rep.	Consumer Finance Law Quarterly Report
Consumer Prod.Saf'y Guide	Consumer Product Safety Guide (CCH)
Contemp. Drug Prob.	Contemporary Drug Problems
Conv	Conveyancer and Property Lawyer
Conv. & Prop. Law	Same
Convey.	Conveyancer
Convey. (N.S.)	Conveyancer & Property Lawyer, New Series
Cooke	Cooke, Cases of Practice, Common Pleas (Eng.)
	Cooke (TN)
Cooke & A.	Cooke & Alcock, King's Bench (Ir.)
cooketn	Cooke's Tennessee Reports
Cook Vice– Adm.	Cook's Vice–Admiralty (Lower Can.)
Cooley L.Rev.	Cooley Law Review
Coop.	Cooper (FL)
	Cooper's Chancery (Eng.)
	Cooper's Chancery (TN)
Coop.C. & P.R.	Cooper's Chancery Practice Reporter (U.S.)
Cooper	Cooper, State Administrative Law
Coop.Pr.Cas.	Cooper's Practice Cases (Eng.)
Coop.t. Brough.	Cooper's Cases tempore Brougham, Chancery (Eng.)
Coop.t.Cott.	Cooper's Cases tempore Cottenham, Chancery (Eng.)
Coop.t.Eldon	Cooper's Reports tempore Eldon, Chancery (Eng.)
Co.P.C.	Coke Pleas of the Crown (Eng.)
Cope	Cope (CA)

Copp Min. Dec.	Copp's Mining Decisions (U.S.)
Copp's Land Owner	Copp's Land Owner
Copy.	Copyright
Copy.Bull.	Copyright Bulletin
Copyright L.Sym.	Copyright Law Symposium (American Society of Composers, Authors, and Publishers)
Cor	Cornell Law Review
Corb. & D.	Corbett & Daniels Election Cases (Eng.)
Cornell Int'l L.J.	Cornell International Law Journal
Cornell J.L. & Pub.Pol'y	Cornell Journal of Law and Public Policy
Cornell L.F.	Cornell Law Forum
Cornell L.J.	Cornell Law Journal
Cornell L.Q.	Cornell Law Quarterly
Cornell L.Rev.	Cornell Law Review
Corp C	Corporations Code (CA)
Corp.Counsel Rev.	Corporate Counsel Review
Corp.Couns. Rep.	Corporate Counsel Reporter
Corp.J.	Corporation Journal
Corp.L.Rev.	Corporation Law Review
Corp.Pract. Comment.	Corporate Practice Commentator
Corp.Pract. Rev.	Corporate Practice Review
Corp.Reorg.	Corporate Reorganizations
Corp.Reorg. & Am.Bank. Rev.	Corporate Reorganization & American Bankruptcy Review
Coup.	Couper's Justiciary (Scot.)
Court. & MacL.	Courtenay & MacLean (Scot.)
Coutlea	Coutlea's Supreme Court Cases
Cow.	Cowen's Reports (NY)
Cow.Cr.	Cowen's Criminal Reports (NY)
Cowp.	Cowper King's Bench (Eng.)
Cowp.Cas.	Cowper (Eng.)
Cox	Cox (AR)
Cox Am.T. Cas.	Cox's American Trademark Cases
Cox & Atk.	Cox & Atkinson, Registration Appeals (Eng.)
Cox C.C.	Cox's Criminal Cases (Eng.)
Cox Ch.	Cox's Chancery (Eng.)
Cox Crim. Cas.	Cox's Criminal Cases
Coxe	Coxe (NJ)

Cox Eq.	Cox's Equity
Cox J.S.Cas.	Cox's Joint Stock Cases (Eng.)
CP	Civil Procedure Reports (NY)
CPA	Court of Customs Appeals Reports
	Court of Customs & Patent Appeals Reports (Customs)
CP(B)	Civil Procedure Reports (NY) (Browne)
C.P.C.	Carswell's Practice Cases
C.P.Coop.	C.P. Cooper, Chancery (Eng.)
CPD	Customs Penalty Decisions
C.P.D.	Law Reports, Common Pleas Division (Eng.)
CP(M)	Civil Procedure Reports (McCarty) (NY)
CPn	Same, New Series
C.P.R.	Canadian Patent Reporter
C.P.Rep.	Common Pleas Reporter (PA)
CR	Columbia Law Review
	Clinical Risk
	California Reporter
C.R.	Criminal Reports (Canada)
crabbe	Crabbe (U.S. District Court)
Crabbe	Same
C.R.A.C.	Canadian Reports, Appeal Cases
Craig & Ph.	Craig & Phillips, Chancery (Eng.)
cranch	Cranch's U.S. Supreme Court Reports
Cranch	Same
Cranch C.C.	Cranch's Circuit Court (U.S.)
Cranch Pat. Dec.	Cranch's Patent Decisions (U.S.)
Cr. & M.	Crompton & Meeson, Exchequer (Eng.)
Cr. & Ph.	Craig & Phillips, Chancery (Eng.)
Crane	Crane (Mont.)
Cr.App.	Criminal Appeals (Eng.)
Cr App Rep (S)	Criminal Appeal Reports (Sentencing)
Cr.App.R.(S.)	Same
Craw.	Crawford (AR)
Crawf. & D. Abr.Cas.	Crawford & Dix's Abridged Cases (Ir.)
Crawf. & Dix's	Crawford & Dix's Circuit Cases (Ir.)
	Crawford & Dix's Criminal Cases (Ir.)
CRC	California Rules of Court
	Decisions of California Railroad Commission

C.R.C.	Canadian Railway Cases	Cro.	Croke's King's Bench (Eng.)
Cr.Cas.Res.	Law Reports, Crown Cases Reserved (Eng.)	C.Rob.	Christopher Robinson's Admiralty (Eng.)
CRD	Customs Rules Decisions	Cro.Car.	Croke tempore Charles I (Eng.)
Creighton L.Rev.	Creighton Law Review	Cro.Eliz.	Croke tempore Elizabeth (Eng.)
Crim.	Criminologie	Cro.Jac.	Croke tempore James I, King's Bench (Eng.)
Crim. & Soc. Just.	Crime and Social Justice		
Crim.App.	Criminal Appeal Reports	Cromp.	Star Chamber Cases (Eng.)
Crim.App. Rep.	Cohen's Criminal Appeals Reports (Eng.)	Cromp. & J.	Crompton & Jervis, Exchequer (Eng.)
Crim.Case & Com.	Criminal Case and Comment	Cromp. & M.	Crompton & Meeson, Exchequer (Eng.)
Crim.Def.	Criminal Defense	Cromp.M. & R.	Crompton, Meeson & Roscoe, Exchequer (Eng.)
Crime & Delin'cy	Crime & Delinquency	Crosw.Pat. Cas.	Croswell's Collection of Patent Cases (U.S.)
Crime & Delin'cy Abst.	Crime and Delinquency Abstracts	Crounse	Crounse (NE)
		C.R.T.C.	Canadian Railway & Transport Cases
Crime & Delin'cy Lit.	Crime and Delinquency Literature	Crumrine	Crumrine (PA)
Crim.Just.	Criminal Justice	CS	Connecticut Supplement
Crim.Just. & Behav.	Criminal Justice and Behavior	C.S.C.R.	Cincinnati Superior Court Reporter
Crim.Just. Ethics	Criminal Justice Ethics	CSD	Customs Service Decisions
		C.S.T.	Capital Stock Tax Division (I.R.B.)
Crim.Just.J.	Criminal Justice Journal	C.T.	Carrier's Taxing Ruling (I.R.B.)
Crim.Just. Newsl.	Criminal Justice Newsletter		
Crim.Just.Q.	Criminal Justice Quarterly	Ct	Connecticut Reports
Crim.Just. Rev.	Criminal Justice Review	CtA	Connecticut Appellate Reports
Crim.L.Bull.	Criminal Law Bulletin	C.T.C.	Canada Tax Cases
Crim.L.F. Int'l J.	Criminal Law Forum: An International Journal	ctcl	U.S. Court of Claims Reports
		Ct.Cl.	Same
Crim.L.J.	Criminal Law Journal	Ct.Cust & Pat.App.	Court of Customs & Patent Appeals
Crim.L.Mag.	Criminal Law Magazine (NJ)	ctcustapp	U.S. Court of Customs Appeals Reports
Crim.L.Mag. & Rep.	Criminal Law Magazine and Reporter		
Crim.L.Q.	Criminal Law Quarterly	Ct.Cust.App.	Same
Crim LR	Criminal Law Review	C.T.L.J.	California Trial Lawyers Journal
Crim.L.Rec.	Criminal Law Recorder		
Crim.L.Rep.	Criminal Law Reporter	CTLR	Computer and Telecommunications Law Review
Crim.L.Rev.	Criminal Law Review (Manhattan)		
Crim.L.Rev. (Eng.)	Criminal Law Review (Eng.)	Ct.Rev.	Court Review
		C.T.S.	Consolidated Treaty Series
Crim.L.Rptr.	Criminal Law Reporter	C.U.	California Unreported Cases
Crim. Prac. L. Rev.	Criminal Practice Law Review	CuCt	Customs Court Reports
		CuD	Customs Court Decisions
Crim.Rep. (N.S.)	Criminal Reports, New Series	Cumb.L.Rev.	Cumberland Law Review
		Cum.Bull.	Cumulative Bulletin
Cripp Ch.Cas.	Cripp's Church & Clergy Cases	Cum.L.Rev.	Cumberland Law Review
Critch.	Critchfield (OH)	Cummins	Cummins (ID)

Cum.Sam.L. Rev.	Cumberland–Samford Law Review
Cunn.	Cunningham King's Bench (Eng.)
Cur.Leg. Thought	Current Legal Thought
Current Com. & Leg.Mis.	Current Comment and Legal Miscellany
Current L.	Current Law
Current L. & Soc.Prob.	Current Law and Social Problems
Current Legal Prob.	Current Legal Problems
Current L.Y.B.	Current Law Yearbook
Current Med. for Atty's	Current Medicine for Attorneys
Currents. Int'l Trade L.J.	Currents. International Trade Law Journal
Curry	Curry (LA)
curt	Curtis Circuit Court (U.S.)
Curt.	Same

Curt. Eccl.	Curtis, Ecclesiastical (Eng.)
Cush.	Cushing's Reports (MA)
cushma	Same
Cust.App.	United States Customs Appeals
Cust.Ct.	Custom Court Reports (U.S.)
C.W.Dud.	C.W. Dudley's Law or Equity (SC)
C.W.Dudl.Eq.	C.W. Dudley's Equity (SC)
C.W.L. Rev.	California Western Law Review
Cy	Connoly's Surrogate's Court Reports (NY)
Cyc.	Cyclopedia of Law & Procedure
Czech.J. Int'l L.	Czechoslovak Journal of International Law
Czech.Y.B. Int'l L.	Czechoslovak Yearbook of International Law

D

D.	Disney (OH)
Dak.	Dakota Reports
Dak.L.Rev.	Dakota Law Review
Dal	Daly's Reports (NY)
Dal.C.P.	Dallson's Common Pleas (Eng.)
Dale	Dale (OK)
Dale Ecc.	Dale's Ecclesiastical (Eng.)
Dale Eccl.	Same
Dale Leg.Rit.	Dale's Legal Ritual (Eng.)
Dalhousie L.J.	Dalhousie Law Journal
Dal. in Keil.	Dallison in Keilway's King's Bench (Eng.)
Dall.	Dallam (TX)
	Dallas (PA)
	Dallas (U.S.)
Dallam	Dallam's Decisions (TX)
dallassc	Dallas' U.S. Supreme Court Reports
Dalr.	Dalrymple's Decisions (S.C.)
daly	Daly's Reports (NY)
Daly	Same
Dan.	Daniell's Exchequer & Equity (Eng.)
Dana	Dana (KY)
D. & B.	Dearsley & Bell's Crown Cases (Eng.)
D. & B.C.C.	Same
D. & C.	Deacon & Chitty's Bankruptcy Cases (Eng.)

	Dow & Clark's Parliamentary Cases (Eng.)
D. & Ch.	Same
D. & Chit.	Same
D. & E.	Dwinford & East's King's Bench, Term Reports (Eng.)
D. & J.	De Gex & Jones, Chancery (Eng.)
D. & J.B.	De Gex & Jones, Bankruptcy (Eng.)
D. & L.	Dowling & Lowndes, Bail Court (Eng.)
D. & M.	Davison & Merivale's Queen's Bench (Eng.)
D. & P.	Denison & Pearce's Crown Cases (Eng.)
D. & R.	Dowling & Ryland's King's Bench (Eng.)
D. & R.Mag. Cas.	Same
D. & R.M.C.	Dowling & Ryland's Magistrates' Cases (Eng.)
D. & R.N.P.	Dowling & Ryland's Nisi Prius Cases (Eng.)
D. & R.N. P.C.	Same
D. & S.	Deane & Swabey's Ecclesiastical (Eng.)
	Drewry & Smale's Chancery (Eng.)
D. & Sm.	Drewry & Smale's Chancery (Eng.)

D. & Sw.	Deane & Swabey Ecclesiastical (Eng.)	DCH	Reports of the United States District Court of Hawaii
D. & W.	Drewry & Walsh's Chancery (Ir.) Drewry & Warren's Chancery (Ir.)	dchip	D. Chipman's Reports (VT)
D. & War.	Drewry & Warren's Chancery (Ir.)	D.Chip.	Same
		D.Chipm.	Same
Dane Abr.	Dane's Abridgment of American Law (Eng.)	D.C.L.Rev.	District of Columbia Law Review
Dann	Dann (AZ) Dann (CA)	D.D.C.	District Court, District of Columbia
Dann.	Danner (AL)	D.Dec.	Dix's School Decisions (NY)
Dans. & L.	Danson & Lloyd's Mercantile Cases (Eng.)	Dea.	Deady, United States Circuit & District Courts (CA & OR)
Dans. & Lld.	Same	Dea. & Chit.	Deacon & Chitty (Eng.)
D'Anv.Abr.	D'Anver's Abridgment (Eng.)	Dea. & Sw.	Deane & Swabey's Ecclesiastical (Eng.) Deane & Swabey's Probate & Divorce (Eng.)
dar	Daily Appellate Report (CA)		
Dass.Ed.	Dassler (KS)	Deac.	Deacon, Bankruptcy (Eng.)
Dauph.Co.	Dauphin County (PA)		
Dav. & M.	Davison & Merivale, Queen's Bench (Eng.)	Deac. & C.	Deacon & Chitty, Bankruptcy (Eng.)
Dav. & Mer.	Same	Deac. & Chit.	Same
Daveis	Daveis (Ware) (U.S.)	Deacon & C.	Same
Davies	Davis, King's Bench (Ir.)	Deacon, Bankr.Cas.	Deacon, Bankruptcy (Eng.)
Davis	Daveis (Ware) (U.S.) Davis (HI) Davis, King's Bench (Ir.)	deady	Deady's United States Circuit Court Reports
Davys	Davys, King's Bench	Deady	Deady, United States Circuit and District Courts (CA & OR)
day	Day's Reports (CT)		
Day	Same		
Dayton	3 Ohio Miscellaneous Decisions	Deane	Deane (VT) Deane & Swabey's Probate & Divorce (Eng.)
Dayton Term Rep.	Iddings' Term Reports (OH)		
Dayton T.R.	Same	Deane & S.Eccl.Rep.	Deane & Swabey's Ecclesiastical (Eng.)
D.B.	Domesday Book	Deane & Sw.	Same
D.B. & M.	Dunlop, Bell & Murray (Scot.)	Deane Ecc.	Same
		Deane Ecc.Rep.	Same
D.C.	District of Columbia Reports Treasury Department Circular (I.R.B.)	Dears.	Dearsley & Bell, Crown Cases (Eng.)
		Dears. & B.	Same
DC2d	Pennsylvania District and County Reports, Second Series	Dears. & B.C.C.	Same
		Dears.C.C.	Same
DC3d	Same, Third Series	Deas & A.	Deas & Anderson (Scot.)
DC4d	Same, Fourth Series		
D.C.A.	Dorion's Queen's Bench (Can.)	Deas & And.	Same
		Decalogue	Decalogue Journal
D.C.App.	District of Columbia Appeals	Dec.Com.Pat.	Decisions of Commissioner of Patents
D.C.B.J.	District of Columbia Bar Journal		
		Dec.Dig.	Decennial Digest
D.C.Cir.	District of Columbia Court of Appeals Cases	Decisions and Reports	Decisions and Reports of European Commission on Human Rights
DCh	Delaware Chancery Reports		
		Dec.Rep.	Ohio Decisions Reprint

Dec.U.S. Compt.Gen.	Decisions of United States Comptroller General	Desaus.Eq.	Same
		Dess.	Same
		Dessaus.	Same
Deering's Gen Laws	Deering's General Laws (CA)	Det.C.L.Rev.	Detroit College of Law Review
Def. Couns. J.	Defense Counsel Journal	Det.Leg.N.	Detroit Legal News
		Det.L.J.	Detroit Law Journal
Def.L.J.	Defense Law Journal	Det.L.Rev.	Detroit Law Review
De G. & J.	De Gex & Jones, Chancery (Eng.)	Detroit Coll L Rev	Detroit College of Law Review
De G. & Sm.	De Gex & Smale, Chancery (Eng.)	Detroit L.Rev.	Detroit Law Review
		Dev	Devereux's Reports
De Gex	De Gex, Bankruptcy (Eng.)	Dev.	Devereux's Equity (NC) Devereux's Law (NC)
De G.F. & J.	De Gex, Fisher & Jones, Chancery (Eng.)		Devereux's United States Court of Claims
De G.J. & S.	De Gex, Jones & Smith, Chancery (Eng.)	Dev. & B.	Devereux & Battle's Equity (NC)
De G.M. & G.	De Gex, Macnaghten & Gordon, Chancery (Eng.)		Devereux & Battle's Law (NC)
del	Delaware Reports	Dev.Ct.Cl.	Devereux's Court of Claims (U.S.)
Del.	Same		
delch	Delaware Chancery Reports	Dew.	Dewey (KS)
		De Witt	De Witt (OH)
Del.Ch.	Same	Di.	Dyer's King's Bench (Eng.)
Del.Co.	Delaware County (PA)		
Del.County	Delaware County Reports	Dice	Dice (IN)
		Dick.	Dickens' Chancery (Eng.)
Del.Cr.Cas.	Delaware Criminal Cases		Dickinson's Equity (NJ)
Del.J.Corp.L.	Delaware Journal of Corporate Law	Dick.J.Envtl. L. & Pol'y	Dickinson Journal of Environmental Law and Policy
Dem.	Demarest's Surrogate Court Reports (NY)	Dick.J.Int'l L.	Dickinson Journal of International Law
Dem.Surr.	Same	Dick. Law.	Dickinson Lawyers
Den.	Denio's Reports (NY) Denis (LA)	Dick.L.Rev.	Dickinson Law Review
		Dicta	Dicta of Denver Bar Association
Den. & P.	Denison & Pearce's Crown Cases (Eng.)		Dicta Magazine, San Diego Bar Association
Den. & P.C.C.	Same		
Den.C.C.	Denison's Crown Cases (Eng.)	Dig.C.L.W.	Digest of Commercial Law of the World (Oceana)
Denio	Denio (NY)		
Denis	Denis (LA)	D.I.L. (Hack.)	Digest of International Law (Hackworth)
Den.J. Int'l L. & Policy	Denver Journal of International Law and Policy	D.I.L. (Moore)	Digest of International Law (Moore)
Den.L.J.	Denver Law Journal	D.I.L. (White.)	Digest of International Law (Whiteman)
Den.L.N.	Denver Legal News		
Denning L.Rev.	Denning Law Review	dill	Dillon's U.S. Circuit Court Reports
Den.U.L.Rev.	Denver University Law Review	Dill.	Same
		Dirl.Dec.	Direlton's Decisions (Scot.)
Denv.J.Int'l L. & Pol'y	Denver Journal of International Law and Policy	Disn.	Disney (OH)
		Disney	Same
Denv.U.L.Rev.	Denver University Law Review	Dispute Res.N.	Dispute Resolution Notes
DePaul Bus.L.J.	DePaul Business Law Journal	Dist.	California District Court
DePaul L.Rev.	DePaul Law Review	distcol	District of Columbia Reports
Dept.State Bull.	Department of State Bulletin (U.S.)		
Des.	Dessaussure's Equity (SC)		

D.L.R.	Dominion Law Reports (Can.)	D.Repr.	Same
		Drew	Drew (FL)
D.L.R.2d	Same, Second Series	Drew.	Drewry's Chancery
D.L.R.3d	Same, Third Series		(Eng.)
Docket	Docket (Lebanon, PA)	Drew. & S.	Drewry & Smale's
	Docket (St. Paul, MN)		Chancery (Eng.)
	Docket Magazine, Sacramento Bar Association	Drinkw.	Drinkwater Common Pleas (Eng.)
		Drug Abuse	Drug Abuse Law
Dod.	Dodson's Admiralty (Eng.)	L.Rev.	Review
		Drug L.J.	Drug Law Journal
Dod.Adm.	Same	Drury	Drury's Chancery (Ir.)
Dods.	Same	D.T.C.	Dominion Tax Cases
Dom.L.R.	Dominion Law Reports (Can.)	Dublin U.L.J.	Dublin University Law Journal
Donaker	Donaker (IN)	Dublin	Dublin University Law
Donn.	Donnelly's Chancery (Eng.)	U.L.Rev.	Review
		Dud	Dudley's Reports (GA)
	Donnelly's Irish Land Cases	Dudl.	Dudley (GA)
			Dudley's Equity (SC)
Donnelly	Same		Dudley's Law (SC)
Dorion	Dorion (Lower Can.)	dudley	Dudley's Georgia
Doshisha L.Rev.	Doshisha Law Review		Reports
		Duer	Duer's Superior Court Reports (NY)
Doug.	Douglas' Reports (MI)		
	Douglas' King's Bench (Eng.)	Duke B. Ass'n J.	Duke Bar Association Journal
dougl	Douglas Reports (MI)	Duke Envtl. L. & Pol'y F.	Duke Environmental Law and Policy Forum
Dougl.	Same		
Dougl.El.Cas.	Douglas, Election Cases (Eng.)	Duke J.Comp. & Int'l L.	Duke Journal of Comparative & International Law
Dougl.K.B.	Douglas, King's Bench (Eng.)		
		Duke L.J.	Duke Law Journal
Dow	Dow's House of Lords Parliamentary Cases (Eng.)	Duke's Charitable Uses	Duke's Charitable Uses (Eng.)
Dow.	Dowling's Practice Cases (Eng.)	Dunc.Ent. Cas.	Duncan Entail Cases (Scot.)
Dow & Cl.	Dow & Clark's House of Lords Cases (Eng.)	Dunc.N.P.	Duncombe, Nisi Prius
		Dunl.	Dunlop, Bell & Murray (Scot.)
Dow. & L.	Dowling & Lowndes' Bail Court (Eng.)		
		Dunl.B. & M.	Same
Dowl. & Lownd.	Dowling & Lowndes' Practice Cases (Eng.)	Dunlop	Dunlop (Scot.)
		Dunn.	Dunning's King's Bench (Eng.)
Dowl. & R.	Dowling & Ryland's King's Bench (Eng.)		
		Duq.L.Rev.	Duquesne Law Review
	Dowling & Ryland's Queen's Bench & Magistrates' Cases (Eng.)	Duq.U.L.Rev.	Duquesne University Law Review
		Durf.	Durfee (RI)
Dowl.P.C. (N.S.)	Dowling, Practice Cases, New Series (Eng.)	Durfee	Same
		Durie	Durie (Scot.)
		Durn. & E.	Durnford & East's King's Bench, Term Report (Eng.)
Dowl.Pr.Cas.	Dowling, Practice Cases (Eng.)		
Down. & Lud.	Downton & Luder's Election Cases (Eng.)	Dutch.	Dutcher's Law (NJ)
		Duv.	Duval's Reports (Can.)
D.P.R.	Decisiones de Puerto Rico		Duval's Supreme Court (Can.)
Drake L.Rev.	Drake Law Review	Dy.	Dyer's King's Bench (Eng.)
Draper	Draper (Upper Can.)		
D.Rep.	Ohio Decisions Reprint	Dyer	Same

E

E.	East's King's Bench (Eng.)
Ea.	Same
E.Afr.L.J.	East African Law Journal
E.Afr.L.R.	East Africa Law Reports
E.Afr.L.Rev.	Eastern Africa Law Review
Eag. & Y.	Eagle & Young's Tithe Cases (Eng.)
Eag.T.	Eagle's Commutation of Tithes (Eng.)
E. & A.	Grant Error & Appeal Reports (Upper Can.)
	Spink's Ecclesiastical & Admiralty (Eng.)
E. & B.	Ellis & Blackburn's Queen's Bench (Eng.)
E. & E.	Ellis & Ellis' Queen's Bench (Eng.)
E. & I.	English & Irish Appeals, House of Lords (Eng.)
Earth L.J.	Earth Law Journal
E.A.S.	Executive Agreement Series (U.S.)
East	East's King's Bench (Eng.)
East.	Eastern Reporter (U.S.)
East.J.Int'l L.	Eastern Journal of International Law
East.L.R.	Eastern Law Reporter (Can.)
East P.C.	East's Pleas of the Crown (Eng.)
East.Rep.	Eastern Reporter (U.S.)
East.T.	Eastern Term (Eng.)
East. U.S. Bus.L.Rev.	Eastern United States Business Law Review
E.A.W.R.	Employment–At–Will Reporter
E.B. & E.	Ellis, Blackburn & Ellis' Queen's Bench (Eng.)
E.B. & S.	Ellis, Best & Smith's Queen's Bench (Eng.)
ebc	Employee Benefits Cases (BNA)
Ebersole	Ebersole (IA)
E.C.	English Chancery
ECA	Temporary Emergency Court of Appeals
Eccl. & Adm.	Spink's Ecclesiastical & Admiralty (Upper Can.)
Eccl.R.	Ecclesiastical Reports (Eng.)
Eccl.Rep.	Same
E.C.L.	English Common Law
E.C.L.R.	European Competition Law Review
Ecology L.Q.	Ecology Law Quarterly
E.C.R.	Reports of Cases before the Court of Justice of the European Communities

Ed.	Eden's Chancery (Eng.)
Ed C	Education Code
Ed.Ch.	Edward's Chancery Reports (NY)
Eden	Eden's Chancery (Eng.)
Edg.	Edgar (Scot.)
Edinb.L.J.	Edinburgh Law Journal
Edm	Edmond's Select Cases (NY)
Edm.Sel.Cas.	Edmond's Select Cases (NY)
EDR	Education Department Reports
E.D.S	E. D. Smith's Reports (NY)
EDSm	Same
E.D.Smith	Same
Educ. C.	Education Code (CA)
Edw.	Edwards (MO)
	Edward's Chancery (NY)
Edw.Abr.	Edward's Abridgment, Prerogative Court Cases
	Edward's Abridgment, Privy Council
Edw.Adm.	Edward's Admiralty (Eng.)
Edw.Ch.	Edward's Chancery (NY)
Edw.Lead. Dec.	Edward's Leading Decisions in Admiralty
Edw.Pr.Cas.	Edward's Prize Cases, Admiralty (Eng.)
Edw.Pr.Ct. Cas.	Edward's Abridgement of Prerogative Court Cases
E.E.	English Exchequer
E.E.C.J.O.	Official Journal of the European Communities
E.E.C.L.	Encyclopedia of European Community Law (Bender)
E.E.O.C.Com pliance Manual	Equal Employment Opportunity Commission Compliance Manual (CCH)
E.E.R.	English Ecclesiastical Reports
Efird	Efird (SC)
EG	Estates Gazette
EGCS	Estates Gazette Case Summaries
E.G.L.	Encyclopedia of Georgia Law
EGLR	Estates Gazette Law Reports
Ehrman 3d	Ehrman & Flavin, Taxing California Property (3d ed.)
EHRR	European Human Rights Reports

EIPR	European Intellectual Property Review
El.	Elchie's Decisions (Scot.)
El. & B.	Ellis & Blackburn's Queen's Bench (Eng.)
El. & Bl.	Same
El. & El.	Ellis & Ellis, Queen's Bench (Eng.)
E.L. & Eq.	English Law & Equity Reports
El.B. & E.	Ellis, Blackburn & Ellis' Queen's Bench (Eng.)
El.B. & El.	Same
El.B. & S.	Ellis, Best & Smith's Queen's Bench (Eng.)
El.Bl. & El.	Ellis, Blackburn & Ellis' Queen's Bench (Eng.)
El.Cas.	Election Cases
Elchies'	Elchies' Decisions (Scot.)
Elec C	Elections Code (CA)
Elect.Cas. (N.Y.)	Election Cases, Armstrong, NY
Elect.Rep.	Election Reports (Ont.)
ELJ	Ecclesiastical Law Journal
Ell. & Bl.	Ellis & Blackburn's Queen's Bench (Eng.)
Ell.Bl. & Ell.	Ellis, Blackburn & Ellis' Queen's Bench (Eng.)
El Paso Trial Law.Rev.	El Paso Trial Lawyers Review
Elr	Environmental Law Reporter
E.L.R.	Eastern Law Reporter (Can.)
Els.W.Bl.	Elsley's Edition of William Blackstone's King's Bench (Eng.)
Em.App.	Emergency Court of Appeals (U.S.)
Emory Int'l L.Rev.	Emory International Law Review
Emory J. Int'l Disp.Resol.	Emory Journal of International Dispute Resolution
Emory L.J.	Emory Law Journal
Empl.Rel.L.J	Employee Relations Law Journal
Empl.Saf'y & Health Guide	Employment Safety and Health Guide (CCH)
Enc.Pl. & Pr.	Encyclopedia of Pleading & Practice
Enc.U.S.Sup. Ct.Rep.	Encyclopedia of United States Supreme Court Reports
Energy Controls	Energy Controls (P–H)
Energy L.J.	Energy Law Journal
Eng.	English (AR)
Eng.Adm.	English Admiralty
Eng.Adm.R.	English Admiralty Reports
Eng.C.C.	English Crown Cases

Eng.Ch.	Condensed English Chancery
	English Chancery
Eng.C.L.	English Common Law Reports
Eng.Com.L.R	Same
Eng.Cr.Cas.	English Crown Cases
Eng.Eccl.	English Ecclesiastical Reports
Eng.Ecc.R.	Same
Eng.Exch.	English Exchequer
Eng.Hist. Rev.	English Historical Review
Eng.Ir.App.	Law Reports English & Irish Appeals
Eng.Judg.	English Judges (Scot.)
Eng.L. & Eq.	English Law & Equity Reports
Eng.L. & Eq.R.	Same
Eng.Rep.	English Reports, Full Reprint
Eng.Rep.R.	Same
Eng.Ry. & C.Cas.	English Railway and Canal Cases
Eng.Sc.Ecc.	English & Scotch Ecclesiastical Reports
Entertainme nt & Med.L.	Entertainment & Media Law
Entertainme nt L.J.	Entertainment Law Journal
Envir.L.	Environmental Law
Envtl.Affairs	Environmental Affairs
Envtl.F.	Environmental Forum
Envtl.L.	Environmental Law
Envtl.L.J.	Environmental Law Journal
Envtl.L.Rev.	Environmental Law Review
Envtl.L.Rptr.	Environmental Law Reporter
Envtl.Pol'y & L.	Environmental Policy and Law
Env't Rptr.	Environment Reporter (BNA)
E.P.D.	Employment Practices Decisions (CCH)
Eq.Cas.Abr.	Equity Cases Abridged (Eng.)
Eq.Rep.	Harper's Equity (SC)
Equity Rep.	English Chancery Appeals Gilbert, Equity (Eng.) Harper's Equity (SC)
E.R.	East's King's Bench (Eng.)
erc	Environment Reporter Cases (BNA)
E.R.C.	English Ruling Cases Environmental Reporter Cases
Err. & App.	Error & Appeals (Upper Can.)
Ersk.	Erskine (U.S. Circuit Court)

E.School L.Rev.	Eastern School Law Review
Esp.	Espinasse's Nisi Prius (Eng.)
Esp.N.P.	Same
Est. & Tr.J.	Estates & Trusts Journal
Est. & Tr.Q.	Estates and Trusts Quarterly
Est. Gifts & Tr.J.	Estates, Gifts & Trusts Journal
Est.Plan.	Estate Planning
Est.Plan.Rev.	Estate Planning Review (CCH)
E.T.	Estate Tax Division (I.R.B.)
E.T.R.	Estates & Trusts Reports
Euer	Euer Doctrina Placitandi (Eng.)
Eur.Consult. Ass.Deb.	Council of Europe Consultative Assembly, Official Report of Debates
Eur.L.Dig.	European Law Digest
Eur.L.Newsl.	European Law Newsletter
Eur.L.Rev.	European Law Review
Eurolaw Com.Intel.	Eurolaw Commercial Intelligence
Europ.T.S.	European Treaty Series
Eur.Parl. Deb.	Debates of the European Parliament
Eur.Parl. Docs.	European Parliament Working Documents
Eur.Tax.	European Taxation
Eur.Trans.L.	European Transport Law
Eur.Y.B.	European Yearbook
Evans	Evans, Washington Territory Reports
Ev C	Evidence Code (CA)
Evid. C.	Same
Ex.	Exchequer Reports (Eng.)
Examiner	Examiner (NY) Examiner (Que.)
Excerpta Crim.	Excerpta Criminologica
Exch.	Exchequer (Scot.) Welsby, Hurlstone & Gordon, Exchequer (Eng.)
Exch.Can.	Exchequer Reports (Can.)
Exch.Cas.	Exchequer Cases (Scot.)
Exch.Rep.	Exchequer Reports
Ex.C.R.	Exchequer Court Reports (Can.)
Ex.D.	Law Reports, Exchequer Division (Eng.)
Ex.Div.	Same
Exec.Order	Executive Order
Eyre	Eyre's King's Bench (Eng.)

F

f	Federal Reporter (U.S.)
F.	Same
F. (Ct.Sess.)	Fraser's Court of Sessions Cases (Scot.)
f2d	Federal Reporter, Second Series (U.S.)
F.2d	Same
f3d	Same, Third Series
F.3d	Same
Fac.L.Rev.	Faculty of Law Review (Toronto)
F.A.D.	Federal Anti–Trust Decisions
Fairf.	Fairfield (ME)
Falc.	Falconer's Court of Sessions Cases (Scot.)
Falc. & F.	Falconer & Fitzherbert's Election Cases (Eng.)
Fam (preceded by date)	Law Reports (Family Division)
Fam C	Family Code (CA)
Family Law Service	California Family Law Service
Family L News	Family Law News
Family LQ	Family Law Quarterly
Fam Law	Family Law (journal)
Fam.L. Commtr.	Family Law Commentator
Fam.L. Newsl.	Family Law Newsletter
Fam.L.Q.	Family Law Quarterly
Fam.L.Rep.	Family Law Reporter (BNA)
Fam.L.Rev.	Family Law Review
F. & F.	Foster & Finlason, Nisi Prius (Eng.)
F & G C	Fish and Game Code
F.App.	West's Federal Appendix
Far.	Farresley's King's Bench (Eng.)
Far East.L.Rev.	Far Eastern Law Review
F.B.C.	Fonblanque's Bankruptcy Cases (Eng.)
FBILEB	Federal Bureau of Investigation Law Enforcement Bulletin
FC	Federal Cases
F.C.	Faculty Collection of Decisions (Scot.) Canada Federal Court Reports
F.C.A.	Federal Code Annotated

F.Carr.Cas.	Federal Carriers Cases (CCH)	Fee Arb Stds	State Bar Guidelines and Minimum Standards for Mandatory Fee Arbitration Programs
fcas	Federal Cases	fep	Fair Employment Practices (BNA)
F.C.C.	Federal Communication Commission Reports	F.E.P.Cas.	Fair Employment Practices Cases
FCCR	Federal Communications Commission Record	ferc	Federal Energy Regulatory Commission Reporter (CCH)
fcdr	Fulton County Daily Report (GA)	Ferg.Cons.	Fergusson's Consistory, Divorce (Scot.)
FCirT	Trade Cases in the U.S. Court of Appeals for the Federal Circuit	Fergusson	Fergusson (of Kilkeran) (Scot.)
FCR	Family Court Reporter	F.H.L.	Fraser, House of Lords (Scot.)
Fd & Ag C	Food and Agricultural Code	Fin C	Financial Code
F.D.Cosm.L. Rep.	Food, Drug, Cosmetic Law Reporter (CCH)	Finch	Finch's Chancery (Eng.)
Fed.	Federal Reporter (U.S.)	Fin. L. R.	Financial Law Reports
fedapp	Federal Appeals	Fin.Tax. & Comp.L.	Finance Taxation and Company Law (Pak.)
Fed.Appx.	West's Federal Appendix	Fire & Casualty Cas.	Fire and Casualty Cases (CCH)
Fed.B.A.J.	Federal Bar Association Journal	Fish & Game C.	Fish and Game Code (CA)
Fed.B.J.	Federal Bar Journal	Fish & G.C.	Same
Fed.B.News	Federal Bar News	fishpatcas	Fisher's U.S. Patent Cases
Fed.Carr. Rep.	Federal Carriers Reporter (CCH)	Fish.Pat.Cas.	Same
Fed.Cas.	Federal Cases (U.S.)	Fish.Pat.R.	Fisher's Patent Reports (U.S.)
fedcir	Federal Circuit Trade Cases	fishpr	Fisher's U.S. Prize Cases
fedcl	Federal Claims Reporter	Fish.Prize Cas.	Same
Fed.Com.B.J.	Federal Communications Bar Journal	Fitzh.	Fitzherbert's Abridgment (Eng.)
Fed.Com.L.J.	Federal Communications Law Journal	Fitzh.N.Br.	Fitzherbert's Natura Brevium (Eng.)
Fed.Crim.L. Rep.	Federal Criminal Law Report	fla	Florida Reports
Fed.Ct.Rep.	Federal Court Reports (Aust.)	Fla.	Same
		Fla. & K.	Flanagan & Kelly, Rolls (Ir.)
Fed.Est. & Gift Tax Rep.	Federal Estate and Gift Tax Reporter (CCH)	Fla.B.J.	Florida Bar Journal
Fed.Juror	Federal Juror	Fla.Int'l L.J.	Florida International Law Journal
Fed.L.Rep.	Federal Law Reports	Fla.J.Int'l L.	Florida Journal of International Law
Fed.L.Rev.	Federal Law Review		
Fed'n Ins. Counsel Q.	Federation of Insurance Counsel Quarterly	Fla.Jur.	Florida Jurisprudence
Fed.Prob.	Federal Probation	Fla. L.J.	Florida Law Journal
Fed RCP	Federal Rules of Civil Procedure	Fla. L. Rev.	Florida Law Review
		Flan. & Kel.	Flanagan & Kelly, Rolls (Ir.)
Fed.Reg.	Federal Register	Fla.St.U. L.Rev.	Florida State University Law Review
Fed.Rules Serv.	Federal Rules Service		
Fed.Rules Serv.2d	Same, Second Series	flasupp	Florida Supplement
Fee Arb Rules	Rules of Procedure for the Hearing of Fee Arbitrations by the State Bar of California	Fla.Supp.	Same
		flasupp2d	Same, Second Series
		Fletcher F. World Aff.	Fletcher Forum of World Affairs

flip	Flippin's U.S. Circuit Court Reports
Flipp.	Same
F.L.J.	Forum Law Journal (U. of Baltimore)
F.L.P.	Florida Law and Practice
FLR	Family Law Reports
FLS	Florida Supplement
FLS2d	Same, Second Series
flw	Florida Law Weekly
flwfeds	Florida Law Weekly–Federal
F.M.C.	Federal Maritime Commission Reports
Fogg	Fogg (NH)
F.O.I.C.R.	Freedom of Information Center Reports
F.O.I.Dig	Freedom of Information Digest
Fonbl.	Fonblanque's Bankruptcy (Eng.)
Food & Ag. C.	Food and Agricultural Code (CA)
Food & Agric. C.	Same
Food Drug Cosm.L.J.	Food, Drug, Cosmetic Law Journal
Fordham Ent.Media & Intell. Prop.L.F.	Fordham Entertainment Media & Intellectual Property Law Forum
Fordham Envtl.L.Rep.	Fordham Environmental Law Report
Fordham Int'l L.F.	Fordham International Law Forum
Fordham Int'l L.J.	Fordham International Law Journal
Fordham L.Rev.	Fordham Law Review
Fordham Urb.L.J.	Fordham Urban Law Journal
Form.	Forman (IL)
Forr.	Forrest's Exchequer (Eng.)
Forrester	Forrester's Chancery Cases Tempore Talbot (Eng.)
For.Sci.	Forensic Science
For.Tax Bull.	Foreign Tax Law Bi–Weekly Bulletin
Fortesc.	Fortescue's King's Bench (Eng.)
Fort.L.J.	Fortnightly Law Journal
Forum	The Forum

Fost.	Foster (HI)
	Foster (NH)
	Foster's Crown Cases (Eng.)
	Foster's Legal Chronicle Reports (PA)
Found.L.Rev.	Foundation Law Review
Fount.Dec.	Fountainhall's Decisions (Scot.)
Fox	Fox's Registration Cases (Eng.)
	Fox's Decisions (ME)
Fox & S.	Fox & Smith's King's Bench (Ir.)
Fox Pat.C.	Fox's Patent, Trade Mark, Design and Copyright Cases
F.P.C.	Federal Power Commission Decisions
FPC	Federal Power Commission Reports
FR	Federal Register
FR	Fordham Law Review
France	France (CO)
Franchise L. Rev.	Franchise Law Review
Fran.Coll.L.J.	Franciso College Law Journal
Fraser	Fraser, Court of Session Cases (Scot.)
FRCh	Freeman's Chancery Reports (MS)
frd	Federal Rules Decisions
F.R.D.	Same
Freem.	Freeman (IL)
freemch	Freeman's Mississippi Chancery Reports
Freem.Ch.	Same
Freem.K.B.	Freeman's King's Bench (Eng.)
French	French (NH)
freserv	Federal Rules of Evidence Service
FS	Federal Supplement
FS2d	Same, Second Series
FSR	Fleet Street Reports
fsupp	Federal Supplement
F.Supp.	Same
F.Supp.2d	Same, 2d
ftc	Federal Trade Commission Decisions
F.T.C.	Same
Fuller	Fuller (MI)

G

ga	Georgia Reports
GA	Decisions of General Appraisers (U.S.)
Ga.	Georgia Reports
GaA	Georgia Appeals Reports
gaapp	Same
Ga.App.	Same
Ga.B.J.	Georgia Bar Journal
Ga.Bus.Law.	Georgia Business Lawyer
Ga.Dec.	Georgia Decisions
gadecpt1; gadecpt2	Same, Part 1; Part 2
Ga.J.Int'l & Comp.L.	Georgia Journal of International & Comparative Law
Galb.	Galbraith (FL)
Galb. & M.	Galbraith & Meek (FL)
Gale	Gale's Exchequer (Eng.)
Gale & D.	Gale & Davison's Queen's Bench (Eng.)
Gale & Dav.	Same
Ga.L.J.	Georgia Law Journal
gall	Gallison's U.S. Circuit Court Reports
Gall.	Same
Ga.L.Rep.	Georgia Law Reports
Ga.L.Rev.	Georgia Law Review
G. & D.	Gale & Davison's Queen's Bench (Eng.)
G. & G.	Goldsmith & Guthrie (MO)
G. & J.	Gill & Johnson (MD) Glyn & Jameson's Bankruptcy (Eng.)
G. & R.	Geldert & Russell (Nova Scotia)
Garden.	Gardenhire (MO)
Gard.N.Y. Reptr.	Gardenier's New York Reporter
GaS	Georgia Reports, Supplement
Ga.St.B.J.	Georgia State Bar Journal
Ga.St.U. L.Rev.	Georgia State University Law Review
gasupp	Lester's Supplement (GA)
Ga.Supp.	Same
Gaz.	Gazette Weekly Law Gazette (U.S.)
Gaz.Bankr.	Gazette of Bankruptcy
Gaz.L.R.	Gazette Law Reports
G.C.M.	General Counsel's Memorandum (I.R.B.)
G.Coop.	G. Cooper's Chancery (Eng.)
GD(1)	Georgia Decisions, Part 1
GD(2)	Same, Part 2

Geld. & M.	Geldart & Maddock's Chancery (Eng.)
Geld. & O.	Geldert & Oxley (Nova Scotia)
Geo	Georgetown Law Journal
Geo.Immigr. L.J.	Georgetown Immigration Law Journal
Geo.Int'l Envtl. L.Rev.	Georgetown International Environmental Law Review
Geo.J.Legal Ethics	Georgetown Journal of Legal Ethics
Geo.L.J.	Georgetown Law Journal
Geo.Mason L. Rev.	George Mason Law Review
Geo.Mason U.Civ.Rts. L.J.	George Mason University Civil Rights Law Journal
Geo.Mason U.L.Rev.	George Mason University Law Review
George	George (MS)
Geo.Wash.J. Int'l L. & Econ.	George Washington Journal of International Law and Economics
Geo.Wash. L.Rev.	George Washington Law Review
ggreene	George Greene's Iowa Reports
gib	Gibbons' Surrogate Court Reports (NY)
Gib	Same
Gibbs	Gibbs (MI)
Gibb.Surr.	Gibbon's Surrogate (NY)
Giff.	Giffard's Chancery (Eng.)
Giff. & H.	Giffard & Hemming's Chancery (Eng.)
Gil.	Gilman (Ill.)
Gilb.	Gilbert's Chancery (Eng.)
Gilb.Cas.	Gilbert's Cases, Law & Equity (Eng.)
Gilb.C.P.	Gilbert's Common Pleas (Eng.)
Gilb.Exch.	Gilbert's Exchequer (Eng.)
Gildr.	Gildersleeve (NM)
Gilf.	Gilfillan (MN)
gill	Gill's Reports (MD)
Gill	Same
gill & j	Gill & Johnson Maryland Reports
Gill & J.	Same
Gill & Johns.	Same
Gilm.	Gilmer (VA)
Gilm. & Falc.	Gilmour & Falconer (Scot.)

gilp	Gilpin's U.S. District Court Reports	Govt. C.	Same
Gilp.	Same	Gov't Cont.Rep.	Government Contracts Reporter (CCH)
GJ	Gill & Johnson Reports (MD)	Gow	Gow's Nisi Prius (Eng.)
Gl. & J.	Glyn & Jameson's Bankruptcy Cases (Eng.)	GR	Grant's Cases (PA)
		Gr.	Grant, Chancery Reports (Upper Can.)
Glanv.	Glanville De Legibus et Consuetudinibus Angliae (Eng.)	Granger	Granger (OH)
		Grant	Grant's Cases (PA)
		grantcas	Same
Glanv.El.Cas.	Glanville's Election Cases (Eng.)	Grant Err. & App.	Grant's Error & Appeal (Upper Can.)
Glasc.	Glascock (Ir.)	Gratt.	Grattan (VA)
Glendale LR	Glendale Law Review	Gray	Gray's Reports (MA)
Glendale L.Rev.	Same		Gray (NC)
Glenn	Glenn (LA)	grayma	Gray's Massachusetts Reports
Glyn & J.	Glyn & Jameson's Bankruptcy Cases (Eng.)	Gre	G. Greene's Reports (IA)
		Green	Green (OK)
			Green (RI)
Glyn & Jam.	Same		Green Equity (NJ)
Godb.	Godbolt's King's Bench (Eng.)		Green Law (NJ)
		Green Cr.	Green's Criminal Law (Eng.)
Godson	Godson, Mining Commissioner's Cases	Greene	Greene (IA)
			Greene's Annotated Cases (NY)
Goebel	Goebel's Probate (OH)	Greenl.	Greenleaf (ME)
Gold. & G.	Goldsmith & Guthrie (MO)	Greenl.Ov. Cas.	Greenleaf's Overruled Cases
Golden Gate LR	Golden Gate Law Review	Grein.Pr.	Greiner, Practice (LA)
		Griffith	Griffith (IN)
Golden Gate L.Rev.	Same	Gris.	Griswold (OH)
		Griswold	Same
Golden Gate U.L.Rev.	Golden Gate University Law Review	Group Legal Rev.	Group Legal Review
Gonz.L.Rev.	Gonzaga Law Review	G.S.R.	Gongwer's State Reports (OH)
Gonz.Pub. Lab.L.Rep.	Gonzaga Special Report: Public Sector Labor Law	Guild Prac.	Guild Practitioner
		Guthrie	Guthrie (MO)
Gottschall	Gottschall (OH)	G.W.D.	Green's Weekly Digest
Gouldsb.	Gouldsborough's King's Bench (Eng.)	Gwill.T.Cas.	Gwillim's Tithe Cases (Eng.)
Gov C	Government Code (CA)		

H

H.	Handy (OH)	Hagg.Adm.	Haggard's Admiralty (Eng.)
Ha.	Hare's Vice–Chancery (Eng.)	Hagn. & M.	Hagner & Miller (MD)
HA	Hawaii Appellate Reports	Hailes Dec.	Hailes' Decisions (Scot.)
		Hale	Hale (CA)
Ha. & Tw.	Hall & Twell's Chancery (Eng.)		Hale's Common Law (Eng.)
HAC	Howard's Appeal Cases (NY)	Hale P.C.	Hale's Pleas of the Crown (Eng.)
Had.	Hadley (NH)	Hall	Hall (NH)
Hadd.	Haddington Manuscript Reports (Scot.)		Hall's Superior Court (NY)
Hadl.	Hadley (NH)	Hall.	Hallett (CO)
Hagan	Hagan (UT)	Hall & Tw.	Hall & Twell's Chancery (Eng.)
Hagans	Hagans (WV)	Halst.	Halsted's Equity (NJ)

	Halsted's Law (NJ)
Ham.	Hammond (GA)
	Hammond (OH)
Ham.A. & O.	Hamerton, Allen & Otter, New Session Cases (Eng.)
Ham. & J.	Hammond & Jackson (GA)
Hamlin	Hamlin (ME)
Hamline J.Pub.L. & Pol'y	Hamline Journal of Public Law and Policy
Hamline L.Rev.	Hamline Law Review
Hammond	Hammond (OH)
Han.	Handy (OH)
Hand	Hand (NY)
H. & B.	Hudson & Brooke's King's Bench (Ir.)
H. & C.	Hurlstone & Coltman's Exchequer (Eng.)
H. & D.	Hill & Denio, Lalor's Supplement (NY)
H. & G.	Harris & Gill (MD)
	Hurlstone & Gordon's Exchequer (Eng.)
H. & H.	Harrison & Hodgin's Municipal Reports (Upper Can.)
	Horn & Hurlstone's Exchequer (Eng.)
H. & J.	Harris & Johason (MD)
	Hayes & Jones' Exchequer (Ir.)
H. & J.Ir.	Same
H. & M.	Hemming & Miller's Vice Chancery (Eng.)
	Hening & Munford (VA)
H. & M.Ch.	Hemming & Miller's Vice Chancery (Eng.)
H. & McH.	Harris & McHenry (MD)
H. & N.	Hurlstone & Norman's Exchequer (Eng.)
H & N C	Harbors and Navigation Code (CA)
H. & R.	Harrison & Rutherford's Common Pleas (Eng.)
H. & S.	Harris & Simrall (MS)
H & S C	Health and Safety Code (CA)
H. & T.	Hall & Twell's Chancery (Eng.)
H. & W.	Harrison & Wollaston's King's Bench (Eng.)
	Hurlstone & Wahnsley's Exchequer (Eng.)
Handy	Handy (OH)
Han.N.B.	Hannay's Reports (N.B.)
Hans.	Hansbrough (VA)
Har.	Harrington (DE)
	Harrington's Chancery (MI)
	Harrison (LA)
	Harrison's Chancery (MI)

Harb. & Nav. C.	Harbors and Navigation Code (CA)
Harc.	Harcarse, Decisions (Scot.)
HarCh	Harrington's Chancery Reports (MI)
Hard.	Hardesty, Term Reports (DE)
Hardes.	Same
Hardin	Hardin (KY)
hardky	Same
Hardres	Hardres' Exchequer (Eng.)
Hare	Hare's Vice–Chancery (Eng.)
Hare & W.	American Leading Cases, Hare & Wallace
Harg.	Hargrove (NC)
Harp.	Harper's Equity (SC)
	Harper's Law (SC)
Harper	Harper's Conspiracy Cases (MD)
Harr.	Harrington's Reports (DE)
	Harrison (IN)
	Harrison (NJ)
harr & g	Harris & Gill's Reports (MD)
Harr. & H.	Harrison & Hodgins' Municipal Reports (Upper Can.)
Harr. & Hodg.	Same
harr & j	Harris & Johnson's Reports (MD)
Harr. & J.	Same
Harr. & M.	Harris & McHenry (MD)
harr & mch	Same
Harr. & R.	Harrison & Rutherford's Common Pleas (Eng.)
Harr. & W.	Harrison & Wollaston's King's Bench (Eng.)
harrch	Harrington's Michigan Chancery Reports
Harr.Ch.	Harrison's Chancery (Eng.)
harrde	Harrington's Delaware Reports
Harris	Harris (PA)
Harris & G.	Harris & Gill (MD)
Harris & S.	Harris & Simrall (MS)
Hart.	Hartley (TX)
Hart. & H.	Hartley & Hartley (TX)
Harv.Blacklett er J.	Harvard Blackletter Journal
Harv.Bus.Rev.	Harvard Business Review
Harv.C.R.– C.L.L.Rev.	Harvard Civil Rights— Civil Liberties Law Review
Harv.Envtl.L. Rev.	Harvard Environmental Law Review
Harv.Hum. Rts.J.	Harvard Human Rights Journal
Harv.Int'l L.J.	Harvard International Law Journal

Harv.J.L. & Pub.Pol'y	Harvard Journal of Law and Public Policy
Harv. J. L. & Tech.	Harvard Journal of Law & Technology
Harv.J. on Legis.	Harvard Journal on Legislation
Harv. L. R.	Harvard Law Review
Harv.L.Rev.	Same
Harv.L.S. Bull.	Harvard Law School Bulletin
Harv.Women's L.J.	Harvard's Women's Law Journal
Harv.W.Tax Ser.	Harvard World Tax Series (CCH)
Hasb.	Hasbrouck (ID)
Hask.	Haskell's Reports for United States Courts in Maine (Fox's Decisions)
haskcc	Haskell's U.S. Circuit Court Reports
Hast.	Hastings (ME)
Hast Comm/Ent LJ	Hastings Communications/Entertainment Law Journal
Hast Const LQ	Hastings Constitutional Law Quarterly
Hastings Comm. & Ent.L.J.	Hastings Communications and Environmental Law Journal
Hastings Const.L.Q.	Hastings Constitutional Law Quarterly
Hastings Int'l & Comp.L. Rev.	Hastings International and Comparative Law Review
Hastings L.J.	Hastings Law Journal
Hastings Women's L.J.	Hastings Women's Law Journal
Hast Intl & Comp LR	Hastings International and Comparative Law Review
Hast LJ	Hastings Law Journal
Havil.	Haviland (P.E.I.)
Haw.	Hawaii Reports
hawaii	Same
Hawaii	Same
Hawaii B.J.	Hawaii Bar Journal
hawapp	Hawaii Appellate Reports
Hawk.	Hawkins' Louisiana Annual
Hawk.P.C.	Hawkins' Pleas of the Crown
Hawks	Hawks (NC)
Hawl.	Hawley (NV)
Hay.	Haywood (NC) Haywood (TN)
Hay & H.	Hay & Hazelton (U.S.)
Hay & M.	Hay & Marriott's Admiralty (Eng.)
Hayes	Hayes (Scot.) Hayes' Exchequer (Ir.)
Hayes & J.	Hayes & Jones' Exchequer (Ir.)
hayw	Haywood's North Carolina Reports
Hayw.	Same Haywood (TN)
haywtn	Haywood's Tennessee Reports
Haz.Reg.	Hazard's Register (PA)
H.Bl.	Henry Blackstone's Common Pleas (Eng.)
hc	Hayward & Hazelton's U.S. Circuit Court Reports
HC	House of Commons Paper
H.C.L.M.	Health Care Labor Manual
HCr	Houston's Criminal Reports (DE)
Head	Head (TN)
headtn	Head's Tennessee Reports
Health & Saf. C.	Health & Safety Code (CA)
Health & S.C.	Same
Health Matrix: J.L.-Med.	Health Matrix: Journal of Law–Medicine
Heath	Heath (ME)
Hedges	Hedges (MT)
heisk	Heiskell's Tennessee Reports
Heisk.	Same
Helm	Helm (NV)
Hem. & M.	Heming & Miller's Vice–Chancery (Eng.)
Heming.	Hemingway (MS)
Hemp.	Hempstead (U.S. Circuit Court)
hempst	Same
Hempst.	Same
Hen. & M.	Hening & Munford (VA)
Henning CLE Rep.	Henning Continuing Legal Education Reporter
Henn.Law.	Hennepin Lawyer (MN)
Hepb.	Hepburn (CO)
Het.	Hetley's Common Pleas (Eng.)
HG	Harris & Gill's Reports (MD)
HH	Hayward and Hazeleton's Reports
Hibb.	Hibbard (NH)
Hight	Hight (IA)
High Tech. L.J.	High Technology Law Journal
Hill	Hill (IL) Hill's Reports (NY) Hill's Equity (SC) Hill's Law (SC)
Hill & D.	Hill & Denio (NY)
Hillyer	Hillyer (CA)
Hil.T.	Hilary Tenn (Eng.)
Hilt.	Hilton's Reports (NY)

Hines	Hines (KY)
Hitotsubashi J.L. & Pol.	Hitotsubashi Journal of Law and Politics
HJ	Harris & Johnson's Reports (MD)
H.L.Cas.	House of Lords Cases (Eng.)
H.L.N.R.	Health Lawyers News Report
HLR	Harvard Law Review
	Housing Law Reports (Eng.)
HM	Harris & McHenry's Reports (MD)
Hob.	Hobart's Common Pleas & Chancery (Eng.)
Hobart	Hobart's King's Bench (Eng.)
Hod.	Hodges' Common Pleas (Eng.)
Hodg.El.	Hodgin's Election (Upper Can.)
Hodges	Hodges' Common Pleas (Eng.)
Hof	Hofstra Law Review
HofCh	Hoffman's Chancery Reports (NY)
hoff	Hoffman's Decisions
Hoff. Dec.	Same
hofflc	Hoffman's Land Cases (U.S. District Court)
Hoff. L. Cas.	Hoffman's Land Cases
Hoffm.	Hoffman's Chancery (NY)
	Hoffman's Land Cases (U.S.)
Hoff. Op.	Hoffman's Opinions
Hofstra Lab.L.F.	Hofstra Labor Law Forum
Hofstra Lab.L.J.	Hofstra Labor Law Journal
Hofstra L.Rev.	Hofstra Law Review
Hofstra Prop. L.J.	Hofstra Property Law Journal
Hog.	Hogan's Rolls Court (Ir.)
Hogoboom & King	Hogoboom & King, California Practice Guide Family Law
Hogue	Hogue (FL)
Holl.	Holligshead (MN)
holmes	Holmes (U.S. Circuit Court)
Holmes	Holmes (OR)
	Holmes (U.S.)
Holt Adm.	Holt's Admiralty Cases (Eng.)
Holt Eq.	Holt's Equity (Eng.)
	Holt's Vice Chancery (Eng.)
Holt K.B.	Holt's King's Bench (Eng.)
Holt N.P.	Holt's Nisi Prius (Eng.)
Home	Home Manuscript, Decisions, Court of Sessions (Scot.)

Hong Kong L.J.	Hong Kong Law Journal
Hook.	Hooker (CT)
Hope Dec.	Hope's Decisions (Scot.)
Hopk.	Hopkins' Chancery Reports (NY)
Hopk.Dec.	Hopkinson's Admiralty Decisions (PA)
Hopw. & C.	Hopwood & Coltman's Registration Appeal Cases (Eng.)
Hopw. & P.	Hopwood & Philbrick's Registration Appeal Cases (Eng.)
Horner	Horner (SD)
Horw.Y.B.	(Horwood) Year Book of Edward I
Hosea	Hosea (OH)
Hoskins	Hoskins (ND)
Hou	Houston's Reports (DE)
Houghton	Houghton (AL)
Housing & Devel.Rep.	Housing and Development Reporter (BNA)
Hous.J.Int'l L.	Houston Journal of International Law
Hous.Law.	Houston Lawyer
Hous.L.Rev.	Houston Law Review
Houst.	Houston (DE)
Houst.Cr.	Houston, Criminal Cases (DE)
houstcrim	Same
houstde	Houston's Delaware Reports
Houst.L.Rev.	Houston Law Review
Houston Law.	Houston Lawyer
Hov.	Hovenden's Supplement, Vesey's Chancery (Eng.)
How.	Howard (MS)
	Howard (U.S.)
	Howell (NV)
How.A.Cas.	Howard's Appeal Cases (NY)
How. & Beat.	Howell & Beatty (NV)
How. & N.	Howell & Norcross (NV)
howard	Howard's U.S. Supreme Court Reporter
Howard Journal	Howard Journal of Criminal Justice
Howard L.J.	Howard Law Journal
How.Ch.	Howard's Chancery (Ir.)
How.L.J.	Howard Law Journal
hownp	Howell, Nisi Prius (MI)
How.N.P.	Same
How.Pr.	Howard's Practice (NY)
How.Pr. (N.S.)	Same, New Series
How.St.Tr.	Howell's State Trials (Eng.)
HP	Howard's Practice Reports (NY)
HPns	Same, New Series
HPr	Same
H.R.J.	Human Rights Journal (Revue des droits de l'homme)

H.R.L.J.	Human Rights Law Journal
Hubb.	Hubbard (ME)
Hud. & B.	Hudson & Brooke's King's Bench (Ir.)
Hughes	Hughes (KY) Hughes (U.S.)
hughescc	Hughes' U.S. Circuit Court Reports
hughesky	Hughes' Kentucky Reports
Hume	Hume's Decisions (Scot.)
Humph.	Humphrey
Humphr.	Humphrey's (TN)
Hum.Rts.	Human Rights
Hum.Rts.J.	Human Rights Journal
Hum.Rts.L.J.	Human Rights Law Journal
Hum.Rts.Q.	Human Rights Quarterly
Hum.Rts.Rev.	Human Rights Review

Hum.Rts. U.S.S.R.	Human Rights in Union of Soviet Socialist Republics
humtn	Humphrey's Tennessee Reports
hun	Hun New York Supreme Court Reports
Hun	Same
Hung.L.Rev.	Hungarian Law Review
Hunt.Torrens	Hunter's Torrens Cases
Hurl. & G.	Hurlstone & Gordon's Exchequer (Eng.)
Hurl. & W.	Hurlstone & Wahnsley's Exchequer (Eng.)
Hutch.	Hutcheson (AL)
Hutt.	Hutton's Common Pleas (Eng.)
H.W.Gr.	H.W. Green's Equity (NJ)

I

Ia	Iowa Reports
I.A.C.	Immigration Appeal Cases
	Industrial Accident Commission Decisions
IALS Bull.	Institute of Advanced Legal Studies, Bulletin
i & ndec	Immigration and Nationality Laws, Administrative Decisions Under Immigration and Naturalization Interim Decisions
I. & N.Dec.	Immigration and Nationality Decisions
I.B.L.	International Business Lawyer
I.Bull.	Interights Bulletin
ICC	Interstate Commerce Commission Reports
ICC2d	Same, Second Series
I.C.C.L.R.	International Company and Commercial Law Review
I.C.C.Pract.J.	Interstate Commerce Commission Practitioners' Journal
ICCR	International Company and Commercial Law Review
I.C.J.	International Court of Justice Reports
ICJ Reports	International Court of Justice Reports

I.C.J.Y.B.	Yearbook of the International Court of Justice
ICLQ	International and Comparative Law Quarterly
I.C.L.R.	International Construction Law Review
ICR	Industrial Cases Reports
ID	Decisions of the Department of the Interior
I.D.	Interior Department Decisions, Public Land
Ida	Idaho Reports
idaho	Same
Idaho	Same
Idaho L.J.	Idaho Law Journal
Idaho L.Rev.	Idaho Law Review
Idding	Idding's Term Reports (Dayton, OH)
Iddings T.R.D.	Same
Idd.T.R.	Same
ier	Individual Employment Rights Cases (BNA)
I.F.L. Rev.	International Financial Law Review
IIC	International Review of Industrial Property and Copyright Law
IlLR	University of Illinois Law Review
I.J.E.C.L.	International Journal of Estuarine and Coastal Law
IlA	Illinois Appellate Court Reports

I.L. & P.	Insolvency Law and Practice	Immig. L. & Bus.News	Immigration Law & Business News
IlCC	Illinois Circuit Court Reports	Immig.Newsl.	Immigration Newsletter
IlCCl	Illinois Court of Claims Reports	InA	Indiana Appellate Court Reports
I.L.C. Newsl.	International Legal Center Newsletter		Indiana Court of Appeals Reports
I.L.E.	Indiana Law Encyclopedia	ind	Indiana Supreme Court Reports
ILJ	Industrial Law Journal	Ind.	Same
ill	Illinois Supreme Court Reports	Ind.Advocate	Indian Advocate
Ill.	Same	Ind. & Intell. Prop.Austl.	Industrial and Intellectual Property in Australia
ill2d	Same, Second Series		
Ill.2d	Same	Ind. & Lab. Rel.Rev.	Industrial and Labor Relations Review
ill3d	Same, Third Series		
illapp	Illinois Appellate Court Reports	indapp	Indiana Appellate Court Reports
Ill.App.	Same	Ind.App.	Same
illapp2d	Same, Second Series	Ind.Cl.Comm.	Indian Claims Commission Decisions
Ill.App.2d	Same		
illapp3d	Same, Third Series		
Ill.App.3d	Same	India Crim.L. J.R.	India Criminal Law Journal Reports
Ill.B.J.	Illinois Bar Journal		
illcc	Illinois Circuit Court Reports	Indian Cas.	Indian Cases
		Indian L.J.	Indian Law Journal
Ill.Cir.	Same	Indian L.R.	Indian Law Reports
Ill.Cont.L.Ed.	Illinois Continuing Legal Education	Indian Rul.	Indian Rulings
		indianterr	Indian Territory Reports
Ill.Cont.Legal Ed.	Same	Indian Terr.	Same
		India S.Ct.	India Supreme Court Reports
Ill.Ct.Cl.	Illinois Court of Claims Reports		
IlD	Illinois Decisions	Ind.Int'l & Comp.L. Rev.	Indiana International & Comparative Law Review
illdec	Same		
Ill.L.B.	Illinois Law Bulletin		
Ill.L.Q.	Illinois Law Quarterly	Ind.J. Int'l L.	Indian Journal of International Law
IlLR	University of Illinois Law Review	Ind.Legal F.	Indiana Legal Forum
		Ind.L.J.	Indiana Law Journal
Ill.L.Rev.	Illinois Law Review	Ind.L.Q.Rev.	Indian Law Quarterly Review
I.L.M.	International Legal Materials		
I.L.P.	Illinois Law and Practice	Ind.L.Rev.	Indian Law Review Indiana Law Review
	International Legal Practitioner	Ind.L.Stud.	Indiana Law Student
		Ind.Prop.	Industrial Property
I.L.R.	Insurance Law Reporter (Can.)	Ind.Prop.Q.	Industrial Property Quarterly
	International Labour Review	Ind.Rel.J. Econ. & Soc.	Industrial Relations: Journal of Economy and Society
	International Law Reports		
I.L.R.M.	Irish Law Reports Monthly	Ind.S.C.	Indiana Superior Court
I.L.W.	Investment Laws of the World (Oceana)	Ind. Sol.	Independent Solicitor
		IndT	Indian Territory Reports
I.M.L.	International Media Law	Indus. & Lab. Rel.Rev.	Industrial and Labor Relations Review
Imm. and Nat. L. & P.	Immigration and Nationality Law and Practice	Indus.L.J.	Industrial Law Journal
		Indus.L.Rev.	Industrial Law Review
		Indus.Rel.L.J.	Industrial Relations Law Journal
Imm AR	Immigration Appeal Reports	Ind.Y.B.Int'l Aff.	Indian Yearbook of International Affairs
Immig.B.Bull.	Immigration Bar Bulletin	Inequal.Ed.	Inequality in Education

INLP	Immigration and Nationality Law and Practice	Int'l & Comp. L.Q.	International and Comparative Law Quarterly
Ins. C.	Insurance Code (CA)	Int'l Arb. Awards	Reports of International Arbitral Awards
Ins.Counsel J.	Insurance Counsel Journal	Int'l Arb.J.	International Arbitration Journal
Ins. L. & P.	Insolvency Law and Practice	Int'l B.J.	International Bar Journal
Ins.Liability Rep.	Insurance Liability Reporter	Int'l Bus. & Trade L.Rep.	International Business & Trade Law Reporter
Ins.L.J.	Insurance Law Journal (PA)	Int'l Bus. Lawyer	International Business Lawyer
Ins.L.Rep.	Insurance Law Reporter (CCH)	Int'l Bus.Ser.	International Business Series (Ernst & Ernst)
Inst.Ad.Legal Stud.Ann.	Institute of Advanced Legal Studies Annual	Int'l Concil.	International Conciliation
Inst.Est.Plan.	Institute on Estate Planning (U. of Miami)	Int'l Crim. Pol.Rev.	International Criminal Police Review
Inst.Lab.Rel. Bull.	Institute for Labor Relations Bulletin	Int'l Dig. Health Leg.	International Digest of Health Legislation
Inst.Min.L.	Institute on Mineral Law (La. State University)	Int'l Encycl. Comp.L.	International Encyclopedia of Comparative Law
Inst. on Fed. Tax'n	Institute on Federal Taxation	Int'l J.	International Journal
Inst.Plan. & Zoning	Institute on Planning and Zoning	Int'l J.Crim. & Pen.	International Journal of Criminology and Penology
Inst.Plan. Zoning & E.D.	Institute on Planning, Zoning and Eminent Domain	Int'l J.L. & Fam.	International Journal of Law and the Family
Inst.Sec.Reg.	Institute on Securities Regulation (PLI)	Int'l J.L. & Psych.	International Journal of Law and Psychiatry
INT	United States Court of International Trade	Int'l J.Legal Res.	International Journal of Legal Research
intdecno	Immigration and Naturalization Interim Decisions	Int'l J.L.Lib.	International Journal of Law Libraries
Int. J. Comp. L.L.I.R.	International Journal of Comparative Law and Industrial Relations	Int'l J.Off. Ther. & Comp.Crim.	International Journal of Offender Therapy and Comparative Criminology
Int. J. Law & Fam.	International Journal of Law and the Family	Int'l J.Pol.	International Journal of Politics
Int. J. Soc. L.	International Journal of the Sociology of Law	Int'l J.Soc.L.	International Journal of the Sociology of the Law
Int. Rel.	International Relations	Int'l Jurid. Ass'n Bull.	International Juridical Association Monthly Bulletin
Int.Rev.Bull.	Internal Revenue Bulletin		
Int.Rev.Code	Internal Revenue Code	Int'l J.World Peace	International Journal on World Peace
Int.Rev.Code of 1954	Internal Revenue Code of 1954	Int'l Lab.Rev.	International Labour Review
Int.Rev.Rec.	Internal Revenue Record	Int'l L. & Trade Persp.	International Law & Trade Perspective
Intell.Prop. L.Rev.	Intellectual Property Law Review		
Inter–Am. L.Rev.	Inter–American Law Review	Int'l Law.	International Lawyer
Interior Dec.	United States Interior Department Decisions	Int'l L.Doc.	International Law Documents
		Int'l Legal Ed.Newsl.	International Legal Education Newsletter
Int'l Aff.	International Affairs		
Int'l & Comp. L.Bull.	International and Comparative Law Bulletin	Int'l Legal Materials	International Legal Materials

Int'l L.News	International Law News
Int'l L.Persp.	International Law Perspective
Int'l L.Q.	International Law Quarterly
Int'l L.Stud.	International Law Studies
Int'l Prop. Inv.J.	International Property Investment Journal
Int'l Rev.Ad. Sci.	International Review of Administrative Sciences
Int'l Rev. Crim.Policy	International Review of Criminal Policy
Int'l Rev.L. & Econ.	International Review of Law and Economics
Int'l Soc'y of Barr.Q.	International Society of Barristers Quarterly
Int'l Surv.L. D.L.L.	International Survey of Legal Decisions on Labour Laws
Int'l Sym. Comp.L.	International Symposium on Comparative Law
Int'l Tax & Bus.Law.	International Tax & Business Lawyer
Int'l Tax J.	International Tax Journal
Int'l Trade L.J.	International Trade Law Journal
Int'l Woman Law.	International Woman Lawyer
Intramural L.J.	Intramural Law Journal
Intramural L.Rev.	Intramural Law Review
I.O.C.C.Bull.	Interstate Oil Compact Commission Bulletin
iowa	Iowa Reports
Iowa	Same
Iowa L.B.	Iowa Law Bulletin
Iowa L.Rev.	Iowa Law Review
I.P.D.	Intellectual Property Decisions
Ir.	Law Reports (Ir.)
IR	Irish Reports
I.R.	Internal Revenue Decisions

irb	Internal Revenue Bulletin
I.R.B.	Same
I.R.C.	Internal Revenue Code
Ir.Ch.	Irish Chancery
Ir.Cir.	Irish Circuit Reports
Ir.C.L.	Irish Common Law
Ir.Eccl.	Irish Ecclesiastical Reports
Ired.	Iredell's Law (NC)
Ired.Eq.	Iredell's Equity (NC)
Ir.Eq.	Irish Equity
Ir.Jur.	Irish Jurist
Ir. Jur. Rep.	Irish Jurist Reports
Ir.L. & Eq.	Irish Law & Equity
I.R.L.I.B.	Industrial Relations Legal Information Bulletin
IRLR	Industrial Relations Law Reports
Ir.L.T.R.	Irish Law Times Reports
Ir.R.	Irish Reports
Ir.R.C.L.	Irish Reports Common Law
Ir.R.Eq.	Irish Reports Equity
I.R.R.Newsl.	Individual Rights and Responsibilities Newsletter
Ir.Soc'y for Lab.L.J.	Irish Society for Labor Law Journal
Irv.Just.	Irvine's Justiciary (Scot.)
ISL L.Rev.	International School of Law Law Review
Israel L.Rev.	Israel Law Review
Israel Y.B. Human Rights	Israel Yearbook on Human Rights
Issues Crim.	Issues in Criminology
I.T.R.	Ridgeway, Lapp & Schoaler, Term Reports (Ir.) Industrial Tribunal Reports
itrd	International Trade Reporter Decisions (BNA)
Iustitia	Iustitia

J

Jac.	Jacob's Chancery (Eng.)
Jac. & W.	Jacob & Walker's Chancery (Eng.)
Jac. & Walk.	Same
J.Accountancy	Journal of Accountancy
Jack.	Jackson (GA)
Jack. & L.	Jackson & Lumpkin (GA)

Jack.Tex. App.	Jackson's Texas Appeals
Jac.L.Dict.	Jacob's Law Dictionary
J.Afr.L.	Journal of African Law
JAG Bull.	Judge Advocate General Bulletin, United States Air Force

JAG J.	Judge Advocate General Journal
JAG L.Rev.	Judge Advocate General Law Review, United States Air Force
J.Agric.Tax. & L.	Journal of Agricultural Taxation and the Law
J.Agr.Tax'n & L.	Same
J.Air L. & Com.	Journal of Air Law and Commerce
J.A.L.	Journal of African Law
JAMA	Journal of the American Medical Association
J.Am.Acad. Matrim. Law.	Journal of American Academy of Matrimonial Lawyers
James	James' Reports (Nova Scotia)
James. & Mont.	Jameson & Montagu's Bankruptcy (Eng.)
J.Am.Jud. Soc'y	Journal of the American Judicature Society
J.Am.Soc'y C.L.U.	Journal of the American Society of Chartered Life Underwriters
J. & C.	Jones & Cary's Exchequer (Ir.)
J. & H.	Johnson & Hemming's Chancery (Eng.)
J. & L.	Jones & La Touche's Chancery (Ir.)
J. & La. T.	Same
J. & S.	Jones & Spencer's Superior Court (NY)
J. & W.	Jacob & Walker's Chancery (Eng.)
Japan Ann.L. & Pol.	Japan Annual of Law and Politics
Jap.Ann.Int'l L.	Japanese Annual of International Law
J.Art & Ent.L.	Journal of Art and Entertainment Law
J.Arts Mgmt.L. Soc'y	Journal of Arts Management, Law and Society
J.Ass'n L.Teachers	Journal of the Association of Law Teachers
J.B.Ass'n D.C.	Journal of the Bar Association of the District of Columbia
J.B.Ass'n St.Kan.	Journal of the Bar Association of the State of Kansas
J.Beverly Hills B.Ass'n	Journal of the Beverly Hills Bar Association
J.B.L.	Journal of Business Law
J.B.Moore	J.B. Moore's Common Pleas (Eng.)
J.Bridg.	Sir John Bridgman's Common Pleas (Eng.)
J.Bridgm.	Same
J.Bus.L.	Journal of Business Law
J.C.	Johnson's Cases (NY)
J.Can.B. Ass'n	Journal of the Canadian Bar Association
J.C. & U.L.	Journal of College & University Law
J.Ceylon L.	Journal of Ceylon Law
JCh	Johnson's Chancery Reports (NY)
J.Ch.	Same
J. Chinese L.	Journal of Chinese Law
J.Church & St.	Journal of Church and State
J.C.L.	Journal of Criminal Law
J.C.L. & Crim.	Journal of Criminal Law and Criminology
J.C.M.S.	Journal of Common Market Studies
J.C.N.P.S.	Journal of Collective Negotiations in the Public Sector
J.Coll. & U.L.	Journal of College and University Law
J.Comm.Mt. Stud.	Journal of Common Market Studies
J.Comp.Leg. & Int'l L.3d	Journal of Comparative Legislation and International Law, Third Series
J.Confl.Res.	Journal of Conflict Resolution
J.Cons.Affairs	Journal of Consumer Affairs
J.Const. & Parl.Stud.	Journal of Constitutional and Parliamentary Studies
J.Contemp. Health L. & Pol'y	Journal of Contemporary Health Law and Policy

J.Contemp.L.	Journal of Contemporary Law
J.Contemp. Legal Issues	Journal of Contemporary Legal Issues
J.Contemp. R.D.L.	Journal of Contemporary Roman–Dutch Law
J.Copyright Entertainment Sports L.	Journal of Copyright Entertainment and Sports Law
J.Corp.L.	Journal of Corporation Law
J.Corp.Tax'n	Journal of Corporate Taxation
J.C.R.	Johnson's Chancery (NY)
J.Crim.Just.	Journal of Criminal Justice
J.Crim.L. (Eng.)	Journal of Criminal Law (Eng.)
J.Crim.L. & Criminology	Journal of Criminal Law and Criminology
J.Crim.L., C. & P.S.	Journal of Criminal Law, Criminology and Police Science
J.Crim.Sci.	Journal of Criminal Science
JCs	Johnson's Cases (NY)
J.D.	Juris Doctor
J.Denning L.Soc'y	Journal of the Denning Law Society
J. Disp.Resol.	Journal of Dispute Resolution
Jebb	Jebb's Crown Cases (Ir.)
Jebb & B.	Jebb & Bourke's Queen's Bench (Ir.)
Jebb & S.	Jebb & Symes' Queen's Bench (Ir.)
Jebb & Sym.	Same
Jebb C.C.	Jebb's Crown Cases (Ir.)
jeff	Jefferson's Reports (VA)
Jeff.	Same
J.Energy & Devel.	Journal of Energy and Development
J.Energy L. & Pol'y	Journal of Energy Law & Policy
Jenk.	Jenkins' Exchequer (Eng.)
Jenk.Cent.	Same
Jenks	Jenks (NH)
Jenn.	Jennison (MI)
J.Env. L.	Journal of Environmental Law

J.Envtl.L. & Litig.	Journal of Environment Law and Litigation
J.E.R.L.	Journal of Energy and Natural Resources Law
J.Eth.L.	Journal of Ethiopian Law
Jew.Y.B.Int'l L.	Jewish Yearbook of International Law
J.Fam.L.	Journal of Family Law
JFK U L Record	John F. Kennedy University Law Record
J.For.Med.	Journal of Forensic Medicine
J.For.Med. Soc'y	Journal of the Forensic Medicine Society
J.For.Sci.	Journal of the Forensic Sciences
J.For.Sci. Soc'y	Journal of the Forensic Science Society
J.Health Pol. Pol'y & L.	Journal of Health, Politics, Policy & Law
JIBFL	Journal of International Banking and Financial Law
J.I.B.L.	Journal of International Banking Law
J.I.F.D.L.	Journal of International Franchising and Distribution Law
J.Ind.L.Inst.	Journal of the Indian Law Institute
J.Int'l Aff.	Journal of International Affairs
J.Int'l Arb.	Journal of International Arbitration
J.Int'l Comm.Jur.	Journal of the International Commission of Jurists
J.Int'l L. & Dipl.	Journal of International Law and Diplomacy
J.Int'l L. & Econ.	Journal of International Law and Economics
J.Int'l L. & Pol.	Journal of International Law and Politics
J.Int'l L. & Prac.	Journal of International Law and Practice
J.Ir.Soc. Lab.L.	Journal of the Irish Society for Labour Law

J.Islam. & Comp.L.	Journal of Islamic and Comparative Law
J.J.	Jersey Judgements
J.J.Mar.	J.J. Marshall (KY)
J.J.Marsh. (KY)	Same
J.Juris.	Journal of Jurisprudence
J.Juv.L.	Journal of Juvenile Law
J Juvenile L	Same
J.Kan.B. Ass'n	Journal of the Kansas Bar Association
J.L.	Journal of Law
J.Land & P.U.Econ.	Journal of Land and Public Utility Economics
J.L. & Com.	Journal of Law and Commerce
J.L. & Econ.	Journal of Law & Economics
J.L. & Educ.	Journal of Law and Education
J.L. & Pol.	Journal of Law and Politics
J.L. & Religion	Journal of Law and Religion
J.L. & Tech.	Journal of Law and Technology
J.Land Use & Envtl.L.	Journal of Land Use & Environmental Law
J.Law & Econ.	Journal of Law and Economics
J.Law & Econ.Dev.	Journal of Law and Economic Development
J.Law & Health	Journal of Law and Health
J.Law & Soc.	Journal of Law and Society
J.Law, Econ. & Org.	Journal of Law, Economics and Organization
J.Law Reform	Journal of Law Reform
J.Legal Educ.	Journal of Legal Education
J.Legal Hist.	Journal of Legal History
J.Legal Med.	Journal of Legal Medicine
J.Legal Prof.	Journal of the Legal Profession
J.Legal Stud.	Journal of Legal Studies
J.Leg. Hist.	Journal of Legal History
J.Legis.	Journal of Legislation
J.L.H.	Journal of Legal History
J.L.Soc'y	Journal of the Law Society of Scotland
J.L.S.S.	Same

J.Mar.J.Prac. & Proc.	John Marshall Journal of Practice and Procedure
J.Mar.L. & Com.	Journal of Maritime Law and Commerce
J.Mar.L.J.	John Marshall Law Journal
J.Mar.L.Q.	John Marshall Law Quarterly
J.Marshall L.Rev.	John Marshall Law Review
J.Min.L. & Pol'y	Journal of Mineral Law and Policy
J.M.L. & P.	Journal of Media Law and Practice
J.M.L.C.	Journal of Maritime Law and Commerce
J Mo Bar	Journal of the Missouri Bar
J.N.A.A.L.J.	Journal of the National Association of Administrative Law Judges at Pepperdine University
Jo. & La T.	Jones & La Touche's Chancery (Ir.)
John.	Johnson's Reports (NY) Johnson's Vice–Chancery (Eng.)
John Mar.J. Prac. & Proc.	John Marshall Journal of Practice and Procedure
John Marsh. L.J.	John Marshall Law Journal
John Marsh. L.Q.	John Marshall Law Quarterly
Johns.	Johnson (NY) Johnson's Vice–Chancery (Eng.)
Johns. & H.	Johnson & Hemming's Chancery (Eng.)
Johns. & Hem.	Same
Johns.Cas.	Johnson's Cases (NY)
Johns.Ch.	Johnson's Chancery (MD) Johnson's Chancery (NY)
Johns.Ct.Err.	Johnson's Court of Errors (NY)
Johns.Dec.	Johnson's Chancery Decisions (MD)
Johns.N.Z.	Johnson's New Zealand Reports
Johns.U.S.	Johnson's United States Circuit Court Decisions
Jon. & L.	Jones & La Touche's Chancery (Ir.)
Jon. & La T.	Same

Jones	Jones (AL)	J.Real Est. Tax.	Journal of Real Estate Taxation
	Jones (MO)	J.Reprints	Journal of Reprints
	Jones (PA)	Antitrust L. &	for Antitrust Law
	Jones, T., King's	Econ.	and Economics
	Bench (Eng.)	JS	Jones and Spencer's
	Jones, W., King's		Superior Court
	Bench (Eng.)		Reports (NY)
	Jones' Exchequer	J.S.Gr. (N.J.)	J.S. Green (NJ)
	(Ir.)	J.Soc.Welfare L.	Journal of Social
	Jones' Law or Equity		Welfare Law
	Jones' Reports	J.Soc'y	Journal of the
	(Upper Can.)	Comp.Leg.	Society of
Jones & C.	Jones & Cary's		Comparative
	Exchequer (Ir.)		Legislation
Jones & L.	Jones & La Touche's	J.Soc'y Pub.	Journal of the
	Chancery (Ir.)	Tchrs.L.	Society of Public
Jones & La T.	Same		Teachers of Law
Jones & McM.	Jones & McMurtrie	J.Space L.	Journal of Space
(PA)	(PA)		Law
Jones & S.	Jones & Spencer's	J.St.Tax'n	Journal of State
	Superior Court		Taxation
	(NY)	JSWFL	Journal of Social
JP	Justice of the Peace		Welfare and
	Reports		Family Law
J.P.	Justice of the Peace	J.Tax'n	Journal of Taxation
	(Eng.)	J.Transnat'l L. &	Journal of
J.Pat. &	Journal of the Patent	Pol'y	Transnational
Trademark	and Trademark		Law and Policy
Off.Soc.	Office Society	Jud.Conduct	Judicial Conduct
J.Pat.Off. Soc'y	Journal of the Patent	Rep.	Reporter
	Office Society	Judd	Judd (HI)
J.Pension Plan.	Journal of Pension	Judge Advoc.J.	Judge Advocate
& Compliance	Planning &		Journal
	Compliance	Judges' J.	Judges' Journal
JP Jo	Justice of the Peace	Judge's J.	Judge's Journal
	Journal	Judicature	Journal of the
J.P.L.	Journal of Planning		American
	and		Judicature Society
	Environmental		Judicature
	Law	Jud Nom Rules	Rules and
J.Plan. & Env.L.	Journal of Planning		Procedures of
	and Environment		Commission on
	Law		Judicial Nominees
J.P.N.	Justice of the Peace		Evaluation (CA
	Journal		State Bar)
J.Pol.Sci. &	Journal of Police	Jur.	Jurist (Eng.)
Admin.	Science and	Jurid.Rev.	Juridical Review
	Administration	Jurimetrics J.	Jurimetrics Journal
J.Prod. & Toxics	Journal of Products	Juris.	Jurisprudence
Liab.	and Toxics	Jurist	Jurist (DC)
	Liability	Jur. (N.S.)	Same, New Series
J.Prod.Liab.	Journal of Products	Just.Cas.	Justiciary Cases
	Liability	Just.L.R.	Justice's Law
J.P.Sm.	J.P. Smith's King's		Reporter (PA)
	Bench (Eng.)	Just.P.	Justice of the Peace
J.Psych. & L.	Journal of Psychiatry		and Local
	and Law		Government
J.Publ.L.	Journal of Public		Review
	Law	Just.Syst.J.	Justice System
J.Quantitative	Journal of		Journal
Criminology	Quantitative	Juv. &	Juvenile and Family
	Criminology	Fam.Courts J.	Courts Journal
J.R.	Johnson (NY)	Juv.Ct.J.	Juvenile Court
J.R.	Judicial Review		Journal
J.Radio L.	Journal of Radio Law		

Juv.Ct.Judges J.	Juvenile Court Judges Journal	J.World Trade L.	Journal of World Trade Law
Juv.Just.	Juvenile Justice	J.W.T.	Journal of Word Trade

K

KA2d	Kansas Court of Appeals Reports, Second Series	Keb.	Keble's King's Bench (Eng.)
Kames Dec.	Kames' Decisions (Scot.)	Keen	Keen's Rolls Court (Eng.)
Kames Elucid.	Kames' Elucidation (Scot.)	Keil.	Keilway's King's Bench (Eng.)
Kames Rem.Dec.	Kames' Remarkable Decisions (Scot.)	Kel.C.C.	Kelyng's Crown Cases (Eng.)
Kames Sel.Dec.	Kames' Select Decisions (Scot.)	Kellen	Kellen (MA)
		Kelly	Kelly (GA)
kan	Kansas Reports	Kelly & C.	Kelly & Cobb (GA)
Kan.	Same	Kel.W.	Kelyng's Chancery (Eng.)
KanA	Kansas Court of Appeals Reports	Kenan	Kenan (NC)
kanapp	Kansas Appeals Reports	Keny.	Kenyon (Lord) King's Bench (Eng.)
Kan.App.	Same		Kenyon's Notes of King's Bench Reports (Eng.)
kanapp2d	Same, Second Series		
Kan.B.Ass'n J.	Kansas Bar Association Journal	Kenya L.R.	Kenya Law Reports
Kan.City L.Rev.	Kansas City Law Review	Keny.Ch.	Kenyon's Chancery (Eng.)
Kan.C.L.Rep.	Kansas City Law Reporter	Kerala L.J.	Kerala Law Journal
K.& G.	Keane & Grant's Registration Appeal Cas	Kern	Kern (MD)
		Kern.	Kernan (NY)
		Kerr	Kerr (IN)
K.& Gr.	Same		Kerr (N.B.)
K.& G.R.C.	Same		Kerr's Civil Procedure (NY)
Kan.J.L. & Pub. Pol'y	Kansas Journal of Law and Public Policy	Key	Keyes' Reports (NY)
Kan.L.J.	Kansas Law Journal	Keyes	Same
Kan.L.Rev.	University of Kansas Law Review	Kilk.	Kilkerran's Decisions (Scot.)
Kan.St.L.J.	Kansas State Law Journal	Kilkerran	Same
Karachi L.J.	Karachi Law Journal (Pak.)	King	King's Civil Practice Cases (CO)
			King's Louisiana Annual
Kay	Kay's Vice–Chancery (Eng.)	Kingston L.R.	Kingston Law Review
Kay & J.	Kay & Johnson's Chancery (Eng.)	Kingston L.Rev.	Same
K.B.	Law Reports King's Bench (Eng.)	K.I.R.	Knight's Industrial Reports
K.C.L.J.	Kings College Law Journal	kirby	Kirby's Reports and Supplement (CT)
K.Counsel	King's Counsel	Kirby	Same
Ke.	Keen's Rolls Court (Eng.)	K.L.R.	Kenya Law Reports
Keane & Gr.	Keane & Grant's Registration Appeal Cases (Eng.)	Knapp	Knapp & Ombler's Election Cases (Eng.)
		Knapp & O.	Same
		Knight's Ind.	Knight's Industrial Reports
Keane & G.R.C.	Same	Knowles	Knowles (RI)
		Knox	Knox (N.S.W.)

Knox & F.	Knox & Fitzhardinge (N.S.W.)
Kn.P.C.	Knapp's Privy Council (Eng.)
Kobe U.L.Rev.	Kobe University Law Review
Korea L.Rev.	Korea Law Review
Korean J.Comp.L.	Korean Journal of Comparative Law
Korean J.Int'l L.	Korean Journal of International Law
Korean L.	Korean Law
Kreider	Kreider (WA)
Kress	Kress (PA)
Kulp	Kulp (PA)
Kwansei Gak.L.Rev.	Kwansei Gaknin Law Review

ky	Kentucky Reports
Ky.	Same
Ky.Bench & B.	Kentucky Bench and Bar
Ky.Comment'r	Kentucky Commentator
Ky.Dec.	Kentucky Decisions
Ky.L.J.	Kentucky Law Journal
kylr	Kentucky Law Reporter
Ky.L.R.	Same
Ky.L.Rptr.	Same
Ky.Op.	Kentucky Opinions
kyops	Kentucky Court of Appeals Opinions
Kyoto L.Rev.	Kyoto Law Review
Ky.St.B.J.	Kentucky State Bar Journal

L

la	Louisiana Reports
La.	Same
LA	Legal Action
laann	Louisiana Annual Reports
La.Ann.	Same
laapp	Louisiana Court of Appeals Reports
La.App.	Same
La.App. (Orleans)	Court of Appeal, Parish of Orleans
Lab.	Labatt's District Court (CA)
Lab. & Auto.Bull.	Labor and Automation Bulletin
Lab.Arb.	Labor Arbitration Reports (BNA)
LA Bar B	Los Angeles Bar Bulletin
Lab C	Labor Code
La.B.J.	Louisiana Bar Journal
L.A.B.J.	Los Angeles Bar Journal
Lab.Law.	Labor Lawyer
Lab.L.J.	Labor Law Journal
Labor C.	Labor Code
Lab.Rel.L.Letter	Labor Relations Law Letter
Lab.Rel.Rep.	Labor Relations Reporter
L.A.C.	Labour Arbitration Cases
Lackawanna B.	Lackawanna Bar (PA)
Lack.Jur.	Lackawanna Jurist (PA)
Lack.Leg.N.	Lackawanna Legal News (PA)
Lack.Leg.Rec.	Lackawanna Legal Record (PA)
Ladd	Ladd (NH)
L.Advertiser	Law Advertiser
L.A.G.Bull.	Legal Act Group Bulletin
L.A.J.P.E.L.	Latin American Journal of Politics, Economics and Law

LA Law	Los Angeles Lawyer
L.A. Lawyer	Same
La.L.J.	Louisiana Law Journal
Lalor	Lalor's Supplement to Hill & Denio (NY)
La.L.Rev.	Louisiana Law Review
Lamar	Lamar (FL)
Lamb	Lamb (WI)
L.Am.Soc'y	Law in American Society
Lan	Lansing's Supreme Court's Reports
LAn	Louisiana Annual Reports
Lanc.Bar	Lancaster Bar (PA)
Lanc.L.Rev.	Lancaster Law Review (PA)
Land & Water L.Rev.	Land and Water Law Review
L. & B.Bull.	Weekly Law and Bank Bulletin (OH)
L. & C.	Lefroy and Cassels' Practice Cases (Ont.) Leigh & Cave's Crown Cases Reserved (Eng.)
L. & Computer Tech.	Law and Computer Technology
Land Dec.	Land Decisions (U.S.)
L. & E.	English Law & Equity Reports (Boston)
L. & E.Rep.	Law & Equity Reporter (NY)
L. & Just.	Law and Justice
L. & Leg. GDR	Law and Legislation in the German Democratic Republic
L. & Lib.	Law and Liberty
L. & M.	Lowndes & Maxwell, Bail Cases (Eng.)
L. & Order	Law and Order
L. & Psych.Rev.	Law and Psychology Review

L. & Soc.Inquiry: J. Am. B. Found.	Law and Social Inquiry: Journal of the American Bar Foundation
Land Use & Env.L.Rev.	Land Use and Environment Law Review
Lane	Lane's Exchequer (Eng.)
Lans.	Lansing (MI)
LAp	Louisiana Courts of Appeal Reports
La Raza L.J.	La Raza Law Journal
Larson	Larson, Workmen's Compensation Practice
Latch	Latch's King's Bench (Eng.)
Lath.	Lathrop (MA)
La.T.R.	Martin's Louisiana Term Reports
Law.	Lawyer
Law.Am.	Lawyer of the Americas
Law & Bk.Bull.	Weekly Law and Bank Bulletin (OH)
Law & Computer Tech.	Law and Computer Technology
Law & Contemp.Probs	Law and Contemporary Problems
Law & Housing J.	Law and Housing Journal
Law & Hum. Behav.	Law and Human Behavior
Law & Just.	Law and Justice
Law. & Magis.Mag.	Lawyer's and Magistrate's Magazine
Law & Phil.	Law & Philosophy
Law & Pol.	Law and Policy
Law & Pol'y Int'l Bus.	Law and Policy in International Business
Law & Pol'y Q.	Law and Policy Quarterly
Law & Psych. Rev.	Law and Psychology Review
Law & Soc. Ord.	Law and the Social Order (Arizona State Law Journal)
Law & Soc'y Rev.	Law and Society Review
Lawasia	Lawasia, Journal of the Law Association for Asia and the Western Pacific
Law Cases	Law Cases, William I to Richard I (Eng.) (Placita Anglo–Normannica)
Law.Committee News	Lawyers Committee News
Law Corp Rules	Law Corporation Rules of State Bar
Law Inst.J.	Law Institute Journal
Law Lib.	Law Librarian

Law Libr.J.	Law Library Journal
Law.Med.J.	Lawyer's Medical Journal
Law Notes	Law Notes
Law Q.Rev.	Law Quarterly Review
Lawr.	Lawrence (OH)
Lawrence	Same
Law Rep.	Law Reporter (MA)
	Law Reports (Eng.)
Law Rep. (N.S.)	Law Reports, New Series (NY)
Law Rev. Com	Law Revision Commission
Law Rev.J.	Law Review Journal
Law Soc'y Gaz.	Law Society Gazette (Toronto)
	Law Society's Gazette (London)
Law Soc'y J.	Law Society Journal (Boston)
	Law Society Journal (N.S.W.)
Lawyer & Banker	Lawyer and Banker and Central Law Journal
Lawyer's Med.J.	Lawyer's Medical Journal
L.Book Adviser	Law Book Adviser
L.C.	Lower Canada
	Lord Chancellor
L.C. News	Law Centres News
LCA	New York Leading Cases Annotated
L.C.D.	Ohio Lower Court Decisions
LCh	Lansing's Chancery Reports
L.Chron.	Law Chronicle
L.Chron. & L.Stud.Mag	Law Chronicle and Law Students' Magazine
L.Chron. & L.Stud.Mag ., (N.S.)	Same, New Series
L.C.Jur.	Lower Canada Jurist
L.C.L.J.	Lower Canada Law Journal
L.Coach	Law Coach
L.Comment'y	Law Commentary
LCP	Law and Contemporary Problems
L.C.R.	Land Compensation Reports
L.C.Rep. S.Qu.	Lower Canada Reports Seignorial Questions
LD	Decisions of the Department of the Interior (Public Land Decisions)
L.D.	Land Office Decisions (U.S.)
L.D.L.R.	Land Development Law Reporter
Ld.Raym.	Lord Raymond's King's Bench (Eng.)

LE	United States Supreme Court Reports, Lawyers' Edition
LE2d	Same, Second Series
Lea	Lea (TN)
Leach C.C.	Leach's Crown Cases, King's Bench (Eng.)
League of Nations Off.J.	League of Nations Official Journal
Learn. & L.	Learning and the Law
L.East.Eur.	Law in Eastern Europe
leatn	Lea's Tennessee Reports
Lect.L.S.U.C.	Special Lectures of the Law Society of Upper Canada
led	Lawyers' Edition, United States Supreme Court Reports
L.Ed.	Same
led2d	Same, Second Series
L.Ed.2d	Same
Lee	Lee (CA)
Lee Eccl.	Lee's Ecclesiastical (Eng.)
Leese	Leese (NE)
Lee t.Hardw.	Lee tempore Hardwicke, King's Bench (Eng.)
Legal Aspects Med.Prac.	Legal Aspects of Medical Practice
Legal Med.Ann.	Legal Medicine Annual
Legal Med.Q.	Legal Medical Quarterly
Legal Obser.	Legal Observer
Legal Res.J.	Legal Research Journal
Legal Resp.Child Adv. Protection	Legal Response: Child Advocacy and Protection
Legal Stud.Forum	Legal Studies Forum
Legal Video Rev.	Legal Video Review
Leg. & Ins.R.	Legal & Insurance Reporter (PA)
Leg.Chron.	Legal Chronicle (PA)
Leg.Gaz.	Legal Gazette Reports (PA)
Leg.Int.	Legal Intelligencer (PA)
Leg.Op.	Legal Opinions (PA)
Leg.Rec.	Legal Record (PA)
Leg.Rep.	Legal Reporter (TN)
Leg.Rev.	Legal Review (Eng.)
Lehigh Co. L.J.	Lehigh County Law Journal (PA)
Lehigh Val. L.R.	Lehigh Valley Law Reporter (PA)
Leigh	Leigh (PA)
Leigh & C.	Leigh & Cave's Crown Cases (Eng.)
Leigh & C.C.C.	Same
Leo.	Leonard, King's Bench, Common Pleas, Exchequer (Eng.)
Leon.	Same

Lester	Lester (GA)
Lester & B.	Lester & Butler's Supplement (GA)
Lev.	Leving, King's Bench, Common Pleas (Eng.)
Lew.C.C.	Lewin's Crown Cases (Eng.)
Lewis	Lewis (MO)
	Lewis (NV)
	Lewis' Kentucky Law Reporter
Lex & Sci.	Lex et Scientia
L. Exec.	Legal Executive
Ley	Ley, King's Bench (Eng.)
	Common Pleas (Eng.)
	Exchequer (Eng.)
	Court of Wards (Eng.)
	Court of Star Chamber (Eng.)
LF	University of Illinois Law Forum
L.G.	Law Glossary
L.Gaz.	Law Gazette
LGR	Local Government Reports
LG Rev	Local Government Review
L.Guard.	Law Guardian
Liberian L.J.	Liberian Law Journal
L.I.E.I.	Legal Issues of European Integration
Life Cas.	Life, Health & Accident Cases (CCH)
Life Cas.2d	Same, Second Series
Lincoln LR	Lincoln Law Review
Lincoln L.Rev.	Same
L. in Soc'y	Law in Society
L.Inst.J.	Law Institute Journal
L.Inst.J.Vict.	Law Institute Journal of Victoria
L. in Trans.Q.	Law in Transition Quarterly
Liquor Liab.J.	Liquor Liability Journal
Lit.	Litigation
Litig.	Same
Livingston's M.L.Mag.	Livingston's Monthly Law Magazine
L.J.	Law Journal
L.J.Adm.	Law Journal, Admiralty (Eng.)
L.Japan	Law in Japan
L.J.Bankr.	Law Journal, Bankruptcy (Eng.)
L.J.Ch.	Law Journal, Chancery, New Series (Eng.)
L.J.Ch.(O.S.)	Same, Old Series
L.J.C.P.	Law Journal, Common Pleas (Eng.)
L.J.C.P. (O.S.)	Same, Old Series
L.J.Eccl.	Law Journal, Ecclesiastical (Eng.)
L.J.Exch.	Law Journal, Exchequer, New Series (Eng.)
L.J.Exch. (O.S.)	Same, Old Series

L.J.H.L.	Law Journal House of Lords, New Series (Eng.)
L.J.K.B.	Law Journal, King's Bench, New Series (Eng.)
L.J.Mag.	Law Journal, New Series Common Law, Magistrates Cases
L.J.M.C.	Law Journal, Magistrate Cases, New Series (Eng.)
L.J.M.C. (O.S.)	Same, Old Series (Eng.)
L.J.N.C.	Law Journal, Notes of Cases (Eng.)
L.J.O.S.	Law Journal, Old Series
L.J.P. & M.	Law Journal, Probate & Matrimonial (Eng.)
L.J.P.C.	Law Journal, Privy Council (Eng.)
L.J.P.C. (N.S.)	Same, New Series
L.J.P.D. & Adm.	Law Journal, Probate, Divorce & Admiralty (Eng.)
L.J.Q.B.	Law Journal, Queen's Bench, New Series (Eng.)
L.J.R.	Law Journal Reports
Ll. & G.t.Pl.	Lloyd & Goold tempore Plunkett, Chancery (Ir.)
Ll. & G.t.S.	Lloyd & Goold tempore Sugden, Chancery (Ir.)
Ll. & W.	Lloyd & Welsby Mercantile Cases (Eng.)
L.Lib.	Law Librarian
L.Libr.J.	Law Library Journal
L.L.J.	Same
Ll.L.Rep.	Lloyd's List Reports (Eng.)
Lloyd's L.Rep.	Lloyd's Law Reports
Lloyds Mar. & Com.L.Q.	Lloyds Maritime and Commercial Law Quarterly
Lloyd's Rep.	Lloyd's List Law Reports Admiralty
llrm	Labor Relations Reference Manual (BNA)
L.Mag. & Rev.	Law Magazine and Review
L.M. & P.	Lowndes, Maxwell & Pollock's Bail Cases (Eng.)
L.M.C.L.Q.	Lloyd's Maritime and Commercial Law Quarterly
L.M.E.L.R.	Land Management and Environmental Law Report
L.Notes Gen. Pract.	Law Notes for the General Practitioner

Lns	Lawyers Reports Annotated, New Series
L.N.T.S.	League of Nations Treaty Series
Local Ct. & Mun.Gaz.	Local Courts and Municipal Gazette
Local Gov't	Local Government and Magisterial Reports
Local Gov't R.Austl.	Local Government Reports of Australia
Lock.Rev.Cas.	Lockwood's Reversed Cases (NY)
L.Off.Econ. & Mgt.	Law Office Economics and Management
Lofft	Lofft's King's Bench (Eng.)
Lois Rec.	Lois Recentes du Canada
London L.Rev.	City of London Law Review
Long & R.	Long & Russell's Election Cases (MA)
Long Beach Bar B	Long Beach Bar Bulletin
Long Beach B.Bull.	Same
Longf. & T.	Longfield & Townsend's Exchequer (Ir.)
Los Angeles Bar J.	Los Angels Bar Journal
Louisville Law.	Louisville Lawyer
low	Lowell's U.S. District Court Reports
Low.Can. Jurist	Lower Canada Jurist
Low.Can.L.J.	Lower Canada Law Journal
Low.Can.R.	Lower Canadian Reports
Lowell	Lowell (U.S.)
Lower Ct.Dec.	Lower Court Decisions (OH)
Loy.Cons. Prot.J.	Loyola of Los Angeles Consumer Protection Journal
Loy. Consumer L. Rep.	Loyola of Los Angeles Consumer Law Reporter
Loy.Dig.	Loyola Digest
Loy. Ent.L. J.	Loyola of Los Angeles Entertainment Law Journal
Loy.L.A.Int'l & Comp.L.Ann.	Loyola of Los Angeles International & Comparative Law Annual
Loy.L.A. Int'l & Comp.L.J.	Loyola of Los Angeles International and Comparative Law Journal
Loy.L.A.L. Rev.	Loyola of Los Angeles Law Review
Loy.Law.	Loyola Lawyer
Loy.L.Rev.	Loyola Law Review (New Orleans)

Loyola Consumer Protection J	Loyola Consumer Protection Journal
Loyola L. Rev.	Loyola University of Los Angels Law Review
Loyola U of LA LR	Loyola University of Los Angeles Law Review
Loy.U.Chi. L.J.	Loyola University of Chicago Law Journal
Loy.U.L.J.	Same
L.Q.	Law Quarterly
LQR	Law Quarterly Review
L.Q.Rev.	Same
L.R.	Law Recorder (Ir.)
	Law Reports (Eng.)
	Ohio Law Reporter
L.R. (N.S.)	Irish Law Recorder, New Series
L.R.A.	Lawyers' Reports Annotated (U.S.)
L.R.A. & E.	Law Reports, Admiralty & Ecclesiastical (Eng.)
L.R.A. (N.S.)	Lawyers' Reports Annotated, New Series (U.S.)
L.R.App.Cas.	Law Reports, House of Lords Appeal Cases (Eng.)
L.R.C.C.	Law Reports, Crown Cases (Eng.)
L.R.C.C.R.	Law Reports, Crown Cases Reserved (Eng.)
L.R.Ch.	Law Reports, Chancery Appeal Cases (Eng.)
L.R.Ch.D.	Law Reports, Chancery Division (Eng.)
L.R.C.P.	Law Reports, Common Pleas Cases (Eng.)
L.R.C.P.D.	Law Reports, Common Pleas Division (Eng.)
L.Record.	Law Recorder
L.R.Eq.	Law Reports, Equity Cases (Eng.)
L.Rev.Dig.	Law Review Digest
L.R.Exch.	Law Reports, Exchequer Cases (Eng.)
L.R.Exch.D.	Law Reports, Exchequer Division (Eng.)
L.R.H.L.	Law Reports, House of Lords (English & Irish Appeal Cases)
L.R.H.L.Sc.	Law Reports, House of Lords (Scotch Appeal Cases)
L.R.Indian App.	Law Reports, Indian Appeals (Eng.)
L.R.Ir.	Law Reports (Ir.)
L.R.N.S.W.	Law Reports, New South Wales
L.R.P. & D.	Law Reports, Probate & Divorce (Eng.)
L.R.P.C.	Law Reports, Privy Council (Eng.)
L.R.Q.B.	Law Reports, Queen's Bench (Eng.)
L.R.Q.B.Div.	Law Reports, Queen's Bench Division (Eng.)
L.R.R.	Labor Relations Reporter
L.R.R.M.	Labor Relations Reference Manual (BNA)
L.R.R.P.	Reports of Restrictive Practices Cases
L.R.S.A.	Law Reports, South Australia
L.S.	Legal Studies
L.S.G.	Law Society Gazette (Eng.)
L.S. Gaz.	Same
LS Gaz Rep	Law Society Gazette Reports
L.Stud.Helper	Law Student's Helper
L.Stud.J.	Law Students' Journal
L.T.	Law Times (PA)
L.T. (N.S.)	Law Times, New Series (Eng.)
L.T. (O.S.)	Same, Old Series (Eng.)
L.T.G.F. Newsl.	Lawyers' Title Guaranty Funds Newsletter
L.T.R. (N.S.)	Law Times, Reports, New Series (Eng.)
L.T.Rep.N.S.	Same
L. Teach.	Law Teacher
L.Teacher	Same
L.Trans.Q.	Law in Transition Quarterly
Ludd.	Ludden (ME)
Lump.	Lumpkin (GA)
Lush.	Lushington's Admiralty (Eng.)
Lutw.	Lutwyche's Common Pleas (Eng.)
Lutw.Reg.Cas.	Lutwyche's Registration Cases (Eng.)
Luz.Leg.Obs.	Luzerne Legal Observer (PA)
Luz.Leg.Reg.	Luzerne Legal Register (PA)
Luz.L.J.	Luzerne Law Journal (PA)
Luz.L.T.	Luzerne Law Times (PA)
Lynd.	Lyndwoode, Provinciale (Eng.)
Lyne	Lyne's Chancery (Ir.)

M

MA	Missouri Appeal Reports
MaA	Massachusetts Appeals Court Reports
Mac.	Macnaghten's Chancery (Eng.)
MacAll.	MacAllister (U.S.)
Mac. & G.	Macnaghten & Gordon's Chancery (Eng.)
Mac. & Rob.	Maclean & Robinson's Appeals, House of Lords (Scot.)
MacAr.	MacArthur (DC)
	MacArthur's Patent Cases (DC)
MacAr. & M.	MacArthur & Mackey's District of Columbia Supreme Court
MacAr. & Mackey	Same
MacAr.Pat. Cas.	MacArthur's Patent Cases (DC)
macarth	MacArthur's Reports (DC)
MacArth.	Same
	MacArthur's Patent Cases (DC)
macarth & m	MacArthur's and Mackey's Reports (DC)
MacArth. & M.	Same
MacFarl.	MacFarlane, Jury Court (Scot.)
mackey	Mackey's Reports (DC)
Mackey	Same
MacL.	MacLean (U.S. Circuit Court)
MacL. & R.	MacLean & Robinson's House of Lords (Eng.)
Macn. & G.	Macnaghten & Gordon's Chancery (Eng.)
Macph.	Macpherson, Court of Sessions (Scot.)
Macph.L. & B.	Macpherson, Lee & Bell (Scot.)
Macph.S. & L.	Macpherson, Shireff & Lee (Scot.)
Macq.	Macqueen's Scotch Appeal Cases
Macr.	Macrory's Patent Cases (Eng.)
Madd.	Maddock (MT)
	Maddock's Chancery (Eng.)
Madd. & B.	Maddock & Back (MT)
Madd.Ch.Pr.	Maddock's Chancery Practice (Eng.)
MADR	Massachusetts Appellate Division Reports
Madras L.J.	Madras Law Journal
Madras L.J. Crim.	Madras Law Journal Criminal
Mag.	Magruder (MD)

Mag. & Const.	Magistrate and Constable
Mag.Cas.	Magisterial Cases
Mag.Mun. Par.Law.	Magistrate and Municipal and Parochial Lawyer
Maine L.Rev.	Maine Law Review
M.A.L.C.M.	Mercantile Adjuster and the Lawyer and Credit Man
Mal.L.J	Malayan Law Journal
Malloy	Malloy's Chancery (Ir.)
Mal.L.Rev.	Malaya Law Review
Malone	Malone's Heiskell (TN)
Man.	Manitoba Law
	Manning (MI)
Man. & G.	Manning & Granger's Common Pleas (Eng.)
Man. & Ry.Mag.	Manning & Ryland's Magistrates' Cases (Eng.)
Man. & S.	Manning & Scott's Common Bench (Old Series) (Eng.)
Man.B.News	Manitoba Bar News
M. & A.	Montagu & Ayrton's Bankruptcy Reports (Eng.)
M. & Ayr.	Same
M. & B.	Montague & Bligh's Bankruptcy (Eng.)
M. & C.	Montague & Chitty's Bankruptcy (Eng.)
	Mylne & Craig's Chancery (Eng.)
M. & Cht.Bankr.	Montague & Chitty's Bankruptcy (Eng.)
M. & G.	Maddock & Geldhart's Chancery (Eng.)
	Manning & Granger's Common Pleas (Eng.)
M. & Gel.	Maddock & Geldhart's Chancery (Eng.)
M. & Gord.	Macnaghten & Gordon's Chancery (Eng.)
M. & H.	Murphy & Hurlstone's Exchequer (Eng.)
M. & K.	Mylne & Keen's Chancery (Eng.)
M. & M.	Moody & Malkin's Nisi Prius (Eng.)
M. & McA.	Montague & McArthur's Bankruptcy (Eng.)
M. & P.	Moore & Payne's Common Pleas & Exchequer (Eng.)
M. & R.	Maclean & Robinson's Appeal Cases (Scot.)
	Manning & Ryland's King's Bench (Eng.)
	Moody & Robinson's Nisi Prius (Eng.)

M. & R.M.C.	Manning & Ryland's Magistrates' Cases, King's Bench (Eng.)
M. & Rob.	Moody & Robinson's Nisi Prius (Eng.)
M. & S.	Manning & Scott's Common Pleas (Eng.)
	Maule & Selwyn's King's Bench (Eng.)
	Moore & Scott's Common Pleas (Eng.)
M. & Scott	Same
M. & W.	Meeson & Welsby's Exchequer (Eng.)
M. & W.Cas.	Mining & Water Cases Annotated (U.S)
M. & Y.	Martin & Yerger (TN)
Man.G. & S.	Manning, Granger & Scott's Common Bench (Eng.)
Man.Gr. & S.	Same
Man.L.J.	Manitoba Law Journal
Mann.	Manning (MI)
Mann. & G.	Manning & Granger's Common Pleas (Eng.)
Mansf.	Mansfield (AR)
Manson	Manson's Bankruptcy (Eng.)
Man.t.Wood	Manitoba tempore Wood
manunrep	Manning's Unreported Cases (LA)
Man.Unrep. Cas.	Same
March	March's King's Bench (Eng.)
MarD	Martin's Decisions in Equity (AR)
Marijuana Rev.	Marijuana Review
Maritime L.J.	Maritime Law Journal
Mark's & Sayre's	Mark's & Sayre's (AL)
Mar.Law.	Maritime Lawyer
Mar.L.Cas. (N.S.)	Maritime Law Cases, New Series
Mar.N. & Q.	Maritime Notes and Queries
Mar.Prov.	Maritime Provinces Reports (Can.)
Marq.L.Rev.	Marquette Law Review
Marq. Sports L.J.	Marquette Sports Law Journal
Mars.Adm.	Marsden's Admiralty (Eng.)
Marsh.	Marshall (U.S.)
	Marshall (UT)
	Marshall, A.K. (KY)
	Marshall, J.J. (KY)
	Marshall's Common Pleas (Eng.)
mart	Martin's Reports (LA)
Mart. & Y.	Martin & Yerger (TN)
martin	Martin's North Carolina Reports
Martin	Martin (GA)
	Martin (IN)

	Martin (LA)
	Martin (U.S.)
	Martin's Decisions (Law) (NC)
Martin Mining	Martin Mining Cases
	Martin's New Series (LA)
martns	Martin's Louisiana Reports, New Series
martyertn	Martin & Yerger's Tennessee Reports
marv	Marvel's Reports (DE)
Marv.	Same
Mas	Massachusetts Reports
Mason	Mason (U.S.)
masoncc	Mason's U.S. Circuit Court Reports
mass	Massachusetts Reports
Mass.	Same
massad	Massachusetts Appellate Division
massapp	Massachusetts Appellate Reports
massappdec	Massachusetts Appellate Decisions
Mass.App. Dec.	Same
Mass.App. Div.	Massachusetts Appellate Division Reports
Mass.App. Rep.	Massachusetts Appeals Court Reports
Mass.L.Q.	Massachusetts Law Quarterly
Mass.L.Rev.	Massachusetts Law Review
Mathews	Mathews (WV)
Matson	Matson (CT)
MC	American Maritime Cases
McA	Michigan Court of Appeals Reports
mcall	McAllister's U.S. Circuit Court Reports
McAll	Same
McBride	McBride (MO)
McC.	McCahon's Reports (KS)
M.C.C.	Mixed Claims Commission
	Motor Carriers' Cases (I.C.C.)
McCah.	McCahon's Reports (KS)
mccahon	Same
McCarter	McCarter's Chancery (NJ)
McCartney	McCartney's Civil Procedure (NY)
McClell.	McClelland's Exchequer (Eng.)
McClell. & Y.	McClelland & Younge's Exchequer (Eng.)
McCook	McCook (OH)
McCord	McCord's Chancery (SC)
McCork.	McCorkle (NC)
McCrary	McCrary (U.S.)
mccrcc	Same

McG.	McGloin's Court of Appeals Reports (LA)
McGill L.J.	McGill Law Journal
mcgloin	McGloin's Court of Appeals Reports (LA)
Mch	Michigan Reports
M.C.J.	Michigan Civil Jurisprudence
McL	McLean's U.S. Circuit Court Reports
mclcc	Same
McLean	Same
MCLE Rules	MCLE Rules and Regulations (CA State Bar)
McMul.	McMullan's Chancery (SC)
	McMullan's Law (SC)
M.C.R.	Montreal Condensed Reports
McWillie	McWillie (MS)
md	Maryland Reports
Md.	Same
M.D.	Master's Decisions (Patents)
MdA	Maryland Appellate Reports
mdapp	Same
Md.App.	Same
Md.B.J.	Maryland Bar Journal
mdch	Maryland Chancery Reports
Md.Ch.	Same
Md.J. Contemp. Legal Issues	Maryland Journal of Contemporary Legal Issues
Md. J. Int'l L. & Trade	Maryland Journal of International Law and Trade
Md.L.F.	Maryland Law Forum
Md.L.Rec.	Maryland Law Record
Md.L.Rep.	Maryland Law Reporter
Md.L.Rev.	Maryland Law Review
me	Maine Reports
Me.	Same
Mean's	Mean's Reports (KS)
Medd.	Meddaugh (MI)
Media L.Notes	Media Law Notes
medialr	Media Law Reporter
Medico–Legal J.	Medico–Legal Journal
Med.L. & Pub.Pol.	Medicine, Law and Public Policy
Med.-Legal Crim.Rev.	Medico–Legal and Criminological Review
Med.-Legal J.	Medico–Legal Journal
Med.-Legal Soc'y Trans.	Medico–Legal Society Transactions
Med LR	Medical Law Reports
Med.Sci. & L.	Medicine, Science and the Law
Med.Trial Tech.Q.	Medical Trial Technique Quarterly
Meg.	Megone Company Cases (Eng.)
Meigs	Meigs (TN)
meigstn	Same
Melanesian L.J.	Melanesian Law Journal (Papua N.G.)
Melb.U.L. Rev.	Melbourne University Law Review
Me.L.Rev.	Maine Law Review
Mem.L.J.	Memphis Law Journal (TN)
Mem.St.U.L. Rev.	Memphis State University Law Review
Menken	Menken's Civil Procedure (NY)
Mercer Beasley L.Rev.	Mercer Beasley Law Review
Mercer L.Rev.	Mercer Law Review
Meredith Lect.	W.C.J. Meredith Memorial Lectures
Meriv.	Merivale's Chancery (Eng.)
met	Metcalf's Reports (MA)
Met.	Metcalf (KY)
	Metcalf (MA)
Metc.	Same
M.F.P.D.	Modern Federal Practice Digest
Miami L.Q.	Miami Law Quarterly
mich	Michigan Reports
Mich.	Same
michapp	Michigan Court of Appeals Reports
Mich.App.	Same
Michie's Jur.	Michie's Jurisprudence of Va. and W.Va.
Mich. J. Int'l L.	Michigan Journal of International Law
Mich.L.Rev.	Michigan Law Review
michnp	Michigan Nisi Prius
Mich.N.P.	Same
Mich.St.B.J.	Michigan State Bar Journal
Mich.T.	Michaelmas Term (Eng.)
Mid.East L.Rev.	Middle East Law Review
Mil & Vet C	Military and Veterans Code
Miles	Miles (PA)
	Miles' Philadelphia District Court
Mill Const.	Mill's Constitutional Reports (SC)
Mill.Dec.	Miller's Decisions (U.S.)
Mil.L.Rev.	Military Law Review
Mills	Mill's Surrogate's Court Reports (NY)
Milw.	Milward's Ecclesiastical (Ir.)
Min	Minnesota Reports
Min.	Minor (AL)
minn	Minnesota Reports
Minn.	Same
Minn.Cont. L.Ed.	Minnesota Continuing Legal Education

Minn.Cont.Legal Ed.	Same	Monag	Monaghan's Reports (PA)
Minn.L.Rev.	Minnesota Law Review	monaghan	Same
minor	Minor's Reports (AL)	Monash U.L. Rev.	Monash University Law Review
Mis	Mississippi Reports	mont	Montana Reports
misc	Miscellaneous (NY)	Mont.	Same
Misc.	Same	Mont. & Ayr.	Montagu & Ayrton's Bankruptcy (Eng.)
misc2d	Same, Second Series	Mont. & M.	Montagu & McArthur's Bankruptcy (Eng.)
Misc.Dec.	Ohio Miscellaneous Decisions	Month.Dig. Tax Articles	Monthly Digest of Tax Articles
miss	Mississippi Reports	Month.Leg. Exam.	Monthly Legal Examiner (NY)
Miss.	Same	Month.L.J.	Monthly Journal of Law (WA)
Miss.C.L.Rev.	Mississippi College Law Review		
Miss.Dec.	Mississippi Decisions (Jackson)	Month.L.Mag.	Monthly Law Magazine (London)
Miss.L.J.	Mississippi Law Journal	Month.L.Rep.	Monthly Law Reporter (Boston)
Miss.St.Cas.	Mississippi State Cases		Monthly Law Reports (Can.)
Mister	Mister (MO)		
Mitchell's Mar.Reg.	Mitchell's Maritime Register	Month.L.Rev.	Monthly Law Review
mj	Military Justice Reporter	Month.West. Jur.	Monthly Western Journal (Bloomington, IN)
MJ	Same		
ML	Judicial Panel on Multidistrict Litigation	Mont.L.Rev.	Montana Law Review
		Montr.Cond. Rep.	Montreal Condensed Reports
Ml.	Miller (Law) (MD)	Montr.Leg.N.	Montreal Legal News
M.L.Dig. & R.	Monthly Digest & Reporter (Que.)	Montr.Q.B.	Montreal Law Reports, Queen's Bench
M.L.E.	Maryland Law Encyclopedia	Mont.Super.	Montreal Law Reports (Superior Court)
M.L.P.	Michigan Law and Practice	Moo.C.C.	Moody's Crown Cases Reserved (Eng.)
M.L.R.	Military Law Reporter Modern Law Review	Mood. & Mack.	Moody & Mackin's Nisi Prius (Eng.)
M.L.R. (Q.B.)	Montreal Law Reports, Queen's Bench	Mood. & Malk.	Moody & Malkin's Nisi Prius (Eng.)
M.L.R. (S.C.)	Montreal Law Reports, Superior Court	Mood. & Rob.	Moody & Robinson's Nisi Prius (Eng.)
mlw	Massachusetts Lawyers Weekly	Moody Cr.C.	Moody's Crown Cases Reserved (Eng.)
MnL	Minnesota Law Review	Moon	Moon (IN)
mo	Missouri Supreme Court Reports	Moo.P.C.	Moore, Privy Council
Mo.	Same	Moo.P.C. (N.S.)	Moore, New Series
Moak	Moak (Eng.)	Moore	Moore (AL)
moapp	Missouri Appeals		Moore (AR)
Mo.App.	Same		Moore (TX)
Mo.A.R.	Missouri Appellate Reporter	Moore & S.	Moore & Scott's Common Pleas (Eng.)
Mo.B.J.	Missouri Bar Journal	Moore & W.	Moore & Walker (TX)
Mod.	Modern (Eng.)	Moore B.B.	Moore's King's Bench (Eng.)
Mo.Dec.	Missouri Decisions		
Mod.L. & Soc'y	Modern Law and Society	Moore C.P.	Moore's Common Pleas (Eng.)
Mod.L.Rev.	Modern Law Review	Moore Indian App.	Moore's Indian Appeals (Eng.)
Mod.Pract. Comm.	Modern Practice Commentator		
Mo.J.Dispute Res.	Missouri Journal of Dispute Resolution	Moore P.C.C.	Moore's Privy Council Cases (Eng.)
Moll.	Molloy's Chancery (Ir.)	Mor	Morris' Reports (IA)
Mo.L.Rev.	Missouri Law Review	Morg.	Morgan's Chancery Acts & Orders (Eng.)
Mon.	B. Monroe (KY) T.B. Monroe (KY)		

Morr.	Morrill's Bankruptcy Cases (Eng.)
	Morris (CA)
	Morris (IA)
	Morris (MS)
morris	Morrissett (AL)
Morris.	Same
Morr. Min. Rep.	Morrison's Mining Reports
Morrow	Morrow (OR)
Morr.St.Cas.	Morris State Cases (MS)
Morr.Trans.	Morrison's Transcript United States Supreme Court Decisions
Morse Exch. Rep.	Morse's Exchequer Reports (Can.)
Mosely	Mosely's Chancery (Eng.)
Moult.Ch.	Moulton's Chancery Practice (NY)
M.P.L.R.	Municipal and Planning Law Reports
M.P.R.	Maritime Province Reports
M.P.T.M.H.	Major Peace Treaties of Modern History
Mrt	Martin's Reports (LA)
MrtN	Same, New Series
mspr	U.S. Merit Systems Protection Board Reporter
Mt	Montana Reports
Mtg Rules	Rules Governing Open Meetings, Closed Sessions and Records of Board of Governors of State Bar (CA)
Mun.	Munford (VA)
Mun.Att'y	Municipal Attorney

Mun.Corp. Cas.	Municipal Corporation Cases
Munf.	Munford (VA)
Munic. & P.L.	Municipal & Parish Law Cases (Eng.)
Mun.L.Ct. Dec.	Municipal Law Court Decisions
Mun.L.J.	Municipal Law Journal
Mun.Ord. Rev.	Municipal Ordinance Review
Mun.Rep.	Municipal Reports (Can.)
Mur.	Murray's New South Wales Reports
	Murray's Scotch Jury Court Reports
Mur. & H.	Murphy & Hurlstone's Exchequer (Eng.)
Mur. & Hurl.	Same
Murph.	Murphy (NC)
Murph. & H.	Murphy & Hurlstone's Exchequer (Eng.)
Murr.	Murray's Scotch Jury Court Reports
Murr.Over. Cas.	Murray's Overruled Cases
M.V.R.	Motor Vehicle Reports
Myer Fed. Dec.	Myer's Federal Decisions
Myl. & C.	Mylne & Craig's Chancery (Eng.)
Myl. & Cr.	Same
Myl. & K.	Mylne & Keen's Chancery (Eng.)
Mylne & K.	Same
Myr.	Myrick's Probate (CA)
Myrick (CA)	Same
Myr.Prob.	Same
Mysore L.J.	Mysore Law Journal

N

NACCA L.J.	National Association of Claimant's Compensation Attorneys Law Journal
N. & Dr.	Nevile & Manning's King's Bench (Eng.)
N. & H.	Nott & Huntington's U.S. Court of Claims
N. & Macn.	Nevile & Macnamara Railway & Canal Cases (Eng.)
N. & Mc.	Nott & McCord (SC)
N. & McC.	Same
N. & P.	Nevile & Perry's King's Bench (Eng.)
Napt.	Napton (MO)

Napton	Same
Narcotics Control Dig.	Narcotics Control Digest
Narcotics L.Bull.	Narcotics Law Bulletin
Nat.Bankr. Reg.	National Bankruptcy Register (U.S.)
Nat.Corp. Rep.	National Corporation Reporter
Nat. Jewish L. Rev.	National Jewish Law Review
N.Atlantic Reg.Bus. L.Rev.	North Altantic Regional Business Law Review
Nat'l Black L.J.	National Black Law Journal
Nat'l Civic Rev.	National Civic Review
Nat.L.F.	Natural Law Forum

Nat'l Income Tax Mag.	National Income Tax Magazine	nchip	North Chipman's Reports (VT)
Nat'l J.Crim. Def.	National Journal of Criminal Defense	N.Chipm.	Same
Nat'l Legal Mag.	National Legal Magazine	N.C.J.Int'l L. & Com. Reg.	North Carolina Journal of International Law and Commercial Regulation
Nat'l Mun. Rev.	National Municipal Review	N.C.L.Rev.	North Carolina Law Review
Nat'l Prison Project J.	National Prison Project Journal	NCr	New York Criminal Reports
Nat.L.Rep.	National Law Reporter	nctermrep	North Carolina Term Reports
Nat'l School L.Rptr.	National School Law Reporter	N.C.T.Rep.	Same
Nat'l Taiwan U.L.J.	National Taiwan University Law Journal	nd	North Dakota Reports
Nat'l Tax J.	National Tax Journal	N.D.	Same
Nat.Munic. Rev.	National Municipal Review	N.D.J.Legis.	North Dakota Journal of Legislation
Nat.Reg.	National Register (Mead)	N.D.L.Rev.	North Dakota Law Review
Nat.Resources & Env't	Natural Resources & Environment	ne	North Eastern Reporter
Nat.Resources J.	Natural Resources Journal	N.E.	Same
		ne2d	Same, Second Series
Nat.Resources Law.	Natural Resources Lawyer	N.E.2d	Same
		neb	Nebraska Reports
Nat.Resources L.Newsl.	Natural Resources Law Newsletter	Neb.	Same
		NebA	Nebraska Advance Reports
Nat U LR	National University Law Review	nebapp	Nebraska Appeals Decisions
N.B.	New Brunswick		
N.Benl.	New Benloe, King's Bench (Eng.)	Neb.L.Bull.	Nebraska Law Bulletin
N.B.Eq.	New Brunswick Equity	Neb.L.Rev.	Nebraska Law Review
N.B.Rep.	New Brunswick Reports	Neb.St.B.J.	Nebraska State Bar Journal
nc	North Carolina Reports	nebunof	Nebraska Unofficial Reports
N.C.	Same	Neb. (Unoff.)	Same
nca	Decisions of Nebraska Court of Appeals	Negl. & Comp.Cas. Ann.	Negligence & Compensation Cases Annotated
NCA	North Carolina Court of Appeals Reports	Negl. & Comp.Cas. Ann. (N.S.)	Same, New Series
		Negl. & Comp.Cas. Ann.3d	Same, Third Series
ncapp	Same	Negl.Cas.	Negligence Cases (CCH)
N.C.App.	Same		
N.C.C.	New Chancery Cases (Eng.)	Negl.Cas.2d	Same, Second Series
N.C.C.A.	Negligence & Compensation Cases Annotated	Negotiation J.	Negotiation Journal
		Negro.Cas.	Bloomfield's Manumission (NJ)
N.C.Cent.L.J.	North Carolina Central Law Journal	Nels.	Nelson's Chancery (Eng.)
N.C.Conf.	North Carolina Conference Reports	Nels.Abr.	Nelson's Abridgment (Lag.)
N.Cent. School L.Rev.	North Central School Law Review	N.Eng.J.Prison L.	New England Journal on Prison Law
		N.Eng.L.Rev.	New England Law Review

Neth.Int'l L.Rev.	Netherlands International Law Review	NJE	New Jersey Equity Reports
Neth.Y.B. Int'l.Law	Netherlands Yearbook of International Law	njeq	Same
		N.J.Eq.	Same
nev	Nevada Reports	njl	New Jersey Law Reports
Nev.	Same	N.J.L.	Same
Nev. & P.	Nevile & Perry's King's Bench (Eng.)	N.J.Law	Same
		N.J.L.J.	New Jersey Law Journal
Nev.St.Bar J.	Nevada State Bar Journal	N.J.L.Rev.	New Jersey Law Review
New.	Newell (IL)	NJM	New Jersey Miscellaneous Reports
newbadm	Newberry's Admiralty (U.S. District Court)		
		njmisc	Same
Newb.Adm.	Same	N.J.Misc.	Same
New Eng.L. Rev.	New England Law Review	NJS	New Jersey Superior Court Reports
New Eng.J. Prison L.	New England Journal of Prison Law	N.J.St.B.J.	New Jersey State Bar Journal
		njsuper	New Jersey Superior and County Court Reports
Newfoundl.	Newfoundland		
Newf.S.Ct.	Newfoundland Supreme Court Decisions	N.J.Super.	Same
		NJT	New Jersey Tax Court Reports
New L.J.	New Law Journal	njtax	Same
New Rep.	New Reports in All Courts (Eng.)	N.Ky.L.Rev.	Northern Kentucky Law Review
New Sess. Cas.	New Session Cases (Eng.)	N.Ky.St.L.F.	Northern Kentucky State Law Forum
New Yugo.L.	New Yugoslav Law	NLADA Brief.	National Legal Aid and Defender Association Briefcase
New Zeal.L.	New Zealand Law		
Nfld. & P.E.I.R.	Newfoundland and Prince Edward Island Reports		
		NLJ	New Law Journal
Nfld.R.	Newfoundland Reports	NLJR	New Law Journal Reports
Nfld.Sel.Cas.	Tucker's Select Cases (Nfld.)	nlrb	National Labor Relations Board Reports
nh	New Hampshire Reports	N.L.R.B.	Same
N.H.	Same	nlrbno	National Labor Relations Board, Decisions and Orders of National Labor Relations Board
N.H.B.J.	New Hampshire Bar Journal		
NI	Northern Ireland Law Reports		
Nigeria L.R.	Nigeria Law Reports	nm	New Mexico Reports
Nigerian Ann.Int'l L.	Nigerian Annual of International Law	N.M.	Same
		NM(J)	New Mexico Reports (Johnson)
Nigerian L.J.	Nigerian Law Journal	N.M.L.R.	Nigerian Monthly Law Reports
N.Ill.U.L. Rev.	Northern Illinois University Law Review	N.M.L.Rev.	New Mexico Law Review
N.I.M.L.O. Mun.L.Rev.	N.I.M.L.O. Municipal Law Review	Noise Reg. Rep.	Noise Regulation Reporter (BNA)
		Nolan	Nolan, Magistrate Cases (Eng.)
N.Ir.L.Q.	Northern Ireland Legal Quarterly	NOLPE Sch.L.J.	National Organization on Problems of Education School Law Journal
N.Ir.L.R.	Northern Ireland Law Reports		
nj	New Jersey Reports		
N.J.	Same		

NOLPE School L. Rep.	National Organization on Problems of Education School Law Reporter	NTR	Northern Territory Reports
Norc.	Norcross (NV)	NU	Nebraska Unofficial Reports
Norris	Norris (PA)	Nuclear L.Bull.	Nuclear Law Bulletin
North	North (IL)		
North.	Northington's Chancery (Eng.)	Nuclear Reg.Rep.	Nuclear Regulation Reporter (CCH)
North & G.	North & Guthrie (MO)	NVAdv	Nevada Advance Opinion Number
North.Co.	Northampton County Legal News (PA)	nw	North Western Reporter
		N.W.	Same
Northrop U.L.J.Aerospace Energy & Env.	Northrop University Law Journal of Aerospace, Energy and the Environment	nw2d	Same, Second Series
		N.W.2d	Same
		Nw.J.Int'l L. & Bus.	Northwestern Journal of International Law & Business
Northumb. Co.Leg. News	Northumberland County Legal News (PA)	NwL	Northwestern University Law Review
Northumb. Legal J.	Northumberland Legal Journal	N.W.Terr.	Northwest Territories Supreme Court Reports
Notes of Cas.	Notes of Cases (Eng.)		
Notre Dame Int'l & Comp.L.J.	Notre Dame International and Comparative Law Journal	N.W.T.L.R.	North West Territories Law Reports
		Nw.U.L.Rev.	Northwestern University Law Review
Notre Dame J.L.Ethics & Pub.Pol'y	Notre Dame Journal of Law, Ethics & Public Policy	ny	New York Reports
		N.Y.	Same
Notre Dame Law.	Notre Dame Lawyer	ny2d	Same, Second Series
Notre Dame L. Rev.	Notre Dame Law Review	N.Y.2d	Same, Second Series
Nova L.J.	Nova Law Journal	NYAD	New York Appellate Division Reports
Nova L.Rev.	Nova Law Review	NYAD2d	Same, Second Series
Noy	Noy, King's Bench (Eng.)	N.Y.Anno. Cas.	New York Annotated Cases
N.P.	Ohio Nisi Prius Reports	N.Y.Anno. Dig.	New York Annotated Digest
N.P. (N.S.)	Same, New Series	N.Y.App.Div.	New York Supreme Court Appellate Division Reports
N.P. & G.T. Rep.	Nisi Prius & General Term Reports (OH)		
		NYC	New York City Court Reports
N.R.	National Reporter	N.Y.Cas.Err.	New York Cases in Error (Claim Cases)
N.R.A.B. (4th Div.)	National Railroad Adjustment Board Awards		
		N.Y.Ch.Sent.	Chancery Sentinel (NY)
N.S.	Nova Scotia		
N.S.Dec.	Nova Scotia Decisions	N.Y.City Ct.	New York City Court
N.S.R.	Nova Scotia Reports	N.Y.City Ct.Supp.	New York City Court Supplement
N.S.W.	New South Wales State Reports	N.Y.City H.Rec.	New York City Hall Recorder
N.S.Wales	New South Wales	N.Y.Civ.Proc.	New York Civil Procedure
N.S.Wales L.	New South Wales Law		
N.S.Wales L.R.Eq.	New South Wales Law Reports Equity	N.Y.Civ.Proc. (N.S.)	Same, New Series
N.S.W.St.R.	New South Wales State Reports	N.Y.Civ.Pro. R.	New York Civil Procedure Reports

N.Y.Civ. Pro.R. (N.S.)	Same, New Series	N.Y.L.Sch. L.Rev.	New York Law School Law Review
N.Y.Code Rep.	New York Code Reporter	NYM	New York Miscellaneous Reports
N.Y.Code Rep. (N.S.)	Same, New Series	N.Y.Misc.	Same
N.Y.Cond.	New York Condensed Reports	N.Y.Misc.2d	Same, Second Series
		N.Y.Month. L.Rep.	New York Monthly Law Reports
N.Y.Cont. L.Ed.	New York Continuing Legal Education	N.Y.Mun. Gaz.	New York Municipal Gazette
N.Y.Cont. Legal Ed.	Same	N.Y.P.R.	New York Practice Reports
N.Y.County Law. Ass'n B.Bull.	New York County Lawyers Association Bar Bulletin	N.Y.Pr.Rep.	Same
		N.Y.Rec.	New York Record
		nys	New York Supplement
N.Y.Cr.R.	New York Criminal Reports	N.Y.S.	Same
		nys2d	Same, Second Series
N.Y.Crim.	Same	N.Y.S.2d	Same
NYCS	New York City Court Reports, Supplement	NYSD	New York State Department Reports
N.Y.Daily L.Gaz.	New York Daily Law Gazette	N.Y.Sea Grant L. & Pol'y J.	New York Sea Grant Law and Policy Journal
N.Y.Daily L.Reg.	New York Daily Law Register	N.Y.St.	New York State Reporter
N.Y.Dep't R.	New York Department Reports	N.Y.St.B.J.	New York State Bar Journal
N.Y.Elec.Cas.	New York Election Cases	N.Y.Super.	New York Superior Court
N.Y.Jud. Repos.	New York Judicial Repository	N.Y.Supp.	New York Supplement
N.Y.Jur.	New York Jurisprudence New York Jurist	N.Y.U.Conf. Charitable	New York University Conference on Charitable Foundations Proceedings
NYL	New York University Law Review		
N.Y.L.Cas.	New York Leading Cases	N.Y.U.Conf. Lab.	New York University Conference on Labor
N.Y.Leg.N.	New York Legal News		
N.Y.Leg.Obs.	New York Legal Observer	N.Y.U. Envtl. L.J.	New York University Environmental Law Journal
N.Y.L.F.	New York Law Forum		
N.Y.L.J.	New York Law Journal	N.Y.U. Inst. on Fed. Tax.	New York University Institute on Federal Taxation
N.Y.L.Rec.	New York Law Record		
N.Y.L.Rev.	New York Law Review	N.Y.U.Intra.L.Rev.	New York Intramural Law Review
N.Y.L.Sch. Int'l L.Soc'y J.	New York Law School International Law Society Journal	N.Y.U.J.Int'l L. & Pol.	New York University Journal of International Law and Politics
N.Y.L.Sch.J. Hum.Rts.	New York Law School Journal of Human Rights		
N.Y.L.Sch.J. Int'l & Comp.L.	New York Law School Journal of International and Comparative Law	N.Y.U.L.Center Bull.	New York University Law Center Bulletin

N,Y.U.L.Q. Rev.	New York University Law Quarterly Review
N.Y.U.L.Rev.	New York University Law Review
N.Y.U.Rev.L. & Soc. Change	New York University Review of Law and Social Change

O

O.	Ohio Oklahoma Oregon
O.A.	Ohio Appellate Reports
OA2d	same, Second Series
OA3d	same, Third Series
OAG	Opinions of the Attorneys General of the United States
oapp	Ohio Appellate Reports
O.App.	Same
oapp2d	Same, Second Series
oapp3d	Same, Third Series
O.A.R.	Ohio Appellate Reports Ontario Appeal Reports
O.B. & F.N.Z.	Olliver, Bell & Fitzgerald's New Zealand Reports
O.Ben.	Old Benloe, Common Pleas (Eng.)
O.Benl.	Same
Obiter Dictum	Obiter Dictum
O.Bridgm.	Orlando Bridgman, Common Pleas (Eng.)
O.C.A.	Ohio Courts of Appeals Reports
O.C.C.	Ohio Circuit Court Decisions Ohio Circuit Court Reports
O.C.C. (N.S.)	Ohio Circuit Court Reports, New Series
OCCns	Same
O.C.D.	Ohio Circuit Decisions
Ocean Dev. & Int'l L.J.	Ocean Development and International Law Journal
OCr	Oklahoma Criminal Reports
O.C.S.	Office of Contract Settlement Decisions

O.D.	Office Decisions (I.R.B.) Ohio Decisions
O.D.C.C.	Ohio Circuit Decisions
O.Dec.Rep.	Ohio Decisions Reprint
Odeneal	Odeneal (OR)
O.D.N.P.	Ohio Decisions, Nisi Prius
O.E.M.	Office of Emergency Management
O.F.D.	Ohio Federal Decisions
Off.Brev.	Officina Brevium
Off.Gaz.	Official Gazette, United States Patent Office
Officer	Officer (MN)
Official Rep. Ill.Courts Commission	Official Reports: Illinois Courts Commission
O.G.	Official Gazette, United States Patent Office
Ogd.	Ogden (LA)
O.G.Pat.Off.	Same
ogr	Oil and Gas Reporter
Oh.	Ohio Reports
Oh.A.	Ohio Court of Appeals
Oh.Cir.Ct.	Ohio Circuit Court
Oh.Cir.Ct. (N.S.)	Same, New Series
Oh.Cir.Dec.	Ohio Circuit Decisions
Oh.Dec.	Ohio Decisions
Oh.Dec. (Reprint)	Same (Reprint)
Oh.F.Dec.	Ohio Federal Decisions
ohio	Ohio Reports
Ohio	Same
Ohio (N.S.)	Same, New Series
Ohio App.	Ohio Appellate Reports
Ohio App.2d	Same, Second Series
Ohio Bar	Ohio State Bar Association Reports
ohiobr	Same

Ohio C.A.	Ohio Courts of Appeals Reports
Ohio C.C.	Ohio Circuit Court Reports
Ohio C.C.R.	Same
Ohio C.C.R. (N.S.)	Same, New Series
Ohio C.Dec.	Ohio Circuit Decisions
Ohio Cir.Ct.	Ohio Circuit Court Decisions
Ohio Cir.Ct. (N.S.)	Ohio Circuit Court Reports, New Series
Ohio Cir.Ct.R.	Ohio Circuit Court Reports
Ohio Cir.Ct.R. (N.S.)	Same, New Series
Ohio Ct.App.	Ohio Courts of Appeals Reports
ohiodec	Ohio Decisions
Ohio Dec.	Same
Ohio Dec. Repr.	Same, Reprint
Ohio F.Dec.	Ohio Federal Decisions
Ohio Fed.Dec.	Same
Ohio Jur.	Ohio Jurisprudence
Ohio Jur.2d	Same, Second Edition
ohiolabs	Ohio Law Abstract
Ohio L.Abs.	Same
Ohio Law Abst.	Same
Ohio Law Bull.	Weekly Law Bulletin (OH)
Ohio Law J.	Ohio Law Journal
Ohio Law R.	Ohio Law Reporter
Ohio L.B.	Weekly Law Bulletin (OH)
Ohio Legal N.	Ohio Legal News
Ohio Leg.N.	Same
Ohio L.J.	Ohio Law Journal
Ohio Lower Dec.	Ohio Lower Court Decisions
Ohio L.R.	Ohio Law Reporter
Ohio Misc.	Ohio Miscellaneous Reports
Ohio Misc. Dec.	Ohio Miscellaneous Decisions
ohionp	Ohio Nisi Prius Reports
Ohio N.P.	Same
ohionpns	Same, New Series
Ohio N.P. (N.S.)	Same
Ohio N.U. L.Rev.	Ohio Northern University Law Review
Ohio Op.	Ohio Opinions
Ohio Op.2d	Same, Second Series
Ohio Prob.	Goebel's Ohio Probate Reports
Ohio R.Cond.	Ohio Reports Condensed
Ohio S. & C.P.Dec.	Ohio Superior & Common Pleas Decisions
Ohio St.	Ohio State Reports
Ohio St. (N.S.)	Same, New Series

Ohio St.2d	Same, Second Series
Ohio St.J. on Disp.Resol.	Ohio State Journal on Dispute Resolution
Ohio St.L.J.	Ohio State Law Journal
Ohio S.U.	Ohio Supreme Court Decisions (Unreported Cases)
Ohio Sup. & C.P.Dec.	Ohio Decisions
Ohio Supp.	Ohio Supplement
Ohio Tax Rev.	Ohio Tax Review
Ohio Unrep. Jud.Dec.	Pollack's Ohio Unreported Judicial Decisions Prior to 1823
Ohio Unrept. Cas.	Ohio Supreme Court Decisions, Unreported Cases
Oh.Jur.	Ohio Jurisprudence
Oh.L.Bull.	Ohio Law Bulletin
Oh.L.Ct.D.	Ohio Lower Court Decisions
Oh.Leg.N.	Ohio Legal News
Oh.L.J.	Ohio Law Journal
Oh.L.Rep.	Ohio Law Reporter
OhM	Ohio Miscellaneous Reports
OhM2d	Same, Second Series
Oh.N.P.	Ohio Nisi Prius
Oh.N.P. (N.S.)	Same, New Series
Oh.Prob.	Ohio Probate
Oh.S. & C.P.	Ohio Superior & Common Pleas Decisions
Oh.S.C.D.	Ohio Supreme Court Decisions (Unreported Cases)
Oh.St.	Ohio State Reports
Oil & Gas Compact Bull.	Oil and Gas Compact Bulletin
Oil & Gas Inst.	Oil and Gas Institute
Oil & Gas J.	Oil and Gas Journal
Oil & Gas L. & Tax.Inst. (Sw.Legal Fdn.)	Oil & Gas Law & Taxation Institute (Southwestern Legal Foundation)
Oil & Gas Rptr.	Oil and Gas Reporter
Oil & Gas Tax Q.	Oil and Gas Tax Quarterly
OJ C	Official Journal of the European Communities– Communications and Information Series
OJ L	Same–Legislation Series
Okl	Oklahoma Reports
okla	Same
Okla.	Same

Okla.B.Ass'n J.	Oklahoma Bar Association Journal
Okla.City U.L.Rev.	Oklahoma City University Law Review
Okla.Cr.	Oklahoma Criminal Reports
oklacrim	Same
Okla.Crim.	Same
Okla.L.J.	Oklahoma Law Journal
Okla.L.Rev.	Oklahoma Law Review
Okla.S.B.J.	Oklahoma State Bar Journal
O.L.A.	Ohio Law Abstract
O.L.B.	Weekly Law Bulletin (OH)
olcott	Olcott (U.S.)
Olcott	Same
O.L.D.	Ohio Lower Court Decisions
O.Legal News	Ohio Legal News
Oliv.B. & L.	Oliver, Beavan & Lefroy, English Railway & Canal Cases
O.L.J.	Ohio Law Journal
O.L.Jour.	Same
Olliv.B. & F.	Olliver, Bell & Fitzgerald (New Zealand)
O.L.N.	Ohio Legal News
O.Lower D.	Ohio (Lower) Decisions
O.L.R.	Ohio Law Reporter Ontario Law Reports
O.L.R.B.	Ontario Labour Relations Board Monthly Report
O.L.Rep.	Ohio Law Reporter
O'M. & H.El. Cas.	O'Malley & Hardcastle, Election Cases (Eng.)
O.M.B.R.	Ontario Municipal Board Reports
omisc	Ohio Miscellaneous Reports; Ohio Miscellaneous Reports
omisc2d	Same, Second Series
O.N.P.	Ohio, Nisi Prius
O.N.P. (N.S.)	Same, New Series
Ont.	Ontario Reports
Ont.A.	Ontario Appeals
Ont.El.Cas.	Ontario Election Cases
Ont.Elec.	Same
Ont.L.	Ontario Law
Ont.L.J.	Ontario Law Journal
Ont.L.J. (N.S.)	Same, New Series
Ont.L.R.	Ontario Law Reports
Ont.Pr.	Ontario Practice

Ont.W.N.	Ontario Weekly Notes
Ont.W.R.Op.	Ontario Weekly Reporter Opinions of Attorneys General (U.S.)
O.O.	Ohio Opinions
oops	Same
oops2d	Same, Second Series
oops3d	Same, Third Series
Op.Att'y Gen.	Opinions of the Attorney General, United States
Op. Leg. Counsel	Opinions of Legislative Counsel (CA)
Ops.Atty. Gen.	Opinions of Attorneys General (U.S.)
Op.Sol.Dept.	Opinions of the Solicitor, U.S. Department of Labor
or	Oregon Reports
Or.	Same
O.R.	Ontario Reports
OrA	Oregon Court of Appeals Reports
Orange County B.J.	Orange County Bar Journal
Orange County Law	Orange County Lawyer
orapp	Oregon Appeals Reports
Ore.	Oregon Reports
Ore.App.	Oregon Court of Appeals Reports
Ore.L.Rev.	Oregon Law Review
Ore.St.B. Bull.	Oregon State Bar Bulletin
Ore.Tax Ct.	Oregon Tax Court Reports
orleansapp	Louisiana Court of Appeals, Parish of Orleans
Orleans' App.	Same
Orleans Tr.	Orleans Term Reports (LA)
Or.L.Rev.	Oregon Law Review
Ormond	Ormond (AL)
os	Ohio State Reports
O.S.	Same
os2d	Same, Second Series
os3d	Same, Third Series
Osaka Pref. Bull.	University of Osaka Prefecture Bulletin
Osaka U.L. Rev.	Osaka University Law Review
oscd	Ohio Supreme Court Decisions (Unreported Cases)
O.S.C.D.	Same
Osgoode Hall L.J.	Osgoode Hall Law Journal

oshc	Occupational Safety and Health Cases (BNA)
O.S.H.Dec.	Occupational, Safety, and Health Decisions (CCH)
O.S.H.Rep.	Occupational, Safety, and Health Reporter (BNA)
O.S.L.J.	Ohio State Law Journal
O.St.	Ohio State Reports
O.Su.	Ohio Supplement
O.S.U.	Ohio Supreme Court Decisions, Unreported Cases
OSUC	Same
Otago L.Rev.	Otago Law Review
otr	Oregon Tax Reports
Ottawa L.Rev.	Ottawa Law Review
otto	Otto (U.S.)
Otto	Same

Out.	Outerbridge (PA)
Outerbridge	Same
Over.	Overton (TN)
Overt.	Same
Overton	Same
overttn	Same
Ow.	Owen's King's Bench (Eng.)
Ow.	Owen's Common Pleas (Eng.)
Owen	Same
O.W.N.	Ontario Weekly Notes
O.W.R.	Ontario Weekly Reporter
Oxford Law.	Oxford Lawyer
Oxley	Oxley, Young's Vice Admiralty Decisions (Nova Scotia)

P

p	Pacific Reporter
P.	Law Reports Probate, Divorce & Admiralty Division, Third Series
	Pacific Reporter
	Pickering (MA)
	Probate
p2d	Pacific Reporter, Second Series
P.2d	Same
P.3d	Pacific Reporter, Third Series
pa	Pennsylvania Reports
Pa.	Same
Pa.B.A.Q.	Pennsylvania Bar Association Quarterly
Pa.B.Brief	Pennsylvania Bar Brief
Pac.	Pacific Reporter
PaC	Pennsylvania Commonwealth Court Reports
Pa.Cas.	Sadler (PA)
Pac. Basin Int'l L.J.	Pacific Basin International Law Journal
Pace Envtl. L.Rev.	Pace Environmental Law Review
Pace J.Int'l & Corp.L.	Pace Journal of International and Comparative Law
Pace L. Rev.	Pace Law Review
Pace Y.B. Int'l L.	Pace Yearbook of International Law
Pacific LJ	Pacific Law Journal

Pac.L.J.	Same
pacmwlth	Pennsylvania Commonwealth Reports
Pa.Co.Ct.	Pennsylvania County Court
Pa.C.P.	Common Pleas Reporter
Pa.C.Pl.	Pennsylvania Common Pleas
Pac.Rim.L. & Pol'y J.	Pacific Rim Law & Policy Journal
pad & c	Pennsylvania District & County Reports
Pa.D. & C.	Same
pad & c2d	Same, Second Series
Pa.D. & C.2d	Same
pad & c3d	Same, Third Series
pad & c4th	Same, Fourth Series
Pa.Dist.	Pennsylvania District Reporter
PaDC	Pennsylvania District and County Reports
Pa.Fid.Reporter	Pennsylvania Fiduciary
Pai	Paige's Chancery Reports (NY)
Paige	Paige's Chancery (NY)
paine	Paine's U.S. Circuit Court Reports
Paine	Same
Pak.Crim. L.J.	Pakistan Criminal Law Journal
Pak.L.R.	Pakistan Law Reports

PaL	University of Pennsylvania Law Review	Pa.State	Pennsylvania State Reports
Pa.L.J.	Pennsylvania Law Journal	pasuper	Pennsylvania Superior Court Reports
Pa.L.J.R.	Clark's Pennsylvania Law Journal Reports	Pa.Super.	Same
Palm.	Palmer (NH) Palmer (VT) Palmer, King's Bench & Common Pleas (Eng.)	Pat. & T.M.Rev.	Patent & Trade Mark Review
		Pat. & Tr.Mk.Rev.	Same
		Pat.Cas.	Reports of Patent, Design and Trade Mark Cases
Pa.L.Rec.	Pennsylvania Law Record	Pater. Ap. Cas.	Paterson's Appeal Cases (Scot.)
Pa.Misc.	Pennsylvania Miscellaneous Reports	Pat.L.Rev.	Patent Law Review
		Pat.Off.Rep.	Patent Office Reports
Pan–Am.T.S.	Pan–American Treaty Series	Paton App. Cas.	Paton's Appeal Cases (Can.)
P. & B.	Pugsley & Burbridge's Reports (N.B.)	Patr.Elec. Ca.	Patrick, Contested Elections (Ont.)
		Patt. & H.	Patton & Heath's Reports (VA)
P. & C.	Prideaux & Cole's New Sessions Cases (Eng.)	PattH	Patton Jr. & Heath's Reports (VA)
P & CR	Property and Compensation Reports	Pat.T.M. & Copy.J.	Patent, Trademark & Copyright Journal
P. & D.	Perry & Davison's Queen's Bench (Eng.)	patton & h	Patton & Heath's Reports (VA)
		P.C.	Price Control Cases (CCH)
P. & F.Radio Reg.	Pike & Fischer's Radio Regulation Reporter	P.C.I.J.	Permanent Court of International Justice Advisory Opinions, Cases, Judgments, Pronouncements
P. & H.	Patton's & Heath's Reports (VA)		
P. & K.	Perry & Knapp, Election Cases (Eng.)	P.C.I.J. Ann.R.	Permanent Court of International Justice Annual Reports
P. & W.	Penrose & Watts (PA)	P.C.L.J.	Pacific Coast Law Journal
Papua & N.G.	Papua and New Guinea Law Reports	P.Coast L.J.	Same
		P.D.	Law Reports, Probate, Divorce & Admiralty Division, Second Series Division Pension and Bounty (U.S. Dept. of Interior)
Papy	Papy (FL)		
Park	Parker's Criminal Reports (NY)		
Park.	Parker's Exchequer (Eng.)		
Park.Cr.	Parker's Criminal Reports (NY)		
Park.Cr.Cas.	Same	P.Div.	Law Reports, Probate Division (Eng.)
Parker	Parker (NH)		
Parker Cr.Cas.	Parker's Criminal Reports (NY)		
Park.Ins.	Parker's Insurance	Peab.L.Rev.	Peabody Law Review
Pars.Dec.	Parson's Decisions (MA)	Peake N.P.	Peake's Nisi Prius (Eng.)
Pars.Eq.Cas.	Parsons' Select Equity Cases (PA)	Peake N.P. Add.Cas.	Peake, Additional Cases, Nisi Prius (Eng.)
PaS	Pennsylvania Superior Court Reports	PEAL	Publishing, Entertainment, Advertising and Allied Fields Law Quarterly
Pasch.	Paschal (TX)		

Pearce C.C.	Pearce's Reports in Dearsley's Crown Cases (Eng.)
Pearson	Pearson, Common Pleas (PA)
peck	Peck (TN)
Peck	Peck (IL)
	Peck (TN)
Peck.El.Cas.	Peckwell's Election Cases (Eng.)
Peeples	Peeples (GA)
Peeples & Stevens	Peeples & Stevens (GA)
Peere Williams	Peere Williams' Chancery (Eng.)
Peere Wms.	Same
P.E.I.	Haszard & Warburton's Reports (Prince Edward Island)
Pel	Pennewill's Reports (DE)
Pen.	Pennington's Law (NJ)
Pen	Pennypacker's Reports (PA)
Pen. & W.	Penrose and Watts (PA)
Pen C	Penal Code (CA)
Penn.B.A.Q.	Pennsylvania Bar Association Quarterly
Penn.Del.	Pennewill (DE)
pennede	Same
pennyp	Pennypacker (PA)
Pennyp.	Same
Pennyp.Col. Cas.	Pennypacker's Colonial Cases
penr & w	Penrose & Watts (PA)
Penr. & W.	Same
Pension Plan. & Tax'n	Pension Planning and Taxation
Pension Rep.	Pension Reporter (BNA)
Pepp. Disp. Res. L.J.	Pepperdine Dispute Resolution Law Journal
Pepperdine LR	Pepperdine Law Review
Pepperdine L.Rev.	Same
Pepp.L.Rev.	Same
Perry & K.	Perry & Knapp's Election Cases (Eng.)
Pers.Finance L.Q.	Personal Finance Law Quarterly Report
Pers.Inj. Comment'r	Personal Injury Commentator
Pers.Inj. Def.Rep.	Personal Injury Defense Reporter
Pet.	Peters (U.S)
Pet.Ab.	Petersdorf's Abridgment
petadm	Peters' Admiralty (U.S.)
Pet.Adm.	Same
Pet.Br.	Petit (or Little) Brook (Brooke) New Cases King's Bench (Eng.)
petcc	Peters' Circuit Court (U.S.)
Pet.C.C.	Same
peters	Peters (U.S.)
Peters	Same
P.F.Smith	P.F. Smith (PA)
P–H	Prentice–Hall
P–H Am.Lab. Arb.Awards	American Labor Arbitration Awards (P–H)
P–H Am.Lab. Cas.	American Labor Cases (P–H)
P–H Corp.	Corporation (P–H)
Pheney Rep.	Pheney's New Term Reports (Eng.)
P–H Est. Plan.	Estate Planning (P–H)
P–H Fed. Taxes	Federal Taxes (P–H)
P–H Fed. Wage & Hour	Federal Wage and Hour (P–H)
Phil.	Phillips' (IL)
	Phillips' Chancery (Eng.)
	Phillips' Equity (NC)
	Phillips' Law (NC)
Phila.	Philadelphia (PA)
Philanthrop.	Philanthropist
Phil.El.Cas.	Phillips Election Cases (Eng.)
Phil.Int'l L.J.	Philippine International Law Journal
Phillim.	Phillimore Ecclesiastical (Eng.)
Phil.L.J.	Philippine Law Journal
P–H Ind. Rel.Lab. Arb.	Industrial Relations, American Labor Arbitration (P–H)
P–H Ind. Rel.Union Conts.	Industrial Relations, Union Contracts and Collective Bargaining (P–H)
P–H Soc.Sec. Taxes	Social Security Taxes (P–H)
P–H State & Local Taxes	State and Local Taxes (P–H)
P–H Tax Ct.Mem.	Tax Court Memorandum Decisions (P–H)
P–H Tax Ct.Rep. & Mem.Dec.	Tax Court Reported and Memorandum Decisions (P–H)
Pick.	Pickering's Reports (MA)
Pickle	Pickle (TN)

Pig. & R.	Pigott & Rodwell's Registration Cases (Eng.)	Pol C	Political Code (CA)
		Police J.	Police Journal
		Police L.Q.	Police Law Quarterly
Pike	Pike's Reports (AR)	Poll.Contr.	Pollution Control
Pin.	Pinney's Reports (WI)	Guide	Guide (CCH)
Pinn.	Same	Pollexf.	Pollexfen, King's Bench (Eng.)
pinney	Same	Pollution Abs.	Pollution Abstracts
Pipe Roll Soc'y	Publications of the Pipe Roll Society	Pol.Sci.Q.	Political Science Quarterly
Pipe Roll Soc'y (N.S.)	Same, New Series	Pol.Y.B.Int'l L.	Polish Yearbook of International Law
PIQR	Personal Injuries and Quantum Reports	Poly L.Rev.	Poly Law Review
		Pomeroy	Pomeroy (CA)
Pitblado Lect.	Isaac Pitblado Lectures on Continuing Legal Education	Poor L. & Local Gov't	Poor Law and Local Government Magazine
		Poph.	Popham, King's Bench (Eng.)
Pittsb.	Pittsburgh (PA)		Chancery (Eng.)
Pittsb.Leg.J.	Pittsburgh Legal Journal (PA)		Common Pleas (Eng.)
Pittsb.R. (PA)	Pittsburgh Reporter (PA)	por	Pending Opinion Reports (OH)
Pitts.Leg.J. (N.S.)	Pittsburgh Legal Journal, New Series (PA)	Por	Porter's Reports (AL)
		port	Porter (IN)
		Port.	Porter (AL)
Pitts.L.J.	Pittsburgh Legal Journal		Porter (IN)
Pitts.Rep.	Pittsburgh Reports (PA)	Portia L.J.	Portia Law Journal
		Portland U.L.Rev.	Portland University Law Review
P.Jr. & H.	Patton, Jr., & Heath (VA)	Porto Rico Fed.	Porto Rico Federal Reports
Plan. & Comp.	Planning and Compensation Reports	Posey	Posey's Unreported Commissioner Cases (TX)
Pl.Ang.-Norm.	Placitca Anglo-Normannica Cases (Bigelow)	poseyunrep	Same
		Posey Unrep. Cas.	Same
Plan.Zoning & E.D.Inst.	Planning, Zoning & Eminent Domain Institute	Post	Post (MI)
			Post (MO)
		Potomac L.Rev.	Potomac Law Review
P.L.E.	Pennsylvania Law Encyclopedia	Potter	Potter (WY)
PLI	Practising Law Institute	Pow	Power's Surrogate's Court Reports (NY)
P.L.M.	Pacific Law Magazine	Pow.Surr.	Same
P.L.Mag.	Same	PQ	United States Patents Quarterly
Plowd.	Plowden, King's Bench (Eng.)	PQ2d	Same, Second Series
PLR	(Estates Gazette) Planning Law Reports	Pr.	Price, Exchequer (Eng.)
		P.R.	Parliamentary Reports
	Pacific Law Reporter		Practice Reports (Ont.)
P.L.Rep.	Pacific Law Reporter		Probate Reports
Plt	Peltier's Orleans Appeals Decisions (LA)		Puerto Rico Supreme Court Reports
plw	Pennsylvania Law Weekly	Prac.Law.	Practical Lawyer
		Prac.Real Est.Law.	Practical Real Estate Lawyer
Pol.	Pollack's Ohio Unreported Judicial Decisions Prior to 1823	P.R. & D.El. Cas.	Power, Rodwell & Dew's Election Cases (Eng.)
	Pollexfen, King's Bench (Eng.)	Prec.Ch.	Precedents in Chancery (Eng.)

Pr.Edw.Isl.	Prince Edward Island
Preview	Preview of United States Supreme Court Cases
P.R.H.	Puerto Rico Federal Reports
Price	Price, Exchequer (Eng.)
	Price's Mining Commissioner's Cases (Ont.)
Price Pr.Cas.	Price's Notes of Practice Cases (Eng.)
Prick.	Prickett (ID)
Prin.Dec.	Sneed's Printed Decisions (KY)
Prison L.Reptr.	Prison Law Reporter
Prob. & Prop.	Probate and Property
Probation & Parole L.Rep.	Probation and Parole Law Reports
Probation & Parole L.Sum.	Probation and Parole Law Summaries
Prob C	Probate Code
Prob.Law.	Probate Lawyer
Prob.L.J.	Probate Law Journal
Prob.Rep.	Probate Reports (OH)
Prod.Liab. Int'l	Product Liability International
Prod.Safety & Liab.Rep.	Product Safety and Liability Reporter (BNA)
Prop. & Comp.	Property and Compensation Reports
Prop.Law.	Property Lawyer
Prouty	Prouty (VT)
P.R.R.	Puerto Rico Reports
Pr.Reg.B.C.	Practical Register, Bail Court (Eng.)
Pr.Reg.Ch.	Practical Register, Chancery (Eng.)
Pr.Reg.C.P.	Practical Register, Common Pleas (Eng.)
Pr.Rep.	Practice Reports (Eng.)

	Practice Reports (Upper Can.)
P.T.	Processing Tax Division (I.R.B.)
Pub.Ad.Rev.	Public Administration Review
Pub Con C	Public Contract Code (CA)
Pub Con LJ	Public Contract Law Journal
Pub.Cont. L.J.	Same
Pub.Cont. Newsl.	Public Contract Newsletter
Pub.Employee Rel.Rep.	Public Employee Relations Reports
Pub. Interest L.J.	Public Interest Law Journal
Pub.Int'l L.	Public International Law
Pub.L.	Public Law
Pub.Land & Res.L.Dig.	Public Land and Resources Law Digest
Pub. Res. C.	Public Resources Code (CA)
Pub. Util. C.	Public Utilities Code (CA)
Pub.Util. Fort.	Public Utilities Fortnightly
P.U.Fort.	Same
Pugs.	Pugsley (N.B.)
Pugs. & B.	Pugsley & Burbridge (N.B.)
Pugs. & T.	Pugsley & Truenian (N.B.)
Puls.	Pulsifer (ME)
Pulsifer	Same
P.U.R.	Public Utilities Reports
P.U.R. (N.S.)	Same, New Series
P.U.R.3d	Same, Third Series
pur4th	Same, Fourth Series
PW	Penrose & Watts' Reports (PA)
P.Wms.	Peere–Williams, Chancery (Eng.)
Pyke	Pyke (Lower Can.)
	Pyke's Reports, King's Bench (Que.)

Q

Q.B.	Law Reports, Queen's Bench
Q.B.D.	Law Reports, Queen's Bench Division
Q.B.L.C.	Queen's Bench (Lower Can.)

Q.B.U.C.	Queen's Bench (Upper Can.)
Q.Intramural L.J.	Queen's Intramural Law Journal
Q.L.	Quebec Law
Q.L.J.	Queen's Law Journal
Q.L.R.	Quebec Law Reports

Q.L.Rev.	Quarterly Law Review	Queensl. S.C.R.	Queensland Supreme Court Reports
Q.Newsl.-Spec.Comm. Env.L.	Quarterly Newsletter–Special Committee on Environmental Law	Queensl. St.Rep.	Queensland State Reports
		Queensl.W.N.	Queensland Weekly Notes
Que.B.R.; Que.C.S.	Quebec Rapports Judicaires Officiels (Banc de la Reine; Cour superieure)	Que.K.B.	Quebec Official Reports, King's Bench
		Que.L.	Quebec Law
		Que.L.R.	Quebec Law Reports
		Que.Pr.	Quebec Practice
Que.C.A.	Quebec Official Reports (Court of Appeal)	Que.Prac.	Quebec Practice Reports
		Que.Q.B.	Quebec Official Reports, Queen's Bench
Queens B.Bull.	Queens Bar Bulletin		
Queensl.	Queensland Reports	Que.Rev.Jud.	Quebec Revised Judicial
Queensl.J.P.	Queensland Justice of the Peace		
		Que.S.C.	Quebec Official Reports, Superior Court
Queensl.J.P. Rep.	Queensland Justice of the Peace Reports		
		Que.Super.	Quebec Reports Superior Court
Queensl.L.	Queensland Law	quincy	Quincy (MA)
Queensl.Law.	Queensland Lawyer	Quincy	Same
Queensl.L.J.	Queensland Law Journal	Quis Cust.	Quis Custodiet
Queensl.L. Soc'y J.	Queensland Law Society Journal		

R

R.	Rawle (PA)	R. & M.	Russell & Mylne's Chancery (Eng.)
	The Reports, Coke's King's Bench (Eng.)	R. & M.C.C.	Ryan & Moody's Crown Cases (Eng.)
R. 1 Cro.	Croke, Elizabeth		
R. 2 Cro.	Croke, James I.	R. & N.L.R.	Rhodesia and Nyasaland Law Reports
R. 3 Cro.	Croke, Charles I.		
RA	Rating Appeals (Eng.)	R. & R.	Russell & Ryan, Crown Cases (Eng.)
R.A.C.	Ramsay's Appeal Cases (Que.)		
		Raney	Raney (FL)
Race Rel.L. Rep.	Race Relations Law Reporter	rawle	Rawle (Pa.)
		Rawle	Same
Rac.Rel.L. Survey	Race Relations Law Survey	Raym.	Raymond (IA)
		R.C.L.	Ruling Case Law
Rader	Rader (MO)	RD	Reappraisement Decisions
Rag.	Ragland California Superior Court Decisions		
		R. de D. McGill	Revue de Droit De McGill
Rand	Rand (OH)		
Rand.	Randall (OH)	R.D.F.Q.	Recueil de droit fiscal Quebecois
	Randolph (KS)		
	Randolph (VA)	R.D.T.	Revue de Droit du Travail
Rand.Ann.	Randolph Annual (LA)		
		Real Est.Fin. L.J.	Real Estate Finance Law Journal
R. & C.	Russell & Chesley (Nova Scotia)		
		Real Est.L.J.	Real Estate Law Journal
R. & Can. Cas.	Railway & Canal Cases (Eng.)		
		Real Est. L.Rep.	Real Estate Law Report
R. & Can. Tr.Cas.	Railway & Canal Traffic Cases (Eng.)	Real Est.Rev.	Real Estate Review

Real Prop. Prob. & Tr.J.	Real Property, Probate and Trust Journal	Res Judic.	Res Judicatae
Reap.Dec.	U.S. Customs Court Reappraisement Decisions	Res.L. & Econ.	Research in Law and Economics
		Res.L. & Soc.	Research in Law and Sociology
Rec.L.	Recent Law	Restric.Prac.	Reports of Restrictive Practices Cases
Rec.Laws	Recent Laws in Canada	Rettie	Rettie, Crawford & Melville's Session Cases (Scot.)
Record of N.Y.C.B.A.	Record of the Association of the Bar of the City of New York	Rev. & T. C.	Revenue and Tax Code (CA)
R.E.D.	Russell's Equity Decisions (Nova Scotia)	Rev & Tax C	Same
		Rev.Bar.	Revue du Barreau
Redf	Redfield's Surrogate's Court Reports	Rev.Barreau Que.	Revue de Barreau de Quebec
Redf. & R.	Redfield & Bigelow's Leading Cases (Eng.)	Rev.C.Abo. Pr.	Revista de Derecho del Colegio de Abogados de Puerto Rico
Redf.Surr.	Redfield's Surrogate (NY)	Rev.Contemp.L.	Review of Contemporary Law
Reding.	Redington (ME)	Rev.Crit.	Revue Critique (Can.)
Reese	Reese, Heiskell's (TN)	Rev. de Legis.	Revue de Legislation (Can.)
Reeve Eng.L.	Reeve's English Law	Rev.D.P.R.	Revista de Derecho Puertorriqueno
Ref.J.	Referees' Journal (Journal of National Association of Referees in Bankruptcy)	Rev.D.U.S.	Revue de Droit Universite de Sherbrooke
		Rev.Gen.D.	Revue Generale de Droit
Ref Svc	Minimum Standards for Lawyer Referral Service in California (State Bar)	Rev.Ghana L.	Review of Ghana Law
		Rev. Int'l Bus. L.	Review of International Business Law
Regent U.L. Rev.	Regent University Law Review	Rev.Int'l Comm.Jur.	Review of the International Commission of Jurists
Rel. & Pub. Order	Religion and the Public Order		
Remy	Remy (IN)	Revised Rep.	Revised Reports (Eng.)
Rep.Atty. Gen.	Attorneys General's Reports (U.S.)	Rev., Jud., & Police J.	Revenue, Judicial, and Police Journal
Reports	Coke's King's Bench (Eng.)	Rev.Jur.U. Inter.P.R.	Revista Juridica de law Universidad Interamericana de Puerto Rico
Rep.Pat.Cas.	Reports of Patent Cases (Eng.)		
Rep.Pat.Des. & Tr.Cas.	Reports of Patents Designs & Trademark Cases	Rev.Jur.U. P.R.	Revista Juridica de la Universidad de Puerto Rico
Reprint	English Reports, Full Reprint	Rev.L. & Soc.Change	Review of Law and Social Change
Rept.t.Finch	Cases tempore Finch, Chancery (Eng.)	Rev.Leg.	Revue Legale (Can.)
Rept.t.Holt	Cases tempore Holt, King's Bench (Eng.)	Rev.Legale	Same
		Rev.Leg. (N.S.)	Same, New Series
		Rev.Leg. (O.S.)	Same, Old Series
Res. & Eq. Judgm.	Reserved & Equity Judgments (N.S.W.)	Rev.Litig.	Review of Litigation
		Rev.Not.	Revue de Notariat Revue du Notariat
Res. Ch.	Resolution Chapter (CA)	Rev.Pol.L.	Review of Polish Law
Res Ipsa	Res Ipsa Loquitur		

Rev.P.R.	Revista de Derecho Puertorriqueno	Ritchie	Ritchie's Equity (Can.)
revproc	Revenue Procedures	R.J.R.Q.	Quebec Revised Reports
Rev.R.	Revised Reports (Eng.)	R.L. & S.	Ridgeway, Lapp & Schoales, King's Bench (Ir.)
Rev.Rep.	Same		
revrul	Revenue Rulings		
Rev.Sec. & Commodities Reg.	Review of Securities and Commodities Regulation	R.L. & W.	Robert, Leaming & Wallis County Court (Eng.)
Rev.Sec.Reg.	Review of Securities Regulation	R.L.B.	United States Railroad Labor Board Decisions
Rev.Sel.Code Leg.	Review of Selected Code Legislation	R.M.C.C.	Ryan & Moody's Crown Cases (Eng.)
Rev.Soc.L.	Review of Socialist Law		
Rev.Stat.	Revised Statutes	R.M.C.C.R.	Same
Rev. Tax'n of Indiv.	Review of Taxation for Individuals	rmcharlt	R.M. Charlton's Reports (GA)
Reyn.	Reynolds (MS)	R.M.Charlt.	Same
Rhodesian L.J.	Rhodesian Law Journal	rob	Robinson (CA)
ri	Rhode Island Reports	Rob.	Robard (MO)
R.I.	Same		Robard, Conscript Cases (TX)
riatcm	U.S. Tax Court Memorandum Decisions (RIA)		Robert's Louisiana Annual
			Robertson (HI)
R.I.B.J.	Rhode Island Bar Journal		Robertson's Marine Court (NY)
Rice	Rice's Equity (SC) Rice's Law (SC)		Robertson's Superior Court (NY)
Rich.	Richardson (NH) Richardson's Equity (SC)		Robinson (CA) Robinson (CO) Robinson's Reports (LA)
	Richardson's Law (SC)		Robinson (NV)
Rich. & H.	Richardson & Hook's Street Railway Decisions		Robinson (Upper Can.)
Rich. & W.	Richardson & Woodbury (NH)		Robinson (VA) Robinson's Annual (LA)
Rich.C.P.	Richardson's Practice, Common Pleas (Eng.)	Rob.Adm.	Robinson, Admiralty (Eng.)
Rich.Ct.Cl.	Richardson's Court of Claims	Rob. & J.	Robard & Jackson (TX)
Ridg.Ap.	Ridgeway's Appeals Parliament Cases (Ir.)		Robertson & Jacob's Marine Court (NY)
Ridg.App.	Same	Robb Pat. Cas.	Robb's Patent Cases (U.S.)
Ridg.L. & S.	Ridgeway, Lapp & Schoales' King's Bench (Ir.)	Rob.Eccl.	Robertson's Ecclesiastical (Eng.)
Ridg.P.C.	Ridgeway's Parliamentary Cases (Ir.)	Robert.App. Cas.	Robertson's Appeal Cases (Scot.)
Ridg.t.Hardw.	Ridgeway tempore Hardwicke, Chancery, King's Bench	Robin.App. Cas.	Robinson's Appeal Cases, House of Lords (Scot.)
Ried.	Riedell (NH)	Rob.L. & W.	Robert, Leaming & Wallis' County Court (Eng.)
Riley	Riley (WV) Riley's Equity (SC)	Rocky Mt. L.Rev.	Rocky Mountain Law Review
	Riley's Law (SC)	Rocky Mt. Miner.L. Rev.	Rocky Mountain Mineral Law Review
rilw	Rhode Island Lawyers Weekly		

Rocky Mt. Min.L. Inst.	Rocky Mountain Mineral Law Institute	RSCR	Robertson's Superior Court Reports (NY)
Rocky Mt. Min.L. Newsl.	Rocky Mountain Mineral Law Newsletter	RTR	Road Traffic Reports
		Rucker	Rucker (WV)
Rodm.	Rodman (KY)	Ruff. & H.	Ruffin & Hawks (NC)
Rogers	Rogers Annual (LA)	Runn.	Runnell (IA)
Roll.	Rolle, King's Bench (Eng.)	Rus.	Russell's Election Cases (Nova Scotia)
Rolle	Same		
Rolle Abr.	Rolle's Abridgment (Eng.)	Rus. & C.Eq. Cas.	Russell & Chesley's Equity Cases (Nova Scotia)
Rom.Cas.	Romilly's Notes of Cases (Eng.)	Russ. & Geld.	Russell & Geldert (Nova Scotia)
root	Root's Reports (CT)	Russ. & M.	Russell & Mylne, Chancery (Eng.)
Root	Same		
Rose	Rose, Bankruptcy (Eng.)	Russ. & Ry.	Russell & Ryan, Crown Cases (Eng.)
Rose's Notes (U.S.)	Rose's Notes on United States Reports	Russ.El.Cas.	Russell's Election Cases (MA) Russell's Election Reports (Can.)
Ross Lead. Cas.	Ross's Leading Cases (Eng.)	Russell	Russell's Chancery (Eng.)
Rot.Chart.	Rotulus Chartarum (The Charter Roll)	Russ.Eq.Cas.	Russell's Equity Cases (Nova Scotia)
Rot.Claus.	Rotuli Clause (The Close Roll)	Russ.t.Eld.	Russell's Chancery tempore Eldon (Eng.)
Rot.Parl.	Rotulae Parliamentarum		
Rot.Pat.	Rotuli Patenes	Rut.Cam.L.J.	Rutgers–Camden Law Journal
Rot.Plac.	Rotuli Placitorum		
Rotuli Curiae Reg.	Rotuli Curiae Regis (Eng.)	Rutgers Computer & Tech. L.J.	Rutgers Computer and Technology Law Journal
Rowe	Rowe, Parliament & Military Cases (Eng.)	Rutgers J. Computers & Law	Rutgers Journal of Computers and the Law
Rowell	Rowell (VT)	Rutgers J. Computers Tech. & L.	Rutgers Journal of Computers, Technology and the Law
Rowell El.Cas.	Rowell, Election Cases (U.S.)		
R.P.	Rapports des Pratique de Quebec/Quebec Practice Reports	Rutgers L.J.	Rutgers Law Journal
		Rutgers L.Rev.	Rutgers Law Review
		Rutgers U.L.Rev.	Rutgers University Law Review
R.P. & W.	Rawle, Penrose & Watt (PA)	RVR	Rating and Valuation Reporter
R.P.C.	Reports of Patent Cases		
R.P.R.	Real Property Reports	Ryan & M.	Ryan & Moody's Nisi Prius (Eng.)
R.P.W.	Rawle, Penrose & Watt	Ry. & M.	Ryan & Moody's Nisi Prius (Eng.)
R.R.	Pike & Fischer Radio Regulation Revised Reports	Ryde	Ryde's Rating Appeals (Eng.)
R.R.2d	Same, Second Series	Ry.M.C.C.	Ryan & Moody's Crown Cases (Eng.)
RRC	Ryde's Rating Cases		
RRR	Special Court Regional Rail Reorganization Act of 1973		

S

S.	Shaw, Dunlop & Bell, Court of Sessions (Scot.)	S. & L.	Schoales & Lefroy's Chancery (Ir.)
	Shaw's Appeal Cases, House of Lords (Scot.)	S. & M.	Smedes & Maclean's Appeal Cases, House of Lords (Scot.)
	Southern Reporter		Smedes & Marshall (MS)
SA	Silvernail's Court of Appeal Reports, (NY)	S. & Mar.	Same
		S. & Mar.Ch.	Smedes & Marshall's Chancery (MS)
	South African Law Reports	S & M.Ch.	Same
Sad	Sadler's Supreme Court Cases (PA)	S. & R.	Sergeant & Rawle's Reports (PA)
sadler	Sadler's Cases (PA)	S. & S.	Sausse & Scully's Rolls Court (Ir.)
Sadler	Same		Simons & Stuart's Vice Chancery (Eng.)
S.Afr.J.Hum. Rts.	South African Journal on Human Rights		
S.Afr.L.J.	South African Law Journal	S. & Sc.	Sausse & Scully's Rolls Court (Ir.)
S.Afr.L.R.	South African Law Reports	S. & Sm.	Searle & Smith's Probate & Divorce Cases (Eng.)
S.Afr.L.R. App.	South African Law Reports Appellate	S. & T.	Swabey & Tristram's Probate & Divorce Cases (Eng.)
S.Afr.L.Rev.	South African Law Review		
S.Afr.L.T.	South African Law Times	Sanf.	Sanford (AL)
S.Afr.Tax Cas.	South African Tax Cases	San Fern.V. L.Rev.	San Fernando Valley Law Review
S.A.G.	Sentencis arbitrales de griefs (Que.)	San Fran.L.Rev.	San Francisco Law Review
Sal.	Salinger (IA)	Santa Clara Computer & High Tech.L.J.	Santa Clara Computer and High Technology Law Journal
Salk.	Salkeld, King's Bench, Common Pleas & Exchequer (Eng.)		
SALT News	Strategic Arms Limitation Treaty News	Santa Clara L.	Santa Clara Lawyer
		Santa Clara Law.	Same
Samoan P.L.J.	Samoan Pacific Law Journal	Santa Clara LR	Santa Clara Law Review
San	Sanford's Chancery Reports (NY)	Santa Clara L.Rev.	Same
S. & B.	Smith & Batty's King's Bench (Ir.)	Santo Tomas L.Rev.	University of Santo Tomas Law Review
S. & C.	Saunders & Cole's Bail Court (Eng.)	Sar.Ch.Sen.	Saratoga Chancery Sentinel
S. & C.P.Dec.	Ohio Decisions	Sask.	Saskatchewan Law Reports
S. & D.	Shaw, Dunlop & Bell, Court of Sessions, 1st Series (Scot.)	Sask.B.Rev.	Saskatchewan Bar Review
Sandf.	Sandford's Superior Court (NY)	Sask.L.	Saskatchewan Law
		Sask.L.Rev.	Saskatchewan Law Review
Sandf.Ch.	Sandford, Chancery Reports (NY)	Sau. & Sc.	Sausee & Scully, Rolls Court (Ir.)
San Diego LR	San Diego Law Review	Sauls.	Saulsbury (DE)
San Diego L.Rev.	Same	Saund.	Saunders, King's Bench (Eng.)
Sand.I.Rep.	Sandwich Islands Reports (HI)	Saund. & Cole	Saunders & Cole, Bail Court (Eng.)
		S.Aust.L.	South Australian Law

S.Austl.	South Australia State Reports
S.Austl.L.R.	South Australian Law Reports
Sav.	Savile, Common Pleas & Exchequer (Eng.)
sawcc	Sawyer's U.S. Circuit Court Reports
Sawy.	Same
Sax.	Saxton's Chancery (NJ)
Say.	Sayer, King's Bench (Eng.)
S. Bar. J.	California State Bar Journal
S.B.J.	Same
sc	South Carolina Reports
S.C.	Court of Session Cases (Scot.)
	South Carolina Reports
	Supreme Court Reporter
SCA	Senate Constitutional Amendment
S.Calif.Law Rev.	Southern California Law Review
S.Cal.L.Rev.	Same
S.Cal.Rev.L. & Women's Stud.	Southern California Review of Law and Women's Studies
Scam.	Scammon (IL)
S.C.Cas.	Cameron's Supreme Court (Can.)
SC–DCA Rule	Rules on Appeal to California Supreme Court and District Courts of Appeal
SCE	South Carolina Equity Reports
sceq	South Carolina Equity
S.C.Eq.	Same
Sch. & Lef.	Schoales & Lefroy, Equity (Ir.)
Scher.	Scherer's Miscellaneous Reports (NY)
Schm.L.J.	Schmidt's Law Journal (New Orleans)
School C.	School Code (CA)
Schuyl.L.Rec.	Schuylkill Legal Record (PA)
scl	South Carolina Law Reports
S.C.L.Q.	South Carolina Law Quarterly
SCLR	Southern California Law Review
	South Carolina Law Reports
S.C.L.Rev.	South Carolina Law Review
Scot.Jur.	Scottish Jurist

Scot.L.J.	Scottish Law Journal and Sheriff Court Record
Scot.L.Mag.	Scottish Law Magazine and Sheriff Court Reporter
Scot.L.Rep.	Scottish Law Report
Scot.L.Rev.	Scottish Law Review and Sheriff Court Report
Scot.L.T.	Scottish Law Times
Scots L.T.R.	Scots Law Times Reports
Scott	Scott, Common Pleas (Eng.)
Scott N.R.	Scott's New Reports, Common Pleas (Eng.)
SCR	Senate Concurrent Resolution (CA)
S.C.R.	Supreme Court Reports (Can.)
Scr.L.T.	Scranton Law Times (PA)
Sc.Sess.Cas.	Scotch Court of Sessions Cases
Sc.St.Crim.	Scandinavian Studies in Criminology
Sc.St.L.	Scandinavian Studies in Law
sct	Supreme Court Reporter (U.S.)
S.Ct.	Same
S.Ct.Rev.	Supreme Court Review
sd	South Dakota Reports
S.D.	Same
SDC	Supreme Court, District of Columbia Reports, New Series
S.D.L.Rev.	South Dakota Law Review
S.D.St.B.J.	South Dakota State Bar Journal
se	South Eastern Reporter
S.E.	Same
se2d	Same, Second Series
S.E.2d	Same
Sea Grant L. & Pol'y J.	Sea Grant Law and Policy Journal
Sea Grant L.J.	Sea Grant Law Journal
S.E.C.	United States Securities and Exchange Commission Decisions
Sec Fd Rules	Rules of Procedure Client Security Fund Matters
Sec.L.Rev.	Securities Law Review
Sec.Reg. & Trans.	Securities Regulation and Transfer Report
Sec.Reg.L.J.	Securities Regulation Law Journal

Sel.Cas.	Yates' Select Cases (NY)
Sel.Cas.Ch.	Select Cases in Chancery (Eng.)
Seld.	Selden's Notes (NY)
Selden	Selden's Court of Appeals (NY)
Sel.Serv. L.Rptr.	Selective Service Law Reporter
Selw.N.P.	Selwyn's Nisi Prius (Eng.)
Senior Law.	Senior Lawyer
Seoul L.J.	Seoul Law Journal
serg & r	Sergeant's & Rawle's Reports (PA)
Serg. & R.	Same
Sess.Ca.	Sessions Cases, King's Bench (Eng.)
Sess.Cas.	Court of Sessions Cases (Scot.)
	Sessions Cases King's Bench (Eng.)
Sess.Laws	Session Laws
Seton Hall Const.L.J.	Seton Hall Constitutional Law Journal
Seton Hall J. Sport L.	Seton Hall Journal of Sport Law
Seton Hall Legis.J.	Seton Hall Legislative Journal
Seton Hall L.Rev.	Seton Hall Law Review
Sex.L.Rep.	Sexual Law Reporter
Sex Prob.Ct. Dig.	Sex Problems Court Digest
S.F.L.J.	San Francisco Law Journal
Shad.	Shadford's Victoria Reports
Shan.	Shannon's Unreported Cases (TN)
Shand	Shand (SC)
Shand Pr.	Shand Practice, Court of Sessions (Scot.)
shannoncas	Shannon's Unreported Tennessee Cases
Shaw	Shaw (VT)
	Shaw, Appeal Cases, English House of Lords from Scotland
	Shaw, Scotch Justiciary Cases
	Shaw, Scotch Teind Reports, Court of Sessions
Shaw & D.	Shaw & Dunlop (Scot.)
Shaw & Dunl.	Same
Shaw & M.	Shaw & MacLean, Appeals, House of Lords (Scot.)
Shaw & Macl.	Same
Shaw App.	Shaw Appeal Cases
Shaw Crim. Cas.	Shaw's Criminal Cases Justiciary Court (Scot.)

Shaw, D. & B.	Shaw, Dunlop & Bell's Court of Sessions (1st Series) (Scot.)
	Shaw, Dunlop & Bell's Session Cases (Scot.)
Shaw, D. & B.Supp.	Shaw, Dunlop & Bell's Supplement, House of Lords Decisions (Scot.)
Shaw Dec.	Shaw's Decisions in Scotch Court of Sessions (1st Series)
Shaw, Dunl. & B.	Shaw, Dunlop & Bell's Sessions Cases (Scot.)
Shaw, W. & C.	Shaw, Wilson & Courtnay, House of Lords (Scot.)
Sheld	Sheldon's Buffalo Superior Court Reports (NY)
Shep.	Shepherd (AL)
Shep.Abr.	Sheppard's Abridgment
Shep.Sel.Cas.	Shepherd's Select Case (AL)
Sher.Ct.Rep.	Sheriff Court Reports (Scot.)
Shingle	The Shingle, Philadelphia Bar Association
Shipp	Shipp (NC)
Shirl.	Shirley (NH)
Shirl.L.C.	Shirley's Leading Crown Cases (Eng.)
Show.	Shower, King's Bench (Eng.)
Show.P.C.	Shower's Parliamentary Cases (Eng.)
Sick.	Sickel's Court of Appeals (Eng.)
Sid.	Siderfin, King's Bench (Eng.)
Sil.	Silver Tax Division (I.R.B.)
S.Ill.U.L.J.	Southern Illinois University Law Journal
S.Ill.U.L.Rev.	Southern Illinois University Law Review
Silv.A.	Silvernail's Appeals (NY)
Silv.Sup.	Silvernail's Supreme Court (NY)
Silv.Unrep.	Silvernail's Unreported Cases (NY)
Sim.	Simmons (WI)
	Simon's Vice– Chancery (Eng.)
Sim. & C.	Simmons & Conover (WI)

Sim. & St.	Simons & Stuart's Vice–Chancery (Eng.)	Smith & B.R.C.	Smith & Bates, American Railway Cases
Simes	Simes, Handbook of the Law of Future Interest (2d ed.)	Smith & G.	Smith & Guthrie (MO)
		Smith & H.	Smith & Heiskell (TN)
Sim. (N.S.)	Simon's Vice–Chancery, New Series (Eng.)	Smith C.C.M.	Smith, Circuit Courts–Martial (ME)
		Smith Cond.	Smith's Condensed Alabama Reports
Singapore L.Rev.	Singapore Law Review	smith(ind)	Smith's Reports (IN)
		Smith K.B.	Smith's King's Bench (Eng.)
SJ	Solicitors' Journal		
SJR	Senate Joint Resolution	Smith Lead. Cas.	Smith's Leading Cases (Eng.)
Skill.Pol.Rep.	Skillman's Police Reports (NY)	Smith L.J.	Smith's Law Journal
		Smith Reg. Cas.	Smith's Registration Cases (Eng.)
Skin.	Skinner, King's Bench (Eng.)	smithtn	Smith's Tennessee Reports
Skink.	Skinker (MO)		
S.I.C.	Stuart's Appeal Cases (Lower Can.)	SmithR	Smith's Reports (III)
		SMU L.Rev.	Southern Methodist University Law Review
S.L.J.R.	Sudan Law Journal and Reports		
SLT	Scots Law Times	Smy.	Smythe, Common Pleas (Ir.)
SLU LJ	Saint Louis University Law Journal	Smythe	Same
		SN	Selden's Notes (NY)
S.M.	Solicitor's Memorandum (Treasury) (I.R.B.)	Sneed	Sneed (TN) Sneed's Decisions (KY)
		Sneed Dec.	Sneed's Kentucky Decisions
Smale & G.	Smale & Gifford's Vice–Chancery (Eng.)	sneedky	Sneed's Kentucky Reports
Small Bus. Tax'n	Small Business Taxation	sneedtn	Sneed's Tennessee Reports
Sm. & M.	Smedes & Marshall (MS)	Snow	Snow (UT)
		so	Southern Reporter
Sm. & M.Ch.	Smedes & Marshall, Chancery (MS)	So.	Same
		so2d	Same, Second Series
Sm. & S.	Smith & Sager's Drainage Cases (Ont.)	So.2d	Same
		SoC	South Carolina Reports
SMCh	Smedes & Marshall's Chancery Reports (MS)	Soc.Action & L.	Social Action and the Law
		So.Calif. L.Rev.	Southern California Law Review
smedes & mch	Smedes & Marshall's Mississippi Chancery	So. Cal. L.R.	Same
		So. Cal. L. Rev.	Same
Smith	Smith (CA)	Soc. & Lab. Bull.	Social and Labour Bulletin
	Smith (Eng.) Smith's Supreme Court Reports (IN)	So.Car.Const.	South Carolina Constitutional Reports
	Smith (ME) Smith (MO) Smith (NH)	So.Car.L.J.	South Carolina Law Journal
	Smith (SD) Smith (WI)	Soc.Just.	Social Justice
	Smith, E.B. (IL)	Soc.Sec.Bull.	Social Security Bulletin
	Smith, E.D., Common Pleas (NY)	Software L.J.	Software Law Journal
	Smith, E.H., Court of Appeals (NY)	Sol.	Solicitor
		Solar L.Rep.	Solar Law Reporter
	Smith, E.P., Court of Appeals (NY)	So.Law T.	Southern Law Times
	Smith, P.F. (PA)	So.L.J.	Southern Law Journal (Nashville)
Smith & B.	Smith & Batty, King's Bench (Ir.)	Sol.J.	Solicitor's Journal (Eng.)

Sol.Op.	Solicitor's Opinions (I.R.B.)	S.R. & O. and S.I.Rev.	Statutory Rules & Orders and Statutory Instruments Revised
So.L.Q.	Southern Law Quarterly		
Sol.Q.	Solicitor Quarterly	SS	Silvernail's Supreme Court Reports (NY)
So.L.Rev.	Southern Law Review (Nashville)	S.S.L.R.	Selective Service Law Reporter
	Southern Law Review (St. Louis)	ssrs	Social Security Reporting Service
So.L.Rev. (N.S.)	Same, New Series	S.S.T.	Social Security Tax Ruling (I.R.B.)
Somerset L.J.	Somerset Legal Journal	S.T.	Sales Tax Division (I.R.B.)
So.Tex.L.J.	South Texas Law Journal	Stafford	Stafford (VT)
So.U.L.Rev.	Southern University Law Review	Stair	Stair (Scot.)
Southard	Southard (NJ)	Stan.Envt'l L.Ann.	Stanford Environmental Law Annual
Southwestern L.J.	Southwestern Law Journal	Stan.Envtl.L.J.	Stanford Environmental Law Journal
Southwestern L. Rev.	Southwestern University Law Review	Stanf. L. Rev.	Stanford Law Review
Southwestern U LR	Same	Stan.J.Int'l L.	Stanford Journal of International Law
Soviet Jewry L.Rev.	Soviet Jewry Law Review	Stan.J.Int'l Stud.	Stanford Journal of International Studies
Soviet L. & Gov't	Soviet Law and Government	Stan.J.L. Gender & Sex. Orient.	Stanford Journal of Law, Gender & Sexual Orientation
Soviet Stat. & Dec.	Soviet Statutes and Decisions	Stan J of Int Studies	Stanford Journal of International Studies
Soviet Y.B. Int'l L.	Soviet Year–Book of International Law	Stan.L. & Pol'y Rev.	Stanford Law & Policy Review
SP	Stewart & Porter's Reports (AL)	Stan LR	Stanford Law Review
S.Pac.L.Rev.	South Pacific Law Review	Stan.L.Rev.	Same
Spaulding	Spaulding (ME)	Stan.Pa.Prac.	Standard Pennsylvania Practice
Spear	Spear's Law (SC)	Stant.	Stanton (OH)
Spear Ch.	Spear's (or Speer) Chancery (SC)	Stanton	Same
Spear Eq.	Spear's Equity (SC)	Star Ch.Cas.	Star Chamber Cases (Eng.)
Speer	Spear's Law (SC)	Stark.	Starkie's Nisi Prius (Eng.)
Spenc.	Spencer (MN) Spencer, Law (NJ)	Stat.	Statutes at Large (U.S.)
Spencer	Same	Stat. at L.	Same
Spinks	Spinks, Ecclesiastical and Admiralty (Eng.)	State Court J.	State Court Journal
		State Gov't	State Government
Spinks Eccl. & Adm.	Same	State Tr.	State Trials (Eng.)
		Stath.Abr.	Statham's Abridgment
Spoon.	Spooner (WI)	St BJ	State Bar Journal (CA)
Spooner	Same	STC	Simon's Tax Cases
Spott.	Spottiswoode (Scot.)	STC (SCD)	Same (Special Commissioners' Decisions)
Spott.C.L. & Eq.Rep.	Common Law & Equity Reports published by Spottiswoode		
		Stetson L.Rev.	Stetson Law Review
Spottis.Eq.	Spottiswoode's Equity (Scot.)	Stev. & G.	Stevens & Graham (GA)
spr	Sprague (U.S. District Court Admiralty)	stew	Stewart's Reports (AL)
Sprague	Same	Stew.	Same Stewart (SD)
SR	Syracuse Law Review		
S.R.	Solicitor's Recommendation (I.R.B.)		

	Stewart's Reports (N.S.)
Stew.Admr.	Stewart's Admiralty (N.S.)
stew & p	Stewart's and Porter's Reporter (AL)
Stew. & P.	Same
Stewart	Stewart's Vice–Admiralty Reports (N.S.)
Stew.Eq.	Stewart's Equity (NJ)
S.Tex.L.J.	South Texas Law Journal
S.Tex.L.Rev.	South Texas Law Review
STI	Simon's Tax Intelligence
Stiles	Stiles (IA)
Still.Eccl.Cas.	Stillingfleet's Ecclesiastical Cases (Eng.)
Stiness	Stiness (RI)
StJ	St. John's Law Review
St. John's J. Legal Comment.	St. John's Journal of Legal Commentary
St. John's L.Rev.	St. John's Law Review
St. Louis L.Rev.	St. Louis Law Review
St. Louis U.L.J.	St. Louis University Law Journal
St. Louis U.Pub.L.F.	St. Louis University Public Law Forum
St. Louis U.Pub.L.Rev.	St. Louis University Public Law Review
St. Mary's L.J.	St. Mary's Law Journal
StnL	Stanford Law Review
Sto	Storey's Reports (DE)
stock	Stockton's New Jersey Equity Reports
Stockett	Stockett (MD)
Stockt.	Stockton's Equity (NJ)
Stockton	Stockton's Vice–Admiralty (N.B.)
Stockt.Vice–Adm.	Same
Story	Story (U.S.)
storycc	Story's U.S. Circuit Court Reports
Story Eq.Jur.	Story on Equity Jurisprudence
Str.	Strange's King's Bench (Eng.)
StR	New York State Reporter
Stra.	Strange's King's Bench (Eng.)
Strahan	Strahan (OR)
Straits L.J. & Rep.	Straits Law Journal and Reporter
Str. & H.C.	Streets and Highways Code (CA)
Stratton	Stratton (OR)
St.Rep.	State Reporter
St.Rep.N. S.W.	State Reports (N.S.W.)
Stringf.	Stringfellow (MO)

Strob.	Strobhart's Law (SC)
Strob.Eq.	Strobhart's Equity (SC)
Sts & H C	Streets and Highways Code
St. Thomas L.Rev.	St. Thomas Law Review
Stuart	Stuart's King's Bench (Lower Can.)
Stuart Vice–Adm.	Stuart's Vice–Admiralty (Lower Can.)
Student Law.	Student Lawyer
Student Law. J.	Student Lawyer Journal
Stud.Int'l Fiscal L.	Studies on International Fiscal Law
Stud.L. & Econ.Dev.	Studies in Law and Economic Development
Stu.M. & P.	Stuart, Milne & Peddie (Scot.)
Stu.Mil. & Ped.	Same
Style	Style, King's Bench (Eng.)
Suffolk Transnat'l L.J.	Suffolk Transnational Law Journal
Suffolk U.L. Rev.	Suffolk University Law Review
S.U.L.Rev.	Southern University Law Review
Summerfield	Summerfield (NV)
Sumn.	Sumner, Circuit Court (U.S.)
sumnercc	Same
Sup. & C.P. Dec.	Ohio Decisions
Sup.Ct.	Superior Court (PA)
Sup.Ct.Hist. Soc'y Q.	Supreme Court Historical Society Quarterly
Sup.Ct.Hist. Soc'y Y.B.	Supreme Court Historical Society Yearbook
Sup.Ct.Rep.	Supreme Court Reporter (U.S.)
Sup.Ct.Rev.	Supreme Court Review
Super.	California Superior Court
Susq.Leg. Chron.	Susquehanna Legal Chronical (PA)
sw	South Western Reporter
S.W.	Same
sw2d	Same, Second Series
S.W.2d	Same
Swab.	Swabey's Admiralty (Eng.)
Swab. & Tr.	Swabey's & Tristram, Probate & Divorce (Eng.)
Swan	Swan (TN)
Swanst.	Swanston, Chancery (Eng.)

swantn	Swan's Tennessee Reports
Sween.	Sweeney's Superior Court (NY)
Swin.	Swinton's Registration Appeal Cases (Scot.)
Swiss Rev.Int'l Competition L.	Swiss Review of International Competition Law
S.W.L.J.	South Western Law Journal (Nashville)
Sw.L.J.	Southwestern Law Journal
Sw.U.L.Rev.	Southwestern University Law Review

Sydney L.Rev.	Sydney Law Review
Syme	Syme's Justiciary Cases (Scot.)
Symposium Jun.B.	Symposium l'Association de Jeune Barreau de Montreal
Syn.Ser.	Synopsis Series of Treasury Decisions (U.S.)
Syracuse J. Int'l L. & Com.	Syracuse Journal of International Law and Commerce
Syracuse L.Rev.	Syracuse Law Review

T

T.	Tappan (OH)
	Tobacco Division (I.R.B.)
Tait	Tait's Manuscript Decisions (Scot.)
Tal.	Cases tempore Talbot, Chancery (Eng.)
Talb.	Same
Tam.	Tamlyn, Rolls Court (Eng.)
Taml.	Same
Tamlyn	Tamlyn's Chancery (Eng.)
Tamlyn Ch.	Same
T. & C.	Thompson & Cook, Supreme Court (NY)
T. & G.	Tyrwhitt & Granger's Exchequer (Eng.)
T. & M.	Temple & Mew's Crown Cases (Eng.)
T. & P.	Turner & Phillips' Chancery (Eng.)
T. & R.	Turner & Russell's Chancery (Eng.)
taney	Taney, Circuit Court (U.S.)
Taney	Same
Tann.	Tanner (IN)
Tanner	Same
Tap	Tappan's Reports (OH)
Tapp.	Tappan (OH)
Tappan	Same
Tasm.	Tasmanian State Reports
Tasm.L.R.	Tasmania Law Reports
Tasm.U.L. Rev.	Tasmania University Law Review
Taun.	Taunton, Common Pleas (Eng.)
Taunt.	Same
Tax A.B.C.	Canada Tax Appeal Board Cases

Tax Adm'rs News	Tax Administrators News
Tax Cas.	Tax Cases (Eng.)
Tax Counselor's Q.	Tax Counselor's Quarterly
Taxes	Taxes, The Tax Magazine (CCH)
Tax. for Law.	Taxation for Lawyers
Tax Law.	Tax Lawyer
Tax L.Rep.	Tax Law Reporter
Tax L.Rev.	Tax Law Review
Tax Mag.	Tax Magazine
Tax Mgmt. Est.Gifts & Tr.J.	Tax Management Estates, Gifts and Trusts Journal
Tax Pract. Forum	Tax Practitioners Forum
Tax.R.	Taxation Reports
Tay.	Taylor's Carolina Reports (NC)
	Taylor's King's Bench (Can.)
	Taylor's Term Reports (NC)
taylor	Taylor's Reports (NC)
Taylor	Same
Taylor, U.C.	Taylor, King's Bench (Ont.)
T.B. & M.	Tracewell, Bowers & Mitchell, Comptroller's Decisions (U.S.)
T.B.M.	Tax Board Memorandum (I.R.B.)
T.B.Mon.	T.B. Monroe (KY)
T.B.R.	Advisory Tax Board Recommendation (I.R.B.)
	Tariff Board Reports
TC	Tax Court of the United States Reports
	Tax Cases (Eng.)

T.C.	Tax Court of the United States Reports
TCh	Tennessee Chancery Reports
TChA	Tennessee Chancery Appeals Reports
tcm	U.S. Tax Court Memorandum Decisions (CCH)
tcmemo	Same (P–H)
TCR	Tribal Court Reporter
TCSR	Thompson & Cook's Supreme Court Reports (NY)
TCSRA	Same, Addenda
TCt	Tax Court of the United States Reports / United States Tax Court Reports
td	Treasury Decisions
T.D.	Same
Tel–Aviv U.Stud.L.	Tel–Aviv University Studies in Law
Temp.	tempore
Temp. & M.	Temple & Mew, Crown Cases (Eng.)
Temp.Envtl. L. & Tech.J.	Temple Environmental Law and Technology Journal
Temp.Geo.II	Cases in Chancery tempore Geo. II. (Eng.)
Temp.Int'l & Comp. L.J.	Temple International and Comparative Law Journal
Temple & M.	Temple & Mew, Crown Cases (Eng.)
Temple L.Q.	Temple Law Quarterly
Temp.L.Q.	Same
Temp.L.Rev.	Temple Law Review
Temp.Pol. & Civ.Rts. L.Rev.	Temple Political and Civil Rights Law Review
Temp.Wood	Manitoba Reports tempore Wood (Can.)
Ten	Tennessee Reports
tenn	Same
Tenn.	Same
tennapp	Tennessee Appeals
Tenn.App.	Same
Tenn.App. Bull.	Tennessee Appellate Bulletin
Tenn.B.J.	Tennessee Bar Journal
Tenn.Cas.	Shannon's Tennessee Cases
tenncca	Tennessee Court of Civil Appeals
Tenn.C.C.A.	Same
tennch	Cooper, Chancery (TN)
Tenn.Ch.	Same
tennchapp	Tennessee Chancery Appeals
Tenn.Ch. App.	Same
Tenn.Civ. App.	Tennessee Court of Civil Appeals
tenncrim	Tennessee Criminal Court
Tenn.Crim. App.	Tennessee Criminal Appeals Reports
Tenn.Leg. Rep.	Tennessee Legal Reporter
Tenn.L.Rev.	Tennessee Law Review
Ter	Terry's Reports (DE)
Term	Durnford & East, Term Reports, King's Bench (Eng.)
Term N.C.	Taylor, Term Reports
Term R.	Durnford and East, Term Reports, King's Bench (Eng.)
Term.Rep.	Same
Terr.	Terrell (TX)
Terr. & Wal.	Terrell & Walker (TX)
Terr.L.R.	Territories' Law Reports (N.W.T.)
tex	Texas Reports
Tex.	Same
Tex.A.Civ. Cas.	White & Wilson's Civil Cases (TX)
Tex.A.Civ. Cas. (Wilson)	Texas Court of Appeal Civil Cases
texapp	Texas Court of Appeals Cases
Tex.App.	Texas Civil Appeals Cases / Texas Court of Appeals Cases
texappciv	Texas Civil Appeals
texbcr	Texas Bankruptcy Court Reporter
Tex.B.J.	Texas Bar Journal
texcivapp	Texas Civil Appeals
Tex.Civ.App.	Same
Tex.Civ.Rep.	Texas Civil Appeals
Tex.Com. App.	Texas Commission Appeals
Tex.Cr.App.	Texas Criminal Appeals
texcrim	Texas Criminal Reports
Tex.Crim.	Same
Tex.Cr.R.	Same
Tex.Ct. App.R.	Texas Court of Appeals Reports
Tex.Dec.	Texas Decisions
Tex.Int.L. Forum	Texas International Law Forum
Tex.Int'l L.F.	Same
Tex.Int'l L.J.	Texas International Law Journal
Tex.Jur.	Texas Jurisprudence
Tex.Jur.2d	Same, Second Series

Tex.J. Women & L.	Texas Journal of Women and the Law	T.I.F.	Treaties in Force
		Tiff.	Tiffany, Court of Appeals (NY)
Tex.Law.	Texas Lawman	Tiffany	Same
Tex.Lawyer	Texas Lawyer	Till.	Tillman (AL)
Tex.L.J.	Texas Law Journal	Tillman	Same
Tex.L.Rev.	Texas Law Review	Timber Tax J.	Timber Tax Journal
Tex. Oil & Gas L.J.	Texas Oil and Gas Journal	Tinw.	Tinwald (Scot.)
Tex.Real Est. L.Rep.	Texas Real Estate Law Reporter	T.Jones	Thomas Jones, King's Bench and Common Pleas (Eng.)
TexS	Texas Supreme Court Reports, Supplement	T.L.R.	Times Law Reports (Eng.)
Tex.S.Ct.	Texas Supreme Court Reporter	T. Marshall L.J.	Thurgood Marshall Law Journal
Tex.So.U. L.Rev.	Texas Southern University Law Review	T. Marshall L.Rev.	Thurgood Marshall Law Review
texsupp	Texas Supplement	T.M.Bull.	Trade Mark Bulletin (U.S.)
Tex.Supp.	Same	T.M.Bull. (N.S.)	Same, New Series
texsupcj	Texas Supreme Court Journal	T.M.M.	Tax Management Memorandum (BNA)
Tex.Tech L.Rev.	Texas Tech Law Review	T.M.Rep.	Trade Mark Reporter
Tex.Unrep. Cas.	Posey Unreported Cases (TX)	TnA	Tennessee Appeals Reports
Th. & C.	Thompson & Cook's (NY) Supreme Court (NY)	TnCr	Tennessee Criminal Appeals Reports
thatchercrim	Thatcher's Criminal Cases (MA)	T.N.E.C.	Temporary National Economic Committee
Thatcher Cr.	Same	tnt	Tax Notes Today
Thayer	Thayer (OR)	Tobey	Tobey (RI)
Themis	La Revue Juridique Themis	Tort L.Rev.	Tort Law Review
		Toth.	Tothill's Chancery (Eng.)
T.Holt	Holt, Modern Cases (Eng.)	Touro J. Transnat'l L.	Touro Journal of Transnational Law
Thom.	Thomson's Reports (Nova Scotia)	Touro L.Rev.	Touro Law Review
Thomas & Fr.	Thomas & Franklin Chancery (MD)	TPR	Official Translations of the Opinions of the Supreme Court of Puerto Rico
Thomp.	Thompson (CA)		
Thompson & C.	Thompson & Cook, Supreme Court (NY)	TR	Taxation Reports
		T.R.	Durnford & East, Term Reports, King's Bench (Eng.)
thomptenn	Thompson's Unreported Tennessee Cases	TrA	Transcript Appeals Reports (NY)
Thomp.Tenn. Cas.	Same	Trace. & M.	Tracefell & Mitchell, Comptroller's Decisions (U.S.)
Thomson	Thomson's Reports (Nova Scotia)		
Thor.	Thorington (AL)	Trade Cas.	Trade Cases (CCH)
Thorpe	Thorpe's Louisiana Annual	Trademark Rep.	Trade–Mark Reporter
		Trade Reg. Rep.	Trade Regulation Reporter (CCH)
Thur.Marsh. L.J.	Thurgood Marshall Law Journal	Trade Reg. Rev.	Trade Regulation Review
T.I.Agree.	Treaties and Other International Agreements of the United States of America	Tr. & Est.	Trusts & Estates
		Tr. & H.Pr.	Troubat & Haly's Practice (PA)
T.I.A.S.	Treaties and Other International Acts Series (U.S.)	Trans. & Wit.	Transvaal & Witswatersrand Reports

Transc.A.	Transcript Appeals (NY)	Tuck.Dist. of Col.	Tucker's Appeals (DC)
Transit L.Rev.	Transit Law Review	Tuck.Sel.Cas.	Tucker's Select Cases (Nfld.)
Transnat'l L.Contemp. Probs.	Transnational Law & Contemporary Problems	Tuck.Surr.	Tucker's Surrogate (NY)
Transp.L.J.	Transportation Law Journal	Tulane L.Rev.	Tulane Law Review
		Tul.Civ.L.F.	Tulane Civil Law Forum
Trauma	Trauma	Tul.Envtl.L. J.	Tulane Environmental Law Journal
T.Raym.	Thomas Raymond, King's Bench (Eng.)		
Tread. Const.	Treadway's Constitutional Reports (SC)	Tul.L.Rev.	Tulane Law Review
		Tul.Mar.L.J.	Tulane Maritime Law Journal
Treas.Dec.	Treasury Decisions (U.S.)	Tulsa L.J.	Tulsa Law Journal
Trem.P.C.	Tremaine, Pleas of Crown (Eng.)	Tul.Tax Inst.	Tulane Tax Institute
		tupcharlt	T.U.P. Charlton's Reports (GA)
Trends L. Libr. Mgmt. & Tech.	Trends in Law Library Management and Technology	T.U.P.Charlt.	Same
		Tupp.App.	Tupper's Appeal Reports (Ont.)
Trent L.J.	Trent Law Journal	Turn.	Turner (AR)
Trial	Trial		Turner (KY)
Trial Advoc.Q.	Trial Advocate Quarterly		Turner & Russell's Chancery (Eng.)
Trial Law. Forum	Trial Lawyers Forum	Turn. & P.	Turner & Phillips' Chancery (Eng.)
Trial Law. Guide	Trial Lawyer's Guide	Turn. & Ph.	Same
		Turn. & R.	Turner & Russell's Chancery (Eng.)
Trial Law.Q.	Trial Lawyers' Quarterly	Turn. & Rus.	Same
Trial Prac. Newsl.	Trial Practice Newsletter	Turn. & Russ.	Same
		Tutt.	Tuttle (CA)
Trin.T.	Trinity Term (Eng.)	Tutt. & C.	Tuttle & Carpenter (CA)
Tripp	Tripp (Dak.Terr.)		
Tru.	Trueman's Equity Cases (N.B.)	Tutt. & Carp.	Same
		TxCi	Texas Civil Appeals Reports
Trust Bull.	Trust Bulletin		
Trust Terr.	Trust Territory Reports	TxCr	Texas Criminal Appeals Reports
T.S.	Treaty Series (U.S.)	TxL	Texas Law Review
TSCR	Tucker's Surrogate's Court Reports (NY)	Tyl	Tyler's Reports (VT)
		tyler	Same
T.T.	Jurisprudence de droit de Travail	Tyler	Same
		Tyng	Tyng (MA)
tuc	Tucker & Clephane	Tyrw.	Tyrwhitt, Exchequer (Eng.)
Tuck.	Tucker (MA)		
Tuck. & C.	Tucker & Clephane (DC)	Tyrw. & G.	Tyrwhitt & Granger, Exchequer (Eng.)

U

U.Ark.Little Rock L.J.	University of Arkansas at Little Rock Law Journal	U.Balt.L.F.	University of Baltimore Law Forum
U.Balt.J. Envtl.L.	University of Baltimore Journal of Environmental Law	U.Balt.L.Rev.	University of Baltimore Law Review
		U.B.C.L.Rev.	University of British Columbia Law Review

U.B.C.Notes	University of British Columbia Legal Notes		Unemployment Compensation Interpretation Service, State Series
U.Bridgeport L.Rev.	University of Bridgeport Law Review	U.C.Jur.	Upper Canada Jurist
U.C.	Upper Canada	U.C.K.B.	Upper Canada King's Bench Reports, Old Series
U.C. (O.S.)	Upper Canada Queen's Bench Reports, Old Series	UCLA–Alaska L.Rev.	UCLA Alaska Law Review
U.C.App.	Upper Canada Appeal Reports	UCLA Intra.L.Rev.	UCLA Intramural Law Review
U.C.App.Rep.	Same	UCLA J.Envtl.L. & Pol'y	UCLA Journal of Environmental Law & Policy
U.C.C.	Uniform Commercial Code		
U.C.Ch.	Upper Canada Chancery Reports	UCLA L.Rev.	UCLA Law Review
U.C.Cham.	Upper Canada Chamber Reports	UCLA Pac. Basin L.J.	UCLA Pacific Basin Law Journal
U.C.Chamb. Rep.	Same	UCLA Women's L.J.	UCLA Women's Law Journal
U.C.Chan.	Upper Canada Chancery Reports	U.C.L.J.	Upper Canada Law Journal
U.C.Ch.Rep.	Same	U.C.L.J. (N.S.)	Same, New Series
U.C.C.Law Letter	Uniform Commercial Code Law Letter	U.Colo.L.Rev.	University of Colorado Law Review
U.C.C.L.J.	Uniform Commercial Code Law Journal	U.C.Pr.	Upper Canada Practice Reports
U.C.C.P.	Upper Canada Common Pleas Reports	U.C.P.R.	Same
		U.C.Q.B.	Upper Canada Queen's Bench Reports
U.C.C.P.D.	Upper Canada Common Pleas Division Reports (Ont.)		
		U.C.Q.B. (O.S.)	Same, Old Series
		U.C.R.	Upper Canada Reports
U.C.C.Rep. Serv.	Uniform Commercial Code Reporting Service		
		UCR2d	Uniform Commercial Code Reporting Service, Second Series
uccrs	Same		
uccrs2d	Same, Second Series		
U.C.Davis L.Rev.	University of California at Davis Law Review	U.C.Rep.	Upper Canada Reports
		Udal	Fiji Law Reports
UCD LR	Same	U.Dayton L.Rev.	University of Dayton Law Review
U.C.E. & A.	Upper Canada Error & Appeals Reports	U.Det.J. Urb.L.	University of Detroit Journal of Urban Law
U.C.Err. & App.	Same		
U.Chi.Legal F.	University of Chicago Legal Forum	U.Det.L.J.	University of Detroit Law Journal
U.Chi.L.Rec.	University of Chicago Law School Record	U.Det.L.Rev.	University of Detroit Law Review
U.Chi.L.Rev.	University of Chicago Law Review	U.Det.Mercy L.Rev.	University of Detroit Mercy Law Review
U.Cin.L.Rev.	University of Cincinnati Law Review	U.East.L.J.	University of the East Law Journal
U.C.I.S.	Unemployment Compensation Interpretation Service, Benefit Series	U.Fla.J.L. & Pub.Pol'y	University of Florida Journal of Law and Public Policy
	Unemployment Compensation Interpretation Service, Federal Series	U.Fla.L.Rev.	University of Florida Law Review
		Uganda L.Foc.	Uganda Law Focus
		U.Ghana L.J.	University of Ghana Law Journal
		U.Hawaii L.Rev.	University of Hawaii Law Review

U.Ill.L.F.	University of Illinois Law Forum	Unif.L.Conf. Can.	Uniform Law Conference of Canada
U.Ill.L.Rev.	University of Illinois Law Review	Uniform L.Rev.	Uniform Law Review
U.I.L.R.	University of IFE Law Reports (Nigeria)	Unif. Prof. C.	Uniform Probate Code
U.Kan.City L.Rev.	University of Kansas City Law Review	Un. Ins. C.	Unemployment Insurance Code (CA)
U.Kan.L.Rev.	University of Kansas Law Review	U.N.Jur.Y.B.	United Nations Juridical Yearbook
U.L.A. (Master Ed.)	Uniform Laws Annotated (Master Ed.)	U.N.M.T.	United Nations Multilateral Treaties
U.Miami Ent. & Sports L.Rev.	University of Miami Entertainment and Sports Law Review	Unof.	Unofficial Reports
		Un.Prac.News	Unauthorized Practice News
U.Miami Inter– Am. L.Rev.	University of Miami Inter–American Law Review	U.N.Res., Ser. I	United Nations Resolutions, Series I
U.Miami L.Rev.	University of Miami Law Review	U.N.R.I.A.A.	United Nations Reports of International Arbitral Awards
U.Miami Y.B.Int'l L.	University of Miami Yearbook of International Law		
U.Mich.J. L.Ref.	University of Michigan Journal of Law Reform	U.N.SCOR	United Nations Security Council Official Records
U.Mo.Bull. L.Ser.	University of Missouri Bulletin Law Series	U.N.T.S.	United Nations Treaty Series
U.N.	United Nations Law Reports	U.Pa.J.Int'l Bus.L.	University of Pennsylvania Journal of International Business Law
U.N.B.L.J.	University of New Brunswick Law Journal	U.Pa.L.Rev.	University of Pennsylvania Law Review
Uncod Meas	Uncodified Initiative Measures and Statutes (CA)	Up.Can.L.J.	Upper Canada Law Journal
U.N.Comm. Int'l Trade L.Y.B.	United Nations Commission on International Trade Law Yearbook	U.Pitt.L.Rev.	University of Pittsburgh Law Review
		U.Puget Sound L.Rev.	University of Puget Sound Law Review
U.N.Doc.	United Nations Documents	U.Queensl. L.J.	University of Queensland Law Journal
U.N.ECOSOC	United Nations Economic and Social Council Records	Urban Affairs Rep.	Urban Affairs Reporter (CCH)
		Urban L.Rev.	Urban Law Review
Unemp. Ins. C.	Unemployment Insurance Code (CA)	Urb.L. & Pol'y	Urban Law and Policy
		Urb.L.Ann.	Urban Law Annual
Unempl.Ins. Rep.	Unemployment Insurance Reporter (CCH)	Urb.Law.	Urban Lawyer
		U.Rich. L.Rev.	University of Richmond Law Review
U.Newark L.Rev.	University of Newark Law Review	us	United States Reports
U.New S.Wales L.J.	University of New South Wales Law Journal	U.S.	Same
		U.S. & Can.Av.	United States and Canadian Aviation Reports
U.N.GAOR	United Nations General Assembly Official Records	U San Fernando V LR	University of San Fernando Valley Law Review
Unific.L.Y.B.	Unification of Law Yearbook		

U.San Fernando V.L.Rev.	Same
U.S.App.	United States Appeals
usappdc	U.S. Circuit Court Reports (D.C. Circuit)
usappx	United States Reports Appendix Cases
USApx	Same
U.S.Aviation	Aviation Reports (U.S.)
U.S.Av.R.	Same
U.S.C.	United States Code
U.S.C. (Supp.)	Same, Supplement
U.S.C.A.	United States Code Annotated
U.S.C.A. Const.	Same, Constitution
U.S.C.Govt'l Rev.	University of South Carolina Governmental Review
U.S.C.M.A.	United States Court of Military Appeals
U.S.Code Cong. & Ad.News	United States Code Congressional & Administrative News
U.S.C.S.	United States Code Service
U.S.Ct.Cl.	United States Court of Claims Reports
U.S.D.C.	United States District Court
U.S. Dept. Int.	United States Department of Interior
USF LR	University of San Francisco Law Review
U.S.F.L.Rev.	Same
U.S.F.Mar. L.J.	University of San Francisco Maritime Law Journal
U.S.I.C.C. V.R.	United States Interstate Commerce Commission Valuation Reports
U.S.Jur.	United States Jurist (DC)
U.S.Law.Ed.	United States Supreme Court Reports, Lawyers' Edition
U.S.L.Ed.	Same
U.S.L.J.	United States Law Journal
U.S.L.Mag.	United States Law Magazine
U.S.L.Rev.	United States Law Review
uslw	U.S. Law Week
U.S.L.W.	Same

U.S.L.Week	Same
U.S.M.C.	United States Maritime Commission
U.S.M.L.Mag.	United States Monthly Law Magazine
U.So. Cal.1955 Tax Inst.	University of Southern California Tax Institute
uspq	U.S. Patents Quarterly,
U.S.P.Q.	Same
uspq2d	Same, Second Series
U.S.S.B.	United States Shipping Board
U.S.S.C.Rep.	United States Supreme Court Reports
U.S.Sup.Ct. Rep.	United States Supreme Court Reporter (West)
U.S.T.	United States Treaties and Other International Agreements
U.S.Tax Cas.	United States Tax Cases (CCH)
ustc	Same
U.S.T.D.	United States Treaty Development
U.S.V.A.A.D.	United States Veterans Administration Administrator's Decisions
U.S.V.B.D.D.	United States Veterans Bureau Director's Decisions
Ut	Utah Reports
Ut2d	Same, Second Series
utah	Utah Reports
Utah	Same
utah2d	Same, Second Series
Utah 2d	Same
utahadvrep	Utah Advance Reports
Utah L.Rev.	Utah Law Review
U.Tasm. L.Rev.	University of Tasmania Law Review (or Tasmania University Law Review)
Util.L.Rep.	Utilities Law Reporter (CCH)
Util.Sect. Newsl.	Utility Section Newsletter
U.Tol.L.Rev.	University of Toledo Law Review
U.Tor.Fac. L.Rev.	University of Toronto Faculty of Law Review

U.Tor.L.Rev.	University of Toronto School of Law Review	U.W.Austl. L.Rev.	University of Western Australia Law Review
U.Toronto Fac.L.Rev.	University of Toronto Faculty of Law Review	U.West L.A. L.Rev.	University of West Los Angeles Law Review
U.Toronto L.J.	University of Toronto Law Journal	U.Windsor L.Rev.	University of Windsor Law Review
U.Toronto Sch.L.Rev.	University of Toronto School of Law Review	UWLA LR	University of West Los Angeles Law Review
U.Wash. L.Rev.	University of Washington Law Review	U.W.L.A. L.Rev.	Same

V

va	Virginia Reports	Van K.	Van Koughnett's Common Pleas (Upper Can.)
Va.	Same		
VaA	Virginia Court of Appeals Reports	vannes	Van Ness, Prize Cases (U.S.)
vaapp	Same	Van Ness Prize Cas.	Same
Va.Bar News	Virginia Bar News		
Va.Cas.	Virginia Cases	Va.R.	Gilmer's Virginia Reports
Va.Ch.Dec.	Chancery Decisions (VA)		
VaD	Virginia Decisions	VATTR	Value Added Tax Tribunal Reports
vadec	Same		
Va.Dec.	Same	Vaug.	Vaughan, Common Pleas (Eng.)
Va.Envtl.L.J.	Virginia Environmental Law Journal	Vaugh.	Same
		Vaughan	Same
Va.J.Int'l L.	Virginia Journal of International Law	Vaux	Vaux, Decisions (PA)
			Vaux, Recorder's Decisions (PA)
Va.J.Nat.Resources L.	Virginia Journal of Natural Resources Law	VCO	Virginia Circuit Court Opinions
Va.J.Soc. Pol'y & L.	Virginia Journal of Social Policy and the Law	V.C.Rep.	Vice Chancellor's Reports (Eng.)
VaL	Virginia Law Review	Ve.	Vesey, Chancery Reports (Eng.)
Va.L.J.	Virginia Law Journal		Vesey, Senior, Chancery (Eng.)
Val.R. (I.C.C.)	Interstate Commerce Commission Valuation Reports	Ve. & B.	Vesey & Beames, Chancery (Eng.)
		Veaz.	Veazey (VT)
Va.L.Reg.	Virginia Law Register	Veazey	Same
		Veh C	Vehicle Code (CA)
Va.L.Reg. (N.S.)	Same, New Series	Vent.	Ventris, Common Pleas (Eng.)
Va.L.Rev.	Virginia Law Review		Ventris, King's Bench (Eng.)
Val.U.L.Rev.	Valparaiso University Law Review	Ventr.	Same
		Ver.	Vermont
		Vern.	Vernon's Cases (Eng.)
Vand.J.Transnat'l L.	Vanderbilt Journal of Transnational Law	Vern. & S.	Vernor & Scriven, King's Bench (Ir.)
Vand.L.Rev.	Vanderbilt Law Review	Vern. & Sc.	Same
		Vern. & Scr.	Same

Vern. & Scriv.	Same	Vict.U.L.Rev.	Victoria University Law Review
Vern.Ch.	Vernon's Chancery (Eng.)	Vict.U.Well. L.Rev.	Victoria University of Wellington Law Review
Ves.	Vesey, Chancery (Eng.)		
	Vesey, Senior, Chancery (Eng.)	Vil. & Br.	Vilas & Bryant's Reports (WI)
Ves. & B.	Vesey & Beames' Chancery (Eng.)	Vilas	Vilas' Criminal Reports (NY)
Ves. & Bea.	Same	Vill.Envtl. L.J.	Villanova Environmental Law Journal
Ves. & Beam.	Same		
Ves.Jr.	Vesey, Junior, Chancery (Eng.)	Vill.L.Rev.	Villanova Law Review
Ves.Jun.	Same	Vin.Abr.	Viner's Abridgment (Eng.)
Ves.Jun. Supp.	Same, Supplement		
Ves.Sen.	Vesey, Senior, Chancery (Eng.)	Vin.Supp.	Same, Supplement
Ves.Sr.	Same	vir	Virginia Law Reports
Ves.Supp.	Vesey, Senior, Supplement, Chancery (Eng.)	Vir.	Virgin (ME)
		Virgin	Same
vetapp	Veterans Appeals Reporter	Virgin Is.	Virgin Islands
Vez.	Vezey, (Vesey) Chancery (Eng.)	VJNRL	Virginia Journal of Natural Resources Law
vi	Virgin Islands Reports	Vr.	Vroom's Law Reports (NJ)
V.I.	Same	VR	Valuation Reports, Interstate Commerce Commission
V.I.B.J.	Virgin Islands Bar Journal		
Vict.	Victoria		Victorian Reports
Vict.Admr.	Victorian Admiralty	Vroom	Vroom's Law Reports (NJ)
Vict.Eq.	Victorian Equity		
Vict.L.	Victorian Law	Vroom (G.D.W.)	G.D.W., Vroom (NJ)
Vict.L.R.	Victorian Law Reports	Vroom (P.D.)	P.D., Vroom (NJ)
Vict.L.R.Min.	Victorian Law Mining Reports	vt	Vermont Reports
		Vt.	Same
Vict.L.T.	Victorian Law Times	Vt.L.Rev.	Vermont Law Review
Vict.Rev.	Victorian Review		
Vict.St.Tr.	Victorian State Trials		

W

W.	Wandell (NY)	Wage & Hour Rep.	Wage & Hour Reporter
	Watts (PA)		
	Wheaton's Supreme Court (U.S.)	Wage–Price L. & Econ.Rev.	Wage–Price Law and Economics Review
	Wright (OH)	Wake Forest Intra.L.Rev.	Wake Forest Intramural Law Review
Wa.	Wage and Hour Reporter		
W.A'B. & W.	Webb, A'Beckett & Williams (Vict.)	Wake Forest L.Rev.	Wake Forest Law Review
W.A.C.A.	Selected Judgments of the West African Court of Appeals	Wake For. L.Rev.	Same
		Wal.By L.	Wallis, Irish Chancery (By Lyne)
W.Afr.App.	West African Court of Appeal Reports	Wal.Jr.	Wallace, Junior (U.S.)
		walk	Walker (MI)
Wage & Hour Cas.	Wage and Hour Cases (BNA)	Walk.	Walker (AL)
			Walker (MS)

	Walker's Supreme Court Reports (PA)
	Walker (TX)
WalkC	Walker's Chancery Reports (MI)
walkch	Same
Walk.Ch.	Same
Walk.Ch.Cas.	Same
Wall.	Wallace (U.S.)(Philadelphia)
	Wallis (Philadelphia)
Wall.C.C.	Wallace, Circuit Court (U.S.)
Wallis	Wallis' Chancery (Ir.)
Wallis by L.	Wallis, Irish Chancery (By Lyne)
walljr	Wallace, Junior (U.S.)
Wall.Jr.	Same
Wall.Rep.	Wallace on the Reporters
	Wallace's Supreme Court Reports (U.S.)
wallsr	Wallace, Senior (U.S.)
Wall.Sr.	Same
Walsh	Walsh's Registry Cases (Ir.)
W. & C.	Wilson & Courtenay's Appeal Cases
W & I C	Welfare and Institutions Code
W. & M.	Woodbury & Minot, Circuit Court (U.S.)
W. & S.	Watts & Sergeant (PA)
	Wilson & Shaw's Appeal Cases (Scot.)
W. & W.	White & Webb's Victorian Reports
W. & W.Vict.	Wyatt & Webb's Victorian Reports
WAp	Washington Appellate Reports
Ward.	Warden (OH)
Ward. & Sm.	Warden & Smith (OH)
Warden's Law & Bk.Bull.	Weekly Law & Bank Bulletin (OH)
ware	Ware, District Court (U.S.)
Ware	Same
wash	Washington Reports
Wash.	Same
	Washington Reports (VA)
wash2d	Washington Reports, Second Series
Wash.2d	Same
Wash. & Haz.P.E.I.	Washburton & Hazard's Reports (P.E.I.)
Wash. & Lee L.Rev.	Washington & Lee Law Review
washapp	Washington Appellate Reports
Wash.App.	Same

Washb.	Washburn (VT)
Washburn L.J.	Washburn Law Journal
washcc	Washington Circuit Court (U.S.)
Wash.C.C.	Same
Wash.L.Rep.	Washington Law Reporter (DC)
Wash.L.Rev.	Washington Law Review
washterr	Washington Territory
Wash.Terr.	Same
Wash.Terr.(N.S.)	Same, New Series
Wash.Ty.	Same
Wash.U.J. Urb. & Contemp.L.	Washington University Journal of Urban and Contemporary Law
Wash.U.L.Q.	Washington University Law Quarterly
Wat	Watts' Reports (PA)
Wat C	Water Code (CA)
Water C.	Same
Water C. App.	Same, Appendix
watts	Watts (PA)
Watts	Same
	Watts (WV)
watts & s	Watts & Sergeant (PA)
Watts & S.	Same
Watts & Ser.	Same
Watts & Serg.	Same
W.Austl.Ind. Gaz.	Western Australia Industrial Gazette
W.Austl.J.P.	Western Australia Justice of the Peace
W.Austl.L.R.	Western Australia Law Reports
Wayne L.Rev.	Wayne Law Review
W.Bl.	Sir William Blackstone's King's Bench & Common Pleas (Eng.)
W.Bla.	Same
W.C.C.	Washington's Circuit Court (U.S.)
	Workmen's Compensation Cases
W.C.Ins.Rep.	Workmen's Compensation & Insurance Reports
W.Coast Rep.	West Coast Reporter
W.C.Rep.	Workmen's Compensation Reports
Webb	Webb (KS)
	Webb (TX)
	Webb's Civil Appeals (TX)
Webb, A'B. & W.	Webb, A'Beckett & Williams' Reports (Austl.)
Webb & D.	Webb & Duval (TX)
Webb & Duval	Same

Webs.Pat. Cas.	Webster's Patent Cases (Eng.)	West.L.Gaz.	Western Law Gazette (OH)
Week.Cin. L.B.	Weekly Law Bulletin (OH)	West.L.J.	Western Law Journal
		West.L.M.	Western Law Monthly (OH)
Week.Dig.	Weekly Digest (NY)		
Week.Jur.	Weekly Jurist (IL)	West.L.Mo.	Same
Week.Law Bull.	Weekly Law Bulletin (OH)	West.L. Month.	Same
		West.L.R.	Western Law Reporter (Can.)
Week.Law Gaz.	Weekly Law Gazette (OH)		
		West.L.Rev.	Western Law Review
Week.L.Gaz.	Same	Westm.	State of Westminster (Eng.)
Week.L.Rec.	Weekly Law Record		
Weekly L.R.	Weekly Law Reports (Eng.)	Westm.L.J.	Westmoreland Law Journal (PA)
Week.Notes Cas.	Weekly Notes of Cases (London)	West.R.	Western Reporter
	Weekly Notes of Cases (PA)	West.School L.Rev.	Western School Law Review
Week.Rep.	Weekly Reporter (Eng.)	West. St. L. R.	Western State Law Review
Week.Trans. Rep.	Weekly Transcript Reports (NY)	West.St.U. L.Rev.	Western State University Law Review
Welf. & Inst. C.	Welfare and Institutions Code (CA)	West t.Hardw.	West tempore Hardwicke, Chancery (Eng.)
Welfare L.Bull.	Welfare Law Bulletin	West Va.	West Virginia
Welfare L.News	Welfare Law News	West.Week. Rep.	Western Weekly Reports (Can.)
Welf. C.	Welfare Code (CA)		
Welf. R. Bull.	Welfare Rights Bulletin	West.Wkly.	Western Weekly (Can.)
Welsb.H. & G.	Welsby, Hurlstone & Gordon's Exchequer (Eng.)	Wethey	Wethey's Queen's Bench (Upper Can.)
Welsby H. & G.	Same	W.F.P.D.2d	West's Federal Practice Digest, Second Series
Welsh (Ir.)	Welsh's Registry Cases	wh	Wages and Hours Cases (BNA)
Wen	Wendell's Reports (NY)		
Wend.	Same	wh2d	Same, Second Series
Wenz.	Wenzell (MN)	W.H. & G.	Welsby, Hurlstone & Gordon's Exchequer (Eng.)
Wes.C.L.J.	Westmoreland County Law Journal		
West	West Publishing or West Group	Whar	Wharton's Reports (PA)
	West's Chancery (Eng.)	whart	Same
West.	Weston (VT)	Whart.	Same
West.Austl.	Western Australian Reports	Whart.Law Dict.	Wharton's Law Lexicon
West Ch.	West's Chancery (Eng.)	Whart.St.Tr.	Wharton's State Trials (U.S.)
Western Res. L.Rev.	Western Reserve Law Review	W.H.Cases	Wage & Hour Cases
		WhCr	Wheeler's Criminal Cases (NY)
Western State L. Rev.	Western State University Law Review	Wheat.	Wheaton (U.S.)
		wheatr	Same
Western St LR	Same	Wheel.	Wheeler's Criminal Cases (NY)
West.Jur.	Western Jurist (Des Moines, IA)		Wheelock (TX)
West L.A. L. Rev.	West Los Angeles Law Review	Wheeler Abr.	Wheeler's Abridgment
		Wheeler C.C.	Wheeler's Criminal Cases (NY)
West.Law J.	Western Law Journal	White	White (TX)
West.Law M.	Western Law Monthly (OH)		White (WV)
			White's Justiciary Cases (Scot.)
West.Legal Obser.	Western Legal Observer		

White & T. Lead.Cas. Eq.	White & Tudor's Leading Cases in Equity (Eng.)
White & W.	White & Wilson (TX)
Whitm.Lib. Cas.	Whitman's Libel Cases (MA)
Whit.Pat.Cas.	Whitman's Patent Cases (U.S.)
Whitt.	Whittlesey (MO)
Whittier LR	Whittier Law Review
Whittier L.Rev.	Same
W.H.Man.	Wages & Hours Manual
W.H.R.	Wage & Hour Reporter
Widener J.Pub.L.	Widener Journal of Public Law
Wight	Wight's Section Cases (Scot.)
Wight.	Wightwick, Exchequer (Eng.)
Wightw.	Same
Wilc.	Wilcox (OH)
Wilc.Cond.	Wilcox, Condensed Ohio Reports
Wilcox	Wilcox (OH) Wilcox (PA)
Wilcox Cond.	Wilcox, Condensed Ohio Reports
Wilk.	Wilkinson (Austl.) Wilkinson, Court of Appeals and Civil Appeals (TX)
Will.	Williams (MA) Willson (TX)
Willamette L.J.	Willamette Law Journal
Willamette L.Rev.	Willamette Law Review
Willes	Willes, King's Bench & Common Pleas (Eng.)
Williams	Peere–Williams' English Chancery Reports Williams (MA) Williams (UT) Williams (VT)
Williams & Bruce Ad.Pr.	Williams & Bruce's Admiralty Practice
Williams P.	Peere–Williams' English Chancery Reports
Williams–Peere	Same
Will.L.J.	Willamette Law Journal
Willm.W. & D.	Willmore, Wollaston & Davison's Queen's Bench (Eng.)
Willm.W. & H.	Willmore, Wollaston & Hodges' Queen's Bench (Eng.)
Wills	Willson's Reports (TX)
Willson	Willson, Civil Cases (TX)

Willson, Civ.Cas.Ct.App.	Same
Will.Woll. & Dav.	Willmore, Wollaston & Davison, Queen's Bench (Eng.)
Will.Woll. & H.	Willmore, Wollaston & Hodges' Queen's Bench (Eng.)
Will.Woll. & Hodg.	Same
Wilm.	Wilmot's Notes (Eng.)
Wils.	Wilson (CA) Wilson (MN) Wilson (OR) Wilson, Superior Court Reports (IN) Wilson's King's Bench & Common Pleas (Eng.)
Wils. & S.	Wilson & Shaw, House of Lords (Scot.)
Wils.Ch.	Wilson's Chancery (Eng.)
Wils.C.P.	Wilson's Common Pleas (Eng.)
Wils.Exch.	Wilson's Exchequer (Eng.)
Wils.K.B.	Wilson's King's Bench (Eng.)
Wils.P.C.	Wilson's Privy Council (Eng.)
wilssuper	Wilson Superior Court Reports (IN)
Winch	Winch, Common Pleas (Eng.)
Winst.	Winston (NC)
W.I.R.	West Indian Reports
wis	Wisconsin Reports
Wis.	Same
wis2d	Same, Second Series
Wis.2d	Same
Wis.B.Bull.	Wisconsin Bar Bulletin
Wis.B.T.A.	Wisconsin Board of Tax Appeals Reports
Wisc.Stud. B.J.	Wisconsin Student Bar Journal
Wis.Int'l L.J.	Wisconsin International Law Journal
Wis.Law.	Wisconsin Lawyer
Wis.L.N.	Wisconsin Legal News
Wis.L.Rev.	Wisconsin Law Review
Wis.Multi–Cultural L.J.	Wisconsin Multi–Cultural Law Journal
Wis.Tax App.C.	Wisconsin Tax Appeals Commission Reports
Wis.Women's L.J.	Wisconsin Women's Law Journal
Withrow	Withrow (IA)

W.Jo.	William Jones King's Bench, Common Pleas, House of Lords and Exchequer (Eng.)
W.Jones	Same
W.Kel.	William Kellynge, King's Bench & Chancery (Eng.)
Wkly.Dig.	Weekly Digest (NY)
Wkly.Law Bull.	Weekly Law Bulletin (OH)
Wkly.L.Bul.	Same
Wkly.L.Gaz.	Weekly Law Gazette (OH)
Wkly.N.C.	Weekly Notes of Cases (PA)
Wkly.Rep.	Weekly Reporter (Eng.)
W.L.A.C.	Western Labour Arbitration Cases
W.L.Bull.	Weekly Law Bulletin
W.L.G.	Weekly Law Gazette (OH)
W.L.Gaz.	Same
W.L.J.	Western Law Journal
W.L.Jour.	Weekly Law Journal
W.L.M.	Western Law Monthly (OH)
WLR	Wisconsin Law Review
W.L.R.	Weekly Law Reports (Eng.)
	Western Law Reporter
	Women Law Reporter
W.L.T.	Western Law Times and Reports
Wm. & Mary Bill Rts.J.	William and Mary Bill of Rights Journal
Wm. & Mary J.Envtl.L.	William & Mary Journal of Environmental Law
Wm. & Mary L.Rev.	William & Mary Law Review
Wm. & Mary Rev.Va.L.	William and Mary Review of Virginia Law
Wm.Mitchell L.Rev.	William Mitchell Law Review
W.N.	Weekly Notes (Eng.)
W.New Eng. L.Rev.	Western New England Law Review
Wol.	Wolcott's Chancery (DE)
	Wollaston's English Bail Court Reports (Eng.)
Wolf. & B.	Wolferstan & Bristow's Election Cases (Eng.)
Wolf. & D.	Wolferstan & Dew's Election Cases (Eng.)
Woll.	Wollaston's English Bail Court Reports (Practice Cases)
Woll.P.C.	Same
Women & L	Women and Law
Woman Offend.Rep.	Woman Offender Report
Women Law.J.	Women Lawyer's Journal
Women's Rights L.Rptr.	Women's Rights Law Reporter
W.Ont.L.Rev.	Western Ontario Law Review
wood	Wood's U.S. Circuit Court Reports
Wood.	Woodbury & Minot, Circuit Court (U.S.)
Wood. & M.	Same
Woodb. & M.	Same
woodm	Same
Woods	Woods, Circuit Court (U.S.)
Woodw.	Woodward's Decisions (PA)
wool	Woolworth's U.S. Circuit Court Reports
Woolw.	Woolworth (NE)
	Woolworth, Circuit Court (U.S.)
Workmen's Comp. L.Rev.	Workmen's Compensation Law Review
World Jurist	World Jurist
World Pol.	World Polity
W.R.	Weekly Reports
W.Res.L.Rev.	Western Reserve Law Review
Wri	Wright's Supreme Court Reports (OH)
Wright	Wright (OH)
	Wright (PA)
W.Rob.	William Robinson's Admiralty (Eng.)
WS	Watts & Sergeant's Reports (PA)
Wsh	Washington State Reports
Wsh2	Same, Second Series
W.St.U. L.Rev.	Western State University Law Review
WT	Washington Territory Reports
WV	West Virginia Reports
wva	Same
W.Va.Crim. Just.Rev.	West Virginia Reports Criminal Justice Review
W.Va.L.Q.	West Virginia Law Quarterly
W.Va.L.Rev.	West Virginia Law Review
WW	White & Willson's Reports (TX)

W.W. & D.	Willmore, Wollaston & Davison, Queen's Bench (Eng.)
W.W. & H.	Willmore, Wollaston & Hodges' Queen's Bench (Eng.)
W.W.D.	Western Weekly Digests
WWH	W. W. Harrington's Reports (DE)
W.W.Harr.	W.W. Harrington (DE)

W.W.R.	Western Weekly Report (Can.)
W.W.R.(N.S.)	Same, New Series
Wy. & W.	Wyatt & Webb (Vict.)
wyo	Wyoming Reports
Wyo.	Same
Wyo.L.J.	Wyoming Law Journal
Wythe	Wythe's Chancery Reports (VA)
wythech	Same
Wy.W. & A'Beck	Wyatt, Webb & A'Beckett (Vict.)

Y

Y.	Yeates (PA)
Y.A.D.	Young's Admiralty Decisions (Nova Scotia)
Yale J.Int'l L.	Yale Journal of International Law
Yale J.L. & Feminism	Yale Journal of Law & Feminism
Yale J.L. & Humanities	Yale Journal of Law & the Humanities
Yale J.L. & Lib.	Yale Journal of Law & Liberation
Yale J. on Reg.	Yale Journal on Regulation
Yale J.World Pub.Ord.	Yale Journal of World Public Order
Yale L. & Pol'y Rev.	Yale Law & Policy Review
Yale L.J.	Yale Law Journal
Yale Rev.Law & Soc.Act'n	Yale Review of Law and Social Action
Yale Stud. World Pub. Ord.	Yale Studies in World Public Order
Y. & C.	Younge & Collyer's Chancery (Eng.)
Y. & C.C.C.	Same
Y. & J.	Younge & Jervis' Exchequer (Eng.)
Yannacone & Cohen	Yannacone & Cohen, Environmental Rights and Remedies
Yates	Yates' Select Cases
Yates Sel. Cas.	Yates' Select Cases (NY)
Y.B.	Year Book, King's Bench (Eng.)
Y.B. (Rolls Series)	Same, Rolls Series (Eng.)
Y.B. (Sel. Soc.)	Same, Selden Society (Eng.)
Y.B.A.A.A.	Yearbook of the Association of Attenders and Alumni of the

	Hague Academy of International Law
Y.B.A.S.L.	Yearbook of Air and Space Law
Y.B.Ed. I	Year Books, Edward I
Y.B.Eur. Conv. on Human Rights	Yearbook of the European Convention on Human Rights
Y.B.Eur.L.	Yearbook of European Law
Y.B.Human Rights	Yearbook on Human Rights
Y.B.Int'l L.Comm'n	Yearbook of the International Law Commission
Y.B.Int'l Org.	Yearbook of International Organizations
Y.B.League of Nations	Yearbook of the League of Nations
Y.B.P.1, Edw. II	Year Books, Part 1, Edward II
Y.B.S.C.	Year Books, Selected Cases
Y.B.U.N.	Yearbook of the United Nations
Y.B.W.A.	Yearbook of World Affairs
Y.B.World Pol.	Yearbook of World Polity
Yea.	Yeates' Reports (PA)
Yearb.	Year Book, King's Bench (Eng.)
Yearb.P.7, Hen.VI	Year Books, Part 7, Henry VI
yeates	Yeates' Reports (PA)
Yeates	Same
Yel.	Yelverton, King's Bench (Eng.)
Yelv.	Same
Yerg.	Yerger (TN)
yertn	Same
Y.L.C.T.	Yearbook of Law, Computers, and Technology

YLJ	Yale Law Journal	Younge & C. Ch.Cas.	Younge & Collyer's Chancery or Exchequer Equity (Eng.)
Yorke Ass.	Clayton Reports, Yorke Assizes		
York Leg. Rec.	York Legal Record (PA)	Younge & C. Exch.	Younge & Collyer's Exchequer Equity (Eng.)
You.	Younge's Exchequer (Eng.)	Younge & Coll.Ex.	Same
You. & Coll. Ch.	Younge & Collyer's Exchequer (Eng.)	Younge & J.	Younge & Jervis, Exchequer (Eng.)
You. & Coll. Ex.	Same	Younge & Je.	Same
You. & Jerv.	Younge & Jervis, Exchequer (Eng.)	Younge Exch.	Younge, Exchequer (Eng.)
Young	Young (MN)	Younge M.L. Cas.	Younge, Maritime Law Cases (Eng.)
Young Adm.	Young, Admiralty (N.S.)	Young Naut. Dict.	Young's Nautical Dictionary
Young Adm. Dec.	Same	Yugo.L.	Yugoslav Law
Younge	Younge's Exchequer (Eng.)		

Z

Zab.	Zabriskie (NJ)
Zambia L.J	Zambia Law Journal
Zane	Zane (UT)

Appendix B

STATE GUIDES TO LEGAL RESEARCH[*]

The various state legal systems in the United States have much in common with each other and with the federal government, including legislative, judicial, and executive departments that, in one way or another, "make law." However, each legal system is the product of a history and culture unique to that state. This leads to differences in the legal resources produced by each state, which will vary depending on methods of legislating, codifying, and court reporting, as well as the scope of executive authority.

Legal researchers must learn and use the sources of law for the states in which their problems arise; effective research is impossible if the correct resources are not consulted. To assist researchers in completing their projects, law librarians and other research professionals have written guides, handbooks, and bibliographies that explain the legal systems and resources of each of the states and the District of Columbia. Many of these publications are listed here.

This state-by-state list includes the more recent printed legal research books (if any) for each state and the District of Columbia and shorter bibliographies from the American Association of Law Libraries (AALL) that focus on the primary legal resources produced by state government. If the need arises to research legal issues that involve the law of any state during its territorial period (prior to formal admission into statehood), an indispensable resource is *Prestatehood Legal Materials: A Fifty-State Research Guide*, 2 v. (Michael Chiorazzi & Marguerite Most eds., 2005).

Many electronic legal research guides are also available, although, like electronic resources generally, whether you can access online legal research guides depends on the licensing terms of the particular resource. In some instances, electronic resources may be available only to the students and faculty at a law school, or only those who come into the library and use the resource on-site. Electronic resources are not included in this list because of the limitations on their general availability.

However, legal researchers should not neglect looking for, or using, a state legal research guide just because the resource is only available electronically. Law school librarians regularly prepare state-specific research guides and advice, and post the resources on their library's website. The bibliographies from AALL are available in the "Spinelli's Law Library Reference Shelf" collection on *HeinOnline*, to which most law school libraries subscribe. The Center for Computer-Assisted Legal Instruction (CALI) provides state legal research tutorials for every state; most law schools are members of CALI and provide passwords for these materials to students and faculty. Checking a law library's catalog or list of databases is the easiest way to locate available electronic research guides.

---

[*] This appendix was revised by Bonnie Shucha, Assistant Director for Public Services, University of Wisconsin Law Library.

Alabama

Blakeley Beals, *State Documents Bibliography: Alabama* (2012) (AALL).

Gary Orlando Lewis, *Legal Research in Alabama: How to Find and Understand the Law in Alabama* (2001).

Alaska

Catherine Lemann, *State Documents Bibliography: Alaska* (2009) (AALL).

Arizona

Tamara S. Herrera, *Arizona Legal Research* (2d ed. 2013).

Ariz. Super. Ct. Law Libr., *A Survey of Arizona State Legal and Law-Related Documents* (2006) (AALL).

Arkansas

Coleen M. Barger, *Arkansas Legal Research* (2007).

Lynn Foster, *Arkansas Legal Bibliography: Documents and Selected Commercial Titles* (1988) (AALL).

California

Larry D. Dershem, *California Legal Research Handbook* (2d ed. 2008).

Janet Fischer & Steven Feller, *California State Documents: A Bibliography of Legal Publications and Related Materials* (2005) (AALL).

John K. Hanft, *Legal Research in California* (6th ed. 2007).

Hether C. Macfarlane, Aimee Dudovizt & Suzanne E. Rowe, *California Legal Research* (2d ed. 2013).

Daniel Martin & Dan F. Henke, *Henke's California Law Guide* (8th ed. 2006).

Colorado

Robert Michael Linz, *Colorado Legal Research* (2010).

Robert C. Richards & Barbara Bintliff, *Colorado Legal Resources: An Annotated Bibliography* (2004) (AALL).

Connecticut

Judith Anspach, Dennis J. Stone & David Voisinet, *Connecticut State Legal Documents: A Selective Bibliography* (1986) (AALL).

Jessica G. Hynes, *Connecticut Legal Research* (2009).

Delaware

Peter J. Egler, *Selective Annotated Bibliography of Delaware State Documents and Other Resources Used in Delaware Legal Research* (2008) (AALL).

District of Columbia

Leah F. Chanin, Pamela J. Gregory & Sarah K. Wiant, *Legal Research in the District of Columbia, Maryland, and Virginia* (2d ed. 2000).

Jennifer Davitt, *State Documents Bibliography: Washington, D.C.* (2008) (AALL).

Florida

Barbara J. Busharis, Jennifer LaVia & Suzanne E. Rowe, *Florida Legal Research* (4th. ed. 2014).

Betsy L. Stupski, *Guide to Florida Legal Research* (7th ed. 2008).

Georgia

Nancy P. Johnson, Elizabeth G. Adelman & Nancy J. Adams, *Georgia Legal Research* (2007).

Nancy P. Johnson & Ronald Wheeler, *State Documents Bibliography: Georgia* (2012) (AALL).

Hawaii

Richard F. Kahle, *How to Research Constitutional Legislative and Statutory History in Hawaii*, (3d ed. 2004).

Leina'ala R. Seeger, *Hawai'i State Documents: A Selective Bibliography of Legal Publications and Related Materials* (2010) (AALL).

Idaho

Tenielle Fordyce-Ruff & Suzanne E. Rowe, *Idaho Legal Research* (2008).

Michael J. Greenlee, *Idaho State Documents: A Bibliography of Legal Publications and Related Materials* (2003) (AALL).

Illinois

Cheryl R. Nyberg, Joyce Olin & Peter Young, *Illinois State Documents: A Selective Annotated Bibliography for Law Librarians* (1986) (AALL).

Laurel Wendt, *Illinois Legal Research Guide* (2d ed. 2006).

Mark E. Wojcik, *Illinois Legal Research* (2d ed. 2009).

Indiana

Linda K. Fariss & Keith A. Buckley, *An Introduction to Indiana State Publications for the Law Librarian* (1986) (AALL).

Iowa

John D. Edwards et al., *Iowa Legal Research* (2011).

Angela K. Secrest, *Iowa Legal Documents Bibliography* (1990) (AALL).

Kansas

Joseph A. Custer, Barbara J. Ginzburg & Robert A. Mead, *Kansas Legal Research and Reference Guide* (3d ed. 2003).

Joseph A. Custer & Christopher L. Steadham, *Kansas Legal Research* (2008).

Martin E. Wisneski, *Kansas State Documents for Law Libraries: Publications Related to Law and State Government* (1984) (AALL).

Kentucky

William A. Hilyerd, Kurt X. Metzmeier & David J. Ensign, *Kentucky Legal Research* (2012).

Kurt X. Metzmeier, Amy Beckham Osborne & Shaun Esposito, *Kentucky Legal Research Manual* (3d ed. 2005).

Ryan Valentin & Michelle Cosby, *Kentucky State Documents: A Bibliography of Legal & Law-Related Material* (2008) (AALL).

Louisiana

Mary Garvey Algero, *Louisiana Legal Research* (2d ed. 2013).

Charlene Cain & Madeline Hebert, *Louisiana Legal Documents and Related Publications* (3d ed. 2001) (AALL).

Maine

Christine I. Hepler & Maureen P. Quinlan, *Maine State Documents: A Bibliography of Legal and Law Related Material* (2003) (AALL).

Maryland

Katherine Baer, *State Documents Bibliography: Maryland* (2013) (AALL).

Leah F. Chanin, Pamela J. Gregory & Sarah K. Wiant, *Legal Research in the District of Columbia, Maryland, and Virginia* (2d ed. 2000).

William L. Taylor, *Maryland State Publications in Law and Related Fields: A Selective Bibliography with Annotations* (1996).

Massachusetts

E. Joan Blum, *Massachusetts Legal Research* (2010).

Leo McAuliffe & Susan Z. Steinway, *Massachusetts State Documents Bibliography* (1985) (AALL).

Handbook of Legal Research in Massachusetts (Mary Ann Neary, ed., 3d ed. 2009).

Virginia J. Wise, *How to Do Massachusetts Legal Research: Maximizing Efficiency in the Print and Online Environment* (3d ed. 2009).

Michigan

Pamela Lysaght & Cristina D. Lockwood, *Michigan Legal Research* (2d ed. 2011).

Christopher T. Bloodworth et al., *Michigan Legal Documents: A Bibliography of Legal & Law-Related Materials* (2006) (AALL).

Minnesota

Deborah K. Hackerson, *A Bibliography of Minnesota Legal Documents* (2d ed. 2010) (AALL).

John Tessner, George R. Jackson & Brenda Wolfe, *Minnesota Legal Research Guide* (2d ed. 2002).

Suzanne Thorpe, *Minnesota Legal Research* (2010).

Mississippi

Ben Cole, *Mississippi Legal Documents and Related Publications: A Selected Annotated Bibliography* (1987) (AALL).

Kristy L. Gilliland, *Mississippi Legal Research* (2014).

Missouri

Judy A. Stark, *State Documents Bibliography: Missouri* (2010) (AALL).

Wanda M. Temm & Julie M. Cheslik, *Missouri Legal Research* (2d ed. 2011).

Introduction to Legal Materials: A Manual for Non-Law Librarians in Missouri (2006).

Montana

Margaret Ann Chansler, *Montana State Documents: A Bibliography of Legal and Law-Related Material* (2004) (AALL).

Robert K. Whelan, Meredith Hoffman & Stephen R. Jordan, *A Guide to Montana Legal Research* (8th ed. 2003).

Nebraska

Kay L. Andrus, *Research Guide to Nebraska Law* (2008).

George Butterfield, Matthew Novak & Brian Striman, *Nebraska State Bibliography of Legal Resources Annotated: A Selective Bibliography* (2012) (AALL).

Patrick H. Charles, *Lexis Publishing's Research Guide to Nebraska Law* (2001).

Nevada

Nevada Legal Research Guide (Jennifer Larraguibel Gross & Thomas Blake Gross, eds., 2012).

Ann S. Jarrell & G. LeGrande Fletcher, *Nevada State Documents Bibliography: Legal Publications and Related Material* (2d ed. 2000) (AALL).

New Hampshire

Linda B. Johnson et al., *State Documents Bibliography: New Hampshire* (2012) (AALL).

New Jersey

Paul Axel-Lute & Molly Brownfield, *New Jersey Legal Research Handbook* (5th ed. 2008).

Karin Johnsrud & Sarah Jaramillo, *New Jersey State Documents: A Bibliography of Legal Resources* (2011) (AALL).

New Mexico

Theresa Strike & Patricia D. Wagner, *Guide to New Mexico State Publications (*3d ed. (2009) (AALL).

New York

Elizabeth G. Adelman, Theodora Belniak & Suzanne E. Rowe, *New York Legal Research* (2d ed. 2012).

Robert Allan Carter, *New York State Constitution: Sources of Legislative Intent* (2d ed. 2001).

William H. Manz, Ellen M. Gibson & Karen L. Spencer, *Gibson's New York Legal Research Guide* (3d ed. 2004).

Gail F. Whittemore, *New York Legal Documents 2007: A Selective Annotated Bibliography* (2007) (AALL).

North Carolina

Scott Childs & Sara Sampson, *North Carolina Legal Research* (2d ed. 2012).

Donna Nixon, Nichelle Perry & Jason R. Sowards, *Guide to North Carolina Legal and Law-Related Materials* (3d ed. 2010) (AALL).

North Dakota

Rhonda R. Schwartz, *North Dakota State Documents: A Selective Bibliography of Legal and Law-related Material* (2009) (AALL).

Ohio

Christine Corcas, *Ohio State Legal Documents and Related Publications: A Selected Annotated Bibliography* (1987) (AALL).

Katherine L. Hall & Sara A. Sampson, *Ohio Legal Research* (2009).

Ann S. McFarland, *Ohio Legal Resources: An Annotated Bibliography and Guide* (4th ed. 1996).

Melanie K. Putnam, Susan M. Schaefgen & Katherine L. Hall, *Ohio Legal Research Guide* (2d ed. 2010).

Oklahoma

Darin K. Fox, *State Documents Bibliography, Oklahoma: A Guide to Legal Research in Oklahoma* (2009) (AALL).

Darin K. Fox, Darla W. Jackson & Courtney L. Selby, *Oklahoma Legal Research* (2013).

Oregon

Stephanie Midkiff & Wendy Schroeder Hitchcock, *State Documents Bibliography, Oregon: A Survey of Oregon State Legal and Law-Related Documents* (2009) (AALL).

Suzanne E. Rowe, *Oregon Legal Research* (3d ed. 2014).

Pennsylvania

Barbara J. Busharis & Bonny L. Tavares, *Pennsylvania Legal Research* (2007).

Joel Fishman, *Pennsylvania State Documents: A Bibliography of Legal and Law-Related Material* (2011) (AALL).

Frank Y. Liu, et al., *Pennsylvania Legal Research Handbook* (2008 ed. 2008).

Rhode Island

Nannette Kelley Balliot, Tom Evans & Colleen McConaghy Hanna, *State Documents Bibliography: Rhode Island* (2013) (AALL).

South Carolina

Paula Gail Benson & Deborah Ann Davis, *A Guide to South Carolina Legal Research and Citation* (2d ed. 2009).

Terrye Conroy, Stacy Etheredge & David Lehmann, *State Documents Bibliography: South Carolina* (2009) (AALL).

South Dakota

Delores A. Jorgensen, *South Dakota Legal Research Guide* (2d ed. 1999).

Candice Spurlin, *State Documents Bibliography: South Dakota* (2011) (AALL).

Tennessee

Reba A. Best, *Tennessee State Documents: A Bibliography of State Publications and Related Materials* (2009) (AALL).

Sibyl Marshall & Carol McCrehan Parker, *Tennessee Legal Research* (2007).

Texas

Malinda Allison & Kay Schleuter, *Texas State Documents for Law Libraries* (1983) (AALL).

Brandon D. Quarles & Matthew C. Cordon, *Researching Texas Law* (2d ed. 2008).

Spencer L. Simons, *Texas Legal Research* (rev. 2012).

Pamela R. Tepper & Peggy N. Kerley, *Texas Legal Research* (2d ed. 1997).

Utah

Jessica Van Buren, Mari Cheney & Marsha C. Thomas, *Utah Legal Research* (2011).

Mari Cheney, *Utah Legal Resources Bibliography* (2009) (AALL).

Vermont

Cynthia Lewis et al., *State Documents Bibliography, Vermont: An Updated Guide to the Vermont Legal System* (3d ed. 2009) (AALL).

Virginia

Leah F. Chanin, Pamela J. Gregory & Sarah K. Wiant, *Legal Research in the District of Columbia, Maryland, and Virginia* (2d ed. 2000).

John D. Eure & Gail F. Zwirner, ed., *A Guide to Legal Research in Virginia* (7th ed. 2012).

Margaret Krause & Sara Sampson, *State Documents Bibliography: Virginia* (2nd rev. ed. 2010) (AALL).

Washington

Penny Hazelton, et al., *Washington Legal Researcher's Deskbook* (3d ed. 2002).

Julie A. Heintz-Cho, Tom Cobb & Mary A. Hotchkiss, *Washington Legal Research* (2d ed. 2009).

Peggy Roebuck Jarrett & Cheryl Rae Nyberg, *Washington State Documents: A Bibliography of Legal and Law-Related Material* (2011) (AALL).

West Virginia

Sandra Stemple, Marjorie Price & June Board, *West Virginia Legal Bibliography* (1990) (AALL).

Hollee Schwartz Temple, *West Virginia Legal Research* (2013).

Wisconsin

Patricia Cervenka & Leslie Behroozi, *Wisconsin Legal Research* (2011).

Barbara Fritschel, *State Documents Bibliography: Wisconsin* (2009) (AALL).

Theodore A. Potter & Jane Colwin, *Legal Research in Wisconsin* (2d ed. 2008).

Wyoming

Debora A. Person & Tawnya K. Plumb, *Wyoming Legal Research* (2013).

Debora A. Person, *Wyoming State Documents: A Bibliography of State Publications and Related Materials* (2006) (AALL).

Appendix C

LEGAL RESEARCH IN TERRITORIES OF THE UNITED STATES*

The United States exercises sovereignty, in varying degrees, over a small number of island jurisdictions in the Caribbean Sea and Pacific Ocean. These jurisdictions can usefully be grouped as either territories or possessions of the United States or states in free association with the United States.[1]

Each of the jurisdictions has substantial local autonomy and lawmaking power. Therefore, legal research requires the use of local materials[2] as well as applicable federal law. This appendix provides a basic introduction to the legal research resources for these jurisdictions.[3]

A. TERRITORIES OF THE UNITED STATES

A territory does not have the status of a state. As a result, a territory is not considered to be fully a part of the United States, and the federal Constitution is held not to apply there fully. Territories are said to be "unincorporated."[4] When Congress has enacted an organic act for the governance of a territory, the territory is said to be organized.[5]

1. American Samoa

American Samoa is an unorganized territory of the United States. The United States gained sovereignty over American Samoa by a treaty in 1899 with Germany and Great Britain,[6] and by cessions in 1900 and 1904 from the indigenous Samoans.

---

* Jonathan Pratter, Foreign and International Law Librarian, Tarlton Law Library, Jamail Center for Legal Research, University of Texas School of Law, revised this appendix.

[1] See STANLEY K. LAUGHLIN, JR., THE LAW OF UNITED STATES TERRITORIES AND AFFILIATED JURISDICTIONS (1995), for a full discussion of the legal status of these jurisdictions.

[2] CONSTITUTIONS OF DEPENDENCIES AND SPECIAL SOVEREIGNTIES (Albert P. Blaustein ed., 1975–) is an important resource for constitutional research in territorial jurisdictions. Its contents are often more current than those published by the several territorial governments.

[3] Several of the jurisdictions discussed in this appendix are in the South Pacific. Readers working with these jurisdictions are advised always to see what resources are available in the website of the Pacific Islands Legal Information Institute, http://www.paclii.org.

[4] One territory, the Palmyra Atoll, is incorporated, through Congressional action. Definitions of Insular Area Political Organizations (U.S. Dept. of Interior, Office of Insular Affairs), at http://www.doi.gov/oia/Island pages/political_types.cfm.

[5] See id.

[6] Convention on Adjustment of Jurisdiction in Samoa, 31 Stat. 1878, T.S. 314, 1 Bevans 276.

American Samoa's status as a territory was confirmed by statute in 1929.[7] The Department of the Interior is responsible for the administration of American Samoa.[8]

a.   *Constitution.* While American Samoa does not have an organic act, it does have a Constitution of 1967 approved by the voters and by the Secretary of the Interior. The text of the Constitution as amended is included at the beginning of the *American Samoa Code Annotated* and at the website of the American Samoa Bar Association.[9] The Constitution provides American Samoa with a legislature, a judiciary, and an executive, so that American Samoa enjoys substantial local lawmaking authority.

b.   *Statutes. American Samoa Code Annotated,* Pago Pago, American Samoa: The Bureau, 2009–. The code is edited, indexed, and published by the Legislative Reference Bureau of American Samoa. It is organized in titles. The code as of 2010 is available online in PDF at the website of the American Samoa Bar Association.

c.   *Court Reports.* All series of the *American Samoa Reports* are available at the website of the American Samoa Bar Association.[10]

(1)   *American Samoa Reports.* Orford, NH: Equity Pub. Corp., 1977–1982. Complete in four volumes and a digest, this series reports the decisions of the High Court of American Samoa from 1900 to 1975.

(2)   *American Samoa Reports, 2d series.* Pago Pago, American Samoa: The Court, 1983–1997. This series, with thirty-one volumes, contains decisions of the Trial, Land and Titles, and Appellate Divisions of the High Court of American Samoa.

(3)   *American Samoa Reports, 3d series.* Pago Pago, American Samoa: The Court, 1997–. As of June 2014, seven volumes have been published.

d.   *Digest. American Samoa Digest.* 2008 ed. Pago Pago, American Samoa: High Court of American Samoa, 2008. This digest covers all three series of the *American Samoa Reports.* It is available on the website of the American Samoa Bar Association.

e.   *Administrative Regulations.* The *American Samoa Administrative Code* is available on the website of the American Samoa Bar Association.

f.   *Court Rules.* Rules of court, including those for the Trial and Appellate Divisions of the High Court, are available on the website of the American Samoa Bar Association.

2.   Guam

Guam is an organized territory of the United States. It was ceded to the United States by treaty following the Spanish–American War.[11]

a.   *Constitution.* Guam received its organic act in 1950[12]; it does not have a constitution. The organic act establishes legislative, judicial, and executive authorities

---

[7] Act of Feb. 20, 1929, ch. 281, 45 Stat. 1253 (1929), codified as amended at 48 U.S.C. § 1661 (2006). Additional foundational documents establishing American Samoa's political status can be found at the website of the American Samoa Bar Association, http://www.asbar.org.

[8] Exec. Order No. 10,264, 16 Fed. Reg. 6419 (1951).

[9] http://www.asbar.org. Click "Legal Resources." (This URL and instruction applies to all legal materials available on the website of the American Samoa Bar Association.)

[10] http://www.asbar.org.

[11] Treaty of Peace, Spain–U.S., December 10, 1898, 30 Stat. 1754, T.S. 343, 11 Bevans 615.

[12] Act of Aug. 1, 1950, ch. 512, 64 Stat. 384, codified as amended at 48 U.S.C. §§ 1421–1428e (2006).

for Guam. In addition to territorial courts, there is a United States District Court of Guam from which appeal lies to the United States Court of Appeals for the Ninth Circuit. Negotiations with Congress and successive administrations on commonwealth status, including the drafting of a constitution, have been underway for years.

    b.   Statutes. The *Guam Code Annotated*, Hagåtña, Guam: Office of Attorney General, Compiler of Laws, 2005–. The *Guam Code Annotated* is available in PDF at the website of the Compiler of Laws.[13] (The *Guam Code Annotated* in hard copy is not as current as the online version.) Both *Westlaw* and *LexisNexis* have the *Guam Code Annotated*. Guam session laws are available at the Compiler of Laws website.

    Guam public laws are available at the website of the Guam Legislature.[14]

    c.   Court Reports. The decisions of the Supreme Court of Guam from 1996 to the present are found on the websites of the Compiler of Laws[15] and the Unified Courts of Guam.[16] Note that the Supreme Court of Guam has adopted format-neutral citation of its decisions. *Westlaw* and *LexisNexis* both include Guam Supreme Court cases (1996–) as well as the decisions of the U.S. District Court of Guam (1951–).

    d.   Administrative Regulations. The *Guam Administrative Rules and Regulations* are available on the website of the Compiler of Laws.[17] *LexisNexis* and *Westlaw* have the Guam administrative regulations, but neither is current as of August 2014.

    e.   Court Rules. Guam court rules are available on the Unified Courts' website.[18] The Local Rules of Practice of the U.S. District Court of Guam are available on that court's website.[19]

3. Northern Mariana Islands.

    This island group in the Pacific, north of Guam, was part of the Trust Territory of the Pacific Islands created in 1947 by the United Nations and administered by the United States. Negotiations on status led to the 1975 signing of the Covenant to Establish a Commonwealth of the Northern Mariana Islands in Political Union with the United States of America, approved by Congress in 1976.[20] Under the Covenant, the Northern Mariana Islands are a self-governing Commonwealth "in political union with and under the sovereignty of the United States." The Commonwealth exercises local self-government, while the United States retains sole responsibility for defense and foreign affairs. Under section 105 of the Covenant, general federal legislation applies in the Northern Mariana Islands. The Covenant establishes a United States District Court of the Northern Mariana Islands, the jurisdiction of which tracks that of its counterpart for Guam. Appeal lies to the Ninth Circuit.

    a.   Constitution. The Covenant calls for the drafting and approval of a Constitution, which was promulgated in 1977. It establishes legislative, judicial, and

---

[13] http://www.guamcourts.org/compileroflaws/gca.html. As of Aug. 13, 2014, it was current through Sept. 11, 2013.

[14] http://www.guamlegislature.com.

[15] http://www.guamcourts.org/compileroflaws/supremeop.html.

[16] http://www.guamsupremecourt.com/Opinions/opinions.html.

[17] http://www.guamcourts.org/compileroflaws/gar.html. As of Aug. 13, 2014, the regulations were current only as of April 2004.

[18] http://www.guamcourts.org/compileroflaws/CourtRules/crtrules.html.

[19] http://www.gud.uscourts.gov/?q=local_rules.

[20] Act of March 24, 1976, Pub.L.No. 94–241, 90 Stat. 263.

executive authorities. The text of the Constitution is contained at the beginning of the *Northern Mariana Islands Commonwealth Code* (below). An annotated text of the Constitution, published in 1995, is available from the Commonwealth Law Revision Commission (CLRC).[21]

    b.   Statutes. The Commonwealth Code, *Northern Mariana Islands Commonwealth Code,* Saipan, MP: Commonwealth Law Revision Commission, 2010–, is also available online at the CLRC website.[22]

Public laws since the Commonwealth was established are on the CLRC's website.[23]

    c.   Court Reports. Decisions of the Commonwealth Supreme Court from 1996 to the present and of the Commonwealth Superior Court from 1989 to the present are on the CLRC's website.[24] Note that the Supreme Court has adopted format-neutral citation.

The *Northern Mariana Islands Reporter*, Saipan, MP: Commonwealth Law Revision Commission, 1997–, publishes decisions of the Supreme Court from 1989 to 1999. The hard copy *Commonwealth Reporter*[25] publishes decisions of the Commonwealth Court (formerly the Trial Court) and the trial and appellate divisions of the District Court for the Northern Mariana Islands from 1979 to 1984.

Westlaw and *LexisNexis* include decisions of the Supreme Court from 1990 and decisions of the U.S. District Court of the Northern Mariana Islands from 1981.

    d.   Administrative Regulations. The CLRC publishes the *Northern Mariana Islands Administrative Code* online.[26]

    e.   Court Rules. Rules of court, including for the Supreme Court and the rules of civil and criminal procedure, are available on the CLRC's website.[27]

4. Puerto Rico

Puerto Rico is the largest of the territories associated with the United States, both in terms of land area and population (approximately 3.7 million in 2014). The United States acquired Puerto Rico from Spain following the Spanish–American War. The law governing Puerto Rico's current political status is found in federal legislation,[28] the Constitution of Puerto Rico, and judicial decisions, both federal and territorial. In its constitution, Puerto Rico is denominated a Commonwealth. Puerto Rico exercises a degree of sovereignty approaching that of a state of the United States. In addition to a fully developed Commonwealth judiciary, there is a United States District Court for Puerto Rico from which appeals lie to the United States Court of Appeals for the First Circuit.

---

[21] http://www.cnmilaw.org. (This URL applies to all legal materials available on the website of the Commonwealth Law Revision Commission.)

[22] http://www.cnmilaw.org/frames/Commonwealth% 20Code.html

[23] http://www.cnmilaw.org/legislativebranch.html

[24] http://www.cnmilaw.org/superiorcourt.html.

[25] http://www.cnmilaw.org/commonwealthreporter.html

[26] http://www.cnmilaw.org/mediawiki–1.21.2/index.php?title=Main_Page

[27] http://www.cnmilaw.org/judicialbranch.html

[28] *See generally* 48 U.S.C. § 731–916 (2006).

  a. *Constitution.* The text of the constitution can be found in the annotated code,[29] in an online unannotated code provided by LexisNexis,[30] and in multiple versions on the Internet.

  b. *Statutes.* Multiple sources are available for Puerto Rican statutes.

  The session laws are found in *Leyes de Puerto Rico / Laws of Puerto Rico.* San Juan, Puerto Rico: LexisNexis of Puerto Rico, 1900–. The session laws are published in separate Spanish and English series. They are also available in *HeinOnline's* Session Laws library and in microfiche from the William S. Hein & Co., Inc. Because of the substantial delay in the publication of bound session law volumes, there are advance session law services through the Internet.

  Leyes de Puerto Rico Anotadas / Laws of Puerto Rico Annotated. San Juan, Puerto Rico: LexisNexis of Puerto Rico, 1954–. This is the standard compilation of the Puerto Rican statutes. It is updated with pocket parts and replacement supplements. The annotations include not only court cases but also cross-references to *Rules and Regulations of Puerto Rico.* There are historical notes to trace the development of various sections. *Laws of Puerto Rico Annotated* is published in separate English and Spanish editions, as both languages are official.

  Westlaw has the Puerto Rico statutes annotated (PR–ST–ANN), both in English and in Spanish, the rules of court, and a legislative database called Recent Laws that purports to have the text of recently passed laws (last two years).

  LexisNexis has a Puerto Rico library that contains files for the annotated statutes, both in English and Spanish, and a file that purports to have the text of recently passed laws, though it does not appear to contain anything more recent than the other statutory databases.

  Biblioteca Legislativa (Legislative Library), Legislative Assembly of Puerto Rico, a free resource, includes bills, resolutions, and statutes in Spanish,[31] statutes from 1997 translated into English, and useful information about the legislative process in Puerto Rico.

  c. *Court Reports.* Puerto Rico has adopted a public domain citation format for cases decided after 1997. Puerto Rican court reports are available from a variety of sources.

  Puerto Rico Reports. San Juan, Puerto Rico: Equity Publishing Corp., vols. 1–100, 1900–1972. This English-language set includes all cases from the Supreme Court of Puerto Rico from 1900 to 1972. The English version suspended publication with volume 100. The decisions of the Supreme Court since 1972 are available in translation, but unpublished, from the Court with the title *Official Translations of the Decisions of the Supreme Court of Puerto Rico.*[32]

  Decisiones de Puerto Rico. San Juan, Puerto Rico: West Group de Puerto Rico, 1900– . The Spanish version of the reports of the Supreme Court of Puerto Rico continues to be

---

[29] The current text in English is found in Title 1, LAWS OF PUERTO RICO.

[30] http://www.lexisnexis.com/hottopics/lawsofpuertorico/.

[31] http://www.oslpr.org/old/BibliotecaLegislativa.asp.

[32] Certified or plain copies of translations prepared by the Court can be requested from Secretaría del Tribunal Supremo, Negociado de Traducciones, Apartado 9022392, San Juan, Puerto Rico 00902–2392, phone (787) 723–6033, ext.2091, Fax number (787)729–8928.

published, but there is approximately a two-year delay before a volume of decisions is published.

Jurisprudencia del Tribunal Supremo de Puerto Rico. San Juan, Puerto Rico: Publicaciones JTS, 1977–. These are weekly advance sheets of the decisions of the Supreme Court, published only in Spanish, with quarterly indexes and case tables.

Avanzadas del Tribunal Supremo. San Juan, Puerto Rico: Colegio de Abogados de Puerto Rico, 1963–. The *Puerto Rico Bar Association* publishes these advance sheets of the decisions of the Supreme Court of Puerto Rico. There is an annual index. The bar association's website[33] includes the complete text of the decisions of the Supreme Court of Puerto Rico since 1998.

Decisiones del Tribunal de Circuito de Apelaciones de Puerto Rico. San Juan, Puerto Rico: Publicaciones JTS, 1995–. These advance sheets of the decisions of the Puerto Rico Appellate Circuit Court are published twice monthly, in Spanish. An annual index is included.

Westlaw includes the decisions of the Supreme Court of Puerto Rico, in Spanish, since 1899 to present in the database (PRS–CS), a selection of translations of the opinions of the Supreme Court of Puerto Rico, in English, since 1973 and the Appellate Circuit Court of Puerto Rico decisions, in Spanish, since September 2001.

LexisNexis has separate case files that contain the decisions of the Supreme Court of Puerto Rico, since 1899, and the decisions of the Appellate Circuit Court of Puerto Rico since 1995, both in Spanish.

d.   *Digests. Digesto de Puerto Rico.* San Juan, Puerto Rico: LexisNexis of Puerto Rico, 1974–1996. This was the topical digest to the decisions of the Supreme Court of Puerto Rico. It was published in Spanish only. Organization is analogous to the West digests. Updating was by cumulative annual pocket parts, but the set has not been updated since 1996.

e.   *Administrative Regulations.* Administrative regulations are no longer published in print. Updated regulations and information can be obtained through commercial databases such as *MicroJuris, Lexjuris, JTS Online, Consulta Legislativa,* described in Section A-4-*i,* and administrative agencies websites, which offer a wealth of information.[34] The *Departamento de Estado (Department of State)* website publishes regulations, searchable by title, number, and agency.[35] The regulations are in Spanish, and some are available in English.

LexisNexis includes the full text of Puerto Rico administrative regulations, although not all the administrative agencies are covered.

f.   *Executive Orders and Opinions.* Pronouncements from Puerto Rico's Governor and its Secretary of Justice, commonly referred to as the Attorney General, are available from several sources.

Executive orders from the governor are available at the *Departamento de Estado* website from 1952, and selectively in the combined resources described in Section B-4-*i.*

---

[33] http://www.capr.org.

[34] http://www.gobierno.pr.

[35] http://www.estado.gobierno.pr.

The opinions of the Secretary of Justice are equivalent to state attorney general opinions. *Opiniones del Secretario de Justicia de Puerto Rico.* San Juan, Puerto Rico: Thomson-West, 1903–. The *opiniones* come out irregularly. They are also published in the William S. Hein & Co., microfiche set of attorney general opinions. The *Departamento de Justicia (Department of Justice)* publishes the opinions, from 2003 to present, online.[36]

    g.   *Law Reviews.* The following law reviews are indexed in *LegalTrac* and in *Index to Legal Periodicals:*

- *Revista de Derecho Puertorriqueño.* Quarterly publication of the Universidad Católica de Puerto Rico, School of Law, Ponce, Puerto Rico, 1961–.

- *Revista del Colegio de Abogados de Puerto Rico.* Quarterly publication of the Colegio de Abogados de Puerto Rico, San Juan, Puerto Rico, 1939–.

- *Revista Jurídica de la Universidad de Puerto Rico.* Quarterly publication of the Escuela de Derecho de la Universidad de Puerto Rico, Rio Piedras, Puerto Rico, 1932–.

- *Revista Jurídica de la Universidad Interamericana de Puerto Rico.* A triennial publication of the Universidad Interamericana de Puerto Rico, Santurce, Puerto Rico, 1964–.

Revista de Derecho Puertorriqueño, Revista del Colegio de Abogados de Puerto Rico, and *Revista Jurídica de la Universidad de Puerto Rico* are available in *Westlaw* and *LexisNexis. Revista Jurídica de la Universidad Interamericana de Puerto Rico* is available in *Microjuris.*[37]

    h.   *Citator. Shepard's Puerto Rico Citations.* Colorado Springs, CO.: LexisNexis, 1968–. This is a complete citation service showing all citations by the Puerto Rico and federal courts to the Puerto Rico cases reported in the various series of Puerto Rico reports. It includes all citations by the Puerto Rico and federal courts to the Constitution of the Commonwealth of Puerto Rico, the Organic Acts, and codes and laws, acts, ordinances, and court rules. All citations by the Puerto Rico courts to the United States Constitution and federal statutes are also shown.

    i.   *Combined resources.* Several free and subscription services include a varying combination of cases, statutes, regulations, and other legal materials.

- The *Colegio de Abogados de Puerto Rico* (Puerto Rico Bar Association)[38] provides a range of legal materials at no cost.

- *LexJuris* de Puerto Rico[39] is a commercial database with free access for the basic collection, which contains the text of Puerto Rico cases, statutes, and regulations and other useful information. They also offer a fee-based subscription for more specialized research.

---

[36] http://www.justicia.gobierno.pr.

[37] http://pr.microjuris.com/home.jsp.

[38] http://www.capr.org.

[39] http://www.lexjuris.com.

- *JTS Online*[40] is a subscription database that includes statutes, cases and regulations in Spanish. *JTS Online* also includes the complete text of various legal books.

- *Consulta Legislativa*[41] is a Spanish-language commercial database with statutes, cases and regulations. *Consulta Legislativa* includes complete information about the legislative process, the text of bills and resolutions, and the legislative calendar, updated daily.

- *Leyes y Reglamentos de Puerto Rico* (West CD-ROM Libraries). Thompson/West 1992–. This is a database in CD-ROM format containing the full text in Spanish of *Leyes de Puerto Rico Anotadas (Laws of Puerto Rico Annotated)* and, in a separate CD, the decisions of the Supreme Court of Puerto Rico, from 1899 to the present. It also contains Puerto Rico administrative regulations, although not all the administrative agencies are covered.

- *Microjuris.*[42] San Juan, Puerto Rico: Microjuris, Inc. 1989–. This database is available on a subscription basis. It contains the opinions of the Supreme Court of Puerto Rico since 1946 and the Appellate Circuit Court of Puerto Rico since 1995. It also includes the *Laws of Puerto Rico Annotated* and the *Opinions of the Attorney General of Puerto Rico*. It includes the most complete collection of government regulations organized by subject and agency names and other useful indexes. The information is in Spanish and is updated on a daily basis. Also included is legislative information: abstracts of the bills and resolutions introduced in the Legislative Assembly of Puerto Rico since 1985, with information about the history and status of the bills, organized by subject, bill number, and other indexes.

- *Rama Judicial de Puerto Rico.* Rama Judicial de Puerto Rico (Puerto Rico Judicial Branch)[43] has information and texts of the Supreme Court cases from 1998. It contains information about the court system, the Canons of Professional Ethics, calendars, Puerto Rico lawyer's directory and more. Case status information is searchable by parties. The information is in Spanish.

    k.   Legal Research Guides. Two recommended legal research guides for Puerto Rico are Garlos I. Gorrín Peralta, *Fuentes y Proceso de Investigación Jurídica.* Orford, NH: Butterworth Legal Publishers, Equity Publishing Division, 1991, and Luis Muñiz Arguelles & Migdalia Fraticelli Torres. *La Investigación Jurídica: Fuentes Puertorriqueñas, Norteamericanas y Españolas.* 4th ed. Bogotá, Colombia: Editorial Temis S.A., 2006. The Law Library of Congress provides a guide to electronic legal materials for Puerto Rico, with links to the constitution and legislative, executive, and judicial sources.[44]

---

[40] http://www.pub-jts.com.

[41] http://www.consultalegislativa.com/.

[42] http://pr.microjuris.com/.

[43] http://www.ramajudicial.pr.

[44] http://www.loc.gov/law/help/guide/states/us-pr.php.

5. Virgin Islands

The United States Virgin Islands were purchased from Denmark in 1916.[45] The Virgin Islands are an organized territory. There is a unicameral legislature, an elected governor, and a supreme court (since 2007). The United States District Court for the Virgin Islands exercises jurisdiction along the lines of other territorial federal courts.

   a.   Constitution. A revised organic act for the U.S. Virgin Islands was adopted in 1954.[46] Efforts to adopt a constitution have proceeded for years; in 2010, Congress adopted a joint resolution to reconvene the Fifth Constitutional Convention. The convention's purpose is to reconsider and amend a draft constitution that the convention had previously approved but that contained provisions of doubtful constitutionality (under the U.S. Constitution).

   b.   Statutes. Session laws and the Virgin Islands Code are available in print and online. The following are readily available sources.

   Session Laws of the Virgin Islands. Charlotte Amalie, Virgin Islands: Law Revision Commission, 1955–. Published annually, the session laws contain the text of laws and resolutions enacted by the legislature and approved by the governor. The session laws are published in the series of state session laws produced in microfiche by William S. Hein & Co., Inc. and in *HeinOnline.*

   Virgin Islands session laws for the current legislature are found in the VI–LEGIS database in *Westlaw.*

   Virgin Islands Code Annotated. Charlottesville, Va.: LexisNexis, 1970–. Annotated and updated annually with pocket parts and replacement volumes, this is the standard commercial edition of the Virgin Islands statutes in compiled form. Unnumbered index and tables volumes, a volume of court rules, and an advance session law service complete the set.

   The *Virgin Islands Code,* unannotated except for basic source information is available freely on the web.[47] *Westlaw* and *LexisNexis* have the current Virgin Islands statutes.

   c.   Court Reports. Virgin Islands Reports. Charlottesville, Va.: LexisNexis, 1959–. Covering the period from 1917, this is the standard series of reports for the courts of the Virgin Islands. The series publishes the decisions of the Supreme Court, the District Court of the Virgin Islands, and the United States Court of Appeals for the Third Circuit (in cases on appeal from the Supreme Court).

   The *Westlaw* database VI–CS has the decisions of the Supreme Court of the Virgin Islands from 2007, the Superior Court (formerly the Territorial Court) from 1996, and the U.S. District Court for the Virgin Islands from 1946. *LexisNexis* has the decisions of the Superior Court back to 1959 and coverage similar to *Westlaw* for the other courts.

   The Supreme Court of the Virgin Islands and the Superior Court, as well as the U.S. District Court, have good websites that include court reports.[48]

---

[45] Convention on Cession of Danish West Indies, Denmark–U.S., Aug. 4, 1916, 39 Stat. 1706, T.S. 629, 7 Bevans 56.

[46] Act of July 22, 1954, ch. 558, 68 Stat. 497, codified as amended at 48 U.S.C. §§ 1541–1645 (2006).

[47] http://www.michie.com/virginislands.

[48] http://www.visupremecourt.org; http://www.visuperiorcourt.org; http://www.vid.uscourts.gov.

d. Administrative Regulations. Virgin Islands Rules and Regulations, marketed by LexisNexis, is the print version of the regulations. *LexisNexis* has a file containing the *Code of U.S. Virgin Island Rules,* along with portions of the *Virgin Islands Government Register.*

e. Digests. Virgin Islands Digest. Charlottesville, Va.: LexisNexis, 1991–. In six volumes, including a descriptive-word index and table of cases, this set gives topical access to decisions published in *Virgin Islands Reports.* Coverage in the bound volumes is through 1990 and updating is done by means of pocket parts.

f. Court Rules. The *Virgin Islands Court Rules Annotated* are published annually by LexisNexis. The volume contains the rules of court for the Supreme Court, the Superior Court, and the local rules of the U.S. District Court of the Virgin Islands. The rules of court can also be found on the websites of the courts, noted above.

B. STATES IN FREE ASSOCIATION WITH THE UNITED STATES

The freely associated states are the Federated States of Micronesia, Palau, and the Republic of the Marshall Islands, all in the western Pacific Ocean. The fundamental distinction between a territory and a freely associated state is that, under international law, the latter has the status of a sovereign nation. Each of the freely associated states is a member of the United Nations.

The freely associated states formerly were part of the Trust Territory of the Pacific Islands created by the United Nations in 1947 and administered by the United States. Negotiations on political status led to the signing and approval of Compacts of Free Association with the United States in the 1980s.[49] The compacts are in the nature of international agreements, and, under the compacts, the United States takes on responsibility for military security and defense and receives exclusive military authority. However, in consultation with the United States, the freely associated states retain their authority to conduct foreign affairs.

1. Federated States of Micronesia

The best place to do research on the law of the Federated States of Micronesia (FSM) is on the web, at the site of the Legal Information System (LIS) of the FSM.[50] The LIS is not current, and the links are not always in working order. Nevertheless, when the site is working, the LIS has primary legal sources for the FSM National Government and for its four states, Chuuk, Kosrae, Pohnpei, and Yap.

a. Constitutions. The Constitutions of the FSM National Government and of the four states are on the LIS.

b. Statutes. The FSM Code, current to August 2001, is on the LIS. Source notes and case notes are included. Recent public laws are on the website of the FSM Congress.[51] A print version of the code has not been published since 1999.

---

[49] For the Marshall Islands and Micronesia, see 48 U.S.C. § 1901–1921h (2006). For Palau, see 48 U.S.C. § 1931–1962 (2006). The texts of the Compacts of Free Association are found in the notes following these sections in the annotated editions of the *United States Code.*

[50] http://fsmsupremecourt.org/WebSite/fsm/index.htm.

[51] http://www.fsmcongress.fm.

c.   Court Reports. Federated States of Micronesia Supreme Court Interim Reporter. Kolonia, Pohnpei, FSM: The Court, 1997–. The *Interim Reporter* publishes decisions of the FSM Supreme Court and selected state court decisions. Volumes 1–16 of the *Interim Reporter,* and selected decisions from other courts, are available in HTML format on the LIS. Decisions of the FSM Supreme Court and some state court decisions are available on the Pacific Islands Legal Information Institute website.[52]

2.   Palau

a.   Constitution. The Constitution of Palau is available in HTML format on the website of the Pacific Islands Legal Information Institute.[53] It is available commercially in *Constitutions of the Countries of the World* and on *Hein Online.*

b.   Statutes. Palau National Code Annotated: PNCA. Koror, Palau: Palau Publication and Law Access Unit, 1995–.The code was prepared by the Palau National Code Commission. It is annotated with case citations and source notes. It has been supplemented to 2003.

c.   Court Reports. Republic of Palau Reports. Koror, Palau: Republic of Palau Supreme Court, 1987–. The former title was *Courts of the Republic of Palau Interim Reporter.* This looseleaf publishes the decisions of the Supreme Court, Appellate Division, and selected decisions of the Supreme Court, Trial Division.

3.   Republic of the Marshall Islands

a.   Constitution. The Constitution of the Marshall Islands is available in PDF on the website of the Republic of the Marshall Islands Judiciary[54] and in HTML on the website of the Pacific Islands Legal Information Network.[55] It is available commercially in *Constitutions of the Countries of the World* and in *HeinOnline.*

b.   Statutes. Marshall Islands Revised Code. 2004 ed. Majuro: Office of Legislative Counsel, Nitijela of the Marshall Islands, 2004–. An unofficial version of the code, containing selective legislation, is available on the website of the Pacific Islands Legal Information Institute.[56] The code as amended to August 2007, which is more recent than will be found elsewhere, is available on the website of the Republic of the Marshall Islands Judiciary.[57] Some session laws for years 2007–2009 are found on the website of the Pacific Islands Legal Information Institute.

c.   Court Reports. Republic of the Marshall Islands Law Reports. Majuro, Marshall Islands: Supreme Court, 1993–. This set contains the decisions of the Supreme Court of the Marshall Islands. The reports are available in PDF on the website of the Republic of the Marshall Islands Judiciary (which also has some more recent decisions) and in HTML on the website of the Pacific Islands Legal Information Institute.

---

[52] http://www.paclii.org.

[53] http://www.paclii.org/pw/constitution.html.

[54] http://rmicourts.org.

[55] http://www.paclii.org/mh/legis/consol_act/cotrotmi490/. The Constitution of the Marshall Islands in Marshallese is available at http://www.paclii.org/mh/constitution.pdf.

[56] http://www.paclii.org/mh/legis/consol_act_2004/.

[57] http://rmicourts.org.

A digest for volumes 1–3 of the reports is on the website of the Republic of the Marshall Islands Judiciary. Selected decisions of the Traditional Rights Court are also there.

Appendix D

STATE REPORTS

A. YEAR OF FIRST REPORTED CASE
DECIDED IN THE STATES' APPELLATE COURTS

Many of the states were colonies or territories when their first appellate decisions were issued. Pennsylvania was a commonwealth. In 1840, what is now the state of Texas was an independent republic.

Although printing began in the colonies in 1638, the first reported case appears to be the *Trial of Thomas Sutherland* for murder, printed in 1692. Prior to the American Revolution, approximately 30 of the 150 English reports were being used in this country as the written case law; only about 35 to 40 legal books or pamphlets had been printed here.

Connecticut was the first state to publish an official law report after a 1784 statute entitled *An Act Establishing the Wages of the Judges of the Superior Court* was enacted requiring judges of the supreme and superior courts to file written opinions. The first volume, known as *Kirby's Reports,* was published in 1789 by Ephraim Kirby in Litchfield, Connecticut; its first case is from 1785. Next to be published were Dallas' *Pennsylvania Cases* (1790), Hopkinson's *Admiralty Reports* (1792), and Chipman's *Vermont Reports* (1793). Through the early 1800s, reports commenced in North Carolina, Virginia, Kentucky, New Jersey, Maryland, Louisiana, New York, and Tennessee. Some of these early reports gathered and published cases much older than the publication date of the reporter. For example, the *Harris & McHenry Reports* from the General Court of Maryland contains a case decided in 1658.

State	Date	State	Date
Alabama	1820	Kansas	1858
Alaska	1869	Kentucky	1785
Arizona	1866	Louisiana	1809
Arkansas	1837	Maine	1820
California	1850	Maryland	1658
Colorado	1864	Massachusetts	1804
Connecticut	1785	Michigan	1805
Delaware	1792	Minnesota	1851
District of Columbia	1801	Mississippi	1818
Florida	1846	Missouri	1821
Georgia	1846	Montana	1868
Hawaii	1847	Nebraska	1860
Idaho	1866	Nevada	1865
Illinois	1819	New Hampshire	1796
Indiana	1817	New Jersey	1789
Iowa	1839	New Mexico	1852

State	Date
New York	1791
North Carolina	1778
North Dakota	1867
Ohio	1821
Oklahoma	1890
Oregon	1853
Pennsylvania	1754
Rhode Island	1828
South Carolina	1783
South Dakota	1867
Tennessee	1791
Texas	1840
Utah	1855
Vermont	1789
Virginia	1729
Washington	1854
West Virginia	1864
Wisconsin	1839
Wyoming	1870

Appendix E

COVERAGE OF THE NATIONAL REPORTER SYSTEM

The entire system, with its beginning year of coverage and its jurisdictional coverage is outlined below:

Reporter	Began in	Jurisdictional Coverage (start date varies by state)
Atlantic Reporter	1885	Conn., Del., Me., Md., N.H., N.J., Pa., R.I., Vt., and D.C.
California Reporter	1959	Calif. Sup. Ct., courts of appeal, and Appellate Division, Superior Ct.
Illinois Decisions	1976	Ill. (all state appellate courts).
New York Supplement	1888	N.Y. (all appellate courts to 1932). Since 1932, the N.Y. Court of Appeals opinions are published here as well as in the North Eastern Reporter.
North Eastern Reporter	1885	Ill., Ind., Mass., N.Y., and Ohio.
North Western Reporter	1879	Iowa, Mich., Minn., Neb., N.D., S.D., and Wis.
Pacific Reporter	1883	Alaska, Ariz., Cal. to 1960, Calif. Sup. Ct. since 1960, Colo., Hawaii, Idaho, Kan., Mont., Nev., N.M., Okla., Or., Utah, Wash., and Wyo.
South Eastern Reporter	1887	Ga., N.C., S.C., Va., and W.Va.
South Western Reporter	1886	Ark., Ky., Mo., Tenn., and Tex.
Southern Reporter	1887	Ala., Fla., La., and Miss.
Supreme Court Reporter	1882	Supreme Court of the United States.
Federal Reporter	1880	From 1880 to 1911: U.S. Circuit Court (abolished in 1912).
		From 1880 to 1932: U.S. district courts (coverage transferred to Federal Supplement).
		1891 to present: U.S. Court of Appeals (formerly U.S. Circuit Court of Appeals).
		1911 to 1913: Commerce Court of the U.S. (abolished in 1913).
		1929 to 1932 and 1960 to 1982: U.S. Court of Claims (abolished in 1982).
		1929 to 1982: U.S. Court of Customs and Patent Appeals.[1]
		1943 to 1961: U.S. Emergency Court of Appeals.
		1972 to 1993: Temporary Emergency Court of Appeals.
Federal Appendix	2001	2001 to present: Unreported cases from the U.S. courts of appeals.
Federal Supplement	1932	1932 to present: U.S. district courts.

---

[1] Since 1983, jurisdiction of the U.S. Court of Customs and Patent Appeals and the appellate division of the U.S. Court of Claims transferred to U.S. Court of Appeals for the Federal Circuit.

Reporter	Began in	Jurisdictional Coverage (start date varies by state)
		1932 to 1960: U.S. Court of Claims.
		1954 to 1980: United States Customs Court (replaced by U.S. Court of International Trade).
		1980 to present: U.S. Court of International Trade.
		1968 to present: Judicial Panel on Multidistrict Litigation.
		1974 to 1997: Special Court under the Regional Rail Reorganization Act of 1973.
Federal Claims Reporter	1982	1982 to 1992: Formerly U.S. Claims Court Reporter through vol. 26, covering U.S. Claims Court.[2]
		1992 to present: U.S. Court of Federal Claims. Commences with vol. 27.
Federal Rules Decisions	1939	1939 to present: U.S. district courts construing Federal Rules of Civil Procedure (1939 to present) and Federal Rules of Criminal Procedure (1946 to present).
Military Justice Reporter	1975	1975 to present: U.S. Court of Appeals for the Armed Forces (formerly the Court of Military Appeals) and courts of criminal appeals (formerly courts of military review) for the Army, Navy–Marine Corps, Air Force, and Coast Guard.
Bankruptcy Reporter	1979	1979 to present: Bankruptcy cases from U.S. bankruptcy courts, U.S. district courts dealing with bankruptcy matters (cases not printed in Federal Supplement), U.S. courts of appeals (reprinted from Federal Reporter), and U.S. Supreme Court (reprinted from Supreme Court Reporter).
Veterans Appeals Reporter	1989	1989 to present: Veterans appeals cases from the U.S. Court of Veterans Appeals, U.S. district courts, U.S. courts of appeals, and U.S. Supreme Court (in review of the Court of Veterans Appeals).

---

[2] This court changed its name in 1992 to the U.S. Court of Federal Claims.

Index

References are to Pages